National Security Law

EDITORIAL ADVISORS

Vicki Been
Elihu Root Professor of Law
New York University School of Law

Erwin Chemerinsky
Alston & Bird Professor of Law
Duke University School of Law

Richard A. Epstein
James Parker Hall Distinguished Service Professor of Law
University of Chicago Law School
Peter and Kirsten Bedford Senior Fellow
The Hoover Institution
Stanford University

Ronald J. Gilson
Charles J. Meyers Professor of Law and Business
Stanford University
Marc and Eva Stern Professor of Law and Business
Columbia Law School

James E. Krier
Earl Warren DeLano Professor of Law
The University of Michigan Law School

Richard K. Neumann, Jr.
Professor of Law
Hofstra University School of Law

David Alan Sklansky
Professor of Law
University of California at Berkeley School of Law

Kent D. Syverud
Dean and Ethan A. H. Shepley University Professor
Washington University School of Law

Elizabeth Warren
Leo Gottlieb Professor of Law
Harvard Law School

ASPEN PUBLISHERS

National Security Law
Fourth Edition

Stephen Dycus
Professor of Law
Vermont Law School

Arthur L. Berney
Professor of Law, Emeritus
Boston College

William C. Banks
Laura J. and L. Douglas Meredith Professor
Syracuse University

Peter Raven-Hansen
Glen Earl Weston Research Professor of Law
George Washington University

AUSTIN   BOSTON   CHICAGO   NEW YORK   THE NETHERLANDS

© 2007 by Stephen Dycus, Arthur L. Berney, William C. Banks, and Peter Raven-Hansen.
Published by Aspen Publishers. All Rights Reserved.

No part of this publication may be reproduced or transmitted in any form or by any means, electronic or mechanical, including photocopy, recording, or any information storage and retrieval system, without permission in writing from the publisher. Requests for permission to make copies of any part of this publication should be mailed to:

Aspen Publishers
Attn: Permissions Department
76 Ninth Avenue, 7th Floor
New York, NY 10011-5201

To contact Customer Care, e-mail customer.care@aspenpublishers.com, call 1-800-234-1660, fax 1-800-901-9075, or mail correspondence to:

Aspen Publishers
Attn: Order Department
PO Box 990
Frederick, MD 21705

Printed in the United States of America.

1 2 3 4 5 6 7 8 9 0

ISBN 0-7355-5614-8

Library of Congress Cataloging-in-Publication Data

National security law / Stephen Dycus . . . [et al.]. — 4th ed.
   p. cm.
Includes bibliographical references and index.
ISBN 0-7355-5614-8 (hardcover : alk. paper)
1. National security — Law and legislation — United States. I. Dycus, Stephen.

KF4651.N377 2007
343.73'01 — dc22   2006036130

About Wolters Kluwer Law & Business

Wolters Kluwer Law & Business is a leading provider of research information and workflow solutions in key specialty areas. The strength of the individual brands of Aspen Publishers, CCH, Kluwer Law International and Loislaw are aligned within Wolters Kluwer Law & Business to provide comprehensive, in-depth solutions and expert-authored content for the legal, professional and education markets.

CCH was founded in 1913 and has served more than four generations of business professionals and their clients. The CCH products in the Wolters Kluwer Law & Business group are highly regarded electronic and print resources for legal, securities, antitrust and trade regulation, government contracting, banking, pension, payroll, employment and labor, and healthcare reimbursement and compliance professionals.

Aspen Publishers is a leading information provider for attorneys, business professionals and law students. Written by preeminent authorities, Aspen products offer analytical and practical information in a range of specialty practice areas from securities law and intellectual property to mergers and acquisitions and pension/benefits. Aspen's trusted legal education resources provide professors and students with high-quality, up-to-date and effective resources for successful instruction and study in all areas of the law.

Kluwer Law International supplies the global business community with comprehensive English-language international legal information. Legal practitioners, corporate counsel and business executives around the world rely on the Kluwer Law International journals, loose-leafs, books and electronic products for authoritative information in many areas of international legal practice.

Loislaw is a premier provider of digitized legal content to small law firm practitioners of various specializations. Loislaw provides attorneys with the ability to quickly and efficiently find the necessary legal information they need, when and where they need it, by facilitating access to primary law as well as state-specific law, records, forms and treatises.

Wolters Kluwer Law & Business, a unit of Wolters Kluwer, is headquartered in New York and Riverwoods, Illinois. Wolters Kluwer is a leading multinational publisher and information services company.

To our teachers

Summary of Contents

Contents		*xi*
Preface		*xxxi*
Acknowledgments		*xxxv*
Editors' Note		*xxxix*
Chapter 1.	Introduction	1

PART I.
Framework — 7

Chapter 2.	Providing for the "Common Defence": The Original Understanding	9
Chapter 3.	The Gloss of History: An Introduction to the Separation of National Security Powers	27
Chapter 4.	The President's National Security Powers	59
Chapter 5.	Congress's National Security Powers	93
Chapter 6.	The Courts' National Security Role	133
Chapter 7.	The Domestic Effect of International Law	157

PART II.
Using Force Abroad — 199

Chapter 8.	War in General	201
Chapter 9.	The War Powers Resolution	240
Chapter 10.	Unilateral Self-Defense and Rescue	255
Chapter 11.	Collective Self-Defense	284
Chapter 12.	Preemptive War	303
Chapter 13.	Humanitarian and Peace/Stability Operations	318

Part III.
Conducting Intelligence Operations Abroad — 337

Chapter 14.	Origins and Evolving Limits of Intelligence Operations	339
Chapter 15.	Covert Action	369
Chapter 16.	Other Legal Problems in the Intelligence Field	430

Part IV.
Fighting Terrorism — 463

Chapter 17.	Defining Terrorism	465
Chapter 18.	The Fourth Amendment and National Security	477
Chapter 19.	Congressional Authority for National Security Surveillance	506
Chapter 20.	Third-Party Records and Data Mining	557
Chapter 21.	Screening for Security	588
Chapter 22.	Organization and Coordination of Counterterrorism Investigations	614
Chapter 23.	Surveillance Abroad	640
Chapter 24.	Civil Detention of Terrorist Suspects	664
Chapter 25.	Suspending the Great Writ	680
Chapter 26.	Military Detention	703
Chapter 27.	Interrogating Terrorist Suspects	759
Chapter 28.	Criminalizing Terrorism and Material Support	817
Chapter 29.	Secret Evidence	848
Chapter 30.	Trial by Military Commission	876
Chapter 31.	Managing a WMD Attack	907
Chapter 32.	The Domestic Role of the Armed Forces	944

Part V.
Obtaining and Protecting National Security Information — 973

Chapter 33.	Regulating Access to National Security Information	975
Chapter 34.	Statutory Access to National Security Information	989
Chapter 35.	Access to National Security Information in Civil Litigation	1020
Chapter 36.	Restraining Unauthorized Disclosures of National Security Information	1051
Chapter 37.	Restraints on Publication of National Security Information	1082

Appendix — Constitution of the United States — 1113

Table of Cases — *1121*
Index — *1129*

Contents

Preface	*xxxi*
Acknowledgments	*xxxv*
Editors' Note	*xxxix*

CHAPTER 1.	*Introduction*	1
A.	Purposes	1
B.	Organization	4

PART I.	**FRAMEWORK**	7

CHAPTER 2.	*Providing for the "Common Defence": The Original Understanding*	9
A.	The Constitutional Text	9
B.	Pre-Constitutional History and Political Theory in Europe	12
C.	The American Experience Prior to 1787	17
D.	The Framers' View	19
	1. The Convention	19
	2. Ratification	22
	Notes and Questions	25

CHAPTER 3.	***The Gloss of History: An Introduction to the Separation of National Security Powers***	27

A. The *Steel Seizure Case* and Its Theories of Presidential Power 28
    Youngstown Sheet & Tube Co. v. Sawyer (The Steel Seizure Case) 28
    Notes and Questions 42
    a. The President's Claim of Lawmaking Authority 43
    b. The President's Claim of Inherent or "Aggregate" Powers in Emergencies 45
    c. The President's Claim of War Powers as Commander in Chief 46
B. Justice Jackson's Grouping of Presidential Powers 47
    1. When the President Acts Pursuant to Delegated Authority 47
    2. When the President Acts with Congressional Acquiescence 48
        Dames & Moore v. Regan 48
        Notes and Questions 54
    3. When the President Takes Measures Incompatible with the Expressed or Implied Will of Congress 55
        Notes and Questions 57

CHAPTER 4.	***The President's National Security Powers***	59

A. The President's Foreign Relations Powers 60
    United States v. Curtiss-Wright Export Corp. 60
    Notes and Questions 65
B. The Commander in Chief's War Powers 67
    1. Defensive War Powers 67
        The Prize Cases 67
        Notes and Questions 70
    2. Customary War Powers 71
        Francis D. Wormuth & Edwin B. Firmage, To Chain the Dog of War 72
        Henry P. Monaghan, Presidential War-Making 74
        Notes and Questions 75
    3. Statutory Limits on the President's War Powers 77
        Little v. Barreme 77
        Notes and Questions 79
C. The President's Emergency Powers 80
    In re Neagle 80
    Notes and Questions 84
D. The President's Power to Protect Information 87
    1. Classified Information 87

	2.	Privileged Information		88
		Notes and Questions		90

CHAPTER 5. *Congress's National Security Powers* — 93

A. Congressional Authorizations for War — 93
    Joint Resolution Declaring War Between Rumania and the United States — 94
    Bas v. Tingy — 94
    Notes and Questions — 97
B. Delegations and Appropriations for National Security — 102
    Lichter v. United States — 102
    Greene v. McElroy — 105
    Notes and Questions — 108
    a. Delegations of National Security Authority — 108
    b. Authorization by Defense Appropriation — 111
    c. Limitation by Defense Appropriation — 112
C. Statutory Emergency Powers — 114
    Proclamation No. 7463, Declaration of National Emergency by Reason of Certain Terrorist Attacks — 114
    Notes and Questions — 115
D. Congressional Investigations — 118
    McGrain v. Daugherty — 118
    Notes and Questions — 121
E. Limitations on Congressional War Powers — 124
    1. Substantive Limits on Congressional National Security Powers — 124
        Notes and Questions — 125
    2. Procedural Limits on Congressional National Security Powers — 128
        Notes and Questions — 129

CHAPTER 6. *The Courts' National Security Role* — 133

    Dellums v. Bush — 134
    Notes and Questions — 143
    a. Political Questions — 144
    b. Standing to Sue — 149
        i. Citizen Plaintiffs — 150
        ii. Taxpayer Standing — 151
        iii. Congressional Plaintiffs — 152
    c. Ripeness — 154

CHAPTER 7.	*The Domestic Effect of International Law*	157

A. The Making and Interpretation of Treaties and Agreements — 158
  1. Making and Interpreting Treaties — 158
      The ABM Treaty Reinterpretation Controversy — 158
      Office of Legal Counsel, Relevance of Senate Ratification History to Treaty Interpretation — 159
      Notes and Questions — 165
    a. Making Treaties — 165
    b. Terminating Treaties — 166
    c. Interpreting Treaties — 167
  2. Executive and Other Agreements — 170
      Dames & Moore v. Regan — 170
      Notes and Questions — 170
B. The Domestic Legal Effect of Treaties and Executive Agreements — 173
      Reid v. Covert — 173
      Committee of U.S. Citizens Living in Nicaragua v. Reagan — 176
      Notes and Questions — 179
C. The Domestic Legal Effect of Customary International Law and *Jus Cogens* — 182
      Committee of U.S. Citizens Living in Nicaragua v. Reagan — 182
      Sosa v. Alvarez-Machain — 187
      Notes and Questions — 194
    a. The Making and Incorporation of Customary International Law — 194
    b. "Controlling" Executive and Legislative Acts and Judicial Decisions — 194
    c. Codifying International Law — 196
    d. *Jus Cogens* — 197

PART II.	**USING FORCE ABROAD**	199

CHAPTER 8.	*War in General*	201

A. Going to War in Vietnam — 202
  1. How the War Began: A Brief History — 202
  2. Legal Foundations for the Commitment of U.S. Forces — 208
      Leonard C. Meeker, The Legality of United States Participation in the Defense of Viet-Nam — 209

		Notes and Questions	213
	3.	Testing the Legitimacy of the War in Court	218
		Orlando v. Laird	219
		Notes and Questions	222
B.	Limiting the Scope of the Vietnam War		225
	1.	Cambodia	226
	2.	Laos	227
		Notes and Questions	228
C.	Ending the Vietnam War		230
	1.	Repeal of the Gulf of Tonkin Resolution	230
		Notes and Questions	231
	2.	Another Congressional Step Back	234
		Notes and Questions	234
	3.	Cutting Off Funding for the War	235
		Holtzman v. Schlesinger	235
		Notes and Questions	238

CHAPTER 9. *The War Powers Resolution* 240

		War Powers Resolution (50 U.S.C. §§1541-1548)	240
		Richard M. Nixon, Veto of the War Powers Resolution	243
		Notes and Questions	246
	a.	The "Substantive" Provisions of Section 2	246
	b.	Consultation	247
	c.	The "Hostilities" Trigger and the Reporting Requirements	248
	d.	The 60-Day Clock	251
	e.	The Concurrent Resolution	253
	f.	The Rule of Construction	253
	g.	Replacing the WPR	254

CHAPTER 10. *Unilateral Self-Defense and Rescue* 255

A.	Pre-Constitutional and Subsequent Experience	256
	Notes and Questions	258
B.	Repelling Sudden Attacks	260
	The Prize Cases	260
	The Gulf of Sidra Incident: Repelling (Or Provoking?) Attack	260
	Statement of Abraham D. Sofaer, The War Powers Resolution and Antiterrorist Operations	262
	Notes and Questions	263
C.	Rescue	264

		In re Neagle	264
		Durand v. Hollins	264
		The Iran Hostage Rescue Mission	266
		Letter of President Jimmy Carter to the Speaker of the House and President Pro Tempore of the Senate	267
		Legal Opinion by Lloyd Cutler on War Powers Consultation Relative to the Iran Rescue Mission	268
		The "Hostage Act"	269
		Notes and Questions	269
D.	Striking First (Or Striking Back?)		273
	1.	The 1998 Attacks on Sudan and Afghanistan	273
		Notes and Questions	274
	2.	Targeted Killing in Anticipatory Self-Defense	277
		Executive Order No. 12,333	277
		W. Hays Parks, Executive Order 12333 and Assassination	278
		Notes and Questions	280

CHAPTER 11. *Collective Self-Defense*   284

A.	Collective Self-Defense Under the United Nations Charter		285
	1.	The Role of the United Nations Security Council	285
		Charter of the United Nations – Chapter VII	285
		Notes and Questions	286
	2.	The Role of the United States Under Chapter VII	287
		United Nations Participation Act (22 U.S.C. §§287-287e-2)	288
		Notes and Questions	289
B.	The Korean "Police Action"		290
	1.	The Outbreak of War	291
	2.	The President's Response	291
		Notes and Questions	293
C.	The Persian Gulf War		294
	1.	The Invasion of Kuwait	294
	2.	Operation Desert Shield	295
	3.	The Buildup	296
	4.	Operation Desert Storm	297
		Letter from President Bush to Congressional Leaders on the Persian Gulf Crisis	297
		Authorization for Use of Military Force Against Iraq (Pub. L. No. 102-01)	298
		Notes and Questions	300
D.	Collective Self-Defense Under Regional Organizations		301
		Charter of the United Nations – Chapter VIII	301

Contents	xvii

CHAPTER 12. *Preemptive War*	303
A. Planning for a Return to the Persian Gulf After 9/11	303
B. Authority for a New War in Iraq	305
Authorization for Use of Military Force Against Iraq Resolution of 2002 (Pub. L. No. 107-243)	305
Notes and Questions	310
C. Justifications for the War	313
Notes and Questions	315
D. Victory in Iraq?	316
Notes and Questions	317

CHAPTER 13. *Humanitarian and Peace/Stability Operations*	318
A. Authority for Humanitarian Operations	319
Humanitarian and Other Assistance (10 U.S.C.A. §§401-405)	319
Notes and Questions	320
B. Crossing the Mogadishu Line: Operation Restore Hope	321
Authority of the President to Use United States Military Forces for the Protection of Relief Efforts in Somalia	323
Letter from President George Bush to Congressional Leaders	327
Notes and Questions	330
C. Stabilization and Reconstruction Operations in Afghanistan and Iraq	334
Notes and Questions	335

PART III. CONDUCTING INTELLIGENCE OPERATIONS ABROAD	337

CHAPTER 14. *Origins and Evolving Limits of Intelligence Operations*	339
A. The Players and Processes of Intelligence	341
Church Committee, Foreign and Military Intelligence	341
Notes and Questions	343
B. Intelligence Operations: Origins and Practice	343
1. National Security Secrecy: The Original Understanding	343
Notes and Questions	345
2. Intelligence Operations: Practice and Inherent Power	347

		Church Committee, Foreign and Military Intelligence	347
		Statement of Mitchell Rogovin	347
		Robert Borosage, Para-Legal Authority and Its Peril	348
		Notes and Questions	349
C.	Intelligence Collection: The "INTS"		349
		Mark M. Lowenthal, Intelligence: From Secrets to Policy	350
		Notes and Questions	353
D.	The National Security Act of 1947		355
		Church Committee, Foreign and Military Intelligence	357
		Statement of Mitchell Rogovin	358
		Robert Borosage, Para-Legal Authority and Its Peril	359
		Notes and Questions	361
E.	Intelligence Reorganization		362
	1.	An Intelligence Czar?	363
	2.	The New Structure	364
		Notes and Questions	366

CHAPTER 15. *Covert Action* 369

A.	The First Public Control — The Neutrality Act			371
B.	Implementing the 1947 Act			372
	1.	From the Cold War Through Vietnam: Intelligence Operations 1947-1973		374
		a.	Intelligence Operations and Executive Branch Decision Making	374
			Notes and Questions	375
			United States v. Lopez-Lima	376
			Notes and Questions	379
		b.	Escalating Use and Review of Intelligence Operations	380
			Notes and Questions	381
			Note on Covert Intervention in Chile	382
			Central Intelligence Agency, CIA Activities in Chile	382
			Notes and Questions	383
C.	Congressional Oversight			384
	1.	From the Cold War Through Vietnam		384
	2.	Budget Oversight		385
		Notes and Questions		386
	3.	Congressional Oversight Reforms		389
		a.	The War Powers Resolution and Covert Action	389
		b.	The Hughes-Ryan Amendment	390
			Notes and Questions	390

		c. The Church Committee and a Proposed Charter	392
		Notes and Questions	393
		d. The Intelligence Oversight Act of 1980	394
		Intelligence Oversight Act of 1980 (Pub. L. No. 96-450, §407(b)(1)	394
		Notes and Questions	395
D.	Executive Branch Reforms		396
		Executive Order No. 12,333	397
		Notes and Questions	400
	a.	Deciding on Intelligence Operations	400
	b.	The Internal Executive Branch Process for Reviewing Intelligence Operations	401
	c.	Implementation of Intelligence Operations	403
	d.	Recording and Reporting Intelligence Operation Decisions	404
E.	The Reforms Tested: A Case Study of the Iran-Contra Affair		404
	1.	The Legality of the Arms Sales	405
		Notes and Questions	407
	2.	Presidents' Rules: Executive Orders and Decision Directives	410
		Notes and Questions	410
	3.	Covert Support for the Contras and the Boland Amendments	411
		Notes and Questions	413
	4.	The Iran-Contra Affair in the Courts	418
		Notes and Questions	419
F.	1991 Oversight Reforms		421
		Intelligence Authorization Act, Fiscal Year 1991 (Pub. L. No. 102-88, §§602-603)	422
		Statement on Signing the Intelligence Authorization Act, Fiscal Year 1991	426
		Notes and Questions	426

CHAPTER 16. *Other Legal Problems in the Intelligence Field*   430

A.	Domestic Collection		431
	1.	The CIA	431
		Church Committee, Foreign and Military Intelligence	431
		Halkin v. Helms	433
		Notes and Questions	436
	2.	The FBI	439
		Church Committee, Intelligence Activities and the Rights of Americans	439
		Notes and Questions	442
	3.	The NSA	443
		Executive Order No. 12,333	444
		Notes and Questions	446

B. Private Assets 447
   1. Proprietaries 447
       Church Committee, Foreign and Military Intelligence 447
       Note on Covert Intervention in Laos 449
       Notes and Questions 450
   2. Dirty Assets 451
       Harbury v. Deutch 451
       Notes and Questions 455
   3. Nonofficial Cover 458
C. Military Special Operations as Intelligence Operations 459
       Notes and Questions 461

PART IV. FIGHTING TERRORISM 463

CHAPTER 17. *Defining Terrorism* 465

       United States v. Yousef 469
       Notes and Questions 471
       People's Mojahedin Organization of Iran v. Department of State 473
       Notes and Questions 476

CHAPTER 18. *The Fourth Amendment and National Security* 477

A. Detection of Terrorist Threats 478
       William C. Banks & M.E. Bowman, Executive Authority for National Security Surveillance 478
       Statement of John Ashcroft, U.S. Federal Efforts to Combat Terrorism 479
       Fact Sheet: Plots, Casings, and Infiltrations 480
B. The Fourth Amendment Framework 481
       William C. Banks & M.E. Bowman, Executive Authority for National Security Surveillance 481
C. A National Security Exception? 483
       Foreign Intelligence Surveillance Act of 1977 483
       United States v. United States District Court (Keith) 485
       Notes and Questions 492
D. A Foreign Intelligence Exception? 495
       Church Committee, Intelligence Activities and the Rights of Americans 495
       United States v. Ehrlichman 495
       Notes and Questions 498
       United States v. Truong Dinh Hung 500
       Notes and Questions 503

CHAPTER 19.	*Congressional Authority for National Security Surveillance*	506

A. The Scope of Fourth Amendment Protection — 507
    Smith v. Maryland — 507
    Notes and Questions — 510
B. Congressional Authority for Surveillance: The Foreign Intelligence Surveillance Act (FISA) — 512
    United States v. Duggan — 513
    Notes and Questions — 519
    a. The Mechanics of FISA — 519
    b. Constitutional Concerns — 530
C. FISA, Law Enforcement, and "The Wall" — 532
    In re Sealed Case No. 02-001, 02-002 — 533
    Notes and Questions — 544
D. FISA Trends — 546
    Case Study: The Terrorist Surveillance Program — 548
    Letter from William E. Moschella, Asst. Attorney General — 548
    Notes and Questions — 552

CHAPTER 20.	*Third-Party Records and Data Mining*	557

A. Finding the Dots — Third-Party Records — 557
   1. Expectations of Privacy Regarding Transactional Data — 557
    Smith v. Maryland — 558
    Notes and Questions — 558
   2. Techniques and Authorities for Collection of Transactional Data — 559
    Doe v. Ashcroft (Doe I) — 562
    Doe v. Gonzales — 575
    Notes and Questions — 577
B. Connecting the Dots — Data Mining — 581
    Notes and Questions — 584

CHAPTER 21.	*Screening for Security*	588

A. Checkpoint Searches — 589
    MacWade v. Kelly — 590
    Notes and Questions — 594
B. Identification and Watch Listing — 595
    Gilmore v. Gonzales — 595
    Watch Lists Maintained by Federal Agencies — 598
    Notes and Questions — 599
    a. Identification Requirements — 599

		b.	Watch Lists and Other Identification-Related Databases	600
		c.	Transparency of Screening Law	604
C.	Profiling			604
			Guidance Regarding the Use of Race by Federal Law Enforcement Agencies	604
			Notes and Questions	607

CHAPTER 22. *Organization and Coordination of Counterterrorism Investigations* — 614

A.	Executive Authority for National Security Investigations			615
			Executive Order No. 12,333	616
			Attorney General's Guidelines on General Crimes, Racketeering Enterprise and Terrorism Enterprise Investigations (Domestic Security Guidelines)	617
			Attorney General's Guidelines for FBI National Security Investigations and Foreign Intelligence Collection (NSI Guidelines)	622
			Notes and Questions	628
		a.	Executive Order No. 12,333	628
		b.	Domestic Security Guidelines	629
		c.	NSI Guidelines	632
B.	Information Sharing and Agency Reforms			634
	1.	Bridging the Law Enforcement/Intelligence Collection Divide		634
	2.	Reforming the FBI		638
			Notes and Questions	638

CHAPTER 23. *Surveillance Abroad* — 640

Reid v. Covert	640
United States v. Verdugo-Urquidez	643
Notes and Questions	649
United States v. Bin Laden	650
Notes and Questions	658

CHAPTER 24. *Civil Detention of Terrorist Suspects* — 664

Affidavit of Michael E. Rolince, In re Ali Abubakr Ali Al-Maqtari	665

	Office of the Inspector General, Dept. of Justice, The September 11 Detainees: A Review of the Treatment of Aliens Held on Immigration Charges	667
	Non-Detention Act (18 U.S.C. §4001(a))	670
	Notes and Questions	671
a.	Constitutional and Statutory Limits on Detention	671
b.	"Spitting on the Sidewalk"	673
c.	Material Witness Detentions	674
d.	Immigration Detentions	676
e.	Military Detentions	679
f.	Profiling?	679

CHAPTER 25. *Suspending the Great Writ* 680

A.	Statutory Basis for Habeas Corpus	681
	Habeas Corpus (28 U.S.C.A. §§2241-2243)	681
B.	Suspending the Writ	682
	Ex parte Milligan	683
	Notes and Questions	689
C.	Availability of the Writ to Nonresident Aliens	690
	Military Order of November 13, 2001, Detention, Treatment, and Trial of Certain Non-Citizens in the War Against Terrorism	691
	Rasul v. Bush	692
	Notes and Questions	700

CHAPTER 26. *Military Detention* 703

A.	Wartime Detention of Noncombatants Before 9/11	703
	Alien Enemy Act (50 U.S.C. §21)	703
	Korematsu v. United States	704
	Notes and Questions	709
B.	Wartime Detention of Combatants Before 9/11	714
	Ex parte Milligan	714
	Ex parte Quirin	714
	Notes and Questions	718
C.	Detention of U.S. Citizens as Enemy Combatants After 9/11	720
	Hamdi v. Rumsfeld	721
	Order by President George W. Bush to the Secretary of Defense	742
	Rumsfeld v. Padilla	743
	Padilla v. Hanft	744
	Notes and Questions	749

D.	Military Detention of Alien Enemy Combatants After 9/11	755
	Notes and Questions	757

CHAPTER 27. *Interrogating Terrorist Suspects*   759

A.	The Evolving History of Detainee Interrogation in the War on Terrorism	759
B.	The Legal Standards and Their Application	764
	Memorandum from John Yoo and Robert J. Delahunty, Application of Treaties and Laws to al Qaeda and Taliban Detainees	764
	Memorandum from Alberto R. Gonzales, Decision re Application of the Geneva Convention on Prisoners of War to the Conflict with Al Qaeda and the Taliban	770
	Memorandum from William H. Taft IV, Comments on Your Paper on the Geneva Convention	773
	Working Group Report on Detainee Interrogations	774
	Memorandum from Donald R. Rumsfeld, Counter-Resistance Techniques in the War on Terrorism	782
	Notes and Questions	785
	a. Torture in General	785
	b. (Incorporated?) International Law on Torture	792
	c. Domestic Law on Torture	798
C.	Extraordinary Rendition	804
	Arar v. Ashcroft	804
	Notes and Questions	812

CHAPTER 28. *Criminalizing Terrorism and Material Support*   817

A.	Treason and Sedition	817
	United States v. Rahman	817
	Notes and Questions	823
B.	Material Support Crimes	824
	Material Support Statutes (18 U.S.C. §§2339A-2339C)	825
	Humanitarian Law Project v. Reno	826
	United States v. Al-Arian	830
	Notes and Questions	834

C.	The Long Arm of the Law: Extraterritorial Criminal Jurisdiction	839
	United States v. Bin Laden	839
	Notes and Questions	844

CHAPTER 29. *Secret Evidence* — 848

A.	Using Secret Evidence Against Terror Suspects	849
	American-Arab Anti-Discrimination Committee v. Reno	849
	Notes and Questions	853
B.	Classified Information Procedures Act	857
	Classified Information Procedures Act (18 U.S.C.A. app. 3 §§1-16)	857
	United States v. Lee	859
	Notes and Questions	862
C.	Handling Secret Exculpatory Testimony	866
	United States v. Moussaoui	866
	Notes and Questions	872

CHAPTER 30. *Trial by Military Commission* — 876

A.	Trial by Military Commission Before 9/11	877
	Ex parte Milligan	877
	Ex parte Quirin	877
	Notes and Questions	877
B.	Trial by Military Commission After 9/11	877
	Military Order of November 13, 2001, Detention, Treatment, and Trial of Certain Non-Citizens in the War Against Terrorism	878
	Hamdan v. Rumsfeld	882
	Notes and Questions	903

CHAPTER 31. *Managing a WMD Attack* — 907

A.	Thinking the Unthinkable: Planning a Response to a Terrorist Attack	908
	Notes and Questions	909
B.	A Hypothetical Worst-Case Scenario	910
	Thomas V. Inglesby, Rita Grossman & Tara O'Toole, A Plague on Your City: Observations from TOPOFF	910
	Notes and Questions	914
C.	First Responders: Roles and Authorities	916

	The 9/11 Commission Report: Final Report of the National Commission on Terrorist Attacks Upon the United States	917
	Notes and Questions	918
D.	Second Responders: The Federal Role	919
	Notes and Questions	922
E.	Quarantines and Like Responses to a Terrorist Attack	924
	1. State and Local Responses to a Terrorist Attack	925
	Jew Ho v. Williamson	925
	Jacobson v. Massachusetts	929
	Notes and Questions	932
	2. A Model State Response: The MSEHPA?	935
	Model State Emergency Health Powers Act	936
	Notes and Questions	938
	3. The Federal Response to a Bioterrorist Attack	939
	Public Health Service Act (42 U.S.C.A. §§243, 264)	939
	Interstate Quarantine Regulations (42 C.F.R. part 70)	940
	Notes and Questions	941

CHAPTER 32. *The Domestic Role of the Armed Forces* — 944

A.	The Military in American Society	945
	1. The Posse Comitatus Act as a Background Principle	945
	Bissonette v. Haig	945
	Notes and Questions	950
	2. Exceptions to the Posse Comitatus Act	953
	Insurrection Act (10 U.S.C. §§331-335)	953
	Military Cooperation with Law Enforcement Officials Act (10 U.S.C. §§371-382)	954
	Notes and Questions	956
B.	The Military's Role in Homeland Security and Disaster Relief	959
	1. The Military's Intelligence Role in Homeland Security	960
	Notes and Questions	962
	2. The Military's Role in Responding to Domestic Crises	963
	a. Leading or Supporting Role?	963
	b. Controlling Authorities	965
	c. Organizing for a Response	966
	d. Preparations for a Natural Disaster	967
	Notes and Questions	968
C.	Martial Law: When Planning Fails	969
	Ex parte Milligan	970
	Notes and Questions	970

Part V. OBTAINING AND PROTECTING NATIONAL SECURITY INFORMATION — 973

Chapter 33. Regulating Access to National Security Information — 975

A. Balancing Secrecy, Security, and Self-Determination — 976
    Arvin S. Quist, Security Classification of Information — 976
    Notes and Questions — 979
B. Classification of National Security Information — 979
    Executive Order No. 13,292, Classified National Security Information — 979
    Notes and Questions — 984

Chapter 34. Statutory Access to National Security Information — 989

A. The Freedom of Information Act — 989
    A Citizen's Guide on Using the Freedom of Information Act and the Privacy Act of 1974 to Request Government Records — 989
  1. The Statutory Text — 990
    Freedom of Information Act (5 U.S.C. §552) — 990
    Notes and Questions — 993
  2. Statutory Exemptions and Judicial Review — 997
    Ray v. Turner — 997
    Bassiouni v. Central Intelligence Agency — 1005
    Notes and Questions — 1007
B. Other Open Government Laws — 1015
  1. Presidential Records Act — 1015
  2. Privacy Act — 1017
  3. Open Meetings Laws — 1018

Chapter 35. Access to National Security Information in Civil Litigation — 1020

A. Common Law Right to Know — 1020
    Schwartz v. United States Department of Justice — 1020
    Notes and Questions — 1021
B. Constitutional Right to Know — 1023
    Nation Magazine v. United States Department of Defense — 1024

	Notes and Questions	1026
	North Jersey Media Group, Inc. v. Ashcroft	1029
	Notes and Questions	1033
C. Protecting "State Secrets" in Litigation		1037
	Halkin v. Helms	1037
	Notes and Questions	1041
	Tenet v. Doe	1045
	Notes and Questions	1048

CHAPTER 36. *Restraining Unauthorized Disclosures of National Security Information*   1051

A. Restraining Leaks by Contract		1052
1. The CIA Precedents		1052
	United States v. Marchetti	1052
	Snepp v. United States	1055
	Notes and Questions	1058
2. Nondisclosure Agreements and Lifetime Prepublication Review		1060
	Classified Information Nondisclosure Agreement (SF 189)	1060
	Sensitive Compartmented Information Nondisclosure Agreement (SF 4193)	1061
	Notes and Questions	1062
B. Restraining Leaks by Espionage Prosecutions		1066
	Espionage and Censorship (18 U.S.C. §§793-798)	1066
	Embezzlement and Theft (18 U.S.C.A. §641)	1068
	United States v. Morison	1068
	Notes and Questions	1072
	Note on a Proposal to Criminalize All Unauthorized Leaks	1077
	Note on "Authorized" Leaks: The Valerie Plame Affair	1079

CHAPTER 37. *Restraints on Publication of National Security Information*   1082

A. Case Study: The Pentagon Papers Litigation		1082
1. The Roles of Lawyers and Journalists		1082
	Notes and Questions	1085
2. The Threat of Criminal Prosecution		1088
	Notes and Questions	1090
3. The Inherent Power of the Executive to Censor		1093
	Notes and Questions	1096

	New York Times Co. v. United States	1098
	Notes and Questions	1105
B.	Nuclear Secrets and *The Progressive*: The Extreme Case?	1107
	Notes and Questions	1110

APPENDIX — *Constitution of the United States*   1113

Table of Cases   *1121*
Index   *1129*

Preface

In the Third Edition of this casebook, which was published shortly after the terrorist attacks of September 11, 2001, we emphasized more than in previous editions the role of law in countering terrorism. Since then, the government has tried to rearrange the disparate programs and tools of counterterrorism into a better coordinated whole. We also have sought in this Fourth Edition to collect the various relevant components of National Security Law and arrange them more systematically to facilitate the teaching and understanding of counterterrorism law. In this edition, for example, we have added new chapters on the data mining and collection of third-party records, screening and profiling at airports and subways, suspension of the writ of habeas corpus, and preemptive war. We also have included some of the growing flood of judicial decisions in the field, including several blockbusters from the Supreme Court.

Because the post-9/11 evolution of National Security Law has been marked by a sharper demarcation of discrete subject areas, we have broken down many of the chapters from earlier editions into shorter, more thematically integrated chapters for this Fourth Edition. The result, we believe, provides a measure of coherence to this still young and somewhat unruly discipline, and makes it easier to teach and learn that discipline in pedagogically digestible units. Thus, the 17 chapters in the Third Edition have given way to 37 shorter chapters here.

Although the content of the "Framework" in Part I is largely unchanged, we have reorganized some materials in it to highlight separation-of-powers analysis for use in later parts of the book. In Part II, "Using Force Abroad," we have distinguished among unilateral defense and rescue, collective self-defense, preemptive war, and humanitarian and peace/stability operations, following chapters on war in general and the War Powers Resolution. In Part III, "Conducting Intelligence Operations Abroad," we have separated the origins and evolution of the law governing intelligence operations from the specific study of covert actions and of other legal problems in the intelligence field. In Part IV, "Fighting Terrorism," we address the definition of terrorism, intelligence activities aimed at detecting and preventing terrorism, the detention and interrogation of terrorist suspects, punishment of terrorists through adjudicative proceedings, and responses to terrorist attacks and insurrection. This part of the book is the most changed from the last edition, as one might expect. Finally, we have streamlined

Part V, "Obtaining and Protecting National Security Information," and have updated it to include materials on the constitutional right of access to "special interest" immigration hearings, state secrets, and leak investigations and laws.

But if the order and priority of topics within National Security Law keep changing, the reasons for studying this discipline remain the same. The subject matter is still complex and difficult, the political and legal issues are perennially contentious, and there are few settled answers. Yet it is hard to think of another topic more current and provocative. Long before the terrorist attacks on September 11, 2001, it offered the opportunity to bring front-page news into the classroom and to better understand the special responsibility that comes with citizenship in a free and open democracy.

National Security Law helps advance other important educational goals, as well. These materials examine the structure and functioning of the government by focusing on the pervasive issue of national defense. They explore every aspect of the domestic legal process, and they integrate experiences from other courses in a new setting. Finally, they offer important insights about the significance of law outside the courtroom and about the interaction of law and politics.

While this book is designed for a course utilizing the "case method" of study, it also serves well as a background reader for lecture courses. In addition to descriptive text, the book includes many primary materials, such as judicial opinions, executive orders, statutes, and legislative history. Because such materials tend to be episodic, disorganized, and incomplete, reading and integrating them places a premium on the student's initiative. Learning from such sources is not passive learning; it is hard but exciting work. This process resembles the work of lawyers and other decision makers in the national security field. Few of the answers to the questions they face every day can be found in a treatise or secondary treatment of the matter; the questions outpace academic production of such reference works. Like national security professionals, therefore, we and our students have to rely on an uneven variety of primary sources, even as the small body of case law grows.

We have tried to fill in some of the blanks with relatively fulsome notes and questions. The notes and questions, however, are not intended as optional addenda to the other materials; they are of equal importance and should be reviewed with equal care in preparing for class. On occasion, answering a question will require review of the "framework" law of Part I. Don't hesitate to go back and reconsider these overarching materials. With the primary sources and notes, we have tried to supply all the information you need to answer these questions — to the extent they are answerable at all.

If you wish to read more or if you are using the book as an initial research source, the notes and questions also mention some of the most important authorities dealing with each topic. It is not necessary to go outside of these pages to get a well-rounded introduction to National Security Law, but an occasional excursion to the library will prove stimulating.

Even more stimulating — and central to a good National Security Law course — will be regular perusal of a national newspaper. National security issues are almost always front-page news, and it is inevitable that several will play themselves out in the news even as you read this book. Follow them and apply the analysis that you learn here. That application is, after all, the object of this study, not just a by-product.

Preface

We cannot claim in what follows that we have always been politically or ideologically neutral. But we have struggled to present a balanced view of every important issue, because we take seriously the persuasive power of the written word. National security is too important to be left to the "conservative" or the "liberal" alone; good legal analysis is neither.

A word about coverage is in order. This book addresses domestic legal issues that arise in providing for the national defense. We have concentrated on what we consider to be the core of this field of study. Unwilling to sacrifice depth of coverage for scope, we have deliberately omitted (except in passing) a number of relevant topics, including restrictions on travel and on transfers of critical technology, defense procurement, the security clearance process, foreign policy initiatives of state and local governments, environmental law and national defense, the draft, military law, and civil disobedience.

We have also provided a good introduction to the domestic recognition and application of public international law—what is sometimes called "foreign relations law." Such law plays an increasingly important part in national security actions. The focus here is on sources of international obligations (treaties, executive agreements, and customary law), the respective roles of Congress and the President in their making, and their effect on domestic National Security Law. The *content* of international law is dealt with only episodically, where it is important to a fuller understanding of particular events, such as the Vietnam War or the alleged torture at Abu Ghraib. A systematic survey of the content of international law is left to other courses.

We have taught courses based on these materials for both two- and three-semester hours in large classroom settings and in seminars. We always do some exercises and simulations along the way. Occasionally we have covered aspects of National Security Law not addressed here. And inevitably we have culled at least one wonderful case study from the newspapers during the course of each term.

The manuscript for this Fourth Edition was completed in July 2006. A number of alterations were made during the editing process, however, to reflect some of the most important breaking developments in this extremely dynamic field, such as the Military Commissions Act of 2006, signed by the President on October 16, 2006. Yet like any work in the field the book is to some degree incomplete. It is truly a work in progress. We invite you to join in this work.

We welcome your reactions, comments, and suggestions.

Stephen Dycus
William C. Banks
Peter Raven-Hansen

November 2006

Acknowledgments

Stephen Dycus owes a special debt of gratitude to Alan B. Sherr and the late Reverend William Sloane Coffin Jr., whose independent, nearly simultaneous suggestions provided the genesis for this book. I am also especially grateful to my wife Elizabeth for her many sacrifices during its preparation. Thanks are due to Dean Jesse H. Choper and the faculty at Boalt Hall and to the late William A. Brockett for their hospitality during a sabbatical leave, to Colonel Dennis R. Hunt and the faculty of the Law Department at the U.S. Military Academy, West Point, and to my colleagues at Vermont Law School. I also want to recognize the contributions of a succession of bright, energetic research assistants: Alexander W. Banks, Sara Baynard, Claude T. Buttrey, Daronda Combs, Charles S. Conerly, Carole L. Conragon, Lewis M. Csedrik, Edward Demetriou, Abigail Doolittle, Matthew T. Einstein, Robin E. Eiseman, Sean C. Flynn, Thomas H. French, Gina M. Godfrey, A. Morgan Goodson, Barbara J. Grabowski, Daniel Patrick Greene, Jessica E. Jay, Byron W. Kirkpatrick, Rhona J. Kisch, Karl M. Kurt, Steven F. Lachman, David C. Lashway, Bernard M. Lewis, Robin Longe, Pamela I. Lundquist, William G. Madsen, William "Trey" Martin, David M. Meezan, Jesse Moorman, Daphne Moritz, Sue Ann M. Orsini, Matthew C. Porterfield, Carole A. Powers, Catherine Rawson, Daniel Richardson, Heather Rider, Alan Roughton, Karen E. Russell, Sam Schneider, Elaine C. Schwartz, Nathaniel Shoaff, Brooks M. Smith, Rebecca Turner, Charles J. Veith, Emily Wetherell, and Karen M. Willis. Finally, I am grateful for the opportunity to undertake this work with three wonderful coauthors, who have become best friends in the process.

William Banks dedicates this edition to the memory of Brady Howell, a former National Security Law student and victim of the September 11 attack on the Pentagon. I also thank the Syracuse University law and graduate students who tested these materials in draft form, reacted to them in the first three editions, and provided many useful suggestions for this revision. I am grateful to my deans, Michael Hoeflich, Daan Bravemen, Hannah Arterian, and Mitchell Wallerstein, for their generous support of this project, and to my colleagues Spike Bowman and William Wiecek for their comments on draft chapters. My research assistants, Diane Exoo, Doug Steele, Charles Fox, Michael Johnson, Christina Zampas, Patricia Adams, Andrew Kanter, Jennifer Morris, Margaret Lyons, Courtland Rae, Shivani Mehta, Ruben Saenz, Bill Dorry, Danielle Raymond, and Laura Pierce, were immensely helpful and supportive along the way. Finally, I want to thank my friends Steve Dycus, Peter Raven-Hansen, and Arthur Berney for involving me in this project. Their intelligence and commitment to exploring this remarkable field continue to be an invaluable source of inspiration to me.

Peter Raven-Hansen thanks Christopher T. Gailu Jr., Robyn D. Herman, Kristine Kassekert, Michael F. Kohler, Douglas J. Lutz, Andrew G. Mergen, Jennifer Riddle, Anne Schwartz, David Silverband, Todd A. Sinkins, Kevin Stack, Jeremy Stein, Ian K. Sweedler, Caroline E. Turner, Earl R. Uehling, Paul C. Vitrano, and Walter L. Williams, all George Washington University Law School students whose energetic and conscientious assistance made prior editions of this book possible. For their enormous help in this edition, I'd like to thank students Alexis Victoria Chapin, Rachel Kramer, Stephan Rice, Kelly Rich, and Justin T. Ryan. I would also like to thank M.E. (Spike) Bowman, William R. Cumming, and Daniel C. Schwartz for their comments and support. I am grateful to my wife Winnie for her patience through another edition, and to my friends and coauthors for keeping it fun. Finally, my special thanks and respect to Steve Dycus, whose leadership and occasional martial law delivered the Fourth Edition, as they did all prior editions. Without him, there would be no book.

This work would not have been started and could not have been completed without the efforts of our esteemed original coauthor, Arthur Berney. Arthur thinks and writes with piercing clarity. His brilliant case study on the *Pentagon Papers* case, which appears in a somewhat modified form at the end of the book, is a perennial favorite of students and of ours. Arthur has provided inspiration and moral leadership for the book. He is kind to a fault, yet stubborn when it comes to speaking the truth. In the Preface to the First Edition he wrote, "I did what little I could" to promote understanding of the work of lawyers as peacemakers. He was far too modest. We remain enormously grateful to Arthur for his original contributions and for his continuing friendship.

Together, the authors deeply appreciate the support and encouragement of the staff at Little, Brown and Aspen, especially Ruth Elvin, Mari Megias, Suzanne W.B. Rapcavage, and Barbara Rappaport, our copy editors, as well as Richard R. Heuser, Carol McGeehan, Jessica Barmack, Melody Davies, Eric Holt, Laurel Ibey, Carmen Corral-Reid, Peggy Rehberger, Elizabeth Kenny, Anne Starr, Kurt Hughes, Heather Shaff, Kathy Yoon, and Michael Gregory.

The authors also gratefully acknowledge permission to reprint excerpts from the following:

Borosage, Robert L., Para-Legal Authority and Its Perils, 40 Law & Contemp. Probs. 166 (1976). Copyright © 1976 by Duke University School of Law. Reprinted by permission of the author and Law and Contemporary Problems.

Carroll Publishing, chart on organization of the intelligence community (2005). Reprinted by permission of Carroll Publishing.

Inglesby, Thomas, Rita Grossman & Tara O'Toole, A Plague on Your City: Observations from TOPOFF, 32 Clinical Infectious Diseases 436 (2001). Copyright © 2001 by The University of Chicago Press. Reprinted by permission of the authors and The University of Chicago Press.

Acknowledgments

Lewis, Anthony, The Constitution and the Press (unpublished course materials, Harvard Law School). Copyright © 1974 by Anthony Lewis. Reprinted by permission of the author.

Lowenthal, Mark M., Intelligence: From Secrets to Policy (3d ed. 2006). Reprinted by permission of the publisher, CQ Press. Copyright © 2006 CQ Press, a division of Congressional Quarterly Inc.

Monaghan, Henry P., Presidential War-Making, 50 B.U.L. Rev. 19 (1970) (special issue). Copyright © 1970 by The Boston University Law Review. Reprinted by permission of the author and The Boston University Law Review.

Shane, Peter M., chart, The Bureaucratic Due Process of Government Watch Lists, 75 Geo. Wash. L. Rev. (forthcoming 2007). Reprinted by permission of the author.

Toles, Tom, cartoon ("Hello, Col. North?"). Reproduced by permission of Mr. Toles and The Buffalo News.

Treverton, Gregory F., Covert Action: The CIA and the Limits of American Intervention in the Postwar World (1987). Copyright © 1987 by Basic Books, Inc. Reprinted by permission of Basic Books, Inc.

Treverton, Gregory F., Reshaping National Intelligence for an Age of Information (2003). Copyright © 2003 by Rand. Reprinted with the permission of Cambridge University Press.

Wormuth, Francis D. & Edwin B. Firmage, To Chain the Dog of War (2d ed. 1989). Copyright © 1989 by Southern Methodist University Press. Reprinted by permission of Southern Methodist University Press and Edwin Firmage.

Editors' Note

In general we have adhered to the rules for citation of authority followed by most lawyers and courts. They are set out in The Bluebook: A Uniform System of Citation (18th ed. 2005). For reasons of economy we have omitted without notation many citations within excerpted materials, and we have removed almost all parallel citations. We have, on the other hand, sought to provide citations that will enable readers to locate and review original sources. Concerning citation to sources on the Internet, we have supplied URLs for harder-to-find materials, but omitted them for materials that can be located easily using Google or another search engine. To make it easier to refer back to materials where they were originally published, we have preserved original footnote numbers in all excerpted materials. Editors' footnotes are numbered consecutively throughout each chapter. Additions to quoted or excerpted materials are enclosed in brackets.

National Security Law

Introduction 1

> The law spoke too softly to be heard amidst the din of arms.
>
> *Plutarch, Lives: Caius Marius*[1]

A. PURPOSES

There is no field of legal study more critical to the well-being of our people or our republic than National Security Law. In a world that bristles with animosity and danger, an inadequate national defense would jeopardize our lives and ideals. Yet measures taken in the name of national security sometimes pose comparable threats to those same ideals of liberty and justice. This irony has not escaped the attention of the Supreme Court:

> [T]his concept of "national defense" cannot be deemed an end in itself, justifying any exercise of legislative power designed to promote such a goal. Implicit in the term "national defense" is the notion of defending those values and ideals which set this Nation apart. For almost two centuries, our country has taken singular pride in the democratic ideals enshrined in its Constitution. . . . It would indeed be ironic if, in the name of national defense, we would sanction the subversion of one of those liberties . . . which make the defense of the Nation worthwhile. [United States v. Robel, 389 U.S. 258, 264 (1968).]

The delicate balance of liberty and security must be appraised and learned, and learned again, by each generation of students of law and public policy. One purpose of this book is to promote the study of that balance.

It might appear that national security issues have only recently taken center stage in our national life. In fact, they have held that position periodically throughout our history. In the first 75 years of the republic, the federal courts unhesitatingly, though infrequently, grappled with core issues of national defense — the existence, legality, and scope of war and military authority. Congress and the executive closely debated questions of war power and foreign policy, not just because they were conscious of setting precedent, but also because each assumed an independent constitutional duty to consider the legality of executive conduct. No one called the resulting body of law — articulated in relatively few judicial opinions and laid bare in a larger number of congressional debates — "national security law." The makers of this law simply applied their

---

1. John Langhorne & William Langhorne, trans. (n.d.).

evolving understanding of the constitutional framework and their ordinary legal skills to the problems of security as these presented themselves.

Six major wars in the last hundred years (including the first one ever lost — or at least not won — by American forces), the prolonged tension of the Cold War, the specter of a nuclear holocaust, and the unstable post-Cold War world have changed the way we approach national security law. So, tragically, have the terrorist attacks on the World Trade Center and the Pentagon on September 11, 2001. Today, the lines between foreign and domestic issues of national security, and even between peace and war, have seriously eroded: Every foreign issue has domestic ramifications, and the country lives in a seemingly permanent "Global War on Terrorism." The front line — the battle zone — is no longer at a safe distance abroad; it is also in Oklahoma City, lower Manhattan, and Arlington, Virginia. And the rules of engagement now must be tailored for use at home as well as abroad.

This state of affairs has empowered and perhaps emboldened the Commander in Chief — the President — to stake out national security as executive domain. Justice Stewart noted as much when he said executive power "in the two related fields of national defense and international relations[,] . . . largely unchecked by the Legislative and Judicial branches, has been pressed to the very hilt since the advent of the nuclear missile age." New York Times Co. v. United States, 403 U.S. 713, 727 (1971) (concurring). A second purpose of our study is therefore to examine the constitutional distribution of decision-making authority among the branches of government in our democracy.

Despite these developments, or perhaps because of them, the judiciary has grown increasingly reluctant to answer questions involving national security claims, even some that it squarely addressed earlier in our nation's history. Congress, too, with but few exceptions, has often shied away from serious debate of the same questions in recent years. Ironically, it has sometimes done so by asserting that such questions are for the courts, not for Congress, to resolve. More often, it has simply avoided the questions by acquiescing in executive conduct. If it is true, as Justice Black said, that "[t]he word 'security' is a broad, vague generality," *id.* at 719 (concurring), it nonetheless has today assumed a talismanic quality that often mesmerizes the courts into inaction, quiets congressional debate, and sometimes persuades the executive to think of national security as an end in itself.

Another major purpose of this book is to demonstrate that national security is no talisman.

> [T]he concept of military necessity is seductively broad, and has a dangerous plasticity. Because they invariably have the visage of overriding importance, there is always a temptation to invoke security "necessities" to justify an encroachment upon civil liberties. For that reason, the military-security argument must be approached with a healthy skepticism. . . . [Brown v. Glines, 444 U.S. 348, 369 (1980) (Brennan, J., dissenting).]

We hope to encourage that skepticism by using ordinary legal skills to help find answers to questions about national security. Not all answers, of course; not always comforting answers either, because security concerns are always factors that weigh in legal analysis.

A. Purposes

Relatively few of these answers are to be found in reported judicial opinions addressing national security. Such opinions are "rare, episodic, and afford little precedential value for subsequent cases," given their typically narrow and contextually limited holdings. Dames & Moore v. Regan, 453 U.S. 654, 661 (1980). We do try to demonstrate, however, that legal analysis is relevant and useful outside of the courtroom and appellate opinions, and that legal questions of national security do not lose their urgency just because courts will not answer them. These legal questions persist in dialogues both within and between the political branches. In that nonjudicial setting, they are not so much answered authoritatively as temporarily negotiated. But legal analysis, with an appreciation for the constitutional framework of our system, is crucial in formulating the negotiating positions, defining terms of the dialogue, and memorializing the bargains that are struck.

The failure of courts to give authoritative answers to many questions of national security law suggests to some that public opinion is what ultimately counts in this field.

> In the absence of governmental checks and balances present in other areas of our national life, the only effective restraint upon executive policy and power in the areas of national defense and international affairs may lie in an enlightened citizenry — in an informed and critical public opinion which alone can here protect the values of democratic government. [New York Times Co. v. United States, 403 U.S. 713, 728 (1971) (Stewart, J., concurring).]

Another facet of our study is therefore to explore the law governing access to the information that would enlighten citizens (and their representatives in Congress) about matters of national security. Again, ordinary legal skills and analysis, here applied by a sometimes less reluctant judiciary, are critical in weighing rights of access against the need to protect truly sensitive information.

Finally, we intend to demonstrate not only that legal skills and analysis *can* be brought to bear on questions of national security but that they *should* be. Our unabashed purpose here is to stimulate wider thought about the appropriate legal framework for national security decisions.

> The general drift of authority and responsibility to the President over the past two centuries is unmistakable. This trend by itself should not be cause for alarm. More threatening is executive activity cut loose from legislative moorings and constitutional restrictions — presidential action no longer tethered by law. To remain consistent with the Constitution, executive authority and administrative discretion should be directed and channeled by legislative policy. [Louis Fisher, *Constitutional Conflicts Between Congress and the President* 326 (1997).]

Without necessarily agreeing that there is no "cause for alarm," we endorse Dr. Fisher's general prescription and continually urge the reader to think about what the controlling legislative policies should be. Indeed, four members of the Supreme Court recently endorsed the same prescription in an important national security law decision. "Where...no emergency prevents consultation with Congress, judicial insistence upon that consultation does not weaken our Nation's ability to deal with danger," they said. Hamdan v. Rumsfeld, 126 S. Ct. 2749, 2799 (2006). "To the contrary," they explained, "that insistence strengthens the Nation's ability to determine — through democratic means — how best to do so. The Constitution places its faith in those democratic means. Our Court today simply does the same." *Id.* Ultimately, the study of national security law is simply the study of how we should deal with danger by democratic means.

Since the time of de Tocqueville, Americans have been criticized for substituting questions about the existence of power for questions about its wise use. Nowhere is this more nearly true than in the field of national security. But this critique assumes that in our system the existence and wise use of power are wholly distinct. Rather, the wise use of national security powers is not a value itself, "it is a condition that allows a nation to maintain its values." Daniel J. Kaufman, Jeffrey S. McKitrick & Thomas J. Leney, *U.S. National Security* 5 (1985). We believe that a central value and ideal of our system is the Rule of Law, and that under the Rule of Law any study of national security power must address its *existence*, as well as its wise *use*.

B. ORGANIZATION

In Part I we begin with a search for sources of authority. The starting point is the text of the U.S. Constitution. As we shall see, two centuries of interpretation have lent meaning to the often cryptic language of the founding document, but questions still outnumber answers. We then systematically examine the role that each branch of the government plays in making decisions about national security matters. A separate chapter addresses the creation and application of international law to domestic national security law. Part I thus establishes a legal and political framework for the study of particular national security subjects in later chapters.

The remainder of the book addresses the most important of these subjects both functionally and categorically. Part II explores our use of force abroad. Beginning with a case study of the Vietnam War and an examination of the War Powers Resolution that the war prompted, this part of the book then successively considers unilateral self-defense and rescue, collective self-defense, preemptive war, and humanitarian and peace/stability operations. Part III deals with intelligence operations abroad. It begins with the origins and historical evolution of limits on intelligence operations and then considers the controversial subset of covert operations, as well as other legal problems in the field. Part IV considers the rapidly growing topic of counterterrorism. Its chapters treat problems of defining terrorism, detecting and preventing terrorism (by surveillance, investigation, and screening), detaining and interrogating terrorist suspects, punishing and deterring terrorism by criminal, immigration, and military adjudication, and responding civilly and militarily to terrorist attacks and insurrection in the homeland. Finally, Part V addresses access to and protection of national security information. It starts by exploring how the classification system regulates access to such information, then turns to issues of public access by statute and by common and constitutional law. The Part closes by treating the regulation of

B. Organization

national security "leaks" and the closely related topic of restraints on the publication of national security information.

Even after more than 200 years of experience, the field of national security law is still evolving rapidly. Patterns for controlling the nation's defense apparatus change from one presidential Administration to the next, and sometimes *within* a single administration, while some of the most fundamental questions about allocation of authority remain unanswered. There are nevertheless some constant analytic approaches and underlying principles in this field. We hope that mastery of these will provide the knowledge, skills, and experience — as well as the encouragement — you need in order to play a role in the development of national security law and policy by "democratic means," as the Justices urged in *Hamdan*.

I
Framework

Providing for the "Common Defence": The Original Understanding —2

The purpose of this chapter is to plumb the original understanding of the Constitution's allocation of national security powers. Because the text alone furnishes an incomplete record, our search for the Framers' intent requires a brief review of English history and European political theory that probably influenced the Framers, the American experience with government prior to the Constitution, records of the 1787 Convention, and the subsequent ratification debates. *See* Louis Fisher, *Presidential War Power* 1-16 (2d ed. 2004). We nevertheless begin with the text, as we must in any quest for the meaning of a written constitution.

A. THE CONSTITUTIONAL TEXT

You should carefully review the excerpts from Articles I-IV of the Constitution found in the Appendix. Focus on the text. Try to suppress what you know about our nation's history since 1787. What are your first impressions? How is the responsibility to "provide for the common defence" allocated among the three branches of government?

Judging simply by the proportion of words, the extensive national security powers given Congress in Article I appear to overwhelm the meager listing for the President in Article II. Article I gives Congress authority to "declare War, grant Letters of Marque and Reprisal, and make Rules concerning Captures on Land and Water," which indicates some legislative role in the commitment of American armed forces to combat. Congress also is empowered to "raise and support" the armed forces and to "make Rules for the Government and Regulation of the land and naval Forces." In addition, Congress is authorized to "regulate Commerce with foreign Nations," to provide for the militia and for calling it forth "to execute the Laws of the Union, suppress Insurrections, and repel Invasions," and "to make all Laws which shall be necessary and proper" for executing any power conferred by the Constitution. Other provisions, particularly the one for impeachment of the President, also suggest legislative dominance. Congress escapes subservience to the executive by the guarantee of meeting "at least once in every Year," by the grant of immunity from arrest during a legislative session and from questioning in any other place about any speech or debate, and by the assignment to each House of control over its membership.

By contrast, the President is provided only one obvious national security power by being designated the "Commander in Chief." Moreover, the President is directed to command the armed forces only when they are "called into the actual Service of the United States." National security powers may be allocated to the President as part of the mandate to "take Care that the Laws be faithfully executed." The other Article II grants that may concern national security seem modest in comparison to powers conferred upon Congress: to appoint and receive ambassadors and ministers, and to make treaties (both powers shared with the Senate).

We now know that the judiciary may have a role in resolving disputes between the other two branches. However, aside from the reference in Article III, §3 to the crime of treason, there is no indication in the constitutional text that the judiciary is to be involved in decisions about the national defense.

Yet both the executive and the courts have played powerful roles in providing for our national security over the last two centuries. How can this history be reconciled with the language of the Constitution? Closer examination of the text reveals the potential for the allocation of national security powers actually reflected in our history. It also demonstrates the futility of trying to divine the Framers' intent from the text alone.

First, Articles I and II assign overlapping functions. For example, the President becomes a legislator of sorts when recommending to Congress "such measures as he shall judge necessary and expedient" and when vetoing bills and resolutions, subject to a two-thirds override by each chamber of Congress. Further, although Congress may tax to "provide for the common Defence" and direct how monies are spent, the President may argue that the "take Care" Clause permits him to act alone in an emergency, using unappropriated or otherwise obligated funds from the Treasury. Similarly, because the President is required to give Congress information "from time to time," he must have been expected to obtain information of interest to Congress. He may obtain the opinion in writing of the principal officer in each of the executive departments, including the Department of Defense, concerning that department's duties. Finally, while the declaration of war is textually committed to Congress, the Commander-in-Chief power could be read to enable the President to use the military to defend against an attack on the United States. Because Article I, §10 allows a state to "engage in War" if "actually invaded, or in such imminent Danger as will not admit of delay," it seems reasonable to claim as much power for the President if the nation is attacked, when consultation with Congress is not possible or practical.

Second, the text itself is anything but precise. Many of its words are general, are not self-defining, and are capable of supporting multiple meanings. Consider the power to "declare War." While the language clearly allocates control over some important aspects of national security decision making to Congress, the text does not say what constitutes a "war" or, for that matter, what it means to "declare" one. Does "war" include small-scale skirmishes, purposefully limited in duration? Does the "Marque and Reprisal" power instead cover these limited

A. The Constitutional Text

hostilities? *See generally* Jules Lobel, *Covert War and Congressional Authority: Hidden War and Forgotten Power*, 134 U. Pa. L. Rev. 1035 (1986). Or should "Marque and Reprisal" be thought of as an anachronism, referring to long-abandoned state-sponsored private battles with pirates? *See* John C. Yoo, *The Continuation of Politics by Other Means: The Original Understanding of War Powers*, 84 Cal. L. Rev. 167, 251 (1996). Should "to declare" be read to give Congress merely a right to recognize an existing state of war? *Id.* at 242. Or is that language intended to confer the general control over initiating war? *See* Michael D. Ramsey, *Textualism and War Powers*, 69 U. Chi. L. Rev. 1543 (2002). Or something in between these polar extremes? *See* Harold H. Koh, *The National Security Constitution: Sharing Power After the Iran-Contra Affair* 69, 79 (1990). What about uses of the military that do not create a state of war? *See* Ramsey, *supra*, at 1546-1547. And what is the meaning of the text that empowers Congress "[t]o make Rules for the Government and Regulation" of the military? There is similar textual uncertainty about the reach of congressional fiscal powers. May Congress exercise its appropriation powers to limit executive powers? To what extent must Congress provide basic operating funds for the executive? May funding be conditioned on compliance with congressional wishes? *See generally* William C. Banks & Peter Raven-Hansen, *National Security Law and the Power of the Purse* (1994).

Concerning presidential authority, there is also vagueness in the language of Article II, most notably the Commander-in-Chief provision. A narrow reading of the Clause indicates no policy-making authority and relegates the President to the status of first general. *See* Louis Henkin, *Constitutionalism, Democracy, and Foreign Affairs* 26 (1990). A broad reading of Article II, on the other hand, combined with a restrictive reading of Article I — the Declaration, Marque and Reprisal, and Rules and Regulation Clauses — would expand the Commander-in-Chief power to include all military actions not unequivocally given to Congress. *See* Yoo, *supra*, at 252-255. A similar range of constructions may be afforded the "take Care" language, the power to "receive Ambassadors and other public Ministers," and the statement in Article II, §1 vesting "[t]he executive Power" in the President. Because the parallel Article I language vests in Congress "[a]ll legislative Powers herein granted," the omission of the words "herein granted" from the text of Article II could be construed to allow the President to do virtually anything "executive" in nature so long as such action is not assigned exclusively to Congress by explicit Article I language. *See* Alexander Hamilton, *Pacificus No. 1*, Gazette of the United States (Philadelphia), June 29, 1793, *reprinted in* 15 *The Papers of Alexander Hamilton* 33-43 (Harold C. Syrett ed., 1969).

Third, the text fails altogether to prescribe or allocate power over some important areas of national security. For example, while Article I, §9 forbids suspending the privilege of the writ of habeas corpus "unless when in Cases of Rebellion or Invasion the public Safety may require it," the text does not say who possesses the power to suspend the writ. In addition, the meager text is by itself inadequate for deciding the scope and locus of authority for deploying American troops abroad or in defense of the homeland, sponsoring private or foreign fighting forces, engaging in covert paramilitary actions (or, for that matter, any intelligence activities), interdicting convoys, engaging in airlifts or blockades, or threatening or promising to do any of the above.

May Congress delegate power to the President? In part because there is no explicit rule in the text forbidding congressional delegations to the executive, such delegations are routinely upheld. But how far may Congress go in delegating its own powers? May the power to declare war be delegated, or would such a wholesale transfer violate the Constitution? The text itself provides little guidance, although the structure of the Constitution may be read to forbid such a sweeping delegation. When Congress merely remains silent while the President takes some national security initiative committed by the Constitution to Congress, is the President acting legally? The answer depends on the construction given to the vague text, since the Constitution fails to describe the effect of legislative inaction. What if the President acts unilaterally in an area not explicitly prescribed or allocated by the Constitution to any branch?

All these uncertainties provoke spirited debates at both ends of Pennsylvania Avenue and among academics. Most national security disputes are resolved in the political process. But when persuasion fails, and the political process will not yield a clear or generally acceptable answer, these disputes end up in court, where the Framers arguably meant for them to be resolved.

Fortunately, the three branches have usually cooperated in making and carrying out national security policy. The practical need for effective administration provides an incentive for Congress to nurture executive branch cooperation. Further, the President's participation in the legislative process is textually assured through his powers to call Congress into special session, to recommend legislation, to provide information about the state of the Union, and to veto any legislative measure. At the same time, any tendency of the President to seek autonomy in the wording of ambiguous text is confined by some explicit and crucial grants to Congress — appropriations and declaration of war to name just two.

Thus, the original understanding of the allocation of national security powers cannot be derived solely from the text of the Constitution. We must broaden our search and consider what is likely to have influenced the delegates to the Philadelphia Convention: British history and European political theory, as well as seminal American events such as the Revolutionary War and earlier efforts at self-government. While the effect of these influences cannot be measured precisely in the Constitution or in the views of any single delegate, it is generally accepted that a combination of theory and practical experience weighed heavily in the plan for a new government.

B. PRE-CONSTITUTIONAL HISTORY AND POLITICAL THEORY IN EUROPE

Many of the Philadelphia delegates were well read in history and political philosophy — from ancient Greece and Rome to contemporary Continental Europe. As erstwhile Englishmen, however, the Framers turned to English ideas and experiences above all others.

It is nonetheless difficult to calculate the British influence on the Constitution and on its national security provisions in particular. The allocation of war-making and foreign affairs powers fluctuated widely in England between the fifteenth and eighteenth centuries, and the unwritten British constitution simply reflected rather than guided this changing relationship. In general,

B. Pre-Constitutional History and Political Theory in Europe

the Crown dominated all foreign and military affairs until the seventeenth century, when Parliament began successfully to assert its constitutional claims to power. Before the surge in parliamentary strength, the "prerogative" powers[1] of the Crown permitted it to exercise unilaterally, among other things, most national security powers—declaring wars, issuing letters of marque and reprisal, making treaties and appointments, and raising armies and navies. The prerogative powers were generally accepted as being free from limitation by Parliament or the courts.

From the mid-seventeenth century onward, Parliament and the Crown alternately dominated decision making about national security matters. When Parliament asserted itself it often relied on its control of the purse and its ability to obtain information from the executive. The Parliament taxed for military programs, controlled the raising and keeping of standing armies in times of peace, and successfully placed restrictive conditions on military appropriations. If the Crown ignored legislation restricting a foreign affairs initiative, the Parliament could and on occasion did resort to impeachment, dismissal, or execution. *See* Banks & Raven-Hansen, *supra* p. 11, at 13-17.

On the other hand, if Parliament was uncooperative, the Crown might secure funding for its ventures from local governments or by borrowing, and it could dismiss Parliament for any reason—if Parliament had not acted first. Further, secret initiatives were sometimes undertaken, and information was often withheld from Parliament under a claim of executive discretion. *See* Abraham D. Sofaer, *War, Foreign Affairs and Constitutional Power: The Origins* 6-15 (1976); W. Taylor Reveley III, *War Powers of the President and Congress: Who Holds the Arrows and Olive Branch?* 53-55 (1981).

In addition to their legacy of shifting royal and parliamentary powers, which had so affected war making and foreign affairs, the British brought with them theoretical principles central to their own constitutional development that greatly influenced the Americans. The most important intellectual contribution was the idea of separation of powers. The theory of separation assigned different powers to different institutions and persons in government in order to forestall

---

1. The royal prerogative was described by John Locke:

   Where the Legislative and Executive Power are in distinct hands, . . . there the good of the Society requires, that several things should be left to the discretion of him, that has the Executive Power. For the Legislators not being able to foresee, and provide, by Laws, for all, that may be useful to the Community, the Executor of the Laws, having the power in his hands, has by the common Law of Nature, a right to make use of it, for the good of the Society, in many Cases, where the municipal Law has given no direction, till the Legislative can conveniently be Assembled to provide for it. . . .

   This Power to act according to discretion, for the publick good, without the prescription of the Law, and sometimes even against it, *is* that which is called *Prerogative*. For since in some Governments the Law-making Power is not always in being, and is usually too numerous, and so too slow, for the dispatch requisite to Execution . . . there is a latitude left to the Executive power, to do many things of choice, which the Laws do not prescribe. . . .

   The old Question will be asked in this matter of *Prerogative*, But *who shall be Judge* when this Power is made a right use of? I Answer: Between an Executive Power in being, with such a Prerogative, and a Legislative that depends upon his will for their convening, there can be no *Judge on Earth:* As there can be none, between the Legislative, and the People, should either the Executive, or the Legislative, when they have got the Power in their hands, design, or go about to enslave, or destroy them. The People have no other remedy in this, as in all other cases where they have no Judge on Earth, but to *appeal to Heaven*. [John Locke, *Two Treatises of Government* 392-393, 397 (Peter Laslett ed., 1967).]

tyranny, to promote the government's legitimacy, and to make government more efficient. *See generally* William Gwynn, *The Meaning of the Separation of Powers* (1965). John Locke, writing between 1679 and 1683, relied on his theory of separation to advance the argument for the Whig view of government. His ideas significantly influenced constitutional development in England and in America.

> In all Cases, whilst the Government subsists, *the Legislative is the Supream Power.* For what can give Laws to another, must needs be superiour to him....
>
> But because the Laws, that are at once, and in a short time made, have a constant and lasting force, and need a *perpetual Execution,* or an attendance thereunto: Therefore 'tis necessary there should be a *Power always in being,* which should see to the *Execution* of the Laws that are made, and remain in force. And thus the *Legislative* and *Executive Power* come often to be separated.
>
> There is another *Power* in every Commonwealth, which one may call *natural,* because it is that which answers to the Power every Man naturally had before he entered into Society. For though in a Commonwealth the Members of it are distinct Persons still in reference to one another, and as such are governed by the Laws of Society; yet in reference to the rest of Mankind, they make one Body, which is, as every Member of it before was, still in the State of Nature with the rest of Mankind. Hence it is, that the Controversies that happen between any Man of the Society with those that are out of it, are managed by the publick; and an injury done to a Member of their Body, engages the whole in the reparation of it. So that under this Consideration, the whole Community is one Body in the State of Nature, in respect of all other States or Persons out of its Community.
>
> This therefore contains the Power of War and Peace, Leagues and Alliances, and all the Transactions, with all Persons and Communities without the Commonwealth, and may be called *Federative,* if any one pleases. So the thing be understood, I am indifferent to the Name.
>
> These two Powers, *Executive* and *Federative,* though they be really distinct in themselves, yet one comprehending the *Execution* of the Municipal Laws of the Society *within* its self, upon all that are parts of it; the other the management of the *security and interest of the publick without,* with all those that it may receive benefit or damage from, yet they are always almost united. And though this *federative Power* in the well or ill management of it be of great moment to the Commonwealth, yet it is much less capable to be directed by antecedent, standing, positive Laws, than the *Executive;* and so must necessarily be left to the Prudence and Wisdom of those whose hands it is in, to be managed for the publick good. For the *Laws* that concern Subjects one amongst another, being to direct their actions, may well enough *precede* them. But what is to be done in reference to *Foreigners,* depending much upon their actions, and the variation of designs and interests, must be *left* in great part *to* the *Prudence* of those who have this Power committed to them, to be managed by the best of their Skill, for the advantage of the Commonwealth.
>
> Though, as I said, the *Executive* and *Federative Power* of every Community be really distinct in themselves, yet they are hardly to be separated, and placed, at the same time, in the hands of distinct Persons. For both of them requiring the force of the Society for their exercise, it is almost impracticable to place the Force of the Commonwealth in distinct, and not subordinate hands; or that the *Executive* and *Federative Power* should be *placed* in Persons that might act separately, whereby the Force of the Publick would be under different Commands: which would be apt sometime or other to cause disorder and ruine. [Locke, *supra,* at 382-386.]

B. Pre-Constitutional History and Political Theory in Europe

The judicial power was born as the third real power in England when Parliament assured the independence of the judges from the King's previously unfettered control over their removal. Yet the judges still were viewed as executive officers while in office. It was Montesquieu in his *Spirit of Laws*, published in 1748, who provided the theoretical challenge to the distinct federative power of the executive described by Locke. Montesquieu's theory subdivided the federative and the law enforcement powers of the executive, treated the judiciary as a distinct branch, and offered the tripartite separation that is reflected in the American Constitution. For Montesquieu, the preservation of liberty required such a separation:

> When the legislative and executive powers are united in the same person, or in the same body of magistracy, there can be no liberty; because apprehensions may arise, lest the same monarch or senate should enact tyrannical laws, to execute them in a tyrannical manner.
>
> Again, there is no liberty, if the power of judging be not separated from the legislative and executive powers. Were it joined with the legislative, the life and liberty of the subject would be exposed to arbitrary control; for the judge would be then the legislator. Were it joined to the executive power, the judge might behave with all the violence of an oppressor. [Charles Louis de Secondat, Baron de Montesquieu, *The Spirit of Laws* 202 (David Wallace Carrithers ed., 1977).]

The problem with the separation of powers theory, however, was that it failed to account for the real class conflicts and overlapping authority that actually characterized the British system. A second theory, that of mixed government, helped to harmonize theory and practice. According to mixed government theory, balance in government could be maintained by mixing classes and institutions of society—kings, lords, and commoners—and combining various primary forms of government, namely monarchy, aristocracy, and democracy. A systematic attempt at creating "counterpoisal pressures...might keep the system stable and healthy." Bernard Bailyn, *The Origins of American Politics* 20 (1970). Thus, separated branches would share all the government's powers, checking against abuses by any single group in society or in government. For example, broad prerogative powers did not necessarily always belong to the King unchecked by the Parliament. The King or his ministers could be criticized or even impeached for their misuse of power. Moreover, either branch could initiate or exercise a prerogative power.

Locke recognized the importance of balancing and mixing powers when he conceded that many things must be left to executive discretion, subject to nullification or modification by legislation. For Locke, both separation of powers and mixed government served to make the King subject to the representative Parliament. Thus, assuming that both the separation and mixed government theories of Locke and Montesquieu influenced the U.S. Constitution, the ambiguities of the American text might be quite intentional reflections of the essential fluidity of these concepts.

General theories of government were not the only European notions to influence the text of the Constitution. The Framers' views of war and peace, in their declared and undeclared forms, seem to be derived especially from Grotius, Pufendorf, Vattel, and Burlamaqui. Charles A. Lofgren, *War-Making Under the Constitution: The Original Understanding*, 81 Yale L.J. 672, 689-697 (1972). For Grotius, declared wars were "perfect," involving committed nations in opposition. Undeclared wars were "imperfect," and occurred in situations where the sovereign authorized private reprisals aimed at claiming property held by subjects of another sovereign. Hugo Grotius, *The Rights of Wars and Peace* 538-549 (Jean Barbeyrac trans., 1738) (1625). Burlamaqui argued that imperfect war and reprisals were often one and the same, but that a sovereign might itself engage in reprisals using its own forces:

> A perfect war is that, which entirely interrupts the tranquillity of the state, and lays a foundation for all possible acts of hostility. An imperfect war, on the contrary, is that, which does not entirely interrupt the peace, but only in certain particulars, the public tranquillity being in other respects undisturbed.
>
> This last species of war is generally called reprisals, of the nature which we shall here give some account. By reprisals then we mean *that imperfect kind of war, or those acts of hostility, which sovereigns exercise against each other, or, with their consent, their subjects, by seizing the persons or effects of the subjects of a foreign commonwealth, that refuseth to do us justice....* [II Jean Jacques Burlamaqui, *The Principles of Natural and Political Law* 180 (Thomas Nugent trans., 5th ed. 1807), *cited with approval in* Miller v. The Resolution, 2 U.S. (2 Dall.) 1, 21 (Ct. App. in Cases of Capture 1781).]

There was no consensus among the theorists about whether a declaration was necessary to initiate war, though no one argued that a declaration was required to wage a defensive war. Before the American Revolution, however, when such "declarations" were made, they were usually only formal, largely ceremonial announcements. Lofgren, *supra*, at 691-693.

Contemporaneous writings indicate that "a nation might 'declare' war, not only by a formal announcement, but also by an act of hostility." Ramsey, *supra* p. 11, at 1590. For example, Locke wrote:

> The State of War is a State of Enmity and Destruction; And therefore declaring by Word or Action, not a passionate or hasty, but a sedate settled Design, upon another Mans Life, puts him in a State of War with him against whom he has declared such an intention. [Locke, *supra* p. 13, at 278.]

According to Professor Ramsey, Locke, Blackstone, and other international law scholars used "declare" to mean "an action (taking up arms) that itself makes a statement." Ramsey, *supra*, at 1592. Launching an attack could constitute "declaring" war. *Id.* at 1636.

War making without a formal declaration was common in the eighteenth century, some of it under the collective noses of the soon-to-be American convention delegates. Between 1754 and 1756 the undeclared beginnings of the Seven Years War between Britain and France occurred mostly on American soil, and Americans were exposed to the undeclared war between Britain and France during the Revolutionary War.

The long-standing European practice of state-sanctioned private reprisals to satisfy private claims during peacetime all but disappeared during the first half of the eighteenth century. Yet sovereign states continued to press their own claims by reprisal, either through use of public forces or private ships, or by the issuance of letters of marque and reprisal. Indeed, recent English history known to the Americans included examples of state reprisals that resulted in general war.

This history underscores the importance of the Declaration and the Marque and Reprisal Clauses in the U.S. Constitution. The Framers knew from the European experience that war might be limited or complete, that limited hostilities were often authorized through letters of marque and reprisal, and that minor skirmishes or even major ones could begin by "Word or Action," as Locke put it. Lofgren, *supra* p. 15, at 693-697. *See generally* Lobel, *supra* p. 11.

C. THE AMERICAN EXPERIENCE PRIOR TO 1787

These British and European influences may have seemed secondary to the Framers compared with the lessons learned firsthand from state, colonial, and national governments prior to the Philadelphia Convention in 1787. Before the Revolution, the mood in the colonies was notoriously antiexecutive. While the structures of colonial governments varied, all but Connecticut and Rhode Island formally placed most of the important powers in their governors, including command of the military, a veto of legislation, authority to raise and spend funds on certain projects, and discretion to delay enforcement of legislation until approved in England. The colonial governors were mostly British agents and were widely disliked in the colonies, even though the colonists' complaints often were traceable to the actions of Parliament. Yet despite the theoretical preeminence of the governors, the legislatures dominated colonial government through fiscal initiatives, investigations, and various other measures, and they effectively controlled the governors, even in the exercise of war and foreign affairs powers. Sofaer, *supra* p. 13, at 15-17.

After the Revolution, constitutional theories of separation and mixed government seem to have been ignored, as seven of the eight state governments formed between 1776 and 1778 adopted constitutions that subordinated the executive to the legislature. A second wave of state constitution making, however, including in New York, Massachusetts, and New Hampshire, provided relatively greater authority for the governors. Yoo, *supra* p. 11, at 228-234. The new state legislatures responded early and often to popular local issues, sometimes restricting interstate commerce and undermining national stability. Eventually, as disorder and instability increased, many began to feel that a stronger national government was needed.

Again, early experiences with a national government had been marked by a pervasive antiexecutive mood. Beginning with the First Continental Congress in 1774, the national legislature was used by the states as a national executive, at first to conduct the Revolutionary War and later to manage other fiscal and national security tasks. But while Congress sought to carry out its policies through committees, boards, and appointed agents, it soon became apparent that the exigencies of the war were beyond the legislature's capacity to manage. Broad powers had to be delegated to the Board of War and to General George Washington. Nevertheless, Washington and other military leaders were often forced to choose between acting on the basis of ambiguous grants of authority or referring questions to Congress for decisions. This arrangement proved to be extremely inefficient.

> The subordination of the military to civilian control was a central axiom of the [English constitutional theory] that had led the colonists into rebellion. But broad agreement on this principle hardly provided Congress with useful guidelines for determining how direct and close its supervision of the army should be. . . . From 1775 to 1781, Congress was intimately concerned with the organization and administration of the army. It established rules of war and discipline, pay scales, terms of enlistment, and detailed regulations governing the procurement of supplies and provisions by the quartermaster and commissary departments; it also seemed to be regularly beset with the incessant complaints — sometimes petty, sometimes substantive, but never forgotten — of its officer corps. [Jack N. Rakove, *The Beginning of National Politics: An Interpretive History of the Continental Congress* 196-197 (1979).]

Congressional direction of the war even threatened the loyalty of its soldiers:

> Loyalty to the Congress was constantly strained but it never snapped; every soldier and officer may have cursed Congress fifty times for every word of praise, and most may have thought their hardships stemmed as much from congressional indifference, ineptness, and corruption as from unavoidable difficulties; but discontent rarely threatened to erupt into mutiny. [Forrest McDonald, *E Pluribus Unum: The Formation of the American Republic 1776-1790* (1965), at 12.]

The Continental Congress's cumbersome executive structures and its inability to raise money for the national government led many influential Americans, including Washington and Hamilton, to urge a strengthened national executive.

One consequence of the Revolutionary War was the emergence of a decidedly American view concerning standing armies. On the one hand, the War served to remind the 1787 Convention delegates that a regular standing army was needed to enable the nation to defend itself against another nation. As Alexander Hamilton later argued, the part-time militia was not an adequate substitute for a regular army:

> These garrisons must either be furnished by occasional detachments from the militia, or by permanent corps in the pay of the government. The first is impracticable; and if practicable, would be pernicious. The militia would not long, if at all, submit to be dragged from their occupations and families to perform that most disagreeable duty in times of profound peace. And if they could be prevailed upon or compelled to do it, the increased expense of a frequent rotation of service, and the loss of labor and disconcertion of the industrious pursuits of individuals, would form conclusive objections to the scheme. It would be as burdensome and injurious to the public as ruinous to private citizens. [*The Federalist No. 24*, at 161 (Alexander Hamilton) (Clinton Rossiter ed., 1961).]

On the other hand, the Americans knew that a standing army could be dangerous if not adequately controlled. They had come to deplore the use of the British army to enforce unpopular policies. The post-Revolutionary War solution, then, was to place responsibility for control of the military in the hands of the legislature. Legislative dominance of the military could be accomplished, it was first thought, by strict control over appropriations. The state assemblies controlled the governors' use of the military by imposing conditions on supply bills and even by specifying the conduct of military operations. *See* Banks & Raven-Hansen, *supra* p. 11, at 18-22; Elias E. Huzar, *The Purse and the Sword: Control of the Army by Congress Through Military Appropriations 1933-1950* (1950), at 18-23.

D. THE FRAMERS' VIEW

The adoption of the Articles of Confederation in 1781 did little to satisfy the demand for a stronger executive. First, the states retained sovereignty except to the extent that powers were "expressly" granted to the United States. Second, while Congress was given significant powers, including "the sole and exclusive right and power of determining on peace and war," the national government had no enforcement power and no independent executive. The business of governing thus continued much as it had before, with increasing delegations over foreign and military affairs to agents such as General Washington. As the national debt grew and the states threatened the national economy by disrupting commerce and issuing paper money, the national government proved unable to maintain order in the fragile Union. By early 1787 the Continental Congress could no longer ignore the demand for change.

Congress called upon the states to send delegates to a convention for the purpose of reforming the government of the Union. The 55 delegates representing all states except Rhode Island ranged from 81-year-old Benjamin Franklin to John Dickinson, who had refused to sign the Declaration of Independence. Most of the delegates had served in the Continental Congress, and most were wealthy. So much a part of the American elite were the delegates that Thomas Jefferson, who was in Paris and did not attend, called the convention "really an assembly of demi-gods." Max Farrand, *The Framing of the Constitution of the United States* 39 (1913).

Widespread demand for a stronger executive forced the Philadelphia delegates to confront basic structural questions: Should the executive be one person or many? Should there be an executive veto? How should the executive be selected, and should the executive serve more than one term? An even bigger issue was how to resolve the federalism question. The federalists wanted a stronger executive than did the states' righters, later known as antifederalists. Compared to these questions, the nature and scope of specific powers for the executive, especially in relation to those of Congress, were peripheral issues in 1787. Indeed, most of the attention given by the Framers and Ratifiers to issues of national security was directed toward national survival and state responsibilities, state incitements of other states and Indians, and state diplomatic activity.

1. The Convention

Unfortunately, records of deliberations at the Constitutional Convention are few and are unreliable. The meetings themselves were secret, and the Convention

Journal recorded only formal motions and votes. Many delegates took notes. The most extensive of these were James Madison's, though his were revised 30 years after the Convention. The various sources are compiled in the four-volume Max Farrand, *The Records of the Federal Convention of 1787* (rev. ed. 1937) (hereinafter *Records*).

There was a general consensus among Convention delegates about the need for a strengthened national government. They approved the so-called Virginia Plan, drafted by Madison, to give Congress the rights vested in it by the earlier Articles of Confederation. 3 *Records, supra,* at 593. They also agreed in principle to a single executive who would have explicit powers of execution and a conditional veto over legislation. It was clear from the start that the delegates wanted to create an executive who would be more than a mere agent of the legislature. They rejected a New Jersey Plan that would have provided for a relatively weak, plural, single-term executive, removable by a majority of the states, yet having the power "to direct all military operations." *Id.* at 611-613.

After additional debate the delegates instructed a Committee on Detail to prepare a draft Constitution. The resulting draft vested "The Executive Power of the United States . . . in a . . . President," who would be "Commander in Chief of the Army and Navy of the United States, and of the Militia of the several States." Congress was given the power to "make war," to appropriate funds, and "to call for the aid of the militia, in order to execute the laws of the Union, enforce treaties, suppress insurrections, and repel invasions." 2 *Records, supra,* at 167-172.

In the ensuing Convention debates on the draft, James Wilson of Pennsylvania opposed granting the House sole power to initiate revenue bills. Wilson's arguments and Edmund Randolph's prevailing response indicate a general understanding that the appropriations power would be employed to control the military. *Id.* at 273-274, 279.

Charles Pinckney of South Carolina complained that requiring the whole Congress to declare war would be cumbersome:

> Mr. Pinckney. . . . Its proceedings were too slow. It wd. meet but once a year. The Hs. of Reps. would be too numerous for such deliberations. The Senate would be the best depositary, being more acquainted with foreign affairs, and most capable of proper resolutions. If the States are equally represented in Senate, so as to give no advantage to large States, the power will notwithstanding be safe, as the small have their all at stake in such cases as well as the large States. It would be singular for one authority to make war, and another peace.
>
> Mr. Butler. The Objections agst the Legislature lie in a great degree agst the Senate. He was for vesting the power in the President, who will have all the requisite qualities, and will not make war but when the Nation will support it.
>
> Mr. M(adison) and Mr. Gerry moved to insert "*declare*," striking out "*make*" war; leaving to the Executive the power to repel sudden attacks.
>
> Mr. Sharman thought it stood very well. The Executive shd. be able to repel and not to commence war. "Make" better than "declare" the latter narrowing the power too much.
>
> Mr. Gerry never expected to hear in a republic a motion to empower the Executive alone to declare war.
>
> Mr. Elseworth. there is a material difference between the cases of making *war*, and making *peace*. It shd. be more easy to get out of war, than into it. War also is a simple and overt declaration. peace attended with intricate & secret negociations.

D. The Framers' View

> Mr. Mason was agst giving the power of war to the Executive, because not (safely) to be trusted with it; or to the Senate, because not so constructed as to be entitled to it. He was for clogging rather than facilitating war; but for facilitating peace. He preferred "*declare*" to "*make*." [*Id.* at 318-319.]

In support of Madison's motion, Rufus King of Massachusetts argued "that 'make' war might be understood to 'conduct' it which was an Executive function." *Id.* at 319.

Eventually, Pinckney's motion to vest the war power solely in the Senate was overwhelmingly rejected and Madison's motion was approved. The Journal records and Madison's notes unfortunately report inconsistent tallies on the two votes taken on Madison's motion, one before and one after King's speech, making it impossible to be certain about the meaning of the change. Madison and Gerry probably wanted the President to be able to respond to "sudden attacks" without a declaration of war, which some delegates thought was intended by the original language. Others, including King, wanted to be certain it was understood that the conduct of a war after its initiation was for the executive. No better consensus from the debate can be safely stated, although nothing in the change suggests an intention to allow the President to "make" war without a declaration. *See* Sofaer, *supra* p. 13, at 31-32. Even Hamilton, ardent advocate of a strong executive, favored limiting the executive in war making and would have given the Senate the declaration power, leaving to the President the "direction of war when authorized or begun," 1 *Records, supra*, at 292, though he knew that many contemporary wars were not technically declared. Lofgren, *supra* p. 15, at 680.

Viewing the larger debate and the process of drafting the Constitution does help place the war powers allocation question in some perspective. First, the draft presented to the Convention by the Committee on Detail assigned the power "to make war" to Congress, though the point had scarcely been debated. The same Committee named the President as Commander in Chief without any record of controversy. The President was to be first general, but was not to initiate hostilities. As for military action short of declared war, the Committee on Detail did not include in the list of powers given to the new legislature the power to issue letters of marque and reprisal, which the old Congress enjoyed under the Articles. At Pinckney's request such language was added and approved without discussion. 2 *Records, supra*, at 324, 326. We cannot ascertain from the Convention records whether this action was meant to ensure congressional primacy over undeclared hostilities. However, the contemporaneous understanding about the use of letters of marque and reprisal suggests that purpose.

Pinckney's motion to vest the war power in the Senate included granting to the Senate the power "to make treaties." 3 *Records, supra*, at 427. As in the debate on the War Declaration Clause, Madison and others eventually cautioned against unfettered Senate power over treaties. After floor discussion, in which Madison urged a role for the President out of fear of parochialism in the Senate, a committee was formed, which reported the following language: "The president, by and with the advice and consent of the Senate, shall have power to make treaties.... But no treaty shall be binding without the consent of two-thirds of the members present." 2 *Records, supra*, at 495. James Wilson proposed adding "and House of Representatives" after the word "Senate," on grounds that treaties should be fully sanctioned as laws if they were to operate as laws. Following objections from Robert Sherman and others that the secrecy that would necessarily attend some treaty negotiations made referral to the House impractical, Wilson's motion was defeated. *Id.* at 538. Among several other failed amendments was a proposal by Madison to permit the Senate alone to make peace treaties. Madison argued that the President "would necessarily derive so much power and importance from a state of war that he might be tempted, if authorized, to impede a treaty of peace." *Id.* at 540.

While the treaty-making powers were being shaped, the eventual Supremacy Clause was drafted to make "all treaties made and ratified under the authority of the United States," along with laws enacted by the Congress, "the supreme law." *Id.* at 28. Supported by Madison's admonition that federal dominance in foreign relations was necessary "to the efficacy and security of the general government," *id.* at 27, the Supremacy Clause became a part of the Constitution, along with the provision in Article I, §10 restricting states from entering into treaties or entering into any "agreement or compact" with a foreign nation without the consent of Congress. Complaints from those who feared the loss of state sovereignty and from others who feared that omission of the House of Representatives from the treaty-making process could lead to abuse of the power did not sway the delegates. Nor did the Framers prescribe any limits on the subject matter of treaties or supply a rule for resolving a conflict between a treaty and the Constitution or the laws.

Meanwhile, the delegates were gradually constructing an executive branch that would be unitary and independent and vested with considerable authority. In keeping with their general interest in balancing the powers of government, the President's selection, vested in the Congress by the Committee on Detail, became an election by state electors for an unrestricted number of four-year terms. The President was also given a conditional veto over legislation. Once the independence of the office was established, the delegates broadened the grounds for impeachment by the legislature to provide a check in the other direction. But they voted down proposals to allow Congress to define the content of "executive power," and no general argument was advanced against Congress's ability to delegate powers to the executive. Sofaer, *supra* p. 13, at 36-38, 56; Reveley, *supra* p. 13, at 98-99. In the end, the delegates themselves did little to define the executive.

2. Ratification

There remained the difficult task of persuading the state ratifying conventions to approve the new Constitution. The ensuing debates in the states, like those in Philadelphia, scarcely addressed the question of how and by which institution the new government would initiate war. Indeed, the Confederation government already had the war-making power, and the question of initiating war was eclipsed by the more immediately volatile issues of federal, state, or civilian-military sovereignty. At the same time, there was debate about supporting an existing war through taxation, about control of the military, and about the use of standing armies.

D. The Framers' View

Despite the limited debates on war-making powers, there is indirect evidence from the ratification period that reveals more clearly how the war-making provisions were understood. Because the Philadelphia debates were secret, the ratifiers themselves had to rely on the words of the Constitution and on the propaganda of the time to establish the meaning of the document.

The Federalist Papers, written by Madison, Hamilton, and Jay to promote ratification, indicate that the new war declaration clause was practically the same as the earlier Articles' grant to Congress of "determining on" war. In *The Federalist No. 41*, Madison wrote: "The existing confederation establishes this power in the most ample form." *The Federalist No. 41*, at 256 (James Madison) (Clinton Rossiter ed., 1961). Delegate Wilson made the same point at the Pennsylvania convention. He rejected the notion of a unilateral presidential power over war making, remarking that the new "system will not hurry us into war.... It will not be in the power of a single man, or a single body of men, to involve us in such distress; for the important power of declaring war is vested in the legislature at large." 1 *Debates in the Several State Conventions on the Adoption of the Federal Constitution* 528 (Jonathan Elliot ed., 1888) (hereinafter *Elliot's Debates*).

There is similar evidence that the Commander-in-Chief power was viewed narrowly. In *The Federalist No. 69*, Hamilton compared the Commander in Chief's prerogative to that of the British Crown, finding the former "much inferior."

> It would amount to nothing more than the supreme command and direction of the military... while that of the British King extends to the *declaring* of war, and to the *raising and regulating* of fleets and armies — all which by the Constitution under consideration, would appertain to the legislature. [*The Federalist No. 69*, at 418 (Alexander Hamilton) (Clinton Rossiter ed., 1961).]

The fact that the authors of the *Federalist Papers* described the assignment of war powers in such terms suggests that they believed this view would be well received in the states.

Madison insisted in general argument that pure separation of the nation's powers was neither desirable nor intended by the theorists. Instead, mixed powers and checks and balances were essential:

> Ambition must be made to counteract ambition.... But what is government itself but the greatest of all reflections on human nature? If men were angels, no government would be necessary. If angels were to govern men, neither external nor internal controls on government would be necessary. In framing a government which is to be administered by men over men, the great difficulty lies in this: you must first enable the government to control the governed; and in the next place oblige it to control itself. A dependence on the people is, no doubt, the primary control on the government; but experience has taught mankind the necessity of auxiliary precautions. [*The Federalist No. 51*, at 322 (James Madison) (Clinton Rossiter ed., 1961).]

For Madison, the balance was completed by having a dominant bicameral legislature and a partial veto in the executive. The House retained the original appropriations power, while the Senate had a special role in treaties and appointments. Similarly, the strong and independent President would be able to prevent legislative tyranny. Thus, separation ensured independence while it divided responsibilities along functional lines.

To be sure, there were arguments during this period that a stronger executive would promote governmental efficiency and dispatch. For example, it might have been inferred from the proposed government's ability to raise and support armed forces, and thereby to deter a surprise attack on the United States, that the President was empowered to respond to such a sudden attack. However, the arguments based on efficiency and dispatch were not made in connection with initiating war. *See, e.g., The Federalist No. 64*, at 12-13 (John Jay) (Clinton Rossiter ed., 1961) (discussing the treaty power).

During the South Carolina debate on the Constitution, convention delegate Major Pierce Butler explained that, while the initial proposal to vest the treaty power solely in the Senate was defeated as "inimical to the genious of a republic, by destroying the necessary balance," a motion to give the power to the President was overcome as "throwing into his hands the influence of a monarch, having an opportunity of involving his country in a war whenever he wished...." 4 *Elliot's Debates, supra,* at 262-263. Only when it was suggested that the House of Representatives join the Senate in approving treaties was it noted that "negotiations always required the greatest secrecy, which could not be expected in a large body." *Id.*

Throughout the ratification process, the objective of the federalists was to defend the entire proposed national government, not one branch of it at the expense of another. For example, Hamilton argued that the two-year limit on military appropriations would prevent the legislature from giving the executive power to build a large standing army. But his objective was to persuade ratifiers to support the proposed new government, not to aggrandize legislative power. Reveley, *supra* p. 13, at 105. In addition, to the extent that the vagueness in describing the President's powers caused fears among the ratifiers, they were substantially mollified by the comforting, though unspoken, assumption that Washington would become the first President, and that he would never abuse his powers.

The ratification debates tend to confirm that the "declare" language could not fairly be read to limit Congress to formal war-initiation. No ratifier argued that the President has unilateral power to engage in hostilities without congressional approval in the absence of a sudden attack. Undeclared wars were thought to be possible, but it is not altogether clear under what circumstances and by whom they could be initiated. *See* Lofgren, *supra* p. 15, at 694-700.

New Hampshire became the necessary ninth state to ratify the Constitution in June 1788, and the new government officially commenced in March 1789. In that year, Jefferson wrote to Madison that "[w]e have already given in example one effectual check to the Dog of War by transferring the power of letting him loose from the Executive to the Legislative body, from those who are to spend to those who are to pay." 15 *The Papers of Thomas Jefferson* 397 (Julian P. Boyd ed., 1958).

Still, careful analysis of the original understanding leaves much unsettled. No provision or argument was made against legislative delegations of military matters to the executive; nor were the required indicia of a valid delegation spelled out. Similarly, there is no evidence that Congress was barred from authorizing hostilities without a declaration of war. The President's authority to "repel sudden attacks" was not clarified; nor was there any indication of what

D. The Framers' View

constitutes an attack or when an attack should be considered imminent. Yet *The Federalist* strongly suggests that the textual uncertainties and overlaps in function and power were intended as an integral part of the overall design. Sofaer, *supra* p. 13, at 58-59.

NOTES AND QUESTIONS

1. *The Preamble.* Does the language of the Preamble to the Constitution help to describe the locus or scope of authority for keeping the nation secure? Suppose that some government action demonstrably harmed the "common defence," or threatened to do so. Could the Preamble be invoked to stop it? *See* Arthur Selwyn Miller, *Nuclear Weapons and Constitutional Law,* in *Nuclear Weapons and Law* 235, 241-243 (Arthur Selwyn Miller & Martin Feinrider eds., 1984).

2. *Textual Conflicts and Silences in the National Security Constitution.* Can you say exactly what provisions of Articles I and II might bring the President and Congress into conflict in providing for the national security, and why?

Various national defense issues are not addressed at all in the text of the Constitution. For example, may the President solicit the financial support of foreign countries for military initiatives not authorized by Congress? May the Congress authorize and appropriate funds for the purchase of military hardware and then restrict its use by the President? May the courts direct the President to disclose sensitive information about foreign affairs to Congress? How should such questions be resolved?

3. *Anti-Executive Sentiments.* Are you clear on the reasons for the strong anti-executive sentiment in America before the 1787 Constitutional Convention? Can you see any of that sentiment reflected in the text of the Constitution or in the ratification debates? Do you see evidence of it in political debates today about national security issues?

4. *A Merely "Juridical" War Power?* Professor John Yoo maintains that the Declaration Clause reflects the Framers' understanding of eighteenth century practice that a declaration of war is not required to authorize combat. Instead, he argues, a declaration simply reflects Congress's "judgment of a current status of relations, not an authorization of war." Yoo, *supra* p. 11, at 248. According to Professor Yoo, in this role Congress performs a judicial function rather than its typical enactment of positive law. *Id.* at 248-249. How would you respond to Professor Yoo's assessment?

Professor Yoo argues further that the Constitution permits the President to initiate wars unless Congress acts through an appropriations restriction or impeachment to stop him. *Id.* at 174. Professor Yoo finds partial support for his conclusion in Article I, §10, which states, "No State shall...engage in war." Thus, "if the Framers intended to require congressional consent before war, they...were perfectly capable of making their wishes known.... Had the Framers intended to prohibit the President from initiating wars, they easily could have incorporated a Section 10 analogue into Article II." *Id.* at 255. What are the strengths and weaknesses of this argument?

5. *Tactical War Powers.* There is ample evidence that the legislature was not meant to make tactical military decisions once war was initiated. But where exactly does the legislature's responsibility stop? Just how much autonomy should the President enjoy as Commander in Chief? If the Framers had addressed these questions, what basic political values would have shaped their debate?

6. *An Obsolete War Power?* "That was then; this is now," the saying goes. Why should we care what the Framers intended? Of what relevance today is the "original understanding" of the Constitution when, from a distance of two centuries, we have to decide whether the President can unilaterally send American warships into the Persian Gulf, or whether Congress can limit the President's ability to use nuclear weapons first, or whether the courts can help decide either question?

7. *Further Reading.* In addition to the sources cited in this chapter, many other scholars have examined the original understanding of the national security provisions of the Constitution. *See, e.g.,* Philip Bobbitt, *War Powers: An Essay on John Hart Ely's War and Responsibility: Constitutional Lessons of Vietnam and Its Aftermath,* 92 Mich. L. Rev. 1364 (1994); Robert H. Bork, *Erosion and the President's Power in Foreign Affairs,* 68 Wash. U. L.Q. 693 (1990); Edward S. Corwin et al., *The President: Office and Powers 1787-1984* (5th rev. ed. 1984); Michael J. Glennon, *Constitutional Diplomacy* (1990); Henry P. Monaghan, *Presidential War-Making,* 50 B.U. L. Rev. 19 (1970); Eugene R. Rostow, *"Once More Unto the Breach": The War Powers Resolution Revisited,* 21 Val. U. L. Rev. 1 (1986); Jane E. Stromseth, *Understanding Constitutional War Powers Today: Why Methodology Matters,* 106 Yale L.J. 845 (1996); William M. Treanor, *Fame, the Founding, and the Power to Declare War,* 82 Cornell L. Rev. 695 (1997); Symposium, *Foreign Affairs and the Constitution: The Roles of Congress, the President, and the Courts,* 43 U. Miami L. Rev. 1 (1988); Symposium, *Foreign Affairs Law at the End of the Century, Part I: History of Foreign Affairs Law,* 70 U. Colo. L. Rev. 1109 (1999); Exchange, *War Powers,* 69 U. Chi. L. Rev. 1543 (2002).

3

The Gloss of History: An Introduction to the Separation of National Security Powers

Almost 200 years after the Constitutional Convention, a leading student of the presidency flatly rejected the supposition that the Convention created a government of separated powers. "It did nothing of the sort. Rather, it created a government of separated institutions *sharing* powers." Richard E. Neustadt, *Presidential Power* 26 (2d ed. 1980). Even those who disagree that the branches share power would today have to agree that they share authority over the same subjects, although they usually exercise it in different forms.

The more astute observers of the proposed constitutional design recognized these truisms from the start. "How is the executive?" asked a delegate to the Virginia ratifying convention. "Contrary to the opinion of all the best writers, blended with the legislative. We have asked for bread, and they have given us a stone." Louis Fisher, *President and Congress* 24 (1972). Indeed, the blending was intended and foreseen by some of the Framers. In any event, the actual experience of government under the Constitution finally wore away any lingering doubts.

In this chapter we introduce the framework of separated institutions sharing national security authority, and its historical gloss, by analyzing Youngstown Sheet & Tube Co. v. Sawyer, 343 U.S. 579 (1952) (*The Steel Seizure Case*), and the grouping of presidential powers that Justice Jackson described in his concurring opinion. *The Steel Seizure Case* is memorable for the apparent simplicity and formalism of Justice Black's opinion for the Court. A careful reading and comparison of the several concurring and dissenting opinions, however, suggests that a majority of the Justices took an approach to the separation of powers that is very different from Justice Black's. As you read the opinions, try to identify each source of power invoked on the President's behalf and to understand how each Justice would limit that power. Count heads, too: how many Justices agree on the limits associated with each source of presidential power? You may find it helpful to list the Justices across the top of a piece of paper and claims of presidential power down the side, and then fill in the blanks as you read.

A. *THE STEEL SEIZURE CASE* AND ITS THEORIES OF PRESIDENTIAL POWER

Youngstown Sheet & Tube Co. v. Sawyer
(*The Steel Seizure Case*)
United States Supreme Court, 1952
343 U.S. 579

Mr. Justice BLACK delivered the opinion of the Court. We are asked to decide whether the President was acting within his constitutional power when he issued an order directing the Secretary of Commerce to take possession of and operate most of the Nation's steel mills. The mill owners argue that the President's order amounts to lawmaking, a legislative function which the Constitution has expressly confided to the Congress and not to the President. The Government's position is that the order was made on findings of the President that his action was necessary to avert a national catastrophe which would inevitably result from a stoppage of steel production, and that in meeting this grave emergency the President was acting within the aggregate of his constitutional powers as the Nation's Chief Executive and the Commander in Chief of the Armed Forces of the United States....

[The facts are set forth in Exec. Order No. 10,340, 17 Fed. Reg. 3139 (1952), which was reproduced in an appendix to the Court's opinion, 343 U.S. at 583-589. A copy of the order as it was originally published is reproduced *infra* pp. 30-31.]

...The Secretary immediately issued his own possessory orders, calling upon the presidents of the various seized companies to serve as operating managers for the United States. They were directed to carry on their activities in accordance with regulations and directions of the Secretary. The next morning the President sent a message to Congress reporting his action.... Twelve days later he sent a second message.... Congress has taken no action.

Obeying the Secretary's orders under protest, the companies brought proceedings against him in the District Court.... Holding against the Government on all points, the District Court on April 30 issued a preliminary injunction restraining the Secretary from "continuing the seizure and possession of the plants...and from acting under the purported authority of Executive Order No. 10340."

The President's power, if any, to issue the order must stem either from an act of Congress or from the Constitution itself. There is no statute that expressly authorizes the President to take possession of property as he did here. Nor is there any act of Congress to which our attention has been directed from which such a power can fairly be implied. Indeed, we do not understand the Government to rely on statutory authorization for this seizure. There are two statutes which do authorize the President to take both personal and real property under certain conditions. However, the Government admits that these conditions were not met and that the President's order was not rooted in either of the statutes. The Government refers to the seizure provisions of one of these statutes (§201(b) of the Defense Production Act) as "much too cumbersome, involved, and time-consuming for the crisis which was at hand."

A. *The Steel Seizure Case* and Its Theories of Presidential Power

Moreover, the use of the seizure technique to solve labor disputes in order to prevent work stoppages was not only unauthorized by any congressional enactment; prior to this controversy, Congress had refused to adopt that method of settling labor disputes. When the Taft-Hartley Act was under consideration in 1947, Congress rejected an amendment which would have authorized such governmental seizures in cases of emergency. Apparently it was thought that the technique of seizure, like that of compulsory arbitration, would interfere with the process of collective bargaining. Consequently, the plan Congress adopted in that Act did not provide for seizure under any circumstances. Instead, the plan sought to bring about settlements by use of the customary devices of mediation, conciliation, investigation by boards of inquiry, and public reports. In some instances temporary injunctions were authorized to provide cooling-off periods. All this failing, unions were left free to strike after a secret vote by employees as to whether they wished to accept their employers' final settlement offer.

It is clear that if the President had authority to issue the order he did, it must be found in some provision of the Constitution. And it is not claimed that express constitutional language grants this power to the President. The contention is that presidential power should be implied from the aggregate of his powers under the Constitution. Particular reliance is placed on provisions in Article II which say that "the executive Power shall be vested in a President..."; that "he shall take Care that the Laws be faithfully executed"; and that he "shall be Commander in Chief of the Army and Navy of the United States."

The order cannot properly be sustained as an exercise of the President's military power as Commander in Chief of the Armed Forces. The Government attempts to do so by citing a number of cases upholding broad powers in military commanders engaged in day-to-day fighting in a theater of war. Such cases need not concern us here. Even though "theater of war" be an expanding concept, we cannot with faithfulness to our constitutional system hold that the Commander in Chief of the Armed Forces has the ultimate power as such to take possession of private property in order to keep labor disputes from stopping production. This is a job for the Nation's lawmakers, not for its military authorities.

Nor can the seizure order be sustained because of the several constitutional provisions that grant executive power to the President. In the framework of our Constitution, the President's power to see that the laws are faithfully executed refutes the idea that he is to be a lawmaker. The Constitution limits his functions in the lawmaking process to the recommending of laws he thinks wise and the vetoing of laws he thinks bad. And the Constitution is neither silent nor equivocal about who shall make laws which the President is to execute. The first section of the first article says that "All legislative powers herein granted shall be vested in a Congress of the United States...." After granting many powers to the Congress, Article I goes on to provide that Congress may "make all laws which shall be necessary and proper for carrying into Execution the foregoing Powers, and all other Powers vested by this Constitution in the Government of the United States, or in any Department or Officer thereof."

The President's order does not direct that a congressional policy be executed in a manner prescribed by Congress — it directs that a presidential policy be executed in a manner prescribed by the President. The preamble of the order itself, like that of many statutes, sets out reasons why the President believes

FEDERAL REGISTER

VOLUME 17 / 1934 / NUMBER 71

Washington, Thursday, April 10, 1952

EXECUTIVE ORDER 10340

DIRECTING THE SECRETARY OF COMMERCE TO TAKE POSSESSION OF AND OPERATE THE PLANTS AND FACILITIES OF CERTAIN STEEL COMPANIES

WHEREAS on December 16, 1950, I proclaimed the existence of a national emergency which requires that the military, naval, air, and civilian defenses of this country be strengthened as speedily as possible to the end that we may be able to repel any and all threats against our national security and to fulfill our responsibilities in the efforts being made throughout the United Nations and otherwise to bring about a lasting peace; and

WHEREAS American fighting men ber 22, 1951, pursuant to Executive Order No. 10233, and a strike has been called for 12:01 A. M. April 9, 1952; and

WHEREAS a work stoppage would immediately jeopardize and imperil our national defense and the defense of those joined with us in resisting aggression, and would add to the continuing danger of our soldiers, sailors, and airmen engaged in combat in the field; and

WHEREAS in order to assure the continued availability of steel and steel products during the existing emergency, it is necessary that the United States take possession of and operate the plants, facilities, and other property of the said companies as hereinafter provided:

that such activities do not interfere with the operation of such plants, facilities, and other properties.

4. Except so far as the Secretary of Commerce shall otherwise provide from time to time, the managements of the plants, facilities, and other properties possession of which is taken pursuant to this order shall continue their functions, including the collection and disbursement of funds in the usual and ordinary course of business in the names of their respective companies and by means of any instrumentalities used by such companies.

5. Except so far as the Secretary of Commerce may otherwise direct, existing rights and obligations of such companies shall remain in full force and

A. *The Steel Seizure Case* and Its Theories of Presidential Power

and fighting men of other nations of the United Nations are now engaged in deadly combat with the forces of aggression in Korea, and forces of the United States are stationed elsewhere overseas for the purpose of participating in the defense of the Atlantic Community against aggression; and

WHEREAS the weapons and other materials needed by our armed forces and by those joined with us in the defense of the free world are produced to a great extent in this country, and steel is an indispensable component of substantially all of such weapons and materials; and

WHEREAS steel is likewise indispensable to the carrying out of programs of the Atomic Energy Commission of vital importance to our defense efforts; and

WHEREAS a continuing and uninterrupted supply of steel is also indispensable to the maintenance of the economy of the United States, upon which our military strength depends; and

WHEREAS a controversy has arisen between certain companies in the United States producing and fabricating steel and the elements thereof and certain of their workers represented by the United Steel Workers of America, CIO, regarding terms and conditions of employment; and

WHEREAS the controversy has not been settled through the processes of collective bargaining or through the efforts of the Government, including those of the Wage Stabilization Board, to which the controversy was referred on December

NOW, THEREFORE, by virtue of the authority vested in me by the Constitution and laws of the United States, and as President of the United States and Commander in Chief of the armed forces of the United States, it is hereby ordered as follows:

1. The Secretary of Commerce is hereby authorized and directed to take possession of all or such of the plants, facilities, and other property of the companies named in the list attached hereto, or any part thereof, as he may deem necessary in the interests of national defense; and to operate or to arrange for the operation thereof and to do all things necessary for, or incidental to, such operation.

2. In carrying out this order the Secretary of Commerce may act through or with the aid of such public or private instrumentalities or persons as he may designate; and all Federal agencies shall cooperate with the Secretary of Commerce to the fullest extent possible in carrying out the purposes of this order.

3. The Secretary of Commerce shall determine and prescribe terms and conditions of employment under which the plants, facilities, and other properties possession of which is taken pursuant to this order shall be operated. The Secretary of Commerce shall recognize the rights of workers to bargain collectively through representatives of their own choosing and to engage in concerted activities for the purpose of collective bargaining, adjustment of grievances, or other mutual aid or protection, provided

effect, and there may be made, in due course, payments of dividends on stock, and of principal, interest, sinking funds, and all other distributions upon bonds, debentures, and other obligations, and expenditures may be made for other ordinary corporate or business purposes.

6. Whenever in the judgment of the Secretary of Commerce further possession and operation by him of any plant, facility, or other property is no longer necessary or expedient in the interest of national defense, and the Secretary has reason to believe that effective future operation is assured, he shall return the possession and operation of such plant, facility, or other property to the company in possession and control thereof at the time possession was taken under this order.

7. The Secretary of Commerce is authorized to prescribe and issue such regulations and orders not inconsistent herewith as he may deem necessary or desirable for carrying out the purposes of this order; and he may delegate and authorize subdelegation of such of his functions under this order as he may deem desirable.

HARRY S. TRUMAN

THE WHITE HOUSE,
April 8th, 1952; 9:50 p. m. e. s. t.

certain policies should be adopted, proclaims these policies as rules of conduct to be followed, and again, like a statute, authorizes a government official to promulgate additional rules and regulations consistent with the policy proclaimed and needed to carry that policy into execution. The power of Congress to adopt such public policies as those proclaimed by the order is beyond question. It can authorize the taking of private property for public use. It can make laws regulating the relationships between employers and employees, prescribing rules designed to settle labor disputes, and fixing wages and working conditions in certain fields of our economy. The Constitution does not subject this lawmaking power of Congress to presidential or military supervision or control.

It is said that other Presidents without congressional authority have taken possession of private business enterprises in order to settle labor disputes. But even if this be true, Congress has not thereby lost its exclusive constitutional authority to make laws necessary and proper to carry out the powers vested by the Constitution "in the Government of the United States, or in any Department or Officer thereof."

The Founders of this Nation entrusted the lawmaking power to the Congress alone in both good and bad times. It would do no good to recall the historical events, the fears of power and the hopes for freedom that lay behind their choice. Such a review would but confirm our holding that this seizure order cannot stand.

The judgment of the District Court is affirmed.

Mr. Justice FRANKFURTER, concurring.... The issue before us can be met, and therefore should be, without attempting to define the President's powers comprehensively....

...We must therefore put to one side consideration of what powers the President would have had if there had been no legislation whatever bearing on the authority asserted by the seizure, or if the seizure had been only for a short, explicitly temporary period, to be terminated automatically unless Congressional approval were given. These and other questions, like or unlike, are not now here....

...No room for doubt remains that the proponents as well as the opponents of the bill which became the Labor Management Relations Act of 1947 clearly understood that as a result of that legislation the only recourse for preventing a shutdown in any basic industry, after failure of mediation, was Congress. Authorization for seizure as an available remedy for potential dangers was unequivocally put aside....

...Previous seizure legislation had subjected the powers granted to the President to restrictions of varying degrees of stringency. Instead of giving him even limited powers, Congress in 1947 deemed it wise to require the President, upon failure of attempts to reach a voluntary settlement, to report to Congress if he deemed the power of seizure a needed shot for his locker. The President could not ignore the specific limitations of prior seizure statutes. No more could he act in disregard of the limitation put upon seizure by the 1947 act.

It cannot be contended that the President would have had power to issue this order had Congress explicitly negated such authority in formal legislation. Congress has expressed its will to withhold this power from the President as though it had said so in so many words. The authoritatively expressed purpose of

Congress to disallow such power to the President and to require him, when in his mind the occasion arose for such a seizure, to put the matter to Congress and ask for specific authority from it, could not be more decisive if it had been written into §§206-210 of the Labor Management Relations Act of 1947....

... The utmost that the Korean conflict may imply is that it may have been desirable to have given the President further authority, a freer hand in these matters. Absence of authority in the President to deal with a crisis does not imply want of power in the Government. Conversely the fact that power exists in the Government does not vest it in the President. The need for new legislation does not enact it. Nor does it repeal or amend existing law....

It is one thing to draw an intention of Congress from general language and to say that Congress would have explicitly written what is inferred, where Congress has not addressed itself to a specific situation. It is quite impossible, however, when Congress did specifically address itself to a problem, as Congress did to that of seizure, to find secreted in the interstices of legislation the very grant of power which Congress consciously withheld. To find authority so explicitly withheld is not merely to disregard in a particular instance the clear will of Congress. It is to disrespect the whole legislative process and the constitutional division of authority between President and Congress....

To be sure, the content of the three authorities of Government is not to be derived from an abstract analysis. The areas are partly interacting, not wholly disjointed. The Constitution is a framework for Government. Therefore the way the framework has consistently operated fairly establishes that it has operated according to its true nature. Deeply embedded traditional ways of conducting government cannot supplant the Constitution or legislation, but they give meaning to the words of a text or supply them. It is an inadmissibly narrow conception of American constitutional law to confine it to the words of the Constitution and to disregard the gloss which life has written upon them. In short, a systematic, unbroken, executive practice, long pursued to the knowledge of the Congress and never before questioned, engaged in by presidents who have also sworn to uphold the Constitution, making as it were such exercise of power part of the structure of our Government, may be treated as a gloss on "executive Power" vested in the President by §1 of Art. II....

... In the *Midwest Oil* case [236 U.S. 459 (1915)], lands which Congress had opened for entry were, over a period of 80 years and in 252 instances, and by Presidents learned and unlearned in the law, temporarily withdrawn from entry so as to enable Congress to deal with such withdrawals. No remotely comparable practice can be vouched for executive seizure of property at a time when this country was not at war, in the only constitutional way in which it can be at war. It would pursue the irrelevant to reopen the controversy over the constitutionality of some acts of Lincoln during the Civil War.... Suffice it to say that he seized railroads in territory where armed hostilities had already interrupted the movement of troops to the beleaguered Capital, and his order was ratified by the Congress.

The only other instances of seizures are those during the periods of the first and second world wars. In his eleven seizures of industrial facilities, President Wilson acted, or at least purported to act, under authority granted by Congress. Thus his seizures cannot be adduced as interpretations by a President of his own powers in the absence of statute.

Down to the World War II period, then, the record is barren of instances comparable to the one before us. Of twelve seizures by President Roosevelt prior to the enactment of the War Labor Disputes Act in June, 1943, three were sanctioned by existing law, and six others were effected after Congress, on December 8, 1941, had declared the existence of a state of war. In this case, reliance on the powers that flow from declared war has been commendably disclaimed by the Solicitor General. Thus the list of executive assertions of the power of seizure in circumstances comparable to the present reduces to three in the six-month period from June to December of 1941. We need not split hairs in comparing those actions to the one before us, though much might be said by way of differentiation. Without passing on their validity, as we are not called upon to do, it suffices to say that these three isolated instances do not add up, either in number, scope, duration or contemporaneous legal justification, to the kind of executive construction of the Constitution revealed in the *Midwest Oil* case. Nor do they come to us sanctioned by long-continued acquiescence of Congress giving decisive weight in a construction by the Executive of its powers....

Mr. Justice DOUGLAS, concurring.... The legislative nature of the action taken by the President seems clear to me. When the United States takes over an industrial plant to settle a labor controversy, it is condemning property. The seizure of the plant is a taking in the constitutional sense....

But there is a duty to pay for all property taken by the Government. The command of the Fifth Amendment is that no "private property be taken for public use, without just compensation."...

The President has no power to raise revenues. That power is in the Congress by Article I, Section 8 of the Constitution.... The branch of government that has the power to pay compensation for a seizure is the only one able to authorize a seizure or make lawful one that the President has effected....

Stalemates may occur when emergencies mount and the Nation suffers for lack of harmonious, reciprocal action between the White House and Capitol Hill. That is a risk inherent in our system of separation of powers. The tragedy of such stalemates might be avoided by allowing the President the use of some legislative authority. The Framers with memories of the tyrannies produced by a blending of executive and legislative power rejected that political arrangement. Some future generation may, however, deem it so urgent that the President have legislative authority that the Constitution will be amended. We could not sanction the seizures and condemnations of the steel plants in this case without reading Article II as giving the President not only the power to execute the laws but to make some....

Mr. Justice JACKSON, concurring in the judgment and opinion of the Court.... A judge, like an executive adviser, may be surprised at the poverty of really useful and unambiguous authority applicable to concrete problems of executive power as they actually present themselves. Just what our forefathers did envision, or would have envisioned had they foreseen modern conditions, must be divined from materials almost as enigmatic as the dreams Joseph was called upon to interpret for Pharaoh. A century and a half of partisan debate and scholarly speculation yields no net result but only supplies more or less apt quotations from respected sources on each side of any question. They largely

A. *The Steel Seizure Case* and Its Theories of Presidential Power

cancel each other. And court decisions are indecisive because of the judicial practice of dealing with the largest questions in the most narrow way.

The actual art of governing under our Constitution does not and cannot conform to judicial definitions of the power of any of its branches based on isolated clauses or even single Articles torn from context. While the Constitution diffuses power the better to secure liberty, it also contemplates that practice will integrate the dispersed powers into a workable government. It enjoins upon its branches separateness but interdependence, autonomy but reciprocity. Presidential powers are not fixed but fluctuate, depending upon their disjunction or conjunction with those of Congress. We may well begin by a somewhat oversimplified grouping of practical situations in which a President may doubt, or others may challenge, his powers, and by distinguishing roughly the legal consequences of this factor of relativity.

1. When the President acts pursuant to an express or implied authorization of Congress, his authority is at its maximum, for it includes all that he possesses in his own right plus all that Congress can delegate.[2] In these circumstances, and in these only, may he be said (for what it may be worth) to personify the federal sovereignty. If his act is held unconstitutional under these circumstances, it usually means that the federal government as an undivided whole lacks power. A seizure executed by the President pursuant to an act of Congress would be supported by the strongest of presumptions and the widest latitude of judicial interpretation, and the burden of persuasion would rest heavily upon any who might attack it.

2. When the President acts in absence of either a congressional grant or denial of authority, he can only rely upon his own independent powers, but there is a zone of twilight in which he and Congress may have concurrent authority, or in which its distribution is uncertain. Therefore, congressional inertia, indifference or quiescence may sometimes, at least as a practical matter, enable, if not invite, measures on independent presidential responsibility. In this area, any actual test of power is likely to depend on the imperatives of events and contemporary imponderables rather than on abstract theories of law.

3. When the President takes measures incompatible with the expressed or implied will of Congress, his power is at its lowest ebb, for then he can rely only upon his own constitutional powers minus any constitutional powers of Congress over the matter. Courts can sustain exclusive presidential control in such a case only by disabling the Congress from acting upon the subject. Presidential claim to a power at once so conclusive and preclusive must be scrutinized with caution, for what is at stake is the equilibrium established by our constitutional system.

Into which of these classifications does this executive seizure of the steel industry fit? It is eliminated from the first by admission, for it is conceded that no congressional authorization exists for this seizure. That takes away also the

---

2. It is in this class of cases that we find the broadest recent statements of presidential power, including those relied on here. United States v. Curtiss-Wright Corp., 299 U.S. 304, involved, not the question of the President's power to act without congressional authority, but the question of his right to act under and in accord with an Act of Congress....

That case does not solve the present controversy. It recognized internal and external affairs as being in separate categories, and held that the strict limitation upon congressional delegations of power to the President over internal affairs does not apply with respect to delegations of power in external affairs. It was intimated that the President might act in external affairs without congressional authority, but not that he might act contrary to an Act of Congress....

support of the many precedents and declarations which were made in relation, and must be confined, to this category.

Can it then be defended under flexible tests available to the second category? It seems clearly eliminated from that class because Congress has not left seizure of private property an open field but has covered it by three statutory policies inconsistent with this seizure. . . .

This leaves the current seizure to be justified only by the severe tests under the third grouping, where it can be supported only by any remainder of executive power after subtraction of such powers as Congress may have over the subject. In short, we can sustain the President only by holding that seizure of such strike-bound industries is within his domain and beyond control by Congress. Thus, this Court's first review of such seizures occurs under circumstances which leave presidential power most vulnerable to attack and in the least favorable of possible constitutional postures.

I did not suppose, and I am not persuaded, that history leaves it open to question, at least in the courts, that the executive branch, like the Federal Government as a whole, possesses only delegated powers. The purpose of the Constitution was not only to grant power, but to keep it from getting out of hand. However, because the President does not enjoy unmentioned powers does not mean that the mentioned ones should be narrowed by a niggardly construction. Some clauses could be made almost unworkable, as well immutable, by refusal to indulge some latitude of interpretation for changing times. I have heretofore, and do now, give to the enumerated powers the scope and elasticity afforded by what seem to be reasonable practical implications instead of the rigidity dictated by a doctrinaire textualism.

The Solicitor General seeks the power of seizure in three clauses of the Executive Article, the first reading, "The executive Power shall be vested in a President of the United States of America." Lest I be thought to exaggerate, I quote the interpretation which his brief puts upon it: "In our view, this clause constitutes a grant of all the executive powers of which the Government is capable." If that be true, it is difficult to see why the forefathers bothered to add several specific items, including some trifling ones.[9] . . .

. . . I cannot accept the view that this clause is a grant in bulk of all conceivable executive power but regard it as an allocation to the presidential office of the generic powers thereafter stated.

The clause on which the Government next relies is that "The President shall be Commander in Chief of the Army and Navy of the United States. . . ." These cryptic words have given rise to some of the most persistent controversies in our constitutional history. Of course, they imply something more than an empty title. But just what authority goes with the name has plagued presidential advisors who would not waive or narrow it by nonassertion yet cannot say where it begins or ends. It undoubtedly puts the Nation's armed forces under presidential command. Hence, this loose appellation is sometimes advanced as support for any presidential action, internal or external, involving use of force, the idea

---

9. ". . . He may require the Opinion, in writing, of the principal Officer in each of the executive Departments, upon any Subject relating to the Duties of their respective Offices. . . ." U.S. Const., Art. II, §2. He ". . . shall Commission all the Officers of the United States." U.S. Const., Art. II, §3. Matters such as those would seem to be inherent in the Executive if anything is.

being that it vests power to do anything, anywhere, that can be done with an army or navy.

That seems to be the logic of an argument tendered at our bar — that the President having, on his own responsibility, sent American troops abroad derives from that act "affirmative power" to seize the means of producing a supply of steel for them. To quote, "Perhaps the most forceful illustrations of the scope of presidential power in this connection is the fact that American troops in Korea, whose safety and effectiveness are so directly involved here, were sent to the field by an exercise of the President's constitutional powers." Thus, it is said he has invested himself with "war powers."

I cannot foresee all that it might entail if the Court should indorse this argument. Nothing in our Constitution is plainer than that declaration of a war is entrusted only to Congress. Of course, a state of war may in fact exist without a formal declaration. But no doctrine that the Court could promulgate would seem to me more sinister and alarming than that a President whose conduct of foreign affairs is so largely uncontrolled, and often even is unknown, can vastly enlarge his mastery over the internal affairs of the country by his own commitment of the Nation's armed forces to some foreign venture. I do not, however, find it necessary or appropriate to consider the legal status of the Korean enterprise to discountenance argument based on it.

Assuming that we are in a war *de facto,* whether it is or is not a war *de jure,* does that empower the Commander in Chief to seize industries he thinks necessary to supply our army? The Constitution expressly places in Congress power "to raise and *support* Armies" and "to *provide* and *maintain* a navy." (Emphasis supplied.) This certainly lays upon Congress primary responsibility for supplying the armed forces. Congress alone controls the raising of revenues and their appropriation and may determine in what manner and by what means they shall be spent for military and naval procurement. I suppose no one would doubt that Congress can take over war supply as a Government enterprise. On the other hand, if Congress sees fit to rely on free private enterprise collectively bargaining with free labor for support and maintenance of our armed forces, can the Executive, because of lawful disagreements incidental to that process, seize the facility for operation upon Government-imposed terms?

There are indications that the Constitution did not contemplate that the title Commander in Chief *of the Army and Navy* will constitute him also Commander in Chief of the country, its industries and its inhabitants. He has no monopoly of "war powers," whatever they are. While Congress cannot deprive the President of the command of the army and navy, only Congress can provide him an army or navy to command. It is also empowered to make rules for the "Government and Regulation of land and naval Forces," by which it may to some unknown extent impinge upon even command functions.

That military powers of the Commander in Chief were not to supersede representative government of internal affairs seems obvious from the Constitution and from elementary American history. Time out of mind, and even now in many parts of the world, a military commander can seize private housing to shelter his troops. Not so, however, in the United States, for the Third Amendment says, "No Soldier shall, in time of peace be quartered in any house, without the consent of the Owner, nor in time of war, but in a manner to be prescribed by law." Thus, even in war time, his seizure of needed military housing must be authorized by Congress. It also was expressly left to Congress to "provide for calling forth the Militia to execute the Laws of the Union, suppress Insurrections and repel Invasions...." Such a limitation on the command power, written at a time when the militia rather than a standing army was contemplated as the military weapon of the Republic, underscores the Constitution's policy that Congress, not the Executive, should control utilization of the war power as an instrument of domestic policy. Congress, fulfilling that function, has authorized the President to use the army to enforce certain civil rights. On the other hand, Congress has forbidden him to use the army for the purpose of executing general laws except when *expressly* authorized by the Constitution or by act of Congress.

While broad claims under this rubric often have been made, advice to the President in specific matters usually has carried overtones that powers, even under this head, are measured by the command functions usual to the topmost officer of the army and navy. Even then, heed has been taken of any efforts of Congress to negate his authority.

We should not use this occasion to circumscribe, much less to contract, the lawful role of the President as Commander in Chief. I should indulge the widest latitude of interpretation to sustain his exclusive function to command the instruments of national force, at least when turned against the outside world for the security of our society. But when it is turned inward, not because of rebellion but because of a lawful economic struggle between industry and labor, it should have no such indulgence. His command power is not such an absolute as might be implied from that office in a militaristic system but is subject to limitations consistent with a constitutional Republic whose law and policy-making branch is a representative Congress. The purpose of lodging dual titles in one man was to insure that the civilian would control the military, not to enable the military to subordinate the presidential office. No penance would ever expiate the sin against free government of holding that a President can escape control of executive powers by law through assuming his military role. What the power of command may include I do not try to envision, but I think it is not a military prerogative, without support of law, to seize persons or property because they are important or even essential for the military and naval establishment.

The third clause in which the Solicitor General finds seizure powers is that "he shall take Care that the Laws be faithfully executed...." That authority must be matched against words of the Fifth Amendment that "No person shall be...deprived of life, liberty, or property, without due process of law...." One gives a governmental authority that reaches so far as there is law, the other gives a private right that authority shall go no farther. These signify about all there is of the principle that ours is a government of laws, not of men, and that we submit ourselves to rulers only if under rules.

The Solicitor General lastly grounds support of the seizure upon nebulous, inherent powers never expressly granted but said to have accrued to the office from the customs and claims of preceding administrations. The plea is for a resulting power to deal with a crisis or an emergency according to the necessities of the case, the unarticulated assumption being that necessity knows no law....

The appeal...that we declare the existence of inherent powers *ex necessitate* to meet an emergency asks us to do what many think would be wise, although it is something the forefathers omitted. They knew what emergencies were, knew the pressures they engender for authoritative action, knew, too, how they afford a ready pretext for usurpation. We may also suspect that they suspected that emergency powers would tend to kindle emergencies. Aside from suspension of the privilege of the writ of habeas corpus in time of rebellion or invasion, when the public safety may require it, they made no express provision for exercise of extraordinary authority because of a crisis.[19] I do not think we rightfully may so amend their work, and, if we could, I am not convinced it would be wise to do so, although many modern nations have forthrightly recognized that war and economic crisis may upset the normal balance between liberty and authority....

In the practical working of our government we already have evolved a technique within the framework of the Constitution by which normal executive powers may be considerably expanded to meet an emergency. Congress may and has granted extraordinary authorities which lie dormant in normal times but may be called into play by the Executive in war or upon proclamation of a national emergency....

In view of the ease, expedition and safety with which Congress can grant and has granted large emergency powers, certainly ample to embrace this crisis, I am quite unimpressed with the argument that we should affirm possession of them without statute. Such power either has no beginning or it has no end. If it exists, it need submit to no legal restraint. I am not alarmed that it would plunge us straightway into dictatorship, but it is at least a step in that wrong direction.

As to whether there is imperative necessity for such powers, it is relevant to note the gap that exists between the President's paper powers and his real powers. The Constitution does not disclose the measure of the actual controls wielded by the modern presidential office. That instrument must be understood as an Eighteenth-Century sketch of a government hoped for, not as a blueprint of the Government that is. Vast accretions of federal power, eroded from that reserved by the States, have magnified the scope of presidential activity. Subtle shifts take place in the centers of real power that do not show on the face of the Constitution.

Executive power has the advantage of concentration in a single head in whose choice the whole Nation has a part, making him the focus of public hopes and expectations. In drama, magnitude and finality his decisions so far overshadow any others that almost alone he fills the public eye and ear. No other personality in public life can begin to compete with him in access to the public mind through modern methods of communications. By his prestige as head of state and his influence upon public opinion he exerts a leverage upon those who are supposed to check and balance his power which often cancels their effectiveness.

Moreover, rise of the party system has made a significant extraconstitutional supplement to real executive power. No appraisal of his necessities is realistic which overlooks that he heads a political system as well as a legal system. Party loyalties and interests, sometimes more binding than law, extend his effective control into branches of government other than his own and he often may win, as a political leader, what he cannot command under the Constitution. Indeed, Woodrow Wilson, commenting on the President as leader both of his party and of the Nation, observed, "If he rightly interpret the national thought and boldly

---

19. I exclude, as in a very limited category by itself, the establishment of martial law....

insist upon it, he is irresistible.... His office is anything he has the sagacity and force to make it." I cannot be brought to believe that this country will suffer if the Court refuses further to aggrandize the presidential office, already so potent and so relatively immune from judicial review, at the expense of Congress.

But I have no illusion that any decision by this Court can keep power in the hands of Congress if it is not wise and timely in meeting its problems. A crisis that challenges the President equally, or perhaps primarily, challenges Congress. If not good law, there was worldly wisdom in the maxim attributed to Napoleon that "The tools belong to the man who can use them." We may say that power to legislate for emergencies belongs in the hands of Congress, but only Congress itself can prevent power from slipping through its fingers....

... With all its defects, delays and inconveniences, men have discovered no technique for long preserving free government except that the Executive be under the law, and that the law be made by parliamentary deliberations.

Such institutions may be destined to pass away. But it is the duty of the Court to be last, not first, to give them up.

Mr. Justice BURTON, concurring in both the opinion and judgment of the Court.... In the case before us, Congress authorized a procedure which the President declined to follow. Instead, he followed another procedure which he hoped might eliminate the need for the first. Upon its failure, he issued an executive order to seize the steel properties in the face of the reserved right of Congress to adopt or reject that course as a matter of legislative policy.

This brings us to a further crucial question. Does the President, in such a situation, have inherent constitutional power to seize private property which makes congressional action in relation thereto unnecessary? We find no such power available to him under the present circumstances. The present situation is not comparable to that of an imminent invasion or threatened attack. We do not face the issue of what might be the President's constitutional power to meet such catastrophic situations. Nor is it claimed that the current seizure is in the nature of a military command addressed by the President, as Commander in Chief, to a mobilized nation waging, or imminently threatened with, total war.[7]...

Mr. Justice CLARK, concurring in the judgment of the Court.... The limits of presidential power are obscure. However, Article II, no less than Article I, is part of "a constitution intended to endure for ages to come, and, consequently, to be adapted to the various *crises* of human affairs." Some of our Presidents, such as Lincoln, "felt that measures otherwise unconstitutional might become lawful by becoming indispensable to the preservation of the Constitution through the preservation of the nation." Others, such as Theodore Roosevelt, thought the President to be capable, as a "steward" of the people, of exerting all power save that which is specifically prohibited by the Constitution or the Congress. In my view — taught me not only by the decision of Mr. Chief Justice Marshall in Little v. Barreme [*infra* pp. 77-79], but also by a score of other pronouncements of distinguished members of this bench — the Constitution

---

7. The President and Congress have recognized the termination of the major hostilities in the total wars in which the nation has been engaged. Many wartime procedures have expired or been terminated.

does grant to the President extensive authority in times of grave and imperative national emergency. In fact, to my thinking, such a grant may well be necessary to the very existence of the Constitution itself. As Lincoln aptly said, "[is] it possible to lose the nation and yet preserve the Constitution?" In describing this authority I care not whether one calls it "residual," "inherent," "moral," "implied," "aggregate," "emergency," or otherwise. I am of the conviction that those who have had the gratifying experience of being the President's lawyer have used one or more of these adjectives only with the utmost of sincerity and the highest of purpose.

I conclude that where Congress has laid down specific procedures to deal with the type of crisis confronting the President, he must follow those procedures in meeting the crisis; but that in the absence of such action by Congress, the President's independent power to act depends upon the gravity of the situation confronting the nation. I cannot sustain the seizure in question because here, as in Little v. Barreme, Congress had prescribed methods to be followed by the President in meeting the emergency at hand.

Mr. Chief Justice VINSON, with whom Mr. Justice REED and Mr. Justice MINTON join, dissenting.... Those who suggest that this is a case involving extraordinary powers should be mindful that these are extraordinary times. A world not yet recovered from the devastation of World War II has been forced to face the threat of another and more terrifying global conflict....

... For almost two full years, our armed forces have been fighting in Korea, suffering casualties of over 108,000 men. Hostilities have not abated. The "determination of the United Nations to continue its action in Korea to meet the aggression" has been reaffirmed. Congressional support of the action in Korea has been manifested by provisions for increased military manpower and equipment and for economic stabilization, as hereinafter described....

... Even ignoring for the moment whatever confidential information the President may possess as "the Nation's organ for foreign affairs," the uncontroverted affidavits in this record amply support the finding that "a work stoppage would immediately jeopardize and imperil our national defense."...

Focusing now on the situation confronting the President on the night of April 8, 1952, we cannot but conclude that the President was performing his duty under the Constitution to "take Care that the Laws be faithfully executed" — a duty described by President Benjamin Harrison as "the central idea of the office."

The President reported to Congress the morning after the seizure that he acted because a work stoppage in steel production would immediately imperil the safety of the Nation by preventing execution of the legislative programs for procurement of military equipment. And, while a shutdown could be averted by granting the price concessions requested by plaintiffs, granting such concessions would disrupt the price stabilization program also enacted by Congress. Rather than fail to execute either legislative program, the President acted to execute both.

Much of the argument in this case has been directed at straw men. We do not now have before us the case of a president acting solely on the basis of his own notions of the public welfare. Nor is there any question of unlimited executive power in this case. The President himself closed the door to any such claim when he sent his Message to Congress stating his purpose to abide by any action of Congress, whether approving or disapproving his seizure action. Here, the President immediately made sure that Congress was fully informed of the temporary action he had taken only to preserve the legislative programs from destruction until Congress could act.

The absence of a specific statute authorizing seizure of the steel mills as a mode of executing the laws — both the military procurement program and the anti-inflation program — has not until today been thought to prevent the President from executing the laws. Unlike an administrative commission confined to the enforcement of the statute under which it was created, or the head of a department when administering a particular statute, the President is a constitutional officer charged with taking care that a "mass of legislation" be executed. Flexibility as to mode of execution to meet critical situations is a matter of practical necessity....

Whatever the extent of presidential power on more tranquil occasions, and whatever the right of the President to execute legislative programs as he sees fit without reporting the mode of execution to Congress, the single Presidential purpose disclosed on this record is to faithfully execute the laws by acting in an emergency to maintain the status quo, thereby preventing collapse of the legislative programs until Congress could act. The President's action served the same purposes as a judicial stay entered to maintain the status quo in order to preserve the jurisdiction of a Court....

In United States v. Midwest Oil Co., this Court approved executive action where, as here, the President acted to preserve an important matter until Congress could act — even though his action in that case was contrary to an express statute. In this case, there is no statute prohibiting the action taken by the President in a matter not merely important but threatening the very safety of the Nation. Executive inaction in such a situation, courting national disaster, is foreign to the concept of energy and initiative in the Executive as created by the Founding Fathers. The Constitution was itself "adopted in a period of grave emergency.... While emergency does not create power, emergency may furnish the occasion for the exercise of power." The Framers knew, as we should know in these times of peril, that there is real danger in Executive weakness. There is no cause to fear Executive tyranny so long as the laws of Congress are being faithfully executed. Certainly there is no basis for fear of dictatorship when the executive acts, as he did in this case, only to save the situation until Congress could act....

NOTES AND QUESTIONS

Counting Heads in Steel Seizure. What exactly is the holding of *The Steel Seizure Case*? Which Justices acknowledge the power of the Commander in Chief to act without statutory authority, and in what circumstances? Which Justices would, in an appropriate case, find general "executive Power" from Article II's Vestiture Clause, as long as there are no statutes to the contrary? Which Justices would endorse a narrower constitutional emergency power in the President, despite the absence of statutory or express constitutional authority? Finally, which Justices join in Justice Black's formalistic view of the separation of powers? Do not proceed through the remaining notes and questions until you have answered these questions as best you can. *See generally* Edward S. Corwin, *The Steel Seizure*

Case: Judicial Brick Without Straw, 53 Colum. L. Rev. 53 (1953); Paul G. Kauper, *The Steel Seizure Case: Congress, the President and the Supreme Court*, 51 Mich. L. Rev. 141 (1952).

a. The President's Claim of Lawmaking Authority

1. *May the President Ever Make Law?* If we take literally Justice Black's description of the separation of powers, can the President ever be a lawmaker? His words are consistent with the nondelegation doctrine noted by the Supreme Court in 1892: "That Congress cannot delegate legislative power to the President is a principle universally recognized as vital to the integrity and maintenance of the system of government ordained by the Constitution." Field v. Clark, 143 U.S. 649, 692 (1892).

However, as early as 1813, the Court declined to apply any such doctrine literally. In The Brig Aurora, 11 U.S. (7 Cranch) 382 (1813), the Court upheld a delegation of power to the President to lift an embargo of European trade if he found that the Europeans had "ceased to violate the neutral commerce of the United States." The Court reasoned that the delegation of legislative power was contingent solely on a finding of facts. In Field v. Clark itself, after paying lip service to the "universally recognized" nondelegation principle, the Court upheld a delegation of power to the President to impose tariffs whenever he was "satisfied" of a need for them. 143 U.S. at 691-692.

Subsequently, reasoning partly from "governmental necessity," the Court suggested that any delegation of legislative power that contains an "intelligible principle" to guide the delegate's discretion could be sustained against a nondelegation attack. J.W. Hampton, Jr. & Co. v. United States, 276 U.S. 394, 409-410 (1928). *See also* Mistretta v. United States, 488 U.S. 361, 371-379 (1989) (applying the foregoing standards in rejecting a nondelegation attack on statute creating Sentencing Commission). In only two cases has the Supreme Court applied the nondelegation doctrine to strike down statutory delegations of power to the executive: Schechter Poultry Corp. v. United States, 295 U.S. 495 (1935), and Panama Refining Co. v. Ryan, 293 U.S. 388 (1935). The Court has not done so since 1935.

Against this background, Justice Black's opinion cannot be taken literally. The President *may* exercise *delegated* law-making power. Indeed, when he does so, "his authority is at its maximum," *The Steel Seizure Case*, 343 U.S. at 635 (Jackson, J., concurring), for he acts not only with his own authority but with all that Congress can delegate. The difficulty in *The Steel Seizure Case* in the majority's view was that there was neither a statutory delegation nor constitutional power for the seizure.

2. *Power Through Practice?* Some scholars have argued that the President makes law severed from any statutory mooring by simply seizing the initiative — going first. *See* Terry M. Moe & William G. Howell, *The Presidential Power of Unilateral Action*, 15 J.L. Econ. & Org. 132, 134 (1999):

> Because presidents are executives, and because of the discretion, opportunities, and resources executives have available to them in politics, presidents are particularly well suited to be first-movers and to reap the agenda powers that go along

> with it. If they want to shift the status quo by taking unilateral action on their own authority, whether or not that authority is clearly established in law, they can simply do it—quickly, forcefully, and (if they like) with no advance notice. The other branches are then presented with a *fait accompli*, and it is up to them to respond. If they are unable to respond effectively, or decide not to, the President wins by default. And even if they do respond, which could take years, he may still get much of what he wants anyway. [*Id.* at 137.]

Justice Frankfurter seemed to agree, at least if the President takes the initiative often enough. Justice Frankfurter asserted that

> a systematic, unbroken, executive practice, long pursued to the knowledge of the Congress and never before questioned, engaged in by Presidents who have also sworn to uphold the Constitution, making as it were such an exercise of power part of the structure of government, may be treated as a gloss on "executive Power" vested in the President by §1 of Art. II. [343 U.S. at 610-611.]

Executive practice in which Congress has acquiesced may evidence an appropriate interpretation of the Constitution and thus ripen into a kind of constitutional common law or custom. "Deeply embedded traditional ways of conducting the government cannot supplant the Constitution or legislation, but they give meaning to the words of a text or supply them." *Id.* at 610. *See generally* William C. Banks & Peter Raven-Hansen, *National Security Law and the Power of the Purse* 114-118 (1994).

Why did the history of plant seizures described by Justice Frankfurter not establish an executive practice in which Congress had acquiesced, creating a constitutional common law or customary authority for the steel seizure? What history would have laid a sufficient predicate for congressional acquiescence in the steel plant seizure?

3. *The Form of the President's Law.* When the President does act properly as lawmaker, what form does his "law" take? The executive order by which President Truman ordered the seizure of the steel plants indicates the usual form of presidential law. *See generally* Phillip J. Cooper, *By Order of the President* (2002); Kenneth R. Mayer, *With the Stroke of a Pen* (2001). Presidential proclamations have also been used as presidential law, *see, e.g.*, United States v. Curtiss-Wright Export Corp., 299 U.S. 304 (1936) (*infra* pp. 60-64), but today they are reserved chiefly for ceremonial announcements.

Presidential national security law often takes the form of a National Security Decision Directive (NSDD), National Security Directive (NSD), Presidential Decision Directive (PDD), or, at this writing, a National Security Presidential Directive (NSPD) (the label varies from administration to administration), rather than an order. *See generally* Cooper, *supra*, at 143-197. One difference is that executive orders and proclamations must be published in *The Federal Register*, 44 U.S.C. §1505 (2000), while national security directives need not be. In fact, only 247 of at least 1,042 presidential directives issued through the National Security Council (NSC) between 1961 and 1988 were publicly released for either congressional or public scrutiny. General Accounting Office, *National Security: The Use of Presidential Directives to Make and Implement U.S. Policy* 2 (Dec. 1988). Legislation has been proposed that would require filing of such directives with

A. *The Steel Seizure Case* and Its Theories of Presidential Power

the Office of the Federal Register and their disclosure to the Speaker of the House and President Pro Tempore of the Senate. H.R. 5092, 100th Cong. (1988). Another difference is that executive orders are usually sent to the U.S. Attorney General "for his consideration as to both form and legality," 1 C.F.R. §19.2(b) (2005), while national security directives are not. No published regulation governs the legal vetting of such directives, although in the first Bush administration the Attorney General attended NSC "meetings pertaining to his jurisdiction, including covert actions." G. Hughes (Exec. Secy. to NSC), *Memorandum re: Description of [NSC] Organization* 1 (April 18, 1989) (unclassified summary of NSD-1 (Jan. 30, 1989)). It is likely today that many national security directives are reviewed by the NSC Legal Adviser or the White House Counsel.

Typically an executive order cites its promulgating authority in its preamble. Eighty-three percent of the executive orders issued from 1945 to 1965 were issued upon specific statutory authority. Ruth P. Morgan, *The President and Civil Rights* 286 n.2 (1970). These presidential laws were thus made with delegated legislative authority and carried the same force and effect as statutes. *See generally* Peter Raven-Hansen, *Making Agencies Follow Orders: Judicial Review of Agency Violations of Executive Order 12,291*, 1983 Duke L.J. 285, 297-301. The rest of the orders were either executive housekeeping orders directed solely at the internal workings of the executive branch or purported exercises of inherent constitutional lawmaking authority in the President. The difficulty of the steel seizure order is laid bare by its preamble. What lawmaking authority did President Truman cite?

4. *Legislative Rules.* Presidential "law" may also take the form of regulations promulgated by presidential subordinates in the executive branch or in the "independent" agencies. Usually these regulations, or "legislative rules" in the administrative lawyer's jargon, are promulgated as exercises of legislative authority delegated directly to the subordinates. The Supreme Court has declared that so "long as [a] regulation remains in force the Executive Branch is bound by it, and indeed the United States as the sovereign composed of the three branches is bound to respect and enforce it." United States v. Nixon, 418 U.S. 683, 696 (1974). Even some regulations issued by the President or his subordinates gratuitously — without statutory compulsion — carry this effect. *See, e.g.*, Service v. Dulles, 354 U.S. 363 (1957). *See generally* Peter Raven-Hansen, *Regulatory Estoppel: When Agencies Break Their Own "Laws,"* 64 Tex. L. Rev. 1 (1985).

b. The President's Claim of Inherent or "Aggregate" Powers in Emergencies

1. *"Inherent Powers" Defined.* The Solicitor General's last resort in *The Steel Seizure Case* was the argument that the seizure was a constitutional exercise of "inherent" presidential powers. As Justice Jackson observed, "Loose and irresponsible use of adjectives colors all non-legal and much legal discussion of presidential powers." 343 U.S. at 646. "Inherent" is sometimes used interchangeably with "implied," "incidental," "plenary," "aggregate," or even "general executive powers" allegedly conferred by the Vestiture, Take Care, and presidential Oath of Office Clauses of Article II. Here we will loosely use

"inherent powers" to differentiate those that are farthest removed from any express grant of constitutional or statutory authority from those that appear to be more closely tied to — "implied" in — express grants of such authority, recognizing that all these powers fall on a continuum.

2. *Constitutional Emergency Powers.* Does the Constitution confer emergency powers? Consider Article I, §8, cls. 15 and 18; Article I, §9, cl. 2; Article I, §10, cl. 3; and Article IV, §4. Does Justice Jackson deny the existence of constitutional emergency powers? How, in his view, can the Republic cope with national emergencies? We explore emergency powers of the President in Chapter 4 and of the Congress in Chapter 5.

3. *Aggregate Authority?* Does the President's responsibility for executing the "mass of legislation" vest him with a whole of executive power that is greater than the sum of the delegated parts, or at least power to "act[] in an emergency to maintain the status quo, thereby preventing collapse of the legislative programs until Congress could act"? See *The Steel Seizure Case,* 343 U.S. at 702 (Vinson, C.J., dissenting). *Cf.* Myers v. United States, 272 U.S. 52, 135 (1926) (The President "may properly supervise and guide [executive officers'] construction of the statutes under which they act in order to secure that unitary and uniform execution of the laws which Article II of the Constitution evidently contemplated in vesting general executive power in the President alone."). Does this aggregate authority and duty to coordinate statutory commands permit a President to choose among conflicting commands? What were the conflicting statutory commands in *The Steel Seizure Case*?

4. *Inherent Emergency Power After Steel Seizure.* After *The Steel Seizure Case,* does the President have *any* inherent constitutional emergency authority? See *infra* pp. 80-87. Recall the lineup of the Justices concerning emergency powers. If the existence of such authority turns on the "gravity of the situation confronting the nation," 343 U.S. at 662 (Clark, J., concurring), who decides that question? How did the dissenters decide the gravity of the situation?

c. The President's Claim of War Powers as Commander in Chief

1. *The Effect of Declaration and Location.* The Korean War was an undeclared war fought overseas. Does the Court's rejection of the Commander-in-Chief Clause as authority for the steel seizure turn on the locus of the war? On the locus of the exercise of presidential power at issue? On the absence of a declared war? How did the different Justices answer these questions? On the legality of the Korean War, see *infra* pp. 290-294. Interestingly, Chief Justice Rehnquist, who was Justice Jackson's law clerk at the time of *The Steel Seizure Case,* believed that the "profound ambivalence" about the undeclared Korean War was a major factor in the decision, which he believes would have come out differently during declared World War II. William H. Rehnquist, *The Supreme Court* 96-97 (2001).

2. *Scope of Commander-in-Chief Power.* What is the scope of the Commander-in-Chief power that emerges by negative inference from these opinions? Where

in the Constitution do the asserted limits of the scope of the Commander-in-Chief power appear? Consider President Truman's assessment of *The Steel Seizure Case:*

> Whatever the six justices of the Supreme Court meant by their differing opinions about the Constitutional powers of the President, he must always act in a national emergency. It is not very realistic for the justices to say that comprehensive powers shall be available to the President only when a war has been declared or when the country has been invaded. We live in an age when hostilities begin without polite exchanges of diplomatic notes. There are no longer sharp distinctions between combatants and noncombatants, between military targets and the sanctuary of civilian areas. Nor can we separate the economic facts from the problems of defense and security....
>
> The President, who is Commander in Chief and who represents the interest of all the people, must [be] able to act at all times to meet any sudden threat to the nation's security. A wise President will always work with Congress, but when Congress fails to act or is unable to act in a crisis, the President, under the Constitution, must use his powers to safeguard the nation. [2 Harry S. Truman, *Memoirs: Years of Trial and Hope* 478 (Doubleday ed. 1956).]

Do you agree?

B. JUSTICE JACKSON'S GROUPING OF PRESIDENTIAL POWERS

Although Justice Black wrote the opinion for the Court in *The Steel Seizure Case,* Justice Jackson's famous grouping of presidential powers is better remembered in separation-of-powers analysis. Chief Justice Rehnquist said it "brings together as much combination of analysis and common sense as there is in this area." Dames & Moore v. Regan, 453 U.S. 654, 661 (1981). We therefore consider each of Justice Jackson's groups in turn.

1. When the President Acts Pursuant to Delegated Authority

Justice Jackson's first group of presidential powers involves situations in which "the President acts pursuant to an express or implied authorization of Congress," and "his authority is [therefore] at its maximum...." 343 U.S. at 635. In these situations, the President purports to act on authority delegated by Congress.

As noted above, the Court has long since ruled that Congress may delegate at least some of its legislative powers to the executive, as long as Congress legislates "intelligible principles" — standards — by which the executive discretion can be channeled and measured. The legality of the President's exercise of delegated authority therefore turns on (a) whether Congress may delegate the specific authority to the executive, (b) whether the delegating statute contains standards for the exercise of the delegated discretion, (c) whether the executive follows the standards, and (d) whether the exercise of delegated authority otherwise violates the Constitution.

For example, a majority of the Supreme Court upheld the President's order for the military detention of a U.S. citizen captured on the battlefield in Afghanistan on the authority of the Authorization for the Use of Military Force that Congress passed after 9/11. *See* Hamdi v. Rumsfeld, 542 U.S. 507 (2004), *infra* p. 721. Although the Authorization, set forth *infra* p. 100, did not expressly delegate detention authority to the President, it impliedly did so by authorizing "all necessary and appropriate force" against "nations, organizations, or persons" associated with the 9/11 attacks. The Authorization thus also contained a standard limiting executive detention discretion just to individuals falling into this category. Moreover, the majority of the Court reasoned that the Constitution poses "no bar to this Nation's holding one of its own citizens as an enemy combatant." *Hamdi*, 542 U.S. at 519. Due process, however, entitled Hamdi to "notice of the factual basis for his classification, and a fair opportunity to rebut the Government's factual assertions before a neutral decisionmaker." *Id.*, 542 U.S. at 533. The Court therefore remanded the case for further proceedings.

2. When the President Acts with Congressional Acquiescence

Justice Jackson's second group of presidential powers falls into a "zone of twilight in which [the President] and Congress may have concurrent authority, or in which its distribution is uncertain [and] congressional inertia, indifference or quiescence may sometimes, at least as a practical matter, enable, if not invite, measures on independent presidential responsibility." *The Steel Seizure Case*, 343 U.S. at 637-638. In the following case, the Supreme Court analyzes authority in this group.

Dames & Moore v. Regan
United States Supreme Court, 1981
453 U.S. 654

Justice REHNQUIST delivered the opinion of the Court.... On November 4, 1979, the American Embassy in Tehran was seized and our diplomatic personnel were captured and held hostage. In response to that crisis, President Carter, acting pursuant to the International Emergency Economic Powers Act, 50 U.S.C. §§1701-1706 (1976 ed., Supp. III) (hereinafter IEEPA), declared a national emergency on November 14, 1979,[1] and blocked the removal or

---

1. Title 50 U.S.C. §1701(a) (1976 ed., Supp. III) states that the President's authority under the Act "may be exercised to deal with any unusual and extraordinary threat, which has its source in whole or substantial part outside the United States, to the national security, foreign policy, or economy of the United States, if the President declares a national emergency with respect to such threat." Petitioner does not challenge President Carter's declaration of a national emergency.

B. Justice Jackson's Grouping of Presidential Powers

transfer of [Iranian assets]. Exec. Order No. 12170, 3 C.F.R. 457 (1980), note following 50 U.S.C. §1701 (1976 ed., Supp. III).[2] . . .

[Pursuant to the Order, the Secretary of the Treasury promulgated regulations nullifying attachments of Iranian assets on or after November 14, 1979, unless licensed by the Treasury Department. The Department subsequently licensed pre-judgment attachments in judicial proceedings against Iran. Dames & Moore sued Iranian defendants for breach of contract and obtained a pre-judgment attachment of Iranian assets.

Thereafter, the American hostages were released pursuant to an agreement obligating the United States to terminate all legal proceedings in U.S. courts involving claims of U.S. nationals against Iran, to nullify all attachments and judgments therein, to terminate such claims through binding arbitration, and to transfer U.S.-held Iranian assets to foreign banks for the satisfaction of any arbitration awards rendered against Iran. President Carter issued a series of executive orders implementing this agreement and "nullif[ying]" all non-Iranian interests in Iranian assets acquired after his initial blocking order. President Reagan subsequently ratified the Carter orders.

Meanwhile, Dames & Moore was granted summary judgment on its claim against the Iranian defendants, but the district court vacated all pre-judgment attachments and stayed further proceedings in light of the executive orders discussed above. Dames & Moore then filed an action in the district court to prevent enforcement of the executive orders and Treasury Department regulations implementing the agreement with Iran on the grounds that they were beyond the statutory and constitutional powers of the executive.]

Although we have in the past found and do today find Justice Jackson's classification [in *The Steel Seizure Case*, 343 U.S. at 635-638] of executive actions into three general categories analytically useful, we should be mindful of Justice Holmes' admonition, quoted by Justice Frankfurter in [that case at 343 U.S. 597] that "[t]he great ordinances of the Constitution do not establish and divide fields of black and white." Springer v. Philippine Islands, 277 U.S. 189, 209 (1928) (dissenting opinion). Justice Jackson himself recognized that his three categories represented "a somewhat over-simplified grouping," and it is doubtless the case that executive action in any particular instance falls, not neatly in one of three pigeonholes, but rather at some point along a spectrum running from explicit congressional authorization to explicit congressional prohibition. This is particularly true as respects cases such as the one before us, involving responses to international crises the nature of which Congress can hardly have been expected to anticipate in any detail.

In nullifying post-November 14, 1979, attachments and directing those persons holding blocked Iranian funds and securities to transfer them to the Federal Reserve Bank of New York for ultimate transfer to Iran, President Carter cited five sources of express or inherent power. The Government, however, has principally relied on §203 of the IEEPA as authorization for these actions. [The

---

2. Title 50 U.S.C. §1702(a)(1)(B) (1976 ed., Supp. III) empowers the President to

investigate, regulate, direct and compel, nullify, void, prevent or prohibit, any acquisition, holding, withholding, use, transfer, withdrawal, transportation, importation or exportation of, or dealing in, or exercising any right, power, or privilege with respect to, or transactions involving, any property in which any foreign country or a national thereof has any interest. . . .

Court concluded that this statute expressly authorized the nullification of the attachments and the transfer of assets.] . . .

. . . [T]here remains the question of the President's authority to suspend claims pending in American courts. Such claims have, of course, an existence apart from the attachments which accompanied them. In terminating these claims through Executive Order No. 12294 the President purported to act under authority of both the IEEPA and 22 U.S.C. §1732, the so-called "Hostage Act."

We conclude that although the IEEPA authorized the nullification of the attachments, it cannot be read to authorize the suspension of the claims. The claims of American citizens against Iran are not in themselves transactions involving Iranian property or efforts to exercise any rights with respect to such property. An in personam lawsuit, although it might eventually be reduced to judgment and that judgment might be executed upon, is an effort to establish liability and fix damages and does not focus on any particular property within the jurisdiction. The terms of the IEEPA therefore do not authorize the President to suspend claims in American courts. This is the view of all the courts which have considered the question.

The Hostage Act, passed in 1868, provides:

> Whenever it is made known to the President that any citizen of the United States has been unjustly deprived of his liberty by or under the authority of any foreign government, it shall be the duty of the President forthwith to demand of that government the reasons of such imprisonment; and if it appears to be wrongful and in violation of the rights of American citizenship, the President shall forthwith demand the release of such citizen, and if the release so demanded is unreasonably delayed or refused, the President shall use such means, not amounting to acts of war, as he may think necessary and proper to obtain or effectuate the release; and all the facts and proceedings relative thereto shall as soon as practicable be communicated by the President to Congress. Rev. Stat. §2001, 22 U.S.C. §1732.

We are reluctant to conclude that this provision constitutes specific authorization to the President to suspend claims in American courts. Although the broad language of the Hostage Act suggests it may cover this case, there are several difficulties with such a view. The legislative history indicates that the Act was passed in response to a situation unlike the recent Iranian crisis. Congress in 1868 was concerned with the activity of certain countries refusing to recognize the citizenship of naturalized Americans traveling abroad, and repatriating such citizens against their will. These countries were not interested in returning the citizens in exchange for any sort of ransom. This also explains the reference in the Act to imprisonment "in violation of the rights of American citizenship." Although the Iranian hostage-taking violated international law and common decency, the hostages were not seized out of any refusal to recognize their American citizenship — they were seized precisely *because* of their American citizenship. The legislative history is also somewhat ambiguous on the question whether Congress contemplated Presidential action such as that involved here or rather simply reprisals directed against the offending foreign country and *its* citizens.

B. Justice Jackson's Grouping of Presidential Powers

Concluding that neither the IEEPA nor the Hostage Act constitutes specific authorization of the President's action suspending claims, however, is not to say that these statutory provisions are entirely irrelevant to the question of the validity of the President's action. We think both statutes highly relevant in the looser sense of indicating congressional acceptance of a broad scope for executive action in circumstances such as those presented in this case.... [T]he IEEPA delegates broad authority to the President to act in times of national emergency with respect to property of a foreign country. The Hostage Act similarly indicates congressional willingness that the President have broad discretion when responding to the hostile acts of foreign sovereigns. As Senator Williams, draftsman of the language eventually enacted as the Hostage Act, put it:

> If you propose any remedy at all, you must invest the Executive with some discretion, so that he may apply the remedy to a case as it may arise. As to England or France he might adopt one policy to relieve a citizen imprisoned by either one of those countries; as to the Barbary powers, he might adopt another policy; as to the islands of the ocean, another. With different countries that have different systems of government he might adopt different means. Cong. Globe, 40th Cong., 2d Sess., 4359 (1868).

Proponents of the bill recognized that it placed a "loose discretion" in the President's hands, id., at 4238 (Sen. Stewart), but argued that "[s]omething must be intrusted to the Executive" and that "[t]he President ought to have the power to do what the exigencies of the case require to rescue [a] citizen from imprisonment." Id., at 4233, 4357 (Sen. Williams). An original version of the Act, which authorized the President to suspend trade with a foreign country and even arrest citizens of that country in the United States in retaliation, was rejected because "there may be a great variety of cases arising where other and different means would be equally effective, and where the end desired could be accomplished without resorting to such dangerous and violent measures." Id., at 4233 (Sen. Williams).

Although we have declined to conclude that the IEEPA or the Hostage Act directly authorizes the President's suspension of claims for the reasons noted, we cannot ignore the general tenor of Congress's legislation in this area in trying to determine whether the President is acting alone or at least with the acceptance of Congress. As we have noted, Congress cannot anticipate and legislate with regard to every possible action the President may find it necessary to take or every possible situation in which he might act. Such failure of Congress specifically to delegate authority does not, "especially... in the areas of foreign policy and national security," imply "congressional disapproval" of action taken by the Executive. Haig v. Agee, [453 U.S. 280 (1981)], at 291. On the contrary, the enactment of legislation closely related to the question of the President's authority in a particular case which evinces legislative intent to accord the President broad discretion may be considered to "invite" "measures on independent presidential responsibility," *Youngstown*, 343 U.S. at 637 (Jackson, J., concurring). At least this is so where there is no contrary indication of legislative intent and when, as here, there is a history of congressional acquiescence in conduct of the sort engaged in by the President. It is to that history which we now turn.

Not infrequently in affairs between nations, outstanding claims by nationals of one country against the government of another country are "sources of friction" between the two sovereigns. United States v. Pink, 315 U.S. 203, 225 (1942). To resolve these difficulties, nations have often entered into agreements settling the claims of their respective nationals. As one treatise writer puts it, international agreements settling claims by nationals of one state against the government of another "are established international practice reflecting traditional international theory." L. Henkin, *Foreign Affairs and the Constitution* 262 (1972). Consistent with that principle, the United States has repeatedly exercised its sovereign authority to settle the claims of its nationals against foreign countries. Though those settlements have sometimes been made by treaty, there has also been a longstanding practice of settling such claims by executive agreement without the advice and consent of the Senate.[8] ... It is clear that the practice of settling claims continues today. Since 1952, the President has entered into at least 10 binding settlements with foreign nations, including an $80 million settlement with the People's Republic of China.

Crucial to our decision today is the conclusion that Congress has implicitly approved the practice of claim settlement by executive agreement. This is best demonstrated by Congress' enactment of the International Claims Settlement Act of 1949, 22 U.S.C. §1621 et seq. (1976 ed. and Supp. IV). The Act had two purposes: (1) to allocate to United States nationals funds received in the course of an executive claims settlement with Yugoslavia, and (2) to provide a procedure whereby funds resulting from future settlements could be distributed. To achieve these ends Congress created the International Claims Commission, now the Foreign Claims Settlement Commission, and gave it jurisdiction to make final and binding decisions with respect to claims by United States nationals against settlement funds. By creating a procedure to implement future settlement agreements, Congress placed its stamp of approval on such agreements. Indeed, the legislative history of the Act observed that the United States was seeking settlements with countries other than Yugoslavia and that the bill contemplated settlements of a similar nature in the future.

Over the years Congress has frequently amended the International Claims Settlement Act to provide for particular problems arising out of settlement agreements, thus demonstrating Congress' continuing acceptance of the President's claim settlement authority.... As with legislation involving other executive agreements, Congress did not question the fact of the settlement or the power of the President to have concluded it.... Finally, the legislative history of the IEEPA further reveals that Congress has accepted the authority of the Executive to enter into settlement agreements. Though the IEEPA was enacted to provide for some limitation on the President's emergency powers, Congress stressed that "[n]othing in this act is intended... to interfere with the authority of the President to [block assets], or to impede the settlement of claims of U.S. citizens against foreign countries." S. Rep. No. 95-466, p. 6 (1977), U.S. Code

---

8. At least since the case of the "Wilmington Packet" in 1799, Presidents have exercised the power to settle claims of United States nationals by executive agreement. In fact, during the period of 1817-1917, "no fewer than eighty executive agreements were entered into by the United States looking toward the liquidation of claims of its citizens." W. McClure, *International Executive Agreements* 53 (1941).

B. Justice Jackson's Grouping of Presidential Powers

Cong. & Admin. News, 1977, pp. 4540, 4544; 50 U.S.C. §1706(a)(1) (1976 ed., Supp. III).[10]

In addition to congressional acquiescence in the President's power to settle claims, prior cases of this Court have also recognized that the President does have some measure of power to enter into executive agreements without obtaining the advice and consent of the Senate. In United States v. Pink, 315 U.S. 203 (1942), for example, the Court upheld the validity of the Litvinov Assignment, which was part of an Executive Agreement whereby the Soviet Union assigned to the United States amounts owed to it by American nationals so that outstanding claims of other American nationals could be paid. The Court explained that the resolution of such claims was integrally connected with normalizing United States' relations with a foreign state:

> Power to remove such obstacles to full recognition as settlement of claims of our nationals...certainly is a modest implied power of the President.... No such obstacle can be placed in the way of rehabilitation of relations between this country and another nation, unless the historic conception of the powers and responsibilities...is to be drastically revised. *Id.* at 229-230....

Just as importantly, Congress has not disapproved of the action taken here. Though Congress has held hearings on the Iranian Agreement itself, Congress has not enacted legislation, or even passed a resolution, indicating its displeasure with the Agreement. Quite the contrary, the relevant Senate Committee has stated that the establishment of the Tribunal is "of vital importance to the United States." S. Rep. No. 97-71, p. 5 (1981).[13] We are thus clearly not confronted with a situation in which Congress has in some way resisted the exercise of Presidential authority.

Finally, we re-emphasize the narrowness of our decision. We do not decide that the President possesses plenary power to settle claims, even as against foreign governmental entities. As the Court of Appeals for the First Circuit stressed, "[t]he sheer magnitude of such a power, considered against the background of the diversity and complexity of modern international trade, cautions against any broader construction of authority than is necessary." Chas. T. Main Intl., Inc. v. Khuzestan Water & Power Authority, 651 F.2d [800], at 814 [(1st Cir. 1980)]. But where, as here, the settlement of claims has been determined to be a necessary

---

10. Indeed, Congress has consistently failed to object to this longstanding practice of claim settlement by executive agreement, even when it has had an opportunity to do so. In 1972, Congress entertained legislation relating to congressional oversight of such agreements. But Congress took only limited action, requiring that the text of significant executive agreements be transmitted to Congress. 1 U.S.C. §112b. In Haig v. Agee, [453 U.S. 280], we noted that "[d]espite the longstanding and officially promulgated view that the Executive has the power to withhold passports for reasons of national security and foreign policy, Congress in 1978, 'though it once again enacted legislation relating to passports, left completely untouched the broad rule-making authority granted in the earlier Act.'" Ante, at 301, quoting Zemel v. Rusk, 381 U.S. 1, 12 (1965). Likewise in this case, Congress, though legislating in the area, has left "untouched" the authority of the President to enter into settlement agreements....

13. Contrast congressional reaction to the Iranian Agreements with congressional reaction to a 1973 Executive Agreement with Czechoslovakia. There the President sought to settle over $105 million in claims against Czechoslovakia for $20.5 million. Congress quickly demonstrated its displeasure by enacting legislation requiring that the Agreement be renegotiated. Though Congress has shown itself capable of objecting to executive agreements, it has rarely done so and has not done so in this case.

incident to the resolution of a major foreign policy dispute between our country and another, and where, as here, we can conclude that Congress acquiesced in the President's action, we are not prepared to say that the President lacks the power to settle such claims....

The judgment of the District Court is accordingly affirmed....

[The opinion of Justice POWELL, concurring in part and dissenting in part, is omitted.]

NOTES AND QUESTIONS

1. *The Sounds of Congressional Silence in Dames & Moore and Steel Seizure.* In both *Dames & Moore* and *The Steel Seizure Case*, the President's authority to take private property was challenged, and in both cases the statutes were silent about that authority. How much weight may properly be assigned to congressional silence or inaction? The Court routinely considers legislative inaction in common law cases, *see* Robert F. Williams, *Statutes as Sources of Law Beyond Their Terms in Common Law Cases*, 50 Geo. Wash. L. Rev. 554 (1982), and in deciding the validity of executive action. *See generally* William N. Eskridge Jr., *Interpreting Legislative Inaction*, 87 Mich. L. Rev. 67 (1988). On the other hand, the Court has admitted in other contexts that "we walk on quicksand when we try to find in the absence of...legislation a controlling legal principle." Helvering v. Hallock, 309 U.S. 106, 121 (1940). Why did congressional inaction in *The Steel Seizure Case* have a different meaning than it did in *Dames & Moore*? Are the two cases consistent in their treatment of legislative silence or inaction?

2. *Article I or Article II Power?* Was it really an Article II rather than an Article I power that the President exercised in *Dames & Moore*? The hostage release agreement with Iran was an executive agreement rather than a treaty. Although the Constitution refers to agreements between states and foreign powers in Article I, §10, it prescribes no procedure for their making by the national government. However, Presidents have long assumed the sole power to make them. *See generally* Louis Henkin, *Foreign Affairs and the Constitution* 176-184 (1972). As noted in *Dames & Moore*, the practice of settling claims by executive agreements is long-standing. In United States v. Belmont, 301 U.S. 324, 330-331 (1937), Justice Sutherland, writing for the Court, upheld such an agreement incident to the recognition of the Soviet Union as well "within the competence of the President," citing his view of the President as "sole organ" of the nation in foreign relations. Does *Dames & Moore* support an inherent power in the President to make executive agreements? See generally Chapter 7.

3. *The Predicate for Acquiescence. Dames & Moore* is significant as an illustration in Justice Jackson's twilight zone of how what Justice Frankfurter called "constitutional common law" and what we have called customary national security law is made by congressional acquiescence in an executive practice. Frankfurter's example in *The Steel Seizure Case* of presidential power by congressional acquiescence was an unbroken 80-year executive practice known to Congress.

B. Justice Jackson's Grouping of Presidential Powers

343 U.S. at 611, citing United States v. Midwest Oil Co., 236 U.S. 459 (1915). This suggests a demanding predicate for such a claim of executive authority. One scholar has proposed that the relevant factors to consider include the consistency, frequency, duration, "density" (the number of times an act is repeated over the course of its duration), continuity, and normalcy (nonattribution to presidential or congressional personality aberrations or unique historical circumstances) of the executive practice, congressional notice of the practice, and meaningful congressional acquiescence. Michael J. Glennon, *The Use of Custom in Resolving Separation of Powers Disputes*, 64 B.U. L. Rev. 109, 128-138 (1984). The last, in turn, is a function of the absence of objection, the institutional opportunity to object, the utility of objection (none for a *fait accompli*), and noninterference with protected freedoms (tantamount to rule of clear statement for acquiescence in executive practices restricting individual freedoms). *Id.* at 139-144.

How were the requirements for making law by acquiescence satisfied in *Dames & Moore*? What congressional action, if any, would have defeated the claim of executive power, according to the Court?

3. When the President Takes Measures Incompatible with the Expressed or Implied Will of Congress

Justice Jackson's third group of presidential powers consists of those that the President asserts in conflict with the express or implied will of Congress. The Supreme Court has decided almost a dozen cases in this group, although none has yet involved national security per se (unless you categorize *The Steel Seizure Case* as such a case). In Public Citizen v. United States Dept. of Justice, 491 U.S. 440 (1989), Justice Kennedy asserted that these cases fall into two groups, each representing a different analytical approach:

> In some of our more recent cases involving the powers and prerogatives of the President, we have employed something of a balancing approach, asking whether the statute at issue prevents the President " 'from accomplishing [his] constitutionally assigned functions.' " Morrison v. Olson, 487 U.S. 654, 695 (1988), quoting Nixon v. Administrator of General Services, 433 U.S. 425, 443 (1977), and whether the extent of the intrusion on the President's powers "is justified by an overriding need to promote objectives within the constitutional authority of Congress." Ibid. In each of these cases, the power at issue was not explicitly assigned by the text of the Constitution to be within the sole province of the President, but rather was thought to be encompassed within the general grant to the President of the "executive Power." U.S. Const., Art. II, §1, cl. 1. Thus, for example, the relevant aspect of our decision in *Morrison* involved the President's power to remove Executive officers, a power we had recognized is not conferred by any explicit provision in the text of the Constitution (as is the appointment power), but rather is inferred to be a necessary part of the grant of the "executive Power." See Myers v. United States, 272 U.S. 52, 115-116 (1926). Similarly, in *Administrator of General Services*, we were confronted with the question of the Executive Branch's power to control the disposition of Presidential materials, a matter which, though vital to the

President's ability to perform his assigned functions, is not given to exclusive Presidential control by any explicit provision in the Constitution itself. We said there that "the proper inquiry focuses on the extent to which [the congressional restriction] prevents the Executive Branch from accomplishing its constitutionally assigned functions," and that we would invalidate the statute only if the potential for disruption of the President's constitutional functions were present and if "that impact [were not] justified by an overriding need to promote objectives within the constitutional authority of Congress." 433 U.S., at 443. See also United States v. Nixon, 418 U.S. 683, 703-707 (1974) (Executive privilege).

In a line of cases of equal weight and authority, however, where the Constitution by explicit text commits the power at issue to the exclusive control of the President, we have refused to tolerate *any* intrusion by the Legislative Branch. For example, the Constitution confers upon the President the "Power to grant Reprieves and Pardons for Offenses against the United States, except in Cases of Impeachment." U.S. Const., Art. II, §2, cl. 1. In United States v. Klein, 13 Wall. 128 (1872), the Court considered a federal statute that allowed citizens who had remained loyal to the Union during the Civil War to recover compensation for property abandoned to Union troops during the War. At issue was the validity of a provision in the statute that barred the admission of a Presidential pardon in such actions as proof of loyalty. Although this provision did not impose direct restrictions on the President's power to pardon, the Court held that the Congress could not in any manner limit the full legal effect of the President's power. As we said there: "[I]t is clear that the legislature cannot change the effect of... a pardon any more than the executive can change a law." Id., at 148....

The justification for our refusal to apply a balancing test in these cases, though not always made explicit, is clear enough. Where a power has been committed to a particular Branch of the Government in the text of the Constitution, the balance already has been struck by the Constitution itself. It is improper for this Court to arrogate to itself the power to adjust a balance settled by the explicit terms of the Constitution. To take an obvious example, it would be improper for us to hold that, although the Constitution sets 35 as the age below which one cannot be President, age 30 would in fact be a permissible construction of this term. *See* U.S. Const., Art. II, §1. And it would be equally improper for us to determine that the level of importance at which a jury trial in a common-law suit becomes available is $1,000 instead of $20, as the Constitution provides. *See* U.S. Const., Amdt. 7. These minor adjustments might be seen as desirable attempts to modernize the original constitutional provisions, but where the Constitution draws a clear line, we may not engage in such tinkering.

However improper would be these slight adjustments to the explicit and unambiguous balances that are struck in various provisions of the Constitution, all the more improper would it be for this Court, which is, after all, one of the three coequal Branches of the Federal Government, to rewrite the particular balance of power that the Constitution specifies among the Executive, Legislative, and Judicial Departments. This is not to say that each of the three Branches must be entirely separate and distinct, for that is not the governmental structure of checks and balances established by the Framers. See Mistretta v. United States, 488 U.S. 361, 380-381 (1989); Humphrey's Executor v. United States, 295 U.S. 602, 629 (1935). But as to the particular divisions of power that the Constitution does in fact draw, we are without authority to alter them, and indeed we are empowered to act in particular cases to prevent any other Branch from undertaking to alter them. [*Id.* at 484-485 (Kennedy, J., with whom the Chief Justice and Justice O'Connor join, concurring in the judgment).]

B. Justice Jackson's Grouping of Presidential Powers

NOTES AND QUESTIONS

1. *Ascertaining the Will of Congress.* We have spoken of congressional inaction as one possible manifestation of congressional acquiescence in the making of customary executive authority. But, as Justice Frankfurter found in *The Steel Seizure Case*, inaction also may manifest Congress's implied will to *deny* the President authority. According to one view, in deciding whether a challenged executive action falls into Jackson's third group because it violates the will of Congress, a court "should assess strong indicia of this will, such as recent congressional denials of executive branch requests for legislation, and is not restricted to language of enacted statutes." Christopher Bryant & Carl Tobias, *Youngstown Revisited*, 29 Hastings Const. L.Q. 373, 425 (2002). Does this insight help reconcile the treatment of legislative silence or inaction in *The Steel Seizure Case* and *Dames & Moore*?

2. *Formalism vs. Functionalism or "Balancing."* One scholar paraphrases Justice Kennedy's distinction as follows:

> At times, [constitutional] text will be sufficient, without necessarily developing an overarching vision of the structure, to decide major cases: thus, the Presentment Clause and the bicamerality requirement furnished the rule of decision in *INS v. Chadha*; . . . and the Appointments Clause did the same for *Buckley v. Valeo, Morrison v. Olson,* and *Freytag v. Commissioner.* Sometimes, however, it will be necessary to extrapolate what amounts to a blueprint of organizational relationships from the fundamental structural postulates one sees as informing the Constitution as a whole. . . . [This] sort of extrapolation . . . is . . . appropriate where explicit constitutional text provides little help in deciding separation of powers issues, such as questions of presidential privilege or immunity. . . . [I Laurence H. Tribe, *American Constitutional Law* 130-131 (3d. ed. 2000).]

Which approach do you think would most often be appropriate to decide national security law conflicts between Congress and the President? Does it depend on how the various national security powers are assigned by the Constitution's "explicit text"? How "explicit" does a textual assignment need to be? If the President orders the detention of enemy combatants in a war in violation of rules for detention set out by statute, how should a court decide the resulting conflict in a proper case? On the one hand, the President is surely within his implied (or "explicit"?) command authority as Commander in Chief in ordering his troops to detain combatants. On the other hand, Congress has explicit authority "to make Rules concerning Captures on Land and Water," U.S. Const. art. I, §8, cl. 11, and to make Rules for the Government and Regulation of the land and naval Forces," *id.* cl. 14, as well as" to Define . . . Offences against the Law of Nations." *Id.* cl. 10.

Unfortunately for predictable constitutional analysis (but perhaps fortunately for the Republic), the President's national security powers are mostly implied in the Commander-in-Chief Clause, and the text often provides little help. This suggests that most national security law conflicts will be subject to the balancing or structural extrapolation approach.

3. *Aggrandizement vs. Encroachment.* Another analytic cut at separation of powers disputes in Justice Jackson's third grouping distinguishes between

legislation by which Congress attempts to aggrandize power for itself (by, for example, appointing one of its members to an executive commission) and legislation that merely "encroaches" on another branch by limiting its power in some fashion or by assigning that power to a third branch. *See, e.g.*, Jonathan T. Molot, *Principled Minimalism: Restriking the Balance Between Judicial Minimalism and Neutral Principles*, 90 Va. L. Rev. 1753, 1823 (2004). Because the Framers were especially concerned about congressional usurpation of executive branch functions, *see* Mistretta v. United States, 488 U.S. 361, 411 n.35 (1989), self-aggrandizing legislation calls for especially careful scrutiny, under which it will almost always fail. Legislation merely limiting another branch, on the other hand, is judged by the balancing test described by Justice Kennedy.

4. *Reconciling the Analyses.* The apparent divergence between these lines of authority can possibly be reconciled by treating the different tests as sequential rather than as alternative. *See, e.g.*, Harold J. Krent, *Separating the Strands in Separation of Powers Controversies*, 74 Va. L. Rev. 1253, 1257 (1988); *cf.* Lee C. Weingart, Note, *Who Keeps the Secrets?: A Framework and Analysis of the Separation of Powers Dispute in American Foreign Service Association v. Garfinkle*, 59 Geo. Wash. L. Rev. 193 (1990). Thus, when deciding a separation of powers challenge to the action of a branch, a court first decides whether the branch has "acted outside the constitutionally prescribed means of conduct," Krent, *supra*, at 1256-1257, or has aggrandized itself by wielding power that is demonstrably and uniquely committed to another branch. If so, then the action is unconstitutional; no further consideration of its particular effects on the other branches or of its justifications is necessary. If not, however, then the court must consider whether the acting branch has exercised power in such a way that it disrupts the functioning of one or both of the other branches, and weigh that disruption against the asserted need for such an exercise of power. How would the steel seizure order have fared by this mode of analysis?

The President's National Security Powers 4

The constitutional text offers little help in tracing the President's national security powers. These powers are nebulously vested in broad and opaque phrases like "executive Power," "take Care that the Laws be faithfully executed," and "Commander in Chief," or secreted between the lines by implication or practical necessity. Building on this spare text, theorists and Presidents have reached sharply contrasting conclusions about the scope of presidential authority.

President Theodore Roosevelt espoused by words and by example the "stewardship" theory of presidential power. "[The President is] a steward of the people bound actively and affirmatively to do all he could for the people. [It is] not only his right but his duty to do anything that the needs of the Nation demand, unless such action [is] forbidden by the Constitution or by the law." Theodore Roosevelt, *Autobiography* 372 (1914). Alexander Hamilton drew support for the same theory from the difference between Article I's opening sentence, conferring only "[a]ll legislative Powers *herein granted*" (emphasis supplied), and Article II's opening sentence, vesting the President with "[t]he executive Power" without express limitation. VII *The Works of Alexander Hamilton* 80 (John C. Hamilton ed., 1851).

By contrast, President William H. Taft asserted that "[t]he true view of the Executive function is... that the President can exercise no power which cannot be fairly and reasonably traced to some specific grant of power or justly implied and included within such express grant as proper and necessary to its exercise." William H. Taft, *Our Chief Magistrate and His Powers* 139-140 (1925).

As Justice Jackson stated in *The Steel Seizure Case*, "a century and a half of partisan debate and scholarly speculation yields no net result but only supplies more or less apt quotations from respected sources on each side of the equation. They largely cancel each other out." 343 U.S. at 634-635 (concurring). Consequently, this chapter uses neither the constitutional text nor political theory to organize the analysis of the President's national security powers, but instead divides these powers into four broad and overlapping functional categories. We look in turn at the President's foreign relations, Commander-in-Chief, and emergency powers, and we then examine the President's power to protect information.

A. THE PRESIDENT'S FOREIGN RELATIONS POWERS

United States v. Curtiss-Wright Export Corp.
United States Supreme Court, 1936
299 U.S. 304

Mr. Justice SUTHERLAND delivered the opinion of the Court. On January 27, 1936, an indictment was returned in the court below, the first count of which charges that appellees, beginning with the 29th day of May, 1934, conspired to sell in the United States certain arms of war, namely, fifteen machine guns, to Bolivia, a country then engaged in armed conflict in the Chaco, in violation of the Joint Resolution of Congress approved May 28, 1934, and the provisions of a proclamation issued on the same day by the President of the United States pursuant to authority conferred by §1 of the resolution. In pursuance of the conspiracy, the commission of certain overt acts was alleged, details of which need not be stated. The Joint Resolution follows:

> *Resolved by the Senate and House of Representatives of the United States of America in Congress assembled*, That if the President finds that the prohibition of the sale of arms and munitions of war in the United States to those countries now engaged in armed conflict in the Chaco may contribute to the reestablishment of peace between those countries, and if after consultation with the governments of other American Republics and with their cooperation, as well as that of such other governments as he may deem necessary, he makes proclamation to that effect, it shall be unlawful to sell, except under such limitations and exceptions as the President prescribes, any arms or munitions of war in any place in the United States to the countries now engaged in that armed conflict, or to any person, company, or association acting in the interest of either country, until otherwise ordered by the President or by Congress.
>
> Sec. 2. Whoever sells any arms or munitions of war in violation of section 1 shall, on conviction, be punished by a fine not exceeding $10,000 or by imprisonment not exceeding two years, or both.

The President's proclamation, after reciting the terms of the Joint Resolution, declares:

> Now, therefore, I, Franklin D. Roosevelt, President of the United States of America, acting under and by virtue of the authority conferred in me by the said joint resolution of Congress, do hereby declare and proclaim that I have found that the prohibition of the sale of arms and munitions of war in the United States to those countries now engaged in armed conflict in the Chaco may contribute to the reestablishment of peace between those countries, and that I have consulted with the governments of other American Republics and have been assured of the cooperation of such governments as I have deemed necessary as contemplated by the said joint resolution; and I do hereby admonish all citizens of the United States and every person to abstain from every violation of the provisions of the Joint Resolution above set forth, hereby made applicable to Bolivia and Paraguay, and I do hereby warn them that all violations of such provisions will be rigorously prosecuted.
>
> And I do hereby enjoin upon all officers of the United States charged with the execution of the laws thereof, the utmost diligence in preventing violations of the

said joint resolution and this my proclamation issued thereunder, and in bringing to trial and punishment any offenders against the same.

And I do hereby delegate to the Secretary of State the power of prescribing exceptions and limitations to the application of the said joint resolution of May 28, 1934, as made effective by this my proclamation issued thereunder....

It is contended that by the Joint Resolution, the going into effect and continued operation of the resolution was conditioned (a) upon the President's judgment as to its beneficial effect upon the reestablishment of peace between the countries engaged in armed conflict in the Chaco; (b) upon the making of a proclamation, which was left to his unfettered discretion, thus constituting an attempted substitution of the President's will for that of Congress; (c) upon the making of a proclamation putting an end to the operation of the resolution, which again was left to the President's unfettered discretion; and (d) further, that the extent of its operation in particular cases was subject to limitation and exception by the President, controlled by no standard. In each of these particulars, appellees urge that Congress abdicated its essential functions and delegated them to the Executive.

Whether, if the Joint Resolution had related solely to internal affairs it would be open to the challenge that it constituted an unlawful delegation of legislative power to the Executive, we find it unnecessary to determine. The whole aim of the resolution is to affect a situation entirely external to the United States, and falling within the category of foreign affairs. The determination which we are called to make, therefore, is whether the Joint Resolution, as applied to that situation, is vulnerable to attack under the rule that forbids a delegation of the lawmaking power. In other words, assuming (but not deciding) that the challenged delegation, if it were confined to internal affairs, would be invalid, may it nevertheless be sustained on the ground that its exclusive aim is to afford a remedy for a hurtful condition within foreign territory?

It will contribute to the elucidation of the question if we first consider the differences between the powers of the federal government in respect of foreign or external affairs and those in respect of domestic or internal affairs. That there are differences between them, and that these differences are fundamental, may not be doubted.

The two classes of powers are different, both in respect of their origin and their nature. The broad statement that the federal government can exercise no powers except those specifically enumerated in the Constitution, and such implied powers as are necessary and proper to carry into effect the enumerated powers, is categorically true only in respect of our internal affairs. In that field, the primary purpose of the Constitution was to carve from the general mass of legislative powers *then possessed by the states* such portions as it was thought desirable to vest in the federal government, leaving those not included in the enumeration still in the states. Carter v. Carter Coal Co., 298 U.S. 238, 294. That this doctrine applies only to powers which the states had, is self evident. And since the states severally never possessed international powers, such powers could not have been carved from the mass of state powers but obviously were transmitted to the United States from some other source. During the colonial period, those powers were possessed exclusively by and were entirely under the control of the Crown. By the Declaration of Independence, "the Representatives of the United States of America" declared the United (not the several) Colonies to be free and independent states, and as such to have "full Power to levy War, conclude Peace, contract Alliances, establish Commerce and to do all other Acts and Things which Independent States may of right do."

As a result of the separation from Great Britain by the colonies acting as a unit, the powers of external sovereignty passed from the Crown not to the colonies severally, but to the colonies in their collective and corporate capacity as the United States of America. Even before the Declaration, the colonies were a unit in foreign affairs, acting through a common agency—namely the Continental Congress, composed of delegates from the thirteen colonies. That agency exercised the powers of war and peace, raised an army, created a navy, and finally adopted the Declaration of Independence. Rulers come and go; governments end and forms of government change; but sovereignty survives. A political society cannot endure without a supreme will somewhere. Sovereignty is never held in suspense. When, therefore, the external sovereignty of Great Britain in respect of the colonies ceased, it immediately passed to the union. See Penhallow v. Doane, 3 Dall. 54, 80-81. That fact was given practical application almost at once. The treaty of peace, made on September 3, 1783, was concluded between his Britannic Majesty and the "United States of America."

The Union existed before the Constitution, which was ordained and established among other things to form "a more perfect Union." Prior to that event, it is clear that the Union, declared by the Articles of Confederation to be "perpetual," was the sole possessor of external sovereignty and in the Union it remained without change save in so far as the Constitution in express terms qualified its exercise. The Framer's Convention was called and exerted its powers upon the irrefutable postulate that though the states were several their people in respect of foreign affairs were one....

It results that the investment of the federal government with the powers of external sovereignty did not depend upon the affirmative grants of the Constitution. The powers to declare and wage war, to conclude peace, to make treaties, to maintain diplomatic relations with other sovereignties, if they had never been mentioned in the Constitution, would have vested in the federal government as necessary concomitants of nationality. Neither the Constitution nor the laws passed in pursuance of it have any force in foreign territory unless in respect of our own citizens; and operations of the nation in such territory must be governed by treaties, international understandings and compacts, and the principles of international law. As a member of the family of nations, the right and power of the United States in that field are equal to the right and power of the other members of the international family. Otherwise, the United States is not completely sovereign. The power to acquire territory by discovery and occupation, the power to expel undesirable aliens, the power to make such international agreements as do not constitute treaties in the constitutional sense, none of which is expressly affirmed by the Constitution, nevertheless exist as inherently inseparable from the conception of nationality. This the court recognized, and in each of the cases cited found the warrant for its conclusions not in the provisions of the Constitution, but in the law of nations....

Not only, as we have shown, is the federal power over external affairs in origin and essential character different from that over internal affairs, but participation in the exercise of the power is significantly limited. In this vast external

A. The President's Foreign Relations Powers

realm, with its important, complicated, delicate and manifold problems, the President alone has the power to speak or listen as a representative of the nation. He *makes* treaties with the advice and consent of the Senate; but he alone negotiates. Into the field of negotiation the Senate cannot intrude; and Congress itself is powerless to invade it. As Marshall said in his great argument of March 7, 1800, in the House of Representatives, "the President is the sole organ of the nation in its external relations, and its sole representative with foreign nations." Annals, 6th Cong., col. 613. The Senate Committee on Foreign Relations at a very early day in our history (February 15, 1816), reported to the Senate, among other things, as follows:

> The President is the constitutional representative of the United States with regard to foreign nations. He manages our concerns with foreign nations and must necessarily be most competent to determine when, how, and upon what subjects negotiation may be urged with the greatest prospect of success. For his conduct he is responsible to the Constitution. The committee considers this responsibility the surest pledge for the faithful discharge of his duty. They think the interference of the Senate in the direction of foreign negotiations calculated to diminish that responsibility and thereby to impair the best security for the national safety. The nature of transactions with foreign nations, moreover, requires caution and unity of design, and their success frequently depends on secrecy and dispatch. U.S. Senate, Reports, Committee on Foreign Relations, vol. 8, p. 24.

It is important to bear in mind that we are here dealing not alone with an authority vested in the President by an exertion of legislative power, but with such an authority plus the very delicate, plenary and exclusive power of the President as the sole organ of the federal government in the field of international relations—a power which does not require as a basis for its exercise an act of Congress, but which, of course, like every other governmental power, must be exercised in subordination to the applicable provisions of the Constitution. It is quite apparent that if, in the maintenance of our international relations, embarrassment—perhaps serious embarrassment—is to be avoided and success for our aims achieved, congressional legislation which is to be made effective through negotiation and inquiry within the international field must often accord to the President a degree of discretion and freedom from statutory restriction which would not be admissible were domestic affairs alone involved. Moreover, he, not Congress, has the better opportunity of knowing the conditions which prevail in foreign countries, and especially is this true in time of war. He has his confidential sources of information. He has his agents in the form of diplomatic, consular and other officials. Secrecy in respect of information gathered by them may be highly necessary, and the premature disclosure of it productive of harmful results. Indeed, so clearly is this true that the first President refused to accede to a request to lay before the House of Representatives the instructions, correspondence, and documents relating to the negotiation of the Jay treaty—a refusal the wisdom of which was recognized by the House itself and has never since been doubted. In his reply to the request, President Washington said:

> The nature of foreign negotiations requires caution, and their success must often depend on secrecy; and even when brought to a conclusion a full disclosure

of all the measures, demands, or eventual concessions which may have been proposed or contemplated would be extremely impolitic; for this might have a pernicious influence on future negotiations, or produce immediate inconveniences, perhaps danger and mischief, in relation to other powers. The necessity of such caution and secrecy was one cogent reason for vesting the power of making treaties in the President, with the advice and consent of the Senate, the principle on which that body was formed confining it to a small number of members. To admit, then, a right in the House of Representatives to demand and to have as a matter of course all the papers respecting a negotiation with a foreign power would be to establish a dangerous precedent.

The marked difference between foreign affairs and domestic affairs in this respect is recognized by both houses of Congress in the very form of their requisitions for information from the executive departments. In the case of every department except the Department of State, the resolution *directs* the official to furnish the information. In the case of the State Department, dealing with foreign affairs, the President is *requested* to furnish the information "if not incompatible with the public interest." A statement that to furnish the information is not compatible with the public interest rarely, if ever, is questioned.

When the President is to be authorized by legislation to act in respect of a matter intended to affect a situation in foreign territory, the legislator properly bears in mind the important consideration that the form of the President's action — or, indeed, whether he shall act at all — may well depend, among other things, upon the nature of the confidential information which he has or may thereafter receive, or upon the effect which his action may have upon our foreign relations. This consideration, in connection with what we have already said on the subject, discloses the unwisdom of requiring Congress in this field of governmental power to lay down narrowly definite standards by which the President is to be governed....

In the light of the foregoing observations, it is evident that this court should not be in haste to apply a general rule which will have the effect of condemning legislation like that under review as constituting an unlawful delegation of legislative power. The principles which justify such legislation find overwhelming support in the unbroken legislative practice which has prevailed almost from the inception of the national government to the present day....

...A legislative practice such as we have here, evidenced not by only occasional instances, but marked by the movement of a steady stream for a century and a half of time, goes a long way in the direction of proving the presence of unassailable ground for the constitutionality of the practice, to be found in the origin and history of the power involved, or in its nature, or in both combined....

Mr. Justice MCREYNOLDS does not agree....

Mr. Justice STONE took no part in the consideration or decision of this case.

NOTES AND QUESTIONS

1. *Holding or Dictum?* What did the Court in *Curtiss-Wright* hold and what is the rationale for the holding? Is the discussion of the President's "plenary and exclusive" foreign affairs power dictum or is it a necessary first principle supporting the holding? *Compare The Steel Seizure Case,* 343 U.S. at 635-636 n.2 (Jackson, J., concurring) ("Much of the Court's opinion [in *Curtiss-Wright*] is dictum...."), *with* Charles A. Lofgren, *United States v. Curtiss-Wright Export Corporation: An Historical Reassessment,* 83 Yale L.J. 1, 12 (1973) (necessary first principle), *and Report of the Congressional Committees Investigating the Iran-Contra Affair, The Minority Report,* H.R. Rep. No. 433, S. Rep. No. 216, 100th Cong. 472 (1987) (hereinafter *Minority Report*) ("The Court's statements about the President's inherent foreign policy powers...were crucial to its final decision.").

2. *Practical Differences Between Foreign and Domestic Powers.* Leaving aside for the moment their sources, what are the practical differences between the federal government's foreign or external powers and its domestic or internal powers? Consider, for example, the government's ability to forecast when and how the powers will come into play, the speed with which they may need to be exercised, the need for flexibility once they have been exercised, their immediate impact on our daily lives, their long-term impact on our daily lives, their relationship to state powers, and the need for secrecy. Do you agree that these considerations, as a practical matter, require broader and less precise delegations of foreign affairs authority from Congress to the President than those appropriate for domestic affairs? *See* Roy E. Brownell II, *The Coexistence of United States v. Curtiss-Wright and Youngstown Sheet & Tube v. Sawyer in National Security Jurisprudence,* 16 J.L. & Pol. 1, 33-34 (2000).

Do the same kinds of practical considerations also require that we recognize broader *constitutional* power in the President in foreign than in domestic affairs? Can such broad foreign affairs power be implied from the spare text of Article II? *See id.* at 29 (asserting that the President draws power from his duty to execute laws in the "unique legal realm which comprises the Law of Nations"). Is such power inherent in the constitutional office of the presidency? Or has it been created by executive custom in which Congress has acquiesced? However created, is it limited? If so, how?

3. *Extra-Constitutional Foreign Relations Power?* Do the same considerations, reinforced by history, require that we recognize *extraconstitutional* power in the President in foreign affairs, as Justice Sutherland argues? Is his theory consistent with the historical account set out in Chapter 2 of the framing of the Constitution? With the itemization of foreign affairs powers vested in Congress by Article I, §8? Does Sutherland's theory necessarily dictate the primacy of the President in foreign affairs, or rather the sovereignty of the federal government as a whole? Does it follow from his theory that the Constitution has no application outside our borders?

On this point, Justice Sutherland's reasoning and authorities have been sharply challenged by constitutional scholars. *See, e.g.,* Michael D. Ramsey, *The Myth of Extraconstitutional Foreign Affairs Power,* 42 Wm. & Mary L. Rev. 379, 381

(2000) (*Curtiss-Wright* "wrongly describes the understanding of the drafters and ratifiers of the Constitution. There was no theory of extraconstitutional power in foreign affairs at the time the Constitution was drafted and ratified."); Lofgren, *supra* Note 1, at 32 ("[T]he history on which [major] segments [of *Curtiss-Wright*] rest is 'shockingly inaccurate.' If good history is a requisite to good constitutional law, then *Curtiss-Wright* ought to be relegated to history.") (citation omitted); David M. Levitan, *The Foreign Relations Power: An Analysis of Justice Sutherland's Theory*, 55 Yale L.J. 467, 489 (1946) (Sutherland's theory "does not harmonize with the [historical] facts."). *But see* Sarah H. Cleveland, *The Plenary Power Background of Curtiss-Wright*, 70 U. Colo. L. Rev. 1127 (1999) (arguing that *Curtiss-Wright* evolved from nineteenth century jurisprudence of inherent plenary power); H. Jefferson Powell, *The Founders and the President's Authority Over Foreign Affairs*, 40 Wm. & Mary L. Rev. 1471 (1999) (asserting that the founders reflected a "coherent pattern of thought that accorded the President central responsibility for the foreign policy of the United States").

4. *The "Sole Organ" Claim.* Sutherland quotes then-Congressman, later Chief Justice, John Marshall for the proposition that "[t]he President is the sole organ of the nation in its external relations, and its sole representative with foreign nations." 299 U.S. at 319. Does it logically follow that the President is solely responsible for the formulation of foreign policy? Or does Marshall's language suggest only that the President is the nation's sole spokesperson and agent for communicating and executing foreign policy made by Congress or by him and the Congress together? One answer is suggested by the rest of John Marshall's statement from which Sutherland quoted. Marshall was defending President John Adams's extradition of a British subject to England pursuant to the Jay Treaty of 1795. He observed:

> The treaty, which is a law, enjoins the performance of a particular object. The person who is to perform this object is marked out by the Constitution, since the person is named who conducts the foreign intercourse, and is to take care that the laws be faithfully executed. The means by which it is to be performed, the force of the nation, are in the hands of this person.... Congress, unquestionably, may prescribe the mode, and Congress may devolve on others the whole execution of the contract; but, till this be done, it seems the duty of the Executive department to execute the contract by any means it possesses. [10 Annals of Cong. 613-614.]

5. *The President as Foreign Policymaker.* As a practical matter, the President cannot be a mere conduit for congressionally made foreign policy. Professor Henkin argues that "the distinction between making foreign policy and conducting foreign relations is essentially empty: the President makes foreign policy by conducting foreign relations, by the way he conducts them and the content and tone he gives them." Louis Henkin, *Foreign Affairs and the Constitution*, 66 Foreign Aff. 284, 294 (Winter 1987/1988). Does it follow that the President alone makes foreign policy or that he can make policy at odds with that set by Congress? Consider Justice Jackson's statement in *The Steel Seizure Case*, 343 U.S. at 635-636 n.2, that *Curtiss-Wright* "intimated that the President might act in

B. THE COMMANDER IN CHIEF'S WAR POWERS

1. Defensive War Power

The Prize Cases
United States Supreme Court, 1863
67 U.S. (2 Black) 635

Mr. Justice GRIER.... [At the beginning of the Civil War, during a congressional recess, President Lincoln issued a proclamation by which he "deemed it advisable to set on foot a blockade of the ports within [certain of the Confederate states], in pursuance of the laws of the United States and of the law of nations.... If, therefore, with a view to violate such blockade, a vessel shall approach or shall attempt to leave either of said ports, she will be duly warned by the commander of one of the blockading vessels, who will endorse on her register the fact and date of such warning, and if the same vessel shall again attempt to enter or leave the blockaded port, she will be captured and sent to the nearest convenient port for such proceedings against her and her cargo, as prize, as may be deemed advisable." The owners of vessels that were captured as prizes during the blockade brought this action challenging the legality of the President's proclamation.]

Had the President a right to institute a blockade of ports in possession of persons in armed rebellion against the Government, on the principles of international law, as known and acknowledged among civilized States?...

The right of prize and capture has its origin in the "*jus belli*," and is governed and adjudged under the law of nations. To legitimate the capture of a neutral vessel or property on the high seas, a war must exist *de facto*, and the neutral must have a knowledge or notice of the intention of one of the parties belligerent to use this mode of coercion against a port, city, or territory, in possession of the other.

Let us enquire whether, at the time this blockade was instituted, a state of war existed which would justify a resort to these means of subduing the hostile force.

War has been well defined to be, "That state in which a nation prosecutes its right by force."...

By the Constitution, Congress alone has the power to declare a national or foreign war. It cannot declare war against a State, or any number of States, by virtue of any clause in the Constitution. The Constitution confers on the President the whole Executive power. He is bound to take care that the laws be faithfully executed. He is Commander-in-Chief of the Army and Navy of the United States, and of the militia of the several States when called into the actual service of the United States. He has no power to initiate or declare a war either against a foreign nation or a domestic State. But by the Acts of Congress of February 28th, 1795, and 3d of March, 1807, he is authorized to call out the militia and use the military and naval forces of the United States in case of invasion by foreign nations, and to suppress insurrection against the government of a State or of the United States.

If a war be made by invasion of a foreign nation, the President is not only authorized but bound to resist force by force. He does not initiate the war, but is bound to accept the challenge without waiting for any special legislative authority. And whether the hostile party be a foreign invader, or States organized in rebellion, it is none the less a war, although the declaration of it be "*unilateral.*" Lord Stowell (1 Dodson, 247) observes, "It is not the less a war on *that account*, for war may exist without a declaration on either side. It is so laid down by the best writers on the law of nations. A declaration of war by one country only, is not a mere challenge to be accepted or refused at pleasure by the other." . . .

This greatest of civil wars was not gradually developed by popular commotion, tumultuous assemblies, or local unorganized insurrections. However long may have been its previous conception, it nevertheless sprung forth suddenly from the parent brain, a Minerva in the full panoply of *war*. The President was bound to meet it in the shape it presented itself, without waiting for Congress to baptize it with a name; and no name given to it by him or them could change the fact. . . .

Whether the President in fulfilling his duties, as Commander-in-Chief, in suppressing an insurrection, has met with such armed hostile resistance, and a civil war of such alarming proportions as will compel him to accord to them the character of belligerents, is a question to be decided *by him*, and this Court must be governed by the decisions and acts of the political department of the Government to which this power was entrusted. "He must determine what degree of force the crisis demands." The proclamation of blockade is itself official and conclusive evidence to the Court that a state of war existed which demanded and authorized a recourse to such a measure, under the circumstances peculiar to the case. . . .

If it were necessary to the technical existence of a war, that it should have a legislative sanction, we find it in almost every act passed at the extraordinary session of the Legislature of 1861, which was wholly employed in enacting laws to enable the Government to prosecute the war with vigor and efficiency. And finally, in 1861, we find Congress "*ex majore cautela*" [out of caution] and in anticipation of such astute objections, passing an act "approving, legalizing, and making valid all the acts, proclamations, and orders of the President, &c., as if they had been *issued and done under the previous express authority* and direction of the Congress of the United States."

Without admitting that such an act was necessary under the circumstances, it is plain that if the President had in any manner assumed powers which it was necessary should have the authority or sanction of Congress, that on the well known principle of law, "*omnis ratihabitio retrotrahitur et mandato equiparatur*" [ratifications relate back and are the equivalent of prior authority] this ratification has operated to perfectly cure the defect. . . .

The objection made to this act of ratification, that it is *ex post facto*, and therefore unconstitutional and void, might possibly have some weight on the trial of an indictment in a criminal Court. But precedents from that source cannot be received as authoritative in a tribunal administering public and international law.

On this first question therefore we are of the opinion that the President had a right, *jure belli,* to institute a blockade of ports in possession of the States in rebellion, which neutrals are bound to regard....

Mr. Justice NELSON, dissenting [in an opinion in which Chief Justice TANEY and Justices CATRON and CLIFFORD concurred].... It is not to be denied... that if a civil war existed between that portion of the people in organized insurrection to overthrow this Government at the time this vessel and cargo were seized, and if she was guilty of a violation of the blockade, she would be lawful prize of war. But before this insurrection against the established Government can be dealt with on the footing of a civil war, within the meaning of the law of nations and the Constitution of the United States, and which will draw after it belligerent rights, it must be recognized or declared by the war-making power of the Government. No power short of this can change the legal status of the Government or the relations of its citizens from that of peace to a state of war, or bring into existence all those duties and obligations of neutral third parties growing out of a state of war. The war power of the Government must be exercised before this changed condition of the Government and people and of neutral third parties can be admitted....

... [W]e find there that to constitute a civil war in the sense in which we are speaking, before it can exist, in contemplation of law, it must be recognized or declared by the sovereign power of the State, and which sovereign power by our Constitution is lodged in the Congress of the United States—civil war, therefore, under our system of government, can exist only by an act of Congress, which requires the assent of two of the great departments of the Government, the Executive and Legislative....

... But we are asked, what would become of the peace and integrity of the Union in case of an insurrection at home or invasion from abroad if this power could not be exercised by the President in the recess of Congress, and until that body could be assembled?

The framers of the Constitution fully comprehended this question, and provided for the contingency. Indeed, it would have been surprising if they had not, as a rebellion had occurred in the State of Massachusetts while the Convention was in session, and which had become so general that it was quelled only by calling upon the military power of the State. The Constitution declares that Congress shall have power "to provide for calling forth the militia to execute the laws of the Union, suppress insurrections, and repel invasions." Another clause, "that the President shall be Commander-in-chief of the Army and Navy of the United States, and of the Militia of the several States when called into the actual service of the United States;" and, again: "He shall take care that the laws shall be faithfully executed." Congress passed laws on this subject in 1792 and 1795. 1 United States Laws, pp. 264, 424. [It also passed a law on the subject in 1807. Act of Mar. 3, 1807, ch. 39, 2 Stat. 443.]...

The Acts of 1795 and 1807 did not, and could not under the Constitution, confer on the President the power of declaring war against a State of this Union, or of deciding that war existed, and upon that ground authorize the capture and confiscation of the property of every citizen of the State whenever it was found on the waters. The laws of war, whether the war be civil or *inter gentes,* as we have seen, convert every citizen of the hostile State into a public enemy, and treat him accordingly, whatever may have been his previous conduct. This great power over the business and property of the citizen is reserved to the legislative department by the express words of the Constitution. It cannot be delegated or surrendered to the Executive. Congress alone can determine whether war exists or should be declared; and until they have acted, no citizen of the State can be punished in his person or property, unless he has committed some offence against a law of Congress passed before the act was committed, which made it a crime, and defined the punishment. The penalty of confiscation for the acts of others with which he had no concern cannot lawfully be inflicted....

... [C]onsequently,... the President had no power to set on foot a blockade under the law of nations, and... the capture of the vessel and cargo in this case, and in all cases before us in which the capture occurred before the 13th of July, 1861 [the date on which Congress first authorized a naval blockade of the Confederacy], for breach of blockade, or as enemies' property, are illegal and void, and... the decrees of condemnation should be reversed and the vessel and cargo restored.

NOTES AND QUESTIONS

1. *The Commander in Chief's Command Authority: First General and Admiral?* One possible interpretation of the Framers' intent is that designation of the President as Commander in Chief merely placed him at the top of the military chain of command, making him First General and Admiral—essentially the top military commander without independent war policy-making authority. At least as late as 1851, the Supreme Court clearly took this position. A unanimous Court held that the military occupation of a Mexican port by order of the President during the congressionally declared Mexican War did not annex it to the United States. Fleming v. Page, 50 U.S. (9 How.) 603 (1851). It reasoned that the President's

> duty and power are purely military. As commander in chief, he is authorized to direct the movements of the naval and military forces *placed by law at his command,* and to employ them in the manner he may deem most effectual to harass and conquer and subdue the enemy. He may invade the hostile country, and subject it to the sovereignty and authority of the United States. But his conquests do not enlarge the boundaries of this Union, nor extend the operation of our institutions and laws *beyond the limits assigned to them by the legislative power.* ... [50 U.S. at 614-615 (emphasis supplied).]

Did the Court pull back from this reading of Article II in *The Prize Cases?* In *Curtiss-Wright?*

2. *Delegated Defensive Power.* In Martin v. Mott, 25 U.S. (12 Wheat.) 19 (1813), the Court for the first time discussed the President's power to repel invasions. It found the President to be "the sole and exclusive judge whether the exigency has arisen" and implied the unsuitability of such a determination for judicial review. Yet *Mott* was decided under a statute that delegated to the President the power to

call forth the militia "as he may judge necessary to repel such invasion [by a foreign nation or Indian tribe]." Act of Feb. 28, 1795, ch. 36, 1 Stat. 424. "Whenever a statute gives a discretionary power to any person, to be exercised by him upon his own opinion of certain facts," the Court explained, "it is a sound rule of construction, that the statute constitutes him the sole and exclusive judge of the existence of those facts." 25 U.S. at 31-32. Into which of Justice Jackson's categories in *The Steel Seizure Case* does the power exercised in *Mott* fall?

3. *Inherent Defensive War Power.* The legal challenge to the naval blockade of the South in *The Prize Cases* presented the Supreme Court for the first time with the question whether the President has the inherent power to repel attacks — to conduct defensive war — without prior congressional authorization. What answer did the Court give? Why did the Court in *The Prize Cases* take such pains to define "war"? On September 12, 2001, President George W. Bush declared that the terrorist attacks on the World Trade Center and the Pentagon were "acts of war." *Remarks by the President in Photo Opportunity with the National Security Team*, Sept. 12, 2001, *at* http://www.whitehouse.gov/news/releases/2001/09/20010912-4.html. Did the circumstances that day or since fit the Court's definition of "war"? Is there any danger that a President might *create* the conditions said to warrant a military response? See *infra* pp. 213-214.

Could the Court in *The Prize Cases* have upheld the President's actions on any narrower ground? Can you argue that it did so? *See generally* Ludwell H. Johnson III, *Abraham Lincoln and the Development of Presidential War-Making Powers: Prize Cases (1863) Revisited*, 35 Civil War Hist. 208 (1989).

The dissenters in *The Prize Cases* did not contest the proposition that a civil war places the nation *in extremis*. Why then did they find the blockade unlawful? Did they conclude that the President's actions were forbidden by Congress? That they exceeded a congressional grant of authority? That the President lacked any inherent authority to order the blockade?

4. *The Scope of the President's Defensive War Power.* What is the scope of the power that the Court recognized? By the logic of the Court, is the President constitutionally empowered to meet *any* threat of force as he determines, without awaiting congressional authorization? Would *The Prize Cases* Court have approved the 1983 invasion of Grenada without prior congressional approval? The deployment of U.S. peacekeeping troops in Lebanon in 1983? The sending of U.S. military advisors to El Salvador in the 1980s? *See generally* Peter Raven-Hansen, *Constitutional Constraints: The War Clause*, in *The U.S. Constitution and the Power to Go to War* 35-43 (Gary M. Stern & Morton H. Halperin eds., 1994). Would *The Prize Cases* Court have approved an extended U.S. military campaign against terrorists and their training facilities in Somalia, Sudan, and Yemen in response to the September 11, 2001, terrorist attacks on the United States?

2. Customary War Powers

Although we have formally declared war only 11 times in our history, we had used armed force abroad on more than 300 occasions through 2004. Richard

F. Grimmett, *Instances of Use of United States Armed Forces Abroad, 1798-2004* (Cong. Res. Serv. RL30172), Oct. 5, 2004. Does this history indicate that the President may use armed force whenever he thinks it necessary to protect national security? That argument was made to support the legality of U.S. participation in the Vietnam War. The Legal Adviser to the State Department inferred from 125 prior congressionally unauthorized uses of armed force abroad that the President has the "power to deploy American forces abroad and commit them to military operations when ... [he] deems such action necessary to maintain the security and defense of the United States...." Leonard C. Meeker, *The Legality of United States Participation in the Defense of Viet-Nam*, 75 Yale L.J. 1085, 1100-1101 (1966), *infra* p. 209. *See also* J. Terry Emerson, *War Powers Resolution*, 74 W. Va. L. Rev. 53, App. A (1971) (citing usage for same proposition). Or does history suggest a narrower claim of presidential war power: that he has acquired some customary war powers with congressional acquiescence?

The answers may turn on the particulars: what uses of armed force were made in what circumstances? In the following excerpt, Professors Wormuth and Firmage argue that the particulars matter, and that after the history is disaggregated, the pieces do not reassemble into an inherent war power in the President. Professor Monaghan disagrees. For him, it is not the particulars but the frequency of the uses of force that has settled the legitimacy of an inherent presidential power to commit the armed forces to hostilities.

Francis D. Wormuth & Edwin B. Firmage, To Chain the Dog of War
pages 145-151 (2d ed. 1989)

The lists [of presidential uses of armed force] are not accurately characterized by their compilers. For the purpose of analysis, the latest official list, that prepared by the State Department in 1967, is used here. The proportions of cases remain fairly constant through all the lists. Sometimes a case might fall under more than one heading, but it is placed here under what appears to be the most appropriate title. The cases in the State Department list can be categorized thus:

1. Actions for which congressional authorization was claimed — 7
2. Naval self-defense — 1
3. Enforcement of law against piracy, no trespass — 1
4. Enforcement of law against piracy, technical trespass — 7
5. Landings to protect citizens before 1862 — 13
6. Landings to protect citizens, 1865-1967 — 56
7. Invasion of foreign or disputed territory, no combat — 10
8. Invasion of foreign or disputed territory, combat — 10
9. Reprisals against aborigines — 9
10. Other reprisals not authorized by statute — 4
11. Minatory demonstrations without combat — 6
12. Intervention in Panama — 1
13. Protracted occupation of Caribbean states — 6
14. Actions anticipating World War II — 1

B. The Commander in Chief's War Powers

15.	Bombing of Laos	1
16.	Korean and Vietnamese Wars	2
17.	Miscellaneous	2
	Total	137

The first category in the list contains three of the limited wars declared by Congress; it includes one of the four conditional declarations of war. It includes two forays into Spanish Florida, purportedly undertaken under statutory authorization, and Woodrow Wilson's seizure of Veracruz on April 21, 1914, said to have been ratified by the joint resolution of April 22, 1914.

A number of other cases can be justified in terms other than presidential initiative. As for category 2, naval vessels have the right of self-defense at international and municipal law. Category 3 is merely obedience to statute. Although his naval commanders did not share his views, President Monroe took the position that the landings in category 4 required statutory authorization. We have no contemporary discussion of the thirteen landings in category 5. As we shall see, some of the fifty-six landings in category 6 enjoy statutory authorization. The invasion of foreign territory in categories 7 and 8 was illegal, but if the United States claimed the territory, the President's action in sending troops was not an act of war. Reprisals, as we have seen, are acts of war, and today naval regulations forbid officers to undertake them. [See *infra* p. 275.] The minatory demonstrations at sea in category 11 were intended to make other states nervous but were not acts of war. Theodore Roosevelt's intervention in Panama was naked aggression, and the United States paid twenty-five million dollars as compensation to Colombia.

Category 13 represents merely an aspect of the involvement of the American executive in the Caribbean area. American forces actually occupied and administered three Caribbean countries: Cuba from 1906 to 1909, Haiti from 1915 to 1934, and the Dominican Republic from 1916 to 1924. On other occasions, forces of marines were permanently stationed in a Caribbean country in order to influence local politics; the longest such interventions were those in Nicaragua from 1912 to 1925 and from 1926 to 1933. In addition, the customshouses of sovereign states were occupied now and again, with or without authorization by treaty, and their finances were administered by the United States for extended periods. On occasion, at the instance of the United States, Latin American countries agreed to put their import duties in the hands of a representative of foreign bankers in case of default on a loan. But in no case was the executive action said to be grounded on a presidential war-making power....

As for category 14, illegal presidential acts of war, as well as a congressional declaration of limited war in the form of the Lend-Lease Act, occurred before the Second World War, as we have already seen. No one would allege that presidential bombing of Laos was authorized by the Constitution or by statute. President Truman's entry into the Korean War was defended by the State Department as authorized by treaty—that is, by the United Nations Charter— and by the executive precedents we have been considering. The Vietnam War was alleged to be authorized by the Southeast Asia Collective Defense Treaty, the Tonkin Gulf Resolution, and the executive precedents....

One cannot be sure, but the number of cases in which Presidents have personally made the decisions, unconstitutionally, to engage in war or in acts of war probably lies between one and two dozen. And in all those cases the Presidents have made false claims of authorization, either by statute or by treaty or by international law. They have not relied on their powers as commander in chief or as chief executive.

In the case of executive wars, none of the conditions for the establishment of constitutional power by usage is present. The Constitution is not ambiguous. No contemporaneous congressional interpretation attributes a power of initiating war to the President. The early Presidents, and indeed everyone in the country until the year 1950, denied that the President possessed such a power. There is no sustained body of usage to support such a claim. It can only be audacity or desperation that leads the champions of recent presidential usurpations to state that "history had legitimated the practice of presidential war-making."

Henry P. Monaghan, Presidential War-Making
50 B.U. L. Rev. 19, 25-27, 30-31 (Special Issue 1970)

The occasions on which presidents have refused to take military action abroad because of a lack of prior congressional authorization are few in number and increasingly rare. From the beginning of our constitutional history, presidents have both deployed the armed forces abroad and committed them to actual hostilities without explicit congressional authorization. In excess of one hundred and twenty instances of such action exist. The precedents extend back to Washington and include that great "strict constructionist" Jefferson; they run through the nineteenth century; and with the emergence of the United States as a global power in this century, they become sharper and more spectacular. The presidencies of the two Roosevelts provide classic examples. Moreover, no recent president has refused to commit the armed forces to actual hostilities because of a lack of congressional approval, as the conduct of Truman in Korea, Johnson in the Dominican Republic, and Kennedy, Johnson and Nixon in Southeast Asia demonstrate. Thus, argues the state department, "practice and precedent have confirmed the constitutional authority of the president to commit the armed forces to battle without a declaration of war."

The strength of the "practice and precedent" has, however, not gone unchallenged. Most writers who seek constitutionally based restrictions on the president's war-making power argue that the precedents are not compelling. Indeed, it has been suggested that there is only one prior illustration of presidential commitment of armed forces to war without congressional authorization, namely, Korea. The other instances cited, it is argued, were simply presidential responses to reprisals, or "relatively minor and short-lived occurrences [that] do not establish precedent for the massive and long-lasting [Vietnam] war...": "minor" and "short-lived" from whose point of view? Certainly not from the perspective of those against whom the armed forces were employed; and certainly not from the presidents' view, since they generally brought about the results intended. To dismiss American interventions in Latin America as "minor" amounts to recognition of presidential power to wage war against weak opponents for limited purposes.

The validity of each of the precedents relied upon by the state department need not be separately defended. Taken as a whole, they seem to me to add up to the following: with ever-increasing frequency, presidents have employed that amount of force that they deemed necessary to accomplish their foreign policy objectives. When little force was needed (e.g., in our incursions in Latin America), little was used; when larger commitments were necessary, they too were forthcoming. Whatever the intention of the Framers, the military machine has become simply an instrument for the achievement of foreign policy goals, which, in turn, have become a central responsibility of the presidency. Congress has seldom objected on legal grounds, and so the only limitation upon presidential power has been that imposed by political considerations. That is the teaching of our history.

To be sure, various legal theories have been advanced in defense of presidential power. In good lawyer-like fashion these theories have been framed in terms no broader than necessary to justify the particular presidential action at issue. For example, in the late nineteenth century, American troop interventions in Latin America were rationalized in terms of "inherent" presidential power "neutrally" to protect the rights of American citizens abroad during foreign disorders — a fiction that did not survive the turn of the century. Since presidential use of armed forces abroad has assumed considerably enlarged dimension in this century, it is hardly surprising that the supporting rationales have been constantly broadened and adjusted. The rationales have, in a word, followed the practice....

In varying degrees the commentators present us with visibly strained efforts to minimize the long and ever-accumulating practice of presidential "war-making," if one prefers that term. For better or worse that practice seems to me clearly established, as I have indicated. To my mind, this historical development of our institutions has settled the legitimacy of "inherent" presidential power to commit the armed forces to hostilities. A practice so deeply embedded in our governmental structure should be treated as decisive of the constitutional issue. History and practice are not here being appealed to in order to freeze forever the scope of a constitutional guarantee framed in terms of individual liberty; rather, this issue deals with the distribution of political power between the legislative and executive branches. Matters of this character are, in the words of Chief Justice Marshall, best left "to the practice of government." ...

NOTES AND QUESTIONS

1. *Usage and Denials of Authority.* If usage is significant, should the relevant list include instances in which the Congress *refused* presidential requests for delegations of authority to use force abroad or *denied funding* for the continued use of force abroad? *See* Wormuth & Firmage, *supra* p. 72, ch. 5 (discussing such instances). Do such instances refute the claim that usage consists of an unbroken line of precedents for unilateral presidential military initiatives? See *supra* pp. 48-55 (executive custom and congressional acquiescence).

2. *Usage and Necessity.* Alexander Hamilton wrote in *The Federalist No. 23* that it was undesirable to impose "constitutional shackles" on "the power to which the care of [the safety of the nation] is committed," because "it is impossible to foresee or define the extent and variety of national exigencies, or the

correspondent extent and variety of means that may be necessary to satisfy them." *The Federalist No. 23*, at 153 (Clinton Rossiter ed., 1961). James Madison also noted in *The Federalist No. 41*, at 257 (Clinton Rossiter ed., 1961), that

> [t]he means of security can only be regulated by the means and the danger of attack. They will, in fact, be ever determined by these rules and no others. It is in vain to oppose constitutional barriers to the impulse of self-preservation. It is worse than in vain; because it places in the Constitution itself necessary usurpations of power; every precedent of which is a germ of unnecessary and multiplied repetitions.

Both observations go only to the necessity of a flexible war power in the government at large, without specifying a branch. Indeed, both Hamilton and Madison made their comments in defense of the *congressional* power to raise armies. *See* Charles A. Lofgren, *War Making Under the Constitution: The Original Understanding*, 81 Yale L.J. 672, 688 (1972). Nevertheless, they gave clear expression to the view that war powers are necessarily adaptive, depending on variable and unforeseeable threats to the national security. From this premise, it is a small step to find the shape of presidential war powers in usage: the accumulation of presidential military initiatives since 1789.

Does the very diversity of usage prove that Madison was right in warning that the "means of security" will be governed only by the rule of necessity "and no others"? Does the President alone not have the practical capacity to respond to that rule? In short, is unpredictability not inherent in the nature of the problem, justifying allocation of war powers to the branch that is able to respond most quickly and flexibly? *See* Eugene V. Rostow, *"Once More Into the Breach": The War Powers Resolution Revisited*, 21 Val. U. L. Rev. 1, 9 (1986).

On the other hand, does the rule of necessity operate with equal force in all instances? If the nation is not itself put at risk and there is time to consider a response to foreign threats, should the President be empowered to fashion that response without first going to Congress?

3. *Customary Law Redux.* Upon what constitutional theory does an historically based claim of inherent presidential power to commit troops to hostilities rest? See generally *supra* pp. 48-55; Raven-Hansen, *supra* p. 71, at 31-32. If the theory is customary law by congressional acquiescence, are the particular circumstances of each military initiative not relevant to the constitutional theory?

4. *Negotiated War Powers.* If Professor Monaghan's theory is that exercise of the war power is negotiated between the branches, what is the point of studying legal limits on war powers? Is what the political branches negotiate not then constitutional per se, and does the President not hold all the cards in the negotiations? *See* Harold H. Koh, *Why the President (Almost) Always Wins in Foreign Affairs: Lessons of the Iran-Contra Affair*, 97 Yale L.J. 1255 (1988). How do constitutional claims, international law doctrines, and past military precedents fit into the next negotiation? *See generally* Abram Chayes, *The Cuban Missile Crisis* 6-7 (1974) (suggesting that law affected the decisional process by acting as a

B. The Commander in Chief's War Powers

constraint, supplying justification or legitimation, and providing organizational structures, procedures, and forums).

5. *Jackson's Third Grouping Again.* If the President has acquired customary war power by congressional acquiescence, does it follow that Congress cannot take it away? Whether or not history establishes that the President may order the use of armed force abroad without prior statutory authority, may he act inconsistently with limits contained in prior statutory authority?

3. Statutory Limits on the President's War Power

Little v. Barreme
United States Supreme Court, 1804
6 U.S. (2 Cranch) 170

MARSHALL, Chief Justice, now delivered the opinion of the Court.... During the hostilities between the United States and France, an act for the suspension of all intercourse between the two nations was annually passed. That under which the *Flying-Fish* was condemned, declared every vessel, owned, hired, or employed wholly or in part by an American, which should be employed in any traffic or commerce with or for any person resident within the jurisdiction or under the authority of the French republic, to be forfeited together with her cargo; the one half to accrue to the United States, and the other to any person or persons, citizens of the United States, who will inform and prosecute for the same.

The 5th section of this act authorizes the President of the United States, to instruct the commanders of armed vessels, "to stop and examine any ship or vessel of the United States on the high sea, which there may be reason to suspect to be engaged in any traffic or commerce contrary to the true tenor of the act, and if upon examination it should appear that such ship or vessel is bound or sailing *to* any port or place within the territory of the French republic or her dependencies, it is rendered lawful to seize such vessel, and send her into the United States for adjudication."

[By this authority, a U.S. frigate commanded by Captain Little intercepted an ostensibly Danish vessel named the *Flying-Fish* as it was returning *from* a French port. The ship's owners subsequently sued Captain Little for trespass.]

It is by no means clear that the president of the United States, whose high duty it is to "take care that the laws be faithfully executed," and who is commander in chief of the armies and navies of the United States, might not, without any special authority for that purpose, in the then existing state of things, have empowered the officers commanding the armed vessels of the United States, to seize and send into port for adjudication, American vessels which were forfeited by being engaged in this illicit commerce. But when it is observed that the... 5th section [of the act] gives a special authority to seize on the high seas, and limits that authority to the seizure of vessels bound or sailing *to* a French port, the legislature seem to have prescribed that the manner in which this law shall be carried into execution was to exclude a seizure of any vessel not bound *to* a French port. Of consequence, however strong the circumstances might be, which induced Captain Little to suspect the *Flying-Fish* to be an American vessel, they could not excuse the detention of her, since he would not have been authorised to detain her had she been really American.

It was so obvious, that if only vessels sailing to a French port could be seized on the high seas, that the law would be very often evaded, that this act of congress appears to have received a different construction from the executive of the United States; a construction much better calculated to give it effect.

A copy of his act was transmitted by the secretary of the navy to the captains of the armed vessels, who were ordered to consider the 5th section as a part of their instructions. The same letter contained the following clause.

> A proper discharge of the important duties enjoined on you, arising out of this act, will require the exercise of a sound and an impartial judgment. You are not only to do all that in you lies, to prevent all intercourse, whether direct or circuitous, between the ports of the *United States* and those of *France* or her dependencies, where the vessels *are apparently as well as really American*, and protected by *American* papers only, but you are to be vigilant that vessels or cargoes really *American*, but covered by *Danish* or other foreign papers, and bound *to* or *from French* ports, do not escape you.

These orders, given by the executive under the construction of the act of congress made by the department to which its execution was assigned, enjoin the seizure of American vessels sailing from a French port. Is the officer who obeys them liable for damages sustained by this misconstruction of the act, or will his orders excuse him? If his instructions afford him no protection, then the law must take its course, and he must pay such damages as are legally awarded against him; if they excuse an act not otherwise excusable, it would then be necessary to inquire whether this is a case in which the probable cause which existed to induce a suspicion that the vessel was American, would excuse the captor from damages when the vessel appeared in fact to be neutral.

I confess the first bias of my mind was very strong in favor of the opinion that though the instructions of the executive could not give a right, they might yet excuse from damages. I was very much inclined to think that a distinction ought to be taken between acts of civil and those of military officers; and between proceedings within the body of the country and those on the high seas. That implicit obedience which military men usually pay to the orders of their superiors, which indeed is indispensably necessary to every military system, appeared to me strongly to imply the principle that those orders, if not to perform a prohibited act, ought to justify the person whose general duty it is to obey them, and who is placed by the laws of his country in a situation which in general requires that he should obey them. I was strongly inclined to think that where, in consequence of orders from the legitimate authority, a vessel is seized with pure intention, the claim of the injured party for damages would be against that government from which the orders proceeded, and would be a proper subject for negotiation. But I have been convinced that I was mistaken, and I have receded from this first opinion. I acquiesce in that of my brethren, which is, that the instructions cannot change the nature of the transaction, or legalize an act which without those instructions would have been a plain trespass. . . .

B. The Commander in Chief's War Powers

Captain Little then must be answerable in damages to the owner of this neutral vessel. . . .

NOTES AND QUESTIONS

1. *Ascertaining the Will of Congress (Again).* The capture at issue in Little v. Barreme took place during the undeclared but congressionally authorized Quasi-War with France. See *infra* p. 94. Why do you think the President interpreted the statute as he did? Had Congress expressly prohibited this capture? Or had Congress simply decided not to authorize the capture? If the latter, why was the capture unlawful? Would it have been unlawful absent any statute on point?

2. *Precedential Value.* What is the precedential value of *Little?* Does the case address the scope of the Commander in Chief's powers or the scope of Congress's power to control the conduct of war? *Compare* Abraham D. Sofaer, *War, Foreign Affairs and Constitutional Power: The Origins* 163 (1976) (*Little* "rests on the notion . . . that declared war involved a delegation to the executive and all citizens of general authority to commit hostilities against the enemy, while the conduct of undeclared or 'imperfect' war was limited to those actions authorized by Congress."), *with* John C. Yoo, *The Continuation of Politics By Other Means: The Original Understanding of War Powers,* 84 Cal. L. Rev. 167, 294-295 n.584 (1996) (*Little* never reached the issue of "the President's inherent constitutional authority to order captures going beyond Congress's commands."), *and* J. Gregory Sidak, *The Quasi War Cases—And Their Relevance to Whether "Letters of Marque and Reprisal" Constrain Presidential War Powers,* 28 Harv. J.L. & Pub. Poly. 465, 492 (2005) ("[The] negative implication [of Chief Justice Marshall's statements in *Little*] was that congressional silence leaves the President free to act"). Can it be distinguished from other cases on the ground that the Constitution provides Congress with express authority to make rules for capture? *See* U.S. Const. art. I, §8, cl. 11. Even more narrowly, does *Little* address just the liability of military subordinates asserting the "I was only following orders" defense?

Or does *Little* stand for the intermediate proposition that when Congress has prescribed the manner in which its authorization for the use of armed force is to be executed, its prescription "occupies the field" and is binding even on the President?

3. *Presidential Declarations of War?* While it is commonly asserted that the United States has not declared war since World War II, it has fought several large, congressionally authorized wars (including those in Viet Nam, Afghanistan, and Iraq). One scholar has argued that these were all, in fact, *declared* wars, in that they were accompanied by official public announcements "that the nation was entering into [or had entered into] sustained military hostilities, together with a statement of the reasons for, and the goals of, the conflict." Michael D. Ramsey, *Presidential Declarations of War,* 37 U.C. Davis L. Rev. 321, 324 (2003). Each, however, was "declared" by the *President,* not by Congress. *Id.* In each case, Congress authorized the use of force, and its authorizations may be viewed as "congressional delegations to the President of the

power to declare war." *Id.* at 325. See *infra* pp. 109-110 (regarding the delegability of the war power).

4. *Command Authority Revisited.* Consider this summary of the President's powers as Commander in Chief in time of war:

> The President, not Congress, makes all day-to-day tactical decisions in the combat deployment of armed forces. Indeed, even when it ends a use of force by cutting off funds, Congress cannot constitutionally interfere with the Commander in Chief's tactical decisions for the safe withdrawal of the armed forces. But as powerful as the command authority is, the framers still intended that the Commander in Chief "would amount to nothing more than the supreme command and direction of the military and naval forces, as first General and Admiral of the Confederacy...," as Alexander Hamilton explained in the *Federalist Papers*. By making the President the Commander in Chief in Article II, the framers addressed what they recognized as a defect in the conduct of the Revolutionary War. They did not compromise their insistence in Article I on collective judgment in the decision for war.
>
> Nor did they give the Commander in Chief any constitutional right to ignore the terms of a congressional authorization for the use of force. When Congress gives the President the authority to conduct war, he or she must conduct it within that authority, just as the President must follow any law that is constitutionally made. [*Deciding to Use Force Abroad: War Powers in a System of Checks and Balances* 15 (The Constitution Project, Peter Raven-Hansen rptr., 2005).]

Can you say what distinguishes uses of force that are tactical from those that are not? Do you think congressional constraints have the same force when the President is fighting a war thrust upon us by attack as when he is fighting one authorized by Congress? Put another way, are you clear about precisely which Commander-in-Chief powers are exclusive? See *generally* Louis Fisher, *Presidential War Power* (2d ed. 2004).

C. THE PRESIDENT'S EMERGENCY POWERS

In re Neagle
United States Supreme Court, 1890
135 U.S. 1

Mr. Justice MILLER, for the Court.... [When David S. Terry and his wife, disappointed litigants, threatened the life of Supreme Court Justice Field, the Attorney General assigned U.S. Marshall David Neagle to protect the Justice while he sat on the circuit court in California. There Neagle shot and killed Terry in the course of an assault on Justice Field. Neagle was then arrested by state authorities and charged with murder. He sought release under a federal habeas corpus statute.]

It is urged... that there exists no statute authorizing any such protection as that which Neagle was instructed to give Judge Field in the present case, and indeed no protection whatever against a vindictive or malicious assault growing

C. The President's Emergency Powers

out of the faithful discharge of his official duties; and that the language of section 753 of the Revised Statutes, that the party seeking the benefit of the writ of *habeas corpus* must in this connection show that he is "in custody for an act done or omitted in pursuance of a law of the United States," makes it necessary that upon this occasion it should be shown that the act for which Neagle is imprisoned was done by virtue of an act of Congress. It is not supposed that any special act of Congress exists which authorizes the marshals or deputy-marshals of the United States in express terms to accompany the judges of the Supreme Court through their circuits, and act as a body-guard to them, to defend them against malicious assaults against their persons....

In the view we take of the Constitution of the United States, any obligation fairly and properly inferrible from that instrument, or any duty of the marshal to be derived from the general scope of his duties under the laws of the United States, is "a law" within the meaning of this phrase. It would be a great reproach to the system of government of the United States, declared to be within its sphere sovereign and supreme, if there is to be found within the domain of its powers no means of protecting the judges, in the conscientious and faithful discharge of their duties, from the malice and hatred of those upon whom their judgments may operate unfavorably....

Where, then, are we to look for the protection which we have shown Judge Field was entitled to when engaged in the discharge of his official duties? Not to the courts of the United States; because, as has been more than once said in this court, in the division of the powers of government between the three great departments, executive, legislative, and judicial, the judicial is the weakest for the purposes of self-protection and for the enforcement of the powers which it exercises....

The legislative branch of the government can only protect the judicial officers by the enactment of laws for that purpose, and the argument we are now combatting assumes that no such law has been passed by Congress.

If we turn to the executive department of the government, we find a very different condition of affairs. The Constitution, section 3, Article 2, declares that the President "shall take care that the laws be faithfully executed"....

Is this duty limited to the enforcement of acts of Congress or of treaties of the United States according to their *express terms*, or does it include the rights, duties and obligations growing out of the Constitution itself, our international relations, and all the protection implied by the nature of the government under the Constitution?

One of the most remarkable episodes in the history of our foreign relations, and which has become an attractive historical incident, is the case of Martin Koszta, a native of Hungary, who, though not fully a naturalized citizen of the United States, had in due form of law made his declaration of intention to become a citizen. While in Smyrna he was seized by command of the Austrian consul general at that place, and carried on board the Hussar, an Austrian vessel, where he was held in close confinement. Captain Ingraham, in command of the American sloop of war St. Louis, arriving in port at that critical period, and ascertaining that Koszta had with him his naturalization papers, demanded his surrender to him, and was compelled to train his guns upon the Austrian vessel before his demands were complied with. It was, however, to prevent bloodshed, agreed that Koszta should be placed in the hands of the French consul subject to the result of diplomatic negotiations between Austria and the United States. The celebrated correspondence between Mr. Marcy, Secretary of State, and Chevalier Hulsemann, the Austrian minister at Washington, which arose out of this affair, and resulted in the release and restoration to liberty of Koszta, attracted a great deal of public attention, and the position assumed by Mr. Marcy met the approval of the country and of Congress, who voted a gold medal to Captain Ingraham for his conduct in the affair. Upon what act of Congress then existing can any one lay his finger in support of the action of our government in this matter?

So, if the President or the Postmaster General is advised that the mails of the United States, possibly carrying treasure, are liable to be robbed, and the mail carriers assaulted and murdered in any particular region of country, who can doubt the authority of the President or of one of the executive departments under him to make an order for the protection of the mail, and of the persons and lives of its carriers, by doing exactly what was done in the case of Mr. Justice Field, namely, providing a sufficient guard, whether it be by soldiers of the army or by marshals of the United States, with a *posse comitatus* [see *infra* p. 945] properly armed and equipped, to secure the safe performance of the duty of carrying the mail wherever it may be intended to go? . . .

We cannot doubt the power of the President to take measures for the protection of a judge of one of the courts of the United States who, while in the discharge of the duties of his office, is threatened with a personal attack which may probably result in his death, and we think it clear that where this protection is to be afforded through the civil power, the Department of Justice is the proper one to set in motion the necessary means of protection. . . .

But there is positive law investing the marshals and their deputies with powers which not only justify what Marshal Neagle did in this matter, but which imposed it upon him as a duty. In chapter fourteen of the Revised Statutes of the United States, which is devoted to the appointment and duties of the district attorneys, marshals, and clerks of the courts of the United States, section 788 declares:

> The marshals and their deputies shall have, in each State, the same powers, in executing the laws of the United States, as the sheriffs and their deputies in such State may have, by law, in executing the laws thereof.

If, therefore, a sheriff of the State of California was authorized to do in regard to the laws of California what Neagle did, that is, if he was authorized to keep the peace, to protect a judge from assault and murder, then Neagle was authorized to do the same thing in reference to the laws of the United States. . . .

. . . That it would be the duty of a sheriff, if one had been present at this assault by Terry upon Judge Field, to prevent this breach of the peace, to prevent this assault, to prevent the murder which was contemplated by it, cannot be doubted. . . . So the marshal of the United States, charged with the duty of protecting and guarding the judge of the United States court against this special assault upon his person and his life, being present at the critical moment, when prompt action was necessary, found it to be his duty, a duty which he had no liberty to refuse to perform, to take the steps which resulted in Terry's death. . . .

We therefore affirm the judgment of the Circuit Court authorizing his discharge from the custody of the sheriff of San Joaquin County.

C. The President's Emergency Powers 83

Mr. Justice LAMAR (with whom concurred Mr. Chief Justice FULLER) dissenting.... The ground on which we dissent, and which in and by itself seems to be fatal to the case of the appellee, is this: That, in treating section 753 of the Revised Statutes as an act of authority for this particular use of the writ a wholly inadmissible construction is placed on the word "law," as used in that statute, and a wholly inadmissible application is made of the clause "in custody in violation of the Constitution... of the United States."...

[The Attorney General maintains]

> that the President... by the very fact that he is made the chief executive of the nation, and is charged to protect, preserve, and defend the Constitution, and to take care that the laws are faithfully executed, is invested with necessary and implied executive powers which neither of the other branches of the government can either take away or abridge; that many of these powers, pertaining to each branch of the government are self-executing, and in no way dependent, except as to the ways and means, upon legislation....

The President is sworn to "preserve, protect, and defend the Constitution." That oath *has* great significance. The sections which follow that prescribing the oath (secs. 2 and 3 of Art. 2) prescribe the duties and fix the powers of the President. But one very prominent feature of the Constitution which he is sworn to preserve, and which the whole body of the judiciary are bound to enforce, is the closing paragraph of sec. 8, Art. 1, in which it is declared that "the Congress shall have power... to make all laws which shall be necessary and proper for carrying into execution the foregoing powers, and all other powers vested by this Constitution in the government of the United States, or in any department or officer thereof."

This clause is that which contains the germ of all the implication of powers under the Constitution. It is that which has built up the Congress of the United States into the most August and imposing legislative assembly in the world; and which has secured vigor to the practical operations of the government, and at the same time tended largely to preserve the equilibrium of its various powers among its co-ordinate departments, as partitioned by that instrument. And that clause alone conclusively refutes the assertion of the Attorney General that it was "the duty of the executive department of the United States to guard and protect, at any hazard, the life of Mr. Justice Field in the discharge of his duty, because such protection is essential to the existence of the government." Waiving the question of the essentiality of any such protection to the existence of the government, the manifest answer is, that the protection needed and to be given must proceed not from the President, but primarily from Congress. Again, while it is the President's duty to take care that the laws be faithfully executed, it is not his duty to *make* laws or a law of the United States. The laws he is to see executed are manifestly those contained in the Constitution, and those enacted by Congress, whose duty it is to make all laws necessary and proper for carrying into execution the powers of those tribunals. In fact, for the President to have undertaken to make any law of the United States pertinent to this matter would have been to invade the domain of power expressly committed by the Constitution exclusively to Congress. That body was perfectly able to pass such laws as it should deem expedient in reference to such matter; indeed, it has passed such laws in reference to elections, expressly directing the United States marshals to attend places of election, to act as peace officers, to arrest with and without process, and to protect the supervisors of election in the discharge of their duties; and there was not the slightest legal necessity out of which to imply any such power in the President....

[The Martin Koszta incident] was justified because it pertained to the foreign relations of the United States, in respect to which the federal government is the exclusive representative and embodiment of the entire sovereignty of the nation, in its united character....

NOTES AND QUESTIONS

1. *The Holding of Neagle.* What is the holding of *Neagle*? Was it necessary for the Court to find that the President had the right and duty to execute "a law" of his own making, at least to protect the officers (and functions) of government? Was it necessary to find that Neagle was executing implied law of any kind, in light of the Court's recognition that his act was justified under a statute incorporating California law? Why was Neagle not simply permitted to stand trial in California? Can you reconcile *Neagle* with *The Steel Seizure Case*?

2. *Neagle and Rescue Abroad.* The *Neagle* Court cited with approval the Koszta episode, in which an American naval captain threatened force to obtain the release of an applicant for U.S. citizenship who was imprisoned by Austria. Unlike Marshal Neagle, the naval captain apparently acted against the instructions of the President and the Secretary of the Navy. *See* Wormuth & Firmage, *supra* p. 72, at 152 ("[H]is action was illegal when undertaken but was later ratified by congressional commendation."). Is *Neagle* authority for military rescue operations without prior congressional authorization? See *infra* pp. 268-270.

3. *Neagle and Emergencies at Home.* The *Neagle* Court also posed the hypothetical case of armed military protection for U.S. mail carriers. Is *Neagle* authority for the domestic use of troops without prior congressional authorization? See *infra* p. 958. Five years after *Neagle,* the President sued on his own authority to enjoin the Pullman Strike on the ground that it threatened the transportation of the mails. The Court upheld an injunction, despite the absence of any statutory authority for such a suit, stating that

> [t]he entire strength of the nation may be used to enforce in any part of the land the full and free exercise of all national powers and security of all rights entrusted by the Constitution to its care. The strong arm of the national government may be put forth to brush away all obstructions to the freedom of interstate commerce or the transportation of the mails. If the emergency arises, the army of the Nation, and all its militia, are at the service of the Nation to compel obedience to its law....
>
> ... [I]t is more to the praise than to the blame of the government, that, instead of determining for itself questions of right or wrong on the part of these petitioners and their associates and enforcing that determination by the club of the policeman and the bayonet of the soldier, it submitted all those questions to the peaceful determination of judicial tribunals.... [In re Debs, 158 U.S. 564, 582-583 (1895).]

C. The President's Emergency Powers

Both *Debs* and *The Steel Seizure Case* involved presidential actions called necessary to protect against the effects of labor strikes. Is *Debs* good law after *The Steel Seizure Case*?

4. *Lincoln's Extra-Constitutional Claims.* Consider President Lincoln's justification for his unilateral issuance of the Emancipation Proclamation:

> [M]y oath to preserve the constitution to the best of my ability, imposed upon me the duty of preserving, by every indispensable means, that government — that nation — of which the constitution was the organic law. Was it possible to lose the nation, and yet preserve the constitution? By general law life *and* limb must be protected; yet often a limb must be amputated to save a life; but a life is never wisely given to save a limb. I felt that measures, otherwise unconstitutional, might become lawful, by becoming indispensable to the preservation of the constitution, through the preservation of the nation. [Letter to Albert G. Hodges (Apr. 4, 1864), in VII *Collected Works* 281 (Roy P. Basler ed., 1953-1955).]

Did Lincoln claim constitutional authority for the Proclamation? If his authority is extra-constitutional, what is its source? If there is some emergency power of self-preservation in the government, does it necessarily follow that it is vested in the President when Congress can act? Note that Congress had previously enacted the Confiscation Act, freeing all slaves put to hostile use by the Confederate forces. Act of Aug. 6, 1861, ch. 60, 12 Stat. 319. *See also* Act of July 17, 1862, ch. 195, 12 Stat. 589.

Lincoln anticipated his defense of the Emancipation Proclamation when he earlier suspended the writ of habeas corpus, asking, "are all the laws, *but one,* to go unexecuted, and the government itself go to pieces, lest the one be violated?" Message to Congress (July 4, 1861), in IV *Collected Works* 429-430 (Roy P. Basler ed., 1953-1955). In that case, however, he claimed no extra-constitutional authority, citing instead the habeas corpus suspension clause of the Constitution. U.S. Const. Art. I, §9.

5. *The Limits of Inherent Emergency Power.* If the inherent executive power recognized in *Neagle* and *Debs* is not unlimited, what is its scope? Can Congress limit such executive power by statute? If it exists only during emergencies, how is the word "emergencies" to be defined? See *infra* p. 116. What emergency was presented in *Debs* that could not have been addressed by legislation? Was the emergency in *Neagle* more acute?

Consider the Court's statement in Home Building & Loan Assn. v. Blaisdell, 290 U.S. 398, 425-426 (1934):

> Emergency does not create power. Emergency does not increase granted power or remove or diminish the restrictions imposed upon power granted or reserved. The Constitution was adopted in a period of grave emergency. Its grants of power to the Federal Government and its limitations of the powers of the States were determined in the light of emergency and they were not altered by emergency. What power was thus granted and what limitations were thus imposed are questions which have always been, and always will be, the subject of close examination under our constitutional system.

In Reid v. Covert, 354 U.S. 1, 5-6 (1957), the Court added, "The United States is entirely a creature of the Constitution. Its power and authority have no other source. It can only act in accordance with all the limitations imposed by the Constitution."

Recall that in *The Steel Seizure Case* the Solicitor General argued that the "customs and claims of preceding administrations" had given rise to an inherent presidential power "to deal with a crisis or an emergency according to the necessities of the case...." 343 U.S. at 646. Justice Jackson responded this way:

> The appeal... that we declare the existence of inherent powers *ex necessitate* to meet an emergency asks us to do what many think would be wise, although it is something the forefathers omitted.... I do not think we rightfully may so amend their work, and, if we could, I am not convinced it would be wise to do so, although many modern nations have forthrightly recognized that war and economic crisis may upset the normal balance between liberty and authority.... [*Id.* at 649-651.]

6. *Delegated Emergency Power.* Suppose the President did not have inherent power to order the protection of Justice Field. Would this mean that the Justice would have had to fend for himself? If the President lacks inherent power, in other words, is the country helpless before a grave emergency?

Justice Jackson gave an answer to this question too. "Absence of authority in the President to deal with a crisis does not imply want of power in the Government," he wrote. 343 U.S. at 603-604. If Congress can anticipate the emergency, it can delegate power to the President to deal with it. If Congress cannot anticipate precisely, it can delegate generally, just as the Court held that it was permitted to do in *Curtiss-Wright*. (And so it had in *Neagle*, by authorizing marshals to exercise the same powers as sheriffs and their deputies could under state law.)

In fact, as *Dames & Moore* discussed, Congress has delegated a wide range of emergency powers to the President. See *supra* pp. 48-54 (discussing International Emergency Economic Powers Act and Hostage Act). If the President foresees the need for some kind of emergency authority, he can seek it from Congress in advance of the particular occasions for its use. In theory, then, the issue of inherent presidential emergency power should only arise when Congress has failed to anticipate the emergency and there is no time for the President to seek advance authorization.

7. *Responding to Unconstitutional Emergency Initiatives.* What if Congress has not anticipated a particular emergency and there is no time for the President to seek authorization? Is the President's unilateral response to the emergency necessarily lawful? According to Professor Lobel, at least until the beginning of the twentieth century the exercise of emergency power by the President was widely believed to be unconstitutional, except to repel attacks or pursuant to congressional authorization. Jules Lobel, *Emergency Power and the Decline of Liberalism*, 98 Yale L.J. 1385, 1388-1397 (1989). Nevertheless, he suggests, such power might be exercised when "universal rules and reasoned disclosure" failed to meet a particular emergency, when law had to be replaced by "discretion and politics." *Id.* at 1390. Thus, in the gravest crisis the President would act unilaterally at his peril, subject to the possibility of impeachment, removal from office, or perhaps ratification by Congress. In other words, emergency rule was

separated from the normal constitutional order, "thereby preserving the Constitution in its pristine form while providing the executive with the power, but not legal authority, to act in an emergency." *Id.*

When the President acts unconstitutionally in an emergency, Congress has the sanction of impeachment and the people have the sanction of the ballot. But as a practical matter, under what circumstances is either sanction likely to be imposed? Note that Congress also has the option of ratifying presidential acts that were statutorily unauthorized when taken. *See* Ex Parte Endo, 323 U.S. 283, 303 n.24 (1944) ("Congress may of course do by ratification what it might have authorized.") (citation omitted); *The Prize Cases*, 67 U.S. (2 Black) at 671. *See generally* Clinton Rossiter, *Constitutional Dictatorship* (1948).

D. THE PRESIDENT'S POWER TO PROTECT INFORMATION

1. Classified Information

The government uses the same basic techniques to keep the nation's secrets that ordinary people use to protect their own secrets. "First, we identify what we wish to keep secret. . . . [Second, we] share the secret only with those we think can be trusted." Harold P. Green, *Espionage and Security Leaks: Diagnosis and Therapy* 102 (George Washington Univ. Grad. Inst. for Poly. Educ. & Research Working Paper No. 5, 1986). The executive branch identifies what we wish to keep secret by *classifying* it. Classification has always been controlled by executive order, which establishes classification levels (basically, confidential, secret, and top secret) and sets out rules for classifying and declassifying. *See* Exec. Order No. 13,292, *Classified National Security Information*, 68 Fed. Reg. 15,315 (Mar. 25, 2003), excerpted *infra* p. 979. We identify and authorize those who can be trusted with the nation's secrets by *clearing* them for access to the secrets. The system of granting and denying security clearances is also established chiefly by executive order. *See id.*; Exec. Order No. 10,450, *Security Requirements for Government Employment*, 18 Fed. Reg. 2489 (Apr. 27, 1953), as amended. The President's orders regarding classification and clearance have often cited statutory authority, but since 1951 they have also purported to rely on "the authority vested in me by the Constitution and statutes, and as President of the United States." See *infra* p. 980.

Does the President need a statute to protect the nation's secrets by classifying them and controlling access to them? In Department of the Navy v. Egan, 484 U.S. 518 (1988), the Supreme Court generally described the system for protecting classified information and suggested in dicta that he does not:

> The President, after all, is the "Commander in Chief of the Army and Navy of the United States." U.S. Const., Art. II, §2. His authority to classify and control access to information bearing on national security and to determine whether an individual is sufficiently trustworthy to occupy a position in the Executive Branch that will give that person access to such information flows primarily from this constitutional investment of power in the President and exists quite apart from any explicit

congressional grant. See *Cafeteria Workers v. McElroy,* 367 U.S. 886, 890 (1961). This Court has recognized the Government's "compelling interest" in withholding national security information from unauthorized persons in the course of executive business. *Snepp v. United States,* 444 U.S. 507, 509 n.3 (1980) [*infra* p. 1055]. The authority to protect such information falls on the President as head of the Executive Branch and as Commander in Chief.

Since World War I, the Executive Branch has engaged in efforts to protect national security information by means of a classification system graded according to sensitivity. After World War II, certain civilian agencies, including the Central Intelligence Agency, the National Security Agency, and the Atomic Energy Commission, were entrusted with gathering, protecting, or creating information bearing on national security. Presidents, in a series of Executive Orders, have sought to protect sensitive information and to ensure its proper classification throughout the Executive Branch by delegating this responsibility to the heads of agencies. Pursuant to these directives, departments and agencies of the Government classify jobs in three categories: critical sensitive, noncritical sensitive, and nonsensitive. Different types and levels of clearance are required, depending upon the position sought. A Government appointment is expressly made subject to a background investigation that varies according to the degree of adverse effect the applicant could have on the national security. [484 U.S. at 527-528.]

Notwithstanding the rhetoric in *Egan,* Congress has enacted extensive legislation limiting the President's ability to withhold government information from public view. These measures and their relation to national security are examined in some depth in Chapter 34.

2. Privileged Information[1]

Early in his second term, President Nixon told White House Domestic Affairs Assistant John Ehrlichman how to respond to inquiries about the growing Watergate scandal: "You should have the most godawful gobbledygook answer prepared. Just put it out on executive privilege. Something that will allow us to do everything that we want." Washington Star, Mar. 17, 1979, at A4 (reporting transcript of taped conversation between Ehrlichman and President Nixon).

"Executive privilege" refers to a group of executive branch justifications for resisting disclosure of information to the public or the other branches. One justification is that the information is a state secret, disclosure of which would jeopardize the nation's security. The Supreme Court recognized this "state secrets privilege" in United States v. Reynolds, 345 U.S. 1 (1952), upholding the assertion of privilege by the government in a wrongful death action brought under the Federal Tort Claims Act. The state secrets privilege is discussed *infra* pp. 1037-1050.

---

1. For an extensive bibliography on executive privilege, *see* Mark J. Rozell, *Executive Privilege: A Bibliographic Essay,* 4 J.L. & Poly. 639 (1988). *See generally* Mark J. Rozell, *Executive Privilege: The Dilemma of Secrecy and Democratic Accountability* (1994); Symposium, *United States v. Nixon: Presidential Power and Executive Privilege Twenty-Five Years Later,* 83 Minn. L. Rev. 1061 (1999).

Another justification is that the information consists of the names of informers or the status of ongoing criminal investigations, disclosure of which would jeopardize law enforcement. *See generally* Ronald L. Claveloux, Note, *The Conflict Between Executive Privilege and Congressional Oversight: The Gorsuch Controversy*, 1983 Duke L.J. 1333, 1346; *Position of the Executive Department Regarding Investigative Reports*, 40 Op. Atty. Gen. 45 (1941) (listing several reasons why disclosure of some materials could frustrate effective law enforcement). This justification anchors the "law enforcement privilege."

A third—and broader—justification is that the information consists of intrabranch deliberative communications, disclosure of which would chill the candor and usefulness of such communications. This justification underlies the "deliberative process privilege."

All three of these justifications for nondisclosure have been incorporated into the exemptions that justify agency withholding of information requested under the Freedom of Information Act and its statutory analogues, considered in Chapter 34. *See* Murl A. Larkin, *Federal Testimonial Privileges* §5.01, at 5-3 to 5-9 (1987).

As the Nixon-Ehrlichman conversation suggests, a fourth justification has also been invoked directly by Presidents to preserve the confidentiality of presidential communications. When the President invokes the "presidential communications privilege" to protect documents he wants to keep confidential, they are presumptively privileged, but the presumption can be overcome by a specific showing of adequate need. *See* In re Sealed Case, 121 F.3d 729, 745 (D.C. Cir. 1997).

One court has described the differences between the presidential communications privilege and the deliberative process privilege as follows:

> While the presidential communications privilege and the deliberative process privilege are closely affiliated, the two privileges are distinct and have different scopes. Both are executive privileges designed to protect executive branch decisionmaking, but one applies to decisionmaking of executive officials generally, the other specifically to decisionmaking of the President. The presidential privilege is rooted in constitutional separation of powers principles and the President's unique constitutional role; the deliberative process privilege is primarily a common law privilege. Consequently, congressional or judicial negation of the presidential communications privilege is subject to greater scrutiny than denial of the deliberative privilege....
>
> Finally, while both the deliberative process privilege and the presidential privilege are qualified privileges, the *Nixon* cases suggest that the presidential communications privilege is more difficult to surmount. In regard to both, courts must balance the public interests at stake in determining whether the privilege should yield in a particular case, and must specifically consider the need of the party seeking privileged evidence. But this balancing is more ad hoc in the context of the deliberative process privilege, and includes consideration of additional factors such as whether the government is a party to the litigation. Moreover, the privilege disappears altogether when there is any reason to believe government misconduct occurred. On the other hand, a party seeking to overcome the presidential privilege seemingly must always provide a focused demonstration of need, even when there are allegations of misconduct by high-level officials. [*Id.* at 745-746.]

NOTES AND QUESTIONS

1. *Historical Basis of Executive Privilege.* As early as 1796, President Washington refused a request by the House of Representatives for all correspondence relating to the Jay Treaty, although he provided it to the Senate.

> The nature of foreign negotiations requires caution; and their success must often depend on secrecy; and even when brought to a conclusion, a full disclosure of all the measures, demands, or eventual concessions which may have been proposed or contemplated would be extremely impolitic. . . . To admit, then, a right in the House of Representatives to demand, and to have, as a matter of course, all the papers respecting a negotiation with a foreign Power, would be to establish a dangerous precedent. [5 Annals of Cong. 760 (1796).]

Presidents have cited the Jay Treaty papers episode as the first invocation of executive privilege by a President. But is it good authority for a general claim of executive privilege? What other basis might Washington have had for withholding treaty correspondence from the House? Washington wrote that the House would be entitled to the correspondence under different circumstances. *Id.* Does the description in Article I of the duties of the House suggest which circumstances?

Former Watergate Special Prosecutor Archibald Cox reviewed 27 additional instances since the Washington administration in which Presidents refused to comply with congressional information requests. Archibald Cox, *Executive Privilege*, 122 U. Pa. L. Rev. 1383, 1395-1405 (1974). *See also History of Refusals by Executive Branch Officials to Provide Information Demanded by Congress*, 6 Op. Off. Legal Counsel 751 (1982); Raoul Berger, *Executive Privilege* (1974). Cox concluded that "[i]f one looks at what was done and confines the words to the events, nothing appears which even approaches a solid historical practice of recognizing claims of executive privilege based upon an undifferentiated need for preserving the secrecy of internal communications within the Executive Branch." Cox, *supra,* at 1404.

2. *Constitutional Basis for a Presidential Communications Privilege?* On a superficial reading, the Supreme Court appeared to confirm Cox's conclusion in United States v. Nixon, 418 U.S. 683 (1974), when it enforced a grand jury subpoena duces tecum for certain Oval Office tapes of conversations with the President against his claim of absolute executive privilege. The Court observed:

> Human experience teaches that those who expect public dissemination of their remarks may well temper candor with a concern for appearances and for their own interest to the detriment of the decision making process. Whatever the nature of the privilege of confidentiality of Presidential communications in the exercise of Art. II powers, the privilege can be said to derive from the supremacy of each branch within its own assigned area of constitutional duties. Certain powers and privileges flow from the nature of enumerated powers; the protection of confidentiality of Presidential communications has similar constitutional underpinnings. . . .
> . . . However, when the privilege depends solely on the broad, undifferentiated claim of public interest in the confidentiality of such conversations, a confrontation with other values arises. Absent a claim of need to protect military,

D. The President's Power to Protect Information

diplomatic, or sensitive national security secrets, we find it difficult to accept the argument that even the very important interest in confidentiality of Presidential communications is significantly diminished by production of such material for *in camera* inspection with all the protection that a district court will be obliged to provide. [*Id.* at 705-706.]

The Court then ruled unanimously, Justice Rehnquist not participating, that "[t]he generalized assertion of privilege must yield to the demonstrated, specific need for evidence in a pending criminal trial." *Id.* at 713.

President Nixon lost the battle, but who won the war? Is the "presumptive" privilege for presidential communications, *id.* at 708, constitutional or is it a product of the common law? Would the Court have balanced interests differently in a civil case? In a case involving national security information not rising to the level of a state secret? In a case involving "sensitive" national security information? *See* Raoul Berger, *The Incarnation of Executive Privilege*, 22 UCLA L. Rev. 4, 26-29 (1974); William Van Alstyne, *A Political and Constitutional Review of United States v. Nixon*, 22 UCLA L. Rev. 116, 117-118 (1974).

3. *Congress and Protected Information.* How would the Supreme Court in *Nixon* have balanced the interests if Congress rather than a grand jury had demanded the tapes? See generally *infra* p. 122. Does *Curtiss-Wright*, 299 U.S. at 320-321 (quoting the statement by George Washington excerpted in Note 1), support the proposition that the President is constitutionally entitled to withhold foreign policy information from Congress? Does this authority extend to all sensitive information at all times, or is its scope more limited?

Egan asserted that the President's power to protect national security information "flows primarily from this constitutional investment of power in the President and exists quite apart from any explicit congressional grant." Does this assertion mean that the President is entitled to withhold such information from Congress? *See infra* pp. 1064-1065, discussing National Federation of Federal Employees v. United States, 688 F. Supp. 671 (D.D.C. 1988), *vacated sub nom.* American Foreign Service Assn. v. Garfinkel, 490 U.S. 153 (1989). Was he justified, for example, in refusing to disclose parts of his Presidential Daily Briefings relevant to Iraq's possession of weapons of mass destruction to the Senate Select Committee on Intelligence during the Committee's investigation of intelligence assessments leading to the war on Iraq? The Committee was forced to conclude in 2004 that it was "unable to determine fully whether the Intelligence Community's judgments were properly disseminated to policymakers in the executive branch." *Report on the U.S. Intelligence Community's Prewar Intelligence Assessments on Iraq*, July 9, 2004, Introduction at 3, *available at* http://intelligence.senate.gov/iraqreport2.pdf.

Usually, conflicts between Congress and the executive branch about information are resolved by negotiation. See *infra* pp. 122-123. *See also* Louis Fisher, *Invoking Executive Privilege: Navigating Ticklish Political Waters*, 8 Wm. & Mary Bill Rts. J. 583 (2000); Neal Devins, *Congressional-Executive Information Access Disputes: A Modest Proposal—Do Nothing*, 48 Admin. L. Rev. 109 (1996); Peter M. Shane, *Legal Disagreement and Negotiation in a Government of Laws: The Case of Executive Privilege Claims Against Congress*, 71 Minn. L. Rev. 462 (1987); 13 Op. Off. Legal

Counsel 190-193 (1989). *But see* Randall K. Miller, *Congressional Inquests: Suffocating the Constitutional Prerogative of Executive Privilege*, 81 Minn. L. Rev. 631 (1997) (advocating earlier judicial resolution in order to provide full protection to the privilege). Why do you think this is so?

4. *Procedure for Invoking the State Secrets or Executive Privilege.* A 1982 memo from President Reagan explained the procedure for invocation of the executive privilege by an executive branch official in response to a congressional request for information. When the official believed that a claim of privilege might be warranted, the head of the relevant agency or department was to consult with the Attorney General and the Counsel to the President. If any of them believed that the privilege should be invoked, the matter was referred to the President for a final decision. *Memorandum for the Heads of Executive Departments and Agencies* (Nov. 4, 1982), *reprinted in* H.R. Rep. No. 99-435, at 1106 (1985). Presidents Kennedy and Johnson also maintained that the executive privilege could be employed only by the President. H.R. Rep. No. 89-1497, at 6 (1966), *reprinted in* 1966 U.S.C.C.A.N. 2419-2420. The courts have similarly insisted on formal invocation of the state secrets privilege by an agency or department head. *See, e.g.*, Halkin v. Helms, 690 F.2d 977, 991 (D.C. Cir. 1982), *infra* p. 1037.

Congress's National Security Powers — 5

Congress, unlike the President, is vested by the Constitution with a host of specific foreign affairs and war powers. Apart from the declaration of war power, however, these powers are rarely considered in isolation. The courts typically review national security legislation from the perspective of the aggregate congressional war powers. *See, e.g.,* Lichter v. United States, 334 U.S. 742 (1948), *infra* p. 102.

In this chapter we begin in Part A with the power to authorize war. In Part B we deal with the delegation of national security powers and with national security appropriations. In Part C we turn to Congress's power to obtain information about national security matters from the executive branch. Finally, in Part D we consider substantive and procedural limits on Congress's national security powers.

A. CONGRESSIONAL AUTHORIZATIONS FOR WAR

John Locke wrote that a nation could "declare" war "by Word or Action." John Locke, *Two Treatises of Government* 278 (Peter Laslett ed., 1967). A nation could declare war, he wrote, "by Word" by issuing a formal declaration of war. It could declare war by "Action" by engaging in an act of war. In our system, of course, Congress may not engage in an act of war, but it can authorize the executive to do so.

The following materials provide an example of each method of "declaring" war: our last formal declaration of war and one of the first statutory authorizations for war (prior authorizations for the use of military force were directed at Indians and pirates). Consider how they differ in scope and whether they exhaust the ways in which Congress can authorize war.

Joint Resolution Declaring That a State of War Exists Between the Government of Rumania and the Government and the People of the United States and Making Provisions to Prosecute the Same

ch. 325, 56 Stat. 307 (June 5, 1942)

Whereas the Government of Rumania has formally declared war against the Government and the people of the United States of America: Therefore be it

Resolved by the Senate and the House of Representatives of the United States of America in Congress assembled, that the state of war between the United States and the Government of Rumania which has thus been thrust upon the United States is hereby formally declared; and the President is authorized and directed to employ the entire naval and military forces of the United States and the resources of the Government to carry on war against the Government of Rumania; and, to bring the conflict to a successful termination, all of the resources of the country are hereby pledged by the Congress of the United States.

Bas v. Tingy
United States Supreme Court, 1800
4 U.S. (4 Dall.) 37

[As relations between France and the United States deteriorated between 1798-1800, Congress enacted a succession of measures approving naval actions against France. Initially, it authorized U.S. armed vessels of the recently established navy to capture French vessels that had "committed depredations" on U.S.-owned vessels or that were "found hovering" off U.S. coasts for that purpose. Act of May 28, 1798, ch. 48, 1 Stat. 561. When this measure did not adequately protect U.S. merchants on the high seas, Congress next authorized such merchants to defend themselves against "any search, restraint or seizure" by vessels operating under French colors. Act of June 25, 1798, ch. 60, 1 Stat. 572. This act also provided for the recapture of U.S.-owned vessels from the French and their restoration to their former owners upon payment of salvage value. Three days later Congress passed another act that provided for the judicial condemnation of captured vessels and for the return of recaptured vessels to their owners for a salvage payment of one-eighth the full value. Act of June 28, 1798, ch. 62, 1 Stat. 574. Eventually, Congress authorized U.S. public and private armed vessels to take any French armed vessels found on the high seas. Act of July 9, 1798, ch. 68, 1 Stat. 578.

The next year Congress passed a set of rules and regulations for its infant navy. This act provided:

> That for the ships or goods belonging to the citizens of the United States, or to the citizens or subjects of any nation, in amity with the United States, if retaken from the enemy within twenty-four hours, the owners are to allow one eighth part of the whole value for salvage, if after twenty-four hours, and under forty-eight, one fifth thereof, if above that and under ninety-six hours, one third part thereof, and if above that, one half, all of which is to be paid without any deduction whatsoever.... [Act of March 2, 1799, ch. 24, §7, 1 Stat. 709, 716.]

A. Congressional Authorizations for War

On April 21, 1799, Captain Tingy, commander of the public armed ship *Ganges,* recaptured the *Eliza,* which belonged to John Bas and had been captured by a French privateer on the high seas on March 31, 1799. After he returned the vessel to Bas, Tingy brought an action in libel for salvage. The question in the case was whether Tingy was entitled to one-eighth the value of the *Eliza,* as provided by the 1798 act, or one-half as provided by the 1799 act. The lower courts ruled that Tingy was entitled to half the value. On appeal to the Supreme Court, the Justices delivered their opinions seriatim. The opinion of Justice MOORE in favor of affirmance is omitted.]

WASHINGTON, Justice.... 1st. [The 1798 Act] relates to re-captures from *the French,* and [the 1799 Act] relates to re-captures from *the enemy;* and, it is said, that "the enemy" is not descriptive of France, or of her armed vessels, according to the correct and technical understanding of the word.

The decision of this question must depend upon another; which is, whether, at the time of passing the act of congress of the 2d of March 1799, there subsisted a state of war between the two nations? It may, I believe, be safely laid down, that every contention by force between two nations, in external matters, under the authority of their respective governments, is not only war, but public war. If it be declared in form, it is called *solemn,* and is of the perfect kind; because one whole nation is at war with another whole nation; and *all* the members of the nation declaring war, are authorised to commit hostilities against all the members of the other, in every place, and under every circumstance. In such a war all the members act under a general authority, and all the rights and consequences of war attach to their condition.

But hostilities may subsist between two nations more confined in its nature and extent; being limited as to places, persons, and things; and this is more properly termed *imperfect war;* because not solemn, and because those who are authorised to commit hostilities, act under special authority, and can go no farther than to the extent of their commission. Still, however, it is *public war,* because it is an external contention by force, between some of the members of the two nations, authorised by the legitimate powers. It is a war between the two nations, though all the members are not authorised to commit hostilities such as in a solemn war, where the government restrain the general power.

Now, if this be the true definition of war, let us see what was the situation of the United States in relation to France. In March 1799, congress had raised an army; stopped all intercourse with France; dissolved our treaty; built and equipt ships of war; and commissioned private armed ships; enjoining the former, and authorising the latter, to defend themselves against the armed ships of France, to attack them on the high seas, to subdue and take them as prize, and to recapture armed vessels found in their possession. Here, then, let me ask, what were the technical characters of an American and French armed vessel, combating on the high seas, with a view the one to subdue the other, and to make prize of his property? They certainly were not friends, because there was a contention by force; nor were they private enemies, because the contention was external, and authorised by the legitimate authority of the two governments. If they were not our enemies, I know not what constitutes an enemy.

2d. But, secondly, it is said, that a war of the imperfect kind, is more properly called acts of hostility, or reprizal, and that congress did not mean to consider the hostility subsisting between France and the United States, as constituting a state of war.

In support of this position, it has been observed, that in no law prior to March 1799, is France styled our enemy, nor are we said to be at war. This is true; but neither of these things were necessary to be done: because as to France, she was sufficiently described by the title of the French republic; and as to America, the degree of hostility meant to be carried on, was sufficiently described without declaring war, or declaring that we were at war. Such a declaration by congress, might have constituted a perfect state of war, which was not intended by the government....

... [T]herefore, in my opinion, the decree of the Circuit Court ought to be affirmed.

CHASE, Justice.... Congress is empowered to declare a general war, or congress may wage a limited war; limited in place, in objects, and in time. If a general war is declared, its extent and operations are only restricted and regulated by the *jus belli*, forming a part of the law of nations; but if a partial war is waged, its extent and operation depend on our municipal laws.

What, then, is the nature of the contest subsisting between America and France? In my judgment, it is a limited, partial, war. Congress has not declared war in general terms; but congress has authorized hostilities on the high seas by certain persons in certain cases. There is no authority given to commit hostilities on land; to capture unarmed French vessels, nor even to capture French armed vessels lying in a French port; and the authority is not given, indiscriminately, to every citizen of America, against every citizen of France; but only to citizens appointed by commissions, or exposed to immediate outrage and violence. So far it is, unquestionably, a partial war; but, nevertheless, it is a public war, on account of the public authority from which it emanates.

There are four acts, authorised by our government, that are demonstrative of a state of war. A belligerent power has a right, by the law of nations, to search a neutral vessel; and, upon suspicion of a violation of her neutral obligations, to seize and carry her into port for further examination. But by the acts of congress, an American vessel is authorised: 1st. To resist the search of a French public vessel: 2d. To capture any vessel that should attempt, by force, to compel submission to a search: 3d. To re-capture any American vessel seized by a French vessel: and 4th. To capture any French armed vessel wherever found on the high seas. This suspension of the law of nations, this right of capture and re-capture, can only be authorized by an act of the government, which is, in itself, an act of hostility. But still it is a restrained, or limited, hostility; and there are, undoubtedly, many rights attached to a general war, which do not attach to this modification of the powers of defence and aggression....

The acts of congress have been analyzed to show, that a war is not openly denounced against France, and that France is no where expressly called the enemy of America: but this only proves the circumspection and prudence of the legislature. Considering our national prepossessions in favour of the French republic, congress had an arduous task to perform, even in preparing for necessary defence, and just retaliation. As the temper of the people rose, however, in resentment of accumulated wrongs, the language and the measures of the government became more and more energetic and indignant; though

A. Congressional Authorizations for War

hitherto the popular feeling may not have been *ripe* for a solemn declaration of war; and an active and powerful opposition in our public councils, has postponed, if not prevented that decisive event, which many thought would have best suited the interest, as well as the honour of the United States. The progress of our contest with France, indeed, resembles much the progress of our revolutionary contest; in which, watching the current of public sentiment, the patriots of that day proceeded, step by step, from the supplicatory language of petitions for a redress of grievances, to the bold and noble declaration of national independence.

Having, then, no hesitation in pronouncing, that a partial war exists between America and France, and that France was an enemy, within the meaning of the act of March 1799, my voice must be given for affirming the decree of the Circuit Court.

PATERSON, Justice. As the case appears on the record, and has been accurately stated by the counsel, and by the judges, who have delivered their opinions, it is not necessary to recapitulate the facts. My opinion shall be expressed in a few words. The United States and the French republic are in a qualified state of hostility. An imperfect war, or a war, as to certain objects, and to a certain extent, exists between the two nations; and this modified warfare is authorized by the constitutional authority of our country. It is a war *quoad hoc* [to this extent]. As far as congress tolerated and authorized the war on our part, so far may we proceed in hostile operations. It is a maritime war; a war at sea as to certain purposes. The national armed vessels of France attack and capture the national armed vessels of the United States; and the national armed vessels of the United States are expressly authorized and directed to attack, subdue, and take, the national armed vessels of France, and also to re-capture American vessels. It is therefore a public war between the two nations, qualified, on our part, in the manner prescribed by the constitutional organ of our country. In such a state of things, it is scarcely necessary to add, that the term "enemy," applies; it is the appropriate expression, to be limited in its signification, import, and use, by the qualified nature and operation of the war on our part. The word enemy proceeds the full length of the war, and no farther....

By the COURT: Let the decree of the Circuit Court be affirmed.

NOTES AND QUESTIONS

1. *Responding to a State of War.* A formal declaration may be used to start a war. As the declaration again Rumania shows, a declaration may also recognize that we are already in a "state of war" by virtue of an attack. Similarly, in response to a declaration of war against the United States by the Bey of Tripoli, Congress enacted a statute in 1802 authorizing the President to instruct American naval commanders to seize Tripolitan vessels "and also to cause to be done all such other acts of precaution or hostility as the *state of war* will justify...." Act approved Feb. 6, 1802, ch. 4, 2 Stat. 129, 130 (emphasis supplied). Moreover, as we have seen, the President need not await a formal declaration or any other

authorization by Congress before responding militarily to an attack. *See The Prize Cases*, 67 U.S. (2 Black) 635 (1863), *supra* p. 67.

2. *The Obsolescent Declaration of War?* Increasing state sensitivity to public diplomacy and world opinion, as well as the decline of opportunities for the lawful use of force occasioned by the proliferation of treaties and the evolution of customary international law, have long made declarations of war impolitic. As a consequence, "[a]lthough conflicts between and among states continue, no state has issued a formal declaration of war [since the 1948 Arab-Israeli War]. Indeed, some argue that a declaration of war today would constitute prima facie evidence of illegal aggression." Robert F. Turner, *The War Powers Resolution: Its Implementation in Theory and Practice* 25 (1983).

In fact, there is evidence that the declaration of war was already obsolete in 1789, by which date the concept of "defensive war" had taken such firm root in the law of nations that it was widely understood that war could be started without the formality of declaration. *See, e.g., The Federalist No. 25*, at 165 (Alexander Hamilton) (Clinton Rossiter ed., 1961); Turner, *supra*, at 16 nn.45-57 (citing sources). In this light, is it likely that the Framers intended to vest Congress with only the increasingly anachronistic formal declaration power, *see* J. Gregory Sidak, *To Declare War*, 41 Duke L.J. 27 (1991), and no other constitutional means to choose war? What answer did the members of the Court give in *Bas*? Regardless of the framing history or current geopolitical realities, does the advent of non-state enemies, such as non-state-sponsored terrorists, now make formal declarations of war obsolete?

3. *Authorizing War Expressly Without Declaring It.* How did Congress express its decision to make war on France at the end of the 18th century? How broad was the resulting authority in the President as Commander in Chief? Could the President have deployed land forces to invade France or French possessions? Could he have deployed the Navy to take the war to French ports? What answers are suggested by Little v. Barreme, 6 U.S. (2 Cranch) 170 (1804), *supra* p. 77?

Less than a year after *Bas*, the Court was again called upon to decide rights of salvage during the naval war with France. Writing for the Court, Chief Justice Marshall concluded that "[t]he whole powers of war being, by the constitution of the United States, vested in congress, the acts of that body can alone be resorted to as our guides in this enquiry." Talbot v. Seeman, 5 U.S. (1 Cranch) 1, 28 (1801). The Court unanimously found that Congress had authorized "partial hostilities" against France.

Do the Quasi-War cases (*Bas, Talbot, Little*) tell us anything about whether the President could have ordered similar hostilities without any congressional authorization at all? *Compare* J. Gregory Sidak, *The Quasi-War Cases — and Their Relevance to Whether "Letters of Marque and Reprisal" Constrain Presidential War Powers*, 28 Harv. J.L. & Pub. Poly. 465, 482, 486 (2005) (asserting that the answer is no, because the cases do not address "how the Constitution divides between Congress and the President the power to commit the nation to waging a limited war"), *with* Campbell v. Clinton, 203 F.3d 19 (D.C. Cir. 2000), at 30 n.7 (Randolph, J., concurring) (citing *Little* for the proposition that executive power in war "was constrained by an absence of legislation"), and 38 (Tatel, J., concurring) (citing *Talbot* for the proposition that Congress possesses the "whole powers of war").

A. Congressional Authorizations for War

4. *The Legal Domino Effects of War.* A formal declaration of war by Congress gives notice to neutrals of the existence of hostilities and of the identity of the belligerents, and it activates certain rights and obligations of neutrals and belligerents alike under international law. It also triggers approximately 30 standby statutory authorities that would not otherwise be available to the President. (Some of them may be activated as well by the President's declaration of a national emergency. See *infra* p. 115.) For example, under the Alien Enemy Act, 50 U.S.C. §21 (2000), "whenever there is a declared war between the United States and any foreign nation or government," citizens of "the hostile nation or government" who are at least 14 years old and not naturalized are subject to summary arrest, internment, and deportation when the President so proclaims. The Trading With the Enemy Act, 50 U.S.C. App. §§1-44 (2000), enables the President to regulate or prohibit commerce with an enemy state or its citizens after "Congress has declared war or the existence of a state of war." And the President may authorize electronic surveillance, physical searches, and the use of pen registers and trap and trace devices to acquire foreign intelligence without a court order for up to 15 days "following a declaration of war by Congress." 50 U.S.C. §§1811, 1829, 1844 (2000).

More than 170 other standby authorities are triggered "in time of war" or "when war is imminent" without requiring a declaration of war. *See generally* David M. Ackerman & Richard F. Grimmett, *Declarations of War and Authorizations for the Use of Military Force: Historical Background and Legal Implications* (Cong. Res. Serv. RL31133), Jan. 14, 2003; J. Gregory Sidak, *War, Liberty, and Enemy Aliens,* 67 N.Y.U. L. Rev. 1402, 1430 & nn.138-145 (1992). These authorize the President to take land for military purposes; commandeer private production lines for war manufacturing; take control of private transportation for war transport; and sequester, hold, and dispose of enemy property, among other powers.

5. *Is Congress's War-Declaring Role Strictly Judicial?* In light of the legal domino effect of a formal declaration of war, some scholars have argued that a declaration is strictly a juridical pronouncement and that Congress's war-declaring role is therefore judicial rather than legislative. *See* John C. Yoo, *The Continuation of Politics by Other Means: The Original Understanding of War Powers,* 84 Cal. L. Rev. 167 (1996). According to this theory, the President manages international relations and, when diplomacy fails, decides unilaterally whether to use military force. *Id.* at 291. Congress only enters into the equation to raise and supply the troops or to provide an "appropriations check" on disfavored military adventures by the President. In short, "the Framers created a framework designed to encourage presidential initiative in war. Congress was given a role in war-making decisions not by the Declare War Clause, but by its powers over funding and impeachment. The courts were given no role at all." *Id.* at 170.

Does this theory square with *Bas, Little* (*supra* p. 77), or *Talbot*? *See* Yoo, *supra*, at 293 (dismissing these cases as implicating only Congress's power to make rules concerning capture). Is it consistent with your understanding of the history of the framing of the Constitution?

6. *Authorizing War on Terrorists.* Formal declarations of war have always named belligerents that were sovereign states. Following the September 2001 terrorist attacks on the World Trade Center and the Pentagon, however, a newspaper columnist wrote, and some members of Congress reportedly agreed,

that "Congress... should immediately declare war. It does not have to name a country. It can declare war against those who carried out [the] attack...." Robert Kagan, Op-Ed., *We Must Fight This War*, Wash. Post, Sept. 12, 2001, at A31. May Congress declare war on a group of people? May it declare war without naming any enemy at all?

In response to the September 11 attacks, Congress passed a joint resolution authorizing the President to

> use all necessary and appropriate force against those nations, organizations, or persons he determines planned, authorized, committed, or aided the terrorist attacks that occurred on September 11, 2001, or harbored such organizations, or persons, in order to prevent any future acts of international terrorism against the United States by such nations, organizations or persons. [Pub. L. No. 107-40, §2(a), 115 Stat. 224 (2001).]

This resolution became law when President Bush signed it on September 18, 2001. Is there any important difference between this law and a formal declaration of war? Do these two different forms of legislative authority affect U.S. relations with other nations differently? Or the domestic powers of the President? Or the legal "dominos" discussed in Note 4?

7. *Impliedly Authorizing War.* How direct must a statute be that authorizes the use of force? In Orlando v. Laird, 443 F.2d 1039 (2d Cir. 1971), *infra* p. 219, the court found congressional authorization for the Vietnam War in, *inter alia*, military appropriations and selective service statutes. It did not cite *Bas*. Is there a difference between the form of authorization found in *Bas* or the September 18, 2001, joint resolution, *supra* Note 6, and authorization by appropriation or selective service legislation? On the authorization for the Vietnam War generally, see Chapter 8. If Congress can indirectly authorize war by appropriating money for it, is there any constitutional or practical limit on the form of war authorization?

Does Congress even need to use a statute? Could it authorize war by separate and substantively different actions in each House? Single-chamber resolutions ("simple resolutions") do not have bicameral approval and are not presented to the President for his signature. See *infra* p. 128 (discussing these requirements for normal legislation that has the force and effect of law). Conceding that without the President's signature (or a veto override) such resolutions lack the force and effect of statutes, Charles Tiefer nonetheless argues that

> [a]ctions by Congress short of enactment may elucidate the intent of congressional appropriations.... Formal and express presidential requests for congressional approval [to use military force]... may [also] bestow or confirm the legal significance of the corresponding congressional "partial" positions. Finally, Congress may take legally significant positions, even apart from a presidential request. [Charles Tiefer, *War Decisions in the Late 1990s by Partial Congressional Declaration*, 36 San Diego L. Rev. 1, 105 (1999).]

Is this theory of "partial congressional declaration" supported by any constitutional text or framing history? If you are skeptical, is the theory strengthened if we require that *each* House pass a "partial declaration" voting to support military action, even though the resulting simple resolutions do not match?

Finally, does either House need to do anything at all to approve war? May Congress authorize war silently by acquiescence in a conflict started by the executive? See *supra* pp. 54-55.

If you have concluded that any of the foregoing forms of indirect authorization is constitutionally sufficient in place of a declaration, what, if any, domino effect (see *supra* Note 4) does this form of authorization risk? It is partly a potential domino effect, as well as the need for accountability for war decisions, that has caused some scholars to insist on the formality of a declaration as a predicate for war. *See* Sidak, *supra* Note 4. Tiefer, in response, notes that the interaction between a President who requests approval for the use of force and the Houses of Congress that respond separately but approvingly "cranks up an elaborate machinery for the democratic inclusion of the nation in the military commitment decision," including "[h]earings, news coverage, briefings, disputes over conditions or demands for assurances, and floor debate." *Id.* at 125. Does this machinery satisfy the need for accountability?

8. *Limitations on Declared War. Bas, Little,* and *Talbot* rest on the principle "that declared war involved a delegation to the executive and all citizens of general authority to commit hostilities against the enemy, while the conduct of undeclared or 'imperfect' war was limited to those actions authorized by Congress." Abraham D. Sofaer, *War, Foreign Affairs and Constitutional Power: The Origins* 1632 (1976). Is there any limitation on declared or "perfect" war? In Brown v. United States, 12 U.S. (8 Cranch) 110 (1814), the issue was whether the declaration of the War of 1812 justified seizure of British-owned timber in Massachusetts. The libellant argued that the President had the authority as Commander in Chief to order confiscation of enemy property in execution of the rights of general war. Chief Justice Marshall, writing for the majority, rejected the argument, citing Congress's express constitutional power to make rules concerning capture. He concluded that "the power of confiscating enemy property is in the legislature, and . . . the legislature has not yet declared its will to confiscate property which was within our territory at the declaration of war." *Id.* at 129. Justice Story disagreed, arguing that the President had the power to order confiscation during a declared war unless Congress or the "rules of warfare established among civilized nations" forbade it. *Id.* at 153-154. Thus, the President may have to await specific congressional authorization to execute at least some of the general war powers recognized by the law of nations.

9. *Area and Use Limitations in War.* Some have argued that the President has plenary power to conduct a constitutionally authorized war and that congressional efforts to control the use of weapons or movement of troops are therefore unconstitutional. See *infra* p. 229. Is this view consistent with *Bas?* With *Little?* Is there any constitutional difference between defining the scope of a limited war in the initial authorization and doing so during the war? Is there a constitutional ratchet that prevents Congress from modifying or rescinding an authorization for war, once granted? If not, what is the difference between such a modification and a statute commanding the conduct of the war — for example, by ordering Platoon *A* to attack Hill *B*? What about a legislative command *not* to attack Hill *B*? Might the answer turn on the location of Hill *B*?

B. DELEGATIONS AND APPROPRIATIONS FOR NATIONAL SECURITY

Lichter v. United States
Supreme Court of the United States, 1948
334 U.S. 742

Mr. Justice BURTON delivered the opinion of the Court.... [The Renegotiation Act was enacted in 1942, 56 Stat. 226, 245-246, and subsequently amended several times during the war. It authorized the government to determine and recapture "excessive profits" by private contractors. Several contractors challenged the constitutionality of this legislation.]

The Renegotiation Act was developed as a major wartime policy of Congress comparable to that of the Selective Service Act. The authority of Congress to authorize each of them sprang from its war powers. Each was a part of a national policy adopted in time of crisis in the conduct of total global warfare by a nation dedicated to the preservation, practice, and development of the maximum measure of individual freedom consistent with the unity of effort essential to success.

With the advent of such warfare, mobilized property in the form of equipment and supplies became as essential as mobilized manpower. Mobilization of effort extended not only to the uniformed armed services but to the entire population. Both Acts were a form of mobilization. The language of the Constitution authorizing such measures is broad rather than restrictive. It says "The Congress shall have Power... To raise and support Armies, but no appropriation of Money to that Use shall be for a longer Term than two Years;..." Art. I, §8, cl. 12. This places emphasis upon the supporting as well as upon the raising of armies. The power of Congress as to both is inescapably express, not merely implied. The conscription of manpower is a more vital interference with the life, liberty and property of the individual than is the conscription of his property or his profits or any substitute for such conscription of them. For his hazardous, full-time service in the armed forces a soldier is paid whatever the Government deems to be a fair but modest compensation. Comparatively speaking, the manufacturer of war goods undergoes no such hazard to his personal safety as does a front-line soldier and yet the Renegotiation Act gives him far better assurance of a reasonable return for his wartime services than the Selective Service Act and all its related legislation give to the men in the armed forces. The constitutionality of the conscription of manpower for military service is beyond question. The constitutional power of Congress to support the armed forces with equipment and supplies is no less clear and sweeping.[1] It is valid, *a fortiori*.

---

[1] "The Constitution grants to Congress power 'to raise and support Armies,' 'to provide and maintain a Navy,' and to make all laws necessary and proper to carry these powers into execution. Under this authority Congress can draft men for battle service. Selective Draft Law Cases, 245 U.S. 366. Its power to draft business organizations to support the fighting men who risk their lives can be no less." United States v. Bethlehem Steel Corp., 315 U.S. 289, 305....

B. Delegations and Appropriations for National Security

In view of this power "To raise and support Armies,..." and the power granted in the same Article of the Constitution "To make all Laws which shall be necessary and proper for carrying into Execution the foregoing Powers,..." the only question remaining is whether the Renegotiation Act was a law "necessary and proper for carrying into Execution" the war powers of Congress and especially its power to support armies.

It is impossible here to picture adequately all that might have been "necessary and proper" in 1942-1944 to meet the unprecedented responsibility facing Congress in this field. We do, however, catch a glimpse of it in authoritative, contemporaneous descriptions of the situation....

... [These] describe a demand for production of war supplies in proportions previously unimagined. They call for production in a volume never before approximated and at an undreamed of speed. The results amply demonstrated the infinite value of that production in winning the war. It proved to be a *sine qua non* condition of the survival of the nation. Not only was it "necessary and proper" for Congress to provide for such production in the successful conduct of the war, but it was well within the outer limits of the constitutional discretion of Congress and the President to do so under the terms of the Renegotiation Act....

The petitioners contend that the Renegotiation Act unconstitutionally attempted to delegate legislative power to administrative officials....

The constitutional argument is based upon the claim that the delegation of authority contained in the Act carried with it too slight a definition of legislative policy and standards. Accordingly, it is contended that the resulting determination of excessive profits which were claimed by the United States amounted to an unconstitutional exercise of legislative power by an administrative official instead of a mere exercise of administrative discretion under valid legislative authority....

... On the basis of (a) the nature of the particular constitutional powers being employed, (b) the current administrative practices later incorporated into the Act and (c) the adequacy of the statutory term "excessive profits" as used in this context, we hold that the authority granted was a lawful delegation of administrative authority and not an unconstitutional delegation of legislative power.

(a) *A constitutional power implies a power of delegation of authority under it sufficient to effect its purposes.* — This power is especially significant in connection with constitutional war powers under which the exercise of broad discretion as to methods to be employed may be essential to an effective use of its war powers by Congress. The degree to which Congress must specify its policies and standards in order that the administrative authority granted may not be an unconstitutional delegation of its own legislative power is not capable of precise definition. In peace or in war it is essential that the Constitution be scrupulously obeyed, and particularly that the respective Branches of the Government keep within the powers assigned to each by the Constitution. On the other hand, it is of the highest importance that the fundamental purposes of the Constitution be kept in mind and given effect in order that, through the Constitution, the people of the United States may in time of war as in peace bring to the support of those purposes the full force of their united action. In time of crisis nothing could be more tragic and less expressive of the intent of the people than so to construe their Constitution that by its own terms it would substantially hinder rather than help them in defending their national safety.

In an address by Honorable Charles E. Hughes, of New York, on "War Powers Under The Constitution," September 5, 1917, 42 A.B.A. Rep. 232, 238-239, 247-248, he said:

> The power to wage war is the power to wage war successfully. The framers of the Constitution were under no illusions as to war. They had emerged from a long struggle which had taught them the weakness of a mere confederation, and they had no hope that they could hold what they had won save as they established a Union which could fight with the strength of one people under one government entrusted with the common defence. In equipping the National Government with the needed authority in war, they tolerated no limitations inconsistent with that object, as they realized that the very existence of the Nation might be at stake and that every resource of the people must be at command....
>
> In the words of the Supreme Court: "It is also settled beyond dispute that the Constitution is not self-destructive. In other words, that the power which it confers on the one hand it does not immediately take away on the other...." This was said in relation to the taxing power. Having been granted in express terms, the Court held it had not been taken away by the due process clause of the Fifth Amendment. As the Supreme Court put it in another case: "the Constitution does not conflict with itself by conferring upon the one hand a taxing power and taking the same power away on the other by the limitations of the due process clause."
>
> Similarly, it may be said that the power has been expressly given to Congress to prosecute war, and to pass all laws which shall be necessary and proper for carrying that power into execution. That power explicitly conferred and absolutely essential to the safety of the Nation is not destroyed or impaired by any later provision of the Constitution or by any one of the amendments. These may all be construed so as to avoid making the constitution self-destructive, so as to preserve the rights of the citizen from unwarrantable attack, while assuring beyond all hazard the common defence and the perpetuity of our liberties. These rest upon the preservation of the nation.
>
> It has been said that the Constitution marches. That is, there are constantly new applications of unchanged powers, and it is ascertained that in novel and complex situations, the old grants contain, in their general words and true significance, needed and adequate authority. So, also, we have a *fighting* Constitution. We cannot at this time fail to appreciate the wisdom of the fathers, as under this charter, one hundred and thirty years old — the constitution of Washington — the people of the United States fight with the power of unity, — as we fight for the freedom of our children and that hereafter the sword of autocrats may never threaten the world.

The war powers of Congress and the President are only those which are to be derived from the Constitution but, in the light of the language just quoted, the primary implication of a war power is that it shall be an effective power to wage the war successfully. Thus, while the constitutional structure and controls of our Government are our guides equally in war and in peace, they must be read with the realistic purposes of the entire instrument fully in mind....

...We believe that the administrative authority there granted was well within the constitutional war powers then being put to their predestined uses....

Accordingly, in each of the cases before us, the judgment of the Circuit Court of Appeals [upholding the Renegotiation Act] is affirmed.

Mr. Justice MURPHY concurs in the result in these cases.

Mr. Justice JACKSON concurs in [one of the three cases consolidated for review, but dissents in two others, including *Lichter*].

Mr. Justice DOUGLAS dissenting in part. [Opinion omitted.]

Greene v. McElroy
United States Supreme Court, 1959
360 U.S. 474

Mr. Chief Justice WARREN delivered the opinion of the Court. This case involves the validity of the Government's revocation of security clearance granted to petitioner, an aeronautical engineer employed by a private manufacturer which produced goods for the armed services. Petitioner was discharged from his employment solely as a consequence of the revocation because his access to classified information was required by the nature of his job. After his discharge, petitioner was unable to secure employment as an aeronautical engineer and for all practical purposes that field of endeavor is now closed to him....

Petitioner contends that the action of the Department of Defense in barring him from access to classified information on the basis of statements of confidential informants made to investigators was not authorized by either Congress or the President and has denied him "liberty" and "property" without "due process of law" in contravention of the Fifth Amendment....

The issue, as we see it, is whether the Department of Defense has been authorized to create an industrial security clearance program under which affected persons may lose their jobs and may be restrained in following their chosen professions on the basis of fact determinations concerning their fitness for clearance made in proceedings in which they are denied the traditional procedural safeguards of confrontation and cross-examination....

The first proffered statute is the National Security Act of 1947, as amended, 5 U.S.C. §171 et seq. That Act created the Department of Defense and gave to the Secretary of Defense and the Secretaries of the armed services the authority to administer their departments. Nowhere in the Act, or its amendments, is there found specific authority to create a clearance program similar to the one now in effect.

Another Act cited by respondents is the Armed Service Procurement Act of 1947, as amended. It provides in 10 U.S.C. §2304 that:

> (a) Purchases of and contracts for property or services covered by this chapter shall be made by formal advertising. However, the head of an agency may negotiate such a purchase or contract, if —....
>> (12) the purchase or contract is for property or services whose procurement he determines should not be publicly disclosed because of their character, ingredients, or components.

It further provides in 10 U.S.C. §2306:

> (a) The cost-plus-a-percentage-of-cost system of contracting may not be used. Subject to this limitation and subject to subsections (b)-(e), the head of an agency may, in negotiating contracts under section 2304 of this title, make any kind of contract that he considers will promote the best interests of the United States.

Respondents argue that these statutes, together with 18 U.S.C. §798, which makes it a crime willfully and knowingly to communicate to unauthorized persons information concerning cryptographic or intelligence activities, and 50 U.S.C. §783(b), which makes it a crime for an officer or employee of the United States to communicate classified information to agents of foreign governments or officers and members of "Communist organizations," reflect a recognition by Congress of the existence of military secrets and the necessity of keeping those secrets inviolate.

Although these statutes make it apparent that Congress recognizes the existence of military secrets, they hardly constitute an authorization to create an elaborate clearance program which embodies procedures traditionally believed to be inadequate to protect affected persons.[29]

Lastly, the Government urges that if we refuse to adopt its "inferred" authorization reasoning, nevertheless, congressional ratification is apparent by the continued appropriation of funds to finance aspects of the program fashioned by the Department of Defense. Respondents refer us to Hearings before the House Committee on Appropriations on Department of Defense Appropriations for 1956, 84th Cong., 1st Sess. 774-781. At those hearings, the Committee was asked to approve the appropriation of funds to finance a program under which reimbursement for lost wages would be made to employees of government contractors who were temporarily denied, but later granted, security clearance. Apparently, such reimbursements had been made prior to that time out of general appropriations. Although a specific appropriation was eventually made for this purpose, it could not conceivably constitute a ratification of the hearing procedures, for the procedures were in no way involved in the special reimbursement program.[30]

Respondents' argument on delegation resolves itself into the following: The President, in general terms, has authorized the Department of Defense to create procedures to restrict the dissemination of classified information and has apparently acquiesced in the elaborate program established by the Secretary of Defense even where application of the program results in

---

29. As far as appears, the most substantial official notice which Congress had of the non-confrontation procedures used in screening industrial workers was embodied in S. Doc. No. 40, 84th Cong., 1st Sess., a 354-page compilation of laws, executive orders, and regulations relating to internal security, printed at the request of a single Senator, which reproduced, among other documents and without specific comment, the Industrial Personnel Security Review Regulation [which established the summary hearing procedures by which Greene's security clearance was revoked].

30. ... [T]he appropriation could not "plainly show a purpose to bestow the precise authority which is claimed." Ex Parte Endo, 323 U.S. 283, 303, n.24. Likewise, appropriations of specific amounts for the Munitions Board or its successors, agencies with multifold objectives, without any mention of the uses to which the funds could be put, cannot be considered as a ratification of the use of the specified hearing procedures.

B. Delegations and Appropriations for National Security

restraints on traditional freedoms without the use of long-required procedural protections. Similarly, Congress, although it has not enacted specific legislation relating to clearance procedures to be utilized for industrial workers, has acquiesced in the existing Department of Defense program and has ratified it by specifically appropriating funds to finance one aspect of it.

If acquiescence or implied ratification were enough to show delegation of authority to take actions within the area of questionable constitutionality, we might agree with respondents that delegation has been shown here. In many circumstances, where the Government's freedom to act is clear, and the Congress or the President has provided general standards of action and has acquiesced in administrative interpretation, delegation may be inferred. Thus, even in the absence of specific delegation, we have no difficulty in finding, as we do, that the Department of Defense has been authorized to fashion and apply an industrial clearance program which affords affected persons the safeguards of confrontation and cross-examination. But this case does not present that situation. We deal here with substantial restraints on employment opportunities of numerous persons imposed in a manner which is in conflict with our long-accepted notions of fair procedures. Before we are asked to judge whether, in the context of security clearance cases, a person may be deprived of the right to follow his chosen profession without full hearings where accusers may be confronted, it must be made clear that the President or Congress, within their respective constitutional powers, specifically has decided that the imposed procedures are necessary and warranted and has authorized their use. Such decisions cannot be assumed by acquiescence or nonaction. Kent v. Dulles, 357 U.S. 116; Peters v. Hobby, 349 U.S. 331; Ex Parte Endo, 323 U.S. 283, 301-302. They must be made explicitly not only to assure that individuals are not deprived of cherished rights under procedures not actually authorized, but also because explicit action, especially in areas of doubtful constitutionality, requires careful and purposeful consideration by those responsible for enacting and implementing our laws. Without explicit action by lawmakers, decisions of great constitutional import and effect would be relegated by default to administrators who, under our system of government, are not endowed with authority to decide them.

Where administrative action has raised serious constitutional problems, the Court has assumed that Congress or the President intended to afford those affected by the action the traditional safeguards of due process. These cases reflect the Court's concern that traditional forms of fair procedure not be restricted by implication or without the most explicit action by the Nation's lawmakers, even in areas where it is possible that the Constitution presents no inhibition.

In the instant case, petitioner's work opportunities have been severely limited on the basis of a fact determination rendered after a hearing which failed to comport with our traditional ideas of fair procedure. The type of hearing was the product of administrative decision not explicitly authorized by either Congress or the President. Whether those procedures under the circumstances comport with the Constitution we do not decide. Nor do we decide whether the President has inherent authority to create such a program, whether congressional action is necessary, or what the limits on executive or legislative authority may be. We decide only that in the absence of explicit authorization from either the President or Congress the respondents were not empowered to deprive petitioner of his job in a proceeding in which he was not afforded the safeguards of confrontation and cross-examination.

Accordingly, the judgment is reversed and the case is remanded to the district court for proceedings not inconsistent herewith....

Mr. Justice FRANKFURTER, Mr. Justice HARLAN and Mr. Justice WHITTAKER concur in the judgment on the ground that it has not been shown that either Congress or the President authorized the procedures whereby petitioner's security clearance was revoked, intimating no views as to the validity of those procedures.

[The opinions of Justices HARLAN, concurring specially, and CLARK, dissenting, are omitted.]

NOTES AND QUESTIONS

a. Delegations of National Security Authority

1. *The Scope of Congressional War Powers.* The Supreme Court has approved the exercise of the defense appropriations power and related congressional war powers to

> control the price of every commodity bought and sold within the national boundaries; to fix the amount of rent to be charged for every room, home, or building and this even though to an individual landlord there may be less than a fair return; to construct extensive systems of public works; to operate railroads; to prohibit the sale of liquor; to restrict freedom of speech in a manner that would be unwarranted in time of peace; to ration and allocate the distribution of every commodity important to the war effort; to restrict the personal freedom of American citizens by curfew orders and the designation of areas of exclusion; and, finally, to demand of every citizen that he serve in the armed forces of the nation. [Spaulding v. Douglas Aircraft Co., 154 F.2d 419, 422-423 (9th Cir. 1946) (citations from Supreme Court decisions omitted).]

These powers may continue after the cessation of hostilities. The Court has recognized that the congressional war power "is not limited to victories in the field.... It carries with it inherently the power to guard against the immediate renewal of the conflict, and to remedy the evils which have arisen from its rise and progress." Stewart v. Kahn, 78 U.S. (11 Wall.) 493, 507 (1871). Do these powers also exist before any conflict arises?

2. *The Clear Statement Requirement.* In light of the sweep of the congressional defense appropriations and the war-supporting authority just described, why did the Court decline to find authority for the security clearance procedures employed by the executive in *Greene*? What is the holding of *Greene*? *See also* Kent v. Dulles, 357 U.S. 116 (1958) (declining to find statutory authority for the Secretary of State to restrict the right of travel absent explicit delegation from Congress). *But see* Haig v. Agee, 453 U.S. 280 (1981) (inferring authority to restrict the right of travel from congressional acquiescence in State Department

policy). The *Greene* Court cited Ex parte Endo, 323 U.S. 283, 303 n.24 (1944), in which the Court said that to authorize or ratify executive action an appropriation must "plainly show a purpose to bestow the precise authority which is claimed." There the Court found no authorization for the continued detention of loyal Japanese Americans during World War II "where a lump appropriation was made for the overall program of the [War Relocation] Authority and no sums were earmarked for the single phase of the total program [there] involved." *Id.*

3. *Standards of National Security Delegation.* National security authority has often been delegated by Congress to the executive branch with only the barest of standards. The inherent variability and unpredictability of national security problems have always placed practical limits on the detail with which Congress could delegate in these areas. Today, the speed of modern communications and executive monopolization of national security information have aggravated the problem. *See generally* Jason A. Rosenberg et al., Note, *Historical and Structural Limitations on Congressional Abilities to Make Foreign Policy*, 50 B.U. L. Rev. 51 (Spec. Issue 1970). As noted above, the Court has not struck down any congressional delegation of lawmaking authority to the executive since 1935. See *supra* p. 43.

Do *Greene* and *Lichter* establish different standards for congressional delegation of national security authority? Can you distinguish the locus and effect of the authorities recognized in those cases? What were the specific constitutional rights allegedly threatened by the government in each case? *Greene* was decided after World War II. Would it have been decided the same way during wartime?

4. *The Delegability of the War Power.* After *Lichter*, is there any limit to delegations of war powers to the executive that do not directly curtail individual constitutional rights? May Congress delegate the power to declare war? Does the impracticality of antecedent standard-setting for the declaration of war suggest that Congress has no choice? Or does it suggest just the opposite: that it cannot? Consider the following argument advanced during the height of the Vietnam War after Congress had, by the Gulf of Tonkin Resolution, allegedly delegated war-making power to the President.

> [I]t seems to me clearly the case that the exclusive responsibility of Congress to resolve the necessity and appropriateness of war as an instrument of national policy at any given time is uniquely not delegable at all. The pursuit of national interest by sustained extraterritorial uses of direct force was textually reserved to Congress alone after alternative formulations were pressed on precisely the grounds that conventionally rationalize a limited power to delegate an interstitial lawmaking authority to the executive, viz., superior expertise in the executive, the need for flexibility in the face of rapidly changing circumstances, the cumbersomeness of parliamentary processes, and a residual power to check the executive in the event of displeasure with the manner in which he might make war. To the extent that such arguments were considered to have merit, they were accommodated by *other* means among the several war-related clauses. To the extent that they were not thus accommodated, the conclusion seems inescapable that they were rejected and correspondingly, that no further latitude of executive control was to be permitted than that already provided for.

To express the same matter less passionately, specific contingencies which give sense and shape to the general doctrine permitting limited delegations of legislative power in other areas of congressional responsibility are *already* provided for in respect to war, *so far as it was felt safe to do so.* Thus, it was contemplated and made possible that peacetime armies might be raised under presidential discretion though this might even increase the risk of war. Similarly, an interim executive capacity to respond to outright emergencies, authorizing the president to resist invasion or repel an attack when war might be thrust upon the nation too quickly for Congress to convene to authorize even such limited defensive measures, was provided. Additionally, executive discretion to make command decisions of tactics and strategy within the express war declaration by Congress was conceded. Further confidence was also reposed of necessity in the President in recognizing that the congressional power would be exercised or not substantially depending upon the information and advice the President would provide in his emergency message of exigent circumstances asking for *their* decision to initiate hostilities, sustain present emergency defensive war actions he had taken, enlarge upon them, or, by doing nothing, require that our extraterritorial forces be immediately disengaged and withdrawn. Finally, although there might have been much to be said for a different view (so to make going to war especially grave and therefore desirably difficult to accomplish), the Constitution does not require that the declaration of war be an all or nothing response....

But precisely because of these various provisions and accommodations, it is even more clearly the case that there is no standing room left for a theory which would transfer to the executive the power to authorize war on his own initiation. When all the accommodations to shared authority otherwise provided by the several war-related clauses are thus aggregated, it becomes quite evident that the determination as to whether circumstances at any given time in fact make it necessary and appropriate to engage in war, however limited in scope or objectives, resides solely in Congress subject to no delegation whatever. [William Van Alstyne, *Congress, the President, and the Power to Declare War: A Requiem for Vietnam*, 121 U. Pa. L. Rev. 1, 16-18 (1972).]

Can Professor Van Alstyne's argument be squared with *Lichter*?

Professor Lobel suggested that some kinds of decisions, including engagement in military hostilities, are uniquely for the Congress to make because "important issues of public policy should be decided by a broadly representative deliberative body." Jules Lobel, *Covert War and Congressional Authority: Hidden War and Forgotten Power*, 134 U. Pa. L. Rev. 1035, 1097-1098 (1986). He found support for his conclusion by analogy in National Cable Television Assn. v. United States, 415 U.S. 336 (1974), which implied that the taxing power was nondelegable. But in Skinner v. Mid-America Pipeline Co., 490 U.S. 212 (1989), the Court declared:

> We discern nothing in this placement of the Taxing clause that would distinguish Congress' power to tax from its other enumerated powers — such as its commerce power, its power to *"raise and support Armies,"* its power to borrow money, or *its power to "make Rules for the government"* — in terms of the scope and degree of discretionary authority that Congress may delegate to the Executive in order that the President may "take Care that the Laws be faithfully executed." [*Id.* at 220-221 (emphasis supplied).]

Indeed, the Court has never expressly held any Article I power to be nondelegable. Does this cast doubt on Professor Lobel's conclusion or on Professor Van Alstyne's analysis?

B. Delegations and Appropriations for National Security

b. Authorization by Defense Appropriation

1. *Appropriation as Acquiescence.* Greene suggests that in some instances appropriations may be regarded as a form of congressional acquiescence in executive practice, discussed *supra* pp. 54-55. Recall that congressional acquiescence presupposes adequate notice of the executive practice to the Congress. Key appropriations hearings in *Greene* were "off the record," in executive session, presumably to protect classified information. *See* 360 U.S. at 521 (Clark, J., dissenting). Why did the Court refuse to infer that Congress received notice during these executive sessions?

2. *Appropriations as "Back-Door Law."* Congress has traditionally distinguished *authorizations*—statutes delegating authority to the executive branch—from *appropriations*—statutes that fund the execution of delegated authority. The former have generally emanated from congressional committees with jurisdiction to oversee the relevant government function or executive agency, while the latter usually come out of the appropriations committees. Academic and occasional judicial efforts to deny the characterization "legislation" to appropriations, *see, e.g.*, Sierra Club v. Andrus, 581 F.2d 895, 910-911 (D.C. Cir. 1978) (MacKinnon, J., concurring in part and dissenting in part), *rev'd*, 442 U.S. 347 (1979), have foundered on the text of Article I, which does not make this distinction. As the product of the Article I legislative process, appropriations are as much legislation as authorizations. Moreover, appropriations "are not only legislative specifications of money *amounts*, but also legislative specifications of the *powers, activities*, and *purposes*—what we may call, simply, 'objects'—for which the appropriated funds may be used." Kate Stith, *Congress' Power of the Purse*, 97 Yale L.J. 1343, 1352 (1988). Both chambers recognize the legislative nature of appropriations by requiring explanation or identification of appropriations bills that change "existing law." *See* House R. XXI, cl. 3; Senate R. XVI, cl. 8.

Nevertheless, the incidental nature of many appropriations measures and the often summary deliberation that attends them properly makes courts more hesitant to infer authority from such "back-door legislation" than from other kinds of legislation, as *Greene* suggests. *See* Neal Devins, *Regulation of Government Agencies Through Limitations Riders*, 1987 Duke L.J. 456, 458, 481, 499. Compare Tennessee Valley Authority v. Hill, 437 U.S. 153, 174-188 (1978) (doctrine that repeals by implication are disfavored applies with special force to repeals by appropriations), *with* United States v. Dickerson, 310 U.S. 554 (1940) (finding repeal by appropriation rider after exhaustive analysis of its legislative history). Moreover, because most appropriations are for a specific term, the purposes for which they are enacted and the limitations they impose are also time-limited and subject to variation. "Court interpretations of limitation riders as amendments to previously enacted legislation, therefore, are inherently unreliable; they may be accurate one day, inaccurate the next, and irrelevant at the end of the fiscal year." Devins, *supra*, at 458. *See also id.* at 465, 498-499. *See generally* Peter Raven-Hansen & William C. Banks, *Pulling the Pursestrings of the Commander in Chief*, 80 Va. L. Rev. 833, 839-848 (1994).

3. *Nullifying Appropriation by Impoundment?* If an appropriation can authorize, does it also mandate? Suppose the President disapproves of the activity for

which Congress has appropriated funds? Of course, in such a case he could veto the appropriation. But if he does not, or if his veto is overridden, may he simply decline to spend — and thus *impound* — the funds? Selective impoundment could give the President the practical equivalent of an item veto. What constitutional theories support or refute presidential impoundment claims? *See generally* Ralph S. Abascal & John R. Kramer, *Presidential Impoundment Part I: Historical Genesis and Constitutional Framework*, 62 Geo. L.J. 1549 (1974). Does it matter whether the impounded funds are for military forces or for nonmilitary foreign relations activities? *See* Timothy R. Harner, *Presidential Power to Impound Appropriations for Defense and Foreign Relations*, 5 Harv. J.L. & Pub. Poly. 131 (1982). The Supreme Court has not yet ruled on the constitutional questions, but it has held that a particular impoundment violated the intent of the relevant statute. *See* Train v. City of New York, 420 U.S. 35 (1975). Congress has attempted to regulate impoundment by enacting the Impoundment Control Act of 1974, 2 U.S.C. §§681-688 (2000), only to have a court of appeals invalidate part of the Act as an unconstitutional, albeit severable, legislative veto. City of New Haven v. United States, 809 F.2d 900 (D.C. Cir. 1987).

c. **Limitation by Defense Appropriation**

1. *Appropriations with "Strings Attached."* The flip side of appropriation as authorization or delegation is appropriation as limitation.

> All appropriations... may be conceived of as lump-sum grants with "strings" attached. These strings, or conditions of expenditure, constitute legislative prescriptions that bind the operating arm of the government. Occasionally, conditions may be stated in an appropriations statute itself. For instance, an appropriations act may provide that "[n]o part of any appropriation contained in this Act shall be used... for publicity or propaganda purposes...." Alternatively, the appropriations act may require that the recipient agency allocate the amount appropriated among certain activities or in accordance with certain conditions. Often, the appropriations act explicitly incorporates other legislation, notably substantive legislation creating particular federal agencies or programs or granting particular agency powers. Moreover, all appropriations legislation effectively incorporates the prescriptions of statutes of general applicability. [Stith, *supra*, at 1353.]

Federal agencies may not use nonappropriated funds because their activities are authorized only to the extent of their appropriations. *Id.* at 1356. *See* Anti-Deficiency Act, 31 U.S.C. §1341(a)(I)(A) (2000) (prohibiting expenditures or obligations in excess of appropriations); U.S. Const. Art. I, §9, cl. 7 ("No money shall be drawn from the Treasury, but in Consequence of Appropriations made by Law.").

In Spaulding v. Douglas Aircraft, 60 F. Supp. 985, 988 (S.D. Cal. 1945), *aff'd*, 154 F.2d 419 (9th Cir. 1946), the court stated that

> Congress in making appropriations has the power and authority not only to designate the purpose of the appropriation, but also the terms and conditions under which the executive department... may expend such appropriations....
>
> The purpose of appropriations, the terms and conditions under which said appropriations were made, is a matter solely in the hands of Congress and it is the plain and explicit duty of the executive branch... to comply with the same.

B. Delegations and Appropriations for National Security

See also 27 Op. Atty. Gen. 259 (1909) (approving constitutionality of bill that conditioned funding of the Marine Corps on the maintenance of a ratio of 8 percent Marines to Navy enlisted men on Navy battleships). Usually limitations in appropriations acts pertain to the particular appropriated funds, but Congress has also used an appropriations rider to limit the executive in ways unrelated to the use or purpose of the appropriation. The Constitution, after all, contains no rule restricting any piece of legislation to a single subject.[1]

2. *The Political Utility of Appropriations Riders.* Why does Congress rely so much on limitations in appropriations bills instead of building them into other legislation? Surely one reason is their comparative effectiveness:

> [A]ppropriations oversight is effective precisely because the statutory controls are so direct, unambiguous, and virtually self-enforcing. While agencies are able to bend the more ambiguous language of authorizing legislation to their own purposes, the dollar figures in appropriations bills represent commands which cannot be bent or ignored except at extreme peril to agency officials. [S. Comm. on Governmental Operations, 95th Cong., *Study of Federal Regulation: Congressional Oversight of Regulatory Agencies* 31 (Comm. Print 1977).]

Another reason is that sponsors of limitations can sometimes avoid the jurisdiction of hostile committees by inserting the limitations in appropriations bills.[2] They can also make it difficult for the President to veto the limitations by embedding them in needed appropriations bills, especially omnibus bills that provide for funding of many different programs.

3. *The History of Defense Appropriations Riders.* Partly out of the foregoing considerations, Congress has often used its defense appropriations power to control national security policy, particularly since World War II. *See generally* Eli E. Nobleman, *Financial Aspects of Congressional Participation in Foreign Relations*, 289 Annals 145 (1953); Stith, *supra* p. 111, at 1360-1361 nn.83-86. For example, Congress used its appropriations power to attempt to control and ultimately to end the Vietnam War, see *infra* pp. 230-239, and to attempt to control military assistance to the Contras fighting in Nicaragua. See *infra* pp. 411-418.

The language and history of the defense appropriations power raise the possibility that these limitations have a specially protected constitutional status. While the power of Congress generally to appropriate monies is implied

---

1. Each house has imposed a limited version of the rule on itself, restricting the use of riders to modify substantive legislation, *see* Senate R. XVI(4) and House R. XXI(2), but a violation of the rule merely makes the rider subject to procedural objection within the Congress and does not invalidate it as law.

2. In both the House and Senate, there are three committees with specific jurisdiction over national security matters: Armed Services, Foreign Relations (International Relations in the House), and Intelligence. The Joint Economic Committee, Governmental Affairs (Government Reform and Oversight in the House), Appropriations, and, to a more general degree, Budget committees all have some oversight responsibilities for national security expenditures. Jurisdictional overlaps are common, however, and many other committees have oversight responsibility for incidental — especially internal — security functions. See generally the current *Congressional Directory* for a description of the jurisdiction and membership of relevant committees.

from the Common Defense Clause, Art. I §8, appropriations for the Army and Navy are separately and expressly authorized in clause 12 of the same section. The Framers were aware of the English Parliament's successful use of the purse in its struggle with the King, *see* Francis L. Coolidge Jr. & Joel David Sharrow, Note, *The War-Making Powers: The Intentions of the Framers in Light of Parliamentary History*, 50 B.U. L. Rev. 5 (Spec. Issue 1970), and of the extensive use of the purse to control the scope and conduct of colonial military operations. *See, e.g.*, Elias Huzar, *The Purse and the Sword* 22-23 (1971). As noted in Chapter 2, the Framers deliberately vested Congress with detailed defense appropriations powers and simultaneously limited the duration of any blank check that Congress might draw to support a standing army. *See* Garry J. Wooters, Note, *The Appropriations Power as a Tool of Congressional Foreign Policy Making*, 50 B.U. L. Rev. 34, 40 (Spec. Issue 1970). Moreover, the difficulty of anticipating precisely and in detail the occasions for exercise of military force arguably increased the practical importance of defense appropriations as at least a post hoc control. *See generally* William C. Banks & Peter Raven-Hansen, *National Security Law and the Power of the Purse* 9-42 (1994); Michael J. Glennon, *Strengthening the War Powers Resolution: The Case for Purse-Strings Restrictions*, 60 Minn. L. Rev. 1 (1975).

C. STATUTORY EMERGENCY POWERS

Proclamation No. 7463, Declaration of National Emergency by Reason of Certain Terrorist Attacks
66 Fed. Reg. 48,199 (Sept. 14, 2001)

A PROCLAMATION

A national emergency exists by reason of the terrorist attacks at the World Trade Center, New York, New York, and the Pentagon, and the continuing and immediate threat of further attacks on the United States.

NOW, THEREFORE, I, GEORGE W. BUSH, President of the United States of America, by virtue of the authority vested in me as President by the Constitution and the laws of the United States, I [sic] hereby declare that the national emergency has existed since September 11, 2001, and, pursuant to the National Emergencies Act (50 U.S.C. 1601 et seq.), I intend to utilize the following statutes: sections 123, 123a, 527, 2201(c), 12006, and 12302 of title 10, United States Code, and sections 331, 359, and 367 of title 14, United States Code.

This proclamation immediately shall be published in the Federal Register or disseminated through the Emergency Federal Register, and transmitted to the Congress.

This proclamation is not intended to create any right or benefit, substantive or procedural, enforceable at law by a party against the United States, its agencies, its officers, or any person.

C. Statutory Emergency Powers

IN WITNESS WHEREOF, I have hereunto set my hand this fourteenth day of September, in the year of our Lord two thousand one, and of the Independence of the United States of America the two hundred and twenty-sixth.

George W. Bush

Congress has enacted at least 40 standby emergency statutes that permit the President to act in ways that would be impermissible in the absence of a crisis. *See* Ackerman & Grimmett (*supra* p. 99), at 68-74 (listing emergency standby statutes). *See also* Harold C. Relyea, *National Emergency Powers* (Cong. Res. Serv. 98-505), Sept. 15, 2005. The statutory authority is activated by a declaration of a national emergency. In Proclamation 7463, the President invoked standby authorities to activate the Ready Reserve and retired officers and enlisted members of the Coast Guard, to suspend separation (retirement) of officers from the armed services, and to suspend certain numerical limitations on numbers of officers at certain ranks. Other standby authorities not there invoked authorize the President to commit troops abroad without congressional approval, 10 U.S.C. §712 (2000), and to enter into defense contracts without following the usual procedures, 50 U.S.C. §§1431-1433 (2000).

During the Vietnam War, it was revealed that President Nixon had relied on one of these emergency statutes, the Feed and Forage Act of 1861, 41 U.S.C. §11 (2000) (intended to provide fodder for cavalry horses), to finance the secret invasion of Cambodia. Nixon based his action on national emergencies, one dating from 1933, that were earlier declared and never revoked. This discovery led to passage in 1976 of the National Emergencies Act, 50 U.S.C. §§1601-1651 (2000 & Supp. III 2003), canceling all existing national emergencies. If a President now wishes to activate standby legislation, she must declare a new national emergency, indicate the statutory authority she intends to exercise, and notify Congress. *Id.* §§1621(a), 1631, 1641. *See* Glenn E. Fuller, Note, *The National Emergency Dilemma: Balancing the Executive's Crisis Powers with the Need for Accountability*, 52 S. Cal. L. Rev. 1453 (1979); Relyea, *supra*.

NOTES AND QUESTIONS

1. *Invoking Standby Authorities.* After Hurricane Katrina hit the Gulf Coast in August 2005, President Bush declared a national emergency and invoked 40 U.S.C. §3147 to suspend the Davis-Bacon Act wage supports for workers in the affected area in order to facilitate recovery construction. Proc. No. 7924, *To Suspend Subchapter IV of Chapter 31 of Title 40, United States Code, Within a Limited Geographic Area in Response to the National Emergency Caused by Hurricane Katrina*, 70 Fed. Reg. 54,227 (Sept. 8, 2005). Oddly, however, he simply found that "the conditions caused by Hurricane Katrina constitute a 'national emergency' within the meaning of section 3147 of title 40, United States Code." *Id.* at 54,227. He appears not to have followed the National Emergencies Act on this occasion. Was the claimed standby authority lawfully invoked? *See* Relyea, *supra*, at 19 ("A more likely course of action seemingly would have been for the

President to declare a national emergency pursuant to the National Emergencies Act and to specify that he was, accordingly, activating the suspension authority."). Should it matter whether the President follows the National Emergencies Act when he seeks to invoke standby statutory emergency authority?

2. *The IEEPA.* In 1917, during World War I, Congress passed the Trading with the Enemy Act, which gives the President authority to regulate a variety of domestic and international economic transactions in wartime. The Act was amended in 1933 to make it applicable during peacetime national emergencies as well. *See* 50 U.S.C. App. §§1-44 (2000), as amended. It has been invoked by a succession of Presidents to take extraordinary foreign and domestic executive actions. A criminal prosecution for violation of the Act is traced in United States v. Plummer, 221 F.3d 1298 (11th Cir. 2000) (defendant apprehended trying to smuggle $50,000 worth of Cuban cigars).

The International Emergency Economic Powers Act (IEEPA), 50 U.S.C. §§1701-1707 (2000 & Supp. III 2003), which was invoked by President Carter and analyzed by the Court in Dames & Moore v. Regan, 453 U.S. 654 (1981), *supra* p. 48, was enacted in 1977 to curb perceived presidential abuses of authority under the Trading with the Enemy Act. Without disturbing the President's wartime authority under the earlier legislation, the IEEPA gives the President the same peacetime emergency economic powers as previously, but those powers may only be exercised following a new national emergency declaration. *See* Mary Margaret Coughlin Bowman, Note, *Presidential Emergency Powers Related to International Economic Transactions: Congressional Recognition of Customary Authority,* 11 Vand. J. Transnatl. L. 515 (1978).

In addition to its use in the Iran hostage crisis, the IEEPA has been invoked by Presidents to limit trade with South Africa, Libya, Panama, Iraq, Haiti, and the Balkans, as well as to restrict activities that threaten the further proliferation of nuclear, chemical, and biological weapons. Executive orders declaring national emergencies invoking the IEEPA are set out in the United States Code following the text of the statute.

3. *Defining "National Emergency."* The President may exercise power under the National Emergencies Act only after declaring a "national emergency." Do you know what a "national emergency" is? According to one commentator, "[n]o statute defines a national emergency.... The test for when a national emergency exists is completely subjective — anything the President says is a national emergency is a national emergency." Fuller, *supra,* 52 S. Cal. L. Rev. at 1458. Should Congress try to provide a definition of the term? Can you suggest suitable language? In the absence of a statutory definition, can you say how and by whom a presidential declaration of a national emergency could be challenged?

In 1985, President Reagan issued Executive Order No. 12,513, 50 Fed. Reg. 18,629 (May 1, 1985), to cut off trade with Nicaragua. The executive order provoked a suit by two U.S. business concerns trading in Nicaragua to enjoin enforcement of the embargo. Beacon Products Corp. v. Reagan, 633 F. Supp. 1191 (D. Mass. 1986), *aff'd,* 814 F.2d 1 (1st Cir. 1987). The plaintiffs argued that the President was not empowered to impose the embargo because Nicaragua did not pose "an unusual and extraordinary

C. Statutory Emergency Powers

threat" as required by §1701(b) of IEEPA. The court found this aspect of the case to be a nonjusticiable political question. The court in United States v. Yoshida Intl., Inc., 526 F.2d 560, 579 (C.C.P.A. 1975), a case testing the President's actions under the Trading with the Enemy Act, observed that "courts will not normally review the essentially political questions surrounding the declaration or continuance of a national emergency."

But in a more recent case, the court found that its review of administrative orders implementing the ban on trading with the Federal Republic of Yugoslavia did not "hamper the executive's conduct of foreign policy by injecting unacceptable sweeping challenges to foreign policy choices." Milena Ship Management Co. v. Newcomb, 804 F. Supp. 846, 850 (E.D. La. 1992), *aff'd*, 995 F.2d 620 (5th Cir. 1993), *cert. denied*, 510 U.S. 1071 (1994). On the other hand, the court observed, before granting a preliminary injunction to suspend the President's blocking orders, it had to "take into account the effect [of its actions] on the executive's ability to conduct foreign affairs, on the congressional policy behind the authorization of blocking orders, and on this country's obligations with respect to the United Nations." 804 F. Supp. at 854.

By avoiding judicial scrutiny of the President's grounds for invoking either the IEEPA or the National Emergencies Act, would a court not effectively nullify the efforts of Congress to regulate the President's emergency powers? *See* Jules Lobel, *Emergency Power and the Decline of Liberalism*, 98 Yale L.J. 1385, 1416-1418 (1989).

4. *Banning Travel.* In 1963, President Kennedy approved a Treasury Department regulation promulgated under the Trading with the Enemy Act that cut off trade and prohibited all economic transactions with Cuba. President Carter relaxed that regulation in early 1977 to allow U.S. citizens to pay ordinary expenses of traveling to Cuba. But in 1982, President Reagan reimposed the ban on most travel without declaring a new national emergency. When it enacted the IEEPA, Congress adopted a grandfather clause providing that "authorities conferred upon the President by section 5(b) of the Trading with the Enemy Act which were being exercised with respect to a country on July 1, 1977" could "continue to be exercised." 91 Stat. 1625, note following 50 U.S.C. App. §5. The Supreme Court decided that the grandfather clause permitted the newly expanded travel ban. Regan v. Wald, 468 U.S. 222 (1984).

The Court also found that the ban did not violate the right to travel guaranteed by the Fifth Amendment's Due Process Clause, because the ban was, in the Court's view, "justified by weighty concerns of foreign policy." Citing the *Curtiss-Wright* decision for a "traditional deference to executive judgment '[i]n this vast external realm,'" the Court said there was an "adequate basis . . . to sustain the President's decision to curtail the flow of hard currency to Cuba — currency that could then be used in support of Cuban adventurism — by restricting travel." *Id.* at 242-243. On similar grounds, the court in Walsh v. Brady, 927 F.2d 1229 (D.C. Cir. 1991), upheld the travel ban against a First Amendment challenge. *See also* Freedom to Travel Campaign v. Newcomb, 82 F.3d 1431 (9th Cir. 1996). Does your reading of earlier decisions reveal such a tradition of deference? If the stated premise of *Curtiss-Wright* is correct, could the Court have decided otherwise?

5. *Takings in Emergencies.* Must the government pay compensation to the owners of claims destroyed by a suspension of dealings under the IEEPA? The *Dames & Moore* Court avoided answering this question when it determined that the plaintiff had an alternative means of at least partial redress. 453 U.S. at 688. In a later case, a landlord found itself unable to sue for past-due rentals or to collect on a related letter of credit from Yugoslav Airlines when President Bush invoked the IEEPA to block "all assets and property interests of Serbia, Montenegro, and the Federal Republic of Yugoslavia . . . in the United States." Exec. Order No. 12,808, 57 Fed. Reg. 23,299 (May 30, 1992). The court found that no compensable taking had occurred, in part because the "President's ability to deal effectively with international events is critical to the safety and prosperity of the nation." Rockefeller Center Properties v. United States, 32 Fed. Cl. 586, 591 (1995). *See also* Paradissiotis v. United States, 49 Fed. Cl. 16, 23 (2001) ("The preservation of the national security interest of the United States . . . greatly outweighs plaintiff's [total] loss."). *See generally* David Meezan, Note, *Forgotten Rights: Takings Claims and the International Emergency Economic Powers Act*, 21 Vt. L. Rev. 591 (1996).

D. CONGRESSIONAL INVESTIGATIONS

McGrain v. Daugherty
United States Supreme Court, 1927
273 U.S. 135

[In the course of investigating the administration of the Department of Justice, a select Senate committee issued a subpoena to compel the testimony of a private witness. When the witness refused to comply, the committee ordered his arrest. After his arrest, he brought a petition for habeas corpus, challenging, *inter alia,* the Senate's constitutional authority to investigate. The lower court granted his petition and this appeal followed.]

Mr. Justice Van Devanter delivered the opinion of the court. . . . The first of the principal questions — the one which the witness particularly presses on our attention — is, as before shown, whether the Senate — or the House of Representatives — both being on the same plane in this regard — has power, through its own process, to compel a private individual to appear before it or one of its committees and give testimony needed to enable it efficiently to exercise a legislative function belonging to it under the Constitution.

The Constitution provides for a Congress consisting of a Senate and House of Representatives and invests it with "all legislative powers" granted to the United States, and with power "to make all laws which shall be necessary and proper" for carrying into execution these powers and "all other powers" vested by the Constitution in the United States or in any department or officer thereof. Article 1, §§1, 8. Other provisions show that, while bills can become laws only after being considered and passed by both houses of Congress, each house is to be distinct from the other, to have its own officers and rules, and to exercise its

D. Congressional Investigations

legislative function independently. Article 1, §§2, 3, 5, 7. But there is no provision expressly investing either house with power to make investigations and exact testimony, to the end that it may exercise its legislative function advisedly and effectively. So the question arises whether this power is so far incidental to the legislative function as to be implied.

In actual legislative practice, power to secure needed information by such means has long been treated as an attribute of the power to legislate. It was so regarded in the British Parliament and in the Colonial legislatures before the American Revolution; and a like view has prevailed and been carried into effect in both houses of Congress and in most of the state Legislatures.

This power was both asserted and exerted by the House of Representatives in 1792, when it appointed a select committee to inquire into the St. Clair expedition and authorized the committee to send for necessary persons, papers and records. Mr. Madison, who had taken an important part in framing the Constitution only five years before, and four of his associates in that work, were members of the House of Representatives at the time, and all voted for the inquiry. 3 Cong. Ann. 494. Other exertions of the power by the House of Representatives, as also by the Senate, are shown in the citations already made. Among those by the Senate, the inquiry ordered in 1859 respecting the raid by John Brown and his adherents on the armory and arsenal of the United States at Harper's Ferry is of special significance. The resolution directing the inquiry authorized the committee to send for persons and papers, to inquire into the facts pertaining to the raid and the means by which it was organized and supported, and to report what legislation, if any, was necessary to preserve the peace of the country and protect the public property....

We are of opinion that the power of inquiry — with process to enforce it — is an essential and appropriate auxiliary to the legislative function. It was so regarded and employed in American Legislatures before the Constitution was framed and ratified. Both houses of Congress took this view of it early in their history — the House of Representatives with the approving votes of Mr. Madison and other members whose service in the convention which framed the Constitution gives special significance to their action — and both houses have employed the power accordingly up to the present time. The acts of 1798 and 1857, judged by their comprehensive terms, were intended to recognize the existence of this power in both houses and to enable them to employ it "more effectually" than before. So, when their practice in the matter is appraised according to the circumstances in which it was begun and to those in which it has been continued, it falls nothing short of a practical construction, long continued, of the constitutional provisions respecting their powers, and therefore should be taken as fixing the meaning of those provisions, if otherwise doubtful.

We are further of opinion that the provisions are not of doubtful meaning, but, as was held by this Court in the cases we have reviewed, are intended to be effectively exercised, and therefore to carry with them such auxiliary powers as are necessary and appropriate to that end. While the power to exact information in aid of the legislative function was not involved in those cases, the rule of interpretation applied there is applicable here. A legislative body cannot legislate wisely or effectively in the absence of information respecting the conditions which the legislation is intended to affect or change; and where the legislative body does not itself possess the requisite information—which not infrequently is true—recourse must be had to others who do possess it. Experience has taught that mere requests for such information often are unavailing, and also that information which is volunteered is not always accurate or complete; so some means of compulsion are essential to obtain what is needed. All this was true before and when the Constitution was framed and adopted. In that period the power of inquiry—with enforcing process—was regarded and employed as a necessary and appropriate attribute of the power to legislate—indeed, was treated as inhering in it. Thus there is ample warrant for thinking, as we do, that the constitutional provisions which commit the legislative function to the two houses are intended to include this attribute to the end that the function may be effectively exercised.

The contention is earnestly made on behalf of the witness that this power of inquiry, if sustained, may be abusively and oppressively exerted. If this be so, it affords no ground for denying the power. The same contention might be directed against the power to legislate, and of course would be unavailing. We must assume, for present purposes, that neither house will be disposed to exert the power beyond its proper bounds, or without due regard to the rights of witnesses. But if, contrary to this assumption, controlling limitations or restrictions are disregarded, the decisions in Kilbourn v. Thompson [103 U.S. 168 (1881)] and Marshall v. Gordon [243 U.S. 521 (1917)] point to admissible measures of relief. And it is a necessary deduction from the decisions in Kilbourn v. Thompson and In re Chapman [166 U.S. 661 (1897)] that a witness rightfully may refuse to answer where the bounds of the power are exceeded or the questions are not pertinent to the matter under inquiry.

We come now to the question whether it sufficiently appears that the purpose for which the witness's testimony was sought was to obtain information in aid of the legislative function. The court below answered the question in the negative and put its decision largely on this ground....

It is quite true that the resolution directing the investigation does not in terms avow that it is intended to be in aid of legislation; but it does show that the subject to be investigated was the administration of the Department of Justice— whether its functions were being properly discharged or were being neglected or misdirected, and particularly whether the Attorney General and his assistants were performing or neglecting their duties in respect of the institution and prosecution of proceedings to punish crimes and enforce appropriate remedies against the wrongdoers—specific instances of alleged neglect being recited. Plainly the subject was one on which legislation could be had and would be materially aided by the information which the investigation was calculated to elicit. This becomes manifest when it is reflected that the functions of the Department of Justice, the powers and duties of the Attorney General and the duties of his assistants are all subject to regulation by congressional legislation, and that the department is maintained and its activities are carried on under such appropriations as in the judgment of Congress are needed from year to year.

The only legitimate object the Senate could have in ordering the investigation was to aid it in legislating; and we think the subject-matter was such that the presumption should be indulged that this was the real object. An express avowal of the object would have been better; but in view of the particular subject-matter was not indispensable....

D. Congressional Investigations

We conclude that the investigation was ordered for a legitimate object; that the witness wrongfully refused to appear and testify before the committee and was lawfully attached; that the Senate is entitled to have him give testimony pertinent to the inquiry, either at its bar or before the committee; and that the district court erred in discharging him from custody under the attachment....

Mr. Justice STONE did not participate in the consideration or decision of the case.

NOTES AND QUESTIONS

1. *Constitutional Basis for Investigation and Oversight.* In a more recent case involving the Navy, a court of appeals asserted that "[t]here is no doubt that Congress constitutionally can act, without recourse to the full legislative procedure of bicameral passage and presentment, to investigate the conduct of executive officials and others outside the legislative branch;... and to influence the executive through the 'illuminating power of investigation.'" Lear Siegler, Inc. Energy Products Div. v. Lehman, 842 F.2d 1102, 1109 (9th Cir. 1988) (dictum) (quoting Ameron, Inc. v. United States Army Corps of Engineers, 809 F.2d 979, 992 (3d Cir. 1986)). What constitutional theories support Congress's power of investigation? In addition to the theories discussed in *McGrain, see* United States v. American Telephone & Telegraph Co., 551 F.2d 384, 394 (D.C. Cir. 1976) (suggesting in dictum that "Congress's power to monitor executive actions is implicit in the appropriations power"). Does *McGrain* suggest any limitations or conditions on this power?

2. *House Resolutions of Inquiry.* Although *McGrain* involved a subpoena to a private witness, an alternative procedure in the House is a *resolution of inquiry,* "a simple resolution making a direct request or demand of the President or the head of an executive department to furnish the House of Representatives with specific factual information in the possession of the executive branch." Louis Fisher, *House Resolutions of Inquiry* (Cong. Res. Serv. RL31909) 1, May 12, 2003, quoting *Deschler's Precedents,* H.R. Doc. No. 94-661, vol. 7, ch. 24, §8 (1977). *See also* Louis Fisher, *Congressional Access to Information: Using Legislative Will and Leverage,* 52 Duke L.J. 323 (2002). However, such resolutions have left broad discretion in the executive concerning what information it must produce. In 1952, for example, the House passed a resolution of inquiry directing the Secretary of State to transmit "full and complete information" regarding any agreements entered into by President Truman and Prime Minister Winston Churchill regarding the deployment of U.S. armed forces beyond the continental limits of the United States or in armed conflict on foreign soil. Fisher, *House Resolutions, supra,* at 9. But even its sponsors said in debate, "We cannot by this resolution make the Executive answer.... All we can do, if we pass this resolution, is to say to the Secretary of State and the Department of State: 'Please try again. That answer you sent down was not very good.'" *Id.,* quoting 98 Stat. 1205, 1208 (1952). Nevertheless, such resolutions were sought often during the Vietnam War to request copies of the Pentagon Papers,

information about U.S. covert operations in Laos, and information on military operations in Cambodia, among other matters. *Id.* at 17-20. Even when such resolutions fail, "a substantial amount of information is usually released to Congress." *Id.* at 25. In fact, arguments that the Administration has complied with a resolution are frequently the reason for reporting a resolution adversely and tabling it." *Id.*

3. *Protecting Secrets in Congress.* May the President refuse to provide national security information to Congress on the grounds that it is classified? See *infra* pp. 1064-1065.

Can Congress keep a secret? Currently there is no requirement that any member of the Congress obtain a security clearance as a condition of gaining access to classified information. *See* Frederick M. Kaiser, *Protection of Classified Information by Congress: Practices and Proposals* (Cong. Res. Serv. RS20748) 5, Jan. 11, 2006. (Neither the President, Vice-President, nor the Justices of the Supreme Court are required to have such clearances either.) Would such a requirement be lawful? In answering this question, consider how the clearance investigation would be conducted (would members be polygraphed?) and who would make the clearance decision. *See* Kaiser, *supra,* at 5-6.

We see in Chapter 15 that intelligence oversight legislation requires the executive to provide notice of covert operations to the Intelligence Committees but permits the President to limit such notice to eight designated congressional leaders in some cases, or to delay notice for some period in others. See *infra* pp. 423-424. House rules require all its members and staff to take a secrecy oath of nondisclosure of "any classified information received in the course of my service with the House of Representatives, except as authorized by the House of Representatives or in accordance with its Rules." House Rule XXIII, cl.13, 108th Cong. The Senate has nothing comparable. The House and Senate Ethics Committees are authorized to investigate breaches of security by members of the chamber or their staff. Kaiser, *supra,* at 3-4.

4. *Enforcing Information Demands.* A witness who refuses to comply with a congressional subpoena may be liable for contempt of Congress. Congress has made contempt a misdemeanor. The House or Senate may certify a citation for contempt to the U.S. Attorney, who is ordinarily expected to bring the matter before the grand jury. 2 U.S.C. §192 (2000). What problems does this scheme pose for enforcing information demands against the executive branch?

In 1982, after Environmental Protection Agency Administrator Ann Gorsuch was cited for contempt by the House for her refusal to comply with a congressional subpoena, the Justice Department not only refused to go before the grand jury but sued the House, seeking a declaratory judgment that she need not comply. The suit was dismissed as premature, because claims of executive privilege could be raised as a defense to a contempt trial, which would be necessary only if the branches could not strike a deal. United States v. United States House of Representatives, 556 F. Supp. 150 (D.D.C. 1983). *See generally* Todd L. Peterson, *Prosecuting Executive Branch Officials for Contempt of Congress,* 66 N.Y.U. L. Rev. 563 (1991); Ronald L. Claveloux, Note, *The Conflict Between Executive Privilege and Congressional Oversight: The Gorsuch Controversy,* 1983 Duke L.J. 1333. The very title of the case suggests why courts are loathe to

D. Congressional Investigations

adjudicate interbranch information disputes and why the political branches typically negotiate a compromise. *See* Joel D. Bush, Note, *Congressional-Executive Access Disputes: Legal Standards and Political Settlements*, 9 J.L. & Pol. 719 (1993); Peter M. Shane, *Legal Disagreement and Negotiation in a Government of Laws: The Case of Executive Privilege Claims Against Congress*, 71 Minn. L. Rev. 462 (1987). *But see* Randall K. Miller, *Congressional Inquests: Suffocating the Constitutional Prerogative of Executive Privilege*, 81 Minn. L. Rev. 631 (1997) (urging earlier judicial resolution). In fact, they reached a compromise in the Gorsuch controversy after the court declined to decide it.

In the *American Telephone & Telegraph* case, *supra*, 551 F.2d 384, a congressional subcommittee subpoened requests made by the FBI to the telephone company for warrantless national security wiretaps. The District Court enjoined the subcommittee. The Court of Appeals, however, was more reluctant to decide the dispute between the branches:

> A court seeking to balance the legislative and executive interests asserted here would face severe problems in formulating and applying standards. Granted that the subpoenas are clearly within the proper legislative investigatory sphere, it is difficult to "weigh" Congress's need for the request letters....
>
> As to the danger to national security, a court would have to consider the Subcommittee's track record for security, the likelihood of a leak if other members of the House sought access to the material. In addition to this delicate and possible unseemly determination, the court would have to weigh the effect of a leak on intelligence activities and diplomatic relations. Finally, the court would have to consider the reasonableness of the alternatives offered by the parties and decide which would better reconcile the competing constitutional interests.
>
> Before moving on to a decision of such nerve-center constitutional questions, we pause to allow for further efforts at a settlement. [*Id.* at 394.]

The court then remanded to the District Court with instructions to seek a settlement. When this effort failed and a second appeal ensued, the Court of Appeals reiterated its reluctance. Although the court declined to invoke the political question doctrine, it decided against deciding as long as any possibility of a compromise remained. The court then suggested procedures for reaching a compromise. 567 F.2d 121 (D.C. Cir. 1977). This time its efforts bore fruit and the branches reached an agreement, ending the litigation.

5. *Resolving a Conflict About Information Demands.* If the political branches do not reach a compromise, however, how should a court decide between a congressional demand for national security information and a claim of executive privilege? See *supra* p. 91. Does the answer depend on the subject of the information demanded? *See generally* Peterson, *supra*, at 616-625; Miller, *supra*, at 679-687.

6. *Congress's Last Resort.* If the Justice Department will not prosecute a contempt of Congress citation against an executive branch official, what recourse does Congress have? *See* Peterson, *supra*, at 625-631; H.R. Rep. No. 93-1305, at 4 (1974) (recommending an article of impeachment against Richard Nixon for his failure to comply with subpoenas issued by the House Committee on the Judiciary as part of its impeachment inquiry).

E. LIMITATIONS ON CONGRESSIONAL WAR POWERS

1. Substantive Limits on Congressional National Security Powers

We have seen that Congress's power to delegate national security powers to the executive branch is, at least theoretically, constrained by the "nondelegation principle." See *supra* p. 43. That principle requires Congress to make fundamental legislative judgments by including "intelligible principles" in any statutory delegation, so that executive discretion can be channeled and, on judicial review, measured. See *supra* pp. 47-48. *Lichter, supra* p. 102, and United States v. Curtiss-Wright Export Corp., 299 U.S. 304 (1936), *supra* p. 60, showed, however, that if the nondelegation principle ever had any teeth, they hardly leave marks on national security and foreign relations delegations.

The nondelegation principle is just one example of a broader substantive constraint: that a statutory delegation not violate any provision of the Constitution. Lovett v. United States, 66 F. Supp. 142 (Ct. Cl. 1945), *aff'd on other grounds*, 328 U.S. 303 (1946), provides an illustration. There Congress had enacted a rider to the Wartime Urgent Deficiency Appropriation of 1943 forbidding the executive branch to disburse salaries to certain identified "subversive" employees unless they were reappointed with the advice and consent of the Senate. Because the House would not approve any appropriation without this provision, the Senate agreed to it. The President reluctantly signed the bill into law, asserting that the rider was unconstitutional. When the employees sued the United States in the Court of Claims for their salaries, the court ruled in favor of the employees on contract grounds. But Judge Whitaker, concurring, found that the provision violated the Bill of Attainder Clause of the Constitution by inflicting punishment without a judicial trial. 66 F. Supp. at 148. He asserted that even an exercise of the appropriation power "is subject to the limitation that it must not be exercised in a way that would nullify another provision of the Constitution." *Id.* Judge Madden acknowledged that Congress has the absolute *power* to withhold appropriations, but not the lawful *authority*.

> I do not think, therefore, that the power of the purse may be constitutionally exercised to produce an unconstitutional result such as taking of a citizen's liberty or property without due process of law, a conviction and punishment of a citizen for wholly innocent conduct, or a trespass upon the constitutional functions of another branch of the Government. [*Id.* at 152.]

The Supreme Court affirmed the judgment for the employees on the ground that the rider constituted an unconstitutional bill of attainder. 328 U.S. at 313-315. "The fact that the punishment is inflicted through the instrumentality of an Act specifically cutting off the pay of certain named individuals found guilty of disloyalty, makes it no less galling or effective than if it had been done by an Act which designated the conduct as criminal." *Id.* at 316.

Lovett does not stand alone. *See also* United States v. Will, 449 U.S. 200, 225-226 (1980) (appropriations act that reduces compensation of federal judges

E. Limitations on Congressional War Powers

violates the Compensation Clause of Article I); Brown v. Califano, 627 F.2d 1221 (D.C. Cir. 1980) (construing an appropriations prohibition of agency support for mandatory busing narrowly to avoid finding it an unconstitutional prohibition of agency enforcement of the constitutional right to equal protection); Blitz v. Donovan, 538 F. Supp. 1119 (D.D.C. 1982) (appropriations provision that denies funds to persons who advocate the overthrow of the government violates the First Amendment).

The limitation on the congressional appropriations power recognized in *Lovett* and its companion cases has found other national security applications as well. *See* 41 Op. Atty. Gen. 507 (1960); 41 Op. Atty. Gen. 230 (1955); 4 Op. Off. Legal Counsel 731 (1980) (all concluding that Congress may not constitutionally use its appropriations power in a manner that violates direct constitutional commands); *cf.* United States v. Robel, 389 U.S. 258, 263-264 (1967) (quoting Home Bldg. & Loan Assn. v. Blaisdell, 290 U.S. 398, 426 (1934): "[T]he phrase 'war power' cannot be invoked as a talismanic incantation to support any exercise of congressional power which can be brought within its ambit. '[E]ven the war power does not remove constitutional limitations safeguarding individual liberties.'"). Presumably what we will call the *Lovett* limitation applies with equal force to legislation enacted under Congress's Necessary and Proper lawmaking authority and is not confined just to appropriations measures.

NOTES AND QUESTIONS

1. *Lovett or Lichter?* How can the *Lovett* limitation be squared with *Lichter*'s approval of the assertion that the congressional war power "is not destroyed or impaired by any later provision of the Constitution or by any one of the amendments"? *Lichter*, 334 U.S. at 781, *supra* p. 102 (quoting Chief Justice Hughes). One answer—or dodge—may be to read an appropriations rider or other statutory limitation narrowly to avoid impairing the executive war power. This principle of avoidance is reflected in the canon of statutory construction that "[w]hen the validity of an act of the Congress is drawn in question, and even if a serious doubt of constitutionality is raised, it is a cardinal principle that this Court will first ascertain whether a construction of the statute is fairly possible by which the question may be avoided." Crowell v. Benson, 285 U.S. 22, 62 (1932). Why didn't this canon apply in *Lovett?*

2. *Lovett and War Powers.* Does *Lovett* also support the proposition that Congress may not use its national security powers to "micro-manage" the conduct of war or foreign policy? Various judicial dicta assert that "Congress cannot direct the conduct of campaigns," Ex parte Milligan, 71 U.S. (4 Wall.) 2, 139 (1866) (dictum) (opinion of Chase, C. J., and Wayne, Swayne, and Miller, JJ., concurring), and that "Congress can not in the disguise of 'rules for the government' of the Army impair the authority of the President as commander in chief." Swaim v. United States, 28 Ct. Cl. 173, 221 (1893) (dictum), *aff'd*, 165 U.S. 553 (1897). *See also* Youngstown Sheet & Tube Co. v. Sawyer, 343 U.S. 579, 644 (1952), *supra* p. 37 (Jackson, J., concurring) ("Congress cannot deprive the President of the command of the army and navy" though "only Congress can provide him an army and navy to command"); Louis Henkin, *Foreign Affairs and*

the Constitution 113, 361-362 n.74 (1972) (quoting Senator Borah, 69 Cong. Rec. 6760 (1928), as saying that "Congress could not, through the power of appropriation, . . . infringe upon the right of the President to command whatever army he might find.").

The Minority Report of the Iran-Contra Committees described its objection to the use of appropriations limitations to manage foreign policy in these terms:

> Congress may not use its control over appropriations, including salaries, to prevent the executive or the judiciary from fulfilling Constitutionally mandated obligations. . . .
>
> Congress does not have to create a State Department or an intelligence agency. Once such departments are created, however, the Congress may not prevent the President from using his executive branch employees from serving as the country's "eyes and ears" in foreign policy. Even if Congress refuses to fund such departments, it may not prevent the President from doing what he can without funds to act as the nation's "sole organ" in foreign affairs. . . .
>
> What Congress grants by statute may be taken away by statute. But Congress may not ask the President to give up a power he gets from the Constitution, as opposed to one he gets from Congress, as a condition for getting something, whether money or some other good or power from Congress. [*Report of the Congressional Committees Investigating the Iran-Contra Affair, The Minority Report*, H.R. Rep. No. 100-433, S. Rep. No. 100-216, at 476 (1987) (hereinafter *Minority Report*).]

See also Assignment of Ground Forces of the United States to Duty in European Areas, S. Rep. No. 93-220, at 92-93 (1973) (statement of former Secretary of State Dean Acheson) ("Not only has the President the authority to use Armed Forces in carrying out the broad foreign policy of the United States and implementing treaties, but it is equally clear that this authority may not be interfered with by the Congress in the exercise of powers which it has under the Constitution.").

Is there any difference between the constitutional commands discussed in *Lovett* or its companion cases and the "Constitutionally mandated obligations" to which the *Minority Report* refers? Does the *Minority Report* critique adequately account for the history of the defense appropriations power? See *supra* p. 113. Or for the reach of the Necessary and Proper Clause? *See War Powers Legislation 1973: Hearings on S. 440 Before the S. Comm. on Foreign Rel.*, 93d Cong. 20 (1973) (statement of Alexander Bickel) ("Nothing in the Constitution does or can empower Congress to do something unconstitutional, but much in the Constitution needs to be clarified or implemented, and except in the limited number of instances where exclusive power is specifically vested elsewhere, the necessary and proper clause authorizes Congress to do so, with respect to its own functions as well as those of the other branches. . . ."). *See generally* Raven-Hansen & Banks, *supra* p. 111, at 884-899.

3. *Lovett and Appropriations Limitations.* On rare occasions, the Supreme Court has struck down legislation for intruding impermissibly on the President's inherent constitutional authority. *See, e.g.*, Myers v. United States, 272 U.S. 52 (1926) (statute requiring Senate consent to removal of a purely executive officer); Ex parte Garland, 71 U.S. 333 (1867) (statute limiting the effect of a presidential pardon). Until 1988, however, no federal court had ever struck

E. Limitations on Congressional War Powers

down an appropriations limitation on the President's exercise of national security powers. In National Federation of Federal Employees v. United States, 688 F. Supp. 671 (D.D.C. 1988), *vacated and remanded sub nom.* American Foreign Service Assn. v. Garfinkel, 490 U.S. 153 (1989), a district court held unconstitutional an appropriations limitation on portions of an executive order regulating disclosure of national security information to Congress by executive branch employees. The court found that Congress's "tug on the purse strings" intruded dramatically and unconstitutionally on the President's constitutionally imposed duty, as Commander in Chief and chief executive, to oversee national security information. 688 F. Supp. at 685. The court noted that the congressional limitation "is merely an appropriations measure by which no substantive rights or causes of action are created. By such a measure, Congress cannot accomplish that which by direct legislative action would be beyond its constitutional authority." *Id.* at 684 n.17. Was the court right in suggesting that "mere" appropriations measures may not create or presumably limit rights?

The Supreme Court subsequently vacated and remanded, chastising the district court for reaching the constitutional question before exhausting non-constitutional grounds for decision. 490 U.S. at 161. For further discussion of the *Garfinkel* case, see *infra* pp. 1064-1065. Congressional access to intelligence information is addressed *infra* pp. 421-429.

4. *A Mandatory Appropriations Power?* If Congress may not use appropriations to control certain executive activities, *must* it appropriate funds for such activities? Judge Madden thought not in *Lovett*. He thought the physical "power of Congress to control expenditures is absolute." 66 F. Supp. at 152. Yet if the President herself is disabled from raising necessary funds for the exercise of an inherent constitutional power, congressional failure to appropriate would carry the same effect as a more direct legislative prohibition. Professor Stith concludes:

> Congress is obliged to provide public funds for constitutionally mandated activities — both obligations imposed upon the government generally [citing the periodic census, U.S. Const. Art. I, §2, cl. 3] and independent constitutional activities of the President. For instance, . . . Congress itself would violate the Constitution if it refused to appropriate funds for the President to receive foreign ambassadors or to make treaties. [Stith, *supra* p. 111, at 1350-1351.]

See also Henkin, *supra* Note 2, at 113. *See generally* Peter Raven-Hansen & William C. Banks, *From Viet Nam to Desert Shield: The Commander in Chief's Spending Power*, 81 Iowa L. Rev. 79, 127-128 (1995).

5. *A Presidential Spending Power?* If you agree that Congress must appropriate funds in some instances, where does a refusal to appropriate leave the executive? May the President transfer funds from other appropriations in disregard of their otherwise valid limitations? *See generally* Louis Fisher, *Presidential Spending Power* (1975); Lucius Wilmerding Jr., *The Spending Power: A History of the Efforts of Congress to Control Expenditures* 3-19 (1943). Logic may suggest an affirmative answer, but the Appropriations Clause seems to provide the opposite answer: "No money shall be drawn from the Treasury, but in Consequence of Appropriations made by law. . . ." U.S. Const. Art. I, §9, cl. 7. When Congress

refuses to appropriate for the President's independent constitutional functions, her constitutional options are seemingly political—to seek the electoral replacement of the recalcitrant Congress or to violate appropriations laws and the Constitution, hoping for congressional ratification after the fact and risking her own replacement or, worse, impeachment.

Yet in this matter, too, custom has overtaken formalism, and the executive has from time to time transferred some funds between accounts without explicit appropriations authority but with apparent congressional acquiescence. *See* Fisher, *supra*, at 99-122. For example, President Nixon financed the Cambodian "incursion," see *supra* p. 115 and *infra* pp. 226-227, by transferring funds from foreign assistance accounts. Fisher, *supra*, at 107. Moreover, executive branch officials have purported to find a distinction

> between the condition subsequent in an appropriation not yet completely spent and new appropriations.... If [the President] has used up all the money appropriated and then Congress refuses to provide any more, I think the Congress has effectively stopped the President from continuing the military action. I don't know how he can go on. If, on the other hand, he still had moneys that were unexpended, he could continue to spend those until such time as there was a court challenge and the court found that he was acting illegally. [*War Powers: A Test of Compliance: Hearings Before the Subcomm. on Intl. Security and Scientific Affairs, H. Comm. on Intl. Relations*, 94th Cong. 92 (1975) (testimony of Monroe Leigh, Legal Adviser to State Dept.).]

On what theory of statutory or constitutional construction does this distinction rest? *See generally* Raven-Hansen & Banks, *supra* Note 4, at 117-126.

2. Procedural Limits on Congressional National Security Powers

The *Lovett* line of cases highlights the substantive constitutional limitation on the congressional national security power. Almost as important are the procedural limitations established by Article I. In Immigration & Naturalization Service v. Chadha, 462 U.S. 919, 952, 958 (1983), the Supreme Court held that to take legislative action—"action that had the purpose and effect of altering the legal rights, duties and relations of persons...outside the legislative branch"—Congress must act "in conformity with the express procedures of the Constitution's prescription for legislative action: passage by a majority of both Houses and presentment to the President." Accordingly, the Court struck down a statutory provision for a "one-house veto" by which Congress reserved to either House the power to veto by resolution an exercise of delegated authority by the Attorney General that would have changed the legal status of an alien. The Court gave short shrift to the argument that the retention of veto authority would be more efficient because it permitted Congress to give the executive needed freedom while preserving needed congressional control of the executive:

> The choices we discern as having been made in the Constitutional Convention impose burdens on governmental processes that often seem clumsy,

inefficient, even unworkable, but those hard choices were consciously made by men who had lived under a form of government that permitted arbitrary governmental acts to go unchecked. There is no support in the Constitution or decisions of this Court for the proposition that the cumbersomeness and delays often encountered in complying with explicit constitutional standards may be avoided, either by the Congress or by the President. *See* Youngstown Sheet & Tube Co. v. Sawyer, 343 U.S. 579 (1952). With all the obvious flaws of delay, untidiness, and potential for abuse, we have not yet found a better way to preserve freedom than by making the exercise of power subject to the carefully crafted restraints spelled out in the Constitution. [462 U.S. at 959.]

Shortly after *Chadha,* the Court summarily affirmed a decision striking down a two-House veto by concurrent resolution (requiring both Houses to veto an executive action, but omitting presentment of the veto resolution to the President). United States Senate v. Federal Trade Commission, 463 U.S. 1216 (1983).

Before *Chadha,* legislative vetoes had been an increasingly popular device for legislative control of executive action, inserted into nearly 200 statutes. Dissenting in *Chadha,* Justice White explained why:

Without the legislative veto, Congress is faced with a Hobson's choice: either to refrain from delegating the necessary authority, leaving itself with a hopeless task of writing laws with the requisite specificity to cover endless special circumstances across the entire policy landscape, or in the alternative, to abdicate its law-making function to the executive branch and independent agencies. To choose the former leaves major national problems unresolved; to opt for the latter risks unaccountable policymaking by those not elected to fill that role. [462 U.S. at 968.]

The special difficulty of writing specific national security laws made the veto particularly appealing. Justice White listed 12 examples of such legislation in an appendix to his opinion, including the War Powers Resolution, *supra* p. 240, various Department of Defense appropriation and authorization acts, the International Security Assistance and Arms Control Act of 1976, and the National Emergencies Act.

NOTES AND QUESTIONS

1. *Are National Security Laws an Exception?* Should the *Chadha* Court have distinguished national security laws from ordinary domestic legislation in declaring the veto unconstitutional? Consider this argument: "Use of the veto as an instrument of the continuing political dialogue between President and Congress, on matters having high and legitimate political interest to both, and calling for flexibility for government generally, does not present the same problems as its use to control, in random and arbitrary fashion, those matters customarily regarded as the domain of administrative law." Peter L. Strauss, *Was There a Baby in the Bathwater? A Comment on the Supreme Court's Legislative Veto Decision,* 1983 Duke L.J. 789, 791-792. Several pre-*Chadha* decisions appeared to leave room for this kind of distinction. *See* Consumer Energy Council of America v. Federal Energy Regulatory Commission, 673 F.2d 425, 459 (D.C. Cir. 1982) ("[T]he foreign affairs veto presents unique problems since in that context there is

the additional question whether Congress or the President or both have inherent power to act."), *summarily aff'd*, 463 U.S. 1216 (1983); American Federation of Government Employees v. Pierce, 697 F.2d 303, 308 (D.C. Cir. 1982) (statement of Judges Wald and Mikva supporting rehearing en banc).

Do you think, based on the brief summary of *Chadha*'s reasoning supplied above, that the Court left room for this distinction? It literally struck down only the veto provision in the Immigration and Nationality Act affecting the domestic power of the Attorney General to suspend the deportation of aliens. But Justice White clearly identified the national security vetoes in his appendix, and the majority opinion made no exception for them, nor is any exception immediately visible in its account of the Article I bicameral/presentment formula for legislative action.

2. *The Special Need for Checks on National Security Delegations.* On the other hand, the majority opinion may rest on the absence of any need for legislative control by veto over the *domestic* executive action at issue there. *See generally* Charles Tiefer, *The FAS Proposal: Valid Check or Unconstitutional Veto?*, in *First Use of Nuclear Weapons: Under the Constitution, Who Decides?* 143 (Peter Raven-Hansen ed., 1987). Explaining why the Attorney General's exercise of legislative authority to change a legal status did not violate the Article I formula, the Court said that

> [e]xecutive action under legislatively delegated authority that might resemble "legislative" action in some respects is not subject to the approval of both houses of Congress and the President for the reason that the Constitution does not so require. *That* kind of executive action is always subject to check by the terms of the legislation that authorized it; and if that authority is exceeded it is open to judicial review. [*Chadha*, 462 U.S. at 953 n.16 (emphasis supplied).]

Curtiss-Wright, Lichter, and *Dames & Moore,* however, all suggest a difference between delegations of domestic power and delegations of foreign affairs and war powers, and suggest further that the latter are not effectively "subject to check by the terms of the legislation" and by "judicial review" because doctrines of nonjusticiability are often invoked to deny judicial enforcement of foreign affairs and war powers legislation. See generally Chapter 6. Moreover,

> *Chadha* allowed no congressional role in decisions after the [Immigration and Nationality Act's] enactment because the [Act] defined the standards for executive action — as it had to, pursuant to the nondelegation doctrine. The Court viewed the subsequent congressional role (the veto resolution) as amending or repealing these previously defined standards.... However, regarding foreign affairs and war powers,... delegation theory from *Curtiss-Wright* to *Dames & Moore* means that the President's sources of authority and funding lack defined standards.... Thus, a mechanism for a congressional role does not amend or repeal a previous standard or limit, because there was none. Rather, it establishes a political check, in place of the domestic-style standards and judicial review which do not apply....
> ... [I]n the foreign sphere, and particularly that of war powers, a more complex and subtle model of authorization applies than the domestic delegation model. Authorization consists of the balance between the claimed inherent presidential powers and any congressional powers of limitation, looking at the various

E. Limitations on Congressional War Powers 131

shades of acquiescence and challenge by each branch in the respective claims and limits....

Many steps in foreign affairs and wartime occur on a level of responsive interaction and cue-following by the executive and Congress, not strict delegation. [Tiefer, *supra*, at 150-152.]

Is this view consistent with *The Steel Seizure Case*? Can an analytic distinction between the "domestic model of delegation" and the "foreign/war powers model of responsive interaction" withstand the changes in communications, markets, and transportation that have steadily shrunk the modern world?

3. *Other Legislative Controls.* Congress, of course, has other devices for legislative control besides the veto. These include durational limits on authorizations ("sunset" provisions), joint resolutions of approval or disapproval (requiring presentment, unlike concurrent resolutions), and report-and-wait rules that require reporting to Congress for some specified period before executive action becomes legally effective. Are these constitutional after *Chadha*? Why or why not? See *Chadha*, 462 U.S. at 955 n.19 ("Beyond the obvious fact that Congress ultimately controls administrative agencies in the legislation that creates them, other means of control, such as durational limits on authorizations and formal reporting requirements, lie well within Congress' constitutional power."). See generally Stephen G. Breyer, *The Legislative Veto After Chadha*, 72 Geo. L.J. 785 (1984); Elliot H. Levitas & Stanley M. Brand, *Congressional Review of Executive and Agency Actions After Chadha: "The Son of Legislative Veto" Lives On*, 72 Geo. L.J. 801 (1984); Jonathan B. Fellows, Note, *Congressional Oversight Through Legislative Veto After INS v. Chadha*, 69 Cornell L. Rev. 1244 (1984).

Congress can also set a "fast track" for legislation in response to certain uses of delegated power. In addition, a veto resolution after *Chadha*, if lacking in legal effect, may still have persuasive impact on a judicial construction of the scope of delegated authority. See *Chadha*, 462 U.S. at 976 n.11 (White, J., dissenting). Perhaps for the latter reason, Congress had enacted 57 new legislative vetoes into 18 statutes as of March 1985, during the first two years *after Chadha* was decided. Louis Fisher, *Legislative Vetoes Enacted After Chadha* 1 (Cong. Res. Serv. RS 22132), Mar. 25, 1985.

4. *The Line-Item Veto.* Notwithstanding the importance of the defense appropriations power as a check on the Executive, in 1996 Congress almost gave away part of the power of the purse in the Line-Item Veto Act, Pub. L. No. 104-130, 110 Stat. 1200. The act permitted the President to cancel, *inter alia*, any "dollar amount of discretionary budget authority." The President could exercise this veto power only if it would reduce the federal budget deficit and would not impair any essential governmental function or harm the national interest. The cancellation took effect upon notice to the House and Senate and could be reversed within 30 days thereafter by passage of a "disapproval bill," which is not subject to the line-item veto authority. Thus, Congress would have to muster two-thirds plus one to ensure that an item of national security spending to which the President objected (for example, spending for a risky peacekeeping operation) would become law.

In Clinton v. City of New York, 524 U.S. 417 (1998), the Court struck down the Line-Item Veto Act because, by its provisions, the President had effectively amended two statutes without following the lawmaking procedure prescribed by Article I. President Clinton, however, had wielded his veto — his "cancellation" authority — against ordinary domestic statutes for ordinary domestic political purposes. Suppose, instead, he had cancelled certain national security expenditures, perhaps because he thought they represented pork-barrel spending to keep open an obsolete military base. Would such a "national security rescission" have been constitutional? *See* Roy E. Brownell II, *The Unnecessary Demise of the Line Item Veto Act: The Clinton Administration's Costly Failure to Seek Acknowledgment of "National Security Rescission,"* 47 Am. U.L. Rev. 1273 (1998) (arguing yes, based on the President's "Olympian powers in the national security realm" and past practice of national security impoundment — that is, the occasional failure of the President to spend all that was appropriated for some national security functions).

6

The Courts' National Security Role

More than a century and a half ago, a visitor to this country had this to say about the way we govern ourselves: "Scarcely any political question arises in the United States that is not resolved, sooner or later, into a judicial question." Alexis DeToqueville, 1 *Democracy in America* 280 (1945). This chapter is about the phenomenon he observed.

In our consideration of the original understanding of the Constitution in Chapter 2, little light was shed on the role intended for the federal courts in resolving national security disputes. The text of Article III provides that the judicial power is "vested in one supreme Court, and in such inferior Courts as the Congress may from time to time ordain and establish." The language suggests an independent judiciary designed to interpret the laws and decide cases. *See generally The Federalist, Nos. 22, 78, 80* (Clinton Rossiter ed., 1961).

Article III extends the potential judicial power to certain categories of cases that could present national security issues. The Supreme Court and the lower federal courts hear all cases "arising under this Constitution, the Laws of the United States, and Treaties made . . . ." The Supreme Court is also given original jurisdiction over "all Cases affecting Ambassadors, other public Ministers and Consuls," and over those "between a State, or the Citizens thereof, and foreign States, Citizens, or Subjects," while it is granted appellate jurisdiction over other categories of cases, subject to Congress's power to make "Exceptions, and . . . Regulations." Congress has also conferred general federal question jurisdiction on the courts in 28 U.S.C. §1331 (2000). Thus, struggles over national security prerogatives seem to meet both constitutional and statutory jurisdictional requirements for resolution in the federal courts.

The principal cases in Chapters 3-5 are illustrative. Recall that in high-stakes disputes such as *The Steel Seizure Case, supra* p. 28, Little v. Bareme, *supra* p. 77, Bas v. Tingy, *supra* p. 94, and Dames & Moore v. Regan, *supra* p. 48, the courts decided important national security law questions. You will encounter judicial resolution of other national security law disputes throughout the book, including some concerning the global war on terrorism. In one prominent lawsuit, American citizen Yaser Hamdi, who allegedly was captured on the battlefield in Afghanistan, challenged his designation by the President as an "enemy combatant" and his indefinite military detention. The government argued that the courts should not question the detention of Hamdi by the Commander in Chief during wartime. In Hamdi v. Rumsfeld, 316 F.3d 450 (4th Cir. 2003), the court conceded that "Article III contains nothing analogous to the specific powers of war carefully enumerated in Articles I and II." *Id.* at 463. Nonetheless, important countervailing interests persuaded the court to review Hamdi's detention:

> The duty of the judicial branch to protect our individual freedoms does not simply cease whenever military forces are committed by the political branches to armed conflict. The Founders "foresaw that troublous times would arise, when rulers and people would ... seek by sharp and decisive measures to accomplish ends deemed just and proper; and that the principles of constitutional liberty would be in peril, unless established by irrepealable law." Ex Parte Milligan, 71 U.S. (4 Wall.) 2, 120 (1866). While that recognition does not dispose of this case, it does indicate one thing: The detention of United States citizens must be subject to judicial review. [316 F.3d. at 464.]

The *Hamdi* case is presented *infra* p. 721.

The courts have nevertheless often avoided deciding the merits of national security cases or have decided the merits in favor of the government after only the most cursory review. In this chapter we explore this limited role of the federal courts and analyze the principal doctrinal devices offered in support of judicial abstention — political question, standing, and ripeness.

We have chosen as the principal case in our study a decision rendered just before the beginning of the 1991 Persian Gulf War. (We defer until Chapter 11 a detailed examination of other legal issues surrounding Operations Desert Shield and Desert Storm.) When the complaint in the following case was filed in November 1990, roughly 430,000 Iraqi troops were deployed in and around Kuwait. While the lawsuit was pending, United States and allied forces amassed a similar number of troops in Saudi Arabia and the Persian Gulf. A U.N. Security Council resolution authorizing the use of force to drive the Iraqis out of Kuwait was also being debated.

Dellums v. Bush
United States District Court, District of Columbia, 1990
752 F. Supp. 1141

HAROLD H. GREENE, J. This is a lawsuit by a number of members of Congress[1] who request an injunction directed to the President of the United States to prevent him from initiating an offensive attack against Iraq without first securing a declaration of war or other explicit congressional authorization for such action.

I.

The factual background is, briefly, as follows. On August 2, 1990, Iraq invaded the neighboring country of Kuwait. President George Bush almost

---

1. The plaintiffs are fifty-three Members of the House of Representatives and one United States Senator.

immediately sent United States military forces to the Persian Gulf area to deter Iraqi aggression and to preserve the integrity of Saudi Arabia. The United States, generally by presidential order and at times with congressional concurrence, also took other steps, including a blockade of Iraq, which were approved by the United Nations Security Council, and participated in by a great many other nations.

On November 8, 1990, President Bush announced a substantial increase in the Persian Gulf military deployment, raising the troop level significantly above the 230,000 then present in the area. At the same time, the President stated that the objective was to provide "an adequate *offensive* military option" should that be necessary to achieve such goals as the withdrawal of Iraqi forces from Kuwait. Secretary of Defense Richard Cheney likewise referred to the ability of the additional military forces "to conduct *offensive* military operations."

The House of Representatives and the Senate have in various ways expressed their support for the President's past and present actions in the Persian Gulf. However, the Congress was not asked for, and it did not take, action pursuant to Article I, Section 8, Clause 11 of the Constitution "to declare war" on Iraq. On November 19, 1990, the congressional plaintiffs brought this action, which proceeds on the premise that the initiation of offensive United States military action is imminent, that such action would be unlawful in the absence of a declaration of war by the Congress, and that a war without concurrence by the Congress would deprive the congressional plaintiffs of the voice to which they are entitled under the Constitution. The Department of Justice, acting on behalf of the President, is opposing the motion for preliminary injunction, and it has also moved to dismiss. Plaintiffs thereafter moved for summary judgment.

The Department raises a number of defenses to the lawsuit—most particularly that the complaint presents a non-justiciable political question, that plaintiffs lack standing to maintain the action, that their claim violates established canons of equity jurisprudence, and that the issue of the proper allocation of the war making powers between the branches is not ripe for decision. These will now be considered seriatim.

II. POLITICAL QUESTION

It is appropriate first to sketch out briefly the constitutional and legal framework in which the current controversy arises. Article I, Section 8, Clause 11 of the Constitution grants to the Congress the power "To declare War."[4] To the extent that this unambiguous direction requires construction or explanation,[5] it is

---

4. Under Article I, Section 8, Congress also has the power to "raise and support armies," "provide and maintain a navy," and "make rules of the government and regulation of the land and naval forces." The Congress also has the power to make "all laws which shall be necessary and proper for carrying into execution" its enumerated powers.

5. While the Constitution itself speaks only of the congressional power to declare war, it is silent on the issue of the effect of a congressional vote that war not be initiated. However, if the War Clause is to have its normal meaning, it excludes from the power to declare war all branches other than the Congress. It also follows that if the Congress decides that the United States forces should not be employed in foreign hostilities, and if the Executive does not of its own volition abandon participation in such hostilities, action by the courts would appear to be the only available means to break the deadlock in favor of the constitutional provision.

provided by the framers' comments that they felt it to be unwise to entrust the momentous power to involve the nation in a war to the President alone; Jefferson explained that he desired "an effectual check to the Dog of war"; James Wilson similarly expressed the expectation that this system would guard against hostilities being initiated by a single man. Even Abraham Lincoln, while a Congressman, said more than half a century later that "*no one man* should hold the power of bringing" war upon us.

The congressional power to declare war does not stand alone, however, but it is accompanied by powers granted to the President. Article II, Section 1, Clause 1 and Section 2 provide that "[t]he executive powers shall be vested in a President of the United States of America," and that "[t]he President shall be Commander in Chief of the Army and Navy...."

It is the position of the Department of Justice on behalf of the President that the simultaneous existence of all these provisions renders it impossible to isolate the war-declaring power. The Department further argues that the design of the Constitution is to have the various war- and military-related provisions construed and acting together, and that their harmonization is a political rather than a legal question. In short, the Department relies on the political question doctrine.

That doctrine is premised both upon the separation of powers and the inherent limits of judicial abilities. *See generally*, Baker v. Carr, 369 U.S. 186 (1962); Chicago & Southern Air Lines, Inc. v. Waterman Steamship Corp., 333 U.S. 103 (1948). In relation to the issues involved in this case, the Department of Justice expands on its basic theme, contending that by their very nature the determination whether certain types of military actions require a declaration of war is not justiciable, but depends instead upon delicate judgments by the political branches. On that view, the question whether an offensive action taken by American armed forces constitutes an act of war (to be initiated by a declaration of war) or an "offensive military attack" (presumably undertaken by the President in his capacity as commander-in-chief) is not one of objective fact but involves an exercise of judgment based upon all the vagaries of foreign affairs and national security. Indeed, the Department contends that there are no judicially discoverable and manageable standards to apply, claiming that only the political branches are able to determine whether or not this country is at war. Such a determination, it is said, is based upon "a political judgment" about the significance of those facts. Under that rationale, a court cannot make an independent determination on this issue because it cannot take adequate account of these political considerations.

This claim on behalf of the Executive[10] is far too sweeping to be accepted by the courts. If the Executive had the sole power to determine that any particular offensive military operation, no matter how vast, does not constitute war-making but only an offensive military attack, the congressional power to declare war will be at the mercy of a semantic decision by the Executive. Such an "interpretation" would evade the plain language of the Constitution, and it cannot stand.

---

10. While the Department refers to the "political branches" in the plural, it is apparent from the context that the claim is that the Executive is deemed to be the branch which will make the decision.

That is not to say that, assuming that the issue is factually close or ambiguous or fraught with intricate technical military and diplomatic baggage, the courts would not defer to the political branches to determine whether or not particular hostilities might qualify as a "war." However, here the forces involved are of such magnitude and significance as to present no serious claim that a war would not ensue if they became engaged in combat, and it is therefore clear that congressional approval is required if Congress desires to become involved.

Mitchell v. Laird, 488 F.2d 611, 614 (D.C. Cir. 1973), is instructive in that regard. In *Mitchell*, the Court of Appeals for this Circuit ruled there is "no insuperable difficulty in a court determining" the truth of the factual allegations in the complaint: that many Americans had been killed and large amounts of money had been spent in military activity in Indo-China. In the view of the appellate court, by looking at those facts a court could determine "whether the hostilities in Indo-China constitute[d] ... a 'war,' ... within ... the meaning of that term in Article I, Section 8, Clause 11." 488 F.2d at 614. Said the Court:

> Here the critical question to be initially decided is whether the hostilities in Indo-China constitute in the Constitutional sense a "war." ... [If the plaintiffs' allegations are true,] then in our opinion, as apparently in the opinion of President Nixon, ... there has been a war in Indo-China. Nor do we see any difficulty in a court facing up to the question as to whether because of the war's duration and magnitude the President is or was without power to continue the war without Congressional approval.

488 F.2d at 614. In short, *Mitchell* stands for the proposition that courts do not lack the power and the ability to make the factual and legal determination of whether this nation's military actions constitute war for purposes of the constitutional War Clause.[12] *See also*, Orlando v. Laird, 443 F.2d 1039 (2d Cir. 1971); Berk v. Laird, 429 F.2d 302 (2d Cir. 1970).

Notwithstanding these relatively straightforward propositions, the Department goes on to suggest that the issue in this case is still political rather than legal, because in order to resolve the dispute the Court would have to inject itself into foreign affairs, a subject which the Constitution commits to the political branches. That argument, too, must fail.

While the Constitution grants to the political branches, and in particular to the Executive, responsibility for conducting the nation's foreign affairs, it does not follow that the judicial power is excluded from the resolution of cases merely because they may touch upon such affairs. The court must instead look at "the particular question posed" in the case. Baker v. Carr, 369 U.S. at 211. In fact, courts are routinely deciding cases that touch upon or even have a substantial impact on foreign and defense policy. Japan Whaling Assn. v. American Cetacean Soc., 478 U.S. 221 (1986); Dames & Moore v. Regan, 453 U.S. 654 (1981);

---

12. The *Mitchell* court found that the hostilities in Vietnam constituted a war for purposes of Article I, Section 8, Clause 11, and that Congress had not authorized the President's unilateral conduct of that war. However, the court went on to hold that under these circumstances the President's only duty was "to bring the war to an end." 488 F.2d at 616. The factual determination of whether at the particular time the President was bringing the war to an end or continuing it was held to be a political question for which there were no judicially manageable standards to apply.

Youngstown Sheet & Tube Co. v. Sawyer, 343 U.S. 579 (1952); United States v. Curtiss-Wright Export Corp., 299 U.S. 304 (1936).

The Department's argument also ignores the fact that courts have historically made determinations about whether this country was at war for many other purposes — the construction of treaties, statutes, and even insurance contracts. These judicial determinations of a de facto state of war have occurred even in the absence of a congressional declaration.[14]

Plaintiffs allege in their complaint that 230,000 American troops are currently deployed in Saudi Arabia and the Persian Gulf area, and that by the end of this month the number of American troops in the region will reach 380,000. They also allege, in light of the President's obtaining the support of the United Nations Security Council in a resolution allowing for the use of force against Iraq, that he is planning for an offensive military attack on Iraqi forces.

Given these factual allegations and the legal principles outlined above, the Court has no hesitation in concluding that an offensive entry into Iraq by several hundred thousand United States servicemen under the conditions described above could be described as a "war" within the meaning of Article I, Section 8, Clause 11, of the Constitution. To put it another way: the Court is not prepared to read out of the Constitution the clause granting to the Congress, and to it alone, the authority "to declare war."

III. STANDING

The Department of Justice argues next that the plaintiffs lack "standing" to pursue this action.

The Supreme Court has established a two-part test for determining standing under Article III of the Constitution. The plaintiff must allege: (1) that he personally suffered actual or threatened injury, and (2) that the "injury 'fairly can be traced to the challenged action' and 'is likely to be redressed by a favorable decision.'" Valley Forge Christian College v. Americans United for Separation of Church and State, Inc., 454 U.S. 464 (1982); Allen v. Wright, 468 U.S. 737 (1984). For the purpose of determining standing on a motion to dismiss, the Court must "accept as true all material allegations of the complaint, and must construe the complaint in favor of the complaining party." Warth v. Seldin, 422 U.S. 490 (1975). Accordingly, plaintiffs' allegations of an imminent danger of hostilities between the United States forces and Iraq must be accepted as true for this purpose.

Plaintiffs further claim that their interest guaranteed by the War Clause of the Constitution is in immediate danger of being harmed by military actions the President may take against Iraq. That claim states a legally-cognizable injury, for as the Court of Appeals for this Circuit stated in a leading case, members of Congress plainly have an interest in protecting their right to vote on matters

---

14. In the Prize Cases, 67 U.S. 635 (1863), the Court was asked to determine whether the Civil War, which Congress had never officially declared to be a war, constituted a war for the purpose of determining whether the right of prize existed. The owners of the captured ships claimed that the Civil War was not a war because it had not been officially declared. The Court responded that they "cannot ask a court to affect a technical ignorance of the existence of a war, which all the world acknowledges to be the greatest civil war known in the history of the human race." 67 U.S. at 669.

entrusted to their respective chambers by the Constitution. Moore v. United States House of Representatives, 733 F.2d 946, 950 (D.C. Cir. 1984). Indeed, *Moore* pointed out even more explicitly that where a congressional plaintiff suffers "unconstitutional deprivations of [his] constitutional duties or rights... if the injuries are specific and discernible," a finding of harm sufficient to support standing is justified. *Id.* at 952 (footnote omitted).

To be sure, *Moore* and other decisions have found standing by members of Congress to challenge the Executive for actions the latter had already taken, and the Department of Justice argues that these precedents do not apply where, as here, the subject of the suit are Executive actions that are only threatened. Especially in view of the extraordinary fact situation that is before the Court, that is a distinction without a difference.

When future harm is alleged as injury-in-fact, the plaintiff must be able to allege harm that is "both 'real and immediate' not 'conjectural' or 'hypothetical.'" O'Shea v. Littleton, 414 U.S. 488 (1974) (citation omitted). Yet that plaintiff does not have to wait for the threatened harm to occur before obtaining standing.

The right asserted by the plaintiffs in this case is the right to vote for or against a declaration of war. In view of that subject matter, the right must of necessity be asserted before the President acts; once the President has acted, the asserted right of the members of Congress—to render war action by the President contingent upon a prior congressional declaration of war—is of course lost.

The Department also argues that the threat of injury in this case is not immediate because there is only a "possibility" that the President will initiate war against Iraq, and additionally, that there is no way of knowing before the occurrence of such a possibility whether he would seek a declaration of war from Congress.

That argument, too, must fail, for although it is not entirely fixed what actions the Executive will take towards Iraq and what procedures he will follow with regard to his consultations with Congress, it is clearly more than "unadorned speculation," Pennell v. San Jose, 485 U.S. 1, 8 (1988) (*quoting* Simon v. Eastern Kentucky Welfare Rights Org., 426 U.S. 26 (1976)), that the President will go to war by initiating hostilities against Iraq without first obtaining a declaration of war from Congress.

With close to 400,000 United States troops stationed in Saudi Arabia, with all troop rotation and leave provisions suspended, and with the President having acted vigorously on his own as well as through the Secretary of State to obtain from the United Nations Security Council a resolution authorizing the use of all available means to remove Iraqi forces from Kuwait, including the use of force, it is disingenuous for the Department to characterize plaintiffs' allegations as to the imminence of the threat of offensive military action for standing purposes as "remote and conjectural" for standing purposes. *But see* Part V.B, *infra*. For these reasons, the Court concludes that the plaintiffs have adequately alleged a threat of injury in fact necessary to support standing....

V. RIPENESS

Although, as discussed above, the Court rejects several of defendant's objections to the maintenance of this lawsuit, and concludes that, in principle, an injunction may issue at the request of Members of Congress to prevent the conduct of a war which is about to be carried on without congressional authorization, it does not follow that these plaintiffs are entitled to relief at this juncture. For the plaintiffs are met with a significant obstacle to such relief: the doctrine of ripeness.

It has long been held that, as a matter of the deference that is due to the other branches of government, the Judiciary will undertake to render decisions that compel action by the President or the Congress only if the dispute before the Court is truly ripe, in that all the factors necessary for a decision are present then and there. The need for ripeness as a prerequisite to judicial action has particular weight in a case such as this. The principle that the courts shall be prudent in the exercise of their authority is never more compelling than when they are called upon to adjudicate on such sensitive issues as those trenching upon military and foreign affairs. Judicial restraint must, of course, be even further enhanced when the issue is one — as here — on which the other two branches may be deeply divided. Hence the necessity for determining at the outset whether the controversy is truly "ripe" for decision or whether, on the other hand, the Judiciary should abstain from rendering a decision on ripeness grounds.

In the context of this case, there are two aspects to ripeness, which the Court will now explore.

A. ACTIONS BY THE CONGRESS

No one knows the position of the Legislative Branch on the issue of war or peace[21] with Iraq; certainly no one, including this Court, is able to ascertain the congressional position on that issue on the basis of this lawsuit brought by fifty-three members of the House of Representatives and one member of the U.S. Senate. It would be both premature and presumptuous for the Court to render a decision on the issue of whether a declaration of war is required at this time or in the near future when the Congress itself has provided no indication whether it deems such a declaration either necessary, on the one hand, or imprudent, on the other.

For these reasons, this Court has elected to follow the course described by Justice Powell in his concurrence in Goldwater v. Carter, 444 U.S. 996 (1979). In that opinion, Justice Powell provided a test for ripeness in cases involving a confrontation between the legislative and executive branches that is helpful here.[23] In *Goldwater*, President Carter had informed Taiwan that the United States would terminate the mutual defense treaty between the two countries

---

21. The "peace" position might more accurately be described as the view that the existing economic embargo of Iraq should be given more time to demonstrate its effectiveness or lack thereof.

23. That is so even though Justice Powell spoke only for himself. The Supreme Court, in a brief order, remanded the *Goldwater* case to the lower court with instructions to dismiss. Four different views were expressed by the various justices. However, several other courts have adopted Justice Powell's reasoning. *See, e.g.*, Lowry v. Reagan, 676 F. Supp. 333, 339 (D.D.C. 1987), *aff'd*, No. 87-5426 (D.C. Cir. Oct. 17, 1988); Sanchez-Espinoza v. Reagan, 770 F.2d 202, 210 (D.C. Cir. 1985) (J.R.B. Ginsburg, concurring statement); Crockett v. Reagan, 558 F. Supp. 893, 899 (D.D.C. 1982), *aff'd*, 720 F.2d 1355 (D.C. Cir. 1983) (per curiam).

within one year. The President made this announcement without the ratification of the Congress, and members of Congress brought suit claiming that, just as the Constitution required the Senate's ratification of the President's decision to enter into a treaty, so too, congressional ratification was necessary to terminate a treaty.

Justice Powell proposed that "a dispute between Congress and the President is not ready for judicial review unless and until each branch has taken action asserting its constitutional authority." *Id.* at 997. He further explained that in *Goldwater* there had been no such confrontation because there had as yet been no vote in the Senate as to what to do in the face of the President's action to terminate the treaty with Taiwan, and he went on to say that the

> Judicial Branch should not decide issues affecting the allocation of power between the President and Congress until the political branches reach a constitutional impasse. Otherwise we would encourage small groups or even individual Members of Congress to seek judicial resolution of issues before the normal political process has the opportunity to resolve the conflict.... It cannot be said that either the Senate or the House has rejected the President's claim. If the Congress chooses not to confront the President, it is not our task to do so.

444 U.S. at 997-998.[25]

Justice Powell's reasoning commends itself to this Court. The consequences of judicial action in the instant case with the facts in their present posture may be drastic, but unnecessarily so. What if the Court issued the injunction requested by the plaintiffs, but it subsequently turned out that a majority of the members of the Legislative Branch were of the view (a) that the President is free as a legal or constitutional matter to proceed with his plans toward Iraq without a congressional declaration of war,[26] or (b) more broadly, that the majority of the members of this Branch, for whatever reason, are content to leave this diplomatically and politically delicate decision to the President?

It would hardly do to have the Court, in effect, force a choice upon the Congress[27] by a blunt injunctive decision, called for by only about ten percent of its membership, to the effect that, unless the rest of the Congress votes in favor of a declaration of war, the President, and the several hundred thousand troops he has dispatched to the Saudi Arabian desert, must be immobilized. Similarly, the President is entitled to be protected from an injunctive order respecting a declaration of war when there is no evidence that this is what the Legislative Branch

---

25. Plaintiffs here, and the American Civil Liberties Union filing as *amicus*, seek to distinguish *Goldwater* on the basis that in that case the issue of Senate affirmation of treaty terminations is not expressly addressed by the Constitution, while in the instant case the power to declare war is expressly reserved to Congress in the Constitution. While this is an important difference between the cases, it has no bearing on the fact that before the Judiciary may review any case, and especially a case between the coordinate branches, there must be an actual conflict between the parties.

26. It might be that these legislators are content to follow some of the historical patterns, including those involving the hostilities in Vietnam and Korea where there was no declaration of war, or that they deem the consultations had in recent months and weeks between the Executive and congressional leaders to constitute adequate compliance with Article I, Section 8, Clause 11 of the Constitution.

27. The plaintiffs argue that "Congress cannot, and should not, be able to read the War Powers Clause out of the Constitution by failure to act." However, plaintiffs are not entitled to receive relief from action or non-action of their colleagues in Congress through a suit for an injunction against the President.

as such — as distinguished from a fraction thereof — regards as a necessary prerequisite to military moves in the Arabian desert.[28]

All these difficulties are avoided by a requirement that the plaintiffs in an action of this kind be or represent a majority of the Members of the Congress: the majority of the body that under the Constitution is the only one competent to declare war, and therefore also the one with the ability to seek an order from the courts to prevent anyone else, i.e., the Executive, from in effect declaring war. In short, unless the Congress as a whole, or by a majority, is heard from, the controversy here cannot be deemed ripe; it is only if the majority of the Congress seeks relief from an infringement on its constitutional war-declaration power that it may be entitled to receive it.[29]

B. ACTIONS TAKEN BY THE EXECUTIVE

The second half of the ripeness issue involves the question whether the Executive Branch of government is so clearly committed to immediate military operations that may be equated with a "war" within the meaning of Article I, Section 8, Clause 11, of the Constitution that a judicial decision may properly be rendered regarding the application of that constitutional provision to the current situation.[30]

Plaintiffs assert that the matter is currently ripe for judicial action because the President himself has stated that the present troop build-up is to provide an adequate offensive military option in the area. His successful effort to secure passage of United Nations Resolution 678, which authorizes the use of "all available means" to oust Iraqi forces remaining in Kuwait after January 15, 1991, is said to be an additional fact pointing toward the Executive's intention to initiate military hostilities against Iraq in the near future.[31]

The Department of Justice, on the other hand, points to statements of the President that the troops already in Saudi Arabia are a peacekeeping force to prove that the President might not initiate more offensive military actions.

---

28. To be sure, Senate Majority Leader George Mitchell has been quoted as stating that "a planned military offensive, which is, by definition, an act of war, must receive the prior authorization of the Congress." However, the statement of one Senator, even one as distinguished as the Majority Leader, is not constitutionally the equivalent of the views of the Congress as an institution. Likewise, the non-binding resolution approved by the House Democratic Caucus stating that Congress give "affirmative approval" before military action is initiated against Iraq, see The Washington Post, December 5, 1990, A32, col. 4, is not the statement of Congress as a whole.

29. Of course, should Congress pass a resolution authorizing the President's proposed actions in the Persian Gulf area, one byproduct would be that the instant action would be mooted.

30. The Court rejects defendant's contention that the issue can never be ripe until hostilities have actually broken out. That argument would insulate the President from even the grossest violations of the War Clause of the Constitution, for a congressional vote after war has begun would likely be without practical effect (as would also be the alternative suggestion that the Congress could always cut off funds for our fighting forces while they are engaged in military operations).

31. On December 3, one day before the hearing in the instant case, Secretary of Defense Dick Cheney testified to the Senate Armed Services Committee that "I do not believe the President requires any additional authorization from the Congress before committing U.S. forces to achieve our objectives in the Gulf." Secretary of State James Baker has asserted similar views on behalf of the Executive: "we do have a constitutionally different view... on the constitutional question of the authority to commit forces."

In addition, and more realistically, it is possible that the meetings set for later this month and next between President Bush and the Foreign Minister of Iraq, Tariq Aziz, in Washington, and Secretary of State James Baker and Saddam Hussein in Baghdad, may result in a diplomatic solution to the present situation, and in any event under the U.N. Security Council resolution there will not be resort to force before January 15, 1991.

Given the facts currently available to this Court, it would seem that as of now the Executive Branch has not shown a commitment to a definitive course of action sufficient to support ripeness.[34] In any event, however, a final decision on that issue is not necessary at this time.

Should the congressional ripeness issue discussed in Part V-A above be resolved in favor of a finding of ripeness as a consequence of actions taken by the Congress as a whole, there will still be time enough to determine whether, in view of the conditions as they are found to exist at that time, the Executive is so clearly committed to early military operations amounting to "war" in the constitutional sense that the Court would be justified in concluding that the remainder of the test of ripeness has been met. And of course an injunction will be issued only if, on both of the aspects of the doctrine discussed above, the Court could find that the controversy is ripe for judicial decision. That situation does not, or at least not yet, prevail, and plaintiffs' request for a preliminary injunction will therefore not be granted.

For the reasons stated, it is this 13th day of December, 1990

ORDERED that plaintiffs' motion for preliminary injunction be and it is hereby denied.

NOTES AND QUESTIONS

1. *The Bottom Line in Dellums.* What is the holding of *Dellums*? Although Judge Greene was unwilling to decide the legality of the anticipated unilateral war making by the President in 1990, the rationale for declining jurisdiction was carefully limited to the facts then before the court. What were the salient facts? Before proceeding to the next set of notes and questions, be sure you understand each argument advanced by the government to urge the court to dismiss the lawsuit. You should also identify which arguments provided the bases for decision.

2. *What if . . . ?* Do you think that a federal judge would decline to decide a lawsuit challenging the President's alleged violation of a statutory restriction on the use of appropriated funds to detain American citizens indefinitely in military custody? How about a challenge to the President's alleged violation of a similar restriction on the treatment of detainees in the war on terrorism? Would such suits present nonjusticiable political questions? Who would have standing to bring these lawsuits? When would they be ripe?

---

34. Obviously, while plaintiffs cannot be expected to pinpoint precisely the time when the Executive will take action that is equivalent to war, constitutional ripeness demands that their submission be more definite and more immediate than it is now.

a. Political Questions

1. *Constitutional Bases.* In Marbury v. Madison, 5 U.S. (1 Cranch) 137, 177 (1803), the Supreme Court stated that it is "emphatically the province and duty of the judicial department to say what the law is." Notwithstanding Chief Justice Marshall's bold enunciation of the doctrine of judicial review in *Marbury*, courts sometimes decline to decide a dispute after concluding that the constitutional issue is better left to the political branches for resolution. This "political question" doctrine is expressed in a holding that the dispute is not justiciable — that is, it is not appropriate for judicial determination. The courts neither approve nor disapprove the action taken by the political branches.

The political question doctrine found expression in dicta in *Marbury* itself. The Chief Justice concluded that the President was bound by law to execute the purely ministerial act of delivering Marbury's judicial commission, but he sought to distinguish a category of conduct that would not be judicially reviewable:

> By the constitution of the United States, the President is invested with certain important political powers, in the exercise of which he is to use his own discretion, and is accountable only to his country in his political character, and to his own conscience. To aid him in the performance of these duties, he is authorized to appoint certain officers, who act by his authority and in conformity with his orders.
>
> In such cases, their acts are his acts; and whatever opinion may be entertained of the manner in which executive discretion may be used, still there exists, and can exist, no power to control that discretion. The subjects are political. They respect the nation, not individual rights, and being entrusted to the executive, the decision of the executive is conclusive.... [*Id.* at 165-166.]

The political question doctrine has profound significance in charting the parameters of national security law. First, when the judiciary declines to entertain disputes about the allocation of powers, one of the political branches may be left to continue behaving unconstitutionally, at least until the other can act decisively to stop it. Or the President and Congress may thus join to act outside their combined constitutional authority without official constraint. Although a President who continues such conduct is theoretically impeachable and, in her first term, vulnerable at the polls, the courts' failure to give an authoritative answer may contribute to a failure of will in the legislature and a failure of knowledge in the electorate. This concern may be tempered only slightly by the oaths of legislators and executive branch officials to act in accordance with the Constitution.

Second, the doctrine may serve to postpone indefinitely any resolution of the meaning of ambiguous constitutional text, for better or for worse. The ambiguity alone may lead the President or Congress astray in good faith, sometimes out of fear that less assertive conduct would abdicate constitutional responsibilities.

The asserted bases for the political question doctrine are both textual and prudential. The text-based argument has been most prominently articulated by Herbert Wechsler:

> [A]ll the doctrine can defensibly imply is that the courts are called upon to judge whether the constitution has committed to another agency of government the

autonomous determination of the issue raised, a finding that itself requires an interpretation....

...Difficult as it may be to make that judgment wisely, whatever factors may be rightly weighed in situations where the answer is not clear, what is involved is in itself an act of constitutional interpretation, to be made and judged by standards that should govern the interpretive process generally. That, I submit, is *toto caelo* different from a broad discretion to abstain or intervene. [Herbert Wechsler, *Toward Neutral Principles of Constitutional Law*, 73 Harv. L. Rev. 1, 7-9 (1959).]

Alexander Bickel rejected Wechsler's argument and maintained instead that the doctrine is prudential, based on

the court's sense of lack of capacity, compounded in unequal parts of the strangeness of the issue and the suspicion that it will have to yield more often and more substantially to expediency than to principle; the sheer momentousness of it, which unbalances judgment and prevents one from subsuming the normal calculations of probabilities; the anxiety not so much that judicial judgment will be ignored, as that perhaps it should be, but won't; finally and in sum ("in a mature democracy"), the inner vulnerability of an institution which is electorally irresponsible and has no earth to draw strength from. [Alexander Bickel, *The Supreme Court, 1960 Term—Foreword: The Passive Virtues*, 75 Harv. L. Rev. 40, 75 (1961).]

See also Fritz W. Scharpf, *Judicial Review and the Political Questions: A Functional Analysis*, 75 Yale L.J. 517 (1966).

2. *Applying the Doctrine in Dellums.* What was the government's political question argument in *Dellums*? One of the government's contentions was that the "simultaneous existence" of the shared war powers set out in Articles I and II "renders it impossible to isolate the war-declaring power." Do you agree? What support is there for this position?

The President's lawyers further maintained that the decision whether a proposed military action requires a declaration of war by its "very nature" is not justiciable. In their view, the determination that a particular use of force constitutes an act of war involves "an exercise of judgment based upon all the vagaries of foreign affairs and national security." Is a judge capable of making that determination?

3. *Textual Commitment.* Is the question of allocation of war powers between the elected branches textually committed to the Congress and President? Judge Greene cites several instances in which the judiciary has reviewed actions having "substantial impact on foreign and defense policy." He also notes that the court must look at the "particular question posed" in deciding whether to reach the merits of a case. Do the cases cited by Judge Greene support his rejection of the textual commitment argument?

4. *Ange v. Bush.* In a lawsuit filed at about the same time as *Dellums*, Army Sergeant Michael Ray Ange claimed that the President's order deploying him to the Persian Gulf—in the face of the realistic threat that the President

might initiate an offensive war against Iraq — exceeded the President's authority. In Ange v. Bush, 752 F. Supp. 509 (D.D.C. 1990), Judge Royce Lamberth found that Ange's claims presented nonjusticiable political questions:

> The determination sought by Ange in each of his three challenges to the President's actions in the Persian Gulf is one which the judicial branch cannot make pursuant to the separation of powers principles embodied in the ... political question doctrine. The conditions triggering unreviewability under the political question doctrine were spelled out by the Supreme Court:
>
>> Prominent on the surface of any case held to involve a political question is found a textually demonstrable constitutional commitment of the issue to a coordinate political department; or a lack of judicially discoverable and manageable standards for resolving it; or the impossibility of deciding without an initial policy determination of a kind clearly for non-judicial discretion; or the impossibility of a court's undertaking independent resolution without expressing lack of respect due coordinate branches of government; or an unusual need for unquestioning adherence to a political decision already made; or the potentiality of embarrassment from multifarious pronouncements by various departments on one question.
>
> Baker v. Carr, 369 U.S. 186, 217 (1962). Most, if not all, of the conditions voiced in Baker v. Carr exist in the present case.
>
> Primary among the conditions [are] the "textually demonstrable constitutional commitment" of the war powers to both political branches and the "respect due" the political branches in allowing them to resolve this long-standing dispute over the war powers by exercising their constitutionally conferred powers.... Resolution of the present conflict in the Gulf, and the proper role of the legislative and executive branches in that resolution, brings the foreign relations and war powers of both political branches into play.
>
> While the Constitution appears to grant the executive and legislative branches certain powers which either directly or indirectly affect the conduct of foreign affairs, the scope of power wielded by either branch is not clearly spelled out in the text of the Constitution....
>
> The judicial branch, on the other hand, is neither equipped nor empowered to intrude into the realm of foreign affairs where the Constitution grants operational powers only to the two political branches and where decisions are made based on political and policy considerations. The far-reaching ramifications of those decisions should fall upon the shoulders of those elected by the people to make those decisions....
>
> By asking the court to determine the constitutionality of the President's actions, Ange asks the court to delve into and evaluate those areas where the court lacks the expertise, resources, and authority to explore. Ange asks the court to find that the President's deployment of U.S. forces in the Persian Gulf constitutes "war," "imminent hostilities," or even the prelude to offensive war. Time and again courts have refused to exercise jurisdiction in such cases and undertake such determinations because courts are ill-equipped to do so.
>
> This court's refusal to exercise jurisdiction under the ... political question doctrine by no means permits the President to interpret the executive's powers as he sees fit, nor does it mean that the legislative branch is helpless without the assistance of the judicial branch. Congress possesses ample powers under the Constitution to prevent Presidential overreaching, should Congress choose to exercise them. If Congress considers the President's current deployment of forces in the Persian Gulf to violate the Constitution, or if Congress considers the country

on the verge of being unconstitutionally brought to war, or if Congress concludes at any time that the President's actions in the Gulf have usurped Congress' constitutional role, Congress has many options to check the President. Congress can itself declare war, exercise its appropriations power to prevent further offensive and/or defensive military action in the Persian Gulf, or even impeach the President.... [752 F. Supp. at 512-514.]

If it is true, as Judge Lamberth insists, that the textual allocation of war powers is unclear, why did he not conclude that such ambiguity demands judicial intervention — to "say what the law is" (Marbury v. Madison)?

Although *Baker* concerned a domestic affairs issue, Justice Brennan supplemented his expansive statement of the political question doctrine with dicta regarding foreign affairs disputes:

[S]uch issues frequently turn on standards that defy judicial application, or involve the exercise of a discretion demonstrably committed to the executive or legislature.... [M]any such questions uniquely demand single-voiced statement of the Government's views.... [However,] it is error to suppose that every case or controversy which touches foreign relations lies beyond judicial cognizance. Our cases in this field seem invariably to show a discriminating analysis of the particular question posed, in terms of the history of its management by the political branches, of its susceptibility to judicial handling in the light of its nature and posture in the specific case, and of the possible consequences of judicial action. [Baker v. Carr, 369 U.S. at 211-212.]

Beyond textual commitment, on what bases did Judge Lamberth conclude that Ange's claim presented a nonjusticiable political question? Is the "lack of standards" argument based on the text of the Constitution or is it prudential? Does it matter?

5. *Fact-Finding Difficulties.* According to Judge Greene, the size of the U.S. force poised to attack the Iraqis, some 380,000 troops, undermined the President's political question argument. Judge Greene implies that some lesser proposed use of military force might prompt the courts to defer to the political branches "to determine whether or not particular hostilities might qualify as a 'war.'" Should the size or scope of a proposed military operation affect a court's willingness to adjudicate its legality? Is the difficulty in deciding about a smaller military operation one of judicially discoverable and manageable standards, or of judicial resources and expertise?

In 1999, 31 members of the House of Representatives sued for a declaration that President Clinton violated the Constitution and the War Powers Resolution when he conducted air strikes in the Federal Republic of Yugoslavia without congressional authorization. In the Court of Appeals, Judges Silberman and Tatel disagreed on the application of the political question doctrine. Judge Silberman maintained that "no one" could challenge the President's actions because of a lack of "judicially discoverable and manageable standards" and because "the War Powers Clause claim implicates the political question doctrine." Campbell v. Clinton, 203 F.3d 19, 24-25 (D.C. Cir. 2000). Judge Tatel opined that "[w]hether the military activity in Yugoslavia amounted to 'war' within the meaning of the Declare War Clause ... is no more standardless than any other question regarding the constitutionality of government action.... Courts have proven no less capable of developing standards to resolve war power challenges [than Fourth or First Amendment actions]." *Id.* at 40. Should the "lack of standards" rationale carry more weight in war powers disputes than it does in individual rights litigation?

6. *Effects of Abstention.* Is Judge Greene correct in asserting that a determination that Representative Dellums's lawsuit presents a nonjusticiable political question would be a ruling for the President? If so, does judicial abstention in such cases always require the court to make a political choice? Is judicial intervention a greater threat to the separation of powers than letting the President have his way through judicial abstention?

7. *Availability of Legislative Remedies.* According to Judges Greene and Lamberth, how does the theoretical availability of legislative devices to thwart presidential initiative — appropriations restrictions and impeachment — affect the justiciability of the war powers claim? How do the two judges come out on the question of which branch has the burden of going forward in war making? Whose views are most in keeping with what you know about the war powers?

8. *Political Questions in the Supreme Court.* Only rarely has the Supreme Court invoked the political question doctrine. In just two of its cases having national security dimensions has the doctrine played an important role. In 1970, members of the Ohio National Guard shot and killed four Kent State University students protesting the Vietnam War. Other students sought a declaratory judgment that the Due Process Clause of the Fourteenth Amendment permitted the federal judiciary to evaluate the "training, weaponry, and orders" of the Guardsmen to determine whether they would inevitably use fatal force in suppressing civil disorders. Reversing a court of appeals order that included ongoing judicial surveillance of the Guard, the Court held that supervision of the Guard was given to Congress alone in the power to "provide for organizing, arming, and disciplining the Militia" in Article I, §8, cl. 16. Gilligan v. Morgan, 413 U.S. 1, 6 (1973). The majority thus apparently adopted Professor Wechsler's view that a political question is determined through interpretation of the Constitution. Even if the Court found a textual commitment to Congress in the Militia Clause, however, why would it deny otherwise available judicial review under the Fourteenth Amendment? In Baker v. Carr, the Court found that the case was justiciable under the Fourteenth Amendment, even though no justiciable question was presented under Article IV, §4 (the Republican Form of Government Clause).

Since *Gilligan*, the closest the Supreme Court has come to finding a political question in a dispute with national security content was its dismissal of a suit filed by Senator Goldwater against President Carter to prevent his abrogation of a mutual defense treaty with Taiwan without Senate authorization. While Article II clearly provides for Senate participation in treaty making, the Constitution says nothing about how to terminate a treaty. In Goldwater v. Carter, 617 F.2d 697 (D.C. Cir. 1979) (en banc), *rev'd,* 444 U.S. 996 (1979), noted *infra* p. 166, the D.C. Circuit found that the President had the authority to withdraw unilaterally from the treaty. In concluding that the lawsuit was nonjusticiable, however, four members of the Supreme Court found that Senator Goldwater's claim presented a political question. A fifth, Justice Powell, concurred in the dismissal, but he thought the lawsuit was not ripe for review by the courts.

b. Standing to Sue

1. *Basic Doctrine.* In Northeastern Florida Chapter, General Contractors of America v. City of Jacksonville, 508 U.S. 656, 663-664 (1993), the Court declared that

> a party seeking to invoke a federal court's jurisdiction must demonstrate three things: (1) "injury in fact," by which we mean an invasion of a legally protected interest that is "(a) concrete and particularized, and (b) actual or imminent, not conjectural or hypothetical," (2) a causal relationship between the injury and the challenged conduct, by which we mean that the injury "fairly can be traced to the challenged action of the defendant," and has not resulted "from the independent action of some third party not before the court," and (3) a likelihood that the injury will be redressed by a favorable decision, by which we mean that the "prospect of obtaining relief from the injury as a result of a favorable ruling" is not "too speculative" (internal citations omitted).

As we saw in earlier chapters, the scope and allocation of national security powers were neither clearly stated by the Framers nor always understood by the political branches. Should Article III be read to deny any litigant a judicial resolution of a national security dispute? Do you see anything in the Article III "case or controversy" requirement, or in its purposes, that would restrict access to the federal courts on the basis of the status of the parties, as distinct from the fitness of the issues for judicial resolution?

2. *Article III Concerns.* The Supreme Court has emphasized that, while Congress may express its intention to allow citizens to sue to vindicate interests protected by statute, the doctrine of standing is "an essential and unchanging part of the case-or-controversy requirement of Article III," Lujan v. Defenders of Wildlife, 504 U.S. 555, 559 (1992), which "defines with respect to the Judicial Branch the idea of separation of powers on which the Federal Government is founded." Allen v. Wright, 468 U.S. 737, 750 (1984). Like the political question doctrine, the law of standing thus has constitutional and prudential components. Unlike the Article III requirements, the prudential limits may be modified or abrogated by Congress. Warth v. Seldin, 422 U.S. 490, 501 (1975). Should the courts be concerned about enhanced judicial power when they determine standing in national security disputes? Or does separation of powers counsel judicial vigilance to prevent intrusions by one elected branch into the proper domain of the other elected branch?

Can you think of a national security context in which Congress might prescribe adjudication that would violate Article III standing requirements? Could Congress require the adjudication of cases that otherwise would be barred by the political question doctrine? *See* Richard H. Fallon Jr., *Of Justiciability, Remedies, and Public Law Litigation: Notes on the Jurisprudence of Lyons,* 59 N.Y.U. L. Rev. 1 (1984).

Alexander Hamilton suggested that the judiciary is the "least dangerous" branch because it "has no influence over either the sword or the purse."

The Federalist No. 78, at 465 (Clinton Rossiter ed., 1961); *see also* Antonin Scalia, *The Doctrine of Standing as an Essential Element of the Separation of Powers*, 17 Suffolk U. L. Rev. 881 (1983). Whatever the Framers intended, do you think Hamilton's statement is true today?

3. *Relationship of Standing to Merits and Political Question.* In theory, the focus in deciding standing is on the fitness of a particular plaintiff to present a case adverse to the defendant, not on the merits of the substantive issues presented in the complaint. As such, the standing doctrine is a narrower and less radical basis for dismissal of a lawsuit than the political question doctrine. A dismissal on standing grounds may simply mean that the wrong plaintiff initiated the action, not that the merits may not be adjudicated in a suit by a different plaintiff.

i. Citizen Plaintiffs

1. *Standing for Concerned Citizens.* Would a concerned citizen have had standing to bring the lawsuit brought by Representative Dellums or Sergeant Ange? In Pietsch v. Bush, 755 F. Supp. 62 (E.D.N.Y. 1991), a citizen sought a court order preventing hostilities between the United States and Iraq. In concluding that Pietsch was not injured in fact, the court distinguished the interest of a concerned citizen from that of members of Congress (who "plainly have an interest in protecting their right to vote in matters entrusted to their respective chambers by the Constitution") or a member of the armed forces deployed to the potential combat area (citing *Ange*). According to the court, Pietsch's claim that he was being made "an accessory to murder against his will," a compulsion causing him emotional distress, was "too abstract" to meet Article III requirements. *Id.* at 65-66.

The court in *Pietsch* also rejected the argument that a citizen has standing to sue the government to enforce obedience to the Constitution:

> [T]he Plaintiff does not have standing merely because as a citizen of the United States he has an "interest" in seeing the Government act constitutionally. In Schlesinger v. Reservists Committee to Stop the War, 418 U.S. 208 (1974), a citizens' group challenged the membership in the National Reserve by United States Congressmen as violative of the Ineligibility Clause of the Constitution (Article I, Section 6, clause 2). The plaintiffs contended that they had standing because as United States citizens they had an interest in insuring "the faithful discharge by members of Congress who are members of the Reserves of their duties as members of Congress, to which all citizens and taxpayers are entitled." Id. at p. 212. The United States Supreme Court rejected this argument, and held: "standing to sue may not be predicated upon an interest of the kind alleged here which is held in common by all members of the public, because of the necessarily abstract nature of the injury all citizens share." Id. at p. 220. The Plaintiff in this case has suffered no more cognizable injury than did the citizens in *Schlesinger*, and, therefore, does not have standing to maintain this action....
>
> ...As the Supreme Court stated in *Schlesinger*: "Our system of government leaves many crucial decisions to the political processes. The assumption that if respondents have no standing to sue, no one would have standing, is not a reason to find standing." Schlesinger v. Reservists Committee to Stop the War, *supra*, 418 U.S. at 227. [755 F. Supp. at 67.]

Is the political process not uniquely appropriate for redress when a citizen alleges an injury common to all citizens? Should the citizen plaintiff be satisfied that he can draft and lobby for passage of legislation to vindicate such common rights?

ii. Taxpayer Standing

1. *Basic Doctrine.* Taxpayer standing doctrine derives from two decisions of the Supreme Court. In Frothingham v. Mellon, 262 U.S. 447 (1923), the Court denied standing to a plaintiff who alleged that an arguably unconstitutional statute would, if implemented, increase her future federal income taxes. The *Frothingham* Court emphasized the "comparatively minute[,] remote, fluctuating and uncertain" impact on the taxpayer, and plaintiff's failure to allege direct injury. *Id.* at 487.

Then in Flast v. Cohen, 392 U.S. 83 (1968), the Court reaffirmed that the principle of *Frothingham* precluded a taxpayer's use of "a federal court as a forum in which to air his generalized grievances about the conduct of government or the allocation of power in the Federal system." *Id.* at 106. At the same time, the Court held that a "taxpayer will have standing consistent with Article III to invoke federal judicial power when he alleges that congressional action under the taxing and spending clause is in derogation of those constitutional provisions which operate to restrict the exercise of the taxing and spending power." *Id.* at 105-106.

Chief Justice Warren elaborated on what is required for taxpayer standing in Flast v. Cohen:

> The nexus demanded of federal taxpayers has two aspects to it. First, the taxpayer must establish a logical link between that status and the type of legislative enactment attacked. Thus, a taxpayer will be a proper party to allege the unconstitutionality only of exercises of congressional power under the taxing and spending clause of Art. I, §8, of the Constitution. It will not be sufficient to allege an incidental expenditure of tax funds in the administration of an essentially regulatory [law].... Secondly, the taxpayer must establish a nexus between that status and the precise nature of the constitutional infringement alleged. Under this requirement, the taxpayer must show that the challenged enactment exceeds specific constitutional limitations imposed upon the exercise of the congressional taxing and spending power and not simply that the enactment is generally beyond the powers delegated to Congress by Art. I, §8. [*Id.* at 102-103.]

Is the War Clause a sufficient predicate to confer injury in fact? Does a citizen's contributions to the public tax coffers constitute a sufficient interest to support a lawsuit challenging the unlawful spending of the same tax dollars? *See* Velvel v. Nixon, 415 F.2d 236 (10th Cir. 1969).

2. *Building a Case.* Can you think of a way to construct the complaint needed to successfully assert standing on the basis of taxpayer status in a challenge to the Gulf War? What "nexus" could you allege between the allegedly unconstitutional spending and some constitutional limit on that spending?

iii. Congressional Plaintiffs

1. *Origins of Congressional Standing.* Should the law of legislator standing be any different from the law of citizen standing? Is Representative Dellums's "interest guaranteed by the War Clause" distinct from your interest or mine?

Members of Congress have often turned to the courts and sought relief for alleged harm to them in their official roles, or, put another way, to protect what they see as interests central to Congress. In Mitchell v. Laird, 488 F.2d 611 (D.C. Cir. 1973), 13 members of Congress sought to enjoin military action in Southeast Asia and requested a declaration that the war was unconstitutional. In rejecting the government's claim that plaintiffs lacked standing, the court stated that, assuming unconstitutional action by the executive, "a declaration to that effect would bear upon the duties of plaintiffs to consider whether to impeach defendants, and upon plaintiffs' quite distinct and different duties to make appropriations to support the hostilities, or to take other legislative actions related to such hostilities...." *Id.* at 614. While the plaintiffs were found to have standing, the court dismissed the suit as presenting a political question.

2. *Nullification.* How did Judge Greene determine that the congressional plaintiffs in *Dellums* had standing? After *Dellums*, the Supreme Court ruled that legislators may not sue in their institutional capacity unless their votes have been "completely nullified" by allegedly illegal action. Raines v. Bird, 521 U.S. 811, 829 (1997). Four Senators and two Representatives sued after voting against the line-item veto statute. They asserted that before the statute was enacted, the expenditure of funds in an appropriations bill would either be approved in its entirety or not at all. Under the line-item veto statute, however, the President could excise a particular spending item after a bill had been enacted. Thus, whether or not the line-item veto was exercised, the members argued that their votes on the appropriations bills would be "less 'effective' than before, and that the 'meaning' and 'integrity' of their vote has changed." *Id.* at 825.

According to Chief Justice Rehnquist's opinion for the Court, the plaintiffs' votes on the line-item veto bill "were given full effect. They simply lost...." *Id.* at 824. The disgruntled members' votes in the future were not "completely nullified" by the Line-Item Veto Act because a majority "may repeal the Act or exempt appropriations bills from its reach." *Id.* at 829. Although the Court did not expressly disavow its only related precedent, Coleman v. Miller, 307 U.S. 433 (1939) (upholding standing for 20 of Kansas's 40 state senators who voted not to ratify a proposed constitutional amendment and argued that a vote cast by the lieutenant governor to break a tie in favor of the amendment was not sufficient for ratification), it is unclear how and to what extent the concept of institutional representation survives beyond the limited context of *Coleman*.

3. *Impact of Raines.* After *Raines*, should the *degree* of a legislator's injury have any effect on a court's willingness to decide a claim that an executive official has injured the legislator in his official capacity?

In Campbell v. Clinton, 52 F. Supp. 2d 34 (D.D.C. 1999), *aff'd*, 203 F.3d 19 (D.C. Cir. 2000), 31 members of the House of Representatives sued President Clinton seeking a declaration that the President's use of United States forces against Yugoslavia was unlawful under the Constitution and the War Powers

Resolution. The lawsuit was filed after President Clinton announced the commencement of NATO air and cruise missile attacks on Yugoslav targets on March 24, 1999, and after House votes on April 28 defeating a declaration of war (427-2), defeating an authorization of the air strikes (213-213), defeating a resolution ordering an immediate end to U.S. participation in the NATO operation (290-139), and approving a restriction on Defense Department appropriations for the deployment of U.S. ground troops in Yugoslavia without specific authorization. On May 20, Congress approved a supplemental appropriations bill for the conflict in Yugoslavia.

The plaintiffs sought to distinguish *Raines* by arguing that President Clinton's commitment of the United States to the air strikes in Yugoslavia "completely nullified" their votes against authorizing the military operation. They further noted that their votes helped defeat an authorization for the air strikes and a declaration of war and that President Clinton ignored the votes and carried on as if Congress had authorized his actions. According to Judge Friedman's opinion denying the plaintiffs standing, however, the two votes emphasized by the plaintiffs "do not provide the President with...an unambiguous directive; neither vote...required the President to do anything or prohibited him from doing anything.... Congressional reaction to the air strikes has sent distinctly mixed messages." 52 F. Supp. 2d at 43-44. Judge Friedman reasoned that if the President had "persisted with air strikes in the face of...votes" against the President's position, there might have been standing to sue, but under the circumstances "there is no confrontation or impasse between the...branches and thus no legislative standing." *Id.*

It was also significant for Judge Friedman that some of the 213 who voted not to authorize the air and missile campaign or declare war then voted to fund the conflict and against ordering the removal of the U.S. forces. Thus, the plaintiffs' position "appears not to be shared by a number of their colleagues the nullification of whose votes they seek to vindicate. While the Court is not suggesting that all 213 representatives who voted to defeat the authorization resolution must join in this lawsuit in order to establish legislative standing, the absence of any indication" that the plaintiffs were authorized to represent "even a substantial number" of the 213 "compels the conclusion" that the plaintiffs lack standing. *Id.* Do you agree that 213 congressional plaintiffs or some "substantial number" would have had standing to sue the President?

The Court of Appeals affirmed on standing grounds and maintained that the nullification standard of *Raines* is not met "whenever the government does something Congress voted against." 203 F.3d at 22. Instead, the *Campbell* court construed *Raines* to require that the plaintiffs have "no legislative remedy." *Id.* at 23. In this case, the court pointed out, Congress could have passed a prohibition on the use of U.S. forces in the Yugoslav campaign. Similarly, Congress could have restricted appropriations for the same end, or it could have sought to impeach the President. Concurring in the judgment, Judge Randolph added that the plaintiffs' votes "were not for naught." *Id.* at 31. The defeat of the declaration of war deprived the President of the authority to expand hostilities against Yugoslavia, and the defeat of the authorization resolution denied the President the right to say that he was prosecuting the bombing campaign with the House's approval. Did the *Campbell* courts correctly apply *Raines*?

In Kucinich v. Bush, 236 F. Supp. 2d 1 (D.D.C. 2002), 32 members of the House sued the President and other executive branch officials challenging President Bush's unilateral withdrawal from the 1972 Anti-Ballistic Missile (ABM) Treaty without the approval of Congress. These plaintiffs voted in the House to prevent the treaty termination but lost the vote. The claim that the House plaintiffs were deprived of a constitutional right and duty to participate in treaty termination was viewed by the court as "like the dilution of legislative power alleged in *Raines*, an institutional injury lacking a personal, particularized nature." 236 F. Supp. 2d at 7. Can you now describe circumstances when members of Congress would have standing to sue?

4. *Should Members Have Standing?* Professor Tribe has argued that, after *Raines*, "[a] finding of standing is proper at least where a legislator demonstrates nullification of a past or future vote that is fairly traceable to the challenged action, and is arguably proper where other core aspects of legislative prerogatives are implicated." I Laurence H. Tribe, *American Constitutional Law* 462 (3d ed. 2000). Do you agree?

Judge Bork and then-Judge Scalia have argued that members of Congress should never be found to have standing to sue in their official capacities. The danger of congressional standing, they claim, is that an unelected judiciary will usurp the roles of the elected branches. Moore v. United States House of Representatives, 733 F.2d 946, 957 (D.C. Cir. 1984) (Scalia, J., concurring), *cert. denied*, 469 U.S. 1106 (1985); Vander Jagt v. O'Neill, 699 F.2d 1166, 1180 (D.C. Cir. 1982) (Bork, J., concurring), *cert. denied*, 464 U.S. 823 (1983). How would you respond to Judge Bork and now-Justice Scalia?

c. Ripeness

The ripeness doctrine allows the judiciary to avoid present adjudication of an issue by determining that future events may affect its shape or even its existence. Like the standing and political question doctrines, ripeness may at least temporarily bar a lawsuit because of Article III case or controversy requirements or for prudential reasons. *See* Reno v. Catholic Social Services, Inc., 509 U.S. 43, 57 n.18 (1993). The doctrine maintains that "federal courts . . . do not render advisory opinions. For adjudication of constitutional issues 'concrete legal issues, presented in actual cases, not abstractions' are requisite." United Public Workers v. Mitchell, 330 U.S. 75, 89 (1947) (internal citations omitted).

1. *Ripeness and Dellums.* On what grounds did Judge Greene determine that Representative Dellums's lawsuit was not ripe for hearing? Does it logically follow that because a majority of Congress is the only body competent to declare war, that majority is the only body with the legal capacity to seek an order from the courts to prevent the President from initiating war? Can you think of a way that Judge Greene could have found that Representative Dellums's lawsuit was not ripe without requiring that a majority of Congress be represented as plaintiffs in the lawsuit?

2. *Making Dellums Ripe.* In Judge Greene's view, when would a congressional challenge to a prospective military strike by the President become ripe? If the

Senate had voted 51-47 in January 1991 to defeat an authorization for the Gulf War, would an injunction have issued? What about a concurrent resolution disapproving the use of offensive force? A joint resolution of disapproval passed by a bare majority but vetoed by the President?

3. *Standing vs. Ripeness.* What are the legal and practical differences between Judge Greene's conclusion that President Bush's pre-attack buildup was not so speculative as to deny his plaintiffs standing, and the judge's conclusion that the lawsuit was not ripe for hearing? Does the *Raines* decision affect how ripeness should be decided when the plaintiffs are members of Congress? *See* Geoffrey S. Corn, *Campbell v. Clinton: The "Implied Consent" Theory of Presidential War Power Is Again Validated*, 161 Mil. L. Rev. 202, 202 (1999) (maintaining that the "true focus" of Judge Friedman's opinion for the District Court in *Campbell* "was the absence of a ripe dispute between the Congress and the President").

How is Judge Greene's ripeness ruling different from his determination that Representative Dellums's lawsuit did not present a nonjusticiable political question?

4. *After Dellums.* President Bush ultimately sought and obtained congressional authorization for the Gulf War. See *infra* pp. 297-300. Some have argued that Judge Greene's *Dellums* opinion influenced the political branches to proceed as they did. *See, e.g.*, Harold Hongju Koh, *Judicial Constraints: The Courts and War Powers*, in *The U.S. Constitution and the Power to Go to War* 127-128 (Gary M. Stern & Morton H. Halperin eds., 1994); Carlin Meyer, *Imbalance of Powers: Can Congressional Lawsuits Serve as Counterweight?*, 54 U. Pitt. L. Rev. 63, 97-98 (1992). By mid-January 1991, it thus appeared that all three branches agreed that it was a congressional prerogative to decide upon war.

On the other hand, President Bush claimed before ("history is replete with examples where the President had to take action," Neil A. Lewis, *Mideast Tensions; Sorting Out Legal War Concerning Real War*, N.Y. Times, Nov. 15, 1990, at A18) and after he decided to seek congressional authorization for the Gulf War that he had no constitutional obligation to do so ("I don't think I need it. . . . I feel that I have the authority to implement the United Nations resolutions." 27 Wkly. Comp. Pres. Doc. 25 (1991).). President Clinton made similar claims concerning the then-anticipated invasion of Haiti ("Like my predecessors of both parties, I have not agreed that I was constitutionally mandated to [obtain congressional authorization to initiate an invasion of Haiti]." *Presidential News Conference; Transcript of Clinton's News Conference at the White House*, N.Y. Times, Aug. 4, 1994, at A16.). President Clinton also declined to seek congressional authorization for the air war against Yugoslavia in 1999, although he did say that "without regard to our differing constitutional views on the use of force, I would ask for Congressional support before introducing U.S. ground forces into Kosovo into a nonpermissive environment." *Crisis in the Balkans; In Clinton's Words: Speak with a Single Voice*, N.Y. Times, Apr. 29, 1999, at A14.

5. *The 2003 War Against Iraq.* In October 2002 Congress passed the Authorization for Use of Military Force Against Iraq Resolution of 2002, Pub. L. No. 107-243, 116 Stat. 1498 (considered *infra* p. 305). In February 2003, a group of active-duty members of the military, parents of military personnel, and members

of Congress sued to enjoin the President from initiating war against Iraq. Doe v. Bush, 323 F.3d 133 (1st Cir. 2003). The plaintiffs argued that the October 2002 resolution was insufficient to authorize an offensive war or, in the alternative, that Congress colluded with the President in the resolution by effectively handing over to the President the power to declare war. The court found that the lawsuit was not ripe and stressed one rationale common to both of plaintiffs' theories: "[B]efore courts adjudicate a case involving the war powers allocated to the two political branches, they must be presented with a case or controversy that clearly raises the specter of undermining the constitutional structure." *Id.* at 135. Does the constitutional text impose such a formidable barrier to judicial consideration of war powers disputes? If not, what is the legal basis for the standard? What do you suppose is the measure of "undermining the constitutional structure"?

The *Doe* plaintiffs argued that the October 2002 resolution only permitted actions sanctioned by the U.N. Security Council. Avoiding interpretation of the resolution, the court found that "important questions remain unanswered about whether there will be a war, and if so, under what conditions." *Id.* at 139. The court's decision was announced on March 13, 2003. The war was launched seven days later. Would the plaintiffs have obtained a ruling on the merits if the court had delayed its decision by a few days?

Responding to the alternative theory that Congress effectively colluded with the President and gave away the war-declaring power, the court found that the October 2002 Resolution met the "intelligible principle" standard from the nondelegation cases (see *supra* p. 43) and that Congress "has been deeply involved in significant debate, activity, and authorization connected to Iraq for over a decade." *Id.* at 144. In addition, the resolution spells out justifications for war and "frames itself as an 'authorization' of such a war." *Id.* Would the court decide the merits if Congress gave absolute discretion to the President to start a war at will? *See id.* at 143.

7

The Domestic Effect of International Law

Charging a grand jury in a 1793 national security case, our first Chief Justice asserted that "the laws of the United States admit of being classed under the three heads of descriptions. 1st. All treaties made under the authority of the United States. 2d. The laws of nations. 3dly. The constitution, and statutes of the United States." Trial of Gideon Henfield (C.C.D. Pa. 1793) (charge to the grand jury by Jay, C.J.), *reprinted in* Francis Wharton, *State Trials of the United States During the Administrations of Washington and Adams* 49, 52-53 (1849). John Jay thus implied that some international agreements and customary international laws are part of our domestic law. But what part? What is their effect in U.S. law?

A thorough study of the framework of national security law must necessarily consider these questions because so many national security actions implicate international law. On the other hand, full study of the sources and content of international law affecting national security and how they impact U.S. foreign relations law is well beyond the scope of this casebook. Indeed, these subjects make up entire courses in international or foreign relations law. This chapter provides an introduction to the making and interpretation of treaties and executive agreements under U.S. law and the effect of conventional and customary international law on (and as) domestic national security law.

The Supremacy Clause seems to supply one answer to the question of the domestic effect of international law by providing that "all Treaties made, or which shall be made, under the Authority of the United States, shall be the supreme Law of the Land...." U.S. Const. art. VI. But this only restates Jay's assertion about treaties; it does not explain the effect of a treaty that requires domestic legislation for its execution or that is inconsistent with a statute, let alone the effect of executive agreements or customary international law.

As necessary background for studying the legal effect of treaties and executive agreements, in Part A we look briefly at the treaty-making process and how treaties and agreements are interpreted under our law. In Part B we consider the domestic legal effect of conventional international law — treaties and executive agreements. In Part C we consider the domestic legal effect of customary international law.

A. THE MAKING AND INTERPRETATION OF TREATIES AND AGREEMENTS

Under international law, an agreement between two or more states is considered to be a treaty—also called convention, pact, protocol, or accord—if (1) the states intend the agreement to be legally binding under international law; (2) the agreement deals with significant matters; (3) it clearly describes the obligations of the parties; and (4) it takes a form consistent with the intent that it be legally binding. Congressional Research Service, *Treaties and Other International Agreements: The Role of the United States Senate, A Study Prepared for the S. Comm. on Foreign Relations*, 106th Cong., 25-28 (Comm. Print 2001) (hereinafter *CRS Treaty Study*). But under our Constitution treaties are only those international agreements approved by a two-thirds vote of the Senate. U.S. Const. art. II, §2.

We consider below a controversy surrounding the Reagan administration's "reinterpretation" of the ABM Treaty and a legal opinion it generated from the Office of Legal Counsel (OLC) to consider how treaties are made under the Constitution. The OLC opinion helpfully summarizes the treaty-making process before making its case for the executive branch's interpretation. Other international agreements may be enacted by the full Congress or made by the President alone. These agreements are addressed subsequently.

1. Making and Interpreting Treaties

The ABM Treaty Reinterpretation Controversy[1]

In 1972, President Nixon and Soviet General Secretary Brezhnev signed the Treaty on the Limitation of Anti-Ballistic Missile Systems (ABM Treaty), which limited strategic defense systems. It was credited with forestalling a costly and destabilizing arms race in ABM technology and even more offensive nuclear missiles. In 1983, however, President Reagan announced the Strategic Defense Initiative (SDI). Its purpose was to develop "Star Wars" technology to defend against nuclear missile attack. After critics argued that testing and eventual implementation of such technology would require amending the ABM Treaty, the Reagan administration announced a reinterpretation of the ABM Treaty that would permit SDI development and testing. When opponents pointed out that the ratification hearings on the Treaty did not support this reinterpretation, the Administration cited a record of secret negotiations to support its reinterpretation. The Legal Adviser to the Department of State, Abraham D. Sofaer, argued that it is "the treaty that was made, irrespective of the explanations [the Senate] is provided." *See The ABM Treaty and the Constitution: Joint*

---

1. Except where otherwise noted, this background is drawn from Symposium, *Arms Control Treaty Reinterpretation*, 137 U. Pa. L. Rev. 1353 (1989); Abram Chayes & Antonia Handler Chayes, *Testing and Development of "Exotic" Systems Under the ABM Treaty: The Great Reinterpretation Caper*, 99 Harv. L. Rev. 1956 (1986).

Hearings Before the S. Comm. on Foreign Relations and S. Comm. on the Judiciary, 100th Cong. 351, 375 (1987) (hereinafter *Joint Hearings*) (statement of State Dept. Legal Adviser Abraham D. Sofaer).

In response, Senator Joseph Biden introduced Senate Resolution 167, which purported to set forth the "constitutional principles" governing treaty interpretation. The resolution provided that "the meaning [of a treaty] is to be determined in light of what the Senate understands the treaty to mean when it gives its advice and consent." That understanding, the resolution stated, is manifested by what the Senate formally expressed and also by "Senate approval or acceptance of, or Senate acquiescence in, interpretations of the treaty by the executive branch communicated to the Senate," but never "by matter of which it is not aware," such as secret negotiations not communicated to it. Eventually, the Senate added a variant on the Biden resolution as a condition to approval of the Intermediate Range Nuclear Forces (INF) Treaty, although the condition technically applied just to that treaty. 134 Cong. Rec. S6724 (May 26, 1988). After he exchanged instruments of ratification of the INF Treaty with the Soviet Union, President Reagan wrote to the Senate disavowing the legal effect of the so-called Biden Condition. Senator Sam Nunn replied, "The Treaty, including this Condition, is now the supreme law of the land. And the President can no more change it with a letter than he can change any other law with a letter."

Relevance of Senate Ratification History to Treaty Interpretation (April 9, 1987)
11 U.S. Op. Off. Legal Counsel 28

I. INTRODUCTION AND SUMMARY

This memorandum responds to your request for the views of this Office concerning the relevance of the Senate's deliberations on ratification of a treaty to subsequent interpretations of ambiguous treaty language by the Executive Branch. We use the term "deliberations" or "ratification record" to encompass sources such as hearings, committee reports, and floor debates, which are generally analogous to the "legislative history" of domestic statutes. Our focus is on the relevance of those sources to interpretation of a treaty as domestic law, i.e., their relevance to the President's constitutional responsibility to "take Care that the Laws be faithfully executed." U.S. Const. art. II, §3. We understand that you are reviewing separately the relevance that would be ascribed under international law to the Senate's ratification record.

The question you raise does not lend itself to any clear or easy answer. As discussed below, the dual nature of treaties as international agreements and as domestic law and the concomitant division of the treaty-making power between the President and the Senate create an inevitable tension. Primarily, treaties are international obligations, negotiated by the President in his capacity as the "sole organ of the federal government in the field of international relations," United States v. Curtiss-Wright Export Corp., 299 U.S. 304, 320 (1936). The most relevant evidence of the meaning of a treaty lies in the mutual exchange of views between the negotiating parties—an exchange in which the Senate does not formally participate unless it explicitly conditions its consent to a treaty and that condition is communicated to and accepted by the other party. Because the advice and consent function of the Senate, however, was designed by the Framers as a constitutional check on the President's otherwise broad authority to make treaties that have the force of law, we believe that the deliberative record that is created when the Senate advises and consents to a treaty cannot be ignored in the interpretative process. Nonetheless, in all but the most unusual case, the ratification record would not be the determinative — or even the primary — source of evidence as to the treaty's meaning under domestic law.

In determining the weight to be assigned to that record, it should be observed that, conceptually, the constitutional division of treaty-making responsibility is essentially the reverse of the division of law-making authority. Congress initially agrees upon and enacts the language of domestic legislation, while the President reserves the right to determine whether that legislation will go into effect (subject, of course, to the override of any veto). Treaties, however, are proposed and negotiated by the President, subject to the approval or disapproval of the Senate. Given this conceptual framework, it is clear that the portions of the treaty ratification record that should be accorded more weight as to the treaty's meaning are the representations of the executive — the draftsman, in effect, of the treaty. Statements by individual Senators, or even groups of Senators, are certainly entitled to no more consideration — and perhaps less — than the limited weight such statements are given in the interpretation of domestic legislation when they are not confirmed by the legislation's sponsor in colloquy or otherwise.

II. CONSTITUTIONAL DIVISION OF TREATY AUTHORITY...

Under [the] separation of powers, the President has a dual role with respect to treaties. First, the President is responsible for "making" treaties, i.e., entering into negotiations with foreign governments and reaching agreement on specific provisions. U.S. Const. art. II, §2, cl. 2. Second, as part of his responsibility to "take Care that the Laws be faithfully executed," and as the "sole organ of the federal government in the field of international relations," the President is responsible for enforcing and executing international agreements, a responsibility that necessarily "involves also the obligation and authority to interpret what the treaty requires." L. Henkin, Foreign Affairs and the Constitution 167 (1972) (Henkin).[4]

The President's authority to make treaties is shared with the Senate, which must consent by a two-thirds vote. This "JOINT AGENCY of the Chief Magistrate of the Union, and of two-thirds of the members of (the Senate)"[6] reflects the Framers' recognition that the negotiation and acceptance of treaties incorporates both legislative and executive responsibilities:

> The particular nature of the power of making treaties indicates a peculiar propriety in that union. Though several writers on the subject of government place

---

4. The President's interpretation of a treaty is, of course, subject to review by the courts in a case or controversy that meets Article III requirements. See U.S. Const. art. III, §2.
6. The Federalist No. 66, at 406 (A. Hamilton) (C. Rossiter ed., 1961).

A. The Making and Interpretation of Treaties and Agreements

that power in the class of executive authorities, yet this is evidently an arbitrary disposition; for if we attend carefully to its operation it will be found to partake more of the legislative than of the executive character, though it does not seem strictly to fall within the definition of either of them. The essence of the legislative authority is to enact laws, or, in other words, to prescribe rules for the regulation of the society; while the execution of the laws and the employment of the common strength, either for this purpose or for the common defense, seem to comprise all the functions of the executive magistrate. The power of making treaties is, plainly, neither the one nor the other.... The qualities elsewhere detailed as indispensable in the management of foreign negotiations point out the executive as the most fit agent in those transactions; while the vast importance of the trust and the operation of treaties as laws plead strongly for the participation of the whole or a portion of the legislative body in the office of making them.

The Federalist No. 75, at 450-51 (A. Hamilton) (C. Rossiter ed., 1961). Rather than vest either Congress or the President with the sole power to make treaties, the Framers sought to combine the judgment of both, providing that the President shall make the treaties, but subject to the "advice and consent" of the Senate. Thus, the Framers included the Senate in the treaty-making process because the result of that process, just as the result of the legislative process, is essentially a law that has "the effect of altering the legal rights, duties and relations of persons...outside the Legislative Branch." INS v. Chadha, 462 U.S. at 952....

III. SENATE PRACTICE

In practice, the Senate's formal participation in the treaty-making process begins after negotiation of the treaty. At that time, the President transmits the treaty to the Senate, with a detailed description and analysis of the treaty, and any protocols, annexes, or other documents that the President considers to be integral parts of the proposed treaty. Under the Senate's rules, treaties are referred to the Senate Foreign Relations Committee, which may hold hearings to develop a record explaining the purposes, provisions, and significance of the agreement. Typically, the principal witnesses at such hearings are representatives of the Executive Branch. The Foreign Relations Committee then issues a report to the full Senate, with its recommendation on approval of the treaty.

The Senate's practice has been to approve, to disapprove, or to approve with conditions, treaties negotiated by the Executive Branch. Express conditions imposed by the Senate may include "understandings," which interpret or clarify the obligations undertaken by the parties to the treaty but do not change those obligations, or "reservations" and "amendments," which condition the Senate's consent on amendment or limitation of the substantive obligations of the parties under the agreement. On occasion, the Senate has accompanied its consent by "declarations," which state the Senate's position, opinion, or intention on issues raised by the treaty, although not on the provisions of the specific treaty itself.

IV. RELEVANCE OF THE SENATE RATIFICATION RECORD

A. EXPRESS CONDITIONS

When the Senate includes express conditions as part of its resolution of consent to ratification, the President may, if he objects, either refuse to ratify the treaty or resubmit it to the Senate with the hope that it will be approved unconditionally the second time. If the President proceeds with ratification, however, such understandings or other conditions expressly imposed by the Senate are generally included by the President with the treaty documents deposited for ratification or communicated to the other parties at the same time the treaty is deposited for ratification. Because such conditions are considered to be part of the United States' position in ratifying the treaty, they are generally binding on the President, both internationally and domestically, in his subsequent interpretation of the treaty.[13]

B. STATEMENTS IN THE RATIFICATION RECORD

The more difficult question is what relevance, if any, the President must give to less formal, contemporaneous indications of the Senate's understanding of the treaty, i.e., statements in committee reports, hearings, and debates which may reflect an understanding of certain treaty provisions by some Senators, but which were not embodied in any formal understanding or condition approved by the entire Senate....

First, it must be observed that a treaty is fundamentally a "contract between or among sovereign nations," and the primary responsibility — whether of the executive or the courts — is "to give the specific words of the treaty a meaning consistent with the shared expectations of the contracting parties." Air France v. Saks, 470 U.S. 392, 399 (1985). International agreements, like "other contracts ... are to be read in the light of the conditions and circumstances existing at the time they were entered into, with a view to effecting the objects and purposes of the States thereby contracting." Rocca v. Thompson, 223 U.S. 317, 331-332 (1912). Necessarily, the best evidence of the intent of the parties is the language and structure of the treaty and, secondarily, direct evidence of the understanding reached by the parties, as reflected in the negotiating record and subsequent administrative construction, rather than unilateral, post-negotiation statements made during the Senate ratification debates.

Moreover, the constitutional role of the Senate is limited to approval or disapproval of the treaty, much as the President's constitutional role in enacting domestic legislation is limited to his veto power. The Senate may, if it chooses,

---

13. This presumes, of course, that the condition is within the Senate's authority to impose as part of its treaty-making authority. The Senate's authority to impose conditions is not unlimited merely because it may withhold its consent. The general principle that Congress cannot attach unconstitutional conditions to a legislative benefit or program merely because it has authority to withhold the benefit or power entirely applies equally to the Senate's advice and consent authority. The Senate may not, for example, use its advice and consent power to impose conditions that affect separate, wholly domestic, statutory schemes.... [W]e do not believe the Senate may impose conditions that interfere with the President's responsibility to execute the laws.

amend or interpret the treaty by attaching explicit conditions to its consent, which are then transmitted to, and either accepted or rejected by, the other parties. Absent such conditions, the Senate does not participate in setting the terms of the agreement between the parties, and therefore statements made by Senators, whether individually in hearings and debates or collectively in committee reports, should be accorded little weight unless confirmed by the Executive....

Indeed, profound foreign policy implications would be raised if the United States were to supplement or alter treaty obligations to foreign governments based on statements made by members of the Senate during its consideration of the treaty that were not communicated to those governments in the form of express conditions. "(F)oreign governments dealing with us must rely upon the official instruments of ratification as an expression of the full intent of the government of the United States, precisely as we expect from foreign governments." Coplin v. United States, 6 [Cl. Ct. 115 (1984),] at 145....

We can well imagine that the United States would be deeply disturbed if the Soviet Union resolved ambiguities in a treaty by reference to deliberations in a Soviet legislative body charged with consenting to its ratification. If individual Senators believe that portions of a treaty are ambiguous, they may resolve that ambiguity in a manner consistent with the mutual process through which treaties are negotiated: either by requesting the Executive to state more clearly the meaning of the agreement it has reached with the foreign country, or by making explicit the Senate's understanding of the provision through a formal reservation or understanding attached to its resolution of approval....

On the other hand, statements made to the Senate by representatives of the Executive Branch as to the meaning of a treaty should have considerably more weight in subsequent interpretations of ambiguous terms of the treaty. Such statements do not present as substantial a threat to the reliance interests of foreign governments, because the Executive Branch negotiated the treaty and is therefore in a position to represent authoritatively the meaning of the agreement that emerged from the negotiating process. Moreover, given that the Senate's constitutional role is limited to approving a treaty already negotiated by the Executive Branch and that much of the extra-textual evidence of a treaty's meaning remains in the control of the Executive Branch, we believe the Senate itself has a substantial reliance interest in statements made by the Executive Branch officials seeking that approval.

Accordingly, consistent with the President's role as the nation's exclusive negotiator of treaties with foreign governments, we believe that statements made to the Senate by the Executive Branch during the ratification debates are relevant in much the same way that contemporaneous statements by congressional draftsmen or sponsors of domestic legislation are relevant to any subsequent interpretation of the statute. We note that because of the primary role played by the Executive Branch in the negotiation of treaties and the implementation of foreign policy, courts generally accord substantial deference—albeit not conclusive effect—to interpretations advanced by the Executive Branch.... Although the courts often rely on interpretative statements made by the Executive Branch prepared well after negotiation and ratification of the treaty, they find particularly persuasive a consistent pattern of Executive Branch interpretation, reflected in the application of the treaty by the Executive and the course of conduct of the parties in implementing the agreement....

The weight to be given to an interpretative statement made by an Executive Branch official to the Senate during the ratification process will likely depend upon such factors as the formality of the statement, the identity and position of the Executive Branch official making the statement, the level of attention and interest focused on the meaning of the relevant treaty provision, and the consistency with which members of the Executive Branch adhered at the time to the view of the treaty provision reflected in the statement. All of these factors affect the degree to which the Senate could reasonably have relied upon the statement and, in turn, the weight that courts will attach to it. At one extreme, a single statement made by a middle-level Executive Branch official in response to a question at a hearing would not be regarded as definitive. Rather, in interpreting the domestic effect of a treaty, the courts would likely accord such a statement in the ratification record a degree of significance subordinate to more direct evidence of the mutual intent of the parties, such as the language and context of the treaty, diplomatic exchanges between the President and the other treaty parties, the negotiating record, and the practical construction of the provision reflected in the parties' course of dealings under the treaty. Moreover, courts often give substantial weight to the Executive Branch's current interpretation of the treaty, in recognition of the President's unique role in shaping foreign policy and communicating with foreign governments, and, accordingly, would be unlikely to bind future chief executives on the basis of an isolated remark of an Executive Branch official in a previous administration....

In contrast, in a case in which the statements by the Executive Branch amount to a formal representation by the President concerning the meaning of a particular treaty provision, the ratification record may be conclusive. If, for example, the ratification record unequivocally shows that the President presented the treaty to the Senate based on specific, official representations regarding the meaning of an ambiguous provision, that the Senate regarded that understanding as important to its consent, and that the Senate relied on the representations made by the Executive Branch in approving the treaty (and thus in refraining from attaching a formal reservation setting forth the understanding), we believe the President would, in effect, be estopped from taking a contrary position in his subsequent interpretation of the treaty, just as he would be bound by a formal reservation or understanding passed by the Senate to the same effect. Obviously, a President could not negotiate a treaty with other nations on the basis of one understanding of its import, submit the treaty to the Senate on a wholly different understanding, and then, in implementing the treaty, rely solely on the understanding he had reached with the other parties. Similarly, he could not reach a secret agreement with the other party that substantially modifies the obligations and authorities created by the text of the treaty submitted to the Senate, and then seek to use the secret agreement as a basis for actions inconsistent with the text of the treaty. Such results would essentially eviscerate the Senate's constitutional advice and consent role, because it would deprive the Senate of a fair opportunity to determine whether, or with what conditions, the treaty should become the "supreme Law of the Land." Accordingly, in such extreme cases, we have little doubt that, as a matter of domestic law, the courts would construe the treaty as presented to and accepted by the Senate, even if as a matter of international law the treaty might have a different meaning.[25]

Charles J. Cooper
Assistant Attorney General

NOTES AND QUESTIONS

a. Making Treaties

1. *Negotiations—A Presidential Monopoly?* The making of a treaty starts with the parties' negotiation of its terms. What are the pros and cons of involving the Senate in treaty negotiations? This was John Jay's answer:

> It seldom happens in the negotiation of treaties, of whatever nature, but that perfect *secrecy* and immediate *dispatch* are sometimes requisite. There are cases where the most useful intelligence may be obtained, if the persons possessing it can be relieved from apprehensions of discovery.... [T]here doubtless are many...who would rely on the secrecy of the President, but who would not confide in that of the Senate, and still less in that of a large popular assembly. The [constitutional] convention have done well, therefore, in so disposing of the power of making treaties that although the President must, in forming them, act by the advice and consent of the Senate, yet he will be able to manage the business of intelligence in such manner as prudence may suggest. [*The Federalist No. 64*, at 392-393 (John Jay) (Clinton Rossiter ed., 1961).]

By the end of the Washington administration, it became the President's custom merely to inform the Senate of proposed negotiations when it consented to his appointment of the negotiator, and to submit his instructions only with the completed treaty. *See* Ralston Hayden, *The Senate and Treaties, 1789-1817*, at 105-106 (1920). Since then, the President has usually dominated the negotiating process and has typically only consulted the Senate after completing negotiations when formally submitting the negotiated treaty to it, *CRS Treaty Study, supra* p. 158, at 87, although the Senate (and sometimes the House) has participated earlier from time to time.

In light of these arguments, may the Senate alone or the Congress direct the President (or his delegate, the Secretary of State) to "initiate negotiations as soon as possible for the development of bilateral or multilateral agreements with other nations" for the protection of sea turtles? *See* 16 U.S.C. §1537 (2000). In an

---

25. Although courts generally seek to construe treaties consistent with their international import, on occasion courts have adopted constructions of particular treaties that conflict with the President's view of the international obligations created by the treaty. Moreover, Congress can enact domestic legislation that is inconsistent with existing treaty obligations, and thus has the effect of tying the President's hands domestically, while leaving the international obligations intact. It would not be unprecedented, therefore, for a court to construe a treaty more narrowly — or more broadly — as a matter of domestic law than the President construes the treaty as a matter of international law. As Professor Henkin has observed, "(i)t could happen...that Congress and the courts would in effect apply treaty provisions different from those that bind the United States internationally — another cost of the separation of powers." Henkin at 167.

opinion dismissing a complaint seeking an injunction to order the President to comply with such a statutory mandate, the court ruled that it

> has not and cannot lawfully order the Executive to comply with the terms of a statute that impinges upon power exclusively granted to the Executive Branch under the Constitution.... Because "the Constitution plainly grants the President the initiative in matters directly involved in the conduct of diplomatic" affairs, we cannot enforce the statute. [Earth Island Inst. v. Christopher, 6 F.3d 648, 653 (9th Cir. 1993) (internal citation omitted).]

Should the Senate be prohibited from dictating terms to be negotiated? From naming the negotiators for the United States? From designating Senators to serve as observers at the negotiations? From insisting on progress reports on negotiations? From forbidding negotiations on certain subjects or with certain states? *See generally CRS Treaty Study, supra,* at 69-82. In *Curtiss-Wright, supra* p. 60, Justice Sutherland claimed that the President "alone negotiates. Into the field of negotiation the Senate cannot intrude; and Congress itself is powerless to invade it." 299 U.S. at 319 (dictum). Was he right? *See* Louis Fisher, *Congressional Participation in the Treaty Process,* 137 U. Pa. L. Rev. 1511, 1512 (1989) (asserting that a presidential monopoly of treaty negotiation is an "historical myth").

2. *Consent.* After a treaty has been negotiated and signed or initialed, it is submitted to the Senate for "advice and consent." *See generally CRS Treaty Study, supra* p. 158, at 87-93. Typically, the treaty is referred to the Senate Foreign Relations Committee for consideration. Should the Administration be required to submit the full negotiating record to the Committee to aid its consideration? Should it hold hearings in secret? What implications, if any, do your answers have for subsequent interpretation of the treaty? As the OLC memorandum states, Senate consent to a treaty is not an all-or-nothing proposition. *See, e.g.,* Michael J. Glennon, *The Senate Role in Treaty Ratification,* 77 Am. J. Intl. L. 257, 263-266 (1983); Curtis A. Bradley & Jack L. Goldsmith, *Treaties, Human Rights, and Conditional Consent,* 149 U. Pa. L. Rev. 399 (2000); *CRS Treaty Study, supra,* at 96-100.

3. *Ratification.* The final stage in the making of a treaty after the Senate consents is the President's ratification of the treaty by transmitting instruments of ratification to the other treaty parties. When these instruments have been exchanged or deposited, the President typically proclaims the treaty to be in force. *CRS Treaty Study, supra,* at 109-113. *Must* the President ratify a treaty that has been unconditionally approved by the Senate? Apparently not, although the constitutional text is silent on the question. *See Restatement (Third) of Foreign Relations Law of the United States* §303 cmt. d (1987).

b. Terminating Treaties

In INS v. Chadha, 462 U.S. 919, 954 (1983), noted *supra* p. 128, the Supreme Court declared that "[a]mendment and repeal of statutes, no less than enactment, must conform to Art[icle] I." By parallel logic, why should not the termination of a treaty conform to Article II? In Goldwater v. Carter,

A. The Making and Interpretation of Treaties and Agreements

617 F.2d 697 (D.C. Cir. 1979), *vacated and remanded*, 444 U.S. 996 (1979), Senator Goldwater challenged the constitutionality of President Jimmy Carter's unilateral termination of the U.S. Mutual Defense Treaty with Taiwan. The Court of Appeals upheld the President, rejecting this "symmetry" logic in a per curiam opinion, and noting, *inter alia*, that the theory has not been applied to the removal of ambassadors and some other executive officials appointed by the President with the advice and consent of the Senate. The Supreme Court subsequently vacated the opinion on justiciability grounds, 444 U.S. 996 (1979), leaving the question of termination authority unsettled.

Dissenting in *Goldwater*, Circuit Court Judge MacKinnon argued that because a constitutional treaty is the "Supreme Law of the Land," it can only be terminated by another law enacted by Congress (absent a superseding treaty). Under his theory, could the Senate alone terminate a treaty? Judge MacKinnon's syllogism was based on the proposition that treaties are like statutes. *See* Michael J. Glennon, *Constitutional Diplomacy* 150 (1990). The per curiam opinion in *Goldwater* dismissed this argument by asserting that the laws designated supreme by the Supremacy Clause "are not necessarily the same in their other characteristics, any more than are the circumstances and terms of their creation the same." 617 F.2d at 704.

Furthermore, the per curiam opinion appealed to practicality and history to uphold the President's power to terminate a treaty unilaterally. The opinion asserted that the Constitution imposes the "special and extraordinary" condition of treaty approval by a supermajority of the Senate because treaties risk tying the nation to "entangling alliances." *Id.* The opinion then implied that the risk to the country from *terminating* an entangling alliance is lower. *Id. See also* Louis Henkin, *Foreign Affairs and the Constitution* 169 (1972) (" 'disentangling' is less risky and may have to be done quickly, and is often done piecemeal, or *ad hoc*, by various means or acts"). Is this logic sound? What if terminating a treaty raised a substantial risk that the erstwhile treaty party would go to war against the United States?

The President *has* terminated treaties unilaterally from time to time. The President's lawyers in *Goldwater* identified 26 instances of treaty termination, in 13 of which the President was said to have acted without Congress. *See Goldwater*, 617 F.2d at 723 (quoting President's brief). Judge MacKinnon responded by asserting that in 5 of the 13, there was a putative legislative basis for termination, and in 4 the treaty was already abrogated by the action of the other party. *Id.* at 733. What sort of history would demonstrate constitutional power in the President to terminate treaties? See *supra* p. 48, describing a theory of constitutional customary law with congressional acquiescence. *See generally* Louis Henkin, *Litigating the President's Power to Terminate Treaties*, 73 Am. J. Intl. L. 647 (1979); David J. Scheffer, *The Law of Treaty Termination as Applied to the United States De-Recognition of the Republic of China*, 19 Harv. Intl. L.J. 931 (1978).

c. Interpreting Treaties

1. *To What Treaty Did the Senate Consent?* An uncontroversial paraphrase of the Treaty Clause is that the President may make a treaty if the Senate has consented to it. A necessary corollary of this proposition is that "the President can only make the treaty to which the Senate consented; he cannot make a treaty

other than the one to which the Senate consented." *See The ABM Treaty and the Constitution, supra* p. 158, at 318 (statement of Professor Louis Henkin).

Does the OLC memorandum support this claim? What is the role of administration testimony to the Senate Foreign Relations Committee about the treaty? Based presumably on the OLC memorandum, the Reagan administration subsequently claimed that "the Executive is, as a matter of domestic law, required to adhere to the interpretation of a treaty authoritatively shared with, and clearly intended, generally understood and relied upon by the Senate at the time of its advice and consent to ratification." Letter from White House Counsel Arthur B. Culvahouse to Senator Richard D. Lugar (Mar. 17, 1988), *reprinted in The INF Treaty*, S. Exec. Rep. No. 100-15, at 443 (1988). Is this consistent with the OLC memorandum? Which witnesses are "authoritative"? How do we know whether an interpretation in their testimony was "clearly intended"? How do we know whether it was "generally understood and relied upon by the Senate"? *See generally* Gary M. Buechler, *Constitutional Limits on the President's Power to Interpret Treaties: The Sofaer Doctrine, the Biden Condition, and the Doctrine of Binding Authoritative Representations*, 78 Geo. L.J. 1983 (1990) (proposing to entrench only "authoritative executive representations" that have not been challenged by the Senate or a significant number of senators).

2. *The Biden Condition.* In what ways does the statement of "constitutional principles" in the Biden Condition differ from that made by the OLC memorandum? Which is more convincing? The supporters of the Biden Condition also argued that "[i]mplicit understandings represent informal—but equally significant—"legislative history," including hearings, committee reports, and floor debates. *The INF Treaty, supra*, at 439. The Condition even provided that the Senate's unenacted "acquiescence" in executive branch interpretations was controlling. Are these "constitutional principles" sound? Since the Senate knows how to formalize its interpretations in amendments and reservations, why should we look past them?

3. *The Importance of the Negotiating Record.* The Reagan administration also contended that when a treaty is ambiguous, the executive may resort to a secret negotiating record to resolve the ambiguity, even though the record has not been disclosed to the Senate. Supporters of the Biden Condition disagreed, asserting that legislative history unknown to the Senate "could not, logically, be part of the 'meeting of the minds' between the President and the Senate extant on the date of Senate consent." *The INF Treaty, supra*, at 439. Thus, Professor Tribe testified during the controversy,

> the President cannot present one treaty to the Senate, accompanied by various formal submittals, obtain the consent of the Senate to that treaty based in part on those submittals, and then unveil a hitherto secret record of negotiations or understandings—either internal to the executive branch or between the executive and the foreign signatory to the treaty—to defend an interpretation of the treaty inconsistent with what the Senate had been led to believe it was accepting. [*The ABM Treaty and the Constitution, supra*, at 417-418.]

A. The Making and Interpretation of Treaties and Agreements

A negotiating record is an ill-defined and uneven collection of plenary statements read and exchanged by the negotiators, draft treaty texts prepared in the negotiations, and often numerous "memoranda of conversations" written after the fact by individual negotiators to summarize discussions. *See* David A. Koplow, *Constitutional Bait and Switch: Executive Reinterpretation of Arms Control Treaties*, 137 U. Pa. L. Rev. 1353, 1385-1386 (1989). *See also* Glennon, *supra* p. 167, at 139 (asserting that the "negotiating record is a term of art used to describe an agreed negotiating record, since it is only the joint intent of the parties that has significance under international law"). If the Administration intends to resolve treaty ambiguities using a secret negotiating record, how would you, as Chief Counsel to the Senate Foreign Relations Committee, advise the Committee to proceed in future hearings on submitted treaties? *See* Koplow, *supra*, at 1377; Michael J. Glennon, *Interpreting "Interpretation": The President, the Senate, and When Treaty Interpretation Becomes Treaty Making*, 20 U.C. Davis L. Rev. 913, 919 (1987). How might your advice affect negotiations? *See* Buechler, *supra* p. 168, at 2000-2001.

4. *Necessary Executive Reinterpretation of Treaties?* No treaty can anticipate every circumstance to which it might apply or every problem that may arise in execution. Must the President therefore return to the Senate every time she encounters an unforeseen circumstance or problem? Or does she have some necessary power of interpretation to fill in the interstices of the treaty and make it work? If so, but you reject the Reagan administration's assertion of the limits of this power, what would you substitute?

Professor Koplow suggests that the executive's power of reinterpretation is a function of the following factors: (a) what the Senate said in providing its advice and consent; (b) what was said to the Senate prior to its consent; (c) the attitude of the treaty partner(s) toward competing treaty interpretations; (d) support in the treaty text and record for competing interpretations; (e) the record of "subsequent practice" by the treaty parties; (f) how different the new interpretation is from the old; (g) whether the new interpretation purports to create new obligations or to release old ones; and (h) whether there are changed circumstances that affect the treaty. Koplow, *supra*, at 1418-1425. Would these factors make it harder or easier for "resourceful lawyers to support a preferred result"? *See* Phillip R. Trimble, *The Constitutional Common Law of Treaty Interpretation: A Reply to the Formalists*, 137 U. Pa. L. Rev. 1461, 1465 (1989) (expressing doubt of the soundness of any analytic approach that would "entrench" the meaning of a treaty).

5. *Deference to the Executive?* Do the factors listed in the preceding note give sufficient weight to the President's role in negotiating and executing a treaty — in other words, sufficient deference to the executive interpretation?

In urging that the Geneva Conventions did not apply to the U.S. conflict in Afghanistan, see *infra* pp. 767-770, Attorney General Ashcroft advised President Bush that "when a President determines that a treaty does not apply, his determination is fully discretionary and will not be reviewed by the federal courts." Letter of Atty. General John Ashcroft to President George W. Bush (Feb. 1, 2002), *available at* http://www.gwu.edu/~nsarchiv/NSAEBB/NSAEBB127/020201.pdf. Is this advice consistent with the deference described by the OLC memorandum? Or the role assigned the courts by Article III? In support of his advice, General Ashcroft cited dicta from Clark v. Allen, 331

U.S. 503, 508-509 (1947) (emphasis added), that during war "the Chief Executive *or* Congress may have formulated a national policy quite inconsistent with the enforcement of a treaty in whole or in part." But the Supreme Court in *Clark* relied for this proposition on an earlier state court opinion in which Judge Cardozo asserted that

> the President and Senate may denounce the treaty, and thus terminate its life. Congress may enact an inconsistent rule, which will control the action of the courts. The treaty of peace itself may set up new relations, and terminate earlier compacts, either tacitly or expressly.... But until some one of these things is done, until some one of these events occurs, while war is still flagrant, and the will of the political departments of the government unrevealed, the courts, as I view their function, play a humbler and more cautious part. It is not for them to denounce treaties generally, en bloc. Their part it is, as one provision or another is involved in some actual controversy before them, to determine whether, alone, or by force of connection with an inseparable scheme, the provision is inconsistent with the policy or safety of the nation in the emergency of war, and hence presumably intended to be limited to times of peace. [*Id.* at 509, quoting Techt v. Hughes, 229 N.Y. 222, 242-243 (1920).]

Does *Clark* support General Ashcroft's advice?

2. Executive and Other Agreements

Dames & Moore v. Regan
United States Supreme Court, 1981
453 U.S. 654

[The opinion is set forth *supra* at p. 48.]

NOTES AND QUESTIONS

1. *The Explosion in Executive Agreements.* In the half-century before World War II, executive agreements outnumbered treaties by a factor of only two to one. In the next 60 years, the discrepancy rose to almost 12 to 1. By the 1980s, the United States was entering into 300 to 400 executive agreements per year, compared to 8 to 26 treaties per year. *CRS Treaty Study, supra* p. 158, at xxxv-xxxvi. The agreements cover such diverse national security subjects as collective security, arms control and disarmament, status of U.S. forces stationed abroad, extradition, human rights, ceasefires, armistices and peace terms, military cooperation, and presumably intelligence collection and sharing. How would you explain the trend in favor of executive agreements?

2. *Types of Executive Agreements.* Executive agreements can be categorized by legal authority. *See Restatement (Third), supra* p. 166, §303. The *first* category consists of *congressional-executive agreements.* Congress either expressly enacts such agreements or, more commonly, delegates the authority to make them to the

A. The Making and Interpretation of Treaties and Agreements

President. *CRS Treaty Study, supra,* at 52-59. We saw in Chapter 5 that the courts have routinely sustained such delegations. *See, e.g.,* Field v. Clark, 143 U.S. 649 (1892) (sustaining a foreign affairs delegation under which reciprocal trade agreements were made by the executive). The *second* category consists of *agreements made pursuant to treaty,* either by express authorization or by reasonable inference. Although the legal authority for treaty agreements has not been fully explored in the cases, in Wilson v. Girard, 354 U.S. 524, 528-529 (1957), the Supreme Court suggested that the Senate's approval of a treaty impliedly authorized the agreements necessary to carry it out.

Into what *third* category of agreements does the 1981 Iranian Hostage Agreement fall? What constitutional authority would you cite for that type of agreement? *See* United States v. Belmont, 301 U.S. 324, 330-331 (1937) (citing President's role as sole organ of foreign relations in finding executive agreement "within [his] competence").

3. *Agreements and the Constitutional Text.* The Constitution expressly mentions treaties and describes the procedure for their making as well as their force and effect. Does the Constitution identify any other kind of international agreement? *See* Ntakirutimana v. Reno, 184 F.3d 419, 426 (5th Cir. 1999) (endorsing the assertion that the Constitution apparently contemplates other kinds of international agreements), *cert. denied,* 528 U.S. 1135 (2000). What textual constitutional arguments can you make for and against the constitutionality in general of executive agreements?

4. *The Interchangeability of Sole Executive Agreements and Treaties.* Are there some putative sole executive agreements for which the treaty process is constitutionally required? If not, what becomes of the Treaty Clause? If so, what differentiates permissible sole executive agreements from agreements for which the treaty process is required? Professor Louis Henkin suggests that "[o]ne is compelled to conclude that there are agreements which the President can make on his sole authority and others which he can make only with the consent of the Senate, but neither Justice Sutherland nor any one else has told us which are which." Henkin, *supra* p. 167, at 179. *See also* Edward Borchard, *Shall the Executive Agreement Replace the Treaty?,* 53 Yale L.J. 664 (1944). Do you think the President has constitutional authority to make a sole executive agreement that would require us to use military force to protect an ally against attack?

5. *The Interchangeability of Congressional-Executive Agreements and Treaties.* Congressional-executive agreements require approval by a simple majority of each House, while treaties require approval by a supermajority of the Senate. Consequently, some multilateral or bilateral national security undertakings that could obtain the requisite approval as congressional-executive agreements might fail as treaties. Are there some putative congressional-executive agreements for which the treaty process is constitutionally required? If so, how do we differentiate those congressional-executive agreements that are permissible from those that are not? Is the differentiating factor their importance, in terms of scope and impact? By this standard, a multilateral trade agreement requiring harmonization of financial, commercial, labor, and environmental laws and regulations for an entire continent would arguably need to be approved by

the treaty process, while an agreement regarding housing for a U.S. military base in a foreign country would not.

In Made in USA Foundation v. United States, 242 F.3d 1300 (11th Cir. 2000), *cert. denied,* United Steelworkers v. United States, 534 U.S. 1039 (2000), however, the court found the "importance" standard unworkable in a challenge to just such a trade agreement (the North American Free Trade Agreement (NAFTA)). Noting that neither the constitutional text nor the case law tells us "what exactly constitutes and distinguishes 'treaties'" from other kinds of agreements, it rejected the "nebulous argument that 'major and significant' agreements require Art. II, §2 ratification," because appellants failed "to supply any analytical framework whatsoever" for classifying agreements as "major and significant." *Id.* at 1315. Furthermore, it asserted that for a court to "adjudicate the 'significance' of an international commercial agreement as the critical determinant of whether or not it constitutes a treaty requiring Senate ratification . . . would . . . unavoidably thrust [it] into making policy judgments of the sort unsuited for the judicial branch." *Id.* at 1317. At the same time, the court conceded that the Treaty Clause does not leave the political branches "unfettered discretion" in deciding whether a particular agreement is subject to the rigors of the Article II treaty process, because otherwise that process would be a "dead letter." *Id.* at 1319. Back to square one.

The State Department lists the following "considerations for selecting among constitutionally authorized procedures": degree of commitment or risk involved, intent to override state laws, need for subsequent legislation, past practice for similar agreements, congressional preference, degree of formality desired, proposed duration, need for prompt conclusion, and general international practice. *Treaties and Other International Agreements,* in II *Foreign Affairs Manual,* Ch. 700 (rev. Feb. 25, 1985), reprinted in *CRS Treaty Study, supra* p. 158, at 301. Professor Steve Charnovitz has recommended that Congress enact a "framework statute" for approving congressional-executive agreements as "a substitute for the Article II procedure." Steve Charnovitz, *Using Framework Statutes to Facilitate U.S. Treaty Making,* 98 Am. J. Intl. L. 969, 702 (2004).

6. *Case-Zablocki Act: A Congressional Limit on Agreements.* Congress has long worried about erosion of the treaty power in light of the increasing number of executive agreements. In 1961, Congress enacted the Arms Control and Disarmament Act, which provides that "no action shall be taken under this chapter or any other law" to commit the United States to reduce or limit arms "except pursuant to the treaty making power of the President under the Constitution or unless authorized by further affirmative legislation by the Congress of the United States." Pub. L. No. 87-297, §33, 75 Stat. 634 (codified as amended at 22 U.S.C. §2573 (2000)). Is this provision constitutional in all its applications?

Concern during the Vietnam War about secret security commitments prompted the Senate to pass a nonbinding resolution expressing its sense that a U.S. national commitment for the use of U.S. armed forces or financial assistance to allies should result "only from affirmative action taken by the executive and legislative branches of the United States Government by means of a treaty, statute, or concurrent resolution of both Houses of Congress specifically providing for such commitment." S. 85, 91st Cong. (1969). Ultimately, however, Congress backed away from any generic challenge to sole executive agreements, settling instead in the Case-Zablocki Act for requiring the President to make a timely submission to Congress of "the text of any international agreement (including text of any oral international agreement, which shall be reduced to writing) other than a Treaty." 1 U.S.C. §112b (2000). The Act provides that the President may submit classified agreements to the Senate Committee on Foreign Relations and the House Committee on International Affairs with an injunction of secrecy. Does the Act validate sole executive agreements by implication? Presidents Nixon, Ford, and Carter made secret agreements regarding South Vietnam, the Sinai, and disarmament, respectively, which they labeled "arrangements" or "accords" to avoid reporting. Does such labeling avoid the Case-Zablocki Act?

B. THE DOMESTIC LEGAL EFFECT OF TREATIES AND EXECUTIVE AGREEMENTS

The Supremacy Clause clearly elevates treaties as the Supreme Law of the Land over state laws. Less clearly, it has been consistently interpreted to give executive agreements that same status, either as a form of "treaty" or as "laws of the United States." But this means only that treaties and executive agreements are supreme over state law, not that they are necessarily equal to one another. William C. Banks, *Treaties and Treaty Power*, in *Oxford Companion to the Supreme Court of the United States* 878 (Kermit L. Hall ed., 1992). If the Constitution is first among equals, why does it differentiate "Laws of the United States which shall be made *in Pursuance thereof*" and "Treaties made, or which shall be made, under the *Authority of the United States*"? U.S. Const. art. VI (emphasis added). And how are we to choose between a statute and a treaty when they are inconsistent?

Reid v. Covert
United States Supreme Court, 1957
354 U.S. 1

[Mrs. Covert killed her husband, a U.S. Air Force sergeant, at an airbase in England. Pursuant to a "status-of-forces" executive agreement with that country, she was tried and convicted by U.S. court-martial without a jury trial under the Uniform Code of Military Justice (UCMJ). On a petition for a writ of habeas corpus, she attacked her conviction on the grounds that it violated her Fifth and Sixth Amendment rights to be tried by a jury after indictment by a grand jury. The District Court granted the petition, and this appeal followed. Mrs. Covert's appeal was consolidated with a like appeal by Mrs. Smith, who had been tried and convicted in similar fashion in Japan.]

Mr. Justice BLACK announced the judgment of the Court and delivered an opinion, in which the Chief Justice, Mr. Justice DOUGLAS, and Mr. Justice BRENNAN join....

I.

[The Supreme Court first held that the Fifth and Sixth Amendments protect American citizens abroad from actions by their government.]

II.

At the time of Mrs. Covert's alleged offense, an executive agreement was in effect between the United States and Great Britain which permitted United States military courts to exercise exclusive jurisdiction over offenses committed in Great Britain by American servicemen or their dependents. For its part, the United States agreed that these military courts would be willing and able to try and to punish all offenses against the laws of Great Britain by such persons. In all material respects, the same situation existed in Japan when Mrs. Smith killed her husband. Even though a court-martial does not give an accused trial by jury and other Bill of Rights protections, the Government contends that Art. 2(11) of U.C.M.J., insofar as it provides for the military trial of dependents accompanying the armed forces in Great Britain and Japan, can be sustained as legislation which is necessary and proper to carry out the United States' obligations under the international agreements made with those countries. The obvious and decisive answer to this, of course, is that no agreement with a foreign nation can confer power on the Congress, or on any other branch of Government, which is free from the restraints of the Constitution.

Article VI, the Supremacy Clause of the Constitution, declares:

> This Constitution, and the Laws of the United States which shall be made in Pursuance thereof; and all Treaties made, or which shall be made, under the Authority of the United States, shall be the supreme Law of the Land; ....

There is nothing in this language which intimates that treaties and laws enacted pursuant to them do not have to comply with the provisions of the Constitution. Nor is there anything in the debates which accompanied the drafting and ratification of the Constitution which even suggests such a result. These debates as well as the history that surrounds the adoption of the treaty provision in Article VI make it clear that the reason treaties were not limited to those made in "pursuance" of the Constitution was so that agreements made by the United States under the Articles of Confederation, including the important peace treaties which concluded the Revolutionary War, would remain in effect. It would be manifestly contrary to the objectives of those who created the Constitution, as well as those who were responsible for the Bill of Rights—let alone alien to our entire constitutional history and tradition—to construe Article VI as permitting the United States to exercise power under an international agreement without observing constitutional prohibitions. In effect, such construction would permit amendment of that document in a manner not sanctioned by Article V. The prohibitions of the Constitution were designed to apply to all branches of the National Government and they cannot be nullified by the Executive or by the Executive and the Senate combined.

B. The Domestic Legal Effect of Treaties and Executive Agreements

There is nothing new or unique about what we say here. This Court has regularly and uniformly recognized the supremacy of the Constitution over a treaty.[33] For example, in Geofroy v. Riggs, 133 U.S. 258, 267, it declared:

> The treaty power, as expressed in the Constitution, is in terms unlimited except by those restraints which are found in that instrument against the action of the government or of its departments, and those arising from the nature of the government itself and of that of the States. It would not be contended that it extends so far as to authorize what the Constitution forbids, or a change in the character of the government or in that of one of the States, or a cession of any portion of the territory of the latter, without its consent.

This Court has also repeatedly taken the position that an Act of Congress, which must comply with the Constitution, is on a full parity with a treaty, and that when a statute which is subsequent in time is inconsistent with a treaty, the statute to the extent of conflict renders the treaty null.[34] It would be completely anomalous to say that a treaty need not comply with the Constitution when such an agreement can be overridden by a statute that must conform to that instrument.

There is nothing in Missouri v. Holland, 252 U.S. 416, which is contrary to the position taken here. There the Court carefully noted that the treaty involved was not inconsistent with any specific provision of the Constitution. The Court was concerned with the Tenth Amendment which reserves to the States or the people all power not delegated to the National Government. To the extent that the United States can validly make treaties, the people and the States have delegated their power to the National Government and the Tenth Amendment is no barrier.

In summary, we conclude that the Constitution in its entirety applied to the trials of Mrs. Smith and Mrs. Covert. Since their court-martial did not meet the requirements of Art. III, §2, or the Fifth and Sixth Amendments we are compelled to determine if there is anything *within* the Constitution which authorizes the military trial of dependents accompanying the armed forces overseas....

[The Court concluded at length that the congressional power to make rules for the government and regulation of the armed forces, U.S. Const. art. I, §8, cl. 14, did not provide the requisite authority. It affirmed the district court judgment releasing Mrs. Covert from custody and reversed the district court judgment against Mrs. Smith, with directions that she also be released.]

[The opinions of Justices HARLAN and FRANKFURTER, concurring in the result, and Justice CLARK, dissenting, are omitted here. Justice WHITTAKER took no part in the consideration or decision of the case.]

[Other parts of this decision are reproduced *infra* p. 640.]

---

33. We recognize that executive agreements are involved here but it cannot be contended that such an agreement rises to greater stature than a treaty.

34. In Whitney v. Robertson, 124 U.S. 190, 194, the Court stated: "By the Constitution a treaty is placed on the same footing, and made of like obligation, with an act of legislation. Both are declared by that instrument to be the supreme law of the land, and no superior efficacy is given to either over the other.... [I]f the two are inconsistent, the one last in date will control the other...."

Committee of U.S. Citizens Living in Nicaragua v. Reagan
United States Court of Appeals, D.C. Circuit, 1988
859 F.2d 929

[In 1986, the International Court of Justice (ICJ) held that the U.S. financial support of paramilitary activities by the Contras against the Sandinista government in Nicaragua violated both a treaty between the countries and customary international law. It concluded that the United States had a duty to refrain from continuing such support. The United States, however, withdrew from the court's jurisdiction before the court's decision, and President Reagan requested and Congress appropriated continued aid after the ICJ decision.

Plaintiffs, organizations, and individuals who opposed this policy brought the instant action for injunctive and declaratory relief against continued U.S. financial support for the Contras contrary to the U.N. Charter and customary international law. The District Court dismissed plaintiffs' entire complaint on political question grounds. The Court of Appeals also expressed serious doubts about the justiciability of plaintiffs' claims but preferred to rest its decision on other grounds. The court's decision on plaintiffs' treaty claim follows.]

MIKVA, Circuit Judge. . . .

B. APPELLANTS HAVE NO BASIS IN DOMESTIC LAW FOR ENFORCING THE ICJ JUDGMENT

1. THE STATUS OF INTERNATIONAL LAW IN THE UNITED STATES' DOMESTIC LEGAL ORDER

Appellants argue that the United States' decision to disregard the ICJ judgment . . . violate[s] part of a United States treaty, namely Article 94 of the U.N. Charter. That article provides that "[e]ach Member of the United Nations undertakes to comply with the decision of the International Court of Justice in any case to which it is a party." . . .

For purposes of the present lawsuit, the key question is not simply whether the United States has violated any . . . legal norms but whether such violations can be remedied by an American court or whether they can only be redressed on an international level. In short, do violations of international law have domestic legal consequences? The answer largely depends on what form the "violation" takes. Here, the alleged violation is the law that Congress enacted and that the President signed, appropriating funds for the Contras. When our government's two political branches, acting together, contravene an international legal norm, does this court have any authority to remedy the violation? The answer is "no" if the type of international obligation that Congress and the President violate is either a treaty or a rule of customary international law. . . .

2. THE EFFECT OF SUBSEQUENT STATUTES UPON PRIOR INCONSISTENT TREATIES

Although appellants' complaint alleges that Congress' funding of the Contras violates Article 94 of the U.N. Charter, appellants seem to concede here that

B. The Domestic Legal Effect of Treaties and Executive Agreements

such a claim is unavailing. They acknowledge, as they must, that "[o]rdinarily, treaty obligations may be overridden by subsequent inconsistent statutes." . . .

In the *Head Money Cases*, 112 U.S. 580 (1884), shipping companies protested payment of a tax on immigrants they had transported to America, arguing that the tax violated treaties of friendship with the immigrants' nations of origin. The Court held that, even if the statute requiring the tax was inconsistent with prior treaties, it necessarily displaced any conflicting treaty provisions for purposes of domestic law.

> A treaty, then, is a law of the land as an act of Congress is, whenever its provisions prescribe a rule by which the rights of the private citizen or subject may be determined. . . .
>
> But even [so] . . . there is nothing in [a treaty] which makes it irrepealable or unchangeable. The Constitution gives it no superiority over an act of Congress in this respect, which may be repealed or modified by an act of a later date. . . .
>
> In short, we are of the opinion that, so far as a treaty made by the United States with any foreign nation can become the subject of judicial cognizance in the courts of this country, it is subject to such acts as Congress may pass for its enforcement, modification, or repeal. [*Id.* at 598-599.]

No American court has wavered from this view in the subsequent century. Indeed, in a comparatively recent case, our court reaffirmed the principle that treaties and statutes enjoy equal status and therefore that inconsistencies between the two must be resolved in favor of the *lex posterior*. In Diggs v. Shultz, 470 F.2d 461 (D.C. Cir. 1972), cert. denied, 411 U.S. 931 (1973), this court reviewed a claim by citizens of what was then Southern Rhodesia, assailing the United States' failure to abide by U.N. Security Council Resolution 232. That resolution directed U.N. members to impose a trade embargo against Rhodesia. The court found that America's contravention of Resolution 232 was required by Congress' adoption of the so-called Byrd Amendment "whose purpose and effect . . . was to detach this country from the U.N. boycott of Southern Rhodesia in blatant disregard of our treaty undertakings." Id. at 466. "Under our constitutional scheme," the court concluded, "Congress can denounce treaties if it sees fit to do so, and there is nothing the other branches of government can do about it . . . [; thus] the complaint [states] no tenable claim in law." Id. at 466-467.

These precedents dispose of any claim by appellants that the United States has violated its treaty obligation under Article 94. It is true, of course, that the facts here differ somewhat from the situation in *Diggs*. Congress has not clearly repudiated the requirement in Article 94 that every nation comply with an ICJ decision "in any case to which it is a party." U.N. Charter, art. 94. Rather, our government asserts that it never consented to ICJ jurisdiction in cases like the Nicaragua dispute. Thus, Congress may well believe that its support for the Contras, while contravening the ICJ judgment, does not violate its treaty obligation under Article 94. And, unless Congress makes clear its intent to abrogate a treaty, a court will not lightly infer such intent but will strive to harmonize the conflicting enactments.

At this stage of the present case, however, the key question is not whether Congress intended to abrogate Article 94. Since appellants *allege* that Congress has breached Article 94, we must determine whether such a claim could ever prevail. The claim could succeed only if appellants could prove that a prior treaty — the U.N. Charter — preempts a subsequent statute, namely the legislation that funds the Contras. It is precisely that argument that the precedents of the Supreme Court and of this court foreclose. We therefore hold that appellants' claims based on treaty violations must fail.

Our conclusion, of course, speaks not at all to whether the United States has upheld its treaty obligations under international law. As the Supreme Court said in the *Head Money Cases*, a treaty "depends for the enforcement of its provisions on the interest and honor of the governments which are parties to it. If these fail, its infraction becomes the subject of international negotiations and reclamations ... [but] with all this the judicial courts have nothing to do and can give no redress." 112 U.S. at 598. This conclusion reflects the United States' adoption of a partly "dualist" — rather than strictly "monist" — view of international and domestic law. "[D]ualists view international law as a discrete legal system [which] ... operates wholly on an inter-nation plane." Louis Henkin, The Constitution and United States Sovereignty: A Century of Chinese Exclusion and Its Progeny, 100 Harv. L. Rev. 853, 864 (1987) (hereinafter Henkin, United States Sovereignty).

It is uncertain whether either our republican form of government or our Constitution's supremacy clause requires this subordination of treaties to inconsistent domestic statutes. Nevertheless, the "[Supreme] Court's jurisprudence about treaties inevitably reflects certain assumptions about the relation between international law and United States law." Henkin, United States Sovereignty, 100 Harv. L. Rev. at 870. Given that dualist jurisprudence, we cannot find — as a matter of *domestic* law — that congressional enactments violate prior treaties.

Finally, we note that even if Congress' breach of a treaty were cognizable in domestic court, appellants would lack standing to rectify the particular breach that they allege here. Article 94 of the U.N. Charter simply does not confer rights on private individuals. Treaty clauses must confer such rights in order for individuals to assert a claim "arising under" them. See U.S. Const. art. III, §2, cl. 1; 28 U.S.C. §1331 (1982). Whether a treaty clause does create such enforcement rights is often described as part of the larger question of whether that clause is "self-executing."

This court has noted that, in "determining whether a treaty is self-executing" in the sense of its creating private enforcement rights, "courts look to the intent of the signatory parties as manifested by the language of the instrument." Diggs v. Richardson, 555 F.2d 848, 851 (D.C. Cir. 1976). The court in Diggs v. Richardson concluded that the U.N. Security Council Resolution that plaintiffs sought to enforce (which barred commercial relations between U.N. members and Namibia) was "not addressed to the judicial branch of our government." Id. The resolution's provisions did not "by their terms confer rights upon individual citizens [but] call[ed] upon governments to take certain actions." Id. Applying the same test to Article 94 of the U.N. Charter, we reach a similar conclusion.

The second paragraph of Article 94 provides that,

> [i]f any party to a case fails to perform the obligations incumbent upon it under a judgment rendered by the [ICJ], the other party may have recourse to the Security

B. The Domestic Legal Effect of Treaties and Executive Agreements

Council, which may, if it deems necessary, make recommendations or decide upon measures to be taken to give effect to the judgment. [U.N. Charter art. 94, ¶2.]

Because only nations can be parties before the ICJ, appellants are not "parties" within the meaning of this paragraph. Clearly, this clause does not contemplate that individuals having no relationship to the ICJ case should enjoy a private right to enforce the ICJ's decision. Our interpretation of Article 94 is buttressed by a related provision in the Statute of the ICJ, which is incorporated by reference in the U.N. Charter. See U.N. Charter art. 92. The Statute provides that "[t]he decision of the Court has no binding force except between the parties and in respect of th[e] particular case." Taken together, these Charter clauses make clear that the purpose of establishing the ICJ was to resolve disputes between national governments. We find in these clauses no intent to vest citizens who reside in a U.N. member nation with authority to enforce an ICJ decision against their own government....

[The court's decision on plaintiffs' customary law claim is reproduced *infra* p. 182.]

NOTES AND QUESTIONS

1. *Missouri v. Holland.* In Missouri v. Holland, 252 U.S. 416 (1920), the Court upheld a statute enacted pursuant to the Migratory Bird Treaty against a Tenth Amendment challenge, even though a federal court had previously sustained such a challenge to an earlier statute that imposed similar restrictions. Referring to the language of the Supremacy Clause highlighted in the introduction to this section, *supra* p. 157, the Court asserted in dicta that "[i]t is obvious that there may be matters of the sharpest exigency for the national well being that an act of Congress could not deal with but that a treaty followed by such an act could...." *Id.* at 433. Does this suggest that the government could by treaty take actions otherwise forbidden by the Constitution? For example, does it mean that the President and the Senate could approve a treaty committing the United States to war in support of an ally without approval by the House? Does *Reid* supply an answer? Is *Holland* distinguishable? *See* Nicholas Quinn Rosenkranz, *Executing the Treaty Power*, 118 Harv. L. Rev. 1868 (2005) (arguing that *Holland* was wrongly decided and that treaties cannot increase the legislative power of Congress).

2. *Self-Executing and Non-Self-Executing Treaties. Committee of U.S. Citizens* quotes *The Head Money Cases*, 112 U.S. 580, 598-599 (1884), for the proposition that a treaty is the legal equivalent of a statute "whenever its provisions prescribe a rule by which the rights of the private citizen or subject may be determined." Chief Justice John Marshall asserted the same proposition more fully:

> Our constitution declares a treaty to be the law of the land. It is, consequently, to be regarded in courts of justice as equivalent to an act of the legislature, whenever it operates of itself, without the aid of any legislative provision. But when the terms of the stipulation import a contract, when either of the parties engages to perform a particular act, the treaty addresses itself to the political, not the judicial

department; and the legislature must execute the contract before it can become the rule for the court. [Foster v. Neilson, 27 U.S. (2 Pet.) 253, 314 (1829).]

Whether a treaty or a provision thereof is "self-executing" or not is therefore significant not only for deciding its enforceability in U.S. courts, but also for deciding whether it authorizes the President to act alone, without further legislation. *See generally* Carlos Manuel Vazquez, *The Four Doctrines of Self-Executing Treaties*, 89 Am. J. Intl. L. 695 (1995).

Although the courts admit the possibility that treaties can be self-executing or non-self-executing, scholars are divided. Some take a dim view of the latter and argue that "the tendency of the Executive branch and in the courts to interpret treaties and treaty provisions as non-self-executing runs counter to the language, and spirit, and history of . . . Constitution." Henkin, *supra* p. 167, at 201. What constitutional text would you cite in support of this view, and why? Others account for the case law recognizing non-self-executing treaties by viewing such treaties as the exception. *See, e.g.*, Vazquez, *supra*, 89 Am. J. Intl. L. 695; Carlos Manuel Vazquez, *Laughing at Treaties*, 99 Colum. L. Rev. 2154, 2176 (1999). Thus, they assert that non-self-executing treaties are either unconstitutional treaties, nonjusticiable precatory or hortatory treaties, treaties that do not create private rights of action, or treaties that expressly require enabling legislation. *Id.* On the other hand, Professor Yoo has vigorously argued that the history of the framing of the Constitution suggests (albeit ambiguously) that, to avoid leaving the people's most direct representatives in the House out of the lawmaking process, no treaty should be construed as self-executing. *Compare* John C. Yoo, *Globalism and the Constitution: Treaties, Non-Self-Execution, and the Original Understanding*, 99 Colum. L. Rev. 1955, 1962 (1999), *with* Martin S. Flaherty, *History Right? Historical Scholarship, Original Understanding, and Treaties as "Supreme Law of the Land,"* 99 Colum. L. Rev. 2095 (1999) (offering rebuttal of Yoo's historical arguments). To give effect to this asserted original intent, Yoo urges the courts to follow "[a] presumption of non-self-execution," at least when the treaty itself is silent. Yoo, *supra*, at 2092-2093. So far, the courts have not sided with either extreme in this academic debate about the domestic legal effect of treaties; they instead continue to find constitutional room for both kinds of treaties.

3. *Subject Matter Limitations on Self-Executing Treaties?* Are there some subjects on which self-executing treaties cannot operate because they fall within the exclusive legislative power of Congress? *See* Edwards v. Carter, 580 F.2d 1055, 1059 (D.C. Cir. 1978) (dictum) (asserting that the Revenue Bill and Appropriations Clauses, U.S. Const. art. I, §7, cl. 1 & §9, cl. 7, respectively, "operate to limit the treaty power because the language of these provisions clearly precludes any method of appropriating money or raising taxes other than through the enactment of laws by the full Congress"), *cert. denied*, 436 U.S. 907 (1978). Many collective defense treaties to which the United States is a party provide that, in the event of an armed attack on a treaty partner, each partner will "act to meet the common danger in accordance with its constitutional processes," or words to that effect. Is this provision self-executing? If it were, would it be constitutional? *See Restatement (Third), supra* p. 166, §111(4)(c) (asserting that an international agreement of the United States is non-self-executing "if implementing legislation is constitutionally required").

B. The Domestic Legal Effect of Treaties and Executive Agreements

4. *Deciding Whether a Treaty Is or Is Not Self-Executing.* How does the court in *Committee of U.S. Citizens* decide whether U.N. Charter article 94 is self-executing? *See also Restatement (Third)* §111(4); Michael A. McKenzie, *Treaty Enforcement in U.S. Courts,* 34 Harv. Intl. L.J. 596, 603 (1993) (adding to factors applied in *Committee of U.S. Citizens,* "the availability and feasibility of alternative enforcement mechanisms, implications of implying self-execution versus non-self-execution, and the existence of appropriate domestic procedures and institutions for the direct implementation of the treaty").

5. *Standing to Enforce.* As *Committee of U.S. Citizens* shows, private litigants are usually held either to lack standing or to have failed to state a cause of action, or both, to enforce non-self-executing international agreements. Courts often reason that private rights are merely "derivative" through their states and that private parties therefore lack standing to invoke international agreements as either swords or shields in the absence of a protest by the signatory state itself. *See, e.g.,* Matta-Ballesteros v. Henman, 896 F.2d 255, 259 (7th Cir.), *cert. denied,* 498 U.S. 878 (1990); United States v. Noriega, 746 F. Supp. 1506, 1533 (S.D. Fla. 1990), *aff'd,* 117 F.3d 1206 (11th Cir. 1997).

6. *Last-in-Time Rule.* If a particular international agreement is the legal equivalent of a statute, it is logical, as a matter of domestic law, that it can be modified or superseded by statute. *Lex posterior*—the last in time—controls. *Restatement (Third)* §115. *See, e.g.,* Whitney v. Robertson, 124 U.S. 190, 193-194 (1888), quoted *supra* p. 175 n.34; The Chinese Exclusion Case, 130 U.S. 581, 600 (1889). *But see* Jordan J. Paust, *Rediscovering the Relationship Between Congressional Power and International Law: Exceptions to the Last in Time Rule and the Primacy of Custom,* 28 Va. J. Intl. L. 392 (1988) (noting case law exceptions to last-in-time rule). Does this mean that Congress can modify or repeal an international agreement? What is the international effect of a subsequent statutory repealer?

7. *Rule of Avoiding Conflict with International Law.* Does your answer to the last question suggest how courts should construe U.S. legislation in light of prior international agreements? *See Restatement (Third)* §114; Ralph G. Steinhardt, *The Role of International Law as a Canon of Domestic Statutory Construction,* 43 Vand. L. Rev. 1103, 1110 (1990) (asserting that "[i]t is plain...that the interpretive role of international law is more common than its controlling role"). Did the court in *Committee of U.S. Citizens* find that Congress intended to violate the U.N. Charter when it appropriated funds for the Contras?

8. *Force and Effect of Executive Agreements.* The Supremacy Clause explicitly equates only treaties with laws of the United States. Do executive agreements have the same domestic legal effect as treaties? In United States v. Pink, 315 U.S. 203, 230 (1942), the Supreme Court declared that a treaty is the law of the land, and that "international compacts and agreements...have a similar dignity." While the case law suggests that congressional-executive agreements and agreements made pursuant to treaties have the same legal effect as constitutional treaties, it is unclear about the effect of sole executive agreements on prior statutory or treaty law. *See CRS Treaty Study, supra* p. 158, at 65-68. In United States v. Guy W. Capps, Inc., 204 F.2d 655, 659-660 (4th Cir. 1953), *aff'd on*

other grounds, 348 U.S. 296 (1955), the court held that a sole executive agreement concerning import limitations does not supersede a prior statute, citing Congress's express authority to regulate foreign commerce. U.S. Const. art. I, §8, cl. 3. How would you explain the difference in the cases? *Cf.* Seery v. United States, 127 F. Supp. 601 (Ct. Cl. 1955) (asserting that it "would indeed be incongruous if the Executive Department alone, without even the limited participation by Congress which is present when a treaty is ratified, could not only nullify ... [an Act of Congress], but, by nullifying that Act ..., destroy the Constitutional right of a citizen."). Does the effect of a sole executive agreement on a prior inconsistent statute depend on the subject matter? *See* Myres S. McDougal & Asher Lans, *Treaties and Congressional-Executive Agreements: Interchangeable Instruments of National Policy: I*, 54 Yale L.J. 181, 317 (1945) (asserting that when a subject is within the President's special competence, he might disregard a prior statute "as an unconstitutional invasion of his own power").

C. THE DOMESTIC LEGAL EFFECT OF CUSTOMARY INTERNATIONAL LAW AND *JUS COGENS*

Committee of U.S. Citizens Living in Nicaragua v. Reagan
United States Court of Appeals, D.C. Circuit, 1988
859 F.2d 929

[The facts of this case are set forth *supra* p. 176.]

MIKVA, J. ...

3. CUSTOMARY INTERNATIONAL LAW AND SUBSEQUENT INCONSISTENT STATUTES

In addition to relying on Article 94 to challenge continued funding of the Contras, appellants also invoke the rule "of customary international law that nations must obey the rulings of an international court to whose jurisdiction they submit." We accept that some version of this rule describes a norm of customary international law. ... For the moment, we assume *arguendo* that Congress' decision to disregard the ICJ judgment violates customary international law.

The question is whether such a violation is cognizable by domestic courts. Once again, the United States' rejection of a purely "monist" view of the international and domestic legal orders shapes our analysis. Statutes inconsistent with principles of customary international law may well lead to international law violations. But within the domestic legal realm, that inconsistent statute simply modifies or supersedes customary international law to the extent of the inconsistency. Although the Supreme Court has never articulated this principle as a firm holding, the Court's persuasive dictum in an important early case established the principle that this and other courts follow.

C. The Domestic Legal Effect of Customary International Law and *Jus Cogens*

In The Paquete Habana, 175 U.S. 677 (1900), the owner of fishing vessels captured and condemned as prize during the Spanish-American War sought compensation from the United States on the ground that customary international law prohibited such seizures. After canvassing prior state practice and the opinions of commentators, the Court concluded that the prohibition against seizure of boats engaged in coastal fishing, which arose at first from considerations of comity between nations, had ripened into "an established rule of international law." Id. at 708. The Court therefore held that the condemnation was improper because "international law is part of our law, and must be ascertained and administered by the courts of justice of appropriate jurisdiction." Id. at 700.

Justice Gray, writing for the Court, qualified this famous statement about the domestic effect of international law with dictum of no less significance: "[W]here there is no treaty, and no controlling executive *or legislative act* or judicial decision, resort must be had to the customs and usages of nations." Id. (emphasis added). Thus, so far as concerned domestic law, the rule was laid down that subsequently enacted statutes would preempt existing principles of customary international law—just as they displaced prior inconsistent treaties....

Few other courts have had occasion to consider the principle that, under domestic law, statutes supersede customary international law. But the principle is implicit in decisions that uphold the statutory abrogation of treaties, "since violation of a treaty is essentially a violation of the principle of customary international law requiring that treaties be observed." Louis Henkin, Foreign Affairs and the Constitution 460 n.61 (1972)....

4. PEREMPTORY NORMS OF INTERNATIONAL LAW (*JUS COGENS*)

Appellants argue that the rule requiring parties who have submitted to an international court to abide by its judgment is not only a principle of customary international law but has become a form of *jus cogens*. Because such peremptory norms are nonderogable and enjoy the highest status within international law, appellants conclude that these norms are absolutely binding upon our government as a matter of domestic law as well. Indeed, appellants assert that "the obligation stemming from the ICJ judgment... is such that it rises to the level of a constitutional obligation, which *cannot* be overridden by statute."

Appellants cite no authority for this assertion that a peremptory norm of international law operates domestically as if it were a part of our Constitution. So far as we know, no federal court has ever considered the concept—much less the domestic effect—of *jus cogens*. The Vienna Convention on the Law of Treaties, which reflects the common understanding of the term, defines *jus cogens* only in relation to *international* law: "A treaty is void if, at the time of its conclusion, it conflicts with a peremptory norm of general international law... [which] is a norm accepted by the international community of States as a whole as a norm from which no derogation is permitted...." Vienna Convention on the Law of Treaties, May 23, 1969, art. 53, U.N. Doc. A/Conf. 39/27, 8 I.L.M. 679 (hereinafter "Vienna Convention").

We need not decide whether an ICJ judgment would restrict Congress' foreign affairs power if that judgment were in fact a peremptory norm of international law. ICJ judgments simply do not meet the Vienna Convention's — or any other authority's — definition of *jus cogens*. To see why, it is useful to clarify the criteria that determine when a rule becomes not only a customary but also a peremptory norm of international law.

"Customary international law results from a general and consistent practice of states followed by them from a sense of legal obligation." Restatement (Third) of Foreign Relations Law §102(2) (1987) (hereinafter "Restatement"). Thus, customary international law is continually evolving. At a crucial stage of that process, "[w]ithin the relevant states, the will has to be formed that the rule will become law if the relevant number of states who share this will is reached." Meijers, How Is International Law Made?, 9 Netherlands Y.B. Intl. L. 3, 5 (1978). As to what constitutes the necessary number of "relevant states," the ICJ has said that "State practice...should have been both extensive and virtually uniform in the sense of the provision invoked." The North Sea Continental Shelf Case (Judgment), 1969 I.C.J. 12, 43. Finally, in order for such a customary norm of international law to become a peremptory norm, there must be a further recognition by "the international community... *as a whole* [that this is] a norm from which no derogation is permitted." Vienna Convention art. 53 (emphasis added).

Given these standards, it is clear that an ICJ judgment of the sort that was rendered against the United States in the Nicaragua case does not rise to the level of *jus cogens*. . . .

Fewer than a third of the U.N.'s member nations have filed unilateral declarations consenting to compulsory jurisdiction, and many of these have imposed significant reservations on the scope of their consent. More to the point, "[i]n the 1970s and 1980s, the Court's compulsory jurisdiction cases have been beset with non-appearing defendants." One scholar concludes that "States do not yet seem to have reached a stage where they are prepared to submit their disputes to international adjudication."... We conclude there is no evidence that an ICJ judgment, in a case of general compulsory jurisdiction, represents "a norm accepted and recognized by the international community of States as a whole as a norm from which no derogation is permitted." Vienna Convention art. 53.

Our conclusion is strengthened when we consider those few norms that arguably do meet the stringent criteria for *jus cogens*. The recently revised Restatement acknowledges two categories of such norms: "the principles of the United Nations Charter prohibiting the use of force," Restatement §102 comment k, and fundamental human rights law that prohibits genocide, slavery, murder, torture, prolonged arbitrary detention, and racial discrimination. Id. §702 & comment n. But see Restatement §331 comment e (doctrine of *jus cogens* is of such "uncertain scope" that a "domestic court should not on its own authority refuse to give effect to an agreement on the ground that it violates a peremptory norm").

Such basic norms of international law as the proscription against murder and slavery may well have the domestic legal effect that appellants suggest. That is, they may well restrain our government in the same way that the Constitution restrains it. If Congress adopted a foreign policy that resulted in the enslavement of our citizens or of other individuals, that policy might well be subject to challenge in domestic court under international law. Such a conclusion was indeed implicit in the landmark decision in Filartiga v. Pena-Irala, 630 F.2d

C. The Domestic Legal Effect of Customary International Law and *Jus Cogens*

876 (2d Cir. 1980), which upheld jurisdiction over a suit by a Paraguayan citizen against a Paraguayan police chief for the death by torture of the plaintiff's brother. The court concluded that "official torture is now prohibited by the law of nations." Id. at 884 (footnote omitted). The same point has been echoed in our own court. Judge Edwards observed in Tel-Oren v. Libyan Arab Republic, 726 F.2d 774 (D.C. Cir. 1984), cert. denied, 470 U.S. 1003 (1985), that "commentators have begun to identify a handful of heinous actions — each of which violates definable, universal and obligatory norms," id. at 781 (Edwards, J., concurring), and that these include, at a minimum, bans on governmental "torture, summary execution, genocide, and slavery." Id. at 791 n.20.

We think it clear, however, that the harm that results when a government disregards or contravenes an ICJ judgment does not generate the level of universal disapprobation aroused by torture, slavery, summary execution, or genocide.... The ICJ judgment does not represent...a peremptory norm....

D. CLAIMS ARISING UNDER THE FIFTH AMENDMENT

Appellants' final argument for enforcing the ICJ judgment is that continued funding of the Contras violates appellants' fifth amendment rights....

1. THE FIFTH AMENDMENT CONJOINED WITH PRINCIPLES OF INTERNATIONAL LAW

Since the Contras' deprivation of appellants' liberty and property is partly funded by the United States government, appellants claim that the government itself has inflicted the deprivation. They further allege that this deprivation "is arbitrary and unreasonable in that it is in violation of Article 94 of the United Nations Charter and is in violation of customary international law as set forth by the ICJ." The allegation of "arbitrary" conduct is crucial to appellants' claim because the "touchstone of [fifth amendment] due process is protection of the individual against arbitrary action of government." Wolff v. McDonnell, 418 U.S. 539, 558 (1974).

This attempt to convert putative violations of international law into violations of the fifth amendment suffers several defects. To begin with, since we have already determined that Congress' violation of a treaty is not cognizable in domestic court, we cannot find that activities that Congress has funded are "arbitrary and unreasonable" (and thus proscribed under the fifth amendment) by virtue of being "in violation of Article 94 of the United Nations Charter." Similarly, we have already determined that (1) even if customary international law requires adherence to ICJ judgments, Congress' violation of that law is not domestically cognizable; [and] (2) an ICJ judgment, by its own terms, operates only between the national governments that are parties to that judgment.... For these very reasons, we must reject appellants' argument that Congress' funding of the Contras violates the fifth amendment solely because it "is in violation of customary international law as set forth by the ICJ." Id.

Even if Congress' contravention of the ICJ judgment were somehow cognizable under the due process clause, such a contravention could not — by itself — transform appellants' injuries into fifth amendment violations. In other words, we disagree with appellants' implicit view that, whenever the government violates a legal norm and that violation coincides with injury to liberty or property interests, a due process violation necessarily results. The standard for what constitutes arbitrary government action under the fifth amendment is by no means so formulaic. Substantive due process doctrine does not protect individuals from all actions that infringe liberty or injure property in violation of some law. Rather, substantive due process prevents "governmental power from being 'used for purposes of oppression,'" or "abuse of government power that shocks the conscience," or action that is "legally irrational [in that] it is not sufficiently keyed to any legitimate state interests.". . .

The circumstances surrounding Congress' decision to disregard the ICJ judgment foreclose any conclusion that Congress thus acted "arbitrarily" against appellants. The United States fully contested the ICJ's jurisdiction in the Nicaragua conflict, invoking applicable principles of international law. When the U.S. government withdrew from the ICJ proceedings in the merits phase of the case, it did so because of a firmly stated view that (1) Nicaragua had not itself consented to, and therefore could not invoke, ICJ jurisdiction; (2) the dispute with Nicaragua was one involving "armed conflict," collective self-defense and preservation of regional stability, and thus fell outside the ICJ's jurisdiction as set forth in the U.N. Charter and in the ICJ's own precedents; and (3) the United States itself had never consented to jurisdiction over this type of conflict since, by reservation, it had expressly excluded "disputes arising under multilateral treaty" from the scope of its consent. See Statement On The U.S. Withdrawal From the Proceedings Initiated By Nicaragua In The International Court of Justice, reprinted in 24 I.L.M. 246 (1985). This objection to the ICJ's jurisdiction was followed by the joint determination of Congress and the President that, notwithstanding the recent ICJ decision, continued funding of the Contras was essential to the national security interests of the United States. See Military Construction Appropriations Act for Fiscal Year 1987, Pub. L. No. 99-500, §101(k), 100 Stat. 1783, 1783-300 (1986).

The United States' justifications for disregarding the ICJ judgment may or may not pass muster under international law. But as a matter of domestic law, these justifications refute any claim that Congress and the President acted so arbitrarily as to transform the resulting harm to appellants into denials of due process. We do not say that, whenever Congress and the President jointly pursue a foreign policy, the impact on individual citizens will inevitably comport with due process. We merely reject appellants' claim that the government acted "arbitrarily" toward them, in violation of their fifth amendment rights, *solely* because it contravened the ICJ judgment.

Finally, appellants' bid to convert a violation of the ICJ judgment into a violation of the fifth amendment fails because the ICJ judgment involves legal principles entirely unrelated to the due process clause. Appellants allege that the United States has injured its own citizens, a claim that the ICJ never considered. Rather, the ICJ held that the United States breached legal duties running between our nation's government and the government of Nicaragua. . . . The discrepancy between these principles of international law and appellants' claims that their government has violated their personal rights underscores the defect in appellants' contention that a violation of the ICJ judgment necessarily constitutes "arbitrary" action that violates their fifth amendment rights. For all of these reasons, we hold that the alleged violation of the ICJ judgment is not a sufficient predicate for a fifth amendment violation....

Sosa v. Alvarez-Machain
United States Supreme Court, 2004
542 U.S. 692

Justice SOUTER delivered the opinion of the Court. The two issues are whether respondent Alvarez-Machain's allegation that the Drug Enforcement Administration instigated his abduction [by José Francisco Sosa and others] from Mexico for criminal trial in the United States supports a claim against the Government under the Federal Tort Claims Act (FTCA or Act), 28 U.S.C. §1346(b)(1), §§2671-2680, and whether he may recover under the Alien Tort Statute (ATS), 28 U.S.C. §1350....

[The Court ruled that Alvarez-Machain had no claim under the FTCA. Under the ATS, Alzarez-Machain asserted a cause of action for violation of international law prohibiting arbitrary arrest and detention. The Court held that the ATS only created subject matter jurisdiction, not a cause of action for violation of international law.]

III...

A...

But holding the ATS jurisdictional raises a new question, this one about the interaction between the ATS at the time of its enactment and the ambient law of the era. Sosa would have it that the ATS was stillborn because there could be no claim for relief without a further statute expressly authorizing adoption of causes of action. *Amici* professors of federal jurisdiction and legal history take a different tack, that federal courts could entertain claims once the jurisdictional grant was on the books, because torts in violation of the law of nations would have been recognized within the common law of the time. We think history and practice give the edge to this latter position....

2

Before there was any ATS, a distinctly American preoccupation with these hybrid international norms had taken shape owing to the distribution of political power from independence through the period of confederation. The Continental Congress was hamstrung by its inability to "cause infractions of treaties, or of the law of nations to be punished," J. Madison, Journal of the Constitutional Convention 60 (E. Scott ed., 1893)....

The Framers responded by vesting the Supreme Court with original jurisdiction over "all Cases affecting Ambassadors, other public ministers and Consuls." U.S. Const., Art. III, §2, and the First Congress followed through. The Judiciary Act reinforced this Court's original jurisdiction over suits brought by diplomats, see 1 Stat. 80, ch. 20, §13, created alienage jurisdiction, §11 and, of course, included the ATS, §9.

3 . . .

The . . . inference to be drawn from the history is that Congress intended the ATS to furnish jurisdiction for a relatively modest set of actions alleging violations of the law of nations. Uppermost in the legislative mind appears to have been offenses against ambassadors, see *id.*, at 118; violations of safe conduct were probably understood to be actionable, *ibid.*, and individual actions arising out of prize captures and piracy may well have also been contemplated. *Id.*, at 113-114. But the common law appears to have understood only those three of the hybrid variety as definite and actionable, or at any rate, to have assumed only a very limited set of claims. . . .

IV

We think it is correct, then, to assume that the First Congress understood that the district courts would recognize private causes of action for certain torts in violation of the law of nations, though we have found no basis to suspect Congress had any examples in mind beyond those torts corresponding to Blackstone's three primary offenses: violation of safe conducts, infringement of the rights of ambassadors, and piracy. We assume, too, that no development in the two centuries from the enactment of §1350 to the birth of the modern line of cases beginning with *Filartiga v. Pena-Irala*, 630 F.2d 876 (C.A.2 1980), has categorically precluded federal courts from recognizing a claim under the law of nations as an element of common law; Congress has not in any relevant way amended §1350 or limited civil common law power by another statute. Still, there are good reasons for a restrained conception of the discretion a federal court should exercise in considering a new cause of action of this kind. Accordingly, we think courts should require any claim based on the present-day law of nations to rest on a norm of international character accepted by the civilized world and defined with a specificity comparable to the features of the 18th-century paradigms we have recognized. This requirement is fatal to Alvarez's claim.

A

A series of reasons argue for judicial caution when considering the kinds of individual claims that might implement the jurisdiction conferred by the early statute. First, the prevailing conception of the common law has changed since 1789 in a way that counsels restraint in judicially applying internationally generated norms. When §1350 was enacted, the accepted conception was of the common law as "a transcendental body of law outside of any particular State but obligatory within it unless and until changed by statute." *Black and White Taxicab & Transfer Co. v. Brown and Yellow Taxicab & Transfer Co.*, 276 U.S. 518, 533 (1928) (Holmes, J., dissenting). Now, however, in most cases where a court is asked to state or formulate a common law principle in a new context, there is a general understanding that the law is not so much found or discovered as it is either made or created. . . .

Second, along with, and in part driven by, that conceptual development in understanding common law has come an equally significant rethinking of the

C. The Domestic Legal Effect of Customary International Law and *Jus Cogens*   189

role of the federal courts in making it. *Erie R. Co. v. Tompkins*, 304 U.S. 64 (1938), was the watershed in which we denied the existence of any federal "general" common law, which largely withdrew to havens of specialty, some of them defined by express congressional authorization to devise a body of law directly. Elsewhere this Court has thought it was in order to create federal common law rules in interstitial areas of particular federal interest. And although we have even assumed competence to make judicial rules of decision of particular importance to foreign relations, such as the act of state doctrine, the general practice has been to look for legislative guidance before exercising innovative authority over substantive law. It would be remarkable to take a more aggressive role in exercising a jurisdiction that remained largely in shadow for much of the prior two centuries.

Third, this Court has recently and repeatedly said that a decision to create a private right of action is one better left to legislative judgment in the great majority of cases....

Fourth, the subject of those collateral consequences is itself a reason for a high bar to new private causes of action for violating international law, for the potential implications for the foreign relations of the United States of recognizing such causes should make courts particularly wary of impinging on the discretion of the Legislative and Executive Branches in managing foreign affairs.... Since many attempts by federal courts to craft remedies for the violation of new norms of international law would raise risks of adverse foreign policy consequences, they should be undertaken, if at all, with great caution. Cf. *Tel-Oren v. Libyan Arab Republic*, 726 F.2d 774, 813 (C.A.D.C.1984) (Bork, J., concurring) (expressing doubt that §1350 should be read to require "our courts [to] sit in judgment of the conduct of foreign officials in their own countries with respect to their own citizens").

The fifth reason is particularly important in light of the first four. We have no congressional mandate to seek out and define new and debatable violations of the law of nations, and modern indications of congressional understanding of the judicial role in the field have not affirmatively encouraged greater judicial creativity. It is true that a clear mandate appears in the Torture Victim Protection Act of 1991, 106 Stat. 73, providing authority that "establish[es] an unambiguous and modern basis for" federal claims of torture and extrajudicial killing, H.R. Rep. No. 102-367, pt. 1, p. 3 (1991). But that affirmative authority is confined to specific subject matter, and although the legislative history includes the remark that §1350 should "remain intact to permit suits based on other norms that already exist or may ripen in the future into rules of customary international law," *id.*, at 4, Congress as a body has done nothing to promote such suits. Several times, indeed, the Senate has expressly declined to give the federal courts the task of interpreting and applying international human rights law, as when its ratification of the International Covenant on Civil and Political Rights declared that the substantive provisions of the document were not self-executing.

B

These reasons argue for great caution in adapting the law of nations to private rights.... Justice SCALIA concludes, however, that two subsequent developments should be understood to preclude federal courts from recognizing any further international norms as judicially enforceable today, absent further congressional action. As described before, we now tend to understand common law not as a discoverable reflection of universal reason but, in a positivistic way, as a product of human choice. And we now adhere to a conception of limited judicial power first expressed in reorienting federal diversity jurisdiction, see *Erie R. Co. v. Tompkins*, 304 U.S. 64 (1938), that federal courts have no authority to derive "general" common law.

Whereas Justice SCALIA sees these developments as sufficient to close the door to further independent judicial recognition of actionable international norms, other considerations persuade us that the judicial power should be exercised on the understanding that the door is still ajar subject to vigilant doorkeeping, and thus open to a narrow class of international norms today. *Erie* did not in terms bar any judicial recognition of new substantive rules, no matter what the circumstances, and post-*Erie* understanding has identified limited enclaves in which federal courts may derive some substantive law in a common law way. For two centuries we have affirmed that the domestic law of the United States recognizes the law of nations. See, *e.g.*, [Banco National de Cuba v. Sabbatino, 376 U.S. 398, 423 (1964)] ("[I]t is, of course, true that United States courts apply international law as a part of our own in appropriate circumstances"); *The Paquete Habana*, 175 U.S. [677, 700 (1900)] ("International law is part of our law, and must be ascertained and administered by the courts of justice of appropriate jurisdiction, as often as questions of right depending upon it are duly presented for their determination"); *The Nereide,* 9 Cranch 388, 423 (1815) (Marshall, C.J.) ("[T]he Court is bound by the law of nations which is a part of the law of the land"); see also *Texas Industries, Inc. v. Radcliff Materials, Inc.,* 451 U.S. 630, 641 (1981) (recognizing that "international disputes implicating...our relations with foreign nations" are one of the "narrow areas" in which "federal common law" continues to exist). It would take some explaining to say now that federal courts must avert their gaze entirely from any international norm intended to protect individuals.

We think an attempt to justify such a position would be particularly unconvincing in light of what we know about congressional understanding bearing on this issue lying at the intersection of the judicial and legislative powers. The First Congress, which reflected the understanding of the framing generation and included some of the Framers, assumed that federal courts could properly identify some international norms as enforceable in the exercise of §1350 jurisdiction. We think it would be unreasonable to assume that the First Congress would have expected federal courts to lose all capacity to recognize enforceable international norms simply because the common law might lose some metaphysical cachet on the road to modern realism. Later Congresses seem to have shared our view. The position we take today has been assumed by some federal courts for 24 years, ever since the Second Circuit decided *Filartiga v. Pena-Irala,* 630 F.2d 876 (C.A.2 1980) .... Congress, however, has not only expressed no disagreement with our view of the proper exercise of the judicial power, but has responded to its most notable instance by enacting legislation supplementing the judicial determination in some detail. See *supra* (discussing the Torture Victim Protection Act).

While we agree with Justice SCALIA to the point that we would welcome any congressional guidance in exercising jurisdiction with such obvious potential to

C. The Domestic Legal Effect of Customary International Law and *Jus Cogens*

affect foreign relations, nothing Congress has done is a reason for us to shut the door to the law of nations entirely. It is enough to say that Congress may do that at any time (explicitly, or implicitly by treaties or statutes that occupy the field) just as it may modify or cancel any judicial decision so far as it rests on recognizing an international norm as such.[19]

C

We must still, however, derive a standard or set of standards for assessing the particular claim Alvarez raises, and for this case it suffices to look to the historical antecedents. Whatever the ultimate criteria for accepting a cause of action subject to jurisdiction under §1350, we are persuaded that federal courts should not recognize private claims under federal common law for violations of any international law norm with less definite content and acceptance among civilized nations than the historical paradigms familiar when §1350 was enacted. See, *e.g., United States v. Smith*, 5 Wheat. 153, 163-180 (1820) (illustrating the specificity with which the law of nations defined piracy). This limit upon judicial recognition is generally consistent with the reasoning of many of the courts and judges who faced the issue before it reached this Court. See *Filartiga, supra*, at 890 ("[F]or purposes of civil liability, the torturer has become — like the pirate and slave trader before him — *hostis humani generis*, an enemy of all mankind"). And the determination whether a norm is sufficiently definite to support a cause of action should (and, indeed, inevitably must) involve an element of judgment about the practical consequences of making that cause available to litigants in the federal courts.[21]

---

19. Our position does not, as Justice SCALIA suggests, imply that every grant of jurisdiction to a federal court carries with it an opportunity to develop common law (so that the grant of federal-question jurisdiction would be equally as good for our purposes as §1350). Section 1350 was enacted on the congressional understanding that courts would exercise jurisdiction by entertaining some common law claims derived from the law of nations; and we know of no reason to think that federal-question jurisdiction was extended subject to any comparable congressional assumption. Further, our holding today is consistent with the division of responsibilities between federal and state courts after *Erie*, as a more expansive common law power related to 28 U.S.C. §1331 might not be.

21. This requirement of clear definition is not meant to be the only principle limiting the availability of relief in the federal courts for violations of customary international law, though it disposes of this case. For example, the European Commission argues as *amicus curiae* that basic principles of international law require that before asserting a claim in a foreign forum, the claimant must have exhausted any remedies available in the domestic legal system, and perhaps in other fora such as international claims tribunals. We would certainly consider this requirement in an appropriate case.

Another possible limitation that we need not apply here is a policy of case-specific deference to the political branches. For example, there are now pending in federal district court several class actions seeking damages from various corporations alleged to have participated in, or abetted, the regime of apartheid that formerly controlled South Africa. See *In re South African Apartheid Litigation*, 238 F. Supp. 2d 1379 (JPML 2002) (granting a motion to transfer the cases to the Southern District of New York). The Government of South Africa has said that these cases interfere with the policy embodied by its Truth and Reconciliation Commission, which "deliberately avoided a 'victors' justice' approach to the crimes of apartheid and chose instead one based on confession and absolution, informed by the principles of reconciliation, reconstruction, reparation and goodwill." The United States has agreed. In such cases, there is a strong argument that federal courts should give serious weight to the Executive Branch's view of the case's impact on foreign policy.

Thus, Alvarez's detention claim must be gauged against the current state of international law, looking to those sources we have long, albeit cautiously, recognized....

To begin with, Alvarez cites two well-known international agreements that, despite their moral authority, have little utility under the standard set out in this opinion. He says that his abduction by Sosa was an "arbitrary arrest" within the meaning of the Universal Declaration of Human Rights (Declaration), G.A. Res. 217A (III), U.N. Doc. A/810 (1948). And he traces the rule against arbitrary arrest not only to the Declaration, but also to article nine of the International Covenant on Civil and Political Rights (Covenant), Dec. 19, 1996, 999 U.N.T.S. 171, to which the United States is a party, and to various other conventions to which it is not. But the Declaration does not of its own force impose obligations as a matter of international law. And, although the Covenant does bind the United States as a matter of international law, the United States ratified the Covenant on the express understanding that it was not self-executing and so did not itself create obligations enforceable in the federal courts. Accordingly, Alvarez cannot say that the Declaration and Covenant themselves establish the relevant and applicable rule of international law. He instead attempts to show that prohibition of arbitrary arrest has attained the status of binding customary international law....

Alvarez... invokes a general prohibition of "arbitrary" detention defined as officially sanctioned action exceeding positive authorization to detain under the domestic law of some government, regardless of the circumstances. Whether or not this is an accurate reading of the Covenant, Alvarez cites little authority that a rule so broad has the status of a binding customary norm today. He certainly cites nothing to justify the federal courts in taking his broad rule as the predicate for a federal lawsuit, for its implications would be breathtaking. His rule would support a cause of action in federal court for any arrest, anywhere in the world, unauthorized by the law of the jurisdiction in which it took place, and would create a cause of action for any seizure of an alien in violation of the Fourth Amendment, supplanting the actions under Rev. Stat. §1979, 42 U.S.C. §1983 and *Bivens v. Six Unknown Fed. Narcotics Agents,* 403 U.S. 388 (1971), that now provide damages remedies for such violations....

Whatever may be said for the broad principle Alvarez advances, in the present, imperfect world, it expresses an aspiration that exceeds any binding customary rule having the specificity we require. Creating a private cause of action to further that aspiration would go beyond any residual common law discretion we think it appropriate to exercise. It is enough to hold that a single illegal detention of less than a day, followed by the transfer of custody to lawful authorities and a prompt arraignment, violates no norm of customary international law so well defined as to support the creation of a federal remedy.

***

The judgment of the Court of Appeals is *Reversed.*

Justice SCALIA, with whom THE CHIEF JUSTICE and Justice THOMAS join, concurring in part and concurring in the judgment. There is not much that I would add to the Court's detailed opinion, and only one thing that I would subtract: its reservation of a discretionary power in the Federal Judiciary to create causes of

C. The Domestic Legal Effect of Customary International Law and *Jus Cogens*

action for the enforcement of international-law-based norms. Accordingly, I join Parts I, II, and III of the Court's opinion in these consolidated cases. Although I agree with much in Part IV, I cannot join it because the judicial lawmaking role it invites would commit the Federal Judiciary to a task it is neither authorized nor suited to perform....

III

The analysis in the Court's opinion departs from my own in this respect: After concluding in Part III that "the ATS is a jurisdictional statute creating no new causes of action," the Court addresses at length in Part IV the "good reasons for a restrained conception of the *discretion* a federal court should exercise in considering a new cause of action" under the ATS (emphasis added). By framing the issue as one of "discretion," the Court skips over the antecedent question of authority. This neglects the "lesson of *Erie*," that "grants of jurisdiction alone" (which the Court has acknowledged the ATS to be) "are not themselves grants of law-making authority." [Daniel J. Meltzer, *Customary International Law, Foreign Affairs, and Federal Common Law*, 42 Va. J. Intl. L. 513 (2002)], at 541. On this point, the Court observes only that no development between the enactment of the ATS (in 1789) and the birth of modern international human rights litigation under that statute (in 1980) "has categorically *precluded* federal courts from recognizing a claim under the law of nations as an element of common law" (emphasis added). This turns our jurisprudence regarding federal common law on its head. The question is not what case or congressional action *prevents* federal courts from applying the law of nations as part of the general common law; it is what *authorizes* that peculiar exception from *Erie's* fundamental holding that a general common law *does not exist*....

Because today's federal common law is not our Framers' general common law, the question presented by the suggestion of discretionary authority to enforce the law of nations is not whether to extend old-school general-common-law adjudication. Rather, it is whether to create new federal common law. The Court masks the novelty of its approach when it suggests that the difference between us is that we would "close the door to further independent judicial recognition of actionable international norms," whereas the Court would permit the exercise of judicial power "on the understanding that the door is still ajar subject to vigilant doorkeeping." The general common law was the old door. We do not close that door today, for the deed was done in *Erie*. Federal common law is a *new* door. The question is not whether that door will be left ajar, but whether this Court will open it....

American law—the law made by the people's democratically elected representatives—does not recognize a category of activity that is so universally disapproved by other nations that it is automatically unlawful here, and automatically gives rise to a private action for money damages in federal court. That simple principle is what today's decision should have announced.

[Concurring opinions of GINSBURG and BREYER, JJ., are omitted.]

NOTES AND QUESTIONS

a. The Making and Incorporation of Customary International Law

1. *The Making of Customary International Law.* How is customary international law made? *See Restatement (Third), supra* p. 166, §102(2) ("Customary international law results from a general and consistent practice of states followed by them from a sense of legal obligation.") (*opinio juris*). *See also* Jordan Paust, *International Law as Law of the United States* 1-5 (1995); Anthony D'Amato, *The Concept of Custom in International Law* (1971). How does the process compare to the process for making common law? *See* Henkin, *supra* p. 167, at 878-886. To the process for establishing constitutional custom? How, once established, is customary international law changed? *See* Phillip R. Trimble, *A Revisionist View of Customary International Law,* 33 UCLA L. Rev. 665, 710-712 (1986). Notwithstanding the holding of The Paquete Habana, some scholars have complained that customary international law is so malleable that it is no more than "a matter of taste, ... [and] [a]s such, ... cannot function as a legitimate source of substantive legal norms...." J. Patrick Kelly, *The Twilight of Customary International Law,* 40 Va. J. Intl. L. 449, 451 (2000). *See also* Jack L. Goldsmith & Eric A. Posner, *A Theory of Customary International Law,* 66 U. Chi. L. Rev. 1113 (1999).

2. *Incorporating Customary International Law as a Rule of Decision.* The Paquete Habana holds that "international law is part of our law" and indicates that it includes "the customs and usages of nations," *supra* p. 183. The statements have become virtually hornbook law, as reflected in the *Restatement (Third)* §111, cmt. d ("customary international law, while not mentioned explicitly in the Supremacy Clause, [is] also federal law.... Customary international law is considered to be like common law in the United States, but it is federal law.").

Sosa, of course, dealt strictly with the scope of the ATS — specifically, which international law claims were enforceable under the ATS. But does it cast doubt on the breadth, if not correctness, of the *Restatement*'s statement of the law?

3. *Enforcing Customary International Law Under the ATS.* Is *Filartiga*, noted in both of the principal cases, still good law after *Sosa*? Would an alien have a claim under the ATS for murder by terrorist attack? For unlawful military detention or abusive military interrogation? For transnational trafficking in women for the purpose of prostitution? If you are not sure, what changes in international law would it take to make these claims actionable under the ATS according to the reasoning of *Sosa*?

b. "Controlling" Executive and Legislative Acts and Judicial Decisions

1. *Controlling Legislative Acts and Customary Law.* As the Supreme Court said in Murray v. The Schooner Charming Betsy, 6 U.S. (2 Cranch) 64, 118 (1804), and as *Committee of U.S. Citizens* reaffirms, *supra* p. 177, our laws should be construed, where fairly possible, to avoid violating customary, no less than conventional, international law. But if reconciliation proves impossible, which prevails? If the conflict cannot be fairly avoided and customary international law is incorporated into our federal common law, does it necessarily follow that Congress

C. The Domestic Legal Effect of Customary International Law and *Jus Cogens*

can override it by statute? *See* Henkin, *supra* p. 167, at 876-877 (no). And if Congress can, will any statute do? Did the Court's reference in The Paquete Habana to "controlling... legislative act" imply that there are some statutes that do not override customary international law? What is the implication of the last-in-time rule, *supra* p. 181, for the domestic effect of customary international law? Because "custom is either constantly reenacted through a process of recognition and behavior involving patterns of expectation and practice or it loses its validity and force as law," is customary law "necessarily 'last in time' "? *See* Paust, *supra* p. 181, at 418, 436-437.

2. *Controlling Judicial Decisions and Customary Law.* The dictum in The Paquete Habana also suggests that controlling judicial decisions can override customary international law. By what theory? Is *Sosa* consistent with this dictum?

3. *Controlling Executive Acts and Customary Law.* The most controversial implication of the *Paquete Habana* dictum is that a controlling executive act may override customary international law. Consider, first, arguments against this proposition. Can you make one based on the *Charming Betsy* rule of avoidance? If you recast this rule as a presumption of congressional intent that the United States abide by international law, what is the implication for presidential power under Justice Jackson's typology, *supra* p. 55? *See* Jules Lobel, *The Limits of Constitutional Power: Conflicts Between Foreign Policy and International Law*, 71 Va. L. Rev. 1071, 1120 (1985).

Another argument against the executive power to override customary international law flows from its selective incorporation into the federal common law.

> Federal common law is binding on every executive branch official, including the President. Congress can by statute create a different rule, however, because federal common law is interstitial; it fills in gaps between the statutes and gives way when an inconsistent law is enacted. Consequently, with congressional authorization, the Chief Executive can disregard any norm of customary international law. But in the face of congressional silence, he is required to respect a clearly defined and widely accepted norm of customary international law. [Michael J. Glennon, *Can the President Do No Wrong?*, 80 Am. J. Intl. L. 923 (1986).]

See also Jordan J. Paust, *The President Is Bound by International Law*, 81 Am. J. Intl. L. 377, 388-389 (1987); Michael J. Glennon, *Raising the Paquete Habana: Is Violation of Customary International Law By the Executive Unconstitutional?*, 80 Nw. U. L. Rev. 321 (1986); Lobel, *supra*, at 1078-1090 (tracing historical relationship between common law, natural law, and the law of nations). *Sosa* stresses the very limited common lawmaking authority of the courts. Does the President have any? *See* Henkin, *supra* p. 167, at 879 (no general lawmaking authority). Finally, consider the potential consequences of a U.S. violation of international law. Do they suggest any practical allocation of the power to violate among the three branches? *See* Glennon, *supra*, 80 Nw. U. L. Rev. at 360-361.

The chief argument for executive power to override customary international law is grounded in the process by which new consensus is forged in the international community.

If a nation or a group of nations seeks to alter an established rule of customary international law, it must forge a new state practice and *opinio juris*. This development does not take place instantaneously; rather it takes time. In order to effect that change, states interested in a new rule of customary law must take action that violates existing law and they must encourage others to do the same....

If customary international law were static, or there were an international legislature capable of changing the law, a required congressional authorization whenever the United States sought to violate international law would be manageable. But in the present system, required congressional approval would place unacceptable obstacles in the way of U.S. participation in the international legal system. The evolution of the community law system would not be amenable to case-by-case authorization by Congress. Just as the international system requires that the President be able to enter into executive agreements and, apparently, to terminate treaties unilaterally, so must the President have the unilateral power to enter into the international lawmaking process. [Jonathan I. Charney, *The Power of the Executive Branch of the United States Government to Violate Customary International Law*, 80 Am. J. Intl. L. 913, 914, 916-917 (1986).]

See also Henkin, *supra* p. 167, at 881-883 (arguing that the President may unilaterally terminate or modify customary international law, and, more problematically, violate such law when his act is "within the confines of his role as sole organ or as commander-in-chief").

4. *Who Performs the Controlling Executive Act?* Assuming that a controlling executive act can supersede customary international law, what officer must perform that act? Does The Paquete Habana give an answer? *See* Glennon, *supra* p. 195, 80 Nw. U. L. Rev. at 338-339. Does Professor Charney's argument for the overriding effect of controlling presidential acts, *supra* p. 195, suggest an answer? In Garcia-Mir v. Meese, 788 F.2d 1446 (11th Cir.), *cert. denied sub nom.* Ferrer-Mazorra v. Meese, 479 U.S. 889 (1986), the court held that an act of the Attorney General overrode presumed international customary law prohibiting prolonged arbitrary detention, although the court acknowledged that The Paquete Habana "suggests that lower level officials cannot by their acts render international law inapplicable." 788 F.2d at 1454.

Recall that courts will not lightly infer a congressional intent to abrogate a treaty. *See Committee of U.S. Citizens, supra* p. 177, 859 F.2d at 936-937. How clear must the *executive* intent be to override customary law? *See* Ralph G. Steinhardt, *Human Rights Litigation and the "One-Voice" Orthodoxy in Foreign Affairs,* in *World Justice? U.S. Courts and International Human Rights* 23, 39 (Mark Gibney ed., 1991) (suggesting that the executive is "oblige[d] at least to overrule a prior position of [international] law specifically and explicitly"). What could be the disadvantages of requiring a clear statement? *See* Charney, *supra,* at 919 ("In the present international system, a state seeking a new rule of customary law justifies its actions by arguing that they are within the law.... [N]o state assert[s] that it [is] violating existing law.").

c. **Codifying International Law**

Codifying International Law. Congress can expressly incorporate customary international law into our own by codifying such law. Congress is vested with

C. The Domestic Legal Effect of Customary International Law and *Jus Cogens*

the constitutional power to "define and punish Piracies and Felonies committed on the high Seas, and Offenses Against the Law of Nations." U.S. Const. art. I, §8, cl. 20. In United States v. Arjona, 120 U.S. 479, 484 (1887), the Court upheld an exercise of this power, explaining that the law of nations requires every state to use due diligence to prevent wrongs done within its territory to another state with which it is at peace. Among the earliest statutes enacted for this purpose were the Neutrality Act, 18 U.S.C. §960 (2000), *infra* p. 371, which criminalizes hostile activities conducted from U.S. territory against nations with which we are at peace, and statutes criminalizing piracy, 18 U.S.C. §§1651-1661 (2000), as well as statutes that authorize the President to use naval force to protect U.S. merchants from pirates. 33 U.S.C. §§381-382, 386 (2000). The Supreme Court has also sustained legislation that merely incorporates international customary law by reference without marking its precise boundaries. *See, e.g.*, Ex parte Quirin, 317 U.S. 1, 30 (1942), *infra* p. 714 (sustaining military trial of German saboteurs under congressionally approved measure referring to "offenders or offenses that . . . *by the law of war* may be triable by military commissions") (emphasis added).

d. Jus Cogens

1. *Jus Cogens.* What is the difference between customary international law and *jus cogens*? In Siderman de Blake v. Republic of Argentina, 965 F.2d 699, 715 (9th Cir. 1992), *cert. denied*, 507 U.S. 1017 (1993), the court explained it as follows:

> Customary international law, like international law defined by treaties and other international agreements, rests on the consent of states. A state that persistently objects to a norm of customary international law . . . is not bound. . . .
> In contrast, *jus cogens* "embraces customary laws considered binding on all nations" and is "derived from values taken to be fundamental by the international community, rather than from the fortuitous or self-interested choices of nations". . . . [T]he fundamental and universal norms constituting *jus cogens* transcend such consent, as exemplified by the theories underlying the judgments of the Nuremberg tribunals following World War II. [Citation omitted.]

Does this basis for *jus cogens* suggest an answer to the question of primacy in our own law that was reserved in *Committee of U.S. Citizens*? Or does *Sosa*, by implication (emphasizing that Congress intended to authorize claims for piracy under the ATS)?

2. *Jus Cogens as Guide to Construction of Constitutional Law.* Even if *jus cogens* is not controlling by its own force, its possible overlap with constitutionally based human rights may give it indirect force as a guide to construction of constitutional law. Why was the court in *Committee of U.S. Citizens* not persuaded by the customary international law in determining whether the government's action violated due process?

What are the advantages, if any, of using international law in this fashion? *See* Harold Hongju Koh, *Is International Law Really State Law?*, 111 Harv. L. Rev. 1824, 1853 (1998) ("When construing customary international law, federal courts arguably exercise less judicial discretion than when making other kinds of federal common law, as their task is not to create rules willy-nilly, but rather to discern rules of decision from an existing corpus of customary international law rules."); Tamela R. Hughlett, *International Law: The Use of International Law as a Guide to Interpretation of the United States Constitution*, 45 Okla. L. Rev. 169, 180-183 (1992) ("The use of international law is even more compelling than most interpretive methods because it is not the subjective decision of a single judge, but a product of years of distillation of principles formed through international consensus.").

What are the disadvantages? *See* Jonathan Turley, *Dualistic Values in the Age of International Jurisprudence*, 44 Hastings L.J. 185, 185 (1993) (arguing that U.S. rejection of monism reflects a distrust of laws that have not undergone the test of a balanced and checked deliberative process); Trimble, *supra* p. 194, at 708-709, 713-714, 716-725 (arguing that courts lack the institutional capacity to participate fully in the development of customary international law and that application of that law by U.S. courts is illegitimate because it is irreconcilable with American political tradition). *See also* Curtis A. Bradley & Jack L. Goldsmith, *Customary International Law as Federal Common Law: A Critique of the Modern Position*, 110 Harv. L. Rev. 815, 857 (1997) ("the modern position that [customary international law] is federal common law is in tension with basic notions of American representative democracy").

How would you judge this debate in light of *Sosa*?

3. *Just Say No?* In alarmed response to the declared willingness of some Justices of the Supreme Court to consider international law in deciding domestic law issues, a bill was introduced in the House in 2003 declaring that "[t]he Supreme Court should base its decisions on the Constitution and the Laws of the United States, and not on the law of any foreign country or any international law." H.R. 446, 108th Cong. (2003). Do you see any legal issues that would be raised by such a measure? Legal issues aside, would it be a good idea?

II
Using Force Abroad

War in General 8

> Perhaps it would not be impossible to write a systematic theory of war, full of intelligence and substance; but the theories we presently possess are very different. Quite apart from their unscientific spirit, they try so hard to make their systems coherent and complete that they are stuffed with commonplaces, truisms, and nonsense of every kind.
>
> *Carl von Clausewitz, c. 1816-1818*[1]

> We are living in a pre-war and not a post-war world.
>
> *Eugene V. Rostow, 1976*[2]

In Bas v. Tingy, 4 U.S. (4 Dall.) 37, 43 (1800), *supra* p. 94, Justice Chase used the label "general war" to describe an armed conflict that is not "limited in place, in objects, and in time" and is restricted and regulated only by the *jus belli*, the law of war. The Vietnam War, which we analyze in this chapter, fits that definition in some respects. The U.S. government poured several hundred billion dollars into that conflict over a period of more than two decades, and 58,000 Americans and more than a million Vietnamese lost their lives in the process. On the other hand, the use of U.S. forces was confined to one fairly small geographical area; there was no general mobilization of military and civilian resources during the Vietnam War, as there had been in the two world wars; no new national emergency was declared, as in the Korean War; and Congress did not formally declare war against another sovereign state.

The commitments of human resources and materiel may be less in "imperfect wars" (again borrowing the term from early cases like Bas v. Tingy), or what are sometimes termed "low-intensity conflicts," and in secret wars, when the United States uses force abroad without disclosing its actions. Still, for various reasons the stakes may be just as high.

The labels attached to particular conflicts are important, because they affect the sources and scope of authority and the decision-making process for sending military forces into battle. Yet the same basic legal principles apply in both big wars and small ones, perfect and imperfect wars, and covert uses of force. This chapter addresses the labels and their significance. It also applies the

---

1. Author's preface to an unpublished manuscript on the theory of war, in Carl von Clausewitz, *On War* 61 (Michael Howard & Peter Paret eds., 1976).

2. Quoted in Robert Scheer, *With Enough Shovels: Reagan, Bush and Nuclear War* 5 (1982), *reprinted in* Thomas Powers & Ruthven Tremain, *Total War: What It Is, How It Got That Way* 136 (1988).

principles introduced in earlier chapters to one conflict that has profoundly shaped our thinking about war in general.

A. GOING TO WAR IN VIETNAM

The Vietnam War was — and remains — extremely controversial. You must not underestimate the complexity of the legal and political issues surrounding America's longest foreign war, nor the depth of feeling in those touched by it. You should also bear in mind that the record is still fragmentary, still being written. Much of what is set out in the following brief report was not known to the American people until long after the events described, and was not known even to members of Congress charged by the Constitution with initiating and supporting the continuation of war.

We begin with a brief historical sketch of the war and then consider a legal justification for U.S. involvement prepared by a lawyer in the Johnson administration. The balance of this section is devoted to a succession of lawsuits testing the legality of the war.

1. How the War Began: A Brief History[3]

The Viet people have a national identity dating back at least to the third century B.C., when they occupied an area comprising much of what came to be known as North Vietnam. Despite a number of interruptions (including occupation by the Chinese at intervals spanning more than a thousand years), Vietnam expanded southward until, at the beginning of the nineteenth century, it included roughly the same geographical area that it does today. Before the end of the century, however, Vietnam, like its neighbors Laos and Cambodia, became a part of French Indochina. It was then taken over by the Japanese at the beginning of World War II.

---

3. This account is drawn from a variety of sources, among them Larry H. Addington, *America's War in Vietnam: A Short Narrative History* (2000); Phillip B. Davidson, *Vietnam at War: The History: 1946-1975* (1988); Daniel Ellsberg, *Secrets: A Memoir of Vietnam and the Pentagon Papers* (2002); Bernard B. Fall, *The Two Viet-Nams* (1963); Frances Fitzgerald, *Fire in the Lake* (1972); George C. Herring, *America's Longest War: The United States and Vietnam, 1950-1975* (2d ed. 1986); David Kaiser, *American Tragedy: Kennedy, Johnson, and the Origins of the Vietnam War* (2000); Stanley Karnow, *Vietnam: A History* (1983); Gabriel Kolko, *Anatomy of a War: Vietnam, the United States, and the Modern Historical Experience* (1985); Robert S. McNamara, *In Retrospect: The Tragedy and Lessons of Vietnam* (1995); John Prados, *Essay: 40th Anniversary of the Gulf of Tonkin Incident*, Aug. 4, 2004, at http://www.gwu.edu/~nsarchiv/NSAEBB/NSAEBB132/essay.htm; John Prados, *The Hidden History of the Vietnam War* (1995); Neil Sheehan, *A Bright Shining Lie: John Paul Vann and America in Vietnam* (1988); *The Pentagon Papers* (Neil Sheehan ed., 1971); *The Pentagon Papers: The Defense Department History of United States Decision-making on Vietnam* (Mike Gravel ed., 1971) (4 vols.); *The Vietnam Reader* (Bernard B. Fall & Marcus G. Raskin eds., 1965); S. Comm. on Foreign Relations, *Hearings on the Causes, Origins, and Lessons of the Vietnam War*, 92d Cong. (1972); and a multivolume report prepared by the Congressional Research Service for the Senate Committee on Foreign Relations, *The U.S. Government and the Vietnam War: Part I, 1945-1961*, and *Part II, 1961-1964*, S. Prt. No. 98-185 (1984); *Part III, January-July 1965*, S. Prt. No. 100-163 (1988).

A. Going to War in Vietnam

Before the French returned to power in 1945, the Viet Minh, a coalition of nationalist groups led by Ho Chi Minh, declared the independent Democratic Republic of Vietnam with its headquarters in Hanoi. The French refused to recognize this indigenous government, however, and repeated appeals by Ho Chi Minh during 1945-1946 for U.S. assistance were ignored. France then became locked in a guerilla war that continued for more than seven years, with the Viet Minh receiving critical support from the Communist Chinese beginning in 1950.

Alarmed at the prospect of a Communist takeover in Vietnam, the U.S. government provided escalating economic and military aid to the French — from $10 million in 1950 to $1.1 billion in 1954 — and even drew up contingency plans for U.S. military intervention that included the use of atomic weapons. Despite French requests, only a small number of U.S. military advisors were sent to Vietnam before the disastrous defeat of French forces at Dienbienphu in May 1954. In July of that year the French, with no realistic military or political alternatives, signed the Geneva Accords, in which they agreed to a cease-fire and withdrawal to the south of a demilitarized zone along the seventeenth parallel. It was understood that no additional troops or equipment would be introduced into either the North or the South except to maintain the status quo. The signatories also agreed that the country would be reunified following elections in 1956. Although neither the United States nor the newly formed State of Vietnam, based in Saigon and supported by the United States as a non-Communist alternative to Ho Chi Minh's government, signed the Accords, the United States pledged that it would not interfere with the agreement.

Yet U.S. leaders were dismayed, fearing (probably correctly) a Communist electoral victory in 1956. Even before the Accords were signed, President Eisenhower dispatched a secret military mission led by Colonel Edward G. Lansdale, a CIA operative, to conduct paramilitary operations and psychological warfare against the North. Soon thereafter, the U.S. began sending direct military aid to the South Vietnamese government of President Ngo Dinh Diem, in violation of the Geneva Accords. Diem was urged by the U.S. government not to participate in the elections contemplated by the Accords, and the elections were never held. In September 1954, the United States signed the Southeast Asia Collective Defense Treaty (SEATO Treaty) and persuaded other SEATO members to extend the treaty's protection to South Vietnam, which was not a signatory. The treaty called for each signer to "act to meet the common danger" posed by an attack on any area covered by the treaty.

As the United States assumed an ever larger role in South Vietnamese affairs, its goals included a strong, stable, constitutional government in the South, the weakening of Communist influence throughout Vietnam, and eventually free elections to reunify the country under non-Communist leadership. However, widespread corruption and nepotism in the Diem regime, the failure of land reform, imprisonment of political opponents, and forced resettlements helped to create an estranged populace and pave the way for a growing insurgency in the South led by the Viet Cong. When Hanoi began to take control of Viet Cong operations in 1959 and infiltrate its own forces into the South in violation of the Geneva Accords, full-scale war began once more. In July 1959 two American servicemen in uniform, the first of many following the French withdrawal, were killed by guerillas at Bien Hoa.

From S. Comm. on Foreign Relations, The U.S. Government and the Vietnam War *(Part I), S. Prt. No. 98-185, at XIII (1984).*

In the spring of 1961, President Kennedy broadened the American commitment by secretly dispatching 400 Special Forces troops and 100 other military advisors to the South, again clearly violating the Geneva agreement. The President also directed clandestine attacks on North Vietnamese and Laotian targets using U.S.-trained South Vietnamese forces. Despite continuing concerns about the ineffectiveness of the Diem government and suggestions from some of his advisors that the United States withdraw entirely, the President was persuaded, like Presidents Truman and Eisenhower before him, that the fall of South Vietnam would quickly result in the Communist domination of all Southeast

Asia — the so-called "domino" theory. In November 1961, President Kennedy accepted the recommendations of his Secretaries of State and Defense to send additional support forces, including helicopters and other airlift equipment, naval patrols, and intelligence units. By the end of 1962 there were 11,000 U.S. troops in South Vietnam, many of them in combat roles, and within another year the number had grown to 16,000.

While control of the countryside slipped more and more from the hands of the Saigon government, Buddhist-led protests in the cities during 1963 were brutally suppressed. Later the same year, the United States encouraged and assisted a coup in which President Diem was killed. The government then changed hands nine times over the next 18 months, before Air Vice Marshall Nguyen Cao Ky assumed control and, in 1967, General Nguyen Van Thieu was elected President. Ky became Vice President, and their government was able to remain in power until a few days before Communist forces entered Saigon in 1975.

After President Kennedy was assassinated in November 1963, President Johnson quickly authorized stepped-up clandestine operations by U.S. and South Vietnamese forces, including commando raids against northern rail and highway targets and bombardment of North Vietnamese coastal installations by PT boats. These operations were approved in Washington and supervised by the chief of the U.S. Military Assistance Command in Saigon. Elaborate secret plans for increased American military involvement, including full-scale bombing of the North in an effort to cut off support for the Viet Cong, were also drawn up, while the deteriorating military situation in the South and in Laos was reportedly concealed from Congress and the public as much as possible. In the early summer of 1964, the President's advisors even drafted a standby congressional resolution intended to be the equivalent of a declaration of war. Privately, President Johnson called the war "the biggest damn mess I ever saw" and lamented that "I don't think it's worth fighting for, and I don't think we can get out." *Tapes Show Johnson Saw Vietnam War As Pointless in 1964*, N.Y. Times, Feb. 15, 1997, §1, at 12.

On the night of July 30, 1964, South Vietnamese commandos at the direction of General William Westmoreland, the U.S. commander in Saigon, launched raids against two North Vietnamese islands in the Gulf of Tonkin at a time when the U.S. destroyer *Maddox* was on patrol in the Gulf. Two days later, on August 2, several North Vietnamese PT boats attacked the *Maddox*. One PT boat was sunk by gunfire from the *Maddox*, while two others were damaged by aircraft from the carrier *Ticonderoga*, which was stationed nearby. The next day, the *Maddox* was ordered back into the Gulf accompanied by the destroyer *C. Turner Joy* at the same time that South Vietnamese naval forces carried out two more attacks on the North. Then, on the night of August 4, North Vietnamese torpedo boats reportedly attacked both U.S. destroyers in what came to be called the "Tonkin Gulf incident." However, there were no confirmed visual sightings of any North Vietnamese craft, and it now seems almost certain that there was no second attack.[4]

---

4. A study by a National Security Agency (NSA) historian released in late 2005, supported by newly declassified signals intelligence (SIGINT) reports, indicates that there was no attack on U.S. ships in the Tonkin Gulf on August 4, 1964, and that evidence pointing to an attack was "skewed" by NSA officials. *See* National Security Archive, *Tonkin Gulf Intelligence "Skewed" According to Official History and Intercepts*, Dec. 1, 2005, *at* http://www.gwu.edu/~nsarchiv/NSAEBB/NSAEBB132/press20051201.htm (with links to relevant documents).

Later the same day, without waiting for further confirmation, President Johnson briefed 16 congressional leaders on the supposed incident and described his plan for reprisal. There is no indication that he told them about U.S. responsibility for the earlier clandestine actions against the North or about recent air strikes against North Vietnamese targets inside Laos. Before the day was over, retaliatory raids, using previously laid contingency plans, were launched against four North Vietnamese PT boat bases and an oil depot holding about 10 percent of the North's petroleum supply. Just before midnight, President Johnson went on television to describe these events to the nation, calling the U.S. response "limited and fitting." "We still seek no wider war," he declared. 2 Pub. Papers 927 (Aug. 4, 1964).

The next day, August 5, a revised draft resolution prepared by the Johnson administration was introduced in Congress by Senator Fulbright and Representative Morgan. In the ensuing brief debate, the Administration acknowledged the July 30 raids (but apparently not the raids on August 3), while it disavowed any connection whatsoever between the raids and the movements of the *Maddox*. The Tonkin Gulf Resolution, as it is now known, was passed on August 7, 1964, with only two dissenting votes in the Senate and none in the House. Pub. L. No. 88-408, 78 Stat. 384 (1964). The resolution provided in part:

> Whereas naval units of the Communist regime in Vietnam, in violation of the principles of the Charter of the United Nations and of international law, have deliberately and repeatedly attacked United States naval vessels lawfully present in international waters, and have thereby created a serious threat to international peace; and
>
> Whereas these attacks are part of a deliberate and systematic campaign of aggression that the Communist regime in North Vietnam has been waging against its neighbors and the nations joined with them in the collective defense of their freedom; and
>
> Whereas the United States is assisting the peoples of southeast Asia to protect their freedom and has no territorial, military or political ambitions in the area, but desires only that these peoples should be left in peace to work out their own destinies in their own way: Now, therefore, be it
>
> Resolved... That the Congress approves and supports the determination of the President, as Commander in Chief, to take all necessary measures to repel any armed attack against the forces of the United States and to prevent further aggression.
>
> Sec. 2.... Consonant with the Constitution of the United States and the Charter of the United Nations and in accordance with its obligations under the Southeast Asia Collective Defense Treaty, the United States is, therefore, prepared, as the President determines, to take all necessary steps, including the use of armed force, to assist any member or protocol state of the Southeast Asia Collective Defense Treaty requesting assistance in defense of its freedom.
>
> Sec. 3. This resolution shall expire when the President shall determine that the peace and security of the area is reasonably assured... except that it may be terminated earlier by concurrent resolution of the Congress.

It is surely no accident that the resolution was drawn in such broad terms. President Johnson is said to have remarked that it was "like grandma's nightshirt—it covered everything." Karnow, *supra* p. 202, at 374.

A. Going to War in Vietnam

Within weeks after passage of the Tonkin Gulf Resolution, a consensus was reached at the White House to initiate a bombing campaign against the North in an effort to prevent the collapse of the Saigon government and to persuade Hanoi to suspend aid to the Viet Cong. But in the midst of a presidential election campaign against Senator Barry Goldwater, who was portrayed by the Democrats as trigger-happy, President Johnson delayed the bombing and instead quietly ordered a resumption of coastal raids, destroyer patrols, and South Vietnamese air strikes on Laotian infiltration routes. Then, in February 1965, following Viet Cong attacks on U.S. forces at Bien Hoa, Pleiku, and Qui Nhon, the President gave the order for a sustained air war against the North, code-named Operation Rolling Thunder. The bombing campaign continued, with only short interruptions, for more than three years.

As the U.S. commitment in Vietnam grew, members of the public and Congress, especially Senator Fulbright, grew increasingly uneasy about the apparent lack of clear military and political objectives there. On April 7, 1965, President Johnson offered this rationale in a speech to the nation:

> Why are we in South Viet-Nam? We are there because we have a promise to keep. Since 1954 every American President has offered support to the people of South Viet-Nam. We have helped to build, and we have helped to defend. Thus, over many years, we have made a national pledge to help South Viet-Nam defend its independence. And I intend to keep that promise. To dishonor that pledge, to abandon this small and brave nation to its enemies, and to the terror that must follow, would be an unforgivable wrong.
>
> We are also there to strengthen world order. Around the globe from Berlin to Thailand are people whose well-being rests in part on the belief that they can count on us if they are attacked. To leave Viet-Nam to its fate would be to shake the confidence of all these people in the value of an American commitment and in the value of America's word. The result would be increased unrest and instability, and even wider war.
>
> We are also there because there are great stakes in the balance. Let no one think for a moment that retreat from Viet-Nam would bring an end to conflict. The battle would be renewed in one country and then another. The central lesson of our time is that the appetite of aggression is never satisfied....
>
> In recent months attacks on South Viet-Nam were stepped up. Thus, it became necessary for us to increase our response and to make attacks by air. This is not a change of purpose. It is a change in what we believe that purpose requires.
>
> We do this in order to slow down aggression. We do this to increase the confidence of the brave people of South Viet-Nam who have bravely borne this brutal battle for so many years with so many casualties. And we do this to convince the leaders of North Viet-Nam — and all who seek to share their conquest — of a simple fact: We will not be defeated. We will not grow tired. We will not withdraw, either openly or under the cloak of a meaningless agreement.... [3 Pub. Papers 395 (Apr. 7, 1965).]

Soon after the air strikes began, it became apparent that they would not materially disrupt North Vietnam's largely agrarian economy and flexible transportation system. Indeed, the bombing only seemed to stiffen Hanoi's resolve to fight on. The day before his April 7 address, the President approved an 18,000-20,000-man increase in U.S. forces in the South. More important, he ordered Marine battalions to leave their coastal enclaves for the first time and go on the offensive against Communist forces. However, these orders were kept secret to avoid the appearance of a change in policy.

In May, the President asked for and Congress approved a $700 million supplemental appropriation to help finance the expanding war effort. Pub. L. No. 89-18, 79 Stat. 109 (1965). Almost immediately thereafter, General Westmoreland began to request large increases in ground forces to carry out the new search-and-destroy strategy and to offset a rapid buildup in Viet Cong recruitment and infiltration by North Vietnamese Army troops from the North. These requests were not made public, but by the end of 1965 there were 184,000 U.S. troops in Vietnam. Approval was given for another 207,000 troops during 1966, and by early 1968 U.S. combat forces there totalled 510,000. It was not enough. Then-Defense Secretary Robert S. McNamara lamented much later that the United States had undertaken "a guerrilla war with conventional military tactics against a foe willing to absorb enormous casualties in a country without the fundamental political stability necessary to conduct effective military and pacification operations. It could not be done, and it was not done." McNamara, *supra* p. 202, at 212.

A major turning point in the war occurred on January 31, 1968, during the Lunar New Year holiday, when Viet Cong and North Vietnamese forces launched the so-called "Tet offensive" against more than 100 cities and bases and the U.S. embassy in Saigon. The attack took U.S. forces completely by surprise. Tactically, the offensive failed, as the Viet Cong suffered devastating losses. Strategically, however, it arguably succeeded, because the massive scale and ferocity of the attacks caused Pentagon planners to rethink their goals and strategies. More important, its initial local successes — such as the siege of the U.S. embassy and the occupation of the historic city of Hue — were prominently featured on television news reports back in the United States, thereby focusing public attention even more closely on the conflict and raising for the first time the specter of defeat.

President Johnson relieved General Westmoreland of his command not long after, and on March 31 announced a cutback in the bombing of the North to the twentieth parallel. In the same speech, the President declared that he would not be a candidate for reelection later that year.

Three days later, North Vietnam agreed to peace talks in Paris. When the bombing of the North was halted altogether in November, the peace talks were expanded to include representatives of the Viet Cong and the Saigon government. The negotiations continued for four more years before further bearing fruit.

2. Legal Foundations for the Commitment of U.S. Forces

The following article by Leonard C. Meeker, who was Legal Adviser to the Department of State during the Johnson administration, contains the clearest and most succinct legal rationale for escalating and continuing the Vietnam war effort. The article provided a framework for analysis of the legality of the war by many scholars in the following years.

Leonard C. Meeker, The Legality of United States Participation in the Defense of Viet-Nam

54 Dept. State Bull. 474 (1966), *reprinted in* 75 Yale L.J. 1085 (1966)

...There can be no question in present circumstances of the President's authority to commit United States forces to the defense of South Viet-Nam. The grant of authority to the President in article II of the Constitution extends to the actions of the United States currently undertaken in Viet-Nam. In fact, however, it is unnecessary to determine whether this grant standing alone is sufficient to authorize the actions taken in Viet-Nam. These actions rest not only on the exercise of Presidential powers under article II but on the SEATO treaty—a treaty advised and consented to by the Senate—and on actions of the Congress, particularly the joint resolution of August 10, 1964....

A. THE PRESIDENT'S POWER UNDER ARTICLE II OF THE CONSTITUTION EXTENDS TO THE ACTIONS CURRENTLY UNDERTAKEN IN VIET-NAM

Under the Constitution, the President, in addition to being Chief Executive, is Commander in Chief of the Army and Navy. He holds the prime responsibility for the conduct of United States foreign relations. These duties carry very broad powers, including the power to deploy American forces abroad and commit them to military operations when the President deems such action necessary to maintain the security and defense of the United States....

In 1787 the world was a far larger place, and the framers probably had in mind attacks upon the United States. In the 20th century, the world has grown much smaller. An attack on a country far from our shores can impinge directly on the nation's security. In the SEATO treaty, for example, it is formally declared that an armed attack against Viet-Nam would endanger the peace and safety of the United States.

Since the Constitution was adopted there have been at least 125 instances in which the President has ordered the armed forces to take action or maintain positions abroad without obtaining prior congressional authorization, starting with the "undeclared war" with France (1798-1800). For example, President Truman ordered 250,000 troops to Korea during the Korean War of the early 1950's. President Eisenhower dispatched 14,000 troops to Lebanon in 1958.

The Constitution leaves to the President the judgment to determine whether the circumstances of a particular armed attack are so urgent and the potential consequences so threatening to the security of the United States that he should act without formally consulting the Congress.

B. THE SOUTHEAST ASIA COLLECTIVE DEFENSE TREATY AUTHORIZES THE PRESIDENT'S ACTIONS

Under article VI of the United States Constitution, "all Treaties made, or which shall be made, under the Authority of the United States, shall be the supreme Law of the Land." Article IV, paragraph 1, of the SEATO treaty establishes as a matter of law that a Communist armed attack against South Viet-Nam endangers the peace and safety of the United States. In this same provision the United States has undertaken a commitment in the SEATO treaty to "act to meet the common danger in accordance with its constitutional processes" in the event of such an attack.

Under our Constitution it is the President who must decide when an armed attack has occurred. He has also the constitutional responsibility for determining what measures of defense are required when the peace and safety of the United States are endangered. If he considers that deployment of U.S. forces to South Viet-Nam is required, and that military measures against the source of Communist aggression in North Viet-Nam are necessary, he is constitutionally empowered to take those measures....

It has recently been argued that the use of land forces in Asia is not authorized under the treaty because their use to deter armed attack was not contemplated at the time the treaty was considered by the Senate. Secretary Dulles testified at that time that we did not intend to establish (1) a land army in Southeast Asia capable of deterring Communist aggression, or (2) an integrated headquarters and military organization like that of NATO; instead, the United States would rely on "mobile striking power" against the sources of aggression. However, the treaty obligation in article IV, paragraph 1, to meet the common danger in the event of armed aggression, is not limited to particular modes of military action. What constitutes an adequate deterrent or an appropriate response, in terms of military strategy, may change; but the essence of our commitment to act to meet the common danger, as necessary at the time of an armed aggression, remains. In 1954 the forecast of military judgment might have been against the use of substantial United States ground forces in Viet-Nam. But that does not preclude the President from reaching a different military judgment in different circumstances, 12 years later.

C. THE JOINT RESOLUTION OF CONGRESS OF AUGUST 10, 1964, AUTHORIZES UNITED STATES PARTICIPATION IN THE COLLECTIVE DEFENSE OF SOUTH VIET-NAM...

Following the North Vietnamese attacks in the Gulf of Tonkin against United States destroyers, Congress adopted, by a Senate vote of 88-2 and a House vote of 416-0, a joint resolution containing a series of important declarations and provisions of law.

Section 1 resolved that "the Congress approves and supports the determination of the President, as Commander in Chief, to take all necessary measures to repel any armed attack against the forces of the United States and to prevent further aggression." Thus, the Congress gave its sanction to specific actions by the President to repel attacks against United States naval vessels in the Gulf of

A. Going to War in Vietnam

Tonkin and elsewhere in the western Pacific. Congress further approved the taking of "all necessary measures ... to prevent further aggression." This authorization extended to those measures the President might consider necessary to ward off further attacks and to prevent further aggression by North Viet-Nam in Southeast Asia. . . .

Section 2 . . . constitutes an authorization to the President, in his discretion, to act — using armed force if he determines that is required — to assist South Viet-Nam at its request in defense of its freedom. The identification of South Viet-Nam through the reference to "protocol state" in this section is unmistakable, and the grant of authority "as the President determines" is unequivocal. . . .

Congressional realization of the scope of authority being conferred by the joint resolution is shown by the legislative history of the measure as a whole. The following exchange between Senators Cooper and Fulbright is illuminating:

Mr. Cooper [John Sherman Cooper]: . . . The Senator will remember that the SEATO Treaty, in article IV, provides that in the event an armed attack is made upon a party to the Southeast Asia Collective Defense Treaty, or upon one of the protocol states such as South Vietnam, the parties to the treaty, one of whom is the United States, would then take such action as might be appropriate, after resorting to their constitutional processes. I assume that would mean, in the case of the United States, that Congress would be asked to grant the authority to act.

Does the Senator consider that in enacting this resolution we are satisfying that requirement of article IV of the Southeast Asia Collective Defense Treaty? In other words, are we now giving the President advance authority to take whatever action he may deem necessary respecting South Vietnam and its defense or with respect to the defense of any other country included in the treaty?

Mr. Fulbright: I think that is correct.

Mr. Cooper: Then, looking ahead, if the President decided that it was necessary to use such force as could lead into war, we will give the authority by this resolution?

Mr. Fulbright: That is the way I would interpret it. If a situation later developed in which we thought the approval should be withdrawn it could be withdrawn by concurrent resolution.

The August 1964 joint resolution continues in force today [1966]. Section [3] of the resolution provides that it shall expire "when the President shall determine that the peace and security of the area is reasonably assured by international conditions created by action of the United Nations or otherwise, except that it may be terminated earlier by concurrent resolution of the Congress." The President has made no such determination, nor has Congress terminated the joint resolution.

Instead, Congress in May 1965 approved an appropriation of $700 million to meet the expense of mounting military requirements in Viet-Nam. (Public Law 89-18, 79 Stat. 109.) The President's message asking for this appropriation stated that this was "not a routine appropriation. For each Member of Congress who supports this request is also voting to persist in our efforts to halt Communist aggression in South Vietnam." The appropriation act constitutes a clear congressional endorsement and approval of the actions taken by the President.

On March 1, 1966, the Congress continued to express its support of the President's policy by approving a $4.8 billion supplemental military authorization by votes of 392-4 and 93-2. An amendment that would have limited the President's authority to commit forces to Viet-Nam was rejected in the Senate by a vote of 94-2.

D. NO DECLARATION OF WAR BY THE CONGRESS IS REQUIRED TO AUTHORIZE UNITED STATES PARTICIPATION IN THE COLLECTIVE DEFENSE OF SOUTH VIET-NAM

No declaration of war is needed to authorize American actions in Viet-Nam. As shown in the preceding sections, the President has ample authority to order the participation of United States armed forces in the defense of South Viet-Nam.

Over a very long period in our history, practice and precedent have confirmed the constitutional authority to engage United States forces in hostilities without a declaration of war. This history extends from the undeclared war with France and the war against the Barbary pirates at the end of the 18th century to the Korean war of 1950-53.

James Madison, one of the leading framers of the Constitution, and Presidents John Adams and Jefferson all construed the Constitution, in their official actions during the early years of the Republic, as authorizing the United States to employ its armed forces abroad in hostilities in the absence of any congressional declaration of war. Their views and actions constitute highly persuasive evidence as to the meaning and effect of the Constitution. History has accepted the interpretation that was placed on the Constitution by the early Presidents and Congresses in regard to the lawfulness of hostilities without a declaration of war. The instances of such action in our history are numerous.

In the Korean conflict, where large-scale hostilities were conducted with an American troop participation of a quarter of a million men, no declaration of war was made by the Congress. The President acted on the basis of his constitutional responsibilities. While the Security Council, under a treaty of this country—the United Nations Charter—recommended assistance to the Republic of Korea against the Communist armed attack, the United States had no treaty commitment at that time obligating us to join in the defense of South Korea. In the case of South Viet-Nam we have the obligation of the SEATO treaty and clear expressions of congressional support. If the President could act in Korea without a declaration of war, a fortiori he is empowered to do so now in Viet-Nam.

It may be suggested that a declaration of war is the only available constitutional process by which congressional support can be made effective for the use of United States armed forces in combat abroad. But the Constitution does not insist on any rigid formalism. It gives Congress a choice of ways in which to exercise its powers. In the case of Viet-Nam the Congress has supported the determination of the President by the Senate's approval of the SEATO treaty, the adoption of the joint resolution of August 10, 1964, and the enactment of the necessary authorizations and appropriations....

NOTES AND QUESTIONS

1. *Inherent Presidential Authority.* Leonard Meeker described the President's foreign relations powers in very broad terms, insisting that the Article II designation as Executive and Commander in Chief enabled the President to commit American forces to military operations "when the President deems such actions necessary to maintain the security and defense of the United States." The same broad claims have been made for the President more recently in connection with the "global war on terrorism." Can you briefly marshal, from your earlier reading, arguments for and against such an expansive reading of the President's powers? See Chapters 2, 3, 4, and 5.

2. *Changing Circumstances and War-Making Authority.* As Mr. Meeker pointed out, strategic considerations in defending the nation today are quite different from those that faced the Framers two centuries ago. Do they require, however, an interpretation of the Constitution that gives greater independence to the President than in the past? Professor Velvel argued that the President's war powers have instead been diminished:

> [I]n the world of today and tomorrow, even small wars can cause a chain of events which could bring mass destruction to the human race.... Such wars have a way of escalating, as has the struggle in Vietnam. They thus carry with them the ultimate risk of nuclear war. If the nation is to run this risk, the decision to do so should be as widely dispersed as the Constitution permits — the decision should be made by 535 federal legislators rather than a tiny handful of executive officials. [Lawrence R. Velvel, *The War in Viet Nam: Unconstitutional, Justiciable, and Jurisdictionally Attackable,* 16 U. Kan. L. Rev. 449, 470-471 (1968).]

How would you compare Professor Velvel's assumptions about the strategic implications of American involvement in Southeast Asia with those of Mr. Meeker?

With the terrorist attacks on the World Trade Center and the Pentagon on September 11, 2001, the world seems smaller still. Extensive media coverage gave an immediate face to the violence and provided an unprecedented intimacy with the suffering of the victims. Americans were left feeling vulnerable at home in a way that they never had during the Cold War. How should a court respond to these developments in interpreting the President's Article II powers today?

3. *The Power to Repel Sudden Attacks.* Has the President's implied "repel attack" authority expanded over time because of advances in military technology? Has his authority changed because of the emergence of stateless terrorists who rely on weapons of mass destruction to threaten the nation?

Abraham Lincoln offered this warning about the President's invocation of his "repel attack" authority to fight the undeclared Mexican War of 1846:

> Allow the President to invade a neighboring nation, whenever he shall deem it necessary to repel an invasion and you allow him to do so, whenever he may choose to say he deems it necessary for such purpose, and you allow him to make war at pleasure. Study to see if you can fix any limit to his power in this respect, after you

have given him so much as you propose. [2 Abraham Lincoln, *The Writings of Abraham Lincoln* 51 (Arthur Brooks Lapsley ed., 1906).]

Do you think President Lincoln's caution was justified in the middle of the nineteenth century? Is it warranted today?

4. *Usage and Presidential War Making.* The spare language of Article II was said by Mr. Meeker to be augmented by usage. He recalled 125 earlier instances when troops were deployed by the President without the approval of Congress. Professor Moore observed that while these incidents represent "a substantial gloss which experience has placed on the Constitution," most of them involved short commitments and few losses; the ones that did not were highly controversial, such as the Korean War and the Mexican War of 1846. John Norton Moore, *Law and the Indo-China War* 542-543 (1972). The historical use of military force by the President alone is carefully traced in Richard F. Grimmett, *Instances of Use of United States Armed Forces Abroad, 1798-2004* (Cong. Res. Serv. RL30172), Oct. 5, 2004; W. Taylor Reveley III, *Presidential War-Making: Constitutional Prerogative or Usurpation?* 55 Va. L. Rev. 1243, 1257-1264 (1969). How do you think Justice Frankfurter would have responded to this "usage" argument based on his opinion in *The Steel Seizure Case, supra* p. 28?

5. *Tonkin Gulf Resolution as a Declaration of War?* Undersecretary of State Nicholas Katzenbach called the Tonkin Gulf Resolution "not a declaration of war" but "the functional equivalent" of such a declaration. *U.S. Commitments to Foreign Powers: Hearings Before the S. Comm. on Foreign Relations on S. Res. No. 151,* 90th Cong. 82, 145 (1967). Recall that in Bas v. Tingy, *supra* p. 94, the Supreme Court decided that Congress could authorize the President to engage in what Justice Washington called an "imperfect war" without a formal declaration. *See also* Talbot v. Seeman, 5 U.S. (1 Cranch) 1, 28 (1801). Indeed, the United States has been engaged in only five "declared" wars. Is there any doubt that in Vietnam the nation was engaged in a "state of war" as that term was defined in *The Prize Cases, supra* p. 67? Can you suggest why Congress did not formally declare war if it intended to authorize hostilities on such a large scale?

In the immediate aftermath of the 2001 terrorist attacks on the World Trade Center and the Pentagon, several members of Congress introduced resolutions that would have formally declared war on an unnamed enemy. Why do you suppose that Congress did not adopt such a resolution?

6. *Scope of the Tonkin Gulf Resolution.* Was the Tonkin Gulf Resolution intended by Congress to vest the President with the broad powers claimed by him? If the language of the resolution was sufficient to authorize the bombing of North Vietnam and the introduction of several hundred thousand American ground troops into the South, would it also have permitted the use of nuclear weapons to halt the spread of Communism in Southeast Asia, as some military leaders recommended? *See* Velvel, *supra* Note 2, at 473.

Are any doubts about the scope of the resolution dispelled by Mr. Meeker's reference to the debate between Senators Fulbright and Cooper at the time of passage? Other exchanges during consideration of the measure indicate a very different understanding. *See id.* at 473-476. Five years later it was recalled:

A. Going to War in Vietnam

The prevailing attitude was not so much that Congress was granting or acknowledging the executive's authority to take certain actions but that it was expressing unity and support for the President in a moment of national crisis and, therefore, that the exact words in which it expressed those sentiments were not of primary importance.

...Although the language of the resolution lends itself to the interpretation that Congress was consenting in advance to a full-scale war in Asia should the President think it necessary, that was not the expectation of Congress at the time. In adopting the resolution Congress was closer to believing that it was helping to *prevent* a large-scale war by taking a firm stand than it was laying the legal basis for the conduct of such a war. [S. Comm. on Foreign Relations, S. Rep. No. 91-129, at 22-23 (1969).]

But does the Committee's statement reflect more than just congressional sour grapes? What should we make of the fact that the Committee then failed to take decisive action to repudiate the President's interpretation of the resolution?

Referring not only to the Tonkin Gulf Resolution but also to the appropriations and draft legislation that followed it, Professor Ely argued that Congress did approve U.S. military activities in Vietnam, although it "invariably did so with enormous ambiguity.... [Congress] lacks the will and/or courage to stop the President from involving us in military ventures, but at the same time has no wish to be held accountable for the wars he gets us into." John Hart Ely, *The American War in Indochina, Part I: The (Troubled) Constitutionality of the War They Told Us About*, 42 Stan. L. Rev. 876, 922 (1990). Professor Ely wanted to devise a "bright-line test of authorization as a way of forcing our representatives in Congress to take a clear stand, up front, on questions of war and peace." *Id.* at 924. Do you think such a bright-line test would be a good idea? Can you articulate such a test?

7. *Authorization of Force Against Terrorism.* Just three days after the September 11, 2001, terrorist attacks on the World Trade Center and the Pentagon, Congress approved, with only one dissenting vote in the House, a joint resolution authorizing the President to

use all necessary and appropriate force against those nations, organizations, or persons he determines planned, authorized, committed, or aided the terrorist attacks that occurred on September 11, 2001, or harbored such organizations or persons, in order to prevent any future acts of international terrorism against the United States by such nations, organizations, or persons. [Pub. L. No. 107-40, §2(a), 115 Stat. 224 (2001).]

Do you think this resolution differs from the Tonkin Gulf Resolution in the scope of the authority it grants to the President? Can Congress have intended to give President George W. Bush as much discretion in the selection of targets and the use of military force as Presidents Johnson and Nixon claimed for themselves during the Vietnam War? How long do you think the authority provided by this resolution was meant to continue? Taking into account as well as you can the popular clamor for an immediate, strong response to the 9/11 attack, can you suggest amending language for the resolution excerpted above that might have preserved for Congress a larger role in formulating an appropriate response?

8. *Sharing Responsibility for the War.* As the Supreme Court noted in *The Prize Cases*, supra p. 67, Martin v. Mott, noted *supra* p. 70, and *Curtiss-Wright*, *supra* p. 60, the executive is uniquely well-equipped to gather and analyze information relevant to the decision to commit the nation to a state of war. But if the President fails or refuses to share that information with Congress, can the legislative branch fairly judge what laws will be "necessary and proper for carrying into Execution" Congress's enumerated powers under Article I, §8?

Not until 1971 was it disclosed that President Johnson and his advisors had kept a great deal from Congress that might have affected its vote on the Gulf of Tonkin Resolution. In that year the New York Times and the Washington Post published parts of a 7,000-page top-secret Pentagon history of the Vietnam conflict, the so-called *Pentagon Papers*, covering the period from World War II to August 1968. (The story of government efforts to prevent its publication is set forth in Chapter 37.) Senator Mike Gravel also read the document into the Congressional Record over the protests of some of his colleagues. *See* Gravel v. United States, 408 U.S. 606 (1972).

Of course, Congress might have voted the same way if it had been told about other U.S. activities in the Tonkin Gulf or about Administration plans for possible escalation of the war effort. Should the withholding of such information affect the force of the resolution as law? Senator Fulbright, who was floor manager of the Tonkin Gulf Resolution in the Senate, suggested this analysis: "Now in contract law, a contract induced by fraud or mistake is voidable. Perhaps some analogous doctrine in constitutional law should apply when statutory authority is given a president on the basis of fraudulent or mistaken representations." J. William Fulbright, *Foreword*, in Michael J. Glennon, *Constitutional Diplomacy* xiii (1990). Is Senator Fulbright's analogy fair or useful?

9. *Treaty Authorization for War?* What is the significance of the reference in Article VI of the Constitution to treaties as part of the supreme law of the land? Was the President obliged as part of his Article II duties to "faithfully execute" the SEATO Treaty as law by sending U.S. troops and equipment to Southeast Asia?

In Article IV of the SEATO Treaty, the United States bound itself in the event of an armed attack in the area covered by the treaty to "act to meet the common danger in accordance with its constitutional processes." Could the treaty itself be taken to satisfy U.S. constitutional processes — to authorize presidential action without additional debate and approval? Was the treaty merely "an international contractual obligation — obliging Congress to make the declaration of war if it intends to fulfill the treaty commitment"? William Van Alstyne, *Congress, the President, and the Power to Declare War: A Requiem for Vietnam*, 121 U. Pa. L. Rev. 1, 14 (1972). If the Tonkin Gulf Resolution is an "act in accordance with its constitutional processes," does the treaty have any further relevance to the debate over presidential authority?

Recall that the Framers rejected a proposal by Charles Pinckney to give the Senate alone the power to commit the nation to a state of war. See *supra* pp. 20-21. Did Mr. Meeker not seek to achieve the same result indirectly, since the power to enter into treaties is given in Article II, §2 to the President, with the advice and consent of two-thirds of the Senators present but without the concurrence of the House of Representatives? *See* John Hart Ely, *War and Responsibility: Constitutional Lessons of Vietnam and Its Aftermath* 13-15 (1993).

Can doubts about the internal authority of the treaty be resolved by reference to the President's independent powers of self-defense? How are those two authorities related in Mr. Meeker's argument? *See generally* Michael Glennon, *United States Mutual Security Treaties: The Commitment Myth*, 24 Colum. J. Transnatl. L. 509 (1986).

10. *Collective Self-Defense and International Law.* As a member of the community of nations, the United States is fundamentally committed to the rule of law that governs relations among sovereign states. Aside from any obligations under the SEATO Treaty, did U.S. involvement in the Vietnam conflict violate international law principles?

Mr. Meeker maintained that the Republic of Viet Nam (R.V.N.) was subjected to armed attack by Communist North Vietnam, and that the United States was engaged in a collective defense of its ally in conformity with settled international law norms and with its obligations under the United Nations Charter. 75 Yale L.J. at 1085. See *infra* pp. 285-286.

Some scholars contended that the Republic of Viet Nam was not a separate sovereign state, and that Vietnam was embroiled in a civil, rather than an international war, making foreign intervention impermissible. Scholars noted also that the 1954 Geneva Accords called for elections and unification of the country in 1956, a scant two years later. Yet when Mr. Meeker wrote his article, the Saigon and Hanoi governments had functioned as separate political and ideological entities for more than a decade, and each had been recognized by a number of other nations. Moreover, neither the Saigon government nor the United States signed the Accords, and each claimed not to be bound by their terms, especially the elections provision.

Defenders of U.S. involvement maintained that the cease-fire line established by the Geneva Accords along the seventeenth parallel was intended to permanently divide Vietnam into two states, even though the Accords provided that "the military demarcation line is provisional and should not in any way be interpreted as constituting a political or territorial boundary." Whatever the intent of the parties to the Accords, they argued further, the movement of North Vietnamese troops and materiel across the cease-fire line, in an effort to disrupt the political and territorial integrity of the Republic of Viet Nam, violated international norms and justified U.S. bombing of the North in response. Earlier U.S. and R.V.N. actions crossing the cease-fire line in the other direction were ignored in the debate or simply were not known until publication of the *Pentagon Papers* in 1971. Finally, it was claimed that even if the conflict in the South could be regarded as entirely indigenous, U.S. support for the Saigon government was warranted because the Viet Cong were materially aided by another state — namely, North Vietnam.

These issues are elaborately described and analyzed in Moore, *supra* p. 214, at 353-478; *The Vietnam War and International Law* (Richard A. Falk ed.) (vol. 1, 1968; vol. 2, 1969; vol. 3, 1972; vol. 4, 1976); Richard A. Falk, *International Law and the United States Role in the Viet Nam War*, 75 Yale L.J. 1122 (1966); Richard A. Falk, *International Law and the United States Role in the Viet Nam War: A Response to Professor Moore*, 76 Yale L.J. 1095 (1967); Edwin Brown Firmage, *Law and the Indochina War: A Retrospective View*, 1974 Utah L. Rev. 1; Wolfgang Friedman, *Law and Politics in the Vietnamese War: A Comment*, 61 Am. J. Intl. L. 776 (1967);

John Norton Moore, *Law and Politics in the Vietnamese War: A Response to Professor Friedman*, 61 Am. J. Intl. L. 1039 (1967); Quincy Wright, *Legal Aspects of the Viet-Nam Situation*, 60 Am. J. Intl. L. 750 (1966).

11. *Delegating War Power.* Assuming that Congress is empowered to delegate at least some of its war powers to the President, is it a legal problem, a practical problem, or both, that in the Gulf of Tonkin Resolution the delegation is described in very broad terms? What about the September 18, 2001, resolution excerpted *supra* Note 7? See generally *supra* pp. 102-110. Or is any risk of executive overreaching minimized by Congress's ability to modify or repeal its authorization at any subsequent time?

Arguing that cases testing delegations of authority in a domestic setting have only limited relevance to delegations of war powers because of the President's substantial independent authority to use the military abroad, Professor Moore suggested as a test "whether there has been meaningful participation by a Congress reasonably informed of the circumstances giving rise to the need for the use of U.S. forces." Moore, *supra* p. 214, at 548-549. Did either the Tonkin Gulf Resolution or the September 18, 2001, resolution meet this test? Does the holding in the *Curtiss-Wright* case support the broad delegations here? *See* Ely, *supra* p. 216, at 23-26; Alexander M. Bickel, *Congress, the President and the Power to Wage War*, 48 Chi.-Kent L. Rev. 131, 138-139 (1971). According to Professor Bickel, the delegation doctrine is concerned with

> the sources of policy, with the crucial joinder between power and broadly based democratic responsibility, bestowed and discharged after the fashion of representative government. Delegation without standards short-circuits the lines of responsibility that make the political process meaningful. [*Id.* at 137.]

Do you agree with Professor Rostow that characterizing the Tonkin Gulf Resolution as an improper delegation would "make foreign affairs even more exclusively the province of the President than is the case today"? Eugene V. Rostow, *Great Cases Make Bad Law: The War Powers Act*, 50 Tex. L. Rev. 833, 890 (1972). Is there a danger that such a holding might make it impossible, as a practical matter, to firmly delineate U.S. interests so as to deter or contain aggression? *Id.* at 892. *See* Raoul Berger, *War-Making by the President*, 121 U. Pa. L. Rev. 29, 45-47 (1972).

3. Testing the Legitimacy of the War in Court

United States involvement in the military conflict in Southeast Asia was challenged in court by a number of plaintiffs on various grounds. All but a few of the suits were dismissed with the statement that the plaintiffs lacked standing to sue or that the issues presented to the court were political and therefore nonjusticiable. Of course, to characterize a question as political is not to diminish either its importance or the difficulty of its resolution. In the case that follows, the court had to assess its own role in the governance process while examining the separation of powers between the political branches. That

Orlando v. Laird

United States Court of Appeals, Second Circuit, 1971
443 F.2d 1039, *cert. denied*, 404 U.S. 869 (1971)

ANDERSON, J. Shortly after receiving orders to report for transfer to Vietnam, Pfc. Malcolm A. Berk and Sp. E5 Salvatore Orlando, enlistees in the United States Army, commenced separate actions in June, 1970, seeking to enjoin the Secretary of Defense, the Secretary of the Army and the commanding officers, who signed their deployment orders, from enforcing them. The plaintiffs-appellants contended that these executive officers exceeded their constitutional authority by ordering them to participate in a war not properly authorized by Congress.

... [I]n Berk v. Laird, 429 F.2d 302 (2nd Cir. 1970) ... [w]e held that the war declaring power of Congress, enumerated in Article I, section 8, of the Constitution, contains a "discoverable standard calling for *some* mutual participation by Congress," and directed that Berk be given an opportunity "to provide a method for resolving the question of when specified joint legislative-executive action is sufficient to authorize various levels of military activity," and thereby escape application of the political question doctrine to his claim that congressional participation has been in this instance, insufficient....

It is the appellants' position that the sufficiency of congressional authorization is a matter within judicial competence because that question can be resolved by "judicially discoverable and manageable standards" dictated by the congressional power "to declare War." See Baker v. Carr, 369 U.S. 186 (1962); Powell v. McCormack, 395 U.S. 486 (1969). They interpret the constitutional provision to require an express and explicit congressional authorization of the Vietnam hostilities though not necessarily in the words, "We declare that the United States of America is at war with North Vietnam." In support of this construction they point out that the original intent of the clause was to place responsibility for the initiation of war upon the body most responsive to popular will and argue that historical developments have not altered the need for significant congressional participation in such commitments of national resources. They further assert that, without a requirement of express and explicit congressional authorization, developments committing the nation to war, as a *fait accompli*, became the inevitable adjuncts of presidential direction of foreign policy, and, because military appropriations and other war-implementing enactments lack an explicit authorization of particular hostilities, they cannot, as a matter of law, be considered sufficient.

Alternatively, appellants would have this court find that, because the President requested accelerating defense appropriations and extensions of the conscription laws after the war was well under way, Congress was, in effect, placed in a straitjacket and could not freely decide whether or not to enact this legislation, but rather was compelled to do so. For this reason appellants claim that such enactments cannot, as a factual matter, be considered sufficient congressional approval or ratification.

The Government on the other hand takes the position that the suits concern a non-justiciable political question; that the military action in South Vietnam was authorized by Congress in [the Tonkin Gulf Resolution] considered in connection with the Seato Treaty; and that the military action was authorized and ratified by congressional appropriations expressly designated for use in support of the military operations in Vietnam.

We held in the first *Berk* opinion that the constitutional delegation of the war-declaring power to the Congress contains a discoverable and manageable standard imposing on the Congress a duty of mutual participation in the prosecution of war. Judicial scrutiny of that duty, therefore, is not foreclosed by the political question doctrine. Baker v. Carr, *supra*; Powell v. McCormack, *supra*. As we see it, the test is whether there is any action by the Congress sufficient to authorize or ratify the military activity in question. The evidentiary materials produced at the hearings in the district court clearly disclose that this test is satisfied.

The Congress and the Executive have taken mutual and joint action in the prosecution and support of military operations in Southeast Asia from the beginning of those operations. The Tonkin Gulf Resolution, enacted August 10, 1964 (repealed December 31, 1970) was passed at the request of President Johnson and, though occasioned by specific naval incidents in the Gulf of Tonkin, was expressed in broad language which clearly showed the state of mind of the Congress and its intention fully to implement and support the military and naval actions taken by and planned to be taken by the President at that time in Southeast Asia, and as might be required in the future "to prevent further aggression." Congress has ratified the executive's initiatives by appropriating billions of dollars to carry out military operations in Southeast Asia[2] and by extending the Military Selective Service Act with full knowledge that persons conscripted under that Act had been, and would continue to be, sent to Vietnam. Moreover, it specifically conscripted manpower to fill "the substantial induction calls necessitated by the current Vietnam buildup."[3]

There is, therefore, no lack of clear evidence to support a conclusion that there was an abundance of continuing mutual participation in the prosecution of the war. Both branches collaborated in the endeavor, and neither could long maintain such a war without the concurrence and cooperation of the other.

---

2. In response to the demands of the military operations the executive during the 1960s ordered more and more men and material into the war zone; and congressional appropriations have been commensurate with each new level of fighting. Until 1965, defense appropriations had not earmarked funds for Vietnam. In May of that year President Johnson asked Congress for an emergency supplemental appropriation "to provide our forces [then numbering 35,000] with the best and most modern supplies and equipment." 111 Cong. Rec. 9283 (May 4, 1965). Congress appropriated $700 million for use "upon determination by the President that such action is necessary in connection with military activities in Southeast Asia." Pub. L. 89-18, 79 Stat. 109 (1965). Appropriation acts in each subsequent year explicitly authorized expenditures for men and material sent to Vietnam. The 1967 appropriations act, for example, declared Congress' "firm intention to provide all necessary support for members of the Armed Forces of the United States fighting in Vietnam" and supported "the efforts being made by the President of the United States...to prevent an expansion of the war in Vietnam and to bring that conflict to an end through a negotiated settlement...." Pub. L. 90-5, 81 Stat. 5 (1967)....

3. In H. Rep. No. 267, 90th Cong., 1st Sess. 38 (1967), in addition to extending the conscription mechanism, Congress continued a suspension of the permanent ceiling on the active duty strength of the Armed Forces, fixed at 2 million men, and replaced it with a secondary ceiling of 5 million....

A. Going to War in Vietnam

Although appellants do not contend that Congress can exercise its war-declaring power only through a formal declaration, they argue that congressional authorization cannot, as a matter of law, be inferred from military appropriations or other war-implementing legislation that does not contain an express and explicit authorization for the making of war by the President. Putting aside for a moment the explicit authorization of the Tonkin Gulf Resolution, we disagree with appellants' interpretation of the declaration clause for neither the language nor the purpose underlying that provision prohibits an inference of the fact of authorization from such legislative action as we have in this instance. The framers' intent to vest the war power in Congress is in no way defeated by permitting an inference of authorization from legislative action furnishing the manpower and materials of war for the protracted military operation in Southeast Asia.

The choice, for example, between an explicit declaration on the one hand and a resolution and war-implementing legislation, on the other, as the medium for expression of congressional consent involves "the exercise of a discretion demonstrably committed to the . . . legislature," Baker v. Carr, *supra* at 211, and therefore, invokes the political question doctrine.

Such a choice involves an important area of decision making in which, through mutual influence and reciprocal action between the President and the Congress, policies governing the relationship between this country and other parts of the world are formulated in the best interests of the United States. If there can be nothing more than minor military operations conducted under any circumstances, short of an express and explicit declaration of war by Congress, then extended military operations could not be conducted even though both the Congress and the President were agreed that they were necessary and were also agreed that a formal declaration of war would place the nation in a posture in its international relations which would be against its best interests. For the judicial branch to enunciate and enforce such a standard would be not only extremely unwise but also would constitute a deep invasion of the political question domain. As the Government says, ". . . decisions regarding the form and substance of congressional enactments authorizing hostilities are determined by highly complex considerations of diplomacy, foreign policy and military strategy inappropriate to judicial inquiry." It would, indeed, destroy the flexibility of action which the executive and legislative branches must have in dealing with other sovereigns. What has been said and done by both the President and the Congress in their collaborative conduct of the military operations in Vietnam implies a consensus on the advisability of *not* making a formal declaration of war because it would be contrary to the interests of the United States to do so. The making of a policy decision of that kind is clearly within the constitutional domain of those two branches and is just as clearly not within the competency or power of the judiciary.

Beyond determining that there has been *some* mutual participation between the Congress and the President, which unquestionably exists here, with action by the Congress sufficient to authorize or ratify the military activity at issue, it is clear that the constitutional propriety of the means by which Congress has chosen to ratify and approve the protracted military operations in Southeast Asia is a political question. The form which congressional authorization should take is one of policy, committed to the discretion of the Congress and outside the power and competency of the judiciary, because there are no intelligible and objectively manageable standards by which to judge such actions. Baker v. Carr, *supra*, 369 U.S. at 217; Powell v. McCormack, *supra*, 395 U.S. at 518....

[The concurring opinion of KAUFMAN, J., is omitted.]

NOTES AND QUESTIONS

1. *The Importance of Being First.* What is the practical political importance of the plaintiffs' "straitjacket" argument that after the President put U.S. resources—and honor—on the line, Congress was hard put to pull them back? Should that argument have affected the court's judgment about compliance with the Declare War Clause in Article I? Do you think the Congress felt so constrained when it voted for the Gulf of Tonkin Resolution? *See* Van Alstyne, *supra* p. 216, at 23.

2. *The Importance of Collaboration.* In a companion case, Berk v. Laird, 429 F.2d 302, 304 (2d Cir. 1970), the government insisted that "the President's authority as Commander in Chief, in the absence of a declared war, is co-extensive with his broad and unitary power in the field of foreign affairs," citing *Curtiss-Wright.* The *Berk* court rejected this contention because "the congressional power to 'declare' a war would be reduced to an antique formality, leaving no executive 'duty' to follow constitutional steps which can be judicially identified." *Id.* at 305.

The *Berk* court went on to say, "Since orders to fight must be issued in accordance with proper authorization from both branches under some circumstances, executive officers are under a threshold constitutional 'duty [that] can be judicially identified and its breach judicially determined,'" *id.*, quoting Baker v. Carr, 369 U.S. 186, 198 (1962). Can you describe the "threshold constitutional duty" that the courts must be prepared to identify? Can you say under what "circumstances" proper authorization from both political branches would *not* be required to fight?

3. *The Adequacy of Collaboration.* What is the source of the *Orlando* court's "mutual participation" standard for prosecution of the war? What is the source of the court's test for determining when there has been "sufficient" mutual participation? Do you see an element of circularity in the test? Does that circularity make this case look "political" and therefore nonjusticiable?

If the standard of "some mutual participation" is discoverable by the courts, will the "highly complex considerations of diplomacy, foreign policy and military strategy" be compromised less than if a single clear act—a declaration of war—were required?

In Massachusetts v. Laird, 451 F.2d 26 (1st Cir. 1971), on facts substantially identical to those in *Orlando*, the court reached the same conclusion as the *Orlando* court but by a different route. The *Massachusetts* court focused instead on the first decisional factor in Baker v. Carr, *supra*—"whether there is a

A. Going to War in Vietnam

'textually demonstrable commitment of the issue to a coordinate political department' of government." *Id.* at 31.

> [T]he war power of the country is an amalgam of powers, some distinct and others less sharply limned. In certain respects, the executive and the Congress may act independently. The Congress may without executive cooperation declare war, thus triggering treaty obligations and domestic emergency powers. The executive may without Congressional participation repel attack, perhaps catapulting the country into a major conflict. But beyond these independent powers, each of which has its own rationale, the Constitutional scheme envisages the joint participation of the Congress and the executive in determining the scale and duration of hostilities....
>
> As to the power to conduct undeclared hostilities beyond emergency defense, then, we are inclined to believe that the Constitution, in giving some essential powers to Congress and others to the executive, committed the matter to both branches, whose joint concord precludes the judiciary from measuring a specific executive action against any specific clause in isolation. [*Id.* at 31-33.]

With the tests in *Orlando* and Massachusetts v. Laird compare this suggested alternative:

> Congressional authorization need not be by formal declaration of war.... A joint resolution, signed by the President, is the most tenable method of authorizing the use of force today. To be meaningful, the resolution should be passed only after Congress is aware of the basic elements of the situation, and has had reasonable time to consider their implications. The resolution should not, as a rule, be a blank check leaving the place, purpose and duration of hostilities to the President's sole discretion. To be realistic, however, the resolution must leave the Executive wide discretion to respond to changing circumstances. [Reveley, *supra* p. 214, at 1289-1290.]

Is Reveley's test constitutionally sound? How difficult would it be for the court to apply in a given case? Would the test be satisfied by the Tonkin Gulf Resolution or the subsequent appropriations and selective service legislation or both? By the September 18, 2001, resolution approving the use of military force against terrorists?

4. *Collaboration by Appropriation.* An important aspect of Congress's collaboration, according to both the First and Second Circuit Courts, was that it approved the expenditure of very large sums of money for the conduct of the war. Is the courts' analysis consistent with Greene v. McElroy, *supra* p. 105? Could the appropriations be said to have ratified the executive's actions? Did they meet the requirements for congressional acquiescence? *See supra* pp. 48, 111. *See also* Ely, *supra* p. 216, at 27-30.

On the same day in September 2001 that Congress adopted its resolution approving the use of military force against terrorists and their sponsors, it appropriated $40 billion for "assistance to victims of the attacks, and to deal with other consequences of the attacks... including for the costs of... (2) providing support to counter, investigate, or prosecute domestic or international terrorism;... and (5) supporting national security." Pub. L. No. 107-38, 115 Stat. 220 (2001).

Do you think this appropriation would bolster a possible presidential claim of authority to act without consulting Congress further?

5. *Political Question?* Invocation of the political question doctrine in many of the Vietnam cases caused great consternation among some commentators. For example, "If the judiciary, the organ of government most fundamentally committed to the vindication of constitutional principle, decides it cannot play its accustomed role in the Vietnam controversy, our basic institutional alternative to lawlessness is lost." Warren F. Schwartz & Wayne McCormack, *The Justiciability of Legal Objections to the American Military Effort in Vietnam*, 46 Texas L. Rev. 1033, 1036 (1968). *See also* Velvel, *supra* p. 213, at 479-485; Louis Henkin, *Is There a Political Question Doctrine?* 85 Yale L.J. 597, 623-624 (1976). Professor Moore, on the other hand, while noting the importance of judicial candor in abstaining in these cases, cautioned against what he called an oversimplification of difficulties inherent in the judicial resolution of such major claims. Moore, *supra* p. 214, at 573.

The nation's highest court maintained sphinx-like silence on the justiciability of the Vietnam War cases. Dissenting from the refusal to rule in Massachusetts v. Laird, Justice Douglas complained, "The question of an unconstitutional war is neither academic nor 'political.' This case has raised the question in an adversary setting. It should be settled here and now." 400 U.S. 886, 900 (1970). *See also* Mitchell v. United States, 386 U.S. 972 (1967) (Douglas, J., dissenting from denial of certiorari); Mora v. McNamara, 389 U.S. 934 (1967) (Douglas and Stewart, JJ., dissenting); and Atlee v. Richardson, 411 U.S. 911 (1973) (Brennan, Douglas, and Stewart, JJ., voting to note probable jurisdiction). Only in *Atlee* did the Court affirm (without opinion) a lower court ruling that a test of the constitutionality of the war presented a nonjusticiable political question. Atlee v. Laird, 347 F. Supp. 689 (E.D. Pa. 1972). Can you guess why the Court decided not even to hear arguments in any of these cases? *See* Rodric B. Schoen, *A Strange Silence: Vietnam and the Supreme Court*, 33 Washburn L.J. 275 (1994).

6. *Standing to Sue?* Despite some uncertainty early on, it seems to have been settled that military personnel with orders for duty in Vietnam had standing to test the legitimacy of the war. *See, e.g.*, Berk v. Laird, 429 F.2d 302, 306 (2d Cir. 1970); *see also* Moore, *supra* p. 214, at 575.

In Massachusetts v. Laird, noted *supra* p. 222, the Commonwealth brought suit alleging impairment of its interest as a sovereign state under the Constitution, since "one branch, the executive, has exercised war-making powers, which the Commonwealth and its sister states had agreed would be exercised only by Congress." 451 F.2d at 28. Massachusetts also sued as *parens patriae*, citing the deaths and injuries of its inhabitants, consequential loss of their prospective civic and tax contributions, increased claims of dependents, additional burdens on its economy, disadvantage to its absentee voters, mass demonstrations, and damage to its public's morale. *Id.* Without deciding the issue of standing, the court expressed doubt about the status of the Commonwealth as protector of the rights of its citizens, since the "federal government is the ultimate *parens patriae* of every American citizen." *Id.* at 29. When the Supreme Court earlier denied leave for the state to file a bill of complaint in the same case, 400 U.S. 886 (1970), Justice Douglas dissented, arguing that only the executive, not the "federal government," represented the citizens in the prosecution of the war. *Id.* at 888.

Standing for members of Congress who brought suit challenging the legitimacy of the war was recognized in one case, Mitchell v. Laird, 488 F.2d 611, 613-614 (D.C. Cir. 1973), but denied in another, Holtzman v. Schlesinger, 484 F.2d 1307, 1315 (2d Cir. 1973), *infra* p. 235. Recent refinements in the law of standing for members of Congress are described *supra* pp. 152-154.

A law professor's suit to test the constitutionality of the war was dismissed on grounds that he had standing neither as an individual citizen nor as a taxpayer. Velvel v. Nixon, 415 F.2d 236 (10th Cir. 1969). Other cases with similar results are analyzed *supra* pp. 150-151.

7. *Challenges Based on International Law.* What result, on a motion to dismiss, if Orlando had asserted that his orders to Vietnam were unlawful because the United States was waging an aggressive war in violation of international law? In United States v. Sisson, 294 F. Supp. 515, 517 (D. Mass. 1968), the court noted that "[f]or argument's sake one may assume that a conscript has a standing to object to induction in a war declared contrary to a binding international obligation." But the court refused to rule on a charge that U.S. operations in Vietnam violated such an obligation, calling the case political and nonjusticiable on grounds that the court (especially a court of the state accused of the violation) was "incapable of eliciting the facts during a war." *Id.* at 517-518. Similarly, in United States v. Berrigan, 283 F. Supp. 336, 342-343 (D. Md. 1968), *aff'd*, 417 F.2d 1009 (4th Cir. 1969), *cert. denied*, 397 U.S. 909 (1970), the court declared in dicta that "'[t]he Nurnberg defense' is premised on a finding that the government is acting in violation of international law in waging an aggressive war, and, as such, cannot be raised here because the question of violations of international law by the government is uniquely a 'political question.'"

More recently, however, in Committee of U.S. Citizens Living in Nicaragua v. Reagan, 859 F.2d 929, 941 (D.C. Cir. 1988), *supra* p. 184, the court indicated that if Congress adopted a foreign policy that violated a peremptory norm of international law, "that policy might well be subject to challenge in domestic court." The court mentioned as examples of such norms the prohibitions on slavery, torture, summary execution, and genocide. And in Nicaragua v. United States, 1986 I.C.J. 14, 100 [para. 190], the World Court declared that "the prohibition of the use of force ... constitutes a conspicuous example of a rule in international law having the character of *jus cojens*." Do you think these rulings make it more likely that a domestic court today would adjudicate a claim of unprovoked U.S. aggression?

B. LIMITING THE SCOPE OF THE VIETNAM WAR

Following the Tet offensive in early 1968, public controversy over U.S. involvement in Indochina grew dramatically. Antiwar demonstrations at the Democratic National Convention in Chicago that year turned violent when police and National Guard troops clashed with protesters, while military intelligence units infiltrated dissident groups for the stated purpose of preventing domestic disorder. *See* Laird v. Tatum, 408 U.S. 1 (1972), noted *infra* p. 960.

Massive demonstrations in cities around the country followed later in the year. Vice President Hubert Humphrey became the Democratic Party nominee for President, first supporting and then renouncing the Johnson administration's policies in Southeast Asia, but not in time to save his candidacy, leaving Richard Nixon to win the election in November by a narrow margin. During the election campaign, candidate Nixon pledged to bring the Vietnam War to an end as quickly as possible. President Nixon described his progress in fulfilling that promise in a speech to the nation on April 7, 1971:

> When I left Washington in January of 1961 after serving 8 years as Vice President under President Eisenhower, there were no American combat forces in Vietnam. No Americans had died in combat in Vietnam.
> When I returned to Washington as President 8 years later, there were 540,000 American troops in Vietnam. Thirty-one thousand had died there. Three hundred Americans were being lost every week and there was no comprehensive plan to end the United States involvement in the war.
> ...In June of 1969, I announced a withdrawal of 25,000 men; in September, 40,000; December, 50,000; April of 1970, 150,000. By the first of next month, May 1, I will have brought home more than 265,000 Americans—almost half of the troops in Vietnam when I took office. [3 Pub. Papers 523.]

The President then announced that he would pull out an additional 100,000 American troops before the end of 1971. *Id.* at 524.

The pace of withdrawal was not quick enough for many. Questions about the moral basis for the war multiplied with the revelation that U.S. troops had massacred 347 civilians in the village of My Lai in 1968.

Key to President Nixon's plans for winding down the war was a process called "Vietnamization." It was hoped that after U.S. troops were withdrawn, U.S. political objectives in Vietnam still might be achieved if only South Vietnamese forces were better able to defend themselves, so in 1969 large quantities of modern military supplies were shipped to the Saigon government for that purpose. However, direct U.S. military support was still to be provided on two new fronts.

1. Cambodia

Like Vietnam, Cambodia was a French colony until 1954, when it achieved independence under the leadership of Prince Norodom Sihanouk. Almost as soon as President Nixon took office, he decided to launch air strikes across the Cambodian border against a massing of North Vietnamese troops there. The extension of U.S. might into new territory was necessary, he reasoned, to assure the safety of U.S. forces in South Vietnam and to signal his resolve to the North Vietnamese. But the bombing was kept secret from the American people, from all but a few members of Congress, and even from many in the Pentagon.

Prince Sihanouk was overthrown by his prime minister, Lon Nol, in March 1970, some say with CIA complicity, and as the Cambodian army came under increasing pressure from Viet Cong, North Vietnamese, and local Communist Khmer Rouge forces, Lon Nol appealed to the United States for help. On April

B. Limiting the Scope of the Vietnam War

30, President Nixon announced to the nation that 20,000 U.S. and South Vietnamese troops supported by U.S. aircraft had attacked Viet Cong and North Vietnamese bases inside Cambodia.

The President's announcement caused a spasm of protest in this country. Demonstrators at Kent State University were met by National Guard troops called out by the Ohio governor, and in the ensuing clash four students were shot and killed. In the days following, hundreds of other universities were forced by student and faculty strikes to close down, and 100,000 protestors marched on government buildings in Washington.

After U.S. combat forces were pulled out of Cambodia in the late summer, the Senate, but not the House, passed the Cooper-Church Amendment to the Foreign Military Sales Act. *See* S. Rep. No. 91-865, at 15 (1970), *reprinted in* 1970 U.S.C.C.A.N. 6054. It would have prohibited expenditures from any source for "retaining United States forces in Cambodia" or "conducting any combat activity in the air above Cambodia in support of Cambodian forces." Then, in January 1971, Congress passed and the President agreed to the following amendment to the Supplemental Foreign Assistance Authorization of 1971:

> In line with the expressed intention of the President..., none of the funds authorized or appropriated pursuant to this or any other Act may be used to finance the introduction of United States ground combat troops into Cambodia, or to provide United States advisers to or for Cambodian military forces in Cambodia. [Pub. L. No. 91-652, §7, 85 Stat. 1942, 1943 (1971).]

United States military action in Cambodia is described in William Shawcross, *Sideshow: Kissinger, Nixon and the Destruction of Cambodia* (1979). *See also* John Hart Ely, *War and Responsibility, supra* p. 216, at 30-32, 34-46, 98-104; Ely, *The American War in Indochina, Part I, supra* p. 215, at 902-905, 908-922; and Ely, *The American War in Indochina, Part II: The Unconstitutionality of the War They Didn't Tell Us About*, 42 Stan. L. Rev. 1093, 1137-1148 (1990).

2. Laos

Like its neighbors, Vietnam and Cambodia, Laos became an independent state in 1954. The Communist Pathet Lao insurgency in that country, with support from North Vietnam, prompted President Kennedy to send a small covert force to Laos in 1961 in an effort to prevent further Communist advances. A second Geneva Agreement the following year called for withdrawal of foreign troops and establishment of a neutral coalition government headed by Prince Souvanna Phouma. Nonetheless, many North Vietnamese forces remained. While the United States withdrew its uniformed military personnel, it continued to support a "secret" army of some 70,000 Hmong tribesmen and as many as 21,000 Thai "volunteers." This large force was financed, trained, supplied, transported, and sometimes accompanied into battle by CIA operatives, many of whom were former U.S. Army Green Berets. In addition, between 1967 and 1972, U.S. military units based in South Vietnam apparently crossed the border more than 1,000 times to fight in Laos.

In June 1964, the United States began bombing operations in northern Laos to support the Laotian "secret" army. The following year the United States commenced bombing of the Ho Chi Minh Trail in the Laotian panhandle. By the time the attacks stopped nine years later, U.S. planes had dropped between 1.6 and 2 million tons of bombs in Laos, more than they dropped on Germany and Japan during all of World War II.

Although the Laotians, North Vietnamese, Soviets, and Chinese were perfectly aware of what was going on, Congress and the American public were kept in substantial ignorance of these developments. President Johnson explained privately that while Souvanna Phouma needed U.S. support to ward off the Pathet Lao, the Laotian leader preferred to maintain the appearance of neutrality. Without revealing the full extent of U.S. military actions in Laos, President Nixon announced that he had ordered U.S. forces to cut off the flow of troops and materiel down the Ho Chi Minh Trail and to force North Vietnamese compliance with the second Geneva Agreement. Richard M. Nixon, *Scope of U.S. Involvement in Laos*, 62 Dept. St. Bull. 405 (1970).

Anxious about apparently increasing U.S. military involvement in Southeast Asia and skeptical about President Nixon's assurances to the contrary, Congress passed this amendment to the Department of Defense Appropriation Act, 1970: "In line with the expressed intention of the President of the United States, none of the funds appropriated by this Act shall be used to finance the introduction of American ground combat troops into Laos or Thailand." Pub. L. No. 91-171, §643, 83 Stat. 469, 487 (1969). In February 1971, President Nixon, observing the strict language of the amendment, approved the invasion of northern Laos by a 30,000-troop South Vietnamese force supported by U.S. helicopters and bombers. Viewed as a major test of the Vietnamization program, this attempt to cut off troops and materiel from the Ho Chi Minh Trail ended in failure, and there was the predictable outcry that the war had been expanded without authorization from Congress.

United States military operations in Laos are recounted in Ely, *War and Responsibility*, supra p. 216, at 68-97; Ely, *The American War in Indochina, Part II*, supra p. 227, at 1094-1137; John M. Orman, *Presidential Secrecy and Deception: Beyond the Power to Persuade* 99-122 (1980); and Christopher Robbins, *The Ravens: The Men Who Flew in America's Secret War in Laos* (1987).

NOTES AND QUESTIONS

1. *Mutual Participation in a Secret War?* What was the source of the President's authority to extend U.S. military might into Cambodia and Laos? Can it be found in the language of the Gulf of Tonkin Resolution, *supra* p. 206? Did other congressional acts constitute "some mutual participation" or "joint concord" between the political branches to authorize these incursions without full knowledge on the part of Congress?

The bombing of Cambodia between March 1969 and April 1970 was conducted almost entirely in secret. Flight records were destroyed. The State Department, the Secretary of the Air Force, and even the Air Force Chief of Staff were kept in the dark, and only a handful of members of Congress were told about the operations. U.S. military involvement in Laos was also concealed from

B. Limiting the Scope of the Vietnam War

Congress until at least 1969. Does this concealment have any bearing on the question of authority? *See* Ely, *War and Responsibility, supra* p. 216, at 68-104; Ely, *The American War in Indochina, Part II, supra* p. 227, at 1105-1148.

2. *Inherent Tactical Authority.* Did the President's Article II powers alone furnish the needed authority? Assistant Attorney General (later Chief Justice) William Rehnquist offered this legal rationale for the introduction of U.S. ground forces into Cambodia:

> The President's determination to authorize incursion into these Cambodian border areas is precisely the sort of tactical decision traditionally confided to the Commander-in-Chief in the conduct of armed conflict.... Faced with a substantial troop commitment to such hostilities made by the previous Chief Executive, and approved by successive Congresses, President Nixon had an obligation as Commander-in-Chief of the Armed Forces to take what steps he deemed necessary to assure their safety in the field.... It is a decision made during the course of an armed conflict already commenced as to how that conflict will be conducted, rather than a determination that some new and previously unauthorized military venture will be taken. [William H. Rehnquist, *The Constitutional Issues — Administration Position,* 45 N.Y.U. L. Rev. 628, 638-639 (1970).]

Do you agree with Rehnquist's analysis? Does it contain a standard for distinguishing between tactical decisions and those that need advance approval from Congress?

3. *Area and Use Limitations.* May Congress properly approve the induction of troops and the purchase of military supplies and then prohibit the President's use of those forces in certain areas? Congress has occasionally purported to do so — for example, in the Selective Service Act of 1940, Pub. L. No. 76-783, 54 Stat. 885 (1940), which prohibited the assignment of U.S. conscriptees to duty outside the Western Hemisphere, except in U.S. possessions.

Drawing on your readings in Chapters 4 and 5, can you make the cases for and against the constitutionality of such congressional "area and use" restrictions during the Vietnam War? Does the Supreme Court's opinion in Little v. Barreme, *supra* p. 77, furnish any guidance? *See generally* Moore, *supra* p. 214, at 561-566; Jason A. Rosenberg, Note, *The Appropriations Power as a Tool of Congressional Foreign Policy Making,* 50 B.U. L. Rev. (Special Issue) 34 (1970).

Professor Moore indicates that in authorizing the use of force Congress "might include limitations as to area of belligerent activities, kinds of activities authorized, and duration of the authorization." Moore, *supra,* at 560. But he warns that such additional requirements "should not be such as to limit needed flexibility of the President to respond to changed circumstances or to interfere with the President's power to make command decisions incident to successful prosecution of the war." *Id.* at 560-561. Can you describe the boundary between proper and inappropriate congressional limitations? Are such practical limits related to any constitutional limits? Would a court ever be in a position to describe either kind of limit?

Professor Moore also suggests that Congress might appropriately restrict the President's use of internationally prohibited chemical or biological weapons, which could involve "profound effects on international relations and the grave risk of escalation and unnecessary suffering." *Id.* at 566. Could the same concerns have justified area restrictions in the Vietnam War? Is there any constitutional basis for distinguishing such international law use restrictions from congressional restrictions?

4. *Appropriations Limitations.* Is it important that the legislation that cut off funds for Cambodian operations omitted the language of the Cooper-Church Amendment, supra p. 227, which would have explicitly prohibited the aerial bombardment of Cambodia? Do you see any practical difference between the language of the respective funding restrictions for Cambodia and for Laos-Thailand?

5. *Border "Incursions" and International Law.* Were U.S. and South Vietnamese military activities in Laos and Cambodia permissible defensive measures incident to the defense of South Vietnam according to international law principles? Or did they represent naked aggression against the territories of two neutral sovereign states? On the one hand, Cambodia was accused of violating its duty as a neutral to expel Viet Cong and North Vietnamese forces operating from its territory, though as a practical matter it hardly seemed capable of doing so. On the other hand, Cambodia was said to be justified by Article 51 of the U.N. Charter in requesting U.S. assistance to defend against attack from those same forces. See *infra* p. 287. For their part, North Vietnam and the Viet Cong were charged with violating Cambodian and Laotian neutrality and with ignoring the requirements of the second Geneva Agreement concerning withdrawal of foreign troops from Laos. These violations, as well as the need to defend South Vietnamese territory, were said to justify the actions in question. The arguments on both sides are rehearsed, for example, in Richard A. Falk, *The Cambodian Operation and International Law*, 65 Am. J. Intl. L. 1 (1971); John Norton Moore, *Legal Dimensions of the Decision to Intercede in Cambodia*, 65 Am. J. Intl. L. 38 (1971).

C. ENDING THE VIETNAM WAR

1. Repeal of the Gulf of Tonkin Resolution

At the end of 1970, spurred by public dissent and frustrated by President Nixon's decision to invade Cambodia, Congress voted to repeal the Gulf of Tonkin Resolution by a single sentence attached to an unrelated measure. Pub. L. No. 91-672, §12, 84 Stat. 2053 (1971). In a case challenging the President's orders for deployment to Vietnam, an Army draftee argued that the repeal eliminated the congressional "mutual participation" on which the *Orlando* court based its finding of presidential authority. DaCosta v. Laird (*DaCosta I*), 448 F.2d 1368 (2d Cir. 1971). The *DaCosta I* court concluded, however, that "there was sufficient legislative action in extending the Selective Service Act and in appropriating billions of dollars to carry on military and naval operations in Vietnam to ratify and approve the measures taken by the Executive, even in the absence of the Gulf of Tonkin Resolution." *Id.* at 1369.

C. Ending the Vietnam War

The court went on to declare:

> It was not the intent of Congress in passing the repeal amendment to bring all military operations in Vietnam to an abrupt halt. The Executive was then endeavoring to unwind the conflict as rapidly as it was feasible to do so. It has steadily pursued that objective up to the present time and has declared it to be its intention to continue the withdrawals of combat forces. If the Executive were now escalating the prolonged struggle instead of decreasing it, additional supporting action by the Legislative Branch over what is presently afforded, might well be required. But that is not the case before us....
>
> As the constitutional propriety of the means by which the Executive and the Legislative branches engaged in mutual participation in prosecuting the military operations in Southeast Asia, is, as we held in *Orlando,* a political question, so the constitutional propriety of the method and means by which they mutually participate in winding down the conflict and disengaging the nation from it, is also a political question and outside of the power and competency of the judiciary. [*Id.* at 1369-1370.]

NOTES AND QUESTIONS

1. *Unwinding the Conflict?* How did the court know that it was not the intent of Congress to halt all military operations? Why was the Gulf of Tonkin Resolution repealed if not to remove that legislative authority for U.S. involvement in Vietnam? Was the repealer a nullity? Why do you think Congress did not express itself more clearly on this issue one way or the other? *Compare* Van Alstyne, *supra* p. 216, at 20-21, 27-28 (authority for war revoked), *with* Ely, *supra* p. 216, at 33 ("just more of Congress's playing Pontius Pilate").

Suppose Congress had wanted to bring the conflict to a prompt halt. Adopting the court's logic, would anything short of a "declaration of peace," a direct order to remove the troops, or a cutoff of funding galvanize the court to intervene?

How did the court know that the executive was endeavoring to unwind the conflict as rapidly as possible? Was it because the President publicly said so? Should the court have decided a case of such moment simply on the assurance of one of the parties to the controversy? In Mitchell v. Laird, 488 F.2d 611, 615-616 (D.C. Cir. 1973), the court observed:

> When on January 20, 1969 President Nixon took office, and when on the same or even later dates the other individual defendants took their present offices, they were faced with a belligerent situation not of their creation. Obviously, the President could not properly execute the duties of his office or his responsibility as Commander-in-Chief by ordering hostilities to cease on the very day he took office. Even if his predecessors had exceeded their constitutional authority, President Nixon's duty did not go beyond trying, in good faith and to the best of his ability, to bring the war to an end as promptly as was consistent with the safety of those fighting and with a profound concern for the durable interests of the nation — its defense, its honor, its morality.
>
> Whether President Nixon did so proceed is a question which at this stage in history a court is incompetent to answer. A court cannot procure the relevant evidence: some is in the hands of foreign governments, some is privileged. Even

> if the necessary facts were to be laid before it, a court would not substitute its judgment for that of the President, who has an unusually wide measure of discretion in this area, and who should not be judicially condemned except in a case of clear abuse amounting to bad faith. Otherwise a court would be ignoring the delicacies of diplomatic negotiation, the inevitable bargaining for the best solution of an international conflict, and the scope which in foreign affairs must be allowed to the President if this country is to play a responsible role in the council of the nations.
>
> In short, we are faced with what has traditionally been called a "political question" which is beyond the judicial power conferred by Article III of the United States Constitution....

What if it could have been demonstrated that the President's statement did not reveal the whole truth, or even that he had deliberately lied? Do you think the court would then have been willing to declare the war effort unconstitutional, since the legitimacy of the war depended on "joint concord" or "some mutual participation" between the President and Congress? Would Congress have ordered the withdrawal of troops from hostilities?

2. *Political Options.* According to one commentator, the court should have been reluctant to intervene because Congress, if it chose to do so, could have cut off funding, censured the President, or even instituted impeachment proceedings against him. *See* Moore, *supra* p. 214, at 583. On the other hand, Justice Douglas observed in his dissent from the Supreme Court's refusal to hear one Vietnam case, "If we determine that the Indochina conflict is unconstitutional because it lacks a congressional declaration of war, the Chief Executive is free to seek one, as was President Truman free to seek congressional approval after our *Steel Seizure* decision." Massachusetts v. Laird, 400 U.S. 886, 899 (1970). How should the *DaCosta I* court have weighed these contrasting political possibilities? Was the court justified in waiting for a clearer expression of congressional intent to end the war more quickly?

3. *The Straightjacket Redux.* Unlike the *DaCosta I* court, the court in Mitchell v. Laird, *supra,* refused to characterize other legislation as "approval or ratification of a war already being waged at the direction of the President alone." 488 F.2d at 615.

> This court cannot be unmindful of what every schoolboy knows: that in voting to appropriate money or to draft men a Congressman is not necessarily approving of the continuation of a war no matter how specifically the appropriation or draft act refers to that war. A Congressman wholly opposed to the war's commencement and continuation might vote for the military appropriations and for the draft measures because he was unwilling to abandon without support men already fighting. An honorable, decent, compassionate act of aiding those already in peril is no proof of consent to the actions that placed and continued them in that dangerous posture. We should not construe votes cast in pity and piety as though they were votes freely given to express consent. [*Id.*]

Does the *Mitchell* court's theory help to explain why Congress continued to pour troops and materiel into the war effort year after year? Is Congress powerless, as a

C. Ending the Vietnam War

practical matter, to stop the process once it is begun by the President? Does the phenomenon described by the court raise doubts about the feasibility of inferring congressional authorization or ratification from "mere" appropriations? See *supra* p. 111.

4. *Winding Up to Wind Down?* Like the war itself, peace talks that began in Paris in 1968 seemed to drag on interminably as first one side and then the other hoped to gain some advantage at the bargaining table from success on the battlefield. In February 1970, direct, secret talks began between National Security Adviser Henry Kissinger and North Vietnamese envoy Le Duc Tho, but those negotiations too moved slowly. At the end of March 1972, North Vietnamese regulars and the Viet Cong launched a new coordinated offensive in the South. Only 6,000 Americans remaining in the country were equipped for combat, and, while more than a million South Vietnamese were under arms, the future of the Vietnamization program seemed to be in jeopardy. President Nixon decided that the only way to conclude peace talks on favorable terms was to finally cut off the flow of war materiel from the Soviet Union and China to North Vietnam—not by a diplomatic initiative but by forcibly closing the northern seaports. To that end, in May the President ordered the mining of the ports and harbors of North Vietnam and the continuation of air and naval strikes against military targets north of the seventeenth parallel.

The expanded use of force produced yet another challenge in court. Recalling the language of *DaCosta I* that "[i]f the Executive were now escalating the prolonged struggle instead of decreasing it, additional supporting action by the Legislative Branch...might well be required," 448 F.2d at 1370, the plaintiff argued that "the President's conduct has so altered the course of hostilities in Vietnam as to make the war as it is currently pursued different from the war...held in *Orlando* and *DaCosta [I]* to have been constitutionally ratified and authorized by Congress." DaCosta v. Laird (*DaCosta III*), 471 F.2d 1146, 1154 (2d Cir. 1973). The court again dismissed on political question grounds, this time citing a lack of discoverable and manageable judicial standards:

> Judges, deficient in military knowledge, lacking vital information upon which to assess the nature of battlefield decisions, and sitting thousands of miles from the field of action, cannot reasonably or appropriately determine whether a specific military operation constitutes an "escalation" of the war or is merely a new tactical approach within a continuing strategic plan.... Are the courts required to oversee the conduct of the war on a daily basis...? [*Id.* at 1155.]

Did the court reverse itself in its assessment of its own fitness to rule on a complicated fact situation—namely, whether the President was trying to wind down the war?

Once the President declared that it was necessary to intensify the war effort in order to wind it down, was there any way for the court to avoid characterizing the President's action as "tactical"? How do you think the *DaCosta III* court would have ruled on a presidential decision to use nuclear weapons in North Vietnam? How about a decision to bomb Beijing?

2. Another Congressional Step Back

The debate about the war was transformed dramatically in June 1971 with publication of the *Pentagon Papers*, which revealed more than two decades of executive concealment and duplicity about U.S. involvement in Southeast Asia. See *supra* p. 216 and Chapter 37. In the late fall of 1971, Congress passed and the President signed the Armed Forces Appropriations Authorization Act of 1971, Pub. L. No. 92-156, 85 Stat. 423 (1971), to which was attached the so-called Mansfield Amendment, 85 Stat. 430, which provided in part:

> Sec. 601. (a) It is hereby declared to be the policy of the United States to terminate at the earliest possible date all military operations of the United States in Indochina, and to provide for the prompt and orderly withdrawal of all United States military forces at a date certain, subject to the release of all American prisoners of war held by the government of North Vietnam and forces allied with such Government and an accounting for all Americans missing in action who have been held by or known to such Government or such forces....

The amendment goes on to "urge and request" the President to implement this policy by negotiating for an immediate cease-fire in Indochina and to set a date certain for the withdrawal of all U.S. forces from the area, contingent on the return of prisoners of war and an accounting for Americans missing in action. Nearly identical language appeared in an earlier measure amending the Military Selective Service Act, Pub. L. No. 92-129, §401, 85 Stat. 348, 360 (1971).

NOTES AND QUESTIONS

1. *A Congressional Commitment?* Why do you think the Mansfield Amendment was not cast in more forceful terms? Should we conclude from the merely aspirational tone of the measure that a majority in Congress still approved of the President's actions in Southeast Asia, albeit grudgingly? Did the amendment serve to diminish the President's authority in any way?

2. *Effect of a Signing Statement.* In a statement on signing the military appropriations bill containing the Mansfield Amendment, President Nixon had this to say:

> Section 601 expresses a judgment about the manner in which the American involvement in the war should be ended. However, it is without binding force or effect, and it does not reflect my judgment about the way in which the war should be brought to a conclusion. My signing of the bill that contains this section, therefore, will not change the policies I have pursued and that I will continue to pursue toward this end. [3 Pub. Papers 1114 (Nov. 17, 1971).]

Should a court testing the continued legitimacy of the war have been influenced by President Nixon's statement? If so, how? *See* T.J. Halstead, *Presidential Signing Statements: Constitutional and Institutional Implications* (Cong. Res. Serv. RL33667), Sept. 20, 2006.

C. Ending the Vietnam War

3. Cutting Off Funding for the War

The Hanoi government was outraged at President Nixon's renewed bombing and mining of its ports, but in the summer of 1972 Le Duc Tho met again in Paris with Dr. Kissinger. In October the two men reached a tentative agreement calling for a cease-fire, withdrawal of all remaining U.S. forces, and an exchange of prisoners. Political matters would be worked out among the various Vietnamese parties utilizing an interim "council of reconciliation." But the Saigon government balked at the agreement, and a number of details proved impossible to resolve quickly. In an effort to break the impasse, President Nixon ordered yet another round of bombing in the North, and in late December U.S. B-52s and other aircraft dropped 40,000 tons of bombs on the area between Hanoi and Haiphong. Then on January 27, 1973, a formal peace agreement was signed in Paris that closely resembled the one agreed to in October. The last U.S. troops left South Vietnam on March 29, 1973, and the last U.S. prisoners of war were allegedly released in Hanoi on April 1.

In Cambodia, air support for the Lon Nol regime had continued after all U.S. ground forces were withdrawn in 1970. When an effort to end fighting between Phnom Penh and Khmer Rouge forces in early 1973 ended in failure, U.S. forces began saturation bombing of Communist positions in that country. But a majority in Congress had finally had enough, and on May 31 a bill was passed containing the following amendment by Senator Thomas Eagleton:

> None of the funds herein appropriated under this act or heretofore appropriated under any other act may be expended to support directly or indirectly combat activities in, over or from off the shores of Cambodia or in or over Laos by United States forces. [29 Cong. Q. Almanac 102 (1973).]

President Nixon vetoed the bill on June 27, however, complaining that it would interfere with chances for a negotiated settlement in Cambodia, and the House failed to override his veto. Then on June 29, in a compromise, Congress approved and the President signed a measure to end all U.S. military involvement in Southeast Asia six weeks later, on August 15, with the result described in the following case.

Holtzman v. Schlesinger
United States Court of Appeals, Second Circuit, 1973
484 F.2d 1307

MULLIGAN, J. This is an appeal from a judgment of the United States District Court [declaring] . . . that "there is no existing Congressional authority to order military forces into combat in Cambodia or to release bombs over Cambodia, and that military activities in Cambodia by American armed forces are unauthorized and unlawful. . . ." The order further enjoined and restrained the named defendants and their officers, agents, servants, employees and attorneys "from participating in any way in military activities in or over Cambodia or releasing any bombs which may fall in Cambodia." . . .

At the outset... we should emphasize that we are not deciding the wisdom, the propriety or the morality of the war in Indo-China and particularly the ongoing bombing in Cambodia. This is the responsibility of the Executive and the Legislative branches of the government. The role of the Judiciary is to determine the legality of the challenged action and the threshold question is whether under the "political question" doctrine we should decline even to do that....

We fail to see how the present challenge involving the bombing in Cambodia is in any significant manner distinguishable from the situation discussed by Judge Kaufman in Da Costa v. Laird [*DaCosta III*].... If we were incompetent to judge the significance of the mining and bombing of North Vietnam's harbors and territories, we fail to see our competence to determine that the bombing of Cambodia is a "basic change" in the situation and that it is not a "tactical decision" within the competence of the President.... While we as men may well agonize and bewail the horror of this or any war, the sharing of Presidential and Congressional responsibility particularly at this juncture is a bluntly political and not a judicial question....

The court below and our dissenting Brother assume that since American ground forces and prisoners have been removed and accounted for, Congressional authorization has ceased as determined by virtue of the so-called Mansfield Amendment, P.L. 92-156, 85 Stat. 430, §601. The fallacy of this position is that we have no way of knowing whether the Cambodian bombing furthers or hinders the goals of the Mansfield Amendment. That is precisely the holding of Da Costa v. Laird [*DaCosta III*]. Moreover, although §601(a)(1) of the Amendment urges the President to remove all military forces contingent upon release of American prisoners, it also in §601(a)(2) urges him to negotiate for an immediate cease fire by all parties in the hostilities in *Indo-China*. (Emphasis added.) In our view, the return and repatriation of American troops only represents the beginning and not the end of the inquiry as to whether such a basic change has occurred that the Executive at this stage is suddenly bereft of power and authority. That inquiry involves diplomatic and military intelligence which is totally absent in the record before us, and its digestion in any event is beyond judicial management....

Since the argument that continuing Congressional approval was necessary, was predicated upon a determination that the Cambodian bombing constituted a basic change in the war not within the tactical discretion of the President and since that is a determination we have found to be a political question, we have not found it necessary to dwell at length upon Congressional participation.... We cannot resist however commenting that the most recent expression of Congressional approval by appropriation, the Joint Resolution Continuing Appropriations for Fiscal 1974 (P.L. 93-52), enacted into law July 1, 1973, contains the following provision:

> Sec. 108. Notwithstanding any other provision of law, on or after August 15, 1973, no funds herein or heretofore appropriated may be obligated or expended to finance directly or indirectly combat activities by United States military forces in or over or from off the shores of North Vietnam, South Vietnam, Laos or Cambodia.

Assuming arguendo that the military and diplomatic issues were manageable and that we were obliged to find some participation by Congress, we cannot see how this provision does not support the proposition that the Congress has approved the Cambodian bombing. The statute is facially clear.... It is [nevertheless] urged that since the Constitution entrusts the power to declare war to a majority of the Congress, the veto exercised makes it possible for the President to thwart the will of Congress by holding one-third plus one of the members of either House....

We cannot agree that the Congress was "coerced" by the President's veto. There was unquestionably a Congressional impasse resulting from the desire of a majority of Congress to stop bombing immediately and the desire of the President that his discretion be unfettered by an arbitrarily selected date. Instead of an acute constitutional confrontation, as Senator Javits noted, an "agreement" was reached. (119 Cong. Rec. S12561 (daily ed. June 29, 1973))....

While the Constitution vests the war declaring authority in the Congress, the Founding Fathers also conferred the veto power upon the President. (Art. I, §7, cl. 2). The suggestion that the veto power is impotent with respect to an authority vested solely in Congress by the Constitution is unsupported by any citation of authority and is hardly persuasive. It of course assumes here that the Cambodian bombing constitutes a new war requiring a new declaration and that it is not part of the extrication of a long suffering nation from an Indo-China war lasting for several years. This again in our view is the nucleus of the issue and we have no way of resolving that question particularly here on a motion for summary judgment....

The judgment is reversed and the case is remanded with instructions to dismiss the complaint. The mandate shall issue forthwith.

> OAKES, J. (dissenting).... Has Congress ratified or authorized the bombing in Cambodia by appropriations acts or otherwise?...
>
> ... [A]n argument could be made that congressional authorization of appropriations with knowledge of our "presence" in Cambodia was ratification. But for authorization on the part of Congress by way of an appropriation to be effective, the congressional action must be based on a knowledge of the facts. Greene v. McElroy, 360 U.S. 474, 506-507 (1959) (appropriation to Defense Department for security program did not ratify procedure denying right of an individual to confront witnesses). I am aware of only one instance in which it has previously been argued that a war was illegal as a result of Congress being misinformed as to the underlying facts surrounding American participation in that war. While the argument was unique and unsuccessful to boot, however, time has vindicated it, I believe. Furthermore, it was advanced by one whose views are worth consideration, even if they were expressed in "dissent," so to speak. I refer of course to Abraham Lincoln and his argument as a lone Congressman on January 12, 1848, in opposition to our "incursion" into Mexico and what later was called the Mexican war. *See* Cong. Globe, 30th Cong. 1st Sess. 93 et seq. (Appendix 1848).
>
> And here, incredibly enough, it appears that neither the American people nor the Congress, at the time it was voting appropriations in aid of the war in Vietnam, were given the facts pertaining to our bombing in Cambodia. Recent disclosures have indicated that Air Force B-52 bombers were secretly attacking Cambodia in 1969, 1970 and even later while the United States was publicly proclaiming respect for Cambodian neutrality....

... But the Congress whose ratification by way of appropriations acts is contended for here did not become aware of these covert bombings until July of 1973. And meanwhile the Congress had declared in the so-called Mansfield Amendment that it was "the policy of the United States to terminate at the earliest practicable date all military operations of the United States in Indochina...." Appropriations Authorization-Military Procurement Act of 1972, Pub. L. No. 92-156, §601, 85 Stat. 423 (92nd Cong., 1st Sess. 1971)....

We come then to the effect of the legislation, following upon a presidential veto of an immediate prohibition against the use of funds to bomb in Cambodia, adopted as a compromise this July 1st: the Continuing Appropriations Act for Fiscal Year 1974, Pub. L. No. 93-52, 93rd Cong. 2nd Sess. (July 1, 1973) which expressly provided that "... on or after August 15, 1973, no funds herein or heretofore appropriated may be obligated or expended to finance directly or indirectly combat activities by United States military forces in or over or from off the shores of North Vietnam, South Vietnam, Laos or Cambodia." §108....

It can be argued that Congress could, if it had so desired, cut off the funds for bombing Cambodia immediately by overriding the Presidential veto. This was indeed championed by those voting against the ultimate compromise Resolution. But it does not follow that those who voted in favor of the Resolution were thereby putting the Congressional stamp of approval on the bombing continuation. While the Resolution constituted a recognition that executive *power* was being exercised, it did not constitute a concession that such exercise was rightful, lawful or constitutional....

... Congress, as I see it, took the only practical way out. It acknowledged the reality of the Executive's exercise of power even while it disputed the Executive's authority for that exercise. It agreed to a final cut-off date as the best practical result but never conceded the legality or constitutionality of interim exercise.

Thus the Resolution of July 1, 1973 cannot be the basis for legalization of otherwise unlawful Executive action. We are talking here about the separate branches of government, and in doing so we must distinguish between the exercise of power on the one hand and authorization for such exercise on the other. That the Executive Branch had the power to bomb in Cambodia, there can be no doubt; it did so, and indeed is continuing to do so. Whether it had the constitutional authority for its action is another question....

NOTES AND QUESTIONS

1. *Vetoing Peace?* Is there any reason to suspect that the presidential veto process described in Article I, §7 of the Constitution does not apply to congressional war making, as it does to other congressional acts? Should it matter that a particular act of Congress could be viewed not as war making, but as peacemaking — that it may take two-thirds of Congress to stop a war already begun? See *supra* p. 21 (remarks of G. Mason); Ely, *supra* p. 216, at 43-46.

2. *Informed Participation.* Judge Oakes suggested that congressional consent is dependent on knowledge, citing Greene v. McElroy, 360 U.S. 474 (1959), *supra* p. 105. Is *Greene* distinguishable? Do you think the court should have taken account of the fact that information about the bombing of Cambodia

was not widely available at the time Congress was voting on military appropriations? Can you imagine some mechanism for Congress to keep itself informed about such developments?

3. *Judicial Realpolitik?* Holtzman v. Schlesinger was heard in a highly charged political atmosphere, as suggested by the series of stays and countermands by members of the Supreme Court during the pendency of the case. *See* 414 U.S. 1316 (1973), 414 U.S. 1321 (1973). Newspaper headlines were filled with the story of secret bombings, and the threat of impeachment proceedings was in the air. Indeed, it was suggested that the Cambodia bombing be one of the impeachment counts. *See Hearings Before the Comm. on the Judiciary Pursuant to H. Res. 803, Resolution Authorizing and Directing the Comm. on the Judiciary to Investigate Whether Sufficient Grounds Exist for the House of Representatives to Exercise Its Constitutional Power to Impeach Richard M. Nixon, Book XI: Bombing of Cambodia*, 93d Cong. (1974). Although the executive protested that Congress had no right to fetter the executive's use of force, the Secretary of State submitted an affidavit to the court committing the government to a termination of the bombing on August 15, only seven days after the *Holtzman* case was decided. Do you think these circumstances influenced the court's decision? Should they have? Do they affect the value of the *Holtzman* decision as precedent for future cases?

4. *Blame or Credit for Congress?* The role of Congress in ending the war is described in Ely, *supra* p. 216, at 32-46; and Thomas M. Franck & Edward Weisband, *Foreign Policy by Congress* 13-33 (1979). For an argument that Congress is at least partly responsible for the U.S. defeat in Vietnam, *see* Douglas Pike, *Congress and the Indochina War*, 11 Geo. Mason L. Rev. 119 (1988). A very different view is expressed in Davidson, *supra* p. 202, at 795-811. An extensive bibliography of writings about the war is found in Herring, *supra* p. 202, at 283-302.

United States bombing in Cambodia was halted on August 14, 1973, in accordance with the congressional mandate. In spite of the cease-fire prescribed in the Paris peace agreement, forces on both sides moved quickly to consolidate their holdings in the South, but by the summer of 1974 Viet Cong and North Vietnamese troops had recaptured all of the ground they had lost earlier. With the withdrawal of U.S. forces, the South Vietnamese economy began to crumble, and the Thieu regime's hold on the population grew more and more tenuous. United States support was reduced sharply after President Nixon resigned in August 1974, while the North Vietnamese poured new troops and supplies into the South for a climactic assault. Finally, Communist troops entered Saigon on April 30, 1975, bringing the war to an end.

The War Powers Resolution — 9

The War Powers Resolution (WPR) was a legislative response to the Vietnam War passed in 1973 over President Richard Nixon's veto. By it, Congress hoped to establish a consensual interbranch procedure for making war powers decisions that would prevent the President alone or both of the political branches together from taking the country to war by stealth or inadvertence. By overriding President Nixon's veto, however, Congress undercut this purpose. *See* Pat M. Holt, *The War Powers Resolution* 1-2 (1978). No President has conceded the constitutionality of the WPR or, many would say, fully complied with it, and its legal and practical effect today is unclear.

After reviewing the provisions of the WPR and President Nixon's veto message, we will analyze the resolution section by section in notes and questions. Case studies of the application of the WPR to specific deployments of U.S. armed forces are presented in Chapters 10-13.

War Powers Resolution
50 U.S.C. §§1541-1548 (2000)

SECTION 1. SHORT TITLE

This joint resolution may be cited as the "War Powers Resolution."

SECTION 2 [§1541]. PURPOSE AND POLICY

(a) It is the purpose of this chapter to fulfill the intent of the framers of the Constitution of the United States and insure that the collective judgment of both the Congress and the President will apply to the introduction of United States Armed Forces into hostilities, or into situations where imminent involvement in hostilities is clearly indicated by the circumstances, and to the continued use of such forces in hostilities or in such situations.

(b) Under article I, section 8, of the Constitution, it is specifically provided that the Congress shall have the power to make all laws necessary and proper for carrying into execution, not only its own powers but also all other powers vested by the Constitution in the Government of the United States, or in any department or officer thereof.

(c) The constitutional powers of the President as Commander-in-Chief to introduce United States Armed Forces into hostilities, or into situations where imminent involvement in hostilities is clearly indicated by the circumstances, are exercised only pursuant to (1) a declaration of war, (2) specific statutory authorization, or (3) a national emergency created by attack upon the United States, its territories or possessions, or its armed forces.

SECTION 3 [§1542]. CONSULTATION

The President in every possible instance shall consult with Congress before introducing United States Armed Forces into hostilities or into situations where imminent involvement in hostilities is clearly indicated by the circumstances, and after every such introduction shall consult regularly with the Congress until United States Armed Forces are no longer engaged in hostilities or have been removed from such situations.

SECTION 4 [§1543]. REPORTING REQUIREMENT

(a) In the absence of a declaration of war, in any case in which United States Armed Forces are introduced—

(1) into hostilities or into situations where imminent involvement in hostilities is clearly indicated by the circumstances;

(2) into the territory, airspace or waters of a foreign nation, while equipped for combat, except for deployments which relate solely to supply, replacement, repair, or training of such forces; or

(3) in numbers which substantially enlarge United States Armed Forces equipped for combat already located in a foreign nation;

the President shall submit within 48 hours to the Speaker of the House of Representatives and to the President pro tempore of the Senate a report, in writing, setting forth—

(A) the circumstances necessitating the introduction of United States Armed Forces;

(B) the constitutional and legislative authority under which such introduction took place; and

(C) the estimated scope and duration of the hostilities or involvement.

(b) The President shall provide such other information as the Congress may request in the fulfillment of its constitutional responsibilities with respect to committing the Nation to war and to the use of United States Armed Forces abroad.

(c) Whenever United States Armed Forces are introduced into hostilities or into any situation described in subsection (a) of this section, the President shall, so long as such Armed Forces continue to be engaged in such hostilities or situation, report to the Congress periodically on the status of such hostilities or situation as well as on the scope and duration of such hostilities or situation, but in no event shall he report to the Congress less often than once every six months.

SECTION 5 [§1544]. CONGRESSIONAL ACTION

(a) Each report submitted pursuant to section 1543(a)(1) of this title shall be transmitted to the Speaker of the House of Representatives and to the President pro tempore of the Senate on the same calendar day. Each report so transmitted shall be referred to the Committee on Foreign Affairs of the House of Representatives and to the Committee on Foreign Relations of the Senate for appropriate action. If, when the report is transmitted, the Congress has adjourned sine die or has adjourned for any period in excess of three calendar days, the Speaker of the House of Representatives and the President pro tempore of the Senate, if they deem it advisable (or if petitioned by at least 30 percent of the membership of their respective Houses) shall jointly request the President to convene Congress in order that it may consider the report and take appropriate action pursuant to this section.

(b) Within sixty calendar days after a report is submitted or is required to be submitted pursuant to section 1543(a)(1) of this title, whichever is earlier, the President shall terminate any use of United States Armed Forces with respect to which such report was submitted (or required to be submitted), unless the Congress (1) has declared war or has enacted a specific authorization for such use of United States Armed Forces, (2) has extended by law such sixty-day period, or (3) is physically unable to meet as a result of an armed attack upon the United States. Such sixty-day period shall be extended for not more than an additional thirty days if the President determines and certifies to the Congress in writing that unavoidable military necessity respecting the safety of United States Armed Forces requires the continued use of such Armed Forces in the course of bringing about a prompt removal of such forces.

(c) Notwithstanding subsection (b) of this section, at any time that United States Armed Forces are engaged in hostilities outside the territory of the United States, its possessions and territories without a declaration of war or specific statutory authorization, such forces shall be removed by the President if the Congress so directs by concurrent resolution.

[Sections 6 & 7, §§1545-1546, Congressional Priority Procedures for Joint Resolution or Bill, and for Concurrent Resolution, respectively, provide for expedited consideration of measures to approve the President's actions under §1544(b) or disapprove them under §1544(c).]

SECTION 8 [§1547]. INTERPRETATION OF JOINT RESOLUTION

(a) Authority to introduce United States Armed Forces into hostilities or into situations wherein involvement in hostilities is clearly indicated by the circumstances shall not be inferred —

(1) from any provision of law (whether or not in effect before November 7, 1973), including any provision contained in any Appropriation Act, unless such provision specifically authorizes the introduction of United States Armed Forces into hostilities or into such situations and states that it is intended to constitute specific statutory authorization within the meaning of this chapter; or

(2) from any treaty heretofore or hereafter ratified unless such treaty is implemented by legislation specifically authorizing the introduction of United States Armed Forces into hostilities or into such situations and stating that it is intended to constitute specific statutory authorization within the meaning of this chapter.

(b) Nothing in this chapter shall be construed to require any further specific statutory authorization to permit members of United States Armed Forces to participate jointly with members of the Armed Forces of one or more foreign countries in the headquarters operations of high-level military commands which were established prior to November 7, 1973, and pursuant to the United Nations Charter or any treaty ratified by the United States prior to such date.

(c) For purposes of this chapter, the term "introduction of United States Armed Forces" includes the assignment of members of such Armed Forces to command, coordinate, participate in the movement of, or accompany the regular or irregular military forces of any foreign country or government when such military forces are engaged, or there exists an imminent threat that such forces will become engaged, in hostilities.

(d) Nothing in this chapter —

(1) is intended to alter the constitutional authority of the Congress or of the President, or the provisions of existing treaties; or

(2) shall be construed as granting any authority to the President with respect to the introduction of United States Armed Forces into hostilities or into situations wherein involvement in hostilities is clearly indicated by the circumstances which authority he would not have had in the absence of this chapter.

SECTION 9 [§1548]. SEPARABILITY OF PROVISIONS

If any provision of this chapter or the application thereof to any person or circumstance is held invalid, the remainder of the chapter and the application of such provision to any other person or circumstance shall not be affected thereby.

Richard M. Nixon, Veto of the War Powers Resolution
5 Pub. Papers 893 (Oct. 24, 1973)

To the House of Representatives:

I hereby return without my approval House Joint Resolution 542 — the War Powers Resolution. While I am in accord with the desire of the Congress to assert its proper role in the conduct of our foreign affairs, the restrictions which this resolution would impose upon the authority of the President are both unconstitutional and dangerous to the best interests of our Nation....

CLEARLY UNCONSTITUTIONAL

House Joint Resolution 542 would attempt to take away, by a mere legislative act, authorities which the President has properly exercised under the

Constitution for almost 200 years. One of its provisions would automatically cut off certain authorities after sixty days unless the Congress extended them. Another would allow the Congress to eliminate certain authorities merely by the passage of a concurrent resolution—an action which does not normally have the force of law, since it denies the President his constitutional role in approving legislation.

I believe that both these provisions are unconstitutional. The only way in which the constitutional powers of a branch of the Government can be altered is by amending the Constitution—and any attempt to make such alterations by legislation alone is clearly without force.

UNDERMINING OUR FOREIGN POLICY

While I firmly believe that a veto of House Joint Resolution 542 is warranted solely on constitutional grounds, I am also deeply disturbed by the practical consequences of this resolution. For it would seriously undermine this Nation's ability to act decisively and convincingly in times of international crisis. As a result, the confidence of our allies in our ability to assist them could be diminished and the respect of our adversaries for our deterrent posture could decline. A permanent and substantial element of unpredictability would be injected into the world's assessment of American behavior, further increasing the likelihood of miscalculation and war.

If this resolution had been in operation, America's effective response to a variety of challenges in recent years would have been vastly complicated or even made impossible. We may well have been unable to respond in the way we did during the Berlin crisis of 1961, the Cuban missile crisis of 1962, the Congo rescue operation in 1964, and the Jordanian crisis of 1970—to mention just a few examples. In addition, our recent actions to bring about a peaceful settlement of the hostilities in the Middle East would have been seriously impaired if this resolution had been in force.

While all the specific consequences of House Joint Resolution 542 cannot yet be predicted, it is clear that it would undercut the ability of the United States to act as an effective influence for peace. For example, the provision automatically cutting off certain authorities after 60 days unless they are extended by the Congress could work to prolong or intensify a crisis. Until the Congress suspended the deadline, there would be at least a chance of United States withdrawal and an adversary would be tempted therefore to postpone serious negotiations until the 60 days were up. Only after the Congress acted would there be a strong incentive for an adversary to negotiate. In addition, the very existence of a deadline could lead to an escalation of hostilities in order to achieve certain objectives before the 60 days expired.

The measure would jeopardize our role as a force for peace in other ways as well. It would, for example, strike from the President's hand a wide range of important peace-keeping tools by eliminating his ability to exercise quiet diplomacy backed by subtle shifts in our military deployments. It would also cast into doubt authorities which Presidents have used to undertake certain humanitarian relief missions in conflict areas, to protect fishing boats from seizure, to deal with ship or aircraft hijackings, and to respond to threats of attack. Not the least of the adverse consequences of this resolution would be the prohibition contained in section 8 against fulfilling our obligations under the NATO treaty as ratified by the Senate. Finally, since the bill is somewhat vague as to when the 60 day rule would apply, it could lead to extreme confusion and dangerous disagreements concerning the prerogatives of the two branches, seriously damaging our ability to respond to international crises.

FAILURE TO REQUIRE POSITIVE CONGRESSIONAL ACTION

I am particularly disturbed by the fact that certain of the President's constitutional powers as Commander in Chief of the Armed Forces would terminate automatically under this resolution 60 days after they were invoked. No overt Congressional action would be required to cut off these powers—they would disappear automatically unless the Congress extended them. In effect, the Congress is here attempting to increase its policymaking role through a provision which requires it to take absolutely no action at all.

In my view, the proper way for the Congress to make known its will on such foreign policy questions is through a positive action, with full debate on the merits of the issue and with each member taking the responsibility of casting a yes or no vote after considering those merits. The authorization and appropriations process represents one of the ways in which such influence can be exercised. I do not, however, believe that the Congress can responsibly contribute its considered, collective judgment on such grave questions without full debate and without a yes or no vote. Yet this is precisely what the joint resolution would allow. It would give every future Congress the ability to handcuff every future President merely by doing nothing and sitting still. In my view, one cannot become a responsible partner unless one is prepared to take responsible action.

STRENGTHENING COOPERATION BETWEEN THE CONGRESS AND THE EXECUTIVE BRANCHES

The responsible and effective exercise of the war powers requires the fullest cooperation between the Congress and the Executive and the prudent fulfillment by each branch of its constitutional responsibilities. House Joint Resolution 542 includes certain constructive measures which would foster this process by enhancing the flow of information from the executive branch to the Congress. Section 3, for example, calls for consultation with the Congress before and during the involvement of the United States forces in hostilities abroad. This provision is consistent with the desire of this Administration for regularized consultations with the Congress in an even wider range of circumstances....

RICHARD NIXON

The White House
October 24, 1973

NOTES AND QUESTIONS

a. The "Substantive" Provisions of Section 2

Under-Inclusiveness of the WPR? The Senate originally took a substantially more specific approach to itemizing the President's constitutional war powers than WPR §2(c). The Senate included the powers "to take necessary and appropriate retaliatory actions in the event of [an armed attack upon the U.S., its territories or possessions]," "to forestall the direct and imminent threat of [an attack against the armed forces of the United States located outside the United States, its territories, and possessions]," and "to protect while evacuating citizens and nationals of the United States, as rapidly as possible, from [certain situations] involving a direct and imminent threat to [their] lives." S. 440, 93d Cong. §3 (1973). Which version more faithfully tracks the constitutional war and emergency powers of the executive recognized in such cases as *The Prize Cases, supra* p. 67, and *Neagle, supra* p. 80? Is even the Senate version complete? Could *any* list be complete? If not, can you think of any other way to frame the "substantive" provision of the WPR that is not under-inclusive? *See* John Hart Ely, *Suppose Congress Wanted a War Powers Act That Worked*, 88 Colum. L. Rev. 1379, 1394 (1988).

In light of the rescue and other war powers asserted by the President, is the WPR unconstitutional? What bearing does WPR §8(d) have on your answer? If these *are* inherent constitutional powers of the President, does Congress have any authority to define them? *See* Stephen L. Carter, *The Constitutionality of the War Powers Resolution*, 70 Va. L. Rev. 101, 117 (1984). To limit them? See *supra* pp. 124-127 (discussing the *Lovett* principle and Congress's appropriations and necessary and proper powers).

Critics of the WPR argue that it unconstitutionally attempts to overturn 200 years of history, during which the President established his claim to war-making authority by usage. *See, e.g.*, J. Terry Emerson, *The War Powers Resolution Tested: The President's Independent Defense Power*, 51 Notre Dame Law. 187, 195-201 (1975); Eugene V. Rostow, *"Once More Unto the Breach": The War Powers Resolution Revisited*, 21 Val. U. L. Rev. 1, 5-18 (1986); Eugene V. Rostow, *Great Cases Make Bad Law: The War Powers Act*, 50 Tex. L. Rev. 833 (1972) (criticizing an early Senate version of the WPR). Defenders of the WPR note that past congressional acquiescence in executive war powers at most establishes that the President may exercise them "*if Congress does not try to stop him.* If Congress *does* try to stop him, then by definition it is no longer acquiescing." Carter, *supra*, at 124 (emphasis in original). Moreover, presidential claims of inherent and exclusive war-making power were first made openly in 1950, and defenders argue that "23 years of deviance" from the pre-1950 understanding of war powers "hardly seem sufficient so definitely to have redefined the constitutional arrangement as to render unconstitutional the [WPR's] attempt to return to the prior understanding." Ely, *supra*, at 1392.

The Senate itemization of these powers was contained not in the "purpose and policy" section of its bill, but in an operational section entitled "Emergency Use of the Armed Forces." This section stated that U.S. troops could be introduced only in certain enumerated instances, the last of which was prior specific congressional authorization. The Conference Committee deliberately moved its itemization to WPR §2 and explained that subsequent sections were not dependent on the language of §2(c). H.R. Rep. No. 93-547, at 8 (1973) (Conf. Rep.).

Why do you suppose the Committee made this change? Does this affect your judgment of the constitutionality of the WPR?

b. Consultation

1. *With Whom?* When does the WPR require the President to consult Congress before introducing U.S. armed forces? Is it satisfied by consultation with a few selected members of Congress? With the relevant congressional leadership? With the leadership plus the membership of relevant committees? With all the members of Congress? What are the practical problems attending each alternative? The WPR's failure to answer these questions has prompted numerous proposed amendments. *See, e.g.,* S.J. Res. 323 & H.R.J. Res. 601, 100th Cong. (1988) (specifying both a small leadership group composed of the Speaker of the House, President pro tempore of the Senate, and the majority and minority leaders of each body, and a larger "permanent consultative group" of these 6 plus 12 committee leaders).

2. *For What?* Does the WPR require advance consultation about exercises of inherent presidential war-making authority? If so, by what authority? *See* Rostow, *supra*, at 41 (Congress may not command the President to "consult" with any of its members because "[a]ny such attempt would interfere with the President's most sensitive executive discretion, that of political leadership.").

3. *How?* What does "consult" mean? The House report on the WPR expressly rejected

> the notion that consultation should be synonymous with merely being informed. Rather, consultation in this provision means that a decision is pending on a problem and that Members of Congress are being asked by the President for their advice and opinions and, in appropriate circumstances, their approval of action contemplated. Furthermore, for consultation to be meaningful, the President must himself participate and all information relevant to the situation must be made available. [H.R. Rep. No. 93-287, at 6-7 (1973).]

Former Secretary of State Cyrus Vance has written that "consultation" means not only advance transmittal of all relevant information to the congressional leadership in sufficient time "to permit a reasonable opportunity to absorb the information, consider its implications, and form a judgment before irrevocable decisions are made by the President," but also "that the congressional leadership should have a real opportunity to communicate its views to the President or at least to his closest advisors." Cyrus R. Vance, *Striking the Balance: Congress and the President Under the War Powers Resolution*, 133 U. Pa. L. Rev. 79, 87-91 (1984).

4. *Why?* Other critics ask what good it would do to consult with Congress about most questions of national security or foreign relations: its members are allegedly parochial, partisan, poorly informed, preoccupied with re-election, and, in a word, collectively unwise about national security and foreign affairs. Indeed, involving them may effectively amount only to involving their staffs, with

a substantially increased risk of leaks that will compromise national security. *See, e.g.*, Robert F. Turner, *Repealing the War Powers Resolution* 110 (1991).

If this critique is correct, does it bear on the constitutionality of the WPR? The Senate Foreign Relations Committee's answer was that the Framers vested the war power in Congress "not primarily because they felt confident that the legislature would necessarily exercise it more wisely but because they expected the legislature to exercise it more *sparingly* than it had been exercised by the Crown, or would be likely to be exercised by the President as successor to the Crown." S. Rep. No. 93-220, at 86 (1973) (emphasis in original). *See also* Carter, *supra* p. 246, at 128 ("policy is not unconstitutional *merely* because it is unwise").

c. The "Hostilities" Trigger and the Reporting Requirements

1. *The Textual Trigger and Its Legislative History.* What is the trigger for application of the WPR's §4(a)(1) reporting and §5(b) 60-day clock provisions? The House Report explained that

> [i]n addition to a situation in which fighting actually has begun, *hostilities* also encompasses a state of confrontation in which no shots have been fired but where there is a clear and present danger of armed conflict. "*Imminent hostilities*" denotes a situation in which there is a clear potential either for such a state of confrontation or for actual armed conflict. [H.R. Rep. No. 93-287, at 7 (1973) (emphasis in original).]

Does this explanation help? What is a "clear potential" for a "clear and present danger"? What does WPR §8(c) add? *See generally* William H. Hardy Jr., Note, *A Tug of War: The War Powers Resolution and the Meaning of "Hostilities,"* 15 Pac. L.J. 265 (1984) (urging broad definition of "hostilities" to prevent presidential *fait accomplis* in committing troops).

2. *Defining "Hostilities" or "War" in the "Tanker War."* In 1988, Iranian attacks on oil tankers in the Persian Gulf prompted President Reagan to deploy U.S. naval vessels as escorts. *See generally* Ely, *supra* p. 246, at 1381-1383 (from which most of the following narrative is drawn). By mid-1988, 31 U.S. vessels were patrolling the Gulf. On April 14, a mine seriously damaged a U.S. frigate, injuring ten members of the crew. Blaming Iran, U.S. forces destroyed two Iranian oil platforms. Two Iranian jets approached an American cruiser but were driven off by anti-aircraft missiles. An Iranian missile boat fired on the cruiser and missed but was then destroyed by return fire from U.S. boats and planes. Meanwhile, in response to attacks by armed Iranian speedboats on a U.S.-flagged supply boat, U.S. planes sank one speedboat and damaged two others. Later the same day, the United States responded to an attack by Iranian frigates on U.S. vessels by sinking one and crippling the other with missiles and aerial bombs. On July 3, 1988, a U.S. cruiser in the Persian Gulf mistook a civilian Iranian airliner for a warplane and downed it with a missile, killing 290 people. The Chairman of the Joint Chiefs of Staff explained that the cruiser's action differed from the Soviet downing of a Korean airliner because the latter did not occur in "a war zone, there was not combat in progress, there was not combat there normally." Statement by Joint Chiefs' Chairman: "U.S. Deeply Regrets This Incident"... but Commanders

on the Scene Believed "Their Units Were in Jeopardy," N.Y. Times, July 4, 1988, at A4. Vice President Bush echoed this explanation: "The Iranians shouldn't be sending an airliner over a combat zone.... A captain is under fire in combat." Richard Halloran, *U.S. Aides Cautious on Airbus Inquiry*, N.Y. Times, Aug. 4, 1988, at A6. Notwithstanding these developments, President Reagan never filed a WPR §4(a)(1) report. Should he have? The Administration's "position seemed to be that we were at war but there was no danger of hostilities." Ely, *supra*, at 1383.

This "Tanker War" in the Persian Gulf generated litigation that produced two strikingly different opinions about the nature of the hostilities. In Lowry v. Reagan, 676 F. Supp. 333 (D.D.C. 1987), the court declined to decide whether the hostilities required the President to file an "imminent hostilities report," partly on grounds that the case presented a political question. In response to the congressional plaintiff's argument that the WPR's legislative history indicated a clear intent to involve Congress in the decision-making process at a relatively early stage of U.S. military involvement abroad, the court said:

> If one were to take this discussion at face value, it might be possible to make a common-sense determination regarding the existence of hostilities. However, two considerations compel the Court to question this approach. First, and most importantly, the very absence of a definitional section in the Resolution, coupled with debate suggesting that determinations of "hostilities" were intended to be political decisions made by the President and Congress, suggest to this Court that fixed legal standards were deliberately omitted from this statutory scheme. Second, the factual evaluation of "hostilities [and] ... situations where imminent involvement in hostilities is clearly indicated by the circumstances" is always hampered, to some degree, by a Court's lack of access to intelligence information and other pertinent expertise. This is exacerbated by the ever-changing intensity of "hostilities," especially when they are in their early stages. The President must have flexibility in executing military and foreign policy on a day to day basis. Thus, this Court is inclined to conclude that this case does not present judicially manageable standards. [*Id.* at 340-341 n.53.]

In Koohi v. United States, 976 F.2d 1328 (9th Cir. 1992), the heirs of deceased passengers and crew of the Iranian airliner shot down by the U.S. cruiser *Vincennes* in the Persian Gulf sued the United States and certain defense contractors for damages under the Federal Tort Claims Act (FTCA), 28 U.S.C. §§1346(b), 2671-2680 (2000). The court had to decide whether the claim fell within the FTCA exception for "[a]ny claim arising out of combatant activities of the military or naval forces, or the Coast Guard during time of war." After noting that the events surrounding the "tanker war" in the Persian Gulf "are a matter of historical record, are supported by documentation in the district court record, and are — to the extent that they are relevant to the outcome of the case before us — beyond reasonable dispute," the court reached the issue whether the hostilities constituted a "time of war."

> We do not express any view concerning the constitutionality of acts of war by American armed forces in the absence of a formal declaration of war. We simply note that such acts have occurred with regularity in recent years, and that from a practical standpoint "time of war" has come to mean periods of significant armed

conflict rather than times governed by formal declarations of war. Since neither the text nor the legislative history of the FTCA expressly states whether Congress intended the combatant activities exception to apply to undeclared conflicts, we must arrive at our conclusion primarily through the use of those techniques to which we have previously adverted — reason and judgment. Here, that process leads us, inexorably, to construe the exception in light of contemporary realities. By giving the term "time of war" its full current meaning rather than a crabbed, artificial, or technical reading we make common sense out of unclear words and best effectuate the purposes of the statute: we shield the government from the type of liability it never intended to assume.

It seems clear that the purpose of the exception we are construing is to ensure that the government will not be liable for negligent conduct by our armed forces in times of combat. Whether that combat is formally authorized by the Congress or follows less formal actions of the Executive and Legislative branches would seem to be irrelevant to Congress's objectives....

In sum, we have no difficulty in concluding that when, as a result of a deliberate decision by the executive branch, United States armed forces engage in an organized series of hostile encounters on a significant scale with the military forces of another nation, the FTCA exception applies. Under those circumstances, a "time of war" exists, at least for purposes of domestic tort law.

There can be no doubt that during the "tanker war" a "time of war" existed. The United States' involvement in naval combat while the Iran-Iraq war was in progress was the result of a deliberate decision on the part of the executive branch to engage in hostile military activities vis-a-vis Iran in order to protect Gulf shipping.... Under the circumstances, we believe that the shooting down of the Airbus by the *Vincennes* falls within the FTCA's exception for combatant activities during time of war. Accordingly, the plaintiffs' FTCA action against the *Vincennes* is barred by the doctrine of sovereign immunity. [976 F.2d at 1334-1335.]

Are these opinions, concerning the same hostilities, reconcilable?

3. *Triggering Reporting.* When does the trigger for reporting to Congress differ from the trigger for consulting with Congress and from the trigger for the 60-day clock under §5(b)? Why? What problems do you foresee arising from any differences? If the President wanted to evade the 60-day clock without openly defying the WPR reporting requirement, what could he do?

The first WPR report was made in 1975. President Ford wrote to the President pro tempore of the Senate, "In accordance with my desire to keep the Congress fully informed on this matter, and taking note of the provision of section 4(a)(2) of the War Powers Resolution (P.L. 93-148), I wish to report to you" that combat-equipped American troops had been dispatched to pick up refugees off the coast of the besieged city of Da Nang, South Vietnam. As authority for this initiative, President Ford cited his "constitutional authority as Commander in Chief and Chief Executive in the conduct of foreign relations and . . . the Foreign Assistance Act of 1961," which authorized humanitarian assistance to refugees of the Vietnam War. Subcomm. on Intl. Security and Scientific Affairs, H. Comm. on Foreign Affairs, 98th Cong., *War Powers Resolution: Relevant Documents, Correspondence, Reports* 40-41 (Comm. Print 1983). One week later, he made a second report "taking note of Section 4" of the WPR, and advising that U.S. air and ground troops were assisting in the evacuation of Phnom Penh, Cambodia, on the eve of its fall to Khmer Rouge forces. *Id.* at 42.

President Carter varied this reporting formula slightly when he advised Congress of the aborted Iran Hostage Rescue Mission "[b]ecause of my desire that Congress be informed on this matter and consistent with the reporting provisions of the War Powers Resolution." *Id.* at 47. Did these reports comply with the WPR? Why didn't the last two reports specify the section of WPR §4 under which they were made? Does the WPR even apply to these uses of the armed forces? For an update of WPR reports through early 2001, *see* Richard F. Grimmett, *War Powers Resolution: Presidential Compliance* (Cong. Res. Serv. RL33532), July 1, 2006.

4. *The Content of WPR Reports.* One student asserts that the intended purposes of a WPR report are triggering the 60-day clock, prompting a dialogue between the branches about the use of force, promoting accountability for the decision to use force, disciplining the decision-making process within the executive branch, and providing Congress with information sufficient for it to legislate concerning the use of force. *See* Daniel L. Richards, *Reporting Under the War Powers Resolution: Section 4*, in George Washington University Law School War Powers Project (GWU Project), *The War Powers Resolution: Origins, History, Criticism and Reform*, 2 J. Natl. Security L. 59 (1998). Which, if any, of these purposes have WPR reports fulfilled? In considering this question, review the required content of the reports. *See* WPR §4, 50 U.S.C. §1543. How would you change the reporting requirement to better fulfill its purposes? In light of the continued refusal of courts to decide WPR questions, does the portion of a WPR report describing the legal authority for a deployment take on any added importance?

d. The 60-Day Clock

1. *A Self-Executing Clock?* Section 5(b) establishes a 60-day (plus 30-day extension) limit on the commitment of troops without congressional authorization. What happens under the WPR if the President refuses to file a §4(a)(1) report or files under the wrong provision? Is §5(b) self-enforcing, or must Congress pull a "second trigger" by declaring that a report is "required to be submitted" within the meaning of the provision? In Crockett v. Reagan, 558 F. Supp. 893, 901 (D.D.C. 1982), *aff'd*, 720 F.2d 1355 (D.C. Cir. 1983), the court found that

> the legislative scheme did not contemplate court-ordered withdrawal when no report has been filed, but rather, it leaves open the possibility for a court to order that a report be filed or, alternatively, withdrawal 60 days after a report was filed or required to be filed by a court or Congress.... [W]here no report has been filed, and the priority procedures would not be invoked, the majority of Congress might not be of the opinion that a specific authorization is necessary for continued involvement and take no action, unaware that this course could result in mandatory withdrawal. In that instance court-ordered withdrawal could thwart the will of the majority of Congress. Therefore, when a report has not been filed, it is consistent with the purposes and structure of the WPR to require further congressional action before the automatic termination provision operates.

But see Steven V. Roberts, *War Powers? What War Powers?* N.Y. Times, Oct. 6, 1987, at A32 (quoting Richard P. Conlon, executive director of the Democratic Study

Group, who protested that "Congress should not have to pass a new law in order to enforce a law already on the books.").

Alternatively, should the courts decide when a §4(a)(1) report is "required to be submitted" under the WPR? Is this question justiciable? If a court reaches the question, what remedy should it give? A declaration of when it should first have been filed (and, if more than 60 days have passed since that time, a concurrent order instructing the President to withdraw the troops)? Or a contemporaneous declaration — not order — that a report is now "required to be submitted" within the meaning of WPR §5(b)? *See* Ely, *supra* p. 246, at 1416-1417. Which remedy would be most consistent with the ultimate purpose of the WPR?

2. *Constitutionality of 60-Day Clock.* Why did President Nixon oppose WPR §5(b)? If §2(c) itemizes the President's inherent *constitutional* powers to introduce U.S. armed forces into hostilities, how can Congress subject those powers to the statutory limitations of §5(b)? What practical impact could §5(b) have on the President's decision to arm U.S. forces? On the degree to which a President might escalate U.S. involvement? On the safety with which a required withdrawal of troops could be carried out? *See* Turner, *supra* p. 248, at 129-155; Bradley Larschan, *The War Powers Resolution: Conflicting Constitutional Powers, the War Powers and U.S. Foreign Policy,* 16 Den. J. Intl. L. & Poly. 33, 71 (1987). Are these consequences of the WPR alone or of any reading of the Constitution that requires congressional approval for nondefensive hostilities abroad? *See* Ely, *supra* p. 246, at 1400. *See also* Walter L. Williams, *The Sixty-Day Rule of the War Powers Resolution: Section 5(b),* in GWU Project, *supra,* at 98-99 (attributing practical problems of warfare under the WPR to the Constitution, not the WPR's 60-day rule, and noting that the President retains the option of obtaining congressional approval for longer deployments).

3. *A Free Pass?* In any case, *within* the 60- (or 90-) day time limit, has not the WPR given the President a free pass to use armed force abroad? Consider the following assessment:

> [T]he defect at the heart of the WPR is that it has given *both* the President and Congress a putative free pass. In the actual contemporary exercise of war powers, perception has become reality as both the media and many members of Congress overlook the WPR's disclaimer of authority [§8(d)(2), 50 U.S.C. §1547(c)(2) (2000).] Thus, some proponents of unilateral presidential action invoke the putative sixty-day free pass as license to use force abroad without constitutionally required advance authorization from Congress. Congress, for its part, takes false comfort that it has somehow fulfilled its constitutional duty to decide on uses of force abroad by doing nothing. [*Deciding to Use Force Abroad: War Powers in a System of Checks and Balances* 33-34 (The Constitution Project, Peter Raven-Hansen rptr., 2005).]

See also Louis Fisher & David Gray Adler, *The War Powers Resolution: Time to Say Goodbye,* 113 Pol. Sci. Q. 1, 11 (1998) (urging repeal of the WPR to "eliminate the concession of 1973 that presidents may use military force anywhere in the world, for whatever reason, for up to ninety days, if not longer"). Although some might quarrel about triggering events, prior to the Operation Allied Force bombing campaign against the Federal Republic of Yugoslavia in 1999, see *infra* p. 302, no combat operation had ever "run the sixty-day clock" without statutory authorization. *See* Geoffrey S. Corn, *Clinton, Kosovo, and the Final Destruction of the War Powers Resolution*, 42 Wm. & Mary L. Rev. 1149, 1154 (2001). Does this history prove that the WPR has become a "free pass"?

e. The Concurrent Resolution

The WPR was a *joint resolution*, which must be presented to the President before becoming law. A *concurrent resolution* is not presented to the President for his signature and, according to *Chadha*, is therefore not law. See *supra* p. 128.

WPR §5(c) authorizes Congress by concurrent resolution to direct the removal of troops from abroad within the 60-day period. Is WPR §5(c) constitutional after *Chadha*? One imaginative argument that it is constitutional relies on the premise that a declaration of war is extraordinary legislation that is not subject to presentment. *See* Carter, *supra* p. 246, at 129-132 (analogizing a declaration to a congressionally proposed constitutional amendment, which the Supreme Court declared exempt from presentment in Hollingsworth v. Virginia, 3 U.S. (3 Dall.) 378 (1798)). If the premise is correct, it follows that any formal expression of the will of the entire Congress (not just one House) — such as the concurrent resolution of WPR §5(c) — should control whether we initiate or continue war. But does the constitutional text support the premise of this argument? *See* Clarence A. Berdahl, *War Powers of the Executive in the United States* 95-96 (1921) (presentment of bill declaring war is necessary). Does history support this argument? *See* Daniel E. Lungren & Mark L. Krotoski, *The War Powers Resolution After the Chadha Decision*, 17 Loy. L.A. L. Rev. 767, 786 n.84 (1984) (every declaration of war has been signed by the President).

Another argument is that *Chadha* is distinguishable because it involved an attempt by Congress to take back authority it had delegated to the President, while WPR §8(d)(2) expressly disclaims delegating any war-making authority to the President. *See, e.g.*, Vance, *supra* p. 247, at 86; G. Sidney Buchanan, *The War Powers Resolution: Chadha Does Not Apply*, 22 Hous. L. Rev. 1155, 1166 (1985). A concurrent resolution of disapproval is merely an expression of congressional will in the "twilight zone" of shared power, when presidential authority depends partly on congruence with the "expressed *or implied* will of Congress." *See* Martin Wald, Note, *The Future of the War Powers Resolution*, 36 Stan. L. Rev. 1407, 1433 (1984) (quoting *The Steel Seizure Case*, 343 U.S. at 637, *supra* p. 28 (Jackson, J., concurring)); Vance, *supra*, at 85 (WPR creates procedure by which Congress expresses "its institutional judgment" on the question of whether President has constitutional authority to act).

f. The Rule of Construction

1. *Inferences of Authorization from Statutes.* WPR §8(a)(1) supplies a rule of construction intended to prevent inferences of authority for the use of armed forces such as those the courts made in Orlando v. Laird, *supra* p. 219, and Holtzman v. Schlesinger, *supra* p. 235. Suppose that Congress passed and the President signed into law a supplemental appropriation providing $2 billion for "the use and support of U.S. armed forces to protect citizens of Darfur

[a region of Sudan] from military and paramilitary aggression." How, if at all, would the rule of construction apply to such an appropriation? How would WPR §8(a)(1) apply if the measure provided, in its entirety, that "the President is authorized to use all necessary means, including armed force, to protect citizens of Darfur from military and paramilitary aggression"?

If the new statute would not satisfy the WPR, which statute would control? How can the intent of the Congress that enacted the WPR in 1973 prevail over the intent of a later Congress that enacted our hypothetical statute? *Compare* William C. Banks & Peter Raven-Hansen, *National Security Law and the Power of the Purse* 130-131 (1994) (asserting that it cannot; when two statutes clash, the clearly expressed intent — if discernible — of the last in time controls), *with* Michael J. Glennon, *Mr. Sofaer's War Powers Partnership*, 80 Am. J. Intl. L. 584, 586 (1986) (asserting "first-in-time" rule of construction by which all post-WPR legislation must be read *in pari materia* with and subordinate to WPR §8), *and* Ely, *supra* p. 246, at 1418 (asserting that WPR creates "a strong rule of construction... telling us how to read the intent of later Congress"). If a later statue controls even when it lacks §8(a)(1)'s "magic words" (what are they?), is WPR §8(a)(1) a dead letter?

2. *Inferences of Authorization from Treaties.* WPR §8(a)(2) prohibits the inference of authorization from treaties such as the Southeast Asia Collective Defense Treaty (SEATO). Does it make all mutual defense treaties non-self-executing, regardless of their language? Does it prevent deployment of U.S. armed forces in U.N. operations without a specific authorization from Congress? *See* WPR §§8(b), 9(d). *See generally* Andrew K. Schiff, Note, *The War Powers Resolution: From the Halls of Congress to the Hills of Bosnia, Inertia Should Give Way to Post-Cold War Reality*, 11 Am. U. J. Intl. L. & Poly. 877 (1996).

g. Replacing the WPR

A study commission recently recommended that

> Congress should replace the War Powers Resolution with legislation that fairly acknowledges the President's defensive war powers, omits any arbitrary general time limit on deployments of force, reasserts the constitutionally-derived clear statement rule for use-of-force bills, and prescribes rules for their privileged and expedited consideration. [*Deciding to Use Force Abroad, supra* p. 252, at 40.]

Do you agree? What bill language would you propose? What would be the likely practical consequence of simply rescinding the WPR? What benefits do you see from leaving it as is?

10
Unilateral Self-Defense and Rescue

If the Framers changed the proposed constitutional text to accommodate a presidential power "to repel sudden attacks," see *supra* p. 20, they were at once prescient and naïve.

They were prescient because in the next 219 years, the United States would fight only five declared and four undeclared large wars.[1] In contrast, the President would unilaterally deploy armed forces on a lesser scale more than 300 times, often asserting inherent defensive authority. From the Korean War until 2004 alone there were more than 145 such deployments, many involving the alleged protection of U.S. nationals or, in the last decade, peacekeeping or "stabilization" operations (see Chapter 13). *See* Richard F. Grimmett, *Instances of Use of United States Armed Forces Abroad, 1798-2004* (Cong. Res. Serv. RL30172), Oct. 5, 2004; *see also* Louis Fisher, *Presidential War Power* (2d ed. 2004).

The Framers were also naïve if they thought that any implied presidential "sudden attack" power could be confined literally to repelling sudden attacks. That power has been invoked repeatedly by Presidents not only to justify an immediate use of defensive force to repel attack, but also to rescue Americans and their property, to retaliate against foreign states and persons, and, more recently, to strike first in anticipatory self-defense. Such acts during peacetime were once called acts of "imperfect war" by international law scholars. See *supra* p. 16.

What is the constitutional authority for these imperfect war powers? One theory is that they are subsumed within the President's defensive war power. Another is that they are supported by customary authority with congressional acquiescence. (Recall the requirements for such authority, discussed *supra* pp. 48-55.) The broadest theory is simply that the President has constitutional authority to use force abroad, subject only to Congress's spending power and its power to decide the juridical consequences of using force. As you read this chapter, consider which of these theories of authority for imperfect war is convincing.

---

1. Korean, Vietnam, and the Persian Gulf Wars. The last two were authorized by statute, but see generally Chapter 8 for counter-arguments regarding authorization. *See generally* Francis D. Wormuth & Edwin B. Firmage, *To Chain the Dog of War* 55, 59 (2d ed. 1989) (noting also several authorizations of limited war).

We begin in Part A by considering what the Framers knew from their own experience and from the law of nations. In Part B, we revisit *The Prize Cases* and the President's power of immediate self-defense. In Part C we explore a relatively uncontroversial extension of this defense power to the rescue of Americans abroad. In Part D, we consider the President's power to strike first or to strike back, and whether it matters which is which. We defer consideration of other uses of armed forces for humanitarian and stabilization operations until Chapter 13.

A. PRE-CONSTITUTIONAL AND SUBSEQUENT EXPERIENCE

The Framers were familiar with the concept of undeclared war, and their allocation to Congress of the power to "declare" war was not intended to deny Congress the power to authorize imperfect war. See *supra* p. 21. At the same time, the textual change from "make" to "declare" war may have reflected in part their intent to allow the President alone to "repel sudden attacks." *Id.*

Some have construed this language as limiting the President's imperfect war powers to responding to an actual attack on the nation. *See* Merlo Pusey, *The Way We Go to War* 45 (1969). But the "sudden attack" language is Madison's, not constitutional text, and therefore cannot bear any extended textual exegesis. In the absence of any further help from the records of the Constitutional Convention or the ratification debates, we turn again to writings of contemporary international law scholars, with whose work we know many of the Framers were familiar. *See* Charles A. Lofgren, *War Making Under the Constitution: The Original Understanding*, 81 Yale L.J. 672, 689 & n.78 (1972).

While these writings do not explore what they called the municipal allocation of war-making powers,[2] they may help frame the allocation question in several ways. First, they suggest acts that were so likely to lead to war that the decision to undertake them must logically have been given to Congress, in which the Framers expressly vested the power to initiate war. Second, they may suggest an appropriate scope for imperfect war powers vested in the President, based on limitations or guidelines derived from international law.

The leading writers on international law described three just causes for using military force: to protect against unjust invasion or attack, to reclaim what is owed by those who refuse to pay, and to obtain reparations or inflict punishment for past injuries. *See, e.g.*, Samuel F.V. Pufendorf, *De Officio Hominis Et Civis Libri Duo* 138 (Frank G. Moore trans., 1927). They also maintained that states have the right to intervene by force to protect their citizens from injury, and possibly to avenge injury to their citizens by a foreign state. Vattel, *supra* note 2, Bk. II, ch. VI, §71, at 137. Many writers distinguished between the use of force against sovereigns and their subjects and against pirates and aborigines, who knew no sovereign and lacked organization as states. *See, e.g.*, Hugo Grotius,

---

2. *See, e.g.*, Emer De Vattel, *The Law of Nations*, Bk. III, ch. XIV, at 359 (1805) (because the different rights that constitute the sovereign authority to make war, "originally resident in the body of the nation, may be separated or limited according to the will of the nation, we are to seek the power of making war in the particular constitution of the state").

The Law of War and Peace 630-631 (Francis W. Kelsey trans., 1925). Both the risk of general war and the opportunity to negotiate peace were smaller when military force was used against such entities than when it was used against a state.

All international law writers were agreed that general attack created a state of war requiring no declaration to defend. What of smaller attacks on forts or border areas? As to these, the commander at the scene had the right to repel the attack and even to drive the attacker from the territory. Whether, beyond such immediate defensive measures, the attack should be avenged by counterattack on the attacker's own territory, be forgiven, or be the occasion of diplomatic negotiations, was not a decision for the local commander. *See, e.g.,* Samuel F.V. Pufendorf, *De Jure Naturae Et Gentium Libri Octo* 1302 (Charles Henry Oldfather & William Abbott trans., 1934). This decision was for the ultimate sovereign power, wherever that power resided as a matter of municipal law.

The early writers recognized a variety of public and private methods for reclaiming property (or hostages) or for inflicting punishment, including seizures of property or hostages and other reprisals.[3] They viewed these uses of force as creating a state of imperfect war, which, unlike perfect war, "does not entirely destroy the public tranquility, but interrupts it only in some particulars, as in the case of reprisal." Miller v. *The Resolution,* 2 U.S. (2 Dall.) 1, 21 (Ct. App. in Cases of Capture 1781) (citing and paraphrasing 2 Jean Jacques Burlamaqui, *The Principles of Natural Law and Politic Law* 258 (Thomas Nugent trans., 1752, 3d ed. 1784)). *See also* Bas v. Tingy, 4 U.S. (4 Dall.) 37, 43 (1800), *supra* p. 94; Talbot v. Seemans, 5 U.S. (1 Cranch) 1, 28 (1800). They also believed that imperfect wars carried the risk of escalation to total war. Professor Lofgren notes that the Framers were aware that English wars with the Netherlands in 1652 and 1664, with Spain in 1739, and with France in 1756 all followed public naval reprisals. Lofgren, *supra* p. 256, at 693.

By the time of the Constitutional Convention, these methods of imperfect war were often collectively considered under the shorthand "general reprisals." Jules Lobel, *Covert War and Congressional Authority: Hidden War and Forgotten Power,* 134 U. Pa. L. Rev. 1035, 1045 (1986). *See also* Gray v. United States, 21 Ct. Cl. 340, 375 (1886) (characterizing the Naval War with France, *supra* p. 94, as "limited war in its nature similar to a prolonged series of reprisals"). For example,

> James McHenry, John Adams' Secretary of War, and Alexander Hamilton, a former Secretary of the Treasury, agreed that any executive exercise of American naval force beyond defending the nation's seacoast, American vessels, or commerce within American waters "come[s] within the sphere of reprisals and . . . require[s] the explicit sanction of the branch of government which is alone constitutionally authorised to grant letters of marque and reprisal." More generally, many statesmen of the period used marque and reprisal to refer to a state of "imperfect war," by which they meant any state of armed hostilities that did not rise to the level of declared war. [Lobel, *supra,* at 1046 (citations omitted).]

" 'The making of a reprisal on a nation was a very serious thing,' often leading to war," Thomas Jefferson observed, "therefore, 'the right of reprisal is *expressly*

---

3. Peacetime reprisals in the nineteenth century came to encompass pacific blockades and military occupations. Today they include embargoes, boycotts, naval bombardments, and other interventions as well. Michael F. Lohr, *Legal Analysis of U.S. Military Responses to State-Sponsored International Terrorism,* 34 Naval L. Rev. 1, 28-30 (1985).

lodged with Congress by the Constitution and not with the Executive.'" *Id.* at 1091 (citation omitted) (emphasis added).

NOTES AND QUESTIONS

1. *The Obsolescence of Marque and Reprisal?* Issuance of letters of marque and reprisal was renounced by signatories to the Declaration of Paris in 1856, II Lassa Oppenheim, *International Law: A Treatise* 262 (Hersch Lauterpacht ed., 7th ed. 1952), and had already fallen into disuse by that time. Is the "letter of marque and reprisal" provision simply obsolete, like the Fugitive Slave Clause? Does the argument that the Framers incorporated elements of international common law into the Constitution in 1787, affecting the war powers of both the President and Congress, suggest any answer?

2. *Allocating Authority for Military "Self-Help."* Should we read the Constitution to confer on Congress only the power to initiate general war and on the President the power to undertake all lesser acts of war, including especially acts of military "self-help"? This allocation of power arguably corresponds to felt necessities, especially the need for rapid action. But it also gives the President the power to risk general war by acts of imperfect war. Even proponents of an expansive presidential war power have acknowledged the danger in ceding to the President all the military self-help initiatives allowed at international law. *See* Eugene V. Rostow, *Great Cases Make Bad Law: The War Powers Act*, 50 Tex. L. Rev. 833, 851 (1972).

3. *Responding to Acts of Imperfect War.* Should the scope of the President's power to respond to general attack or invasion be different from the scope of his power to respond to an act of imperfect war? Consider this answer: "In the case of individual acts of war, such as seizure of a seaman or a ship, nothing is lost by resorting to diplomacy and delaying a military response until Congress has acted. But when an enemy has launched a general war, as by invasion, it may be necessary to meet this danger by immediate recourse to all the practices of war that international law and municipal law permit." Wormuth & Firmage, *supra* p. 255 n.1, at 22. *Cf.* Bas v. Tingy, 4 U.S. (4 Dall.) 37, 43 (1800), *supra* p. 94 ("If a general war is declared, its extent and operations are only restricted and regulated by the *jus belli*, forming a part of the law of nations; but if a partial war is waged, its extent and operation depend on our municipal laws.").

The point was made by Justice Paterson, author of the New Jersey plan at the Constitutional Convention, in an early criminal case. *See* United States v. Smith, 27 F. Cas. 1192 (C.C.N.Y. 1806) (No. 16,342). There defendants were charged with violating the Neutrality Act, 18 U.S.C. §960 (2000), *infra* p. 371, by mounting a military expedition against Spanish territory. In their defense they pleaded that the expedition was done "with the knowledge and approbation of the president of the United States." The court responded that not even the President had a unilateral power to change peace into war.

> There is a manifest distinction between our going to war with a nation at peace, and a war being made against us by an actual invasion, or a formal declaration. In the

former case, it is the exclusive province of congress to change a state of peace into a state of war. A nation, however, may be in such a situation as to render it more prudent to submit to certain acts of a hostile nature, and to trust to negotiations for redress, than to make an immediate appeal to arms. Various considerations may induce to a measure of this kind; such as motives of policy, calculations of interest, the nature of the injury and provocation, the relative resources, means and strength of the two nations, &c., and, therefore, the organ intrusted with the power to declare war, should first decide whether it is expedient to go to war, or to continue in peace.... [27 F. Cas. at 1230-1231.]

4. *Customary Authority.* Review the listing of presidential uses of force abroad without express congressional approval, *supra* p. 72. Does such use on more than 300 occasions (and counting) now add up to a customary authority for the President to make such use in the future, subject to Congress's power to cut off funds? See *supra* pp. 48-55. Does the answer depend on the circumstances of the various uses, in light of the disaggregated history? If so, which kinds of use of force abroad have been sufficiently frequent and similar, with congressional acquiescence, to vest a customary authority in the President?

5. *Negotiated War Powers.* Is the exercise of the imperfect war power simply negotiated between the political branches? If so, what is the point of studying legal limits on the imperfect war powers? Isn't whatever is negotiated constitutional, and doesn't the President hold all the cards in the negotiations? *See* Harold H. Koh, *Why the President (Almost) Always Wins in Foreign Affairs: Lessons of the Iran-Contra Affair,* 97 Yale L.J. 1255 (1988). How do constitutional claims, international law doctrines, and past military precedents fit into the next negotiation? *See generally* Abram Chayes, *The Cuban Missile Crisis* 6-7 (1974) (suggesting that law affected the decisional process by acting as a constraint, supplying justification or legitimation, and providing organizational structures, procedures, and forums).

6. *A Sliding Scale of War Powers?* Is the real lesson of a nuanced listing of uses of force that constitutional war powers operate on a sliding scale ranging from immediate self-defense to general de jure war? The President necessarily has the authority to repel sudden attack by ordering immediate acts of self-defense. Only Congress has the authority to give de jure effect to general war by making a formal declaration. Between these extremes, the necessity and *form* of the constitutionally required authorization depends on the size, frequency, and nature of the threat at which the use of force is directed. For example, recurring small-scale military initiatives against pirates and over non-sovereigns do not require individualized authorizations from Congress; a general delegation of authority to the President is sufficient. *See, e.g.,* 33 U.S.C. §381 (2000) (authorizing the President to use naval force against "piratical aggressions and depredations"). Recurring military initiatives against American Indians posed somewhat greater risks, and also sometimes implicated entities recognized as sovereign under the Constitution. Thus, although they did not require declarations of war, authorizations by appropriation at least were necessary. *See, e.g.,* 5 Stat. 7 (1836) (appropriating funds "to defray the expenses attending the

suppression of hostilities with the Seminole Indians in Florida"). Larger-scale hostilities against sovereign states required even more formal authorization by statute, but not declaration as long as they did not contemplate the full range of de jure consequences. See *supra* p. 99. Is this a persuasive theory of war powers or just a post hoc rationalization of usage? Does it sufficiently promote public accountability for the use of force? *See* J. Gregory Sidak, *To Declare War*, 41 Duke L.J. 27 (1991) (arguing for formal declaration as the only clear instrument of accountability). Does it have predictive value for determining the legality of future uses of force?

B. REPELLING SUDDEN ATTACKS

The Prize Cases
United States Supreme Court, 1863
67 U.S. (2 Black) 635

[The opinion is set forth *supra* p. 67.]

THE GULF OF SIDRA INCIDENT: REPELLING (OR PROVOKING?) ATTACK[4]

In 1973, Libya claimed as its territorial waters the entire Gulf of Sidra, a body of water that extends roughly 90 to 150 miles north of the Libyan coast and measures about 275 miles across. The United States has generally refused to recognize claims of territorial waters running more than 12 miles offshore. Accordingly, it formally rejected Libya's claim to the Gulf of Sidra in February 1974. 1974 Dig. U.S. Prac. Intl. L. 293-294.

Libyan leader Muammar el-Qadhafi declared a "line of death" across the northern boundary of the Gulf, and two Libyan fighters fired at American planes operating inside it in 1981. Both Libyan aircraft were shot down in return fire. After the 1981 incident, U.S. naval forces conducted exercises inside the line drawn by Qadhafi on seven or eight occasions through January 1986.

In March 1986, the U.S. began an unusual build-up of carrier forces in the area of the line. United States carrier-based planes flew 375 flights south of the line and a naval task force crossed it for 75 hours. On March 24, Libyan shore-based batteries fired on U.S. planes inside the line.

---

4. Except where otherwise noted, the background for this account is drawn from *War Powers, Libya, and State-Sponsored Terrorism: Hearing Before the Subcomm. on Arms Control, Intl. Security and Science of the H. Comm. on Foreign Aff.*, 99th Cong. (1986) (hereinafter *Libya Hearings*); Pat Towell, *Military Strikes Against Libya Receive Capitol Hill Support*, 44 Cong. Q. 699-702 (March 29, 1986); and Stephen R. Ratner, *The Gulf of Sidra Incident of 1981: The Lawfulness of Peacetime Aerial Engagements*, in *International Incidents* 181 (W. Michael Reisman & Andrew R. Willard eds., 1988).

B. Repelling Sudden Attacks

News of these events prompted Chairman Dante Fascell of the House Committee on Foreign Affairs to complain that the administration had failed to comply with the War Powers Resolution. Chairman Fascell wrote President Reagan:

> [T]hese deployments constituted from the outset a situation where imminent involvement in hostilities was a distinct possibility clearly indicated by the circumstances even prior to today's development.
>
> Under the circumstances, prior consultation with Congress was required under the War Powers Act.
>
> In view of these circumstances, I respectfully urge you to comply fully with the provisions of the War Powers Resolution before the situation evolves further. [Letter from Chairman Fascell to President Reagan (March 24, 1986), *reprinted in Libya Hearings, supra* note 4, at 207-208.]

On the afternoon of March 24, U.S. carrier-based aircraft returned the Libyan shore-based fire with missiles designed to home in on anti-aircraft radar. The missiles apparently struck home. At the same time, U.S. planes and ships attacked five and sank at least two Libyan missile-armed ships that had approached the U.S. fleet too closely. Two days later, the Pentagon announced the end of the naval exercise.

As these events unfolded, the Administration made the following reply to Chairman Fascell:

> First, our maneuvers in the Gulf have long been planned, as part of a global freedom-of-navigation program by which the United States preserves its rights to use international waters and airspace. Numerous similar prior operations did not provoke a response. We obviously cannot be deterred from exercising our rights by Qadhafi's legally baseless claims or by his threats.
>
> We disagree with your claim that our "actions in the Gulf of Sidra have failed to adequately satisfy the requirements of the War Powers Resolution." Nor do we believe that the Resolution was intended to require consultation before conducting naval maneuvers in international waters or airspace. We considered this question carefully and concluded that conducting the operations did not place U.S. forces into hostilities or into a situation in which imminent hostilities were clearly indicated by the circumstances. Contrary to your letter's suggestion, it is not enough under the statute that an operation create "a distinct possibility" of hostilities. After Libya attacked our forces, we notified congressional leaders.
>
> Our plans in this instance have been known to all, including Qadhafi himself. The very purpose of the present operation has been to exercise our rights, openly and unambiguously. [Letter from W. Ball (Assistant to President Reagan) to Chairman Fascell (March 26, 1986), *reprinted in Libya Hearings, supra* note 4, at 209.]

Newspaper reports asserted that the naval maneuvers were intended to provoke Libyan attacks and thus justify U.S. counterattacks, apparently planned at least as early as March 14. Responding to these reports in part and to Chairman Fascell's complaint, the Legal Adviser to the State Department gave the following testimony in congressional hearings.

Statement of Abraham D. Sofaer, Legal Adviser to the Department of State, The War Powers Resolution and Antiterrorist Operations (April 29, 1986)

reprinted in Libya Hearings, supra p. 260 n. 4, at 22-26

Issues under the War Powers Resolution have also been raised where U.S. forces have engaged in a military exercise in conformity with international law. The incident in the Gulf of Sidra in late March illustrates the situation. Does the resolution require the President to consult and report in this kind of case?...

The War Powers Resolution was not intended to require consultation before conducting maneuvers in international waters or airspace in the context of this global freedom of navigation program. We are aware of no previous suggestion that the resolution would require consultation in such situations. This question was carefully considered in connection with the Sidra exercise in March, and the decision was made that the conduct of those operations did not place U.S. forces into hostilities or into a situation in which imminent involvement in hostilities was "clearly indicated by the circumstances." The United States has conducted its exercises not only in Sidra but around the world, not only in March but for years — and, in most instances, without hostile response. We have, in fact, been in the Gulf of Sidra area 16 times since 1981, and we have crossed Qadhafi's so-called line of death seven times before the operation last March. Only once before did Qadhafi respond with military action, and, in that instance, he was singularly unsuccessful. While we must always be aware of the risks and be prepared to deal with all contingencies, we have every right to expect that neither Libya nor any other country will take hostile action against U.S. forces while they are lawfully in and over areas of the high seas. The threat of a possible hostile response is not sufficient to trigger the consultation requirement of section 3, which refers only to actual hostilities and to situations in which imminent involvement in hostilities is "clearly indicated" by the circumstances.

Where a peaceful, lawful exercise does, in fact, result in hostile action to which U.S. forces must respond in immediate self-defense, such an isolated engagement should not normally be construed as constituting the introduction of U.S. Armed Forces into a situation of actual or imminent hostilities for the purpose of the reporting requirement of section 4 of the resolution. No report was submitted in the case of the 1981 Sidra incident, in which two Libyan aircraft were shot down after they fired at U.S. aircraft. Similarly, during the period in which U.S. peacekeeping forces were deployed in the Beirut area in 1983, many incidents occurred in which hostile forces attacked and U.S. peacekeeping forces responded in immediate self-defense. Yet, *no* separate war powers report was submitted for each of these incidents. Of course, a different situation might be presented if U.S. forces withdrew from an area and subsequently returned for the purpose of undertaking further military action....

B. Repelling Sudden Attacks

NOTES AND QUESTIONS

1. *Authority for Minatory Deployments.* Arguably, many historical deployments with congressional acquiescence (but without prior congressional approval) establish presidential authority to order minatory demonstrations in support of foreign policy. Freedom of navigation has always been our policy, even if not always formally declared by that name. Congress presumably has approved that policy by acquiescence, as well as by naval appropriations. Doesn't any such tacit congressional authorization satisfy the War Powers Resolution and justify disregard of its consultation and reporting provisions?

In addition, doesn't the President have inherent authority — indeed, the duty — to enforce that established policy as he sees fit, short of actually engaging in acts of war? If so, does the constitutional savings clause of the War Powers Resolution place the Gulf of Sidra deployment outside the Resolution, whether or not it involved "imminent hostilities"?

2. *The Caroline Standard: Necessity for Self-Defense. The Prize Cases* involved the President's authority to respond to force with force in a war. Does it support the same authority to respond immediately to attack, even when it is not part of any larger scale conflict? What answer does the "sudden attack" language in Madison's notes of the framing of the Declaration Clause suggest? How important is "sudden"? Consider Secretary of State Daniel Webster's classic statement that under the law of nations, a valid plea of self-defense must rest on a showing of "a necessity of self-defense, instant, overwhelming, leaving no choice of means, no moment for deliberation." VI *The Works of Daniel Webster* 261 (1851). Are these also the conditions for a valid plea of inherent presidential power to repel attack? If so, has the advent of the missile age, with its rapidly unfolding technological warfare, changed the meaning of "no moment for deliberation"?

3. *Immediate Self-Defense and the WPR.* In the 1981 Gulf of Sidra incident fire was exchanged and two Libyan fighters were shot down. In the five succeeding years seven or eight comparable freedom of navigation exercises did not draw fire. Given this history, was the 1986 exercise a situation "where imminent involvement in hostilities is clearly indicated by the circumstances"? *See* War Powers Resolution §4(a)(1), 50 U.S.C. §1543(a)(1), *supra* p. 241. Legal Adviser Sofaer asserts that the situation "should not normally be construed as" a triggering event under the WPR. *See also* Robert F. Turner, *The War Powers Resolution: Its Implementation in Theory and Practice* 79-80 (1983) (noting that the United States did not initiate fire). Do you agree?

4. *Provoking Attack?* If our forces were lawfully deployed over the "line of death," then surely their return of Libyan fire fits even the narrowest definition of a presidential power to repel sudden attacks. Or does it? Some experts have written that the 1981 Libyan attack had no chance of success because of the great margin of technological superiority enjoyed by the American F-14s over the export version Soviet SU-22s used by the Libyans. Letter to the Editor from J. McFaul, Proc. U.S. Naval Inst. 42 (May 1982). Was the 1981 U.S. response defensive or retaliatory? In 1986, U.S. forces attacked Libyan vessels for approaching too closely, even though the Libyans had not attacked. Was this

later U.S. action defensive or retaliatory? *See* David Blundy & Andrew Lycett, *Qaddafi and the Libyan Revolution* 7 (1986) (alleging that in the 1986 incident American planes crossed the 12-mile limit and flew over Libyan land to provoke a Libyan military response). *See also* George P. Politakis, *From Action Stations to Action: U.S. Naval Deployment, "Non-Belligerency," and "Defensive Reprisals" in the Final Year of the Iran-Iraq War*, 25 Ocean Dev. & Intl. L. 31 (1994) (arguing that U.S. attacks against Iranian oil platforms and patrol boats during the Tanker War, *supra* p. 248, went beyond internationally permissible self-defense to constitute unlawful armed reprisals). If either action was not defensive, what was the source of presidential authority to order it?

C. RESCUE

In re Neagle
United States Supreme Court, 1890
135 U.S. 1

[The opinion is set forth *supra* p. 80.]

Durand v. Hollins
United States Circuit Court,
Southern District of New York, 1860
8 F. Cas. 111 (No. 4186)

[In 1852, a group of adventurers seeking to corner the business of conducting travelers over the Central American isthmus established the "state" of Greytown in what is now Nicaragua. The United States backed a rival transit company partly owned by Nicaraguans. Wormuth & Firmage, *supra* p. 255 n.1, at 38. In the ensuing friction between the companies, a Greytown mob threatened the American minister to Central America and hit him with a bottle. The U.S. Secretary of the Navy then sent Captain Hollins of the U.S.S. *Cyane* to Greytown to obtain redress for damages done to property of the U.S.-backed company and an apology for the attack on the minister. When Greytown authorities did not comply with his demands, Hollins shelled the town and then burned what remained. An American owner of property destroyed by Hollins's actions subsequently sued him, and Hollins asserted in his defense that he was merely following orders.]

NELSON, Circuit Justice.... The executive power, under the constitution, is vested in the president of the United States (article 2, §1). He is commander-in-chief of the army and navy, (Id. §2), and has imposed upon him the duty to "take care that the laws be faithfully executed" (Id. §3).... There was also established another executive department, denominated the "Department of the Navy," the chief officer of which is called the "Secretary of the Navy," "whose duty it

C. Rescue

shall be to execute such orders as he shall receive from the president of the United States...." Act Cong. April 30, 1798, §1 (1 Stat. 553).

As the executive head of the nation, the president is made the only legitimate organ of the general government, to open and carry on correspondence or negotiations with foreign nations, in matters concerning the interests of the country or of its citizens. It is to him, also, the citizens abroad must look for protection of person and of property, and for the faithful execution of the laws existing and intended for their protection. For this purpose, the whole executive power of the country is placed in his hands, under the constitution, and the laws passed in pursuance thereof; and different departments of government have been organized, through which this power may be most conveniently executed, whether by negotiation or by force....

Now, as it respects the interposition of the executive abroad, for the protection of the lives or property of the citizen, the duty must, of necessity, rest in the discretion of the president. Acts of lawless violence, or of threatened violence to the citizen or his property, cannot be anticipated and provided for; and the protection, to be effectual or of any avail, may, not unfrequently, require the most prompt and decided action. Under our system of government, the citizen abroad is as much entitled to protection as the citizen at home. The great object and duty of government is the protection of the lives, liberty, and property of the people composing it, whether abroad or at home; and any government failing in the accomplishment of the object, or the performance of the duty, is not worth preserving.

I have said, that the interposition of the president abroad, for the protection of the citizen, must necessarily rest in his discretion; and it is quite clear that, in all cases where a public act or order rests in executive discretion neither he nor his authorized agent is personally civilly responsible for the consequences. As was observed by Chief Justice Marshall, in Marbury v. Madison, 1 Cranch [5 U.S.] 165: "By the constitution of the United States, the president is invested with certain important political powers, in the exercise of which he is to use his own discretion, and is accountable only to his country in his political character, and to his own conscience. To aid him in the performance of these duties, he is authorized to appoint certain officers, who act by his authority, and in conformity with his orders. In such cases, their acts are his acts, and, whatever opinion may be entertained of the manner in which executive discretion may be used, still there exists, and can exist, no power to control that discretion. The subjects are political. They respect the nation, not individual rights, and, being intrusted to the executive, the decision of the executive is conclusive." This is a sound principle, and governs the present case. The question whether it was the duty of the president to interpose for the protection of the citizens at Greytown against an irresponsible and marauding community that had established itself there, was a public political question, in which the government, as well as the citizens whose interests were involved, was concerned, and which belonged to the executive to determine; and his decision is final and conclusive, and justified the defendant in the execution of his orders given through the secretary of the navy.

Judgment for defendant.

THE IRAN HOSTAGE RESCUE MISSION[5]

In November 1979, Iranian militants stormed the American Embassy in Teheran and took the Americans inside it hostage. By March 1980, diplomatic initiatives to gain their release had failed, and the Carter administration considered its military options. The Chairman of the Joint Chiefs of Staff outlined the details of a proposed rescue mission, contemplating a series of discrete and reversible but incredibly complex and difficult steps.

First, troops and materials would be pre-positioned in the Middle East and the Indian Ocean under cover of routinely scheduled activities. Second, eight helicopters and eight C-130 aircraft were to fly below Iranian radar coverage across 500 miles of desert at night to a rendezvous inside Iran, "Desert One," for refueling and reloading of the helicopters. Third, the helicopters would proceed to a second mountain rendezvous, where they would remain concealed throughout the following day. Fourth, the rescue team would proceed to Teheran by local vehicles on the second night to undertake the actual rescue. Fifth, the helicopters would reappear just long enough to pick up the team and the hostages, and then fly to an abandoned airfield near Teheran to rendezvous again with the transport aircraft. Finally, helicopters abandoned, the group would fly to safety under an umbrella of heavy U.S. air power.

Secretary of State Cyrus Vance opposed any military initiative at that time. He reasoned that

> the hostages would be freed only when Khomeini was certain that all the institutions of the Islamic republic were in place.... Our only realistic course was to keep up the pressure on Iran while we waited for Khomeini to determine that the revolution had accomplished its purpose, and that the hostages were of no further value.

President Carter did not immediately approve the mission, preferring instead to exhaust all peaceful means for obtaining release of the hostages. But United States allies refused to adopt meaningful sanctions against Iran, and by April hopes of a negotiated release had dimmed even further. On April 9, National Security Adviser Brzezinski advised the President that, in his view, "a carefully planned and boldly executed rescue operation represents the only realistic prospect that the hostages — any of them — will be freed in the foreseeable future.... It is time for us to act now."

On April 11, during a National Security Council (NSC) meeting from which Secretary of State Vance was absent, President Carter decided that a rescue mission should be launched on April 24. On his return, Vance objected vociferously and was permitted to present his case at another NSC meeting. He noted that intelligence reports indicated that the hostages were in no physical danger and in satisfactory health, and that any rescue was almost certain to lead to deaths among them, as well as among the rescuers and the Iranians. He also noted that the Iranians could simply react by taking American journalists hostage and turning towards the Soviet Union. He reaffirmed his belief that time

---

5. Except where otherwise noted, this background is based upon Gary Sick, *All Fall Down* (1985); *American Hostages in Iran: The Conduct of a Crisis* (Warren Christopher ed., 1985); and Cyrus R. Vance, *Hard Choices* (1983).

C. Rescue

would lead to the release of the hostages. No one else supported his position, however, and the President reaffirmed his decision to go ahead. On April 17, Vance advised President Carter that he would have to resign if the mission went forward. He subsequently did resign after the mission was made public.

On the night of April 23, President Carter met with Senate Majority Leader Robert Byrd to develop a short list for congressional notification concerning "possible military action." He did not inform Byrd that the rescue mission would be launched just hours later, at 10:30 A.M. on April 24, 1980, Washington time.

The mission ran into difficulty when several of the helicopters failed. Advised that there were too few helicopters to carry out the remainder of the mission, President Carter ordered it aborted. In the ensuing rush to evacuate Desert One, a helicopter and a C-130 transport collided, killing eight persons, and the dead were abandoned with their equipment and sundry documents bearing on the mission.

Only after the mission was aborted were other congressional leaders informed by telephone late on April 24th and during the following morning. Within 48 hours of the time that U.S. units first entered Iranian air space, but well after the mission was aborted, President Carter sent the following message to Congress.

Letter of President Jimmy Carter to the Speaker of the House and President Pro Tempore of the Senate (April 26, 1980)
reprinted in 4 Pub. Papers 777

Because of my desire that Congress be informed on this matter and consistent with the reporting provisions of the War Powers Resolution of 1973 (Public Law 93-148), I submit this report.

On April 24, 1980, elements of the United States Armed Forces under my direction commenced the positioning stage of a rescue operation which was designed, if the subsequent stages had been executed, to effect the rescue of the American hostages who have been held captive in Iran since November 4, 1979, in clear violation of international law and the norms of civilized conduct among nations. The subsequent phases of the operation were not executed. Instead, for the reasons described below, all these elements were withdrawn from Iran and no hostilities occurred.

The sole objective of the operation that actually occurred was to position the rescue team for the subsequent effort to withdraw the American hostages. The rescue team was under my overall command and control and required my approval before executing the subsequent phases of the operation designed to effect the rescue itself....

The remote desert area was selected to conceal this phase of the mission from discovery. At no time during the temporary presence of United States Armed Forces in Iran did they encounter Iranian forces of any type....

At one point during the period in which United States Armed Forces elements were on the ground at the desert landing site a bus containing forty-four Iranian civilians happened to pass along a nearby road. The bus was stopped and then disabled. Its occupants were detained by United States Armed Forces elements until their departure, and then released unharmed. One truck closely followed by a second vehicle also passed by while United States Armed Forces elements were on the ground. These elements stopped the truck by a shot into its headlights. The driver ran to the second vehicle which then escaped across the desert. Neither of these incidents affected the subsequent decision to terminate the mission.

Our rescue team knew, and I knew, that the operation was certain to be dangerous. We were all convinced that if and when the rescue phase of the operation had been commenced, it had an excellent chance of success....

The mission on which they were embarked was a humanitarian mission. It was not directed against Iran. It was not directed against the people of Iran. It caused no Iranian casualties.

This operation was ordered and conducted pursuant to the President's powers under the Constitution as Chief Executive and as Commander-in-Chief of the United States Armed Forces, expressly recognized in Section 8(d)(1) of the War Powers Resolution. In carrying out this operation, the United States was acting wholly within its rights, in accordance with Article 51 of the United Nations Charter, to protect and rescue its citizens where the government of the territory in which they are located is unable or unwilling to protect them.

Sincerely,
Jimmy Carter

Legal Opinion by Lloyd Cutler, President's Counsel, on War Powers Consultation Relative to the Iran Rescue Mission (May 9, 1980)

reprinted in Subcomm. on Intl. Security and Scientific Aff. of the H. Comm. on Foreign Aff., 98th Cong., War Powers Resolution: Relevant Documents, Correspondence, Reports 50 (1983)

1. In my opinion, the President's decision to use the armed forces in an attempt to rescue the American hostages in Iran, without consulting Congress before taking this action, was a lawful exercise of his constitutional powers as President and Commander-in-Chief, and did not violate the War Powers Resolution of 1973.

2. The President's constitutional power to use the armed forces to rescue Americans illegally detained abroad is clearly established. In re Neagle, 135 U.S. 1, Durand v. Hollins, 8 Fed. Cases 111. This power was expressly recognized in the Senate version of the War Powers Resolution, and is not negated by the final version of the Resolution, especially where, as here, those to be rescued include United States Marines.

3. His inherent constitutional power to conduct this kind of rescue operation, which depends on total surprise, includes the power to act before consulting Congress, if the President concludes, as he did in this case, that to do so would unreasonably endanger the success of the operation and the safety of those to be rescued.

C. Rescue

4. Section 3 of the War Powers Resolution does require consulting with Congress "in every possible instance" before introducing United States Armed Forces into "hostilities or into situations where imminent involvement in hostilities is clearly indicated by the circumstances." In this case, the first stage of the operation—introducing the rescue team into Iran during the night of April 24—did not involve any hostilities. The rescue effort itself was not to be initiated before the following night, and could have been aborted before any involvement in hostilities was "clearly indicated," and this is in fact what occurred.

5. In any event, Section 8(d)(1) of the War Powers Resolution provides that nothing in it "is intended to alter the constitutional authority of the Congress or of the President." If Section 3 were read to require prior consultation in these precise circumstances—where the President has inherent constitutional authority to conduct a rescue operation dependent on surprise and reasonable ground to believe that prior consultation would unreasonably endanger the success of the operation and the safety of those to be rescued—this would raise grave issues as to the constitutionality of Section 3. Since statutes and joint resolutions are to be read where possible in a manner that does not raise such grave constitutional issues, Section 3 and Section 8(d)(1), read together, should not be construed to require prior consultation under the precise circumstances of this case.

The "Hostage Act"
22 U.S.C. §1732 (2000)

[The text is set forth in the opinion in Dames & Moore v. Regan, *supra* p. 48.]

NOTES AND QUESTIONS

1. *Protecting Government Functions.* Neagle plainly holds that, under the Supremacy Clause, a United States employee "cannot be guilty" of a state law crime for performing a task within the general scope of his employment. 135 U.S. at 75. *See* Peter M. Shane & Harold H. Bruff, *The Law of Presidential Power* 460 (1988). Does it mean more than that? *See* Henry P. Monaghan, *The Protective Powers of the President*, 93 Colum. L. Rev. 1, 66 (1993) (arguing that *Neagle* suggests that the President may use force without express statutory authority not only to defend the United States against sudden attack, but also to protect the personnel and property interests of the United States). In its opinion the Court noted with approval an intervention—without congressional authorization—by an American naval captain on behalf of a Hungarian applicant for U.S. citizenship who had been illegally detained abroad. 135 U.S. at 64 (the case of Martin Koszta). Can we assume from this reference and the facts of *Neagle* that the President is inherently empowered to do only what is immediately necessary to repel attacks on Americans or those waiting to become Americans? If the holding is not limited at least in this respect, then what limit is there on inherent presidential power to repel attacks and protect Americans? *See* Monaghan, *supra*,

at 70 (distinguishing between protection of U.S. government personnel and private Americans).

2. *Durand's Holding.* Durand has been cited for the proposition that rescue and reprisal are powers vested exclusively in the President. Did the court address, or need to address, the exclusivity of the President's rescue power? What is the actual holding? Some observers have found *Durand*'s reliance on the rescue power ironic. The property protected by the American intervention was that of a Nicaraguan corporation, and the U.S. citizen Durand's property was destroyed by the shelling.

3. *Judicial Precedent.* Mr. Cutler's opinion cites *Neagle* and *Durand* as judicial authority for the President's constitutional authority to order rescue missions. Are they really apposite? Would you agree with the Iran-Contra Committee minority, who claimed, "the *Durand* case stands for the proposition that the President has the discretion to take whatever steps may be necessary, short of a full-scale war, to protect American citizens"? *Report of the Congressional Committees Investigating the Iran-Contra Affair, Minority Report,* H.R. Rep. No. 100-433, S. Rep. No. 100-216, at 474 (1987).

4. *Effect of the Hostage Act.* Does either case address the scope of the President's authority when Congress *has* enacted legislation on this point? Is the Hostage Act such legislation?

In the wake of the agreement by which the hostages were released, the Supreme Court held the Hostage Act inapplicable because the "hostages were not seized out of any refusal to recognize their American citizenship — they were seized precisely *because* of their American citizenship." Dames & Moore v. Regan, 453 U.S. 654, 677 (1981), *supra* p. 48 (emphasis in original). Analysis of the legislative history of the Act suggests that the Court was wrong; the Act was intended to include *any* "unfounded" or pretextual arrest of American citizens abroad. *See* Abner J. Mikva & Gerald L. Neuman, *The Hostage Crisis and the "Hostage Act,"* 49 U. Chi. L. Rev. 292, 330-332 (1982). Congress apparently agreed; it amended the Hostage Act in 1989 to insert "and otherwise not prohibited by law" after "acts of war" in response to administration initiatives to free American hostages during the Iran-Contra Affair, reflecting Congress's assumption that the Act applied to such hostages. *See* Anti-Terrorism and Arms Export Control Act Amendments of 1989, Pub. L. No. 101-222, 103 Stat. 1892 (codified at 22 U.S.C. §1732 (2000)).

The bill that became the Hostage Act originally would have authorized a President to take hostages in reprisal, but this provision was dropped as an improper delegation of the war-making power. Mikva & Neuman, *supra,* at 319-327. Even the restricted delegation of authority in the final bill was criticized by legislators who were concerned that it "would permit the President to perform further preliminary acts of hostility whose inevitable tendency would be to precipitate war, even if those acts did not technically come into the ban of the proviso." *Id.* at 335.

Given this history and the Act's careful circumscription of delegated authority to use "means not amounting to acts of war," what exactly is the lawful scope of a President's authority to rescue hostages? Is the Act constitutional?

C. Rescue

What is the relationship, if any, between the President's authority under the Hostage Act and international law? If, for example, customary international law allows armed intervention to rescue citizens held hostage abroad and does not treat such intervention as an act of war, what is the President's authority under the Act?

5. *Rescue and the War Powers Resolution.* The original Senate version of the War Powers Resolution authorized the President to make a carefully limited use of military force to "protect while evacuating" American citizens and nationals. S. 440, 93d Cong., §3(3) (1973). See *supra* p. 246. Does the omission of this provision from the final War Powers Resolution suggest that Congress intended to deny the President rescue authority? Could Congress constitutionally do so?

6. *Differentiating Rescue and Repelling Attack.* The only authority cited by the Senate Foreign Relations Committee for the "protection" provision in its version of the War Powers Resolution was Madison's notation about the power to repel sudden attacks. S. Rep. No. 93-220, at 2-3 (1975). If the rescue authority is predicated on the implied power to repel sudden attacks, consider the following argument:

> With respect to sudden attacks, there is a textual constitutional presumption that Congress will not be able [as an institution to address the unanticipated emergency]. Such a general presumption is not applicable to rescue operations. These operations involve emerging crises or they may involve relatively static and predictable situations. Once it is conceded in a particular context that there is or has been a substantial opportunity to contemplate action, the authority to decide whether to proceed devolves back to Congress. Congress may then delegate authority to the President, but the President is without authority, under such circumstances, to act in the absence of some action by Congress. [Allan Ides, *Congress, Constitutional Responsibility and the War Power*, 17 Loy. L.A. L. Rev. 599, 636-637 (1984).]

What constitutional *text* creates this presumption? Do you agree with Professor Ides' conclusion? How would the Iran hostage rescue mission fare under his proposed analysis?

Is the capture of American citizens by itself a sufficient legal predicate for exercise of any implied presidential rescue power? If *Neagle* is legal authority for rescue missions, does it presuppose at least the threat of *imminent* harm to Americans? *Cf.* Jeffrey A. McCredie, *The April 14, 1986 Bombing of Libya: Act of Self-Defense or Reprisal?*, 19 Case W. Res. J. Intl. L. 215, 235 (1987) (noting that the right of rescue at international law is predicated upon "an imminent threat of injury to nationals").

7. *Rules for Rescue.* Congress, in the exercise of its constitutional authority to "make Rules for the Government and Regulation of the land and naval Forces," U.S. Const. art. I, §8, cl. 14, has delegated rule-making authority to the Secretary of the Navy. 10 U.S.C. §§5013(g)(3) & 6011 (2000). Any regulations made with this authority have the force and effect of law. *See, e.g.*, Cafeteria and Restaurant Workers Union v. McElroy, 367 U.S. 886, 890-891 (1961). The first such regulations required naval commanders to aid U.S. diplomatic agents who requested

help "for the protection of lives and property of American citizens." *See* Wormuth & Firmage, *supra* p. 255 n.1, at 156-157. Although the current Navy regulations still delegate decisional responsibility to the naval commander at the scene, they strictly limit the use of force to acts of self-defense, "exercised only as a last resort, and then only to the extent which is absolutely necessary to accomplish the end required." U.S. Navy Regs. art. 0915(2) (1990) (rev. Jan. 24, 2003).

8. *Consultation.* Was President Carter required to consult with Congress or to report the rescue mission under §4(a)(1) of the War Powers Resolution, *supra* p. 241? Mr. Cutler concluded that the rescuers were not placed in a situation where imminent involvement in hostilities was clearly indicated by the circumstances. Representative Zablocki, co-sponsor of the Resolution and then-Chairman of the House Committee on Foreign Affairs, called the Cutler opinion "perhaps the most serious affront ever exercised against [the Resolution's] implementation." Clement J. Zablocki, *The War Powers Resolution: Its Past Record and Future Promise*, 17 Loy. L.A. L. Rev. 579, 585 (1984). Who was right?

Mr. Cutler cites concerns about possible leaks as one reason for not informing Congress of the mission in advance. *See generally Minority Report, supra* p. 270, at 575 (attributing the Reagan administration's withholding of information about the Iran-Contra Affair to concerns about congressional leaks). Is this a sufficient reason for failing to report to Congress under the War Powers Resolution? For failing to obtain prior congressional authorization for a military initiative? Does the size of Congress alone pose such a security risk that wider consultation is inappropriate? The General Counsel to the Defense Department reported that "less than 2,000, including less than 100 non-military personnel," were briefed in advance about some phase of the Iran hostage rescue mission, and that the number of significant decision makers and planners generally involved in sensitive operations "varies and could range from 75 upward." *Libya Hearings, supra* p. 260 n.4, at 85. Do these facts weaken the security argument for withholding information from Congress, or are they distinguishable?

What good would it have done to consult the congressional leaders? What expertise could they have brought to the rescue problem? For example, what could members of Congress have added to the Iran hostage rescue mission decision that Secretary of State Vance had not already argued without success? President Carter has written of his failure to inform Senator Byrd during their talk on April 23 that "[a]fter he left the White House, I wondered if it would have been better to involve him more directly in our exact plans for the mission. His advice would have been valuable to me then — and also twenty-four hours later." Jimmy Carter, *Keeping Faith: Memoirs of a President* 513-514 (1982). Political scientists have since argued that classic "groupthink" — in which "pressures internal to the group result in an overriding concern with maintaining a sense of an amiable in-group, at the cost of individual members ignoring or suppressing their doubts over policy options" — contributed significantly to the rescue mission fiasco. *See* Steve Smith, *Groupthink and the Hostage Rescue Mission*, 15 Brit. J. Pol. Sci. 117 (1984); Steve Smith, *Policy Preferences and Bureaucratic Position: The Case of the American Hostage Rescue Mission*, 61 Intl. Aff. 9 (1984-1985).

Former Secretary of State Vance has speculated that if President Carter had consulted in advance with congressional leaders, "some of them would have expressed reasonable doubts that could have affected the President's decision.... Presidents, mired in the executive responsibilities of government, sometimes lose touch with the tide of domestic political opinion. The unadorned views of wise individuals outside the executive branch can play an important and useful role." Cyrus R. Vance, *Striking the Balance: Congress and the President Under the War Powers Resolution*, 133 U. Pa. L. Rev. 79, 91 (1984). Do you believe that launching a mission to rescue Americans held hostage by foreign terrorists or a foreign nation would ever be inconsistent with the "tide of domestic political opinion"?

D. STRIKING FIRST (OR STRIKING BACK?)

1. The 1998 Attacks on Sudan and Afghanistan[6]

On August 7, 1998, truck bombs exploded at the U.S. embassies in Kenya and Tanzania, killing nearly 300 people, including 12 Americans. Two weeks later, on August 20, the United States launched 79 Tomahawk cruise missiles against terrorist training camps in Afghanistan and a Sudanese pharmaceutical plant that the United States alleged to be a chemical weapons facility. President Clinton explained that he ordered the attacks because "we have convincing evidence that [Islamic terrorist groups, including that of Osama bin Laden] ... played the key role in the Embassy bombings ... and compelling information that they were planning additional terrorist attacks against our citizens...." He had notified certain congressional leaders on August 19 that the attacks were coming and had sent Congress a letter the day after the attacks reporting, "consistent with the War Powers Resolution," that

> [t]he United States acted in exercise of our inherent right of self-defense consistent with Article 51 of the United Nations Charter [*infra* p. 286]. These strikes were a necessary and proportionate response to the imminent threat of further terrorist attacks against U.S. personnel and facilities. These strikes were intended to prevent and deter additional attacks by a clearly identified terrorist threat. [Letter to Congressional Leaders Reporting on Military Action Against Terrorist Sites in Afghanistan and Sudan, 34 Weekly Comp. Pres. Doc. 1650 (Aug. 21, 1998).]

The President's National Security Adviser explained that it was "appropriate" not only under Article 51, but also "under a 1996 statute in Congress, for us to try to disrupt and destroy those kinds of military terrorist targets." The statute

---

6. Except as otherwise noted, the background on the 1998 cruise missile attacks on Sudan and Afghanistan is drawn from Sara N. Scheideman, *Standards of Proof in Forcible Responses to Terrorism*, 50 Syracuse L. Rev. 249 (2000); Sean Murphy, *Contemporary Practice of the United States Relating to International Law*, 93 Am. J. Intl. L. 161-166 (1999); Jules Lobel, *The Use of Force to Respond to Terrorist Attacks: The Bombing of Sudan and Afghanistan*, 24 Yale J. Intl. L. 537 (1999); Ruth Wedgwood, *Responding to Terrorism: The Strikes Against bin Laden*, 24 Yale J. Intl. L. 559 (1999); William C. Banks, *To "Prevent and Deter" International Terrorism: The U.S. Response to the Kenya and Tanzania Embassy Bombings* (National Security Studies CS 0699-12, 1999). Background for the notes on the 2001 military campaign against al Qaeda and the Taliban in Afghanistan are drawn from contemporaneous media accounts.

was apparently the Antiterrorism and Effective Death Penalty Act of 1996 (AEDPA). Pub. L. No. 104-132, 110 Stat. 1255 (1996). In the AEDPA, Congress prohibited various kinds of assistance to countries that sponsor or harbor terrorists. In the preamble to these prohibitions, it made the following "finding," among others: "the President should use all necessary means, including covert action and military force, to disrupt, dismantle, and destroy international infrastructure used by international terrorists, including overseas terrorist training facilities and safe havens." *Id.* §324(4). The finding was not codified, but it appears instead in the annotations to a codified prohibition on assistance to countries that aid terrorist states. 22 U.S.C. §2377 (2000).

Reports on the results of the attacks varied. A spokesman for bin Laden reported that 28 people were killed in the attacks on the camps. Sudan reported that ten were injured in the attack on the pharmaceutical plant. The U.S. government subsequently asserted that a soil sample from the plant revealed the presence of a precursor chemical for the production of VX, a nerve agent. Other evidence suggested that the plant was an unguarded pharmaceutical producer, which had often been visited by foreign dignitaries, and that the soil sample contained a chemical structure resembling an agricultural insecticide. It was subsequently reported that the Defense Intelligence Agency had reviewed the evidence and concluded that the attack was based on bad intelligence and bad science. *See ABC World News Tonight: Last Summer's Attack in the Sudan, Was It Based on Faulty Evidence?* (ABC television broadcast Feb. 10, 1999), *available at* 1999 WL 6800665. *But see* Benjamin & Steven Simon, *A Failure of Intelligence?*, N.Y. Rev. of Books, Dec. 20, 2001, at 7 (asserting that the attack was correctly based on classified evidence).

NOTES AND QUESTIONS

1. *Congressional Authorization for the Attacks.* Did either law cited by the administration supply authority for the attacks? Would they authorize an attack against bin Laden himself? See *infra* p. 277 for a discussion of assassination.

In April 1986, the United States conducted an air strike against Libya in response to its alleged involvement in a terrorist bombing in Berlin that took the life of an American soldier. Does this earlier attack suggest any other source of authority? Consider this testimony by the Legal Adviser to the State Department in support of the 1986 air strike:

> It is also important to note, in this regard, that the President is not simply acting alone, under this inherent constitutional authority, when taking the types of actions we are discussing today. The Congress has, over the years, learned of, considered, and effectively endorsed in principle the use of U.S. forces for a variety of purposes through its adoption of laws and other actions. Most significantly, Congress has authorized and appropriated money for creation of forces specifically designed for anti-terrorist tasks. For example, Section 1453 of the 1986 Department of Defense Authorization Act specifically states that it is the duty of the government to safeguard the safety and security of U.S. citizens against a rapidly increasing terrorist threat, and that U.S. special operations forces provide the immediate and primary capability to respond to such terrorism; and the Congress has appropriated funds for the specific purpose of improving U.S. capabilities to

carry out such operations.... In this sense, Congress has participated in the creation and maintenance of the forces whose function, at least in part, is to defend Americans from terrorism through the measured use of force. The President has openly discussed and explained the need for and propriety of these uses of force, which he has correctly assumed are widely supported by Congress and the American people. All of the actions undertaken were clearly signaled well in advance, and therefore posed no threat to the role of Congress under the Constitution in military and foreign affairs.... [*Libya Hearings, supra* p. 260 n.4, at 26-31 (statement of Abraham D. Sofaer, Legal Adviser to the Department of State).]

What theory of legal authority was the Legal Adviser invoking? Was he right?

2. *Striking First or Striking Back: Does It Make a Legal Difference?* The 1998 attacks (like the 1986 air strike on Libya) can be characterized either as striking first (in anticipatory self-defense) or striking back (in reprisal). Does the proper characterization of the attacks make any difference to their constitutionality, assuming that there is no congressional authorization for them? *See* U.S. Const. art. I, §8, cl. 11 (Declare War Clause).

Does the characterization of the attacks make any difference to their legality at international law and, therefore, perhaps derivatively at U.S. law? Professor Bowett has argued that, "coming after the event and when the harm has already been inflicted, reprisals cannot be characterized as a means of protection." D. Bowett, *Reprisals Involving Recourse to Armed Force*, 66 Am. J. Intl. L. 1, 3 (1972). Recall also Daniel Webster's statement of the conditions for self-defense. See *supra* p. 263.

An immediate response to a terrorist attack is often impossible. Terrorist targets are unpredictable and therefore difficult to protect, and attribution of responsibility is typically problematic and time-consuming. David Turndorf, *The U.S. Raid on Libya: A Forceful Response to Terrorism*, 14 Brook. J. Intl. L. 187, 216 (1988). Was the statutory or constitutional legitimacy of the 1998 attacks diminished by the fact that they were conducted after the embassy bombings, or the legitimacy of the 1986 attack that it came nine days after the Berlin bombing?

These same issues were presented even more starkly by the June 1993 missile raid on the Iraqi Intelligence Service Headquarters in Baghdad. President Clinton ordered the raid in response to a failed Iraqi assassination attempt against former President Bush during the latter's visit to Kuwait months before. *See* John Quigley, *Missiles with a Message: The Legality of the United States Raid on Iraq's Intelligence Headquarters*, 17 Hastings Intl. & Comp. L. Rev. 241 (1994); Politakis, *supra* p. 264, at 42. Defending this strike, the U.S. Ambassador to the United Nations cited U.S. rights under U.N. Charter article 51, *infra* p. 286, and emphasized that the strike was aimed at a target directly linked to the assassination plan. Was this strike an exercise of self-defense or a reprisal? *See* Stuart G. Baker, *Comparing the 1993 U.S. Airstrike on Iraq to the 1986 Bombing of Libya: The New Interpretation of Article 51*, 24 Ga. J. Intl. & Comp. L. 99 (1994).

3. *Attacking Stateless Terrorists and the WPR.* Was the 1998 attack on bin Laden's terrorist training camps in Afghanistan subject to the War Powers Resolution (WPR)? If Congress had not later authorized military action against those responsible for the September 11, 2001, attacks, see *supra* p. 100, would

the use of special forces against bin Laden and his network in Afghanistan in 2001 be subject to the WPR?

Professor Cox has suggested that the War Powers Resolution does not apply to military action to "directly repel immediate acts of terrorists and promptly capture terrorists without encounter with the armed forces of a *de jure* [or] *de facto* government." *See Libya Hearings, supra* p. 260 n.4, at 247. According to the Legal Adviser to the State Department:

> We have substantial doubt that the Resolution should, in general, be construed to apply to the deployment of ... antiterrorist units, where operations of a traditional military character are not contemplated and where no confrontation is expected between our units and forces of another state. To be sure, the language of the resolution makes no explicit exception for activities of this kind, but such units can reasonably be distinguished from "forces equipped for combat" and their actions against terrorists differ greatly from the "hostilities" contemplated by the Resolution.
>
> Nothing in the legislative history indicated, moreover, that the Congress intended the Resolution to cover deployments of such antiterrorist units. These units are not conventional military forces. A rescue effort or an effort to capture or otherwise deal with terrorists, where the forces of a foreign nation are not involved, is not a typical military mission, and our *antiterrorist forces are not equipped to conduct sustained combat with foreign armed forces.* Rather, these units operate in secrecy to carry out precise and limited tasks designed to liberate U.S. citizens from captivity or to attack terrorist kidnappers and killers. *When used, these units are not expected to confront the military forces of a sovereign state.* In a real sense, therefore, action by an antiterrorist unit constitutes a use of force that is more analogous to law enforcement activity by police in the domestic context than it is to the "hostilities" between states contemplated by the War Powers Resolution. [*Id.* at 20-21 (statement of Abraham D. Sofaer, Legal Adviser to the Department of State) (emphasis in original).]

Do you agree? Can you find these distinctions in the Constitution? In the War Powers Resolution? Suppose bin Laden and his network were intertwined with the Taliban (which ruled most of Afghanistan before the September 11 attacks), sharing resources and engaging in joint planning and defense. On this supposition, were the attackers stateless or state-sponsored? Should the President's legal authority for attacks in anticipatory self-defense turn on nice distinctions about the sponsorship of the terrorists?

4. *The Evidentiary Standard for Anticipatory Self-Defense.* When a state defends itself against ongoing attack, "the factual predicate for self-defense is clear and observable." Lobel, *supra* p. 273 n.6, at 543. But when a state uses force in anticipatory self-defense against a stateless terrorist group operating abroad or against a state that gives such a group sanctuary, the factual predicate is more ambiguous. If unsubstantiated, self-serving claims by the counterterrorist state are not deemed sufficient justification, what sort of proof must be supplied, and to whom?

Some scholars have argued that, because death may ensue from such attacks, the appropriate evidentiary standard is a criminal one — beyond a reasonable doubt. *Id.* at 551; Scheideman, *supra* p. 273 n.6. That is, the preemptively attacking state must make public for international scrutiny evidence that shows beyond a reasonable doubt that the terrorist group was responsible for terrorist attacks or that the state attacked knowingly harbored the group. Another

D. Striking First (or Striking Back?)

scholar suggests instead that responsible decision makers must consider a host of "prudential considerations," including

> whether [the use of force] will make a martyr of the leader of the target organization, or deeply offend good relations with affected countries, or waste military assets that are not limitless..., whether the use of force will save the lives of innocent victims and prevent future attacks; whether it is the only realistic way to achieve deterrence by signaling that the responsible country will strike back hard; or whether a leader who has come to power by brutal means is likely to scoff at words and remonstrations that are not backed by force. [Wedgwood, *supra* p. 273 n.6, at 563.]

Wedgwood notes that the counterterrorist state will often be unable to disclose its evidence in public without compromising its intelligence sources, but that sometimes it may take this risk in order to influence world opinion or obtain foreign support. *Id.* at 574.

Who is right? How would these conflicting standards apply to the 1998 attacks on Sudan and Afghanistan? Bin Laden and several of his associates were eventually indicted for the embassy bombings. The indictment alleged that these defendants, "together with other members and associates of al Qaeda and others known and unknown to the Grand Jury, unlawfully, willfully, and knowingly combined, conspired, confederated and agreed to kill nationals of the United States," including those who served in the U.S. embassies in Tanzania and Kenya. *See* Murphy, *supra* p. 273 n.6, at 166. Although bin Laden was not apprehended, the defendants who were tried were all convicted of various crimes and sentenced to life in prison without the possibility of parole. The convictions, however, came after lengthy trials and almost three years after the embassy bombings.

5. *Authority for the 2001 Military Campaign Against Al Qaeda and the Taliban in Afghanistan.* Congress quickly took up bills to authorize military force against those who were involved in the September 11, 2001, attacks or who gave them support or sanctuary. The White House reportedly first proposed a joint resolution that would have authorized force against those involved in the attacks "*and to deter and preempt any future acts of terrorism and aggression against the United States.*" David Abramowitz, *The President, the Congress and Use of Force: Legal and Political Considerations in Authorizing Use of Force Against International Terrorism*, 43 Harv. Intl. L.J. 71 (2002) (emphasis added). Why do you suppose Congress did not enact this authorization? Instead it enacted the authorization set out *supra* p. 100. Does the scope of the enacted measure match the administration's rhetorical commitment to combating terrorists wherever they can be found and states that give them support? Does its last clause serve as a limitation on the authority it bestows?

2. Targeted Killing in Anticipatory Self-Defense

Executive Order No. 12,333
46 Fed. Reg. 59,941 (1981)

2.11 Prohibition on Assassination. No person employed by or acting on behalf of the United States Government shall engage in, or conspire to engage in, assassination.

2.12 Indirect Participation. No agency of the Intelligence Community shall participate in or request any person to undertake activities forbidden by this Order....

W. Hays Parks, Memorandum of Law: Executive Order 12333 and Assassination

Department of the Army Pamphlet 27-50-204
from The Army Lawyer 4 (Dec. 1989)

1. *Summary.* Executive Order 12333 prohibits assassination as a matter of national policy, but does not expound on its meaning or application. This memorandum explores the term and analyzes application of the ban to military operations at three levels: (a) conventional military operations; (b) counterinsurgency operations; and (c) peacetime counterterrorist operations. It concludes that the clandestine, low visibility, or overt use of military force against legitimate targets in time of war, or against similar targets in time of peace where such individuals or groups pose an immediate threat to United States citizens or the national security of the United States, as determined by competent authority, does not constitute assassination or conspiracy to engage in assassination, and would not be prohibited by the proscription in EO 12333 or by international law....

3. a. *Assassination in General.* ...While assassination generally is regarded as an act of murder for political reasons, its victims are not necessarily limited to persons of public office or prominence. The murder of a private person, if carried out for political purposes, may constitute an act of assassination. For example, the 1978 "poisoned-tip umbrella" killing of Bulgarian defector Georgi Markov by Bulgarian State Security agents on the streets of London falls into the category of an act of murder carried out for political purposes, and constitutes an assassination. In contrast, the murder of Leon Klinghoffer, a private citizen, by the terrorist Abu el Abbas during the 1985 hijacking of the Italian cruise ship *Achille Lauro,* though an act of murder for political purposes, would not constitute an assassination. The distinction lies not merely in the purpose of the act and/or its intended victim, but also under certain circumstances in its covert nature.[1] Finally, the killings of Martin Luther King and Presidents Abraham Lincoln, James A. Garfield, William McKinley and John F. Kennedy generally are regarded as assassination because each involved the murder of a public figure or national leader for political purposes accomplished through a surprise attack.

b. *Assassination in Peacetime.* ...Peacetime assassination...would seem to encompass the murder of a private individual or public figure for political purposes, and in some cases also require that the act constitute a covert activity, particularly when the individual is a private citizen. Assassination is unlawful killing, and would be prohibited by international law even if there were no executive order proscribing it.

---

1. *Covert operations* are defined as "operations which are planned and executed so as to conceal the identity of or permit plausible denial by the sponsor. They differ from clandestine operations in that emphasis is placed on concealment of identity of [the] sponsor rather than on concealment of the operation." In contrast, low visibility operations are...undertaken with the knowledge that the action and or sponsorship of the operation may preclude plausible denial by the initiating power. JCS Pub. 1, *Dictionary of Military and Associated Terms* (1 June 1987).

D. Striking First (or Striking Back?)

c. *Assassination in Wartime*. . . . In wartime the role of the military includes the legalized killing (as opposed to murder) of the enemy, whether lawful combatants or unprivileged belligerents, and may include in either category civilians who take part in the hostilities.

The term *assassination* when applied to wartime military activities against enemy combatants or military objectives does not preclude acts of violence involving the element of surprise. Combatants are liable to attack at any time or place, regardless of their activity when attacked. Spaight, *War Rights on Land* (1911), pp. 86, 88; U.S. Army Field Manual 27-10, *The Law of Land Warfare* (1956), para. 31. . . . An individual combatant's vulnerability to lawful targeting (as opposed to assassination) is not dependent upon his or her military duties, or proximity to combat as such. Nor does the prohibition on assassination limit means that otherwise would be lawful; no distinction is made between an attack accomplished by aircraft, missile, naval gunfire, artillery, mortar, infantry assault, ambush, land mine or boobytrap, a single shot by a sniper, a commando attack, or other, similar means. All are lawful means for attacking the enemy and the choice of one vis-a-vis another has no bearing on the legality of the attack. If the person attacked is a combatant, the use of a particular lawful means for attack (as opposed to another) cannot make an otherwise lawful attack either unlawful or an assassination.

Likewise, the death of noncombatants ancillary to the lawful attack of a military objective is neither assassination nor otherwise unlawful. Civilians and other noncombatants who are within or in close proximity to a military objective assume a certain risk through their presence in or in proximity to such targets. . . .

The scope of assassination in the U.S. military was first outlined in U.S. Army General Orders No. 100 (1863). Paragraph 148 states

> *Assassination.* The law of war does not allow proclaiming either an individual belonging to the hostile army, or a citizen, or a subject of the hostile government, an outlaw, who may be slain without trial by any captor, any more than the modern law of peace allows such international outlawry; on the contrary, it abhors such outrage. . . .

This provision, consistent with the earlier writings of Hugo Grotius (*Cf.* Bk, III, Sec. XXXVIII(4)), has been continued in U.S. Army Field Manual 27-10, *The Law of Land Warfare* (1956), which provides (paragraph 31):

> (Article 23b, Annex to Hague Convention IV, 1907) is construed as prohibiting assassination, proscription, or outlawry of an enemy, or putting a price upon an enemy's head, as well as offering reward for an enemy "dead or alive." . . .

5. *Peacetime Operations.* The use of force in peacetime is limited by the previously cited article 2(4) of the Charter of the United Nations. However, article 51 of the Charter of the United Nations recognizes the inherent right of self defense of nations. Historically, the United States has resorted to the use of military force in peacetime where another nation has failed to discharge its international responsibilities in protecting U.S. citizens from acts of violence originating in or launched from its sovereign territory, or has been culpable in aiding and abetting international criminal activities. . . .

The Charter of the United Nations recognizes the inherent right of self defense and does not preclude unilateral action against an immediate threat.

In general terms, the United States recognizes three forms of self defense:

a. Against an actual use of force, or hostile act.

b. Preemptive self defense against an imminent use of force.

c. Self defense against a continuing threat.[8]

A national decision to employ military force in self defense against a legitimate terrorist or related threat would not be unlike the employment of force in response to a threat by conventional forces; only the nature of the threat has changed, rather than the international legal right of self defense. The terrorist organizations envisaged as appropriate to necessitate or warrant an armed response by U.S. military forces are well-financed, highly-organized paramilitary structures engaged in the illegal use of force.[9]

NOTES AND QUESTIONS

1. *The Origins of the Executive Order Ban on Assassination.* In 1976, a congressional committee found evidence of CIA involvement in assassination plots against foreign leaders but was unable to determine whether such involvement had been approved by senior officials. *See* Select Comm. to Study Governmental Operations with Respect to Intelligence Activities (Church Comm.), *Alleged Assassination Plots Involving Foreign Leaders: An Interim Report*, 94th Cong. (1976). The committee then proposed a bill to criminalize the assassination or attempted assassination of "any foreign official because of such official's political views, actions, or statements, while such official is outside the United States." *Id.* at App. A. "Foreign official" was defined as "Chief of State or the political equivalent...of a foreign government...or of a foreign political group, party, military force, movement or other association with which the United States is not at war pursuant to a declaration of war or against which the United States Armed Forces have not been introduced into hostilities or situations pursuant to the provisions of the War Powers Resolution." *Id.*

However, President Ford headed off such legislation by adopting Executive Order No. 11,905, 41 Fed. Reg. 7703 (1976), prohibiting U.S. employees from engaging in "political assassination." In 1978, President Carter replaced this order with Executive Order No. 12,036, 43 Fed. Reg. 3674, which expanded the prohibition to include agents of the United States and dropped, without explanation, the modifier "political." President Reagan retained Carter's

---

8. ...This right of self defense would be appropriate to the attack of terrorist leaders where their actions pose a continuing threat to U.S. citizens or the national security of the United States. As with an attack on a guerrilla infrastructure, the level to which attacks could be carried out against individuals within a terrorist infrastructure would be a policy rather than a legal decision.

9. In a conventional armed conflict, such individuals would be regarded as unprivileged belligerents, subject to attack, but not entitled to prisoner of war protection or exemption from prosecution for their crimes. Employment of military force against terrorists does not bestow prisoner of war protection upon members of the terrorist organization.

language as sections 2.11 and 2.12 in the still-current Executive Order No. 12,333. *See generally* William C. Banks & Peter Raven-Hansen, *Targeted Killing and Assassination: The U.S. Legal Framework*, 37 U. Rich. L. Rev. 667, 717-726 (2003); Jonathan M. Fredman, *Covert Action, Loss of Life, and the Prohibition on Assassination*, 1 Studies in Intelligence 15 (1997 unclassified ed.).

2. *The Applicability of the Executive Order Prohibition.* Would the executive order have barred the killing of Saddam Hussein, leader of Iraq, in 1991 during the first Gulf War, or in 2003, during the invasion of Iraq? *See* Stuart Taylor Jr., *Should We Just Kill Saddam?*, Legal Times, Feb. 4, 1991.

Would the prohibition have applied to General Manuel Antonio Noriega, leader of Panama? In 1989 the CIA was approached for help by Panamanian military officers who proposed a coup against Noriega after he nullified a national election that he had lost. The officers sought nonlethal assistance in the form of money and equipment, but they admitted that Noriega might be killed in the coup. Could the U.S. have legally furnished assistance? *See* David B. Ottaway & Don Oberdorfer, *Administration Alters Assassination Ban*, Wash. Post, Nov. 4, 1989, at A1; David B. Ottaway, *CIA Aides Call Hill Rules No Hindrance*, Wash. Post, Oct. 18, 1989, at A14.

How about targeting a Columbian drug trafficker who has embarked on a campaign of narco-terror and assassination against the government of Columbia, and who has been indicted in the United States for drug-trafficking and multiple drug-related murders?

After the September 11, 2001, terrorist attacks, President Bush intimated that Osama bin Laden, who was alleged to have been behind both the 1998 embassy bombings and the September 11 attacks, should be taken "dead or alive." *Guard and Reserves "Define Spirit of America": Remarks by the President to Employees at the Pentagon*, Sept. 17, 2001. Could he legally order the killing of bin Laden? *See, e.g.*, Robert F. Turner, *In Self-Defense, U.S. Has Right to Kill Terrorist bin Laden*, USA Today, Oct. 26, 1998, at 17A. In this regard, consider the following recommendation:

> The United States should adopt a[n assassination] program aimed not only at the heads of the [terrorist] networks, but also at the arms and the fingers. It should locate and assassinate the killers, the planners, and the trainers. It should go beyond the organizations to target those who finance them and those who tend to communications and logistics. The program should target officials of the governments that give terrorists shelter. None should feel safe who knowingly aid these organizations — whether they launder their money or their clothes. [Lawrence J. Siskind, *Our Killer Instinct*, Legal Times, Oct. 8, 2001.]

Would such a program be lawful under the executive order? Would it be wise, now that we have learned that apparently the "arms and fingers" of the group that executed the September 11 attacks made significant preparations in Germany and that they had financing from institutions in Switzerland and Saudi Arabia? *See* Barton Gellman, *CIA Weighs "Targeted Killing" Missions*, Wash. Post, Oct. 28, 2001, at A01 (reporting that senior managers in the CIA's Directorate of Operations urged targeting not just Al Qaeda's commanders, but also its financiers — "the Gucci guys, the guys who write the checks," because they are easier to find and because "it would have a tremendously chilling effect"). *See* Daniel Byman, *Do Targeted Killings Work?* 85 For. Aff. 95 (2006).

3. *Force and Effect of the Executive Order Ban.* We have seen that an executive order can have the same force and effect as a statute. See *supra* p. 45. But it is not a statute. How, if at all, do you think the legal force of the executive order ban was affected by President Reagan's secret intelligence findings authorizing lethal operations against Qadhafi (*see* Bob Woodward, *1984 Order Gave CIA Latitude; Reagan's Secret Move to Counter Terrorists Called "License to Kill,"* Wash. Post, Oct. 5, 1988, at A1), or by President Clinton's (*see* James Risen, *Bin Laden Was Target of Afghan Raid, U.S. Confirms*, N.Y. Times, Nov. 14, 1998, at A3) and President George W. Bush's findings authorizing lethal operations against bin Laden? *See* Memorandum from Acting Asst. Attorney General Randolph D. Moss to the President, *Legal Effectiveness of a Presidential Directive as Compared to an Executive Order*, Jan. 29, 2000 (concluding that presidential directives — and, by implication, findings — can have the same substantive legal effect as an executive order, and that any such presidential decision, however it is memorialized, remains effective upon a change in administration and until subsequent presidential action is taken). *See also* Banks & Raven-Hansen, *supra* p. 281, at 725-726.

In the wake of the September 11 attacks, Rep. Bob Barr introduced the Terrorist Elimination Act of 2001, which provided that sections 2.11 and 2.12 of Executive Order No. 12,333 "shall have no further force or effect." H.R. 19, 107th Cong. (2001). Is such a law necessary to permit the military to use military strikes to remove a terrorist leader, as the bill's proposed findings indicate? Would it be constitutional? *See* Banks & Raven-Hansen, *supra*, at 745-747.

4. *Assassination and International Law.* As the Parks memorandum suggests, assassination in peacetime is unlawful at international law, but the use of military force in self-defense arguably is not. *See generally* Vincent-Joël Proulx, *If the Hat Fits, Wear It, If the Turban Fits, Run for Your Life: Reflections on the Indefinite Detention and Targeted Killing of Suspected Terrorists*, 56 Hastings L.J. 801 (2005); Jami Melissa Jackson, *The Legality of Assassination of Independent Terrorist Leaders: An Examination of National and International Implications*, 24 N.C. J. Intl. & Com. Reg. 669 (1999); Michael N. Schmitt, *State-Sponsored Assassination in International and Domestic Law*, 17 Yale J. Intl. L. 609 (1992); Patricia Zengel, *Assassination and the Law of Armed Conflict*, 43 Mercer L. Rev. 615 (1992). Even if a particular killing were unlawful at international law, however, would that make it unlawful under our law? Suppose the President has ordered it?

5. *Deciding to Assassinate.* If assassination is legal, should it be treated as a covert action, requiring a prior written presidential finding? See *infra* p. 423. What evidentiary standard, if any, should the administration use in making a decision to assassinate? *See* Byman, *supra*, at 108 (faulting the United States for the absence of "clear, transparent, and legitimate procedures for deciding when targeted killings are appropriate"). Since the decision is to kill someone, is the appropriate standard the one that would be used in a capital criminal case: beyond a reasonable doubt? A student has argued that "[t]argeted killings *do not* substitute for apprehension, prosecution, and court-ordered punishment... [;] they substitute for *overt use of military or paramilitary force.*"

D. Striking First (or Striking Back?)

Brian P. Finnegan, *Assassination, U.S. Law, and the International Use of Lethal Force* 33 (Nov. 17, 2000) (on file with authors) (emphasis in original). Should the standard turn on the risk posed by the target rather than on evidence of responsibility for a completed terrorist act? Would your answer change if assassination were used as a tool of policy not just against terrorists, but also against other transnational criminals, such as drug-traffickers?

6. *Assassination at Home?* It is important to keep in mind that the executive order and all the discussion about it contemplate only targeted killings or assassinations of foreign persons *abroad*. A variety of laws, in addition to ordinary criminal laws, seemingly prohibit the use of such tools against any person in the United States. *See, e.g.*, U.S. Const. amend. V (providing that "no person" shall be deprived of life "without due process of law"); Posse Comitatus Act, 18 U.S.C. §1385 (2000), *infra* p. 945 (prohibiting the Army or Air Force from executing the laws without express constitutional or statutory authority); the National Security Act of 1947, 50 U.S.C. §403-3(d) (2000) (prohibiting the CIA from performing "internal security functions"); Idaho v. Horiuchi, 253 F.3d 359, 377 (9th Cir. 2001) (asserting, in a suit growing out of the Ruby Ridge killing by an FBI sharpshooter, that "wartime rules" of engagement permitting targeting of suspects who pose no "immediate threat...[are] patently unconstitutional for a police action").

Collective Self-Defense — 11

The world's sovereign states solemnly declared in Article 2(4) of the U.N. Charter that they would not engage in unprovoked aggression: "All Members shall refrain in their international relations from the threat or use of force against the territorial integrity or political independence of any state...." Yet the drafters of the Charter understood that no such commitment could ensure that war would never again break out. They therefore provided for a variety of measures, including the authorized use of military force, to preserve or restore the peace, and especially to prevent a limited conflict from spreading.

How does this development bear on the domestic separation of powers relating to national security?

> Any adequate contemporary theory of the division of war powers between Congress and the President must take account of the growing role of the United Nations Security Council in responding to threats to international peace and security. In 1945, drafters of the U.N. Charter responded to the devastation of World War II by seeking to limit the unilateral use of force as a method for resolving international disputes and by creating a mechanism to prevent war and resolve disputes peacefully. If threats to the peace or acts of aggression did occur, however, the U.N. Security Council could recommend or decide to take action, including imposing economic and diplomatic sanctions. If necessary, it could authorize collective military enforcement action to restore international peace and security.
> [Jane E. Stromseth, *Rethinking War Powers: Congress, the President, and the United Nations*, 81 Geo. L.J. 597, 598 (1993).]

In this chapter we first examine provisions of the U.N. Charter that provide for collective uses of force under certain circumstances, as well as domestic legislation intended to guide the U.S. use of force in reliance on those provisions. We then consider two large-scale conflicts—the Korean War and the Persian Gulf War—as examples of collective self-defense, by which we mean the use of force by one or more states to assist another state that is the victim of unprovoked aggression. In both conflicts the President relied in part on the U.N. Charter and U.N. Security Council resolutions as authority for commitments of U.S. troops. Both raise important questions of legitimacy under international as well as domestic law. And both offer important lessons about the interactions of these two sources of law.

A. COLLECTIVE SELF-DEFENSE UNDER THE UNITED NATIONS CHARTER

1. The Role of the United Nations Security Council

Charter of the United Nations
June 26, 1945, 59 Stat. 1031, T.S. No. 993

CHAPTER VII. ACTION WITH RESPECT TO THREATS TO THE PEACE, BREACHES OF THE PEACE, AND ACTS OF AGGRESSION

ARTICLE 39

The Security Council shall determine the existence of any threat to the peace, breach of the peace, or act of aggression and shall make recommendations, or decide what measures shall be taken in accordance with Articles 41 and 42, to maintain and restore international peace and security.

ARTICLE 40

In order to prevent an aggravation of the situation, the Security Council may, before making the recommendations or deciding upon the measures provided for in Article 39, call upon the parties concerned to comply with such provisional measures as it deems necessary or desirable. Such provisional measures shall be without prejudice to the rights, claims, or position of the parties concerned. The Security Council shall duly take account of failure to comply with such provisional measures.

ARTICLE 41

The Security Council may decide what measures not involving the use of armed force are to be employed to give effect to its decisions, and it may call upon the Members of the United Nations to apply such measures. These may include complete or partial interruption of economic relations and of rail, sea, air, postal, telegraphic, radio, and other means of communication, and the severance of diplomatic relations.

ARTICLE 42

Should the Security Council consider that measures provided for in Article 41 would be inadequate or have proved to be inadequate, it may take such action by air, sea, or land forces as may be necessary to maintain or restore international peace and security. Such actions may include demonstrations, blockade, and other operations by air, sea, or land forces of Members of the United Nations.

ARTICLE 43

1. All Members of the United Nations, in order to contribute to the maintenance of international peace and security, undertake to make available to the Security Council, on its call and in accordance with a special agreement or agreements, armed forces, assistance, and facilities, including rights of passage, necessary for the purpose of maintaining international peace and security.

2. Such agreement or agreements shall govern the numbers and types of forces, their degree of readiness and general location, and the nature of the facilities and assistance to be provided.

3. The agreement or agreements shall be negotiated as soon as possible on the initiative of the Security Council. They shall be concluded between the Security Council and Members or between the Security Council and groups of Members and shall be subject to ratification by the signatory states in accordance with their respective constitutional processes....

ARTICLE 51

Nothing in the present charter shall impair the inherent right of individual and collective self-defense if an armed attack occurs against a Member of the United Nations, until the Security Council has taken measures necessary to maintain international peace and security....

NOTES AND QUESTIONS

1. *Force as a Last Resort.* Recognizing the provisions of Chapter VII of the U.N. Charter as exceptional, can you describe the sequence of events that might provoke the invocation of each respective article, from Article 39 to Article 42, leading to eventual authorization for the use of military force? Do you think an individual state or group of states might find it extremely inconvenient, even dangerous, to have to persuade a majority of the U.N. Security Council members to authorize such use (and to persuade all of the permanent members not to veto it)? Can you imagine why every member state agreed to abide by these provisions?

2. *Article 42: Actions "It May Take."* In more than half a century, not a single Article 43 agreement has been signed.

> The tensions of the Cold War soon eclipsed efforts to negotiate any special agreements, leaving the Security Council dependent on the willingness of member states to provide troops on an ad hoc basis. Moreover, with the notable exception of Korea, superpower disagreement essentially barred the United Nations from authorizing collective military action in response to acts of aggression—until the Persian Gulf War following Iraq's invasion of Kuwait in August 1990. Instead, during the Cold War, the United Nations developed a more limited capacity for responding to conflict, namely, consensual deployment of "peacekeeping" forces to perform tasks such as monitoring ceasefires and observing the demobilization of opposing forces. [Stromseth, *supra* p. 284, at 598-599.]

A. Collective Self-Defense Under the United Nations Charter

The operation of the U.N. Security Council without special agreements is explained in Frederic L. Kirgis Jr., *The Security Council's First Fifty Years*, 89 Am. J. Intl. L. 506 (1995).

According to one view, "the central idea of a globally sanctioned police action was never abandoned; . . . the failure to implement Article 43 merely led to organic growth and the alternative creation of police action through Article 42, which does not require special agreements." Thomas M. Franck & Faiza Patel, *UN Police Action in Lieu of War: "The Old Order Changeth,"* 85 Am. J. Intl. L. 63, 66 (1991). Does the language of Article 42 support this reading of it? Or is the Article 42 provision for the use of force by the Security Council necessarily qualified by Article 43? *See* Michael J. Glennon, *The Constitution and Article VII of the United Nations Charter*, 85 Am. J. Intl. L. 74, 77-80 (1991) (citing extensive evidence that the use of force under Article 42 was understood to be dependent on the existence of an Article 43 agreement); Stromseth, *supra*, at 612-614 (same).

3. *Military Actions Outside the U.N. Charter.* Suppose a state or group of states decides that a development somewhere in the world requires the use of military force. Suppose further that efforts to secure the approval of the U.N. Security Council are unsuccessful or that the Security Council's response is ambiguous. Does the U.N. Charter permit such use of force without clear approval from the Security Council? Does customary international law permit it? These questions are squarely presented by NATO's bombing of the Federal Republic of Yugoslavia in 1999, *see* Sean D. Murphy, *Legal Regulation of the Use of Force*, 93 Am J. Intl. L. 628 (1999), and by the March 2003 invasion of Iraq by the United States and its coalition partners. See *infra* pp. 303-317.

4. *Individual and Collective Self-Defense.* The use of force may be permissible without Security Council approval, at least for a time, as an exercise of every state's inherent right of individual and collective self-defense, as set forth in Article 51. If such use is consistent with the requirements of Article 51, of course, it may also be regarded as consistent with the requirements of the Charter generally.

Some commentators argue that Article 51 was meant to replace traditional self-help measures, providing for an immediate response to aggression until — but only until — the Security Council has had time to act. *See* Franck & Patel, *supra*, at 64. Others maintain that Article 51 simply restates the right of individual and collective self-defense that is inherent in sovereignty, and that that right remains intact until the Security Council has dealt *successfully* with an international conflict. Eugene V. Rostow, *Until What? Enforcement Action or Collective Self-Defense?*, 85 Am. J. Intl. L. 506, 511 (1991). Can you tell from the text what was intended? Can you see practical difficulties with each claimed meaning?

2. The Role of the United States Under Chapter VII

In 1945, during debate on the United Nations Charter, some Senators argued for a reservation to the Charter that would have allowed Congress to approve or reject each use of American armed forces under an Article 43 special agreement. Otherwise, they insisted, the Charter represented an unconstitutional delegation of war-making authority to the U.N. Security Council. But a majority in the Senate were persuaded to approve the Charter without reservation, partly on grounds that: (1) Congress would have an opportunity to approve the terms of any special agreement, and (2) the United States could veto any Security Council resolution invoking the special agreement. *See* Stromseth, *supra*, at 604-612.

Within months of ratification of the Charter, however, Congress undertook to spell out more clearly the respective roles of the executive and legislative branches in fulfilling U.S. obligations under Chapter VII. The United Nations Participation Act, 22 U.S.C. §§287-287e-2 (2000 & Supp. III 2003), instructs U.S. representatives at the United Nations to vote in accordance with instructions from the President, and it directs the President to report any Security Council enforcement actions to the Congress. It also authorizes the President to implement any economic sanctions approved by the Security Council. Concerning the use of United States military force pursuant to a resolution of the Security Council under Article 42, the Act provides as follows:

United Nations Participation Act
22 U.S.C. §§287-287e-2 (2000 & Supp. III 2003)

§287d. USE OF ARMED FORCES; LIMITATIONS

The President is authorized to negotiate a special agreement or agreements with the Security Council which shall be subject to the approval of the Congress by appropriate Act or joint resolution, providing for the numbers and types of armed forces, their degree of readiness and general location, and the nature of facilities and assistance, including rights of passage, to be made available to the Security Council on its call for the purpose of maintaining international peace and security in accordance with article 43 of said Charter. The President shall not be deemed to require the authorization of the Congress to make available to the Security Council on its call in order to take action under article 42 of said Charter and pursuant to such special agreement or agreements the armed forces, facilities, or assistance provided for therein: Provided, That, except as authorized in section 287d-1 of this title, nothing herein contained shall be construed as an authorization to the President by the Congress to make available to the Security Council for such purpose armed forces, facilities, or assistance in addition to the forces, facilities, and assistance provided for in such special agreement or agreements.

§287d-1. NONCOMBATANT ASSISTANCE TO UNITED NATIONS

(a) Armed forces details; supplies and equipment; obligation of funds; procurement and replacement of requested items. Notwithstanding the provisions of any other law, the President, upon the request by the United Nations for cooperative action, and to the extent that he finds that it is consistent with the national interest to comply with such request, may authorize, in support of such activities of the United Nations as are specifically directed to the peaceful settlement of disputes and not involving the employment of armed forces contemplated by chapter VII of the United Nations Charter—

(1) the detail to the United Nations, under such terms and conditions as the President shall determine, of personnel of the armed forces of the United States to serve as observers, guards, or in any non-combatant capacity, but in no event shall more than a total of one thousand of such personnel be so detailed at any one time....

NOTES AND QUESTIONS

1. *The U.N. Charter as U.S. Law?* Article 2(5) of the United Nations Charter provides that "[a]ll Members shall give the United Nations every assistance in any action it takes in accordance with the present Charter." Article 25 of the Charter provides that "Members of the United Nations agree to accept and carry out the decisions of the Security Council...." As a treaty approved by the Senate, the U.N. Charter is part of the "Law of the Land" under Article VI of the U.S. Constitution. Is the President not therefore empowered—indeed obliged—to "execute" the terms of the Charter, just as he would any other law under the Take Care Clause, by enforcing resolutions of the Security Council? *See generally* James A.R. Nafziger & Edward M. Wise, *The Status in United States Law of Security Council Resolutions Under Chapter VII of the United Nations Charter*, 46 Am. J. Comp. L. 421 (1998).

According to one commentator,

> The Charter was seen as conferring no additional authority on the President to use United States armed forces in hostilities; the President could not, by an affirmative vote in the Security Council, confer upon himself power to use armed force that he would not otherwise possess. The text of the UNPA [United Nations Participation Act] makes that clear, as does a review of its legislative history. [Glennon, *supra* p. 287, at 78.]

A dramatically different reading of the same history may be found in Robert F. Turner, *Truman, Korea, and the Constitution: Debunking the "Imperial President" Myth*, 19 Harv. J.L. & Pub. Poly. 533 (1996).

2. *Delegation of War-Making Authority.* Does Congress's ability to shape the terms of a special agreement under Article 43 preserve its proper constitutional role in committing U.S. forces to combat? Would it be easier to answer if the agreement could specify not only the number of troops, their equipment, and the geographical scope of their deployment, but also rules for their engagement of an enemy force? As a practical matter, should Congress seek to impose such restrictions on the use of a standby force before placing it at the disposal of the U.N. Security Council? *See* Stromseth, *supra*, at 606-607.

Should Congress reserve the ability to order withdrawal of U.S. troops from a particular conflict after they have been deployed by the Security Council? *See* Franck & Patel, *supra* p. 287, at 67-68. May Congress not cut off funding for any military action at any time? *See* William C. Banks & Peter Raven-Hansen, *National Security Law and the Power of the Purse* 144-148 (1994). If it may, is there any reason to worry about Congress's surrender of its proper constitutional role?

As a permanent member of the Security Council, the United States may veto any Security Council resolution with which it disagrees. Does that veto power allay any fears about an improper delegation of war-making authority?

3. *Categorizing Uses of U.S. Troops.* During debate on approval of the U.N. Charter, a majority in the Senate were persuaded that special agreement forces would be used only in a "police action" of such limited scope and duration that it would not constitute a "war" in either an international or constitutional sense. Secretary of State John Foster Dulles testified that Congress's war powers would not be implicated if "we are talking about a little bit of force to be used as a police demonstration.... [But] if this is going to be a large volume of force which is going to put a big drain on the resources of the United States or commit us to great and costly adventures, then the Congress ought to have a voice in this matter." *The Charter of the United Nations: Hearings Before the Senate Committee on Foreign Relations,* 79th Cong. 655 (1945), *quoted in* Stromseth, *supra,* at 609. Can this explanation be squared with the text of the Constitution or with your understanding of the Framers' intent?

Can you define "police action"? If your answer is that it is "not a war," are you prepared to say what a "war" is? Is the Supreme Court's definition in *The Prize Cases, supra* p. 67 ("that state in which a nation prosecutes its right by force"), hopelessly outdated for this purpose? *See generally* Peter Raven-Hansen, *Constitutional Constraints: The War Clause,* in *The U.S. Constitution and the Power to Go to War* 40-41 (Gary M. Stern & Morton H. Halperin eds., 1993). However the terms are defined, would Congress need to be consulted if a conflict in which U.S. forces were deployed escalated from "police action" to "war"?

Congressional committee reports accompanying the U.N. Participation Act also indicated that the use of U.S. special agreement forces would not require ad hoc approval by Congress. "Preventative or enforcement action by these forces on order of the Security Council would not be an act of war," they asserted, "but would be international action for the preservation of the peace and for the purpose of preventing war. Consequently, the provisions of the Charter do not affect the exclusive power of the Congress to declare war." H. Rep. No. 79-1383 (1945), *reprinted in* 1945 U.S.C.C.A.N. 927; S. Rep. No. 79-717 (1945). Do you know how to distinguish between an action for the preservation of the peace or the prevention of war and an "act of war"?

Who should be able to make an authoritative pronouncement about the character of a particular conflict?

B. THE KOREAN "POLICE ACTION"[1]

In 1966, early in the Vietnam War, the State Department Legal Adviser cited the Korean War as precedent for the President's exercise of inherent Article II

---

1. Except where otherwise noted, background for this study is drawn from Max Hastings, *The Korean War* (1987); Burton I. Kaufman, *The Korean War: Challenge in Crisis, Credibility, and Command* (1986); Callum A. MacDonald, *Korea: The War Before Vietnam* (1986); Glenn D. Paige, *The Korean*

B. The Korean "Police Action"

power to send U.S. forces into battle without formally consulting Congress. See *supra* p. 209. Professor Moore called it "a poor precedent." John Norton Moore, *Law and the Indo-China War* 557 (1972). The Korean War was cited again in 1990 by members of the first Bush administration, who argued that the President did not need Congress's approval for offensive military action in the Persian Gulf War.

In this part of the chapter we consider domestic and international law justifications for U.S. involvement in the Korean War, and, in the process, the importance of that war as a precedent for future uses of force abroad.

1. The Outbreak of War

In 1943, while Korea was still occupied by the Japanese, President Roosevelt, Prime Minister Churchill, and Generalissimo Chiang Kai-shek announced in the Cairo Declaration that Korea would "in due course" be free and independent. Two years later, at the Potsdam Conference in July 1945, it was agreed that at war's end the United States would occupy the Korean peninsula south of the thirty-eighth parallel, while the Soviets would take over the area north to Korea's border with China. United Nations-sponsored efforts to establish a unified democratic government soon broke down, leaving the two major powers to sponsor their own politically sympathetic governments led, respectively, by Syngman Rhee in the South and Kim Il Sung in the North. Each one eventually claimed to represent all of Korea.

Early on the morning of Sunday, June 25, 1950 (local time), without any warning, North Korean troops launched a massive invasion of the South. Later the same day, the United States presented a resolution to the U.N. Security Council calling on North Korea to stop its aggression and asking member states to "render every assistance to the United Nations in the execution of this resolution." S.C. Res. 82, U.N. Doc. S/INF/4/Rev. 1 (1950). The Soviet Union, which presumably would have vetoed the resolution, was boycotting the United Nations at the time to protest Nationalist Chinese representation of China. The vote was 9-0 in favor of the resolution, with one abstention.

2. The President's Response

Before the day ended, President Truman ordered U.S. air and naval forces to assist in the evacuation of American dependents and noncombatants from Korea. The next day, June 26, as the military situation quickly deteriorated, U.S. forces were directed to provide support for South Korean troops. The President

---

Decision, June 24-30, 1950 (1968); David Rees, *Korea: The Limited War* (1964); James L. Stokesbury, *A Short History of the Korean War* (1988); Jane E. Stromseth, *Rethinking War Powers: Congress, the President, and the United Nations*, 81 Geo. L.J. 597, 621-640 (1993); A. Kenneth Pye, *The Legal Status of the Korean Hostilities*, 45 Geo. L.J. 45 (1956); and Dean Acheson, *Review of U.N. and U.S. Action to Restore Peace*, 23 Dept. St. Bull. 43 (1950).

announced his decision to the American people the day after that. It was not until later on June 27, however, that the U.N. Security Council adopted a second resolution in which it "recommended" that member states "furnish such assistance to the Republic of Korea as may be necessary to repel the armed attack and to restore international peace and security in the area." S.C. Res. 83, U.N. Doc. S/INF/4/Rev. 1 (1950).

Although Congress was in session at the time of the North Korean invasion, President Truman waited until June 27 to brief congressional leaders on the conflict — after he had ordered U.S. forces into combat. On June 29 and 30, the President approved U.S. air strikes against North Korea and directed the deployment of U.S. ground combat forces. But he elected not to ask Congress to approve any of these actions, fearing that an extended public debate might weaken the American effort to blunt this first major Communist aggression in the Far East.

Almost every member of Congress publicly supported the substance of the President's decision to act promptly to repel the North Korean attack. Still, some worried about Congress's exclusion from the commitment to go to war. Responding to that concern, a July 3 State Department memorandum declared:

> The President, as Commander in Chief of the Armed Forces of the United States, has full control over the use thereof. He also has authority to conduct the foreign relations of the United States. Since the beginning of United States history, he has, upon numerous occasions, utilized these powers in sending armed forces abroad. The preservation of the United Nations for the maintenance of peace is a cardinal interest of the United States. Both traditional international law and Article 39 of the United Nations Charter and the resolution pursuant thereto authorize the United States to repel the armed aggression against the Republic of Korea. [23 Dept. St. Bull. 173 (1950).]

The memorandum called North Korean defiance of the Security Council resolutions "a threat to the peace and security of the United States and to the security of United States forces in the Pacific." The memorandum also cited 85 earlier instances in which presidents had used military force abroad without a declaration of war. The President's supporters referred to the Korean conflict as a "police action" rather than a war, to suggest that congressional approval was not required.

Despite some members' misgivings about the process for going to war, in the days and weeks that followed, Congress tacitly approved President Truman's actions. As early as June 27, it voted overwhelmingly to approve an extension of the draft, a matter on which it earlier had been sharply divided. Congress also lifted the ceiling on the size of the armed forces, increased taxes to help pay for the war, and gave the President extensive powers over the management of defense production.

United States warplanes were sent into the battle on June 26. The first U.S. ground forces arrived in Korea on July 1. One week later, the Security Council adopted a third resolution placing all forces defending South Korea under the unified command of the United States. The fighting ended three years later where it had started, with a cease-fire along the thirty-eighth parallel. The United States had suffered 33,629 killed and more than 100,000 wounded.

B. The Korean "Police Action"

Some 50,000 South Korean troops were killed. The exact extent of North Korean losses is still unknown.

NOTES AND QUESTIONS

1. *Korean and Vietnam Wars Compared.* The Korean conflict was different from the one in Indochina, see *supra* Chapter 8, in several ways that might bear on the legitimacy of President Truman's actions. Can you say how?

2. *Source of Presidential Authority?* If you had written the July 3, 1950, State Department memorandum excerpted above, what authority would you have cited for the President's claim to have "full control" over the use of the armed forces? Could you argue that Congress lacked authority to stop him from sending U.S. troops to Korea? *See* John Hart Ely, *War and Responsibility: Constitutional Lessons of Vietnam and Its Aftermath* 10-11 (1993) (recalling contemporary discussion of this issue).

If the "preservation of the United Nations for the maintenance of peace" was really at stake in Korea, did characterizing it as a "cardinal interest of the United States" provide the President with authority that he otherwise lacked? How could that characterization have been tested?

3. *A Role for Congress or the Courts?* What is the significance of President Truman's decision not to ask Congress for its approval of his actions, even retrospectively? *See* Louis Fisher, *The Korean War: On What Legal Basis Did Truman Act?*, 89 Am. J. Intl. L. 21, 33 (1995) (arguing that "Truman's legal authority was nonexistent").

Did subsequent legislation extending the draft and financing the war effort cure any constitutional deficiency? Is there any doubt in your mind that there was "some mutual participation" between the President and Congress, such as in Orlando v. Laird, *supra* p. 219?

Do you think any court would have entertained a challenge to the legitimacy of the war? If not, can you describe the probable reason or reasons for judicial abstention? If the answer is yes, can you say who would have had standing to sue?

4. *A Paradigm Shift?* Professor Ely suggested that the "position taken by the Truman administration respecting Korea ruptured [a] long-standing consensus" about Congress's proper role in foreign affairs. Ely, *supra*, at 62. Can you point to evidence of such a "long-standing consensus"? What are the implications of his argument for future assertions of Korea as precedent for the unilateral executive use of force? What effect, if any, do you think enactment of the War Powers Resolution, *supra* pp. 240-243, had on this precedent?

5. *U.N. Security Council "Recommendations."* Recall the exceptions in Chapter VII of the U.N. Charter to the general prohibition in Article 2(4) on the threat or use of force by one state against another. *Supra* p. 285. Which provisions of Chapter VII do you think authorized the U.N. Security Council resolutions responding to the North Korean invasion?

The June 27, 1950, U.N. Security Council resolution "recommended" that member states furnish military assistance to South Korea. Why do you suppose its resolution took the form of a recommendation rather than an "authorization" or an "order"? *See* Stromseth, *supra* p. 284, at 602 n.20 (indicating that member states would be obligated if the Security Council "'decides' to take action" rather than simply "recommending"). Do you think the choice of words had any legal significance? *See* Glennon, *supra* p. 287, at 75 (arguing that use of the term "authorizes" in Security Council Resolution 678 in advance of the 1991 Persian Gulf War imposed "no obligation on the United States to use armed force").

According to one view, the President had no choice but to comply with the recommendation: "'Military assistance, in case of aggression, ceases to be a *recommendation* made to member states; it becomes for us an *obligation* which none can shirk.'" Franck & Patel, *supra* p. 287, at 65, quoting the rapporteur of the committee that drafted Article 42; *see also* Turner, *supra* p. 289; *contra* Glennon, *supra*, at 78.

Does it matter that President Truman ordered U.S. military forces into action *before* adoption of the June 27 Security Council resolution? *Compare* Fisher, *supra*, at 22-33 (Truman administration did not act pursuant to U.N. authority), *with* Turner, *supra*, at 564 ("so what?").

6. *Collective Self-Defense?* Did President Truman get the authority he needed from Article 51, which approves acts of collective self-defense "until" the Security Council can act? See *supra* p. 286. Might Article 51 have provided justification for President Truman's sending troops into Korea even *after* the June 27 Security Council resolution? Professor Rostow argues that "the forces which finally prevailed in Korea were national forces carrying out a mission of collective self-defense under American direction, not a Security Council enforcement action." Rostow, *supra* p. 287, at 508; *contra* Glennon, *supra*, at 81.

7. *Police Action?* While the conflict raged in Korea, it was referred to by many as a "police action" rather than a war. *See* Fisher, *supra*, at 33-34; Stromseth, *supra*, at 630-631. Do you think this characterization of the conflict had any legal significance? *Compare* Franck & Patel, *supra*, at 71 (reporting that a majority in Congress approved the President's unilateral use of force in Korea on the basis that it was a "police action"), *with* Stromseth, *supra*, at 604 ("Congress expected U.N. 'police actions' to be limited in size; if a conflict escalated and required a large-scale commitment of U.S. troops, it would be 'war' under the U.S. Constitution even if it was authorized by the U.N. Security Council.").

C. THE PERSIAN GULF WAR[2]

1. The Invasion of Kuwait

In 1990, Iraq boasted the world's second largest oil reserves and fourth largest army, which had been battle-tested in a multiyear war with Iran.

---

2. Except as otherwise noted, the facts in this study are drawn from Rick Atkinson, *Crusade* (1993); Bob Woodward, *The Commanders* (1991); Lawrence Freedman & Efraim Karsh, *The Gulf Conflict, 1990-1991: Diplomacy and War in the New World Order* (1993); *Gulf War Legal and Diplomatic Documents*, 13 Hous. J. Intl. L. 281 (1991); *Iraqi Symposium*, 15 S. Ill. U. L.J. 411 (1991).

C. The Persian Gulf War

Iraq and Kuwait had long disputed drilling rights in the large oil fields that lie near their common border. Asserting that Kuwait was extracting oil from fields that lay partly in Iraq, that Kuwait was not paying its fair share of the costs of defending the area from Iran, and that some Kuwaiti territory belonged to Iraq, Iraq invaded Kuwait on August 2, 1990. More than 100,000 Iraqi troops quickly occupied Kuwait and detained many foreigners, including some 2,500 Americans. Eventually, the Iraqi troop level in the Kuwait theater reached 450,000, substantially more than were needed to garrison Kuwait, posing a serious threat to the adjacent kingdom of Saudi Arabia, a long-time U.S. ally in the Mideast.

2. Operation Desert Shield

"For forty years after the United Nations authorized the use of force in Korea, Cold War tensions rendered the collective security machinery of the U.N. Charter largely unusable. On August 2, 1990, however, . . . the Security Council took united action." Stromseth, *supra*, at 640. The Security Council promptly adopted Resolution 660, which condemned the invasion and demanded Iraq's immediate and unconditional withdrawal, S.C. Res. 660, U.N. Doc. S/RES/660 (Aug. 2, 1990). Four days later the Security Council approved Resolution 661, which imposed a trade embargo on Iraq. S.C. Res. 661, U.N. Doc. S/RES/661 (Aug. 6, 1990). Determined not to appease Saddam Hussein, Iraq's military leader, President George H. W. Bush acted quickly to enforce the embargo. He dispatched elements of the 82nd Airborne Division and the U.S. Air Force to Saudi Arabia on August 8, commencing what became known as "Operation Desert Shield." Although he asserted that the mission of the U.S. forces was "wholly defensive," he noted that the United States sought "the immediate and unconditional withdrawal of all Iraqi forces from Kuwait," restoration of the legitimate Kuwaiti government, security in the Gulf, and protection of Americans in Kuwait. He also advised that "to assume that Iraq will not attack again would be unwise and unrealistic."

Congress was not in session at the time, and the President did not call it back. On August 10, however, he sent a letter to the Speaker of the House and the President Pro Tempore of the Senate "in accordance with my desire that Congress be fully informed and consistent with the War Powers Resolution." The letter stated that he had dispatched U.S. forces "equipped for combat" to respond to the Iraqi "threat" along the Kuwaiti-Saudi Arabian border, "pursuant to my constitutional authority to conduct our foreign relations and as Commander in Chief." He added that he did "not believe that involvement in hostilities is imminent." 26 Weekly Comp. Pres. Docs. 1225 (Aug. 9, 1990)

On August 28, President Bush briefed selected members of Congress at the White House about Operation Desert Shield. By the time Congress returned, the United Nations Security Council had passed additional resolutions condemning Iraq's actions and calling for trade sanctions. Operation Desert Shield had also expanded, as American commanders nervously eyed the growing number of Iraqis poised at the Saudi border and expressed open concern about the threat if they crossed. On October 1, the House of Representatives passed a simple resolution condemning Iraq, reaffirming the objectives asserted by President Bush, affirming its support for the Security Council resolutions and noting the requirements of the War Powers Resolution. The House also expressed support for

> the President's emphasis on diplomatic efforts, international sanctions, and negotiations under the auspices of the United Nations to achieve the United States objectives.... The United States shall continue to emphasize the use of diplomatic and other nonmilitary means in order to achieve those objectives and policies, while maintaining credible United States and multinational deterrent military force. [H.R.J. Res. 658, §3, 101st Cong. (1990).]

Representative Dante Fascell, Chairman of the House Foreign Affairs Committee, explained that the House resolution was "not a declaration of war," but was intended "to show that the Congress has acted affirmatively." 136 Cong. Rec. H8441 (Oct. 1, 1990). The Senate passed its own resolution the following day, "strongly approv[ing] the leadership of the President," and supporting

> continued action by the President in accordance with the decisions of the United Nations Security Council and in accordance with United States constitutional and statutory processes, including authorization and appropriation of funds by the Congress, to deter Iraqi aggression and to protect American lives and vital interests in the region. [S. Con. Res. 147, 101st Cong. (1990).]

Neither resolution was voted on by both Houses.

On October 1, 1990, Congress voted supplemental appropriations for Operation Desert Shield, which included lines for "military personnel" and "operation and maintenance," without further detail. Pub. L. No. 101-403, 104 Stat. 867 (1990). Five weeks later, on November 5, Congress passed the Iraq Sanctions Act of 1990. Pub. L. No. 101-513, 104 Stat. 1979 (1990). In the Act, Congress declared its support for "the actions that have been taken by the President in response to... [the] invasion," required continued consultation with Congress, and approved economic and trade sanctions against Iraq, as well as a trade embargo.

3. The Buildup

United States and Saudi forces were augmented by forces of other U.N. members who were persuaded (chiefly by U.S. diplomatic efforts) to join the "coalition." United States naval forces patrolled the Persian Gulf, intercepting vessels bound to or from Iraq and Kuwait, in order to enforce the trade embargo. By early November, President Bush had deployed approximately 230,000 U.S. armed forces in Saudi Arabia and the Persian Gulf. Although Iraq had by that time released Americans and other foreigners it had earlier detained and the threat of further invasion had apparently receded, on November 8 the Administration announced its intention to deploy an additional 150,000 U.S. troops to provide the United States and its allies with what President Bush called an "adequate offensive military option" to oust Iraq from Kuwait. The decision was apparently made a week earlier, on October 30, just before the mid-term

C. The Persian Gulf War

congressional elections. Secretary of Defense Richard Cheney also rationalized the buildup by emphasizing the coalition forces' ability "to conduct offensive military operations."

On November 29, in a vote widely attributed to the diplomatic efforts of the Bush administration, the Security Council passed Resolution 678. S.C. Res. 678, U.N. Doc. S/RES/678 (Nov. 29, 1990). The resolution declared that the Security Council:

> ACTING under Chapter VII of the Charter of the United Nations,
> 1. DEMANDS that Iraq comply fully with Resolution 660 (1990) and all subsequent relevant resolutions and decides, while maintaining all its decisions, to allow Iraq one final opportunity, as a pause of good will, to do so;
> 2. AUTHORIZES member states cooperating with the Government of Kuwait, unless Iraq on or before Jan. 15, 1991, fully implements, as set forth in paragraph 1 above, the foregoing resolutions, to use all necessary means to uphold and implement the Security Council Resolution 660 and all subsequent relevant Resolutions and to restore international peace and security in the area;
> 3. REQUESTS all states to provide appropriate support for the actions undertaken in pursuance of paragraph 2 of this resolution....

In short, Resolution 678 established a deadline for Iraqi compliance with Resolution 660 and "all subsequent relevant resolutions," and ominously threatened the use of "all necessary means" to enforce them thereafter.

During this period, the President did not request any authorization for the use of force from Congress. Asked at a press conference on January 9, 1991, whether he thought he needed such authorization, he replied, "No, I don't think I need it.... I feel that I have the authority to fully implement the United Nations resolutions." 27 Weekly Comp. Pres. Docs. 17-18 (Jan. 14, 1991). The following year President Bush remarked, "I didn't have to get permission from some old goat in the United States Congress to kick Saddam Hussein out of Kuwait." 28 Weekly Comp. Pres. Docs. 1120-1121 (June 29, 1992). He did go to Congress with a request, however.

4. Operation Desert Storm

Following the decision in Dellums v. Bush, 752 F. Supp. 1141 (D.D.C. 1990), *supra* p. 134, the President sent the following letter to congressional leaders:

Letter to Congressional Leaders on the Persian Gulf Crisis
27 Weekly Comp. Pres. Doc. 17 (January 8, 1991)

Dear Mr. Speaker:

The current situation in the Persian Gulf, brought about by Iraq's unprovoked invasion and subsequent brutal occupation of Kuwait, threatens vital U.S. interests. The situation also threatens the peace. It would, however, greatly enhance the chances for peace if Congress were now to go on record supporting the position adopted by the UN Security Council on twelve separate occasions.

Such an action would underline that the United States stands with the international community and on the side of law and decency; it also would help dispel any belief that may exist in the minds of Iraq's leaders that the United States lacks the necessary unity to act decisively in response to Iraq's continued aggression against Kuwait.

Secretary of State Baker is meeting with Iraq's Foreign Minister on January 9. It would have been most constructive if he could have presented the Iraqi government a Resolution passed by both houses of Congress supporting the UN position and in particular Security Council Resolution 678. As you know, I have frequently stated my desire for such a Resolution. Nevertheless, there is still opportunity for Congress to act to strengthen the prospects for peace and safeguard this country's vital interests.

I therefore request that the House of Representatives and the Senate adopt a Resolution stating that Congress supports the use of all necessary means to implement UN Security Council Resolution 678. Such action would send the clearest possible message to Saddam Hussein that he must withdraw without condition or delay from Kuwait. Anything less would only encourage Iraqi intransigence; anything else would risk detracting from the international coalition arrayed against Iraq's aggression.

Mr. Speaker, I am determined to do whatever is necessary to protect America's security. I ask Congress to join with me in this task. I can think of no better way than for Congress to express its support for the President at this critical time. This truly is the last best chance for peace.

Sincerely,
George Bush

After a dramatic debate four days later, Congress responded by passing the following joint resolution, by a vote of 52-47 in the Senate and 250-183 in the House:

Authorization for Use of Military Force Against Iraq
Pub. L. No. 102-01, 105 Stat. 3
January 12, 1991

To authorize the use of United States Armed Forces pursuant to United Nations Security Council Resolution 678.

Whereas the Government of Iraq without provocation invaded and occupied the territory of Kuwait on August 2, 1990; and

Whereas both the House of Representatives (in H.J. Res. 658 of the 101st Congress) and the Senate (in S. Con. Res. 147 of the 101st Congress) have condemned Iraq's invasion of Kuwait and declared their support for international action to reverse Iraq's aggression; and

Whereas, Iraq's conventional, chemical, biological, and nuclear weapons and ballistic missile programs and its demonstrated willingness to use weapons of mass destruction pose a grave threat to world peace; and

C. The Persian Gulf War

Whereas the international community has demanded that Iraq withdraw unconditionally and immediately from Kuwait and that Kuwait's independence and legitimate government be restored; and

Whereas the United Nations Security Council repeatedly affirmed the inherent right of individual or collective self-defense in response to the armed attack by Iraq against Kuwait in accordance with Article 51 of the United Nations Charter; and

Whereas, in the absence of full compliance by Iraq with its resolutions, the United Nations Security Council in Resolution 678 has authorized member states of the United Nations to use all necessary means, after January 15, 1991, to uphold and implement all relevant Security Council resolutions and to restore international peace and security in the area; and

Whereas Iraq has persisted in its illegal occupation of, and brutal aggression against Kuwait: Now, therefore, be it

Resolved by the Senate and House of Representatives of the United States of America in Congress assembled,

SECTION 1. SHORT TITLE

This joint resolution may be cited as the "Authorization for Use of Military Force Against Iraq Resolution."

SECTION 2. AUTHORIZATION FOR USE OF UNITED STATES ARMED FORCES

(a) AUTHORIZATION. The President is authorized, subject to subsection (b), to use United States Armed Forces pursuant to United Nations Security Council Resolution 678 (1990) in order to achieve implementation of Security Council Resolutions 660, 661, 662, 664, 665, 666, 667, 669, 670, 674, and 677.

(b) REQUIREMENT FOR DETERMINATION THAT USE OF MILITARY FORCE IS NECESSARY. Before exercising the authority granted in subsection (a), the President shall make available to the Speaker of the House of Representatives and the President pro tempore of the Senate his determination that—

(1) the United States has used all appropriate diplomatic and other peaceful means to obtain compliance by Iraq with the United Nations Security Council resolutions cited in subsection (a); and

(2) that those efforts have not been and would not be successful in obtaining such compliance.

(c) WAR POWERS RESOLUTION REQUIREMENTS.

(1) SPECIFIC STATUTORY AUTHORIZATION. Consistent with section 8(a)(1) of the War Powers Resolution, the Congress declares that this section is intended to constitute specific statutory authorization within the meaning of section 5(b) of the War Powers Resolution.

(2) APPLICABILITY OF OTHER REQUIREMENTS. Nothing in this resolution supersedes any requirement of the War Powers Resolution.

SECTION 3. REPORTS TO CONGRESS

At least once every 60 days, the President shall submit to the Congress a summary on the status of efforts to obtain compliance by Iraq with the resolutions adopted by the United Nations Security Council in response to Iraq's aggression.

On January 16, 1991, President Bush reported to Congress that the United Nations had exhausted diplomatic and other peaceful means of obtaining compliance by Iraq with the Security Council's resolutions. The next day, at 2:38 A.M. Riyadh, Saudi Arabia, time, Army Apache helicopters carrying rockets, missiles, and extra fuel tanks commenced Operation Desert Storm by hitting Iraqi radar sites to help clear the way for more massive coalition air attacks. For the next six weeks, coalition air forces bombed Iraqi military and infrastructure targets, including dug-in Iraqi armor, until February 24, when coalition forces launched a ground attack into southern Iraq and Kuwait. By February 26, Iraqi forces were fleeing Kuwait City under fire, and the city was liberated the next day. On February 28, a halt in the fighting was ordered. The Iraqis had been expelled. The war officially ended with Iraqi acceptance of cease-fire terms in U.N. Security Council Resolution 687, S.C. Res. 687, U.N. Doc. S/RES/687 (Apr. 3, 1991).

NOTES AND QUESTIONS

1. *Role of the U.N. Security Council.* Beginning on August 2, 1990, the U.N. Security Council adopted a series of resolutions in response to the Iraqi invasion of Kuwait. Upon what authority did each resolution described here rest?

2. *Authority for Operation Desert Shield.* Upon what authority did President Bush deploy U.S. military forces equipped for combat to the Gulf beginning on August 8, 1990? Did that deployment start the 60-day clock ticking under War Powers Resolution §5(b), *supra* p. 242? Do you think the President complied with the War Powers Resolution? What authorization, if any, did congressional actions or the U.N. Security Council resolutions give the President during the fall of 1990?

3. *Authority for Operation Desert Storm.* Would President Bush have had constitutional authority to launch Operation Desert Storm unilaterally, as he contended? How would you compare his powers with those of President Truman at the beginning of the Korean War? Consider not only each President's inherent war powers, but also the effect, if any, of various U.N. Security Council resolutions.

Why do you suppose President Bush, after maintaining so emphatically that he needed no congressional approval to order U.S. troops into battle, finally decided to send the January 8, 1991, letter to Congress set out above? Do you think he was influenced by the opinion in Dellums v. Bush, 752 F. Supp. 1141 (D.D.C. 1990), *supra* p. 134? What exactly did the letter request? Did the President get what he asked for?

Why do you think §2(c) of the January 12, 1991, resolution was written the way it was? Were the requirements of the War Powers Resolution satisfied?

D. Collective Self-Defense Under Regional Organizations

How, if at all, do you think the January 12, 1991, resolution might have affected the precedent set in Korea for unilateral presidential war power? For presidential authority based on U.N. Security Council resolutions?

4. *Dellums and the Decision to Seek Congressional Approval.* In light of the facts set forth in this case study, was Dellums v. Bush, *supra* p. 134, correctly decided? Does the court's determination that the congressional plaintiffs' claims were not ripe for hearing support the assertion that the courts play no meaningful role in war powers disputes?

5. *The Joint Resolution for the Use of Force.* Why do you think Congress did not formally declare war on Iraq? What, precisely, did it authorize instead? Did it give President Bush the authority to annihilate the Iraqi Republican Guards? To carpet-bomb Baghdad? Did that authority change after the Iraqis were driven out of Kuwait?

For years after the cease-fire, coalition planes flew over Iraqi territory to enforce "no-fly zones" intended to protect Kurdish and Shiite groups from Iraqi repression. See *infra* p. 304. These planes also attacked Iraqi ground installations from time to time. Were these flights authorized by Public Law No. 102-01? *See* Richard F. Grimmett, *The War Powers Resolution: Presidential Compliance* 6-7 (Cong. Res. Serv. RL30308) (Sept. 11, 2001); Michael N. Schmitt, *Clipped Wings: Effective and Legal No-Fly Zone Rules of Engagement*, 20 Loy. L.A. Intl. & Comp. L.J. 727, 733-737 (1998); *cf.* Louis Fisher & David Gray Adler, *The War Powers Resolution: Time to Say Goodbye*, 113 Pol. Sci. Q. 1, 19 (1998) (questioning authority to use air strikes to force Iraq to permit U.N. weapons inspections).

Did the authority for the use of force conferred by Public Law No. 102-01 continue for longer still? Can you make an argument that it extended to the spring of 2003? See *infra* p. 310.

6. *"Mutual Participation"?* Did Congress play the role envisioned for it by the Framers in approving the use of force in the Persian Gulf? Did the courts? If not, what do you think can be done to restore them to their intended roles?

D. COLLECTIVE SELF-DEFENSE UNDER REGIONAL ORGANIZATIONS

The U.N. Charter is not the only international agreement providing for the use of force in collective self-defense or for humanitarian purposes. In fact, the Charter contemplates other agreements.

Charter of the United Nations
June 26, 1945, 59 Stat. 1031, T.S. No. 993

CHAPTER VIII. REGIONAL ARRANGEMENTS

ARTICLE 52

1. Nothing in the present Charter precludes the existence of regional arrangements or agencies for dealing with such matters relating to the

maintenance of international peace and security as are appropriate for regional action, provided that such arrangements or agencies and their activities are consistent with the Purposes and Principles of the United Nations.

2. The Members of the United Nations entering into such arrangements or constituting such agencies shall make every effort to achieve pacific settlement of local disputes through such regional arrangements or by such regional agencies before referring them to the Security Council.

3. The Security Council shall encourage the development of pacific settlement of local disputes through such regional arrangements or by such regional agencies either on the initiative of the states concerned or by reference from the Security Council....

ARTICLE 53

1. The Security Council shall, where appropriate, utilize such regional arrangements or agencies for enforcement action under its authority. But no enforcement action shall be taken under regional arrangements or by regional agencies without the authorization of the Security Council....

A number of regional alliances around the world have been organized to address breaches or threatened breaches of the peace. In the Western Hemisphere the Organization of American States was used to enforce a quarantine of Cuba during the missile crisis there in 1962 and to send peacekeeping forces into the Dominican Republic in 1965. The Organization of Eastern Carribean States was said to have requested the U.S. invasion of Grenada in 1983. One of the most controversial uses of force without U.N. Security Council approval was NATO's bombing of the Federal Republic of Yugoslavia in 1999. *See, e.g.,* Mary Ellen O'Connell, *The UN, NATO, and International Law After Kosovo,* 22 Hum. Rts. Q. 57 (2000). Elsewhere, the Organization of African Unity has deployed peacekeeping forces a number of times, most recently in the Darfur region of Sudan.

Preemptive War 12

The war that began with the invasion of Iraq by U.S.-led coalition forces in March 2003 gives us an opportunity to apply almost everything we have learned up to this point about how we decide to go to war. It lets us consider in a new setting the respective roles of the political branches of our government and of the United Nations in making that decision. In particular, it brings sharply into focus questions about the ability of any nation legally to engage in either anticipatory self-defense or preemptive war.

A. PLANNING FOR A RETURN TO THE PERSIAN GULF AFTER 9/11

The Persian Gulf War of 1991, analyzed *supra* pp. 294-301, ended with a formal cease-fire when Iraq accepted the terms of U.N. Security Council Resolution 687, S.C. Res. 687, U.N. Doc. S/RES/687 (Apr. 3, 1991). Iraq agreed that it would allow a Special Commission (UNSCOM) to destroy and remove all of its chemical and biological weapons, as well as longer-range missiles, together with any facilities for research, development, and production of such weapons. *Id.* ¶¶8, 9. *See United Nations Special Commission (UNSCOM)* (n.d.), *at* http://www.un.org/Depts/unscom/General/basicfacts.html. A similar commitment was made concerning nuclear weapons, to be carried out by the Director General of the International Atomic Energy Agency with the assistance of UNSCOM. S.C. Res. 687, ¶¶9(b)(iii), 12, 13. Iraq also promised not to develop or acquire any such weapons in the future and to submit to monitoring to assure compliance. *Id.* ¶¶10, 12. In addition, it agreed that it would "not commit or support any act of international terrorism or allow any organization directed towards commission of such acts to operate within its territory." *Id.* ¶32.

With the withdrawal of coalition forces from Iraq, the Iraqi government reacted to internal rebellions by attacking Kurdish dissidents in the north and Shias in the southern part of the country. The U.N. Security Council responded by adopting Resolution 688, S.C. Res. 688, U.N. Doc. S/RES/688 (Apr. 5, 1991), which demanded that Iraq end its repression of its own population and allow immediate access by humanitarian organizations. *Id.* ¶¶1-3. *See* Mary Ellen O'Connell, *Continuing Limits on UN Intervention in Civil War,* 67 Ind. L.J. 903, 904-909 (1992). Relying principally on this resolution, the United States, Great Britain, and France established "no-fly" zones in the north and south to prevent Iraqi attacks on civilian populations from the air, and the three countries carried out repeated air strikes on anti-aircraft installations and other targets within these zones over the next ten years. *See* Sean D. Murphy, *Assessing the Legality of Invading Iraq,* 92 Geo. L.J. 173, 215-216 (2004).

In late 1991, Congress approved "sense of the Congress" resolutions supporting the use of "all necessary means" to achieve the goals of Security Council Resolutions 687 and 688. National Defense Authorization Act for Fiscal Years 1992 and 1993, Pub. L. No. 102-190, §§1095, 1096, 105 Stat. 1290, 1488-1489 (1991).

A year and a half later, when the United States uncovered an Iraqi plot to assassinate former President Bush in Kuwait, President Clinton authorized a retaliatory response that targeted Iraq's intelligence headquarters in Baghdad with 23 cruise missiles. *See* Gwen Ifill, *U.S. Fires Missiles at Baghdad, Citing April Plot to Kill Bush,* N.Y. Times, June 27, 1993, §1, at 1.

During the next seven years UNSCOM destroyed large quantities of chemical weapons and precursors, chemical and biological weapons facilities, and missile components. But Iraq violated its obligations repeatedly by interfering with UNSCOM inspectors and by failing to disclose information about its weapons programs. *See UNSCOM: Chronology of Main Events,* Dec. 1999, *at* http://www.un.org/Depts/unscom/Chronology/chronologyframe.htm.

In August 1998, Congress adopted a measure declaring that Iraq was in "material and unacceptable breach" of various U.N. Security Council resolutions and urging the President to "take appropriate action, in accordance with the Constitution and relevant laws of the United States, to bring Iraq into compliance with its international obligations." Pub. L. No. 105-235, 112 Stat. 1538, 1541 (1998). Two months later, in response to Saddam Hussein's threat to terminate weapons-monitoring activities of the International Atomic Energy Agency (IAEA) and UNSCOM, Congress passed the Iraq Liberation Act of 1998, Pub. L. No. 105-338, 112 Stat. 3178. Included was a "sense of Congress" provision declaring, "It should be the policy of the United States to support efforts to remove the regime headed by Saddam Hussein from power in Iraq and to promote the emergence of a democratic government to replace that regime." *Id.* §3, 112 Stat. 3179. The measure also provided cash and military assistance for "Iraqi democratic opposition organizations." *Id.* §4, 112 Stat. 3179.

Matters finally came to a head in late 1998, when Iraq formally ended all cooperation with UNSCOM on October 31, and UNSCOM withdrew its staff from Iraq on December 16. *See UNSCOM: Chronology of Main Events, supra.* The following day, U.S. and British forces launched a three-day air and missile attack code-named "Operation Desert Fox" against more than one hundred military and industrial targets throughout Iraq. *See* Steven Lee Myers, *U.S. and Britain End Raids on Iraq, Calling Mission a Success,* N.Y. Times, Dec. 20, 1998, §1, at 1.

Immediately after 9/11, according to one intelligence insider, President Bush pushed hard to identify a link between Saddam Hussein and the terrorist attacks on the World Trade Center and the Pentagon. *Clarke's Take on Terror,* 60 Minutes, CBS, Mar. 21, 2004. In the late summer of 2002, the Bush administration launched a campaign to generate public support for an invasion by describing Iraq as a threat to the United States. Vice President Cheney declared on August 26, for example, "Simply stated, there is no doubt that Saddam Hussein now has weapons of mass destruction." *In Cheney's Words: The Administration Case for Removing Saddam Hussein*, N.Y. Times, Aug. 27, 2002, at A8. National Security Advisor Condoleezza Rice warned, "We don't want the smoking gun to be a mushroom cloud." *Top Bush Officials Push Case Against Saddam*, CNN.com, Sept. 8, 2002. And in a speech to the United Nations General Assembly President Bush stated,

> Saddam Hussein's regime is a grave and gathering danger. To suggest otherwise is to hope against the evidence. To assume this regime's good faith is to bet the lives of millions and the peace of the world in a reckless gamble. And this is a risk we must not take. [President's Remarks at the United Nations General Assembly (Sept. 12, 2002).]

B. AUTHORITY FOR A NEW WAR IN IRAQ

Thirteen months after the terrorist attacks on the World Trade Center and the Pentagon, and just three weeks before the mid-term congressional elections in 2002, Congress approved the following measure:

Authorization for Use of Military Force Against Iraq Resolution of 2002
Pub. L. No. 107-243, 116 Stat. 1498
October 16, 2002

Whereas in 1990 in response to Iraq's war of aggression against and illegal occupation of Kuwait, the United States forged a coalition of nations to liberate Kuwait and its people in order to defend the national security of the United States and enforce United Nations Security Council resolutions relating to Iraq;

Whereas after the liberation of Kuwait in 1991, Iraq entered into a United Nations sponsored cease-fire agreement pursuant to which Iraq unequivocally agreed, among other things, to eliminate its nuclear, biological, and chemical weapons programs and the means to deliver and develop them, and to end its support for international terrorism;

Whereas the efforts of international weapons inspectors, United States intelligence agencies, and Iraqi defectors led to the discovery that Iraq had large stockpiles of chemical weapons and a large scale biological weapons program, and that Iraq had an advanced nuclear weapons development program that was much closer to producing a nuclear weapon than intelligence reporting had previously indicated;

Whereas Iraq, in direct and flagrant violation of the cease-fire, attempted to thwart the efforts of weapons inspectors to identify and destroy Iraq's weapons of mass destruction stockpiles and development capabilities, which finally resulted in the withdrawal of inspectors from Iraq on October 31, 1998;

Whereas in Public Law 105-235 (August 14, 1998), Congress concluded that Iraq's continuing weapons of mass destruction programs threatened vital United States interests and international peace and security, declared Iraq to be in "material and unacceptable breach of its international obligations" and urged the President "to take appropriate action, in accordance with the Constitution and relevant laws of the United States, to bring Iraq into compliance with its international obligations";

Whereas Iraq both poses a continuing threat to the national security of the United States and international peace and security in the Persian Gulf region and remains in material and unacceptable breach of its international obligations by, among other things, continuing to possess and develop a significant chemical and biological weapons capability, actively seeking a nuclear weapons capability, and supporting and harboring terrorist organizations;

Whereas Iraq persists in violating resolution[s] of the United Nations Security Council by continuing to engage in brutal repression of its civilian population thereby threatening international peace and security in the region, by refusing to release, repatriate, or account for non-Iraqi citizens wrongfully detained by Iraq, including an American serviceman, and by failing to return property wrongfully seized by Iraq from Kuwait;

Whereas the current Iraqi regime has demonstrated its capability and willingness to use weapons of mass destruction against other nations and its own people;

Whereas the current Iraqi regime has demonstrated its continuing hostility toward, and willingness to attack, the United States, including by attempting in 1993 to assassinate former President Bush and by firing on many thousands of occasions on United States and Coalition Armed Forces engaged in enforcing the resolutions of the United Nations Security Council;

Whereas members of al Qaida, an organization bearing responsibility for attacks on the United States, its citizens, and interests, including the attacks that occurred on September 11, 2001, are known to be in Iraq;

Whereas Iraq continues to aid and harbor other international terrorist organizations, including organizations that threaten the lives and safety of United States citizens;

Whereas the attacks on the United States of September 11, 2001, underscored the gravity of the threat posed by the acquisition of weapons of mass destruction by international terrorist organizations;

Whereas Iraq's demonstrated capability and willingness to use weapons of mass destruction, the risk that the current Iraqi regime will either employ those weapons to launch a surprise attack against the United States or its Armed Forces or provide them to international terrorists who would do so, and the extreme magnitude of harm that would result to the United States and its citizens from such an attack, combine to justify action by the United States to defend itself;

Whereas United Nations Security Council Resolution 678 (1990) authorizes the use of all necessary means to enforce United Nations Security Council Resolution 660 (1990) and subsequent relevant resolutions and to compel Iraq to cease certain activities that threaten international peace and security, including the development of weapons of mass destruction and refusal or obstruction of

B. Authority for a New War in Iraq

United Nations weapons inspections in violation of United Nations Security Council Resolution 687 (1991), repression of its civilian population in violation of United Nations Security Council Resolution 688 (1991), and threatening its neighbors or United Nations operations in Iraq in violation of United Nations Security Council Resolution 949 (1994);

Whereas in the Authorization for Use of Military Force Against Iraq Resolution (Public Law 102-1), Congress has authorized the President "to use United States Armed Forces pursuant to United Nations Security Council Resolution 678 (1990) in order to achieve implementation of Security Council Resolutions 660, 661, 662, 664, 665, 666, 667, 669, 670, 674, and 677";

Whereas in December 1991, Congress expressed its sense that it "supports the use of all necessary means to achieve the goals of United Nations Security Council Resolution 687 as being consistent with the Authorization of Use of Military Force Against Iraq Resolution (Public Law 102-1)," that Iraq's repression of its civilian population violates United Nations Security Council Resolution 688 and "constitutes a continuing threat to the peace, security, and stability of the Persian Gulf region," and that Congress "supports the use of all necessary means to achieve the goals of United Nations Security Council Resolution 688";

Whereas the Iraq Liberation Act of 1998 (Public Law 105-338) expressed the sense of Congress that it should be the policy of the United States to support efforts to remove from power the current Iraqi regime and promote the emergence of a democratic government to replace that regime;

Whereas on September 12, 2002, President Bush committed the United States to "work with the United Nations Security Council to meet our common challenge" posed by Iraq and to "work for the necessary resolutions," while also making clear that "the Security Council resolutions will be enforced, and the just demands of peace and security will be met, or action will be unavoidable";

Whereas the United States is determined to prosecute the war on terrorism and Iraq's ongoing support for international terrorist groups combined with its development of weapons of mass destruction in direct violation of its obligations under the 1991 cease-fire and other United Nations Security Council resolutions make clear that it is in the national security interests of the United States and in furtherance of the war on terrorism that all relevant United Nations Security Council resolutions be enforced, including through the use of force if necessary;

Whereas Congress has taken steps to pursue vigorously the war on terrorism through the provision of authorities and funding requested by the President to take the necessary actions against international terrorists and terrorist organizations, including those nations, organizations, or persons who planned, authorized, committed, or aided the terrorist attacks that occurred on September 11, 2001, or harbored such persons or organizations;

Whereas the President and Congress are determined to continue to take all appropriate actions against international terrorists and terrorist organizations, including those nations, organizations, or persons who planned, authorized, committed, or aided the terrorist attacks that occurred on September 11, 2001, or harbored such persons or organizations;

Whereas the President has authority under the Constitution to take action in order to deter and prevent acts of international terrorism against the United States, as Congress recognized in the joint resolution on Authorization for Use of Military Force (Public Law 107-40); and

Whereas it is in the national security interests of the United States to restore international peace and security to the Persian Gulf region: Now, therefore, be it

Resolved by the Senate and House of Representatives of the United States of America in Congress assembled...

SEC. 2. SUPPORT FOR UNITED STATES DIPLOMATIC EFFORTS

The Congress of the United States supports the efforts by the President to—

(1) strictly enforce through the United Nations Security Council all relevant Security Council resolutions regarding Iraq and encourages him in those efforts; and

(2) obtain prompt and decisive action by the Security Council to ensure that Iraq abandons its strategy of delay, evasion and noncompliance and promptly and strictly complies with all relevant Security Council resolutions regarding Iraq.

SEC. 3. AUTHORIZATION FOR USE OF UNITED STATES ARMED FORCES

(a) AUTHORIZATION—The President is authorized to use the Armed Forces of the United States as he determines to be necessary and appropriate in order to—

(1) defend the national security of the United States against the continuing threat posed by Iraq; and

(2) enforce all relevant United Nations Security Council resolutions regarding Iraq.

(b) PRESIDENTIAL DETERMINATION—In connection with the exercise of the authority granted in subsection (a) to use force the President shall, prior to such exercise or as soon thereafter as may be feasible, but no later than 48 hours after exercising such authority, make available to the Speaker of the House of Representatives and the President pro tempore of the Senate his determination that—

(1) reliance by the United States on further diplomatic or other peaceful means alone either (A) will not adequately protect the national security of the United States against the continuing threat posed by Iraq or (B) is not likely to lead to enforcement of all relevant United Nations Security Council resolutions regarding Iraq; and

(2) acting pursuant to this joint resolution is consistent with the United States and other countries continuing to take the necessary actions against international terrorist and terrorist organizations, including those nations, organizations, or persons who planned, authorized, committed or aided the terrorist attacks that occurred on September 11, 2001.

(c) WAR POWERS RESOLUTION REQUIREMENTS—

(1) SPECIFIC STATUTORY AUTHORIZATION—Consistent with section 8(a)(1) of the War Powers Resolution, the Congress declares that

B. Authority for a New War in Iraq

this section is intended to constitute specific statutory authorization within the meaning of section 5(b) of the War Powers Resolution.

(2) APPLICABILITY OF OTHER REQUIREMENTS—Nothing in this joint resolution supersedes any requirement of the War Powers Resolution....

The U.S. government worked hard to obtain a resolution from the U.N. Security Council approving an invasion of Iraq—one at least as clear as Resolution 678, which on November 29, 1990, authorized the expulsion of Iraqi forces from Kuwait. See *supra* p. 297. On November 8, 2002, the Security Council adopted Resolution 1441, "deploring" that Iraq had not made full disclosure of or granted the U.N. inspectors unconditional access to its programs and sites for weapons of mass destruction. The Security Council found Iraq to be in "material breach of its obligations under relevant resolutions, including resolution 687," which brought the 1991 Persian Gulf War to a close, but it decided to afford Iraq "a final opportunity to comply." S.C. Res. 1441, U.N. Doc. S/RES/1441 (2002). Perhaps most pertinent, in Resolution 1441 the Security Council recalled "that the Council has repeatedly warned Iraq that it will face serious consequences as a result of its continued violations of its obligations," and the Council pledged to reconvene immediately following any report of future breaches "to consider the situation and the need for full compliance." *Id.*

On February 5, 2003, Secretary of State Colin Powell delivered an address to the Security Council, punctuated by photographic exhibits, insisting, "There can be no doubt that Saddam Hussein has biological weapons and the capability to rapidly produce more, many more.... If biological weapons seem too terrible to contemplate, chemical weapons are equally chilling." *Powell's Address, Presenting "Deeply Troubling" Evidence on Iraq,* N.Y. Times, Feb. 6, 2003, at A18. Powell added, "These are not assertions. What we're giving you are facts and conclusions based on solid evidence." *Id.* But the United States was unable to procure a more forceful resolution.

On the home front, President Bush and members of his administration continued to press the case for war. In his State of the Union address, the President declared, "Saddam Hussein has gone to elaborate lengths, spent enormous sums, taken great risks to build and keep weapons of mass destruction." State of the Union Address (Jan. 28, 2003). "If Saddam Hussein does not fully disarm," he continued, "for the safety of our people and for the peace of the world, we will lead a coalition to disarm him." *Id.*

Iraq's formal declaration on December 7, 2002, that it had no weapons of mass destruction was deemed inadequate by the head of a new U.N. inspection team, Hans Blix, and others. Meanwhile, U.N. weapons inspectors had resumed their search for weapons of mass destruction (WMD) in Iraq on November 27, 2002. But aside from some intermediate range missiles, which were destroyed, no such weapons were found before inspectors were forced to leave on March 17, 2003, in the face of the impending invasion.

Members of a U.S.-led coalition asserted that even without another meeting of the U.N. Security Council and without waiting for the inspection process to be completed, Resolution 1441 had cleared the way for coalition forces to "take their own steps" to secure Iraq's disarmament. These developments are traced in UN News Service stories, *at* http://www.un.org/news/dh/infocus/iraq/chronology-02-04.htm.

On March 18, 2003, President Bush sent the "determination" required by §3(b) of the October 16, 2002, joint resolution to congressional leaders. Letter from the President to the Speaker of the House of Representatives and the President Pro Tempore of the Senate (Mar. 19, 2003). The next day, Operation Iraqi Freedom was launched with missile and aircraft attacks on Iraqi targets. The President addressed the nation in these words: "My fellow citizens, at this hour, American and coalition forces are in the early stages of military operations to disarm Iraq, to free its people, and to defend the world from grave danger." President Bush Addresses the Nation (Mar. 19, 2003). "Our nation enters this conflict reluctantly — yet, our purpose is sure," he declared. "The people of the United States and our friends and allies will not live at the mercy of an outlaw regime that threatens the peace with weapons of mass murder. We will meet that threat now . . . so that we do not have to meet it later with armies of firefighters and police and doctors on the streets of our cities." *Id.*

Less than a month later, with 135,000 U.S. troops deployed in Iraq, the last stronghold of forces loyal to Saddam Hussein was captured. On May 1, 2003, President Bush, standing in front of a banner proclaiming "Mission Accomplished," declared that "[m]ajor combat operations in Iraq have ended." President Bush Announces Major Combat Operations in Iraq Have Ended (May 1, 2003). Day-by-day reports on the progress of the war may be found on the website of Global Security.org, *at* http://www.globalsecurity.org/military/ops/iraqi_freedom.htm. For official news releases and press briefings, see the website of the Defense Department's Central Command, *at* http://www.centcom.mil/.

NOTES AND QUESTIONS

1. *War Without the 2002 Joint Resolution?* Prior to Congress's approval of the October 16, 2002, joint resolution, some maintained that the President already had the domestic authority needed to send troops into battle. *See* Mike Allen & Juliet Eilperin, *Bush Aides Say Iraq War Needs No Hill Vote; Some See Such Support as Politically Helpful*, Wash. Post, Aug. 26, 2002, at A1. What theories might support this argument? Are any of these theories suggested by the "whereas" clauses of the resolution? For an exceptionally aggressive assertion of plenary presidential authority to wage war, see John C. Yoo's opinion for the Justice Department's Office of Legal Counsel, *The President's Constitutional Authority to Conduct Military Operations Against Terrorists and Nations Supporting Them*, Sept. 25, 2001, *at* http://www.usdoj.gov/olc/warpowers925.htm.

Did the President already have Congress's approval to go to war? Could he have relied, for example, on the 1991 Authorization for Use of Military Force Against Iraq, *supra* p. 298? Would such reliance have been dependent on the continued viability of U.N. Security Council Resolution 678, *supra* p. 297? Did either the Iraq Liberation Act of 1998 or Pub. L. No. 105-235, described in the October 16 resolution and *supra* p. 304, provide the needed authority? What about the resolution approved by Congress three days after the September 11, 2001, terrorist attack, *supra* p. 215?

B. Authority for a New War in Iraq

Could the President have taken the country to war solely on the strength of his implied "repel attack" authority, based on the imminence and gravity of an Iraqi threat? If so, what facts would have justified the unilateral use of force? What legal procedures, if any, should have been followed before the President gave the order to attack?

2. *United Nations Involvement.* The United States asserted that no subsequent Security Council resolution was necessary to make war with Iraq legal under international law. On March 27, 2003, for example, the U.S. Permanent Representative to the United Nations, John Negroponte, declared that

> Resolution 687 (1991) imposed a series of obligations on Iraq that were the conditions of the ceasefire. It has long been recognized and understood that a material breach of those obligations removes the basis of the ceasefire and revives the authority to use force under resolution 678 (1990). Resolution 1441 (2002) explicitly found Iraq in continuing material breach. In view of Iraq's additional material breaches, the basis for the existing ceasefire has been removed and the use of force is authorized under resolution 678 (1990). [U.N. SCOR, 58th Sess., 4726th mtg. at 25, U.N. Doc. S/PV.4726 (Resumption 1).]

What arguments can you marshal to rebut this assertion? *See* Murphy, *supra* p. 304, at 178-229 (arguing that assertion was not justified); Miriam Sapiro, *Preempting Prevention: Lessons Learned*, 37 N.Y.U. J. Intl. L. & Pol. 357, 360-365 (2005) (same).

3. *Preemptive War.* The September 2002 *National Security Strategy of the United States of America, available at* http://www.whitehouse.gov/nsc/nss.html, embraced for the first time as a public policy "the option of preemptive actions to counter a sufficient threat to our national security.... We must be prepared to stop rogue states and their terrorist clients before they are able to threaten or use weapons of mass destruction against the United States and our allies and friends." *Id.* at 9-10. It pointed to international law recognizing that "nations need not suffer an attack before they can lawfully take action to defend themselves against forces that present an imminent danger of attack," *id.* at 9, an apparent reference to Article 51 of the U.N. Charter, *supra* p. 286.

There was speculation that a U.S. invasion of Iraq would represent the first application of the newly announced preemption policy. Almost two months before coalition forces invaded Iraq, President Bush declared:

> Some have said we must not act until the threat is imminent. Since when have terrorists and tyrants announced their intentions, politely putting us on notice before they strike? If this threat is permitted to fully and suddenly emerge, all actions, all words, and all recriminations would come too late. [State of the Union Address, Jan. 28, 2003.]

The President did not "explicitly characterize his military action as an implementation of the expansive concept of preemptive use of military force against rogue states with WMD." Richard F. Grimmett, *U.S. Use of Preemptive Military Force* 6 (Cong. Res. Serv. RS21311), Apr. 11, 2003. It was nevertheless widely viewed that way.

If the U.S. preemption policy is consistent with Article 51 and other requirements of the U.N. Charter, what factual predicates must be satisfied before the policy can be invoked? Were those predicates satisfied in the run-up to Operation Iraqi Freedom? How, if at all, is your answer affected by the U.N. Security Council's refusal to explicitly authorize the invasion of Iraq? *Compare* David M. Ackerman, *International Law and the Preemptive Use of Force Against Iraq* 6 (Cong. Res. Serv. RS21314), Apr. 11, 2003 ("[I]t seems doubtful that the use of force against Iraq could be deemed to meet the traditional legal tests justifying preemptive attack."), *and* Thomas M. Franck, *What Happens Now? The United Nations After Iraq*, 97 Am. J. Intl. L. 607 (2003) (invasion not justified under Article 51), *with* John Yoo, *International Law and the War in Iraq*, 97 Am. J. Intl. L. 563 (2003) (invasion warranted as act of anticipatory self-defense).

If a preemptive attack was justified, might the U.S. use of nuclear weapons also have been warranted? *See* William M. Arkin, *The Nuclear Option in Iraq; The U.S. Has Lowered the Bar for Using the Ultimate Weapon*, L.A. Times, Jan. 26, 2003, at M1.

4. *Scope of Delegation.* Consider the operative language of §3 in the October 16, 2002, resolution. Did Congress set out "intelligible principles" to guide the President's exercise of discretion in using military force? Or is the resolution vulnerable to attack under the nondelegation doctrine? See generally *supra* pp. 102-110, and 218, and consider again Justice Sutherland's analysis in United States v. Curtiss-Wright Export Corp., 299 U.S. 304 (1936), *supra* p. 60. Doesn't the very unpredictability of armed conflict and the corresponding need for speed, flexibility, and secrecy in fighting a war impose practical limits on Congress's ability to furnish the guidance required by the doctrine? How would you describe those limits? Did the October 16, 2002, resolution satisfy your test?

5. *A Judicial Challenge to the War.* Just days before the war in Iraq began, the First Circuit Court of Appeals affirmed the dismissal of a suit by military personnel, their parents, and several members of the U.S. House of Representatives to enjoin the initiation of hostilities. Doe v. Bush, 323 F.3d 133 (1st Cir. 2003). The plaintiffs had argued that the President was about to violate conditions placed by the October 16, 2002, resolution on his use of force and that the resolution delegated excessive authority to the President, rendering it constitutionally inadequate as a vehicle for Congress to declare war.

The court based its decision in part on ripeness grounds. It rejected the government's assertion, citing Ange v. Bush, 752 F. Supp. 509 (D.D.C. 1990), noted *supra* p. 145, that no claim could ever be ripe until an attack had actually occurred. 323 F.3d at 138 n.4. Nevertheless, the court decided that the case was not fit for review, because either the President, Congress, or the U.N. Security Council might change course or Saddam might surrender before the shooting started.

In addition, the court rejected the plaintiffs' nondelegation doctrine arguments, recalling its own Vietnam-era decision in Massachusetts v. Laird, 451 F.2d 26 (1st Cir. 1971), noted *supra* p. 222, when the court declared that the Constitution overall "envisions the joint participation of the Congress and the executive in determining the scale and duration of hostilities." *Id.* at 32. "An extreme case might arise," said the court in 2003, "if Congress gave absolute discretion to the President to start a war at his or her own will.... The mere fact that the October Resolution grants some discretion to the President fails to raise a sufficiently clear constitutional issue." 323 F.3d at 143. Besides, the court observed, "Congress has been deeply involved in significant debate, activity, and authorization connected to our relations with Iraq for over a decade...." *Id.* at 144.

Do you think the court might have reached a different conclusion if it had been presented with evidence that information given to Congress to justify the war was wrong?

C. JUSTIFICATIONS FOR THE WAR

Both the October 16 congressional resolution and claims of unilateral presidential authority for the use of force were based on the existence of a serious, continuing threat to the national security of the United States. According to the resolution, the threat was posed, in part, by a "significant" chemical, biological, and nuclear weapons capability, by the risk that the current Iraqi regime would "employ those weapons to launch a surprise attack against the United States or its Armed Forces," and by "the extreme gravity of harm that would result to the United States and its citizens from such an attack." In his 2003 State of the Union message, President Bush described Iraq as "a serious and mounting threat to our country," and he called Saddam Hussein a "dictator who is assembling the world's most dangerous weapons." State of the Union Address (Jan. 28, 2003.)

More than two years after coalition forces invaded Iraq, however, no chemical, biological, or nuclear weapons had been found. A detailed account of the fruitless search for WMD appears in *Comprehensive Report of the Special Advisor to the DCI on Iraq's WMD (Duelfer Report)*, Sept. 30, 2004, *available at* http://www.cia.gov/cia/reports/iraq_wmd_2004. The President then adjusted his emphasis on WMD as a justification for the war:

> Although we haven't found stockpiles of weapons, I believe we were right to go into Iraq. And America is safer today because we did. We removed a declared enemy of America who had the capability of producing weapons of mass destruction and could have passed that capability to terrorists bent on acquiring them. In the world after September the 11th, that was a risk we could not afford to take. [President's Remarks at York, Pennsylvania, Rally (July 9, 2004).]

Concerning the ongoing threat of terrorism, President Bush asserted before the war that "Saddam Hussein aids and protects terrorists, including members of al Qaeda." State of the Union Address, *supra.* Some members of his administration claimed or implied a link between Saddam and the September 11 attacks. National Security Advisor Condoleeza Rice, for example, declared, "Oh, indeed there is a tie between Iraq and what happened on 9/11." Morning Show, CBS, Nov. 28, 2003. She then went on to add, "It's not that Saddam Hussein was somehow himself and his regime involved in 9/11, but, if you think about what caused 9/11, it is the rise of ideologies of hatred that lead people to drive airplanes into buildings in New York." *Id.* Other government officials were not so sure. *See, e.g.,* James Risen & David Johnston, *Split at C.I.A. and F.B.I. on Iraqi Ties to Al Qaeda,* N.Y. Times, Feb. 2, 2003, §1, at 13 (quoting one analyst as saying the intelligence was "obviously being politicized"). The independent 9/11 Commission found "no evidence [of] a collaborative operational relationship" between Iraq and al Qaeda, National Commission on Terrorist Attacks Upon the United States, *The 9/11 Commission Report* 66 (July 22, 2004), while the Senate Select Committee on Intelligence found no "established formal relationship" between the two. *Report on the U.S. Intelligence Community's Prewar Intelligence Assessments on Iraq,* July 9, 2004, at Conclusion 93, *available at* http://intelligence.senate.gov/iraqreport2.pdf. The Senate committee also cited a CIA assessment that there was "no evidence proving Iraqi complicity or assistance in an al-Qaida attack." *Id.* at 347.

The failure to locate WMD or to uncover clear links to terrorists was blamed in part on bad intelligence. According to the Senate Select Committee on Intelligence, most of the information available in the CIA's October 2002 *National Intelligence Estimate* concerning Iraq's WMD program was either "overstated" or "not supported by" the underlying intelligence reporting. *Id.* at 14. *See also* Commission on the Intelligence Capabilities of the United States Regarding Weapons of Mass Destruction (Silberman/Robb Commission), *Report to the President of the United States,* Mar. 31, 2005.

One key piece of intelligence about Iraq's training of al Qaeda members in the use of WMD reportedly came from Ibn al-Shaykh al-Libi. Libi was captured in Pakistan, then "rendered" to Egypt, where he says he was tortured to compel statements that he later recanted. *See* Douglas Jehl, *Qaeda-Iraq Link U.S. Cited Is Tied to Coercion Claim,* N.Y. Times, Dec. 9, 2005, at A1. See *infra* p. 804. An Iraqi exile code-named Curveball apparently provided fabricated information about Iraqi mobile bioweapons labs. *See* David Barstow, *Doubts on Source for Key Piece of Data Were Suppressed, Report Says,* N.Y. Times, Apr. 1, 2005, at A1. Both of these sources were widely discredited within the intelligence community, yet the information they supplied found its way into speeches given by the President and others.

Some suggested that the 2002 *National Intelligence Estimate* was crafted to support the President's determination to attack Iraq, while others concluded that the Bush administration had simply misled Congress and the American people, as well as the international community, about the existence of WMD. *See, e.g.,* John Prados, *Hoodwinked: The Documents That Reveal How Bush Sold Us a War* (2004); Joseph Cirincionne, Jessica T. Matthews & George Perkovich, *WMD in Iraq: Evidence and Implications* (Carnegie Endowment for Intl. Peace 2004); Spencer Ackerman & John B. Judis, *The First Casualty,* New Republic, June 30, 2003, at 14.

New concerns were raised in 2005 by the report of a meeting of top British officials, including Prime Minister Tony Blair, some three months before Congress voted to authorize the use of force in Iraq. Memorandum from Matthew Rycroft to David Manning, *Iraq: Prime Minister's Meeting, 23 July,* July 23, 2002, *reprinted in The Secret Downing Street Memo,* Sunday Times (London), May 1, 2005, *available at* http://www.timesonline.co.uk/article/0,,2087-1593607,00.html. The head of the British Secret Intelligence Service (MI6), just returned from talks with Director of Central Intelligence George Tenet and other Washington officials, reported that "[m]ilitary action was now seen as inevitable. Bush wanted to remove Saddam, through military action, justified by the conjunction of terrorism and WMD. But the intelligence and facts were being fixed around the policy." *Id. See also* Mark Danner, *The Secret Way to War*, N.Y. Rev. of Books, June 9, 2005, at 70.

When the Senate Intelligence Committee issued its report in July 2004, it decided to postpone until after the November presidential election a separate report on how the Bush administration used intelligence to shape policy. *See* Douglas Jehl, *Senators Assail C.I.A. Judgments on Iraq's Arms as Deeply Flawed*, N.Y. Times, July 10, 2004, at A1. That question was not addressed, however, in a second report issued by the committee more than two years later. *Postwar Findings About Iraq's WMD Programs and Links to Terrorism and How They Compare with Prewar Assessments*, Sept. 8, 2006.

By fall of 2005, some congressional critics of the war claimed that the Bush administration's use of pre-war intelligence was deliberately misleading. *See, e.g.,* Walter Pincus, *Newly Released Data Undercut Prewar Claims; Source Tying Bagdhad, Al Qaeda Doubted*, Wash. Post, Nov. 6, 2005, at A22. The President countered that "it is irresponsible for Democrats to now claim that we misled them and the American people. Leaders in my administration and members of the United States Congress from both political parties looked at the same intelligence on Iraq, and reached the same conclusion: Saddam Hussein was a threat." *President Delivers Remarks at Elmendorf AFB on War on Terror,* Nov. 14, 2005.

NOTES AND QUESTIONS

1. *War Based on False Premises?* Based on the language of the October 16, 2002, joint resolution, how important would you say the perceived WMD threat was in justifying the war? The terrorist connection? If one or both of these factual predicates for the war did not actually exist, would that affect the legal authority conferred by the 2002 joint resolution? Would it have any bearing on the President's exercise of his inherent "repel attack" power? Would it matter how the mistakes arose? Compare the debate about the Tonkin Gulf Resolution, *supra* p. 206. Senator Fulbright, one of the 1964 resolution's sponsors, later remarked, "I was hoodwinked." *Quoted in* John Hart Ely, *The American War in Indochina, Part I: The (Troubled) Constitutionality of the War They Told Us About*, 42 Stan. L. Rev. 877, 889 (1990).

2. *What Members of Congress Knew and When They Knew It.* Do you think members of Congress had access to the same intelligence that the President had when they voted to authorize the use of force in Iraq? What bearing, if any, does your answer have on the legitimacy of the October 16 resolution?

3. *Setting the Record Straight.* What could Congress do (if it chose to) to obtain information about the origins of the war that the President did not wish to disclose? What role or roles of Congress would be implicated by such an inquiry? What justifications would you expect the President to offer in

withholding the requested data? How would you expect the dispute to be resolved? See *supra* pp. 122-123.

D. VICTORY IN IRAQ?

Beginning in October 2003, the U.N. Security Council, acting under Chapter VII of the U.N. Charter, authorized the deployment of a Multinational Force (MNF) in Iraq to assist in rebuilding the country's infrastructure, restoring order, and training Iraqi police and military personnel. *See* S.C. Res. 1637, U.N. Doc. S/RES/1637 (Nov. 11, 2005) (extending the mandate to December 31, 2006, or until terminated by the Iraqi government). In late 2005, the United States provided some 160,000 of the nearly 180,000 MNF troops.

But with continuing, organized attacks by "insurgent" forces on MNF and Iraqi military personnel as well as on civilian targets, the goal of establishing a secure environment in Iraq proved elusive. By mid-2006, more than 2,300 U.S. military personnel had been killed, and more than 17,000 were wounded. Perhaps 30,000 Iraqis, some say many more, had also died; many of these were civilians.

With mounting U.S. combat deaths and continuing questions about justifications for the war, public support for continued U.S. military involvement in Iraq began to erode. In the summer of 2005, President Bush described Iraq as the "latest battlefield" in the war on terror. President Addresses Nation, Discusses Iraq, War on Terror (June 28, 2005). "There is only one course of action" against the terrorists, he said: "to defeat them abroad before they attack us at home." *Id.*

> Our mission in Iraq is clear. We're hunting down the terrorists. We're helping Iraqis build a free nation that is an ally in the war on terror. We're advancing freedom in the broader Middle East. We are removing a source of violence and instability, and laying the foundation of peace for our children and our grandchildren. [*Id.*]

In November 2005, the National Security Council published *Victory in Iraq*. It called Iraq "the central front in our war on terror," and it noted a continuing U.S. commitment to make Iraq "peaceful, united, stable, democratic, and secure." *Id.* at 3-4. And on the eve of the first post-war parliamentary elections in Iraq, President Bush declared that "[w]e are in Iraq today because our goal has always been more than the removal of a brutal dictator; it is to leave a free and democratic Iraq in its place." Remarks on the War on Terrorism (Dec. 14, 2005). The result, he said, would be "an example for the broader Middle East." *Id.*

By late 2005, however, some members of Congress in both parties had begun calling for a withdrawal, or at least a plan for withdrawal, of U.S. troops from Iraq. *See, e.g.*, Patrick D. Healy, *Clinton Calls for Iraq Plan to Start Withdrawal by '06*, N.Y. Times, Nov. 30, 2005, §B, at 6. But while the White House insisted that the United States would not "cut and run," others in the administration

D. Victory in Iraq?

signaled that planning for a drawdown of U.S. forces was underway. *See* David S. Cloud, *U.S. Considers Troop Cuts After Iraq Holds Elections*, N.Y. Times, Nov. 25, 2005, at A14.

NOTES AND QUESTIONS

1. *Continuing Authority for the War?* If the reasons for military action changed over time, was the President's mandate under the October 16, 2002, resolution still good? Was the continued deployment merely a tactical decision properly entrusted to the President? See *supra* p. 229. Was the earlier mandate extended by Congress's recurring votes of appropriations for the war? *See, e.g.,* Department of Defense Appropriations Act, 2005, Pub. L. No. 108-287, tit. IX, 118 Stat. 951, 1005 (2004) (appropriating $3.8 billion for an "Iraq Freedom Fund" to support "operations in Iraq or Afghanistan and classified activities"). See *supra* p. 223. Or should the President have sought new authority from Congress?

2. *War Without End?* In August 2005, President Bush declared:

> An immediate withdrawal of our troops in Iraq, or the broader Middle East, as some have called for, would only embolden the terrorists and create a staging ground to launch more attacks against America and free nations. So long as I'm the President, we will stay, we will fight, and we will win the war on terror. [President Addresses Military Families, Discusses War on Terror (Aug. 24, 2005).]

If the President is determined to maintain U.S. forces in Iraq, would anything short of a "declaration of peace" — a joint resolution approved by a veto-proof majority in both houses of Congress — suffice to require their withdrawal? Would such a resolution be constitutional?

During confirmation hearings for Chief Justice John Roberts, the following colloquy took place between the nominee and Vermont Senator Patrick Leahy:

Senator Leahy: We [Congress] have the power to declare war. Do we have the power to terminate a war?

Judge Roberts: Senator, that's a question that I don't think can be answered in the abstract. You need to know the particular circumstances and exactly what the facts are and what the legislation would be like. . . .

U.S. Senate Judiciary Committee Holds a Hearing on the Nomination of John Roberts to Be Chief Justice of the Supreme Court, Wash. Post Online, Sept. 13, 2005. Do you agree with the Chief Justice?

If a congressional resolution to terminate hostilities were constitutional, would a court issue an order to enforce it? Recall one court's response on similar facts three decades earlier in Holtzman v. Schlesinger, 484 F.2d 1307 (2d Cir. 1973), *supra* p. 235.

13

Humanitarian and Peace/Stability Operations

An increasingly frequent and important use of U.S. armed forces abroad is their deployment in circumstances where their engagement in armed conflict is not the objective, or at least is not the primary objective. Some of these missions, including those responding to famines and other natural disasters, are strictly humanitarian. Others are mainly concerned with establishing or preserving the peace or stability. These missions are variously described as relief efforts; peace operations; nation-building; stabilization and reconstruction operations; stability operations; and security, transition, and reconstruction operations, among other terms. We opt here for the hybrid "peace/stability operations."

Some missions are carried out in conjunction with the United Nations or regional organizations. At the end of 1995, for example, some 2,800 U.S. military personnel participated in seven U.N. operations. *See generally* Marjorie Ann Browne, *United Nations Peacekeeping: Issues for Congress* (Cong. Res. Serv. IB90103), Sept. 24, 2003. Ten years later, U.S. participation in U.N. peace operations had shrunk to 29 individuals, although the net number of U.S. forces engaged in peacekeeping missions had increased substantially, with large deployments in Afghanistan and Iraq in the wake of successful military campaigns in those countries. *See* Nina M. Serafino, *Peacekeeping and Related Stability Operations: Issues of U.S. Military Involvement* (Cong. Res. Serv. IB94040), May 18, 2006.

Peace/stability operations may encounter armed resistance or run the risk of hostilities. The military occupation of Iraq, for example, has experienced "a level of instability that many define as low-intensity conflict rather than peace enforcement." *Id.* at 4. Thus, it is sometimes useful to distinguish between "peacekeeping" and "peacemaking." "Peacekeeping" interventions — in "transition situations where a state lacks capacity to manage affairs to assure domestic or international tranquility, yet the use of force in the traditional sense of armed conflict is not contemplated"[1] — pose the lesser risk. These often attend the cessation of armed hostilities and usually involve the use of unarmed

---

1. *See* George K. Walker, *United States National Security Law and United Nations Peacekeeping or Peacemaking Operations*, 29 Wake Forest L. Rev. 435, 445-446 (1994) (making the distinction and citing examples); Rajendra Ramlogan, *Towards a Vision of World Security: The United Nations Security Council and the Lessons of Somalia*, 16 Hous. J. Intl. L. 213, 248-250 (1993) (making the distinction).

or lightly armed forces to police or "observe" cease-fires or armistices with the consent of the parties involved. "Peacemaking" (or "peace-enforcing") interventions—in "situation[s] where the use of force in the traditional sense of armed conflict may be employed to restore tranquility"[2]—pose greater risks. These involve the deployment of armed forces into hostilities with the mission of using force to halt or limit the fighting, usually without the consent of all the contending parties.

Unfortunately, the terminology is as unstable as the operations. The lines between strictly humanitarian intervention and peacemaking, or between peacekeeping and peacemaking, often erode during the course of an operation. Furthermore, post-conflict deployments aimed at achieving stability and reconstruction—such as those in Afghanistan and Iraq—may meet armed opposition from remnants of defeated armies or groups, or from insurgents.

In the first part of this chapter we examine some authorities for the use of U.S. military forces in humanitarian operations abroad. We then look closely at one operation—the intervention in Somalia—that began as a humanitarian mission and quickly "crossed the Mogadishu line" into something else. Finally, we look briefly at the still evolving "stabilization and reconstruction operations" in Afghanistan and Iraq.

A. AUTHORITY FOR HUMANITARIAN OPERATIONS

Humanitarian and Other Assistance
10 U.S.C.A. §§401-405 (West 1998 & Supp. 2006)

10 U.S.C. §401. HUMANITARIAN AND CIVIC ASSISTANCE PROVIDED IN CONJUNCTION WITH MILITARY OPERATIONS

(a) (1) Under regulations prescribed by the Secretary of Defense, the Secretary of a military department may carry out humanitarian and civic assistance activities in conjunction with authorized military operations of the armed forces in a country if the Secretary concerned determines that the activities will promote—

(A) the security interests of both the United States and the country in which the activities are to be carried out; and

(B) the specific operational readiness skills of the members of the armed forces who participate in the activities....

---

2. Walker, *supra*, at 445-446. Professor Walker acknowledges that "there is an elusive sliding scale between peacekeeping and peacemaking." *Id.* at 446. *See also* Michael O'Hanlon, *Saving Lives With Force: Military Criteria for Humanitarian Intervention* 7 (Brookings Inst. Press 1997) ("[I]t is probably better to leave the modifier 'peace' entirely out of the terminology and describe it as intervention to restore order."); Jon E. Fink, *From Peacekeeping to Peace Enforcement: The Blurring of the Mandate for the Use of Force in Maintaining International Peace and Security*, 19 Md. J. Intl. L. & Trade 1, 42 (1995) (noting that the distinction is "fading" as peacekeeping missions evolve into peace enforcement).

(e) In this section, the term "humanitarian and civic assistance" means any of the following:

(1) Medical, surgical, dental, and veterinary care provided in areas of a country that are rural or are underserved by medical, surgical, dental, and veterinary professionals, respectively, including education, training, and technical assistance related to the care provided.

(2) Construction of rudimentary surface transportation systems.

(3) Well drilling and construction of basic sanitation facilities.

(4) Rudimentary construction and repair of public facilities.

(5) Detection and clearance of landmines and other explosive remnants of war, including activities relating to the furnishing of education, training, and technical assistance with respect to the detection and clearance of landmines and other explosive remnants of war.

10 U.S.C. §402. TRANSPORTATION OF HUMANITARIAN RELIEF SUPPLIES TO FOREIGN COUNTRIES

(a) Notwithstanding any other provision of law, and subject to subsection (b), the Secretary of Defense may transport to any country, without charge, supplies which have been furnished by a nongovernmental source and which are intended for humanitarian assistance. Such supplies may be transported only on a space available basis....

10 U.S.C. §404. FOREIGN DISASTER ASSISTANCE

(a) In general. — The President may direct the Secretary of Defense to provide disaster assistance outside the United States to respond to manmade or natural disasters when necessary to prevent loss of lives or serious harm to the environment.

(b) Forms of assistance. — Assistance provided under this section may include transportation, supplies, services, and equipment....

NOTES AND QUESTIONS

1. *Congressional Authority for Humanitarian Operations.* Can you say precisely what is authorized by the foregoing statutes? What prerequisites must be satisfied before these statutes are invoked?

Other possibly relevant statutes include 10 U.S.C. §2561 (2000 & Supp. III 2003), which allows the Defense Department to use appropriated funds for "transportation of humanitarian relief and for other humanitarian purposes worldwide," *id.* §2561(a)(1), and 22 U.S.C. §2292 (2000), which authorizes the President to "furnish assistance to any foreign country, international organization, or private voluntary organization, on such terms and conditions as he may determine, for international disaster relief and rehabilitation." *Id.* §2292(b). Can you think of additional statutory authorities that might be needed for deployment of the military on humanitarian missions?

What if the purely humanitarian missions outlined in the statutes cannot be carried out without the support of troops equipped for combat? Do these statutes authorize their deployment? If so, might the President have to comply with the consultation, reporting, and other requirements of the War Powers Resolution, *supra* p. 240?

2. *Presidential Authority for Humanitarian Operations?* Suppose Congress had not enacted legislation to authorize humanitarian operations. Does the President have the constitutional authority unilaterally to deploy military forces in such cases? If he does, may Congress restrict such deployments? *See* Matthew D. Berger, *Implementing a United Nations Security Council Resolution: The President's Power to Use Force Without Authorization of Congress*, 15 Hastings Intl. & Comp. L. Rev. 83, 100 (1991) (asserting that "the President has exclusive control over all peacetime deployments which do not threaten war") (citation omitted). How do the foregoing statutes indicate that Congress has sought to restrict the President's authority? Omitted sections require detailed reporting to Congress regarding exercises of the delegated authority. May Congress require the President to make such reports?

3. *Additional Authority for Peace/Stability Operations?* What additional statutory authority, if any, do you think is required for the humanitarian deployment of U.S. military forces in situations where they may have to engage in armed combat? Does your answer turn on the likelihood that hostilities will erupt? On the fact that hostilities do erupt during the mission? If so, can you articulate a bright-line standard to indicate when that authority must be invoked?

B. CROSSING THE MOGADISHU LINE: OPERATION RESTORE HOPE[3]

With the fall of the Siad Barre government in 1991, Somalia plunged into a civil war among rival clans. The war not only directly threatened the population, it also disrupted food production and transportation. As the Secretary-General of the United Nations reportedly said, "There are more arms than food in Somalia." By early 1993, some 350,000 Somalians had died from famine and civil strife, and 2 million remained at risk. More than 1 million fled into refugee camps.

The U.N. Security Council responded with a series of resolutions urging the clans to cease hostilities and dispatching a U.N. security force of 500 lightly armed Pakistani troops to provide security for humanitarian relief operations. Congress acted in April 1992 by passing the Horn of Africa Recovery and Food Security Act, Pub. L. No. 102-274, 106 Stat. 115 (1992). Noting that armed

---

3. Except where otherwise noted, this background is drawn from Terrence Lyons & Ahmed I. Samatar, *Somalia* (1995); Office of U.S. Foreign Disaster Assistance, Agency for Intl. Dev., *Situation Report No. 19* (Mar. 12, 1993); John R. Bolton, *Wrong Turn in Somalia*, 73 Foreign Aff. 266 (Jan./Feb. 1994); Ramlogan, *supra* note 1; Charles Ernest Edgar, *United States Use of Armed Force Under the United Nations... Who's in Charge?*, 10 J.L. & Pol. 299, 329-333 (1994).

groups in Somalia were eroding "food security," it expressed the "sense of the Congress" that the President should, *inter alia*, "ensure, to the maximum extent possible and in conjunction with other donors, that emergency humanitarian assistance is being made available to those in need...." *Id.* §3(b)(3). It also stated that it should be U.S. policy

> to redouble its commendable efforts to secure safe corridors of passage for emergency food and relief supplies in affected areas ... [and] to lend the full support of the United States to all aspects of relief operations in the Horn of Africa, and to work in support of [the] United Nations ... in breaking the barriers currently threatening the lives of millions of refugees.... [*Id.* §4(b)(1), (4).]

Beginning in August 1992, U.S. planes helped airlift humanitarian relief supplies to Somalia. In the same month, the Senate urged the President to work with the U.N. Security Council "to deploy security guards [to protect relief shipments and workers], with or without the consent of the Somalia factions, in order to assure that humanitarian relief gets to those most in need...." S. Con. Res. 132, 102d Cong. (1992). The House followed suit in October 1992 by expressing "the willingness of the United States to participate, consistent with applicable United States legal requirements, in the deployment of armed United Nations security guards, as authorized by the Security Council, in order to secure emergency relief activities," and emphasizing that the deployment should proceed "even in the event that an invitation by the various warring Somali factions cannot be obtained." H.R. Con. Res. 370, 102d Cong. (1992).

The full Congress then declared that

> [i]nternational peacekeeping activities take many forms and include observer missions, ceasefire monitoring, human rights monitoring, refugee and humanitarian assistance, monitoring and conducting elections, monitoring of police in the demobilization of former combatants, and reforming judicial and other civil and administrative systems of government. [Pub. L. No. 102-484, §1342(a)(2), 106 Stat. 2315, 2556 (1992).]

It also authorized the transfer of funds from Department of Defense appropriations to meet "unexpected and urgent" budget shortfalls for "international peacekeeping activities of the United Nations." 10 U.S.C. §403, *repealed* Pub. L. No. 104-106, §1061(g)(1), 110 Stat. 443 (1996).

But clan militias continued to imperil the relief workers and intercept relief convoys. In December 1992, the Security Council condemned continued "violations of international humanitarian law" in Somalia. It called for the deployment of 3,500 U.N. personnel there to coordinate humanitarian relief and to provide a secure environment for relief operations, and, pursuant to Chapter VII, see *supra* p. 285, authorized member states to use "all necessary means" to achieve these ends. S.C. Res. 794, U.N. Doc. S/RES/794 (Dec. 3, 1992). President George Bush responded on December 4, 1992, by ordering U.S. military forces to secure the airfield and port facility of Mogadishu and to provide a secure environment for the relief effort. The troops were deployed on December 8 and 9, and the President reported the deployment to Congress two days later. See *infra* p. 327. Within a month, 28,000 U.S. troops were deployed on

Authority of the President to Use United States Military Forces for the Protection of Relief Efforts in Somalia

13 Op. Off. Legal Counsel 8
Dec. 4, 1992

MEMORANDUM FOR THE ATTORNEY GENERAL

You have asked for our opinion whether the President has the legal authority to commit United States Armed Forces to assist the United Nations in ensuring the safe delivery of food, medicine and other relief to the population in affected regions of Somalia. We understand that the mission of those troops will be to restore as quickly as possible the flow of humanitarian relief to those areas of Somalia most affected by famine and disease, and to facilitate the safe and orderly deployment of United Nations peacekeeping forces in Somalia in the near future. We also understand that private United States nationals are currently involved in relief operations in Somalia and United States military personnel are engaged in humanitarian supply flights into Somalia. We further understand that the efforts of the United States and other nations and of private organizations to deliver humanitarian relief to those areas of Somalia are being severely hampered by the breakdown of governmental authority in Somalia and, in particular, by armed bands who steal relief commodities for their own use.[1]

In our opinion, the President's role under our Constitution as Commander in Chief and Chief Executive vests him with the constitutional authority to order United States troops abroad to further national interests such as protecting the lives of Americans overseas. Accordingly, where, as here, United States government personnel and private citizens are participating in a lawful relief effort in a foreign nation, we conclude that the President may commit United States troops to protect those involved in the relief effort. In addition, we believe that long-standing precedent supports the use of the Armed Forces to protect Somalians and other foreign nationals in Somalia. We also believe that the President, in determining to commit the Armed Forces to this operation, may lawfully look to the importance to the national interests of the United States of upholding the recent United Nations resolutions regarding Somalia. Finally, we note that Congress has expressed its tacit approval for the President's exercise of his constitutional authority in this matter.

---

1. We note at the outset that the deployment of troops to Somalia appears primarily aimed at providing humanitarian assistance, and will only involve combat as an incident to that humanitarian mission. Thus, the current situation poses two questions: is there legal authority for United States Armed Forces to perform humanitarian tasks, and if so, may the President authorize those troops to engage in more purely military actions, such as self-defense and the creation of safe corridors for the provision of aid. We understand from the General Counsel of the Department of Defense that there is clear statutory authority for the use of the Armed Forces to support and to perform humanitarian tasks in Somalia. E.g., 10 U.S.C. §2551 [now §2561]; see also 22 U.S.C. §§2292, 2292*l*. We conclude in this opinion that in these circumstances the President's constitutional authority to authorize the troops to engage in various related military actions is also clear. We do not address issues raised by the proposed operation under the War Powers Resolution.

I

From the instructions of President Jefferson's Administration to Commodore Richard Dale in 1801 to "chastise" Algiers and Tripoli if they continued to attack American shipping, to the present, Presidents have taken military initiatives abroad on the basis of their constitutional authority. Against the background of this repeated past practice under many Presidents, this Department and this Office have concluded that the President has the power to commit United States troops abroad for the purpose of protecting important national interests. See, e.g., Training of British Flying Students in the United States, 40 Op. Atty. Gen. 58, 62 (1941) ("the President's authority has long been recognized as extending to the dispatch of armed forces outside of the United States, either on missions of good will or rescue, or for the purpose of protecting American lives or property or American interests") (Jackson, A.G.). As the Supreme Court noted in United States v. Verdugo-Urquidez, 494 U.S. 259, 273 (1990), "[t]he United States frequently employs armed forces outside this country—over 200 times in our history—for the protection of American citizens or national security."

At the core of this power is the President's authority to take military action to protect American citizens, property, and interests from foreign threats. See, e.g., Presidential Powers Relating to the Situation in Iran, 4A Op. OLC 115, 121 (1979) ("It is well established that the President has the constitutional power as Chief Executive and Commander-in-Chief to protect the lives and property of Americans abroad."); Presidential Power to Use the Armed Forces Abroad Without Statutory Authorization, 4A Op. OLC 185, 187 (1980) ("Presidents have repeatedly employed troops abroad in defense of American lives and property."); see also Memorandum of William H. Rehnquist, Assistant Attorney General, Office of Legal Counsel, Re: The President and the War Power: South Vietnam and the Cambodian Sanctuaries, 8 (May 22, 1970) (President as Commander in Chief has authority "to commit military forces of the United States to armed conflict... to protect the lives of American troops in the field"). In Durand v. Hollins, 8 Fed. Cas. 111 (No. 4186) (C.C.S.D.N.Y. 1860) [*supra* p. 264], an American naval officer, under orders of the President and the Secretary of the Navy, bombarded Greytown, Nicaragua in retaliation for the Nicaraguan government's refusal to make reparations for attacks against United States citizens and property. In a suit brought against the naval officer, Justice Nelson held that the officer properly took this action, observing that such an attack on American citizens and property required the sort of swift and effective response that only the Executive could make.

> Acts of lawless violence, or of threatened violence to the citizen or his property, cannot be anticipated and provided for; and the protection, to be effectual or of any avail, may, not unfrequently, require the most prompt and decided action.

Id. at 112. Justice Nelson also stated that whether the President had a duty to act to protect the citizens involved "was a public political question... which belonged to the executive to determine." Id. See also Youngstown Sheet & Tube Co. v. Sawyer, 343 U.S. 579, 645 (1952) [*supra* p. 28] (Jackson, J., concurring) ("I should indulge the widest latitude of interpretation to sustain [the

B. Crossing the Mogadishu Line

President's] exclusive function to command the instruments of national force, at least when turned against the outside world for the security of our society.").

Applying these principles to the present case, we conclude that the President can reasonably determine that the proposed mission is necessary to protect the American citizens already in Somalia. We understand that these include private United States citizens engaged in relief operations, and United States military personnel conducting humanitarian supply flights. The United Nations has determined that existing conditions in Somalia pose a threat to the lives and safety of these individuals and of non-Americans also engaged in efforts to deliver food, medicine and other relief to over two million Somalis. See Security Council Resolution No. 794 (December 3, 1992) (determining that the Somali situation "constitutes a threat to international peace and security," and expressing alarm at "reports of violence and threats of violence against personnel participating lawfully in impartial humanitarian relief activities").

It is also essential to consider the safety of the troops to be dispatched as requested by Resolution 794. The President may provide those troops with sufficient military protection to insure that they are able to carry out their humanitarian tasks safely and efficiently. He may also decide to send sufficient numbers of troops so that those who are primarily engaged in assisting the United Nations in noncombatant roles are defended by others who perform a protective function. See, e.g., Memorandum of William H. Rehnquist, Assistant Attorney General, Office of Legal Counsel, Re: The President and the War Power: South Vietnam and the Cambodian Sanctuaries 8 (May 22, 1970).

Nor is the President's power strictly limited to the protection of American citizens in Somalia. Past military interventions that extended to the protection of foreign nationals provide precedent for action to protect endangered Somalians and other non-United States citizens. For example, in 1965, President Lyndon Johnson explained that he had ordered United States military intervention in the Dominican Republic to protect both Americans and the citizens of other nations. "An Assessment of the Situation in the Dominican Republic," 53 Dept. State Bull. 19, 20 (1965) ("to preserve the lives of American citizens and citizens of a good many other nations — 46 to be exact, 46 nations"). During the 1900-01 Boxer Rebellion in China, President McKinley, without prior congressional authorization, sent about 5,000 United States troops as part of a multi-national contingent to lift the siege of the foreign quarters in Peking after the Chinese government proved unable to control rebels. J. Richardson, Compilation of the Messages and Papers of the Presidents 1789-1902 (Supp.) 113, 120 (1904).[3]

The United States has an additional important national interest arising from the involvement of the United Nations in the Somalian situation. In a 1950 opinion supporting President Truman's decision to support the

---

3. A case of intervention on behalf of a foreign national, one Martin Koszta, was cited approvingly by the Supreme Court in In re Neagle, 135 U.S. 1, 64 (1890) [*supra* p. 80], as an example of the legitimate exercise of Executive power "growing out of the Constitution itself, our international relations, and all the protection implied by the nature of the government under the Constitution." Id. Although Koszta had expressed his intention of becoming naturalized, at the time of the events in question he was not an American citizen. He was seized by the Austrian government while in Smyrna and confined in an Austrian vessel. A United States naval officer demanded Koszta's surrender, and "was compelled to train his guns upon the Austrian vessel before his demands were complied with." Id. The Court noted that no Act of Congress sanctioned this armed intervention.

United Nations in repelling the invasion of South Korea, the State Department concluded that "[t]he continued existence of the United Nations as an effective international organization is a paramount United States interest." Authority of the President to Repel the Attack on Korea, 23 Dept. State Bull. 173, 177 (1950). We adopt that conclusion. Here, too, maintaining the credibility of United Nations Security Council decisions, protecting the security of United Nations and related relief efforts, and ensuring the effectiveness of United Nations peacekeeping operations can be considered a vital national interest, and will promote the United States' conception of a "new world order."

In Resolution 794, which was adopted pursuant to Chapter VII of the United Nations Charter, the Security Council has authorized the United States and other member States to use "all necessary means" to establish a secure environment for the delivery of essential humanitarian aid in Somalia. The President is entitled to rely on this Resolution, and on its finding that the situation in Somalia "constitutes a threat to international peace and security," in making his determination that the interests of the United States justify providing the military assistance that Resolution 794 calls for. Moreover, American assistance in giving effect to this and other Security Council resolutions pertaining to Somalia would in itself strengthen the prestige, credibility and effectiveness of the United Nations—which the President can legitimately find to be a substantial national foreign policy objective, and which will tend further to guarantee the lives and property of Americans abroad.

This conclusion accords with our prior opinions. During the Korean War, for example, we took the position that a Security Council resolution authorizing the use of force by member States to protect international peace and security could furnish a new ground for a decision by the President to use troops abroad....

> In the presence of such a resolution the President is bound to consider what the interests of the United States require. He will necessarily weigh the nature of the breach of the peace which has occurred, what its consequences will be for the United Nations if it goes unchallenged, and what it foreshadows in the way of an ultimate threat to the vital interests of the United States. In the light of these and other considerations he will then make the decisions which he, as President, must make.

F. Pollak, Power of the President to Send Troops Abroad, 35 (Apr. 27, 1951).[5]

II

Finally, we note that the available evidence strongly suggests that Congress believes that the President's use of military force to assist United Nations relief and peacekeeping efforts in Somalia does not exceed his constitutional powers. In recent legislation, Congress appears to have recognized the President's

---

5. We do not conclude that a Security Council resolution calling on member States to provide troops to assist the United Nations by itself imposes any legal duty on the President to act in accordance with the resolution. But, as we explained in our 1951 memorandum, such a resolution can be an important factor on which the President may rely in determining whether national interests require such military action.

authority to make use of military personnel, should he deem it necessary to carry out or protect humanitarian missions in Somalia. Section 3(b)(3) of the Horn of Africa Recovery and Food Security Act, Pub. L. No. 102-274, 106 Stat. 115 (1992) [noted *supra* p. 321], states that "[i]t is the sense of the Congress that the President should... ensure, to the maximum extent possible and in conjunction with other donors, that emergency humanitarian assistance is being made available to those in need...." Section 4(a)(1) of the Act states in part that U.S. policy should be "to assure noncombatants... equal and ready access to all food, emergency, and relief assistance," and section 4(b)(1) states that pursuant to the United States policy of "seeking to maximize relief efforts" the United States should "redouble its commendable efforts to secure safe corridors of passage for emergency food and relief supplies in affected areas." Moreover, in section 2(3), Congress explicitly found that the actions of the government and armed opposition groups in Somalia "erode[d] food security" in that country.

Thus, Congress appears to have contemplated that the President might find it necessary to make use of military forces to ensure the safe delivery of humanitarian relief in Somalia, and to have assumed in such circumstances that the President possessed constitutional authority to do so.[6] See also *Dames & Moore* [v. Regan], 453 U.S. [654 (1981),] at 678-79 [*supra* p. 48].

Please let us know if we may be of further assistance.

Timothy E. Flanigan
Assistant Attorney General

Letter from President George Bush to Congressional Leaders
28 Weekly Comp. Pres. Doc. 2338 (Dec. 10, 1992)

Dear Mr. [Speaker/President]:...

On November 29, 1992, the Secretary General of the U.N. reported to the Security Council that the deteriorating security conditions in Somalia had severely disrupted international relief efforts and that an immediate military operation under U.N. authority was urgently required. On December 3, the Security Council adopted Resolution 794, which determined that the situation in Somalia constituted a threat to international peace and security, and, invoking Chapter VII of the U.N. Charter, authorized Member States to use all necessary means to establish a secure environment for humanitarian relief operations in Somalia. In my judgment, the deployment of U.S. Armed Forces under U.S. command to Somalia as part of this multilateral response to the Resolution is necessary to address a major humanitarian calamity, avert related threats to international peace and security, and protect the safety of Americans and others engaged in relief operations.

In the evening, Eastern Standard Time, on December 8, 1992, U.S. Armed Forces entered Somalia to secure the airfield and port facility of Mogadishu.

---

6. As noted above, the quoted provisions of the Act are part of a "sense of Congress" resolution. A "sense of Congress" resolution does not, of course, give the President authority he does not otherwise possess. Nonetheless, we believe that the Congressional views expressed in the quoted portions of the Act are evidence that Congress recognized that the President has authority to use military force to accomplish the goals of the Act.

Other elements of the U.S. Armed Forces and the Armed Forces of other Members of the United Nations are being introduced into Somalia to achieve the objectives of U.N. Security Council Resolution 794. No organized resistance has been encountered to date.

U.S. Army Forces will remain in Somalia only as long as necessary to establish a secure environment for humanitarian relief operations and will then turn over the responsibility of maintaining this environment to a U.N. peacekeeping force assigned to Somalia. Over 15 nations have already offered to deploy troops. While it is not possible to estimate precisely how long the transfer of responsibility may take, we believe that prolonged operations will not be necessary.

We do not intend that U.S. Armed Forces deployed to Somalia become involved in hostilities. Nonetheless, these forces are equipped and ready to take such measures as may be needed to accomplish their humanitarian mission and defend themselves, if necessary; they also will have the support of any additional U.S. Armed Forces necessary to ensure their safety and the accomplishment of their mission.

I have taken these actions pursuant to my constitutional authority to conduct our foreign relations and as Commander in Chief and Chief Executive, and in accordance with applicable treaties and laws. In doing so, I have taken into account the views expressed in H. Con. Res. 370, S. Con. Res. 132, and the Horn of Africa Recovery and Food Security Act, Public Law 102-274, on the urgent need for action in Somalia.

I am providing this report in accordance with my desire that Congress be fully informed and consistent with the War Powers Resolution. I look forward to cooperating with Congress in the effort to relieve human suffering and to restore peace and stability to the region.

Sincerely,
George Bush

On February 4, 1993, the Senate approved Senate Joint Resolution 45, noting President Bush's letter and asserting that he was "authorized to use United States armed forces pursuant to United Nations Security Council Resolution 794 in order to implement the resolution...within the meaning of section 5(b) of the War Powers Resolution." S.J. Res. 45, 103d Cong. (1993). The House, however, did not immediately follow suit.

In March 1993, the Security Council noted the continuing threat to peace and security in Somalia and called for a "prompt, smooth, and phased transition" from the U.S.-led Unified Task Force in Somalia to the U.N. Operation in Somalia (UNOSOM II). S.C. Res. 814, U.N. Doc. S/RES/814 (Mar. 26, 1993). The United States turned over command of the Unified Task Force to UNOSOM II in May, although it continued to support U.N. efforts by providing approximately 3,000 U.S. logistics and other support personnel under UNOSOM II control. In addition, approximately 1,100 U.S. troops remained in the area as part of a Quick Reaction Force (QRF) for emergency operations under the operational control of U.S. commanders. By then, however, Congress had begun to have second thoughts. When the House finally approved a modified version of Senate Joint Resolution 45 on May 25, 1993, it added a 12-month

B. Crossing the Mogadishu Line

time limit on the authorization. S.J. Res. 45, 103d Cong., §4(c)(1) (1993) (as modified and approved by the House).

On June 5, 1993, forces of Somali warlord Mohammed Farah Hassan Aidid ambushed a U.N. convoy, killing 24 Pakistani troops and injuring three U.S. soldiers. The following day the Security Council adopted Resolution 837, which authorized UNOSOM II to take "all necessary measures against all those responsible" for the attack and to secure "their arrest and detention for prosecution, trial, and punishment." S.C. Res. 837, U.N. Doc. S/RES/837 (June 6, 1993).

On June 10, 1993, President Clinton reported these events to Congress and reaffirmed the deployment of U.S. armed forces to Somalia to accomplish their humanitarian mission "and to defend themselves." Approximately a week later, elements of the QRF launched air and ground strikes against Aidid's headquarters in a search for Aidid. This phase of the operations concluded in a bloody firefight with Aidid's forces on October 3-4, 1993, in which 17 U.S. soldiers were killed and 84 wounded. The disaster prompted speculation that the Administration had under-equipped the QRF to avoid inflaming congressional and public opinion. The press subsequently popularized the phrase "crossing the Mogadishu line" to describe a change in mission from peacekeeping to peacemaking.

President Clinton then reported to Congress that he would withdraw the troops by March 31, 1994. *Report on Military Operations in Somalia — Message from the President*, 139 Cong. Rec. H7796 (daily ed. Oct. 13, 1993). But a majority in Congress were not satisfied by these assurances. In the defense appropriation for 1994, Congress found that

> neither the expanded United Nations mission of national reconciliation, nor the broad mission of disarming the clans, nor any other mission not essential to the performance of the humanitarian mission has been endorsed or approved by the Senate; [and] the expanded mission of the United Nations was, subsequent to an attack on the United Nations force, diverted into a mission aimed primarily at capturing certain persons.... [Department of Defense Appropriations Act, 1994, Pub. L. No. 103-139, §8151(a)(4)-(5), 107 Stat. 1418, 1476 (1993).]

Accordingly, Congress authorized appropriations for U.S. forces in Somalia only through March 31, 1994, and required that they be placed under U.S. command and control. *Id.* §8151(b)(2)(B), 107 Stat. 1476-1477. Beyond that date, it authorized the obligation of funds for forces "sufficient only to protect American diplomatic facilities and American citizens, and noncombat personnel to advise the United Nations commander in Somalia," and to protect themselves. *Id.*, 107 Stat. 1476.

More generally, in the same Act, Congress expressed its sense that no funds appropriated by the Act should be spent for costs incurred by U.S. forces in "international peacekeeping or peace-enforcement operations" under the authority of Chapters VI or VII of the U.N. Charter or of a U.N. Security Council Resolution, or in "any significant... peacekeeping, or peace-enforcement operations," unless the President consulted with Congress prior to the operation, whenever possible, regarding the goals, mission, cost, funding, and anticipated duration and scope of the operation. *Id.* §8153(1)(a), 107 Stat. 1477.

Taking another swipe at the United Nations, Congress found that the United Nations had not acquired the expertise or infrastructure to manage "peace enforcement" operations effectively. *Id.* §9001(5), 107 Stat. 1479. Congress expressed the sense that the President should consult with it before placing U.S. combat forces under the operational control of foreign commanders, and that he should describe the justification for foreign command, command and control arrangements, rules of engagement, and other details. *Id.* §9002, 107 Stat. 1479-1480.

Three weeks later, Congress revisited the Somalia issue in the National Defense Authorization Act for Fiscal Year 1994, Pub. L. No. 103-160, 107 Stat. 1547 (1993). The Act required the President to submit detailed reports about operations in Somalia, and it expressed the sense that he "should by November 15, 1993, seek and receive Congressional authorization in order for the deployment of United States Forces to Somalia to continue." *Id.* §1512(b)(3)-(4), 107 Stat. at 1841. The President signed this measure into law on November 30, 1993. Less than three months later, on February 26, 1994, all U.S. forces were withdrawn from Somalia. The remaining UNOSOM II forces followed shortly thereafter.

NOTES AND QUESTIONS

1. *Making Peace, Not War?* Does a peace operation involve the war power at all? One commentator has speculated that "[s]ince the United Nations approached the United States requesting assistance in Somalia where there was no defined 'enemy' or 'aggression,' the subsequent commitment might be viewed as falling fully within Presidential police powers and not requiring Congressional authorization." Edgar, *supra* p. 321 n.3, at 331. See *supra* p. 290. Do you agree? *See* Byron F. Burmester, *Humanitarian Intervention*, 1994 Utah L. Rev. 269, 295-296 (arguing that humanitarian intervention to stop human rights violations by force is war under international law).

Should it make any difference whether the government (if there is one) of the country to which troops are to be deployed invites their intervention? Can an invited intervention be a war? *See* Jane E. Stromseth, *Collective Force and Constitutional Responsibility: War Powers in the Post-Cold War Era*, 50 U. Miami L. Rev. 145, 161 (1995) (arguing that the President does not require Congress's authorization if "all the parties to a conflict (not just some of them) consent to and support" a peacekeeping operation, because the chances of significant combat risks are then low); Letter from Walter Dellinger (Asst. Attorney General, Office of Legal Counsel) to Senator Robert Dole et al. (Sept. 27, 1994), at 5-7, 1994 OLC LEXIS 16.

Does it matter whether the deployment is primarily for humanitarian purposes, or whether its goal is either peacekeeping or peacemaking? Is there a meaningful distinction among these missions? Clarke and Herbst express doubt:

> When U.S. troops intervened in December 1992 to stop theft of food, they disrupted the political economy and stepped deep into the muck of Somali politics. By reestablishing some order, the U.S. operation inevitably affected the direction

of Somali politics and became nation-building because the most basic component of nation-building is an end to anarchy. The current conventional wisdom that draws the distinctions between different types of intervention and stresses the desire to avoid nation-building may be analytically attractive, but it is not particularly helpful. How could anyone believe that landing 30,000 troops in a country was anything but a gross interference in its politics? The Mogadishu line was crossed as soon as troops were sent in. [Walter Clarke & Jeffrey Herbst, *Somalia and the Future of Humanitarian Intervention*, 75 Foreign Aff. 70, 74 (Mar./Apr. 1996).]

They conclude that "there is no such thing as a humanitarian surgical strike." *Id.* at 82. If they are right, what implication, if any, does this conclusion carry for the President's authority to order a humanitarian intervention into a politically unstable area?

2. *Mission Creep and the Commander in Chief's Tactical Authority.* By what statutory authority, if any, did President George Bush initially deploy U.S. armed forces in Somalia? If there was statutory authority for the initial deployment of U.S. forces, did it also authorize subsequent deployments and mission changes? If the troops were lawfully deployed at the outset, did the President *need* any further authority to order them to find warlord Aidid? To put it differently, is "mission creep" inherently within the tactical discretion of the Commander in Chief? *See* Mark T. Uyeda, *Presidential Prerogative Under the Constitution to Deploy U.S. Military Forces in Low-Intensity Conflict*, 44 Duke L.J. 777, 813 n.187 (1995).

3. *Retail or Wholesale Uses of Force?* Statutes aside, what constitutional authority did the President claim in deploying U.S. armed forces in Somalia? How, if at all, is that authority limited? *See* Jane E. Stromseth, *Rethinking War Powers: Congress, the President, and the United Nations*, 81 Geo. L.J. 597, 660-664 (1993).

Recall the debate in the Senate about approval of the U.N. Charter, *supra* p. 290. During that debate, a distinction was repeatedly drawn between what might be called retail and wholesale uses of force. Stromseth, *supra*, at 607-612. Early on, Senator Vandenberg responded to concerns about protecting Congress's war powers by emphasizing the distinction between presidential authority to use "the armed forces in preliminary national defense action... to stop a dispute before it graduate[d] into war" and Congress's authority to declare war. 91 Cong. Rec. 7957 (1945). Later, he elaborated on the former authority by suggesting that Congress used force "in a summary, preliminary, policing way...." *Id.* at 7992. Senator Pepper said that the distinction was between the use of "limited force" and "the whole force and strength of the United States." *Id.* at 8075. Can you articulate the distinction more clearly? How would you classify the naval war with France (the so-called Quasi-War) at the end of the eighteenth century? See *supra* p. 94. The Korean War? See *supra* p. 290. The Vietnam War? *See generally* Stromseth, *supra*, at 666; Peter Raven-Hansen, *Constitutional Constraints: The War Clause*, in *The U.S. Constitution and the Power to Go to War* 29, 41 (1994).

If you can make the distinction, does it justify presidentially ordered peace operations like Operation Restore Hope? Where does the President get authority to use "preliminary," "limited," or "summary" force for such operations? Senator Milliken suggested one possible answer during a colloquy with Secretary of State John Foster Dulles when he urged that "[t]he policing powers *traditionally exercised by the President* might possibly be kept in mind, and the war powers might be kept in Congress, thus preserving in symmetry all of constitutional powers of the Congress and the President." 91 Cong. Rec. 7987 (1945) (emphasis added). What limits, if any, does his answer suggest for presidentially ordered peace operations?

4. *Operation Restore Hope and the War Powers Resolution.* Did the deployments of U.S. armed forces in Somalia satisfy the War Powers Resolution, *supra* p. 240? Is 22 U.S.C. §287d-1, part of the U.N. Participation Act, *supra* p. 288, pertinent to this question? *See* Walker, *supra* p. 318 n.1, at 483. Congress has authorized the President to give up to $5 million of assistance to friendly countries and international organizations "for peacekeeping operations and other programs carried out in furtherance of the national security interests of the United States," including noncombatant assistance to the United Nations under the U.N. Participation Act. 22 U.S.C. §2348 (2000). But further assistance presumably requires additional legislation, unless the President has the constitutional authority to order assistance without prior congressional approval. Does this authorization satisfy the War Powers Resolution?

5. *Required Consultation.* Section 8153(1)(a) of the Defense Appropriations Act, 1994, *supra* p. 329, states the sense of Congress to forbid any use of the funds it appropriates for peacekeeping or peace-enforcing operations unless the President consults with Congress before the deployment, if possible, or immediately after. Is this provision constitutional? If you conclude that it is, does it necessarily follow that the consultation provision of the War Powers Resolution is also constitutional?

6. *United States Troops Under Foreign Command.* The first U.S. troops in Somalia were apparently placed under UNOSOM II command. The Clinton administration later asserted that "[o]n a case by case basis, the President will consider placing appropriate U.S. forces under the operational control of a competent UN commander for specific UN operations authorized by the Security Council." *The Clinton Administration's Policy on Reforming Multilateral Peace Operations*, May 1994, at 9 (summarizing key elements of a Presidential Decision Directive). By what authority may the President place U.S. armed forces under non-U.S. command? *See* James W. Houck, *The Commander in Chief and United Nations Charter Article 43: A Case of Irreconcilable Differences?*, 12 Dickinson J. Intl. L. 1, 14-28 (1993). United States forces have previously been placed under foreign command a number of times, especially during the world wars. *See generally* Andrew J. Bacevich, *The Use of Force in the Clinton Era: Continuity or Discontinuity?* 1 Chi. J. Intl. L. 375, 377-378 (2000) (asserting, with examples, that "the notion that American troops as a matter of principle do not serve under foreign command is simply ahistorical"); David Kaye, *Are There Limits to Military Alliance? Presidential Power to Place American Troops Under Non-American Commanders*, 5 Transnatl. L. & Contemp. Probs. 399 (1995); Walker, *supra*, at 441 n.53. Some have argued that the practice poses constitutional problems by ignoring constitutional limitations on delegations of federal power outside the national government and by

B. Crossing the Mogadishu Line

undermining accountability both to the President as Commander in Chief and, indirectly, to Congress. *See* John C. Yoo, *UN Wars, US War Powers*, 1 Chi. J. Intl. L. 355, 367-368 (2000). But could the President's deployment of U.S. troops under foreign command ever surrender his power to call them back or to override foreign commands?

Section 8151(b)(2)(B) of the Department of Defense Appropriations Act, 1994, *supra*, required the President to place the U.S. forces in Somalia under U.S. command and control. Is this requirement constitutional? The proposed Peace Powers Act of 1995, S. 5, 104th Cong. (1995), would have prohibited the President from "subordinat[ing] to the command or operational control of any foreign national" any U.S. forces participating in U.N. peacekeeping activity unless Congress enacts legislation specifically approving such subordination, or the President first submits to designated congressional committees documents showing that U.S. unit commanders retain certain identified command prerogatives and explaining why the proposed subordination does not violate the Constitution. Would this provision of the proposed Act violate the Constitution? *See* Office of Legal Counsel, *Placing of United States Armed Forces Under United Nations Operational or Tactical Control*, 20 Op. Off. Legal Counsel 182 (1996) (finding such restrictions unconstitutional).

7. *International Law and Peacemaking Interventions.* Most arguments defending the legality of presidentially ordered peace operations start with Security Council resolutions that these operations support. But is it self-evident that the resolutions themselves are lawful under international law, i.e., that the United Nations may lawfully intervene in a strictly civil war? *See* U.N. Charter art. 2, para. 7 ("Nothing contained in the present Charter shall authorize the United Nations to intervene in matters which are essentially within the domestic jurisdiction of any state . . . ; but this principle shall not prejudice the application of enforcement measures under Chapter VII.").

The U.N. peace operations in Iraq, Somalia, and Bosnia may "point to an emerging customary norm of U.N. humanitarian intervention in member states where humanitarian violations are severe and have the slightest transboundary effect." Fink, *supra* p. 319 n.2, at 45. Professor John Norton Moore has suggested that such intervention is permissible if: (a) there is an immediate threat of genocide or other widespread deprivation of human life in violation of international law; (b) peaceful techniques for protecting threatened rights have been exhausted; (c) effective action by international agencies or the United Nations is unavailable; (d) the contemplated use of force is the minimum necessary to protect the threatened rights and proportionate to the threat; (e) the intervention is promptly concluded consistent with its purpose; and (f) the intervention is promptly and fully reported to the Security Council. John N. Moore, *Toward an Applied Theory for the Regulation of Intervention*, in *Law and Civil War in the Modern World* 3, 24-25 (John Norton Moore ed., 1974). *See also* Nicholas J. Wheeler, *Saving Strangers: Humanitarian Intervention in International Society* (2000); Sean D. Murphy, *Humanitarian Intervention* (1996). What effect, if any, does the international legality of such operations have on the question of domestic U.S. authority for them?

C. STABILIZATION AND RECONSTRUCTION OPERATIONS IN AFGHANISTAN AND IRAQ[4]

Following the terrorist attacks of September 11, 2001, U.S. military forces and CIA special operations officers were deployed in Afghanistan in Operation Enduring Freedom to hunt down members of Al Qaeda and remove the Taliban government that had harbored them. On May 1, 2003, Secretary of Defense Donald Rumsfeld declared major combat operations in Afghanistan ended. The United States continued efforts through the United Nations to establish a broad-based Afghani government, leading to presidential elections in 2004.

Doing so, however, required provision of a secure environment and control or suppression of warlords and armed regional factions. Although security in Kabul, the capital, was left to an International Security Assistance Force (ISAF) of troops primarily from NATO nations, by mid-2005 11,000 U.S. soldiers were still hunting members of Al Qaeda and providing some security in areas outside Kabul, helping to form an Afghani military force, and deploying mixed military-civilian "Provincial Reconstruction Forces" in the countryside. At the same time, the United States engaged in an ambitious reconstruction effort under the auspices of USAID and the Department of State. In the interim, Taliban remnants—some of them apparently returned from or operating from across the border in Pakistan—mounted a low-level insurgency that continues (and may be expanding) at this writing.

Following the 2003 invasion of Iraq, President George W. Bush declared an end to major combat operations there on May 1, 2003. Although the Administration initially denied that there was any organized resistance, the CENTCOM commander eventually acknowledged that the United States was facing "a classical guerilla-type campaign," which caused 1,397 hostile fire deaths among U.S. troops between the May 1, 2003, "end" of major combat operations and January 16, 2006 (out of 2,242 total hostile fire deaths through that date). As of early 2006, there were still 153,000 U.S. troops deployed in Iraq, together with more than 20,000 military support personnel and 21,000 non-U.S. troops from a variety of foreign nations, and Congress had appropriated more than $250 billion cumulatively through fiscal year 2005 for military operations in Iraq. As of 2006, it was widely believed that the continued deployment of substantial U.S. military forces in Iraq would be needed for several more years. (By comparison, in the comparatively benign Bosnia and Kosovo regions, 7,000 NATO troops were still deployed nine years after the end of major hostilities there.)

Although the U.S. military inevitably has been engaged in some reconstruction efforts—sometimes as part of counter-insurgency campaigns—the lead responsibility for reconstruction of Iraq was assumed by the U.N.-recognized Coalition Provisional Authority from May 2003 to June 2004, and thereafter by the Department of State through the U.S. ambassador to Iraq, working with the Iraqi interim government. Through early 2005, $60 billion in U.S.

---

4. Except as otherwise noted, the background for this account is drawn from Serafino, *supra* p. 318; Steve Bowman, *Iraq: U.S. Military Operations* (Cong. Res. Serv. RL31701), May 9, 2006; U.S. Govt. Accountability Office, *Rebuilding Iraq: Actions Needed to Improve Use of Private Security Providers* (GAO-05-737), July 2005; Kenneth Katzman, *Afghanistan: Post-War Governance, Security, and U.S. Policy* (Cong. Res. Serv. RL30588), Aug. 23, 2006.

appropriations, Iraqi revenues and assets, and international donor pledges was made available to support relief and reconstruction.

While the U.S. military was tasked to protect Department of Defense civilians and contractors who directly support the military's mission in Iraq, for the most part civilian contractors who were engaged in reconstruction efforts, and even individual U.S. government agencies, had to contract for their own private security forces. It was estimated that by the end of 2005, one in every ten foreign soldiers in Iraq was an employee of a private military firm, although the lack of oversight of such firms makes such estimates guesswork. *See* Heather Carney, *Prosecuting the Lawless: Human Rights Abuses and Private Military Firms*, 74 Geo. Wash. L. Rev. 317, 327 (2006). Between the declared end of combat operations in May 2003 and mid-2005, more than 200 contractor personnel were killed in Iraq.

NOTES AND QUESTIONS

1. *Legal Authority for Stability Operations.* Recall the authorities for "necessary and appropriate" force in Afghanistan, *supra* p. 100, and Iraq, *supra* p. 305. *See also* 10 U.S.C. §401, *supra* p. 319. Do these authorities extend beyond the declared end of major combat operations? If so, for how long? Of course, any prolonged stability operation will require supplemental appropriations, as the operations in Afghanistan and Iraq have several times. Do such appropriations impliedly authorize or reauthorize the operations they fund? How, if at all, does the War Powers Resolution address these questions?

2. *Legal Controls for Private Security Contractors.* If the deployment of U.S. armed forces in stability operations is authorized, most of the remaining issues posed by such deployments are political issues, such as the need for the deployments; the division of labor for stability operations and reconstruction among U.S. military forces, private civilian contractors, and international forces; the effects of such deployments on U.S. war-fighting capability ("readiness"); and the desirability of reorganizing and training U.S. forces for such operations. One common answer to the last three concerns is that stability operations should be "privatized" by contracting them out to private contractors and third-party nationals. Indeed, such contractors may even be engaged to conduct traditionally governmental or even military functions, such as maintaining prisons and security checkpoints or interrogating prisoners.

Privatizing, however, poses its own legal problems. What law controls the contractors? U.S. domestic laws will rarely apply, given the presumption against extraterritoriality, and U.S. courts often may lack jurisdiction in disputes involving such contractors anyway. The Uniform Code of Military Justice applies to civilians accompanying armed forces only in declared wars. 10 U.S.C. §802(a)(10) (2000). Congress attempted to address the jurisdictional problem by enacting the Military Extraterritorial Jurisdiction Act of 2000 (MEJA). 18 U.S.C. §§3261-3267 (2000). MEJA provides for federal jurisdiction over crimes committed abroad by civilians who are "employed by or accompanying" the U.S. military, but it may leave significant gaps. *Id.* §3261(a)(1). We address MEJA's scope and related problems in the context of investigatory torture, *infra* p. 802.

A sense of the scope of problems that may arise from privatization is conveyed by a statutory requirement that the Department of Defense promulgate guidelines for dealing with private contractors in Iraq. Ronald W. Reagan National Defense Authorization Act for Fiscal Year 2005, Pub. L. No. 108-375, §1205, 118 Stat. 1811, 2083 (2004). The statute required the guidelines to address at least the following matters:

(1) Warning contractor security personnel of potentially hazardous situations.

(2) Coordinating the movement of contractor security personnel, especially through areas of increased risk or planned or ongoing military operations.

(3) Rapidly identifying contractor security personnel by members of the Armed Forces.

(4) Sharing relevant threat information with contractor security personnel and receiving information gathered by contractor security personnel for use by United States and coalition forces.

(5) Providing appropriate assistance to contractor personnel who become engaged in hostile situations.

(6) Providing medical assistance for, and evacuation of, contractor personnel who become casualties as a result of enemy actions.

(7) Investigating background and qualifications of contractor security personnel and organizations.

(8) Establishing rules of engagement for armed contractor security personnel, and ensuring proper training and compliance with the rules of engagement.

(9) Establishing categories of security, intelligence, law enforcement, and criminal justice functions that are —

    (A) inherently governmental functions under Subpart 7.5 of the Federal Acquisition Regulation; or

    (B) although not inherently governmental functions, should not ordinarily be performed by contractors in areas of operations.

(10) Establishing procedures for making and documenting determinations about which security, intelligence, law enforcement, and criminal justice functions will be performed by military personnel and which will be performed by private companies. [*Id.*]

But how should such "guidelines" be enforced? If they are made part of the private contracts, is monitoring and enforcement left to a contracting officer? What then happens to "unity of command" in the field? *See generally* Frank Camm & Victoria A. Greenfield, *How Should the Army Use Contractors on the Battlefield?* (Rand Arroyo Center 2005); Karen L. Douglas, *Contractors Accompanying the Force: Empowering Commanders With Emergency Change Authority*, 55 A.F. L. Rev. 127 (2004); David Isenberg, British American Security Information Council, *A Fistful of Contractors: The Case for a Pragmatic Assessment of Private Military Companies in Iraq* (2004).

III
Conducting Intelligence Operations Abroad

14

Origins and Evolving Limits of Intelligence Operations

The purpose of the three chapters in this part of the book is to examine the authority for and control of intelligence operations. According to Judge Posner,

> The goal of intelligence is to learn about the intentions and capabilities of potential enemies.... Intelligence data are collected by spies, by scrutiny of publicly available ("open source") materials such as newspapers, magazines, the Web, and scientific and technical journals, and by technical means of surveillance, such as imagery (aerial and satellite photography) and signals (electronic surveillance) intelligence. The data are given to analysts to collate and interpret, and the results of their analysis are forwarded to the officials responsible for policy. So there are three levels: *collection, analysis,* and *action,* the last being the response to analysis by the officials who are authorized to act in accordance with what intelligence reveals. [Richard A. Posner, *Preventing Surprise Attacks: Intelligence Reform in the Wake of 9/11* (2005), at 99-100.]

Changes in technology and in the ways of the world have added a dizzying capacity to gather information through technical means, while the explosion of information sources has made information easier to come by and less trustworthy. As collection has become more complex, protection of intelligence processes from penetration has also become a major activity within the intelligence community. (The parameters of information security are considered in Chapters 33-37.) At the other end of the spectrum, covert paramilitary operations—undertaken to influence events in another nation in a way that is not attributable to the United States—add new dimensions to the allocation of war powers addressed in earlier chapters.

For most of our post-World War II history, the CIA and other members of the intelligence community targeted the former Soviet Union or perceived communist threats around the world—in Southeast Asia, the Middle East, Latin America, and the Caribbean. The U.S. intelligence agencies conducted propaganda and various political actions in an effort to influence other governments. Support was given to overthrowing governments, for example, in Iran,

Guatemala, Cuba, and Chile. Even political assassination was planned, and unsavory assets and groups, who were later revealed to be engaged in drug-trafficking and human rights abuses, were used to further U.S. objectives.

Revelations about secret aspects of the Vietnam War and related disruption of domestic protest groups, along with congressional investigations into intelligence operations excesses around the world through the early 1970s, began a reform process that truly took root only after the collapse of the Soviet Union. Another event that provoked reforms was the Iran-Contra Affair, explored in Chapter 15, which showed that rogue covert operations are sometimes still undertaken.

The end of the Cold War and the emergence of "asymmetric" attacks on the United States presented unprecedented challenges for our intelligence agencies. Instead of a single-minded focus on the Soviet Union, intelligence has had to confront a wide range of targets across the globe, including states and potentially lethal non-state actors intent on doing harm to the United States. As technology ushered in an information era, the intelligence challenge of digging for secrets has been replaced by the need to sift through masses of data in pursuit of a reliable understanding of an intelligence target. That terrorists would infiltrate our cities and then succeed in doing catastrophic harm to our nation on 9/11 underscored our vulnerability, while it caused significant re-thinking about how our intelligence structure is organized and how our assets are deployed.

Intelligence operations and objectives are currently experiencing a remarkable change. Covert operations now seek to disrupt terrorist groups and ward off their planned attacks, to foil narcotics shipments, and to thwart financial transactions of black market weapons traders. Computer technology is used increasingly to disrupt financial activities of hostile governments and to mine masses of data in pursuit of suspicious persons and groups. Activities like influencing elections abroad or spreading democratic ideas and programs, once covert, are carried out in the open, either by government programs or privately.

What do intelligence operations look like? What forms do they take? According to Gregory Treverton, intelligence operations are "kindred" but "separable":

> Liaison activity involves sharing information and working with foreign intelligence and police services. The CIA maintains liaisons with 400 different foreign intelligence, security, and police services around the world. These connections involve varying degrees of cooperation and competition.... In the CIA's relations with traditional counterparts where the relationship is of long standing, the equation is weighted toward cooperation: no spying on each other, though nothing requires that each partner tell the other the whole truth.... Other liaisons, though, are "marriages of convenience" rife with "infidelity." The CIA uses such arrangements to get access to a foreign service and its operatives, while the foreign service seeks something from the CIA as well, usually help or information. Liaison services carry risk (the extent depending on the country) because they associate the CIA with the actions of those foreign services and the foreigners who staff them.
>
> [Liaison may be distinguished] from espionage—persuading with money, ideology, or other inducements to provide information secretly on their policies and institutions. Common usage labels CIA officers as "spies," but they are not. The spying is done by foreigners whom those CIA officers recruit. The CIA

spymasters, known as "case officers," then manage (or "run") their "assets," or "cases"—the foreigners who do the spying.

Covert action is the obverse of espionage. Both depend on secret links to foreigners. But espionage requires case officers to be patient, passive, and quiet as they wait for the information to flow from the foreign spy to them.... The aim of covert action, by contrast, is to influence events in the short run in foreign countries. The case officer asks the foreign connection to act and to do so in a specified time frame. With timely action, the risk that the secret connection to the CIA and to the United States will be revealed goes up. These differences—action versus passivity, short-run versus long-range goals—lead to organizational cultures for spying and covert action. At the CIA's beginning, the United States had for a time two clandestine services, one for spying and one for covert action. That proved unwise, as the two services found themselves competing for agents, but the tension between the two clandestine tasks is inherent.

Finally, most spy novels... are not about either espionage or covert action but about counterespionage; not about seeking information or influencing events but about detecting when one's own service has been penetrated by a "mole" or double agent, pretending... to be a loyal officer but in fact working for an enemy service. [Gregory F. Treverton, *Reshaping National Intelligence for an Age of Information* 137-138 (2003).]

In this chapter we trace the origins and sources of intelligence operations authority. We consider whether the executive branch is empowered by the Constitution or by legislation to act alone in this sphere, and we return to the arguments for authority derived from usage and inherent power. Then we bring our study forward through a discussion of the evolution of legal controls over the intelligence community, including those enacted in intelligence reform legislation in 2004. Examples of twenty-first century intelligence operations are given to provide context and better understanding of the legal controls. In Chapter 15 covert operations are examined separately, as we assess the category of intelligence operation that most nearly calls into question the constitutional separation of war powers. In Chapter 16 a range of new and continuing problems in the field are addressed, including the domestic collection of intelligence, the use of so-called dirty assets, and the conduct of intelligence operations by military agencies.

A. THE PLAYERS AND PROCESSES OF INTELLIGENCE

Select Committee to Study Governmental Operations with Respect to Intelligence Activities (Church Committee), Foreign and Military Intelligence
S. Rep. No. 94-755, Book I, at 17-19 (1976)

In theory at least [intelligence] operations can be described in simple terms by the following cycle:

— Those who use intelligence, the "consumers," indicate the kind of information needed.

— These needs are translated into concrete "requirements" by senior intelligence managers.
— The requirements are used to allocate resources to the "collectors" and serve to guide their efforts.
— The collectors obtain the required information or "raw intelligence."
— The finished intelligence is distributed to the consumer and the intelligence managers who state new needs, define new requirements, and make necessary adjustments in the intelligence programs to improve effectiveness and efficiency.

In reality this pattern is barely recognizable.

There are many different consumers, from the President to the weapons designer. Their needs can conflict. Consumers rarely take the time to define their intelligence needs and even if they do so there is no effective and systematic mechanism for translating them into intelligence requirements.

Therefore, intelligence requirements reflect what intelligence managers think their organizations can produce. Since there are many managers and little central control, each is relatively free to set his own requirements. Resources therefore tend to be allocated according to the priorities and concerns of the various intelligence bureaucracies. Most intelligence collection operations are part of other organizations—the Department of Defense, the Department of State—and so their requirements and their consumers are often the first to be served.

Collecting intelligence is not an automatic process. There are many different kinds of intelligence, from a radar return to an indiscreet remark, and the problems in acquiring it vary greatly. Information that is wanted may not be available, or years may be required to develop an agency or a technical device to get it. Meanwhile intelligence agencies collect what they can.

In the world of bureaucracy, budgets, programs, procurement, and managers, the needs of the analyst can be lost in the shuffle. There has been an explosion in the volume and quality of raw intelligence but no equivalent increase in the capacity of analytical capabilities. As a result, "raw" intelligence increasingly dominates "finished" intelligence; analysts find themselves on a treadmill where it is difficult to do more than summarize and put in context the intelligence flowing in. There is little time or reward for the task of providing insight.

In the end the consumer, particularly at the highest levels of the government, finds that his most important questions are not only unanswered, but sometimes not even addressed.

To some extent, all this is in the nature of things. Many questions cannot be answered. The world of intelligence is dominated by uncertainty and chaos, and those in the intelligence bureaucracy, as elsewhere in the Government, try to defend themselves against uncertainties in ways which militate against efficient management and accountability.

Beyond this is the fact that the organizations of the intelligence community must operate in peace but be prepared for war. This has an enormous impact on the kind of intelligence that is sought, the way resources are allocated, and the way the intelligence community is organized and managed.

Equally important, the instruments of intelligence have been forged into weapons of psychological, political, and paramilitary warfare. This has had a profound effect on the perspective and preoccupations of the leadership of the intelligence community, downgrading concerns for intelligence in relation to the effective execution of operations.

These problems alone would undermine any rational scheme, but it is also important to recognize that the U.S. intelligence community is not the work of a single author. It has evolved from an interaction of the above internal factors and the external forces that have shaped America's history since the end of the Second World War.

NOTES AND QUESTIONS

1. *Setting Requirements.* Intelligence serves policymakers and helps to shape policy. That policy in turn determines the need for additional intelligence and guides intelligence operations. There is, however, no formal mechanism for translating policy into intelligence requirements. Who should set intelligence objectives? How should those objectives be communicated to intelligence officials, following what kind of process?

2. *Collection.* Technical means offer tremendous advantages in collecting large volumes of information. Technical collection is, however, very expensive. Human intelligence is cheaper and may be more narrowly focused. How should these collection trade-offs be made, and by whom? If the mass of data collected through technical means cannot realistically be processed and analyzed, how should collection priorities be modified?

3. *Analysis, Delivery, and Consumption.* Some intelligence products are widely known—the President's Daily Briefings (PDBs), for example, and National Intelligence Estimates (NIEs). Analysis of intelligence and other, less well-known products are discussed in this and the next two chapters. How do you suppose it is decided which material collected is important enough to report, in whatever form? Who should receive intelligence reports—in the executive branch and in Congress? How rapidly should the information be provided, in how much detail, and in what form?

4. *Keeping the Players Straight.* The structure and principal players in the intelligence community have changed over time. The chart on p. 365 reflects the arrangement in late 2005. Consult the chart whenever you are not sure of who the players are or when you want to know their relationship to each other and to other actors in the executive branch.

B. INTELLIGENCE OPERATIONS: ORIGINS AND PRACTICE

1. National Security Secrecy: The Original Understanding

Events in eighteenth century England and America reflected a trend toward publicity and away from secrecy in government. In England, press licensing was abandoned and libel law became more permissive. Parliament's proceedings began to be legally reported, and Parliament often asserted its power as a "grand inquest of the nation" successfully to make inquiries of the Crown. The American colonies and then the states likewise typically reported legislative proceedings, and eight states explicitly provided that the legislature could obtain records maintained by the executive.

On the other hand, sessions and records of the Continental Congress were initially kept secret, a response to wartime conditions. Daniel Hoffman, *Governmental Secrecy and the Founding Fathers* 13-14 (1981). Publication of congressional proceedings began in 1777, although regular public sessions were not held, and some diplomatic, financial, and military matters were handled by congressional boards or committees in secret. *Id.* at 14-18.

The 1787 Constitutional Convention was itself conducted secretly; the debates were not officially recorded, and the official journal of formal motions and roll call votes was available only to the delegates. Although the delegates agreed that secrecy was essential until a complete plan could be developed, there was "a torrent of wild speculation about what was afoot, until rumors that a foreign prince was to be offered the crown had to be countered by denials leaked to the press." *Id.* at 21.

There was an extended debate among the Convention delegates over congressional secrecy. Indeed, Elbridge Gerry and George Mason gave as one reason for their refusal to sign the completed Constitution the provision in Article I, Section 5, which permitted each House of Congress to keep its proceedings secret. *Id.* at 30.

There seemed to be less concern about presidential secrecy.

> Among the many advantages of a single executive, delegates repeatedly mentioned the greater secrecy with which one man could conduct the nation's foreign affairs. Yet the framers realized that this capability posed a threat to the democratic concept of accountability. On June 4, for example, George Mason said:
>
>> The chief advantages which have been urged in favor of unity in the Executive, are the secrecy, the dispatch, the vigor and energy which the government will derive from it, especially in time of war. That these are great advantages I will most readily allow.... Yet perhaps a little reflection may incline us to doubt whether these advantages are not greater in theory than in practice, or lead us to enquire whether there is not some pervading principle in republican government which sets at naught & tramples upon that boasted superiority....
>
> ... The primary safeguard against tyranny was that the president's power to take independent initiatives was carefully circumscribed. His main duty was to execute the laws passed by Congress, and his discretion was further limited by congressional control of the purse strings. In fact, for the most part the framers were less concerned with restraining the president than with making it possible for him to provide a modicum of leadership. They feared that a Congress jealous of its prerogatives would not respond favorably to legislative proposals coming from the executive branch. It was the desire to legitimize such proposals that called forth an explicit statement of the president's right and duty to keep Congress informed. [*Id.* at 31-32.]

Thus, Article II, Section 3 includes the requirement that the President "shall from time to time give to the Congress Information of the State of the Union,

B. Intelligence Operations: Origins and Practice

and recommend to their Consideration such Measures as he shall judge necessary and expedient." This provision, with its mandatory language, was reportedly adopted by the Framers without controversy. *Id.* at 32.

NOTES AND QUESTIONS

1. *Keeping Congress in the Dark?* If intelligence operations must necessarily be kept secret from the public to accomplish their goals, must they also be kept secret from Congress? May the President constitutionally refuse to divulge information about such operations — or even the fact of their existence — to Congress? What, if any, importance should we attach to the Framers' failure to prescribe a rule for congressional requests for information from the executive?

2. *Executive Privilege.* One decidedly pro-executive view of the President's right to withhold information from the Congress concerns the doctrine of executive privilege, considered *supra* p. 88. The argument is that the Framers were aware of the existence of an executive privilege and that they did nothing to cast doubt on its vitality when it was invoked by President Washington to withhold from the House papers relating to negotiation of the Jay Treaty. *See* Hoffman, *supra,* at 4; Louis Henkin, *Foreign Affairs and the Constitution* 116 (2d. ed. 1996); Arthur Schlesinger, *The Imperial Presidency* 333 (1973). But of course the House has no explicit role in treaty approval. U.S. Const. art. II, §2. Does the doctrine of executive privilege suggest a broader claim of national security secrecy for the executive today? A vigorous defense of presidential secrecy generally and of the executive privilege in particular may be found in Robert F. Turner, *The Constitution and the Iran-Contra Affair: Was Congress the Real Lawbreaker?,* 11 Hous. J. Intl. L. 83 (1988). *See also* John Lehman, *Making War* 185-199 (1992).

3. *Congressional Power.* Professor Berger makes the opposing case for the congressional prerogative:

> One to whom a duty runs, said Chief Justice Marshall, has a correlative right to require performance of the duty;[137] what the President is under a duty to furnish to Congress "from time to time" could be requested at its convenience. That the President was given no discretion as to what to furnish or refuse emerges from the next following clause of Article II, §3: "and recommend to their consideration such measures as he shall judge necessary and expedient." No such discretion limits his duty to supply information and it is reasonable to conclude that none was conferred.
>
> The "State of the Union" clause has too mechanically been associated with annual presidential messages, but Justice Story properly read it more broadly. The President, he stated,

---

137. Marbury v. Madison, 5 U.S. (1 Cranch) 137, 162-166 (1803).

must possess more extensive sources of information, as well in regard to domestic as foreign affairs, than can belong to Congress. The true working of the laws... [is] more readily seen, and more constantly under the view of the executive.... There is great wisdom, therefore... in requiring the President to lay before Congress all facts and information which may assist their deliberations.[139]

An annual message does not exhaust the duty to furnish information "from time to time": the duty to furnish such information is the reciprocal of the familiar legislative power to inquire.... [Raoul Berger, *Executive Privilege: A Constitutional Myth* 37-38 (1974).]

Are you persuaded by Berger's interpretation? If the text does not limit executive discretion explicitly, is there any reason that it should be read in the context of national security disputes as Berger interprets it? Would it make more sense to resolve disputes concerning congressional access to executive branch information by employing the sort of balancing process reserved for shared powers disputes? *See* Peter Raven-Hansen & William C. Banks, *Pulling the Purse Strings of the Commander in Chief*, 80 U. Va. L. Rev. 833, 923-942 (1994). See also *supra* p. 57.

4. *Solutions in the Political Process?* Yet another interpretation of the original understanding is that the Framers did not want a constitutional rule for secrecy. Instead, they wanted disputes to be decided in the political process. *See* Schlesinger, *supra,* at 396, 410. This interpretation presumes that the judiciary would not participate in such disputes, there being no rule for decision. Is this a fair reading of Articles I and II? Is the secrecy system that would emerge under this view harmonious with other provisions in the Constitution? *See* United States v. American Tel. & Tel. Co., 551 F.2d 384 (D.C. Cir. 1976), 567 F.2d 121 (D.C. Cir. 1977), noted *supra* p. 121.

5. *Secrecy and Ratification.* During the ratification debates, secrecy issues received relatively little attention. *See* Hoffman, *supra,* at 34-38; Abraham Sofaer, *War, Foreign Affairs, and Constitutional Power* 53-56 (1976). The only explicit mention of secrecy in the *Federalist Papers* was Jay's reference in Number 64 to the need for "perfect *secrecy* and immediate dispatch" in the negotiation of treaties. *The Federalist No. 64,* at 392 (John Jay) (Clinton Rossiter ed., 1961). Jay also referred to "the business of intelligence," when "the most useful intelligence may be obtained if the persons possessing it can be relieved of the apprehensions of discovery." *Id.* Of course, ratification would not have occurred without the promise of the addition of a bill of rights to the Constitution. Should we infer that the First Amendment's speech, press, assembly, and petition freedoms have a role to play in assuring the free flow of government information? See generally Chapters 35-37.

---

139. 2 Joseph Story, *Commentaries on the Constitution of the United States* §1561 (Boston, 1905).

B. Intelligence Operations: Origins and Practice

2. Intelligence Operations: Practice and Inherent Power

Select Committee to Study Governmental Operations with Respect to Intelligence Activities (Church Committee), Foreign and Military Intelligence

S. Rep. No. 94-755, Book I, at 15 (1976) [hereinafter Church Comm. Rep.]

Permanent institutions for the conduct of secret foreign and military intelligence activities are a relatively new feature of American government. Secure behind two oceans and preoccupied with the settlement of a continent, America had no permanent foreign intelligence establishment for more than a century and a half. In times of crisis, Americans improvised their intelligence operations. In times of peace, such operations were not needed and were allowed to lie fallow.

Despite the experience of the First World War, Americans believed they could continue this pattern well into the Twentieth Century. The military services developed important technical intelligence capabilities, such as the breaking of the Japanese code, but the American public remained unaware of the importance of effective intelligence for its security. As a world power, the United States came late to intelligence. It came on December 7, 1941, when Japan attacked Pearl Harbor.

Consider the following arguments from the nation's history for and against intelligence operations authority for the President.

Statement of Mitchell Rogovin, Special Counsel to the Director of Central Intelligence

Hearings Before the House Select Committee on Intelligence, 94th Cong., Part 5, at 1729, 1732-1733 (1976) [hereinafter Rogovin Memorandum]

...Beginning with George Washington, almost every President has appointed special agents to engage in certain activities with, or against, foreign countries.... In the first century of the Nation's existence alone, more than 400 such agents were appointed by the President.

Early examples of covert action performed by these agents are legion. The following three are typical: One, in 1843, President Tyler secretly dispatched an agent to Great Britain to meet privately with individual government and opposition leaders and to attempt to influence public opinion with respect to matters affecting the two countries, without ever disclosing that he was a representative of the U.S. Government; two, in 1845, when President Polk feared that Mexico was on the verge of ceding California to Great Britain, he secretly dispatched an agent to California for the purpose of "defeating any attempt which may be made by foreign governments to acquire a control over that country"; and three, in 1869, when the United States had territorial designs on central and western Canada, President Grant sent an agent to that area to foment sentiment for separation from Canada and union with the United States. These examples show that the practice of appointment of special agents by the President for the purpose of conducting covert action in foreign countries is deeply rooted in our national history....

... Consequently, when the CIA was established in 1947, and when, shortly thereafter, it was delegated the responsibility for covert action, there was no attempt by the President to assert or exercise any new or theretofore unrecognized executive authority; he was merely delegating to the CIA various executive functions which were previously assigned to ad hoc special agents and other executive agencies....

Robert Borosage, Para-Legal Authority and Its Peril
40 Law & Contemp. Probs. 166, 173-174 (Summer 1976)

What of the 400 agents in the first hundred years or the "legion" of precedents cited in the [Rogovin] Memorandum? These refer to special agents selected by Presidents to represent them abroad.... [T]hey are agents of the President rather than officials of the government— "They have an employment, not an office"; their duties are generally special and temporary.

The "characteristic situations" in which special agents have been used include: "ceremonial occasions"; to speak for the President personally; international conferences and delegations;...contacts with unrecognized states; technical matters requiring a high degree of expertness. In effect, then, the Rogovin Memorandum would have us consider the dispatch of Chief Justice Warren to DeGaulle's funeral as a precedent for covert action....

This is the longstanding practice from which the Rogovin Memorandum would derive a constitutional power for the President to employ a secret agency in widespread covert operations abroad. More than a difference of degree reaching a difference in kind, it is rather a simple form of sophistry to justify this dangerous agency on the basis of an inapposite tradition. The tortured logic of the Memorandum was not forwarded without reason, however. The CIA traces its birth back to an executive order issued by President Roosevelt in 1941, establishing the Office of Coordination and Information in the White House. Roosevelt issued the order four months before Pearl Harbor on the basis of "the authority vested in me as President of the United States...." Eleven months later, OCI became the Office of Strategic Services, a transformation directed by "military order," and OSS undertook both clandestine intelligence collection and para-military operations (covert action) throughout the war.

In 1945, OSS was disbanded by executive order, but four months later President Truman established the National Intelligence Authority and the Central Intelligence Group by a "Presidential Directive" issued without any proclaimed basis in law. The directive authorized the CIG to plan, develop and coordinate "such other functions and duties related to intelligence affecting the national security as the President...may from time to time direct." Thus, the CIA's immediate forebears were established by executive orders issued in peacetime. Although the CIG reportedly had no covert action arm, the Rogovin Memorandum claims...that it did engage in such activities. Only some notion of inherent power can legitimate this activity *post facto*. The Rogovin Memorandum seeks to legitimate this ancestry by inventing a birthright in inherent power.

NOTES AND QUESTIONS

1. *Secrecy and Inherent Power.* General claims for inherent presidential power in national security affairs are reviewed in Chapters 3 and 4. Arguments to support the more specific claim that the President may unilaterally engage the nation in covert intelligence operations, including paramilitary warfare, typically rely on the perceived need for secrecy. *See* Rogovin Memorandum, *supra* p. 347, at 1731-1733. Is there an inherent executive power to act secretly? *See* John N. Moore & Robert F. Turner, *The Legal Structure of Defense Organization* 94-97 (1986). Does the Declare War Clause represent a check on that power? *See* Charles Lofgren, *War-Making Under the Constitution: The Original Understanding,* 81 Yale L.J. 672, 689-697 (1972); Jules Lobel, *Covert War and Congressional Authority: Hidden War and Forgotten Power,* 134 U. Pa. L. Rev. 1035, 1078-1085 (1986); Louis Fisher, *Presidential War Power* 236-239 (2d ed. 2004).

2. *A Variable Power?* To what extent does the authority to act secretly depend on the nature of the intelligence activity at issue? Is there constitutional authority to collect intelligence? If so, what is the source of that authority?

3. *Custom and Secrecy.* Recall the theories of congressional acquiescence and executive usage from Chapters 3, 8, and 10. What is the significance of executive usage for the legality of intelligence operations?

C. INTELLIGENCE COLLECTION: THE "INTS"

Although all of the intelligence activities reviewed below were conducted during the Cold War years, the law of intelligence grew up chiefly around several covert action issues: authorities, spending, assassination, and oversight. Covert operations are examined separately in Chapter 15.

The Cold War and a preoccupation with the Soviet Union dominated the intelligence agenda until the fall of the Berlin Wall in 1989. From 1989 until the September 11 terrorist attacks in 2001, there was no comparably focused intelligence mission. September 11 provided a mission. The dominant role and most important legal questions concerning intelligence now revolve around countering the ongoing threat of terrorism.

Intelligence collection has been the core of the intelligence function. Depending on the nature of the information sought, differing means are employed to collect it. In this section, we survey briefly the range of intelligence collection disciplines and how intelligence activities evolved from 1947 to the present.

Intelligence collection is engaged in by people — human intelligence or espionage (HUMINT) — and by machines — imagery intelligence (IMINT), signals intelligence (SIGINT), and measurement and signatures intelligence (MASINT). Except for open-source intelligence (OSINT), each of the INTs has a self-contained process, from collection to delivery. This tendency toward "stovepipes" is exacerbated by an intentional redundancy in the separate INTs. By sending different collection systems in pursuit of the same intelligence we hope to learn from the shared perspectives they offer. We also compensate in one INT for a shortcoming in another.

Mark M. Lowenthal, Intelligence: From Secrets to Policy
pp. 80-102 (3d ed. 2006)

IMINT

...is a direct descendant of the brief practice of sending soldiers up in balloons during the U.S. Civil War. In World War I and World War II, both sides used airplanes to obtain photos. Airplanes are still employed, but several nations now utilize imagery satellites. In the United States, the National Reconnaissance Office (NRO) develops these satellites. The National Geospatial-Intelligence Agency (which was the National Imagery and Mapping Agency, NIMA, until 2003) is responsible for processing and exploiting imagery. Some imagery also comes via the Defense Department's airborne systems, such as unmanned aerial vehicles (UAVs), or drones....

Imagery offers a number of advantages over other collection means. First, it is sometimes graphic and compelling. When shown to policymakers, an easily interpreted image can be worth a thousand words. Second, imagery is easily understood much of the time by policymakers. Even though few of them, if any, are trained imagery analysts, all are accustomed to seeing and interpreting images....

Imagery also suffers from a number of problems. The very graphic quality that is an advantage is also a disadvantage. An image can be too compelling, leading to hasty or ill-formed decisions or to the exclusion of other, more subtle intelligence that is contradictory. Also, the intelligence on an image may not be self-evident; it may require interpretation by trained photo interpreters who can see things that the untrained person cannot. At times, the policymakers must take on faith that the skilled analysts are correct.

Another disadvantage of imagery is that it is a snapshot, a picture of a particular place at a particular time.... Imagery is a static piece of intelligence, revealing something about where and when it was taken but nothing about what happened before or after....

Because details about U.S. imagery capabilities have become better known, states can take steps to deceive collection — through the use of camouflage or dummies — or to preclude collection by conducting certain activities at times when they are unlikely or less likely to be observed.

The war against terrorism led to two major developments in the use of imagery. First, the government greatly expanded its use of commercial imagery. In October 2001, the NGA (then known as NIMA) bought exclusive and perpetual rights to all imagery of Afghanistan taken by IKONOS satellite, operated by the Space Imaging Company.... [This] expanded the overall collection capability of the United States and allowed it to reserve more sophisticated imagery capabilities for those areas where they were most needed, while IKONOS took up other collection tasks.... At the same time, foreign governments that may be hostile to the United States or may see the Afghanistan campaign as a means of gauging U.S. military capabilities were denied access to imagery. This purchase also denied the use of this commercial imagery to news media, which might be eager to use it as a means of reporting and assessing the conduct and success of the war....

SIGNALS INTELLIGENCE

SIGINT is a twentieth-century phenomenon. British intelligence pioneered the field during World War I, successfully intercepting German communications by tapping underwater cables. The most famous product of this work was the Zimmermann Telegram, a German offer to Mexico of an anti-U.S. alliance that Britain made available to the United States without revealing how it was obtained. With the advent of radio communications, cable taps were augmented by the ability to pluck signals from the air. The United States also developed a successful signals intercept capability that survived World War I. Prior to World War II the United States broke Japan's Purple code; Britain, via ULTRA, read German codes.

Today signals intelligence can be gathered by Earth-based collectors—ships, planes, ground sites or satellites. Again, U.S. SIGINT satellites are built by the NRO. The National Security Agency is responsible for both carrying out U.S. signals intelligence activities and protecting the United States against hostile SIGINT.

SIGINT consists of several different types of intercepts. The term is often used to refer to the interception of communications between two parties, which is also known as communications intelligence (COMINT). SIGINT can also refer to the pickup of data relayed by weapons during tests which is sometimes called telemetry intelligence (TELINT). Finally, SIGINT can refer to the pickup of electronic emissions from modern weapons and tracking systems (military and civil), which are useful means of gauging their capabilities, such as range and frequencies on which systems operate. This is sometimes referred to as electronic intelligence (ELINT).

The ability to intercept communications is highly important, since it gives insight into what is being said, planned, and considered. It comes as close as one can, from a distance, to reading the other side's mind, a goal that cannot be achieved by imagery. Reading the actual messages and analyzing what they mean is called *content analysis*. Tracking communications also gives a good indication *and warning*. ...

COMINT has some weaknesses. First and foremost, it depends on the presence of communications that can be intercepted. If the target goes silent or opts to communicate via secure landlines instead of through the air, then the ability to undertake COMINT ceases to exist. Perhaps the landlines can be tapped, but doing so is a more difficult task than remote interception from a ground site or satellite. The target can also begin to *encrypt*—or code—its communications. Within the offensive/defensive struggle over SIGINT is a second struggle, that between encoders and codebreakers, or *cryptographers*.... Computers greatly increase the ability to construct complex, one-time use codes. Meanwhile, computers also make it more possible to attack these codes. Finally, the target can use false transmissions as a means of creating less compromising patterns or of subsuming important communications amid a flood of meaningless ones—in effect, increasing the ratio of noise to signals.

Another issue is the vast quantity of communications now available: telephones of all sorts, faxes, e-mails, and so on.... Even a focused collection plan collects more COMINT than can be processed and exploited. One means of coping with this is the *key-word search*, in which the collected data are fed into computers that look out for specific words or phrases. The words are used as indicators of the likely value of an intercept.... The war against terrorism has underscored a growing concern for SIGINT. As with the other collection disciplines, SIGINT was developed to collect intelligence on the Soviet Union and other nations. Terrorist cells offer much smaller signatures, which may not be susceptible to interception by remote SIGINT sensors. Therefore, a growing view is that future SIGINT will have to rely on sensors that have been physically placed close to the target by humans. In effect, HUMINT will become the enabler for SIGINT....

HUMAN INTELLIGENCE

HUMINT is espionage—spying—and is sometimes referred to as the world's second-oldest profession. It is as old as the Bible. Joshua sent two spies into Canaan before leading the Jewish people across the Jordan River. Spying is what most people think about when they hear the word "intelligence," whether they conjure up famous spies from history such as Nathan Hale or Mata Hari (both failures) or the many fictional spies such as James Bond. In the United States HUMINT is largely the responsibility of the CIA, through its Directorate of Operations (DO). DIA [Defense Intelligence Agency] also has a HUMINT capability with the Defense Humint Service, which it has sought to expand since the war in Afghanistan.

HUMINT largely involves sending agents to foreign countries, where they attempt to recruit foreign nationals to spy.... [Agents must] identif[y] individuals who have access to the information that the United States may desire... gain[] their confidence and assess[] their weaknesses and susceptibility to being recruited... [and] mak[e] a *pitch* to them, suggesting a relationship. A source may accept a pitch for a variety of reasons: money, disaffection with their own government, blackmail, or thrills. Once the pitch has been accepted, the agent must meet with his sources [assets] regularly to receive information, holding meetings in a manner and in places that will reduce the risk of being caught and then transmitting the information back home....

In addition to gaining the skills required for this activity, agents have to maintain their cover stories—the overt lives that give them a plausible reason for being in that foreign nation....

In addition to recruiting foreign nationals, HUMINT agents may undertake more direct spying, such as stealing documents or planting sensors. Some of their information may come through direct observation of activity....

An important adjunct to one's own HUMINT capabilities are those of allied or friendly services. Known as foreign liaison relationships, they offer several important advantages. First, the friendly service has greater familiarity with its own region. Second, its government may maintain a different pattern of relations with other states, more friendly in some cases or even having diplomatic relations where one's own government does not. These HUMINT-to-HUMINT

C. Intelligence Collection: The "INTS"

relationships are somewhat formal in nature and tend to be symbiotic. They also entail risks, as one can never be entirely sure of the liaison partner's security procedures.... Furthermore, some liaison relationships may be with intelligence services that do not have the same standards in terms of operational limits, acceptable activities, and other criteria. A choice therefore has to be made between the value of the information being sought or exchanged and the larger question of the propriety of a relationship with this service....

Espionage provides a very small part of the intelligence that is collected. IMINT and SIGINT produce a greater volume of intelligence. But HUMINT, like SIGINT, has the major advantage of affording access to what is being said, planned, and thought. Moreover, clandestine human access to another government also may offer opportunities to influence that government by feeding it false or deceptive information. For intelligence targets where the technical infrastructure may be irrelevant as a fruitful target—such as terrorism, narcotics, or international crime, where the "signature" of activities is rather small—HUMINT may be the only available source.

HUMINT also has disadvantages. First, it cannot be done remotely, as is the case with various types of technical collection. It requires proximity and access and therefore must contend with the counterintelligence capabilities of the other side. It is also far riskier, as it jeopardizes individuals, and, if they are caught, could have political ramifications that are less likely to occur with technical collectors....

Like all the other collection INTs, HUMINT is susceptible to deception....

OPEN-SOURCE INTELLIGENCE

To some, OSINT may seem like a contradiction in terms. How can information that is openly available be considered intelligence?... OSINT includes a wide variety of information and sources:

- Media: newspapers, magazines, radio, television, and computer-based information.
- Public data: government reports, official data such as budgets, demographics, hearings, legislative debates, press conference speeches.
- Professional and academic: conferences, symposia, professional associations, academic papers, and experts....

The major advantage of OSINT is its accessibility, although it still requires collection....

The main disadvantage of OSINT is its volume. In many ways, it represents the worst wheat and chaff problem. Some argue that the so-called information revolution has made OSINT more difficult without a corresponding increase in usable intelligence. Computers have increased the ability to manipulate information; however, the amount of derived intelligence has not increased apace....

NOTES AND QUESTIONS

1. *The Players.* An intelligence community organization chart showing the various member agencies as they existed in mid-2006 is set forth *infra*

p. 365. You may find it helpful in relating the INTs to the agencies that conduct them and in understanding the relationships among the agencies. These relationships, as well as the INTs described above, feature prominently in our examination of intelligence operations issues in Chapters 15 and 16 and in the terrorism chapters that follow.

2. *Redundancy.* Recall that one aim of intelligence collection is redundancy: send as many INTs as possible to pursue the same issue. Can you see the value in this purposeful overkill? Do you see particular strengths or weaknesses in any of the INTs that would cause you to emphasize or reduce its role in collection?

3. *Open Sources.* During the Cold War, "open source" intelligence consisted simply of what could be collected outside the other INTs. Open source intelligence is potentially quite useful. Open sources might have been helpful in anticipating the Iranian revolution in 1979, for example, when our collectors apparently neglected to read about the collapse of support for the Shah, even though it was widely reported in the popular press in Iran.

More recently, the volume of open source intelligence far outstrips anyone's capacity to collect it, much less to analyze or make assessments on the basis of it. Yet if an analyst or collector inside the CIA or DIA or NSA limits her universe of intelligence to SIGINT or another INT, she is likely to have missed significant publicly available information. How do you think this problem should be managed?

4. *Human Sources vs. Technical Sources.* A frequent criticism of U.S. intelligence in the post-Cold War period, and in particular since September 11, 2001, has been that we have invested too heavily in technology at the expense of developing effective HUMINT in critical places. Do you understand why the priorities developed the way they did? Do you think that placing more HUMINT in selected places would better advance intelligence than working to improve technical collection?

5. *IMINT to OSINT?* In the last few years, commercial satellite companies have begun to sell high-resolution images of almost any place on earth. These images are used by geographers, land use planners, and many others. But their ready availability has raised serious concerns among several governments, including that of the United States, who worry about their military value. *See* Katie Hafner & Saritha Rai, *Google Offers a Bird's-Eye View, and Some Governments Tremble*, N.Y. Times, Dec. 20, 2005, at A1. Do you think the United States or any other government can do anything to halt or restrict the distribution of these images? May they forbid coverage of certain areas, such as the White House; require a degradation in quality; or force a time delay in their release? Should they do any of these things? High-resolution images of many sensitive sites around the world may be found at http://www.globalsecurity.org/eye/index.html.

6. *Intelligence Support for Military Operations.* According to one commentator, U.S. soldiers in the future will fight on a radically transformed battlefield, where they will be more dispersed and will operate "sensors capable of seeing

and weapons capable of striking over long distances." Treverton, *supra* p. 340, at 62. From the military's point of view, the mission of intelligence during the Cold War was "*national*—finding out about and keeping tabs on the Soviet Union. Now it is becoming *tactical*—especially supporting American warriors around the globe." *Id.* at 64.

Do you think the radically transformed battlefield in the war on terrorism requires the military to conduct surveillance inside the United States? Can you point to authority for a domestic intelligence role for the military? See *infra* p. 960.

D. THE NATIONAL SECURITY ACT OF 1947

The National Security Act of 1947, Pub. L. No. 80-253, 61 Stat. 495 (codified as amended in scattered sections of 10 & 50 U.S.C.), was slightly amended and recodified in 1992, 1993, 1996, and 2001. More significant changes, including the creation of the Director of National Intelligence (DNI), were made in the Intelligence Reform and Terrorism Prevention Act of 2004, Pub. L. No. 108-458, 118 Stat. 3638. References to the Act in the following text are to its current codification.

The Act describes the authority of the recently created DNI and of the CIA only in the most general terms. Regarding the DNI, 50 U.S.C. §403-1 provides:

(a) Provision of intelligence

(1) The Director of National Intelligence shall be responsible for ensuring that national intelligence is provided—

(A) to the President;

(B) to the heads of departments and agencies of the executive branch;

(C) to the Chairman of the Joint Chiefs of Staff and senior military commanders;

(D) to the Senate and House of Representatives and the committees thereof; and

(E) to such other persons as the Director of National Intelligence determines to be appropriate.

(2) Such national intelligence should be timely, objective, independent of political considerations, and based upon all sources available to the intelligence community and other appropriate entities....

(b) Access to intelligence. Unless otherwise directed by the President, the Director of National Intelligence shall have access to all national intelligence and intelligence related to the national security which is collected by any Federal department, agency, or other entity, except as otherwise provided by law or, as appropriate, under guidelines agreed upon by the Attorney General and the Director of National Intelligence....

(f) Tasking and other authorities

(1) (A) The Director of National Intelligence shall—

(i) establish objectives, priorities, and guidance for the intelligence community to ensure timely and effective collection, processing, analysis, and dissemination (including access by users to collected data consistent with applicable law and, as appropriate, the guidelines referred to in subsection (b) and analytic products generated by or within the intelligence community) of national intelligence;

(ii) determine requirements and priorities for, and manage and direct the tasking of, collection, analysis, production, and dissemination of national intelligence by elements of the intelligence community, including —

(I) approving requirements (including those requirements responding to needs provided by consumers) for collection and analysis; and

(II) resolving conflicts in collection requirements and in the tasking of national collection assets of the elements of the intelligence community; and

(iii) provide advisory tasking to intelligence elements of those agencies and departments not within the National Intelligence Program....

(4) The Director of National Intelligence shall ensure compliance with the Constitution and laws of the United States by the Central Intelligence Agency and shall ensure such compliance by other elements of the intelligence community through the host executive departments that manage the programs and activities that are part of the National Intelligence Program....

(6) The Director of National Intelligence shall establish requirements and priorities for foreign intelligence information to be collected under the Foreign Intelligence Surveillance Act of 1978 (50 U.S.C. 1801 et seq.), and provide assistance to the Attorney General to ensure that information derived from electronic surveillance or physical searches under that Act is disseminated so it may be used efficiently and effectively for national intelligence purposes, except that the Director shall have no authority to direct or undertake electronic surveillance or physical search operations pursuant to that Act unless authorized by statute or Executive order.

(7) The Director of National Intelligence shall perform such other functions as the President may direct....

(h) Analysis. To ensure the most accurate analysis of intelligence is derived from all sources to support national security needs, the Director of National Intelligence shall —

(1) implement policies and procedures —

(A) to encourage sound analytic methods and tradecraft throughout the elements of the intelligence community;

(B) to ensure that analysis is based upon all sources available; and

(C) to ensure that the elements of the intelligence community regularly conduct competitive analysis of analytic products, whether such products are produced by or disseminated to such elements;...

(i) Protection of intelligence sources and methods

(1) The Director of National Intelligence shall protect intelligence sources and methods from unauthorized disclosure....

D. The National Security Act of 1947

Concerning the CIA, §403-4a of title 50 provides:

(a) Director of Central Intelligence Agency. There is a Director of the Central Intelligence Agency who shall be appointed by the President, by and with the advice and consent of the Senate.

(b) Supervision. The Director of the Central Intelligence Agency shall report to the Director of National Intelligence regarding the activities of the Central Intelligence Agency.

(c) Duties. The Director of the Central Intelligence Agency shall —
  (1) serve as the head of the Central Intelligence Agency; and
  (2) carry out the responsibilities specified in subsection (d).

(d) Responsibilities. The Director of the Central Intelligence Agency shall —
  (1) collect intelligence through human sources and by other appropriate means, except that the Director of the Central Intelligence Agency shall have no police, subpoena, or law enforcement powers or internal security functions;
  (2) correlate and evaluate intelligence related to the national security and provide appropriate dissemination of such intelligence;
  (3) provide overall direction for and coordination of the collection of national intelligence outside the United States through human sources by elements of the intelligence community authorized to undertake such collection and, in coordination with other departments, agencies, or elements of the United States Government which are authorized to undertake such collection, ensure that the most effective use is made of resources and that appropriate account is taken of the risks to the United States and those involved in such collection; and
  (4) perform such other functions and duties related to intelligence affecting the national security as the President or the Director of National Intelligence may direct. . . .

As the following excerpts indicate, those who have examined the history of the CIA's creation differ about what activities Congress intended the Agency to conduct.

Select Committee to Study Governmental Operations with Respect to Intelligence Activities (Church Committee), Foreign and Military Intelligence
S. Rep. No. 94-755, Book I, at 128-131 (1976)

A. CLANDESTINE COLLECTION OF INTELLIGENCE

While the National Security Act of 1947 authorizes correlation, evaluation, and dissemination of national security intelligence by the CIA, nowhere does it specify that the Agency is authorized to engage in the direct collection of intelligence. As its authority to engage in the direct collection, the CIA has relied upon Section 102(d)(4) and (5) [currently codified as amended at 50 U.S.C. §403-4a(d)(4)] of the Act. . . .

The legislative history of the 1947 Act does not indicate clearly that the full Congress specifically intended by these provisions to authorize direct clandestine collection by the CIA. The legislating committee discussed the issue in some detail in executive session, but it was mentioned only briefly in public hearings and floor debates. However, the public record does suggest that the full Congress had access to information which indicated that the Act could be construed as authorizing direct collection. No action was taken to prohibit such activity. Moreover, the 1949 enactment of the Central Intelligence Agency Act demonstrates congressional intent to facilitate clandestine activities, and thus congressional endorsement of the view that such activities were the legitimate function of the CIA....

Public references to collection are too obscure and in some cases too ambiguous for the inference to be drawn that the full Congress specifically intended to authorize direct collection by the CIA. It would require an attentive legislator, alert to the full record, to be apprised of the possibility of CIA participation in this activity through the public hearings and debates. But the language of Section 102(d)(4) and (5) [now 50 U.S.C. §403-4a(d)(4)] indicates that the Congress intended some flexibility in the operations of the CIA. These provisions are sufficiently broad that clandestine collection of information could reasonably fall within the range of activities which they describe....

Two years after the enactment of the National Security Act, Congress passed the Central Intelligence Agency Act of 1949, 50 U.S.C. 403a-403j. The 1949 legislation was an enabling act: technically it contributed nothing to the kinds of activities which the Agency was authorized to carry out. Its enactment, however, sheds some light upon what Congress thought it had authorized in 1947.

There is no doubt that the purpose of certain provisions of the 1949 Act was to protect clandestine activities of the CIA. The Act waives the normal restrictions placed on government acquisition of materiel, hiring, and accounting for funds expended. If Congress did not believe that some type of clandestine activity had been authorized by the National Security Act, these provisions would not have been necessary.

Further, the Congress had reason to believe that the CIA was already engaged in espionage. Prior to passage of the Act, there had been discussion in the press of CIA involvement in direct clandestine collection. Clandestine collection was specifically discussed in closed hearings on the Act, and finally, in floor debates. Members of Congress referred to the legislation as "an espionage bill." While there was much debate on the floor of both Houses as to the wisdom of specific provisions of the bill and the general need for secrecy in the enactment process, no one suggested that the provisions of the bill were unwarranted because the operations which they were designed to facilitate were not authorized by law....

Statement of Mitchell Rogovin, Special Counsel to the Director of Central Intelligence

Hearings Before the House Select Committee on Intelligence,
94th Cong., Part 5, at 1729, 1734-1735 (1976)

Heading the [Central Intelligence Group (CIG) in 1946] was a Director of Central Intelligence, whose duties were to: "...perform such other functions and duties related to intelligence affecting the national security as the President and the national intelligence authority may from time to time direct" [later referred to as the "Fifth Function," after §102(d)(5) of the 1947 Act, now 50 U.S.C. §403-4a(d)(4)]. The National Security Act of 1947 called for the CIA to have the same powers and responsibilities as were accorded the CIG under the 1946 Presidential directive. Accordingly, when the House Committee on Expenditures in the Executive Departments held hearings on the 1947 act, it paid special attention to the broad authority delegated to the CIG by subsection (d). During these hearings, for example, Representative Clarence Brown questioned Lt. Gen. Hoyt S. Vandenberg, Director of Central Intelligence, about the authority which subparagraph (d) conveyed:...

Representative Brown. This other section — that is, subparagraph (d) — was so broad that you could do about anything that you decided was either advantageous or beneficial, in your mind?
Lieutenant General Vandenberg. Yes, sir.
Representative Brown. In other words, if you decided you wanted to go into direct activities of any nature, almost, why, that could be done?
Lieutenant General Vandenberg. Within the foreign intelligence field, if it was agreed upon by all of the three agencies concerned — that is, State, War, and Navy....

A subsequent witness, Peter Visher, the draftsman of the Presidential directive establishing the CIG, recommended to the committee that it pass the act without authority for the CIA to perform any "other functions related to intelligence affecting the national security." He called this provision a loophole because it enabled the President to direct the CIG to perform almost any operation.... It is significant, then, that when the bill was reported out, and when it was passed, it... conferred the identical powers and responsibilities on the CIA. This legislative history indicates that the committee, by including section 102(d)(5) in the final bill, intended that the CIA have the authority, subject to directions from the National Security Council, to conduct a broad range of direct operational assignments.

Robert Borosage, Para-Legal Authority and Its Peril
40 Law & Contemp. Probs. 166, 175-177 (Summer 1976)

CIG was an interim agency, a "short-term pip-squeak thing," noted Arthur Macy Cox, a former employee of both CIG and CIA. There is no historical evidence that CIG had any covert action programs. Cox and Lawrence Houston, General Counsel of the CIA for over twenty years, both stated that the CIG had no such projects. In both the House and the Senate, CIG was described in public record[s] as a coordinating and analytical agency. There were rare and passing references to intelligence collection; covert action was not mentioned.

The same descriptions were provided for the proposed functions of the CIA in the public hearings of the House and Senate — scattered reference[s] to intelligence collection, no mention at all of covert action. The Rogovin Memorandum quotes an exchange between Representative Brown and Lt. General

Hoyt Vandenberg, then Director of Central Intelligence, as authority for imputing congressional knowledge of and intent to authorize covert action. The Memorandum fails to indicate that the exchange took place in executive session, the minutes of which are classified to this day.... In fact, the exchange referred only to the covert collection of intelligence. Walter Pforzheimer, legislative counsel with the OSS, CIG, and CIA, stated that Vandenberg testified in executive session about intelligence collection, because Army Intelligence (G-2) was opposed to the CIA undertaking any collection activities. According to Pforzheimer, covert action was not mentioned. Lawrence Houston, who drafted the 1946 executive order, stated that the policy within the administration was "completely unclear" about covert action, and the fifth function clause was to "leave a door open" in case of the "unforeseen." The first director of the CIA, Admiral Roscoe Hillenkoetter, stated he had no interest in covert action, and intended the CIA to be purely an "intelligence outfit." The language of the fifth function clause itself, as well as the entire public legislative record, may be taken at least as easily against, as for, the notion that Congress intended to authorize covert action in 1947.

The National Security Council (NSC) was created in the 1947 Act "to advise the President with respect to the integration of domestic, foreign, and military policies relating to the national security." National Security Act of 1947, Pub. L. No. 80-253, §101, 61 Stat. 495, 496. Its statutory members were and still are the President, the Vice President, the Secretary of State, and the Secretary of Defense. 50 U.S.C. §402(a)(2000).

The statutory functions of the NSC include the following:

> (b) ...In addition to performing such other functions as the President may direct, for the purpose of more effectively coordinating the policies and functions of the departments and agencies of the Government relating to the national security, it shall... be the duty of the Council—
>
> (1) to assess and appraise the objectives, commitments, and risks of the United States in relation to our actual and potential military power, in the interest of national security, for the purpose of making recommendations to the President in connection therewith; and
>
> (2) to consider policies on matters of common interest to the departments and agencies of the Government concerned with the national security, and to make recommendations to the President in connection therewith.... [*Id.* §402(b).]

Originally, the 1947 Act authorized an executive secretariat to serve as staff to the NSC. In 1953, however, President Eisenhower created the position of Assistant to the President for National Security Affairs, now known as National Security Adviser, pursuant to a statute that authorized the appointment of "employees in the White House Office." 3 U.S.C. §105(a)(1) & (2) (2000). Although the National Security Adviser's role has varied widely since then, *see* Office of the Historian, Bureau of Pub. Affairs, United States Dept. of State, *History of the National Security Council 1947–1997* (1997), *available at* http://www.fas.org/irp/offdocs/NSChistory.htm, the position was created to supervise the NSC staff and to brief the President on national security affairs. *See generally* Thomas Franck, *The Constitutional and Legal Position of the National Security Adviser and Deputy Adviser,* 74 Am. J. Intl. L. 634 (1980).

The role for intelligence agencies in support of military intelligence was less than clear in the 1947 Act:

> The 1947 Act provided no explicit charter for military intelligence. The charter and mission of military intelligence activities was established either by executive orders... or various National Security Council directives. These National Security Council Intelligence Directives (NSCIDs) were the principal means of establishing the roles and functions of all the various entities in the intelligence community. They composed the so-called "secret charter" for the CIA. However, most of them also permitted "departmental" intelligence activities, and in this way also provided the executive charter for the intelligence activities of the State Department and the Pentagon. However, the intelligence activities of the Department of Defense remained with the military rather than with the new Defense Department civilians. [Church Comm. Rep., *supra* p. 341, Book I, at 21.]

NOTES AND QUESTIONS

1. *Why a Statute?* Why should President Truman have sought statutory authority for the government's intelligence function? If the President's goal was to keep the wartime intelligence machine in operation, why did he not simply promulgate an executive order on his own authority? When statutory authority is asserted, what are the consequences for nonstatutory claims of executive power to conduct intelligence operations?

2. *Relevance of the CIG in Understanding the Intent of Congress.* Of what relevance is the 1946 presidential directive in establishing what was intended by the 1947 Act? Are the historical facts important? That is, in deciding the scope of CIA authority after 1947, would it matter whether the CIG had undertaken intelligence collection or covert actions abroad or whether the congressional committees knew of such actions?

3. *Covert Collection vs. Covert Action.* Borosage emphasized the distinction between covert intelligence collection and covert action. Is it always possible to distinguish between the two types of CIA operations, particularly when the methods employed are similar? *See* Treverton, *supra* p. 340, at 137-138.

4. *The Varying Roles of Military Intelligence.* Why would Congress have omitted any explicit reference to military intelligence activities in the National Security Act? Could Congress have subjected the intelligence activities of the Department of Defense to the control of the CIA Director, or, more recently, of the DNI? To what extent do you think that the DNI has effective control over intelligence support for military operations? Is your answer the same, or should it be, when military intelligence is used in support of homeland security? The activities of military intelligence agencies in various settings are examined *infra* pp. 459, 960.

5. *The NSC, CIA, and Intelligence Policy.* It is clear from the 1947 Act that the NSC was created neither to make national security decisions nor to carry them out.

The same may be said of the later-created National Security Adviser. In fact, both the NSC staff and the National Security Adviser have engaged in operations. See *infra* pp. 412-418. It is equally clear from the 1947 Act that the CIA was not meant to formulate intelligence policy, especially given the requirement that the CIA act at the direction of the NSC. However, the CIA has on occasion been the driving force in intelligence operations policy-making, notwithstanding the 1947 Act.

E. INTELLIGENCE REORGANIZATION

The September 11, 2001, attacks on the World Trade Center and the Pentagon prompted numerous critiques of what some regarded as massive failures of intelligence. *See, e.g.,* S. Select Comm. on Intelligence & H. Permanent Select Comm. on Intelligence, Joint Inquiry into Intelligence Community Activities Before and After the Terrorist Attacks of September 11, 2001, S. Rep. No. 107-351, H.R. Rep. No. 107-792 (2002); *9/11 Commission Report: Final Report of the National Commission on Terrorist Attacks Upon the United States* (2004). How could such a devastating attack have been planned and carried out under our collective noses? Why did our intelligence agencies not know the attack was coming? The two intelligence committees and the 9/11 Commission found that inadequate organization and management of the intelligence community prevented the DCI from ensuring that information about the hijackers' plans was shared with agency analysts, who could have "connected the dots" and uncovered the plot in advance. The 9/11 Commission also noted that limited legal authority forced the DCI to "direct agencies without controlling them." *9/11 Commission Report, supra,* at 357. The Commission pointed out that, especially for intelligence elements within the Department of Defense (DOD), the DCI "does not receive an appropriation for their activities, and therefore does not control their purse strings." *Id.* Similarly, the congressional joint inquiry found that even after DCI George J. Tenet ordered the intelligence community to give the Osama bin Laden network its highest priority, his words had little effect beyond the CIA. *Joint Inquiry, supra,* at 236.

Meanwhile, the Bush administration case for the 2003 Iraq war relied heavily on intelligence-based assertions that the Saddam Hussein regime had stockpiles of weapons of mass destruction (WMD) that would imminently be used against the United States and its allies. After President Bush declared an end to major combat operations in Iraq and investigators cleared the battlefield rubble, no WMD were found. In March 2005, a presidentially appointed commission found "that the Intelligence Community was dead wrong in almost all of its pre-war judgments about Iraq's weapons of mass destruction." Commission on the Intelligence Capabilities of the United States Regarding Weapons of Mass Destruction (Silberman/Robb Commission), *Report to the President of the United States* (transmittal letter), Mar. 31, 2005. The Commission found an "inability to collect good information," "serious errors in analyzing" the information collected, and a failure to distinguish assumptions from evidence in its analysis. *Id.* But the commission reached no conclusions about how the flawed intelligence was actually used in deciding to invade Iraq. See *supra* p. 313.

E. Intelligence Reorganization

The intelligence failures of September 11 and Iraq appeared to many observers as symptomatic of a larger struggle by our nation's intelligence agencies to confront the post-Cold War environment. Instead of focusing on the Soviet Union as the dominant threat, as it had since the origins of the CIA in 1947, the intelligence community today faces dozens of high-priority targets that include not only states but also highly diffuse transnational terrorism, crime, and proliferation networks. Worse yet, advances in technology and potential dual uses of goods have made detection of weapons and facilities harder and made their concealment easier.

In its July 2004 report, the 9/11 Commission recommended several changes in the structure of the intelligence community:

- unify strategic intelligence and operational planning against Islamist terrorists across the foreign-domestic divide with a National Counterterrorism Center;
- unify the intelligence community with a National Intelligence Director;
- unify the many participants in the counterterrorism effort and their knowledge in a network-based information-sharing system that transcends traditional governmental boundaries;
- unify and strengthen congressional oversight to improve quality and accountability; and
- strengthen the FBI and homeland defenders.

See 9/11 Commission Report, supra, at 399-400.

1. An Intelligence Czar?

In December 2004, Congress approved the most extensive reorganization of U.S. intelligence in more than half a century. Intelligence Reform and Terrorism Prevention Act of 2004, Pub. L. No. 108-458, 118 Stat. 3638 [hereinafter Intelligence Reform Act]. (Unless otherwise noted, references in the following description are to sections of the National Security Act of 1947 as amended by the Intelligence Reform Act and as currently codified.) The 2004 Act responded—at least in part—to those who sought the creation of a cabinet-level intelligence czar. The Act created the position of DNI, appointed by the President and confirmed by the Senate and subject to the "authority, direction, and control of the President." 50 U.S.C. §403(b). The DNI serves as "head of the intelligence community" and as principal adviser to the President, National Security Council, and Homeland Security Council "for intelligence matters related to the national security." *Id.* §403(b)(1), (2). She also oversees and directs implementation of the National Intelligence Program. *Id.* §403(b)(3). The DNI may not simultaneously serve as Director of the CIA or as head of any other component of the intelligence community. *Id.* §403(c).

The DNI has direct authority over a Senate-confirmed Principal Deputy and up to four additional deputy directors appointed by the DNI, a National Counterterrorism Center, a National Counterproliferation Center, a General Counsel, a Director of Science and Technology, and a National Intelligence Council. *Id.* §403-3a(b), (c), (e). The former DCI post was eliminated, and the job of running the CIA was given to a Director of the CIA. *Id.* §403-4a.

The DNI must "develop and determine" the annual consolidated National Intelligence Program budget. *Id.* §403-1(c)(1). She also directs the allocation of appropriations through the heads of departments containing agencies or organizations within the intelligence community and through the Director of the CIA. *Id.* §403-1(c)(5)(A). (Component intelligence agencies and lines of reporting are shown in the chart on p. 365.) Although the DNI has thus been given considerable new budgetary authority with which to manage the intelligence community, the DNI has no direct prescriptive authority over intelligence support to military operations through the Department of Defense Joint Military Intelligence Program (JMIP) and Tactical Intelligence and Related Activities (TIARA) program. *Id.* §403-1(c)(3)(A).

After consultation with the Secretary of Defense, the DNI must ensure that National Intelligence Program budgets for components of the intelligence community within DOD are adequate for the intelligence needs of DOD, including the intelligence needs of the service branches. *Id.* §403-1(c). The DNI, after consulting with the Secretary of Defense and Director of the CIA, must develop joint procedures to "improve the coordination and deconfliction" of operations that involve the U.S. armed forces and the CIA. *Id.* §403-1 note.

The DNI is responsible for establishing "objectives, priorities, and guidance" for elements of the intelligence community. *Id.* §403-1(f)(1)(A). She also must "determine requirements and priorities for, and manage and direct the tasking of" intelligence collection, analysis, production, and dissemination by entities of the intelligence community. *Id.* These authorities do not extend to the DNI if the President so directs or if the DNI and Secretary of Defense agree otherwise, or to dissemination of information to state and local governments and the private sector under the Homeland Security Act. *Id.* §403-1(f)(1)(B).

2. The New Structure

Within the office of the DNI, a National Intelligence Council (NIC), composed of senior analysts and other experts appointed by the DNI, is charged with producing national intelligence estimates, evaluating intelligence collection and production performance, and otherwise assisting the DNI. *Id.* §403-3b. A Senate-confirmed General Counsel was created, as was a Civil Liberties Protection Officer and a Director of Science and Technology, both appointed by the DNI. *Id.* §§403-3c, 3d, 3e.

The Director of the CIA reports to the DNI, and the DNI remains responsible for intelligence collection, evaluation, and dissemination by the CIA, as well as for performing "such other functions and duties related to intelligence affecting the national security" as the President or DNI may direct. *Id.* §403-4a(d)(4). Thus, the original "fifth function," which was the putative statutory basis for covert operations by the CIA, has been retained.

The DNI oversees the National Counterterrorism Center (NCTC), created by the Act, and any other national intelligence centers determined necessary by the Director. *Id.* §404o. The Director of the NCTC is a Senate-confirmed presidential appointee who reports to the DNI generally but to the President on the planning and implementation of joint counterterrorism operations. *Id.*

E. Intelligence Reorganization

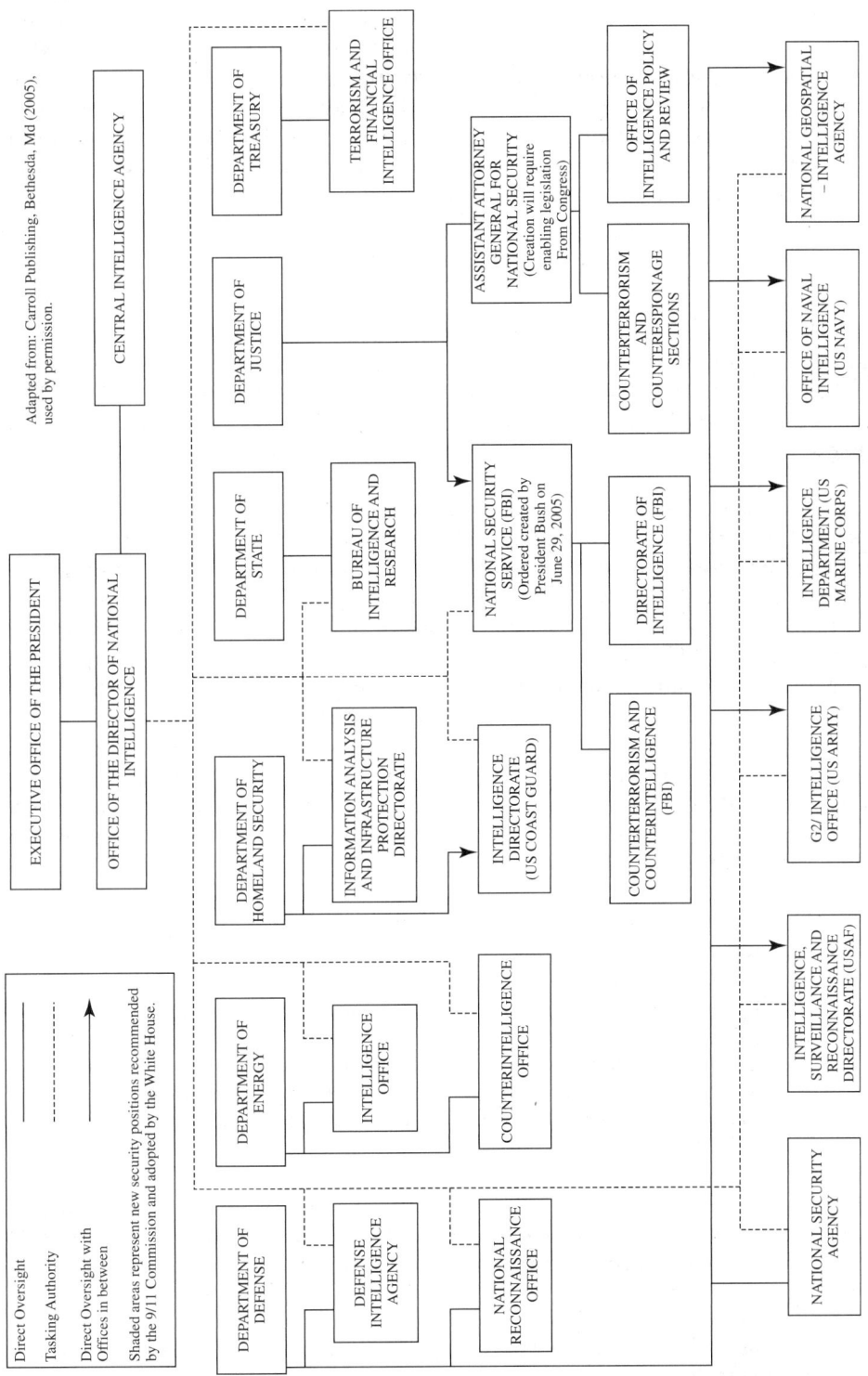

A Privacy and Civil Liberties Oversight Board, appointed by the President, was established within the Executive Office of the President and charged with ensuring that privacy and civil liberties concerns are appropriately considered in the implementation of policies designed to protect against terrorism. The Board provides oversight of regulations and policies, advises the President and agencies in the executive branch, and reports to Congress. The Board has no power to compel production of information, but it may request such assistance from the Attorney General. 5 U.S.C. §601 note.

NOTES AND QUESTIONS

1. *Authorities of the DNI.* Based on the 2004 legislation, could you write a job description for the DNI? Why would Congress and the President have determined to create an intelligence official superior to the Director of the CIA? The structure created by the 2004 Intelligence Reform Act is further described and assessed *infra* p. 438.

2. *The DNI and the Intelligence Community.* The "intelligence community" headed by the DNI consists of all the entities depicted in the chart on p. 365 except the President and the six listed cabinet departments. Intelligence Reform Act §1073, 118 Stat. 3693. The National Intelligence Program directed by the DNI includes "all programs, projects, and activities of the intelligence community," 50 U.S.C. §401a(6), but "does not include programs, projects, or activities of the military departments to acquire intelligence solely for the planning and conduct of tactical military operations of United States Armed Forces." *Id.* In what respects does the DNI constitute a "Secretary of Intelligence," and how specifically does the new post fall short of the Secretary model? Does the Intelligence Reform Act give the DNI the authority he needs to be effective? May she hire or fire agency heads? Does the Act tell the CIA or other agencies within the National Intelligence Program what to do?

3. *Defining the Scope of the Mission.* The terms "national intelligence" and "intelligence related to national security" are defined to include

> all intelligence, regardless of the source from which derived and including information gathered within or outside the United States, that pertains . . . to more than one . . . agency; and that involves threats to the United States, its people, property, or interests; the development, proliferation, or use of weapons of mass destruction; or any other matter bearing on United States national or homeland security. [50 U.S.C. §401a(5).]

Are these definitions useful to the DNI in understanding the scope of her responsibilities? What categories of intelligence are outside the definition? How does this expansive definition affect the geographical boundaries of intelligence activities of the CIA? Of the FBI?

4. *The Fifth Function.* Several authorities and responsibilities given to the DNI by the Intelligence Reform Act of 2004 previously belonged to the Director of Central Intelligence (DCI), who was also the Director of the CIA. For

E. Intelligence Reorganization

example, the DNI must "ensure compliance with the Constitution and laws of the United States" by the CIA and other elements of the intelligence community. 50 U.S.C. §403-1(f)(4). The DNI "shall perform such other functions as the President may direct." *Id.* §403-1(f)(7). The new Director of the CIA continues to "perform such other functions and duties related to intelligence affecting the national security as the President or National Security Council may direct." *Id.* §403-4a(d)(4), 118 Stat. 3661. Do you suppose the differences in what used to be referred to as the fifth function are purposeful? If so, how do the authorities of the two offices differ in this regard? Parallel authorities for the DNI and Director of the CIA extend to "protect[ing] intelligence sources and methods from unauthorized disclosure." *Id.* §403-1(i)(1); 50 U.S.C. §403-3(c)(7).

5. *The Budget and its Control.* The roughly $40 billion intelligence budget is divided between agencies within the National Intelligence Program (one-half to two-thirds of the total) and intelligence programs to support military operations (JMIP and TIARA). Within the NIP, about three-fourths of the total is also for various DOD agencies, most for NSA and NRO. The rest, perhaps $5 to 10 billion, is shared among the CIA, the FBI, and other agencies. *See* Stephen Daggett, *The U.S. Intelligence Budget: A Basic Overview* (Cong. Res. Serv. RS21945), Oct. 4, 2004.

Does the DNI now control the purse strings of the intelligence agencies? Although intelligence budgets will continue to be developed in various individual agencies, the DNI has discretion under the Act to reject or revise items or programs and to direct that funds be spent or withheld. 50 U.S.C. §403-1c. Can you see how this budget and spending authority could make the DNI the final decision maker in the agencies of the NIP?

6. *The NCTC.* The 9/11 Commission proposal to create the NCTC was adopted by President Bush before it was approved by Congress. On August 27, 2004, the President signed Executive Order No. 13,354, *National Counterterrorism Center*, 69 Fed. Reg. 53,589 (2004). A similar NCTC was provided for in the Intelligence Reform Act a few months later. In the Intelligence Reform Act, the Director of the NCTC reports to the DNI regarding intelligence operations, while the DNI reports to the President regarding the "planning and progress of joint counterterrorism operations (other than intelligence operations)." 50 U.S.C. §404o(c)(3). What kinds of operations do you think are included among those that require direct reports to the President by the Director of the NCTC? Why would someone other than the DNI make those reports to the President? (The relationship of the NCTC to other information-sharing and terrorism assessment entities is considered in Chapter 22.)

7. *Additional Reforms and a Report Card.* The President also acted to implement other recommendations of the Silberman/Robb Commission by establishing a National Counter Proliferation Center to manage and coordinate intelligence community activities related to nuclear, biological, and chemical weapons and delivery systems; by signing an executive order to combat trafficking in WMDs and related materials by blocking the assets of persons engaged in proliferation activities and their supporters; and by clarifying authorities concerning information sharing by expanding the authority and control of

the DNI. In addition, a new center at the CIA will focus on the collection of open-source intelligence. *See President Bush Administration Actions to Implement WMD Commission Recommendations*, June 29, 2005. These reforms are considered further in Chapter 16.

Almost one year after enactment of the Intelligence Reform Act, members of the 9/11 Commission issued their *Final Report on 9/11 Commission Recommendations*, Dec. 5, 2005, *available at* http://www.9-11pdp.org/press/2005-12-05_report.pdf. Their report card on the status of a range of recommendations from the 2004 *9/11 Commission Report* gave B grades to the DNI and NCTC, a C for the creation of an FBI national security workforce (progress "is too slow"), and Ds for information-sharing initiatives (changes in incentives that favor sharing "have been minimal," and policies and procedures "that compel sharing" must be implemented). *Id.*

8. *Conforming Amendments.* In several sections of the National Security Act of 1947, Central Intelligence Agency Act of 1949, *supra*, p. 340, Foreign Intelligence Surveillance Act, *infra* pp. 512-556, Classified Information Procedures Act, *infra* pp. 857-859, and several intelligence authorization acts, "DNI" is inserted by the Intelligence Reform Act in place of "DCI," and similar changes are made to reflect the structure of the new office of the DNI, including the Principal Deputy.

9. *The National Intelligence Strategy.* In late 2005, DNI John D. Negroponte issued a new strategy document, *The National Intelligence Strategy of the United States of America*, Oct. 26, 2005, *available at* http://www.dni.gov/release_letter_102505.html. The top two "mission objectives" identified in the *Strategy* are countering terrorism and halting weapons proliferation. The third listed objective is to "bolster the growth of democracy" by having "collectors, analysts and operators" within the intelligence agencies seek to "forge relationships with new and incipient democracies" in order to help "strengthen the rule of law and ward off threats to representative government." Why would the DNI promulgate a strategy document? Is this task more properly performed by the Department of State or the Department of Defense? Which agencies are legally authorized to work toward the democracy-building task? Do you see any legal problems with this assignment? In the Foreword to the *Strategy* document, DNI Negroponte stated that "the time has come for our domestic and foreign intelligence cultures to grow stronger by growing together." *Id.* at 1. In the same vein, he claimed that a first priority for intelligence is to "inform and warn the President, the Cabinet, the Congress, the Joint Chiefs of Staff and commanders in the field, domestic law enforcement and homeland security authorities in the heartland, and our international allies." *Id.* Do you find support for all these roles in the legal authorities assessed in this chapter?

Covert Action ────15

Covert action is intended to influence people and events without revealing the source, or perhaps even the existence, of the influence. Like the secret collection of information using human intelligence (HUMINT), covert action requires access and local resources. Collection and covert action are nonetheless distinct.

> The history of covert action might be loosely grouped into three categories. *Propaganda* can be no more than a little money distributed secretly to a few journalists in country X to get them to write articles favorable to the United States — a "project," in CIA practice, but one that might have a budget of only a few thousand dollars. At the other extreme are covert *paramilitary operations*, secret military aid and training. Most though not all of these are large; the "secret" war in Laos, for instance, was not so much secret as unacknowledged, consuming several million dollars a day as a second front to the war in Vietnam but one managed by the CIA. In between, *political action* attempts to change the balance of political forces in a particular country, most often by secretly providing money to particular groups. [Gregory F. Treverton, *Covert Action: The CIA and the Limits of American Intervention in the Postwar World* 13 (1987).]

Propaganda operations can produce "blowback" — when a false story planted overseas by the CIA is reported in the United States. With worldwide 24-hour news outlets, blowback is inevitable. When it happens, must the CIA inform the media that the story is false? What if doing so would compromise the overseas operation?

Political action can also pose problems. If the CIA supports a foreign group for particular purposes — say, the Guatemalan military in a fight with Central American radicals — is the CIA legally responsible if its support is used instead to abuse the human rights of Guatemalan citizens? This chapter and Chapter 16 assess the legal dimensions of these questions.

Paramilitary covert actions have always been controversial. Such actions take a variety of forms:

> At one extreme, paramilitary operations have been tantamount to full-scale wars — "covert" only in the sense that the United States wanted to be able to deny that it was directly involved. Witness the "secret war" in Laos, an unadmitted war

on the cheap, with CIA paramilitary specialists providing the advice and Laotian hill tribesmen doing the fighting.... Like earlier CIA paramilitary campaigns in Korea, Laos was part of an open American war; if the campaigns were meant to be secret, neither the war nor its purposes were.

At the other end of the spectrum, some paramilitary operations have amounted to little more than the clandestine transfer of a few weapons or of small amounts of training—for instance, for "palace guards" to protect friendly heads of state who would prefer not to be widely known as protected by the United States....

All these paramilitary operations involved the same elements: money and weaponry for groups and movements the United States was supporting, plus clandestine ways to transfer both, plus CIA officers and others to provide training and advice. The weaponry was "sterile"—that is, not easy to identify as coming from the United States....

To backstop these paramilitary operations, the CIA has developed networks of air carriers, some CIA "fronts," and some contractors to move arms and supplies—if not secretly, then at least as less visibly "American." During the Vietnam war, that network, centered on Air America, amounted to a large air force. After Vietnam, the CIA divested itself of these "proprietaries" but retained contacts with those companies; in many cases, the "new" private managers were the "old" CIA managers, now retired. Nor did even the names change: Southern Air Transport, a CIA company during the Vietnam war, shipped supplies to the CIA-sponsored Contras in Nicaragua two decades later as a "private" company.

Transferring weapons and training both require bases. Nicaraguan dictator Somoza provided bases for CIA-supported operations against both Guatemala in 1954 and Cuba in 1961.... By the 1980s, when Nicaragua was the target, Honduras served as the host, however nervously, for the main Contra training bases. Indeed, for one Nicaragua port town, covert war came full circle: having served as a base for the CIA-sponsored invasion of Guatemala in 1954, it was a target of the CIA-sponsored Contras three decades later. [*Id.* at 26-28.]

Who performs paramilitary operations? They do not, of course, involve the use of uniformed U.S. military personnel in combat roles. Is covert action a mission for military Special Operations Forces, or should such missions be run by the CIA using its paramilitary capabilities? Who controls covert action, whichever entities carry it out? Does it matter who carries out such operations in determining whether they are acts of war?

For the United States, the historic core of covert action was the idea of "plausible deniability"—that if such an action were detected, our denial of involvement in it would appear plausible. As the materials in this chapter show, the threats to accountability and law presented by plausible deniability led to reforms and an end to the practice in the 1970s. The chapter begins by introducing early congressional control of the use of a private military force. Then we examine how executive branch practice and congressional oversight of covert action evolved in the decades after passage of the National Security Act of 1947. Abuses involving covert action uncovered by investigations in the early 1970s produced a series of reforms, and structures and procedures were set up for covert-action decision making that continue to provide important legal guidance. Next we examine briefly the Iran-Contra Affair of the mid-1980s. That scandal revealed the inadequacy of some reforms and the continuing possibilities for abuse of covert action capabilities. In the final section, we assess more recent oversight reforms, including important legislation enacted in 1991.

A. THE FIRST PUBLIC CONTROL — THE NEUTRALITY ACT

The original understanding of the use of private armies to meet sovereign objectives is considered in Chapters 2 and 10. The Marque and Reprisal Clause may have been intended to vest in Congress all control over privateers. See *supra* p. 9. The Neutrality Act was passed in 1794, arguably to cement congressional control over private armies. In its current form, the Neutrality Act provides:

> Whoever, within the United States, knowingly begins or sets on foot or provides or prepares a means for or furnishes the money for, or takes part in, any military or naval expedition or enterprise to be carried on from thence against the territory or dominion of any foreign prince or state, or of any colony, district, or people with whom the United States is at peace, shall be fined under this title or imprisoned not more than three years, or both. [18 U.S.C. §960 (2000).]

The original purpose of the Neutrality Act has been described this way:

> One of the aims of the Neutrality Act was to protect the sovereignty of the United States by keeping United States citizens aloof from the intrigues of foreign government. Moreover, strict laws preventing U.S. citizens from encroaching on foreign disputes were seen as the quid pro quo for the non-interference by foreign governments in our affairs....
>
> The fundamental purpose of the Neutrality Act, however, lay not in asserting state sovereignty with respect to other states but in strengthening the authority of the central government vis-à-vis its citizens, particularly with respect to warfare. Thus Jefferson noted that:
>
>> If one citizen has a right to go to war of his own authority, every citizen has the same. If every citizen has that right, then the nation (which is composed of all its citizens) has a right to go to war, by the authority of its individual citizens. But this is not true either on the general principles of society, or by our Constitution, which gives that power to Congress alone and not to the citizens individually.[134]
>
> Congress passed the Act, then, to help secure government control over the power to make war. In order to ensure that control Congress enacted a statute which had as its object "to repress and punish all enterprises of private war, one of the last relics of medieval barbarism." By outlawing private warfare, the Act would insure that national policy would be made by the government acting through Congress, and not by the acts of individuals. [Jules Lobel, *The Rise and Decline of the Neutrality Act: Sovereign and Congressional War Powers in United States Foreign Policy*, 24 Harv. Intl. L.J. 1, 24-25 (1983).]

---

134. Letter from Thomas Jefferson, Secretary of State, to Gouverneur Morris, U.S. Minister to France (Aug. 16, 1793), *reprinted in* 6 J. Moore, *A Digest of International Law* 917 (1906). *See also* Jefferson's Third Annual Message to Congress (Oct. 17, 1803), *reprinted in* 1 Richardson, *Messages & Papers of the Presidents* 357, 361 (1896). Similarly, Congressman Ames, in considering the Neutrality Act legislation, observed that the general authority of the United States was very weak, and that a purpose of the bill was thus to prevent being "driven into war by the licentious behavior of some individuals." 1 Annals of Cong. 743 (1794). *See also id.* at 744, 746 (remarks of Reps. Wadsworth and Hillhouse).

See also United States v. Smith, 27 F. Cas. 1192 (C.C.D.N.Y. 1806) (Neutrality Act prosecution).

Does covert support for a paramilitary operation abroad by the President or his subordinates violate the Neutrality Act? *See* Dellums v. Smith, 797 F.2d 817 (9th Cir. 1986); United States v. Terrell, 731 F. Supp. 473 (S.D. Fla. 1989), *infra* p. 134.

What about U.S. companies training foreign military forces that are fighting governments abroad? See *infra* p. 451.

In a similar vein, Congress passed the Logan Act in 1799 to criminalize unauthorized efforts by U.S. citizens to "influence the measures or conduct of any foreign government or of any officer or agent thereof, in relation to any disputes or controversies with the United States...." 18 U.S.C. §953 (2000). *See* Kevin M. Kearney, Comment, *Private Citizens in Foreign Affairs: A Constitutional Analysis*, 36 Emory L.J. 285 (1987). Although apparently not enforced, the Logan Act has been "periodically brandished by Administrations embarrassed by activists displaying in foreign capitols their opposition to U.S. policies." Brad R. Roth, *The First Amendment in the Foreign Affairs Realm: "Domesticity" and the Restrictions on Citizen Participation*, 2 Temple Pol. & Civ. Rts. L. Rev. 255, 266 (1993). Like the Neutrality Act, the Logan Act was designed to foster the government's control over its foreign relations. Unlike the Neutrality Act, the Logan Act is presumably not enforced because of potential First and Fifth Amendment problems with any prosecution. *Id.* at 268-274. *See generally* Michael V. Seitzinger, *Conducting Foreign Relations Without Authority: The Logan Act* (Cong. Res. Serv. RL33265), Feb. 1, 2006.

B. IMPLEMENTING THE 1947 ACT

In Chapter 14 we saw that the National Security Act provides especially open-ended authority for the CIA to engage in intelligence operations. The public legislative history of the 1947 Act indicates that the issue of covert action was not raised during enactment. Because the underlying purpose of the legislation was to unify the intelligence function of the armed services and thereby to sustain the intelligence capability during peacetime, the text did not detail the CIA's functions or its relationship with the rest of the executive branch. *See* Thomas F. Troy, *Donovan and the CIA: A History of the Establishment of the Central Intelligence Agency* 377-410 (1981); John Ranelagh, *The Agency: The Rise and Decline of the CIA* 104-111 (1986). However, while the records of hearings, floor debates, and committee meetings in executive session suggest that Congress as a whole did not contemplate that the CIA would conduct covert operations, a few nagging questions about the 1947 Act record persist. First, some statements in the record suggest that witnesses and legislators did not always engage in a full and frank discussion of intelligence needs, apparently out of fear that the national security might be compromised by such a discussion. *See, e.g.*, 93 Cong. Rec. 9605 (1947) (statement of Rep. Manasco). Second, it has been argued that the ambiguous language of the so-called fifth function—authorizing the CIA to "perform such other functions and duties related to intelligence affecting the national security as the President or the Director of National Intelligence may

B. Implementing the 1947 Act

direct," 50 U.S.C. §403-4a(d)(4) — was chosen so as not to advertise to the world that the nation was planning to conduct covert operations. Select Committee to Study Governmental Operations with Respect to Intelligence Activities, *Foreign and Military Intelligence (Church Committee Report)*, S. Rep. No 94-755, Book I, at 485-486 (1976). Finally, the contemporary term "covert action" had no clearly understood forebear in 1947. While the terms "operational activities," "special operations," and "direct activities" were all used, they were employed to refer to secret collection of intelligence as well as to covert action. *Id.* at 486-487.

On the other hand, a 1947 memorandum from the CIA General Counsel to the Director offered this opinion of the new CIA authority:

> Taken out of context and without knowledge of its history, these Sections [50 U.S.C. §403-4a(d)(4)] could bear almost unlimited interpretation, provided that the services performed could be shown to be of benefit to an intelligence agency or related to national intelligence.... Even certain forms of S.O. [special operations] work could be held to benefit intelligence by establishment of W/T [wireless telegraph] teams in accessible areas, and by opening penetration points in confusion following sabotage or riot. *In our opinion, however, either activity would be an unwarranted extension of the functions authorized in Sections* [403-4a(d)(4)]. This is based on our understanding of the intent of Congress at the time these provisions were enacted. [*Quoted in id.* at 478.]

Similar conclusions about the 1947 Act were reached by the General Counsel in a 1962 memorandum to the Director. *Id.* at 478-479.

How should we interpret the "fifth function"? To begin, we know that activities authorized by §403-4a(d)(4) must be "related to intelligence affecting the national security." Does the language require that the *purpose* of the operation be to gather intelligence or simply that there be *a relationship* between intelligence and the operation, such as the use of similar sources or methods? For example, in 1948 the National Security Council (NSC) relied on §403-4a(d)(4) and this similarity of operational methods to instruct the Director of Central Intelligence (DCI) to conduct covert psychological operations designed to counteract similar Soviet actions. *Id.* at 490-491, further described *infra* p. 431. If §403-4a(d)(4) requires a purpose to collect intelligence, many covert paramilitary actions undertaken in pursuit of military objectives would not be authorized by this section. If only a connection to intelligence must exist, even assassination of foreign leaders would be permitted if, for example, the agent-assassins previously supplied intelligence to the CIA. *See id.* at 131-132.

The second condition that must be met before activities authorized by the fifth function may begin is that the NSC must "direct" the CIA to perform the "other functions and duties." If Congress literally meant to require NSC approval for each covert action, several questions arise. First, may Congress delegate covert-actions decision making if military force is to be used? On the other hand, may Congress force the President to convene the NSC before ordering the CIA to act? Finally, may the NSC subdelegate whatever approval authority it possesses or approve categories of covert actions in advance? According to the *Church Committee Report*, through the 1960s the actual CIA practice was that

> all politically risky or costly covert action projects would be brought before a Committee of the National Security Council ... for approval. However, low-risk projects could be approved within the CIA. During some periods of time only a quarter of

all covert action projects undertaken by the CIA — the high-risk, high-cost covert actions — were approved by the NSC....

If Congressional authorization is claimed then the procedures established by Congress must be honored. If Congress intended covert actions to be undertaken on an ad hoc basis as specifically directed by the NSC then that procedure must be followed.... [*Id.* at 480-481.]

Are the Church Committee's legal conclusions constitutionally sound? Does the claim for statutory authorization then require case-by-case NSC approval? Consider again the holding of the Supreme Court in Little v. Barreme, 6 U.S. (2 Cranch) 170 (1804), *supra* p. 77.

1. From the Cold War Through Vietnam: Intelligence Operations 1947-1973

a. *Intelligence Operations and Executive Branch Decision Making*

Post-enactment events quickly converted the National Security Act of 1947 from an academic debate about legislative intent into a real instrument of foreign policy. As the Church Committee reported:

> At its first meeting in December, 1947, the National Security Council approved NSC-4[/]A, which empowered the Secretary of State to coordinate information activities designed to counter communism. A top secret annex took cognizance of the "vicious psychological efforts of the USSR, its satellite countries, and Communist groups to discredit and defeat the activities of the U.S. and other Western powers." The NSC determined that "in the interests of world peace and U.S. national security the foreign information activities of the U.S. government must be supplemented by covert psychological operations."
>
> The CIA was already engaged in clandestine collection of intelligence and, as the NSC put it, "The similarity of operational methods involved in covert psychological and intelligence activities and the need to ensure their secrecy and obviate costly duplication renders the CIA the logical agency to conduct such operations." Therefore, acting under the authority of section [403-4a(d)(4)] of the National Security Act of 1947, the NSC instructed the Director of Central Intelligence to initiate and conduct covert psychological operations that would counteract Soviet and Soviet-inspired covert actions and which would be consistent with U.S. foreign policy and overt foreign information activities.
>
> In the following months, the CIA was involved in a number of covert actions. As the Soviet threat loomed larger and larger, the need for covert action, beyond psychological operations, seemed more pressing. On June 18, 1948, the NSC issued NSC-10/2 which superseded NSC-4[/]A, and vastly expanded the range of covert activities. The CIA was authorized to undertake economic warfare, sabotage, subversion against hostile states (including assistance to guerrilla and refugee liberation groups), and support of indigenous anti-communist elements in threatened countries.... [U]nder the authority of 50 U.S.C. §[403-4a(d)(4)], the NSC ordered the establishment in CIA of the Office of Special Projects (OSP), to conduct covert action. The Chief of OSP was to receive policy guidance from the Secretary of State and the Secretary of Defense. OSP (later, OPC) [Office of Policy

B. Implementing the 1947 Act

Coordination] was to operate independently of all components of the CIA to the maximum degree consistent with efficiency.... [*Church Committee Report, supra* p. 341, Book I, at 490-491.]

NOTES AND QUESTIONS

1. *NSC-4/A.* NSC-4/A was the President's first formal authorization of covert operations in the post-war period. The CIA used this authority to try to influence the outcome of the 1948 Italian national elections. *Church Committee Report, supra,* Book I, at 49; John Prados, *Presidents' Secret Wars* 27-28, 33 (1986). If you had been counsel to President Truman, would you have advised him to approve NSC-4/A? If so, on what authority? Should it matter that Congress appropriated the funds to carry out these covert actions?

2. *NSC-10/2.* According to Prados, NSC-10/2 had three distinct features that were important in shaping the post-war evolution of American covert operations:

> For the first time in a government decisional document, there appeared a mechanism designated by the President to approve and manage secret operations, and make them responsible to him. Second, and also for the first time, there appeared a comprehensive definition of covert operations. Finally, the CIA was again given primary responsibility for the mission, confirming the arrangement begun with NSC-4/A. [Prados, *supra,* at 29.]

Why require presidential approval for covert operations? What is the purpose and practical effect of the NSC-10/2 requirement that operations be conducted so that the United States can deny responsibility for them?

3. *Deniability for the President?* If the President denies having undertaken an operation that he approved and that was in fact carried out, to whom is the President accountable? The Church Committee argued against extending deniability as far as the President:

> Whatever can be said in defense of the original purpose of plausible denial — a purpose which intends to conceal United States involvement from the outside world — the extension of the doctrine to the internal decisionmaking process of the Government is absurd. Any theory which, as a matter of doctrine, places elected officials on the periphery of the decision-making process is an invitation to error, an abdication of responsibility, and a perversion of democratic government. The doctrine is the antithesis of accountability.
> Permitting specific acts to be taken on the basis of general approvals of broad strategies... blurs responsibility and accountability. Worse still, it increases the danger that subordinates may take steps which would have been disapproved if the policymakers had been informed. A further danger is that policymakers might intentionally use loose general instructions to evade responsibility for embarrassing activities. [*Alleged Assassination Plots Involving Foreign Leaders, An Interim Report of the Select Committee to Study Governmental Operations with Respect to Intelligence Activities,* S. Rep. No. 94-465, at 277-278 (1975).]

This controversial policy of "plausible deniability" was officially terminated in 1974 by the enactment of a statutory requirement that the President execute a predicate finding authorizing the action. See *infra* p. 390.

4. *Authority for Post-World War II Operations.* Consider the range of covert operations permitted by NSC-10/2. Which of these are authorized by statute? Which by the Constitution? Which, if any, are prohibited by the Constitution? Management of covert operations during the Truman administration is also reviewed in XII *Foreign Relations of the United States, 1964-1968, Western Europe,* XXXI-XXXV (2001) [hereinafter *Note on Covert Programs*], *available at* http://www.state.gov/r/pa/ho/frus/johnson/b/xii/2961.htm.

United States v. Lopez-Lima
United States District Court, Southern District of Florida, 1990
738 F. Supp. 1404

RYSKAMP, District Judge.... The indictment against Reinaldo Juan Lopez-Lima charges him with aircraft piracy in violation of Title 49, United States Code App., Section 1472(i). Specifically, the indictment charges that on or about February 18, 1964, Lopez-Lima "did unlawfully commit aircraft piracy in that [he and codefendant Enrique Castillo-Hernandez] did seize and exercise control by threat of force and violence, and with wrongful intent, of an aircraft... that is, the defendant did force Richard L. Wright at gunpoint to fly from Monroe County, Florida, to the Republic of Cuba."...

Lopez-Lima returned to the United States in 1987. In 1989, the U.S. State Department approached him as a possible source of information about Cuba, at which point the outstanding indictment against him was discovered. This prosecution then ensued.

Lopez-Lima's defense to the air piracy charge is that the hijacking was authorized by the Central Intelligence Agency ("CIA"), as part of its activities to destabilize the communist regime of Fidel Castro. According to Lopez-Lima, he and Castillo-Hernandez were to pose as defectors from the Cuban exile community who intended to reenter Cuba and support Castro. Once inside Cuba, the codefendants were to assist anti-Castro activists. Lopez-Lima claims that this CIA operation was designed to look like a hijacking, so that Cuban authorities would not suspect CIA involvement....

The issue presented... is whether Lopez-Lima has a legally cognizable defense based on classified information, so as to make that information relevant at trial. [Concerning the discovery and admissibility of classified information in a criminal trial, see *infra* pp. 859-866.]...

Lopez-Lima seeks to use the classified information included in the notices in two ways: (1) as an affirmative defense to show his reliance on the real authority of the CIA to sanction the hijacking; and (2) to rebut the government's proof on the intent element of the air piracy offense. The government challenges the use of this classified information on grounds of relevancy and admissibility....

... This court holds that to establish a public authority affirmative defense, the defense must show that the governmental entity involved had the real authority to sanction conduct that would violate the laws under which the defendant is charged; and that the defendant acted in reasonable reliance on an actual U.S. government agent. The court now considers whether the version of events put forth by Lopez-Lima constitutes such a public authority defense.

1. CIA AUTHORITY IN 1964...

... Executive Order 12,333, signed by President Reagan on Dec. 4, 1981, outlines U.S. intelligence activities but specifically provides that "[n]othing in this Order shall be construed to authorize any activity in violation of the Constitution or statutes of the United States." Exec. Order No. 12,333, Part 2.8, 46 Fed. Reg. 59,941 (1981). In 1964, the time of the offense with which Lopez-Lima is charged, Executive Order 12,333 did not exist. Thus, the CIA was not precluded explicitly from authorizing Lopez-Lima and his codefendant to hijack a plane to Cuba, even if that act were illegal according to U.S. statutes....

The first question is whether Executive Order 12,333 changed existing practice or merely codified practice that existed in 1981 and before. The answer to this question is revealed unequivocally in the public record, in the final report of what is popularly known as the Church Committee. Senate Select Committee to Study Governmental Operations with Respect to Intelligence Activities, S. Rept. No. 94-755, 94th Congress, 2nd Session, Book I (1976) [hereinafter "Church Committee Report"]. The Church Committee documented numerous activities undertaken by the intelligence community that violated declared policy and law, noting that "these abuses cannot be regarded as aberrations." *Id.* at 4. Clearly, Executive Order No. 12,333 was a corrective measure designed to stop intelligence agencies from engaging in covert activities that violated U.S. law.

The second question concerning Executive Order No. 12,333 is whether in its absence the CIA had the authority to authorize illegal activity. The answer to this question requires consideration of the laws and directives that created the CIA and cloaked it with the authority to engage in covert activities.

The CIA was established under the National Security Act of 1947. National Security Act of 1947, ch. 343, 61 Stat. 495 (1947) (codified as amended at 50 U.S.C. §§401-405 (1982)). Under the 1947 act, Congress empowered the agency to perform various intelligence functions, such as advising the National Security [Council] and correlating intelligence related to national security. 50 U.S.C. §403(d)(1), (3). Significantly, Congress also granted the CIA a broad, nonspecific power "to perform such other functions and duties related to intelligence affecting the national security as the National Security Council may from time to time direct." *Id.* §403(d)(5).

From the broad, nonspecific grant of power in section 403(d)(5), the National Security Council, with presidential approval, issued various directives that eventually provided the CIA with the license to exercise vast power. In 1948, Directive 10-2 formally authorized the CIA to conduct covert operations, which were defined as those "which are so planned and executed that any US [sic] Government responsibility for them is not evident to unauthorized persons and that if uncovered the US [sic] Government can plausibly disclaim any responsibility for them." *See* National Security Council Directive 10-2, §5, June 18, 1948. These covert operations were specified to include propaganda campaigns and economic subversion of hostile states.

In 1955, the National Security Council expanded CIA authority to conduct covert operations, allowing such operations necessary to meet the goals and objectives of the agency. *See* National Security Council Directive 5412-1, §6, March 12, 1955. The Council retained the concept of plausible deniability but broadened the catalogue of listed covert activities to include:

> any covert activities related to: propaganda, political action; economic warfare; preventative direct action, including sabotage, anti-sabotage, demolition; escape and evasion and evacuation measures; subversion against hostile states or groups including assistance to underground resistance movements, guerrillas and refugee liberation groups; support of indigenous and anti-communist elements in threatened countries of the free world; deception plans and operations; and all activities compatible with this directive necessary to accomplish the foregoing.

Although this directive was amended, its definition of covert activities did not change. *See* National Security Council Directive 5412-2, §6, Dec. 28, 1955.

The catalogue of covert activities included in the 5412 Directives was that which the CIA was empowered to pursue in 1964, the year of the offense with which Lopez-Lima is charged. Until Executive Order 12,333 was signed in 1981, the CIA was under no limitation that its activities could not violate U.S. law. Significantly, nothing required the CIA to clear its activities with the Department of Justice, even though the directives of the National Security Council required clearance with the Departments of State and Defense. *See* National Security Council Directive 10-2, §3(d)(1), June 18, 1948; National Security Council Directive 5412-1, §4(a), March 12, 1955; National Security Council Directive 5412-2, §4(a), Dec. 28, 1955.

Not only was there no requirement that the CIA comply with the law in 1964, according to the Church Committee Report the agency routinely violated the law during the time period of the offense in question. Congressional oversight of intelligence activities during this time period was extremely limited. Church Committee Report, Book I, at 447. This situation began to change only in 1974, when Congress passed the Hughes-Ryan Amendment, which established presidential accountability for covert activities and statutory reporting requirements. Pub. L. No. 87-195, Pt. III, §662, as added Pub. L. No. 93-559, §32, 88 Stat. 1804 (1974) (codified as amended at 22 U.S.C. §2422 (1988)). Thereafter, the Senate empaneled the Church Committee, which issued its final report in 1976. Following that report, a number of executive orders were issued that limited covert operations, including Executive Order No. 12,333.

Yet, the situation was far different in 1964. At that time, the CIA operated with broad authority, emanating from successive National Security Council directives issued pursuant to a vague congressional grant of authority in section 403(d)(5). Accordingly, the court holds that in 1964 the CIA had the real authority to authorize a hijacking to Cuba, as one of its "deception plans and operations." The court does not accept the government's argument that even if the CIA used its authority to authorize the illegal activity with which Lopez-Lima is charged, the use of that authority would be not real but illegitimate. According to this argument, if the CIA acted in a vacuum of authority to authorize illegal covert activities, it cannot be said to have possessed the real authority to authorize those activities. Yet, the Church Committee did not so conclude. If the court

B. Implementing the 1947 Act

were to accept the government's argument, it would be impossible for a defendant to establish a real authority defense. Even if the CIA's authority to authorize illegal covert activities in 1964 was not specifically provided in law, it was exercised as a very real authority.

2. REASONABLE RELIANCE ON A GOVERNMENT AGENT

Although the CIA as an entity had the real authority to authorize an illegal hijacking in 1964, Lopez-Lima still must show that he reasonably relied on the authorization of government agents acting in their individual capacities. According to CIA records, the individuals named in Lopez-Lima's notices as having sanctioned the hijacking were actual CIA assets at the time....

Lopez-Lima must be allowed to introduce evidence to establish whether he reasonably relied on the sanction of actual government assets. While the named assets might "have no authority themselves [to sanction the hijacking of an airplane], they undoubtedly have authority to communicate decisions made by those in the CIA hierarchy who have authority." [United States v.] Smith, 592 F. Supp. [424 (E.D. Va. 1984),] at 432 n.10....

For the reasons articulated, the court concludes that Lopez-Lima's version of events, if credited by a jury, establishes an affirmative defense to the aircraft piracy charge against him and negates the wrongful intent necessary to secure a conviction on that charge. The classified information Lopez-Lima seeks to introduce clearly is relevant to his defense, as it would tend to show that the CIA sanctioned the hijacking or that he reasonably believed that it did. Of course, while the classified information is relevant, it may not prove persuasive before a jury. Notwithstanding, Lopez-Lima is entitled to have a jury consider the theories and evidence that he marshals in his defense....

NOTES AND QUESTIONS

1. *Legal Effect of Executive Order No. 12,333 on 1964 Actions.* The court relies heavily on the provision of Executive Order No. 12,333 which expressly disclaims any authority "in this Order" to violate the Constitution or laws. Does it follow logically or legally that in 1964 the CIA "was not precluded explicitly from authorizing Lopez-Lima . . . to hijack a plane to Cuba, even if that act were illegal according to U.S. statutes"? Executive Order No. 12,333 is excerpted *infra* p. 397.

2. *Sources of CIA Authority in 1964.* Of what relevance to the CIA's authority in 1964 are the Church Committee findings in the mid-1970s that there were numerous abuses of declared law and policy by the intelligence agencies during the period at issue, and that Executive Order No. 12,333 was a "corrective measure"?

3. *Legal Effect of the NSC Directives.* Consider the activities permitted by NSC Directives 10-2 and 5412. What activities by the CIA would not have been within the scope of those directives? Were the directives authorized by the National Security Act?

4. *Rights of the Criminal Defendant.* Do you suppose that the court was influenced in finding that the CIA had "real authority" to authorize a hijacking to Cuba in 1964 by the implications of a contrary finding for the criminal defendant's chances of mounting a defense of authorization? The parameters of authorization and "following orders" defenses are explored *supra* p. 65 and *infra* p. 419.

b. *Escalating Use and Review of Intelligence Operations*

The size and scope of covert actions grew dramatically after the first few years:

> As a result of the upsurge of paramilitary action and contingency planning, OPC's manpower almost trebled during the first year of the Korean War. A large part of this increase consisted of paramilitary experts, who were later to be instrumental in CIA paramilitary operations in the Bay of Pigs, the Congo, and Laos, among others.... By 1953, there were major covert operations in 48 countries, consisting primarily of propaganda and political action....
>
> The post-Korean War period did not see a reduction in CIA covert activities. Indeed, the communist threat was now seen to be world-wide, rather than concentrated on the borders of the Soviet Union and mainland China. In response, the CIA, at the direction of the National Security Council, expanded its European and crisis-oriented approach into a world-wide effort to anticipate and meet communist aggression, often with techniques equal to those of the Soviet clandestine services....
>
> The Bay of Pigs disaster in 1961 prompted a reorganization of CIA covert action and the procedures governing it. A new form of covert action—counterinsurgency—was now emphasized. Under the direction of the National Security Council, the CIA rapidly expanded its counterinsurgency capability, focusing on Latin America, Africa, and the Far East.... The Laos operation eventually became the largest paramilitary effort in post-war history....
>
> The CIA's paramilitary effort continued to expand throughout the decade. The paramilitary budget reached an all-time high in 1970. It probably would have continued to climb, had not the burden of the Laos program been transferred to the Department of Defense in 1971.... [*Church Committee Report, supra* p. 359, Book I, at 145-147.]

As covert action capability evolved, so did the processes for deciding whether to engage in such actions. Between 1948 and 1955, no formal process existed for reviewing or approving covert proposals. The DCI approved some projects on his own authority; others were brought to the President's attention at the DCI's initiative. A 1955 NSC directive authorized the CIA to "develop underground resistance and facilitate covert and guerilla operations" through projects that would be reviewed and approved by a "Special Group" consisting of "designated representatives" of the President and the State and Defense Departments. This directive did not spell out substantive review criteria, however, and while control procedures for covert action were tightened after the failure of the Bay of Pigs in 1962, operational decisions were made by informal meetings of NSC principals throughout the 1960s. The review process changed in 1970, when National Security Decision Memorandum (NSDM) 40 was issued, creating

B. Implementing the 1947 Act

the "40 Committee" (made up of the DCI, the National Security Adviser, the Deputy Secretary of Defense, and the Under Secretary of State for Political Affairs) to review covert action proposals:

> NSDM 40 assigned the DCI responsibility for coordinating and controlling covert operations. The Director was instructed to plan and conduct covert operations in a manner consistent with United States foreign and military policies and to consult with and obtain appropriate coordination from any other interested agencies or officers on a need-to-know basis. The directive also spelled out the role of the 40 Committee. It stated that the DCI was responsible for obtaining policy approval for all major and/or politically sensitive covert action programs through the 40 Committee.... Guidelines for the submission of covert action proposals to the 40 Committee were spelled out in an internal CIA directive. The [DCI] decided whether an operational program or activity should be submitted to the 40 Committee for policy approval. The paramount consideration was political sensitivity, but it was also significant if a program involved large sums of money.... After a proposal was approved by the DCI, it was distributed in memorandum form to the 40 Committee principals. Except in emergencies, distribution to the principals was to occur at least 72 hours in advance of a meeting. Normally, the written proposal, as contained in the 40 Committee memorandum, was formally considered following an oral presentation by the CIA. This presentation was usually given by the Agency Division Chief having action responsibility. In addition to the principals, participants at 40 Committee meetings included, on occasion, the CIA's Deputy Director for Operations, a representative from the State Department's Bureau of Intelligence and Research, and the Assistant Secretary of State for the region involved.... The President would become involved, formally, only if there was disagreement within the Committee, or if the Chairman or another member thought a proposal was sufficiently important.... [*Church Committee Report, supra*, Book I, at 53-55.]

NOTES AND QUESTIONS

1. *Reconciling Covert Actions and Policy.* The justification for covert operations shifted sharply between the immediate post-war years and the early 1970s, from containing international communism to serving more broadly as an instrument of U.S. foreign policy. But while the rationale for covert operations evolved, attempts to harmonize the rationale with public policy were halting and controversial. Center for National Security Studies (CNSS), *Covert Operations and the Democratic Process: The Implications of the Iran/Contra Affair* 9 (1987) (hereinafter *CNSS*). Though the intelligence community has, of course, endorsed the broad goal of conducting covert programs in support of the interests of the United States, many officials have argued that a range of covert activities should be undertaken that may seem at odds with American principles. A 1954 report on CIA activities reflected this view:

> It is now clear that we are facing an implacable enemy whose avowed objective is world domination by whatever means and at whatever cost. There are no rules in such a game. Hitherto acceptable norms of human conduct do not apply. If the U.S. is to survive, long-standing American concepts of "fair play" must be reconsidered. We must develop effective espionage and counterespionage services and must learn to subvert, sabotage, and destroy our enemies by more clever, more

sophisticated, and more effective methods than those used against us. It may become necessary that the American people be made acquainted with, understand and support this fundamentally repugnant philosophy. [*Quoted in Church Committee Report, supra* p. 359, Book I, at 50.]

One alternative strategy would be to require that covert operations form some part of a larger overt program. *CNSS, supra*, at 9. Even more broadly, "consistency with American principles" has been suggested as a test for covert operations, requiring that both the aims and methods of particular operations be capable of winning public support if the operations were overt. *Id.* Do you think the early CIA initiatives would have met this test? Would political assassinations? Efforts to subvert democratic governments? Support for internal security forces that engage in the systematic violation of human rights?

2. *Measuring Accountability.* Accountability for covert operations was an important issue from the beginning. According to one theory, accountability would be best ensured by requiring a full debate within the executive branch about all covert action proposals. Full internal debate would protect against different executive branch actors working at cross purposes, and it would substitute for the normal public debate on policy issues by including officials with expertise and with different perspectives. *CNSS, supra*, at 28. To what extent did the early directives further this principle? In fact, State and Defense Department representatives were included from the beginning, but the Office of the President was not formally involved until 1955. Even then, the Special Group met infrequently, and only some covert operations proposals were submitted to it for review. Additional detail on executive review during this period is supplied by *Note on Covert Programs, supra* p. 376. What weaknesses can you identify in the structures and processes for reviewing covert action proposals? What reforms could you suggest?

NOTE ON COVERT INTERVENTION IN CHILE

Central Intelligence Agency, CIA Activities in Chile
September 18, 2000
http://www.cia.gov/cia/publications/chile

In the 1960s and the early 1970s, as part of the US Government policy to try to influence events in Chile, the CIA undertook specific covert action projects in Chile.... The overwhelming objective—firmly rooted in the policy of the period—was to discredit Marxist-leaning political leaders, especially Dr. Salvador Allende, and to strengthen and encourage their civilian and military opponents to prevent them from assuming power.

Overview of Covert Actions. At the direction of the White House and interagency policy coordination committees, CIA undertook...sustained propaganda efforts, including financial support for major news media, against Allende and other Marxists. Political action projects supported selected parties before and after the 1964 elections and after Allende's 1970 election....

B. Implementing the 1947 Act

Support for Coup in 1970. . . . CIA sought to instigate a coup to prevent Allende from taking office after he won a plurality in the 4 September election and before, as Constitutionally required because he did not win an absolute majority, the Chilean Congress reaffirmed his victory. CIA was working with three different groups of plotters. All three groups made it clear that any coup would require the kidnapping of Army Commander Rene Schneider, who felt deeply that the Constitution required that the Army allow Allende to assume power. CIA agreed with that assessment. Although CIA provided weapons to one of the groups, we have found no information that the plotters' or CIA's intention was for the general to be killed. Contact with one group of plotters was dropped early on because of its extremist tendencies. CIA provided tear gas, submachine-guns and ammunition to the second group. The third group attempted to kidnap Schneider, mortally wounding him in the attack. CIA had previously encouraged this group to launch a coup but withdrew support four days before the attack because, in CIA's assessment, the group could not carry it out successfully.

Awareness of Coup Plotting in 1973. Although CIA did not instigate the coup that ended Allende's government on 11 September 1973, it was aware of coup-plotting by the military, had ongoing intelligence collection relationships with some plotters, and — because CIA did not discourage the takeover and had sought to instigate a coup in 1970 — probably appeared to condone it. There was no way that anyone, including CIA, could have known that Allende would refuse the putchists' offer of safe passage out of the country and that instead — with *La Moneda* Palace under bombardment from tanks and airplanes and in flames — would take his own life.

Knowledge of Human Rights Violations. CIA officers were aware of and reported to analysts and policymakers in 1973 that General Pinochet and the forces that overthrew the Allende Government were conducting a severe campaign against leftists and perceived political enemies in the early months after the coup. Activities of some security services portended a long-term effort to suppress opponents. In January 1974, CIA officers and assets were tasked to report on human rights violations by the Chilean government.

NOTES AND QUESTIONS

1. *Authorization to Uncover the U.S. Role.* The report, *CIA Activities in Chile*, was created in response to §311 of the Intelligence Authorization Act for Fiscal Year 2000, Pub. L. No. 106-120, 113 Stat. 1606, 1614 (1999), to answer lingering questions about the U.S. role in the coup that brought General Pinochet to power in Chile, and in human rights violations committed during the early Pinochet rule. *See generally* National Security Archive, *Chile Documentation Project*, Nov. 13, 2000, *at* http://www.gwu.edu/~nsarchiv/latin_america/chile.htm.

2. *Secret Executive Decisions.* According to the report, "[e]fforts by the United States to support anti-Communist forces in Chile date back to the late 1950s and reflect the rivalry between the United States and the Soviet Union for influence throughout the Third World." *CIA Activities in Chile, supra,* at 5. The Church Committee reported that at a September 15, 1970, meeting

between President Nixon, National Security Adviser Henry Kissinger, and DCI Richard Helms, Nixon and Kissinger directed the CIA to prevent Allende from taking power. According to Helms's notes, they were "not concerned [about the] risks involved," and they wanted Helms to "make the economy scream." *Id.* President Nixon instructed the CIA not to inform the 40 Committee, the State or Defense Departments, or the ambassador in Santiago. Staff of the S. Select Comm. to Study Governmental Operations with Respect to Intelligence Activities, 94th Cong., *Covert Action in Chile 1963-1973* (1975), at 41. Were the instructions to Helms lawful? Whether they were or not, do you think the executive review process outlined above functioned properly?

3. *The Role of Dirty Assets.* The CIA has admitted that its clandestine assets in Chile were involved in human rights abuses. What legal mechanisms, if any, could make it less likely that future assets will commit such abuses? See *infra* p. 451.

C. CONGRESSIONAL OVERSIGHT

1. From the Cold War Through Vietnam

For the first thirty years of its existence the agency's relationship with Congress was very informal indeed. In essence, the DCI and his close colleagues dealt personally and informally with the chairmen of the important and relevant Senate and House committees... and other senators and congressmen who were "friends" or who had significant political influence in areas important to the agency in Washington. This worked because the agency was trusted, its directors were respected, and it was seen as being America's principal defense against the subterranean machinations of world communism....

The reluctance of the legislators to press the CIA for information about operations... was entirely understandable.... They preferred to be able to plead ignorance of specific information so that they would not find themselves compromised politically. CIA officials were content with this arrangement; they made it clear that they would provide the information asked of them, and if it was not asked, so be it. For over twenty-five years the system worked. [Ranelagh, *supra* p. 372, at 281-285.]

The Church Committee described congressional oversight during this period by recounting the example of covert operations in Chile:

Of the 33 covert action projects undertaken in Chile between 1963 and 1974 with 40 Committee approval, Congress was briefed in some fashion on eight. Presumably the 25 others were undertaken without congressional consultation. Of the more than $13 million spent in Chile on covert action projects between 1963 and 1974, Congress received briefings (sometimes before and sometimes after the fact) on projects totaling about $9.3 million. Further, congressional oversight committees were not consulted about projects which were not reviewed by the full 40 Committee.... [*Church Committee Report, supra* p. 358, Book I, at 150-151.]

C. Congressional Oversight

The events in Chile, along with Watergate and the Southeast Asia war, all served to focus public attention on the CIA. They also had a corrosive effect on the historical pattern of informal congressional oversight of the intelligence community. The fact that Congress acted to formalize that oversight indicates the delicacy of the relationship and the need for bipartisan trust to make oversight effective. *See* Prados, *supra* p. 375, at 331-334; Daniel B. Silver, *The Uses and Misuses of Intelligence Oversight*, 11 Hous. J. Intl. L. 7 (1988). For an argument that such an increasingly "legalesque" relationship between the President and Congress is ill-advised and perhaps unconstitutional, *see* David Everett Colton, *Speaking Truth to Power: Intelligence Oversight in an Imperfect World*, 137 U. Pa. L. Rev. 571 (1988).

2. Budget Oversight

The importance of the defense appropriations power as a means of ensuring congressional participation in national security decision making was established in Chapters 5 and 8. Once funds are appropriated for covert actions, however, the open-ended authority given to the CIA in the National Security Act, along with the secret nature of intelligence operations, may make oversight of the expenditure of those funds especially difficult.

An adage from the Watergate era — "follow the money" — reminds us of one way for Congress and citizens to learn about covert action and other intelligence operations, albeit after the fact. Article I, Section 9, Clause 7 states that "a regular Statement and Account of the Receipts and Expenditures of all public Money shall be published from time to time." Does the Constitution thus require that spending for intelligence programs, including covert action, be made public? If the "from time to time" qualifier affords some discretion to delay disclosure, is permanent budget secrecy foreclosed by the Constitution? If publication of budget details for intelligence programs, such as covert action, could compromise security, upon what legal basis may publication be avoided? Is there a lawful middle ground, such as required publication of the aggregate spending for intelligence programs without any detail?

Beginning in 1967, U.S. citizen-taxpayer William B. Richardson wrote a series of letters to the Treasury Department seeking information concerning detailed expenditures of the CIA. Richardson was provided copies of the "Combined Statement of Receipts, Expenditures, and Balances of the United States Government." But in accordance with the Central Intelligence Agency Act of 1949, which permits the Agency to account for its expenditures "solely on the certificate of the Director," 50 U.S.C. §403j(b) (2000), the Combined Statement did not provide information on the budget of the CIA. Richardson sued, claiming that §403j(b) violates the Statement and Account Clause of Article I, Section 9, Clause 7. The Supreme Court eventually found that Richardson lacked standing as a citizen because his grievance was "generalized" and "common to all members of the public," while his claim as a taxpayer failed because there was no challenge to an enactment under the Taxing and Spending Clause and no claim based on a "specific constitutional limitation" on the taxing and spending power. United States v. Richardson, 418 U.S. 166, 175-177 (1974). See Chapter 6.

The Third Circuit Court of Appeals, sitting en banc, had found standing in Richardson v. United States, 465 F.2d 844 (3d Cir. 1972), and had this to say about the Statement and Account Clause:

> A responsible and intelligent taxpayer and citizen, of course, wants to know how his tax money is being spent. Without this information he cannot intelligently follow the actions of the Congress or of the Executive. Nor can he properly fulfill his obligations as a member of the electorate. The Framers of the Constitution deemed fiscal information essential if the electorate was to exercise any control over its representatives and meet their new responsibilities as citizens of the Republic. [*Id.* at 853.]

The framing history was reviewed by Judge Adams, dissenting:

> The debates regarding Article I, Section 9, Clause 7 . . . that occurred during the Constitutional Convention, shed light on the relative importance of that stipulation. . . . Farrand indicates that the discussion began with a statement by George Mason that "he did not conceive that the receipts and expenditures of the public money ought ever to be concealed. The people, he affirmed, had a right to know the expenditures of their money." 3 Farrand, The Records of the Federal Convention of 1787, at 326 (Rev. ed. 1966). James Madison disagreed only with Mason's proposal of a fixed reporting period, stating that reports based on short periods:
>
>> would not be so full and connected as would be necessary for a thorough comprehension of them and detection of any errors. But by giving them [the reporting officials] an opportunity of publishing them from time to time, as might be found easy and convenient, they would be more full and satisfactory to the public, and would be sufficiently frequent. *Id.*
>
> Rufus King objected to a full accounting on the ground that it would be "impracticable" to report "every minute shilling." 2 Farrand 618.
>
> The argument that the duty to report the accounting runs to the public is based on a comparison of Article I, Section 9, Clause 7 with Article II, Section 3. . . . [T]he impact of the distinction between "shall be published" and "shall from time to time give to the Congress" becomes apparent. Furthermore, the Articles of Confederation, drafted by many of the same persons as the Constitution, required only that Congress inform the states of its indebtedness, as opposed to the requirement of publication of the receipt and expenditures of all public money. *Compare* U.S. Const. Art. I, §9, cl. 7 *with* Articles of Confederation, Art. IX, ¶5 (requiring Congress to account to the states for "sums of money . . . borrowed or emitted"). . . .
>
> Nevertheless, without denigrating the importance of Article I, Section 9, Clause 7, it would appear fair to conclude that it does not rise to the paramount stature of other constitutional provisions, such as those contained in the Bill of Rights. [465 F.2d at 871-872.]

NOTES AND QUESTIONS

1. *Congressional Authority to Change the Rules.* The Supreme Court stated in *Richardson* that "Congress has plenary power to exact any reporting and accounting requirement it considers appropriate." 418 U.S. at 178 n. 11. Indeed, no court has enforced Article I, Section 9 by striking down an act of Congress

C. Congressional Oversight

requiring an accounting for or reporting of spending. Kate Stith, *Congress' Power of the Purse*, 97 Yale L.J. 1343, 1392 (1988). Does the grant of the appropriations power to Congress necessarily include the power to interpret Article I, Section 9? *Cf.* Powell v. McCormack, 395 U.S. 486 (1969), holding that Congress's power to construe Article I, Section 5 is limited. Would repeal of the Central Intelligence Agency Act of 1949, *supra* p. 358, be constitutional? Would a statutory requirement to publish the CIA budget be constitutional? In other words, *must* the Congress keep the CIA budget secret in the interest of national security? Do you think a federal court would decide this issue? *See generally* Stith, *supra*; William C. Banks & Peter Raven-Hansen, *National Security Law and the Power of the Purse* 105 (1994) (arguing that such a requirement would be constitutional).

2. *Merits of the Richardson Suit.* If the merits had been reached in *Richardson*, what should have been the holding? That "all public Money" means what it says and applies to the CIA? That the CIA budget is one of those matters that the Framers understood might require secrecy? That whatever the Framers' intentions, the "from time to time" language provides Congress with discretion to shield CIA funds from public view indefinitely? In the No-Transfer Act of 1811, Congress secretly empowered the President to seize any part of Florida if any foreign power attempted to occupy the area, but the Act was not published until 1818. Act of Jan. 15, 1811, 3 Stat. 471 (1818). *See* Louis Fisher, *Presidential Spending Power* 214 (1975). Does the existence of an implied executive privilege in Article II, in addition to Congress's discretion in Article I, Section 9, provide authority for the government to keep any financial information from the public?

In the Virginia ratification debate, George Mason conceded that while "some matters, such as ongoing diplomatic negotiations and military operations, might require secrecy, he did not conceive that the receipts and expenditures of the public money ought ever to be concealed." 3 Jonathan Elliot, *Debates on the Federal Constitution* 459 (1836). Does the CIA budget simply reflect a situation not contemplated by the Framers—that disclosing expenses could undermine an ongoing covert paramilitary operation?

3. *Secret Journal Clause.* Does the Secret Journal Clause of Article I, Section 5 lend support to the argument that a plain meaning construction of the Statement and Account Clause requires publication of intelligence spending? Or does the express recognition of the need for secrecy for the congressional journal reflect a more general acknowledgment that national security concerns might justify keeping information from the people?

4. *How the Money Game Works.* The 1949 Central Intelligence Agency Act grants expansive authority to the CIA concerning the transfer and use of public funds. The Act states that sums made available to the CIA "may be expended without regard to the provisions of law and regulations relating to the expenditure of Government funds." 50 U.S.C. §403j(b) (2000). Moreover, instead of direct appropriations to the CIA, the 1949 Act authorizes the Agency to transfer to and receive from other government agencies "such sums as may be approved" by the Office of Management and Budget (OMB) for any of the functions or activities authorized by the National Security Act of 1947. 50 U.S.C. §403f(a) (2000). Other agencies are also permitted to transfer or receive from the CIA

such sums "without regard to any provisions of law limiting or prohibiting transfers between appropriations." *Id.* Thus, funds for the intelligence community are first concealed in various inflated appropriation bills and then secretly transferred by OMB to the intelligence agencies after the bills are enacted.

> In the formulation of the president's budget, the requests of the intelligence agencies are first coordinated by representatives of sponsoring agencies before being submitted to OMB for careful review of justifications and further coordination within the intelligence community. Once the president's budget is submitted to Congress, the portion for the intelligence agencies is segregated from the rest and discussed by members of the House and Senate Intelligence Committees and the relevant defense appropriations subcommittees meeting in executive session. The committees hold closed hearings at which agency staff answer questions and supply additional detail for the written budget justifications.
>
> Once an NFIP [National Foreign Intelligence Program] budget is approved by the intelligence and defense appropriation committees, a classified schedule of the authorizations and an explanation of the budget issues considered by the intelligence committees is made available to the executive branch and to the appropriations and armed services committees. This classified schedule lists the recommended allocation for all intelligence programs. When floor debate on the larger appropriation bills begins, the NFIP budget is hidden within the recommended appropriations for other agencies, recently DOD. These appropriation accounts are inflated to reflect the pending budget transfers, but the members of Congress who are debating the budget and voting on appropriations do not know which figures are inflated or by how much. Congress is thus only mechanically involved in approving the budget... and its action in approving the remainder of the budget is clouded with the shell game of hiding the intelligence figures within other accounts.
>
> After a budget is approved by Congress and the president, OMB receives instructions from the chair of the House Appropriations Committee as to the amounts and sources of budget transfers to be made to the intelligence agencies. OMB then carries out the transfers through its own highly secretive process. [Banks & Raven-Hansen, *supra* p. 387, at 52 (footnotes omitted)].

5. *Small Steps Toward Openness.* The budget for the intelligence community remains officially secret. However, beginning in 1991 all members of Congress were granted access to the classified annex to the defense appropriations bill that contains detailed information about appropriations for the intelligence community. Pub. L. No. 102-172, §6035, 105 Stat. 1150 (1991). At about the same time, Congress took tentative steps toward more openness in the intelligence budget. Until conferees compromised in the face of a threatened veto by President Bush, the fiscal 1992 intelligence authorization would have required publication of the aggregate budget figure. *See* H.R. Rep. No. 102-2038 (1991); H.R. Rep. No. 102-65 (1991).

In 1997, the CIA yielded to a Federation of American Scientists (FAS) Freedom of Information Act (FOIA) lawsuit and disclosed that the fiscal year 1997 aggregate budget for intelligence-related activities was $26.6 billion. *Statement of the Director of Central Intelligence Regarding the Disclosure of the Aggregate Intelligence Budget for Fiscal Year 1997,* Oct. 15, 1997, *available at* http://www.fas.org/sgp/foia/victory.html. DCI George J. Tenet said that the disclosure was authorized by President Clinton and that it "does not jeopardize" national security and "serves

C. Congressional Oversight

to inform the American people." *Id.* A 1998 FAS FOIA request produced a similar statement from the DCI that the fiscal year 1998 figure was $26.7 billion. *Statement by the Director of Central Intelligence Regarding the Disclosure of the Aggregate Intelligence Budget for Fiscal Year 1998,* Mar. 20, 1998, *available at* http://www.fas.org/sgp/foia/intel98.html.

Later in 1998, however, the FAS filed another lawsuit seeking disclosure when DCI Tenet declined to release the fiscal year 1999 aggregate intelligence budget figure. Tenet argued that mandatory disclosure of 1999 spending after two years of voluntary disclosure "provides too much trend information and too great a comparison and analysis for our adversaries." Vernon Loeb, *Intelligence Budget Can Be Secret, Judge Rules,* Wash. Post, Nov. 23, 1999, at A4. In November 1999, the district court granted a CIA motion for summary judgment that the budget information is properly classified in the interest of national security and that release of the information might compromise intelligence sources and methods. Aftergood v. Central Intelligence Agency, No. 1:98CV02107 (TFH) (D.D.C. 1999), *available at* http://www.fas.org/sgp/foia/hogan.html. Congressional efforts to compel publication since 1999 have lacked sufficient support. *See, e.g.,* Intelligence Authorization Act for Fiscal Year 2001, H.R. 4392, 106th Cong., §306 (2000); 146 Cong. Rec. H3496-3509 (May 22, 2000). At a November 2005 conference, the deputy director of national intelligence for collection stated that the annual budget for intelligence was $44 billion, an apparent slip. Scott Shane, *Official Reveals Budget for U.S. Intelligence,* N.Y. Times, Nov. 8, 2005, at A18.

3. Congressional Oversight Reforms

a. *The War Powers Resolution and Covert Action*

The War Powers Resolution, 50 U.S.C. §§1541-1548 (2000), a product of the Vietnam War, was meant to limit unilateral executive war making. Yet it appears that Congress failed to address what may be the dominant form of military action in modern times. As we saw in Chapter 9, many short-term military operations escape the time limits of the resolution or are arguably not subject to its strictures for other reasons. More important for our immediate purposes, the resolution applies only to "United States Armed Forces," 50 U.S.C. §§1542-1543, and so appears to exempt covert paramilitary operations conducted by U.S. agents other than members of the armed forces. Indeed, the legislative history seems to confirm that exemption. An amendment proposed by Senator Eagleton that would have extended the measure to private armies "employed by, under contract to, or under the direction of" the government failed to pass. 119 Cong. Rec. 25,079-25,092 (1973). *See* Newell L. Highsmith, *Policing Executive Adventurism: Congressional Oversight of Military and Paramilitary Operations,* 19 Harv. J. Legis. 327, 353-354 (1982). Thus, the War Powers Resolution may have inadvertently driven war making even farther underground. *See* Harold Hongju Koh, *Why the President (Almost) Always Wins in Foreign Affairs: Lessons of the Iran-Contra Affair,* 97 Yale L.J. 1255, 1273 (1988); Douglas Steele, Note, *Covert Action and the War Powers Resolution: Preserving the Constitutional Balance,* 39 Syracuse L. Rev. 1139 (1988).

b. *The Hughes-Ryan Amendment*

Any remaining doubt that Congress had by legislation recognized the CIA's covert action function ended in 1974, when Congress passed the Hughes-Ryan Amendment to the Foreign Assistance Act, Pub. L. No. 93-559, §32, 88 Stat. 1804, which provided in part:

> Limitation on Intelligence Activities. (a) No funds appropriated under the authority of this or any other Act may be expended by or on behalf of the Central Intelligence Agency for operations in foreign countries, other than activities intended solely for obtaining necessary intelligence, unless and until the President finds that each such operation is important to the national security of the United States and reports, in a timely fashion, a description and scope of such operation to the appropriate committees of the Congress, including the Committee on Foreign Relations of the United States Senate and the Committee on Foreign Affairs of the United States House of Representatives.

NOTES AND QUESTIONS

1. *Legal Effect of Hughes-Ryan.* Did Hughes-Ryan constitute congressional authorization for covert operations, including CIA sponsorship of paramilitary action? If so, what is your opinion of the constitutionality of the statute?

Soon after Hughes-Ryan was passed, CIA General Counsel Rogovin maintained that the amendment "clearly implies that the CIA is authorized to plan and conduct covert action." Rogovin Memorandum, *supra* p. 358, at 1737. The same conclusion was reached by two committees of the Association of the Bar of the City of New York. Committee on Civil Rights and the Committee on International Human Relations, Association of the Bar of the City of New York, *The Central Intelligence Agency: Oversight and Accountability* 15 (1975). During floor debates, Representative Holtzman argued that the amendment would permit the CIA to "subvert or undermine foreign governments." 120 Cong. Rec. 39,165 (1974). On the other hand, Senator Hughes and others viewed the amendment as the beginning of a reform process. Information about the CIA's activities generated by the reporting requirement would inform Congress, so that Congress could determine what permanent controls to impose. 120 Cong. Rec. 39,488-39,490 (1974) (Sen. Hughes); *id.* at 39,491 (Sen. Baker and Sen. Symington). *See generally* Americo R. Cinquegrana, *Dancing in the Dark: Accepting the Invitation to Struggle in the Context of "Covert Action," the Iran-Contra Affair and the Intelligence Oversight Process*, 11 Hous. J. Intl. L. 177, 182-187 (1988).

If Congress learns after several Hughes-Ryan reports that covert actions are not to its collective liking, may it simply ban, say, all activities described in NSC-10/2, *supra* p. 374?

2. *Exemption for the Military.* Subsection (b) of the Hughes-Ryan Amendment exempted military actions in a declared war or "an exercise of powers by the President under the War Powers Resolution" from the law's requirements. Pub. L. No. 93-559, 88 Stat. 1804, *repealed,* Pub. L. No. 96-450, §407(a)(3), 94 Stat. 1981 (1980). Do you think the second exemption was needed?

C. Congressional Oversight

3. *Expanding the Number Who Receive Notice.* One who was not happy with the new oversight contemplated by Hughes-Ryan was President Gerald Ford. As he later commented:

> When I served in the House the system we had for monitoring the CIA worked well. Under that arrangement, eight Representatives and six Senators were designated as overseers. We met with the CIA director and his top staff people on a regular basis. No staff members ever joined us and there were no leaks. It was in one of those sessions, for example, that I was informed about our plans to build the U-2 and I was kept abreast of every development from the inception of the program. Only a handful of people knew about the planned overflights of the USSR and we kept the secret to ourselves. That couldn't happen today.
>
> The reason is the Hughes-Ryan amendment of 1974. Congress decided that the "appropriate committees" that had to be informed of CIA activities totalled eight with a combined membership of 163 Senators and Representatives. That's not including the dozens of top staff members who would be privy to reports. Anytime you tell some 200 people in Washington, D.C., the details of a "secret" operation, the odds are overwhelming that they'll be in the media soon. Rather than risk exposure and embarrassment, the intelligence agency will simply decide not to undertake the operation it planned. That's what happened to the CIA. [Gerald R. Ford, *A Time To Heal* xxv (1980).]

Before Hughes-Ryan, the CIA reported to the Armed Services Committees and the Appropriations Committees of both Houses. Hughes-Ryan added the House Foreign Affairs and the Senate Foreign Relations committees. The seventh and eighth oversight committees were added following the Church Committee investigations in 1975-1976, when each House established a special committee for oversight of intelligence. Scott Breckenridge, *The CIA and the U.S. Intelligence System* 266 (1986). Was President Ford fair in his criticism of Hughes-Ryan? Can oversight be effectively performed without such a wide distribution of information about covert activities? Does the improvement in oversight outweigh the risk of disclosure? The wide distribution of reports complained of by President Ford was changed in 1980. See *infra* p. 394. The organization and operation of the current intelligence oversight committees are described in Select Committee on Intelligence, United States Senate, *Legislative Oversight of Intelligence Activities: The U.S. Experience*, S. Prt. No. 103-88, at 6-19 (1994).

4. *Satisfying the Hughes-Ryan Requirements.* Consider the threshold for invoking Hughes-Ryan, that an operation be "important to the national security." What showing must the President have made to satisfy this standard? Should Congress have substituted "essential" or "grave threats" for "important"? What, if any, practical difference would it have made?

Could Congress have required the reports to be in writing prior to implementing a covert operation? Could it have required that each project be approved by Congress in advance? Note that Hughes-Ryan was an exercise of Congress's defense appropriations power. How, if at all, does that fact affect your answer to these questions?

5. *Ending "Plausible Deniability."* One clear purpose of Hughes-Ryan was to end the practice of "plausible deniability" for the President, at least in his

relations with the Congress. *See Church Committee Report, supra* p. 359, Book I, at 58 ("The concept of plausible denial . . . is dead."). In addition to ensuring accountability for covert operations, requiring the President's approval was supposed to assure the President's careful review of proposals and promote effective internal debate in the executive branch. *CNSS, supra* p. 381, at 37-41.

c. *The Church Committee and a Proposed Charter*

By 1977 the climate had clearly changed. In addition to passage of the War Powers Resolution and Hughes-Ryan, both the House and Senate had established intelligence oversight committees. For the CIA, "it was as if they were in the position of the medical staff in a hospital waking up one morning to find their board of governors consisted of Christian Scientists and herbalists." Ranelagh, *supra* p. 372, at 616.

Perhaps the largest single contribution to the changed climate was the Senate's 1975 creation of the Select Committee to Study Governmental Operations (later known as the Church Committee after its Chair, Senator Frank Church of Idaho). The Committee was charged with determining "the extent, if any, to which illegal, improper, or unethical activities were engaged in by the intelligence agencies." S. Res. 21, 94th Cong. (1975). In its final report, issued in 1976,

> the Committee gave serious consideration to proposing a total ban on all forms of covert action. The Committee has concluded, however, that the United States should maintain the option of reacting in the future to a grave, unforeseen threat to United States national security through covert means. . . .
>
> (1) . . . [C]overt action must be seen as an exceptional act, to be undertaken only when the national security requires it and when overt means will not suffice. . . . [T]he policy and procedural barriers are presently inadequate to insure that any covert operation is absolutely essential to the national security. These barriers must be tightened and raised or covert action should be abandoned as an instrument of foreign policy.
>
> (2) . . . [C]overt action must in no case be a vehicle for clandestinely undertaking actions incompatible with American principles. . . . [T]he standards of acceptable covert activity should also exclude covert operations in an attempt to subvert democratic governments or provide support for police or other internal security forces which engage in the systematic violation of human rights.
>
> (3) Covert operations must be based on a careful and systematic analysis of a given situation, possible alternative outcomes, the threat to American interests of these possible outcomes, and above all, the likely consequences of an attempt to intervene. . . .
>
> (5) . . . [T]he appropriate oversight committee should be informed of all significant covert operations *prior* to their initiation and . . . all covert action projects should be reviewed by the committee on a semi-annual basis. Further, the oversight committee should require that the annual budget submission for covert action programs be specific and detailed as to the activity recommended. Unforeseen covert action projects should be funded only from the Contingency Reserve Fund which could be replenished only after the concurrence of the oversight and any other appropriate congressional committees. The . . . oversight committee should be notified prior to any withdrawal from the Contingency Reserve Fund. [*Church Committee Report, supra*, Book I, at 159-161.]

C. Congressional Oversight

Presidents Ford and Carter responded to the Church Committee by imposing revised structures and processes for covert action decision making by executive order, complicating efforts to legislate new rules in the Congress.

Eventually, Senator Huddleston introduced a proposed comprehensive charter for the intelligence community, the National Intelligence Reorganization and Reform Act of 1978, S. 2525, 95th Cong. (1978). Its principal goal was to replace the 1947 National Security Act with more specific lines of responsibility and limits of authority. In addition to incorporating the Hughes-Ryan reporting requirement for covert action, S. 2525 would have imposed an array of structural and process constraints on the intelligence community that by and large incorporated measures already in place under President Carter's Executive Order No. 12,036 (described *infra* p. 396).

In the area of operational controls, however, the proposed charter diverged from executive branch rules. Covert action would have been specifically authorized "in support of national foreign policy objectives." §111(a), but it would have prohibited the assassination of foreign officials in peacetime, §134, and would have prohibited covert action if it had as its objective or was likely to result in —

(1) the support of international terrorist activities;
(2) the mass destruction of property;
(3) the creation of food or water shortages or floods;
(4) the creation of epidemics or diseases;
(5) the use of chemical, biological, or other weapons in violation of treaties or other international agreements to which the United States is a party;
(6) the violent overthrow of the democratic government of any country;
(7) the torture of individuals; or
(8) the support of any action, which violates human rights, conducted by the police, foreign intelligence, or internal security forces of any foreign country. [§135(a).]

NOTES AND QUESTIONS

1. *Perils of Authorization?* Was it wise to try to authorize covert action? Is the 1947 Act preferable in that respect?

2. *Perils of Listing?* Is the list of prohibitions in §135 desirable? Complete? Is Congress empowered to so restrict the intelligence community? Compare the activities permitted by NSC-10/2, *supra* p. 374. How would permissible covert action have changed if Senate bill 2525 had been enacted?

3. *Reform Efforts Fizzle.* Efforts in the Senate to enact a comprehensive charter for the intelligence community ended in frustration. Senate Bill 2525 was never passed. Indeed, it was attacked by almost everyone with an interest in the subject. For example, the American Civil Liberties Union and the Center for National Security Studies objected to such broad authorization of covert and counterintelligence activities without adequate explicit controls. Intelligence professionals objected to the loss of flexibility imposed by the operational

constraints, in light of what they perceived as a growing Soviet threat and the need for effective intelligence as an instrument of national security policy.

When the American embassy in Teheran was seized and 52 American hostages were imprisoned in the embassy compound by Iranian militants on November 4, 1979, there was widespread feeling that there had been an "intelligence failure," that we should have detected signs of the revolution and anti-American unrest in Iran. Then, when the Soviet Union invaded Afghanistan on December 27, 1979, the tide effectively swung away from regulation and toward an enhanced intelligence capability. A successor to Senate bill 2525 was introduced in the Senate in February 1980, but the debate focused more on whether to legislate than on particular structures and controls. By May of that year, the Senate Intelligence Committee saw the handwriting on the wall and shelved the charter proposal in favor of a modest bill revising Hughes-Ryan. The story of the rise and fall of the charter proposal is told in John M. Oseth, *Regulating U.S. Intelligence Operations* 122-131 (1985).

The Intelligence Oversight Act of 1980, adding §501 of the National Security Act of 1947, Pub. L. No. 96-450, §407(b), 94 Stat. 1975, 1981 (1980), represented what the Senate Intelligence Committee was able to salvage of its 263-page proposed charter.

d. *The Intelligence Oversight Act of 1980*

Intelligence Oversight Act of 1980
Pub. L. No. 96-450, §407(b)(1), 94 Stat. 1975, 1981 (1980)

(a) To the extent consistent with all applicable authorities and duties, including those conferred by the Constitution upon the executive and legislative branches of the Government, and to the extent consistent with due regard for the protection from unauthorized disclosure of classified information and information relating to intelligence sources and methods, the [DCI] and the heads of all departments, agencies, and other entities of the United States involved in intelligence activities shall—

(1) keep the Select Committee on Intelligence of the Senate and the Permanent Select Committee on Intelligence of the House of Representatives (hereinafter in this section referred to as the "intelligence committees") fully and currently informed of all intelligence activities which are the responsibility of, are engaged in by, or are carried out for or on behalf of, any department, agency, or entity of the United States, including any significant anticipated intelligence activity, except that (A) the foregoing provision shall not require approval of the intelligence committees as a condition precedent to the initiation of any such anticipated intelligence activity, and (B) if the President determines it is essential to limit prior notice to meet extraordinary circumstances affecting vital interests of the United States, such notice shall be limited to the chairman and ranking minority members of the intelligence committees, the Speaker and minority leader of the House of Representatives, and the majority and minority leaders of the Senate;

C. Congressional Oversight

(2) furnish any information or material concerning intelligence activities which is in the possession, custody, or control of any department, agency, or entity of the United States and which is requested by either of the intelligence committees in order to carry out its authorized responsibilities; and

(3) report in a timely fashion to the intelligence committees any illegal intelligence activity or significant intelligence failure and any corrective action that has been taken or is planned to be taken in connection with such illegal activity or failure.

(b) The President shall fully inform the intelligence committees in a timely fashion of intelligence operations in foreign countries, other than activities intended solely for obtaining necessary intelligence, for which prior notice was not given under subsection (a) and shall provide a statement of the reasons for not giving prior notice.

(c) The President and the intelligence committees shall each establish such procedures as may be necessary to carry out the provisions of subsections (a) and (b).

(d) The House... and the Senate, in consultation with the [DCI], shall each establish, by rule or resolution of such House, procedures to protect from unauthorized disclosure all classified information and all information relating to intelligence sources and methods furnished to the intelligence committees or to Members of the Congress under this section....

(e) Nothing in this Act shall be construed as authority to withhold information from the intelligence committees on the grounds that providing the information to the intelligence committees would constitute the unauthorized disclosure of classified information or information relating to intelligence sources and methods.

NOTES AND QUESTIONS

1. *Responding to the Shortcomings of Hughes-Ryan?* In the same legislation, Congress amended Hughes-Ryan, *supra* p. 390, by striking out "and reports, in a timely fashion" and the remainder of subsection (a) and inserting this new second sentence in the subsection: "Each such operation shall be considered a significant anticipated intelligence activity for the purpose of section 501 of the National Security Act of 1947." Pub. L. No. 96-450, §407(a), 94 Stat. 1975, 1981 (1980). How did the Oversight Act change what Hughes-Ryan required? How did Congress respond to the concern expressed by President Ford, *supra* p. 391, that such widespread notice would effectively end covert action?

A useful catalogue of "core questions" for determining when a proposed government action requires a presidential finding and a prior or "timely" report to the congressional intelligence committees appears in Cinquegrana, *supra* p. 390, at 206-208.

2. *What Did the 1980 Act Accomplish?* The 1980 Act appears to be an especially modest product, considering the protracted legislative deliberation. Moreover, its provisions largely repeated oversight measures in President Carter's

Exec. Order No. 12,036, §§3-4, 43 Fed. Reg. 3678 (Jan. 24, 1978). What practical importance can be ascribed to the measure?

3. *Did Congress Surrender Control?* Note that the 1980 Act made no provision for congressional controls on operations, and it allowed the President to avoid prior notice. Can the Act therefore be read as a surrender of congressional authority over such operations?

4. *Closing the Loop?* Recall the so-called paramilitary loophole in the War Powers Resolution, *supra* p. 389. Did the 1980 Act do anything to close the hole?

5. *Continuing Reforms.* More recent amendments to oversight mechanisms are assessed *infra* Section F.

D. EXECUTIVE BRANCH REFORMS

The Church Committee found that, notwithstanding improvements over the years, the procedures for executive branch review of covert operations were inadequate and had on occasion been entirely circumvented. *See Church Committee Report, supra* p. 359, Book I, at 159. The Committee recommended that a group consisting of the Secretaries of State and Defense, the National Security Adviser, the DCI, the Attorney General, the Chairman of the Joint Chiefs of Staff, and the Director of the OMB (as an observer) be required to approve each covert action proposal and review all covert projects at least annually.

To a large extent the Church Committee's recommendations were implemented by executive orders. President Ford's Executive Order No. 11,905, 41 Fed. Reg. 7707 (Feb. 18, 1976), created an Operations Advisory Group (OAG) with the membership recommended by the Church Committee, except that the Attorney General was made an observer rather than a member of the group. *Id.* §3(c). The OAG was charged with making a recommendation for each special activity and forwarding it, along with any dissents, to the President. *Id.* An Intelligence Oversight Board (IOB) was also created. *Id.* §6. The three-member Board would review, at the instance of members of the intelligence community, "activities that raise questions of legality or propriety." *Id.*

President Carter's Executive Order No. 12,036, 43 Fed. Reg. 3675 (Jan. 24, 1978), replaced the OAG with the Special Coordination Committee (SCC). The Carter order incorporated most of the provisions for high-level review of operational proposals from President Ford's order. However, the Attorney General became a full member of the SCC, *id.* §1-302, and her oversight role grew to include the responsibility to receive reports from intelligence agency heads and forward to the President information about possible unlawful activity by subordinate agency officials. *Id.* §§1-706, 3-302. The order also foreshadowed the 1980 Intelligence Oversight Act by including requirements that the DCI keep the intelligence committees "fully and currently" informed of ongoing activities, as well as "any significant anticipated activities." *Id.* §3-401. The order was replaced in 1981 by another signed by President Reagan.

D. Executive Branch Reforms

Executive Order No. 12,333
46 Fed. Reg. 59,941 (Dec. 4, 1981)

Timely and accurate information about the activities, capabilities, plans, and intentions of foreign powers, organizations, and persons and their agents, is essential to the national security of the United States. All reasonable and lawful means must be used to ensure that the United States will receive the best intelligence available. For that purpose, by virtue of the authority vested in me by the Constitution and statutes of the United States of America, including the National Security Act of 1947, as amended, and as President of the United States of America, in order to provide for the effective conduct of United States intelligence activities and the protection of constitutional rights, it is hereby ordered as follows:...

1.2 The National Security Council.

(a) Purpose. The National Security Council (NSC) was established by the National Security Act of 1947 to advise the President with respect to the integration of domestic, foreign and military policies relating to the national security. The NSC shall act as the highest Executive Branch entity that provides review of, guidance for and direction to the conduct of all national foreign intelligence, counterintelligence, and special activities, and attendant policies and programs.

(b) Committees. The NSC shall establish such committees as may be necessary to carry out its functions and responsibilities under this Order. The NSC, or a committee established by it, shall consider and submit to the President a policy recommendation, including all dissents, on each special activity and shall review proposals for other sensitive intelligence operations....

1.4 The Intelligence Community. The agencies within the Intelligence Community shall, in accordance with applicable United States law and with the other provisions of this Order, conduct intelligence activities necessary for the conduct of foreign relations and the protection of the national security of the United States, including:

(a) Collection of information needed by the President, the National Security Council, the Secretaries of State and Defense, and other Executive Branch officials for the performance of their duties and responsibilities;...

(c) Collection of information concerning, and the conduct of activities to protect against, intelligence activities directed against the United States, international terrorist and international narcotics activities, and other hostile activities directed against the United States by foreign powers, organizations, persons, and their agents;

(d) Special activities;

(e) Administrative and support activities within the United States and abroad necessary for the performance of authorized activities; and

(f) Such other intelligence activities as the President may direct from time to time.

1.5 Director of Central Intelligence. In order to discharge the duties and responsibilities prescribed by law, the Director of Central Intelligence shall be responsible directly to the President and the NSC and shall:

(a) Act as the primary adviser to the President and the NSC on national foreign intelligence and provide the President and other officials in the Executive Branch with national foreign intelligence;...

(d) Ensure implementation of special activities;

(e) Formulate policies concerning foreign intelligence and counterintelligence arrangements with foreign governments, coordinate foreign intelligence and counterintelligence relationships between agencies of the Intelligence Community and the intelligence or internal security services of foreign governments, and establish procedures governing the conduct of liaison by any department or agency with such services on narcotics activities;

(f) Participate in the development of procedures approved by the Attorney General governing criminal narcotics intelligence activities abroad to ensure that these activities are consistent with foreign intelligence programs;...

(s) Facilitate the use of national foreign intelligence products by Congress in a secure manner....

1.7 Senior Officials of the Intelligence Community. The heads of departments and agencies with organizations in the Intelligence Community or the heads of such organizations, as appropriate, shall:

(a) Report to the Attorney General possible violations of federal criminal laws by employees and of specified federal criminal laws by any other person as provided in procedures agreed upon by the Attorney General and the head of the department or agency concerned, in a manner consistent with the protection of intelligence sources and methods, as specified in those procedures;...

(c) Furnish the Director of Central Intelligence and the NSC, in accordance with applicable law and procedures approved by the Attorney General under this Order, the information required for the performance of their respective duties;

(d) Report to the Intelligence Oversight Board, and keep the Director of Central Intelligence appropriately informed, concerning any intelligence activities of their organizations that they have reason to believe may be unlawful or contrary to Executive order or Presidential directive;

(e) Protect intelligence and intelligence sources and methods from unauthorized disclosure consistent with guidance from the Director of Central Intelligence;...

(i) Ensure that the Inspectors General and General Counsels for their organizations have access to any information necessary to perform their duties assigned by this Order.

1.8 The Central Intelligence Agency. All duties and responsibilities of the CIA shall be related to the intelligence functions set out below. As authorized by this Order; the National Security Act of 1947, as amended; the CIA Act of 1949, as amended; appropriate directives or other applicable law, the CIA shall:

(a) Collect, produce and disseminate foreign intelligence and counterintelligence, including information not otherwise obtainable. The collection of foreign intelligence or counterintelligence within the United States shall be coordinated with the FBI as required by procedures agreed upon by the Director of Central Intelligence and the Attorney General;

(b) Collect, produce and disseminate intelligence on foreign aspects of narcotics production and trafficking;

(c) Conduct counterintelligence activities outside the United States and, without assuming or performing any internal security functions, conduct counterintelligence activities within the United States in coordination with

D. Executive Branch Reforms

the FBI as required by procedures agreed upon by the Director of Central Intelligence and the Attorney General;

(d) Coordinate counterintelligence activities and the collection of information not otherwise obtainable when conducted outside the United States by other departments and agencies;

(e) Conduct special activities approved by the President. No agency except the CIA (or the Armed Forces of the United States in time of war declared by Congress or during any period covered by a report from the President to the Congress under the War Powers Resolution) may conduct any special activity unless the President determines that another agency is more likely to achieve a particular objective;...

(i) Conduct such administrative and technical support activities within and outside the United States as are necessary to perform the functions described in sections (a) through (h) above, including procurement and essential cover and proprietary arrangements....

2.2 Purpose.... Set forth below are certain general principles that, in addition to and consistent with applicable laws, are intended to achieve the proper balance between the acquisition of essential information and protection of individual interests. Nothing in this Order shall be construed to apply to or interfere with any authorized civil or criminal law enforcement responsibility of any department or agency....

2.6 Assistance to Law Enforcement Authorities. Agencies within the Intelligence Community are authorized to:...

(b) Unless otherwise precluded by law or this Order, participate in law enforcement activities to investigate or prevent clandestine intelligence activities by foreign powers, or international terrorist or narcotics activities;...

2.7 Contracting. Agencies within the Intelligence Community are authorized to enter into contracts or arrangements for the provision of goods or services with private companies or institutions in the United States and need not reveal the sponsorship of such contracts or arrangements for authorized intelligence purposes. Contracts or arrangements with academic institutions may be undertaken only with the consent of appropriate officials of the institution.

2.8 Consistency with Other Laws. Nothing in this Order shall be construed to authorize any activity in violation of the Constitution or statutes of the United States....

2.11 Prohibition on Assassination. No person employed by or acting on behalf of the United States Government shall engage in, or conspire to engage in, assassination.

2.12 Indirect Participation. No agency of the Intelligence Community shall participate in or request any person to undertake activities forbidden by this Order.

3.1 Congressional Oversight. The duties and responsibilities of the Director of Central Intelligence and the heads of other departments, agencies, and entities engaged in intelligence activities to cooperate with the Congress in the conduct of its responsibilities for oversight of intelligence activities shall be as provided in title 50, United States Code, section 413. The requirements of section 662 of the Foreign Assistance Act of 1961, as amended (22 U.S.C. 2422), and section 501 of the National Security Act of 1947, as amended (50 U.S.C. 413), shall apply to all special activities as defined in this Order....

3.4 Definitions. For the purposes of this Order, the following terms shall have these meanings:...

(f) Intelligence Community and agencies within the Intelligence Community refer to the following agencies or organizations:

(1) The Central Intelligence Agency (CIA);
(2) The National Security Agency (NSA);
(3) The Defense Intelligence Agency (DIA);
(4) The offices within the Department of Defense for the collection of specialized national foreign intelligence through reconnaissance programs;
(5) The Bureau of Intelligence and Research of the Department of State;
(6) The intelligence elements of the Army, Navy, Air Force, and Marine Corps, the Federal Bureau of Investigation (FBI), the Department of the Treasury, and the Department of Energy; and
(7) The staff elements of the Director of Central Intelligence....

(h) Special activities means activities conducted in support of national foreign policy objectives abroad which are planned and executed so that the role of the United States Government is not apparent or acknowledged publicly, and functions in support of such activities, but which are not intended to influence United States political processes, public opinion, policies, or media and do not include diplomatic activities or the collection and production of intelligence or related support functions....

3.5 Purpose and Effect. This Order is intended to control and provide direction and guidance to the Intelligence Community. Nothing contained herein or in any procedures promulgated hereunder is intended to confer any substantive or procedural right or privilege on any person or organization....

NOTES AND QUESTIONS

The preamble to Executive Order No. 12,333 is directed at intelligence information and its importance to the national security. Covert action is not mentioned. Is this omission legally significant? Preamble language typically sets forth the presumed authority for the prescriptions that follow. Precisely what constitutional or statutory authority empowered the President to promulgate this executive order?

a. Deciding on Intelligence Operations

1. *Who Initiates and Who Approves?* According to the executive order, which official or entity must approve an intelligence operation? Which officials or entities may originate proposals for covert action?

2. *Comparing Prior Assignments of Responsibility.* How is the assignment of responsibility for deciding on covert operations under the Reagan executive order different from the requirements of prior executive orders and from the recommendations of the Church Committee?

3. *Role of the NSC.* Consider the role of the NSC. As the "highest executive branch entity" involved in covert operations, the NSC appears to be the primary

D. Executive Branch Reforms

link between the intelligence community and the President in deciding on intelligence policy and individual operations. According to the executive order, how does the NSC obtain the information it needs to fulfill its statutory role?

The NSC principals are, of course, not as familiar with intelligence operations as the professionals in the intelligence community. Thus,

> Regular NSC review may dull the effectiveness of intelligence operations, especially those involving high risk but also high payoff. Since NSC members are not as familiar with intelligence operations as the director, sometimes they do not appreciate the potential benefits of high-risk operations.... Timidity and parochial interests may supplant sound judgment. There is a compensating advantage.... [NSC review] strengthens the DCI's control in areas where decisions are not black or white and where there exist enormous pressures to take high risks.... NSC review... [forces the advocates of an operation] to do their homework better than they might otherwise because a rejection from the NSC is more difficult to appeal than one from the director. The requirement also forces the director... to think the proposal through rigorously. [Stansfield Turner & George Thibault, *Intelligence: The Right Rules*, 48 Foreign Poly. 125-126 (Fall 1982).]

What advantages and disadvantages do you see in NSC review and approval of covert operations? According to the executive order, is such review limited to the policies or criteria that inform decisions about individual operations, or is each proposal subject to the NSC review process?

4. *Management vs. Operations.* The long-standing practice prior to the Iran-Contra Affair was not to use the NSC to conduct covert operations. The CIA was the primary operational entity for covert action, and the NSC was chiefly a consumer and coordinator of intelligence. *See* Peter Raven-Hansen & William C. Banks, *Pulling the Purse Strings of the Commander in Chief*, 80 Va. L. Rev. 833, 867 (1994). Former National Security Adviser Zbigniew Brzezinski explained:

> Membership on the NSC staff by definition confers a staff role — to plan strategy, to coordinate, to supervise, and, for the national security adviser, to advise the president. Active and sustained involvement in bureaucratic operations or covert intelligence activity militates against fulfilling these roles. Fortunately, that danger has been recognized throughout most of the NSC's history, and deviations from that rule have been few, the Iran-contra scandal notwithstanding. [Zbigniew Brzezinski, *The NSC's Midlife Crisis*, 69 Foreign Poly. 80, 97-98 (Winter 1987-1988).]

b. The Internal Executive Branch Process for Reviewing Intelligence Operations

1. *Changing Internal Review.* Executive Order No. 12,333 cut back substantially on the procedures for internal review prescribed by the Ford and Carter orders. *See* Part 1.2(b). These procedures changed again later in the Reagan administration:

> President Reagan appointed several additional members to his National Security Council and allowed staff attendance at meetings. The resultant size of

the meetings led the President to turn increasingly to a smaller group (called the National Security Planning Group or "NSPG"). Attendance at its meetings was more restricted but included the statutory principals of the NSC. The NSPG was supported by the SIGs, and new SIGs were occasionally created to deal with particular issues. These were frequently chaired by the National Security Advisor. But generally the SIGs and many of their subsidiary groups (called Interagency Groups or "IGs") fell into disuse.

As a supplement to the normal NSC process, the Reagan Administration adopted comprehensive procedures for covert actions. These are contained in a classified document, NSDD-159, establishing the process for deciding, implementing, monitoring, and reviewing covert activities. [President's Special Review Board, *The Tower Commission Report* II-5 (1987).]

What are the important differences between the Reagan order and the earlier executive order? How have the prescribed roles of the President, the Attorney General, and the NSC in the structure and process for making intelligence operations decisions changed? Can you tell who is now in charge of operational controls? How do you think these changes have affected the speed with which decisions are made about covert actions? The quality of those decisions?

2. *Sorting Out the Players and Their Roles.* In light of the developments in the Reagan administration decision-making process for intelligence matters, can you describe the roles of the DCI, National Security Advisor, and Attorney General, as well as their relationships to each other and to the President and NSC?

3. *Changed Definition and Omitting the Lawyers.* President Carter's Executive Order No. 12,036, 43 Fed. Reg. 3675 (Jan. 24, 1978), defined "covert activities" as secret "activities conducted in support of national foreign policy objectives abroad *which are designed to further official United States programs and policies abroad.*" *Id.* §3-212. The italicized part of this language was omitted from Executive Order No. 12,333, §3.4(h). Is the difference legally significant?

The Ford and Carter executive orders, unlike the Reagan order, formally included the Justice Department in the covert action decision-making process. Does the presence or absence of lawyers really matter if the President is free to ignore the lawyers' advice?

4. *Intelligence Oversight Board (IOB).* Executive Order No. 12,334, 46 Fed. Reg. 59,955 (Dec. 4, 1981), was promulgated the same day as Executive Order No. 12,333. It reconstituted the IOB "to enhance the security of the United States by assuring the legality of activities of the intelligence community." *Id.* Like the earlier IOB, Executive Order No. 12,334 is activated by internal intelligence community requests. Unlike the Carter IOB, the Reagan IOB was designed to scrutinize the legality but not necessarily the propriety of activities. Compare Executive Order No. 12,334, §2(a), with Executive Order No. 12,036, §3-403.

5. *President's Foreign Intelligence Advisory Board (PFIAB).* A third Reagan order created the President's Foreign Intelligence Advisory Board, which is maintained within the Executive Office of the President. Executive Order No. 12,331, 46 Fed. Reg. 51,705 (Oct. 20, 1981). Its several members serve at the pleasure of the President and are appointed from among citizens outside

D. Executive Branch Reforms

government. The Board reviews the performance of all government agencies engaged in the collection, evaluation, or production of intelligence or in the execution of intelligence policy. It also assesses the adequacy of management, personnel, and organization in intelligence agencies and advises the President concerning the objectives, conduct, and coordination of the activities of these agencies. The PFIAB is specifically charged with making appropriate recommendations for actions to improve and enhance the performance of the intelligence efforts of the United States. This advice may be passed directly to the CIA or to other agencies engaged in intelligence activities.

c. Implementation of Intelligence Operations

1. *What Are "Special Activities"?* Consider the range of intelligence activities permitted by §1.4. Covert action, or "special activities," is defined in §3.4(h) as "activities conducted in support of national foreign policy objectives abroad which are planned and executed so that the role of the United States Government is not apparent or acknowledged publicly." Can you ascertain from the executive order how and by whom it should be determined that particular intelligence activities conform to U.S. law? That they support national foreign policy objectives?

2. *Comparing Earlier Mechanisms.* How do the standards in Executive Order No. 12,333 differ from those suggested by the Church Committee and those recommended in the proposed charter for the intelligence community? Which standards should guide intelligence operations decision making?

3. *Who May Conduct Covert Operations?* Which entities in the intelligence community may legally conduct covert operations? Note that the armed forces are permitted to engage in covert operations "during a period covered by a report from the President" under the War Powers Resolution. Do you see the ambiguity in this exception? See the discussion *supra* p. 389. What are the implications of the armed forces exception? Should §1.8(e) be amended?

4. *Support for Covert Operations?* What is contemplated by the authority granted in §1.8(i) to "conduct...support activities...including procurement and essential cover and proprietary arrangements"? Similarly, what kinds of "contracts or arrangements for the provision of goods or services" are contemplated by §2.7?

5. *What Other Agencies are Covered?* Other executive branch agencies are recognized by Executive Order No. 12,333 as having a role in intelligence activities. For example, the Departments of State and Treasury are assigned overt collection and dissemination tasks relevant to their policy areas. *See* §§1.9, 1.10. The Department of Energy (DOE) also is charged with overt collection relevant to foreign energy matters and with "formulating intelligence collection and analysis requirements where the special expert capability of the Department can contribute." §1.13(a), (b). The provisions in Executive Order No. 12,333 governing the role of the FBI are examined in Chapter 22. Provisions pertaining to DOD agencies are discussed in Chapter 32.

6. *Summing Up the Requirements.* Compare the definition of "special activities" quoted above with the limitations in §§2.8, 2.11, 2.12, and 3.5. Can you synthesize these various requirements into a workable set of criteria for deciding what activities may be approved as covert operations?

d. Recording and Reporting Intelligence Operation Decisions

1. *Making a Record.* Does the executive order require that intelligence operation decisions be made in writing? What considerations would enter into deciding whether to impose such a requirement within the executive branch? If such decisions are made in writing, should or must the writing be done before the operation is carried out?

2. *The Lawyers' Role.* What is the role of the Attorney General in reviewing the form and legality of intelligence operations, either before or after implementation? Can you think of ways to improve the lawyers' role in the intelligence operation decision-making process?

3. *Making Reports to Congress.* What requirements does the executive order impose for reporting intelligence operations to Congress? Do such requirements apply to the NSC or its staff?

E. THE REFORMS TESTED: A CASE STUDY OF THE IRAN-CONTRA AFFAIR

On November 3, 1986, Al-Shiraa, a Beirut weekly, reported that the United States had secretly sold arms to Iran, using Israel as an intermediary. Reports soon followed that linked the arms sales to a desire to gain the release of American hostages in Lebanon. After a brief investigation by the Justice Department, it was also revealed that some proceeds from the arms sales to Iran had been diverted to the administration-supported Contras fighting the Sandinista government of Nicaragua, at a time when U.S. military aid to the Contras had been prohibited by Congress. A major scandal suddenly burst upon the scene: the Iran-Contra Affair. A member of the staff of the NSC, Lt. Col. Oliver L. North, was effectively in charge of both operations. He was supported by National Security Advisers Robert McFarlane and Vice Admiral John Poindexter and by CIA Director William Casey.

The principal congressional and executive branch investigations of the Iran-Contra Affair shared a basic conclusion—that the scandal was not due to the patchwork legal controls of the national security system. The Tower Commission, appointed by President Reagan and made up of former Senator John Tower, former Senator/Secretary of State Edmund Muskie, and former National Security Adviser Brent Scowcroft, emphasized human failings, criticized the President's lax "management style," and concluded that, while systemic problems were found, "their solution does not lie in revamping the

E. A Case Study of the Iran-Contra Affair

National Security Council system." President's Special Review Board, *The Tower Commission Report* (1987), at 1-4. The congressional committees looking into the affair, formed in January 1987 in the Senate and House, merged to conduct a ten-month investigation that included 40 days of public hearings, review of more than 300,000 documents, and examination or interview of more than 500 witnesses. Their final report concluded "that the Iran-Contra Affair resulted from the failure of individuals to observe the law, not from deficiencies in existing law or in our system of governance." H. Select Comm. to Investigate Covert Arms Transactions with Iran and S. Select Comm. on Secret Military Assistance to Iran and the Nicaraguan Opposition, *Report of the Congressional Committees Investigating the Iran-Contra Affair (Iran-Contra Report)*, S. Rep. No. 100-216/H.R. Rep. No. 100-433, at 423 (1987). As you read the following materials, consider whether you agree with these assessments. Are there significant structural reforms that would make such an affair less likely in the future, given the human failings just described?

In this section we examine briefly executive branch compliance with Congress's rules for covert action and with its own rules for decision making, focusing on the parallel arms sales and Contra resupply initiatives. The Boland Amendments—appropriations measures enacted to restrict aid to the Contras—allow us to revisit the limits and utility of the appropriations power. We conclude by considering the special problems of using the courts to prosecute those accused of wrongdoing in the scandal, and reforms in intelligence operations decision making prompted by the Iran-Contra Affair.

It would be inaccurate—and unfair to many dedicated professionals in the intelligence community—to depict the Iran-Contra Affair as typical, and we do not. It was an aberration. We assume that most intelligence operations—and certainly the vast majority of ordinary intelligence collection efforts—comply with all applicable U.S. laws and executive requirements. But the Affair teaches us important lessons of statutory drafting and construction. It also suggests what can go wrong when national security decision making is done without informed outside (or inside) scrutiny. Most important, it tests the limits of the rule of law in this branch of national security.

For a detailed day-by-day account of the Iran-Contra events, *see* Scott Armstrong, Malcolm Byrne, Tom Blanton & The National Security Archive, *The Chronology: The Documented Day-by-Day Account of Secret Military Assistance to Iran* (1987); *see also* Theodore Draper, *A Very Thin Line: The Iran-Contra Affairs* (1991).

1. The Legality of the Arms Sales

A central issue in the Iran-Contra Affair is whether the President had authority to transfer arms to Iran. There are three possible sources of presidential authority for the transfer of arms to a foreign country. First, the President may seek to rely on Article II or on inherent constitutional powers. President Reagan's incentive to send arms to Iran was at least in part humanitarian in nature—he wanted to secure the return of the American hostages held in Lebanon. Thus, the arms transactions were something more than arms sales. Each was calculated to be a trade: arms for hostages. The President may therefore have been acting pursuant to implied constitutional powers to rescue Americans held abroad (see Chapter 10). In addition, the President's constitutional authority may have been enhanced by the Hostage Act, *supra* p. 269, if the Act is read as "necessary and proper for carrying into execution" the President's Article II powers.

If the President cannot find authority in the Constitution, it must come from Congress. The Arms Export Control Act, codified as amended at 22 U.S.C. §§2751-2796 (2000) (hereinafter AECA), allows the President to sell arms to foreign countries under certain conditions, including advance notice to Congress, but it gives Congress the opportunity to veto sales over certain dollar amounts. When Israel sent missiles to Iran in 1985, the administration promised to replenish Israel's stockpile. Israel had obtained the missiles from the United States pursuant to the AECA, which also required an agreement between Israel and the United States that the United States give its written consent to any retransfer of the missiles. *Iran-Contra Report, supra* p. 405, at 418. Yet, according to the Iran-Contra Report,

> The President's authorization of the 1985 transfers to Iran [was] made without even a pretense of compliance with the AECA or Israel's written agreements with the United States. No written consent was sought or given; and even if Israel had sought a written consent, this government could not have given it without changing its own regulations. This is so because Iran, which was considered a terrorist nation by the United States and which was the subject of a U.S. arms embargo, was not eligible for direct sales. [*Id.*]

Furthermore, Iran never agreed not to retransfer the missiles, as the AECA required, and the President never reported the sales to Congress.

The President also may have had the power to transfer arms as part of a covert intelligence operation, subject to the finding and reporting requirements of §501 of the National Security Act, added by the Intelligence Oversight Act of 1980, *supra* p. 394. Could characterizing the sales this way excuse compliance with the AECA? Events leading up to the sales were described by the congressional committees as follows:

> In 1981, Attorney General William French Smith had taken the position — based on an analysis by the State Department Legal Adviser — that the restrictions of [the arms export] statutes applied only to transfers undertaken pursuant to them; the President, however, could approve a transfer "outside the context of those statutes" by utilizing the Economy Act and the National Security Act. Nonetheless, the Smith opinion recognized the Congressional reporting requirements applicable in any event, and specifically concluded that "the House and Senate Intelligence Committees should be informed of this proposal and the President's determinations."
>
> When the Smith opinion was considered in the context of the Iran Finding in January 1986, its requirement of at least some form of prior Congressional notification was ignored. Instead, a memorandum from Poindexter to the President describing the Finding characterized that opinion as concluding "that under an appropriate finding you could authorize the CIA to sell arms to countries outside of the provisions of laws and reporting requirements for foreign military sales." Poindexter's memorandum recommended to the President "that you exercise your statutory prerogative to withhold notification... to the Congressional

E. A Case Study of the Iran-Contra Affair

oversight committees until such time as you deem it to be appropriate." [*Iran-Contra Report, supra*, at 380.]

NOTES AND QUESTIONS

1. *Applying the Rescue Power.* Does the rescue power, like the repel power, require some immediate threat of harm? Or is rescue a longer-term power? The *Minority Report* of the congressional investigators of the Iran-Contra Affair maintained that "the *Durand* case [*supra* p. 264] stands for the proposition that the President has the discretion to take whatever steps may be necessary, short of a full scale war, to protect American citizens." *Iran-Contra Report, supra*, at 474 (*Minority Report*). Does this statement accurately reflect the holding of *Durand?* More generally, does it correctly state the scope of the President's constitutional rescue powers?

2. *Applying the Hostage Act.* Whatever the role of constitutional rescue and reprisal powers, is there any constitutional bar to Congress legislating in this sphere? Did the Hostage Act apply to the arms-for-hostages deals? One view is that the Act is confined to naturalized citizens who are forcibly repatriated. *See Dames & Moore, supra* p. 48. Should it matter that the hostages were actually held in Lebanon, while the deals were struck with Iran? If the Hostage Act did apply, did its terms permit the activities undertaken by the President on behalf of the hostages?

There was apparently no effort to comply with the Hostage Act's requirement that "all facts and proceedings relative thereto shall as soon as practicable be communicated by the President to Congress." Is this statutory reporting requirement constitutional? If it is, may it credibly be argued that the requirements of the Hostage Act were superseded by subsequent statutes? Consider the next notes.

3. *Applying the AECA.* Under the AECA, the President may not consent to transfer arms to "any country or international organization" unless he finds that the transfer "will strengthen the security of the United States and promote world peace," and unless the transferee agrees in writing not to further transfer the items without obtaining the consent of the President. 22 U.S.C. §2753(a). In addition, the President is required to inform Congress of arms transfers above a monetary threshold, which was met with respect to the Iran transfers. *Id.* §2753(d). Is there any way to reconcile the transfers from Israel with the AECA? *See* David Scheffer, *U.S. Law and the Iran-Contra Affair*, 81 Am. J. Intl. L. 696, 699-700 (1987).

Secretary of State Schultz determined in 1984 "that Iran is a country which has repeatedly provided support for acts of international terrorism." 49 Fed. Reg. 2836 (1984). Schultz's determination thus stood throughout the period in 1985 and 1986 when the Reagan administration transferred arms to Iran. The AECA requires that a transferee be "otherwise eligible" to receive a transfer, 22 U.S.C. §2753(a)(4), and that any sales to "any government which aids or abets...international terrorism" must be terminated unless the President finds that the national security requires otherwise and reports his finding to

Congress. *Id.* §2753(f). If the President had found that "national security" reasons nonetheless justified sales to Iran, there was no report of such a finding to the Congress.

4. *Burdening the Foreign Relations Power.* Do the restrictions on transferring arms to nations that support international terrorism unconstitutionally burden the President's foreign relations powers?

5. *Arms for Hostages as a Covert Operation?* The *Minority Report* argues that the National Security Act provided an "alternative legal route" for the 1985 arms shipments to Iran:

> Like the AECA and FAA, the National Security Act presupposes some kind of Presidential determination. Specifically, the determination must be that an action—in this case a retransfer—would "affect" the national security. If the CIA is involved, the so-called Hughes-Ryan Amendment requires a more emphatic Presidential determination. Instead of saying an activity must "affect" national security, Hughes-Ryan says it must be "important." More significantly, this determination must be made personally by the President, and reported in a "timely fashion" to Congress.
>
> We believe that the terms under which the President may use the National Security Act in fact meet all underlying purposes of the AECA and FAA, and that is why Congress has been satisfied to let the one approach be a substitute or alternative route to the other. The fact is that the 1985 Israeli transactions essentially—and legally—were equivalent to ones in which the United States sold the weapons directly to Iran. [*Iran-Contra Report, supra,* at 540.]

Do you find this analysis persuasive?

When Attorney General Meese was asked by the Tower Commission whether the CIA's activities in arranging the November 1985 shipment by the Israelis should have been preceded by a finding, he replied in a letter that "a finding under the Hughes-Ryan amendment would be required." *Tower Commission Report, supra* p. 405, at Appendix H. How would you answer?

6. *Using the Economy Act.* On January 17, 1986, President Reagan signed a finding that was a slight revision of one executed ten days earlier. The earlier finding, authorizing more shipments of missiles through Israel, was abandoned at CIA General Counsel Sporkin's urging, when he advised that the approval of Israeli sales would violate the AECA. The new finding, based on the National Security Act, would, according to Sporkin, permit the CIA to take Defense Department weapons and sell them to Israel or Iran directly under the Economy Act, Pub. L. No. 314-212, 47 Stat. 382 (1932). The Economy Act permits the President to transfer functions and property from one executive agency to another. *Id.,* 47 Stat. 413. But may the President avoid the AECA simply by labeling an arms transfer as a covert action? If so, did the revised finding comply with the National Security Act?

7. *Oral Findings?* Were findings for the arms sales to Iran required by Hughes-Ryan or §501 of the Intelligence Oversight Act? If so, what form should those findings have taken? Attorney General Meese testified that President

E. A Case Study of the Iran-Contra Affair

Reagan's tacit oral approval of the early Israeli shipments established legal authorization for the covert direct sales. *Iran-Contra Report, supra,* at 379. Was the Meese opinion sound in light of §501? In light of the Hughes-Ryan Amendment, *supra* p. 390?

8. *Constitutional Limits on Oversight?* Section 501 states that its notice requirements apply "to the extent consistent with all applicable authorities and duties, including those conferred by the Constitution upon the executive and legislative branches of the government." CIA General Counsel Sporkin testified to the congressional committees that the alleged failures to comply with Hughes-Ryan and §501 could be defended as an exercise of constitutional power:

[*Sporkin:*] The argument I'm making is... that §501 specifically recognizes that there are constitutional prerogatives which are not going to be dealt with by the notification.... I'm saying it is both a statutory matter as well as a constitutional matter because if the statute recognizes it, then the statute must mean that there are times when there will be non-notification....

Representative Louis Stokes: ...Do you believe that if covert action involves possible risk to life, but also involves significant policy changes, that such an operation still can be kept from the Congress for months, and perhaps years?

A: I think it would be wrong to do so, but I, again, I'm not going to say it would be illegal.

Q: Judge Sporkin, during the Jan. 16, 1986, meeting that you attended in the White House, when was it suggested by those attending there that Congress would be told about the Iran initiative?

A: It was suggested, my recollection as soon as the hostages were out.

Q: Did someone at the meeting advance the suggestion that Congress might not be told until the President left office, that is, if all the hostages had not been freed by that time?

A: I don't think it was put that way. It was put a different way. It was saying this President is going to have to make a report to this Congress to justify what he did even if it means the last day in office. That's the way it was put, not the other way. [*Joint Hearings Before the H. Select Comm. to Investigate Covert Arms Transactions with Iran and the S. Select Comm. on Secret Military Assistance to Iran and the Nicaraguan Opposition,* 100th Cong. 194-199 (1987) (testimony of Stanley Sporkin).]

Do you agree with Judge Sporkin's interpretation of §501? *See generally* Lawrence L. Block & David B. Rivkin Jr., *The Battle to Control the Conduct of Foreign Intelligence and Covert Operations: The Ultra-Whig Counterrevolution Revisited,* 12 Harv. J.L. & Pub. Poly. 303, 342 (1989) (supporting that interpretation). How could Hughes-Ryan or §501 be rewritten to remove any apparent ambiguities regarding the timing of congressional notification?

9. *Delayed Reporting.* The President's January 17, 1986, finding that authorized direct arms sales to Iran was never reported to Congress. Like the rest of us, Congress learned of the sales through a November 1986 Beirut newspaper story. At a news conference shortly after the story broke, President Reagan said, "I have the right under the law to defer reporting to Congress...and defer it until such time as I believe it can safely be done with no risk to others." *See* David Marcus, *Intelligence Law: What Notice Does It Require?,* Wash. Post, Dec. 21, 1986, at A21. Do you agree with the President's interpretation?

2. Presidents' Rules: Executive Orders and Decision Directives

The Reagan administration model of decision making for covert action differed significantly from those of the Ford and Carter administrations. For example, President Reagan's National Security Decision Directive 159 required written findings for all covert actions, even if "undertaken by components other than the CIA." NSDD 159, *Covert Action Policy Approval and Coordination Procedures*, Jan. 18, 1985, *available at* http://www.fas.org/irp/offdocs/nsdd/23-2543a.gif. In addition, NSDD 159 required a specific designation by the President when an agency other than the CIA conducted a covert action, as well as a provision in any finding that "substantial support" would be provided "by one government component to another" in a covert action. *Id.* Even so, according to the Tower Commission, the executive branch failed to follow its own rules and policies in both the Iran and the Nicaraguan operations.

The Tower Commission found that the Iran arms transfer initiative was developed within the NSC staff and was the subject of only two or three cabinet-level reviews in a 17-month period. In addition, because of an "obsession with secrecy, interagency consideration of the initiative was limited to the cabinet level." *Tower Commission Report, supra* p. 405, at IV-4. Thus, there was no staff-level vetting of the initiative, where those with relevant expertise and a capacity for critical review might have affected the plan. *Id.* There was also "little effort to face squarely the legal restrictions and notification requirements applicable to the operation. . . . [Q]uestions about violations of law or regulations . . . were dismissed without . . . investigating them with the benefit of legal counsel." *Id.*

The President received reviews of the Iran initiative prepared by NSC staff who were proponents of the initiative. The dissenting views of other NSC principals were not pursued, and there was no interagency review of Lt. Col. North's activities. North "worked largely in isolation, keeping first Mr. McFarlane and then VADM Poindexter informed." *Id.* at IV-6.

NOTES AND QUESTIONS

1. *Executive Order No. 12,333 and the NSC.* Review the structure and processes for making covert action decisions prescribed by Exec. Order No. 12,333, *supra* p. 397. Which provisions are applicable? The order stipulates that only agencies within the intelligence community may conduct special activities. *Id.* §1.4(d). The order also states that the CIA shall conduct all special activities unless the President determines that "another agency is more likely to achieve a particular objective." *Id.* §1.8(e). Could the NSC legitimately have carried out the arms sales and Contra supply missions without such a presidential determination?

2. *Must the Executive Follow Its Own Rules?* Section 1.4 of Executive Order No. 12,333 directs compliance with "applicable United States law," presumably including the National Security Act and its reporting requirements. The order

E. A Case Study of the Iran-Contra Affair

also specifically states that nothing in the order "shall be construed to authorize any activity in violation of the Constitution or statutes of the United States." *Id.* §2.8. NSDD 159 provides that no foreign covert activity may be conducted unless the President signs a finding authorizing the activity. *Iran-Contra Report,* supra p. 405, at 416.

Is it legally possible for an activity authorized by the President to violate an executive order or NSDD? Justice Department lawyers defended activities that appeared to do so by arguing that presidential "authorization creates a valid modification of, or exception to [the executive order or NSDD]." Memorandum from Assistant Attorney General Charles J. Cooper, Dec. 17, 1986, at 14, *cited in Iran-Contra Report, supra,* at 542 (*Minority Report*). Is this argument persuasive? In United States v. Nixon, 418 U.S. 683, 695-696 (1974), the President's lawyers sought unsuccessfully to defeat the Watergate Special Prosecutor's subpoena in part on grounds that the President was not bound by Justice Department regulations, which conferred authority on the Special Prosecutor to contest the invocation of executive privilege. *See also* United States v. North, 708 F. Supp. 375, 378 (D.D.C. 1988). If the President could have changed the executive order or NSDD to permit oral findings, is it simply nitpicking to argue that he should have obeyed his own rule? See generally *supra* p. 45.

3. Covert Support for the Contras and the Boland Amendments

We have seen that many of our nation's most important national security disputes are aired in the appropriations process. Indeed, because of Congress's reluctance to exercise its war declaration and marque and reprisal powers, the appropriations power has become the primary congressional lever for checking the national security initiatives of the executive branch. *See* Louis Fisher, *Constitutional Conflicts Between Congress and the President* 221-251, 318-323 (1985); Michael J. Glennon, *Strengthening The War Powers Resolution: The Case for Purse-Strings Restrictions,* 60 Minn. L. Rev. 1 (1975). At the same time, there has been ongoing statutory support for activities of the intelligence community. Thus, appropriations legislation has served at different times either to ratify national security actions (e.g., the 1949 Central Intelligence Agency Act) or to control them (e.g., the 1973 and 1974 funding restrictions on the Southeast Asia War). See *supra* p. 235. See generally *supra* pp. 102-114.

United States aid to the Nicaraguan Contra forces and CIA involvement in their fight became two of the most contentious issues in American politics in the early 1980s. On December 1, 1981, President Reagan signed a finding that authorized the CIA to "[s]upport and conduct...paramilitary operations against the Cuban presence and Cuban Sandinista support infrastructure in Nicaragua and elsewhere in Central America." *Iran-Contra Report,* supra, at 386 n.41. The finding was presented to the intelligence committees. The stated purpose of this early covert program was the interdiction of arms shipments from Nicaragua to the leftist insurgents in El Salvador. However, the CIA relied on this finding to assist Sandinista forces throughout Nicaragua. *Id.* at 32.

Beginning in 1982, Congress enacted a series of measures, dubbed Boland Amendments for their sponsor, Representative Edward P. Boland, designed to limit that assistance. However, Congress was anything but steadfast in its opposition to supporting the Contras. On the one hand, chastened by its failure to assert its powers during the Vietnam War until very late, Congress was eager to act assertively to forestall a repeat of the Southeast Asia tragedy. On the other hand, many members of Congress felt that Central America presented a different kind of political and strategic situation, and that it might be imprudent to tie the President's hands. *See Iran-Contra Report, supra,* at 395-407; *id.* at 489-499 (*Minority Report*).

The most restrictive of these Contra aid measures, commonly referred to as "Boland II," was part of the DOD appropriations legislation for fiscal year 1985 and was in place during the most critical period of clandestine support by the Reagan administration. Boland II provided:

> [N]o funds available to the Central Intelligence Agency, the Department of Defense, or any other agency or entity of the United States involved in intelligence activities may be obligated or expended for the purpose or which would have the effect of supporting, directly or indirectly, military or paramilitary operations in Nicaragua by any nation, group, organization, movement, or individual. [Foreign Assistance and Related Programs Appropriations Act, 1985, Pub. L. No. 98-473, §8066(a), 98 Stat. 1837, 1935 (1984).]

This prohibition came after it was revealed that the CIA had participated in the mining of Nicaraguan harbors and in military attacks on Nicaraguan oil facilities with only scant notice given to the intelligence committees. *See* John Prados, *Presidents' Secret Wars* 392-397 (1986); *see also* 1984 Cong. Q. Almanac 89. However, in spite of a growing congressional determination to terminate covert war making in Nicaragua, Senate conferees agreed to the House prohibition only by coupling it with a promise to consider the aid issue again four months later. Remarking on the successful conference compromise, Representative Boland stated that "[t]he compromise...clearly ends United States support for the war in Nicaragua.... [It] can only be renewed if the President can convince the Congress that this very strict prohibition should be overturned." 130 Cong. Rec. H11974 (daily ed. Oct. 10, 1984).

Boland II presents three discrete problems of interpretation. First, does the language "any other agency or entity" cover only agencies traditionally involved in intelligence operations, or does it also apply to any entity that is actually so involved? It was Lt. Col. North and other members of the NSC staff, not CIA officials (except for DCI Casey) or others traditionally active in covert operations, who were principally responsible for managing the resupply operation, including the diversion of arms sales funds to the Contras and the solicitation of donations for the Contras from private citizens and officials of foreign nations. Second, does "involved" encompass indirect support? Third, does the phrase "no funds available" apply only to the then-current DOD appropriation or to all government funds? Apart from the formal statutory construction, consider two more basic questions. Was there ever any serious doubt of the spirit, if not the articulated intent, of Boland II, given its origins? If not, are the President's lawyers nevertheless permitted, if not obliged, to read such legislation narrowly

E. A Case Study of the Iran-Contra Affair

BY TOLES FOR THE BUFFALO NEWS

and legalistically on the theory that legislation in derogation of the President's national security authority must be construed strictly? *See* Banks & Raven-Hansen, *supra* p. 387, at 137-157.

NOTES AND QUESTIONS

1. *Was the Language Clear?* The congressional investigators found the "any other agency or entity" language "clear on its face." *Iran Contra Report, supra* p. 405, at 399. Do you agree? In other years the various Boland amendments were more or less restrictive but always controversial, prompting arguments that Boland II was so vague that its requirements could not be determined. "Some claimed that the Boland amendments were convenient fig leaves for Congressmen who wanted to be against 'another Vietnam' in Central America and at the same time did not want to be accused of allowing another country to fall under Soviet control." Eugene Rostow, *President, Prime Minister, or Constitutional Monarch?* 22-23 (Inst. for Natl. Strategic Studies 1989). How do you think the executive branch should have responded to such legislative vacillation?

Is that vacillation evidence of institutional incompetency on the part of Congress to make policy for covert operations? Of a congressional failure of nerve? Is it important that Congress appears generally to have tightened the Boland restrictions in the belief that earlier versions were being disregarded by the executive branch? *See Iran-Contra Report, supra,* at 396.

2. *Application of Boland II to the NSC and Its Staff.* While the NSC and its staff were established in the National Security Act of 1947 to advise the President and to provide coordination of national security policies, see *supra* p. 359, the President's actual use of the NSC and its staff has varied considerably over time. *See generally History of the NSC 1947-1997, supra* p. 360; John Prados, *Keeper of the Keys: A History of the National Security Council from Truman to Bush* (1991); Christopher C. Shoemaker, *The NSC Staff: Counseling the Council* (1991); Carnes Lord, *The Presidency and the Management of National Security* (1988); *Decisions of the Highest Order: Perspectives on the National Security Council* (Karl F. Inderfurth & Loch K. Johnson eds., 1988).

President Reagan's Executive Order No. 12,333 directs that the NSC provide "review of, guidance for, and direction to the conduct of" covert operations, §1.2, while the CIA shall "ensure implementation" of covert action. *Id.* §1.5(d).

Notwithstanding details of the NSC charter in the National Security Act of 1947, how should the actual historical use of the NSC affect our interpretation of the language in Boland II? Can that question be answered without knowing what Congress, or at least the intelligence committees, knew about that historical practice? *See* Ed Jenkins & Robert H. Brink, *The National Security Council and the Iran-Contra Affair,* 18 Ga. J. Intl. & Comp. L. 19, 22-27 (1988).

3. *NSC Staff and the National Security Act.* In the period covered by Boland II, the NSC staff raised money and organized a private resupply operation for the Contras. President Reagan told the Tower Board that he did not know that the NSC staff was directly helping the Contras, and there was no presidential finding explicitly authorizing these activities. Did any or all of these activities violate Hughes-Ryan? The National Security Act? Were they authorized by the National Security Act?

4. *"No funds available."* In 1987, the Reagan administration asserted that Boland II restricted only funds appropriated under the DOD appropriation, and that because none of those funds were earmarked for the NSC, the NSC was unaffected by Boland. *See* Philip M. Seib, *White House Case Against Boland Amendment Attempts End Run Around Charges of Violation,* Wall St. J., May 18, 1987, at 56. According to the congressional committees, the "prohibition against employment of CIA funds 'available' to it precluded that agency from using its contingency reserve or any funds at its disposal." *Iran-Contra Report, supra,* at 401. Consider this General Accounting Office (GAO) assessment of general appropriations act provisions:

> Appropriation acts, in addition to making appropriations, frequently contain a variety of provisions either restricting the availability of the appropriations or making them available for some particular use. Such provisions come in two forms: (a) "provisos" attached directly to the appropriating language, and (b) general provisions. A general provision may apply solely to the act in which it is contained ("No part of any appropriation contained in this Act shall be used"), . . . or it may

E. A Case Study of the Iran-Contra Affair

have general applicability ("No part of any appropriation contained in this or any other Act shall be used").... Provisions of this type are no less effective merely because they are contained in appropriation acts. General provisions may be phrased in the form of restrictions or positive authority. [Office of General Counsel, General Accounting Office, I *Principles of Federal Appropriations Law* 2-33 (3d ed. 2004).]

Boland II contains neither form of restriction described by the GAO. Does the "no funds available" language nonetheless imply a prohibition of general application? With respect to CIA support for the Contras, does the secret nature of CIA funding, see *supra* p. 387, help to explain why Boland II says "no funds available," instead of "no appropriations contained in this or any other Act"? Or could the CIA have legally assisted the Contras with funds available to it from sources other than the Defense Department?

5. *CIA Contingency Fund.* The Reagan administration's decision to provide assistance to the Nicaraguan Contras through a covert CIA program was made and carried out without public or congressional debate and without a specific appropriation for that purpose. The CIA contingency fund, a secret fund within the secret CIA budget, financed the Contras early on. In line with the CIA's 1949 statutory authority, the only "publication" of the costs of the operation came when President Reagan submitted a report to Congress and thus complied with the Hughes-Ryan reporting requirements. Thus, "there was no public accounting or even notice to most members of Congress of the actual investment in the Contras' cause." Banks & Raven-Hansen, *supra* p. 401, at 104.

In 1983, Congress explicitly prohibited the use of the CIA contingency fund to augment the appropriation in support of the Contras. *Iran-Contra Report, supra,* at 397. Nonetheless, the congressional investigators found that the administration continued to rely on the contingency fund even after the cut-off of appropriated funds in 1984. *Id.* at 399-401.

Like the Central Intelligence Agency Act of 1949, the DOD appropriation measure each year permits certain spending solely on the certificate of the Secretary of Defense. "Special forces" is one type of military operation for which funds are permitted to be spent in this way. When appropriations for the Contras ran out in 1984, the Administration relied on DOD special forces budget authority to purchase equipment, which was then made available to the NSC and CIA staff who were supplying the Contras. *See* Kenneth Sharpe, *The Post-Vietnam Formula Under Siege: The Imperial Presidency and Central America,* 102 Pol. Sci. Q. 549, 561-562 (1987).

6. *Congressional Limits on Solicitation of Unappropriated Funds.* One of the most contentious issues surrounding Boland II concerns its application to the executive branch solicitation of funds from other countries. According to the congressional committees, it was understood that such solicitation was forbidden, even though Boland did not specifically address the matter. *Iran-Contra Report, supra,* at 403-404.

In spite of this understanding, between June 1984 and the beginning of 1986, $34 million was raised from foreign countries by administration officials for the Contras. Although the earliest third-country contributions went directly to the Contras, beginning in July 1985 Oliver North and others effectively ran an "off-the-shelf" covert operation with unappropriated funds. At the criminal trial of North, it was revealed that at least ten countries were solicited for contributions to the Contras and that several of the countries were later rewarded with increased U.S. foreign aid. Stipulation of Facts, United States v. North, No. 88-0080-02 (D.D.C. Apr. 6, 1989); *Iran-Contra Report, supra*, at 16, 19-27.

The contributions given to the United States were not "funds available" from an appropriation or budget transfer. Do you understand why some officials of the State Department, CIA, and NSC nevertheless internally took the position that Boland II prohibited solicitation and use of such contributions to support the Contras?

7. *An Impeachable Offense?* Would efforts by the President or his staff to circumvent Boland II by third-party solicitation of funds for the Contras violate the obligation to "take care that the laws be faithfully executed," imposed by Article II, Section 3 of the Constitution? *See* Laurence H. Tribe, *Reagan Ignites a Constitutional Crisis*, Harv. L. Bull. 7, 8 (Autumn 1987) (maintaining that the President's failure to "take care" to execute Boland "may well entail an impeachable abuse of power").

8. *The President's First Amendment Rights.* May Congress properly prohibit solicitation of third-party contributions? Would a broad reading of the ban on solicitation unconstitutionally burden the President's alleged First Amendment right to, for example, talk with the King of Saudi Arabia? *Compare* Gordon Crovitz, *Boland Laws May Be the Real "Crime,"* Wall St. J., June 4, 1987, at 30 (asserting the First Amendment right), *with* Michael Kinsley, *In Defense of the Boland Amendment*, Wall St. J., June 18, 1987, at 31 ("It may be that no law can prevent the President from talking to King Fahd or the President of Honduras, though it is fanciful to assert . . . that any such conversation was Mr. Reagan's First Amendment right. There is no First Amendment right to say, 'I'll pay you $5,000 to kill my wife,' and there is no First Amendment right to knowingly further a conspiracy by others in violation of the Boland amendment, even if that amendment doesn't apply to you personally.").

9. *The President's Foreign Relations Power.* Does the President have implied power, incident to his power of diplomatic communication, to encourage third parties to pursue the policies he favors? Could Congress prohibit the President from exercising this power by talking with King Fahd or the President of Honduras about the Contras? Professor Rostow insists that "Presidents have used unorthodox channels in diplomacy, usually for important reasons of policy, since Washington's day. . . . A diplomatic exploration conducted under the direction of the President can never be 'outside the normal government framework' and Congress has no power to regulate such Presidential activities." Rostow, *supra* p. 413, at 18. See also *supra* pp. 59-67.

Professor Stith, on the other hand, argues that a denial of appropriated funds forecloses the executive from

> all means of engaging in the prohibited activity because employees' salaries and other overhead costs are almost invariably paid out of appropriated funds. . . . In

E. A Case Study of the Iran-Contra Affair

principle, a government employee acting in an official capacity — including the President — may not spend one minute to make one phone call to solicit private funds (for use of the government or directly for a third party) for an activity explicitly denied appropriated funds. [Kate Stith, *Congress' Power of the Purse*, 97 Yale L.J. 1343, 1361-1362 (1988).]

Which conclusion best reflects your understanding of the constitutional powers in dispute?

10. *Congressional Limits on Spending Third-Party Contributions.* Whether or not the Boland Amendment applied, use of third-party contributions to support the Contras may have been restricted by other statutes:

> The Government may, of course, receive gifts. However, consistent with Congress' constitutionally exclusive power of the purse, gifts like all other "miscellaneous receipts" must, by statute (31 U.S.C. Section 484) be placed directly into the Treasury of the United States, and may be spent only pursuant to a Congressional appropriation....
>
> The Constitutional process that lodges control of Government expenditures exclusively in Congress is further enforced by the Anti-Deficiency Act (31 U.S.C. Section 1341), which prohibits an officer of the United States from authorizing an expenditure that has not been the subject of a Congressional appropriation, or that exceeds the amount of any applicable appropriation. Thus it provides: "An officer or employee of the United States government may not make or authorize an expenditure or obligation exceeding an amount available in an appropriation or fund for the expenditure or obligation; or involve [the] government in a contract or obligation for the payment of money before an appropriation is made unless authorized by law." Violations of the Anti-Deficiency Act are made crimes by 31 U.S.C. Section 1350. [*Iran-Contra Report, supra* p. 405, at 412.]

The gift authority noted above was repealed in 1990. Pub. L. No. 101-403, §2608(b), 104 Stat. 874.

At least as early as June 25, 1984, months before Boland II was enacted, at a National Security Planning Group meeting attended by President Reagan, Secretary of State George Schultz reported an opinion of White House Chief of Staff James Baker that it would be an "impeachable offense" if the United States served as a conduit for third-country funding to the Contras. *Iran-Contra Report, supra,* at 39. In response to a suggestion that the possible U.S. solicitation of third-country support for the Contras should not be made public, President Reagan remarked: "If such a story gets out, we'll all be hanging by our thumbs in front of the White House until we find out who did it." National Security Council, *National Security Planning Group Meeting, June 25, 1984, Minutes* at 14.

11. *The President's Commander-in-Chief Power.* Does the Commander in Chief Clause empower the President to conduct covert operations without regard for the strictures of Boland II? To what extent do the terms of Boland II determine an answer to this question? Of what relevance is Justice Jackson's dictum in *The Steel Seizure Case* that, though the President's power of command is plenary, "only Congress can provide him an army or navy to command"? Youngstown Sheet & Tube Co. v. Sawyer, 343 U.S. 579, 644 (1952). Does Justice Jackson's proposition apply as much to proxy armies as to public armies?

During floor debate, Representative Wilbur Daniel stated that "[t]he Boland Amendment makes clear that *no matter what happens*—even if the Sandinistas seize our Embassy or round up all Americans in Nicaragua—the President of the United States is not allowed to use the U.S. Armed Forces to protect American citizens." 133 Cong. Rec. 16,007 (1987) (emphasis added). If this reading of Boland is correct, does Boland II violate the President's repel attack authority? *See* Durand v. Hollins, *supra* p. 264.

The President's Commander in Chief Clause power to conduct covert operations overlaps with the foreign relations power discussed above. It may include the discrete element of intelligence collection and exchange, perhaps augmenting the power to negotiate treaties. *See* Louis Henkin, *Constitutionalism, Democracy, and Foreign Affairs* 32 (1990). As Justice Sutherland maintained in *Curtiss-Wright,*

> [the President,] not Congress, has the better opportunity of knowing the conditions which prevail in foreign countries, and especially is this true in time of war. He has his confidential sources of information. He has his agents in the form of diplomatic, consular and other officials. Secrecy in respect of information gathered by them may be highly necessary.... [*Curtiss-Wright, supra* p. 60, 299 U.S. at 320.]

Does Boland II intrude on this implied constitutional power of intelligence gathering and exchange?

12. *A Role for the Marque and Reprisal Clause?* On Congress's side of the ledger, reconsider the Marque and Reprisal Clause. May the Boland Amendment be viewed as an assertion of congressional control over imperfect war powers vested in Congress by this forgotten war clause? In light of various claims for presidential and congressional authority, according to which separation of powers analysis should the constitutional dispute be resolved? See *supra* pp. 256-260. However you come out on the separation of powers question, can you fashion a construction of Boland II "by which the [constitutional] question may be avoided"? Crowell v. Benson, 285 U.S. 22, 62 (1932). *See* Raven-Hansen & Banks, *supra* p. 401, at 909-911.

4. The Iran-Contra Affair in the Courts

Soon after the public disclosure of the Iran-Contra Affair, Attorney General Edwin Meese requested the appointment of an Independent Counsel pursuant to the Ethics in Government Act of 1978, Pub. L. No. 95-521, 92 Stat. 1824. A panel of judges appointed former federal judge Lawrence E. Walsh as Independent Counsel. Walsh and his staff conducted a 15-month investigation, and on March 16, 1988, a grand jury returned a 101-page, 23-count indictment against R. Adm. Poindexter, Lt. Col. North, and two co-conspirators. The indictment charged the defendants with three categories of crimes: so-called political or foreign affairs crimes (conspiracy to violate the Boland Amendment and Executive Order No. 12,333), information crimes (obstruction of inquiries and proceedings, false statements, and falsification, destruction, and removal

E. A Case Study of the Iran-Contra Affair

of documents), and garden-variety money crimes (illegal gratuities, embezzlement, and diversion of funds).

After the original four-defendant case was assigned, the defense filed more than 100 pretrial motions. The defendants challenged the validity of the indictment itself and the application of the Classified Information Procedures Act (CIPA), which governs the disclosure of classified information in trials (discussed *infra* p. 857), while they made demands for the discovery of hundreds of thousands of documents. Perhaps the most vexing problem for the prosecution was the fact that some defendants had been granted immunity from prosecution based on their testimony at congressional hearings. Rules restricting the use of such testimony are set out in Kastigar v. United States, 406 U.S. 331 (1972). After a motion and argument, Judge Gerhard A. Gesell agreed in June 1988 to sever the four trials, based on the defendants' contentions that their planned use of the immunized testimony of their codefendants in their own defenses prevented a fair joint trial.

Independent Counsel Walsh elected to try North first. Going first permitted North to present himself as a patriotic fall guy and to blame his superiors and others for his law breaking. The severed trials also delayed by a year the completion of the questioning and other investigative steps in the remaining cases.

NOTES AND QUESTIONS

1. *United States v. North.* Judge Gesell upheld Count One of the indictment, which described the Iran-Contra conspiracy as one intended to defraud the United States by deceitfully conducting a covert action in violation of executive orders and laws of the United States. United States v. North, 708 F. Supp. 375 (D.D.C. 1988). In subsequent preliminary rulings, Judge Gesell dismissed charges of theft and conspiracy to defraud the government when the White House refused to allow the disclosure of classified documents that were viewed by North's lawyers as essential to their defense. (This aspect of the Iran-Contra prosecutions is discussed *infra* pp. 420-421.)

As a policy matter, should we compel faithful execution of national security policy by using criminal sanctions? Does such a conspiracy charge simply constitute "the criminalization of policy differences," as later charged by President Bush in his statement pardoning several Iran-Contra figures?

2. *Following Orders.* In his defense, North claimed that his superiors in the White House authorized his acts. Does a criminal defendant have a duty to ascertain the authority of the authorizer? Does *Curtiss-Wright, supra* p. 60, support North's claim of his superiors' authority? Does the decision in Durand v. Hollins, *supra* p. 264, purportedly recognizing an inherent presidential rescue power, support North in this instance? Should it matter that the President claimed not to have authorized the diversion that underlay the indictment against North? Is Little v. Barreme, *supra* p. 77, relevant to the resolution of these questions?

The district court in North's case refused to instruct the jury that authorization was a complete defense, and the court of appeals affirmed. The latter concluded that North's suggested instruction

> goes so far as to conjure up the notion of a "Nuremberg" defense, a notion from which our criminal justice system, one based on individual accountability and responsibility, has historically recoiled. In the absence of clear and comprehensible Circuit authority that we must do so, we refuse to hold that following orders, without more, can transform an illegal act into a legal one. [United States v. North, 910 F.2d 843, 881 (D.C. Cir. 1990).]

However, the court of appeals also found that a defendant's belief in authorization might relieve him of criminal liability if the statutory scienter standard requires knowledge that the act is unlawful, and not merely specific intent to do the act. *Id.* at 884. Is "I was only following orders" therefore still a backdoor defense in the D.C. Circuit?

3. *The Neutrality Act.* In United States v. Terrell, 731 F. Supp. 473 (S.D. Fl. 1989), Terrell and his companions were charged with supplying weapons to the Contras between October 1984 and mid-March 1985, thereby violating the Neutrality Act by providing the means for "a military . . . enterprise against a country with whom the United States is at peace." 18 U.S.C. §960 (2000). *See supra* p. 371. The defendants argued successfully that the United States was not "at peace" with Nicaragua during the relevant period. The charges were dismissed. The court found that the "at peace" inquiry was factual, not dependent on the existence of formal or declared war.

> The facts demonstrate the unceasing efforts of the executive branch to support the Contra cause, as well as Congressional support immediately before and also after Boland II. That the executive and legislative branches came into conflict regarding foreign policy is indisputable. That such conflict, and Congress' initial response to such conflict (Boland II), means that the United States was "at peace" with Nicaragua for the six months in the indictment after October 12, 1984, is absurd. [731 F. Supp. at 477.]

Because declarations of war have become anachronistic, what should the measure be of a state of peace or war for purposes of the Neutrality Act? Should Boland II be relevant in construing the critical text of the Neutrality Act? Should the prior or subsequent history of congressional support for the Contras be taken into account?

4. *Conviction and Reversal.* Between his December 1986 appointment and the termination of the investigation in 1993, Independent Counsel Walsh charged 14 persons with criminal offenses. Eleven persons were convicted. One case was dismissed when the Bush administration refused to declassify information necessary for trial. See *infra* p. 857.

North was convicted of accepting an illegal gratuity, aiding and abetting in the obstruction of a congressional inquiry, and destruction of documents. Poindexter was convicted of five charges related to obstruction of inquiries, false statements, and destruction of documents. A court of appeals panel vacated both convictions and ordered proceedings to determine whether North's or Poindexter's immunized testimony before the congressional committees influenced witnesses in their trials. On remand, the obligation of the Independent Counsel was to prove by a preponderance of the evidence that each witness's testimony was independently derived. If it was not possible to separate out "unspoiled memory" from that influenced by the congressional testimony, evidence presented by the witness would be excluded. United States v. North, 910 F.2d at 862; United States v. Poindexter, 951 F.2d 369, 389-390 (D.C. Cir. 1991). The cases were subsequently dismissed on the motion of the Independent Counsel, who concluded that the required proofs would be impossible to make.

F. 1991 OVERSIGHT REFORMS

The congressional committees investigating the Iran-Contra Affair determined that the "Administration's conduct in the Iran-Contra Affair was inconsistent" with §501 of the 1980 Oversight Act because the Intelligence Committees were never informed by the President of the arms sales to Iran. *Iran-Contra Report, supra* p. 405, at 415. House and Senate Intelligence Committees introduced several bills seeking generally to strengthen the oversight process. *See* William Cohen, *Congressional Oversight of Covert Actions: The Public's Stake in the Forty-Eight Hour Rule,* 12 Harv. J.L. & Pub. Poly. 285 (1989).

Congressional advocates of oversight reform differed sharply with administration officials concerning the timing for notification of congressional leaders of a presidential finding authorizing a covert action. Instead of the "in a timely fashion" language first incorporated into the Hughes-Ryan Amendment, *supra* p. 390, the congressional reformers wanted presidential notification within 48 hours of a finding.

In a 1986 opinion, Assistant Attorney General Charles J. Cooper took the position that the President enjoys "unfettered discretion" in interpreting the "timely" notification requirement. President Bush sought to mollify members of the intelligence committees in an October 30, 1989, letter:

Dear Mr. Chairman:
 I am aware of your concerns regarding the provision of notice to Congress of covert action and the December 17, 1986 opinion of the Office of Legal Counsel of the Department of Justice, with which you strongly disagree primarily because of the statement that "a number of factors combine to support the conclusion that 'timely notice' language should be read to leave the President with virtually unfettered discretion to choose the right moment for making the required notification."
 I can assure you that I intend to provide notice in a fashion sensitive to congressional concerns. The statute requires prior notice or, when no prior notice is given, timely notice. I anticipate that in almost all instances where prior notice is not provided, notice will be provided within a few days. Any withholding beyond this period would be based upon my assertion of the authorities granted this office by the Constitution. [Letter from President Bush to Intelligence Committees (Oct. 30, 1989), *reprinted in* H.R. Rep. No. 102-166, at 27 (1991).]

A major intelligence oversight reform bill, without the 48-hour notice requirement, was passed by both houses of Congress in 1990. But the President withheld his signature, and a pocket veto was recorded on November 30, 1990. *Memorandum of Disapproval for the Intelligence Authorization Act, Fiscal Year 1991,* Pub. Papers 1729 (1990). *See* William E. Conner, *Reforming Oversight of Covert Actions After the Iran-Contra Affair: A Legislative History of the Intelligence Authorization Act for FY 1991,* 32 Va. J. Intl. L. 871, 910-912 (1992).

In 1991, the intelligence committees agreed to revise the bill in light of the President's objections and concerns. After repealing the Hughes-Ryan Amendment, they substituted the following provisions for the Intelligence Oversight Act of 1980, *supra* p. 394:

Intelligence Authorization Act, Fiscal Year 1991
Pub. L. No. 102-88, 105 Stat. 441, Aug. 14, 1991

SECTION 602. OVERSIGHT OF INTELLIGENCE ACTIVITIES

[Replacing Section 501 of the National Security Act of 1947, 50 U.S.C. §413, with the following new sections:]

Sec. 501. (a)
(1) The President shall ensure that the intelligence committees are kept fully and currently informed of the intelligence activities of the United States, including any significant anticipated intelligence activity as required by this title.
(2) As used in this title, the term "intelligence committees" means the Select Committee on Intelligence of the Senate and the Permanent Select Committee on Intelligence of the House of Representatives.
(3) Nothing in this title shall be construed as requiring the approval of the intelligence committees as a condition precedent to the initiation of any significant anticipated intelligence activity.
(b) The President shall ensure that any illegal intelligence activity is reported promptly to the intelligence committees, as well as any corrective action that has been taken or is planned in connection with such illegal activity.
(c) The President and the intelligence committees shall each establish such procedures as may be necessary to carry out the provisions of this title.
(d) The House of Representatives and the Senate shall each establish, by rule or resolution of such House, procedures to protect from unauthorized disclosure all classified information, and all information relating to intelligence sources and methods, that is furnished to the intelligence committees or to Members of Congress under this title. Such procedures shall be established in consultation with the Director of Central Intelligence. In accordance with such procedures, each of the intelligence committees shall promptly call to the attention of its respective House, or to any appropriate committee or committees of its respective House, any matter relating to intelligence activities requiring the attention of such House or such committee or committees.

F. 1991 Oversight Reforms

(e) Nothing in this Act shall be construed as authority to withhold information from the intelligence committees on the grounds that providing the information to the intelligence committees would constitute the unauthorized disclosure of classified information or information relating to intelligence sources and methods.

(f) As used in this section, the term "intelligence activities" includes covert actions as defined in section 503(e).

REPORTING OF INTELLIGENCE ACTIVITIES OTHER THAN COVERT ACTIONS

Sec. 502. To the extent consistent with due regard for the protection from unauthorized disclosure of classified information relating to sensitive intelligence sources and methods or other exceptionally sensitive matters, the Director of Central Intelligence and the heads of all departments, agencies, and other entities of the United States Government involved in intelligence activities shall —

(1) keep the intelligence committees fully and currently informed of all intelligence activities, other than a covert action (as defined in section 503(e)), which are the responsibility of, are engaged in by, or are carried out for or on behalf of, any department, agency, or entity of the United States Government, including any significant anticipated intelligence activity and any significant intelligence failure; and

(2) furnish the intelligence committees any information or material concerning intelligence activities, other than covert actions, which is within their custody or control, and which is requested by either of the intelligence committees in order to carry out its authorized responsibilities.

PRESIDENTIAL APPROVAL AND REPORTING OF COVERT ACTIONS

Sec. 503. (a) The President may not authorize the conduct of a covert action by departments, agencies, or entities of the United States Government unless the President determines such an action is necessary to support identifiable foreign policy objectives of the United States and is important to the national security of the United States, which determination shall be set forth in a finding that shall meet each of the following conditions:

(1) Each finding shall be in writing, unless immediate action by the United States is required and time does not permit the preparation of a written finding, in which case a written record of the President's decision shall be contemporaneously made and shall be reduced to a written finding as soon as possible but in no event more than 48 hours after the decision is made.

(2) Except as permitted by paragraph (1), a finding may not authorize or sanction a covert action, or any aspect of any such action, which already has occurred.

(3) Each finding shall specify each department, agency, or entity of the United States Government authorized to fund or otherwise participate in any significant way in such action. Any employee, contractor, or contract agent of

a department, agency, or entity of the United States Government other than the Central Intelligence Agency directed to participate in any way in a covert action shall be subject either to the policies and regulations of the Central Intelligence Agency, or to written policies or regulations adopted by such department, agency, or entity, to govern such participation.

(4) Each finding shall specify whether it is contemplated that any third party which is not an element of, or a contractor or contract agent of, the United States Government, or is not otherwise subject to United States Government policies and regulations, will be used to fund or otherwise participate in any significant way in the covert action concerned, or be used to undertake the covert action concerned on behalf of the United States.

(5) A finding may not authorize any action that would violate the Constitution or any statute of the United States.

(b) To the extent consistent with due regard for the protection from unauthorized disclosure of classified information relating to sensitive intelligence sources and methods or other exceptionally sensitive matters, the Director of Central Intelligence and the heads of all departments, agencies, and entities of the United States Government involved in a covert action—

(1) shall keep the intelligence committees fully and currently informed of all covert actions which are the responsibility of, are engaged in by, or are carried out for or on behalf of, any department, agency, or entity of the United States Government, including significant failures; and

(2) shall furnish to the intelligence committees any information or material concerning covert actions which is in the possession, custody, or control of any department, agency, or entity of the United States Government and which is requested by either of the intelligence committees in order to carry out its authorized responsibilities.

(c)(1) The President shall ensure that any finding approved pursuant to subsection (a) shall be reported to the intelligence committees as soon as possible after such approval and before the initiation of the covert action authorized by the finding, except as otherwise provided in paragraph (2) and paragraph (3).

(2) If the President determines that it is essential to limit access to the finding to meet extraordinary circumstances affecting vital interests of the United States, the finding may be reported to the chairmen and ranking minority members of the intelligence committees, the Speaker and minority leader of the House of Representatives, the majority and minority leaders of the Senate, and such other member or members of the congressional leadership as may be included by the President.

(3) Whenever a finding is not reported pursuant to paragraph (1) or (2) of this section, the President shall fully inform the intelligence committees in a timely fashion and shall provide a statement of the reasons for not giving prior notice.

(4) In a case under paragraph (1), (2), or (3), a copy of the finding, signed by the President, shall be provided to the chairman of each intelligence committee. When access to a finding is limited to the Members of Congress specified in paragraph (2), a statement of the reasons for limiting such access shall also be provided.

(d) The President shall ensure that the intelligence committees, or, if applicable, the Members of Congress specified in subsection (c)(2), are notified of any significant change in a previously approved covert action, or any significant undertaking pursuant to a previously approved finding, in the same manner as findings are reported pursuant to subsection (c).

(e) As used in this title, the term "covert action" means an activity or activities of the United States Government to influence political, economic, or military conditions abroad, where it is intended that the role of the United States Government will not be apparent or acknowledged publicly, but does not include —

(1) activities the primary purpose of which is to acquire intelligence, traditional counterintelligence activities, traditional activities to improve or maintain the operational security of United States Government programs, or administrative activities;

(2) traditional diplomatic or military activities or routine support to such activities;

(3) traditional law enforcement activities conducted by United States Government law enforcement agencies or routine support to such activities; or

(4) activities to provide routine support to the overt activities (other than activities described in paragraph (1), (2), or (3)) of other United States Government agencies abroad.

(f) No covert action may be conducted which is intended to influence United States political processes, public opinion, policies, or media....

SEC. 603. LIMITATIONS ON USE OF FUNDS

Section 504 of the National Security Act of 1947 (50 U.S.C. 414), as redesignated by section 602(a) and amended by section 602(c), is further amended —

(1) by redesignating subsection (c) as subsection (e); and

(2) by inserting after subsection (b) the following new subsections:

(c) No funds appropriated for, or otherwise available to, any department, agency, or entity of the United States Government may be expended, or may be directed to be expended, for any covert action, as defined in section 503(e), unless and until a Presidential finding required by subsection (a) of section 503 has been signed or otherwise issued in accordance with that subsection.

(d) (1) Except as otherwise specifically provided by law, funds available to an intelligence agency that are not appropriated funds may be obligated or expended for an intelligence or intelligence-related activity only if those funds are used for activities reported to the appropriate congressional committees pursuant to procedures which identify —

(A) the types of activities for which non-appropriated funds may be expended; and

(B) the circumstances under which an activity must be reported as a significant anticipated intelligence activity before such funds can be expended.

(2) Procedures for purposes of paragraph (1) shall be jointly agreed upon by the intelligence committees and, as appropriate, the Director of Central Intelligence or the Secretary of Defense....

Statement on Signing the Intelligence Authorization Act, Fiscal Year 1991

27 Wkly. Comp. Pres. Docs. 1127, Aug. 14, 1991

Today I have signed H.R. 1455, the "Intelligence Authorization Act, Fiscal Year 1991."

I am pleased that the Congress has eliminated the most serious problems identified in my Memorandum of Disapproval of November 30, 1990, regarding its predecessor, S. 2834 (101st Congress). In particular, I am pleased that the Act, as revised, omits any suggestion that a "request" by the United States to third parties may constitute "covert action" as defined by the Act. In addition, I am pleased that the revised provision concerning "timely" notice to the Congress of covert actions incorporates without substantive change the requirement found in existing law. I reiterate my intention to proceed in this area as outlined in my letters to Senators Boren and Cohen of October 30, 1989; I am glad that the Congress has accepted that statement of intention and, in the spirit of comity in which it was offered, has not added any restrictions beyond those that the executive and legislative branches have agreed are found in existing law.

I remain concerned about legislatively directed policy determinations in the Act and provisions that are without effect because they are unconstitutional under the Supreme Court decisions in INS v. Chadha, 462 U.S. 919 (1983). I reiterate that the inclusion of such provisions is inappropriate.

Several provisions in the Act requiring the disclosure of certain information to the Congress raise constitutional concerns. These provisions cannot be construed to detract from the President's constitutional authority to withhold information the disclosure of which could significantly impair foreign relations, the national security, the deliberative processes of the Executive, or the performance of the Executive's constitutional duties.

I believe that the Act's definition of "covert action" is unnecessary. In determining whether particular military activities constitute covert actions, I shall continue to bear in mind the historic missions of the Armed Forces to protect the United States and its interests, influence foreign capabilities and intentions, and conduct activities preparatory to the execution of operations.

I am confident that this Act will lay to rest disputes that in the past have arisen between some Members of Congress and the executive branch, and I look forward to continued cooperation with the Intelligence Committees.

George Bush
August 14, 1991

NOTES AND QUESTIONS

1. *Responding to the Iran-Contra Affair.* As the congressional reformers struggled to maintain their original goals in a revised bill, the Iran-Contra Affair was fading from the news, replaced by widespread public support for President Bush's handling of Operations Desert Shield and Desert Storm in the Gulf War. *See* Conner, *supra* p. 422, 32 Va. J. Intl. L. at 916. Examine the provisions

of the 1991 Act carefully. Can you assign a reason for each change in the 1980 Intelligence Oversight Act? Specifically, can you see how Congress addressed the questions of presidential accountability, NSC involvement in covert actions, surrogate agents, notice to Congress, government-sponsored propaganda, and expenditure of unappropriated funds?

2. *Definitions.* Consider the definition of "covert action." Is the revised definition clear and unambiguous? Is it an improvement over no definition at all? Does it contain all the relevant categories of activities? *See* W. Michael Reisman & James E. Baker, *Regulating Covert Action: Practices, Contexts, and Policies of Covert Coercion Abroad in International and American Law* 124 (1992). Is this definition an improvement over that contained in Exec. Order 12,333? Why or why not?

3. *Legislative Veto?* President Bush had objected to any provision that required prior approval of the intelligence committees before the President could take certain actions, on the grounds that it would violate INS v. Chadha, noted *supra* p. 128. Is the 1991 Act constitutionally suspect for that reason?

4. *Notice to Congress?* In December 2005, a newspaper revealed the existence of a four-year, large-scale, warrantless surveillance program that intercepted communications of some U.S. citizens. James Risen & Eric Lichtblau, *Bush Lets U.S. Spy on Callers Without Courts*, N.Y. Times, Dec. 16, 2005, at A1. The Administration defended the controversial program in part by claiming that it had briefed selected members of Congress, including some members of the intelligence committees, about the program. *See* Suzanne E. Spaulding, Op-Ed., *Power Play: Did Bush Roll Past the Legal Stop Signs?*, Wash. Post, Dec. 25, 2005, at B1. Did the intelligence oversight legislation require a report on such a program to the intelligence committees? If not, did the legislation require reporting to anyone else? If notice was required, how much information about the program should have been included?

Would reporting to the intelligence committees constitute notice to Congress? If all the members of the committees were not notified, could committee members who were briefed inform other members of the committees or colleagues outside the committees? In any case, if the program violated the Foreign Intelligence Surveillance Act, as its critics charged (see *infra* pp. 483-495), would notice to any part or even all of Congress make the program lawful?

5. *Inspectors General.* The Iran-Contra Affair raised substantial doubts about the effectiveness of the internally appointed, nonstatutory IG for the CIA. "[The] inspectors general apparently never knew about the Iran-contra affair. Agency directors and other senior officials simply by-passed the multiple checks on their actions." Loch Johnson, *Controlling the CIA: A Critique of Current Safeguards,* 12 Harv. J.L. & Pub. Poly. 371, 378 (1989).

In 1989, Congress amended the Central Intelligence Agency Act of 1949 to create a presidentially appointed IG who is subject to Senate confirmation and who will initiate and conduct independent audits, investigations, and inspections of the CIA, and keep the DCI (and now the DNI) and the Intelligence Committees "fully and currently informed about problems and deficiencies."

Intelligence Authorization Act, Fiscal Year 1990, Pub. L. No. 101-193, §17(a)(3) & (4), 103 Stat. 1701, 1711-1712 (1989) (codified as amended at 50 U.S.C. §403q(a)(3) & (4) (2000 & Supp. IV 2004)). The new IG is not given the power to issue subpoenas to other federal government agencies, but she is given her own staff and statutory access to CIA employees, who must cooperate on penalty of dismissal. 50 U.S.C.A. §403q(e)(2), (5).

If this legislation had been enacted a decade earlier, do you think it would have changed the course of the Iran-Contra Affair? Why do you think the CIA strongly resisted its passage? *See* Stephen Engelberg, *C.I.A. Mounts Drive to Defeat Plan for an Outside Inspector*, N.Y. Times, Sept. 29, 1989, at A1; Stephen Engelberg, *Senate Debates Independent C.I.A. Inspector*, N.Y. Times, Nov. 8, 1989, at A22.

6. *Executive Oversight Reforms.* In 1993, President Clinton reconstituted the President's Foreign Intelligence Advisory Board (PFIAB). Exec. Order No. 12,863, 58 Fed. Reg. 48,441 (Sept. 15, 1993). The PFIAB consists of not more than 16 members who are appointed by and serve at the pleasure of the President from among citizens outside the government. The PFIAB reports directly to the President and advises him "concerning the objectives, conduct, management, and coordination of the various activities of the agencies of the Intelligence Community." *Id.* §1.3. In the same executive order, President Clinton established the Intelligence Oversight Board (IOB) as a standing committee of no more than four members from within the PFIAB. *Id.* §2.1. The IOB conducts investigations and makes reports to the President through the PFIAB concerning intelligence activities that the IOB believes "may be unlawful or contrary to Executive order or Presidential directive." *Id.* §2.2.

In 1996, the IOB released its first public report on an investigation of alleged improprieties in the conduct of intelligence activities. In *Report on the Guatemala Review*, June 28, 1996, *available at* http://www.us.net/cip/iob.htm, the IOB reported in response to a request from President Clinton on allegations bearing on the torture, disappearance, or death of U.S. citizens in Guatemala since 1984. The *Guatemala Review* is discussed *infra* p. 451.

How do you rate the potential effectiveness of these oversight mechanisms? Can you think of revisions that would make them more likely to be effective?

7. *Renewed Budget Oversight.* In addition to the oversight mechanisms enacted in 1991, Congress also exercised its power of the purse to better ensure a legislative role in national security decision making. According to Louis Fisher, accepting funds for the Contras from foreign governments meant that "[i]nstead of national policy being articulated by Congress through an open legislative process, it became the net product of secret agreements." Fisher, *supra* p. 411, at 295.

> Congress tackled this issue in 1989. Compromises between President Bush and congressional leaders produced the 1989 Foreign Operations, Export Financing, and Related Programs Appropriations Act of 1990, Pub. L. No. 101-167, 103 Stat. 1195, which in part regulates quid pro quo arrangements without forbidding solicitation of foreign leaders. The 1989 provision declares that any future Boland-like prohibition that is "express" may not be circumvented by third-party funding if the third party is acting "in exchange for" U.S. foreign aid funds. *Id.* §582(a), 103

F. 1991 Oversight Reforms

Stat. 1251. The act does not purport to regulate solicitations, even though earlier bills had criminalized quid pro quos and solicitations alike. President Bush also persuaded sponsor Congressman Obey to record his view on the floor of the House that "the word 'exchange' should be understood to refer to a direct verbal or written agreement." For the president, this version of the bill avoided the "serious constitutional problems" and "unacceptable risk... [of chilling] the conduct of our Nation's foreign affairs" presented by earlier versions. [Banks & Raven-Hansen, *supra* p. 387, at 165-166 (footnotes omitted).]

Does the 1991 oversight legislation address this issue?

16
Other Legal Problems in the Intelligence Field

Intelligence mistakes in advance of the Iraq War illustrate a familiar truth about the intelligence function: failures, when they are revealed, attract widespread attention, while successes are rarely acknowledged publicly and seldom counted by critics of intelligence activities. Less familiar is the fact that the intelligence world has changed and continues to change in dramatic ways following the end of the Cold War. Advances in technology and worldwide communications have complicated intelligence gathering beyond the imaginations of those who had a hand in creating the CIA in 1947.

In Chapters 14 and 15 we saw that legal limits are important in intelligence. The law authorizes intelligence activities, prescribes procedures for approval, implementation, and oversight of those activities, and limits their exercise. This chapter goes beyond the legal overview of those activities and samples a few practical problems that bedevil intelligence in the field.

In Part A we explore problems attendant on the conduct of intelligence operations inside the United States. As September 11 demonstrated with a vengeance, external enemies can do grave damage to the homeland. At the same time, the 1995 Oklahoma City bombing reminded us that threats to our security can as likely be homegrown as foreign. We nevertheless resist as a culture the idea of a Big Brother-like intelligence presence among us. What should the rules be for domestic intelligence collection, and what parts of government should do the collecting?

We then turn in Part B to a range of problems that arise with the employment of private assets in intelligence operations. Proprietary firms — real or fictitious — are sometimes sponsored by the United States and then engage in unlawful or otherwise abhorrent conduct. Similarly, so-called "dirty assets" may be recruited by intelligence agencies, despite their unsavory records, because of their ability to perform tasks considered important by their U.S. handlers. Problems may also arise when journalists or others assume non-official cover (NOC). Are there legal or other limits on such "outsourcing" of intelligence functions? Should we, for example, tolerate the employment of "dirty assets"? Is such tolerance lawful?

Finally, in Part C, we explore briefly some ongoing questions about the relationship of intelligence to military operations. When nonmilitary intelligence operatives act in support of military operations, to whom do they report and according to which laws? If military planners engage their own intelligence collectors or covert actors, are they subject to the intelligence laws? To Defense Department rules?

A. DOMESTIC COLLECTION

In the United States, domestic intelligence collection is regarded as a task for law enforcement. For the FBI and state and local police, the term "intelligence" traditionally refers to information that may be pertinent in solving crimes, including crimes that affect national security. After World War II, fear of a Gestapo or Soviet KGB-style secret police led Congress to withhold internal security authority from the CIA when it passed the National Security Act of 1947. Congress declared that the "Agency shall have no police, subpoena, or law enforcement powers or internal security functions." 50 U.S.C.A. §403-4a(d)(1) (West Supp. 2006). Still, the CIA has conducted domestic operations. In addition, the FBI has on occasion strayed from its lawful domestic role and has undertaken efforts to disrupt domestic groups. Both of these developments are explored below.

1. The CIA

Select Committee to Study Governmental Operations with Respect to Intelligence Activities (Church Committee), Foreign and Military Intelligence
S. Rep. No. 94-755, Book I, at 136-139 (1976)

The National Security Act of 1947 defines the duties of the CIA in terms of "intelligence" or "intelligence relating to the national security." The legislative history of the Act clearly shows that Congress intended the activities authorized by this language to be related to foreign intelligence. This construction is aided by the statute's provision that "the Agency shall have no police, subpoena, law enforcement power, or internal-security functions," 50 U.S.C. [§403-4a(d)(1), *supra* p. 357]....

The legislative history of the Act shows that in establishing the CIA Congress contemplated an agency which not only would be limited to foreign intelligence operations but one which would conduct very few of its operations within the

United States. It was contemplated that the Agency would have its headquarters here, and in House Committee hearings in executive session the possibility of seeking foreign intelligence information from private American citizens who traveled abroad was discussed with approval. But in public and in private it was generally agreed among legislators and representatives of the Executive that the CIA would be "confined out of the continental limits of the United States and in foreign fields," that it should have no "police power or anything else within the confines of this country," and that it was "supposed to operate only abroad."...

The CIA... has interpreted the internal security prohibition narrowly to exclude investigations of domestic activities of American groups for the purpose of determining foreign associations. But history indicates that at the time of enactment of the National Security Act, threats to "internal security" were widely understood to include domestic groups with foreign connections. Investigations by the FBI of American groups with no such connections, in fact, have been a recent phenomenon. The original order from President Roosevelt to J. Edgar Hoover to begin internal security operations was to investigate foreign communist and fascist influence within the United States. There is no evidence that by 1947 these investigations were considered foreign intelligence....

...As authority for some of its operations within the United States, the Agency has relied upon Section 102(d)(3) of the National Security Act, [50 U.S.C. §403-3(c)(7)], which charges the Director of Central Intelligence with responsibility to protect intelligence sources and methods from unauthorized disclosure.

The CIA has construed the sources and methods language broadly to authorize investigation of domestic groups whose activities, including demonstrations, have potential, however remote, for creating threats to CIA installations, recruiters or contractors. In the course of carrying out these investigations the Agency has collected general information about the leadership, funding activities, and policies of targeted groups....

The sources and methods language was discussed only briefly in the recorded legislative history of the National Security Act. As originally drafted, the proposed Act had charged the Director with "fully" protecting sources and methods. In the House Committee executive session, however, General Vandenburg suggested that the Director could not possibly "fully" protect sources and methods, and the word "fully" was subsequently dropped. According to the former General Counsel to the CIA, who was privy to many of the discussions and debates on the legislation as it was being prepared, the purpose of the sources and methods provision was essentially to allay concern in the military services that the Agency would not operate with adequate safeguards to protect the services' intelligence secrets. Despite congressional concern, expressed again and again during hearings and floor debates on the bill, that the CIA was to have no potential for infringing upon the rights of American citizens and that it was to be virtually excluded from acting within the United States, no one questioned whether the sources and methods language would raise problems in this area. The lack of interest in the provision suggests that it was not viewed as conveying new authority to investigate; rather it charged the Director of the Central Intelligence Agency with responsibility to use the authority which he already had to protect sensitive intelligence information....

Halkin v. Helms
United States Court of Appeals, District of Columbia Circuit, 1982
690 F.2d 977

MacKinnon, J. Plaintiffs appeal several orders of the district court which resulted in the dismissal of their complaint for legal and equitable relief on claims arising out of certain activities of the Central Intelligence Agency (CIA) in the period from 1967 to 1974. The complaint alleged violations of plaintiffs' first, fourth, fifth and ninth amendment rights, and of section 102(d)(3) of the National Security Act of 1947, 50 U.S.C. §403(d)(3). For the reasons set forth below, the judgment of the district court is affirmed.

Appellants are 21 individuals and 5 organizations who in the late 1960's and early 1970's were involved in various activities seeking to protest and secure an end to the involvement of the United States in the Vietnam War. The individual appellees are seven named persons and an unspecified number of John Does who at the time plaintiffs' claims arose were officials of the CIA or were otherwise agents or employees of the United States government. The seven appellees referred to hereinafter as the "individual appellees"[1] were sued for damages in their individual capacities. The appellees also include the heads of the CIA, FBI, Department of Defense and Secret Service, who were sued in their official capacities and with respect to whom plaintiffs sought injunctive and declaratory relief only.

Plaintiffs filed suit in October 1975, after disclosures by the press and by the President's Commission on CIA Activities Within the United States[6] (the Rockefeller Commission) revealed that government agencies, including the FBI and the CIA, had conducted intelligence operations that resulted in surveillance of United States citizens who opposed the war in Vietnam. These operations included intelligence gathering activities both within and without the United States. Two such intelligence gathering programs are the focus of the present litigation.

A. OPERATION CHAOS

The first program, designated by the CIA as Operation CHAOS, was an intelligence-gathering activity conducted by the CIA originally at the request of President Johnson which sought to determine the extent to which foreign governments or political organizations[8] exerted influence on or provided

---

1. The individual appellees are Richard Helms (former Director of Central Intelligence), William E. Colby (same), James R. Schlesinger (same and also former Secretary of Defense), Cord Meyer, Jr. (Assistant Director for Plans of the CIA), James J. Angleton (Chief of CIA Counterintelligence Staff), Richard Ober (CIA Counterintelligence Staff), and Howard Osborn (Director of Security of the CIA).

6. The Commission was established by Executive Order of President Ford on January 4, 1975, Executive Order No. 11828 (1975) and filed its final Report in June 1975.

8. Early CHAOS documents indicate the program's concern with the influence of "Soviets, Chicoms [Chinese Communists], Cubans and other Communist countries.... Of particular interest is any evidence of foreign direction, control, training or funding."

support to domestic critics of the government's Vietnam policies.[9] CHAOS was begun in 1967 by appellee Helms, who at the time was Director of Central Intelligence.[10] ...

Over the course of several years, Operation CHAOS produced six reports for the White House and some thirty-four reports for cabinet-level officials, dealing with the subject of foreign influence on the domestic antiwar movement. In the normal course of its operations, CHAOS also produced a steady stream of reports to the FBI and other agencies detailing the results of its various intelligence activities with respect to the antiwar movement.

Discovery conducted by plaintiffs in the district court revealed that among the several thousand computerized files it maintained on Americans involved in various aspects of the antiwar movement,[12] Operation CHAOS ultimately developed files on 15 of the individual appellants and the five appellant organizations. The gravamen of plaintiffs' claims with respect to Operation CHAOS concerned the several known methods whereby the CIA compiled information on plaintiffs' activities....

... [B]eginning in late 1969, the CHAOS office developed its own network of informants for the purposes of infiltrating various foreign antiwar groups located in foreign countries that might have had ties to domestic antiwar activity. Although the principal focus of such infiltration was foreign groups, it is now known that informants destined for such assignments were directed to infiltrate antiwar circles within the United States for the purpose of gaining knowledge of their operations and credibility as antiwar activists. In the course of these preliminary associations, CHAOS agents apparently supplied information on the activities of domestic antiwar groups, and this information was placed in the general CHAOS data base.[16]

... Operation CHAOS made use of the facilities of other ongoing CIA surveillance programs. These included: (1) the CIA letter-opening program, which was directed at letters passing between the United States and the Soviet Union, and involved the examination of correspondence to and from individuals or organizations placed on a "watchlist";[17] (2) the Domestic Contact Service, a CIA office which solicits foreign intelligence information overtly from willing sources within the United States; (3) the CIA's "Project 2," which was directed at the infiltration of foreign intelligence targets by agents posing as dissident sympathizers and which, like CHAOS, had placed agents within domestic radical

---

9. According to early CHAOS documents, the domestic groups suspected of receiving such support included "radical students, anti-Vietnam war activists, draft resisters and deserters, black nationalists, anarchists, and assorted 'New Leftists.'"

10. Helms testified before the Rockefeller Commission that although the President never specifically directed the CIA to institute a program devoted to gathering this information, "the setting up of this unit [CHAOS] was what I conceived to be a proper action" to respond to "almost daily and weekly" requests of the President.

12. In addition to files containing information on the subject individual or group, the CIA's computer system indexed over 100,000 names of persons upon whom separate files were not maintained.

16. The CIA admitted that CHAOS agents associated with at least one plaintiff within the United States and with an unspecified number of plaintiffs traveling in foreign countries; however, it refused to identify these plaintiffs.

17. In addition to the mail of persons who had been "watchlisted," the letter-opening program also examined randomly-selected letters moving between the United States and the Soviet Union.

A. Domestic Collection

organizations for the purposes of training and establishment of dissident credentials; (4) the CIA's Project MERRIMAC, operated by the Office of Security, which was designed to infiltrate domestic antiwar and radical organizations thought to pose a threat to the security of CIA property and personnel; and (5) Project RESISTANCE, also a creature of the Office of Security, which gathered information on domestic groups without any actual infiltration.

From its inception, CHAOS also regularly received information from the FBI on that agency's investigations of the domestic antiwar movement.

B. INTERNATIONAL ELECTRONIC COMMUNICATIONS

In addition to the surveillance activities carried out under the aegis of Operation CHAOS, plaintiffs complained of the CIA's practice of obtaining the contents of international communications (telephone, telegraph and radio transmissions) by submitting subjects' names on "watchlists" to the National Security Agency (NSA). NSA possesses the technology to scan the mass of signals transmitted through various communications systems and then to select out by computer those messages in which certain words or phrases occur. It is thereby possible for that agency to acquire all communications over a monitored system in which, for example, a person's name is mentioned. Between 1967 and 1973, the FBI, the Secret Service, and military intelligence agencies, as well as the CIA, submitted the names of domestic individuals and organizations on watchlists to NSA, and ultimately acquired through NSA the international communications of over a thousand American citizens....

C. HISTORY OF THE LITIGATION

1. DISCOVERY

Since this action was filed in October 1976, the parties have fought the bulk of their dispute on the battlefield of discovery. Shortly after filing their complaint, plaintiffs sought the production of documents concerning (1) the conduct of Operation CHAOS in general, and (2) CHAOS surveillance of plaintiff individuals and organizations in particular. A large number of documents responsive to plaintiffs' request were produced, but with portions claimed to disclose sensitive information redacted. Approximately 200 responsive documents were withheld in their entirety.[27] Subsequently, as public reports further disclosed the extent of CIA domestic activities, plaintiffs in July 1977 sought additional discovery in the form of (3) requests for admissions that the CIA or foreign "liaison services" had conducted various types of surveillance against each plaintiff or against nonparty organizations to which plaintiffs belonged; (4) further interrogatories seeking more detailed justification of the redaction and withholding of documents previously requested; (5) a request for the production of [other] documents....

---

27. The CIA furnished brief descriptions of documents that were entirely withheld (e.g., "Dispatch dated 1 August 1968, information on dissident activity abroad, mentions [plaintiff] in passing").

The CIA declined to supply all of the information requested by plaintiffs. With respect to the identification of plaintiffs who had been the subjects of surveillance under the CHAOS program or by virtue of watchlists submitted by the CIA to NSA, the CIA claimed that more than the limited disclosure already given[28] would reveal the identities of covert sources and disclose the existence of liaison relationships with foreign intelligence services, and that therefore this information was privileged from discovery. The CIA declined... to answer plaintiffs' interrogatories seeking more detailed explanations of the redactions in the documents it had produced.... Finally, it refused to disclose whether any plaintiffs' names had been submitted on watchlists to NSA by the Special Operations Group.

In January 1978, plaintiffs pursuant to Fed. R. Civ. P. 37 filed a motion to compel the Director of the CIA to respond to plaintiffs' interrogatories and requests for production of documents. The CIA responded with two affidavits by then-Director Stansfield Turner formally claiming that the requested information was protected from discovery by the state secrets privilege....

In a memorandum opinion filed August 30, 1978, the district court upheld the CIA's claim of the state secrets privilege and denied plaintiffs' motion to compel....

Plaintiffs explicitly conceded in the district court that the successful invocation of the state secrets privilege by the Director of Central Intelligence made it impossible for them to go forward with their claims for *damages* based on statutory and constitutional violations occurring as a result of Operation CHAOS. Without access to the facts about the identities of particular plaintiffs who were subjected to CIA surveillance (or to NSA interception at the instance of the CIA), direct injury in fact to any of the plaintiffs would not have been susceptible of proof....

... The district court was on solid ground in refusing to compel production of documents on the basis of the Director's claim as asserted in the public affidavit without resort to any more detailed justification.... [The court also refused to compel the defendants to answer interrogatories or appear for oral depositions. The opinion is continued *infra* p. 1037.]

NOTES AND QUESTIONS

1. *State Secrets Privilege.* Additional discussion of the state secrets privilege is presented *infra* p. 1037.

---

28. The CIA had admitted in the course of discovery that various identified and unidentified plaintiffs were on several occasions the targets of CHAOS surveillance or were subjected to surveillance in the course of CHAOS operations directed at other subjects. Specifically, it appears that under Operation CHAOS, the CIA (1) opened and copied the mail of three identified plaintiffs within the United States; (2) targeted the mail of at least two identified plaintiffs for opening; (3) had CHAOS agents attend private meetings of unidentified plaintiff organizations; (4) collected nonpublic information on nine other identified plaintiffs; (5) electronically surveilled two unidentified plaintiffs abroad in the course of operations directed at other persons; (6) had two agents who "were associated" with at least one unidentified plaintiff within the United States; and (7) had agents who "associated" with an undisclosed number of unidentified plaintiffs abroad, in the course of operations directed at other persons.

A. Domestic Collection

2. *Authority for Operation CHAOS?* Did the domestic activities of Operation CHAOS exceed the statutory authority of the CIA? If the mission was to ascertain foreign influence on domestic dissident activities, was CIA accumulation of information on Americans needed to assess fairly whether the activities had foreign connections? Was CHAOS a legitimate program to protect CIA "sources and methods"? If you believe the operation exceeded statutory limits, does the Constitution supply the needed authority?

If you were responsible for approving staff requests to engage in surveillance of Americans, what criteria would you apply in deciding?

3. *Weighing Government Misconduct and National Security Concerns.* In *Halkin*, the court's ruling against disclosure of the disputed evidence apparently made it impossible for individual plaintiffs to demonstrate any personal injury from government misconduct, resulting in dismissal of their claims for damages. Moreover, while several plaintiffs identified as subjects of CHAOS surveillance could establish standing to sue, they could not demonstrate such a cognizable danger of recurrent violation of their rights as to entitle them to injunctive or declaratory relief. *Halkin*, 690 F.2d at 1003-1009.

Has the court concluded, in effect, that foreign policy considerations may excuse violations of the plaintiffs' statutory or constitutional rights? If the plaintiffs would otherwise have been entitled to damages under the Federal Tort Claims Act, is this an instance of uncompensated injury by the government without due process, in violation of the Fifth Amendment to the Constitution? *See* Logan v. Zimmerman Brush Co., 455 U.S. 422, 428-431 (1982). The *Halkin* court observed:

> As in the other cases in which the need to protect sensitive information affecting the national security clashes with fundamental constitutional rights of individuals, we believe that "[t]he responsibility must be where the power is." New York Times Co. v. United States, 403 U.S. 713, 728 (1971) (Stewart, J., concurring). In the present context, where the Constitution compels the subordination of appellants' interest in the pursuit of their claims to the executive's duty to preserve our national security, this means that remedies for constitutional violations which cannot be proven under existing legal standards, if there are to be such remedies, must be provided by Congress. That is where the government's power to remedy wrongs is ultimately reposed. Consequently, that is where the responsibility for compensating those injured in the course of pursuing the ends of state must lie. [690 F.2d at 1001.]

If responsibility is where the power is, what authority did the executive have to launch Operation CHAOS without congressional authority? *See The Steel Seizure Case* (*supra* p. 28), 343 U.S. at 630-632 (Douglas, J., concurring).

Is it clear, as the court suggests, that the Constitution "compels" subordination of individual constitutional claims in cases like this one, or that the court in enforcing the organic law must prefer one part of it over another? In United States Dept. of Justice v. Julian, 486 U.S. 1, 13 (1988), the Supreme Court indicated that the state secrets privilege arises "as a result of judicial decision."

4. *Interpreting the 1947 Act.* What does it mean to say that "the Agency shall have no police, subpoena, or law enforcement powers or internal security

functions"? There is no express geographic limitation in the Act. To what extent may the CIA act within the United States? Are CIA authorities greater when operating abroad? Absent definitions in the Act, how should the CIA interpret the key terms "police," "law enforcement," and "internal security"?

5. *Executive Order No. 12,333.* Recall from our examination of covert action in Chapter 15 that Executive Order No. 12,333, *supra* p. 397, anticipates that the CIA will engage in the "collection of foreign intelligence or counterintelligence within the United States," §1.8(a), and "participate in law enforcement activities to investigate or prevent clandestine intelligence activities by foreign powers or international terrorist or narcotics activities." §2.6(b). Can you reconcile these authorities with the "no police . . . or internal security" proviso in the 1947 Act?

6. *Redefining the Scope of the Mission?* When Congress enacted the 2004 Intelligence Reform Act, *supra* p. 363, the terms "national intelligence" and "intelligence related to national security" were defined to include "all intelligence, regardless of the source from which derived and including information gathered within or outside the United States, that pertains . . . to more than one . . . agency; and that involves threats to the United States, its people, property, or interests; the development, proliferation, or use of weapons of mass destruction; or any other matter bearing on United States national or homeland security." Intelligence Reform and Terrorism Prevention Act of 2004, Pub. L. No. 108-458, §1012, 118 Stat. 3638, 3662. How does this expansive definition affect the geographical boundaries of intelligence activities by the CIA? By the FBI?

Read in isolation, the broadened definition of what counts as intelligence and where it might be sought could be read to permit unfettered CIA intelligence collection in the United States. To clarify that the FBI conducts domestic collection of intelligence and that the CIA does not direct those FBI activities, the Intelligence Reform Act amends the domestic authority of the CIA by adding the qualifier "outside the United States" to the Agency's collection mandate: "The Director of the Central Intelligence Agency shall . . . provide overall direction for and coordination of the collection of national intelligence outside the United States through human sources by elements of the intelligence community authorized to undertake such collection . . . ." Intelligence Reform Act §1011, 50 U.S.C.A. §403-4a(d)(3) (West 2003 & Supp. 2005). Note that this amended tasking refers only to human intelligence collection. Is the implication of the amended Act that the CIA may lawfully collect intelligence through technical means inside the United States? Can you say what limits exist on such authority after the Intelligence Reform Act?

7. *The Director of National Intelligence and Internal Security.* Although the CIA internal security proviso remains after the enactment of the 2004 Intelligence Reform Act, no such constraint was imposed on the Director of National Intelligence (DNI) by the act. What are the legal and practical implications of omitting the internal security prohibition for the DNI? Does the expanded definition of "national intelligence" noted above undercut the internal security prohibition for the CIA?

8. *Is Further Reform Needed?* Do the continuing ambiguities in the law concerning the domestic role of the CIA and its relationship to the FBI suggest

A. Domestic Collection

a need for further statutory reform? Would it be preferable to list activities that the CIA may lawfully perform inside the United States, rather than to maintain a blanket prohibition of uncertain scope? Reviewing the 1947 Act and its 2004 amendments, along with Executive Order 12,333, can you come up with such a list? How would you describe the justifications for CIA collection activities inside the United States? Which methods of collection should be authorized and which ones prohibited, if any? Can you add language that would ensure coordination of CIA activities with those of the FBI and provide a mechanism for ensuring respect for the rights of U.S. persons? Should the no "internal security" proviso be amended to say "except as otherwise permitted by law?" *See* Grant T. Harris, *The CIA Mandate and the War on Terror*, 23 Yale L. & Poly. Rev. 529, 571-576 (2005) (suggesting such changes).

2. The FBI

Select Committee to Study Governmental Operations with Respect to Intelligence Activities (Church Committee), Intelligence Activities and the Rights of Americans
S. Rep. No. 94-755, Book II, at 86-89 (1976)

The FBI's initiation of COINTELPRO operations against the Ku Klux Klan, "Black Nationalists" and the "New Left" brought to bear upon a wide range of domestic groups the techniques previously developed to combat Communists and persons who happened to associate with them.

The start of each program coincided with significant national events. The Klan program followed the widely-publicized disappearance in 1964 of three civil rights workers in Mississippi. The "Black Nationalist" program was authorized in the aftermath of the Newark and Detroit riots in 1967. The "New Left" program developed shortly after student disruption of the Columbia University campus in the spring of 1968. While the initiating memoranda approved by Director Hoover do not refer to these specific events, it is clear that they shaped the context for the Bureau's decisions.

These programs were not directed at obtaining evidence for use in possible criminal prosecutions arising out of those events. Rather, they were secret programs — "under no circumstances" to be "made known outside the Bureau" — which used unlawful or improper acts to "disrupt" or "neutralize" the activities of groups and individuals targeted on the basis of imprecise criteria.

(1) *Klan and "White Hate" COINTELPRO.* — The expansion of Klan investigations, in response to pressure from President Johnson and Attorney General Kennedy, was accompanied by an internal Bureau decision to shift their supervision from the General Investigative Division to the Domestic Intelligence Division. One internal FBI argument for the transfer was that the Intelligence Division was "in a position to launch a disruptive counterintelligence program" against the Klan with the "same effectiveness" it had against the Communist Party.

Accordingly, in September 1964 a directive was sent to seventeen field offices instituting a COINTELPRO against the Klan and what the FBI considered to be other "White Hate" organizations (e.g., American Nazi Party, National States Rights Party) "to expose, disrupt, and otherwise neutralize" the activities of the groups, "their leaders, and adherents."

During the 1964-1971 period, when the program was in operation, 287 proposals for COINTELPRO actions against Klan and "White Hate" groups were authorized by FBI headquarters. Covert techniques used in this COINTELPRO included creating new Klan chapters to be controlled by Bureau informants and sending an anonymous letter designed to break up a marriage.

(2) *"Black Nationalist" COINTELPRO.* — The stated strategy of the "Black Nationalist" COINTELPRO instituted in 1967 was "to expose, disrupt, misdirect, discredit, or otherwise neutralize" such groups and their "leadership, spokesmen, members, and supporters." The larger objectives were to "counter" their "propensity for violence" and to "frustrate" their efforts to "consolidate their forces" or to "recruit new or youthful adherents." Field offices were instructed to exploit conflicts within and between groups; to use news media contacts to ridicule and otherwise discredit groups; to prevent "rabble rousers" from spreading their "philosophy" publicly; and to gather information on the "unsavory backgrounds" of group leaders.

In March 1968, the program was expanded from twenty-three to forty-one field offices and the following long-range goals were set forth:

(1) prevent the "coalition of militant black nationalist groups";
(2) prevent the rise of a "messiah" who could "unify and electrify" the movement, naming specifically Dr. Martin Luther King, Jr., Stokely Carmichael, and Elijah Muhammed;
(3) prevent violence by pinpointing "potential troublemakers" and "neutralizing" them before they "exercise their potential for violence";
(4) prevent groups and leaders from gaining "respectability" by discrediting them to the "responsible" Negro community, the "responsible" white community, "liberals" with "vestiges of sympathy" for militant black nationalist and "Negro radicals"; and
(5) "prevent these groups from recruiting young people."

After the Black Panther Party emerged as a group of national stature, FBI field offices were instructed to develop "imaginative and hard-hitting counterintelligence measures aimed at crippling the BPP." Particular attention was to be given to aggravating conflicts between the Black Panthers and rival groups in a number of cities where such conflict had already taken on the character of "gang warfare with attendant threats of murder and reprisals."

During 1967-1971, FBI headquarters approved 379 proposals for COINTELPRO actions against "black nationalists." These operations utilized dangerous and unsavory techniques which gave rise to the risk of death and often disregarded the personal rights and dignity of the victims.

(3) *"New Left" COINTELPRO.* — The most vaguely defined and haphazard of the COINTELPRO operations was that initiated against the "New Left" in

A. Domestic Collection

May 1968. It was justified to the FBI Director by his subordinates on the basis of the following considerations:

> The nation was "undergoing an era of disruption and violence" which was "caused to a large extent" by individuals "generally connected with the New Left."
>
> Some of these "activists" were urging "revolution" and calling for "the defeat of the United States in Vietnam."
>
> The problem was not just that they committed "unlawful acts," but also that they "falsely" alleged police brutality, and that they "scurrilously attacked the Director and the Bureau" in an attempt to "hamper" FBI investigations and to "drive us off the college campuses."

Consequently, the COINTELPRO was intended to "expose, disrupt, and otherwise neutralize" the activities of "this group" and "persons connected with it." The lack of any clear definition of "New Left" meant, as an FBI supervisor testified, that "legitimate" and nonviolent antiwar groups were targeted because they were "lending aid and comfort" to more disruptive groups.

Further directives issued soon after initiation of the program urged field offices to "vigorously and enthusiastically" explore "every avenue of possible embarrassment" of New Left adherents. Agents were instructed to gather information on the "immorality" and the "scurrilous and depraved" behavior, "habits, and living conditions" of the members of targeted groups. This message was reiterated several months later, when the offices were taken to task for their failure to remain alert for and seek specific data depicting the "depraved nature and moral looseness of the New Left" and to "use this material in a vigorous and enthusiastic approach to neutralizing them."

In July 1968, the field offices were further prodded by FBI headquarters to:

(1) prepare leaflets using "the most obnoxious pictures" of New Left leaders at various universities;
(2) instigate "personal conflicts or animosities" between New Left leaders;
(3) create the impression that leaders are "informants for the Bureau or other law enforcement agencies" (the "snitch jacket" technique);
(4) send articles from student or "underground" newspapers which show "depravity" ("use of narcotics and free sex") of New Left leaders to university officials, donors, legislators, and parents;
(5) have members arrested on marijuana charges;
(6) send anonymous letters about a student's activities to parents, neighbors and the parents' employers;
(7) send anonymous letters about New Left faculty members (signed "A Concerned Alumni" or "A Concerned Taxpayer") to university officials, legislators, Board of Regents, and the press;
(8) use "cooperative press contacts";
(9) exploit the "hostility" between New Left and Old Left groups;
(10) disrupt New Left coffee houses near military bases which are attempting to "influence members of the Armed forces";
(11) use cartoons, photographs, and anonymous letters to "ridicule" the New Left;
(12) use "misinformation" to "confuse and disrupt" New Left activities, such as by notifying members that events have been cancelled.

During the period 1968-1971, 291 COINTELPRO actions against the "New Left" were approved by headquarters. Particular emphasis was placed upon preventing the targeted individuals from public speaking or teaching and providing "misinformation" to confuse demonstrators.

NOTES AND QUESTIONS

1. *Legislative Authority?* Unlike the CIA, the FBI has no legislative charter. The FBI operates on the basis of the Attorney General's authority in 28 U.S.C. §533 (2000 & Supp. III 2003) to appoint officials:

(1) to detect and prosecute crimes against the United States;
(2) to assist in the protection of the person of the President; and...
(4) to conduct such other investigations regarding official matters under the control of the Department of Justice and the Department of State as may be directed by the Attorney General.

Does this statute indicate any limits to FBI investigative activities? Can you outline the elements of a proposed charter for the FBI? Should such a charter be enacted?

2. *Suing the FBI over COINTELPRO.* In 1976, several Washington area residents who had been politically active in anti-war and civil rights activities in the 1960s and early 1970s brought suit against the FBI and District of Columbia officials for alleged violations of constitutional rights related to the FBI COINTELPRO program. In Hobson v. Wilson, 737 F.2d 1, 10 (D.C. Cir. 1984), *cert. denied sub nom.* Brennan v. Hobson, 470 U.S. 1084 (1985), the plaintiffs prevailed against most of the defendants. The Court of Appeals stated, "Government action taken with the intent to disrupt or destroy lawful organizations, or to deter membership in those groups, is absolutely unconstitutional." 737 F.2d at 29. What likely explains the different outcomes in *Halkin* and *Hobson*?

3. *The FBI Role in Fighting Domestic National Security Crime and Terrorism.* Putting aside the abuses of the COINTELPRO program, the FBI has an important domestic, as well as international, role in fighting national security crimes and terrorism. Part IV of this book explores that role in depth. In particular, Part IV examines the statutory surveillance authorities available for FBI use in domestic investigations as well as executive branch rules that shape contemporary FBI practice in domestic intelligence.

4. *Intelligence Reform and the FBI.* On March 31, 2005, the Silberman/Robb Commission, co-chaired by Judge Laurence Silberman and former Senator Charles Robb, recommended that the President create a new National Security Service within the FBI under a new Executive Assistant Director. Commission on the Intelligence Capabilities of the United States Regarding Weapons of Mass Destruction (Silberman/Robb Commission), *Report to the President of the United States* 465, Mar. 31, 2005, *available at* http://www.wmd.gov/report/. The new service would include the Counterterrorism and Counterintelligence Divisions

A. Domestic Collection

and the Directorate of Intelligence, and it would be subject to the coordination and budget authorities of the DNI. Appointment of a new Executive Assistant Director would be subject to approval by the DNI. *Id.* The Commission also recommended that the primary Department of Justice national security elements — the Office of Intelligence Policy and Review (OIPR) and the Counterterrorism and Counterespionage Sections — be placed under a new Assistant Attorney General for National Security. *Id.* at 471. On June 29, 2005, President Bush accepted these recommendations, directed the Attorney General to implement them, and asked Congress to create the new Assistant Attorney General position. Memorandum for the Vice President et al., *Strengthening the Ability of the Department of Justice to Meet Challenges to the Security of the Nation,* available at http://www.whitehouse.gov/news/releases/2005/06/20050629-1.html. Congress did so in March 2006 in the Patriot Reauthorization Act, *infra* pp. 527-528.

The restructuring was "intended to break down old walls between foreign and domestic intelligence activities." Douglas Jehl, *Bush to Create New Unit in F.B.I. for Intelligence,* N.Y. Times, June 30, 2005, at A1. How do you suppose the new organization will break down walls? Do you see any downside risk in tearing down the wall between foreign and domestic intelligence? In lowering the historic barrier between the FBI and the CIA? To what extent will the FBI now be subject to the authority of the DNI? Whose job is it to determine that the new National Security Service does not undertake activities that violate U.S. laws? The legal consequences of these FBI reforms are considered further in Chapter 22.

5. *Creation of a U.S. MI5?* In recent years, some have suggested that the United States create a domestic intelligence service, perhaps patterned after the Security Service in the United Kingdom, more commonly known as MI5. *See, e.g.,* William E. Odom, *Fixing Intelligence for a More Secure America* 180-182 (2d ed. 2003). Instead of relying on the FBI to perform domestic intelligence gathering, an MI5-type agency might be separate from the FBI and CIA and, like them, report to the DNI. The FBI could do what it has historically done best — fight crime by building cases against criminals. The domestic intelligence agency would look for what has not yet happened by gathering intelligence in the United States about espionage or terrorist plots that are inchoate. The potential targets of the new agency could be wholly homegrown, like the Ku Klux Klan or domestic terrorists, or those with foreign origins or connections, such as al Qaeda.

Would creation of a such a new agency be a good idea? If our "MI5" reported to the DNI instead of directly to the President, are you satisfied that the agency would not be prone to performing the politically driven operations that bedeviled the nation in the Nixon years?

3. The NSA

The National Security Agency (NSA) is the largest agency within the intelligence community. It is devoted to communications security and to collecting and disseminating signals intelligence (SIGINT). See *supra* p. 351. NSA's predecessor, the Armed Forces Security Agency (AFSA), was established within the Department of Defense in 1949, but because each military service branch continued to collect SIGINT for its own use, AFSA proved ineffectual in coordinating SIGINT activities. In October 1952, President Truman signed a secret directive to create the NSA in order to provide an effective structure for coordinating SIGINT activities for civilian and military consumers. Richard A. Best Jr., *The National Security Agency: Issues for Congress* (Cong. Res. Serv. RL30740) 16, Jan. 16, 2001. Apart from annual appropriations for the NSA based on secret briefings about SIGINT activities before the appropriations committees, the first major legislation dealing with NSA was the National Security Agency Act of 1959, Pub. L. No. 86-36, 73 Stat. 63. It authorized the Secretary of Defense to "establish such positions, and to appoint ... such officers and employees, in the National Security Agency, as may be necessary to carry out the functions of such agency." *Id.* §2. However, this measure dealt mostly with housekeeping matters inside the agency and did not describe the functions of NSA.

Until it was revealed that U.S. intelligence agencies were spying on domestic groups opposed to the Vietnam War, there was little interest in NSA among members of Congress or the public and little knowledge about the secretive agency. During the Church Committee hearings in 1976, NSA Director Lt. Gen. Lew Allen Jr. provided the first open-session congressional testimony about NSA SIGINT activities and the NSA practice of establishing "watch lists," discussed in *Halkin, supra* p. 433. Although the Church Committee and its House counterpart, known as the Pike Committee, acknowledged the continuing importance of NSA's foreign intelligence collection activities, both committees also recommended specific authorizing legislation for NSA that would include strict limits on the monitoring of communications by U.S. citizens. *See* Church Committee, *supra* p. 431, Book I, at 464; *Recommendations of the Final Rpt. of the House Select Comm. on Intelligence*, H.R. Rep. No. 94-833, at 3 (1976). The congressional initiative toward a "legislative charter" for the intelligence agencies, including NSA, died in the 1979-1980 congressional session amidst partisan disputes, when the Soviet invasion of Afghanistan caught the United States by surprise and provoked new efforts to invigorate intelligence capabilities. *See supra* p. 394.

In 1992, the National Security Act of 1947 was amended to state that

> the Secretary of Defense shall ensure ... through the National Security Agency (except as otherwise directed by the President or the National Security Council), the continued operation of an effective unified organization for the conduct of signals intelligence activities and shall ensure that the product is disseminated in a timely manner to authorized recipients. [Intelligence Authorization Act for Fiscal Year 1993, Pub. L. No. 102-496, §706, 106 Stat. 3180, 3194-3195 (1992) (codified as amended at 50 U.S.C.A. §403-5(b)(1) (West 2003 & Supp. 2006)).]

Additional guidance for NSA has been provided by executive order.

Executive Order No. 12,333
46 Fed. Reg. 59,941 (Dec. 4, 1981)

1.12 Intelligence Components Utilized by the Secretary of Defense.... [T]he Secretary of Defense is authorized to utilize the following: ...

A. Domestic Collection

(b) National Security Agency, whose responsibilities shall include:

(1) Establishment and operation of an effective unified organization for signals intelligence activities, except for the delegation of operational control over certain operations that are conducted through other elements of the Intelligence Community. No other department or agency may engage in signals intelligence activities except pursuant to a delegation by the Secretary of Defense;

(2) Control of signals intelligence collection and processing activities, including assignment of resources to an appropriate agent for such periods and tasks as required for the direct support of military commanders;

(3) Collection of signals intelligence information for national foreign intelligence purposes in accordance with guidance from the Director of Central Intelligence;

(4) Processing of signals intelligence data for national foreign intelligence purposes in accordance with guidance from the Director of Central Intelligence;

(5) Dissemination of signals intelligence information for national foreign intelligence purposes to authorized elements of the Government, including the military services, in accordance with guidance from the Director of Central Intelligence;

(6) Collection, processing and dissemination of signals intelligence information for counterintelligence purposes;

(7) Provision of signals intelligence support for the conduct of military operations in accordance with tasking, priorities, and standards of timeliness assigned by the Secretary of Defense. If provision of such support requires use of national collection systems, these systems will be tasked within existing guidance from the Director of Central Intelligence;

(8) Executing the responsibilities of the Secretary of Defense as executive agent for the communications security of the United States Government;...

(10) Protection of the security of its installations, activities, property, information, and employees by appropriate means, including such investigations of applicants, employees, contractors, and other persons with similar associations with the NSA as are necessary;...

The power of NSA computers to collect massive amounts of data is staggering. NSA "employs more mathematicians than any other organization in the world and [its facilities contain] the densest concentration of computer power on the planet." Patrick Radden Keefe, *Chatter: Dispatches from the Secret World of Global Eavesdropping* 8 (2005). Its technical capacity actually far outstrips the human capacity to evaluate or use all the information it collects.

The agency does not act upon the intelligence it collects. Instead, NSA provides intelligence to other civilian and military agencies and officials. *Id.* Still, NSA uses sophisticated key-word searching and other techniques (often lumped together and referred to as "data mining") to perform some analysis on large amounts of material before it is delivered to other agencies.

An NSA program called ECHELON allegedly used data-mining techniques aimed at telecommunications from Europe for economic espionage. *Id.* at 194-208. Sophisticated listening stations in the United States and Great Britain allegedly tracked these communications. *Id.* at 52-54. European leaders claimed that ECHELON was employed to steal secrets from European countries and pass them on to U.S. competitors. European Parliament, *Report of the Existence of a Global System for the Interception of Private and Commercial Communications (ECHELON Interception System)*, July 11, 2001, *available at* http://www.fas.org/irp/program/process/rapport_echelon_en.pdf. The privacy implications of data mining are considered further *infra* p. 581.

In its communications security role, NSA uses its SIGINT capabilities to detect espionage and other intelligence activities directed against the United States. For example, early in the Cold War NSA conducted a program codenamed VENONA that used signal intercepts to detect Soviet espionage in the United States. Between 1943 and 1957, VENONA helped identify Alger Hiss, Julius Rosenberg, Klaus Fuchs, and others who served as Soviet agents. *See* Robert L. Benson, *The Venona Story*, National Security Agency/Central Security Service (n.d.), *available at* http://www.nsa.gov/publications/publi00039.cfm. Many of the released intercepts may be viewed at http://www.nsa.gov/venona/. Additional background on the NSA may be found in two books by James Bamford, *Body of Secrets: Anatomy of the Ultra-Secret National Security Agency* (2001), and *Puzzle Palace* (1982).

NOTES AND QUESTIONS

1. *Authority to Create the NSA?* What authority did President Truman have to establish the NSA in 1952? The National Security Act of 1947, *supra* p. 355, creates a Secretary of Defense and states that "[u]nder the direction of the President and subject to the provisions of this Act he shall ... [e]stablish general policies and programs for the National Military Establishment and for all the departments and agencies therein." Pub. L. No. 80-253, §202(a)(1), 61 Stat. 495, 500. If this provision is insufficient, does the President possess constitutional authority to create an agency to collect SIGINT for foreign intelligence purposes? To collect SIGINT in the United States? What was the legal effect of annual appropriations for the NSA on its authority to perform SIGINT activities before the 1992 amendment to the National Security Act? *See supra* pp. 111-114.

2. *Watch Lists.* If the *Halkin* court had reached the merits, how should it have ruled on the plaintiffs' complaints concerning the NSA's use of watch lists? Watch lists were developed by identifying individual names, subjects, locations, and the like within a mass of communications to separate useful intelligence from background "noise." Watch lists were thus precursors to contemporary data-mining techniques, including those at issue in the post-September 11 NSA domestic eavesdropping program. *See infra* pp. 548-556.

During the Vietnam War period, congressional investigators learned of an NSA project known as Shamrock in which copies of international telegrams were provided on a daily basis to NSA by three telegraph companies.

Church Committee, *supra* p. 341, Book III, at 765-776. Pursuant to what legal authority would this project have been conducted? The congressional desire to bring practices such as these under legislative control helped assure the enactment of the Foreign Intelligence Surveillance Act of 1978 (FISA). FISA is examined *infra* p. 483.

3. *Contemporary Authorities.* To what extent, if at all, does the 1959 National Security Agency Act, *supra* p. 444, authorize the activities of the NSA? Does the 1992 amendment to the National Security Act of 1947 constitute an adequate legislative charter for the NSA's activities? If not, what changes or additions would you recommend? To what extent do the provisions of Executive Order No. 12,333 supply the necessary details? What questions do you have about what the NSA may and may not do after reading these two measures?

4. *ECHELON.* Does the NSA have the authority to conduct the ECHELON program? Some in the United States countered the European complaints by maintaining that ECHELON was used to observe bribes by European companies of government officials in furtherance of their commercial interests. Keefe, *supra,* at 194-198. Do you see any legal problems with these techniques or with their objectives?

B. PRIVATE ASSETS

To some degree, U.S. intelligence operations have always had a private component. Washington and other early American leaders hired spies to carry out intelligence operations. *See generally* Henry Merritt Wriston, *Executive Agents in Foreign Relations* (1929). In the more recent past, especially throughout the Vietnam War years, the CIA relied on proprietaries—business entities wholly owned by the CIA—either to do business or to appear to do business as an adjunct to the conduct of intelligence operations.

1. Proprietaries

Select Committee to Study Governmental Operations with Respect to Intelligence Activities (Church Committee), Foreign and Military Intelligence
S. Rep. No. 94-755, Book I, at 205-209 (1976)

Proprietaries... are part of the "arsenal of tools" the CIA believes it must have to be an effective intelligence component. In recent years, particularly during the Vietnam War, serious questions were raised about this proprietary capability.
... Some of the criticism arose from the suspected entrance of proprietaries into areas where they would be in competition with legitimate business interests,

such as the airline industry. It has been feared that their profits were used to provide secret funding for covert operations, thus avoiding scrutiny by the Executive and the Congress through a "back door" funding process.

In addition, there have been allegations that the domestic impact of these entities has effectively violated the Agency's charter, which generally proscribes domestic activity of a police or internal security nature.... Questions have arisen about whether Agency policy included using these entities to engage in illegal activities to make profits which could be used to fund clandestine operations. Most notably, the latter charges have involved allegations that the Agency's air proprietaries were involved in drug trafficking....

Acting under broad authority granted them by the National Security Act of 1947 and Central Intelligence Act of 1949, the various Directors of Central Intelligence have established proprietaries (Government-owned business enterprises, foundations and quasi-business enterprises) to serve a variety of intelligence and covert action purposes. Chief among those purposes have been:

1. PROVISION OF COVER FOR INTELLIGENCE COLLECTION AND ACTION PROJECTS

Commercial firms established in foreign countries provide plausible reasons for the presence of CIA case officers. Agency-funded foundations serve as conduits of funds for a variety of purposes, including clandestine activities and contributions to scholars conducting research which supports United States foreign policy positions.

2. EXTENSION OF AGENCY INFLUENCE AND INFORMATION NETWORK IN OVERSEAS BUSINESS COMMUNITY

The very act of establishing a proprietary firm requires banking, insurance, and other services. Acquiring these services entails support, communications, and intimate business relationships with bona fide commercial entities here and abroad. At a minimum, these relationships require the clearance of those in top management positions for access to CIA business. On occasion this relationship includes the Agency using commercial contacts for information or assistance.

3. PROVISION OF SUPPORTING SERVICES FOR COVERT OPERATIONS

In paramilitary operations, airlift and sealift by Agency-owned carriers has many advantages: flexibility, security, ability to implant technical collection devices, etc. CIA agents, who engage in hazardous activities which would ordinarily make them uninsurable, can obtain commercial insurance at standard or subsidized rates via a conglomerate of CIA-owned insurance companies. In foreign locations where actual contact with the nearest CIA station is not operationally discreet, proprietaries provide payroll channels and other administrative services for Agency personnel. Firms based in locations with permissive corporate laws and regulations can also engage in many activities unrelated

B. Private Assets

to their charters. For example, insurance firms can acquire real estate for operational purposes on a non-attributed basis.

4. *OPERATION OF PROPAGANDA MECHANISMS*

In establishing the clandestine radios (Radio Free Europe and Radio Liberty) in the 1950s, the CIA acquired a means of directly influencing populations behind the Iron Curtain. These proprietaries were eventually disposed of and placed under the aegis of the Department of State.

5. *MANAGEMENT OF PRIVATE INVESTMENTS*

The Agency would deny that private investment is a *purpose* of proprietaries. Agency officials state that standing policy prohibits the investment of CIA operational funds in the private sector without explicit authorization by the DCI. Actually, the existence of proprietary enterprises which occasionally returned sizable profits, indicates that private investment may indeed have been a widespread Agency policy. Moreover, the Agency has specifically authorized its insurance complex to act as an institutional investor for its own funds and those of other proprietaries. Thus, the extent of private investment by the Agency is actually a question of definition and shading....

Air America, the Agency's largest proprietary, provided air support for CIA operations in Southeast Asia. This support was under cover of a commercial flying service fulfilling United States Government contracts. Corporate headquarters were in Washington, D.C., with field headquarters in Taipei, Taiwan....

NOTE ON COVERT INTERVENTION IN LAOS[1]

After the 1962 Geneva agreements "neutralized" Laos and required all "foreign military personnel" to leave the country, the CIA took over a U.S. paramilitary operation for control of northern and central Laos in support of the government and against Communist Pathet Lao and North Vietnamese forces. William Colby organized L'Armée Clandestine with a handful of CIA case officers and ran what became the largest paramilitary operation in U.S. history from across the border in Thailand. Tens of thousands of Hmong and other tribesmen were recruited for the CIA's private army. Upwards of 20,000 of them were U.S.-paid "volunteers" who had resigned from the Thai army. Colby and other case officers (substantially made up of Army Special Forces troops who joined the CIA payroll after the 1962 accords) trained and supplied these volunteers, transported and directed and sometimes participated in battles with them against the Pathet Lao, and supported them with bombing raids.

Nearly all of the equipment for the Armée Clandestine was supplied by the United States, typically delivered under the cover of the Agency for

---

1. Background and sources on U.S. involvement in Laos are supplied *supra* p. 380. In addition, *see* John Prados, *Presidents' Secret Wars* 261-296 (1986).

International Development (AID). The CIA also engaged in food drops and various other nation-building activities in Laos, in pursuit of Laotian support for American policies. As the costs of the program mounted, CIA briefs to subcommittees of the appropriations committees in Congress persuaded members to support ever-increasing spending for the covert program.

By the mid-1960s, about 250 Americans were either in Laos or commuting to their assignments there. Air America pilots flew in support of the Laos program during time off from their regular flight routes. The pilots were paid bonuses, given tax breaks, and could earn $40,000 or more. Flying out of its Thailand bases, the 1969 Air America fleet had 29 helicopters, 20 light planes, and 19 medium transport planes. Ironically, the demand for transport in support of the Laos operation led to competition for the USAID contracts from a rival company, Continental Air Services. To avoid revealing the real nature of Air America, Continental Air was given some of the Laotian contract work. The air combat task was carried out by Air Force planes and pilots, not Air America. The U.S. Air Force role eventually grew to 100 fighter-bombers and supporting gunships.

By the late 1960s, CIA veterans grew tired and leery of the Laos operation, not due to the growing dissatisfaction with the larger war, but because the program was cumbersome and mostly overt rather than smoothly run and secret. Still, until the New York Times reported on the U.S. role in Laos in 1969, most Americans and members of Congress were unaware of the paramilitary program there.

NOTES AND QUESTIONS

1. *The Legal Propriety of Proprietaries.* Do you see any legal problems with the government's use of proprietaries in conducting intelligence operations? If the CIA has authority to violate laws, see *supra* p. 376, is that authority delegable? What control mechanisms or reforms would you propose to respond to the problems?

2. *The CIA in Laos.* In Laos, the CIA supported a "secret" army of tens of thousands of Hmong tribesmen and Thai "volunteers." This force was financed, trained, supplied, transported, and sometimes accompanied into battle by CIA operatives, many of whom were former U.S. Army Green Berets. Pursuant to what legal authority was this operation conducted? See *supra* pp. 372-380. *See also* John Hart Ely, *War and Responsibility: Constitutional Lessons of Vietnam and Its Aftermath* 68-97 (1993) (concluding that the "secret war" in Laos was unconstitutional). What purpose was served by keeping this operation secret from members of Congress and from the American people?

3. *The CIA and Constitutional War Powers.* Does the fact that the CIA, rather than the uniformed military, conducted the operation in Laos mean that it should not count as a "war" under the Constitution? *See* Ely, *supra*, at 73-75 (no).

4. *The CIA and the Drug Trade.* It was widely known that the CIA and Air America were passive participants in the lucrative and pervasive drug trade in

Laos and Thailand. It was passive only in the sense that intelligence reported on the movement of drugs, sometimes by CIA-paid operatives and on proprietary aircraft, but did nothing to stop it. Reporting about these linkages to less savory elements helped spur congressional hearings and the eventual end of the Laotian secret war. *See* Prados, *supra*, at 284-287. Legal problems with such "dirty assets" are explored below.

5. *The CIA and Contracting for Services.* In the post-Cold War environment for intelligence operations, privatization has taken on new meaning. For example, U.S. participation in Plan Colombia and related anti-drug efforts in Bolivia and Peru have been contracted out in part to DynCorp, a private company that supplies pilots and mechanics for U.S.-owned aircraft sponsored by the State Department's International Narcotics and Law Enforcement Bureau. Media attention focused on the program in April 2001, when innocent civilians flying in a private plane were mistakenly shot down and killed by anti-drug surveillance aircraft operating over Peru. Although the attacking aircraft was Peruvian and was piloted by Peruvians, the program they were participating in was underwritten by the United States.

In Colombia, DynCorp and other contractors have flown drug-crop fumigation missions, ferried battalions into combat, served as mechanics and logistical personnel, performed reviews of local armed forces, and gathered intelligence. DynCorp contract personnel also engaged in a firefight with Colombian Revolutionary Armed Forces (FARC) guerillas during a search and rescue mission. *See Drug Policy and Human Resources: Hearing Before the Subcomm. on Crim. Justice of the H. Government Reform Comm.*, 107th Cong. (2001) (statement of Adam Isacson), *available at* http://www.ciponline.org/colombia/050103.htm.

2. Dirty Assets

One of the risks of employing private intelligence operatives (assets) is the relative inability to control an asset's behavior through the employment relationship or through thorough vetting prior to employment. The intelligence asset typically is a foreign national sought out by U.S. intelligence officials because of the asset's potential ability to fulfill an intelligence objective. Suppose such an asset behaves unlawfully in the extreme and causes serious injury to the rights of a U.S. citizen or others. Is the injured party entitled to recover in the courts? If so, against whom?

Harbury v. Deutch
United States Court of Appeals, District of Columbia Circuit, 2000
233 F.3d 596

TATEL, Circuit Judge.... Since this appeal comes here on a motion to dismiss, we accept the facts as alleged in the complaint. Emphasizing that defendants have not yet answered Harbury's charges and that her claims have been subject to neither discovery nor cross-examination, we set out the facts as she pleads them, borrowing liberally from her complaint.

In 1991, Harbury, an American citizen, married Efrain Bamaca-Velasquez, a Guatemalan citizen and high-ranking member of the Guatemalan National Revolutionary Union, a Guatemalan rebel organization. Several months after their Texas wedding, Bamaca returned to Guatemala where, on or around March 12, 1992, he disappeared. The Guatemalan army reported that during a skirmish with its troops, Bamaca committed suicide and was buried nearby. This was false. In fact, Bamaca had been captured and secretly detained by members of the Guatemalan military, including, Harbury alleges, CIA "assets"—members of Guatemalan Security Forces or Intelligence Services paid by the CIA to obtain information about the Guatemalan resistance.

According to the complaint, over the next twelve to eighteen months, Bamaca's captors psychologically abused and physically tortured him. They chained and bound him naked to a bed, beat and threatened him, and encased him in a fullbody cast to prevent escape. Eventually, probably some time around September of 1993, they executed him.

About a year after Bamaca disappeared, in early 1993, Harbury learned from a prisoner who had escaped from a Guatemalan interrogation camp that her husband was alive and being tortured. Harbury immediately contacted several State Department officials, reported what she had learned, and asked for information about her husband's status. Although officials to whom she spoke promised to look into the matter, they never provided her with any information....

... [B]ecause of the "failure of the [State Department and NSC] defendants to inform her of her husband's fate," Harbury announced that she would begin a hunger strike in front of the White House on March 12, 1995, the third anniversary of her husband's disappearance. State Department and NSC officials then met with her again, telling her this time that they believed Bamaca was dead because so many years had passed without evidence that he was alive. Unconvinced, Harbury began her hunger strike. Twelve days into the strike, Congressman Robert Torricelli announced publicly that years earlier, Bamaca had been killed at the order of a paid CIA asset.

On her own behalf and as administratrix of Bamaca's estate, Harbury brought suit in the U.S. District Court here against various named and unnamed officials of the CIA, the State Department, and the NSC. She based her claims on two broad factual allegations. First, she alleged that CIA officials at all levels "knowingly engaged in, directed, collaborated and conspired in, and otherwise contributed to [her husband's] secret imprisonment, torture and extrajudicial murder." Many of the Guatemalan military officers who tortured and killed Bamaca, she alleged, were paid CIA agents. Two had been trained in torture and interrogation techniques at the School of the Americas, a U.S. Army facility located in Georgia. According to Harbury, CIA officials who did not participate directly in Bamaca's torture not only paid Agency assets for information about Bamaca's rebel organization, knowing that the information had been extracted through torture, but also requested further intelligence, knowing it too would be obtained in the same manner. And as a general matter, Harbury alleged that CIA officials knew of other gross human rights violations in Guatemalan interrogation centers—including beatings with cement blocks, burials of prisoners

B. Private Assets

alive, and electrical shocks to the testicles and legs—and that CIA officials up the chain of command, from the operations and intelligence divisions to the Director himself, expressly authorized their assets to use torture to obtain information from Guatemalan rebel leaders.

Second, Harbury alleged that while Bamaca was still alive, State Department and NSC officials, including Ambassador McAfee and NSA Lake, made "fraudulent statements and intentional omissions" that prevented her from "effectively seeking adequate legal redress, petitioning the appropriate government authorities, and seeking to publicize her husband's true plight." According to the complaint, when Harbury first contacted State Department officials to follow up on what she had learned from the escaped prisoner, they actually knew that her husband was alive and being tortured. They knew this, she alleged, because a week after Bamaca's capture, the CIA informed both State Department and White House officials that Guatemalan military forces would "probably fabricate his combat death in order to maximize their ability to extract information from [him]." Yet State Department officials, including Ambassador McAfee, revealed none of this information to Harbury. Instead, they repeatedly reassured her that although they were investigating Bamaca's fate, they had discovered nothing. . . .

After Bamaca's death, the pattern of deception and nondisclosure allegedly continued. . . . Based on these factual allegations, Harbury pleaded [a variety of claims against the defendants in both their official and individual capacities, seeking injunctive relief and damages.] . . . Only Harbury's *Bivens* claims are directly at issue in this appeal. These claims rest on three alleged constitutional violations: (1) by contributing to Bamaca's torture, CIA defendants violated his Fifth Amendment substantive due process rights; (2) by participating in and concealing information about Bamaca's torture and murder, all defendants violated Harbury's constitutional right to familial association; and (3) by concealing information and misleading her about her husband's fate, NSC and State Department defendants violated her right of access to courts.

The district court dismissed Harbury's *Bivens* claims, finding with respect to each not only that she failed to allege a deprivation of an actual constitutional right, but also that even if she had, defendants were entitled to qualified immunity because the scope of the alleged right was not clearly established. . . .

. . . [W]e must address the validity of Harbury's constitutional allegations before reaching the question of qualified immunity. It is to that task that we now turn.

FIFTH AMENDMENT

Government conduct that "shocks the conscience" violates the Fifth Amendment guarantee against deprivation of "life, liberty, or property, without due process of law." *See* Rochin v. California, 342 U.S. 165, 172-73 (1952). No one doubts that under Supreme Court precedent, interrogation by torture like that alleged by Harbury shocks the conscience. The difficult question, and the one presented by this case, is whether the Fifth Amendment prohibits torture of non-resident foreign nationals living abroad. Before reaching that question, however, we must consider Harbury's claim that because many of the CIA, NSC, and State Department officials who she says conspired to torture her husband did so within the United States, this case does not require extraterritorial application of the Fifth Amendment....

Harbury fails to notice the relevance of United States v. Verdugo-Urquidez, 494 U.S. 259 (1990) [*infra* p. 643]... where the Supreme Court held that a warrantless search and seizure of an alien's property in Mexico did not violate the Fourth Amendment. The search was conceived, planned, and ordered in the United States, carried out in part by agents of the United States Drug Enforcement Agency, and conducted for the express purpose of obtaining evidence for use in a United States trial. Still, the Court treated the alleged violation as having "occurred solely in Mexico." In reaching this conclusion, the Court never mentioned that the search was both planned and ordered from within the United States. Instead, it focused on the location of the primary constitutionally significant conduct at issue: the search and seizure itself.

We think *Verdugo-Urquidez* controls this case.... We thus turn to Harbury's primary claim — that Bamaca was entitled to Fifth Amendment protection even though the torture occurred in Guatemala.

Acknowledging that aliens are entitled to fewer constitutional protections than citizens, *see* Mathews v. Diaz, 426 U.S. 67, 77-79 (1976), and that constitutional protections (even for citizens) diminish outside the U.S., Harbury argues that the Constitution's most fundamental protections, like the Fifth Amendment prohibition of torture, apply even to foreign nationals located abroad....

Although [various] cases demonstrate that aliens abroad may be entitled to certain constitutional protections against mistreatment by the U.S. Government, we do not agree that they establish that Bamaca's torture ran afoul of the Fifth Amendment. To begin with, in adjudicating the application of constitutional rights to aliens, the Supreme Court has looked — among other factors — to whether the aliens have "come within the territory of the United States and developed substantial connections with this country." *See Verdugo-Urquidez*, 494 U.S. at 271....

...Though that case involved extraterritorial application of the Fourth Amendment, the Court also dealt with the extraterritorial application of the Fifth:

> Indeed, we have rejected the claim that aliens are entitled to Fifth Amendment rights outside the sovereign territory of the United States. In Johnson v. Eisentrager... the Court held that enemy aliens arrested in China and imprisoned in Germany after World War II could not obtain writs of habeas corpus in our federal courts on the ground that their convictions for war crimes had violated the Fifth Amendment.... The *Eisentrager* opinion acknowledged that in some cases constitutional provisions extend beyond the citizenry; "the alien... has been accorded a generous and ascending scale of rights as he increases his identity with our society." But our rejection of the extraterritorial application of the Fifth Amendment was emphatic:
>
>> "Such extraterritorial application of organic law would have been so significant an innovation in the practice of governments that, if intended or apprehended, it could scarcely have failed to excite contemporary comment. Not one word can be cited. No decision of this Court supports such a view.... None of the learned commentators on our Constitution has even hinted at it. The practice of every modern government is opposed to it."

B. Private Assets

Id. at 269 (quoting Johnson v. Eisentrager, 339 U.S. 763, 770 (1950)). To be sure, as Harbury points out, this language is dict[um]. But it is firm and considered dict[um] that binds this court.... For these reasons, we agree with the district court that Harbury failed to allege a valid claim for deprivation of her husband's Fifth Amendment due process rights....

NOTES AND QUESTIONS

1. *The Holding and Its Reversal.* In contrast to its Fifth Amendment ruling, the Court of Appeals agreed with Harbury that NSC and State Department defendants had, by giving her "false and deceptive information related to her husband and otherwise concealing whether he was alive, ... deprived Plaintiff of her right... to adequate, effective, and meaningful access to the courts." 233 F.3d at 609. The court also found that, by affirmatively misleading Harbury, the defendants enjoyed no qualified immunity from suit. *Id.* at 611.

The Supreme Court granted review and unanimously reversed. Christopher v. Harbury, 536 U.S. 403 (2002). In finding that Harbury's complaint did not state a constitutional denial-of-access claim upon which relief could be granted, the Court declared that an access claim is merely ancillary to an underlying claim, without which a plaintiff cannot have suffered injury by being shut out of court. Thus, the underlying claim must be described in the complaint, and the complaint must identify a remedy that could be awarded and that would not be available in some future lawsuit. In this case, because the acts alleged by Harbury "raise concerns for the separation of powers in trenching on matters committed to other branches," the Court said, it was all the more important for the district court to know whether the denial-of-access allegations stated a claim. The best she could offer, accepted by the Court of Appeals as sufficient, was that she would have brought an action for intentional infliction of emotional distress, and that a lawsuit seeking injunctive relief for that wrong might have saved Bamaca's life. The Supreme Court found Harbury's claim inadequate:

> [E]ven on the assumption that Harbury could surmount all difficulties raised by treating the underlying claim as one for intentional infliction of emotional distress, she could not satisfy the requirement that a backward-looking denial-of-access claim provide a remedy that could not be obtained on an existing claim.

536 U.S. at 420-421.

2. *Surviving Claims?* Harbury's counts naming CIA defendants, including the Guatemalan "asset" who allegedly tortured and killed Bamaca, were among the tort claims that survived the original motion to dismiss in the district court. According to the Supreme Court, Harbury could still seek damages and injunctive relief for emotional distress, although she could not obtain an order that might have saved Bamaca. Her access claim did not support such an order, and it could not compensate her for the loss claimed due to her inability to bring the tort action earlier. What is the likely outcome of the remaining tort claims? What obstacles are most likely to stand in Harbury's way?

3. *Necessary Cover-ups?* The government alleged that cover-ups of the type alleged by Harbury are sometimes "necessary in order to protect the national security or to maintain secrecy of classified intelligence sources or methods." Appellees' Petition for Reh'g at 2, *quoted in* Harbury v. Deutch, 244 F.3d at 957. What do you think of this argument? On what authority would such a cover-up be permitted?

4. *Elements of an Earlier Claim?* Can you outline the elements of a lawsuit for injunctive relief on behalf of Harbury that could have saved Bamaca's life if it had been filed earlier, based on truthful responses to Harbury's inquiries? How would the government likely have responded to such a lawsuit?

5. *The Bill of Rights Abroad.* The extraterritorial application of Bill of Rights protections in national security cases is considered *infra* p. 640.

6. *Claims Involving Torture.* One of Harbury's claims was that the individual defendants violated international law against torture. As the court noted in dicta in Committee of United States Citizens Living in Nicaragua v. Reagan, 859 F.2d 929, 941 (D.C. Cir. 1988), *supra* p. 176, fundamental human rights law rising to the level of *jus cogens* prohibits torture. What should Harbury have argued to avoid dismissal of this claim for failure to state a claim? *See* Filartiga v. Pena-Irala, 630 F.2d 876 (2d Cir. 1980). What argument, if any, could she have made from Executive Order No. 12,333, *supra* p. 397? *See also infra* pp. 616-617.

7. *Extraordinary Rendition.* Since the September 11, 2001, terrorist attacks, U.S. military operations in Afghanistan and elsewhere against the Taliban and al Qaeda have been supported by intelligence operatives, who have detained and interrogated captives in pursuit of intelligence. It has been alleged that the CIA has also engaged in the practice of "extraordinary rendition," in which the Agency has rendered some captives to third nations, whose intelligence services interrogate the detainees unburdened by the constraints of U.S. laws. What legal issues are presented by this form of intelligence outsourcing? The practice of extraordinary rendition is analyzed *infra* pp. 804-816.

8. *Follow-on Investigations of CIA Activities in Guatemala.* In 1995 President Clinton directed the Intelligence Oversight Board (IOB) to review allegations regarding the disappearance of Bamaca, the death of U.S. citizen Michael DeVine, and related matters bearing on the torture, disappearance, or death of U.S. citizens in Guatemala since 1984. The IOB *Report on the Guatemala Review,* June 28, 1996, *available at* http://www.ciponline.org/iob.htm, found that intelligence officials in Guatemala had laudable goals and that "achieving them and maintaining influence in Guatemala required that the CIA deal with some unsavory groups and individuals. The human rights records of the Guatemala security services were widely known to be reprehensible." *Id.* at 4. The IOB found two areas where the CIA's "performance was unacceptable.... [U]ntil late 1994, insufficient attention was given to allegations of serious human rights abuse made against several station assets or liason contacts. Second, the CIA failed to provide enough information on this subject to policy-makers and the Congress to permit proper policy and Congressional

B. Private Assets

oversight." *Id.* What legal reforms might make these mistakes less likely to occur in the future?

9. *New Guidelines and their Rescission.* In response to headlines generated by accusations that the CIA conspired with Guatemalan military officers in the Bamaca torture and murder and in other atrocities in Guatemala, the CIA issued guidelines in June 1995 to make case officers more selective in their recruiting. Apparently the guidelines required case officers to obtain a waiver from CIA headquarters before employing any asset whose background includes assassinations, torture, or other serious criminal activities.

The June 2000 report of the National Commission on Terrorism, *Countering the Changing Threat of International Terrorism,* available at http://www.fas.org/irp/threat/commission.html, maintained that the guidelines "have deterred and delayed vigorous efforts to recruit potentially useful informants. The CIA has created a climate that is overly risk averse." *Id.* at 10. The Commission recommended that the DCI "issue a directive that the 1995 guidelines will no longer apply to recruiting terrorist informants." *Id.* On June 4, 2000, however, a CIA spokesperson defended the guidelines and said that they had not impeded investigations of potential terrorism:

> No one knows better than we do that when combating terrorism it is often necessary to deal with unsavory individuals. But we do so with eyes wide open and with appropriate notification to senior officials.... [The CIA] has never... turned down a request to use someone, even someone with a record of human rights abuses, if we thought that person could be valuable in our overall counterterrorism program. [*Quoted in* Secrecy News, Sept. 14, 2001, *at* http://www.fas.org/sgp/news/secrecy/2001/09/091401.html.]

In the wake of the September 11, 2001, terrorist attacks on the World Trade Center and the Pentagon, Congress enacted legislation directing the DCI to rescind the portions of the 1995 guidelines pertaining to recruitment of counterterrorism assets. Intelligence Authorization Act for Fiscal Year 2002, Pub. L. No. 107-108, §403, 115 Stat. 1394, 1402 (2001). Would you have advised Congress to pass the rescission instruction? Former CIA Inspector General Frederick Hitz wrote that new guidelines issued since the legislation have "retained the requirement of an audit trail in . . . recognition of a need for some explanation to headquarters why a dirty asset ought to be on the payroll." Frederick P. Hitz, *Unleashing the Rogue Elephant: September 11 and Letting the CIA Be the CIA*, 25 Harv. J.L. & Pub. Poly. 765, 769 (2002). Does this assurance compensate for whatever was lost in the rescission?

10. *To Regulate or Not to Regulate?* In the early 1970s, the CIA managed to penetrate what was then the most feared terrorist organization that had targeted the United States and U.S. citizens in the Middle East — the Palestine Liberation Organization (PLO). Through a secret arrangement with Ali Hassan Salameh, the PLO's chief of intelligence, the CIA obtained extensive information about terrorist activities and groups, and Salameh himself intervened to stop planned attacks. Part of Salameh's motivation was his belief that working for the CIA could help the PLO achieve its political goals in the Middle East. Salameh was a

terrorist, a member of Yasir Arafat's "Black September" organization, and he may have helped plan the slaughter of Israeli athletes at the Munich Olympics in 1972. Although the CIA targeted Salameh for assassination, agents continued to work with him until the Israelis killed him in 1979. *See* David Ignatius, *Penetrating Terrorist Networks*, Wash. Post, Sept. 16, 2001, at B7. What lesson should we take from the Salameh experience? Does law have any role to play in deciding what to do with dirty assets in counterterrorism? Do you think the answer to this question has changed in the wake of the 9/11 terrorist attacks?

Would any guidelines for intelligence assets like Salameh be constrained by the provisions of Executive Order No. 12,333, *supra* p. 397? If so, which provisions?

11. *The Value of Vetting.* After U.S. and coalition forces failed to find the weapons of mass destruction (WMD) that were part of the justification for the invasion of Iraq in 2003, see *supra* p. 313, President Bush appointed a commission to investigate the failure. Silberman/Robb Commission, *supra* p. 314. The commission reported in 2005 that "the Intelligence Community was dead wrong in almost all of its pre-war judgments about Iraq's weapons of mass destruction. This was a major intelligence failure. Its principal causes [included] the Intelligence Community's inability to collect good information about Iraq's WMD programs...." *Id.* at 2.

The commission found that the story of a "pivotal source" code-named "Curveball," who lied to intelligence officials about Iraq's biological weapons program, was "an all-too-familiar one." *Id.* at 27, 367. The commission recommended that the CIA "take the lead in systematizing and standardizing the Intelligence Community's asset validation procedures... ways in which intelligence collectors ensure that the information provided to them is truthful and accurate." *Id.* at 372. Should lawyers play any role in such a system for vetting? Would dirty assets plausibly survive the vetting?

3. Nonofficial Cover

Intelligence collection abroad through human intelligence (HUMINT) depends on case officers operating in two ways to maintain their "covers" and thus hide their intelligence-gathering roles. Some have official covers — they have real jobs in the government, typically in U.S. embassies abroad. Although these posts facilitate the case officers' communications with higher-ups in intelligence, their credibility is compromised due to the widespread suspicion that the embassy staffs are intelligence operatives. A nonofficial cover (NOC) avoids the taint of embassy or other U.S. government employment. Instead, the NOC, sometimes referred to as an "angel asset," has another job overseas that explains her presence. One of the most common and plausible jobs for an NOC is journalist, because a journalist can explain her presence and be expected to ask a lot of questions. Other NOCs pretend to work for businesses or for nongovernmental organizations (NGOs).

> According to former DCI Robert Gates, after the end of the Cold War the biggest challenge [is]... how to move the clandestine service away from the embassy to a

more independent status, without the protection of diplomatic cover or a diplomatic passport.... The risks are different and much higher. You no longer want people who can do tea and cookies in the afternoon. You have to look for a new kind of personality... you need a guy walking into Tripoli or Pyongyang who doesn't look like he just left Iowa. [Tim Weiner, *The CIA's Most Important Mission: Itself*, N.Y. Times, Dec. 10, 1995, §6 (Magazine), at 67.]

Following the Church and Pike Committees' investigations, then-DCI George H.W. Bush issued regulations in 1976 limiting the CIA employment but not the "voluntary" use of clergy and journalists for intelligence gathering. When DCI John Deutch revealed in 1996 that the CIA had skirted the Bush regulations on some occasions by using "voluntary" journalists as assets and by taking advantage of an "emergency conditions" loophole in the regulations, Congress prohibited such use absent a waiver by the DCI or President finding that such use is in the "overriding national security interest of the United States." Intelligence Authorization Act for Fiscal Year 1997, §309, Pub. L. No. 104-293, 110 Stat. 3461, 3467 (codified at 50 U.S.C. §403-7 (2000)). The prohibition does not apply to CIA operatives posing as journalists. Hitz, *supra*, 25 Harv. J.L. & Pub. Poly. at 778-779.

Review the relevant sections of the National Security Act, *supra* p. 355, and Executive Order No. 12,333, *supra* p. 444. To what extent do these laws set limits on the use of NOCs for intelligence collection? What practical and legal problems do you see with the use of NOCs for this purpose? Are the problems outweighed by the potential advantages?

C. MILITARY SPECIAL OPERATIONS AS INTELLIGENCE OPERATIONS

As we saw in our survey of intelligence activities and responsibilities in Chapter 14, the Department of Defense exercises effective control over much of the intelligence that is collected, analyzed, and distributed throughout the government. Under Executive Order No. 12,333, *supra* p. 444, the Defense Department is given responsibility for signals intelligence (SIGINT) and communications security activities (COMINT), "except as otherwise directed by the NSC." §1.11(e). The Secretary of Defense must also "[d]irect, operate, control, and provide fiscal management for the National Security Agency and for defense and military intelligence and national reconnaissance entities." §1.11(j). DOD's Defense Intelligence Agency (DIA) collects and provides military and military-related intelligence for the Secretary and for other agencies, §1.12(a), while the NSA is given exclusive authority to engage in SIGINT activities, subject to express exceptions granted by the Secretary. §1.12(b)(1). The Secretary is also given responsibility for "Offices for the collection of specialized intelligence through reconnaissance programs," §1.12(c), more recently identified publicly as the National Reconnaissance Office (NRO).

Finally, the Secretary oversees collection and dissemination of military and military-related foreign intelligence and counterintelligence by the intelligence elements of the U.S. Army, Navy, Air Force, and Marine Corps. §1.12(d).

In recent years, intelligence support for special military operations, or SMO, has generated continuing controversy and ongoing legal problems. After the 1979 revolution in Iran and the seizure of American hostages in Tehran, military planners for an eventual hostage rescue operation needed human intelligence on the ground — to learn about the embassy compound where the hostages were held and to provide assistance before and during a rescue operation. The CIA had no agents who could provide the necessary intelligence. The Department of Defense responded by creating an Intelligence Support Activity (ISA) to collect intelligence and conduct covert military operations. The ISA consisted of Army Special Forces personnel and intelligence case officers. Although the hostage rescue operation ended in failure, *supra* p. 266, the Army decided to retain ISA. *See* Odom, *supra* p. 443, at 145.

During the 1980s, cooperation between the Army and the CIA increased, and the ISA became a permanent entity within DOD. After September 11, the ISA, code-named Gray Fox, invigorated by Defense Secretary Donald Rumsfeld to participate in the war on terrorism, began reporting to a new Under Secretary of Defense for Intelligence. But Gray Fox operated independently of the rest of the intelligence community. *See* William M. Arkin, *The Secret War: Frustrated by Intelligence Failures, the Defense Department Is Dramatically Expanding Its "Black World" of Covert Operations*, L.A. Times, Oct. 27, 2002, at M1.

DOD reportedly has expanded the ISA role in the war on terrorism to include "special access programs" (SAPs), defined by an Army regulation as "a security program...approved by the Deputy Secretary of Defense to apply extraordinary security measures to protect extremely sensitive information." Army Regulation 380-381, *Special Access Programs (SAPs) and Sensitive Activities*, Apr. 21, 2004, at 11, *available at* http://www.fas.org/irp/doddir/army/ar380-381.pdf. In addition, a Strategic Support Branch was reportedly created by Defense Secretary Rumsfeld in 2003 as part of the Defense Intelligence Agency (DIA) Human Intelligence Service, designed to provide human intelligence for military operations, ending what he called his "near total dependence on CIA" for HUMINT. Barton Gellman, *Secret Unit Expands Rumsfeld's Domain*, Wash. Post, Jan. 23, 2005, at A1. The Strategic Support Branch apparently includes the unit formerly known as Gray Fox, as well as other Army, Air Force, and Navy units. These units provide the Defense Department with a clandestine service capable of conducting covert operations in "friendly or unfriendly states, when conventional war is a distant or unlikely prospect." *Id.*

Although the Strategic Support Branch was established with funds reprogrammed from other Pentagon accounts, the 2005 Defense Appropriations Act authorized the Secretary to spend up to $25 million during a fiscal year "to provide support to foreign forces, irregular forces, groups, or individuals engaged in supporting or facilitating ongoing military operations by United States special operations forces to combat terrorism." Department of Defense Appropriations Act, Fiscal Year 2005, Pub. L. No. 108-375, §1208(a), 118 Stat. 1811, 2086 (2004).

C. Military Special Operations as Intelligence Operations

NOTES AND QUESTIONS

1. *Legal Wiggle Room?* The fiscal 2005 Defense Appropriations Act provision requires that the Secretary "notify the congressional defense committees expeditiously, and in any event in not less than 48 hours" when funds are spent for the approved purposes. *Id.* §1208(c), 118 Stat. 2086. The notice must be in writing and need be given only once for each operation. *Id.* What is the purpose of such a notification procedure?

   The Act also states that the authority granted "does not constitute authority to conduct a covert action" as that term is defined in the National Security Act, *supra* p. 355. Do you understand the meaning of this apparent restriction? Is it a restriction? What is the implication of not labeling a secret military operation a "covert action"? When is a clandestine operation not a covert action? *See* Chapter 15.

2. *Paramilitary or Military?* If Army Special Forces participate in covert actions under the direction of the CIA, are its personnel bound by Army regulations? Is a Special Forces covert operation an intelligence activity or a military operation? Does the distinction matter?

3. *An Iraq SAP.* One SAP reportedly was diverted from its original purpose of interrogating Taliban and al Qaeda detainees in the war on terrorism to staffing detention and interrogation operations at the Abu Ghraib prison in Iraq. Seymour Hersh, *The Gray Zone: How a Secret Pentagon Program Came to Abu Ghraib*, New Yorker, May 24, 2004, at 38. When the prisoner abuse scandal broke in the spring of 2004, the commander of the 800th Military Police Brigade, the unit ostensibly in charge of the Abu Ghraib facility, stated that she could not always be sure who was who among the persons in civilian clothes managing interrogations. *Id.* The interrogation and treatment of detainees for investigative purposes is considered further *infra* pp. 759-804. Do you think it matters whether those in charge of investigative interrogations are from the DOD, rather than the CIA?

4. *Two Paramilitary Organizations or One?* Are there good reasons for the United States to have two paramilitary organizations — one managed by the CIA and one run by DOD? Is there a legal problem with this redundancy? Consider this view:

   > The military's strength is in military skills and operations. These are not the strength of the [CIA] DO [Directorate of Operations]. Not surprisingly, DO paramilitary operations have generally been looked on by army officers as amateurish at best, usually designed to fail. A close comparative look at the record of army and...DO paramilitary operations would, in all likelihood, show that the [DOD] has more justification for disdaining DO paramilitary capabilities than the DO has.... This raises the question of whether or not the DO should drop its paramilitary capabilities and depend largely on those of the Department of Defense.... [T]he experience with Special Forces teams in Afghanistan seems to have convinced the secretary of defense that such a change is now desirable. [Odom, *supra* p. 443, at 148-149.]

Is this proposal workable? Lawful? Would the legal basis change between peacetime and wartime operations? In the war in Afghanistan after September 11, Special Forces teams were able to cooperate with anti-Taliban Afghan groups, but not through the efforts of the CIA, because initially the CIA had no contacts there. Instead, Russian intelligence services provided the sources that put the U.S. military in contact with the Afghans. In many cases, the Special Forces teams struck out on their own and formed alliances with Afghan groups without intelligence support. *Id.* at 25-26. Are there legal problems with Special Forces conducting such covert operations? In coordinating operations with Russian intelligence personnel?

IV
Fighting Terrorism

Defining Terrorism ─────17

Long before September 11, 2001, the growing threat of terrorism was a serious concern in the United States. Fifteen years earlier, a government task force characterized the threat this way:

> Terrorism is a phenomenon that is easier to describe than to define. It is the unlawful use or threat of violence against persons or property to further political or social objectives. It is generally intended to intimidate or coerce a government, individuals, or groups to modify their behavior or policies.
>
> Some experts see terrorism as the lower end of the warfare spectrum, a form of low-intensity, unconventional aggression....
>
> ...Americans...realize that terrorism needs an audience; that it is propaganda designed to shock and stun them; that it is behavior that is uncivilized and lacks respect for human life. They also believe that terrorism constitutes a growing danger to our system, beliefs, and policies worldwide. [*Public Report of the Vice President's Task Force on Combating Terrorism* 1, 21 (1986).]

Unlike war, terrorism often deliberately targets noncombatants. Unlike the ordinary murderer or mugger, who directs his violence against the victim alone without wanting to alert others, a terrorist uses violence "to instill fear in the targeted population...[in a] deliberate evocation of dread." Jessica Stern, *The Ultimate Terrorists* 11 (1999).

Terrorism has ancient roots. At least since the first century, terrorists have wrought destruction in furtherance of religious or secular ends. Sometimes by assassinating individual targets, at other times by fomenting mass uprisings or forming into marauding bands of roving thugs, early terrorists probably inflicted more harm than any modern equivalent group. *See* Stern, *supra,* at 15. In the United States, where terrorism is generally considered a modern phenomenon, terrorist acts have in fact occurred throughout our history. From presidential and other political assassinations, to Civil War-related terrorist violence, to anarchist and other radical group actions, our nation has experienced its share of lethal and usually politically motivated terrorism. *Id.* at 17.

Still, terrorism has emerged as a central national security concern in the United States only since the end of the Cold War. At first, the vulnerability of U.S. interests abroad dominated the policy agenda. Not long after terrorist Abu

Nidal killed 19 tourists at airports in Rome and Vienna in December 1985, President Reagan issued NSDD-207, establishing a comprehensive counterterrorism policy for the United States and noting that terrorists use or threaten violence against innocents "to achieve a political objective through coercion or intimidation of an audience beyond the immediate victims." NSDD-207 (Jan. 20, 1986) (partly classified), *reprinted in* Christopher Simpson, *National Security Directives of the Reagan & Bush Administrations* 656 (1995).

The bombings of the World Trade Center in 1993 and the Oklahoma City federal building in 1995, along with the 1995 Aum Shinrikyo nerve gas attack in Tokyo, shifted attention toward homeland security and domestic terrorist threats. In 1994, President Clinton found "that the proliferation of nuclear, biological, and chemical weapons ('weapons of mass destruction'), and of the means for delivering such weapons, constitutes an unusual and extraordinary threat to the national security," and he declared "a national emergency to deal with that threat." Exec. Order No. 12,938, 59 Fed. Reg. 58,099 (Nov. 14, 1994). After the September 11, 2001, attacks on the World Trade Center and the Pentagon, President George W. Bush also declared a national emergency, citing "the continuing and immediate threat of further attacks on the United States." Proclamation No. 7463, 66 Fed. Reg. 48,199 (Sept. 14, 2001).

Beginning in the 1990s, terrorism changed in important ways:

> As the 1990s began, the conventional wisdom that terrorists employed violence in discriminate and proportionate ways was called into question. A new, more ruthless breed of terrorists began to leave its mark on the world. The first sharp departure from their predecessors was that many terrorists who became active in this time period did not necessarily espouse political causes or aim to take power. The second distinguishing feature was that a fair share of 1990s terrorists were intent on harming a maximum number of people. Instead of kidnapping an ambassador, the 1990s-vintage terrorists took a whole embassy hostage. Rather than hijack an aircraft, terrorists plotted to blow planes out of the sky. Terrorists upped the ante from pipe bombs to truck bombs capable of blowing up entire buildings, peppering the decade with headlines about the World Trade Center in 1993, the Murrah Federal Building in Oklahoma City in 1995, the Khobar Towers barracks in Saudi Arabia in 1997, and U.S. embassies in Kenya and Tanzania in 1998. [Amy E. Smithson, *Grounding the Threat in Reality*, in *Ataxia: The Chemical and Biological Terrorism Threat and the U.S. Response* 15 (Amy E. Smithson & Leslie-Anne Levy eds., Henry L. Stimson Center 2000).]

The September 11 attacks vividly displayed these terrorism trends and catapulted the United States into what the Bush administration has called a "global war on terror." Five years' sustained efforts to combat Al Qaeda "have degraded the ability of the core [Al Qaeda] leadership group... to mount global acts of terrorism.... [However,] terrorists continue[] to attempt to adapt to improved countermeasures and evolve new approaches in response to a less permissive operating environment." U.S. Dept. of State, Office of the Coordinator for Counterterrorism, *Country Reports on Terrorism 2005*, at 11-12 (2006). Although Al Qaeda and its affiliates remain the most prominent terrorist threat, the general trends in terrorism show that micro-actors — small autonomous cells and individuals enabled by technologies and international commerce — are increasingly worrisome and difficult to counter. *Id.* at 11. Some of these small groups are ethnically defined, others are mixed, and some meet and organize virtually, using the Internet for training and communications. *Id.* at 13. Trends also point toward ever-greater sophistication by terrorists in using global mechanisms to share "information, finance, and ideas [and] improved... technological sophistication across many areas of operational planning, communications, targeting, and propaganda," *id.*, while the same groups may overlap in their planning and operations with transnational crime. *Id.* The Department of State concluded in 2006 that Al Qaeda, although weakened, is "adaptive and resilient," and that "we are still in the first phase of a potentially long war." *Id.* at 14-15.

Although "terrorism" is universally a pejorative term today, the inevitable politicization of terrorism renders any search for a consensus definition futile. Some view terrorism as violence or the threat of violence against noncombatants intended to exact revenge, intimidate, and cause fear, in pursuit of political, religious, or economic objectives. *See* Bruce Hoffman, *Inside Terrorism* 43 (1998); Stern, *supra*, at 11. The State Department defines terrorism as "premeditated, politically motivated violence perpetrated against noncombatant targets by subnational groups or clandestine agents." *Country Reports on Terrorism, supra*, at 9. *See also* 22 U.S.C.A. §2656f(d)(2) (West 2004). However, the State Department definition is only one of nearly 150 definitions of the term "terrorism" in U.S. federal law. *See* Nicholas J. Perry, *The Numerous Federal Legal Definitions of Terrorism: The Problem of Too Many Grails*, 30 J. Legis. 249 (2004).

In the summer of 2005, after ten years of negotiations, it appeared that the United Nations might reach agreement on key principles, including a definition of "terrorism," that would lead to adoption of a Comprehensive Convention on International Terrorism. A draft version of the Convention contained this statement: "The targeting and deliberate killing of civilians and non-combatants cannot be justified or legitimized by any cause or grievance." *See Advanced Unedited Version*, Aug. 5, 2005, *at* http://www.un.org/ga/59/hlpm_rev.2.pdf. The U.S. Ambassador urged that the words "by terrorists" be inserted between "killing" and "of." *See* Letter from John R. Bolton (n.d.), *at* http://www.un.int/usa/reform-un-jrb-ltr-terror-8-05.pdf. Some governments sought to exclude from the definition of "terrorism" actions that are taken in "resistance to occupation," and to add language that would reach collateral damage caused by military action. When government leaders gathered in September, they approved an agenda-setting document in anticipation of the 60th session of the General Assembly that avoided these controversies by simply deleting all of the definitional language. *See Draft Outcome Document*, Sept. 13, 2005, *at* http://www.un.org/summit2005/Draft_Outcome130905.pdf.

If the definition of "terrorism" is difficult, it is also legally important. As one federal appeals court has explained:

> Under the Anti-Terrorism and Effective Death Penalty Act of 1996, 8 U.S.C. §1189, the Secretary of State is empowered to designate an entity as a "foreign terrorist organization." The consequences of designation are dire. The designation by the Secretary results in blocking any funds which the organization has on deposit with any financial institution in the United States. 18 U.S.C. §2339B(a)(2). Representatives and certain members of the organization are barred from entry into the United States. 8 U.S.C. §1182(a)(3)(B)(i)(IV & V). Perhaps most importantly, all persons within or subject to jurisdiction of the United States are forbidden from "knowingly providing material support or resources" to the organization.

18 U.S.C. §2339B(a)(1). [National Council of Resistance of Iran v. Department of State, 251 F.3d 192, 196 (D.C. Cir. 2001).]

Such knowing provision of material support or resources is a crime punishable by up to 15 years' imprisonment, or life if the death of any persons results. See *infra* p. 825.

Under the 1996 statute, the Secretary of State may designate an organization as a terrorist organization if it engages in "terrorist activity" that threatens "the security of United States nationals or the national security of the United States." 8 U.S.C. §1189(a)(1) (2000). Under a different part of the statute, an alien is deemed inadmissible to the United States if he engages in "terrorist activity," defined as activity that is

unlawful...where it is committed...and which involves any of the following:
(I) The hijacking or sabotage of any conveyance....
(II) The seizing or detaining, and threatening to kill, injure, or continue to detain, another individual in order to compel a third person (including a governmental organization) to do or abstain from doing any act as an explicit or implicit condition for the release of the individual seized or detained.
(III) A violent attack upon an internationally protected person... or upon the liberty of such a person.
(IV) An assassination.
(V) The use of any—
  (a) biological agent, chemical agent, or nuclear weapon or device, or
  (b) explosive, firearm, or other weapons or dangerous device (other than for mere personal monetary gain),
with intent to endanger, directly or indirectly, the safety of one or more individuals or to cause substantial damage to property.
(VI) A threat, attempt, or conspiracy to do any of the foregoing. [8 U.S.C. §1182(a)(3)(B)(iii) (2000 & Supp. III 2003).]

A different federal statute provides criminal sanctions for "international terrorism," defined as activities that—

(A) involve violent acts or acts dangerous to human life that are a violation of the criminal laws of the United States or of any State, or that would be a criminal violation if committed within the jurisdiction of the United States or of any State;
(B) appear to be intended—
  (i) to intimidate or coerce a civilian population;
  (ii) to influence the policy of a government by intimidation or coercion; or
  (iii) to affect the conduct of a government by mass destruction, assassination or kidnaping; and
(C) occur primarily outside the territorial jurisdiction of the United States, or transcend national boundaries in terms of the means by which they are accomplished, the persons they appear intended to intimidate or coerce, or the locale in which their perpetrators operate or seek asylum. [18 U.S.C. §2331(1) (2000 & Supp. III 2003).]

See also 18 U.S.C.A. §2332b(g)(5) (West 2000 & Supp. 2006), as amended by Pub. L. No. 109-177, §§110(b)(3)(A), 112(a) and (b), 120 Stat. 192, 208, 209 (2006) (defining "Federal crime of terrorism"). In addition, if the Secretary of State finds that a country has "repeatedly provided support for acts of international terrorism," she is required to cut off U.S. foreign aid to the offending country. 22 U.S.C. §2371(a) (2000). Criminal sanctions are addressed in greater detail in Chapter 28.

The USA PATRIOT Act (Providing Appropriate Tools Required to Intercept and Obstruct Terrorism Act), passed in response to the September 11 attacks, borrows from the foregoing definition of "international terrorism" to define as "domestic terrorism" such acts that occur primarily *within* the jurisdiction of the United States. Pub. L. No. 107-56, §802(5), 115 Stat. 560 (2001) (codified at 18 U.S.C. 2331(5) (Supp. III 2003)). The same definition is used (with one change) to identify permissible targets of electronic surveillance or surreptitious physical searches under the Foreign Intelligence Surveillance Act (FISA). 50 U.S.C. §1801(c) (2000). See Chapter 19.

United States v. Yousef
United States Court of Appeals, Second Circuit, 2003
327 F.3d 56

JOHN M. WALKER, JR., Chief Judge, RALPH K. WINTER and JOSÉ A. CABRANES, Circuit Judges....

[Ramzi Yousef and others were convicted of conspiracy to bomb United States commercial airliners in Southeast Asia and of involvement in the 1993 bombing of the World Trade Center. They appealed on the ground that the courts lacked extraterritorial jurisdiction over the charged offenses. The District Court had rested jurisdiction in part on the concept of "universal jurisdiction," which "permits a State to prosecute an offender of any nationality for an offense committed outside of that State and without contacts to that State, but only for a few, near-unique offenses uniformly recognized by the 'civilized nations' as an offense against the 'Law of Nations.'" 327 F.3d at 103. This case presents the question whether "terrorism" is such an offense.]

Unlike those offenses supporting universal jurisdiction under customary international law—that is, piracy, war crimes, and crimes against humanity—that now have fairly precise definitions and that have achieved universal condemnation, "terrorism" is a term as loosely deployed as it is powerfully charged. Judge Harry T. Edwards of the District of Columbia Circuit stated eighteen years ago in *Tel-Oren v. Libyan Arab Republic*, 726 F.2d 774 (D.C. Cir. 1984), that "[w]hile this nation unequivocally condemns all terrorist acts, that sentiment is not universal. Indeed, the nations of the world are so divisively split on the legitimacy of such aggression as to make it impossible to pinpoint an area of harmony or consensus." *Id.* at 795 (Edwards, J., concurring). Similarly, Judge Robert H. Bork stated in his opinion in *Tel-Oren* that the claim that a defendant "violated customary principles of international law against terrorism[ ] concerns an area of international law in which there is little or no consensus and in which the disagreements concern politically sensitive issues.... [N]o consensus has developed on how properly to define 'terrorism' generally." *Id.* at 806-07 (Bork, J., concurring).

Finally, in a third concurring opinion, Judge Roger Robb found the question of assigning culpability for terrorist acts to be "non-justiciable" and outside of the competency of the courts as inextricably linked with "political question[s]." *Id.* at 823 (Robb, J., concurring). Judge Robb stated that

> [I]nternational "law", or the absence thereof, renders even the search for the least common denominators of civilized conduct in this area [defining and punishing acts of terrorism] an impossible-to-accomplish judicial task. Courts ought not to engage in it when that search takes us towards a consideration of terrorism's place in the international order. Indeed, when such a review forces us to dignify by judicial notice the most outrageous of the diplomatic charades that attempt to dignify the violence of terrorist atrocities, we corrupt our own understanding of evil.

Id.

We regrettably are no closer now than eighteen years ago to an international consensus on the definition of terrorism or even its proscription;[41] the mere existence of the phrase "state-sponsored terrorism" proves the absence of agreement on basic terms among a large number of States that terrorism violates public international law. Moreover, there continues to be strenuous disagreement among States about what actions do or do not constitute terrorism, nor have we shaken ourselves free of the cliché that "one man's terrorist is another man's freedom fighter."[42] We thus conclude that the statements of Judges

---

41. For example, each side of the Israeli-Palestinian conflict charges the other with "terrorism," sentiments echoed by their allies. *See, e.g.,* Todd S. Purdum, *What Do You Mean, "Terrorist"?,* N.Y. Times, Apr. 7, 2002, Week in Review, at 1 ("If Israel sees its military campaign in the West Bank as a justifiable echo of Mr. Bush's assault on Al Qaeda, Palestinians claim affinity with the American colonists' revolt against an occupying power."). The Organization of the Islamic Conference met in Kuala Lumpur, Malaysia, in April 2002, to define terrorism; the host of the conference, Malaysian Prime Minister Mahathir Mohamad, proposed a definition of terrorism as "all attacks on civilians"; the conference's final declaration, however, stated that terrorism consists only of attacks on civilians perpetrated by non-Palestinians, stating that the Conference " 'rejects any attempt to link terrorism to the struggle of the Palestinian people in the exercise of their inalienable right to establish their independent state.' " *Id.* (quoting statements by Mohamad and contained in the conference's final declaration). Sentiments at the conference were far from uniform, however: The deputy foreign minister of Bosnia-Herzegovina stated that "if a person kills or harms a civilian . . . he is a terrorist" irrespective of the "race or religion" of the perpetrator and the victims. *Terrorism Issue Splits Muslim Conferees,* Chi. Trib., April 2, 2002, at 10 (quoting statements of Bosnian-Herzegovinian delegate to conference).

42. Confusion on the definition of "terrorism" abounds. *See, e.g.,* Craig S. Smith, *Debate Over Iraq Raises Fears of a Shrinking Role for NATO,* N.Y. Times, Jan. 26, 2003, at L26 (quoting Celeste A. Wallander, senior fellow at the Center for Strategic and International Studies, as stating that even among members of the North Atlantic Treaty Alliance ("NATO") there is no consensus "on how to define transnational terrorism"). Terrorism is defined variously by the perpetrators' motives, methods, targets, and victims. Motive-based definitions suffer from confusion because of the attempt to carve out an exception for assertedly legitimate armed struggle in pursuit of self-determination. For example, under one of the various United Nations resolutions addressing terrorism, armed and violent acts do not constitute "terrorism" if committed by peoples seeking self-determination in opposition to a violently enforced occupation. *See, e.g.,* Declaration on Principles of International Law Concerning Friendly Relations Among Co-operating States in Accordance with the Charter of the United Nations, Oct. 24, 1970, G.A. Res. 2625, 25 U.N. GAOR Supp. (No. 28) at 21, U.N. Doc. A/8028 (1971), *reprinted in* 9 I.L.M. 1292 (1970). This attempt to distinguish "terrorists" from "freedom fighters" potentially could legitimate as non-terrorist certain groups nearly universally recognized as terrorist, including the Irish Republican Army, Hezbollah, and Hamas. *See Boim v. Quranic Literacy Inst. & Holy Land Found. for Relief & Dev.,* 291 F.3d 1000, 1002 (7th Cir. 2002) (describing Hamas); *Stanford v. Kuwait Airways Corp.,* 89 F.3d 117, 120 (2d Cir. 1996) (describing Hezbollah); *Matter of Requested Extradition of Smyth,* 863 F. Supp. 1137, 1139-1140 (N.D. Cal. 1994) (describing the Irish Republican Army).

By contrast, the European Convention on the Suppression of Terrorism defines terrorism solely based on the methods of violence the perpetrator employs, and explicitly removes political

Edwards, Bork, and Robb remain true today, and that terrorism — unlike piracy, war crimes, and crimes against humanity — does not provide a basis for universal jurisdiction....

NOTES AND QUESTIONS

1. *Crime or War?* Is terrorism a crime, or is it better viewed as a species of armed conflict? What are the legal and practical implications of characterizing terrorism as one or the other? *See* Tyler Raimo, *Winning at the Expense of Law: The Ramifications of Expanding Counter-Terrorism Law Enforcement Jurisdiction Overseas,* 14 Am. U. Intl. L. Rev. 1473, 1481-1485 (1999).

In an October 31, 2003, speech, then-National Security Adviser Condoleezza Rice stated that "Iraq is the central front in the war on Terror." *Remarks by National Security Adviser Dr. Condoleezza Rice to the National Legal Center for the Public Interest, available at* http://www.whitehouse.gov/news/releases/2003/10/20031031-5.html. In the same week, former National Security Adviser Zbigniew Brzezinski argued that the "war on terrorism" is a misleading phrase, because its abstractness obscures the nature of the enemy: "[T]errorism is a technique for killing people. That doesn't tell us who the enemy is. It's as if we said that World War II was not against the Nazis but against the blitzkrieg." Zbigniew Brzezinski, *Remarks, New American Strategies for Security and Peace Conference,* Oct. 28, 2003, *available at* http://www.prospect.org/webfeatures/2003/10/brzezinski-z-10-31.html.

Why would the White House capitalize "Terror" in Dr. Rice's speech? What harm is there in fixing the "war" label to terrorism?

2. *Differences in Legal Definitions.* How do the statutory definitions of "terrorism" differ? Why do you think they are different?

---

judgment of the acts by defining most violent acts as "non-political" (regardless of the perpetrator's claimed motive). European Convention on the Suppression of Terrorism, Nov. 10, 1976, Europ. T.S. No. 90. Thus, in Article I, the Convention defines as terrorism any offenses, *inter alia,* "involving the use of a bomb, grenade, rocket, automatic firearm, or letter or parcel bomb if this use endangers persons," a definition that may fail to circumscribe the offense adequately. The Arab Convention on the Suppression of Terrorism (Cairo, Apr. 22, 1998), *reprinted in* International Instruments Related to the Prevention and Suppression of International Terrorism, 152-73 (United Nations 2001), while condemning terrorism, takes a uniquely restrictive approach to defining it, stating that offenses committed against the interests of Arab states are "terrorist offenses," while offenses committed elsewhere or against other peoples or interests are not. *Id.* at Art. I.3 (defining "terrorist offence" as any of several defined violent actions that occur "in any of the Contracting States, or against their nationals, property or interests"). The Convention further defines as legitimate (non-terrorist) "[a]ll cases of struggle by whatever means, including armed struggle," unless such struggles "prejudic[e] the territorial integrity of any Arab State." *Id.* at Art. II(a).

United States legislation has adopted several approaches to defining terrorism, demonstrating that, even within nations, no single definition of "terrorism" or "terrorist act" prevails. [The court surveyed several of these approaches, some of which are set out at pp. 468-469.]

Still other definitions of "terrorism" may focus on the victims of the attacks or the relationship between the perpetrators and the victims. *See, e.g.,* Alex P. Schmid & Albert J. Jongman, Political Terrorism 1-2 (1988) ("Terrorism is a method of combat in which...symbolic victims serve as an instrumental target of violence. These instrumental victims share group or class characteristics which form the basis for their selection for victimization. Through previous use of violence or the credible threat of violence other members of that group or class are put in a state of chronic fear (terror).").

3. *Domestic Terrorism.* Note that by adapting the definition of "international terrorism" to acts that occur primarily inside the United States, the USA PATRIOT Act defines as "domestic terrorism" some acts attributed to Operation Rescue (an anti-abortion group), the Environmental Liberation Front, Greenpeace, and PETA (People for the Ethical Treatment of Animals). Should members of these groups be defined as terrorists? What legal issues would arise if a member of one of those groups were charged with "domestic terrorism"?

4. *The Politics of Designation.* Do any of the definitions of "terrorism" set out above permit us to distinguish among the following: the attack on the World Trade Center on September 11, 2001; the attack on the Pentagon on the same day; the 1995 bombing of the federal building in Oklahoma City; acts of violence by Nelson Mandela and the ANC — carried out for the political purpose of fighting apartheid; the 1946 bombing of the King David Hotel, which housed civilian as well as military guests, for political purposes by Menachem Begin (later Prime Minster of Israel); and the 2001 Palestinian suicide bombing that killed more than a dozen Israeli teenagers at a discotheque to avenge Israeli attacks on other Palestinians who allegedly had participated in bombings?

Could you argue that some of these acts were not terrorism? Which ones, and why not? Note that our courts have sometimes refused to extradite members of the IRA who have killed British troops in Northern Ireland, on grounds that they were engaged in "political" acts.

Does it matter that Mandela and Begin succeeded in their political purposes, while the Palestinians have not? *See* Symposium, *Post-Cold War International Security Threats: Terrorism, Drugs, and Organized Crime,* 21 Mich. J. Intl. L. 527, 569 (2000) (so suggesting).

Is it legally significant for this purpose that we have a political relationship with South Africa and Israel that is different from the one we have with the Palestinian Authority? Does the electoral victory of Hamas in the January 2006 elections in the Palestinian Authority permit, or even require, the United States to designate the Palestinian Authority as a state supporter of terrorism? *See* Michael Herzog, *Can Hamas Be Tamed?* Foreign Aff., Mar.-April 2006, at 83. How should the law and politics of designation account for participation in democratic processes of designated terrorist organizations? Does politics alone account for the Bush administration's reported reluctance, during its effort to build an anti-terrorist coalition after the September 11 attacks, to include Syria on the list of countries that support terrorism? *See* Karen DeYoung, *Definitions of Terrorism Dog U.S. Officials,* Wash. Post, Oct. 25, 2001, at A9.

5. *The Procedures for Designation.* Even this brief overview shows that there are many serious legal consequences of a designation as terrorist or terrorist organization. Should a designee therefore be given notice and an opportunity to be heard?

The answer for foreign entities not connected to the United States is no. "A foreign entity without property or presence in this country has no constitutional rights, under the due process clause or otherwise." People's Mojahedin Organization of Iran v. United States Department of State, 182 F.3d 17, 22 (D.C. Cir. 1999). A fortiori, no foreign state is entitled to any process before it is listed as a country that supports terrorism and is therefore cut off from foreign aid. "No one would suppose that a foreign nation had a due process right to notice and a hearing before the Executive imposed an embargo on it for the purpose of coercing a change in policy." *Id.*

But entities and persons with substantial connections to the United States stand on a different constitutional footing. They are entitled to due process before their property or liberty rights can be curtailed by the government. *National Council of Resistance of Iran, supra* p. 468, at 203. The D.C. Circuit Court of Appeals has ruled that such an entity must be given notice that the designation is impending (at least absent a showing that prior notice would "impinge on security and other foreign policy goals of the United States"), disclosure of the nonclassified administrative record on which the designation relies, and the opportunity to present a written rebuttal of that administrative record. *Id.* at 208-209.

People's Mojahedin Organization of Iran v. Department of State

United States Court of Appeals, District of Columbia Circuit, 2003
327 F.3d 1238

SENTELLE, Circuit Judge. The People's Mojahedin Organization of Iran ("PMOI" or "Petitioner") seeks review of 1999 and 2001 decisions of the Secretary of State ... designating Petitioner as a foreign terrorist organization....

I. BACKGROUND

We note at the outset that this is PMOI's third petition to this court to review designations of the PMOI as a foreign terrorist organization. *See* People's Mojahedin Org. of Iran v. Dep't. of State, 182 F.3d 17 (D.C. Cir. 1999) ("*PMOI*"); Nat'l Council of Resistance of Iran v. Dep't. of State, 251 F.3d 192 (D.C. Cir. 2001) ("*NCOR*")....

II. ANALYSIS

A. DUE PROCESS AND SUFFICIENCY OF EVIDENCE

Petitioner raises several arguments. First, it contends that its redesignation as a terrorist organization under 8 U.S.C. §1189 is unconstitutional under the Due Process Clause of the Fifth Amendment of the Constitution because the statute permitted the Secretary to rely upon secret evidence—the classified information that respondents refused to disclose and against which PMOI could therefore not effectively defend. We reject this contention.... [T]hat statute authorizes designation of a foreign terrorist organization when the Secretary finds three elements. As to the first, that is that the organization is a foreign organization, there is not and cannot be any dispute. The People's Mojahedin is so assuredly a foreign organization that until the Secretary's designation of the

NCOR as its alias, it could not even establish a presence in the United States. Nothing has changed in that regard since our prior decisions on the subject.

As to the second element, the PMOI advances a colorable argument: that the Secretary was able under §1189(a)(3)(B) to "consider classified information in making [this designation]" and that the classified information was not "subject to disclosure" except to the court ex parte and in camera for purposes of this judicial review. Petitioner contends that this violates the due process standard set forth in Abourezk v. Reagan, 785 F.2d 1043, 1061 (D.C. Cir. 1986), "that a court may not dispose of the merits of a case on the basis of ex parte, in camera submissions." While colorable, this argument will not carry the day.

First, we have already set forth in *NCOR* the due process standards that the Secretary must meet in making designations under the statute. We held that the Constitution requires the Secretary in designating foreign terrorist organizations to provide to the potential designees, "notice that the designation is impending." *NCOR*, 251 F.3d at 208. We further required that the Secretary must afford the potential designee an "opportunity to be heard at a meaningful time and in a meaningful manner." *Id.* at 209. The record reflects that the Secretary complied with our instructions.

Granted, petitioners argue that their opportunity to be heard was not meaningful, given that the Secretary relied on secret information to which they were not afforded access. The response to this is twofold. We already decided in *NCOR* that due process required the disclosure of only the unclassified portions of the administrative record. 251 F.3d at 207-09. We made that determination informed by the historically recognized proposition that under the separation of powers created by the United States Constitution, the Executive Branch has control and responsibility over access to classified information and has "'compelling interest' in withholding national security information from unauthorized persons in the course of executive business." Dep't. of the Navy v. Egan, 484 U.S. 518, 527 (1988) (quoting Snepp v. United States, 444 U.S. 507, 509 n.3 (1980)). In the context of another statutory scheme involving classified information, we noted the courts are often ill-suited to determine the sensitivity of classified information. United States v. Yunis, 867 F.2d 617, 623 (D.C. Cir. 1989) ("Things that did not make sense to [a judge] would make all too much sense to a foreign counter intelligence specialist...."). The Due Process Clause requires only that process which is due under the circumstances of the case. We have already established in *NCOR* the process which is due under the circumstances of this sensitive matter of classified intelligence in the effort to combat foreign terrorism. The Secretary has complied with the standard we set forth therein, and nothing further is due.

However, even if we err in describing the process due, even had the Petitioner been entitled to have its counsel or itself view the classified information, the breach of that entitlement has caused it no harm. This brings us to Petitioner's statutory objection. Petitioner argues that there is not adequate record support for the Secretary's determination that it is a foreign terrorist organization under the statute. However, on this element, even the unclassified record taken alone is quite adequate to support the Secretary's determination. Indeed, as to this element — that is, that the organization engages in terrorist activities — the People's Mojahedin has effectively admitted not only the adequacy of the unclassified record, but the truth of the allegation....

By its own admission, the PMOI has

(1) attacked with mortars the Islamic Revolutionary Prosecutor's Office; (2) assassinated a former Iranian prosecutor and killed his security guards; (3) killed the Deputy Chief of the Iranian Joint Staff Command, who was the personal military adviser to Supreme Leader Khamenei; (4) attacked with mortars the Iranian Central Command Headquarters of the Islamic Revolutionary Guard Corps and the Defense Industries Organization in Tehran; (5) attacked and targeted with mortars the offices of the Iranian Supreme Leader Khamenei, and of the head of the State Exigencies Council; (6) attacked with mortars the central headquarters of the Revolutionary Guards; (7) attacked with mortars two Revolutionary Guards Corps headquarters; and (8) attacked the headquarters of the Iranian State Security Forces in Tehran.

Were there no classified information in the file, we could hardly find that the Secretary's determination that the Petitioner engaged in terrorist activities is "lacking substantial support in the administrative record taken as a whole," even without repairing to the "classified information submitted to the court." 8 U.S.C. §1189(b)(3)(D)....

The remaining element under §1189(a)(1) is that "the terrorist activity or terrorism of the organization threatens the security of United States nationals or the national security of the United States." Id. §1189(a)(1)(C). The thrust of Petitioner's argument is that its allegedly terrorist acts were not acts of terrorism under the statute, because they do not meet the requirement of subsection (C). Petitioner argues that the attempt to overthrow the despotic government of Iran, which itself remains on the State Department's list of state sponsors of terrorism, is not "terrorist activity," or if it is, that it does not threaten the security of the United States or its nationals. We cannot review that claim. In *PMOI* we expressly held that that finding "is nonjusticiable." 182 F.3d at 23. As we stated in that decision, "it is beyond the judicial function for a court to review foreign policy decisions of the Executive Branch." *Id.* (citing Chicago & Southern Air Lines v. Waterman Steamship Corp., 333 U.S. 103, 111 (1948)).... In short, we find neither statutory nor due process errors in the Secretary's designation of petitioner as a foreign terrorist organization.

B. PETITIONER'S OTHER CLAIMS

Petitioner raises several other arguments to the effect that the designation violates its constitutional rights. Those warranting separate discussion fall under the general heading of First Amendment claims. Petitioner's argument that its First Amendment rights have been violated rests on the consequences of the designation. Petitioner argues that by forbidding all persons within or subject to the jurisdiction of the United States from "knowingly provid[ing] material support or resources," 18 U.S.C. §2339B(a)(1), to it as a designated foreign terrorist organization, the statute violates its rights of free speech and association guaranteed by the First Amendment. We disagree.

As the Ninth Circuit held in Humanitarian Law Project v. Reno, 205 F.3d 1130, 1135 (9th Cir. 2000), the statute "is not aimed at interfering with the expressive component of [the organization's] conduct but at stopping aid to terrorist groups." It is conduct and not communication that the statute controls. We join the Ninth Circuit in observing that "there is no constitutional right to facilitate terrorism by giving terrorists the weapons and explosives with which to carry out their grisly missions. Nor, of course, is there a right to provide resources with which terrorists can buy weapons and explosives." *Id.* at 1133....

III. CONCLUSION

For the reasons set forth above, we conclude that in the designation and redesignation of the People's Mojahedin of Iran as a foreign terrorist organization, the Secretary of State afforded all the process that the organization was due, and that this designation violated neither statutory nor constitutional rights of the Petitioner. We therefore deny the petitions for review.

So ordered.

[The concurring opinion of EDWARDS, J., is omitted.]

NOTES AND QUESTIONS

1. *Process without Access?* If PMOI is entitled to the protections of the Due Process Clause, how can the process due include denying to PMOI access to the evidence upon which its designation is based? On what basis did the court justify a process that was admittedly not "meaningful"?

2. *Result-oriented?* The consequences of designation are dire, as the court noted in its 2001 decision, *supra* pp. 467-468. Under the circumstances, why do you suppose the process obligations of the government are so scant? Would you say that the outcome in PMOI was determined primarily by the State Department, Congress, or the court?

3. *The Statutory Argument.* Are you persuaded by PMOI's statutory argument? Why should the statutory question be any less amenable to judicial resolution than the constitutional claim?

4. *First Amendment Issues.* The First Amendment consequences of designation are explored *infra* pp. 835-836.

The Fourth Amendment and National Security

Since the birth of our nation, Americans have worried about espionage committed by hostile foreign agents. In recent times, we have also become the targets of violent terrorist acts at home and abroad. To gather information about these threats to national security, we have employed many of the same techniques that are used in ordinary criminal investigations, including wiretaps, undercover agents and informants, physical searches of persons and places, and, more recently, sophisticated computer technologies, including e-mail intercepts and data mining.

In almost every instance, these measures have succeeded in protecting the American people from harm. In the process, however, government officials have occasionally lost sight of their mission, or strayed from it, and have violated individual privacy rights, just as in any criminal investigation gone awry. Where the subject of a probe is a possible terrorist act, which may be politically motivated, First Amendment freedoms of assembly and expression may be implicated as well. Special care is thus required in sorting out protected activities from those that could lead to violence or serious disruption of society and in selecting appropriate investigative techniques for each.

This sorting-out process is often complicated by a lack of information about the exact nature of suspected threats. While no one argues that a mere hunch about anticipated violent acts or subversion will justify surveillance of potential targets, something less than a completed illegal act must suffice. Thus, the development of standards for approval of investigations into national security threats is a critical legal issue.

In this and the succeeding five chapters we focus on intelligence collection operations within the United States and abroad—electronic surveillance; physical searches; infiltration of groups by informants; the collection of tangible and electronic transactional records, such as travel records, telephone dialing and billing information, bank records, and library records; and datamining of the resulting databases, among others. In this chapter we start with a short primer on the Fourth Amendment, then examine the Supreme Court's seminal analysis of the President's claim of inherent authority to conduct warrantless electronic surveillance in domestic security investigations. We then consider subsequent lower court case law exploring the contours of an inherent executive authority for such surveillance in foreign intelligence investigations. In Chapter 19, we turn to statutory authority for electronic foreign intelligence surveillance in the Foreign Intelligence Surveillance Act (FISA) and related legislation. In Chapter 20, we take up statutory authority for investigatory collection of tangible and electronic transactional records from third parties, using court orders, National Security Letters, and subpoenas. In Chapter 21, we consider a range of other surveillance and collection techniques used to profile and "watchlist" terrorist suspects and to screen access to transportation systems, critical infrastructure, and other possible targets for terrorism. In Chapter 22 we assess self-imposed executive branch rules for internal security investigations, and we examine how counterterrorism investigations are coordinated among various agencies and overseen by Congress and the Executive. Our primary focus throughout the foregoing chapters is on domestic surveillance, but the "Global War on Terror," as its name suggests, is also conducted abroad. In Chapter 23 we therefore turn to the U.S. law, if any, governing national security surveillance abroad.

A. DETECTION OF TERRORIST THREATS

William C. Banks & M.E. Bowman, Executive Authority for National Security Surveillance
50 Am.U. L. Rev. 1, 92-94 (2001)

Terrorism presents a unique set of challenges in the United States. First, current criminal laws and traditional law enforcement processes cannot provide absolute protection against terrorist acts. While arrest, prosecution, and incarceration serve well to help prevent most crimes from occurring, the risk of catastrophic harm from terrorist attacks forces us to consider other means of prevention. Moreover, traditional Fourth Amendment requirements may thwart many investigations of terrorism, which depend on stealth to prevent terrorist plans before they are carried out.

Second, while terrorism is at its core a national security problem, it represents an unusual confluence of phenomena for the investigative community — the primary purpose of the investigation may be simultaneously and in equal measure law enforcement and national security. With few exceptions, the rules for gathering intelligence about terrorism in the United States are no different from the rules for ordinary criminal investigations.

Third, most prognostications are for more threats of terrorism in the United States in coming years, largely due to the perception that our defenses against conventional attacks are so formidable. Greater threats thus place an additional premium on greater intelligence resources and successes.

The tradition of liberty in the United States casts a shadow over all national security surveillance, and is an overriding problem in addressing terrorism concerns. The core openness of our society permits all of us, including the potential terrorist, considerable freedom to move about, to associate with others, and to act in furtherance of political aims. As recent terrorist incidents in the United

A. Detection of Terrorist Threats

States have created a sense of urgency among citizens and government officials to find better preventive strategies, reflection has also reminded us that hasty actions to thwart terrorism may threaten the freedoms that permit an open society. Thus, in seeking ways to investigate potential terrorist activity, just as in fashioning better responses to terrorist incidents, the measures adopted must not undermine our basic freedoms.

Statement of John Ashcroft, Attorney General, U.S. Federal Efforts to Combat Terrorism
Hearing Before the Subcomm. on Commerce, Justice, and State, the Judiciary, and Related Agencies of the S. Comm. on Appropriations, 107th Cong. (2001)

...The Department of Justice is responsible for the investigation and prosecution of terrorist acts that violate U.S. law, wherever they occur. It has been involved in responding to overseas terrorist acts against U.S. interests for more than a decade and a half and has been involved in addressing terrorist acts at home for an even longer period. While we continue to make adjustments designed to improve our law enforcement response and to prepare for the challenges presented by the evolving nature of terrorist activity, the fact is that the Department's enforcement program related to terrorism is one which has had an opportunity to be fine tuned through experience....

It goes without saying that the paramount objective of U.S. counterterrorism policy is the prevention of terrorist acts. This requires both intelligence and investigative capabilities working together to detect and react effectively to incipient terrorist threats. By making effective use of intelligence information, we seek to involve the FBI in the investigation of terrorist plots as early in the chain of conspiratorial events as possible. In this way, the terrorist plot can not only be disrupted, but the conspirators can also be apprehended, preventing them from recycling their terrorist plans for use at some unknown future time and place.

This objective of preventing terrorist acts before they occur requires the collection and effective use of foreign intelligence and foreign counterintelligence to detect and to react to terrorist threats before they occur. The Department of Justice supports the collection efforts of U.S. intelligence agencies by representing them at the Foreign Intelligence Surveillance Court and obtaining the necessary warrants under the Foreign Intelligence Surveillance Act (FISA). In addition, under Executive Order 12333, the Attorney General approves the proposals of U.S. intelligence agencies to collect against U.S. persons overseas who are suspected of international terrorist activities. To enable effective use of the intelligence collected on terrorists under FISA and the Executive Order, the Attorney General also approves the passage of such intelligence to authorities in a position to prevent the planning, movement, or other actions of terrorists....

Some of our successes in prevention must necessarily remain secret. But some can be described. Several international terrorist plots have been prevented through effective law enforcement efforts.

1. For example, overseas, the Department worked with other U.S. agencies and our foreign counterparts to disrupt a bomb plot in 1995 which, if carried to completion, would have resulted in the destruction of a dozen U.S. commercial jumbo jets flying Asian-Pacific routes. Three terrorists involved in the plot were arrested in distant countries, brought to the U.S., and convicted in federal court.

2. Within the United States, investigative efforts resulted in the arrest, and subsequent conviction, of Sheik Omar Abdel Rahman and a number of his followers in 1993 before they could carry out a deadly plot to bomb buildings, tunnels, and a bridge in Manhattan. Prevention of these two terrorist plots alone probably averted the death or serious injury of tens of thousands of Americans.

3. More recently, on December 14, 1999, Ahmed Ressam was arrested entering the United States from Canada with powerful explosives and timing devices. He has just been convicted of all counts of a nine count indictment, including the charge of an act of terrorism transcending national boundaries.

Similarly, a number of potentially deadly terrorist acts planned by domestic terrorists have been prevented....

Fact Sheet: Plots, Casings, and Infiltrations Referenced in President Bush's Remarks on the War on Terror

Oct. 6, 2005

Overall, the United States and our partners have disrupted at least ten serious al-Qaida terrorist plots since September 11 — including three al-Qaida plots to attack inside the United States. We have stopped at least five more al-Qaida efforts to case targets in the United States or infiltrate operatives into our country.

10 PLOTS

The West Coast Airliner Plot: In mid-2002 the U.S. disrupted a plot to attack targets on the West Coast of the United States using hijacked airplanes. The plotters included at least one major operational planner involved in planning the events of 9/11.

The East Coast Airliner Plot: In mid-2003 the U.S. and a partner disrupted a plot to attack targets on the East Coast of the United States using hijacked commercial airplanes.

The Jose Padilla Plot: In May 2002 the U.S. disrupted a plot that involved blowing up apartment buildings in the United States. One of the plotters, Jose Padilla, also discussed the possibility of using a "dirty bomb" in the U.S.

The 2004 UK Urban Targets Plot: In mid-2004 the U.S. and partners disrupted a plot that involved urban targets in the United Kingdom. These plots involved using explosives against a variety of sites.

The 2003 Karachi Plot: In the Spring of 2003 the U.S. and a partner disrupted a plot to attack Westerners at several targets in Karachi, Pakistan.

The Heathrow Airport Plot: In 2003 the U.S. and several partners disrupted a plot to attack Heathrow Airport using hijacked commercial airliners. The planning for this attack was undertaken by a major 9/11 operational figure.

The 2004 UK Plot: In the Spring of 2004 the U.S. and partners, using a combination of law enforcement and intelligence resources, disrupted a plot to conduct large-scale bombings in the UK.

The 2002 Arabian Gulf Shipping Plot: In late 2002 and 2003 the U.S. and a partner nation disrupted a plot by al-Qa'ida operatives to attack ships in the Arabian Gulf.

The 2002 Straits of Hormuz Plot: In 2002 the U.S. and partners disrupted a plot to attack ships transiting the Straits of Hormuz.

The 2003 Tourist Site Plot: In 2003 the U.S. and a partner nation disrupted a plot to attack a tourist site outside the United States.

5 CASINGS AND INFILTRATIONS

The U.S. Government & Tourist Sites Tasking: In 2003 and 2004, an individual was tasked by al-Qa'ida to case important U.S. Government and tourist targets within the United States.

The Gas Station Tasking: In approximately 2003, an individual was tasked to collect targeting information on U.S. gas stations and their support mechanisms on behalf of a senior al-Qa'ida planner.

Iyman Faris & the Brooklyn Bridge: In 2003, and in conjunction with a partner nation, the U.S. government arrested and prosecuted Iyman Faris, who was exploring the destruction of the Brooklyn Bridge in New York. Faris ultimately pleaded guilty to providing material support to al-Qa'ida and is now in a federal correctional institution.

2001 Tasking: In 2001, al-Qa'ida sent an individual to facilitate post-September 11 attacks in the U.S. U.S. law enforcement authorities arrested the individual.

2003 Tasking: In 2003, an individual was tasked by an al-Qa'ida leader to conduct reconnaissance on populated areas in the U.S.

B. THE FOURTH AMENDMENT FRAMEWORK

William C. Banks & M.E. Bowman, Executive Authority for National Security Surveillance
50 Am. U. L. Rev. 1, 2-4 (2001)

The British general warrant was a search tool employed without limitation on location, and without any necessity to precisely describe the object or person sought. British authorities were simply given license to "break into any shop or place suspected" wherever they chose. With that kind of unfettered discretion, the general warrant could be, and often was, used to intimidate. General warrants executed during the reign of Charles I sought to intimidate dissidents, authors, and printers of seditious material by ransacking homes and seizing personal papers. In 1765, the courts declared general warrants illegal, and Parliament followed a year later.

In the colonies, complaints that royal officials were violating the privacy of colonists through the use of writs of assistance, equivalent to general warrants, grew. Because English law did not, as yet, recognize a right of personal privacy, the crown's abuses in the colonies were not remediable at law. It was thus no surprise that the new American Constitution and the government it created would respect a series of individual freedoms....

Although the Fourth Amendment eliminated the abuses of general warrants, its commands remain unclear, especially in the face of technological progress. Moreover, the Fourth Amendment was designed to protect against overreaching in investigations of criminal enterprises. Investigations of politically motivated threats to our national security, such as terrorism or espionage, were simply not contemplated.

The Fourth Amendment to the U.S. Constitution provides:

> The right of the people to be secure in their persons, houses, papers, and effects, against unreasonable searches and seizures shall not be violated, and no Warrants shall issue, but upon probable cause, supported by Oath or affirmation, and particularly describing the place to be searched, and the persons or things to be seized.

The Fourth Amendment limits governmental authority to conduct searches for various purposes, from criminal law enforcement to safety and health inspections of homes and businesses. The Fourth Amendment concern in this chapter arises because the techniques used in enforcing the criminal laws are also used in gathering intelligence for national security or counterterrorism, and because some such intelligence is obtained for use in criminal prosecutions. In this setting, most Fourth Amendment challenges to intelligence gathering concern electronic surveillance or the physical entry required for the installation of electronic, audio, or video equipment.

Apart from the fact that the Framers could not have foreseen problems of adapting the Amendment to electronic communication, the Fourth Amendment's two clauses — the protection against "unreasonable searches and seizures" and the warrant requirement — present a threshold problem of interpretation. Is a warrantless search *per se* unreasonable? In 1967, the Supreme Court held that warrantless searches "are *per se* unreasonable — subject only to a few specifically established and well-delineated exceptions." Katz v. United States, 389 U.S. 347, 357 (1967). Thus, exceptions are recognized for searches incident to arrest, *see, e.g.*, United States v. Robinson, 414 U.S. 218 (1973); automobile searches, Michigan v. Long, 463 U.S. 1032 (1983); "stop and frisk" searches, Terry v. Ohio, 392 U.S. 1 (1968); searches of persons and things entering and leaving the United States, United States v. Montoya de Hernandez, 473 U.S. 531 (1985), United States v. Duncan, 693 F.2d 971 (9th Cir. 1982); searches of boats on navigable waters, United States v. Villamonte-Marquez, 462 U.S. 579 (1983); and searches of airplanes. United States v. Nigro, 727 F.2d 100 (6th Cir. 1984) (*en banc*). The Supreme Court has also maintained that warrantless searches may be conducted to prevent railroad accidents that cause "great human loss," Skinner v. Railway Labor Executives' Assn., 489

U.S. 602, 628 (1989), or to address the potential spread of disease or contamination during a public health crisis. Camara v. Municipal Court, 387 U.S. 523, 539 (1967).

In view of the devastation wrought by the airline hijackings on September 11, 2001, any effort to defend warrantless preboarding airplane searches appears almost prosaic:

> When the risk is the jeopardy to hundreds of human lives and millions of dollars of property inherent in the pirating or blowing up of a large airplane, that danger alone meets the test of reasonableness, so long as the search is conducted in good faith for the purpose of preventing hijacking or like damage and with reasonable scope, and the passenger has been given notice of his liability to such a search so that he can avoid it by choosing not to travel by air. [United States v. Edwards, 498 F.2d 496, 500 (2d Cir. 1974).]

See also John Rogers, *Bombs, Borders, and Boarding: Combating International Terrorism at United States Airports and the Fourth Amendment*, 20 Suffolk Transnatl. L. Rev. 501 (1997); *infra* Chapter 21.

The reasoning in the decisions noted above might be thought to excuse the warrant requirement for surveillance in other kinds of cases implicating national security. It might, for example, be used to justify warrantless electronic surveillance of Americans suspected in some way of being connected to terrorist threats. Or it might provide the basis for video surveillance of streets, parks, and other public places. But if there is an exception to the warrant requirement when surveillance involves national security concerns, what procedures should substitute for the warrant process? The existence of a possible national security exception to the warrant requirement, and the effects of new technologies on this constitutional doctrine, are the primary issues explored in the following section.

C. A NATIONAL SECURITY EXCEPTION?

Foreign Intelligence Surveillance Act of 1977

S. Rep. No. 95-604, at 9-12 (1977)
[hereinafter *Senate Report No. 604*]

... In 1928, the Supreme Court in Olmstead v. United States [277 U.S. 468] held that wiretapping was not within the coverage of the Fourth Amendment. Three years later, Attorney General William D. Mitchell authorized telephone wiretapping, upon the personal approval of bureau chiefs, of syndicated bootleggers and in "exceptional cases where the crimes are substantial and serious, and the necessity is great and [the bureau chief and the Assistant Attorney General] are satisfied that the persons whose wires are to be tapped are of the criminal type." These general guidelines governed the Department's practice through the thirties and telephone wiretapping was considered to be an important law enforcement tool.

Congress placed the first restrictions on wiretapping in the Federal Communications Act of 1934, which made it a crime for any person "to intercept and divulge or publish the contents of wire and radio communications." [48 Stat. 1103.] The Supreme Court construed this section to apply to Federal agents and held that evidence obtained from the interception of wire and radio communications and the fruits of the evidence, were inadmissible to court. [Nardone v. United States, 302 U.S. 379 (1937); 308 U.S. 338 (1939).] However, the Justice Department did not interpret the Federal Communications Act or the *Nardone* decision as prohibiting the interception of wire communications per se; rather only the interception and divulgence of their contents outside the Federal establishment was considered to be unlawful. Thus, the Justice Department found continued authority for its national security wiretaps.

In 1940, President Roosevelt issued a memorandum to the Attorney General stating his view that electronic surveillance would be proper under the Constitution where "grave matters involving defense of the nation" were involved. The President authorized and directed the Attorney General "to secure information by listening devices [directed at] the conversation or other communications of persons suspected of subversive activites against the Government of the United States, including suspected spies." The Attorney General was requested "to limit these investigations so conducted to a minimum and to limit them insofar as possible to aliens."

This practice was continued in successive administrations....

In the early fifties, however, Attorney General J. Howard McGrath took the position that he would not approve or authorize the installation of microphone surveillances by means of trespass. This policy was quickly reversed by Attorney General Herbert Brownell in 1954 in a sweeping memorandum to FBI Director Hoover instructing him that the Bureau was indeed authorized to conduct such trespassory surveillances regardless of the fact of surreptitious entry, and without the need to first acquire the Attorney General's authorization. Such surveillance was simply authorized whenever the Bureau concluded that the "national interest" so required....

In Katz v. United States, 389 U.S. 347 (1967), the Supreme Court finally discarded the *Olmstead* doctrine and held that the Fourth Amendment's warrant provision did apply to electronic surveillance. The Court explicitly declined, however, to extend its holding to cases "involving the national security." 389 U.S. at 358 n.23. The next year, Congress followed suit: responding to the *Katz* case, Congress enacted the Omnibus Crime Control and Safe Streets Act (18 U.S.C. §§2510-2520). Title III of that Act established a procedure for the judicial authorization of electronic surveillance for the investigation and prevention of specified types of serious crimes and the use of the product of such surveillance in court proceedings. It prohibited wiretapping and electronic surveillance by persons other than duly authorized law enforcement officers, personnel of the Federal Communications Commission, or communication common carriers monitoring communications in the normal course of their employment.

Title III, however, disclaimed any intention of legislating in the national security area....

C. A National Security Exception?

United States v. United States District Court (*Keith*)[1]
United States Supreme Court, 1972
407 U.S. 297

Mr. Justice POWELL delivered the opinion of the Court. The issue before us is an important one for the people of our country and their Government. It involves the delicate question of the President's power, acting through the Attorney General, to authorize electronic surveillance in internal security matters without prior judicial approval.... This case brings the issue here for the first time. Its resolution is a matter of national concern, requiring sensitivity both to the Government's right to protect itself from unlawful subversion and attack and to the citizen's right to be secure in his privacy against unreasonable Government intrusion.

This case arises from a criminal proceeding in the United States District Court for the Eastern District of Michigan, in which the United States charged three defendants with conspiracy to destroy Government property in violation of 18 U.S.C. §371. One of the defendants, Plamondon, was charged with the dynamite bombing of an office of the Central Intelligence Agency in Ann Arbor, Michigan.

During pretrial proceedings, the defendants moved to compel the United States to disclose certain electronic surveillance information and to conduct a hearing to determine whether this information "tainted" the evidence on which the indictment was based or which the Government intended to offer at trial. In response, the Government filed an affidavit of the Attorney General, acknowledging that its agents had overheard conversations in which Plamondon had participated. The affidavit also stated that the Attorney General approved the wiretaps "to gather intelligence information deemed necessary to protect the nation from attempts of domestic organizations to attack and subvert the existing structure of the Government." The logs of the surveillance were filed in a sealed exhibit for in camera inspection by the District Court.

On the basis of the Attorney General's affidavit and the sealed exhibit, the Government asserted that the surveillance was lawful, though conducted without prior judicial approval, as a reasonable exercise of the President's power (exercised through the Attorney General) to protect the national security. The District Court held that the surveillance violated the Fourth Amendment, and ordered the Government to make full disclosure to Plamondon of his overheard conversations.

...[T]he Court of Appeals for the Sixth Circuit...held that the surveillance was unlawful and that the District Court had properly required disclosure of the overheard conversations....

I

Title III of the Omnibus Crime Control and Safe Streets Act, 18 U.S.C. §§2510-2520, authorizes the use of electronic surveillance for classes of crimes

---

[1. This case is commonly referred to by the name of the district court judge who first heard it, Damon J. Keith.]

carefully specified in 18 U.S.C. §2516. Such surveillance is subject to prior court order. Section 2518 sets forth the detailed and particularized application necessary to obtain such an order as well as carefully circumscribed conditions for its use. The Act represents a comprehensive attempt by Congress to promote more effective control of crime while protecting the privacy of individual thought and expression. Much of Title III was drawn to meet the constitutional requirements for electronic surveillance enunciated by this Court in Berger v. New York, 388 U.S. 41 (1967), and Katz v. United States, 389 U.S. 347 (1967).

Together with the elaborate surveillance requirements in Title III, there is the following proviso, 18 U.S.C. §2511(3):

> Nothing contained in this chapter or in section 605 of the Communications Act of 1934 (48 Stat. 1143; 47 U.S.C. 605) shall limit the constitutional power of the President to take such measures as he deems necessary to protect the Nation against actual or potential attack or other hostile acts of a foreign power, to obtain foreign intelligence information deemed essential to the security of the United States, or to protect national security information against foreign intelligence activities. *Nor shall anything contained in this chapter be deemed to limit the constitutional power of the President to take such measures as he deems necessary to protect the United States against the overthrow of the Government by force or other unlawful means, or against any other clear and present danger to the structure or existence of the Government.* The contents of any wire or oral communication intercepted by authority of the President in the exercise of the foregoing powers may be received in evidence in any trial hearing, or other proceeding only where such interception was reasonable, and shall not be otherwise used or disclosed except as is necessary to implement that power. (Emphasis supplied.)

The Government relies on §2511(3). It argues that "in excepting national security surveillances from the Act's warrant requirement Congress recognized the President's authority to conduct such surveillances without prior judicial approval." The section thus is viewed as a recognition or affirmance of a constitutional authority in the President to conduct warrantless domestic security surveillance such as that involved in this case.

We think the language of §2511(3), as well as the legislative history of the statute, refutes this interpretation. The relevant language is that: "Nothing contained in this chapter... shall limit the constitutional power of the President to take such measures as he deems necessary to protect..." against the dangers specified. At most, this is an implicit recognition that the President does have certain powers in the specified areas. Few would doubt this, as the section refers — among other things — to protection "against actual or potential attack or other hostile acts of a foreign power." But so far as the use of the President's electronic surveillance power is concerned, the language is essentially neutral.

Section 2511(3) certainly confers no power, as the language is wholly inappropriate for such a purpose. It merely provides that the Act shall not be interpreted to limit or disturb such power as the President may have under the Constitution. In short, Congress simply left presidential powers where it found them....

...[I]t would have been incongruous for Congress to have legislated with respect to the important and complex area of national security in a single brief and nebulous paragraph. This would not comport with the sensitivity of the

C. A National Security Exception?

problem involved or with the extraordinary care Congress exercised in drafting other sections of the Act. We therefore think the conclusion inescapable that Congress only intended to make clear that the Act simply did not legislate with respect to national security surveillances....

... [V]iewing §2511(3) as a congressional disclaimer and expression of neutrality, we hold that the statute is not the measure of the executive authority asserted in this case. Rather, we must look to the constitutional powers of the President.

II

It is important at the outset to emphasize the limited nature of the question before the Court. This case raises no constitutional challenge to electronic surveillance as specifically authorized by Title III of the Omnibus Crime Control and Safe Streets Act of 1968. Nor is there any question or doubt as to the necessity of obtaining a warrant in the surveillance of crimes unrelated to the national security interest. Further, the instant case requires no judgment on the scope of the President's surveillance power with respect to the activities of foreign powers, within or without this country. The Attorney General's affidavit in this case states that the surveillances were "deemed necessary to protect the nation from attempts of *domestic organizations* to attack and subvert the existing structure of Government" (emphasis supplied). There is no evidence of any involvement, directly or indirectly, of a foreign power.[8]

Our present inquiry, though important, is therefore a narrow one. It addresses a question left open by *Katz*: "Whether safeguards other than prior authorization by a magistrate would satisfy the Fourth Amendment in a situation involving the national security...." The determination of this question requires the essential Fourth Amendment inquiry into the "reasonableness" of the search and seizure in question, and the way in which that "reasonableness" derives content and meaning through reference to the warrant clause.

... [T]he President of the United States has the fundamental duty, under Art. II, §1, of the Constitution, to "preserve, protect and defend the Constitution of the United States." Implicit in that duty is the power to protect our Government against those who would subvert or overthrow it by unlawful means. In the discharge of this duty, the President—through the Attorney General—may

---

8. Section 2511(3) refers to "the constitutional power of the President" in two types of situations: (i) where necessary to protect against attack, other hostile acts or intelligence activities of a "foreign power"; or (ii) where necessary to protect against the overthrow of the Government or other clear and present danger to the structure or existence of the Government. Although both of the specified situations are sometimes referred to as "national security" threats, the term "national security" is used only in the first sentence of §2511(3) with respect to the activities of foreign powers. This case involves only the second sentence of §2511(3), with the threat emanating—according to the Attorney General's affidavit—from "domestic organizations." Although we attempt no precise definition, we use the term "domestic organization" in this opinion to mean a group or organization (whether formally or informally constituted) composed of citizens of the United States and which has no significant connection with a foreign power, its agents or agencies. No doubt there are cases where it will be difficult to distinguish between "domestic" and "foreign" unlawful activities directed against the Government of the United States where there is collaboration in varying degrees between domestic groups or organizations and agents or agencies of foreign powers. But this is not such a case.

find it necessary to employ electronic surveillance to obtain intelligence information on the plans of those who plot unlawful acts against the Government. The use of such surveillance in internal security cases has been sanctioned more or less continuously by various Presidents and Attorneys General since July 1946....

Though the Government and respondents debate their seriousness and magnitude, threats and acts of sabotage against the Government exist in sufficient number to justify investigative powers with respect to them. The covertness and complexity of potential unlawful conduct against the Government and the necessary dependency of many conspirators upon the telephone make electronic surveillance an effective investigatory instrument in certain circumstances. The marked acceleration in technological developments and sophistication in their use have resulted in new techniques for the planning, commission, and concealment of criminal activities. It would be contrary to the public interest for Government to deny to itself the prudent and lawful employment of those very techniques which are employed against the Government and its law-abiding citizens....

But a recognition of these elementary truths does not make the employment by Government of electronic surveillance a welcome development—even when employed with restraint and under judicial supervision. There is, understandably, a deep-seated uneasiness and apprehension that this capability will be used to intrude upon cherished privacy of law-abiding citizens. We look to the Bill of Rights to safeguard this privacy. Though physical entry of the home is the chief evil against which the wording of the Fourth Amendment is directed, its broader spirit now shields private speech from unreasonable surveillance. Our decision in *Katz* refused to lock the Fourth Amendment into instances of actual physical trespass. Rather, the Amendment governs "not only the seizure of tangible items, but extends as well to the recording of oral statements... without any 'technical trespass under... local property law.'"... *Katz,* supra, at 353....

National security cases, moreover, often reflect a convergence of First and Fourth Amendment values not present in cases of "ordinary" crime. Though the investigative duty of the executive may be stronger in such cases, so also is there greater jeopardy to constitutionally protected speech. "Historically the struggle for freedom of speech and press in England was bound up with the issue of the scope of the search and seizure power," Marcus v. Search Warrant, 367 U.S. 717, 724 (1961). History abundantly documents the tendency of Government—however benevolent and benign its motives—to view with suspicion those who most fervently dispute its policies. Fourth Amendment protections become the more necessary when the targets of official surveillance may be those suspected of unorthodoxy in their political beliefs. The danger to political dissent is acute where the Government attempts to act under so vague a concept as the power to protect "domestic security." Given the difficulty of defining the domestic security interest, the danger of abuse in acting to protect that interest becomes apparent....

III

As the Fourth Amendment is not absolute in its terms, our task is to examine and balance the basic values at stake in this case: the duty of Government to

C. A National Security Exception?

protect the domestic security, and the potential danger posed by unreasonable surveillance to individual privacy and free expression. If the legitimate need of Government to safeguard domestic security requires the use of electronic surveillance, the question is whether the needs of citizens for privacy and free expression may not be better protected by requiring a warrant before such surveillance is undertaken. We must also ask whether a warrant requirement would unduly frustrate the efforts of Government to protect itself from acts of subversion and overthrow directed against it.

Though the Fourth Amendment speaks broadly of "unreasonable searches and seizures," the definition of "reasonableness" turns, at least in part, on the more specific commands of the warrant clause....

... [W]here practical, a governmental search and seizure should represent both the efforts of the officer to gather evidence of wrongful acts and the judgment of the magistrate that the collected evidence is sufficient to justify invasion of a citizen's private premises or conversation. Inherent in the concept of a warrant is its issuance by a "neutral and detached magistrate." The further requirement of "probable cause" instructs the magistrate that baseless searches shall not proceed.

These Fourth Amendment freedoms cannot properly be guaranteed if domestic security surveillances may be conducted solely within the discretion of the Executive Branch.... The historical judgment, which the Fourth Amendment accepts, is that unreviewed executive discretion may yield too readily to pressures to obtain incriminating evidence and overlook potential invasions of privacy and protected speech.

It may well be that, in the instant case, the Government's surveillance of Plamondon's conversations was a reasonable one which readily would have gained prior judicial approval. But this Court "has never sustained a search upon the sole ground that officers reasonably expected to find evidence of a particular crime and voluntarily confined their activities to the least intrusive means consistent with that end." *Katz,* supra, at 356-357. The Fourth Amendment contemplates a prior judicial judgment, not the risk that executive discretion may be reasonably exercised. This judicial role accords with our basic constitutional doctrine that individual freedoms will best be preserved through a separation of powers and division of functions among the different branches and levels of Government. The independent check upon executive discretion is not satisfied, as the Government argues, by "extremely limited" post-surveillance judicial review. Indeed, post-surveillance review would never reach the surveillances which failed to result in prosecutions....

It is true that there have been some exceptions to the warrant requirement. But those exceptions are few in number and carefully delineated; in general, they serve the legitimate needs of law enforcement officers to protect their own wellbeing and preserve evidence from destruction. Even while carving out those exceptions, the Court has reaffirmed the principle that the "police must, whenever practicable, obtain advance judicial approval of searches and seizures through the warrant procedure," Terry v. Ohio, [392 U.S. 1, 20 (1968)].

The Government argues that the special circumstances applicable to domestic security surveillances necessitate a further exception to the warrant requirement. It is urged that the requirement of prior judicial review would obstruct the President in the discharge of his constitutional duty to protect domestic security. We are told further that these surveillances are directed primarily to the collecting and maintaining of intelligence with respect to subversive forces, and are not an attempt to gather evidence for specific criminal prosecutions. It is said that this type of surveillance should not be subject to traditional warrant requirements which were established to govern investigation of criminal activity, not ongoing intelligence gathering.

The Government further insists that courts "as a practical matter would have neither the knowledge nor the techniques necessary to determine whether there was probable cause to believe that surveillance was necessary to protect national security." These security problems, the Government contends, involve "a large number of complex and subtle factors" beyond the competence of courts to evaluate.

As a final reason for exemption from a warrant requirement, the Government believes that disclosure to a magistrate of all or even a significant portion of the information involved in domestic security surveillances "would create serious potential dangers to the national security and to the lives of informants and agents.... Secrecy is the essential ingredient in intelligence gathering; requiring prior judicial authorization would create a greater 'danger of leaks ... because in addition to the judge, you have the clerk, the stenographer and some other officer like a law assistant or bailiff who may be apprised of the nature' of the surveillance." ...

... There is, no doubt, pragmatic force to the Government's position.

But we do not think a case has been made for the requested departure from Fourth Amendment standards.... Security surveillances are especially sensitive because of the inherent vagueness of the domestic security concept, the necessarily broad and continuing nature of intelligence gathering, and the temptation to utilize such surveillances to oversee political dissent. We recognize, as we have before, the constitutional basis of the President's domestic security role, but we think it must be exercised in a manner compatible with the Fourth Amendment. In this case we hold that this requires an appropriate prior warrant procedure.

We cannot accept the Government's argument that internal security matters are too subtle and complex for judicial evaluation. Courts regularly deal with the most difficult issues of our society. There is no reason to believe that federal judges will be insensitive to or uncomprehending of the issues involved in domestic security cases.... If the threat is too subtle or complex for our senior law enforcement officers to convey its significance to a court, one may question whether there is probable cause for surveillance.

Nor do we believe prior judicial approval will fracture the secrecy essential to official intelligence gathering. The investigation of criminal activity has long involved imparting sensitive information to judicial officers who have respected the confidentialities involved. Judges may be counted upon to be especially conscious of security requirements in national security cases. Title III of the Omnibus Crime Control and Safe Streets Act already has imposed this responsibility on the judiciary in connection with such crimes as espionage, sabotage, and treason, §2516(1)(a) and (c), each of which may involve domestic as well as foreign security threats. Moreover, a warrant application involves no public or adversary proceedings: it is an *ex parte* request before a magistrate or judge. Whatever security dangers clerical and secretarial personnel may pose can be

C. A National Security Exception?

minimized by proper administrative measures, possibly to the point of allowing the Government itself to provide the necessary clerical assistance.

Thus, we conclude that the Government's concerns do not justify departure in this case from the customary Fourth Amendment requirement of judicial approval prior to initiation of a search or surveillance. Although some added burden will be imposed upon the Attorney General, this inconvenience is justified in a free society to protect constitutional values. Nor do we think the Government's domestic surveillance powers will be impaired to any significant degree. A prior warrant establishes presumptive validity of the surveillance and will minimize the burden of justification in post-surveillance judicial review. By no means of least importance will be the reassurance of the public generally that indiscriminate wiretapping and bugging of law-abiding citizens cannot occur.

IV

... [W]e do not hold that the same type of standards and procedures prescribed by Title III are necessarily applicable to this case. We recognize that domestic security surveillance may involve different policy and practical considerations from the surveillance of "ordinary crime." The gathering of security intelligence is often long range and involves the interrelation of various sources and types of information. The exact targets of such surveillance may be more difficult to identify than in surveillance operations against many types of crime specified in Title III. Often, too, the emphasis of domestic intelligence gathering is on the prevention of unlawful activity or the enhancement of the Government's preparedness for some possible future crisis or emergency. Thus, the focus of domestic surveillance may be less precise than that directed against more conventional types of crime.

Given these potential distinctions between Title III criminal surveillances and those involving the domestic security, Congress may wish to consider protective standards for the latter which differ from those already prescribed for specified crimes in Title III. Different standards may be compatible with the Fourth Amendment if they are reasonable both in relation to the legitimate need of Government for intelligence information and the protected rights of our citizens. For the warrant application may vary according to the governmental interest to be enforced and the nature of citizen rights deserving protection....

...We...hold...that prior judicial approval is required for the type of domestic security surveillance involved in this case and that such approval may be made in accordance with such reasonable standards as the Congress may prescribe.

V

As the surveillance of Plamondon's conversations was unlawful, because conducted without prior judicial approval, the courts below correctly held that Alderman v. United States, 394 U.S. 165 (1969), is controlling and that it requires disclosure to the accused of his own impermissibly intercepted conversations. As stated in *Alderman,* "the trial court can and should, where appropriate, place a defendant and his counsel under enforceable orders against unwarranted disclosure of the materials which they may be entitled to inspect." 394 U.S. at 185.

The judgment of the Court of Appeals is hereby affirmed.

The Chief Justice concurs in the result.

[The concurring opinions of DOUGLAS and WHITE, JJ., are omitted.]

NOTES AND QUESTIONS

1. *The Nature of the Privacy Interest.* Has your phone ever been tapped, or have you suspected that it was? Ever had your mail opened? Your e-mail or the history of your Internet use read by others without your permission? How did you feel (or how do you think you would feel) upon discovering such an intrusion? Would you feel better knowing that a judge had issued a warrant to authorize it?

While acknowledging that "physical entry of the home is the chief evil" addressed by the Fourth Amendment, the Court found in *Keith,* as it had in *Katz,* that the "broader spirit" of the amendment protects telephone conversations as well. But what is it about electronic surveillance that the Court found objectionable? Is it that a "search" of private conversations is being conducted, or is it the "convergence of First and Fourth Amendment values"?

Arguably, a physical search may be less intrusive than a wiretap, especially if the electronic surveillance continues for weeks or months after the initial intrusion. *See* Olmstead v. United States, 277 U.S. 438, 473 (1928) (Brandeis, J., dissenting); Berger v. New York, 388 U.S. 41, 60 (1967).

Why is this form of privacy important to individuals? What purpose does it serve in society? *See generally* Alan Westin, *Privacy and Freedom* (1967).

2. *Inherent Surveillance Authority?* Does Article II, Section 1 implicitly authorize the President to conduct electronic surveillance? *See* In re Neagle, 135 U.S. 1 (1890), *supra* p. 80. Does Article II distinguish between domestic and foreign national security threats?

If the President possesses some independent constitutional authority to engage in domestic electronic surveillance, why, according to the Court, is an exception to the warrant requirement not appropriate?

3. *Balancing Away the Warrant Requirement.* Does the warrant clause of the Fourth Amendment adequately protect privacy interests? What is the function of a "neutral and detached magistrate" in a warrant proceeding? Why did the government object to the warrant procedure for electronic surveillance in *Keith*?

How did the Supreme Court balance the President's Article II powers against the Fourth Amendment warrant requirement for domestic subjects? Did the Court fairly reconcile "the Government's right to protect itself from unlawful subversion and attack" with "the citizen's right to be secure in his privacy against unreasonable Government intrusion"? Should the Court have attached more importance to the fact that a magistrate's role could be

C. A National Security Exception?

performed more efficiently by after-the-fact judicial review where surveillance abuses are alleged?

In December 2005, the New York Times revealed the existence of a four-year, large-scale warrantless electronic surveillance program that intercepted communications of some U.S. citizens. James Risen & Eric Lichtblau, *Bush Lets U.S. Spy on Callers Without Courts*, N.Y. Times, Dec. 16, 2005, at A1. At a White House press conference, President Bush offered this explanation for the warrantless surveillance:

> ...We know that a two-minute phone conversation between somebody linked to al Qaeda here and an operative overseas could lead directly to the loss of thousands of lives. To save American lives, we must be able to act fast and to detect these conversations so that we can prevent new attacks.
>
> So, consistent with U.S. law and the Constitution, I authorized the interception of international communications of people with known links to al Qaeda and related terrorist organizations....
>
> ...I've reauthorized this program more than 30 times since the September 11th attacks, and I intend to do so for so long as our nation...faces the continuing threat of an enemy that wants to kill American citizens. [Press Conference of the President, Dec. 19, 2005.]

Assuming, arguendo, that Congress has enacted no applicable statute, would you agree, based on *Keith*, that the program described by the President is constitutional? Other aspects of this program are considered in Chapter 19.

4. *Domestic vs. Foreign Surveillance.* Justice Powell's interpretation of §2511(3) may have been crucial to the outcome of the case. His willingness to draw a sharp distinction between a "domestic organization" and "foreign" activities in the United States became the predicate for establishing the Fourth Amendment warrant requirement for "domestic" national security investigations. Why is the power to protect "domestic security" viewed with greater skepticism by the Court than the power to protect against foreign perils? Are the two concepts really different? Does §2511(3) clearly reflect such a sharp distinction in the origin of national security threats?

Justice Powell also concluded that §2511(3) "is essentially neutral" regarding presidential power. Do you agree? Consider the provision's last sentence.

5. *Title III (Ordinary Criminal) Electronic Surveillance.* Title III requires that an application for authorization to conduct electronic surveillance contain detailed information about the alleged criminal offense, the facilities and communication sought to be intercepted, the identity of the target (if known), the period of time sought for surveillance, and an explanation of whether other investigative methods have failed or why they are unlikely to succeed or are too dangerous. 18 U.S.C. §2518(1)(b)-(d) (2000). A court may issue an order for electronic surveillance only if it finds probable cause that communications related to the commission of a crime will be obtained through the surveillance. *Id.* §2518(3)(b). Can you see why intelligence agencies would seek to avoid the strictures of Title III in conducting electronic surveillance for intelligence purposes?

Title III also requires a warrant before the government may obtain access to stored communications, such as e-mail, during the first 180 days of storage. 18 U.S.C. §2703(a) (2000 & Supp. III 2003). After 180 days, the government may obtain access to stored communications pursuant to a search warrant or, after notice to the subscriber, pursuant to an administrative or grand jury subpoena or a court order. *Id.* §2703. See *infra* Chapter 20. Likewise, cell phones, display pagers, and voice pagers are protected by Title III. 18 U.S.C. §§2510(1), (12) (2000 & Supp. III. 2003).

6. *Post-Keith Case Law on Warrantless Foreign Intelligence Surveillance.* Several lower courts have taken up the important question, reserved by the Supreme Court in *Keith,* of surveillance to obtain foreign intelligence.

> ...The Fifth Circuit in United States v. Brown, 484 F.2d 418 (5th Cir. 1973), *cert. denied,* 415 U.S. 960 (1974), upheld the legality of a surveillance in which the defendant, an American citizen, was incidentally overheard as a result of a warrantless wiretap authorized by the Attorney General for foreign intelligence purposes. The court found that on the basis of "the President's constitutional duty to act for the United States in the field of foreign affairs, and his inherent power to protect national security in the conduct of foreign affairs...the President may constitutionally authorize warrantless wiretaps for the purpose of gathering foreign intelligence." [484 F.2d at 426.]
>
> In United States v. Butenko, 494 F.2d 593 (3d Cir. 1974) (en banc), *cert. denied sub nom.* Ivanov v. United States, 419 U.S. 881 (1974), the Third Circuit similarly held that electronic surveillance conducted without a warrant would be lawful so long as the primary purpose was to obtain foreign intelligence information. The court found that such surveillance would be reasonable under the Fourth Amendment without a warrant even though it might involve the overhearing of conversations.
>
> However, in Zweibon v. Mitchell, 516 F.2d 594 (D.C. Cir. 1975), *cert. denied,* 425 U.S. 944 (1976), the Circuit Court of Appeals for the District of Columbia, in the course of an opinion requiring that a warrant must be obtained before a wiretap is installed on a domestic organization that is neither the agent of, nor acting in collaboration with, a foreign power, questioned whether any national security exception to the warrant requirement would be constitutionally permissible.
>
> Although the holding of *Zweibon* was limited to the case of a domestic organization without ties to a foreign power, the plurality opinion of the court — in legal analysis closely patterned on *Keith* — concluded "that an analysis of the policies implicated by foreign security surveillance indicates that, absent exigent circumstances, all warrantless electronic surveillance is unreasonable and therefore unconstitutional." [*Senate Report No. 604, supra* p. 483, at 14, 15.]

Note that the Supreme Court declined to decide the appeals in the above cases.

Zweibon was a suit for damages by members of the Jewish Defense League (JDL) for unlawful electronic surveillance. Although the JDL is a U.S. organization, JDL protest actions directed against Soviet facilities inside the United States risked a significant foreign relations problem with the Soviet Union. Despite the fact that "Soviet officials vigorously and continuously protested these activities, for which they held the United States Government responsible," 516 F.2d at 608, 609, the D.C. Circuit refused to rule that this foreign affairs tension was cause to waive the Fourth Amendment warrant requirement. 516 F.2d at 614. A similar result was reached in Berlin Democratic Club v. Rumsfeld, 410 F. Supp. 144 (D.D.C. 1976), where a warrant was required to wiretap Americans living in West Germany despite Department of Defense arguments about dangers to United States forces and to American foreign policy. *Id.* at 157.

7. *Implications of Keith?* In the principal case, Justice Powell suggested that national security wiretaps may not have to meet all the Fourth Amendment requirements applicable in criminal investigations, but he did not specify what alternative processes might be appropriate in such cases. Nor did the Court refer to the constitutional requirements for other forms of surveillance, such as searches of the home and person. Meanwhile, the agencies within the intelligence community had, since their inception after World War II, been developing their own guidelines for national security surveillance. A post-Watergate investigation revealed widespread abuses within the intelligence community and prompted significant reform efforts by Congress and the executive branch. The next section examines some of these abuses.

D. A FOREIGN INTELLIGENCE EXCEPTION?

Select Committee to Study Governmental Operations with Respect to Intelligence Activities (Church Committee), Intelligence Activities and the Rights of Americans
S. Rep. No. 94-755, Book III, at 355 (1976)

... Before 1966, the FBI conducted over two hundred "black bag jobs." These warrantless surreptitious entries were carried out for intelligence purposes *other than* microphone installation, such as physical search and photographing or seizing documents.

... [T]here is no indication that the FBI informed any Attorney General about its use of "black bag jobs."

Surreptitious entries were performed by teams of FBI agents with special training in subjects such as "lock studies." Their missions were authorized in writing by FBI Director Hoover or his deputy, Clyde Tolson. A "Do Not File" procedure was utilized, under which most records of surreptitious entries were destroyed soon after an entry was accomplished.

The use of surreptitious entries against domestic targets dropped drastically after J. Edgar Hoover banned "black bag jobs" in 1966. . . .

United States v. Ehrlichman
United States District Court, District of Columbia, 1974
376 F. Supp. 29, *aff'd*, 546 F.2d 910 (D.C. Cir. 1976),
cert. denied, 429 U.S. 1120 (1977)

GESELL, J. Five defendants stand indicted for conspiring to injure a Los Angeles psychiatrist [Dr. Lewis Fielding] in the enjoyment of his Fourth Amendment rights by entering his offices without a warrant for the purpose of obtaining the doctor's medical records relating to one of his patients, a Daniel

Ellsberg, then under Federal indictment for revealing top secret documents. They now claim that broad pretrial discovery into the alleged national security aspects of this case is essential to the presentation of their defense, in that it will establish (1) that the break-in was legal under the Fourth Amendment because the President authorized it for reasons of national security, and (2) that even in the absence of such authorization the national security information available to the defendants at that time led them to the good-faith, reasonable belief that the break-in was legal and justified in the national interest. The Court has carefully considered these assertions, which have been fully briefed and argued over a two-day period, and finds them to be unpersuasive as a matter of law....

The Fourth Amendment protects the privacy of citizens against unreasonable and unrestrained intrusion by Government officials and their agents. It is not theoretical. It lies at the heart of our free society. As the Supreme Court recently remarked, "no right is held more sacred." Terry v. Ohio, 392 U.S. 1, 9 (1968). Indeed, the American Revolution was sparked in part by the complaints of the colonists against the issuance of writs of assistance, pursuant to which the King's revenue officers conducted unrestricted, indiscriminate searches of persons and homes to uncover contraband. James Otis' famous argument in Lechmere's Case, challenging the writ as a "monster of oppression" and a "remnant of Star Chamber tyranny," sowed one of the seeds of the coming rebellion. The Fourth Amendment was framed against this background; and every state in the Union, by its own constitution, has since reinforced the protections and the security which that Amendment was designed to achieve.

Thus the security of one's privacy against arbitrary intrusion by governmental authorities has proven essential to our concept of ordered liberty. When officials have attempted to justify law enforcement methods that ignore the strictures of this Amendment on grounds of necessity, such excuses have proven fruitless, for the Constitution brands such conduct as lawless, irrespective of the end to be served. Throughout the years the Supreme Court of the United States, regardless of changes in its composition or contemporary issues, has steadfastly applied the Amendment to protect a citizen against the warrantless invasion of his home or office, except under carefully delineated emergency circumstances. No right so fundamental should now, after the long struggle against governmental trespass, be diluted to accommodate conduct of the very type the Amendment was designed to outlaw.

The break-in charged in this indictment involved an unauthorized entry and search by agents of the Executive branch of the Federal Government. It is undisputed that no warrant was obtained and no Magistrate gave his approval. Moreover, none of the traditional exceptions to the warrant requirement are claimed and none existed; however desirable the break-in may have appeared to its instigators, there is no indication that it had to be carried out quickly, before a warrant could have been obtained. On the contrary, it had been meticulously planned over a period of more than a month. The search of Dr. Fielding's office was therefore clearly illegal under the unambiguous mandate of the Fourth Amendment.

Defendants contend that even though the Fourth Amendment would ordinarily prohibit break-ins of this nature, the President has the authority, by reason of his special responsibilities over foreign relations and national defense, to suspend its requirements, and that he did so in this case. Neither assertion is

D. A Foreign Intelligence Exception?

accurate. Many of the landmark Fourth Amendment cases in this country and in England concerned citizens accused of disloyal or treasonous conduct, for history teaches that such suspicions foster attitudes within a government that generate conduct inimical to individual rights. See United States v. United States District Court, 407 U.S. 297, 314 (1972). The judicial response to such Executive overreaching has been consistent and emphatic: the Government must comply with the strict constitutional and statutory limitations on trespassory searches and arrests even when known foreign agents are involved. To hold otherwise, except under the most exigent circumstances, would be to abandon the Fourth Amendment to the whim of the Executive in total disregard of the Amendment's history and purpose.

Defendants contend that, over the last few years, the courts have begun to carve out an exception to this traditional rule for purely intelligence-gathering searches deemed necessary for the conduct of foreign affairs. However, the cases cited are carefully limited to the issue of wiretapping, a relatively nonintrusive search, United States v. Butenko, 494 F.2d 593 (3d Cir. 1974); United States v. Brown, 484 F.2d 418 (5th Cir. 1973); Zweibon v. Mitchell, 363 F. Supp. 936 (D.D.C. 1973), and the Supreme Court has reserved judgment in this unsettled area. United States v. United States District Court, 407 U.S. 297, 322 n.20 (1972). The Court cannot find that this recent, controversial judicial response to the special problem of national security wiretaps indicates an intention to obviate the entire Fourth Amendment whenever the President determines that an American citizen, personally innocent of wrongdoing, has in his possession information that may touch upon foreign policy concerns.[4] Such a doctrine, even in the context of purely information-gathering searches, would give the Executive a blank check to disregard the very heart and core of the Fourth Amendment and the vital privacy interests that it protects. . . .

The facts presented pretrial lead the Court to conclude as a matter of law that the President not only lacked the authority to authorize the Fielding break-in but also that he did not in fact give any specific directive permitting national security break-ins, let alone this particular intrusion. The President has repeatedly and publicly denied prior knowledge or authorization of the Fielding break-in, and the available transcripts of the confidential tape recordings support that claim. . . . [The evidence reflected] intense Presidential concern with the need to plug the national security leaks and a belief that Dr. Ellsberg might be involved, but no specific reference either to Dr. Fielding or to trespassory searches. . . .

Defendants adopt the fall-back position that even if the President did not specifically authorize the Fielding break-in, he properly delegated to one or more of the defendants or unindicted co-conspirators the authority to approve national security break-ins. Of course, since the President had no such authority

---

4. The doctrine of the President's inherent authority as "the sole organ of the nation in its external relations," 10 Annals of Cong. 613 (1800) (remarks of John Marshall), has been developed by a series of Supreme Court decisions dealing with the President's power to enter into international agreements and to prohibit commercial contracts which impede American foreign policy. United States v. Curtiss-Wright Export Corp., 299 U.S. 304 (1936). None of these cases purport to deal with the constitutional rights of American citizens or with Presidential action in defiance of congressional legislation. When such issues have arisen, Executive assertions of inherent authority have been soundly rejected. See Kent v. Dulles, 357 U.S. 116 (1958); Youngstown Sheet & Tube Co. v. Sawyer, 343 U.S. 579 (1952).

in the first place, he could not have delegated it to others. Beyond this, however, the Court rejects the contention that the President could delegate his alleged power to suspend constitutional rights to non-law enforcement officers in the vague, informal, inexact terms noted above. Even in the wiretap cases the courts have stressed the fact that the President had specifically delegated the authority over "national security" wiretaps to his chief legal officer, the Attorney General, who approved each such tap. See, e.g., Katz v. United States, 389 U.S. 347, 364 (1967) (White, J., concurring). Whatever accommodation is required between the guarantees of the Fourth Amendment and the conduct of foreign affairs, it cannot justify a casual, ill-defined assignment to White House aides and part-time employees granting them an uncontrolled discretion to select, enter and search the homes and offices of innocent American citizens without a warrant. Cf. Ex parte Milligan, 71 U.S. (4 Wall.) 2 (1866); Ex parte Merryman, 17 Fed. Cas. p. 144, 151 (No. 9,487) (C.C. Md. 1861)....

NOTES AND QUESTIONS

1. *Comparing Searches and Electronic Surveillance.* Is physical entry of the home more threatening to civil liberties than a wiretap? Microphone surveillance requires entry to install the device, which will, like a wiretap, transmit all conversations, including those not subject to the investigation. If a physical search is controlled, it will take less time and may focus only on material relevant to the investigation. Yet for many of us, invasion of our physical space is more threatening than the prospect of electronic surveillance. Why is that so?

2. *Accountability for the Exception.* While the D.C. Circuit Court affirmed the conviction in United States v. Ehrlichman, 546 F.2d 910 (1976), *cert. denied,* 429 U.S. 1120 (1977), the panel was more circumspect than Judge Gesell. The court merely held that no "national security" exception to the warrant requirement could be invoked without specific authorization by the President or Attorney General. *Id.* at 925. Judge Wilkey elaborated:

> The danger of leaving delicate decisions of propriety and probable cause to those actually assigned to ferret out "national security" information is patent, and is indeed illustrated by the intrusion undertaken in this case, without any more specific Presidential direction than that ascribed to Henry II vexed with Becket.[68] As a constitutional matter, if Presidential approval is to replace judicial approval for foreign intelligence gathering, the personal authorization of the President — or his alter ego for these matters, the Attorney General — is necessary to fix accountability and centralize responsibility for insuring the least intrusive surveillance necessary and preventing zealous officials from misusing the President's prerogative. [*Id.* at 926.]

3. *Executive Approval as a Warrant Substitute?* Would the substitution of the President's or Attorney General's approval for a search compensate for the loss

---

68. Attributed as "Who will free me from this turbulent priest?"

D. A Foreign Intelligence Exception?

of the warrant procedure? The Attorney General at the time of the Fielding break-in was John N. Mitchell, who was subsequently sent to prison for perjury and conspiracy in connection with efforts to cover up the burglary of the Democratic National Committee headquarters at the Watergate in Washington. The President was Richard M. Nixon, who was named an unindicted co-conspirator in the same affair. *See* United States v. Haldeman, 559 F.2d 31, 51 (D.C. Cir. 1976).

4. *A Domestic Intelligence Exception?* At the time of the break-in, Ellsberg had been indicted for disclosing the *Pentagon Papers* (a classified account of American involvement in the Vietnam War) to reporters. See *supra* p. 216 and *infra* p. 1082. Ehrlichman and his co-defendants argued that "the search was legal because [it was] undertaken pursuant to a delegated Presidential power to authorize such a search in the field of foreign affairs." *Ehrlichman*, 546 F.2d at 913. However, there was no accusation that Ellsberg or his psychiatrist had any relationship to a foreign power. What does Judge Wilkey's dictum, *supra* Note 2, suggest about the parameters of any such "national security" exception to the warrant requirement?

Consider again the warrantless surveillance program described by President Bush, *supra* p. 493. Does the *Ehrlichman* decision change your view about the constitutionality of the more recent surveillance program, again assuming no controlling legislative authority?

5. *Applying the Exception to Other Searches.* If there is some "national security" exception to the warrant requirement, is there a principled basis for limiting the exception to electronic surveillance? *See* United States v. Ehrlichman, 546 F.2d at 938 (Leventhal, J., concurring); David S. Eggert, Note, *Executive Order 12,333: An Assessment of the Validity of Warrantless National Security Searches*, 1983 Duke L.J. 611, 627-628. *See also* Banks & Bowman, *supra* p. 481, at 67 ("In light of the potentially greater intrusiveness of electronic surveillance, it may be reasonable to expect greater executive discretion to conduct warrantless searches than warrantless wiretaps."). In addition to the degree of intrusion, what factors should be taken into account in deciding whether the warrant requirement applies? *See id.* at 67-68.

Unlike a physical search, most computer searches involve the remote collection of digital electronic data. Is a computer search therefore a "search" under the Fourth Amendment? Under what circumstances are computer data "seized," and when would such a search or seizure be "reasonable"? Computer searches "challenge several of the basic assumptions underlying Fourth Amendment doctrine. Computers are like containers in a physical sense, homes in a virtual sense, and vast warehouses in an informational sense." Orin S. Kerr, *Searches and Seizures in a Digital World*, 119 Harv. L. Rev. 531, 533 (2005). Which perspective do you find most helpful in thinking about application of the Fourth Amendment to Internet and computer searches?

United States v. Truong Dinh Hung
United States Court of Appeals, Fourth Circuit, 1980
629 F.2d 908, *cert. denied*, 454 U.S. 1144 (1982)

WINTER, J. Truong Dinh Hung, more familiarly known as David Truong, and Ronald Humphrey were convicted of espionage, conspiracy to commit espionage and several espionage-related offenses for transmitting classified United States government information to representatives of the government of the Socialist Republic of Vietnam. In these appeals, they seek reversal of their convictions because of warrantless surveillance and searches....

We hold that the warrantless searches and surveillance did not violate the Fourth Amendment....

David Truong, a Vietnamese citizen and son of a prominent Vietnamese political figure, came to the United States in 1965. At least since his arrival in the United States, Truong has pursued an active scholarly and political interest in Vietnam and the relationship between Vietnam and the United States. In 1976, Truong met Dung Krall, a Vietnamese-American, the wife of an American Naval Officer, who had extensive contacts among the Vietnamese community in Paris. Truong persuaded Krall to carry packages for him to Vietnamese in Paris. The recipients were representatives of the Socialist Republic of Vietnam at the time of the 1977 Paris negotiations between that country and the United States. The packages contained copies of diplomatic cables and other classified papers of the United States government dealing with Southeast Asia. Truong procured the copies from Ronald Humphrey, an employee of the United States Information Agency, who obtained the documents surreptitiously, copied them, removed their classification markings and furnished the copies to Truong. In a statement given after his arrest, Humphrey said that his motive was to improve relations between the North Vietnamese government and the United States so that he could be reunited with a woman whom he loved who was a prisoner of the North Vietnamese government.

Unknown to Truong, Krall was a confidential informant employed by the CIA and the FBI. Krall kept these agencies fully informed of Truong's activities and presented the packages Truong had given her to the FBI for inspection, copying and approval before she carried the documents to Paris. The FBI permitted this operation to continue, while monitoring it closely, from approximately September, 1976, until January 31, 1978.

When the intelligence agencies first learned that Truong was transmitting classified documents to Paris, they were understandably extremely anxious to locate Truong's source for his data. Toward that end, the government conducted a massive surveillance of Truong. Truong's phone was tapped and his apartment was bugged from May, 1977 to January, 1978. The telephone interception continued for 268 days and every conversation, with possibly one exception, was monitored and virtually all were taped. The eavesdropping device was operative for approximately 255 days and it ran continuously. No court authorization was ever sought or obtained for the installation and maintenance of the telephone tap or the bug. The government thus ascertained that Humphrey was providing Truong with the copies of secret documents. This leak of sensitive information of course ceased when Truong and Humphrey were arrested on January 31, 1978....

D. A Foreign Intelligence Exception?

The defendants raise a substantial challenge to their convictions by urging that the surveillance conducted by the FBI violated the Fourth Amendment and that all the evidence uncovered through that surveillance must consequently be suppressed. As has been stated, the government did not seek a warrant for the eavesdropping on Truong's phone conversations or the bugging of his apartment. Instead, it relied upon a "foreign intelligence" exception to the Fourth Amendment's warrant requirement. In the area of foreign intelligence, the government contends, the President may authorize surveillance without seeking a judicial warrant because of his constitutional prerogatives in the area of foreign affairs. On this basis, the FBI sought and received approval for the surveillance from the President's delegate, the Attorney General. This approval alone, according to the government, is constitutionally sufficient to authorize foreign intelligence surveillance such as the surveillance of Truong....

...Although the Supreme Court has never decided the issue which is presented to us, it formulated the analytical approach which we employ here in an analogous case, United States v. United States District Court (*Keith*), 407 U.S. 297 (1972)....

For several reasons, the needs of the executive are so compelling in the area of foreign intelligence, unlike the area of domestic security, that a uniform warrant requirement would, following *Keith*, "unduly frustrate" the President in carrying out his foreign affairs responsibilities. First of all, attempts to counter foreign threats to the national security require the utmost stealth, speed, and secrecy. A warrant requirement would add a procedural hurdle that would reduce the flexibility of executive foreign intelligence initiatives, in some cases delay executive response to foreign intelligence threats, and increase the chance of leaks regarding sensitive executive operations.

More importantly, the executive possesses unparalleled expertise to make the decision whether to conduct foreign intelligence surveillance, whereas the judiciary is largely inexperienced in making the delicate and complex decisions that lie behind foreign intelligence surveillance. The executive branch, containing the State Department, the intelligence agencies, and the military, is constantly aware of the nation's security needs and the magnitude of external threats posed by a panoply of foreign nations and organizations. On the other hand, while the courts possess expertise in making the probable cause determination involved in surveillance of suspected criminals, the courts are unschooled in diplomacy and military affairs, a mastery of which would be essential to passing upon an executive branch request that a foreign intelligence wiretap be authorized. Few, if any, district courts would be truly competent to judge the importance of particular information to the security of the United States or the "probable cause" to demonstrate that the government in fact needs to recover that information from one particular source.

Perhaps most crucially, the executive branch not only has superior expertise in the area of foreign intelligence, it is also constitutionally designated as the pre-eminent authority in foreign affairs. The President and his deputies are charged by the constitution with the conduct of the foreign policy of the United States in times of war and peace. See United States v. Curtiss-Wright Corp., 299 U.S. 304 (1936). Just as the separation of powers in *Keith* forced the executive to recognize a judicial role when the President conducts domestic security surveillance, so the separation of powers requires us to acknowledge the principal responsibility of the President for foreign affairs and concomitantly for foreign intelligence surveillance....

However, because individual privacy interests are severely compromised any time the government conducts surveillance without prior judicial approval, this foreign intelligence exception to the Fourth Amendment warrant requirement must be carefully limited to those situations in which the interests of the executive are paramount. First, the government should be relieved of seeking a warrant only when the object of the search or the surveillance is a foreign power, its agent or collaborators. In such cases, the government has the greatest need for speed, stealth, and secrecy, and the surveillance in such cases is most likely to call into play difficult and subtle judgments about foreign and military affairs. When there is no foreign connection, the executive's needs become less compelling; and the surveillance more closely resembles the surveillance of suspected criminals, which must be authorized by warrant. Thus, if the government wishes to wiretap the phone of a government employee who is stealing sensitive documents for his personal reading or to leak to a newspaper, for instance, the absence of a foreign connection and the importance of individual privacy concerns contained within the Fourth Amendment lead to a requirement that the executive secure advance judicial approval for surveillance....

Second... the executive should be excused from securing a warrant only when the surveillance is conducted "primarily" for foreign intelligence reasons. We think that the district court adopted the proper test, because once surveillance becomes primarily a criminal investigation, the courts are entirely competent to make the usual probable cause determination, and because, importantly, individual privacy interests come to the fore and government foreign policy concerns recede when the government is primarily attempting to form the basis for a criminal prosecution. We thus reject the government's assertion that, if surveillance is to any degree directed at gathering foreign intelligence, the executive may ignore the warrant requirement of the Fourth Amendment.

The defendants urge that the "primarily" test does not go far enough to protect privacy interests. They argue that the government should be able to avoid the warrant requirement only when the surveillance is conducted "solely" for foreign policy reasons. The proposed "solely" test is unacceptable, however, because almost all foreign intelligence investigations are in part criminal investigations. Although espionage prosecutions are rare, there is always the possibility that the targets of the investigation will be prosecuted for criminal violations. Thus, if the defendants' "solely" test were adopted, the executive would be required to obtain a warrant almost every time it undertakes foreign intelligence surveillance, and, as indicated above, such a requirement would fail to give adequate consideration to the needs and responsibilities of the executive in the foreign intelligence area.

In this case, the district court concluded that on July 20, 1977, the investigation of Truong had become primarily a criminal investigation. Although the Criminal Division of the Justice Department had been aware of the investigation from its inception, until summer the Criminal Division had not taken a central role in the investigation. On July 19 and July 20, however, several memoranda circulated between the Justice Department and the various intelligence and national security agencies indicating that the government had begun to assemble a criminal prosecution....

D. A Foreign Intelligence Exception?

Therefore, because there was more than enough evidence to indicate that Truong had collaborated with the Vietnamese government and because the district court did not err in choosing July 20 as the date when the investigation became primarily a criminal investigation, we do not disturb the decision of the district court to exclude all evidence obtained through the surveillance after July 20 but to permit the government to introduce evidence secured through the surveillance before July 20.

Because the Fourth Amendment warrant requirement is a critical constitutional protection of individual privacy, this discussion should conclude by underscoring the limited nature of this foreign intelligence exception to the warrant requirement which we recognize in the instant case. The exception applies only to foreign powers, their agents, and their collaborators. Moreover, even these actors receive the protection of the warrant requirement if the government is primarily attempting to put together a criminal prosecution....

NOTES AND QUESTIONS

1. *Deciding Reasonableness.* The court also found that intercepting Truong's phone calls and listening to conversations with visitors to Truong's apartment were "reasonable" efforts to locate the source of the purloined documents. 629 F.2d at 916-917. In light of the court's conclusion that no warrant was required for the surveillance, does it necessarily follow that the surveillance was reasonable? According to what criteria should reasonableness be determined?

2. *Package Searches.* Although the discussion of surveillance in *Truong* is not specifically directed to either electronic or non-electronic surveillance as such, the court did independently consider the constitutionality of the searches of packages Truong sent to Paris with Krall. A letter and package searched with executive authorization but without a warrant before the July 20 date at which the surveillance became, in the court's view, criminal in nature, were treated as governed by the foreign intelligence exception to the warrant requirement. *Id.* at 916-917. Another package searched without either the authorization of the Attorney General or a warrant was not covered by the foreign intelligence exception to the warrant requirement but was nonetheless constitutional, according to the court, because Truong had no reasonable expectation of privacy in the package. *Id.*

3. *Reconciling the Cases?* Is there any way to square the reasoning of the court in *Truong* with the holding of the Supreme Court in *Keith*? With the holding by Judge Gesell in *Ehrlichman*? Does the *Truong* court's reasoning apply equally to inspection of sealed parcels and to installation of surveillance cameras in a target's workplace or home?

4. *Less Intrusive Surveillance.* First and Fourth Amendment interests have not always received such extensive judicial protection where arguably less intrusive information collection techniques are employed. For example, in an area that is open to visual surveillance, the monitoring of beeper signals from a radio transmitter placed in contraband material and picked up by a police radio

receiver does not trigger Fourth Amendment protections, because the target has no legitimate expectation of privacy. United States v. Knotts, 460 U.S. 276, 284-285 (1983). The same result applies when the police use the beeper signal to monitor movements, so long as visual surveillance could have performed the monitoring. *Id.* at 285.

What are the implications of this extension of *Katz*—that someone who "knowingly exposes" her movements to others in a public place has no reasonable expectation of privacy—when others, including police or intelligence officials, take note of or record those movements? Katz v. United States, 389 U.S. 347, 351 (1967). Does this reduced expectation insulate from constitutional challenge the use of evolving technologies such as video cameras, video tracking devices, radio transmitting devices, visual magnification, and biometrics and face recognition for surveillance in public places? *See* Marc Jonathan Blitz, *Video Surveillance and the Constitution of Public Space: Fitting the Fourth Amendment to a World that Tracks Image and Identity*, 82 Tex. L. Rev. 1349, 1375-1398 (2004). Can you say which places are public and which are private? If privacy is a personal freedom, why do its existence and scope vary so much with the location of the individual?

In Laird v. Tatum, 408 U.S. 1, 10 (1972), the Supreme Court dismissed on standing grounds a complaint against an Army program that investigated civil disturbances by collecting personal information about individuals and organizations. See *infra* p. 948. *See also* Socialist Workers Party v. Attorney General, 510 F.2d 253 (2d Cir. 1974) (approving undercover FBI surveillance of convention of Young Socialists of America). *But see* Philadelphia Yearly Meeting of the Religious Society of Friends v. Tate, 519 F.2d 1335 (3d Cir. 1975) (approving photography and compilation of records on political demonstrators but not the sharing of information with private employers or broadcasters). Constitutional protections generally have not been extended to investigations based on the use of informants and the examination of financial records held by third parties. *See* John Elliff, *The Attorney General's Guidelines for FBI Investigations*, 69 Cornell L. Rev. 785, 788-789 (1984). Should the courts be more solicitous of individual rights in these cases?

5. *Effect of New Technologies on Fourth Amendment Law.* Evolving surveillance technologies continue to raise civil liberties concerns. In Kyllo v. United States, 533 U.S. 27 (2001), the police used thermal imaging technology to measure the heat radiating from the exterior walls of a private home to verify suspicions that high-intensity lamps were being used indoors to grow marijuana. Because the sense-enhancing technology permitted intrusion into the home that would not otherwise have been possible without physical intrusion, and because the thermal imaging technique is not in general public use, the Court found that the homeowner had a reasonable expectation of privacy that was violated. *Id.* at 34-35. Although the Court has declined to speculate generally about the effects of changing technologies on Fourth Amendment protections, it has noted that expectations of privacy changed dramatically when air flight permitted new forms of observation. *See* Dow Chemical Co. v. United States, 476 U.S. 227, 234-235 (1986) (advanced aerial photography of business activities not a "search" for Fourth Amendment purposes).

In many cities today, public cameras are ubiquitous, and video surveillance in stores, banks, mass transit facilities, and other places where crowds gather is

D. A Foreign Intelligence Exception?

now commonplace. Do individuals have important privacy interests in these public places that are threatened by the new surveillance systems? What predictions can you make about constitutional challenges to these new surveillance technologies? *See* Blitz, *supra*, 82 Tex. L. Rev. at 1406-1407.

6. *The "Primary Purpose" Doctrine.* At what point in a national security investigation would you advise the Attorney General to seek a Title III warrant? Recall that the court in *Truong* concluded that the standard for deciding the constitutionality of warrantless foreign intelligence surveillance that eventually became a criminal investigation was whether the "primary purpose" of the search was in fact to obtain foreign intelligence information. At what point does an investigation change from "primarily" foreign intelligence to "primarily" law enforcement? Does the "primary purpose" rule adequately accommodate the competing interests? The "primary purpose" problem also arises in connection with statutory authorization for intelligence surveillance. See Chapter 19.

19

Congressional Authority for National Security Surveillance

Communications technology has undergone explosive growth since the digital and dot-com revolutions of the 1980s and 1990s. Both ordinary and Internet communications can be intercepted, and cell phone calls can be traced to the phone's location. Hidden recorders may preserve conversations, while parabolic microphones can capture conversations at long distances. Video surveillance cameras permit government officials to monitor public areas by closed-circuit television. Computer-driven scanners can search through millions of e-mail messages in a heartbeat.

By providing the means to watch and listen to people and to trace their movements, electronic surveillance can help to detect and prevent terrorism. Surveillance may also help to find those responsible for terrorism-related crimes after the fact.

Yet unlike physical searches for particular information or things, electronic surveillance records everything a target says or does. Especially when undertaken over a long period on a 24/7 basis, electronic surveillance casts a wide and open-ended net, capturing data that may be at best irrelevant and at worst deeply personal.

The Constitution contains two provisions that can guard against government abuses of such advanced technology. The Fourth Amendment was included in our Bill of Rights to counter any tendency government might have toward the kind of intimidation practiced by the English Crown against its citizens. The First Amendment was added as a bulwark against government intrusions that could dampen political expression.

This chapter extends our review, begun in Chapter 18, of the evolution of Fourth Amendment and electronic surveillance law in the courts, as we turn here to legislative efforts in this field. In the aftermath of the Vietnam War, there was widespread concern about reports of government abuses of warrantless electronic surveillance that targeted civil rights leaders, war protesters, and political opponents. Congress responded by enacting measures that regulate the approval of such surveillance. Yet it remained for the courts to explore the scope of constitutional privacy protection recognized in *Katz v. United States*, 389 U.S. 347 (1967), and Justice Harlan's concurrence in that case. In what settings and under which circumstances is there a reasonable expectation of privacy? More recent litigation testing statutory requirements also examines

A. THE SCOPE OF FOURTH AMENDMENT PROTECTION

Smith v. Maryland
United States Supreme Court, 1979
442 U.S. 735

Mr. Justice BLACKMUN delivered the opinion of the Court. This case presents the question whether the installation and use of a pen register[1] constitutes a "search" within the meaning of the Fourth Amendment, made applicable to the States through the Fourteenth Amendment.

On March 5, 1976, in Baltimore, Md., Patricia McDonough was robbed. She gave the police a description of the robber and of a 1975 Monte Carlo automobile she had observed near the scene of the crime. After the robbery, McDonough began receiving threatening and obscene phone calls from a man identifying himself as the robber. On one occasion, the caller asked that she step out on her front porch; she did so, and saw the 1975 Monte Carlo she had earlier described to police moving slowly past her home. On March 16, police spotted a man who met McDonough's description driving a 1975 Monte Carlo in her neighborhood. By tracing the license plate number, police learned that the car was registered in the name of petitioner, Michael Lee Smith.

The next day, the telephone company, at police request, installed a pen register at its central offices to record the numbers dialed from the telephone at petitioner's home. The police did not get a warrant or court order before having the pen register installed. The register revealed that on March 17 a call was placed from petitioner's home to McDonough's phone. On the basis of this and other evidence, the police obtained a warrant to search petitioner's residence. The search revealed that a page in petitioner's phone book was turned down to the name and number of Patricia McDonough; the phone book was seized. Petitioner was arrested, [convicted, and sentenced to six years' imprisonment.] . . .

. . . In determining whether a particular form of government-initiated electronic surveillance is a "search" within the meaning of the Fourth Amendment, our lodestar is *Katz v. United States*, 389 U.S. 347 (1967). . . .

In applying the *Katz* analysis to this case, it is important to begin by specifying precisely the nature of the state activity that is challenged. The activity here

---

1. "A pen register is a mechanical device that records the numbers dialed on a telephone by monitoring the electrical impulses caused when the dial on the telephone is released. It does not overhear oral communications and does not indicate whether calls are actually completed." United States v. New York Tel. Co., 434 U.S. 159, 161 n.1 [(1977)]. A pen register is "usually installed at a central telephone facility [and] records on a paper tape all numbers dialed from [the] line" to which it is attached. United States v. Giordano, 416 U.S. 505, 549 n.1 (1974).

took the form of installing and using a pen register. Since the pen register was installed on telephone company property at the telephone company's central offices, petitioner obviously cannot claim that his "property" was invaded or that police intruded into a "constitutionally protected area." Petitioner's claim, rather, is that, notwithstanding the absence of a trespass, the State, as did the Government in *Katz*, infringed a "legitimate expectation of privacy" that petitioner held. Yet a pen register differs significantly from the listening device employed in *Katz*, for pen registers do not acquire the *contents* of communications. This Court recently noted:

> "Indeed, a law enforcement official could not even determine from the use of a pen register whether a communication existed. These devices do not hear sound. They disclose only the telephone numbers that have been dialed—a means of establishing communication. Neither the purport of any communication between the caller and the recipient of the call, their identities, nor whether the call was even completed is disclosed by pen registers." *United States v. New York Tel. Co.*, 434 U.S. 159, 167 (1977).

Given a pen register's limited capabilities, therefore, petitioner's argument that its installation and use constituted a "search" necessarily rests upon a claim that he had a "legitimate expectation of privacy" regarding the numbers he dialed on his phone.

This claim must be rejected. First, we doubt that people in general entertain any actual expectation of privacy in the numbers they dial. All telephone users realize that they must "convey" phone numbers to the telephone company, since it is through telephone company switching equipment that their calls are completed. All subscribers realize, moreover, that the phone company has facilities for making permanent records of the numbers they dial, for they see a list of their long-distance (toll) calls on their monthly bills. In fact, pen registers and similar devices are routinely used by telephone companies "for the purposes of checking billing operations, detecting fraud and preventing violations of law." *United States v. New York Tel. Co.*, 434 U.S., at 174-175. . . .

. . . Most phone books tell subscribers, on a page entitled "Consumer Information," that the company "can frequently help in identifying to the authorities the origin of unwelcome and troublesome calls." Telephone users, in sum, typically know that they must convey numerical information to the phone company; that the phone company has facilities for recording this information; and that the phone company does in fact record this information for a variety of legitimate business purposes. Although subjective expectations cannot be scientifically gauged, it is too much to believe that telephone subscribers, under these circumstances, harbor any general expectation that the numbers they dial will remain secret. . . .

. . . [E]ven if petitioner did harbor some subjective expectation that the phone numbers he dialed would remain private, this expectation is not "one that society is prepared to recognize as 'reasonable.'" This Court consistently has held that a person has no legitimate expectation of privacy in information he voluntarily turns over to third parties. E.g., *United States v. Miller*, 425 U.S. [435] at 442-444 [1976]. In *Miller*, for example, the Court held that a bank depositor has no "legitimate 'expectation of privacy'" in financial information "voluntarily

A. The Scope of Fourth Amendment Protection

conveyed to... banks and exposed to their employees in the ordinary course of business." 425 U.S. at 442. The Court explained:

> "The depositor takes the risk, in revealing his affairs to another, that the information will be conveyed by that person to the Government.... This Court has held repeatedly that the Fourth Amendment does not prohibit the obtaining of information revealed to a third party and conveyed by him to Government authorities, even if the information is revealed on the assumption that it will be used only for a limited purpose and the confidence placed in the third party will not be betrayed." *Id.* at 443.

Because the depositor "assumed the risk" of disclosure, the Court held that it would be unreasonable for him to expect his financial records to remain private.

This analysis dictates that petitioner can claim no legitimate expectation of privacy here. When he used his phone, petitioner voluntarily conveyed numerical information to the telephone company and "exposed" that information to its equipment in the ordinary course of business. In so doing, petitioner assumed the risk that the company would reveal to police the numbers he dialed. The switching equipment that processed those numbers is merely the modern counterpart of the operator who, in an earlier day, personally completed calls for the subscriber. Petitioner concedes that if he had placed his calls through an operator, he could claim no legitimate expectation of privacy. We are not inclined to hold that a different constitutional result is required because the telephone company has decided to automate....

... We therefore conclude that petitioner in all probability entertained no actual expectation of privacy in the phone numbers he dialed, and that, even if he did, his expectation was not "legitimate." The installation and use of a pen register, consequently, was not a "search," and no warrant was required....

Mr. Justice POWELL took no part in the consideration or decision of this case.

Mr. Justice STEWART, with whom Mr. Justice BRENNAN joins, dissenting.... The numbers dialed from a private telephone — although certainly more prosaic than the conversation itself — are not without "content." Most private telephone subscribers may have their own numbers listed in a publicly distributed directory, but I doubt there are any who would be happy to have broadcast to the world a list of the local or long distance numbers they have called. This is not because such a list might in some sense be incriminating, but because it easily could reveal the identities of the persons and the places called, and thus reveal the most intimate details of a person's life....

Mr. Justice MARSHALL, with whom Mr. Justice BRENNAN joins, dissenting.... [E]ven assuming... that individuals "typically know" that a phone company monitors calls for internal reasons, it does not follow that they expect this information to be made available to the public in general or the government in particular. Privacy is not a discrete commodity, possessed absolutely or not at all. Those who disclose certain facts to a bank or phone company for a limited business purpose need not assume that this information will be released to other persons for other purposes.

The crux of the Court's holding, however, is that whatever expectation of privacy petitioner may in fact have entertained regarding his calls, it is not one "society is prepared to recognize as 'reasonable.'" In so ruling, the Court determines that individuals who convey information to third parties have "assumed the risk" of disclosure to the government. This analysis is misconceived in two critical respects.

Implicit in the concept of assumption of risk is some notion of choice. At least in the third-party consensual surveillance cases, which first incorporated risk analysis into Fourth Amendment doctrine, the defendant presumably had exercised some discretion in deciding who should enjoy his confidential communications. By contrast here, unless a person is prepared to forgo use of what for many has become a personal or professional necessity, he cannot help but accept the risk of surveillance. It is idle to speak of "assuming" risks in contexts where, as a practical matter, individuals have no realistic alternative.

More fundamentally, to make risk analysis dispositive in assessing the reasonableness of privacy expectations would allow the government to define the scope of Fourth Amendment protections. For example, law enforcement officials, simply by announcing their intent to monitor the content of random samples of first-class mail or private phone conversations, could put the public on notice of the risks they would thereafter assume in such communications. Yet, although acknowledging this implication of its analysis, the Court is willing to concede only that, in some circumstances, a further "normative inquiry would be proper." No meaningful effort is made to explain what those circumstances might be, or why this case is not among them.

In my view, whether privacy expectations are legitimate within the meaning of *Katz* depends not on the risks an individual can be presumed to accept when imparting information to third parties, but on the risks he should be forced to assume in a free and open society. . . .

The use of pen registers, I believe, constitutes such an extensive intrusion. To hold otherwise ignores the vital role telephonic communication plays in our personal and professional relationships, as well as the First and Fourth Amendment interests implicated by unfettered official surveillance. Privacy in placing calls is of value not only to those engaged in criminal activity. The prospect of unregulated governmental monitoring will undoubtedly prove disturbing even to those with nothing illicit to hide. Many individuals, including members of unpopular political organizations or journalists with confidential sources, may legitimately wish to avoid disclosure of their personal contacts. Permitting governmental access to telephone records on less than probable cause may thus impede certain forms of political affiliation and journalistic endeavor that are the hallmark of a truly free society. Particularly given the Government's previous reliance on warrantless telephonic surveillance to trace reporters' sources and monitor protected political activity, I am unwilling to insulate use of pen registers from independent judicial review. . . .

NOTES AND QUESTIONS

1. *Pen Registers and Trap and Trace vs. Wiretaps.* What is it about a pen register or trap and trace device that makes it so different from a wiretap?

A. The Scope of Fourth Amendment Protection

Should the differences have such constitutional significance? Consider the analogy to a mailed letter. The letter contains protected content, while the envelope contains only the mailing and return addresses and postage information. Thus, the contents of the letter are afforded protection, but the envelope is not. *See* Orin S. Kerr, *Internet Surveillance Law After the USA Patriot Act: The Big Brother That Isn't*, 97 Nw. U. L. Rev. 607, 611-616 (2003). Does the same contents/envelope distinction fit the pen register/trap and trace scenarios? Consider the views of Justices Stewart and Marshall. What "content" is arguably revealed by a pen register? *See* Daniel J. Solove, *Reconstructing Electronic Surveillance Law*, 72 Geo. Wash. L. Rev. 1264, 1286-1287 (2004).

2. *Comparing Katz.* Is the privacy interest recognized by the Court in *Katz* different in any appreciable way from the interest asserted in *Smith*? If the telephone company had the technical means to listen in on the phone calls in both cases, why protect one caller but not the other? Are the phone numbers dialed private? Should they be? *See* Patricia Bellia, *Surveillance Law Through Cyberlaw's Lens*, 72 Geo. Wash. L. Rev. 1375, 1405 (2004). Why should providing that information to a private third party matter so much in deciding what information the government can acquire? When you provide phone numbers to the phone company, do you expect that it will turn them over to Big Brother? Have you knowingly and willingly "assumed the risk" of such disclosure?

Alternatively, is the outcome in *Smith* best understood as reflecting a judgment that it doesn't really matter much, because the phone numbers were not of much value to the individual? *See* Daniel J. Solove, *Digital Dossiers and the Dissipation of Fourth Amendment Privacy*, 75 S. Cal. L. Rev. 1083 (2002).

3. *Extending Smith to the Internet.* Is *Smith* authority for searching e-mail subject lines and URLs without a warrant? See *infra* p. 520.

4. *A Statutory Remedy?* After *Smith*, Congress enacted the Pen Register Act, 18 U.S.C. §§3121-3127 (2000 & Supp. III 2003). The Act imposes a warrant requirement before the government may obtain a pen register. *Id.* §3121(a). However, in contrast to a traditional Fourth Amendment warrant based on probable cause, the government may obtain an order for a pen register simply by showing that its use is "relevant to an ongoing investigation." *Id.* §3123(a). The USA PATRIOT Act extended the pen register and trap and trace authorities to addressing information on e-mail and to ISP and URL addresses. Pub. L. No. 107-56, §216, 115 Stat. 272, 288-290 (2001) (amending 18 U.S.C. §3127(3), (4)). *See infra* p. 520. Are these statutory provisions constitutional?

5. *Comparing Keith.* *Smith* is like United States v. United States District Court (*Keith*), 407 U.S. 297 (1972), *supra* p. 485, in that both decisions of the Court prompted federal legislation. Recall, however, that the problem addressed in *Keith* was wiretapping for domestic security investigations. Although Justice Powell's opinion for the Court suggested that something other than traditional law enforcement warrant requirements might be appropriate for such investigations, the Court did not suggest what a satisfactory judicial approval scheme might look like. When Congress responded with legislation a few years later, the resulting statute did nothing to guide domestic intelligence

investigations. Instead, Congress created a scheme for the collection of foreign intelligence inside the United States.

B. CONGRESSIONAL AUTHORITY FOR SURVEILLANCE: THE FOREIGN INTELLIGENCE SURVEILLANCE ACT (FISA)

The Supreme Court's decision in the *Keith* case, *supra* p. 485, was only one part of a unique set of circumstances that led to the enactment in 1978 of the Foreign Intelligence Surveillance Act (FISA), 50 U.S.C.A §§1801-1862 (West 2003 & Supp. 2005). In addition to the Watergate scandal, see *supra* p. 89, the early 1970s saw startling revelations of illegal spying and other activities by U.S. intelligence agencies, including the FBI and CIA, and by the IRS and the military. These agencies sought to target and disrupt politically active domestic groups (principally civil rights and anti-war organizations), see *supra* pp. 433-436, and they engaged in widespread warrantless surveillance. The Senate Select Committee to Study Government Operations with Respect to Intelligence Activities, known as the Church Committee for its chairman, Senator Frank Church, summarized the effects of these domestic intelligence abuses in a 1976 report:

> FBI headquarters alone has developed over 500,000 domestic intelligence files, and these have been augmented by additional files at FBI Field Offices. The FBI opened 65,000 of these domestic intelligence files in 1972 alone. In fact, substantially more individuals and groups are subject to intelligence scrutiny than the number of files would appear to indicate, since typically, each domestic intelligence file contains information on more than one individual or group, and this information is readily retrievable through the FBI General Name Index.
>
> The number of Americans and domestic groups caught in the domestic intelligence net is further illustrated by the following statistics:
>
> - Nearly a quarter of a million first class letters were opened and photographed in the United States by the CIA between 1953-1973, producing a CIA computerized index of nearly one and one-half million names.
> - At least 130,000 first class letters were opened and photographed by the FBI between 1940-1966 in eight U.S. cities.
> - Some 300,000 individuals were indexed in a CIA computer system and separate files were created on approximately 7,200 Americans and over 100 domestic groups during the course of CIA's Operation CHAOS (1967-1973).
> - Millions of private telegrams sent from, to, or through the United States were obtained by the National Security Agency from 1947 to 1975 under a secret arrangement with three United States telegraph companies.
> - An estimated 100,000 Americans were the subjects of United States Army intelligence files created between the mid-1960's and 1971.
> - Intelligence files on more than 11,000 individuals and groups were created by the Internal Revenue Service between 1969 and 1973 and tax investigations were started on the basis of political rather than tax criteria.

B. Congressional Authority for Surveillance: FISA

- At least 26,000 individuals were at one point catalogued on an FBI list of persons to be rounded up in the event of a "national emergency."

[Select Committee to Study Government Operations with Respect to Intelligence Activities (Church Committee), *Intelligence Activities and the Rights of Americans,* S. Rep. No. 94-755, Book II, at 6-7 (1976).]

Two years later, Congress enacted FISA. Consider how that statute applied to the defendants in the following case and whether it is constitutional.

United States v. Duggan
United States Court of Appeals, Second Circuit, 1984
743 F.2d 59

KEARSE, J. The principal issues raised in this appeal by alleged agents of the Provisional Irish Republican Army ("PIRA") concern the constitutionality and proper application of the Foreign Intelligence Surveillance Act ("FISA" or the "Act"), 50 U.S.C. §§1801-1811 (Supp. V 1981). Defendants Andrew Duggan, Eamon Meehan, Gabriel Megahey, and Colm Meehan appeal from judgments of conviction... [on a series of charges relating to export, transportation, and delivery of explosives and firearms].... On July 27, 1982, pursuant to the provisions of FISA, 50 U.S.C. §1806(b), the Acting Attorney General of the United States, Edward C. Schmults, authorized the use at trial of tape recordings and information obtained pursuant to the FISA surveillance of the activities of the defendants. Shortly thereafter, pursuant to 50 U.S.C. §1806(c), the government notified the court and the defendants of its intention to introduce evidence from the FISA surveillance at trial. In the following months, the government provided the defendants with copies of all tape recordings, transcripts, surveillance logs, and pen register tapes of all telephone conversations resulting from the surveillance.

Defendants moved to suppress the fruits of the FISA surveillance on a variety of grounds....

ISSUES ON APPEAL...

Enacted in 1978, FISA generally allows a federal officer, if authorized by the President of the United States acting through the Attorney General (or the Acting Attorney General or the Deputy Attorney General) of the United States, to obtain from a judge of the specially created FISA Court, see 50 U.S.C. §1803, an order "approving electronic surveillance of a foreign power or an agent of a foreign power for the purpose of obtaining foreign intelligence information." *Id.* §1802(b).

FISA contains several definitions of "foreign power" and "agent of a foreign power." Most pertinently to this case, FISA defines "foreign power" to include "a group engaged in international terrorism or activities in preparation therefor." *Id.* §1801(a)(4). An "agent of a foreign power" is defined to include both "any person other than a United States person, who... acts in the United States as...a member of a foreign power as defined in [§1801(a)(4)]," *id.* §1801(b)(1)(A), and "any person who...knowingly engages in...international terrorism, or activities that are in preparation therefor, for or on behalf of a foreign power," *id.* §1801(b)(2)(C). Section 1801(i) defines "United States person" to include a citizen of the United States, an alien lawfully admitted for permanent residence (as defined in section 1101(a)(20) of title 8), [and] an unincorporated association a substantial number of members of which are citizens of the United States or aliens lawfully admitted for permanent residence.

The Act defines "foreign intelligence information," in part, as

(1) information that relates to, and if concerning a United States person is necessary to, the ability of the United States to protect against— ...
   (B) sabotage or international terrorism by a foreign power or an agent of a foreign power; or...
(2) information with respect to a foreign power or foreign territory that relates to, and if concerning a United States person is necessary to—
   (A) the national defense or security of the United States; or
   (B) the conduct of the foreign affairs of the United States. *Id.* §1801(e).

"International terrorism" is defined to include activities that—

(1) involve violent acts or acts dangerous to human life that...would be a criminal violation if committed within the jurisdiction of the United States or any State;
(2) appear to be intended
   (A) to intimidate or coerce a civilian population;
   (B) to influence the policy of a government by intimidation or coercion; or
   (C) to affect the conduct of a government by assassination or kidnapping; and
(3) occur totally outside the United States, or transcend national boundaries in terms of the means by which they are accomplished, the persons they appear intended to coerce or intimidate, or the locale in which their perpetrators operate or seek asylum. *Id.* §1801(c).

A federal officer making application for a FISA order approving electronic surveillance must include in his application, *inter alia*, "the identity, if known, or a description of the target of the electronic surveillance," *id.* §1804(a)(3); "a statement of the facts and circumstances relied upon by the applicant to justify his belief that...the target of the electronic surveillance is a foreign power or an agent of a foreign power," *id.* §1804(a)(4); and a certification by the Assistant to the President for National Security Affairs, or an executive branch designee of the President that, *inter alia*, the certifying official deems the information sought to be foreign intelligence information and that the purpose of the surveillance is to obtain foreign intelligence information, together with a statement of the basis for the certification that the information sought is the type of foreign intelligence information designated, *id.* §1804(a)(7). When the target is a United States person, the government is required to minimize the acquisition and retention of nonpublicly available information and to prohibit its dissemination, consistent with the need of the United States to obtain,

B. Congressional Authority for Surveillance: FISA

produce, and disseminate foreign intelligence information, *id.* §1801(h); and the application must set out what minimization procedures are proposed, *id.* §1804(a)(5).

The FISA Judge is authorized to enter an order approving electronic surveillance if he finds, *inter alia*, that on the basis of the facts submitted by the applicant there is probable cause to believe that—

> (A) the target of the electronic surveillance is a foreign power or an agent of a foreign power: *Provided*, That no United States person may be considered a foreign power or an agent of a foreign power solely upon the basis of activities protected by the first amendment to the Constitution of the United States,

id. §1805(a)(3), and finds that the applying official has obtained the requisite authorization and has submitted the required information, *id.* §1805(a)(1), (2), (5). If the target is a United States person, the FISA Judge is not to approve surveillance unless he finds that the certifications submitted pursuant to §1804(a)(7)(E) are not clearly erroneous on the basis of the data before him. *Id.* §1805(a)(5).

Defendants mount two types of challenge with regard to FISA. First, they contend that the Act is unconstitutional on several grounds. In addition, they contend that even if FISA is not unconstitutional, its requirements were not met in this case.

A. THE CONSTITUTIONALITY OF FISA

Defendants contend that FISA is unconstitutional principally on the grounds that... it violates the probable cause requirement of the Fourth Amendment....

2. THE PROBABLE CAUSE REQUIREMENT OF THE FOURTH AMENDMENT

...Defendants argue principally (1) that the Amendment applies to all proposed surveillances, including those in national security cases, and (2) that even if there were an exception for national security matters, it would not apply to terrorism cases where the objects of the terrorism are entirely outside of the United States. We reject these contentions.... Congress passed FISA to settle what it believed to be the unresolved question of the applicability of the Fourth Amendment warrant requirement to electronic surveillance for foreign intelligence purposes, and to "remove any doubt as to the lawfulness of such surveillance." H.R. Rep. 1283, pt. I, 95th Cong., 2d Sess. 25 (1978) ("House Report"). FISA reflects both Congress's "legislative judgment" that the court orders and other procedural safeguards laid out in the Act "are necessary to insure that electronic surveillance by the U.S. Government within this country conforms to the fundamental principles of the fourth amendment," S. Rep. No. 701, 95th Cong., 2d Sess. 13, *reprinted in* 1978 U.S. Code Cong. & Ad. News 3973, 3982 ("Senate Report 95-701"), and its attempt to fashion a "secure framework by which the Executive Branch may conduct legitimate electronic surveillance for foreign intelligence purposes within the context of this Nation's commitment to privacy and individual rights." S. Rep. No. 604, 95th Cong., 1st Sess. 15, *reprinted in* 1978 U.S. Code Cong. & Ad. News 3904, 3916 ("Senate Report 95-604"). In constructing this framework, Congress gave close scrutiny to departures from those Fourth Amendment doctrines applicable in the criminal-investigation context in order

> to ensure that the procedures established in [FISA] are reasonable in relation to legitimate foreign counterintelligence requirements and the protected rights of individuals. Their reasonableness depends, in part, upon an assessment of the difficulties of investigating activities planned, directed, and supported from abroad by foreign intelligence services and foreign-based terrorist groups. The differences between ordinary criminal investigations to gather evidence of specific crimes and foreign counterintelligence investigations to uncover and monitor clandestine activities have been taken into account. Other factors include the international responsibilities of the United States, the duties of the Federal Government to the States in matters involving foreign terrorism, and the need to maintain the secrecy of lawful counterintelligence sources and methods. Senate Report 95-701, at 14-15, *reprinted in* 1978 U.S. Code Cong. & Ad. News 3973, 3983.

We regard the procedures fashioned in FISA as a constitutionally adequate balancing of the individual's Fourth Amendment rights against the nation's need to obtain foreign intelligence information. The governmental concerns... make reasonable the adoption of prerequisites to surveillance that are less stringent than those precedent to the issuance of a warrant for a criminal investigation. Against this background, the Act requires that the FISA Judge find probable cause to believe that the target is a foreign power or an agent of a foreign power, and that the place at which the electronic surveillance is to be directed is being used or is about to be used by a foreign power or an agent of a foreign power; and it requires him to find that the application meets the requirements of the Act. These requirements make it reasonable to dispense with a requirement that the FISA Judge find probable cause to believe that surveillance will in fact lead to the gathering of foreign intelligence information. Further, if the target is a United States person, the Act requires the FISA Judge to determine that the executive branch's certifications pursuant to §1804(a)(7) are not clearly erroneous in light of the application as a whole, and to find that the application properly proposes, as required by §1801(h), to minimize the intrusion upon the target's privacy.

We conclude that these requirements provide an appropriate balance between the individual's interest in privacy and the government's need to obtain foreign intelligence information, and that FISA does not violate the probable cause requirement of the Fourth Amendment.

Nor is there any merit to defendants' contention that the national security interests of the United States are not implicated by acts of terrorism directed wholly outside the United States. The government points out that if other nations were to harbor terrorists and give them safe haven for staging terrorist activities against the United States, United States national security would be threatened. As a reciprocal matter, the United States cannot afford to give safe haven to terrorists who seek to carry out raids against other nations. Thus, international terrorism conducted from the United States, no matter

B. Congressional Authority for Surveillance: FISA

where it is directed, may well have a substantial effect on United States national security and foreign policy. In recognition of these considerations, Senate Report 95-701 noted:

> The committee intends that terrorists and saboteurs acting for foreign powers should be subject to surveillance under this bill when they are in the United States, even if the target of their violent acts is within a foreign country and therefore outside actual Federal or State jurisdiction. This departure from a strict criminal standard is justified by the international responsibility of government to prevent its territory from being used as a base for launching terrorist attacks against other countries. We demand that other countries live up to this responsibility and it is important that in our legislation we demonstrate a will to do so ourselves. Senate Report 95-701, at 30, *reprinted in* 1978 U.S. Code Cong. & Ad. News 3973, 3999.

We find highly persuasive the conclusions of Congress and the executive branch, the two branches most often concerned with foreign intelligence and national security questions, that international terrorist organizations are legitimate and important targets for foreign intelligence surveillance. . . .

B. COMPLIANCE WITH THE REQUIREMENTS OF FISA . . .

1. THE ALLEGED USE OF FISA SURVEILLANCE TO CONDUCT A CRIMINAL INVESTIGATION

Defendants contend that the surveillance of Megahey's telephone was not authorized by FISA because the information was sought as part of a criminal investigation. We see no grounds for concluding that the requirements of FISA were not met.

FISA permits federal officials to obtain orders authorizing electronic surveillance "for the purpose of obtaining foreign intelligence information." 50 U.S.C. §1802(b). The requirement that foreign intelligence information be the primary objective of the surveillance is plain not only from the language of §1802(b) but also from the requirements in §1804 as to what the application must contain. The application must contain a certification by a designated official of the executive branch that the purpose of the surveillance is to acquire foreign intelligence information, and the certification must set forth the basis for the certifying official's belief that the information sought is the type of foreign intelligence information described. *Id.* §1804(a)(7).

Once this certification is made, however, it is, under FISA, subjected to only minimal scrutiny by the courts. Congress deemed it a sufficient check in this regard to require the FISA Judge (1) to find probable cause to believe that the target of the requested surveillance is an agent of a foreign power; (2) to find that the application is complete and in proper form; and (3) when the target is a United States person, to find that the certifications are not "clearly erroneous." The FISA Judge, in reviewing the application, is not to second-guess the executive branch official's certification that the objective of the surveillance is foreign intelligence information. Further, Congress intended that, when a person affected by a FISA surveillance challenges the FISA Court's order, a reviewing court is to have no greater authority to second-guess the executive branch's certifications than has the FISA Judge:

> [I]n determining the legality of a surveillance ... the trial judge ... [is] not to make determinations which the issuing judge is not authorized to make. Where the bill specifies the scope or nature of judicial review in the consideration of an application, any review under these subsections is similarly constrained. For example, when reviewing the certifications required by [§1804(a)(7)], unless there is a prima facie showing of a fraudulent statement by a certifying officer, procedural regularity is the only determination to be made if a non-U.S. person is the target.... House Report at 92-93.

We see no basis for any suggestion in the present case that the application to the FISA Court did not meet the statutory requirement for certifying that the information sought was foreign intelligence information. At the time of the FISA application, the executive branch was aware that PIRA was an international terrorist organization and that Megahey played a leadership role in PIRA activities. In such circumstances, the foreign intelligence value of a FISA wiretap on Megahey's telephone would be plain: he would likely be a prime source of information relating to PIRA membership, goals, methods, and operations. The publicly filed government affidavits in this case make clear that the FISA surveillance was instituted as part of an investigation of international terrorism. Moreover, we have reviewed the in camera submissions to the FISA Judge, and we agree with the district court's finding that "the purpose of the surveillance in this case, both initially and throughout, was to secure foreign intelligence information and was not, as [the] defendants assert, directed towards criminal investigation or the institution of a criminal prosecution." *Megahey*, 553 F. Supp. at 1190.

Finally, we emphasize that otherwise valid FISA surveillance is not tainted simply because the government can anticipate that the fruits of such surveillance may later be used, as allowed by §1806(b), as evidence in a criminal trial. Congress recognized that in many cases the concerns of the government with respect to foreign intelligence will overlap those with respect to law enforcement. Thus, one Senate Report noted that

> [i]ntelligence and criminal law enforcement tend to merge in [the area of foreign counterintelligence investigations].... [S]urveillances conducted under [FISA] need not stop once conclusive evidence of a crime is obtained, but instead may be extended longer where protective measures other than arrest and prosecution are more appropriate. Senate Report 95-701, at 11, *reprinted in* 1978 U.S. Code Cong. & Ad. News 3973, 3979-80 (footnote omitted)....

2. THE DISTRICT COURT'S REFUSAL TO DISCLOSE THE SUBSTANCE OF THE FISA APPLICATIONS

Defendant's contention that the district court erred in refusing to disclose the substance of the affidavits and certifications that accompanied the FISA applications need not detain us long. Section 1806(f) of FISA provides for *in camera, ex parte* review of the documents where the Attorney General has filed an affidavit stating that disclosure of the FISA applications and orders would harm the national security of the United States. The judge has the discretion to disclose portions of the documents, under appropriate protective procedures, only if he decides that such disclosure is "necessary to make an accurate determination of the legality of the surveillance." 50 U.S.C. §1806(f). Such a need might arise if the judge's initial review revealed potential irregularities such as "possible misrepresentation of fact, vague identification of the persons to be surveilled, or surveillance records which include a significant amount of non-foreign intelligence information, calling into question compliance with the minimization standards contained in the order." Senate Report 95-604, at 58, *reprinted in* 1978 U.S. Code Cong. & Ad. News 3904, 3960. In general, however, "*ex parte, in camera* determination is to be the rule."

We see no error in Judge Sifton's determination that disclosure was not necessary for an accurate determination of the legality of the surveillance of Megahey. Defendants have made no showing of misrepresented facts; they do not argue that Megahey was not clearly identified as a target. They have made no other presentation warranting disclosure. Under the circumstances, Judge Sifton did not abuse his discretion....

[In omitted portions of the opinion, the court also upheld FISA against challenges that the Act is unconstitutionally overbroad and vague, that the Act raises nonjusticiable political questions, and that the differing treatment of U.S. persons and others in FISA violates the Equal Protection Clause.]

The judgments of conviction are affirmed....

NOTES AND QUESTIONS

After reading *Duggan*, would you say that FISA supplies a constitutionally adequate substitute for the traditional law enforcement warrant? What advantages does FISA provide for intelligence officials? What drawbacks are there to the FISA process from the investigators' point of view? If FISA had not been enacted, how and pursuant to what authority would investigators have learned about the alleged criminal activities of the PIRA operatives charged in *Duggan*? To what extent does the legality of FISA surveillance turn on whether the objective of the investigation is a criminal prosecution?

a. The Mechanics of FISA

1. *Information Subject to FISA Surveillance.* Review the definitions of "foreign intelligence information" and "international terrorism" quoted in *Duggan*. Can you think of some kinds of information that investigators of possible terrorism would be interested in having that could not be collected pursuant to FISA?

2. *Surveillance Methods*

a. *Electronic Surveillance.* The surveillance in *Duggan* was conducted using conventional wiretaps of telephone landlines. However, FISA defines four categories of electronic surveillance, some of which go beyond conventional telephone wiretaps and hidden microphones:

(f) "Electronic surveillance" means—

(1) the acquisition by an electronic, mechanical, or other surveillance device of the contents of any wire or radio communication sent by or intended to be received by a particular, known United States person who is in the United States, if the contents are acquired by intentionally targeting that United States person, under circumstances in which a person has a reasonable expectation of privacy and a warrant would be required for law enforcement purposes;

(2) the acquisition by an electronic, mechanical, or other surveillance device of the contents of any wire communication to or from a person in the United States, without the consent of any party thereto, if such acquisition occurs in the United States...;

(3) the intentional acquisition by an electronic, mechanical, or other surveillance device of the contents of any radio communication, under circumstances in which a person has a reasonable expectation of privacy and a warrant would be required for law enforcement purposes, and if both the sender and all intended recipients are located within the United States; or

(4) the installation or use of an electronic, mechanical, or other surveillance device in the United States for monitoring to acquire information, other than from a wire or radio communication, under circumstances in which a person has a reasonable expectation of privacy and a warrant would be required for law enforcement purposes. [50 U.S.C. §1801(f)(1)-(4)].

Does this definition cover surveillance by hidden microphones installed in a person's home or office? What about a listening device in a person's car? Is video surveillance covered? *See* United States v. Koyomejian, 946 F.2d 1450, 1451 (9th Cir. 1991), *aff'd in part, rev'd in part,* 970 F.2d 536 (9th Cir. 1992) (en banc), *cert. denied,* 506 U.S. 1005 (1992) (yes).

b. *Traditional Pen Registers and Trap and Trace Devices.* In 1998, Congress amended FISA to permit the FBI to use pen registers and trap and trace devices in foreign intelligence investigations. Intelligence Authorization Act for Fiscal Year 1999, Pub. L. No. 105-272, §601, 112 Stat. 2396, 2404 (1998) (codified at 50 U.S.C. §§1841-1846 (2000 & Supp. III 2003)).

c. *Internet and E-Mail Intercepts.* The pen register and trap and trace authorities were amended within weeks of the September 11, 2001, terrorist attacks when Congress enacted the USA PATRIOT Act, Pub. L. No. 107-56, 115 Stat. 272 (2001). First, the definitions of "pen register" and "trap and trace device" were changed to include "dialing, routing, addressing, or signaling information transmitted by an instrument or facility from which a wire or electronic communication is transmitted, provided... that such information shall not include the contents of any communication." *Id.* §216(c), 115 Stat. 290 (amending 18 U.S.C. §3127(3), (4)). What new forms of communication do these provisions reach?

In Internet or e-mail communications, trap and trace and pen register devices record the e-mail or Web page addresses of incoming and outgoing communications of the target of surveillance. Does FISA's "contents" restriction really protect the substantive content of these communications? If the FBI can record search terms used at a given Web site visited by the target, how will it sort "addressing" information from contents? Is government access to e-mail

B. Congressional Authority for Surveillance: FISA

and Web addresses any more threatening to privacy interests than access to telephone numbers? How so?

d. *Collection of Business Records.* In 1998, FISA procedures were extended to hotel, car rental, bus, airline, and other business records. Intelligence Authorization Act for Fiscal Year 1999, Pub. L. No. 105-272, §602, 112 Stat. 2396, 2404 (1998) (codified at 50 U.S.C. §§1861-1863 (2000)). In the 2001 amendments, this 1998 provision was struck down in favor of broader authorization under FISA for orders that may require the production of "any tangible things (including books, records, papers, documents, and other items)." USA PATRIOT Act §215, 115 Stat. 287. Concerning the collection of business records and other information held by third parties, see generally Chapter 20.

e. *Physical Searches.* In 1994, as part of the Intelligence Authorization Act for Fiscal Year 1995, Congress amended FISA to permit physical searches in the United States for the purpose of collecting "foreign intelligence information" of the "premises, property, information or material of a foreign power or agent of a foreign power." Pub. L. No. 103-359, §807, 108 Stat. 3423, 3442 (codified at 50 U.S.C. §§1821-1829 (2000 & Supp. III 2003)). The substantive provisions for physical searches track those for electronic surveillance. The procedures are somewhat different.

A physical search may be approved "for the period necessary to achieve its purpose, or for ninety days, whichever is less." 50 U.S.C. §1824(d)(1). But a search may continue for up to one year if it is directed against a foreign power," or up to one hundred twenty days if the target is an agent of a foreign power. *Id.* §1824(d)(1)(A) and (B). Unlike the usual procedure for a search pursuant to a warrant, FISA does not require that agents knock before entry, supply notice of the search, particularize the object of the search, or inventory what is found for the target. The difference is based on practical considerations:

> Physical searches to gather foreign intelligence information depend upon stealth. If the targets of such searches discover that the United States Government had obtained significant information about their activities, those activities would likely be altered, rendering the information useless. [William F. Brown & Americo R. Cinquegrana, *Warrantless Physical Searches for Foreign Intelligence Purposes: Executive Order 12,333 and the Fourth Amendment,* 35 Cath. L. Rev. 97, 131 (1985).]

Does this explanation provide constitutional justification either for the FISA procedure or for the wholly untethered warrantless search? *See* Daniel J. Malooly, *Physical Searches Under FISA: A Constitutional Analysis,* 35 Am. Crim. L. Rev. 411, 420-423 (1998).

3. *The Geographical Scope of FISA Surveillance.* Are there geographical limits to the communications subject to FISA electronic surveillance? See the definition of "electronic surveillance," *supra* Note 2a. Does FISA cover the surveillance of communications from Afghanistan to the United States? From the United States to Afghanistan? From one city to another within Afghanistan? If not the latter, why do you think Congress did not require FISA authorization for such communications?

4. *Who May Be Targeted?* Is the PIRA in *Duggan* a "foreign power"? Do the alleged PIRA assets fall within the definition of "agent of a foreign power"? FISA sets out several categories of potential targets, in addition to those described in *Duggan*:

§1801. Definitions. As used in this subchapter:

(a) "Foreign power" means—

(1) a foreign government or any component thereof, whether or not recognized by the United States;

(2) a faction of a foreign nation or nations, not substantially composed of United States persons;

(3) an entity that is openly acknowledged by a foreign government or governments to be directed and controlled by such foreign government or governments;

(4) a group engaged in international terrorism or activities in preparation therefor;

(5) a foreign-based political organization, not substantially composed of United States persons; or

(6) an entity that is directed and controlled by a foreign government or governments.

(b) "Agent of a foreign power" means—

(1) any person other than a United States person, who—

(A) acts in the United States as an officer or employee of a foreign power, or as a member of a foreign power as defined in subsection (a)(4) of this section;

(B) acts for or on behalf of a foreign power which engages in clandestine intelligence activities in the United States contrary to the interests of the United States, when the circumstances of such person's presence in the United States indicate that such person may engage in such activities in the United States, or when such person knowingly aids or abets any person in the conduct of such activities or knowingly conspires with any person to engage in such activities; or

(C) engages in international terrorism or activities in preparation therefore [sic]; or

(2) any person who—

(A) knowingly engages in clandestine intelligence gathering activities for or on behalf of a foreign power, which activities involve or may involve a violation of the criminal statutes of the United States;

(B) pursuant to the direction of an intelligence service or network of a foreign power, knowingly engages in any other clandestine intelligence activities for or on behalf of such foreign power, which activities involve or are about to involve a violation of the criminal statutes of the United States;

(C) knowingly engages in sabotage or international terrorism, or activities that are in preparation therefor, for or on behalf of a foreign power;

(D) knowingly enters the United States under a false or fraudulent identity for or on behalf of a foreign power or, while in the United States,

B. Congressional Authority for Surveillance: FISA

knowingly assumes a false or fraudulent identity for or on behalf of a foreign power; or

(E) knowingly aids or abets any person in the conduct of activities described in subparagraph (A), (B), or (C) or knowingly conspires with any person to engage in activities described in subparagraph (A), (B), or (C).

Can you now describe the categories of targets that may be subjected to electronic surveillance or a physical search pursuant to FISA? Can you think of examples of a "foreign power" or "agent of foreign power"? Under what circumstances could a "United States person" be treated as an agent of a foreign power? Does the availability of wiretaps for some categories of targets threaten constitutional freedom? Alternatively, do the prescribed categories of targets unreasonably limit needed flexibility for the intelligence agencies to conduct investigations?

The so-called lone-wolf provision, 50 U.S.C. §1801(b)(1)(C), was added by §6001 of the Intelligence Reform and Terrorism Prevention Act of 2004, Pub. L. No. 108-458, 118 Stat. 3638, 3742. Like several other Patriot Act changes, this lone-wolf authority was set to expire at the end of 2005. If the lone wolf need not be linked in any way to a foreign power, has the "foreign agent" requirement effectively been eliminated for foreign intelligence surveillance? Is the lone-wolf provision constitutional? Why would the lone-wolf provision have been sought by the government? Can you identify any downside risks to the expanded definition? *See* Patricia L. Bellia, *The "Lone Wolf" Amendment and the Future of Foreign Intelligence Surveillance Law,* 50 Vill. L. Rev. 425, 428-429, 455-456 (2005); Elizabeth B. Bazan, *Intelligence Reform and Terrorism Prevention Act of 2004: "Lone-Wolf" Amendment to the Foreign Intelligence Surveillance Act* (Cong. Res. Serv. RS22011), Dec. 29, 2004. After short-term extensions were approved in December 2005 and January 2006, in March 2006 Congress enacted the USA PATRIOT Improvement and Reauthorization Act of 2005, Pub. L. No. 109-177, 120 Stat. 192 (2006), extending the sunset date for the lone-wolf provision to December 31, 2009, but permitting its continued application to investigations begun or offenses or potential offenses committed before that date. *Id.* §103, 120 Stat. 195. Why has Congress again "sunsetted" this provision?

Before the FBI obtained an order under FISA authorizing electronic surveillance of Megahey's home telephone, a seller of surveillance and other electronic equipment contacted the FBI and reported that he had been sought out by some of the eventual defendants, who explained that they were members of PIRA and wanted to buy equipment for use against the British in Northern Ireland. The equipment maker became an informant and cooperated with the FBI in arranging to meet Megahey, who introduced himself as the leader of PIRA operations in the United States. Over several months, the defendants contacted the informant several times, seeking to arrange the purchase of equipment that could be used as fusing mechanisms for bombs. *Duggan,* 743 F.2d at 65-66. Absent such a fortuitous availability of an informant, how would investigators make a "foreign agency" determination before seeking FISA surveillance? In the usual situation, can the FBI make such a determination without the surveillance permitted by FISA? *See infra* pp. 622-627.

5. *The Special Court.* Congress relied on its Article III power to "ordain and establish" the lower federal courts when it created the Foreign Intelligence Surveillance Court (FISC). The FISC consists of 11 U.S. District Court judges designated by the Chief Justice for terms of up to seven years. These judges operate in secret and are empowered "to hear applications for and grant orders approving electronic surveillance anywhere within the United States under the procedures set forth" in FISA. USA PATRIOT Act §208, 115 Stat. 283 (amending 50 U.S.C. §1803(a). Similarly, FISA provides for designation by the Chief Justice of three District or Court of Appeals judges to sit as a special Court of Review to hear appeals by the government from denial of an application by one of the FISC judges. *Id.* §1803(b). The government may then appeal to the Supreme Court.

6. *What Must an Application Contain?* What are the essential components of an application for FISA surveillance? How do they differ from the elements of an application for a traditional warrant for law enforcement purposes? Why do you suppose that FISA requires a target to be identified only "if known"?

In *Duggan* the defendants argued that the FISA applications were flawed and that the eventual surveillance was thus unlawful because Duggan was not identified as a target. Why was it legally permissible for the fruits of that surveillance to be used as evidence in his criminal prosecution?

In addition to the requirements summarized in *Duggan*, the U.S. Attorney General must find that "each of the facilities or places at which the... surveillance is directed is being used, or is about to be used, by a foreign power or an agent of a foreign power," 50 U.S.C. §1804(a)(4)(B), and that the information sought "cannot reasonably be obtained by normal investigative techniques." *Id.* §1804(a)(7)(C). The application also must describe any past surveillance involving the target, the surveillance devices to be employed, the means of installation (including whether physical entry will be required), and the period of time for conducting the surveillance. *Id.* §1804(a)(8), (9), (10).

In 2000, FISA was amended to require the Attorney General personally to review and to justify in writing any decision not to approve an application for a FISA order. Pub. L. No. 106-567, §§602(a), 603(b), 114 Stat. 2831, 2851-2853, amending 50 U.S.C. §1804(e)(2)(A). What is the likely purpose of this change? What is likely to be its effect?

In 2002, the presiding judge of the FISC complained that several applications to the court contained factual inaccuracies. In re All Matters Submitted to the Foreign Intelligence Surveillance Court, 218 F. Supp. 2d 611 (FISA Ct. 2002), noted *infra* p. 538. In response, the FBI developed FISA verification procedures (the so-called Woods Procedures, named for their author, FBI lawyer Michael J. Woods) to better ensure the accuracy of the facts in each FISA application, particularly concerning what FISA calls "probable cause," and the existence and nature of any parallel criminal processes or prior or ongoing asset relationship involving the target. The procedures include FBI computer database searches and requirements to check the status of the proposed target with the Asset and Informant Unit and Criminal Division. The Woods Procedures were declassified in 2002 and are available at http://www.fas.org/irp/agency/doj/fisa/woods/pdf. Are these likely to improve the accuracy of the FISA process? How will Congress or the public know of their success or failure?

B. Congressional Authority for Surveillance: FISA

FBI Director Robert Mueller responded to Senate Judiciary Committee questions about the new procedures in August 2003. He stated that FBI field offices had, among other things, mistakenly reported that there were no criminal investigations ongoing concerning a target when in fact there were, and that the Bureau had failed to report that a proposed FISA target was also an FBI informant. *See* Written Questions of Senator Leahy to the Honorable Robert S. Mueller, III, Aug. 29, 2003, *at* http://www.fas.org/irp/agency/doj/fisa/fbi082903.pdf. Responding to a Freedom of Information Act (FOIA) request, in October 2005 the FBI released documents detailing hundreds of instances over three years in which procedural requirements of FISA may not have been met. Dan Eggen, *FBI Papers Indicate Intelligence Violations; Secret Surveillance Lacked Oversight*, Wash. Post, Oct. 24, 2005, at A1; Eric Lichtblau, *Tighter Oversight of F.B.I. Is Urged After Investigation Lapses*, N.Y. Times, Oct. 25, 2005, at A16. A March 2006 report by the Department of Justice confirmed that the FBI had violated its own procedures in conducting electronic surveillance and other intelligence activities, including wiretaps that were broader in scope and longer in duration than approved by a court. Eric Lichtblau, *Justice Dept. Report Cites Intelligence-Rule Violations by F.B.I.*, N.Y. Times, Mar. 9, 2006, at A21.

7. The FISA Order.

a. *Probable Cause.* The general standard for searches in criminal investigations is set out in Federal Rule of Criminal Procedure 41. Among other things, Rule 41 permits warrants for a search and seizure of property that constitutes evidence of or is related to the commission of a crime.

In contrast, FISA requires the FISC judge to find that

> (1) the President has authorized the Attorney General to approve applications for electronic surveillance for foreign intelligence information;
>
> (2) the application has been made by a Federal officer and approved by the Attorney General;
>
> (3) on the basis of the facts submitted by the applicant there is probable cause to believe that—
>
>> (A) the target of the electronic surveillance is a foreign power or an agent of a foreign power: Provided, That no United States person may be considered a foreign power or an agent of a foreign power solely upon the basis of activities protected by the first amendment to the Constitution of the United States; and
>>
>> (B) each of the facilities or places at which the electronic surveillance is directed is being used, or is about to be used, by a foreign power or an agent of a foreign power;
>
> (4) the proposed minimization procedures meet the definition of minimization procedures under section 1801(h) of this title; and
>
> (5) the application which has been filed contains all statements and certifications required by section 1804 of this title and, if the target is a United States person, the certification or certifications are not clearly erroneous on the basis of the statement made under section 1804(a)(7)(E) of this title and any other information furnished under section 1804(d) of this title. [50 U.S.C. §1805(a) (2000).]

Is this a more onerous or less onerous probable cause standard than the general criminal standard? For probable cause, both FISA and federal criminal laws require something like the probability of a certain fact. But unlike criminal law, under FISA orders are based "upon the probability of a possibility; the probability to believe that the foreign target of the order *may* engage in spying, or the probability to believe that the American target of the order *may* engage in criminal spying activities." Charles Doyle, *Memorandum to Senate Select Committee On Intelligence, Probable Cause, Reasonable Suspicion, and Reasonableness Standards in the Context of the Fourth Amendment and the Foreign Intelligence Surveillance Act* (Cong. Res. Serv.), Jan. 30, 2006. Under what circumstances and according to what standard may the FISC question the determinations made in the application for surveillance? *See* William C. Banks & M.E. Bowman, *Executive Authority for National Security Surveillance*, 50 Am. U. L. Rev. 1, 83 (2001); Brown & Cinquegrana, *supra* p. 521, at 129-131.

In 2000, the definition of "probable cause" was expanded to allow consideration of "past activities of the target, as well as facts and circumstances relating to current or future activities of the target." Pub. L. No. 106-567, §§602(b), 603(b), 114 Stat. 2831, 2851-2853 (2000) (codified at 50 U.S.C. §1805(b)). Why do you suppose this change was adopted?

Rule 41 also requires that the target receive a copy of the warrant and an inventory of seized property and that the investigator show "reasonable cause" for serving the warrant at night rather than in daylight. Would such requirements make sense in national security investigations? Under FISA, notice to the target of surveillance is not required until the government determines to introduce intelligence gathered through FISA surveillance in a judicial or other proceeding, 50 U.S.C. §1806(c)-(d), or if the U.S. Attorney General approves emergency surveillance and a court later denies a request for an order. *Id.* §1806(j).

b. *Relevancy to a Terrorism Investigation.* FISA "probable cause" is not required for an order for pen registers or trap and trace devices, as now broadly defined in FISA. Instead, the 2001 amendments to FISA require only a certification by the applicant

> that the information likely to be obtained is foreign intelligence information not concerning a United States person or is relevant to an ongoing investigation to protect against international terrorism or clandestine intelligence activities, provided that such investigation of a United States person is not conducted solely upon the basis of activities protected by the first amendment.... [USA PATRIOT Act §214(a)(2), 115 Stat. 286.]

How is the "relevant" standard different from FISA "probable cause"? Does the "relevant" standard satisfy constitutional requirements?

The amendment was made at the same time that language was deleted that had required an investigation to be in pursuit of "foreign intelligence information or information concerning international terrorism," substituting a requirement that the investigation serve instead "to obtain foreign intelligence information not concerning a United States person or to protect against international terrorism or clandestine intelligence activities...." *Id.* §214(a)(1). Can you see what operational effect the changed targeting language will have? Who may be targeted by pen register or trap and trace devices now?

c. *Intelligence Collection vs. Law Enforcement.* What justifies the lesser probable cause requirement in FISA? The purpose of law enforcement is to prosecute those guilty of committing a crime, while intelligence investigations have a broader scope: they seek to protect the nation from foreign enemies. Foreign intelligence investigations are often more open-ended. Consider this comparison:

> The hallmarks of a law enforcement investigation are repeated conferences with the appropriate criminal prosecutor, concerted efforts to acquire specific information needed to prove each element of every charged offense at trial, and the deliberate collection of the evidence required to sustain the prosecutorial theory of the case. In contrast, the primary use of counterintelligence information is the conduct of United States foreign and national defense policies. [Louis A. Chiarella & Michael A. Newton, *So Judge, How Do I Get That FISA Warrant?: The Policy and Procedure for Conducting Electronic Surveillance*, Army Law. 25, 27 (Oct. 1997).]

Do these differences justify the FISA probable cause standard? What are the legal implications if law enforcement and intelligence surveillance objectives blur or even merge when intelligence information produces evidence that is used in a criminal prosecution? What answer does *Duggan* suggest?

d. *Keeping Up with Technology.* Among the many changes in surveillance authorities wrought by the 2001 USA PATRIOT Act, Federal Rule of Criminal Procedure 41(a) was amended to permit a single law enforcement warrant to be used "in any district in which activities related to the terrorism may have occurred" in conducting "an investigation of domestic terrorism or international terrorism." USA PATRIOT Act §219, 115 Stat. 291. Can you see why this change was sought?

FISA was also amended in 2001 to permit the FISC to order so-called roving wiretaps. A roving wiretap permits investigators to listen in on any phone a target might use. If the judge "finds that the actions of the target of the application may have the effect of thwarting" the ability of the investigators to identify a specific communications carrier, Internet service provider, or other person needed to assist in the effective and secret execution of the surveillance, the order may authorize such assistance from multiple parties. USA PATRIOT Act §206, 115 Stat. 282 (amending 50 U.S.C. §1805(c)(2)(B)).

The FISA requirement that the FISC "specify . . . the nature and location of each of the facilities or places at which the electronic surveillance will be directed" was also amended by adding "if known" at the end. Intelligence Authorization Act for Fiscal Year 2002, Pub. L. No. 107-108, §314(a)(2)(A), 115 Stat.1394, 1402 (amending 50 U.S.C. §1805(c)(1)(B). Why was this change needed?

These provisions do not require that investigators first determine that the target is using the phone to be tapped. Does this authority permit investigators to tap a homeowner's phone if the target enters the home? Could they monitor the Internet use at the public library if the target enters the library?

In the USA PATRIOT Improvement and Reauthorization Act of 2005, Congress added a provision for orders when the "nature and location of . . . the facilities or places at which the surveillance will be directed is unknown." Within ten days after surveillance begins, investigators must provide the FISC with a description of the facility or place brought under surveillance, the reasons to believe that it is being used by the target, and any necessary minimization procedures. Pub. L. No. 109-177, §108, 120 Stat. 192, 203 (2006) (amending 50 U.S.C. §1805(c)).

8. *Minimization Requirements.* In an effort to reduce the risk that FISA surveillance could interfere with the rights of U.S. persons, the Act prescribes "minimization procedures" that must be adopted by the U.S. Attorney General and followed to the satisfaction of a FISC judge in order to "minimize the acquisition and retention, and prohibit the dissemination" of nonpublic information about U.S. persons. 50 U.S.C. §§1801(h), 1805(a)(4), 1805(b)(2). What role should lawyers play in the preparation or review of minimization procedures? How effective do you suppose the minimization procedures are?

The minimization procedures are classified, "although the internal review mechanisms include standard goals for all applications, as well as for situation-specific assessments for individual applications." Banks & Bowman, *supra* p. 526, at 89. *See also* James E. Meason, *The Foreign Intelligence Surveillance Act: Time for Reappraisal*, 24 Intl. Law. 1043, 1048-1050 (1990) (describing the review process). FISA prohibits disclosure of information obtained from FISA surveillance except as provided by the minimization procedures. 50 U.S.C. §1806(a). While even after-the-fact notice to a surveillance target may be omitted if the FISC judge so orders after an ex parte showing of good cause, *id.* §1806(j), intelligence information that is also evidence of a crime may be disseminated for law enforcement purposes. *Id.* §1801(h)(3). Minimization requirements are considered further in an opinion by the Foreign Intelligence Surveillance Court of Review, *infra* p. 533.

9. *Provisions for Emergency Surveillance.* FISA authorizes electronic surveillance without a court order in certain emergency circumstances. Such surveillance is permitted for up to a year when directed solely at communications between or among foreign powers or focused on their property, when there is "no substantial likelihood" that a communication involving a U.S. person will be acquired. 50 U.S.C.A. §1802 (West 2003 & Supp. 2005).

More important, FISA includes this provision:

[W]hen the Attorney General reasonably determines that—
    (1) an emergency situation exists with respect to the employment of electronic surveillance to obtain foreign intelligence information before an order authorizing such surveillance can with due diligence be obtained; and
    (2) the factual basis for issuance of an order under this subchapter to approve such surveillance exists;
he may authorize the emergency employment of electronic surveillance if a judge [of the FISC] is informed by the Attorney General or his designee at the time of such authorization that the decision has been made to employ emergency electronic surveillance and if an application in accordance with this subchapter is made to that judge as soon as practicable, but not more than 72 hours after the Attorney General authorizes such surveillance. If the Attorney General authorizes such emergency employment of electronic surveillance, he shall require that the minimization procedures required by this

B. Congressional Authority for Surveillance: FISA

subchapter for the issuance of a judicial order be followed. In the absence of a judicial order approving such electronic surveillance, the surveillance shall terminate when the information sought is obtained, when the application for the order is denied, or after the expiration of 72 hours from the time of authorization by the Attorney General, whichever is earliest. In the event that such application for approval is denied, or in any other case where the electronic surveillance is terminated and no order is issued approving the surveillance, no information obtained or evidence derived from such surveillance shall be received in evidence or otherwise disclosed in any trial, hearing, or other proceeding in or before any court, grand jury, department, office, agency, regulatory body, legislative committee, or other authority of the United States, a State, or political subdivision thereof, and no information concerning any United States person acquired from such surveillance shall subsequently be used or disclosed in any other manner by Federal officers or employees without the consent of such person, except with the approval of the Attorney General if the information indicates a threat of death or serious bodily harm to any person.... [50 U.S.C. §1805(f)].

Provision for physical searches in emergency circumstances is made on a basis parallel to that for electronic surveillance; the authority lasts for up to 72 hours, by which time an application for approval must be made to the FISC. 50 U.S.C. §§1822(a), 1824(e), (f). *See also* 50 U.S.C. §1843(a), (b) (pen register and trap and trace devices).

Between FISA's enactment in 1978 and September 11, 2001, Attorneys General issued 47 emergency authorizations under FISA. In the 18 months after September 11, 2001, the Attorney General authorized more than 170 emergency wiretaps and/or physical searches under FISA. Dan Eggen & Robert O'Harrow Jr., *U.S. Steps Up Secret Surveillance*, Wash. Post, Mar. 23, 2003, at A1.

Are you troubled by the absence of a prior judicial check on these executive decisions? How can responsible officials be certain that these decisions satisfy statutory and constitutional norms?

With the availability of these FISA emergency provisions, can you envision any emergency that would justify foreign intelligence surveillance in the United States without complying with FISA? This question is addressed *infra* p. 548.

The Homeland Security Act authorizes law enforcement officials to use pen registers and trap and trace devices without seeking a court order in emergencies involving "an immediate threat to a national security interest." Pub. L. No. 107-296, §225(i)(3), 116 Stat. 2135, 2158 (2002) (amending 18 U.S.C. §3125). It also allows an Internet service provider to disclose the content of electronic communications to any government agency if the ISP in "good faith" believes that the communication relates to information that involves the risk of death or serious physical injury. *Id.* §225(d)(1)(D) (amending 18 U.S.C. §2702).

10. *Judicial Review of FISA Surveillance.* The *Duggan* defendants learned that FISA surveillance had been conducted of their activities only when the government notified them that evidence from the surveillance would be introduced at their criminal trial. If no criminal prosecution is initiated following FISA surveillance, how would an individual subjected to unlawful surveillance under FISA be able to challenge the illegal conduct in court? The FISC does not publish its decisions, and its orders are sealed. Proceedings are ex parte and

are thus normally not known to the targets of surveillance. 50 U.S.C. §§1802(a)(3), 1806(f)-(g). As the *Duggan* defendants learned, even if targets of surveillance do find out, they may not be able to examine materials related to the surveillance if the Attorney General files a claim of privilege under FISA §1806(f). FISA does permit a district court to review FISC-ordered surveillance, although the review is ex parte and may be in camera if the claim of privilege is filed. *Id.*

Can you see why FISA permits the government to withhold the applications and accompanying affidavits and certifications from discovery in an adversarial proceeding? If the reviewing judge exercises his statutory discretion not to disclose portions of the documents, how will the targets of surveillance be able to appeal the judge's decision? If Megahey could not see the affidavits that formed the basis for the probable cause determination and eventual FISA surveillance, how could he make a showing of misrepresented facts or that he was not clearly identified as a target? On what basis could a court of appeals overturn the nondisclosure decision? *See* ACLU v. Barr, 952 F.2d 457 (D.C. Cir. 1991) (reviewing court may overturn a nondisclosure decision if the certifications of compliance with FISA requirements are clearly erroneous). *See also* United States v. Rahman, 189 F.3d 88 (2d Cir. 1999), *cert. denied,* 528 U.S. 982 (2000).

b. Constitutional Concerns

1. *Article III Case or Controversy?* The FISC receives applications and issues orders solely on an ex parte basis without any adversarial proceedings. Do such matters meet the Article III case or controversy requirements? United States v. Megahey, 553 F. Supp. 1180 (E.D.N.Y. 1982), held that FISA proceedings before the FISC "involve concrete questions respecting the application of the Act and are in a form such that a judge is capable of acting on them." 553 F. Supp. at 1197. *See also* United States v. Cavanaugh, 807 F.2d 787 (9th Cir. 1987); In re Kevork, 788 F.2d 566 (9th Cir. 1986); United States v. Falvey, 540 F. Supp. 1306, 1313 (E.D.N.Y. 1982); United States v. Johnson, 952 F.2d 565 (2d Cir. 1991), *cert. denied,* 506 U.S. 816 (1992).

2. *Political Question Doctrine.* The courts that have reviewed challenges to FISA surveillance orders have not been persuaded that their review itself is barred by the political question doctrine on the theory that the surveillance decision is for the President alone to make. *See, e.g.,* an omitted portion of *Duggan,* 743 F.2d at 74-75 (limited judicial role in determining whether the target of a warrant is properly subject to the prescribed procedure does not threaten political question values and does not inject courts into the making of foreign policy).

3. *Does FISA Occupy the Field?* In an effort to prevent the executive branch from bypassing the FISA procedures, in 1988 Congress enacted an amendment to Title III expressly eliminating the §2511(3) disclaimer that was central to the *Keith* decision and stating that FISA and Title III are intended to be "the exclusive means" for the conduct of electronic surveillance by the government. 18 U.S.C. §2511(2)(f) (2000 & Supp. III 2003). Is Congress empowered to so restrict the President's conduct of national security surveillance? If it is, does the

B. Congressional Authority for Surveillance: FISA

1988 provision affect the constitutionality of surveillance undertaken outside the prescriptions of FISA? The exclusivity of FISA and Title III are considered in a case study of warrantless surveillance *infra* p. 548.

After September 11, the Department of Justice maintained that "FISA... is not required by the Constitution." Letter from Daniel J. Bryant, Asst. Attorney General, to Senator Bob Graham, Chairman, S. Select Comm. on Intelligence (Aug. 6, 2002) (copy on file with authors). Do you agree?

4. *Confrontation.* Although the Supreme Court has never decided a FISA appeal, the Court did deny review in a challenge to the government's refusal to disclose materials that supported an application for FISA surveillance. In United States v. Squillicote, 221 F.3d 542 (4th Cir. 2000), *cert. denied*, 532 U.S. 971 (2001), a married couple were convicted of conspiring to commit espionage on behalf of East Germany, the Soviet Union, Russia, and South Africa. The FBI obtained 20 separate FISA orders for surveillance that lasted 550 days. Based almost exclusively on the FISA-derived evidence, the parties were sentenced to 22 and 17 years in prison, respectively. Although FISA and the Due Process Clause entitled the accused to question the basis for the government's surveillance, counsel for the accused spies were never permitted to see the underlying documentation that supported the applications for surveillance, because the government invoked §1806(f) and filed a claim of privilege. Does §1806(f) comply with the Due Process Clause? Why do you think that the Supreme Court has declined to review a conviction on this basis?

5. *Fourth Amendment.* Although the Supreme Court has not considered the constitutionality of FISA, the lower courts have uniformly followed *Duggan* in upholding the FISA procedures. *See, e.g.*, United States v. Johnson, 952 F.2d 565, 575 (1st Cir. 1991) (FISA satisfies Fourth Amendment requirements); United States v. Pelton, 835 F.2d 1067, 1075 (4th Cir. 1987) (same); United States v. Ott, 827 F.2d 473, 475-477 (9th Cir. 1987) (ex parte review procedures do not violate Fourth or Fifth Amendments); United States v. Cavanaugh, *supra*, at 790 (FISA satisfies the Fourth Amendment).

The *Duggan* court found that the FISA probable cause standard is properly relaxed for the gathering of foreign intelligence and that requiring judicial approval of a FISA request adequately protects against government abuses and safeguards individual liberties. Do you agree that FISA provides a "constitutionally adequate" substitute for a criminal warrant?

Professor Bellia argues that "FISA reflected a compromise between national security and privacy interests at a crucial moment of political awareness of abuses of executive power.... [T]he inherent indeterminacy of *Keith*'s 'reasonableness' inquiry makes it difficult for courts not to defer to Congress's assessment of the statute's constitutionality." Bellia, *supra* p. 523, at 452. How does this "FISA as compromise" view compare to your understanding of the constitutionality of FISA?

6. *First Amendment.* What protections does FISA provide against surveillance that would burden expressive freedoms? What is meant by the prohibition against finding a U.S. person to be an agent of a foreign power "solely upon the basis of activities protected by the first amendment?" 50 U.S.C. §1805(a)(3)(A).

The 1978 Senate Judiciary Committee report on FISA stated that activities protected by the First Amendment may not "form *any part* of the basis" for identifying a FISA target. *See Foreign Intelligence Surveillance Act of 1978: Hearing Before the Subcomm. on Criminal Laws and Procedures of the S. Comm. on the Judiciary*, 95th Cong. 23 (1977) (emphasis added). How does this legislative history affect the rules for identifying a potential FISA target?

Can you think of situations where a potential target's expressive activities might form the basis for a FISA application? In such instances, what other information could be available to investigators that would permit the application to go forward without being "solely" based on protected First Amendment activities?

Review the definition of "agent of a foreign power" set out *supra* p. 522. Could the FISC grant a surveillance order based on an investigators' assessment that advocacy or fundraising on the part of a potential target constitutes "activities that are in preparation" for terrorism? Problems of profiling targets on the basis of their expressive activities are considered *infra* p. 632.

C. FISA, LAW ENFORCEMENT, AND "THE WALL"

The defendants in United States v. Duggan contended that the FISA surveillance of Megahey's telephone was not lawful because the information was sought as part of a criminal investigation. The government answered that the investigators sought foreign intelligence information. Is it possible, indeed likely, that both sides are correct? Given the role allegedly played by the *Duggan* defendants in the PIRA, it is hard to muster much enthusiasm for their argument that the FISA requirements were not met. However, if, as the *Duggan* court concluded, "otherwise valid FISA surveillance is not tainted" simply because the government anticipates that its fruits may be used in a criminal prosecution, it may be difficult for judges to determine that the government has not used FISA as an end run around Rule 41. *See* United States v. Rahman, 861 F. Supp. 247 (S.D.N.Y. 1994), *aff'd*, 189 F.2d 88 (2d Cir. 1999).

Before 2002, courts followed United States v. Truong Dinh Hung, 629 F.2d 908 (4th Cir. 1980), *supra* p. 500, and allowed evidence gathered during FISA surveillance to support a criminal conviction after finding that intelligence was the "primary" purpose of the surveillance, United States v. Johnson, 952 F.2d 565 (1st Cir. 1991), *cert. denied*, 506 U.S. 816 (1992), or at least a purpose (not necessarily primary), United States v. Sarkissian, 841 F.2d 959, 964 (9th Cir. 1988). The assumption seemed to be that if the original purpose of the surveillance was intelligence gathering, there was no reason not to use the information collected in a criminal prosecution. But the assumption raises some important questions. One question is the ability of officials who authorize surveillance to verify its intelligence purpose. Another is the obligation of such officials to do so. Consider this observation:

> The net effect of FISA has been to confuse intelligence gathering with criminal law, and to enmesh intelligence in procedures which are wholly inappropriate to it. In law enforcement the purpose of surveillance is to prosecute the guilty.

C. FISA, Law Enforcement, and "The Wall"

> In intelligence, the purpose of surveillance is to gather information which should not be used for or against any individual, but to safeguard the country from foreign enemies. The proper cure for abuses of surveillance for purposes of intelligence is examination after the fact, and punishment of those who abuse their trust. But it is nonsense to think one can draw up a formula beforehand which will ensure that everyone is surveilled who should be. [S. Select Comm. on Intelligence, *Implementation of the Foreign Intelligence Surveillance Act of 1978*, S. Rep. No. 97-691, at 9-10 (1982) (supporting views of Sen. Wallop).]

In the days and weeks after the September 11, 2001, terrorist attacks, it was widely reported that an investigative failure may have permitted a twentieth hijacker to escape pre-attack detection because of a concern based on "primary purpose." Zacarias Moussaoui was arrested on immigration charges a few weeks before the attacks. Officials at a flight training school had grown suspicious when Moussaoui said that he wanted to learn to fly large jet aircraft, but that he had no interest in becoming a commercial pilot. At about the same time, a French intelligence agency warned the FBI in a classified cable that Moussaoui had "Islamic extremist beliefs." David Johnston & Philip Shenon, *F.B.I. Curbed Scrutiny of Man Now a Suspect in Attacks*, N.Y. Times, Oct. 6, 2001, at A1. When FBI field agents sought headquarters approval for a FISA search, they were turned down, apparently because there was insufficient indication that Moussaoui was an agent of a foreign power. The field agents then failed to persuade headquarters to open a criminal investigation that would have employed grand jury subpoenas and law enforcement warrants to examine Moussaoui's computer and telephone records. Apparently, this request was denied because senior FBI officials worried that an open criminal investigation might thwart a later FISA application by defeating the primary purpose requirement. FISC Chief Judge Royce Lamberth had recently questioned the candor of Justice Department officials who sought FISA orders for targets who were already the subjects of criminal investigations. A criminal case was eventually opened and a FISA order was obtained, but only after the September 11 attacks. *Id.*

The belief that a full investigation of Moussaoui before September 11 might have led to exposure of the hijackers' plot helped spur enactment of the USA PATRIOT Act and, three years later, the lone-wolf provision in the Intelligence Reform and Terrorism Prevention Act of 2004. See *supra* p. 523. The criminal prosecution of Moussaoui is considered *infra* p. 866.

Concerns about the primary purpose requirement produced an amendment to FISA in the USA PATRIOT Act, which led in turn to the following case.

In re: Sealed Case No. 02-001, 02-002
Foreign Intelligence Surveillance Court of Review, 2002
310 F.3d 717

Guy, Senior Circuit Judge, presiding; Silberman and Leavy, Senior Circuit Judges.

Per Curiam: This is the first appeal from the Foreign Intelligence Surveillance Court to the Court of Review since the passage of the Foreign Intelligence

Surveillance Act (FISA), 50 U.S.C. §§1801-1862 (West 1991 and Supp. 2002), in 1978. The appeal is brought by the United States from a FISA court surveillance order which imposed certain restrictions on the government. . . .

I.

The court's decision from which the government appeals imposed certain requirements and limitations accompanying an order authorizing electronic surveillance of an "agent of a foreign power" as defined in FISA. There is no disagreement between the government and the FISA court as to the propriety of the electronic surveillance. . . . [T]he court ordered that

> law enforcement officials shall not make recommendations to intelligence officials concerning the initiation, operation, continuation or expansion of FISA searches or surveillances. Additionally, the FBI and the Criminal Division [of the Department of Justice] shall ensure that law enforcement officials do not direct or control the use of the FISA procedures to enhance criminal prosecution, and that advice intended to preserve the option of a criminal prosecution does not inadvertently result in the Criminal Division's directing or controlling the investigation using FISA searches and surveillances toward law enforcement objectives.

To ensure the Justice Department followed these strictures the court also fashioned what the government refers to as a "chaperone requirement"; that a unit of the Justice Department, the Office of Intelligence Policy and Review (OIPR) (composed of 31 lawyers and 25 support staff), "be invited" to all meetings between the FBI and the Criminal Division involving consultations for the purpose of coordinating efforts "to investigate or protect against foreign attack or other grave hostile acts, sabotage, international terrorism, or clandestine intelligence activities by foreign powers or their agents." If representatives of OIPR are unable to attend such meetings, "OIPR shall be appri[s]ed of the substance of the meetings forthwith in writing so that the Court may be notified at the earliest opportunity."

These restrictions are not original to the order appealed. They were actually set forth in an opinion written by the former Presiding Judge of the FISA court on May 17 of this year. [*See* In re All Matters Submitted to the Foreign Intelligence Surveillance Court, 218 F. Supp. 2d 611 (2002).] . . .

We think it fair to say, however, that the May 17 opinion of the FISA court does not clearly set forth the basis for its decision. It appears to proceed from the assumption that FISA constructed a barrier between counterintelligence/intelligence officials and law enforcement officers in the Executive Branch — indeed, it uses the word "wall" popularized by certain commentators (and journalists) to describe that supposed barrier.

The "wall" emerges from the court's implicit interpretation of FISA. The court apparently believes it can approve applications for electronic surveillance only if the government's objective is *not* primarily directed toward criminal prosecution of the foreign agents for their foreign intelligence activity. But the court neither refers to any FISA language supporting that view, nor does it reference the Patriot Act amendments, which the government contends

C. FISA, Law Enforcement, and "The Wall"

specifically altered FISA to make clear that an application could be obtained even if criminal prosecution is the primary counter mechanism.

Instead the court relied for its imposition of the disputed restrictions on its statutory authority to approve "minimization procedures" designed to prevent the acquisition, retention, and dissemination within the government of material gathered in an electronic surveillance that is unnecessary to the government's need for foreign intelligence information. 50 U.S.C. §1801(h)....

II.

The government makes two main arguments. The first... is that the supposed pre-Patriot Act limitation in FISA that restricts the government's intention to use foreign intelligence information in criminal prosecutions is an illusion; it finds no support in either the language of FISA or its legislative history. The government does recognize that several courts of appeals, while upholding the use of FISA surveillances, have opined that FISA may be used only if the government's primary purpose in pursuing foreign intelligence information is not criminal prosecution, but the government argues that those decisions, which did not carefully analyze the statute, were incorrect in their statements, if not incorrect in their holdings.

Alternatively, the government contends that even if the primary purpose test was a legitimate construction of FISA prior to the passage of the Patriot Act, that Act's amendments to FISA eliminate that concept. And as a corollary, the government insists the FISA court's construction of the minimization procedures is far off the mark both because it is a misconstruction of those provisions *per se*, as well as an end run around the specific amendments in the Patriot Act designed to deal with the real issue underlying this case. The government, moreover, contends that the FISA court's restrictions, which the court described as minimization procedures, are so intrusive into the operation of the Department of Justice as to exceed the constitutional authority of Article III judges.

The government's brief, and its supplementary brief requested by this court, also set forth its view that the primary purpose test is not required by the Fourth Amendment....

THE 1978 FISA

We turn first to the statute as enacted in 1978.... [The court reviewed the definitions of "foreign intelligence information" and "agent of a foreign power" and noted that each is concerned with national security crimes.]

In light of these definitions, it is quite puzzling that the Justice Department, at some point during the 1980s, began to read the statute as limiting the Department's ability to obtain FISA orders if it intended to prosecute the targeted agents — even for foreign intelligence crimes. To be sure, section 1804, which sets forth the elements of an application for an order, required a national security official in the Executive Branch — typically the Director of the FBI — to certify that "the purpose" of the surveillance is to obtain foreign intelligence information (amended by the Patriot Act to read "a significant purpose").

But as the government now argues, the definition of foreign intelligence information includes evidence of crimes such as espionage, sabotage or terrorism. Indeed, it is virtually impossible to read the 1978 FISA to exclude from its purpose the prosecution of foreign intelligence crimes, most importantly because, as we have noted, the definition of an agent of a foreign power — if he or she is a U.S. person — is grounded on criminal conduct.

It does not seem that FISA, at least as originally enacted, even contemplated that the FISA court would inquire into the government's purpose in seeking foreign intelligence information. Section 1805, governing the standards a FISA court judge is to use in determining whether to grant a surveillance order, requires the judge to find that

> the application which has been filed contains all statements and certifications required by section 1804 of this title and, if the target is a United States person, the certification or certifications are not clearly erroneous on the basis of the statement made under section 1804(a)(7)(E) of this title and any other information furnished under section 1804(d) of this title.

50 U.S.C. §1805(a)(5). And section 1804(a)(7)(E) requires that the application include "a statement of the basis of the certification that — (i) the information sought is the type of foreign intelligence information designated; and (ii) such information cannot reasonably be obtained by normal investigative techniques." That language certainly suggests that, aside from the probable cause, identification of facilities, and minimization procedures the judge is to determine and approve (also set forth in section 1805), the only other issues are whether electronic surveillance is necessary to obtain the information and whether the information sought is actually foreign intelligence information — not the government's proposed use of that information.

Nor does the legislative history cast doubt on the obvious reading of the statutory language that foreign intelligence information includes evidence of foreign intelligence crimes....

The government argues persuasively that arresting and prosecuting terrorist agents of, or spies for, a foreign power may well be the best technique to prevent them from successfully continuing their terrorist or espionage activity. The government might wish to surveil the agent for some period of time to discover other participants in a conspiracy or to uncover a foreign power's plans, but typically at some point the government would wish to apprehend the agent and it might be that only a prosecution would provide sufficient incentives for the agent to cooperate with the government....

Congress was concerned about the government's use of FISA surveillance to obtain information not truly intertwined with the government's efforts to protect against threats from foreign powers. Accordingly, the certification of purpose under section 1804(a)(7)(B) served to

> prevent the practice of targeting, for example, a foreign power for electronic surveillance when the true purpose of the surveillance is to gather information about an individual for other than foreign intelligence purposes. It is also designed to make explicit that the sole purpose of such surveillance is to secure "foreign intelligence information," as defined, and not to obtain some other type of information.

C. FISA, Law Enforcement, and "The Wall"

[H.R. Rep. No. 95-1283 (hereinafter "H. Rep.")] at 76; *see also* [S. Rep. No. 95-701 (hereinafter "S. Rep.")] at 51. But Congress did not impose any restrictions on the government's use of the foreign intelligence information to prosecute agents of foreign powers for foreign intelligence crimes. Admittedly, the House, at least in one statement, noted that FISA surveillances "are not primarily for the purpose of gathering evidence of a crime. They are to obtain foreign intelligence information, which when it concerns United States persons must be necessary to important national concerns." H. Rep. at 36. That, however, was an observation, not a proscription. And the House as well as the Senate made clear that prosecution is one way to combat foreign intelligence crimes. *See id.*; S. Rep. at 10-11.

The origin of what the government refers to as the false dichotomy between foreign intelligence information that is evidence of foreign intelligence crimes and that which is not appears to have been a Fourth Circuit case decided in 1980. United States v. Truong Dinh Hung, 629 F.2d 908 (4th Cir. 1980). That case, however, involved an electronic surveillance carried out prior to the passage of FISA and predicated on the President's executive power. In approving the district court's exclusion of evidence obtained through a warrantless surveillance subsequent to the point in time when the government's investigation became "primarily" driven by law enforcement objectives, the court held that the Executive Branch should be excused from securing a warrant only when "the object of the search or the surveillance is a foreign power, its agents or collaborators," and "the surveillance is conducted 'primarily' for foreign intelligence reasons." *Id.* at 915....

... [S]ome time in the 1980s—the exact moment is shrouded in historical mist—the Department [of Justice] applied the *Truong* analysis to an interpretation of the FISA statute. What is clear is that in 1995 the Attorney General adopted "Procedures for Contacts Between the FBI and the Criminal Division Concerning Foreign Intelligence and Foreign Counterintelligence Investigations."

Apparently to avoid running afoul of the primary purpose test used by some courts, the 1995 Procedures limited contacts between the FBI and the Criminal Division in cases where FISA surveillance or searches were being conducted by the FBI for foreign intelligence (FI) or foreign counterintelligence (FCI) purposes. The procedures state that "the FBI and Criminal Division should ensure that advice intended to preserve the option of a criminal prosecution does not inadvertently result in either the fact or the appearance of the Criminal Division's *directing or controlling* the FI or FCI investigation toward law enforcement objectives." 1995 Procedures at 2, ¶6 (emphasis added). Although these procedures provided for significant information sharing and coordination between criminal and FI or FCI investigations, based at least in part on the "directing or controlling" language, they eventually came to be narrowly interpreted within the Department of Justice, and most particularly by OIPR, as requiring OIPR to act as a "wall" to prevent the FBI intelligence officials from communicating with the Criminal Division regarding ongoing FI or FCI investigations....

THE PATRIOT ACT AND THE FISA COURT'S DECISION

The passage of the Patriot Act altered and to some degree muddied the landscape. In October 2001, Congress amended FISA to change "the purpose" language in 1804(a)(7)(B) to "a significant purpose." It also added a provision allowing "Federal officers who conduct electronic surveillance to acquire foreign intelligence information" to "consult with Federal law enforcement officers to coordinate efforts to investigate or protect against" attack or other grave hostile acts, sabotage or international terrorism, or clandestine intelligence activities, by foreign powers or their agents. 50 U.S.C. §1806(k)(1). And such coordination "shall not preclude" the government's certification that a significant purpose of the surveillance is to obtain foreign intelligence information, or the issuance of an order authorizing the surveillance. *Id.* §1806(k)(2). Although the Patriot Act amendments to FISA expressly sanctioned consultation and coordination between intelligence and law enforcement officials, in response to the first applications filed by OIPR under those amendments, in November 2001, the FISA court for the first time adopted the 1995 Procedures, as augmented by the January 2000 and August 2001 Procedures, as "minimization procedures" to apply in all cases before the court.

The Attorney General interpreted the Patriot Act quite differently. On March 6, 2002, the Attorney General approved new "Intelligence Sharing Procedures" to implement the Act's amendments to FISA. The 2002 Procedures supersede prior procedures and were designed to permit the complete exchange of information and advice between intelligence and law enforcement officials. They eliminated the "direction and control" test and allowed the exchange of advice between the FBI, OIPR, and the Criminal Division regarding "the initiation, operation, continuation, or expansion of FISA searches or surveillance." On March 7, 2002, the government filed a motion with the FISA court, noting that the Department of Justice had adopted the 2002 Procedures and proposing to follow those procedures in all matters before the court. The government also asked the FISA court to vacate its orders adopting the prior procedures as minimization procedures in all cases and imposing special "wall" procedures in certain cases.

Unpersuaded by the Attorney General's interpretation of the Patriot Act, the court ordered that the 2002 Procedures be adopted, *with modifications*, as minimization procedures to apply in all cases. The court emphasized that the definition of minimization procedures had not been amended by the Patriot Act, and reasoned that the 2002 Procedures "cannot be used by the government to amend the Act in ways Congress has not." . . .

Undeterred, the government submitted the application at issue in this appeal on July 19, 2002, and expressly proposed using the 2002 Procedures *without modification.* In an order issued the same day, the FISA judge hearing the application granted an order for surveillance of the target but modified the 2002 Procedures consistent with the court's May 17, 2002 *en banc* order. It is the July 19, 2002 order that the government appeals. . . .

Essentially, the FISA court took portions of the Attorney General's augmented 1995 Procedures—adopted to deal with the primary purpose standard—and imposed them generically as minimization procedures. In doing so, the FISA court erred. . . .

. . . [M]inimization procedures are designed to protect, as far as reasonable, against the acquisition, retention, and dissemination of nonpublic information which is not foreign intelligence information. If the data [are] not foreign intelligence information as defined by the statute, the procedures are to ensure

C. FISA, Law Enforcement, and "The Wall"

that the government does not use the information to identify the target or third party, unless such identification is necessary to properly understand or assess the foreign intelligence information that is collected. *Id.* §1801(h)(2)....

The minimization procedures allow, however, the retention and dissemination of non-foreign intelligence information which is evidence of *ordinary crimes* for preventative or prosecutorial purposes. *See* 50 U.S.C. §1801(h)(3). Therefore, if through interceptions or searches, evidence of "a serious crime totally unrelated to intelligence matters" is incidentally acquired, the evidence is "*not*...required to be destroyed." H. Rep. at 62 (emphasis added). As we have explained, under the 1978 Act, "evidence of certain crimes like espionage would itself constitute 'foreign intelligence information,' as defined, because it is necessary to protect against clandestine intelligence activities by foreign powers or their agents." H. Rep. at 62; *see also id.* at 49. In light of these purposes of the minimization procedures, there is simply no basis for the FISA court's reliance on section 1801(h) to limit criminal prosecutors' ability to advise FBI intelligence officials on the initiation, operation, continuation, or expansion of FISA surveillances to obtain foreign intelligence information, even if such information includes evidence of a foreign intelligence crime.

The FISA court's decision and order not only misinterpreted and misapplied minimization procedures it was entitled to impose, but as the government argues persuasively, the FISA court may well have exceeded the constitutional bounds that restrict an Article III court. The FISA court asserted authority to govern the internal organization and investigative procedures of the Department of Justice which are the province of the Executive Branch (Article II) and the Congress (Article I). Subject to statutes dealing with the organization of the Justice Department, however, the Attorney General has the responsibility to determine how to deploy personnel resources....

We also think the refusal by the FISA court to consider the legal significance of the Patriot Act's crucial amendments was error. The government, in order to avoid the requirement of meeting the "primary purpose" test, specifically sought an amendment to section 1804(a)(7)(B) which had required a certification "that the purpose of the surveillance is to obtain foreign intelligence information" so as to delete the article "the" before "purpose" and replace it with "a." The government made perfectly clear to Congress why it sought the legislative change. Congress, although accepting the government's explanation for the need for the amendment, adopted language which it perceived as not giving the government quite the degree of modification it wanted. Accordingly, section 1804(a)(7)(B)'s wording became "that a *significant* purpose of the surveillance is to obtain foreign intelligence information" (emphasis added). There is simply no question, however, that Congress was keenly aware that this amendment relaxed a requirement that the government show that its primary purpose was other than criminal prosecution....

...[T]here can be no doubt as to Congress' intent in amending section 1804(a)(7)(B). Indeed, it went further to emphasize its purpose in breaking down barriers between criminal law enforcement and intelligence (or counterintelligence) gathering by adding section 1806(k):

> (k) Consultation with Federal law enforcement officer
> (1) Federal officers who conduct electronic surveillance to acquire foreign intelligence information under this title may consult with Federal

law enforcement officers to coordinate efforts to investigate or protect against

(A) actual or potential attack or other grave hostile acts of a foreign power or an agent of a foreign power; or

(B) sabotage or international terrorism by a foreign power or an agent of a foreign power; or

(C) clandestine intelligence activities by an intelligence service or network of a foreign power or by an agent of a foreign power.

(2) Coordination authorized under paragraph (1) shall not preclude the certification required by section [1804](a)(7)(B) of this title or the entry of an order under section [1805] of this title....

... [W]hen Congress explicitly authorizes consultation and coordination between different offices in the government, without even suggesting a limitation on who is to direct and control, it necessarily implies that either could be taking the lead....

Accordingly, the Patriot Act amendments clearly disapprove the primary purpose test. And as a matter of straightforward logic, if a FISA application can be granted even if "foreign intelligence" is only a significant — not a primary — purpose, another purpose can be primary. One other legitimate purpose that could exist is to prosecute a target for a foreign intelligence crime....

... [I]t is our task to do our best to read the statute to honor congressional intent. The better reading, it seems to us, excludes from the purpose of gaining foreign intelligence information a sole objective of criminal prosecution. We therefore reject the government's argument to the contrary. Yet this may not make much practical difference. Because, as the government points out, when it commences an electronic surveillance of a foreign agent, typically it will not have decided whether to prosecute the agent (whatever may be the subjective intent of the investigators or lawyers who initiate an investigation). So long as the government entertains a realistic option of dealing with the agent other than through criminal prosecution, it satisfies the significant purpose test.

The important point is — and here we agree with the government — the Patriot Act amendment, by using the word "significant," eliminated any justification for the FISA court to balance the relative weight the government places on criminal prosecution as compared to other counterintelligence responses. If the certification of the application's purpose articulates a broader objective than criminal prosecution — such as stopping an ongoing conspiracy — and includes other potential non-prosecutorial responses, the government meets the statutory test. Of course, if the court concluded that the government's sole objective was merely to gain evidence of past criminal conduct — even foreign intelligence crimes — to punish the agent rather than halt ongoing espionage or terrorist activity, the application should be denied.

... It can be argued, however, that by providing that an application is to be granted if the government has only a "significant purpose" of gaining foreign intelligence information, the Patriot Act allows the government to have a primary objective of prosecuting an agent for a non-foreign intelligence crime. Yet we think that would be an anomalous reading of the amendment. For we see not the slightest indication that Congress meant to give that power to the Executive Branch. Accordingly, the manifestation of such a purpose, it seems to us, would continue to disqualify an application. That is not to deny

C. FISA, Law Enforcement, and "The Wall"

that ordinary crimes might be inextricably intertwined with foreign intelligence crimes. For example, if a group of international terrorists were to engage in bank robberies in order to finance the manufacture of a bomb, evidence of the bank robbery should be treated just as evidence of the terrorist act itself. But the FISA process cannot be used as a device to investigate wholly unrelated ordinary crimes.

One final point; we think the government's purpose as set forth in a section 1804(a)(7)(B) certification is to be judged by the national security official's articulation and not by a FISA court inquiry into the origins of an investigation nor an examination of the personnel involved. It is up to the Director of the FBI, who typically certifies, to determine the government's national security purpose, as approved by the Attorney General or Deputy Attorney General. This is not a standard whose application the FISA court legitimately reviews by seeking to inquire into which Justice Department officials were instigators of an investigation....

III.

Having determined that FISA, as amended, does not oblige the government to demonstrate to the FISA court that its primary purpose in conducting electronic surveillance is not criminal prosecution, we are obliged to consider whether the statute as amended is consistent with the Fourth Amendment.... The FISA court indicated that its disapproval of the Attorney General's 2002 Procedures was based on the need to safeguard the "privacy of Americans in these highly intrusive surveillances and searches," which implies the invocation of the Fourth Amendment. The government, recognizing the Fourth Amendment's shadow effect on the FISA court's opinion, has affirmatively argued that FISA is constitutional....

The FISA court expressed concern that unless FISA were "construed" in the fashion that it did, the government could use a FISA order as an improper substitute for an ordinary criminal warrant under Title III. That concern seems to suggest that the FISA court thought Title III procedures are constitutionally mandated if the government has a prosecutorial objective regarding an agent of a foreign power. But in United States v. United States District Court (*Keith*), 407 U.S. 297, 322 (1972) — in which the Supreme Court explicitly declined to consider foreign intelligence surveillance — the Court indicated that, even with respect to domestic national security intelligence gathering for prosecutorial purposes where a warrant was mandated, Title III procedures were not constitutionally required: "[W]e do not hold that the same type of standards and procedures prescribed by Title III are necessarily applicable to this case. We recognize that domestic security surveillance may involve different policy and practical considerations from the surveillance of 'ordinary crime.'" Nevertheless, in asking whether FISA procedures can be regarded as reasonable under the Fourth Amendment, we think it is instructive to compare those procedures and requirements with their Title III counterparts. Obviously, the closer those FISA procedures are to Title III procedures, the lesser are our constitutional concerns.

COMPARISON OF FISA PROCEDURES WITH TITLE III

... [W]hile Title III contains some protections that are not in FISA, in many significant respects the two statutes are equivalent, and in some, FISA contains additional protections. Still, to the extent the two statutes diverge in constitutionally relevant areas — in particular, in their probable cause and particularity showings — a FISA order may not be a "warrant" contemplated by the Fourth Amendment.... We do not decide the issue but note that to the extent a FISA order comes close to meeting Title III, that certainly bears on its reasonableness under the Fourth Amendment.

DID TRUONG ARTICULATE THE APPROPRIATE CONSTITUTIONAL STANDARD?

Ultimately, the question becomes whether FISA, as amended by the Patriot Act, is a reasonable response based on a balance of the legitimate need of the government for foreign intelligence information to protect against national security threats with the protected rights of citizens....

It will be recalled that the case that set forth the primary purpose test *as constitutionally required* was *Truong*. The Fourth Circuit thought that *Keith*'s balancing standard implied the adoption of the primary purpose test. We reiterate that *Truong* dealt with a pre-FISA surveillance based on the President's constitutional responsibility to conduct the foreign affairs of the United States. 629 F.2d at 914. Although *Truong* suggested the line it drew was a constitutional minimum that would apply to a FISA surveillance, *see id.* at 914 n.4, it had no occasion to consider the application of the statute carefully. The *Truong* court, as did all the other courts to have decided the issue, held that the President did have inherent authority to conduct warrantless searches to obtain foreign intelligence information. It was incumbent upon the court, therefore, to determine the boundaries of that constitutional authority in the case before it. We take for granted that the President does have that authority and, assuming that is so, FISA could not encroach on the President's constitutional power. The question before us is the reverse, does FISA amplify the President's power by providing a mechanism that at least approaches a classic warrant and which therefore supports the government's contention that FISA searches are constitutionally reasonable.

The district court in the *Truong* case had excluded evidence obtained from electronic surveillance after the government's investigation — the court found — had converted from one conducted for foreign intelligence reasons to one conducted primarily as a criminal investigation.... The court of appeals endorsed that approach, stating:

> We think that the district court adopted the proper test, because once surveillance becomes primarily a criminal investigation, the courts are entirely competent to make the usual probable cause determination, and because, importantly, individual privacy interests come to the fore *and government foreign policy concerns recede* when the government is primarily attempting to form the basis of a criminal prosecution.

Id. at 915 (emphasis added).

C. FISA, Law Enforcement, and "The Wall"

That analysis, in our view, rested on a false premise and the line the court sought to draw was inherently unstable, unrealistic, and confusing. The false premise was the assertion that once the government moves to criminal prosecution, its "foreign policy concerns" recede. As we have discussed in the first part of the opinion, that is simply not true as it relates to counterintelligence. In that field the government's primary purpose is to halt the espionage or terrorism efforts, and criminal prosecutions can be, and usually are, interrelated with other techniques used to frustrate a foreign power's efforts....

Recent testimony before the Joint Intelligence Committee amply demonstrates that the *Truong* line is a very difficult one to administer. Indeed, it was suggested that the FISA court requirements based on *Truong* may well have contributed, whether correctly understood or not, to the FBI missing opportunities to anticipate the September 11, 2001 attacks. That is not to say that we should be prepared to jettison Fourth Amendment requirements in the interest of national security. Rather, assuming *arguendo* that FISA orders are not Fourth Amendment warrants, the question becomes, are the searches constitutionally reasonable. And in judging reasonableness, the instability of the *Truong* line is a relevant consideration....

SUPREME COURT'S SPECIAL NEEDS CASES

The distinction between ordinary criminal prosecutions and extraordinary situations underlies the Supreme Court's approval of entirely warrantless and even suspicionless searches that are designed to serve the government's "special needs, beyond the normal need for law enforcement." Vernonia School Dist. 47J v. Acton, 515 U.S. 646, 653 (1995) (quoting Griffin v. Wisconsin, 483 U.S. 868, 873 (1987) (internal quotation marks omitted)) (random drug-testing of student athletes). Apprehending drunk drivers and securing the border constitute such unique interests beyond ordinary, general law enforcement. *Id.* at 654 (citing Michigan Dep't of State Police v. Sitz, 496 U.S. 444 (1990), and United States v. Martinez-Fuerte, 428 U.S. 543 (1976)).

A recent case, City of Indianapolis v. Edmond, 531 U.S. 32 (2000), is relied on by both the government and amici. In that case, the Court held that a highway check point designed to catch drug dealers did not fit within its special needs exception because the government's "primary purpose" was merely "to uncover evidence of ordinary criminal wrongdoing." *Id.* at 41-42. The Court rejected the government's argument that the "severe and intractable nature of the drug problem" was sufficient justification for such a dragnet seizure lacking any individualized suspicion. *Id.* at 42. *Amici* particularly rely on the Court's statement that "the gravity of the threat alone cannot be dispositive of questions concerning what means law enforcement officers may employ to pursue a given purpose." *Id.*

But by "purpose" the Court makes clear it was referring not to a subjective intent, which is not relevant in ordinary Fourth Amendment probable cause analysis, but rather to a programmatic purpose. The Court distinguished the prior check point cases *Martinez-Fuerte* (involving checkpoints less than 100 miles from the Mexican border) and *Sitz* (checkpoints to detect intoxicated motorists) on the ground that the former involved the government's "longstanding concern for the protection of the integrity of the border," *id.* at 38 (quoting United States v. Montoya de Hernandez, 473 U.S. 531, 538 (1985)), and the latter was "aimed at reducing the immediate hazard posed by the presence of drunk drivers on the highways." *Id.* at 39. The Court emphasized that it was decidedly not drawing a distinction between suspicionless seizures with a "non-law-enforcement primary purpose" and those designed for law enforcement. *Id.* at 44 n.1. Rather, the Court distinguished general crime control programs and those that have another particular purpose, such as protection of citizens against special hazards or protection of our borders. The Court specifically acknowledged that an appropriately tailored road block could be used "to thwart an imminent terrorist attack." *Id.* at 44. The nature of the "emergency," which is simply another word for threat, takes the matter out of the realm of ordinary crime control.

CONCLUSION

FISA's general programmatic purpose, to protect the nation against terrorists and espionage threats directed by foreign powers, has from its outset been distinguishable from "ordinary crime control." After the events of September 11, 2001, though, it is hard to imagine greater emergencies facing Americans than those experienced on that date.

We acknowledge, however, that the constitutional question presented by this case—whether Congress's disapproval of the primary purpose test is consistent with the Fourth Amendment—has no definitive jurisprudential answer. The Supreme Court's special needs cases involve random stops (seizures) not electronic searches. In one sense, they can be thought of as a greater encroachment into personal privacy because they are not based on any particular suspicion. On the other hand, wiretapping is a good deal more intrusive than an automobile stop accompanied by questioning.

... Our case may well involve the most serious threat our country faces. Even without taking into account the President's inherent constitutional authority to conduct warrantless foreign intelligence surveillance, we think the procedures and government showings required under FISA, if they do not meet the minimum Fourth Amendment warrant standards, certainly come close. We, therefore, believe firmly, applying the balancing test drawn from *Keith*, that FISA as amended is constitutional because the surveillances it authorizes are reasonable.

Accordingly, we reverse the FISA court's orders in this case to the extent they imposed conditions on the grant of the government's applications, vacate the FISA court's Rule 11, and remand with instructions to grant the applications as submitted and proceed henceforth in accordance with this opinion.

NOTES AND QUESTIONS

1. *Defending the FISC (and the Public?) on Appeal.* No target of a FISC surveillance order ever learns about the issuance of the order, unless the information collected is later used in a criminal prosecution, as in *Duggan,* or turns up in

C. FISA, Law Enforcement, and "The Wall"

a FOIA or Privacy Act request. See Chapter 34. As a practical matter, therefore, there was no one who had a legally protected interest to process an appeal of the *FISCR* decision to the Supreme Court—or at least no one who knew she had such an interest. Nonetheless, public interest groups led by the ACLU filed a petition for leave to intervene and a petition for certiorari in the Supreme Court. Can you outline their likely positions, both on their right to intervene and on the merits? On March 24, 2003, the Supreme Court dismissed the petition. American Civil Liberties Union v. United States, 538 U.S. 920 (2003) (mem.). *See* Linda Greenhouse, *Opponents Lose Challenge to Government's Broader Use of Wiretaps to Fight Terrorism*, N.Y. Times, Mar. 25, 2003, at A12.

Should Congress amend FISA to provide for public and FISC representation on appeals to the FISCR?

2. *The Holding.* What is the holding of the *FISCR* decision? Is the holding based on FISA, on the Constitution, or both? Can you reconcile the holding in the *FISCR* decision with *Keith*? With *Truong*?

3. *Purpose vs. Use.* Are the FISA limits addressed in the principal case concerned with the objective of the surveillance or with the nature and subsequent uses of the information to be obtained? The *FISCR* decision emphasized the importance of preserving the foreign intelligence objectives of FISA. In view of those objectives, on what basis did the FISCR object to forbidding the Criminal Division from directing or controlling the use of FISA procedures? Is the alleged flaw in the FISC order based on the PATRIOT Act amendments to FISA, or would the infirmity have been present even if FISA had not been amended?

Is the FBI now permitted to conduct a secret search or wiretap for the primary purpose of investigating a crime even though there is no probable cause to suspect the commission of a crime? Although terrorism itself is criminal, terrorists may also engage in common criminal activities—credit card fraud, for example. If the primary purpose standard is still followed in criminal investigations, the existence of an ongoing credit card investigation might make it difficult to obtain a FISA order for surveillance of the same targets, even if there were some indication of plans for a terrorist act. If the PATRIOT Act amendment makes it easier for the FBI to manage parallel criminal and intelligence investigations, is the gain in effectiveness worth the risk of misuse of the process? Who will ensure that the FISA process is not employed as an end-run around Title III? Does the amendment "have the effect of changing the statute to more closely track the constitution"? *See* Letter from Daniel J. Bryant, *supra* p. 531 (arguing that it does). If so, is it because the constitutional "track" changed after September 11? *See id.* (arguing that it did).

Can you now describe the significance of the PATRIOT Act amendment to the "purpose" requirement? Did the information-sharing additions to FISA in the PATRIOT Act contribute to the result? If so, how? Should Congress revisit the "purpose" standard in FISA? If so, should Congress codify the "primary purpose" requirement, or should it more clearly abandon any required foreign intelligence objectives in shaping requests to the FISC?

Absent intervention by Congress, do you think the *FISCR* decision represents the last word on the issues it addresses? Can you see how these same issues might be addressed by other courts in the future?

4. *The Minimization Requirements.* Why did the FISC err in relying on the minimization requirements of FISA to justify its order? Do the minimization procedures imply a "wall" between law enforcement and intelligence investigators?

5. *The "Special Needs" Precedents.* Are you persuaded that the Supreme Court's "special needs" cases are based on considerations analogous to the Justice Department procedures at issue in the principal case?

6. *The Aftermath.* Approximately six months after the *FISCR* decision, Justice Department officials reported to the House Judiciary Committee that the procedures approved by the FISCR have

> allowed the Department of Justice to investigate cases in a more orderly, efficient, and knowledgeable way, and ha[ve] permitted all involved personnel, both law enforcement and intelligence, to discuss openly legal, factual, and tactical issues arising during the course of investigations.... The Department has developed counterterrorism tools and methods that plainly would not have been possible under the previous standards. [Letter from Jamie E. Brown, Acting Asst. Attorney General, Off. of Legis. Affairs, U.S. Dept. of Justice, to F. James Sensenbrenner Jr., Chair, H. Comm. on the Judiciary, May 13, 2003, at 15-16.]

The Department also reported that approximately 4,500 open intelligence files were shared with criminal prosecutors since October 2002 to allow the law enforcement personnel to determine whether criminal investigations of any of those intelligence targets should be initiated. *Id.*

In 2003, the FBI issued a classified field directive to further dismantle the wall between law enforcement and intelligence investigations. The directive spells out the Model Counterterrorism Investigations Strategy (MCIS) and new requirements that criminal and intelligence investigators physically work as part of the same teams investigating terrorism. All terrorism investigations are now treated as intelligence investigations, are formally run by the counterterrorism division at FBI headquarters, and will be able to use FISA procedures and methods. Dan Eggen, *FBI Applies New Rules to Surveillance*, Wash. Post, Dec. 13, 2003, at A1. FBI officials stated that the new system will deemphasize criminal prosecution in favor of longer-term intelligence surveillance. When a criminal case is brought, however, prosecutors will be able to use the FISA-derived evidence at trial. *Id.* Does the MCIS satisfy the requirements outlined in the *FISCR* decision? Is the new strategy constitutional?

D. FISA TRENDS

The FISC has been active. More than 12,000 applications for surveillance or searches have been approved by the FISC since 1979. Brief annual FISA reports from the Attorney General, including the volume of applications approved for the year, are posted at http://www.usdoj.gov/oipr/readingroom/2005fisa-ltr.pdf. During calendar year 2005, 2,074 applications were made, and 2,072

D. FISA Trends

were approved by the FISC. Two applications were withdrawn by the government prior to a FISC ruling. The FISC did not deny any application submitted by the Government in 2005. By comparison, an average of about 1,100 requests for electronic surveillance are submitted by law enforcement officials under 18 U.S.C. §2518 annually. What do the numbers suggest?

Section 6002 of the Intelligence Reform and Terrorism Prevention Act of 2004, Pub. L. No. 108-458, 118 Stat. 3742, expanded the reporting under FISA to require semiannual reports to the intelligence and judiciary committees of the House and Senate that include the aggregate number of persons targeted and breakdowns for electronic surveillance, physical searches, pen registers, access to records, and lone-wolf orders. The new reports must also indicate the number of times the Attorney General has approved the use in criminal proceedings of information derived from FISA surveillance, provide summaries of significant legal interpretations of FISA by DOJ before the FISC or FISCR, and include copies of all decisions or opinions of the FISC or FISCR that include "significant construction or interpretation" of FISA. *Id.* During 2005, the government made 155 applications for business records, including requests for pen registers. Two proposed orders were modified substantively by the FISC, but none were denied. In the same period, the government requested 9,254 national security letters (NSLs) involving 3,501 U.S. persons. No mention was made of lone-wolf orders, and none of the other information mentioned above was included. Why do you suppose the record is incomplete?

Notwithstanding the ever-increasing use of FISA and the FISC, foreign intelligence surveillance of suspected terrorists under the terms and conditions of FISA has not been a panacea. In part, this is because

> experience demonstrates three harsh realities: first, it is often difficult to isolate U.S. persons from one or more foreign surveillance targets in a place or through electronic monitoring; second, it is often impossible to determine the relationship of a potential terrorist to a foreign power early in an investigation; and third... U.S. persons are as capable as any other of wreaking catastrophic havoc. [Banks & Bowman, *supra* p. 526, at 95.]

The lone-wolf provision, *supra* p. 523, is supposed to address the second of these concerns.

Enactment of the Intelligence Reform and Terrorism Prevention Act of 2004, *supra*, affected FISA in a number of ways. In addition to the lone-wolf and reporting provisions noted above, the new Director of National Intelligence (DNI) was given responsibility "to establish requirements and priorities for foreign intelligence information to be collected" under FISA and assist the Attorney General to ensure that FISA intelligence "may be used efficiently and effectively for foreign intelligence purposes, except that the Director shall have no authority to direct, manage, or undertake" surveillance or search operations under FISA "unless otherwise authorized by statute or Executive order." *Id.* §102(A)(f)(6), 118 Stat. 3650. Another section of the Intelligence Reform Act provides that "[n]othing in this act shall be construed as affecting the role of the Department of Justice or the Attorney General with respect to applications under" FISA. *Id.* §102(A)(f)(8), 118 Stat. 3650. The authorities and duties of the DNI generally are considered in Chapter 14. The precise role of this new player in the FISA processes is not yet clear. Neither is it clear what legal issues might be raised by an executive order authorizing the DNI to direct or undertake FISA surveillance.

CASE STUDY: THE TERRORIST SURVEILLANCE PROGRAM

On December 16, 2005, the New York Times reported that, according to government officials, "President Bush secretly authorized the National Security Agency to eavesdrop on Americans and others inside the United States to search for evidence of terrorist activity without the court-approved warrants ordinarily required for domestic spying." James Risen & Eric Lichtblau, *Bush Lets U.S. Spy on Callers Without Courts*, N.Y. Times, Dec. 16, 2005, at A1. Pursuant to a secret executive order signed by the President in 2002, the NSA has monitored the telephone and e-mail communications of thousands of persons inside the United States where one end of the communication is outside the United States, without warrants, to learn more about possible terrorist plots. *Id.* Later called the Terrorist Surveillance Program by the Administration, the NSA surveillance has created a major controversy, drawing out prominent critics and proponents alike, provoking hearings in Congress, prompting lawsuits by civil liberties organizations and by defendants in criminal cases who have challenged their previous pleas or convictions, and generating countless op-ed pieces, blog debates, and commentary.

The Bush administration has vigorously defended the Terrorist Surveillance Program. The Justice Department's Office of Legislative Affairs immediately prepared the following letter for congressional leaders summarizing its legal rationale for the NSA surveillance:

Letter from William E. Moschella, Asst. Attorney General, to The Honorable Pat Roberts, Chairman, Senate Select Committee on Intelligence, et al.

Dec. 22, 2005
available at http://www.fas.org/irp/agency/doj/fisa/doj122205.pdf

As you know, in response to unauthorized disclosures in the media, the President has described certain activities of the National Security Agency ("NSA") that he has authorized since shortly after September 11, 2001. As described by the President, the NSA intercepts certain international communications into and out of the United States of people linked to al Qaeda or an affiliated terrorist organization. The purpose of these intercepts is to establish an early warning system to detect and prevent another catastrophic terrorist attack on the United States. The President has made clear that he will use his constitutional and statutory authorities to protect the American people from further terrorist attacks, and the NSA activities the President described are part of that effort. Leaders of the Congress were briefed on these activities more than a dozen times.

The purpose of this letter is to provide an additional brief summary of the legal authority supporting the NSA activities described by the President.

D. FISA Trends

As an initial matter, I emphasize a few points. The President stated that these activities are "crucial to our national security." The President further explained that "the unauthorized disclosure of this effort damages our national security and puts our citizens at risk. Revealing classified information is illegal, alerts our enemies, and endangers our country." These critical national security activities remain classified. All United States laws and policies governing the protection and nondisclosure of national security information, including the information relating to the activities described by the President, remain in full force and effect. The unauthorized disclosure of classified information violates federal criminal law. The Government may provide further classified briefings to the Congress on these activities in an appropriate manner. Any such briefings will be conducted in a manner that will not endanger national security.

Under Article II of the Constitution, including in his capacity as Commander in Chief, the President has the responsibility to protect the Nation from further attacks, and the Constitution gives him all necessary authority to fulfill that duty. *See, e.g., Prize Cases,* 67 U.S. (2 Black) 635, 668 (1863) (stressing that if the Nation is invaded, "the President is not only authorized but bound to resist by force . . . without waiting for any special legislative authority"); *Campbell v. Clinton,* 203 F.3d 19, 27 (D.C. Cir. 2000) (Silberman, J., concurring) ("[T]he *Prize Cases* . . . stand for the proposition that the President has independent authority to repel aggressive acts by third parties even without specific congressional authorization, and courts may not review the level of force selected."); *id.* at 40 (Tatel, J., concurring). The Congress recognized this constitutional authority in the preamble to the Authorization for the Use of Military Force ("AUMF") of September 18, 2001, 115 Stat. 224 (2001) ("[T]he President has authority under the Constitution to take action to deter and prevent acts of international terrorism against the United States."), and in the War Powers Resolution, *see* 50 U.S.C. §1541(c) ("The constitutional powers of the President as Commander in Chief to introduce United States Armed Forces into hostilities [] . . . [extend to] a national emergency created by attack upon the United States, its territories or possessions, or its armed forces.").

This constitutional authority includes the authority to order warrantless foreign intelligence surveillance within the United States, as all federal appellate courts, including at least four circuits, to have addressed the issue have concluded. *See, e.g., In re Sealed Case,* 310 F.3d 717, 742 (FISA Ct. of Rev. 2002) ("[A]ll the other courts to have decided the issue [have] held that the President did have inherent authority to conduct warrantless searches to obtain foreign intelligence information. . . . We take for granted that the President does have that authority. . . ."). The Supreme Court has said that warrants are generally required in the context of purely *domestic* threats, but it expressly distinguished *foreign* threats. *See United States v. United States District Court,* 407 U.S. 297, 308 (1972). As Justice Byron White recognized almost 40 years ago, Presidents have long exercised the authority to conduct warrantless surveillance for national security purposes, and a warrant is unnecessary "if the President of the United States or his chief legal officer, the Attorney General, has considered the requirements of national security and authorized electronic surveillance as reasonable." *Katz v. United States,* 389 U.S. 347, 363-364 (1967) (White, J., concurring).

The President's constitutional authority to direct the NSA to conduct the activities he described is supplemented by statutory authority under the AUMF. The AUMF authorizes the President "to use all necessary and appropriate force against those nations, organizations, or persons he determines planned, authorized, committed, or aided the terrorist attacks of September 11, 2001,... in order to prevent any future acts of international terrorism against the United States." §2(a). The AUMF clearly contemplates action within the United States, *see also id.* pmbl. (the attacks of September 11 "render it both necessary and appropriate that the United States exercise its rights to self-defense and to protect United States citizens both at home and abroad"). The AUMF cannot be read as limited to authorizing the use of force against Afghanistan, as some have argued. Indeed, those who directly "committed" the attacks of September 11 resided in the United States for months before those attacks. The reality of the September 11 plot demonstrates that the authorization of force covers activities both on foreign soil and in America.

In *Hamdi v. Rumsfeld*, 542 U.S. 507 (2004), the Supreme Court addressed the scope of the AUMF. At least five Justices concluded that the AUMF authorized the President to detain a U.S. citizen in the United States because "detention to prevent a combatant's return to the battlefield is a fundamental incident of waging war" and is therefore included in the "necessary and appropriate force" authorized by the Congress. *Id.* at 518-519 (plurality opinion of O'Connor, J.); *see id.* 587 (Thomas, J., dissenting). These five Justices concluded that the AUMF "clearly and unmistakably authorize[s]" the "fundamental incident[s] of waging war." *Id.* at 518-19 (plurality opinion); *see id.* at 587 (Thomas, J., dissenting).

Communications intelligence targeted at the enemy is a fundamental incident of the use of military force. Indeed, throughout history, signals intelligence has formed a critical part of waging war. In the Civil War, each side tapped the telegraph lines of the other. In the World Wars, the United States intercepted telegrams into and out of the country. The AUMF cannot be read to exclude this long-recognized and essential authority to conduct communications intelligence targeted at the enemy. We cannot fight a blind war. Because communications intelligence activities constitute, to use the language of *Hamdi*, a fundamental incident of waging war, the AUMF *clearly and unmistakably authorizes* such activities directed against the communications of our enemy. Accordingly, the President's "authority is at its maximum." *Youngstown Sheet & Tube Co. v. Sawyer*, 343 U.S. 579, 635 (1952) (Jackson, J., concurring); *see Dames & Moore v. Regan*, 453 U.S. 654, 668 (1981); *cf. Youngstown*, 343 U.S. at 585 (noting the absence of a statute "from which [the asserted authority] c[ould] be fairly implied").

The President's authorization of targeted electronic surveillance by the NSA is also consistent with the Foreign Intelligence Surveillance Act ("FISA"). Section 2511(2)(f) of title 18 provides, as relevant here, that the procedures of FISA and two chapters of title 18 "shall be the exclusive means by which electronic surveillance... may be conducted." Section 109 of FISA, in turn, makes it unlawful to conduct electronic surveillance, "except as authorized by statute." 50 U.S.C. §1809(a)(1). Importantly, section 109's exception for electronic surveillance "authorized by statute" is broad, especially considered in the context of surrounding provisions. *See* 18 U.S.C. §2511(1) ("Except as

D. FISA Trends

otherwise specifically provided *in this chapter* any person who — (a) intentionally intercepts...any wire, oral or electronic communication [ ]...shall be punished....") (emphasis added); *id.* §2511(2)(e) (providing a defense to liability to individuals "conduct[ing] electronic surveillance,...as authorized by *that Act [FISA]*") (emphasis added).

By expressly and broadly excepting from its prohibition electronic surveillance undertaken "as authorized by statute," section 109 of FISA permits an exception to the "procedures" of FISA referred to in U.S.C. §2511(2)(f) where authorized by another statute, even if the other authorizing statute does not specifically amend section 2511(2)(f). The AUMF satisfies section 109's requirement for statutory authorization of electronic surveillance, just as a majority of the Court in *Hamdi* concluded that it satisfies the requirement in 18 U.S.C. §4001(a) that no U.S. citizen be detained by the United States "except pursuant to an Act of Congress." *See Hamdi*, 542 U.S. at 519 (explaining that "it is of no moment that the AUMF does not use specific language of detention"); *see id.* at 587 (Thomas, J., dissenting).

Some might suggest that FISA could be read to require that a subsequent statutory authorization must come in the form of an amendment to FISA itself. But under established principles of statutory construction, the AUMF and FISA must be construed in harmony to avoid any potential conflict between FISA and the President's Article II authority as Commander in Chief. *See, e.g., Zadvydas v. Davis*, 533 U.S. 678, 689 (2001); *INS v. St. Cyr*, 533 U.S. 289, 300 (2001). Accordingly, any ambiguity as to whether the AUMF is a statute that satisfies the requirements of FISA and allows electronic surveillance in the conflict with al Qaeda without complying with FISA procedures must be resolved in favor of an interpretation that is consistent with the President's long-recognized authority.

The NSA activities described by the President are also consistent with the Fourth Amendment and the protection of civil liberties. The Fourth Amendment's "central requirement is one of reasonableness." *Illinois vs. McArthur*, 531 U.S. 326, 330 (2001) (internal quotation marks omitted). For searches conducted in the course of ordinary criminal law enforcement, reasonableness generally requires securing a warrant. *See Bd. of Educ. v. Earls*, 536 U.S. 822, 828 (2002). Outside the ordinary criminal law enforcement context, however, the Supreme Court has, at times, dispensed with the warrant, instead adjudging the reasonableness of a search under the totality of circumstances. *See United States v. Knights*, 534 U.S. 112, 118 (2001). In particular, the Supreme Court has long recognized that "special needs, beyond the normal need for law enforcement," can justify departure from the usual warrant requirement. *Vernonia School Dist. 47J v. Acton*, 515 U.S. 646, 653 (1995); *see also City of Indianapolis v. Edmond*, 531 U.S. 32, 41-42 (2000) (striking down checkpoint where "primary purpose was to detect evidence of ordinary criminal wrongdoing").

Foreign intelligence collection, especially in the midst of an armed conflict in which the adversary has already launched catastrophic attacks within the United States, fits squarely within the "special needs" exception to the warrant requirement. Foreign intelligence collection undertaken to prevent further devastating attacks on our Nation serves the highest purpose through means other than traditional law enforcement. *See In re Sealed Case*, 310 F.3d at 745; *United States v. Duggan*, 743 F.2d 59, 72 (2d Cir. 1984) (recognizing that the Fourth Amendment implications of foreign intelligence surveillance are far different from ordinary wiretapping, because they are not principally used for criminal prosecution).

Intercepting communications into and out of the United States of persons linked to al Qaeda in order to detect and prevent a catastrophic attack is clearly *reasonable.* Reasonableness is generally determined by "balancing the nature of the intrusion on the individual's privacy against the promotion of legitimate governmental interests." *Earls,* 536 U.S. at 829. There is undeniably an important and legitimate privacy interest at stake with respect to the activities described by the President. That must be balanced, however, against the Government's compelling interest in the security of the Nation, *see, e.g., Haig v. Agee,* 453 U.S. 280, 307 (1981) ("It is obvious and unarguable that no governmental interest is more compelling than the security of the Nation.") (citation and quotation marks omitted). The fact that the NSA activities are reviewed and reauthorized approximately every 45 days to ensure that they continue to be necessary and appropriate further demonstrates the reasonableness of these activities.

As explained above, the President determined that it was necessary following September 11 to create an early warning system. FISA could not have provided the speed and agility required for the early warning detection system. In addition, any legislative change, other than the AUMF, that the President might have sought specifically to create such an early warning system would have been public and would have tipped off our enemies concerning our intelligence limitations and capabilities. Nevertheless, I want to stress that the United States makes full use of FISA to address the terrorist threat, and FISA has proven to be a very important tool, especially in longer-term investigations. In addition, the United States is constantly assessing all available legal options, taking full advantage of any developments in the law.

We hope this information is helpful.

Sincerely,
William E. Moschella
Assistant Attorney General

NOTES AND QUESTIONS

1. *Nature of the Terrorist Surveillance Program.* What is the NSA actually doing, as best you can tell from the DOJ letter? Are there any internal procedural controls? If so, what are they? Do they adequately safeguard any privacy rights that may be implicated?

2. *Applicability of FISA.* Although FISA's scope is summarized in *Duggan* and the Notes and Questions following that case, in considering the applicability of FISA to this program you will want to look in particular at the language of §1801(f), quoted *supra* p. 520. Consider also the complete text of 18 U.S.C. §2511(2)(e) and (f), governing ordinary criminal warrants:

> (e) Notwithstanding any other provision of this title or section 705 or 706 of the Communications Act of 1934, it shall not be unlawful for an officer, employee, or agent of the United States in the normal course of his official duty to conduct electronic surveillance, as defined in section 101 of the Foreign Intelligence Surveillance Act of 1978, as authorized by that Act.

D. FISA Trends

(f) Nothing contained in this chapter or chapter 121 or 206 of this title, or section 705 of the Communications Act of 1934, shall be deemed to affect the acquisition by the United States Government of foreign intelligence information from international or foreign communications, or foreign intelligence activities conducted in accordance with otherwise applicable Federal law involving a foreign electronic communications system, utilizing a means other than electronic surveillance as defined in section 101 [50 U.S.C. section 1801] of the Foreign Intelligence Surveillance Act of 1978, and procedures in this chapter or chapter 121 and the Foreign Intelligence Surveillance Act of 1978 shall be the exclusive means by which electronic surveillance, as defined in section 101 of such Act, and the interception of domestic wire, oral, and electronic communications may be conducted.

Finally, consider §1809(a)(1) of FISA (making unauthorized electronic surveillance a criminal offense):

A person is guilty of an offense if he intentionally—
(1) engages in electronic surveillance under color of law except as authorized by statute; or
(2) discloses or uses information obtained under color of law by electronic surveillance, knowing or having reason to know that the information was obtained through electronic surveillance not authorized by statute. [50 U.S.C. §1809(a)(1).]

Are you persuaded by the DOJ analysis that FISA is inapplicable to the Terrorist Surveillance Program?

3. *Why Not FISA?* The government has an enviable track record in the Foreign Intelligence Surveillance Court. See *supra* p. 533. Why did it not seek a FISA order(s) for the Terrorist Surveillance Program? In a January 2006 address, Attorney General Alberto R. Gonzales defended the decision not to rely on FISA:

We have to remember that we're talking about a wartime foreign intelligence program. It is an "early warning system" with only one purpose: To detect and prevent the next attack on the United States from foreign agents hiding in our midst. It is imperative for national security that we can detect RELIABLY, IMMEDIATELY, and WITHOUT DELAY whenever communications associated with al Qaeda enter or leave the United States. That may be the only way to alert us to the presence of an al Qaeda agent in our country and to the existence of an unfolding plot.

Consistent with the wartime intelligence nature of this program, the optimal way to achieve the necessary speed and agility is to leave the decisions about particular intercepts to the judgment of professional intelligence officers, based on the best available intelligence information. They can make that call quickly. If, however, those same intelligence officers had to navigate through the FISA process for each of these intercepts, that would necessarily introduce a significant factor of DELAY, and there would be critical holes in our early warning system.

Some have pointed to the provision in FISA that allows for so-called "emergency authorizations" of surveillance for 72 hours without a court order. There's a serious misconception about these emergency authorizations. People should know that we do not approve emergency authorizations without knowing that we will receive court approval within 72 hours. FISA requires the Attorney General to determine IN ADVANCE that a FISA application for that particular intercept will be fully supported and will be approved by the court before an emergency authorization may be granted. That review process can take precious time. Thus, to initiate surveillance under a FISA emergency authorization, it is not enough to rely on the best judgment of our intelligence officers alone. Those intelligence officers would have to get the sign-off of lawyers at the NSA that all provisions of FISA have been satisfied, then lawyers in the Department of Justice would have to be similarly satisfied, and finally as Attorney General, I would have to be satisfied that the search meets the requirements of FISA. And we would have to be prepared to follow up with a full FISA application within the 72 hours. [*Prepared Remarks for Attorney General Alberto R. Gonzales,* Georgetown University Law Center, Jan. 24, 2006, available at http://www.usdoj.gov/ag/speeches/2006/ag_speech_0601241.html.]

In evaluating the Attorney General's statement, consider FISA's emergency surveillance provisions, quoted *supra* p. 528. Do you believe he was justified in bypassing the FISA procedures?

4. *The AUMF.* The September 18, 2001, Authorization for the Use of Military Force (AUMF) is set forth *supra* p. 215. Did it authorize the Terrorist Surveillance Program? (The Supreme Court's construction of the AUMF appears in the *Hamdi* case, *infra* p. 721.) Is it relevant to your answer that in the USA Patriot Act, enacted in October 2001, Congress amended FISA by, *inter alia,* extending the period of emergency surveillance from 24 hours to 72 hours, or that it left in place the following FISA provision?

Notwithstanding any other law, the President, through the Attorney General, may authorize electronic surveillance without a court order under this subchapter to acquire foreign intelligence information for a period not to exceed fifteen calendar days following a declaration of war by the Congress. [50 U.S.C. §1811 (2000).]

5. *Inherent Constitutional Authority?* In light of all the foregoing, does President Bush have inherent constitutional authority to order the Terrorist Surveillance Program? Consider the President's exchange with a reporter at a December 19, 2005, press conference:

Q... [W]hy did you skip the basic safeguards of asking courts for permission for the intercepts?
THE PRESIDENT: First of all, I — right after September the 11th, I knew we were fighting a different kind of war. And so I asked people in my administration to analyze how best for me and our government to do the job people expect us to do, which is to detect and prevent a possible attack. That's what the American people want. We looked at the possible scenarios. And the people responsible for helping us protect and defend came forth with the current program, because it enables us to move faster and quicker. And that's important. We've got to be fast on our feet, quick to detect and prevent.
   We use FISA still — you're referring to the FISA court in your question — of course, we use FISAs. But FISA is for long-term monitoring. What is needed in order to protect the American people is the ability to move quickly to detect.
   Now, having suggested this idea, I then, obviously, went to the question, is it legal to do so? I am — I swore to uphold the laws. Do I have the legal

D. FISA Trends

authority to do this? And the answer is, absolutely. As I mentioned in my remarks, the legal authority is derived from the Constitution, as well as the authorization of force by the United States Congress.

Are you persuaded by the President's statement? Consider first the case law regarding national security surveillance. What unilateral authority does it recognize in the President? Then consider the statutes. If you think there is a clash between the President's claim of authority and the statutes — placing the program in Justice Jackson's third category — how should we resolve it?

6. *The Fourth Amendment.* If the President has inherent constitutional authority for the Terrorist Surveillance Program, notwithstanding any statute, does he also escape the strictures of the Fourth Amendment? If not, is the program constitutional?

7. *Amending FISA.* Some have argued that FISA should be amended "to provide for programmatic approvals of cutting-edge technologies — including automated monitoring of suspected terrorist communications." K.A. Taipale & James Jay Carafano, *Fixing Surveillance,* Wash. Times, Jan. 25, 2006, at A15. Taipale goes farther and asserts that FISA *must* be amended to permit orders for "electronic surveillance" to capture the data and voice communications inside modern networks:

> Thirty years ago ... it made sense to speak exclusively about the interception of targeted communication — one in which there were usually two known ends and a dedicated ("circuit-based") communication channel that could be "tapped." In modern networks, however, data and increasingly voice communications are broken into discrete packets that travel along independent routes between point of origin and destination where these fragments are then reassembled into the original whole message. Not only is there no longer a dedicated circuit, but individual packets from the same communication may take completely different paths to their destination. To intercept these kinds of communications, filters ("packet-sniffers") and search strategies are deployed at various communication nodes to scan and filter all passing traffic with the hope of finding and extracting those packets of interest and reassembling them into a coherent message.... Were FISA to be applied strictly according to its terms prior to any "electronic surveillance" of foreign communication flows passing through the US or where there is a substantial likelihood of intercepting US persons, then no automated monitoring of any kind could occur. [K.A. Taipale, *Whispering Wires and Warrantless Wiretaps: Data Mining and Foreign Intelligence Surveillance,* 8 N.Y.U. Rev. L. & Security (forthcoming 2006).]

How would you respond to this claim? Are the FISA definitions of "electronic surveillance," limitations regarding "U.S. persons," and inapplicability to international communications relics that simply fail to reflect changing technologies and realities? Taipale also maintains that the retroactive warrant procedures in FISA could not provide a remedy for these problems because the communications intercepted would not meet the probable cause predicate in FISA. *Id.* How do you suppose the recommended pre-approved monitoring programs would operate? What legal issues would remain unresolved and what new legal issues would arise if such a change were enacted?

A number of bills were introduced in Congress in 2006 to address issues raised by the Terrorist Surveillance Program. One, sponsored by Senator Robert Byrd, would establish a Surveillance Activities Commission to further investigate and monitor the Terrorist Surveillance Program. S. 2362, 109th Cong. (2006). Another, sponsored by Senator Specter, would revise FISA procedures to accommodate the NSA activities. National Security Surveillance Act of 2006, S. 2453, 109th Cong. (2006). Senator Schumer introduced a bill to provide judicial remedies for those aggrieved by warrantless surveillance, S. 2468, 109th Cong. (2006); and Senator DeWine introduced the Terrorist Surveillance Act of 2006 to authorize the President to order warrantless surveillance for periods up to 45 days upon the filing of presidential findings and meeting other requirements. S. 2455, 109th Cong. (2006). Would any of these measures address whatever practical or constitutional concerns you have about the program?

8. *References.* In addition to the DOJ letter excerpted here, an extensive collection of documents that include administration arguments for the legality of the Terrorist Surveillance Program, arguments against, legal filings, and congressional letters and testimony may be found at Center for Democracy & Technology, *NSA Domestic Snooping—Resources* (n.d.), *at* http://www.cdt.org/security/nsa/briefingbook.php.

9. *Challenging the Legality of the Program in Court.* Several lawsuits have been filed challenging the legality of the program. In August 2006, Judge Anna Diggs Taylor ruled that the Terrorist Surveillance Program violates FISA, the separation of powers, and the First and Fourth Amendments. American Civil Liberties Union v. National Security Agency, 438 F. Supp. 2d 754 (E.D. Mich. 2006). Judge Taylor found that the burden on plaintiffs' expressive freedom to engage in conversations with persons abroad established standing to sue. On the merits, the court found that FISA effectively decided any separation of powers question, that no inherent executive power could overcome congressional regulation of surveillance, and that the AUMF could not overcome the constitutional limits on surveillance in the First and Fourth Amendments. The court dismissed the plaintiffs' claims regarding data mining, however, finding that a test of the merits of those claims could expose state secrets (see *infra* p. 1037). Can you predict how Judge Taylor's decision will fare on appeal? Other cases pending at this writing include Center for Constl. Studies v. Bush, No. 06-CV-00313 (S.D.N.Y. 2006); Hepting v. AT&T Corp., 439 F. Supp. 2d 974 (N.D. Cal. 2006) (ruling that the suit was not categorically barred by the state secrets privilege); Pascazi v. Verizon Comm., 06-Civ. 1221 (S.D.N.Y. 2006); and Terkel v. AT&T Corp., 441 F. Supp. 2d 899 (N.D. Ill. 2006) (dismissing on the ground that, because the state secrets privilege barred discovery, plaintiffs could not establish standing to sue).

Third-Party Records and Data Mining 20

The conventional wisdom after 9/11 was that U.S. national security agencies failed to "connect the dots" before the attacks. But some experts have noted that while there "certainly was a lack of dot-connecting before September 11," the more critical failure was that "[t]here were too few useful dots." Robert Bryant et al., *America Needs More Spies*, The Economist, July 12, 2003, at 30. In this chapter, we explore both parts of this insight.

We first consider how so-called national security letters(NSLs) and Foreign Intelligence Surveillance Act (FISA) §215 orders are used to collect dots in quantity—transactional data—from third-party record holders like banks, telephone companies, Internet service providers, and travel agencies. Later in the chapter we look at how dots are connected by computer "data mining" to perform link analysis or pattern recognition.

A. FINDING THE DOTS—THIRD-PARTY RECORDS

1. Expectations of Privacy Regarding Transactional Data

As we saw in the last chapter, in Smith v. Maryland, 442 U.S. 735 (1979), *supra* p. 507, the Supreme Court reasoned that people have no "legitimate expectation of privacy" in the telephone numbers they dial—merely "numerical information" they "voluntarily convey[] . . . to the phone company . . . in the normal course of business." *Id.* at 735, 744. The Court therefore rejected a Fourth Amendment challenge to evidence obtained by police use of a pen register on Smith's phone (recording the numbers of outgoing calls) and laid the legal foundation for both pen registers and trap and trace devices as police investigatory tools.

But *Smith* laid the foundation for more than just pen registers. If people have no legitimate expectation of privacy in information they voluntarily convey to the phone company in the normal course of business, then they also arguably have no such expectation in the transactional information they convey to hundreds of other third parties in the ordinary course of business. Congress therefore authorized the Foreign Intelligence Surveillance Court (FISC) to issue §215 orders for transactional records pursuant to FISA and enacted several statutes authorizing the FBI to obtain transactional data by issuing NSLs without prior court order to third-party record holders. In calendar year 2005, the government reported that it had obtained 155 §215 orders and issued 9,254 NSLs related to U.S. persons (excluding NSLs for subscriber information), Letter from William E. Moschella (Asst. Attorney General, Dept. of Justice) to J. Dennis Hastert (Speaker, House of Representatives), Apr. 28, 2006, while the media claim that the FBI now issues more than 30,000 NSLs a year. Barton Gellman, *The FBI's Secret Scrutiny*, Wash. Post, Nov. 6, 2005, at A1.

We begin here by exploring further the scope and implications of *Smith*. Then, after reviewing a redacted national security letter, we consider one of two 2004 court decisions declaring parts of the NSL statutes unconstitutional. In response to these decisions, Congress amended the NSL statutes when it passed the USA Patriot Improvement and Reauthorization Act of 2005, Pub. L. No. 109-177, 120 Stat. 192 (2006) (hereinafter "Patriot Improvement Act"). *See generally* Brian T. Yeh, *USA PATRIOT Improvement and Reauthorization Act of 2005: A Legal Analysis* (Cong. Res. Serv. RL33332), Mar. 24, 2006. Relevant parts of those statutes are described in the notes and questions at the end of the chapter.

Smith v. Maryland
United States Supreme Court, 1979
442 U.S. 735

[The opinion is set forth *supra* p. 507.]

NOTES AND QUESTIONS

1. *Some of the Dots: Transactional Data.* " 'Transactional' information broadly describes information that documents financial or communications transactions without necessarily revealing the substance of those transactions." Michael J. Woods, *Counterintelligence and Access to Transactional Records: A Practical History of USA PATRIOT Act Section 215*, 1 J. Natl. Security L. & Poly. 37, 41 (2005). Such information includes telephone billing records that list numbers dialed, an Internet service provider's records showing a customer's Internet use, records of banking transactions and money transfers, credit card records, and travel records. It has proven invaluable in counterterrorist investigations. Terrorists can try to encrypt or otherwise disguise the substance of their communications, but "[i]t is far more difficult for them to cover their transactional footsteps." *Id.* at 41-42. Counterterrorist analysts can use transactional information to perform "link analysis" to tie suspects together and thus help identify terror cells. *See* McCormick Tribune Foundation, *Counterterrorism Technology and Privacy*

A. Finding the Dots—Third-Party Records

(Cantigny Conf. Rpt.) 53 (Patrick J. McMahon Rep., 2005). An example is the retrospective link analysis of the 9/11 hijackers. Woods, *supra*, at 42. It can also be used for pattern recognition and data matching to identify suspects. See *infra* pp. 581-584.

2. *The Expectation of Privacy in Transactional Records.* In United States v. Miller, 425 U.S. 435 (1976), the Court held that police seizure of bank records under a defective subpoena duces tecum was lawful because the depositor had no protected Fourth Amendment privacy interest in checks, deposit slips, and other financial information that she voluntarily conveyed to banks. "The depositor takes the risk, in revealing his affairs to another, that the information will be conveyed by that person to the Government." *Id.* at 443. The Court used the same logic three years later in Smith v. Maryland, *supra*.

Is this logic sound? Do you, subjectively, have any expectation of privacy when you convey data to a bank or commercial vendor, dial a telephone number, or transmit an e-mail message? Of course, you do not expect to keep the information private from the bank, vendor, phone company, or Internet service provider. The entities with which you deal directly need the data to complete the transaction that you initiate. But do you also expect those entities to share the information with others? In fact, don't some vendors promise you just the opposite, and sometimes even provide a box to check or button to indicate whether you want such data to be shared?

Under Katz v. United States, 389 U.S. 347 (1967), a subjective expectation of privacy for Fourth Amendment purposes is legitimate—protectible—only if it is also "one that society is prepared to recognize as 'reasonable.'" *Id.* at 361. If your expectation is that transactional information will be disclosed by the bank, vendor, or phone company only as needed to complete a transaction, would society recognize it as reasonable? In the late 1970s, the Court thought not. Have the dramatic changes in patterns of commercial activity and communications in the decades since then also made such an expectation reasonable? *See* Christopher Slobogin & Joseph E. Schumacher, *Reasonable Expectations of Privacy and Autonomy in Fourth Amendment Cases: An Empirical Look at "Understandings Recognized and Permitted by Society,"* 42 Duke L.J. 727 (1993) (reporting a survey suggesting that the public finds government perusal of bank records highly invasive). Was the reasonableness of such an expectation altered by the events of September 11, 2001?

2. Techniques and Authorities for Collection of Transactional Data

Building on the privacy theory of *Smith*, Congress enacted several statutes that authorized the FBI to use NSLs—issued without any prior judicial order—to obtain transactional records from third-party record holders. Here is a redacted example of such a letter, followed by a judicial decision in a case testing its legitimacy.

ALL INFORMATION CONTAINED
HEREIN IS UNCLASSIFIED EXCEPT
WHERE SHOWN OTHERWISE

U.S. Department of Justice

Federal Bureau of Investigation

In Reply, Please Refer to
File No

[Drafting] Field Division
[Street Address]
[City, State, Zip]

[Month Date, Year]

[Mr /Mrs.] [COMPANY POINT OF CONTACT]
[TITLE]
[COMPANY]
[STREET ADDRESS]
[CITY, STATE No Zip Code]

Dear [Mr /Mrs] [LAST NAME]:

Under the authority of Executive Order 12333, dated December 4, 1981, and pursuant to Title 18, United States Code (U S.C), Section 2709 (as amended, October 26, 2001), you are hereby directed to provide the Federal Bureau of Investigation

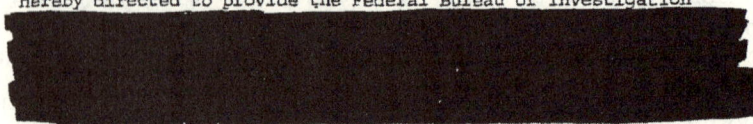

b2-2
b7E-1

In accordance with Title 18, U.S.C., Section 2709(b), I certify that the information sought is relevant to an authorized investigation to protect against international terrorism or clandestine intelligence activities, and that such an investigation of a United States person is not conducted solely on the basis of activities protected by the first amendment of the Constitution of the United States

You are further advised that Title 18, U.S C , Section 2709(c), prohibits any officer, employee or agent of yours from disclosing to any person that the FBI has sought or obtained access to information or records under these provisions.

b2-2
b7E-1

CLASSIFIED DECISIONS FINALIZED BY
DEPARTMENT REVIEW COMMITTEE (DRC)
DATE: 07-01-2004
CA# 03-2522

CLASSIFIED BY 65179 dmk/bce/amw 6/5/2004
REASON: 1, (c)
DECLASSIFY ON: X 6/5/2029
Patriot Act II-828

SECRET

DECLASSIFIED BY 65179 dmk/bce/amw
ON 8/3/2004

A. Finding the Dots — Third-Party Records

SECRET

[Mr /Mrs] [COMPANY POINT OF CONTACT]

Your cooperation in this matter is greatly appreciated

Sincerely,

[ADIC/SAC Name]
Assistant Director/Special
Agent in Charge

CLASSIFIED DECISIONS FINALIZED BY
DEPARTMENT REVIEW COMMITTEE (DRC)
DATE: 01-01-2004

CA# 03-2522

ALL INFORMATION CONTAINED
HEREIN IS UNCLASSIFIED EXCEPT
WHERE SHOWN OTHERWISE

CLASSIFIED BY 65/79 dmh/bc4/smw 6/30/2004
REASON: 1.4 (c)
DECLASSIFY ON: 6/30/2029

Patriot Act II-829

SECRET
DECLASSIFIED BY 65/29 dmh/bc4/smw
ON 8/3/2004

Doe v. Ashcroft (*Doe I*)
United States District Court, Southern District of New York, 2004
334 F. Supp. 2d 471
vacated and remanded sub nom. Doe v. Gonzales,
449 F.3d 415 (2d Cir. 2006)

MARRERO, J. . . .

I. INTRODUCTION

Plaintiffs in this case challenge the constitutionality of 18 U.S.C. §2709 ("§2709").[1] That statute authorizes the Federal Bureau of Investigation ("FBI") to compel communications firms, such as internet service providers ("ISPs") or telephone companies, to produce certain customer records whenever the FBI certifies that those records are "relevant to an authorized investigation to protect against international terrorism or clandestine intelligence activities." [*Id.*] The FBI's demands under §2709 are issued in the form of national security letters ("NSLs"), which constitute a unique form of administrative subpoena cloaked in secrecy and pertaining to national security issues. The statute bars all NSL recipients from ever disclosing that the FBI has issued an NSL.

The lead plaintiff, called "John Doe" ("Doe") for purposes of this litigation, is described in the complaint as an internet access firm that received an NSL. . . .

II. BACKGROUND . . .

A. DOE'S RECEIPT OF AN NSL

After receiving a call from an FBI agent informing him that he would be served with an NSL, Doe received a document, printed on FBI letterhead, which stated that, "pursuant to Title 18, United States Code (U.S.C.), Section 2709" Doe was "directed" to provide certain information to the Government. As required by the terms of §2709, in the NSL the FBI "certif[ied] that the information sought [was] relevant to an authorized investigation to protect against international terrorism or clandestine intelligence activities." Doe was "further advised" that §2709(c) prohibited him, or his officers, agents, or employees, "from disclosing to *any person* that the FBI has sought or obtained access to information or records under these provisions." Doe was "requested to provide records responsive to [the] request *personally*" to a designated individual, and to not transmit the records by mail or even mention the NSL in *any* telephone conversation. . . .

. . . Doe has not complied with the NSL request, and has instead engaged counsel to bring the present lawsuit.

[1. This section was amended by the Patriot Improvement Act in 2006, *supra* p. 558, as explained in the following Notes and Questions.]

A. Finding the Dots—Third-Party Records

B. §2709 IN GENERAL

As stated above, §2709 authorizes the FBI to issue NSLs to compel communications firms to produce certain customer records whenever the FBI certifies that those records are relevant to an authorized international terrorism or counterintelligence investigation, and the statute also categorically bars NSL recipients from disclosing the inquiry. In relevant part, it states:

> (a) Duty to provide.—A wire or electronic communication service provider shall comply with a request for subscriber information and toll billing records information, or electronic communication transactional records in its custody or possession made by the Director of the Federal Bureau of Investigation under subsection (b) of this section.
>
> (b) Required certification.—The Director of the Federal Bureau of Investigation, or his designee in a position not lower than Deputy Assistant Director at Bureau headquarters or a Special Agent in Charge in a Bureau field office designated by the Director, may—(1) request the name, address, length of service, and local and long distance toll billing records of a person or entity if the Director (or his designee) certifies in writing to the wire or electronic communication service provider to which the request is made that the name, address, length of service, and toll billing records sought are relevant to an authorized investigation to protect against international terrorism or clandestine intelligence activities, provided that such an investigation of a United States person is not conducted solely on the basis of activities protected by the first amendment to the Constitution of the United States....
>
> (c) Prohibition of certain disclosure.—No wire or electronic communication service provider, or officer, employee, or agent thereof, shall disclose to any person that the Federal Bureau of Investigation has sought or obtained access to information or records under this section....

Section 2709 is one of only a handful of statutes authorizing the Government to issue NSLs. The other NSL statutes authorize the Government to compel disclosure of certain financial and credit records which it certifies are relevant to international terrorism or counter-intelligence investigations, and to compel disclosure of certain records of current or former government employees who have (or have had) access to classified information.[17]

C. LEGISLATIVE HISTORY

Section 2709 was enacted as part of Title II of the Electronic Communications Privacy Act of 1986 ("ECPA"),[19] which sought to "protect privacy interests" in "stored wire and electronic communications" while also "protecting the Government's legitimate law enforcement needs."[20] ...

... As first enacted, §2709 required electronic communication service providers to produce "subscriber information," "toll billing records information," or "electronic communication transactional records," upon the FBI's internal

---

17. *See* 12 U.S.C. §3414 (financial records); 15 U.S.C. §§1681u, 1681v (credit records); 50 U.S.C. §436 (government employee records).
19. Pub. L. No. 99-508, §201, 100 Stat. 1848, 1867 (1986).
20. S. Rep. No. 99-541, at 3 (1986), *reprinted in* 1986 U.S.C.C.A.N. 3555, 3557.

certification that (1) the information was "relevant to an authorized foreign counterintelligence investigation" and that (2) there were "specific and articulable facts giving reason to believe that the person or entity to whom the information sought pertains [was] a foreign power or an agent of a foreign power."...

The ... most recent major revision to §2709 occurred in October 2001,[2] as part of the USA PATRIOT Act of 2001 ("Patriot Act").[39] In short, the Patriot Act removed the previous requirement that §2709 inquiries have a nexus to a foreign power, replacing that prerequisite with a broad standard of relevance to investigations of terrorism or clandestine intelligence activities. In hearings before the House Judiciary Committee on September 24, 2001, the Administration submitted the following explanation for the proposed change:

> NSL authority requires both a showing of relevance and a showing of links to an "agent of a foreign power." In this respect, [it is] substantially more demanding than the analogous criminal authorities, which require only a certification of relevance. Because the NSLs require documentation of the facts supporting the "agent of a foreign power" predicate and because they require the signature of a high-ranking official at FBI headquarters, they often take months to be issued. This is in stark contrast to criminal subpoenas, which can be used to obtain the same information, and are issued rapidly at the local level. In many cases, counterintelligence and counterterrorism investigations suffer substantial delays while waiting for NSLs to be prepared, returned from headquarters, and served. The section would streamline the process of obtaining NSL authority....

The House Judiciary Committee agreed that "[s]uch delays are unacceptable" and stated in its October 11, 2001, report that the Patriot Act would "harmonize[ ]" §2709 "with existing criminal law where an Assistant United States Attorney may issue a grand jury subpoena for all such records in a criminal case."

D. NSLS AND OTHER INFORMATION-GATHERING AUTHORITY

It is instructive to place the Government's NSL authority in the context of other means by which the Government gathers information of the type covered by §2709 because Congress (in passing and amending the NSL statutes) and the parties here (in contesting §2709's constitutionality) have drawn analogies to those other authorities as grounds for or against its validity. The relationship of §2709 to other related statutes supplies a backdrop for assessing congressional intent and judging the validity of the law on its face and as applied. In addition, an analysis of these analogous information-gathering methods indicates that NSLs such as the ones authorized by §2709 provide fewer procedural protections to the recipient than any other information-gathering technique the Government employs to procure information similar to that which it obtains pursuant to §2709.

[2. The statute was amended again in 2006 by the Patriot Improvement Act, *supra* p. 558, as explained in the following Notes and Questions.]

39. *See* Pub. L. No. 107-56, §505, 115 Stat. 272, 365 (2001)....

A. Finding the Dots — Third-Party Records

1. Administrative Subpoenas

The most important set of statutes relevant to this case are those authorizing federal agencies to issue administrative subpoenas for the purpose of executing the particular agency's function. Ordinary administrative subpoenas, which are far more common than NSLs, may be issued by most federal agencies, as authorized by the hundreds of applicable statutes in federal law. For example, the Internal Revenue Service (IRS) may issue subpoenas to investigate possible violations of the tax code, and the Securities Exchange Commission (SEC) may issue subpoenas to investigate possible violations of the securities laws....

There is a wide body of law which pertains to administrative subpoenas generally. According to the Government's central theory in this case, those standing rules would presumably also apply to NSLs, even if not so explicitly stated in the text of the statute. Where an agency seeks a court order to enforce a subpoena against a resisting subpoena recipient, courts will enforce the subpoena as long as: (1) the agency's investigation is being conducted pursuant to a legitimate purpose, (2) the inquiry is relevant to that purpose, (3) the information is not already within the agency's possession, and (4) the proper procedures have been followed. The Second Circuit has described these standards as "minimal." Even if an administrative subpoena meets these initial criteria to be enforceable, its recipient may nevertheless affirmatively challenge the subpoena on other grounds, such as an allegation that it was issued with an improper purpose or that the information sought is privileged.

Unlike the NSL statutes, most administrative subpoena laws either contain no provision requiring secrecy, or allow for only limited secrecy in special cases. For example, some administrative subpoena statutes permit the investigating agency to apply for a court order to temporarily bar disclosure of the inquiry, generally during specific renewable increments or for an appropriate period of time fixed by the court, where such disclosure could jeopardize the investigation....

2. Subpoena Authority in the Criminal Context

In its role as a party to a federal criminal proceeding (including a grand jury proceeding), the Government has broad authority to issue a subpoena to obtain witness testimony or "*any* books, papers, documents, data, or other objects the subpoena designates."[52] Although such subpoenas "are issued in the name of the district court over the signature of the clerk, they are issued pro forma and in blank to anyone requesting them," and the "court exercises no prior control whatsoever upon their use."[53]

The court becomes involved in the subpoena process only if the subpoenaed party moves to quash the request as "unreasonable or oppressive,"[54] or if the Government seeks to compel compliance with the subpoena. The reasonableness of a subpoena depends on the context. For example, to survive a motion to quash, a subpoena issued in connection with a criminal trial "must make a reasonably specific request for information that would be both relevant and admissible at trial."[55] By contrast, a grand jury subpoena is

---

52. Fed. R. Crim. P. 17(a), (c)(1) (emphasis added).
53. In re Grand Jury Proceedings, 486 F.2d 85, 90 (3d Cir. 1973).
54. Fed. R. Crim. P. 17(c)(2).
55. United States v. R. Enters., Inc., 498 U.S. 292, 299 (1991) (*citing* United States v. Nixon, 418 U.S. 683, 700 (1974)).

generally enforced as long as there is a "reasonable possibility that the category of materials the Government seeks will produce information relevant to the general subject of the grand jury's investigation."[56] Considering the grand jury's broad investigatory power and minimal court supervision, it is accurate to observe, as the Second Circuit did long ago, that "[b]asically the grand jury is a law enforcement agency."[57]

While materials presented in a criminal trial setting are generally public, the federal rules impose stringent secrecy requirements on certain grand jury participants, including the attorneys, court reporters, and grand jurors.[59] ...

In certain contexts, the Government may issue subpoenas related to criminal investigations even without initiating a formal criminal proceeding. For example, the United States Attorney General is authorized to issue administrative subpoenas, without convening a grand jury, to investigate federal narcotics crimes, racketeering crimes, health care related crimes, and crimes involving the exploitation of children. In each of these instances, the administrative process is governed by the general rules described above, providing safeguards of judicial review.

3. Background Rules Governing Disclosure of Stored Electronic Communications

Title II of the ECPA [also called the Stored Communications Act], in which §2709 was enacted, sets forth an intricate framework by which electronic communications providers, such as ISPs and phone companies, may be compelled to disclose stored electronic information to the Government. The framework described below operates independently of the rules governing NSLs issued pursuant to §2709, but may aid with interpretation of §2709.

The Government may obtain basic subscriber information[69] merely by issuing an authorized administrative subpoena, trial subpoena, or grand jury subpoena, and the Government need not notify the subscriber of the request.

If the Government gives prior notice to the subscriber, or otherwise complies with certain delayed notice procedures, the Government may also subpoena the *contents* of electronic communications which are either (1) retained on a system for storage purposes (*e.g.,* opened email which remains on an ISP's server), or (2) retained, for more than 180 days, in intermediate or temporary storage (*e.g.,* unopened email on an ISP's server). For the Government to obtain the contents of electronic communications kept for 180 days or less in intermediate or temporary storage (*e.g.,* unopened email on an ISP's server), it must obtain a search warrant under Federal Rule of Criminal Procedure 41, or the state equivalent. In other words, the Government would have to appear before a neutral magistrate and make a showing of probable cause.

---

56. *Id.* at 301.
57. United States v. Cleary, 265 F.2d 459, 461 (2d Cir. 1959).
59. *See* Fed. R. Crim. P. 6(e).
69. Basic subscriber information includes: (1) a subscriber's name and (2) address; (3) the subscriber's local and long distance telephone connection records, or records of session times and durations; (4) the subscriber's length of service and types of service he has utilized; (5) any telephone or instrument number or other subscriber number or identity, including any temporarily assigned network address; and (6) the subscriber's means and source of payment for the service. *See* 18 U.S.C. §2703(c)(2).

A. Finding the Dots — Third-Party Records 567

The Government may also obtain a court order requiring an electronic communications service provider to turn over transactional and content information by setting forth "specific and articulable facts showing that there are reasonable grounds to believe that" the information sought is "relevant and material to an ongoing criminal investigation."[75]

The ECPA permits the Government to seek a court order prohibiting the communications provider from revealing the Government's inquiry "for such period as the court deems appropriate" if the court determines that such disclosure, among other things, would result in "destruction of or tampering with evidence" or "seriously jeopardizing an investigation or unduly delaying a trial."[76]

4. Mail

Government law enforcement agencies are authorized to request the Postal Inspector to initiate a so-called "mail cover" to obtain any information appearing on the outside of a particular piece of mail.[77] Among other grounds, the law enforcement agency can obtain a mail cover by "specify[ing] the reasonable grounds to demonstrate the mail cover is necessary" to "[p]rotect the national security" or to "[o]btain information regarding the commission or attempted commission of a crime." There is no requirement that the mail sender or recipient be notified of the mail cover.

The Government must obtain a warrant based upon probable cause to open and inspect sealed mail because the contents of mail are protected by the Fourth Amendment. As the Supreme Court established long ago: "Whilst in the mail, [a person's papers] can only be opened and examined under like warrant, issued upon similar oath or affirmation, particularly describing the thing to be seized, as is required when papers are subjected to search in one's own household."[80]

5. Pen Registers and Trap and Trace Devices

Pen registers and trap and trace devices record certain electronic communications data indicating the origins and destinations of various "dialing, routing, addressing, or signaling information," *e.g.*, the phone numbers dialed to and from a telephone.[81] In criminal investigations, the Government must apply for a court order, renewable in 60-day increments, to install or collect data from such devices, though the standard for issuing such an order is relatively low. The Government need only show that "the information likely to be obtained by such installation and use is relevant to an ongoing criminal investigation."[83]

The person owning the communications device is prohibited, unless otherwise directed by court order, from disclosing the fact that a pen register or trap and trace device is in effect.

---

75. 18 U.S.C. §2703(d).
76. *Id.* §2705(b).
77. *See* 39 C.F.R. §233.3.
80. *See* Ex parte Jackson, 96 U.S. 727, 733 (1877).
81. *See* 18 U.S.C. §3127(3)-(4).
83. *Id.* §3123(a).

6. Wiretaps and Electronic Eavesdropping

The Fourth Amendment protects against warrantless Government wiretapping. Federal legislation specifies the procedures by which law enforcement officials may obtain a court order to conduct wiretaps and other forms of electronic eavesdropping. The requirements are rigorous. Among other things, the Government must show that: (1) "there is probable cause for belief that an individual is committing, has committed, or is about to commit" one of a list of enumerated crimes; (2) "there is probable cause for belief that particular communications concerning that offense will be obtained through such interception"; and (3) "normal investigative procedures have been tried and have failed or reasonably appear to be unlikely to succeed if tried or to be too dangerous."[87] Such orders are not available "for any period longer than is necessary to achieve the objective of the authorization," subject to a renewable maximum of 30 days.[88] The communications provider is prohibited from disclosing that a wiretap or electronic surveillance is in place, "except as may otherwise be required by legal process and then only after prior notification" to the appropriate law enforcement authorities.[89]

7. Foreign Intelligence Surveillance Act...

[The court summarized the procedures for obtaining an order from the Foreign Intelligence Surveillance Court for electronic surveillance under FISA.]

The FISA also authorizes the Government to apply to the FISA court "for an order requiring the production of any tangible things (including books, records, papers, documents, and other items) for an investigation to obtain foreign intelligence information not concerning a United States person or to protect against international terrorism or clandestine intelligence activities...."[99] Such an application need only specify that the inquiry is part of an authorized investigation and in accordance with the appropriate guidelines. Recipients of such an order are prohibited from disclosing to anyone (except those whose assistance is necessary to comply with the subpoena) that the inquiry was made.

Finally, FISA authorizes the Government to apply to the FISA court for an order, renewable in 90-day increments, to install a pen register or trap and trace device as part of "any investigation to obtain foreign intelligence information not concerning a United States person or to protect against international terrorism or clandestine intelligence activities." The Government need only certify to the court that it will likely obtain information relevant to a proper inquiry. Just as in the criminal context, the person owning the communications device is prohibited, unless otherwise directed by court order, from disclosing the fact that a pen register or trap and trace device is in effect....

---

87. *Id.* §2518(3).
88. *Id.* §2518(5).
89. *Id.* §2511(2)(a)(ii).
99. 50 U.S.C. §1861(a). [This authority was added by §215 of the USA PATRIOT Act, Pub. L. No. 107-108, §215, 115 Stat. 272, 287-288 (2001), and is therefore sometimes called a "Section 215 Order." This authority was amended by the Patriot Improvement Act, as explained in the Notes and Questions that follow this decision.]

A. Finding the Dots—Third-Party Records

IV. DISCUSSION...

B. AS APPLIED HERE, SECTION 2709 LACKS PROCEDURAL PROTECTIONS NECESSARY TO VINDICATE CONSTITUTIONAL RIGHTS

1. Section 2709 and The Fourth Amendment[118]...

... The Fourth Amendment's protection against unreasonable searches applies to administrative subpoenas, even though issuing a subpoena does not involve a literal physical intrusion or search. In so doing, the Supreme Court explained that the Fourth Amendment is not "confined literally to searches and seizures as such, but extends as well to the orderly taking under compulsion of process."[122]

However, because administrative subpoenas are "at best, constructive searches," there is no requirement that they be issued pursuant to a warrant or that they be supported by probable cause. Instead, an administrative subpoena needs only to be "reasonable," which the Supreme Court has interpreted to mean that (1) the administrative subpoena is "within the authority of the agency;" (2) that the demand is "not too indefinite;" and (3) that the information sought is "reasonably relevant" to a proper inquiry.[124]

While the Fourth Amendment reasonableness standard is permissive in the context of administrative subpoenas, the constitutionality of the administrative subpoena is predicated on the availability of a neutral tribunal to determine, after a subpoena is issued, whether the subpoena actually complies with the Fourth Amendment's demands. In contrast to an actual physical search, which must be justified by the warrant and probable cause requirements occurring *before* the search, an administrative subpoena "is regulated by, and its justification derives from, [judicial] process" available *after* the subpoena is issued.[125]

Accordingly, the Supreme Court has held that an administrative subpoena "may not be made and enforced" by the administrative agency; rather, the subpoenaed party must be able to "obtain judicial review of the reasonableness of the demand prior to suffering penalties for refusing to comply."[126] In sum, longstanding Supreme Court doctrine makes clear that an administrative

---

118. To be clear, the Fourth Amendment rights at issue here belong to the person or entity receiving the NSL, not to the person or entity to whom the subpoenaed records pertain. Individuals possess a limited Fourth Amendment interest in records which they voluntarily convey to a third party. *See* [Smith v. Maryland, 442 U.S. 735, 742-746 (1979), *supra* p. 507]; United States v. Miller, 425 U.S. 435, 440-443 (1976).] Nevertheless, as discussed below, many potential NSL recipients may have particular interests in resisting an NSL, *e.g.*, because they have contractually obligated themselves to protect the anonymity of their subscribers or because their own rights are uniquely implicated by what they regard as an intrusive and secretive NSL regime. For example, since the definition of "wire or electronic communication service provider," 18 U.S.C. §2709(a), is so vague, the statute could (and may currently) be used to seek subscriber lists or other information from an association that also provides electronic communication services (e.g., email addresses) to its members, or to seek records from libraries that many, including the *amici* appearing in this proceeding, fear will chill speech and use of these invaluable public institutions....

122. [See United States v. Morton Salt Co., 338 U.S. 632, 651-652 (1950).]

124. *Id.* at 652.

125. United States v. Bailey (In re Subpoena Duces Tecum), 228 F.3d 341, 348 (4th Cir. 2000).

126. See v. City of Seattle, 387 U.S. 541, 544-45 (1967); *see also* Oklahoma Press Publishing Co. v. Walling, 327 U.S. 186, 217 (1946).

subpoena statute is consistent with the Fourth Amendment when it is subject to "judicial supervision" and "surrounded by every safeguard of judicial restraint."[127]

Plaintiffs contend that §2709 violates this Fourth Amendment process-based guarantee because it gives the FBI alone the power to issue as well as enforce its own NSLs, instead of contemplating some form of judicial review. Although Plaintiffs appear to concede that the statute does not authorize the FBI to literally enforce the terms of an NSL by, for example, unilaterally seizing documents or imposing fines, Plaintiffs contend that §2709 has the *practical* effect of coercing compliance....

The crux of the problem is that the form NSL, like the one issued in this case, which is preceded by a personal call from an FBI agent, is framed in imposing language on FBI letterhead and which, citing the authorizing statute, orders a combination of disclosure *in person* and in complete secrecy, essentially coerces the reasonable recipient into immediate compliance. Objectively viewed, it is improbable that an FBI summons invoking the authority of a certified "investigation to protect against international terrorism or clandestine intelligence activities," and phrased in tones sounding virtually as biblical commandment, would not be perceived with some apprehension by an ordinary person and therefore elicit passive obedience from a reasonable NSL recipient. The full weight of this ominous writ is especially felt when the NSL's plain language, in a measure that enhances its aura as an expression of public will, prohibits disclosing the issuance of the NSL to "any person." Reading such strictures, it is also highly unlikely that an NSL recipient reasonably would know that he may have a right to contest the NSL, and that a process to do so may exist through a judicial proceeding.

Because neither the statute, nor an NSL, nor the FBI agents dealing with the recipient say as much, all but the most mettlesome and undaunted NSL recipients would consider themselves effectively barred from consulting an attorney or anyone else who might advise them otherwise, as well as bound to absolute silence about the very existence of the NSL....

The evidence in this case bears out the hypothesis that NSLs work coercively in this way. The ACLU obtained, via the Freedom of Information Act ("FOIA"), and presented to the Court in this proceeding, a document listing all the NSLs the Government issued from October 2001 through January 2003. Although the entire substance of the document is redacted, it is apparent that hundreds of NSL requests were made during that period. Because §2709 has been available to the FBI since 1986 (and its financial records counterpart in RFPA since 1978), the Court concludes that there must have been hundreds more NSLs issued in that long time span. The evidence suggests that, until now, none of those NSLs was ever challenged in any court....

...The Court thus concludes that in practice NSLs are essentially unreviewable because, as explained, given the language and tone of the statute as carried into the NSL by the FBI, the recipient would consider himself, in virtually every case, obliged to comply, with no other option but to immediately obey and stay quiet....

Accordingly, the Court concludes that §2709, as applied here, must be invalidated because in all but the exceptional case it has the effect of authorizing coercive searches effectively immune from any judicial process, in violation of the Fourth Amendment....

---

127. *Oklahoma Press*, 327 U.S. at 217.

2. NSLs May Violate ISP Subscribers' Rights

Plaintiffs have focused on the possibility that §2709 could be used to infringe subscribers' First Amendment rights of anonymous speech and association. Though it is not necessary to precisely define the scope of ISP subscribers' First Amendment rights, the Court concludes that §2709 may, in a given case, violate a subscriber's First Amendment privacy rights, as well as other legal rights, if judicial review is not readily available to an ISP that receives an NSL....

The Supreme Court has recognized the First Amendment right to anonymous speech at least since *Talley v. California*,[161] which invalidated a California law requiring that handbills distributed to the public contain certain identifying information about the source of the handbills. The Court stated that the "identification requirement would tend to restrict freedom to distribute information and thereby freedom of expression."[162] The Supreme Court has also invalidated identification requirements pertaining to persons distributing campaign literature, persons circulating petitions for state ballot initiatives, and persons engaging in door-to-door religious advocacy.

In a related doctrine, the Supreme Court has held that "compelled disclosure of affiliation with groups engaged in advocacy" amounts to a "restraint on freedom of association" where disclosure could expose the members to "public hostility."[166] Laws mandating such disclosures will be upheld only where the Government interest is compelling.

The Court concludes that such First Amendment rights may be infringed by application of §2709 in a given case. For example, the FBI theoretically could issue to a political campaign's computer systems operator a §2709 NSL compelling production of the names of all persons who have email addresses through the campaign's computer systems. The FBI theoretically could also issue an NSL under §2709 to discern the identity of someone whose anonymous online web log, or "blog," is critical of the Government. Such inquiries might be beyond the permissible scope of the FBI's power under §2709 because the targeted information might not be relevant to an authorized investigation to protect against international terrorism or clandestine intelligence activities, or because the inquiry might be conducted solely on the basis of activities protected by the First Amendment. These prospects only highlight the potential danger of the FBI's self-certification process and the absence of judicial oversight.

Other rights may also be violated by the disclosure contemplated by the statute; the statute's reference to "transactional records" creates ambiguity regarding the scope of the information required to be produced by the NSL recipient. If the recipient—who in the NSL is called upon to exercise judgment in determining the extent to which complying materials constitute transactional records rather than content—interprets the NSL broadly as requiring production of all e-mail header information, including subject lines, for example, some disclosures conceivably may reveal information protected by the subscriber's attorney-client privilege, *e.g.*, a communication with an attorney where the subject line conveys privileged or possibly incriminating information. Indeed,

---

161. 362 U.S. 60 (1960).
162. *Id.* at 64.
166. NAACP v. State of Alabama ex rel. Patterson, 357 U.S. 449, 462 (1958).

the practical absence of judicial review may lead ISPs to disclose information that is protected from disclosure by the NSL statute itself, such as in a case where the NSL was initiated solely in retaliation for the subscriber's exercise of his First Amendment rights, as prohibited by §2709(b)(1)-(b)(2). Only a court would be able to definitively construe the statutory and First Amendment rights at issue in the "First Amendment retaliation" provision of the statute, and to strike a proper balance among those interests.

The Government asserts that disclosure of the information sought under §2709 could not violate a subscriber's rights (and thus demands no judicial process) because the information which a §2709 NSL seeks has been voluntarily conveyed to the ISP who receives the NSL. According to the Government, an internet speaker relinquishes any interest in any anonymity, and any protected claim to that information, as soon as he releases his identity and other information to his ISP. In support of its position, the Government cites the Supreme Court's holding [in *Smith* and *Miller*] that, at least in the Fourth Amendment context involving the Government installing a pen register or obtaining bank records, when a person voluntarily conveys information to third parties, he assumes the risk that the information will be turned over to the Government....

The evidence on the record now before this Court demonstrates that the information available through a §2709 NSL served upon an ISP could easily be used to disclose vast amounts of anonymous speech and associational activity. For instance, §2709 imposes a duty to provide "electronic communication transactional records," a phrase which, though undefined in the statute, certainly encompasses a log of email addresses with whom a subscriber has corresponded and the web pages that a subscriber visits. Those transactional records can reveal, among other things, the anonymous message boards to which a person logs on or posts, the electronic newsletters to which he subscribes, and the advocacy websites he visits. Moreover, §2709 imposes a duty on ISPs to provide the names and addresses of subscribers, thus enabling the Government to specifically identify someone who has written anonymously on the internet.[175] As discussed above, given that an NSL recipient is directed by the FBI to turn over all information "*which you consider to be* an electronic communication transactional record," the §2709 NSL could also reasonably be interpreted by an ISP to require, at minimum, disclosure of all e-mail header information, including subject lines.

In stark contrast to this potential to compile elaborate dossiers on internet users, the information obtainable by a pen register is far more limited. As the Supreme Court in *Smith* was careful to note:

> [Pen registers] disclose only the telephone numbers that have been dialed—a means of establishing communication. Neither the purport of any communication between the caller and the recipient of the call, their identities, nor whether the call was even completed is disclosed by pen registers.[177]

---

175. NSLs can potentially reveal far more than constitutionally-protected associational activity or anonymous speech. By revealing the websites one visits, the Government can learn, among many other potential examples, what books the subscriber enjoys reading or where a subscriber shops. As one commentator has observed, the records compiled by ISPs can "enable the government to assemble a profile of an individual's finances, health, psychology, beliefs, politics, interests, and lifestyle." Daniel J. Solove, *Digital Dossiers and the Dissipation of Fourth Amendment Privacy*, 75 S. Cal. L. Rev. 1083, 1084 (2002).

177. *Smith*, 442 U.S. at 741 (citation omitted).

A. Finding the Dots — Third-Party Records

The Court doubts that the result in *Smith* would have been the same if a pen register operated as a key to the most intimate details and passions of a person's private life.

The more apt Supreme Court case for evaluating the assumption of risk argument at issue here is *Katz v. United States*,[178] the seminal decision underlying both *Smith* and *Miller*. *Katz* held that the Fourth Amendment's privacy protections applied where the Government wiretapped a telephone call placed from a public phone booth. Especially noteworthy and pertinent to this case is the Supreme Court's remark that: "The Government's activities in electronically listening to and recording the petitioner's words violated the privacy upon which he justifiably relied while using the telephone booth and thus constituted a 'search and seizure' within the meaning of the Fourth Amendment."[180] The Supreme Court also stated that a person entering a phone booth who "shuts the door behind him" is "surely entitled to assume that the words he utters into the mouthpiece will not be broadcast to the world," and held that, "[t]o read the Constitution more narrowly is to ignore the vital role that the public telephone has come to play in private communication."[181]

Applying that reasoning to anonymous internet speech and associational activity is relatively straightforward. A person who signs onto an anonymous forum under a pseudonym, for example, is essentially "shut[ting] the door behind him," and is surely entitled to a reasonable expectation that his speech, whatever form the expression assumes, will not be accessible to the Government to be broadcast to the world absent appropriate legal process. To hold otherwise would ignore the role of the internet as a remarkably powerful forum for private communication and association. Even the Government concedes here that the internet is an "important vehicle for the free exchange of ideas and facilitates associations."

To be sure, the Court is keenly mindful of the Government's reminder that the internet may also serve as a vehicle for crime. The Court equally recognizes that circumstances exist in which the First Amendment rights of association and anonymity must yield to a more compelling Government interest in obtaining records from internet firms. To this end, the Court re-emphasizes that it does not here purport to set forth the scope of these First Amendment rights in general, or define them in this or any other case. The Court holds only that such fundamental rights are certainly implicated in some cases in which the Government may employ §2709 broadly to gather information, thus requiring that the process incorporate the safeguards of some judicial review to ensure that if an infringement of those rights is asserted, they are adequately protected through fair process in an independent neutral tribunal. Because the necessary procedural protections are wholly absent here, the Court finds on this ground additional cause for invalidating §2709 as applied.

C. CONSTITUTIONALITY OF THE NON-DISCLOSURE PROVISION

Finally, the Court turns to the issue of whether the Government may properly enforce §2709(c), the non-disclosure provision, against Doe or any other

---

178. 389 U.S. 347 (1967).
180. *Id.* at 353.
181. *Id.* at 352.

person who has previously received an NSL. Section 2709(c) states: "No wire or electronic communication service provider, or officer, employee, or agent thereof, shall disclose to any person that the Federal Bureau of Investigation has sought or obtained access to information or records under this section."

A threshold question concerning this issue is whether, as Plaintiffs contend, §2709(c) is subject to strict scrutiny as either a prior restraint on speech or a content-based speech restriction, or whether, as the Government responds, §2709(c) is subject to the more relaxed judicial review of intermediate scrutiny. The difference is crucial. A speech restriction which is either content-based or which imposes a prior restraint on speech is presumed invalid and may be upheld only if it is "narrowly tailored to promote a compelling Government interest." If "less restrictive alternatives would be at least as effective in achieving the legitimate purpose that the statute was enacted to serve," then the speech restriction is not narrowly tailored and may be invalidated. Under intermediate scrutiny, a speech restriction may be upheld as long as "it advances important governmental interests unrelated to the suppression of free speech and does not burden substantially more speech than necessary to further those interests."

The Court agrees with Plaintiffs that §2709(c) works as both a prior restraint on speech and as a content-based restriction, and hence, is subject to strict scrutiny. First, axiomatically the categorical non-disclosure mandate embodied in §2709(c) functions as prior restraint because of the straightforward observation that it prohibits speech before the speech occurs. As the Supreme Court articulated the threshold inquiry: "The relevant question is whether the challenged regulation authorizes suppression of speech in advance of its expression."[189] . . .

Second, the Court considers §2709(c) to be a content-based speech restriction. . . .

The Government . . . argues that §2709(c) is content-neutral because it prohibits certain disclosures irrespective of any particular speaker's views on NSLs, terrorism, or anything else. . . .

The Government's argument is unpersuasive. It fails to recognize that even a *viewpoint*-neutral restriction can be *content*-based, if the restriction pertains to an entire category of speech. . . .

The Government's claim to perpetual secrecy surrounding the FBI's issuance of NSLs, by its theory as advanced here an authority neither restrained by the FBI's own internal discretion nor reviewable by any form of judicial process, presupposes a category of information, and thus a class of speech, that, for reasons not satisfactorily explained, must forever be kept from public view, cloaked by an official seal that will always overshadow the public's right to know. In general, as our sunshine laws and judicial doctrine attest, democracy abhors undue secrecy, in recognition that public knowledge secures freedom. Hence, an unlimited government warrant to conceal, effectively a form of secrecy *per se*, has no place in our open society. Such a claim is especially inimical to democratic values for reasons borne out by painful experience. Under the mantle of secrecy, the self-preservation that ordinarily impels our government to censorship and secrecy may potentially be turned on ourselves as a weapon of self-destruction. When withholding information from disclosure is no longer justified, when it ceases to foster the proper aims that initially may have supported confidentiality, a categorical and uncritical extension of non-disclosure

---

189. Ward v. Rock Against Racism, 491 U.S. 781, 795 n.5 (1989) (emphasis omitted).

may become the cover for spurious ends that government may then deem too inconvenient, inexpedient, merely embarrassing, or even illicit to ever expose to the light of day. At that point, secrecy's protective shield may serve not as much to secure a safe country as simply to save face....

... Section 2709(c) does not countenance the possibility that the FBI could permit modification of the NSL's no-disclosure order even in those or any other similar situations no longer implicating legitimate national security interests and presenting factual or legal issues that any court could reasonably adjudicate. Bluntly stated, the statute simply does not allow for that balancing of competing public interests to be made by an independent tribunal at any point. In this regard, it is conceivable that "less restrictive alternatives would be at least as effective in achieving the legitimate purpose that the statute was enacted to serve." For instance, Congress could require the FBI to make at least *some* determination concerning need before requiring secrecy, and ultimately it could provide a forum and define at least *some* circumstances in which an NSL recipient could ask the FBI or a court for a subsequent determination whether continuing secrecy was still warranted....

In this Court's judgment,... authorities persuasively confirm that the Government should be accorded a due measure of deference when it asserts that secrecy is necessary for national security purposes in a *particular situation* involving *particular persons* at a *particular time*. Here, however, the Government cites no authority supporting the open-ended proposition that it may universally apply these general principles to impose perpetual secrecy upon an entire category of future cases whose details are unknown and whose particular twists and turns may not justify, for all time and all places, demanding unremitting concealment and imposing a disproportionate burden on free speech....

VI. CONCLUSION

To summarize, the Court concludes that the compulsory, secret, and unreviewable production of information required by the FBI's application of 18 U.S.C. §2709 violates the Fourth Amendment, and that the non-disclosure provision of 18 U.S.C. §2709(c) violates the First Amendment. The Government is therefore enjoined from issuing NSLs under §2709 or from enforcing the non-disclosure provision in this or any other case, but enforcement of the Court's judgment will be stayed pending appeal, or if no appeal is filed, for 90 days....

A different district court also found that the nondisclosure provisions of the NSL legislation violated the First Amendment. Doe v. Gonzales, 386 F. Supp. 2d 66 (D. Conn. 2004) (*Doe II*). The two cases were consolidated on appeal.

Doe v. Gonzales
United States Court of Appeals for the Second Circuit, 2006
449 F.3d 415

[While consolidated appeals from the two district court cases were pending in the Second Circuit, Congress passed the Patriot Improvement Act, *supra*

p. 558, and the government inadvertently revealed the names of the plaintiffs in *Doe II*. The Court of Appeals, in a per curiam opinion, dismissed *Doe II* as moot and vacated *Doe I* in part as moot, remanding the remainder for reconsideration in light of the Patriot Improvement Act. Judge Cardamone concurred in the following separate opinion.]

CARDAMONE, Circuit Judge, concurring:.... A permanent ban on speech seems highly unlikely to survive the test of strict scrutiny, one where the government must show that the statute is narrowly tailored to meet a compelling government interest.

It seems to me that courts resolve the tension between the government's interest in maintaining the integrity of its investigative process and the First Amendment in favor of the government so long as the ban on disclosure is limited. The cases also hold that a ban on speech is not constitutionally permissible once the investigation ends....

The government advanced the "mosaic theory" as one of the reasons to support a permanent ban on speech. That theory envisions thousands of bits and pieces of apparently innocuous information, which when properly assembled create a picture. At bottom the government's assertion is simply that antiterrorism investigations are different from other investigations in that they are derivative of prior or concurrent investigations. Thus, permanent non-disclosure is necessary because, implicitly in the government's view, all terrorism investigations are permanent and unending.

The government's urging that an endless investigation leads logically to an endless ban on speech flies in the face of human knowledge and common sense: witnesses disappear, plans change or are completed, cases are closed, investigations terminate. Further, a ban on speech and a shroud of secrecy in perpetuity are antithetical to democratic concepts and do not fit comfortably with the fundamental rights guaranteed American citizens. Unending secrecy of actions taken by government officials may also serve as a cover for possible official misconduct and/or incompetence.

Moreover, with regard to having something be secret forever, most Americans would agree with Benjamin Franklin's observation on our human inability to maintain secrecy for very long. He wrote "three may keep a secret, if two of them are dead." Benjamin Franklin, *Poor Richard's Almanack* 8 (Dean Walley ed., Hallmark 1967) (1732). In fact, what happened in the Connecticut case bears out Franklin's astute observation. While striving to keep the identities of the Connecticut plaintiffs secret, the government inadvertently revealed their identities through public court filings. This revelation was widely reported in the media. Thus, the case assumed the awkward posture where the identities of the Connecticut plaintiffs were published, yet the government continued to insist that the Connecticut plaintiffs may not identify themselves and that their identities must still be kept secret. This is like closing the barn door after the horse has already bolted.

Since the passage of the [Patriot Improvement Act, *supra* p. 558], the government asserts that we should vacate the District of Connecticut's preliminary injunction rather than leaving it unreviewed on appeal. To me, the government's request for vacatur in the Connecticut case is not surprising, but right

A. Finding the Dots—Third-Party Records

in line with the pervasive climate of secrecy. It sought to prevent, through §2709(c), the Doe plaintiffs from ever revealing that they were subjects of an NSL, effectively keeping that fact secret forever. Then, by requesting vacatur of the decision below, the government attempts to purge from the public record the fact that it had tried and failed to silence the Connecticut plaintiffs.

While everyone recognizes national security concerns are implicated when the government investigates terrorism within our Nation's borders, such concerns should be leavened with common sense so as not *forever* to trump the rights of the citizenry under the Constitution. . . .

Although I concur in the *per curiam* that declines to resolve the novel First Amendment issue before us on this appeal, that does not mean I think that issue unworthy of comment. Hence, this concurrence.

NOTES AND QUESTIONS

1. *Matching Legal Thresholds and Processes with Government Surveillance and Collection Techniques.* Professor Orin Kerr identifies the following legal thresholds (standards for obtaining the information) and attendant processes (administrative or judicial or both) for government surveillance, in ascending order of strictness:

   a. No standard or legal process. The government just gets the information it seeks.

   b. Internal administrative process. There is no bifurcation between the issuing and enforcing authority.

   c. Grand jury or administrative subpoena. The issuing and enforcing authority are bifurcated.

   d. Certification court order. The government needs a court order, but gets it simply by certifying relevancy. The court does not decide whether the certification is justified.

   e. Articulable facts court order. The government needs a court order and must offer specific and articulable facts to establish relevancy.

   f. Probable cause search warrant. The traditional criminal law standard and the predicate preferred by the Fourth Amendment.

   g. "Super" search warrant. Same, but government must first exhaust all other investigatory techniques or meet some other "plus" requirement beyond showing probable cause.

   h. Prohibition. The government is forbidden from getting the information.

Adapted from Orin Kerr, *Internet Surveillance Law After the USA Patriot Act: The Big Brother That Isn't*, 97 Nw. U. L. Rev. 607, 620-621 (2003). Match one of these thresholds to each of the surveillance and collection techniques catalogued in Doe v. Ashcroft.

Recall that FISA electronic surveillance has its own unique threshold. See *supra* p. 525. Where would you place it in the hierarchy of thresholds? What about the threshold for national security surveillance ordered by the President on the basis of his own claimed unilateral authority? See *supra* p. 500. You may need to prepare a table of techniques and standards to do this exercise. Is there any logic or pattern to the matches reflected in your table?

Should one have to make a table to figure all this out? Looking just at electronic surveillance techniques, Professor Daniel Solove remarks, "The intricacy of electronic surveillance law is remarkable because it is supposed to apply not just to the FBI, but to state and local police — and even to private citizens. Given its complexity, however, it is unfair to expect these varying groups to comprehend what they can and cannot do." Daniel J. Solove, *Reconstructing Electronic Surveillance Law*, 72 Geo. Wash. L. Rev. 1264, 1293 (2004). If you agree, and if you believe that inclusion of nonelectronic surveillance techniques only compounds the complexity, should the law be simplified? How?

2. *The Relevancy Standard.* Prior to the USA PATRIOT Act, FISA orders for selected business records required a showing of a counterintelligence purpose and of "specific and articulable facts giving reason to believe that the person to whom the records pertain is a foreign power or agent of a foreign power." Pub. L. No. 105-272, §602, 112 Stat. 2396, 2411. The USA PATRIOT Act broadened eligible information to "tangible things," and it substituted a showing that the production was for an authorized investigation to protect against international terrorism, and that such an investigation of a U.S. person was not based solely upon activities protected by the First Amendment. USA PATRIOT Act, Pub. L. No. 107-56, §215, 115 Stat. 287. See *supra* p. 526. This was effectively a relevancy standard. The same criteria were adopted for NSLs. *Id.* §214, 112 Stat. 286. See *supra* p. 563.

How did the substitution of the relevancy standard for the FISA probable cause standard affect the scope of government surveillance authority? Consider the following assessment.

> Previously, the FBI could get the credit card records of anyone suspected of being a foreign agent. Under the PATRIOT Act, broadly read, the FBI can get the entire database of the credit card company. Under prior law, the FBI could get library borrowing records only with a subpoena in a criminal investigation, and generally had to ask for the records of a specific patron. Under the PATRIOT Act, broadly read, the FBI can go into a public library and ask for the records on everybody who ever used the library, or who used it on a certain day, or who checked out certain kinds of books. It can do the same at any bank, telephone company, hotel or motel, hospital, or university — merely upon the claim that the information is... sought for... an investigation to protect against international terrorism or clandestine intelligence activities. [*Terrorism Investigations and the Constitution: Hearing Before the Subcomm. on the Constitution of the H. Comm. on the Judiciary*, 108th Cong. (2003) (statement of James X. Dempsey, Executive Director, Center for Democracy & Technology), *available at* 2003 WL 21153545.]

The relevancy standard has been defended on the basis of the Supreme Court's reasoning in *Smith* and *Miller* that a person who voluntarily conveys information to a third party to consummate a transaction has no legitimate privacy interest in the information. Section 215, however, is not on its face limited to transactional information; it applies to "any tangible things (including books, records, papers, documents, and other items)...." 50 U.S.C. §1861(a)(1). Does the Court's reasoning, even if correct, support the full breadth of §215? Suppose you entrust your personal diary to your brother. Would a §215 order to your brother be supported by the Court's reasoning?

3. *Tightening the Relevancy Standard?* Although FISA §215 requires a prior FISC order for FBI access to "tangible things," its relevancy standard is so low that the order is arguably boilerplate. The government itself has suggested that the FISC's role is simply to ascertain that the government has made the required certification of relevancy, not to determine that the certification is justified. *See* Letter from Jamie E. Brown, Acting Asst. Attorney General, Off. of Legislative Affairs, U.S. Dept. of Justice, to F. James Sensenbrenner Jr., Chair, House Comm. on the Judiciary, May 13, 2003.

In the Patriot Improvement Act, *supra* p. 558, §106, Congress amended FISA §215 to clarify the relevancy standard. The government must now supply a "statement of facts" demonstrating that there are "reasonable grounds" to believe that the order is relevant to a counterterrorist investigation, although a requested order is deemed "presumptively relevant" to an authorized foreign intelligence or counterterrorist investigation if the government can show that the tangible things pertain to a foreign power or agent or suspected agent of a foreign power under FISA, or to "an individual in contact with, or known to, a suspected agent of a foreign power who is the subject of such authorized investigation." *Id.* The request must also provide a particularized description of the records sought. *Id.* Does this amendment make it easier or harder for the government to obtain a §215 order?

4. *Judicial Review of NSLs.* NSLs have been described as "the intelligence corollary to... administrative subpoena[s]." Lee S. Strickland, *New Information-Related Laws and the Impact on Civil Liberties*, Bull. Am. Soc. for Info. Sci. & Tech., Feb./Mar. 2002, *available at* http://www.asis.org/Bulletin/Mar-02/strickland2.html. Neither administrative subpoenas nor NSLs require a prior court order. *See* Charles Doyle, *Administrative Subpoenas in Criminal Investigations: A Brief Legal Analysis* (Cong. Res. Serv. RL33321), Mar. 17, 2006; Charles Doyle, *Administrative Subpoenas and National Security Letters in Criminal and Foreign Intelligence Investigations: Background and Proposed Adjustments* (Cong. Res. Serv. RL 32880), Apr. 15, 2005. Why are the former lawful under the Fourth Amendment but not the latter, according to the court in Doe v. Ashcroft? How, if at all, can the infirmity of NSLs be cured without compromising national security?

In the Patriot Improvement Act, *supra*, §115, Congress for the first time authorized a recipient of an NSL to petition a federal court to modify or set aside the letter "if compliance would be unreasonable, oppressive, or otherwise unlawful." (It also authorized the government to seek enforcement of an NSL from a federal court.) Does the opportunity for judicial review now afforded the NSL recipient satisfy the Fourth Amendment concern identified in the principal case? The plaintiffs there seemingly thought so; they abandoned their Fourth Amendment claims, mooting that part of the case on appeal. Doe v. Gonzales, 449 F.3d 415, 419 (2d. Cir. 2006).

5. *First Amendment Issues.* In Doe v. Ashcroft, the court found that NSLs for electronic communications records may impermissibly infringe First Amendment rights. Whose rights? (Hint: more than one category of person.) How are they infringed? How is this infringement different from that resulting from pen registers? How, if at all, could this infirmity be cured without compromising national security?

A former chief of the FBI's National Security Law Unit writes that the pre-9/11 "regulatory scheme governing counterintelligence, the higher legal standards for counterintelligence authorities, and even the 'wall' separating intelligence and criminal law enforcement have all functioned to counterbalance and contain a tendency toward excessive secrecy in this area." Woods, *supra* p. 558, at 67. Does the post-9/11 lowering of the legal standards and dismantling of the wall, see *supra* p. 538, upset that balance, supporting the conclusion that the nondisclosure provisions of the NSL statutes fail strict scrutiny? What answer does Judge Cardamone suggest?

In partial response to *Doe I* and *II*, in §§115-116 of the Patriot Improvement Act Congress authorized a recipient of an NSL to disclose the letter for the purpose of obtaining legal advice regarding her response and to petition a court to challenge the NSL, as noted above. A recipient also may seek a judicial order setting aside the nondisclosure requirement by showing "that there is no reason to believe that disclosure may endanger the national security of the United States, interfere with a criminal, counterterrorism, or counterintelligence investigation, interfere with diplomatic relations, or endanger the life or physical safety of any person." The government's certification to the contrary is conclusive, however. If, on the other hand, the petition is filed more than a year after the NSL is delivered, then the government must permit disclosure within 90 days unless it recertifies that disclosure would so endanger or interfere. A recertification is also treated as conclusive.

The *Doe I* plaintiffs did not think that this amendment laid the First Amendment issues to rest, and the Court of Appeals remanded for further consideration in light of the Patriot Improvement Act. What First Amendment arguments would you make for the plaintiffs on remand? Does the "conclusive" treatment of government certifications render this First Amendment protection toothless? *See* Yeh, *supra* p. 558, at 14.

6. *Library Records.* You have to tell the library what book you are borrowing. Do you intend that the library, in turn, will tell the government? Although as of April 2005, the government denied having yet used NSLs for library records, *see Attorney General Defends Patriot Act,* CNN.com, Apr. 5, 2005, *at* http://www.cnn.com/2005/POLITICS/04/05/patriot.act/, "John Doe II" turned out to be four Connecticut librarians who had received an NSL demanding library records. American Library Assn., *Library Connection Is "John Doe"—Board Speaks About NSL Order for Library Records,* May 30, 2006, *available at* http://www.ala.org/PrinterTemplate.cfm?Template=/ContentManagement/HTMLDisplay.cfm&ContentID=128280.

No potential application of §215 has drawn more criticism than its possible use to obtain library records. Can you guess why? Do you think the Fourth Amendment and/or the First Amendment are implicated? If library records enjoy a distinct First Amendment protection, should they be excluded from §215 authority?

In 2006, Congress excluded libraries from the definition of "wire or electronic communication service provider" for purposes of NSLs issued to obtain subscriber information and toll billing records information or electronic communication transactional records. Pub. L. No. 109-178, §§4(b) and 5, 120 Stat. 280, 281 (2006), *codified at* 18 U.S.C. §2709(f). *See* Yeh, *supra,* at 14-15 (describing dispute over construction of library exemption from "ISP" definition). It left libraries subject to §215 orders, however, although it also limited the number of FBI officials who could approve §215 applications for library records, as well as "book sales records, book customer lists, firearms sales records, tax return records, educational records, or medical records containing information that would identify a person." Patriot Improvement Act, *supra* p. 558, §106. Do all of these different kinds of information present the same constitutional issues?

7. *Internet Surveillance.* As *Doe I* indicates, an important legal framework for Internet surveillance is the Electronic Communications Privacy Act of 1986 (ECPA), Pub. L. No. 99-508, 100 Stat. 1848, in addition to the pen register provisions of FISA. See *supra* p. 520. ECPA's intricacies are reviewed in Kerr, *supra* p. 577.

B. CONNECTING THE DOTS — DATA MINING

In May 2006, a news article asserted that the National Security Agency had been secretly collecting telephone call data (external or "envelope" data, but not internal or "content" data) on "tens of millions of Americans" in order (in the words of an anonymous source) to "create a database of every call ever made" within the nation's borders. Leslie Cauley, *NSA Has Massive Database of Americans' Phone Calls,* USA Today, May 11, 2006. The information collected may include calling and called phone numbers, dates, times, and perhaps lengths of completed calls. The details are unknown at this writing, but the data may be used in programs that identify patterns of calling that could indicate particular activity of interest to investigators. For example, a computer using these programs to search phone calls by members of the Yemeni immigrant community in Buffalo might identify several phone numbers of interest. The calling records of these numbers would then be searched, yielding perhaps 100 other numbers with which each phone number of interest had repeated contact.

> If we began with 100 interesting phone numbers from the community under inspection, we now have 10,000 active phone taps. Everything is computer-driven so far, and a single workday at Fort Meade is not yet over....
> Social nets of people whom the computers think make "interesting phone calls" to each other are defined and stored, presumably forever, as persons of interest. Computers compare these government lists to others....
> Establishing the social networks within communities and among individuals requires tapping phones without probable cause. Computers must be free to crawl through their databases and open every phone line along the way. Of necessity, many phone taps are brief and will be discarded. After all, only four "degrees of

separation" will get you to all 100 million households in the United States when each phone has 100 contacts, all of them available in phone bill records.

Finding groups is a good way to find conspiracies. Unfortunately and despite attempts to be selective, a system with geometrical expansion will yield many false positives. At some point, therefore, human analysts inspect the computer harvest we have been discussing. It is possible that a court might be asked for a paper-based search warrant.... [J.I. Nelson, *How the NSA Warrantless Wiretap System Works: An Educated Guess*, revised June 9, 2006, *available at* http://wiretapfacts.notlong.com/.]

This outline of a massive domestic intelligence program, including warrantless wiretaps, is, of course, simply an educated guess, as its author acknowledges. The government has not yet admitted the existence of the program, much less its details.

The use of pen registers and trap and trace devices contemplated in Smith v. Maryland represents a relatively limited, "retail" form of surveillance. The NSA call data program, by contrast, apparently involves a "wholesale" collection effort to create a megadatabase of domestic calls by everyone in the United States. Such a database can be analyzed or "mined" to create new, more useful sets of information.

> Data mining involves the use of sophisticated data analysis tools to discover previously unknown, valid patterns and relationships in large data sets....
>
> Data mining applications can use a variety of parameters to examine the data. They include association (patterns where one event is connected to another event, such as purchasing a pen and purchasing paper), sequence or path analysis (patterns where one event leads to another event, such as the birth of a child and purchasing diapers), classification (identification of new patterns, such as coincidences between duct tape purchases and plastic sheeting purchases), clustering (finding and visually documenting groups of previously unknown facts, such as geographic location and brand preferences), and forecasting (discovering patterns from which one can make reasonable predictions regarding future activities, such as the prediction that people who join an athletic club may take exercise classes). [Jeffrey W. Seifert, *Data Mining and Homeland Security: An Overview* (Cong. Res. Serv. RL 31798) 1, Jan. 27, 2006.]

Data mining is widely used in the private sector as a means for fraud detection, risk assessment, and product retailing. The credit card industry uses it, for example, to detect fraud by revealing unusual patterns of credit card use. *See* Peter P. Swire, *Privacy and Information Sharing in the War on Terrorism*, 51 Vill. L. Rev. (forthcoming 2006).

In a counterterrorism effort, "data mining can be a potential means to identify terrorist activities, such as money transfers and communications, and to identify and track individual terrorists themselves, such as through travel and immigration records." Seifert, *supra*, summary. *See generally* K.A. Taipale, *Data Mining and Domestic Security: Connecting the Dots to Make Sense of Data*, 5 Colum. Sci. & Tech. L. Rev. 2 (2003) (describing and assessing the technology).

B. Connecting the Dots — Data Mining

The NSA call data program is only the latest example of data mining for counterterrorim purposes. The following data-mining programs have also come to light:

- *The Total (Later Terrorist) Information Awareness Program (TIA).* This was a research project of the Defense Advanced Research Projects Agency (DARPA) in 2002 to develop technology programs to "counter asymmetric threats by achieving *total information awareness* useful for preemption, national security warning, and national security decision making." Dept. of Defense, *Report to Congress Regarding the Terrorism Information Awareness Program, Detailed Information* 1, May 20, 2003 (emphasis added). Serious public relations mistakes (placing TIA under the direction of a principal in the Iran-Contra scandal and adopting a logo with an all-seeing eye atop a pyramid over the globe with the motto "*scientia est potentia*" (knowledge is power)), *see* http://www.richardgingras.com/tia/, contributed to Congress's decision to cut off funding for TIA in its original form. *See generally* Seifert, *supra*, at 5-7; Gina Marie Stevens, *Privacy: Total Information Awareness Programs and Related Information Access* (Cong. Res. Serv. RL31730), Mar. 21, 2003.

- *Computer-Assisted Passenger Prescreening System (CAPPS II).* CAPPS II was an airline passenger prescreening program that used computer-generated profiles to select passengers for additional security screening — technically data-matching. It would have relied on commercial data to calculate "scores" for passengers. In fact, the Transportation Security Administration obtained such data from at least four airlines and two travel companies. But litigation made airlines wary of voluntarily sharing such data, the European Union objected, and Congress became concerned about false positives and a lack of procedures for correcting errors. In 2005, Congress prohibited the use of appropriated funds for CAPPS II or its successor, Secure Flight, until the Government Accountability Office certified that the system met certain privacy requirements. Seifert, *supra*, at 7-11; Office of Inspector General Audit Division, Dept. of Justice, *Review of the Terrorist Screening Center's Efforts to Support the Secure Flight Program* (Aug. 2005).

- *Multistate Anti-Terrorism Information Exchange (MATRIX) Pilot Project.* A private contractor developed MATRIX, a query-based search system that used a dynamic database of over 3.9 billion public records collected from thousands of sources, including FAA pilot licenses and aircraft ownership records, property ownership records, state sexual offender lists, corporation filings, criminal history information, driver's license information and photo images, motor vehicle registration information, bankruptcy filings, and information from commercial sources that "are generally available to the public or legally permissible under federal law." Seifert, *supra*, at 12 (quoting website no longer available). Although initially as many as 16 states were reported as participating or considering participation in MATRIX, after critics raised concerns about law enforcement actions being taken on the basis of data mining performed privately without public or legislative input, only four states remained as of April

2005. The pilot project was then reportedly discontinued. *See generally id.* at 11-15; William J. Krouse, *Multi-State Anti-Terrorism Information Exchange (MATRIX) Pilot Project* (Cong. Res. Serv. RL 32536), Aug. 18, 2004.

NOTES AND QUESTIONS

1. *Just Finding Clues?* Police investigators have always conducted "link analysis" when they interview witnesses who saw a crime committed or who know the victim, then looked for connections in the information obtained in the interviews. "Data mining is no more than the computational automation of traditional investigative skills — that is, the intelligent analysis of myriad 'clues' in order to develop a theory of the case." Taipale, *supra*, at 21. Does it follow that "using computers to analyze data is similar to a police officer examining the same information and does not violate personal privacy"? *Counterterrorism Technology and Privacy, supra* p. 558, at 27. Do the two processes have different implications for personal privacy or expectations of privacy? Should we distinguish, for example, between subject-specific searches and generalized undirected data mining to derive or to match patterns? If so, how is computerized pattern matching different, from a privacy perspective, from a police officer's observation of a masked individual running on a public street? *See* Taipale, *supra*, at 64.

2. *The Question Smith and Miller Did Not Ask.* Attorney General Alberto R. Gonzales defended the NSA call data program, without admitting its existence, by arguing that "[t]here is no reasonable expectation of privacy in those kinds of records," citing *Smith.* Walter Pincus, *Gonzales Defends Phone-Data Collection*, Wash. Post, May 24, 2006, at A6. But the Supreme Court focused in *Smith* and *Miller* on the surveillance and collection techniques (pen registers recording dialed numbers and subpoenas for bank records), not on what became of the information they yielded. The Court's focus was understandable from the perspective of traditionally reactive "retail" criminal law enforcement, which builds one case at a time.

But in the fight against terrorism, reactive law enforcement has given way to proactive and preventive law enforcement. *See* Peter Raven-Hansen, *Security's Conquest of Law Enforcement*, in *In Democracy's Shadow* ch. 12 (Marcus G. Raskin & A. Carl LeVan eds., 2005); Daniel J. Steinbock, *Data Matching, Data Mining, and Due Process*, 40 Ga. L. Rev. 1, 16-17 (2005). Data are collected and stored in databases, perhaps indefinitely, for the continuing "wholesale" preventive effort. Even if they are not immediately archived with other data, they can be "virtually aggregated" at any moment to create a dynamic megadatabase. *See* Taipale, *supra*, at 42.

Does the prospect of such indefinite retention and aggregation have any bearing on the expectation of privacy? Do you have a greater expectation of privacy in your aggregated data than in their parts? For example, are you willing to risk that airlines will disclose your travel plans to the government, yet not want those data linked to your other consumer and credit information? Should courts gauge the legitimacy of privacy expectations in each collected item of personal

B. Connecting the Dots—Data Mining

information by the possibility that it will be aggregated for data mining to establish personal behavior patterns and profiles?

> [W]hen combined together, bits and pieces of data begin to form a portrait of a person. The whole becomes greater than the parts. This occurs because combining information creates synergies. When analyzed, aggregated informaton can reveal new facts about a person that she did not expect would be known about her when the original, isolated data was collected. [Daniel J. Solove, *A Taxonomy of Privacy*, 154 U. Pa. L. Rev. 477, 507 (2006).]

Does your answer depend on the length of time that information may be maintained by a government agency? On the purpose for which the information was originally collected? *See* Laurence H. Tribe, Op-Ed., *Bush Stomps on Fourth Amendment*, Boston Globe, May 16, 2006, at A15 ("Even if one trusts the president's promise not to connect all the dots to the degree the technology permits, the act of collecting all those dots in a form that *permits* their complete connection at his whim is a 'search,'" and "[d]oing it to all Americans...is an 'unreasonable search' if those Fourth Amendment words have any meaning at all.").

In United States Dept. of Justice v. Reporters Comm. for Freedom of the Press, 489 U.S. 749 (1989), Justice Stevens, writing for the Court, acknowledged that even public personal data enjoy a certain "practical obscurity" that may be altered by its aggregation into an easily searched database. Posing the issue as "whether the compilation of otherwise hard-to-obtain information alters the privacy interest implicated by disclosure of that information," he asserted that "there is a vast difference between the public records" accessible by diligent effort in sundry locations throughout the country and "a computerized summary located in a single clearinghouse of information." *Id.* at 764. But today many public records exist in easily searchable computer databases. Are any computerized records still "practically obscure," in the same sense that hard copy records at the courthouse or land office once were? Does the ever-increasing use of data mining—in both the public and private sectors—suggest a diminishing expectation of privacy in data? *See* Kyllo v. United States, 533 U.S. 27, 34 (2001) (finding that the use of heat-sensing technology was an unreasonable search, "*at least where (as here) the technology in question is not in general public use*") (emphasis added)).

3. *False Positives.* Credit card data have several attributes that contribute to the success of data mining: a large number of valid transactions, a large number of fraudulent transactions, repetitive fraudulent use that generates common data patterns, and a relatively low cost to "false positives"—valid purchases that are incorrectly flagged as fraudulent—since they usually simply trigger a confirming phone call to the credit card holder. *See* Swire, *supra* p. 582. In contrast, the number of terrorist attacks is extremely low, terrorist attacks are far less likely to be repetitive, rather than one of a kind, and the cost of false positives is far higher, both to the falsely identified innocent person and to the government, which must use substantial resources to investigate that person. *Id.* But see Paul Rosenzweig, *Proposals for Implementing the Terrorist Information Awareness System* (Heritage Found. Legal Memorandum), Aug. 7, 2003, at 4

(suggesting that costs of false positives are "relatively modest"). These differences do not rule out data mining for counterterrorism purposes, but they might suggest the need for special rules for dealing with false positives. *See* Rosenzweig, *supra* (suggesting that "robust" mechanisms to correct false positives from counterterrorist data mining would make the high false positive rate acceptable in light of the consequences of failing to data mine); Steinbock, *supra* p. 584 (suggesting due process protections for persons against whom government action will be taken because of data matching, such as persons denied boarding because of a match on a terrorist watch list). Can you think of special rules to address these differences?

4. *Mission Creep.* CAPPS II ran afoul, in part, of the fear of mission creep. Originally justified as a screening device for foreign terrorists, CAPPS II could also be used to identify individuals with outstanding federal or state arrest warrants, or linked to the U.S. Visitor and Immigrant Status Indicator Technology to identify illegal or out-of-status aliens. Seifert, *supra* p. 582, at 10. Presumably, with a little tweaking, it could also be used to identify deadbeat dads or tax delinquents. So what? If the decision to use data mining involves a balancing of privacy interests in the data against security concerns, then the balance shifts with each intended use of the data. Americans who are willing to give up privacy to protect against terrorism may feel differently about giving it up to trace tax delinquents.

5. *Profiling.* A Department of Defense report suggests that concerns about mission creep may extend beyond privacy if information is used for "targeting an individual solely on the basis of religion or expression, or...in a way that would violate the constitutional guarantee against self-incrimination." Technology and Privacy Advisory Comm., Dept. of Defense, *Safeguarding Privacy in the Fight Against Terrorism* 39 (Mar. 2004). After all, pattern matching *is* profiling of a sort when it is used predictively. Racial and ethnic profiling is discussed *infra* pp. 604-613.

6. *Statutory Protection?* In Whalen v. Roe, 429 U.S. 589 (1977), the Court upheld a state law requiring disclosure of certain prescription information to the state, which could enter it into an electronic database. The Court stated, however,

> We are not unaware of the threat to privacy implicit in the accumulation of vast amounts of personal information in computerized data banks or other massive government files.... The right to collect and use such data for public purposes is typically accompanied by a concomitant statutory or regulatory duty to avoid unwarranted disclosures. Recognizing that in some circumstances that duty arguably has its roots in the Constitution, nevertheless New York's statutory scheme, and its implementing administrative procedures, evidence a proper concern with, and protection of, the individual's interest in privacy. [*Id.* at 605.]

Congress has required inter-agency agreements for computer-matching among federal agencies, *see* Computer Matching and Privacy Protection Act of 1988, Pub. L. No. 100-153, §1, 102 Stat. 2507 (1988), but it has also enacted Privacy Act

B. Connecting the Dots — Data Mining

exemptions for computer-matching and inter-agency data sharing for national security and law enforcement purposes. *See* 5 U.S.C. §§552a(a)(8)(B)(vi), 552a(b)(7), 552a(j) (2000). Numerous other statutes regulate particular databases, usually with broad exemptions for law enforcement. *See* Taipale, *supra*, at 53 n.223.

In 2006, Congress deferred regulating data mining and instead required the Attorney General to provide a report on any initiatives to "develop pattern-based data-mining technology." Patriot Improvement Act, *supra* p. 558, §126(b)(1), 120 Stat. 228. It defined "data mining" as

> a query or search or other analysis of one or more electronic databases, where (A) at least one of the databases was obtained from or remains under the control of a non-Federal entity, or the information was acquired initially by another department or agency of the Federal Government for purposes other than intelligence or law enforcement; (B) the search does not use personal identifiers of a specific individual or does not utilize inputs that appear on their face to identify or be associated with a specified individual to acquire information; and (C) a department or agency of the Federal Government is conducting the query or search or other analysis to find a pattern indicating terrorist or other criminal activity. [*Id.*]

How much counterterrorist data mining falls outside this definition? The definition expressly excludes "telephone directories, information publicly available via the Internet or available by any other means to any member of the public, any databases maintained, operated, or controlled by a State, local, or tribal government (such as a State motor vehicle database), or databases of judicial and administrative opinions." Even for what remains within the definition, however, Congress merely required the executive branch to give it a report.

What protections, if any, should Congress enact with respect to data mining by the government for counterterrorism purposes? *See* Report of the Technology and Privacy Advisory Comm., *supra* (recommending, *inter alia*, that Congress authorize the FISC to oversee government data mining but excluding data mining not involving U.S. persons or based on particularized suspicion); Rosenzweig, *supra*.

Screening for Security — 21

On September 11, 2001, Mohamed Atta and Abdul Aziz al Omari boarded a 6 A.M. flight from Portland, Maine, to Boston's Logan International Airport to catch a connecting flight bound for Los Angeles.[1] A program called Computer Assisted Passenger Prescreening System (CAPPS) (see *supra* p. 583) selected Atta for special security measures, which consisted at the time of holding his checked bags until he was on board the airplane. At Logan, Atta and al Omari, and eight colleagues who joined them, went through security checkpoints at which they were screened by metal detectors calibrated to detect items with the metal content of at least a .22-caliber handgun. Some of these men are now thought to have carried box cutters or pocket utility knives (defined as having blades less than four inches long and permitted on flights at the time).

In the meantime, four more colleagues were flagged by CAPPS at Dulles International Airport en route to board a flight bound for Los Angeles. Two of them — brothers — were selected for extra scrutiny by the airline customer representative at the check-in counter because one of the brothers lacked a photo identification and could not speak English, and they seemed suspicious. Both brothers had dark hair and swarthy complexions, and one had a dark mustache. Again the consequence was that their bags were held until they were on board the airplane. Several of the men at Dulles set off the metal detectors at the security checkpoint and were hand-wanded before being passed. One had his carry-on bag swiped by an explosive trace detector. All were videotaped at the checkpoint.

Of the 19 men who eventually boarded the fateful flights on September 11 in this fashion, 7 used Virginia driver's licenses as their identification at check-in. None of them lived in Virginia. They had obtained the licenses there because they had learned that one can get a genuine driver's license in Virginia in one day for approximately $100 cash, with no questions asked.

The *9/11 Commission Report* tells the rest of the story.

---

1. These and other details in this introduction are drawn from *Final Report of the National Commission on Terrorist Attacks Upon the United States* (*9/11 Report*) (2004) and *Protecting Our National Security From Terrorist Attacks: A Review of Criminal Terrorism Investigations and Prosecutions: Hearing Before the S. Comm. on the Judiciary*, 108th Cong. (2003) (statement of Paul McNulty, U.S. Attorney, E.D. Va.).

A. Checkpoint Searches

The 19 men were aboard four transcontinental flights. They were planning to hijack these planes and turn them into large guided missiles, loaded with up to 11,400 gallons of jet fuel. By 8:00 A.M. on the morning of Tuesday, September 11, 2001, they had defeated all the security layers that America's civil aviation system then had in place to prevent a hijacking. [*9/11 Report* at 4 (footnotes omitted).]

This chapter explores some of the legal issues raised by this defeat of what was and still is essentially a system designed to screen terrorists from entry to transportation systems and other high-risk targets. All 19 of the hijackers passed through the passenger prescreening system (which then used CAPPS and a Federal Aviation Administration (FAA) watch list) and checkpoint security. In part A we explore issues of checkpoint searches. In part B we consider the narrower concerns of identification and watch list screening. Finally, in part C we examine the difficult question of profiling.

A. CHECKPOINT SEARCHES

The government has been screening persons seeking entry into the country since the first Congress passed a customs statute exempting border searches from probable cause requirements. *See* 5 Wayne R. LaFave, *Search and Seizure* §10.5(a) (4th ed. 2004), *citing* Act of July 31, 1789, ch. 5, 1 Stat. 29, 43 (1789). Border searches without warrant or probable cause have consistently been held reasonable as tools of national self-protection that are justified by "considerations specifically related to the need to police the border." City of Indianapolis v. Edmond, 531 U.S. 32, 38 (2000) (dictum). Such searches are often conducted at airports at which international flights land.

Airplane hijacking — "skyjacking" — in the 1960s gave a reason to conduct searches of outbound, and even domestic, air travelers. At first, passengers were selected for frisking if they fit a skyjacker profile and activated a metal detector. LaFave, *supra*, §10.6(a). Courts measured the reasonableness of this early selective screening program by balancing the probability that the selectee was armed and dangerous against the manner and extent of the intrusion on the passenger and the risk of air piracy if he slipped through. *Id.* §10(b) (citing Terry v. Ohio, 392 U.S. 1 (1968) (approving brief stop-and-frisk)).

But the selective screening program gave way after 1973 to a program requiring *all* passengers to go through a metal detector and to submit to a search and usually an x-ray scan of all carry-on items. *See* United States v. Davis, 482 F.2d 893, 897-904 (9th Cir. 1973) (reciting history of airplane hijacking, early "profiling" by the FAA, and a 1972 order by the President for screening of passengers and inspection of carry-on baggage); LaFave, *supra*, §§10.6(a)-(b). The old balancing rationale could no longer be used to justify entirely suspicionless screening of all passengers. Instead, the courts justified the new all-passenger screening as an administrative or "regulatory" search.

[S]creening searches of airline passengers are conducted as part of a general regulatory scheme in furtherance of an administrative purpose, namely, to prevent the carrying of weapons or explosives aboard aircraft, and thereby to prevent hijackings. The essential purpose of the scheme is not to detect weapons or explosives or to apprehend those who carry them, but to deter persons carrying such material from seeking to board at all. [*Davis*, 482 F.2d at 908.]

The intrusiveness of the screening program had to match the administrative need, leading to the conclusion that there was no justification for compelled search of a person who elected not to board the plane. *Id. See generally* LaFave, *supra*, §10.6(c).

Entry control by screening is a counterterrorist tool that is not confined to airports alone. The following post-9/11 case concerns its use on subway passengers. Does the airport screening model fit the subway case? Could the law the case discusses also be used to justify screening at government buildings and national monuments?

MacWade v. Kelly
United States District Court, Southern District of New York, 2005
2005 WL 3338573, *aff'd*, 460 F.3d 260 (2d Cir. 2006)

BERMAN, J. . . . [The New York City subway system, with 26 interconnected lines and 468 passenger stations operating 24 hours a day, is the most heavily used subway in the United States. Experts assert that transportation systems like it are attractive targets for terrorist bombings because they carry large numbers of people. An attack could produce huge casualties, as well as causing widespread economic consequences and public fear. Following the March 11, 2004, Madrid commuter train bombings that killed more than 200 persons, another 2004 train bombing in Moscow that killed 40, and the London subway bombings in July 2005 killing 52 persons, the New York City subway system adopted a random "container inspection program" to address the threat of an explosive device being taken into the subway in a carry-on container or backpack. Inspectors randomly stop passengers to inspect containers. An individual may refuse to permit an inspection at the cost of being denied entrance to the subway with the uninspected item, but a refusal does not subject the individual to arrest. Officials concede that the inspection program does not secure the transit system, but they reason that it would deter some terrorists. On the following Fourth Amendment challenge to the program, a plaintiff's expert testified, on the contrary, that the program's deterrent effect is close to zero, because any would-be terrorist can simply walk away from a random inspection.]

IV. CONCLUSIONS OF LAW

(i) THE FOURTH AMENDMENT AND THE "SPECIAL NEEDS" DOCTRINE...

"[T]he ultimate measure of the constitutionality of a governmental search is 'reasonableness.'" Veronia Sch. Dist. 47J v. Acton, 515 U.S. 646, 652 (1995). "To be reasonable under the Fourth Amendment, a search ordinarily must be based on individualized suspicion of wrongdoing." Chandler v. Miller, 520 U.S. 305, 313 (1997) (citing *Acton*, 515 U.S. at 652-53). "'[I]n certain limited

A. Checkpoint Searches

circumstances, the Government's need to discover such latent or hidden conditions, or to prevent their development, is sufficiently compelling to justify the intrusion on privacy entailed by conducting such searches without any measure of individualized suspicion.'" Bd. of Educ. of Indep. Sch. Dist. No. 92 v. Earls, 536 U.S. 822, 829 (2002) (quoting [National Treasury Employees Union v. Von Raab, 489 U.S. 656, 668 (1989)]). "Therefore, in the context of safety and administrative regulations, a search unsupported by probable cause may be reasonable 'when special needs, beyond the normal need for law enforcement, make the warrant and probable-cause requirement impracticable.'" *Earls*, 536 U.S. at 829 (quoting Griffin v. Wisconsin, 483 U.S. 868, 873 (1987)); *see also Chandler*, 520 U.S. at 323 ("Where the risk to public safety is substantial and real, blanket suspicionless searches calibrated to the risk may rank as 'reasonable'—for example, searches now routine at airports and at entrances to courts and other official buildings.").

Where a special need exists, "what is required is 'a fact-specific balancing of the intrusion... against the promotion of legitimate governmental interests'" to determine if the program is reasonable under the Fourth Amendment. N.G. v. Connecticut, 382 F.3d 225, 231 (2d Cir. 2004) (quoting *Earls*, 536 U.S. at 830). Courts weigh "[1] the gravity of the public concerns served by the [challenged governmental conduct], [2] the degree to which the [challenged conduct] advances the public interest, and [3] the severity of the interference with individual liberty." Illinois v. Lidster, 540 U.S. 419, 427 (2004) (internal quotation omitted).

(ii) THE CONTAINER INSPECTION PROGRAM ADDRESSES A SPECIAL NEED

The "risk to public safety" of a terrorist bombing of New York City's subway system "is substantial and real." *Chandler*, 520 U.S. at 323.

The special need addressed by the Container Inspection Program is the need to reduce (deter and detect) the risk of a terrorist attack on the subways. It is not "to detect evidence of ordinary criminal wrongdoing." *See* City of Indianapolis v. Edmond, 531 U.S. 31, 41 (2000). The Program addresses a problem well beyond the "normal need for law enforcement" or a "general interest in crime control." *See Edmond*, 531 U.S. at 37-38, 47-48; [Michigan Dep't of State Police v. Sitz, 496 U.S. 444, 450 (1990)].

(iii) THE GOVERNMENTAL INTEREST BEHIND THE CONTAINER INSPECTION PROGRAM IS COMPELLING

The need to prevent a terrorist bombing of the New York City subway system is a governmental interest of the very highest order.

(iv) THE CONTAINER INSPECTION PROGRAM IS (REASONABLY) EFFECTIVE

"[T]he effectiveness inquiry involves only the question whether the [search] is a 'reasonable method of deterring the prohibited conduct;' the test does not require that the checkpoint be 'the most effective measure.'" [Mollica v. Volker, 229 F.3d 366, 370 (2d Cir. 2000) (quoting Maxwell v. City of New York, 102 F.3d 644, 667 (2d Cir. 1996))]. And, as noted, the United States Supreme Court has counseled against a "searching examination of 'effectiveness'" by the Court. *See Sitz*, 496 U.S. at 454. Consideration of the effectiveness of a special needs program

> was not meant to transfer from politically accountable officials to the courts the decision as to which among reasonable alternative law enforcement techniques should be employed to deal with a serious public danger.... [F]or purposes of Fourth Amendment analysis, the choice among such reasonable alternatives remains with the governmental officials who have a unique understanding of, and a responsibility for, limited public resources, including a finite number of police officers....

Id. at 453-54....

In the Court's view, there is no doubt that the Container Inspection Program is a reasonable method of deterring (and detecting) a terrorist bombing of the New York City subway system. *See Earls*, 536 U.S. at 877; *Von Raab*, 489 U.S. at 676 (finding that, although an employee could avoid detection under drug testing policy through various techniques, these techniques were "fraught with uncertainty and risks for those employees who venture to attempt them"); *see also id.* at 675 n.3 & 676 n.4 (citing *Von Raab*, 816 F.2d at 180); United States v. Marquez, 410 F.3d 612, 618 (9th Cir. 2005) (the "very randomness" of selection for additional screening procedure at airports furthers goals of "detection and deterrence of airborne terrorism"); United States v. Green, 293 F.3d 855, 862 (5th Cir. 2002) (upholding suspicionless checkpoint on military installation which stopped every sixth car because "[s]topping vehicles at regular intervals, rather than every one, first husbands the resources of law enforcement. It also reasonably advances the purposes of the checkpoint because it deters individuals from driving while unlicensed and or transporting weapons and thereby endangering base personnel. It provides a gauntlet, random as it is, that persons bent on mischief must traverse.").

(v) THE CONTAINER INSPECTION PROGRAM ONLY MINIMALLY INTRUDES UPON PRIVACY INTERESTS

Against the compelling governmental interest in preventing a terrorist attack, the Court has weighed the (relatively limited) level of intrusion imposed upon subway riders. *See, e.g., Sitz*, 496 U.S. at 452 (objective intrusion measured by duration and intensity, subjective intrusion measured by potential for creating fear and surprise). To be reasonable under the Fourth Amendment, a search program need not employ the least intrusive means practicable. *See Earls*, 536 U.S. at 837 ("this Court has repeatedly stated that reasonableness under the Fourth Amendment does not require employing the least intrusive means, because '[t]he logic of such elaborate less-restrictive-alternative arguments could raise insuperable barriers to the exercise of virtually all search-and-seizure powers.'") (quoting [United States v. Martinez-Fuerte, 428 U.S. 543, 556 (1976)]). At the same time, "the means employed must bear 'a close and

A. Checkpoint Searches

substantial relation,' to the government's interest in pursuing the search." United States v. Lifshitz, 369 F.3d 173, 192 (2d Cir. 2004) (citing *Earls,* 536 U.S. at 837; *Von Raab,* 489 U.S. at 676); *see id.* at 190 (search should not "sweep so broadly as to draw a wide swath of extraneous material into its net").

The Court finds that the Container Inspection Program is narrowly tailored and only minimally intrudes upon privacy interests. For one thing, passengers are given notice of the Program by, among other things, a prominently displayed sign and by public announcements. *See* [American-Arab Anti-Discrimination Comm. v. Massachusetts Bay Transp. Auth., Civil Action No. 04-11652, 2004 U.S. Dist. Lexis 14345, at *8-9 (D. Mass. July 28, 2004)] (notice "tends to reduce the subjective anxiety that MBTA riders might otherwise experience upon being asked to submit to the inspection of their bags if they had no reason to anticipate the inspection."). Second, inspections are conducted at openly viewable, fixed checkpoints relatively close to subway entrances by uniformed police officers. *See Martinez-Fuerte,* 428 U.S. at 558-59 ("motorist can see that other vehicles are being stopped, he can see visible signs of the officers' authority, and he is much less likely to be frightened or annoyed by the intrusion") (internal quotation omitted). Subway passengers are randomly selected for bag search pursuant to a selection formula the ratio for which is determined by a supervisor based upon neutral factors. Officers have little or no discretion in selecting individuals for inspection except to determine whether a bag or container is large enough to contain an explosive device. *See* Brown v. Texas, 443 U.S. 47, 51 (1979) (Fourth Amendment requires that suspicionless searches and seizures must be "carried out pursuant to a plan embodying explicit, neutral limitations on the conduct of individual officers"). Third, individuals may refuse inspection under the Program.[33] *See* [United States v.] *Edwards,* 498 F.2d [496 (2d Cir. 1974),] at 500-01 (holding airport searches reasonable because, among other reasons, "the passenger has been given advance notice of his liability to such a search so that he can avoid it by choosing not to travel by air"). Fourth, the searches are limited in scope and duration. The goal is to determine whether a container contains an explosive device. Officers are instructed to inspect those containers and areas of containers capable of containing an explosive device, not to look for contraband or to read written or printed material, and to open or manipulate the contents of bags themselves only "if necessary." *See Lifshitz,* 369 F.3d at 192; Downing v. Kunzig, 454 F.2d 1230, 1232 (6th Cir. 1972) (upholding bag searches upon entry to federal building which were "cursory in nature and made for the strictly limited purpose of determining that no explosives or dangerous weapons were transported into the building."). The inspections generally are brief (a matter of seconds not minutes). *See Lidster,* 540 U.S. at 425 (fact that highway checkpoint stop to gather information was "likely brief" diminished intrusion).

V. CONCLUSION AND ORDER

The Court finds that the governmental interest in preventing a terrorist bombing of New York City's subway system is vitally important, that the

---

33. Or they may opt not to travel with (uninspected) containers.

Container Inspection Program is effective in deterring such an attack, and the minimal intrusion entailed by subway searches is justified.

For the reasons set forth above, Plaintiffs' application for a declaratory judgment and a permanent injunction is denied....

NOTES AND QUESTIONS

1. *Consent.* Some of the airport screening cases argue that by electing to travel by air, after notice of the screening programs, a passenger impliedly consents to the screening. LaFave, *supra* p. 589, §10.6(g). If she consents, she waives her privacy interest. Is this logic compelling for subway travelers? For air travelers? *See* United States v. Davis, 482 F.2d at 905 (asserting that it would violate the principle that government cannot "avoid the restrictions of the Fourth Amendment by notifying the public that all telephone lines would be tapped or that all homes would be searched"); LaFave, *supra*, §10.6(g) (theory of implied consent "diverts attention from the more fundamental question of whether the nature of the regulation undertaken by the government is in fact reasonable under the Fourth Amendment"). Does *MacWade* rely on the consent theory? What is the significance of notice to subway passengers under the court's reasoning?

2. *The Walk-Away Option.* Closely related to the consent theory is the logic that subway passengers have notice of the inspection and therefore can always refuse inspection and take alternative transportation. A few courts condition their finding that a screening program is reasonable upon the program's inclusion of this option. *See* United States v. Davis, 482 F.2d at 910. Does this logic take into account the impact of the walk-away option on the government's security interest? A few courts have reasoned that "such an option would constitute a one-way street for the benefit of a party planning airplane mischief, since there is no guarantee that if he were allowed to leave he might not return and be more successful" and that "the very fact that a safe exit is available if apprehension is threatened would, by diminishing risk, encourage attempts." United States v. Skipwith, 482 F.2d 1272, 1282 (5th Cir. 1973) (Aldrich, J., dissenting, but this discussion adopted by majority). Does the apparently heightened risk of terrorism to transportation systems after 9/11 now justify finding that a screening system without this option can still be reasonable? Then-Circuit Judge Alito, writing for the Third Circuit Court of Appeals, thought so in United States v. Hartwell, 436 F.3d 174, 182 (3d Cir. 2006) (upholding a nonconsensual hand-wanding of Hartwell after he set off the metal detector at an airport).

3. *Building Entry Screening.* The balancing test articulated in the airport screening cases and adapted for the container-inspection program in *MacWade* is fact-sensitive. Do the factors carry the same weight when the government screens entry into a building? How is that different? In Barrett v. Kunzig, 331 F. Supp. 266, 274 (M.D. Tenn. 1971), the court found that "[w]hen the interest in protection of the government property and personnel from destruction is balanced against any invasion to the entrant's personal dignity, privacy, and

constitutional rights, the government's substantial interest in conducting the cursory [article] inspection [at building entry] outweighs the personal inconvenience suffered by the individual." But there the court also emphasized the relatively unobtrusive nature of the article inspection and its neutral application to all entrants. Suppose the screening includes frisks? Body searches? Suppose, using a watch list, the security personnel select particular entrants for a second search? Does it matter whether the search is conducted at the Pentagon or the Smithsonian Museum of Natural History? Professor LaFave's answer is that "what is required is a judicial assessment of the magnitude of the danger and a judicial determination of what screening procedures will suffice to meet it." LaFave, *supra*, at §10.7(a). How would you perform this requirement for these building searches?

B. IDENTIFICATION AND WATCH LISTING

Two of the 9/11 hijackers had been identified as possible terrorist suspects by the CIA before 9/11 and added to a State Department watch list of such suspects called "TIPOFF" on August 24, 2001. *9/11 Report, supra* p. 588 n.1, at 270. TIPOFF was intended primarily to keep terrorists from getting visas to the United States. It was not shared with the FAA, which maintained a separate "no-fly list" of persons banned for air travel because of the threat they were thought to pose to civil aviation, as well as a "selectee list" of persons selected for further screening, such as hand-wanding and questioning. None of the hijackers were on either FAA list. *The 9/11 Investigations* 27 (Steve Strasser ed., 2004).

What authority does the government have to require identification in the screening process? The following case provides some answers, and subsequent notes and questions address the related question of whether we should adopt and require a national identifier. We also review a listing of currently known federal watch lists as a backdrop to discussing their creation and the problems they may pose of misidentification and other false positives.

Gilmore v. Gonzales
United States Court of Appeals, Ninth Circuit, 2006
435 F.3d 1125

PAEZ, Circuit Judge. John Gilmore ("Gilmore") sued Southwest Airlines and the United States Attorney General, Alberto R. Gonzales, among other defendants, alleging that the enactment and enforcement of the Government's civilian airline passenger identification policy is unconstitutional. The identification policy requires airline passengers to present identification to airline personnel before boarding or be subjected to a search that is more exacting than the routine search that passengers who present identification encounter. Gilmore alleges that when he refused to present identification or be subjected to a more thorough search, he was not allowed to board his flights to Washington,

D.C. Gilmore asserts that because the Government refuses to disclose the content of the identification policy, it is vague and uncertain and therefore violated his right to due process. He also alleges that when he was not allowed to board the airplanes, Defendants violated his right to travel, right to be free from unreasonable searches and seizures, right to freely associate, and right to petition the government for redress of grievances....

[The government contended that the Security Directive authorizing the Transportation Security Administration to require passenger identification as a condition of boarding was "sensitive security information" that could not be shown to Gilmore or disclosed to the public. The court accepted this claim, but reviewed the Directive in camera.]

III. RIGHT TO TRAVEL

Gilmore alleges that the identification policy violates his constitutional right to travel because he cannot travel by commercial airlines without presenting identification, which is an impermissible federal condition. We reject Gilmore's right to travel argument because the Constitution does not guarantee the right to travel by any particular form of transportation....

...Gilmore does not possess a fundamental right to travel by airplane even though it is the most convenient mode of travel for him. Moreover, the identification policy's "burden" is not unreasonable. The identification policy requires that airline passengers either present identification or be subjected to a more extensive search. The more extensive search is similar to searches that we have determined were reasonable and "consistent with a full recognition of appellant's constitutional right to travel." *United States v. Davis,* 482 F.2d 893, 912-13 (9th Cir. 1973).

...Additionally, Gilmore was free to decline both options and use a different mode of transportation. In sum, by requiring Gilmore to comply with the identification policy, Defendants did not violate his right to travel.

IV. FOURTH AMENDMENT

Gilmore next alleges that both options under the identification policy—presenting identification or undergoing a more intrusive search—are subject to Fourth Amendment limitations and violated his right to be free from unreasonable searches and seizures.

REQUEST FOR IDENTIFICATION

Gilmore argues that the request for identification implicates the Fourth Amendment because "the government imposes a severe penalty on citizens

B. Identification and Watch Listing

who do not comply." Gilmore highlights the fact that he was once arrested at an airport for refusing to show identification and argues that the request for identification "[i]mposes the severe penalty of arrest." Gilmore further argues that the request for identification violates the Fourth Amendment because it constitutes "a warrantless general search for identification" that is unrelated to the goals of detecting weapons or explosives.

The request for identification, however, does not implicate the Fourth Amendment. "[A] request for identification by the police does not, by itself, constitute a Fourth Amendment seizure." INS v. Delgado, 466 U.S. 210, 216 (1984). Rather, "[a]n individual is seized within the meaning of the fourth amendment only if, in view of all of the circumstances surrounding the incident, a reasonable person would have believed that he was not free to leave." United States v. $25,000 U.S. Currency, 853 F.2d 1501, 1504 (9th Cir. 1988) (internal quotation marks omitted). In *Delgado,* the Supreme Court held that INS agents' questioning of factory workers about their citizenship status did not constitute a Fourth Amendment seizure. In *$25,000 U.S. Currency,* we held that a DEA agent's request for identification from a person waiting to board a flight was not a Fourth Amendment seizure.

Similarly, an airline personnel's request for Gilmore's identification was not a seizure within the meaning of the Fourth Amendment. Gilmore's experiences at the Oakland and San Francisco airports provide the best rebuttal to his argument that the requests for identification imposed a risk of arrest and were therefore seizures. Gilmore twice tried to board a plane without presenting identification, and twice left the airport when he was unsuccessful. He was not threatened with arrest or some other form of punishment; rather he simply was told that unless he complied with the policy, he would not be permitted to board the plane. There was no penalty for noncompliance.

REQUEST TO SEARCH

[The Court rejected the Fourth Amendment challenge to the selectee search option, relying on the balancing analysis of United States v. Davis, 482 F.2d 893 (9th Cir. 1973), noted *supra* p. 589.]

CONCLUSION

In sum, we conclude that Defendants did not violate Gilmore's constitutional rights by adopting and implementing the airline identification policy. Therefore, his claims fail on the merits and we deny his petition for review....

WATCH LISTS MAINTAINED BY FEDERAL AGENCIES
from Peter M. Shane, *The Bureaucratic Due Process of Government Watch Lists*, 75 Geo. Wash. L. Rev. (forthcoming 2007)

Dept.	Agency	List	Purposes	Further Background
State	Bureau of Consular Affairs	Consular Lookout & Support System	Vetting foreign nationals seeking visas	Receives information from TIPOFF
	Bureau of Intelligence and Research	TIPOFF	Tracking known and suspected international terrorists	Created in 1987, transferred to NCTC in 2003, which plans to create new Terrorist Identities Datamart Identities watch list
Homeland Security	U.S. Customs and Border Protection	Interagency Border Inspection System	Primary database for border management and Customs law enforcement functions	Part of Treasury Enforcement Communications System (TECS)
	Transportation Security Agency	No-Fly List	Identify threats to civil aviation	
		Selectee List	Selecting passengers for additional screening	
	U.S. Immigration and Customs Enforcement	National Automated Immigration Lookout System	Biographical and case date for aliens who may be inadmissible to US	Created originally by INS, now absorbed into DHS systems in 2005; also housed in the TECS
		Automated Biometric Identification System	Tracking aliens entering US illegally or suspected of crimes	Created by INS, transferred to DHS
Justice	U.S Marshals Service	Warrant Information Network	Tracking persons with existing federal warrants	Does not perform any independent watch list function regarding terrorism
	FBI	Violent Gang and Terrorist Organization File	Tracking individuals associated with gangs, terrorist organizations	Created in 1995 as a component of the National Crime Information Center
		Integrated Automated Fingerprint ID System	National fingerprint and criminal history database	
	U.S. National Central Bureau of Interpol	Interpol Terrorism Watch List	Assistance for global police operations	Created in 2002; contains about 100 names also in other watch lists
Defense	Air Force Office of Special Investigations	Top 10 Fugitive List	Retrieving Air Force fugitives	Performs no independent terrorist watch list function

NOTES AND QUESTIONS

a. Identification Requirements

1. *Identification for Screening Purposes and the Fourth Amendment.* "Effective checking of names against watch lists...requires that every person carry an accurate and secure form of identification." Daniel J. Steinbock, *Designating the Dangerous: From Blacklists to Watch Lists,* 30 Seattle L. Rev. (forthcoming 2006). Watch-listing is thus linked closely to the asserted need for more secure identification and to more frequent identification stops or checkpoints. *Id.*

Identification is mandatory for boarding flights. As *Gilmore* suggests, the Fourth Amendment poses no barrier to suspicionless government requests for identification at check-in or the security checkpoint, provided that a reasonable requested person would feel free to terminate the encounter. Daniel J. Steinbock, *National Identity Cards: Fourth and Fifth Amendment Issues,* 56 Fla. L. Rev. 697, 711-714 (2004). Furthermore, the *MacWade* analysis suggests that "regulatory" (administrative) demands for identification at airport, transit system, and many building checkpoints would pass Fourth Amendment muster as well. *Id.* at 725-743. How would you apply that analysis to mandatory identification at the entrance to a federal building? What about a random demand for "your papers, please" made by police in a public street?

Of course, good identification serves not just a governmental interest, but also an individual interest in avoiding wrong matching. *See* Paul Rosenzweig & Jeff Jonas, *Correcting False Positives: Redress and the Watch List Conundrum,* 17 Legal Mem. (Heritage Found.) 10-11, June 17, 2005, *available at* http://www.heritage.org/Research/HomelandDefense/lm17.cfm. For this reason in part but, more important, as a personal convenience, most persons voluntarily provide identification. That is, we voluntarily show our government-issued identification — usually a driver's license — to cash checks, to register for classes, and to obtain other privileges. Such voluntary disclosure presents no Fourth Amendment concern. Why not?

2. *A National Identity Card or Other Identifier?* Some have argued that after 9/11, we need a national identity card system. *See* Alan Dershowitz, *Why Fear National ID Cards?,* N.Y. Times, Oct. 13, 2001, at A23. *See generally* Steinbock, *Designating the Dangerous, supra* (citing proponents). An effective system "necessitates mandatory participation, both in the sense of having an identity within the system and in presenting identification when required." Steinbock, *National Identity Cards, supra,* at 708.

A mandatory national identifier requirement would pose at least three kinds of legal issues. First, there may be a Fourth Amendment question if identification is demanded randomly in some places, such as public streets, as suggested above. "[O]ne of the primary reasons that governments created passports and identity cards was to restrict movement, alter patterns of migration, and control the movements of poor people and others viewed as undesirable." Daniel J. Solove, *A Taxonomy of Privacy,* 154 U. Pa. L. Rev. 477, 514 n.183 (2006).

Second, the "main point of identity checking is to make a connection between the identified individual and collection of data." Steinbock, *National Identity Cards, supra,* at 699. A national identifier "would likely be but one component of a large and complex nationwide identity system, the core of which could be a database of personal information on the U.S. population." Computer Science and Telecommunications Board, National Research Council, *IDs—Not That Easy: Questions About Nationwide Identity Systems* 7 (Stephen T. Kent & Lynette I. Millet eds., 2002). The legality of a national identifier system thus turns in part on the legality of the associated database or watch list. *See infra* pp. 581-587.

Third, identity checking may also generate data that can be used to track movements and purchases (e.g., subject was identified at 11:06 A.M. on June 20, 2006, at Constitution Ave. entrance to Department of Justice). The use of such data in a computer database raises some of the same privacy concerns created by government access to and use of third-party records. See *supra* Chapter 20. By providing identification on demand, does a person waive her privacy interest in the data? *See* Steinbock, *National Identity Cards, supra,* at 748-752 (no, because identification is different from providing telephone numbers or banking information). Even if a single identification encounter does not offend privacy, does its aggregation into a database do so?

3. *The Real ID Act—A Step in the Direction of a National ID Card?* In 2005, Congress enacted the "Real ID" Act. Emergency Supplemental Appropriations Act for Defense, the Global War on Terror, and Tsunami Relief, Pub. L. No. 109-13, §202, 119 Stat. 231, 311, *codified at* 49 U.S.C.A. §3301 note (West Supp. 2005). The Real ID Act forbids any federal agency, three years after the Act's enactment, from accepting for any official purpose a state-issued driver's license or identification card unless it meets certain requirements. The identification must include name, address, date of birth, gender, a digital photo, signature, anti-tampering security features, and "[a] common machine-readable technology, with defined minimum data elements." In addition, the state must insist on and verify certain identifying information and evidence of lawful status to issue such an identification. Finally, each state must "provide electronic access to all other States to information contained in the motor vehicle database of the States," which must include, at a minimum, "all data fields printed on drivers' licenses and identification cards issued by the State." *Id.* How is the Real ID different from a national identity card? Which poses the larger privacy concern, the Real ID or the database the Act requires? In Whalen v. Roe, 429 U.S. 589 (1977), noted *supra* p. 586, the Supreme Court found reasonable a mandatory prescription-reporting system tied to a centralized database, but only because the system limited access to the database and criminalized unauthorized disclosures. What protections, if any, are necessary to make the motor vehicle database contemplated by the Real ID Act reasonable?

b. Watch Lists and Other Identification-Related Databases

1. *Blacklists and Watch Lists.* Watch lists are automated databases used to identify individuals or entities for consequences (such as denial of entry or boarding) based solely on their inclusion ("listing") in the database. *See*

B. Identification and Watch Listing

Government Accounting Office, *Terrorist Watch Lists Should Be Consolidated to Promote Better Integration and Sharing* (GAO-03-322) 3, Apr. 15, 2003; Steinbock, *Designating the Dangerous, supra.* Their use did not start with the counterterrorist efforts of the 1990s and later. The infamous "blacklists" of the McCarthy Era — listing "known" Communists and their "fellow travelers" — are a disturbing antecedent. Professor Steinbock summarizes the blacklists and the loyalty screening programs with which they were associated, as follows:

> Little or no effort was made to identify particular workers whose presence would actually pose some realistic threat to national security. Because Communist Party membership or "sympathetic association" with "subversive organizations," even long in the past, were deemed to be adequate proxies for dangerousness, large numbers of people were labeled disloyal or security threats who factually were not. In practice these programs often amounted, instead, to widespread punishment for the exercise of rights of belief, speech, and association. More broadly, they were also about public shaming and enforcing ideological conformity. [*Id.*]

Some procedural protections were eventually required by the courts or by Congress to protect victims of blacklisting and loyalty screening programs. Remarkably, "even [these] are wholly absent from twenty-first century listing. The result [today], in all likelihood, is a glut of both false positives and false negatives." *Id.* See *infra* p. 585.

2. *Generating Watch Lists.* Although the process obviously varies with the watch list, potential terrorists are "nominated" for what is now supposed to be a consolidated "Terrorist Screening Database" by various contributing government agencies through the National Counterterrorism Center (NCTC) and the Terrorist Watch and Warning Unit (TWWU) of the FBI, often based on intelligence. Nominee names are then forwarded to the Terrorist Screening Center (TSC), the agency established in 2003 for consolidating the 12 original watch lists. The TSC codes each name to specify how the individual is associated with international terrorism. *See* Steinbock, *Designating the Dangerous, supra.* The standards applied are not public, although some anecdotal evidence suggests that they are at least partly subjective, may rest on indirect and possibly innocent connections to suspected terrorists as well as informant information of doubtful reliability, and err on the side of inclusion. *Id.*

3. *Mission Creep?* Watch lists are already used to control visa eligibility, entry, and departure, to screen airline passengers, to screen employees for sensitive jobs, and to trigger surveillance. *See id.* "Mission creep" — using lists for more and more purposes, including ordinary criminal and regulatory purposes, such as denial of firearms purchases — is a continuing risk. The Japanese-American internment experience suggests a more frightening mission — preventive detention in a perceived emergency. Indeed, the Japanese Americans who were detained in World War II were selected from a "custodial detention list" prepared by the FBI. *Id.* The FBI also prepared lists for use under the Emergency Detention Act of 1950, Pub. L. No. 81-831, 64 Stat. 1019. See *infra* pp. 672-673. By 1966, the FBI's "Security Index" had grown to 26,000 names. Steinbock, *Designating the Dangerous, supra.* Does the reasonableness of a watch

list turn in part on some statutory control of the purposes for which it may be used? *See* Whalen v. Roe, 429 U.S. 589 (1977), noted *supra* p. 586; Solove, *supra* p. 599, at 520-522.

4. *False Positives and Protected Interests.* When an innocent person is erroneously included on a watch list or has the same name as someone on the list, the listing generates a "false positive." With approximately 8 percent of all air travelers being stopped each day and an estimated 70 million secondary screening searches being conducted annually, even a small rate of false positives will snare many innocent travelers. *See* Rosenzweig & Jonas, *supra* p. 599, at 2 n.3.

Does a person have a right to due process in the no-fly decision, or, more plausibly, in the making or correction of the no-fly list? To establish a claim to due process, a person must first show that the challenged government action deprives her of life or a constitutionally protected liberty or property interest. *See* American Manufacturers Mutual Insurance Co. v. Sullivan, 526 U.S. 40, 59 (1999). The Supreme Court has held that something more than a mere reputational injury or "stigma" from the government action is required to make out a liberty interest. It requires "stigma-plus," the plus being some tangible burden such as loss of employment or of the opportunity to purchase alcohol. *See* Wisconsin v. Constantineau, 400 U.S. 433 (1971); Paul v. Davis, 424 U.S. 693 (1976). Does a person who is singled out for further screening or barred from boarding by his identification on a no-fly list meet the requirement? The court in Green v. Transportation Security Administration, 351 F. Supp. 2d 1119 (W.D. Wash. 2005), held no.

> As Plaintiffs point out, there can be little doubt that association with a government terrorist watch-list "might seriously damage [Plaintiffs'] standing and associations in [their] community," Vanelli [v. Reynolds Sch. Dist. No. 7, 667 F.2d 773, 777 n.5 (9th Cir. 1982)], and Defendants have not argued otherwise.
>
> However, Plaintiffs fail to satisfy the "plus" prong of the stigma-plus doctrine....
>
> Plaintiffs, in the present matter, argue that their status has been altered because they are no longer able to travel like other airline passengers because of their alleged association with the No-Fly List. While Plaintiffs have a right to travel throughout the United States "uninhibited by statutes, rules, and regulations which unreasonably burden or restrict movement," Saenz v. Roe, 526 U.S. 489, 499 (1999), it is also true that "burdens on a single mode of transportation do not implicate the right to interstate travel." Miller v. Reed, 176 F.3d 1202, 1205 [(9th Cir. 1999)]. Thus, Plaintiffs do not have a right to travel without any impediments whatsoever. Indeed, Plaintiffs do not allege that they have suffered impediments different than the general traveling public.
>
> Plaintiffs also argue that their status has been altered because they have been publicly associated with the No-Fly List in full view of co-workers and the general traveling public. However, "injury to reputation alone is insufficient to establish a deprivation of a liberty interest protected by the Constitution." Ulrich [v. City and County of San Francisco, 308 F.3d 968, 982 (9th Cir. 2002)]. Plaintiffs have not alleged any tangible harm to their personal or professional lives that is attributable to their association with the No-Fly List, and which would rise to the level of a Constitutional deprivation of a liberty right. Furthermore, Plaintiffs have not alleged any injury to a property interest as a result of the disclosure of allegedly stigmatizing statements. Plaintiffs have not plead[ed] any tangible harm that

B. Identification and Watch Listing

satisfies the "plus" prong. Therefore, Plaintiffs have failed to state a stigma-plus Fifth Amendment claim. [*Id.* at 1129-1130.]

Do you agree? If you are denied boarding on a transcontinental flight because of your misidentification on a no-fly list, have you suffered any tangible burden? Suppose you have to get to the other coast as quickly as possible to see a dying relative? Is the court confusing the right to travel with the burden constituting a "plus factor"? *See* Shane, *supra* p. 598 ("court's analysis seems flatly wrong"); Justin Florence, Note, *Making the No Fly List: A Due Process Model for Terrorist Watchlists*, 115 Yale L.J. 2148, 2161 (2006) (asserting that the right to travel by plane is a liberty interest).

5. *Process Due in Watch List Making or Correction.* If, notwithstanding the *Green* decision, you think a watch-listed traveler has a constitutionally protected liberty interest, what process is due her? *See* Matthews v. Eldridge, 424 U.S. 319 (1976) (which is discussed so often in national security cases, see *infra* pp. 850-852, that we do not repeat it here.)

Critics of watch lists have suggested several procedural fixes for false positives and misidentification. A "front-end" fix is to institute more careful vetting procedures for placing a name on the list and tighter, more transparent standards. *See* Shane, *supra*, at 19-26. Professor Steinbock, however, raises the question whether the cost of such additional procedure and/or higher evidentiary standards for watch-listing may be too high for effective prevention of terrorist entry. Given the magnitude of the risk, shouldn't doubts be resolved in favor of inclusion? *See* Steinbock, *Designating the Dangerous*, *supra* p. 599.

Another fix is "back-end": providing some procedure for the victim of misidentification or other false positive to clear his name from the list. *See* Rosenzweig & Jonas, *supra* (suggesting administrative procedures for deciding passenger complaints, with a right of appeal to federal court, as well as "wrong matching" procedures for full attribution of list entries and for a wrongly matched person to supply additional information to correct an error); Shane, *supra*, at 31; Florence, *supra*, at 2166-2178 (suggesting that passengers be given "advance notice" of watch-listing on inquiry and a right to an administrative hearing about the alleged listing error through a government-appointed and security-cleared "compensatory counsel"). Professor Steinbock suggests a different and simpler kind of back-end protection: restricting the consequences of being listed just to selection for further investigation, thus "putting the *watch* back in watch lists." Steinbock, *Designating the Dangerous*, *supra*.

Congress has conditioned implementation of "Secure Flight," a new watch list-based passenger screening program, on development of procedures for protecting privacy and providing redress for victims of false positives. Department of Homeland Security Appropriations Act of 2006, Pub. L. No. 109-90, tit. XLIX, §518(a)-(e), 119 Stat. 2064. *See generally* Office of Inspector General, Dept. of Justice, *Review of the Terrorist Screening Center's Efforts to Support the Secure Flight Program* (Aug. 2005), *available at* http://www.usdoj.gov/oig/reports/FBI/a0534/index.htm.

c. Transparency of Screening Law

Secret Screening Law? Congress has generally authorized screening of airline passengers and baggage. *See* 49 U.S.C.A. §§114(h)(1)-(3), 44901 (West 1997 & Supp. 2005). In *Gilmore,* the government asserted that it had implemented that authority by an unpublished Security Directive requiring Gilmore to show a government-issued identification, but it refused to show the directive to him or make it public. Instead, it showed it to the court in camera. The court rejected Gilmore's due process challenge to this secret law by finding that he had "actual notice" of the identification rule because airline personnel told him it was the rule and because he "saw a sign in front of United Airlines' ticketing counter that read "PASSENGERS MUST PRESENT IDENTIFICATION UPON INITIAL CHECK-IN." 435 F.3d at 1136. The court also found that the Security Directive embodied clear standards applicable to all passengers, which prevented its arbitrary application.

Why should such a rule be secret? What are the dangers, if any, of keeping it secret from the public? Should both identification and watch list law (though not necessarily every particular of watch list standards) be made with public participation and transparency—if not by Congress as part of the normal legislative process, then by agencies with public participation in notice-and-comment rulemaking?

C. PROFILING

Guidance Regarding the Use of Race by Federal Law Enforcement Agencies [*DOJ Guidance*]
U.S. Department of Justice, Civil Rights Division, June, 2003

THE CONSTITUTIONAL FRAMEWORK

"[T]he Constitution prohibits selective enforcement of the law based on considerations such as race." *Whren v. United States,* 517 U.S. 806, 813 (1996). Thus, for example, the decision of federal prosecutors "whether to prosecute may not be based on 'an unjustifiable standard such as race, religion, or other arbitrary classification.'"[4] *United States v. Armstrong,* 517 U.S. 456, 464 (1996) (quoting *Oyler v. Boles,* 368 U.S. 448, 456 (1962)). The same is true of Federal law enforcement officers. Federal courts repeatedly have held that any general policy of "utiliz[ing] impermissible racial classifications in determining whom to stop, detain, and search" would violate the Equal Protection Clause. *Chavez v. Illinois State Police,* 251 F.3d 612, 635 (7th Cir. 2001). As the Sixth Circuit has explained, "[i]f law enforcement adopts a policy, employs a practice, or in a given situation takes steps to initiate an investigation of a citizen based solely

---

4. These same principles do not necessarily apply to classifications based on alienage. For example, Congress, in the exercise of its broad powers over immigration, has enacted a number of provisions that apply only to aliens, and enforcement of such provisions properly entails consideration of a person's alien status.

C. Profiling

upon that citizen's race, without more, then a violation of the Equal Protection Clause has occurred." *United States v. Avery*, 137 F.3d 343, 355 (6th Cir. 1997). "A person cannot become the target of a police investigation solely on the basis of skin color. Such selective law enforcement is forbidden." *Id.* at 354.

As the Supreme Court has held, this constitutional prohibition against selective enforcement of the law based on race "draw[s] on 'ordinary equal protection standards.'" *Armstrong*, 517 U.S. at 465 (quoting *Wayte v. United States*, 470 U.S. 598, 608 (1985)). Thus, impermissible selective enforcement based on race occurs when the challenged policy has "'a discriminatory effect and ... was motivated by a discriminatory purpose.'" *Id.* (quoting *Wayte*, 470 U.S. at 608). Put simply, "to the extent that race is used as a proxy" for criminality, "a racial stereotype requiring strict scrutiny is in operation." *Cf. Bush v. Vera*, 517 U.S. at 968 (plurality).

I. GUIDANCE FOR FEDERAL OFFICIALS ENGAGED IN LAW ENFORCEMENT ACTIVITIES

A. ROUTINE OR SPONTANEOUS ACTIVITIES IN DOMESTIC LAW ENFORCEMENT

> In making routine or spontaneous law enforcement decisions, such as ordinary traffic stops, Federal law enforcement officers may not use race or ethnicity to any degree, except that officers may rely on race and ethnicity in a specific suspect description. This prohibition applies even where the use of race or ethnicity might otherwise be lawful. . . .

Some have argued that overall discrepancies in certain crime rates among racial groups could justify using race as a factor in general traffic enforcement activities and would produce a greater number of arrests for non-traffic offenses (e.g., narcotics trafficking). We emphatically reject this view. The President has made clear his concern that racial profiling is morally wrong and inconsistent with our core values and principles of fairness and justice. Even if there were overall statistical evidence of differential rates of commission of certain offenses among particular races, the affirmative use of such generalized notions by federal law enforcement officers in routine, spontaneous law enforcement activities is tantamount to stereotyping. It casts a pall of suspicion over every member of certain racial and ethnic groups without regard to the specific circumstances of a particular investigation or crime, and it offends the dignity of the individual improperly targeted. Whatever the motivation, it is patently unacceptable and thus prohibited under this guidance for Federal law enforcement officers to act on the belief that race or ethnicity signals a higher risk of criminality. This is the core of "racial profiling" and it must not occur.

The situation is different when an officer has specific information, based on trustworthy sources, to "be on the lookout" for specific individuals identified at least in part by race or ethnicity. In such circumstances, the officer is not acting based on a generalized assumption about persons of different races; rather, the officer is helping locate specific individuals previously identified as involved in crime. . . .

B. LAW ENFORCEMENT ACTIVITIES RELATED TO SPECIFIC INVESTIGATIONS

> In conducting activities in connection with a specific investigation, Federal law enforcement officers may consider race and ethnicity only to the extent that there is trustworthy information, relevant to the locality or time frame, that links persons of a particular race or ethnicity to an identified criminal incident, scheme, or organization. This standard applies even where the use of race or ethnicity might otherwise be lawful.

As noted above, there are circumstances in which law enforcement activities relating to particular identified criminal incidents, schemes or enterprises may involve consideration of personal identifying characteristics of potential suspects, including age, sex, ethnicity or race. Common sense dictates that when a victim describes the assailant as being of a particular race, authorities may properly limit their search for suspects to persons of that race. Similarly, in conducting an ongoing investigation into a specific criminal organization whose membership has been identified as being overwhelmingly of one ethnicity, law enforcement should not be expected to disregard such facts in pursuing investigative leads into the organization's activities.

Reliance upon generalized stereotypes is absolutely forbidden. Rather, use of race or ethnicity is permitted only when the officer is pursuing a specific lead concerning the identifying characteristics of persons involved in an *identified* criminal activity. The rationale underlying this concept carefully limits its reach....

II. GUIDANCE FOR FEDERAL OFFICIALS ENGAGED IN LAW ENFORCEMENT ACTIVITIES INVOLVING THREATS TO NATIONAL SECURITY OR THE INTEGRITY OF THE NATION'S BORDERS

> In investigating or preventing threats to national security or other catastrophic events (including the performance of duties related to air transportation security), or in enforcing laws protecting the integrity of the Nation's borders, Federal law enforcement officers may not consider race or ethnicity except to the extent permitted by the Constitution and laws of the United States.

... "It is 'obvious and unarguable' that no governmental interest is more compelling than the security of the Nation." *Haig v. Agee*, 453 U.S. 280, 307 (1981) (quoting *Aptheker v. Secretary of State*, 378 U.S. 500, 509 (1964)).

The Constitution prohibits consideration of race or ethnicity in law enforcement decisions in all but the most exceptional instances. Given the incalculably high stakes involved in such investigations, however, federal law enforcement officers who are protecting national security or preventing catastrophic events (as well as airport security screeners) may consider race, ethnicity, and other relevant factors to the extent permitted by our laws and the Constitution. Similarly, because enforcement of the laws protecting the Nation's borders may necessarily involve a consideration of a person's alienage in certain circumstances, the use of race or ethnicity in such circumstances is properly governed by existing statutory and constitutional standards. *See, e.g., United States*

C. Profiling

v. Brignoni-Ponce, 422 U.S. 873, 886-87 (1975). This policy will honor the rule of law and promote vigorous protection of our national security.

As the Supreme Court has stated, all racial classifications by a governmental actor are subject to the "strictest judicial scrutiny." *Adarand Constructors, Inc. v. Pena*, 515 U.S. 200, 224-25 (1995). The application of strict scrutiny is of necessity a fact-intensive process. *Id.* at 236. Thus, the legality of particular, race-sensitive actions taken by Federal law enforcement officials in the context of national security and border integrity will depend to a large extent on the circumstances at hand. In absolutely no event, however, may Federal officials assert a national security or border integrity rationale as a mere pretext for invidious discrimination. Indeed, the very purpose of the strict scrutiny test is to "smoke out" illegitimate use of race, *Adarand*, 515 U.S. at 226 (quoting *Richmond v. J.A. Croson Co.*, 488 U.S. 469, 493 (1989)), and law enforcement strategies not actually premised on *bona fide* national security or border integrity interests therefore will not stand....

> *Example:* The FBI receives reliable information that persons affiliated with a foreign ethnic insurgent group intend to use suicide bombers to assassinate that country's president and his entire entourage during an official visit to the United States. Federal law enforcement may appropriately focus investigative attention on identifying members of that ethnic insurgent group who may be present and active in the United States and who, based on other available information, might conceivably be involved in planning some such attack during the state visit.

> *Example:* U.S. intelligence sources report that terrorists from a particular ethnic group are planning to use commercial jetliners as weapons by hijacking them at an airport in California during the next week. Before allowing men of that ethnic group to board commercial airplanes in California airports during the next week, Transportation Security Administration personnel, and other federal and state authorities, may subject them to heightened scrutiny.

Because terrorist organizations might aim to engage in unexpected acts of catastrophic violence in any available part of the country (indeed, in multiple places simultaneously, if possible), there can be no expectation that the information must be specific to a particular locale or even to a particular identified scheme.

Of course, as in the example below, reliance solely upon generalized stereotypes is forbidden.

> *Example:* At the security entrance to a Federal courthouse, a man who appears to be of a particular ethnicity properly submits his briefcase for x-ray screening and passes through the metal detector. The inspection of the briefcase reveals nothing amiss, the man does not activate the metal detector, and there is nothing suspicious about his activities or appearance. In the absence of any threat warning, the federal security screener may not order the man to undergo a further inspection solely because he appears to be of a particular ethnicity.

NOTES AND QUESTIONS

1. *Fourth Amendment Analysis: Mere "Relevance"?* The Fourth Amendment "special needs" (administrative search) analysis of racial profiling in security

screening asks whether the race or ethnic factor in the profile is "clearly...relevant to the law enforcement need to be served." *See* United States v. Martinez-Fuerte, 428 U.S. 543, 564 n.17 (1976). That it may constitute purposeful discrimination does not make the search or seizure unreasonable under the Fourth Amendment. Whren v. United States, 517 U.S. 806, 813 (1996). Thus, the Supreme Court has upheld secondary screening of persons at a border checkpoint made largely on the basis of apparent Mexican ancestry. United States v. Martinez-Fuerte, 428 U.S. 543, 563 (1976). The Court relied in part on its earlier decision in United States v. Brignoni-Ponce, 422 U.S. 873 (1975), where it noted that "[t]he likelihood that any given person of Mexican ancestry is an alien is high enough to make Mexican appearance a relevant factor...." *Id.* at 886-887. In *Brignoni-Ponce*, however, the Court held that apparent Mexican ancestry could not *alone* create the reasonable suspicion required for a roving-patrol stop. *Id.* The *Martinez-Fuerte* Court also noted that "[d]ifferent considerations would arise if...reliance were put on apparent Mexican ancestry at a checkpoint operated near the Canadian border." 428 U.S. at 564.

2. *Equal Protection Analysis: Stricter Scrutiny and Necessity?* Given the foregoing analysis, the constitutional basis for challenges to racial profiling is the Equal Protection Clause rather than the Fourth Amendment. *Id.* The former subjects purposeful race discrimination to a probing strict scrutiny form of judicial review. At least as early as 1944, the Supreme Court declared that "all legal restrictions which curtail the rights of a single racial group are immediately suspect" and therefore subject to the "most rigid scrutiny." Korematsu v. United States, 323 U.S. 214, 216 (1944), *infra* p. 704. The scrutiny actually applied by the Court, however, did not overturn the government's program to intern 120,000 Japanese Americans following the attack on Pearl Harbor. Although the Court acknowledged that "[n]othing short of apprehension by the proper military authorities of the gravest imminent danger to the public safety can constitutionally justify" race-based confinement or exclusion, the Court deferred to the judgment of such military authorities and found that exclusion of Japanese Americans from threatened areas "has a definite and close relationship to the prevention of crime and sabotage." 323 U.S. at 218.

Since *Korematsu*, the Court has refined equal protection analysis. When government action is challenged on equal protection grounds, "the issue is whether the government can identify a sufficiently important objective for its discrimination. What is a sufficient justification depends entirely on the type of discrimination." Erwin Chemerinsky, *Constitutional Law* 669-670 (3d ed. 2006). When the government discriminates on the basis of race, national origin, or, for some actions, alienage, its justification will be subject to "strict scrutiny" and upheld only "if it is proven necessary to achieve a compelling government purpose." *Id.* at 529 (footnote omitted). Other classifications may require only "rational basis" review, under which the law need only be rationally related to a legitimate government purpose, or "intermediate scrutiny." *Id.*

The *DOJ Guidance* apparently authorizes airport screening selection based on "ethnic selection" and alienage. Can you formulate an argument for the legality of such profiling under modern equal protection analysis? Can you justify the selection of the two brothers at Logan Airport for further screening on September 11? Could you justify that selection if it had been based only on

C. Profiling

the gate agent's suspicion of their "Middle Eastern" appearance? See *supra* p. 588. If your answers to these questions differ, can you see how the difference helps explain the final example given in the *DOJ Guidance*? Assuming that the computerized CAPPS air passenger screening system described in part B profiles using both racial or ethnic characteristics *and* behavioral factors, would it satisfy the equal protection analysis? *See* Sharon L. Davies, *Profiling Terror,* 1 Ohio St. J. Crim. L. 45, 60-61 (2003) (noting that courts have required profiles to be based on more than racial or ethnic elements alone to withstand equal protection challenge).

3. *The Easy Case: Individualized Description.* The *DOJ Guidance* reflects general agreement that law enforcement agents may use race or an ethnic characteristic when it is part of the description of a particular suspect. *See* Davies, *supra,* at 54 & n.38 (citing decisions). "To act on the basis of a particular suspect's description as belonging to a given race is certainly to take race into account," Professor Ellman explains, "but it is not to take *generalizations* about race into account." Stephen J. Ellman, *Racial Profiling and Terrorism,* 46 N.Y.U. L. Rev. 675, 676 n.4 (2003). But the *DOJ Guidance*'s approval of profiling in some counterterrorism investigations may suggest how easily "the identification of a group of offenders by race tends to transform the physical description into a negative predictor and then into a mark of social status." Albert W. Alshuler, *Racial Profiling and the Constitution,* 2002 U. Chi. Legal F. 163, 265-266. Is being on the lookout for "Middle Eastern men" in their early twenties merely taking into account the fact that the original Al Qaeda membership seems overwhelmingly to have included such men, or is it also a prediction that they are more likely to commit future terrorist acts than Swedish grandmothers? And does the "look-out" profile stigmatize all Middle Eastern men?

4. *What Is "Race"?* In Saint Francis College v. Al Khazraji, 481 U.S. 604 (1987), the Supreme Court's earlier construction of 42 U.S.C. §1981 as forbidding all "racial" discrimination in the making of private and public contracts, *see* Runyon v. McCrary, 427 U.S. 160, 168 (1976), was extended to protect a citizen of the United States born in Iraq. The Court conceded that "a variety of ethnic groups, including Arabs, are now considered to be within the Caucasian race." *Id.* at 610. When §1981 became law in the 19th century, however, it was clear that "Congress intended to protect from discrimination identifiable classes of persons who are subjected to intentional discrimination solely because of their ancestry or ethnic characteristics." *Id.* at 613. Although *Saint Francis College* did not involve a constitutional claim, the Court's discussion of the concept of "race" is instructive, particularly because it relates to a statute that was enacted at about the same time as the adoption of the Fourteenth Amendment. Does "race" for equal protection purposes now encompass the "ethnic" characteristics mentioned by the *DOJ Guidance* in its examples of permissible counterterrorist discrimination?

5. *Applying Racial and Ethnic Classifications in Screening.* The *DOJ Guidance* is (calculatingly?) vague about the classification for profiling in counterterrorism cases: it refers just to "ethnic groups." But "defenses of racial and ethnic profiling depend upon the ability of law enforcement officers to do it — to

distinguish racial and ethnic groups from one another." Alschuler, *supra*, at 224. Doesn't the legality depend partly on how the "ethnic group" is described and what discretion that leaves checkpoint screeners or law enforcement officers?

One prominent conservative journalist has characterized *MacWade*'s random container inspection as an "obvious absurdity" and an "appalling waste of effort." Charles Krauthammer, *Give Grandma a Pass: Politically Correct Screening Won't Catch Jihadists*, Wash. Post, July 29, 2005, at A23. Since "jihadist terrorism has been carried out . . . by young Muslim men," he reasons, we should give "special scrutiny to young Islamic men." *Id. See also* Milton Hirsch & David O. Markus, *Fourth Amendment Forum*, 27 Champion 34 (Mar. 2003) ("since 9/11 attacks were perpetrated by "Arab Muslim men," there "exists a demonstrable, verifiable nexus between" such characteristics when used to select travelers for high-level screening "and conduct that American officials have a public duty to interdict").

Could you explain to subway security officers how to identify "Islamic men"? What about persons "of Middle Eastern appearance"? *See* John Derbyshire, *At First Glance: Racial Profiling, Burning Hotter*, Natl. Rev. Online, Oct. 5, 2001, *at* http://www.nationalreview.com/derbyshire/derbyshire100501.shtml. What about "Arab-looking"? *See* Stuart Taylor Jr., *D.C. Dispatch: Politically Incorrect Profiling: A Matter of Life or Death*, Natl. J., Nov. 6, 2001. *See* Davies, *supra*, at 51 n.29 ("It is a common misconception that all Arabs are racially identifiable by their darker skin. In fact, Arabs may have white skin and blue eyes, olive or dark skin and brown eyes, and hair in a variety of textures.").

One danger of vague classifications is that they leave the screeners too much discretion, creating space for conscious or unconscious application of the screeners' own classifications. The same may be true even of profiling that includes behavioral factors, such as unusual passenger nervousness or sweating or failure to make eye contact, in a profile together with racial or ethnic factors. After 9/11, for example, the American Civil Liberties Union reported that 67 percent of airline passengers subjected to personal searches upon entering the United States were people of color; Black and Latino Americans were four to nine times as likely as white Americans to be x-rayed after being frisked or patted down; and black women were more likely than any other U.S. citizens to be strip-searched. *See* R. Spencer McDonald, Note, *Rational Profiling in America's Airports*, 17 BYU J. Pub. L. 113, 136 (2002) (citing American Civil Liberties Union press release, Mar. 26, 2002). Is this kind of profiling justified under the *DOJ Guidance*? If not, does it simply illustrate the need for closer supervision of the TSA security personnel or an inherent risk of racial or ethnic screening profiles? Does the container inspection program in *MacWade* avoid this danger?

6. *Empirical Nexus?* In United States v. Lopez, 328 F. Supp. 1077 (E.D.N.Y. 1971), the court initially upheld the use of a passenger profile in the pre-1973 selective anti-skyjacking screening program and follow-up frisk. But when discovery revealed that the airline had unilaterally eliminated one element of the FAA-established profile and added "an ethnic element for which there was no experimental basis, thus raising serious equal protection problems," the court suppressed the evidence from the frisk. *Id.* at 1101. "The approved [FAA] system survives constitutional scrutiny only by its careful adherence to absolute objectivity and neutrality," the court explained. "When elements of discretion and prejudice are interjected it becomes constitutionally impermissible." *Id.*

C. Profiling

Does this mean than any ethnic, religious, or national origin element of a screening profile must have at least "an experimental basis" to find a nexus between the element and the probability of a terrorist act? If so, does "Islamic men" or "Middle Eastern appearance" have such a nexus to terrorism, in light of the fact that the 19 9/11 hijackers were apparently Muslims from the Middle East? *Compare* Thomas W. Joo, *Presumed Disloyal: Executive Power, Judicial Deference, and the Construction of Race Before and After September 11*, 34 Colum. Hum. Rts. L. Rev. 1, 41-42 (2002) (the "categories of 'Arab' and 'Muslim' are simply too broad"; "even if a man of Arab descent is relatively more likely to be a terrorist than a non-Arab, the likelihood that any given Arab man is a terrorist remains negligible"), *with* Ellman, *supra* p. 609, at 698 ("People sharing all of Al Qaeda's background characteristics still seem more likely to be our adversaries than most of the people who share none of them — even though the great majority of people sharing all of these characteristics have no connection to terrorism whatsoever.").

Professor Alshuler suggests that "when a police practice systematically subjects the members of a race to searches and seizures at a higher rate than their rate of offending, a court should hold the practice unconstitutional unless it is appropriately tailored to advance a significant state interest." Alshuler, *supra* p. 609, at 223. Would profiling of "Middle Eastern men" satisfy this test? *See id.* at 265 ("special screening of people of Arab ethnicity at airports...should be impermissible"). How would we measure their "rate of offending"?

Professor Harcourt suggests that the success and justification of profiling depend on more than "identifying a stable group trait that correlates with higher offending." It also depends on "how responsive different groups are to the targeted policing and whether they engage in forms of substitution" by recruiting from nonprofiled groups or substituting different types of attacks that are more immune to profiling. *See* Bernard E. Harcourt, *Muslim Profiles Post 9/11: Is Racial Profiling an Effective Counterterrorist Measure and Does It Violate the Right to Be Free From Discrimination?*, Univ. of Chicago Law School, John M. Olin Law & Economics Working Paper No. 288 (2d Series), at 9-10 (Mar. 2006), *available at* http://ssrn.com/abstract=893905.

> The central question [is] whether racial profiling of young Muslim men in the New York subways will likely detect a terrorist attack or instead lead to the recruitment of non-profiled persons and the substitution of other acts for subway attacks — in other words, whether profiling will detect or increase terrorist attacks. The answer to this question is pure speculation. In the end, then, there is no need or reason to engage in a rights trade-off by racial profiling as part of any subway screening. [*Id.* at 27-28.]

That is, without empirical evidence that racial profiling works, there is no need for it. Do you agree?

7. *Costs and Benefits of Profiling.* Proponents of counterterrorism profiling have argued that the cost to a victim of frequent false positives "is minuscule," while the cost to society of a false negative (letting a terrorist through) could be enormous. They conclude that racial profiling is justified by a cost-benefit analysis. *See* LaFave, *supra* p. 589 (summarizing arguments of some proponents);

Ellman, *supra*, at 698-707. Does this analysis consider all the costs? What about the risk that Al Qaeda will respond to the profile by selecting terrorists who do not look "Islamic" or "Middle Eastern" (if you can figure out what this means), including Americans like Jose Padilla (see *infra* p. 742), thus increasing the rate of false negatives? What about the cost of creating hostility and anxiety in the U.S. community of persons from the Middle East, and discouraging its members from voluntary cooperation? *See generally* Ellman, *supra*, at 705-707; Davies, *supra* p. 609, at 73-74. How would you inventory and balance all the benefits and costs of racial profiling in security screening and counterterrorism investigations?

8. *National Origin Profiling of Post-9/11 Detainees and Interviewees.* Following the September 11 attacks, law enforcement and immigration authorities detained more than 1,100 persons as part of their investigation. *See generally* Chapter 24. On November 27, 2001, the Bush administration provided a breakdown of some 600 persons still being held. According to the report, 548 detained on immigration charges hailed from 47 countries, including more than 200 from Pakistan, and smaller numbers from Egypt, Turkey, Yemen, and India. Dan Eggen, *About 600 Still Held in Connection with Attacks, Ashcroft Says*, Wash. Post, Nov. 28, 2001, at A15. An earlier newspaper investigation of 235 detainees found that the largest numbers were from Saudi Arabia, Egypt, and Pakistan, and that almost all of them were men in their twenties and thirties. Amy Goldstein, *A Deliberate Strategy of Disruption*, Wash. Post, Nov. 4, 2001, at A1. When these figures were reported, none of the detainees had been charged with any terrorist activity. Subsequently, the administration conducted "voluntary" interviews targeting 5,000 mostly Middle Eastern aliens holding tourist, student, or business visas. *See* Allan Lengel, *Arab Men in Detroit to Be Asked to See U.S. Attorney*, Wash. Post, Nov. 27, 201, at A5.

Did these actions constitute constitutionally suspect profiling? *Compare* Davies, *supra*, at 80-81, *and* Ellman, *supra*, at 726-727 (because mass interviews were based on stigmatizing racial generalization that promoted public stereotypes, created great resentment in the targeted community, and probably generated few, if any leads, they were "unjustifiable discrimination"), *with* Samuel R. Gross & Debra Livingston, *Racial Profiling Under Attack*, 102 Colum. L. Rev. 1413, 1436 (2002) (concluding that the interview campaign was profiling to the extent that the FBI assumed that Middle Eastern men were more likely than others to commit acts of terror but was not profiling to the extent that FBI agents were "pursuing case-specific information about the September 11 attacks, albeit in dragnet fashion"). Does it matter? Professors Gross and Livingston suggest that how the FBI selects its interviewees matters less than how they carry out the interviews. *Id.* at 1436-1437 ("Are the interviews conducted respectfully...?"). Do you agree?

A court has refused to dismiss equal protection and First Amendment (freedom of religion) challenges to the pretextual post-9/11 detentions of Muslim men arrested for non-terrorist criminal offenses. *See* Elmaghraby v. Ashcroft, 2005 WL 2375202, at *28-29 (E.D.N.Y. 2005). But the same court dismissed claims by Muslim men that they had been selectively detained for

C. Profiling

immigration violations and identified as persons of "high interest" (to the 9/11 investigation) based on their national origin. The court explained:

> As a tool fashioned by the executive branch to ferret out information to prevent additional terrorist attacks, this approach may have been crude, but it was not so irrational or outrageous as to warrant judicial intrusion into an area in which courts have little experience and less expertise. See [Reno v. American-Arab Anti-Discrimination Committee, 525 U.S. 471, 490-91 (1999)]; Mathews [v. Diaz, 426 U.S. 67, 81-82 (1976)] ("The reasons that preclude judicial review of political questions also dictate a narrow standard of review of decisions made by the Congress or the President in the area of immigration and naturalization."); see also Zadvydas [v. Davis, 533 U.S. 678, 696 (2001)] (stating that "terrorism" might warrant "special arguments" for "heightened deference to the judgments of the political branches with respect to matters of national security"). I note, however, that the extraordinary circumstances of September 11 are by no means a prerequisite to the deference owed the political branches in this area. Such national emergencies are not cause to relax the rights guaranteed in our Constitution. Yet regarding immigration matters such as this, the Constitution assigns to the political branches all but the most minimal authority in making the delicate balancing judgments that attend all difficult constitutional questions; "nothing in the structure of our Government or the text of our Constitution would warrant judicial review by standards which would require [courts] to equate [their] political judgment with that of" the executive or the Congress. Harisiades [v. Shaughnessy, 342 U.S. 580, 590 (1952)].
> [Turkmen v. Ashcroft, 2006 WL 1662663, at *43 (E.D.N.Y. 2006).]

Can you articulate the difference between the claims in the two cases? *See DOJ Guidance, supra* p. 604. (Of course, profiling in terrorism investigations did not begin with the 9/11 attacks. *See* William C. Banks, *The "L.A. Eight" and Investigation of Terrorist Threats in the United States*, 31 Colum. Hum. Rts. L. Rev. 481 (2000).)

9. *Profiling and National Identity Cards.* One commentator has argued that "[a] national identity card could facilitate greater civil liberties for groups targeted by racial and ethnic stereotyping and profiling. Membership would alleviate harassment because presentation of the card would result in an immediate check of one's identity with the national computerized data system." John Dwight Ingram, *Racial and Ethnic Profiling*, 29 T. Marshall L. Rev. 55, 83 (2003). Do you agree?

Organization and Coordination of Counterterrorism Investigations

22

The constitutional and statutory framework established by the judiciary and by Congress in the Foreign Intelligence Surveillance Act (FISA) and other statutes tells only part of the story of the law concerning counterterrorism investigations. Particularly for investigative techniques other than electronic surveillance and physical searches, the discretion in the executive branch to initiate and then conduct investigations is largely governed by executive branch rules, not by statute, and the courts have had little to say to provide guidance for these investigations.

Nevertheless, important legal determinations must be made—such as whether to approve an agent's request to follow the daily routine of a potential suspected terrorist, whether sufficient suspicion exists to launch even a preliminary investigation, and when informants may be placed inside a targeted organization. Once intelligence is collected, say by the FBI, under what circumstances should the information be shared, and with what other agencies?

In this chapter we first probe the executive branch organization for counterterrorism investigations. An executive order supplies an overarching template for the conduct of intelligence operations by executive agencies, including the FBI and CIA. Then we explore the rules that govern how the FBI—the principal federal intelligence agency for countering terrorism—conducts its terrorism detection activities. Post-September 11 evaluations by the Department of Justice have produced important revisions to longstanding FBI Guidelines governing a range of investigative activities.

Second, it is now common knowledge that some of the September 11 hijackers lived openly in the United States when their names or names of their close associates were on intelligence "watch lists." The watch list information was not shared in a timely fashion with the FBI or state and local law enforcement agencies, which might have been able to detect the hijackers' plot before it was implemented. Because intelligence about would-be terrorists might be obtained by the FBI, CIA, NSA, or agencies inside the Defense Department, or by a state or local law enforcement agency, the challenges of sharing intelligence are staggering. Moreover, the FBI, long embedded in its role as the federal government's law enforcement agency, has struggled to reshape its mission to incorporate a vigorous counterterrorism component. How should information classified by one agency be shared with another agency? How should a federal agency share with a state or local agency? How can information be shared in a secure way without jeopardizing the privacy interests of those identified in the intelligence? Here we survey the efforts toward information sharing that have been made in the counterterrorism area, and we examine briefly the state of reforms at the FBI.

A. EXECUTIVE AUTHORITY FOR NATIONAL SECURITY INVESTIGATIONS

The Attorney General is expressly vested with "primary investigative authority for all Federal crimes of terrorism." 18 U.S.C. §2332b(f) (2000 & Supp. III 2003). The FBI, in contrast, has scant statutory authority to carry out its mission. Lacking a legislative charter, the FBI operates on the basis of the Attorney General's authority in 28 U.S.C. §533 (2000 & Supp. III 2003) to appoint officials:

(1) to detect and prosecute crimes against the United States;
(2) to assist in the protection of the person of the President; and ...
(4) to conduct such other investigations regarding official matters under the control of the Department of Justice and the Department of State as may be directed by the Attorney General.

The FBI also draws investigative authority from statutes like FISA.

All FBI investigations are conducted according to guidelines promulgated by the Attorney General and a 1981 executive order that directs the activities of all the agencies that make up the intelligence community. The *Attorney General's Guidelines on General Crimes, Racketeering Enterprise and Domestic Security/Terrorism Investigations*, Mar. 7, 1983, 32 Crim. L. Rep. 3087 (hereinafter *Domestic Security Guidelines*), "provide guidance for all investigations by the FBI of crimes and crime-related activities." *Id.*, Preamble. On May 30, 2002, the FBI issued three new sets of guidelines for investigations that significantly revise the 1983 *Domestic Security Guidelines*. They are the *Attorney General's Guidelines on General Crimes, Racketeering Enterprise and Terrorism Enterprise Investigations*; the *Attorney General's Guidelines on the Use of Confidential Informants*; and the *Attorney General's Guidelines on Federal Bureau of Investigation Undercover Operations*, available at http://www.usdoj.gov/olp/index.html#agguide. The 1983 *Attorney General Foreign Counterintelligence (FCI) Guidelines* were replaced on November 5, 2003, by the *Attorney General's Guidelines for FBI National Security Investigations and Foreign Intelligence Collection (NSI Guidelines)*. These guidelines support FBI collection of foreign intelligence and national security information. Excerpts of the current guidelines, as revised, along with a portion of Executive Order No. 12,333, are set out below.

Executive Order No. 12,333[1]
46 Fed. Reg. 59,941 (Dec. 4, 1981)

1.8 The Central Intelligence Agency. All duties and responsibilities of the CIA shall be related to the intelligence functions set out below. As authorized by this Order; the National Security Act of 1947, as amended; the CIA Act of 1949, as amended; appropriate directives or other applicable law, the CIA shall:

(a) Collect, produce and disseminate foreign intelligence and counterintelligence, including information not otherwise obtainable. The collection of foreign intelligence or counterintelligence within the United States shall be coordinated with the FBI as required by procedures agreed upon by the [DCI] and the Attorney General; ...

(c) Conduct counterintelligence activities outside the United States and, without assuming or performing any internal security functions, conduct counterintelligence activities within the United States in coordination with the FBI as required by procedures agreed upon by the [DCI] and the Attorney General; ...

2.3 Collection of Information. Agencies within the Intelligence Community are authorized to collect, retain or disseminate information concerning United States persons only in accordance with procedures established by the head of the agency concerned and approved by the Attorney General. . . . Those procedures shall permit collection, retention and dissemination of the following types of information: ...

(b) Information constituting foreign intelligence or counterintelligence, including such information concerning corporations or other commercial organizations. Collection within the United States of foreign intelligence not otherwise obtainable shall be undertaken by the FBI or, when significant foreign intelligence is sought, by other authorized agencies of the Intelligence Community, provided that no foreign intelligence collection by such agencies may be undertaken for the purpose of acquiring information concerning the domestic activities of United States persons; ...

2.5 Attorney General Approval. The Attorney General hereby is delegated the power to approve the use for intelligence purposes, within the United States or against a United States person abroad, of any technique for which a warrant would be required if undertaken for law enforcement purposes, provided that such techniques shall not be undertaken unless the Attorney General has determined in each case that there is probable cause to believe that the technique is directed against a foreign power or an agent of a foreign power. Electronic surveillance, as defined in the Foreign Intelligence Surveillance Act of 1978, shall be conducted in accordance with that Act, as well as this Order.

2.6 Assistance to Law Enforcement Authorities. Agencies within the Intelligence Community are authorized to: ...

(b) Unless otherwise precluded by law or this Order, participate in law enforcement activities to investigate or prevent clandestine intelligence activities by foreign powers, or international terrorist or narcotics activities; ...

[1. Portions of Executive Order No. 12,333 are reproduced *supra* pp. 397, 444.]

2.8 Consistency With Other Laws. Nothing in this Order shall be construed to authorize any activity in violation of the Constitution or statutes of the United States.

2.9 Undisclosed Participation in Organizations Within the United States. No one acting on behalf of agencies within the Intelligence Community may join or otherwise participate in any organization in the United States on behalf of any agency within the Intelligence Community without disclosing his intelligence affiliation to appropriate officials of the organization, except in accordance with procedures established by the head of the agency concerned and approved by the Attorney General. Such participation shall be authorized only if it is essential to achieving lawful purposes as determined by the agency head or designee. No such participation may be undertaken for the purpose of influencing the activity of the organization or its members except in cases where:

(a) The participation is undertaken on behalf of the FBI in the course of a lawful investigation; or

(b) The organization concerned is composed primarily of individuals who are not United States persons and is reasonably believed to be acting on behalf of a foreign power....

Attorney General's Guidelines on General Crimes, Racketeering Enterprise and Terrorism Enterprise Investigations [*Domestic Security Guidelines*]

Department of Justice, May 2002
http://www.usdoj.gov/olp/generalcrimes2.pdf

I. GENERAL PRINCIPLES

Preliminary inquiries and investigations governed by these Guidelines are conducted for the purpose of preventing, detecting, or prosecuting violations of federal law. The FBI shall fully utilize the methods authorized by these Guidelines to maximize the realization of these objectives....

All preliminary inquiries shall be conducted pursuant to the General Crime Guidelines. There is no separate provision for preliminary inquiries under the Criminal Intelligence guidelines.... A preliminary inquiry shall be promptly terminated when it becomes apparent that a full investigation is not warranted. If, on the basis of information discovered in the course of a preliminary inquiry an investigation is warranted, it may be conducted as a general crimes investigation, or a criminal intelligence investigation, or both. All such investigations, however, shall be based on a reasonable factual predicate and shall have a valid law enforcement purpose.

In its efforts to anticipate or prevent crime, the FBI must at times initiate investigations in advance of criminal conduct. It is important that such investigations not be based solely on activities protected by the First Amendment or on the lawful exercise of any other rights secured by the Constitution or laws of the United States. When, however, statements advocate criminal activity or indicate an apparent intent to engage in crime, particularly crimes of violence, an investigation under these Guidelines may be warranted unless it is apparent, from the circumstances or the context in which the statements are made, that there is no prospect of harm....

II. GENERAL CRIMES INVESTIGATIONS...

B. PRELIMINARY INQUIRIES

(1) On some occasions the FBI may receive information or an allegation not warranting a full investigation — because there is not yet a "reasonable indication" of criminal activities — but whose responsible handling requires some further scrutiny beyond the prompt and extremely limited checking out of initial leads. In such circumstances, though the factual predicate for an investigation has not been met, the FBI may initiate an "inquiry" involving some measured review, contact, or observation activities in response to the allegation or information indicating the possibility of criminal activity.

This authority to conduct inquiries short of a full investigation allows the government to respond in a measured way to ambiguous or incomplete information and to do so with as little intrusion as the needs of the situation permit. This is especially important... when an allegation or information is received from a source of unknown reliability....

(2) The FBI supervisor authorizing an inquiry shall assure that the allegation or other information which warranted the inquiry has been recorded in writing....

(4) The choice of investigative techniques in an inquiry is a matter of judgment, which should take account of: (i) the objectives of the inquiry and available investigative resources, (ii) the intrusiveness of a technique, considering such factors as the effect on the privacy of individuals and potential damage to reputation, (iii) the seriousness of the possible crime, and (iv) the strength of the information indicating its existence or future commission. Where the conduct of an inquiry presents a choice between the use of more or less intrusive methods, the FBI should consider whether the information could be obtained in a timely and effective way by the less intrusive means. The FBI should not hesitate to use any lawful techniques consistent with these Guidelines in an inquiry, even if intrusive, where the intrusiveness is warranted in light of the seriousness of the possible crime or the strength of the information indicating its existence or future commission. This point is to be particularly observed in inquiries relating to possible terrorist activities.

(5) All lawful investigative techniques may be used in an inquiry except:

(a) Mail openings; and

(b) Nonconsensual electronic surveillance or any other investigative technique covered by chapter 119 of title 18, United States Code (18 U.S.C. 2510-2522).

(6) The following investigative techniques may be used in an inquiry without any prior authorization from a supervisory agent:

(a) Examination of FBI indices and files;

(b) Examination of records available to the public and other public sources of information;

(c) Examination of available federal, state and local government records;

(d) Interview of the complainant, previously established informants and confidential sources;

(e) Interview of the potential subject;

(f) Interview of persons who would readily be able to corroborate or deny the truth of the allegation, except this does not include pretext interviews or interviews of a potential subject's employer or co-workers unless the interviewee was the complainant;

(g) Physical or photographic surveillance of any person.

The use of any other lawful investigative technique in an inquiry shall require prior approval by a supervisory agent, except in exigent circumstances....

(7) Where a preliminary inquiry fails to disclose sufficient information to justify an investigation, the FBI shall terminate the inquiry and make a record of the closing....

III. TERRORISM ENTERPRISE INVESTIGATIONS

This section authorizes the FBI to conduct criminal intelligence investigations of certain enterprises who seek either to obtain monetary or commercial gains or profits through racketeering activities or to further political or social goals through activities that involve criminal violence. These investigations differ from general crimes investigations, authorized by Section II, in several important respects. As a general rule, an investigation of a completed criminal act is normally confined to determining who committed that act and with securing evidence to establish the elements of the particular offense. It is, in this respect, self-defining. An intelligence investigation of an ongoing criminal enterprise must determine the size and composition of the group involved, its geographic dimensions, its past acts and intended criminal goals, and its capacity for harm. While a standard criminal investigation terminates with the decision to prosecute or not to prosecute, the investigation of a criminal enterprise does not necessarily end, even though one or more of the participants may have been prosecuted....

B. DOMESTIC SECURITY/TERRORISM INVESTIGATIONS...

1. General Authority

a. A terrorism enterprise investigation may be initiated when facts or circumstances reasonably indicate that two or more persons are engaged in an enterprise for the purpose of: (i) furthering political or social goals wholly or in part through activities that involve force or violence and a violation of federal criminal law, (ii) engaging in terrorism as defined in 18 U.S.C. 2331(1) or (5) that involves a violation of federal criminal law, or (iii) committing any offense described in 18 U.S.C. 2332b(g)(5)(B). A terrorism enterprise investigation may also be initiated when facts or circumstances reasonably indicate that two or more persons are engaged in a pattern of racketeering activity as defined in the RICO statute, 18 U.S.C. 1961(5), that involves an offense or offenses described in 18 U.S.C. 2332b(g)(5)(B). The standard of "reasonable indication" is identical to that governing the initiation of a general crimes investigation under Part II. In determining whether an investigation should be conducted, the FBI shall consider all of the circumstances including: (i) the magnitude of the threatened harm; (ii) the likelihood it will occur; (iii) the immediacy of the threat; and (iv) any danger to privacy or free expression posed by an investigation....

c. Mere speculation that force or violence might occur during the course of an otherwise peaceable demonstration is not sufficient grounds for initiation of an investigation under this Subpart, but where facts or circumstances reasonably indicate that a group or enterprise has engaged or aims to engage in activities involving force or violence or other criminal conduct described in paragraph (1)(a) in a demonstration, an investigation may be initiated in conformity with the standards of that paragraph.... This does not limit the collection of information about public demonstrations by enterprises that are under active investigation pursuant to paragraph (1)(a) above....

4. Authorization and Renewal

a. A terrorism enterprise investigation may be authorized by the Special Agent in Charge, with notification to FBIHQ, upon a written recommendation setting forth the facts or circumstances reasonably indictating the existence of an enterprise as described in paragraph (1)(a)....

IV. INVESTIGATIVE TECHNIQUES

A. When conducting investigations under these guidelines the FBI may use any lawful investigative technique.... When the conduct of an investigation presents a choice between the use of more or less intrusive methods, the FBI should consider whether the information could be obtained in a timely and effective way by less intrusive means....

B. All requirements for use of a technique set by statute, Department regulations and policies, and Attorney General Guidelines must be complied with. The investigative techniques listed below are subject to the noted restrictions:

    1. Informants and confidential sources must be used in compliance with the Attorney General's Guidelines on the Use of Informants and Confidential Sources;

    2. Undercover operations must be conducted in compliance with the Attorney General's Guidelines of FBI Undercover Operations;...

    4. Nonconsensual electronic surveillance must be conducted pursuant to the warrant procedures and requirements of Title III....

    7. Consensual electronic monitoring must be authorized pursuant to Department policy....

    8. Searches and seizures must be conducted under the authority of a valid warrant unless the search or seizure comes within a judicially recognized exception to the warrant requirements....

V. DISSEMINATION OF INFORMATION

A. The FBI may disseminate information during investigations conducted pursuant to these guidelines to another Federal agency or to a State or local criminal justice agency when such information:

A. Executive Authority for National Security Investigations

      1. falls within the investigative or protective jurisdiction or litigative responsibility of the agency;

      2. may assist in preventing a crime or the use of violence or any other conduct dangerous to human life; ...

      4. is required to be disseminated by statute, interagency agreement approved by the Attorney General, or Presidential Directive;

and to other persons and agencies as permitted by Sections 552 and 552a of Title V, U.S.C. ...

VI. COUNTERTERRORISM ACTIVITIES AND OTHER AUTHORIZATIONS

A. COUNTERTERRORISM ACTIVITIES

1. Information Systems

The FBI is authorized to operate and participate in identification, tracking, and information systems for the purpose of identifying and locating terrorists. ... Systems within the scope of this paragraph may draw on and retain pertinent information from any source permitted by law, including information derived from past or ongoing investigative activities; other information collected or provided by governmental entities, such as foreign intelligence information and lookout list information; publicly available information, whether obtained directly or through services or resources (whether nonprofit or commercial) that compile or analyze such information; and information voluntarily provided by private entities. Any such system operated by the FBI shall be reviewed periodically for compliance with all applicable statutory provisions, Department regulations and policies, and Attorney General Guidelines.

2. Visiting Public Places and Events

For the purpose of detecting or preventing terrorist activities, the FBI is authorized to visit any place and attend any event that is open to the public, on the same terms and conditions as members of the public generally. No information obtained from such visits shall be retained unless it relates to potential criminal or terrorist activity.

VII. RESERVATION ...

      C. These guidelines are set forth solely for the purpose of internal Department of Justice guidance. They are not intended to, do not, and may not be relied upon to create any rights, substantive or procedural, enforceable at law by any party in any manner, civil or criminal, nor do they place any limitation on otherwise lawful investigative and litigative prerogatives of the Department of Justice.

Attorney General's Guidelines for FBI National Security Investigations and Foreign Intelligence Collection (U)[2] [*NSI Guidelines*]

Department of Justice, October 2003
http://www.usdoj.gov/olp/nsiguidelines.pdf

INTRODUCTION (U)

... These Guidelines generally authorize investigation by the FBI of threats to the national security of the United States; investigative assistance by the FBI to state, local, and foreign governments in relation to matters affecting the national security; the collection of foreign intelligence by the FBI; the production of strategic analysis by the FBI; and the retention and dissemination of information resulting from the foregoing activities. This includes guidance for the activities of the FBI pursuant to Executive Order 12333, "United States Intelligence Activities" (Dec. 4, 1981). (U)

The general objective of these Guidelines is the full utilization of all authorities and investigative techniques, consistent with the Constitution and laws of the United States, so as to protect the United States and its people from terrorism and other threats to the national security. (U)...

The activities of the FBI under these Guidelines are part of the overall response of the United States to threats to the national security, which includes cooperative efforts and sharing of information with other agencies, including other entities in the Intelligence Community and the Department of Homeland Security. The overriding priority in these efforts is preventing, preempting, and disrupting terrorist threats to the United States. In some cases, this priority will dictate the provision of information to other agencies even where doing so may affect criminal prosecutions or ongoing law enforcement or intelligence operations. To the greatest extent possible that is consistent with this overriding priority, the FBI shall also act in a manner to protect other significant interests, including the protection of intelligence and sensitive law enforcement sources and methods, other classified information, and sensitive operational and prosecutorial information. (U)

A. NATIONAL SECURITY INVESTIGATIONS (U)

... The investigations authorized by these Guidelines serve to protect the national security by providing the basis for, and informing decisions concerning, a variety of measures to deal with threats to the national security. These measures may include, for example, recruitment of double agents and other assets; excluding or removing persons involved in terrorism or espionage from the United States; freezing assets of organizations that engage in or support terrorism; securing targets of terrorism or espionage; providing threat information and warnings to other federal agencies and officials, state and local governments, and private entities; diplomatic or military actions; and actions by

[2. The guidelines are partly classified. "(U)" means that a particular provision is unclassified.]

A. Executive Authority for National Security Investigations

other intelligence agencies to counter international terrorism or other national security threats. In addition, the matters identified by these Guidelines as threats to the national security, including international terrorism and espionage, almost invariably involve possible violations of criminal statutes. Detecting, solving, and preventing these crimes — and in many cases, arresting and prosecuting the perpetrators — are crucial objectives of national security investigations under these Guidelines. Thus, these investigations are usually both "counterintelligence" investigations and "criminal" investigations. (U)

The authority to conduct national security investigations under these Guidelines does not supplant or limit the authority to carry out activities under other Attorney General guidelines or pursuant to other lawful authorities of the FBI. (U)...

Part II of these Guidelines authorizes three levels of investigative activity in national security investigations: (1) threat assessments, (2) preliminary investigations, and (3) full investigations: (U)

(1) *Threat assessments.* To carry out its central mission of preventing the commission of terrorist acts against the United States and its people, the FBI must proactively draw on available sources of information to identify terrorist threats and activities. It cannot be content to wait for leads to come in through the actions of others, but rather must be vigilant in detecting terrorist activities to the full extent permitted by law, with an eye towards early intervention and prevention of acts of terrorism before they occur. (U)

Part II.A of these Guidelines accordingly authorizes the proactive collection of information concerning threats to the national security, including information on individuals, groups, and organizations of possible investigative interest, and information on possible targets of international terrorist activities or other national security threats (such as infrastructure and computer systems vulnerabilities). (U)...

In addition to allowing proactive information collection for national security purposes, the authority to conduct threat assessments may be used in cases in which information or an allegation concerning possible terrorist (or other national security-threatening) activity by an individual, group, or organization is received, and the matter can be checked out promptly through the relatively non-intrusive techniques authorized in threat assessments. This can avoid the need to open a formal preliminary or full investigation, if the threat assessment indicates that further investigation is not warranted. In this function, threat assessments under these Guidelines are comparable to the checking of initial leads in ordinary criminal investigations. (U)

(2) *Preliminary investigations....* Preliminary investigations may relate to individuals, groups, organizations, and possible criminal violations, as specified in Part II.B....

(3) *Full investigations.* Like preliminary investigations, full investigations may relate to individuals, groups, or organizations and possible criminal violations, as specified in Part II.B....

Part II.E. of these Guidelines sets out conditions and approval requirements for extraterritorial activities. As provided in Part II.E, these activities require a request from or approval of the Director of Central Intelligence or a designee. This requirement ensures that extraterritorial activities under these Guidelines are properly coordinated with other agencies in the Intelligence

Community, so that their authorities and capabilities are also brought to bear as appropriate to protect the national security, consistent with Executive Order 12333 or a successor order.

The FBI may also provide assistance to state and local governments, and to foreign law enforcement, intelligence, and security agencies, in investigations relating to threats to the national security. Part III of these Guidelines specifies standards and procedures for the provision of such assistance. (U) . . .

B. FOREIGN INTELLIGENCE COLLECTION (U)

The FBI's functions pursuant to Executive Order 12333 §§1.6, 1.14, 2.3, and 2.4 include engaging in foreign intelligence collection and providing operational support for other components of the U.S. Intelligence Community. This role is frequently critical in collecting foreign intelligence within the United States because the authorized domestic activities of other intelligence agencies are more constrained than those of the FBI under applicable statutory law and Executive Order 12333. (U) . . .

I. GENERAL AUTHORITIES AND PRINCIPLES (U)

A. GENERAL AUTHORITIES (U)

1. The FBI is authorized to conduct investigations to obtain information concerning or to protect against threats to the national security, including investigations of crimes involved in or related to threats to the national security, as provided in Parts II and V of these Guidelines. Threats to the national security are:

    a. International terrorism.
    b. Espionage and other intelligence activities, sabotage, or assassination, conducted by, for, or on behalf of foreign powers, organizations, or persons.
    c. Foreign computer intrusions.
    d. Other matters as determined by the Attorney General, consistent with Executive Order 12333 or a successor order. (U) . . .

B. USE OF AUTHORITIES AND METHOD (U) . . .

2. Choice of Methods (U)

The conduct of investigations and other activities authorized by these Guidelines may present choices between the use of information collection methods that are more or less intrusive, considering such factors as the effect on the privacy of individuals, and potential damage or reputation. As Executive Order 12333 §2.4 provides, "the latest intrusive collection techniques feasible" are to be used in such situations. It is recognized, however, that the choice of techniques is a matter of judgment. The FBI shall not hesitate to use any lawful techniques consistent with these Guidelines, even if intrusive, where the degree

A. Executive Authority for National Security Investigations

of intrusiveness is warranted in light of the seriousness of a threat to the national security or the strength of the information indicating its existence. This point is to be particularly observed in investigations relating to terrorism. (U)

3. Respect for Legal Rights (U)

These Guidelines do not authorize investigating or maintaining information on United States persons solely for the purpose of monitoring activities protected by the First Amendment or the lawful exercise of other rights secured by the Constitution or laws of the United States. Rather, all activities under these Guidelines must have a valid purpose consistent with these Guidelines, and must be carried out in conformity with the Constitution and all applicable statutes, executive orders, Department of Justice regulations and policies, and Attorney General Guidelines....

C. DETERMINATION OF UNITED STATES PERSON STATUS (U) ...

3. Determination Whether Certain Groups are Substantially Composed of United States Persons (U)

In determining whether a group or organization in the United States that is affiliated with a foreign-based international organization is substantially composed of United States persons, the relationship between the two shall be considered. If the U.S.-based group or organization operates directly under the control of the international organization and has no independent program or activities in the United States, the membership of the entire international organization shall be considered in determining if it is substantially composed of United States persons. If, however, the U.S.-based group or organization has programs or activities separate from, or in addition to, those directed by the international organization, only its membership in the United States shall be considered in determining whether it is substantially composed of United States persons. (U)

D. NATURE AND APPLICATION OF THE GUIDELINES (U)

1. Status as Internal Guidance (U)

These Guidelines are set forth solely for the purpose of internal Department of Justice guidance. They are not intended to, do not, and may not be relied upon to create any rights, substantive or procedural, enforceable by law by any party in any matter, civil or criminal, nor do they place any limitation on otherwise lawful investigative and litigative prerogatives of the Department of Justice. (U)

2. Departures from the Guidelines (U)

Departures from these Guidelines must be approved by the Attorney General, the Deputy Attorney General, or an official designated by the Attorney

General. If a departure from these Guidelines is necessary without such prior approval because of the immediacy or gravity of a threat to the national security or to the safety of persons or property and the need to take immediate action to protect against such a threat, the Attorney General, the Deputy Attorney General, or an official designated by the Attorney General shall be notified as soon thereafter as practicable. The FBI shall provide timely written notice of departures from these Guidelines to the Office of Intelligence Policy and Review. Notwithstanding this paragraph, all activities in all circumstances must be carried out in a manner consistent with the Constitution and laws of the United States. (U) . . .

II. NATIONAL SECURITY INVESTIGATIONS (U) . . .

B. COMMON PROVISIONS FOR PRELIMINARY AND FULL INVESTIGATIONS (U) . . .

3. Investigations of Groups and Organizations (U)

a. Preliminary and full investigations of groups and organizations should focus on activities related to threats to the national security, not on unrelated First Amendment activities. . . .

E. EXTRATERRITORIAL OPERATIONS (U)

1. The FBI may conduct investigations abroad, participate with foreign officials in investigations abroad, or otherwise conduct activities outside the United States with the written request or approval of the Director of Central Intelligence and the Attorney General or their designees. . . . The involvement of the Director of Central Intelligence or designee in the authorization of these extraterritorial activities reflects the coordinating and liaison roles of the Director of Central Intelligence and the Central Intelligence Agency in this area in accordance with the National Security Act of 1947 and Executive Order 12333, including §§1.5(e), 1.8(c)-(d), 1.14(b) of that Order, and helps to ensure that the collective resources and capabilities of the broader Intelligence Community will be used in the most effective manner to protect the national security. . . .

IV. FOREIGN INTELLIGENCE COLLECTION AND ASSISTANCE TO INTELLIGENCE AGENCIES (U)

A. FOREIGN INTELLIGENCE COLLECTION (U)

1. The FBI may collect foreign intelligence in response to requirements of topical interest published by an entity authorized by the Director of Central Intelligence to establish such requirements, including, but not limited to, the National HUMINT Requirements Tasking Center. When approved by the Attorney General, the Deputy Attorney General, or an official designated by the Attorney General, the FBI may collect other foreign intelligence in response

A. Executive Authority for National Security Investigations

to tasking specifically levied on the FBI by an official of the Intelligence Community designated by the President. Upon a request by an official of the Intelligence Community designated by the President, the FBI may also collect foreign intelligence to clarify or complete foreign intelligence previously disseminated by the FBI. Copies of such requests shall be provided to the Office of Intelligence Policy and Review. (U)

2. The FBI may also collect foreign intelligence, if consistent with Executive Order 12333 or a successor order, as directed by the Attorney General, the Deputy Attorney General, or an official designated by the Attorney General. (U) ...

B. OPERATIONAL SUPPORT (U)

1. When approved by the Attorney General, the Deputy Attorney General, or an official designated by the Attorney General, the FBI may provide operational support to authorized intelligence activities of other entities of the Intelligence Community upon a request made or confirmed in writing by an official of the Intelligence Community designated by the President. The request shall describe the type and duration of support required, the reasons why the FBI is being requested to furnish the assistance, and the techniques that are expected to be utilized, and shall certify that such assistance is necessary to an authorized activity of the requesting entity. (U)

2. The support may include techniques set forth in the approved request and, with the approval of FBI headquarters, any other technique that does not substantially alter the character of the support. The FBI shall promptly notify the Office of Intelligence Policy and Review of the utilization of any such additional techniques. (U)

3. The FBI may recruit new assets to obtain information or services needed to furnish the requested support, subject to the same standards and procedures applicable to other FBI assets. (U) ...

VII. RETENTION AND DISSEMINATION OF INFORMATION ...

B. INFORMATION SHARING (U)

Legal rules and Department of Justice policies regarding information sharing and interagency coordination have been significantly modified since the September 11, 2001, terrorist attack by statutory reforms and new Attorney General guidelines. The general principle reflected in current laws and policies is that information should be shared as consistently and fully as possible among agencies with relevant responsibilities to protect the United States and its people from terrorism and other threats to the national security, except as limited by specific constraints on such sharing. Under this general principle, the FBI shall provide information expeditiously to other agencies in the Intelligence Community, so that these agencies can take action in a timely manner to protect the national security in accordance with their lawful functions. (U) ...

NOTES AND QUESTIONS

a. Executive Order No. 12,333

1. *Investigatory Authorizations Under Executive Order No. 12,333.* What constitutes a "lawful" FBI investigation within the meaning of Executive Order No. 12,333? What are the likely elements of a probable cause determination under §2.5? How does such a probable cause decision differ from those made pursuant to either FISA or Federal Rule of Criminal Procedure 41? See *supra* p. 525.

According to the executive order, the most important factor in assessing executive power to conduct national security investigations is the presence or absence of a connection between the target of surveillance and a foreign power. To this extent, the executive order tracks FISA. The 1994 amendments to FISA extended the FISA procedures to applications for a physical search for foreign intelligence information where the target is a foreign power or agent of a foreign power. In Executive Order No. 12,949, 60 Fed. Reg. 8169 (Feb. 9, 1995), President Clinton updated Executive Order No. 12,333 to authorize the Attorney General to approve applications to the Foreign Intelligence Surveillance Court (FISC) for physical searches for foreign intelligence purposes, following the certifications required by FISA. *Id.* §2. Bearing in mind the provisions of FISA, what "technique[s] for which a warrant would be required if undertaken for law enforcement purposes" (§2.5) continue to be governed by Executive Order No. 12,333 and FBI guidelines?

2. *Infiltration.* Is CIA or FBI infiltration of domestic organizations permitted by Executive Order No. 12,333? On the basis of what information will the "agency head or designee" determine that infiltration is "essential to achieving lawful purposes"? If infiltration is authorized outside the limits of the order, what redress would be available to aggrieved persons? *See* Seth Kreimer, *Watching the Watchers: Surveillance, Transparency, and Political Freedom in the War on Terror,* 7 U. Pa. J. Const. L. 133 (2004).

3. *12,333 and the National Security Act of 1947.* Compare §§1.8 and 2.3(b) of Executive Order No. 12,333, *supra* p. 397, to the National Security Act of 1947, *supra* p. 355. Does the order adequately respect the statutory mandate that the CIA not engage in "internal security functions"? How may the CIA "conduct counterintelligence activities within the United States in coordination with the FBI" without performing any "internal security functions"? In what ways will the reorganization of the intelligence community and the creation of the Director of National Intelligence (DNI), as prescribed in the Intelligence Reform and Terrorism Prevention Act of 2004, described *supra* p. 355, affect the CIA/FBI relationship in national security investigations?

4. *Making of Guidelines for Investigation.* Several sections of Executive Order No. 12,333 provide that procedures for intelligence collection are to be independently established by each agency, subject to approval by the Attorney General. Should a citizen be able to participate in setting such procedures? Where would they be published?

b. Domestic Security Guidelines

1. *Authority for Guidelines.* Does the FBI have statutory authority to promulgate the guidelines set out above? In addition to the authority granted by 28 U.S.C. §533, the Attorney General "may from time to time make such provisions as he considers appropriate authorizing the performance by any other officer, employee, or agency of the Department of Justice of any function of the Attorney General." *Id.* §510. Do you think Congress should provide more explicit statutory authority for the FBI to conduct national security investigations? *See* Tom Lininger, *Sects, Lies, and Videotape: The Surveillance and Infiltration of Religious Groups*, 89 Iowa L. Rev. 1201 (2004).

2. *The Guidelines and FISA.* What purposes are served by these guidelines that are not met by FISA? Can you see where the prescriptions in FISA end and those of the two sets of guidelines begin?

3. *Application.* Compare the coverage of the two sets of guidelines. How can you tell which set applies to a potential investigation?

4. *Preliminary Investigation.* Are the standards for beginning a preliminary inquiry in the domestic security setting clear? What purpose is served by the preliminary inquiry? Can you predict when agents might opt for a preliminary inquiry instead of a full investigation? Are the rights of the targets of an inquiry safeguarded adequately by the *Domestic Security Guidelines*?

The Introduction to the *2002 Domestic Security Guidelines* describes and explains the checking of leads and preliminary inquiries:

> The lowest level of investigative activity is the "prompt and extremely limited checking out of initial leads," which should be undertaken whenever information is received of such a nature that some follow-up as to the possibility of criminal activity is warranted. This limited activity should be conducted with an eye toward promptly determining whether further investigation (either a preliminary inquiry or a full investigation) should be conducted.
>
> The next level of investigative activity, a preliminary inquiry, should be undertaken when there is information or an allegation which indicates the possibility of criminal activity and whose responsible handling requires some further scrutiny beyond checking initial leads. This authority allows FBI agents to respond to information that is ambiguous or incomplete. Even where the available information meets only this threshold, the range of available investigative techniques is broad....
>
> Whether it is appropriate to open a preliminary inquiry immediately, or instead to engage first in a limited checking out of leads, depends on the circumstances presented. If, for example, an agent receives an allegation that an individual or group has advocated the commission of criminal violence, and no other facts are available, an appropriate first step would be checking out of leads to determine whether the individual, group, or members of the audience have the apparent ability or intent to carry out the advocated crime. A similar response would be appropriate on the basis of non-verbal conduct of an ambiguous character—for example, where a report is received that an individual has accumulated explosives that could be used either in a legitimate business or to commit

a terrorist act. Where the limited checking out of leads discloses a possibility or reasonable indication of criminal activity, a preliminary inquiry or full investigation may then be initiated. However, if the available information shows at the outset that the threshold standard for a preliminary inquiry or full investigation is satisfied, then the appropriate investigative activity may be initiated immediately, without progressing through more limited investigative stages.

The application of these Guidelines' standards for inquiries merits special attention in cases that involve efforts by individuals or groups to obtain, for no apparent reason, biological, chemical, radiological, or nuclear materials whose use or possession is constrained by such statutes as 18 U.S.C. 175, 229, or 831. For example, FBI agents are not required to possess information relating to an individual's intended criminal use of dangerous biological agents or toxins prior to initiating investigative activity. On the contrary, if an individual or group has attempted to obtain such materials, or has indicated a desire to acquire them, and the reason is not apparent, investigative action, such as conducting a checking out of leads or initiating a preliminary inquiry, may be appropriate to determine whether there is a legitimate purpose for the possession of the materials by the individual or group. Likewise, where individuals or groups engage in efforts to acquire or show an interest in acquiring, without apparent reason, toxic chemicals or their precursors or radiological or nuclear materials, investigative action to determine whether there is a legitimate purpose may be justified.

Upon what authority do FBI agents check leads or conduct preliminary inquiries? Do you see a risk that this authority could be exercised in a way that burdens constitutional liberties?

5. *Full Investigation.* How would you describe the threshold test for initiating a full investigation under the *Domestic Security Guidelines*? The guidelines define "reasonable indication" as: "substantially lower than probable cause.... [T]he standard does require specific facts or circumstances indicating a post, current, or impending violation. There must be an objective, factual basis for initiating the investigation; a mere hunch is insufficient." *2002 Domestic Security Guidelines*, §II.C.1. Does the definition clarify or muddy "reasonable indication"? The 2002 guidelines add that a full investigation "may be conducted to prevent, solve, or prosecute" criminal activity. *Id.* Does the "reasonable indication" standard continue to provide an adequate benchmark for preserving privacy or First Amendment interests?

6. *Informants.* Compare the provisions for the use of informants in the executive order with those in the *Domestic Security Guidelines*. While interviews and photographic surveillance in a domestic security investigation do not require prior authorization, the use of an informant to infiltrate a group "in a manner that may influence the exercise of rights protected by the First Amendment" must be approved by FBI headquarters with notice to the Department of Justice. *Domestic Security Guidelines* §IV.B.3. By contrast, during a preliminary "inquiry," informants and infiltrators may be used based on uncorroborated allegations; no reasonable suspicion of an illegal act is required. *Id.* §§I, IIB. What accounts for the differing treatment of the use of informants in these rules? Do the guidelines provide sufficient protection for individual liberties in this respect?

A. Executive Authority for National Security Investigations

The 2002 guidelines change the "undisclosed participation" strictures, providing instead that any such investigation that could raise "potential constitutional concerns relating to activities of the organization protected by the First Amendment" must comply with the *Attorney General's Guidelines on FBI Undercover Operations* and the *Attorney General's Guidelines Regarding the Use of Informants*. 2002 *Domestic Security Guidelines* §IV.B.3.

An undercover operation uses a government employee whose relationship with the FBI is concealed from third parties in the course of an investigation, *Undercover Operations Guidelines, supra,* §§II.B, C, while a confidential informant is any person who provides useful and credible information. *Confidential Informants Guidelines* §I.B.6. The *Confidential Informants Guidelines* do not mention the First Amendment interests of groups that may be infiltrated by an informant or undercover agent, and the *Undercover Operations Guidelines* simply say that any official empowered to authorize an undercover operation should give "careful consideration" to the "risk of invasion of privacy or interference with privileged or confidential relationships and any potential constitutional concerns or other legal concerns" in deciding whether to approve an application. *Undercover Operations Guidelines* §IV.A.(3). Do you think that these provisions are constitutional?

7. *Mail Covers and New Techniques.* The 2002 *Domestic Security Guidelines* removed mail covers from the list of forbidden techniques during preliminary inquiries. §II.B.5. Mail covers consist of viewing and recording information on the outside covers of mail. The Postal Inspector is authorized by regulation to initiate a mail cover at the request of a law enforcement agency. 39 C.F.R. §233.3 (2005). Is this change lawful? The 2002 guidelines also added potentially important and constitutionally controversial new authority for FBI investigations in counterterrorism in reaction to September 11 and the continuing threat of terrorism. Three broad investigative activities are authorized: (1) surfing the Internet to identify Web sites, bulletin boards, chat rooms, and the like where terrorist or other criminal activities might be detected; (2) attending public events and visiting public places for the purpose of detecting terrorist activity; and (3) using data-mining services to search for terrorists and terrorist activities. *See Domestic Security Guidelines* §§VI.A.1, 2; VI.B. According to DOJ officials, the decision to spell out the authorities in these three areas was based on the fact that the prior guidelines were widely regarded as exclusive; if something was not explicitly permitted, it was viewed as barred. *See New Rules Allow FBI Greater Use of Web, Visits to Public Places in Terrorism Probes,* 70 U.S.L.W. 2779 (June 11, 2002). What are the implications of the DOJ explanation for the scope and meaning of the new guidelines?

Some groups reacted by claiming that the new authorities would permit "fishing expeditions" and would chill protected expression in places like mosques, libraries, and Internet chat rooms, and at public gatherings in support of Palestinian or Islamic causes. *See* Center for Democracy & Technology, *CDT's Analysis of New FBI Guidelines,* May 30, 2002, *available at* http://www.cdt.org/wiretap/020530guidelines.shtml; Adam Liptak, *Changing the Standard: Despite Civil Liberties Fears, FBI Faces No Legal Obstacles on Domestic Spying,* N.Y. Times, May 31, 2002, at A1.

Section VI.B of the 2002 *Domestic Security Guidelines* authorizes the FBI to carry out "general topical research" online, defined as

> concerning subject areas that are relevant for the purpose of facilitation or supporting the discharge of investigative responsibilities... [but] does not include online searches for information by individuals' names or other individual identifiers, except where such searches are incidental to topical research, such as searching to locate writings on a topic by searching under the names of authors who write on the topic, or searching by the name of a party to a case in conducting legal research.

But if a private citizen can search the Internet using someone's name, why can't the FBI?

8. *Pretext Interviews?* In advance of the 2004 Republican and Democratic party conventions in New York and Boston, the FBI interviewed dozens of members of antiwar groups. One FBI field office memorandum characterized the effort as "pretext interviews" in pursuit of general information about possible criminal activity at the party conventions. While FBI officials claimed that the interviews were based on undisclosed, specific threat information, critics claimed that the FBI was treating dissent as a form of terrorism. Dan Eggen, *FBI Memos Show Agents Conducting "Pretext Interviews,"* Wash. Post, May 18, 2005, at A4. An internal Justice Department review concluded that the interviews were conducted for legitimate law enforcement purposes, not to inhibit the exercise of First Amendment rights. Inspector General, U.S. Dept. of Justice, *A Review of the FBI's Investigative Activities at the 2004 Democratic and Republican National Political Conventions*, Apr. 27, 2006. Upon what authority would these "pretext interviews" have been conducted?

9. *Enforceability of Guidelines.* The *Domestic Security Guidelines* explain that they are "solely for the purpose of internal Department of Justice guidelines" and are thus not judicially enforceable. §VII.C. If the guidelines are not judicially enforceable, do they serve any useful purpose? Would they have any importance in a judicial proceeding?

c. NSI Guidelines

1. *Comparing the Guidelines.* What are the principal differences between the *Domestic Security* and *NSI Guidelines*? What best explains the need for a separate set of *NSI Guidelines*? What guidance to investigators is supplied by the *NSI Guidelines* that is not already available under Executive Order No 12,333, FISA, other statutes, and the Constitution?

2. *Threat Assessments.* The authorization for conducting threat assessments is new in the 2003 *NSI Guidelines*. Roughly equivalent to the checking of leads in the *Domestic Security Guidelines*, the threat assessment activity is designed to

A. Executive Authority for National Security Investigations 633

permit early intervention and prevention of terrorist attacks. The authorization for "proactive collection" of publicly available information was not part of the previous *FCI Guidelines*. Why do you think the *Guidelines* were changed in this way? The predicate criteria for conducting threat assessments are redacted from the *Guidelines*, as is the threshold for initiating such an assessment. Can you imagine what the redactions say?

3. *Initiating and Conducting NSI Investigations.* Like the prior *FCI Guidelines*, significant portions of the *NSI Guidelines* are classified. Review the threshold for opening and the techniques for conducting an investigation under the *Domestic Security Guidelines*. Based on those guidelines and what you know from FISA and Executive Order 12,333, can you predict the triggering requirements for opening an NSI investigation? Can you say what techniques are permitted or foreclosed?

4. *Choice of Methods.* Note that the *NSI Guidelines* contain language roughly similar to the *Domestic Security Guidelines* stating that the FBI should "not hesitate to use any lawful techniques" if warranted by the circumstances. Of what value is such an instruction?

5. *United States Persons.* What is the idea behind the presumption that the entire membership of an international organization with no independent activities in the United States be counted in determining whether the organization is substantially composed of United States persons? Why is making the "U.S. persons" determination important under the *NSI Guidelines*?

6. *Extraterritorial Investigations.* Why is the written request or approval of the Director of the CIA and the Attorney General required before the FBI conducts investigations abroad? Does Executive Order No. 12,333 further prescribe the standards for extraterritorial investigations by the FBI? If not, what limits are there on such investigations? See generally Chapter 23.

7. *CIA and DOD Activities in the United States?* One entirely redacted section in the *NSI Guidelines* is entitled "Central Intelligence Agency and Department of Defense [DOD] Activities Within the United States." In light of the National Security Act and Executive Order No. 12,333, can you imagine what the redacted language says? What CIA or DOD activities would be legally permissible in the United States? See *supra* p. 431, *infra* p. 960.

8. *Enforceability.* Like the *Domestic Security Guidelines*, the *NSI Guidelines* state that they are not judicially enforceable. Do the *NSI Guidelines* serve any useful purpose? Would they ever be relevant in a judicial proceeding?

9. *Departures.* What is the purpose of providing a process for exceeding the authority given by the Guidelines? What is the legal effect, if any, of a departure that is approved by or noticed to the Attorney General?

B. INFORMATION SHARING AND AGENCY REFORMS

1. Bridging the Law Enforcement/Intelligence Collection Divide

The chapters in this part of the book have traced the increased intermingling of intelligence and law enforcement activities in support of counterterrorism objectives. While the FBI has expanded its extraterritorial role to acquire information about transnational threats, the CIA and agencies inside the Departments of Homeland Security and Defense have also stepped up their efforts in support of counterterrorism. In theory, at least, law enforcement and intelligence collection roles, activities, and methods had been legally and functionally separated to protect the integrity of their tasks and to protect the civil liberties of those targeted for investigation by the government. *See* Jonathan M. Fredman, *Intelligence Agencies, Law Enforcement, and the Prosecution Team*, 16 Yale L. & Poly. Rev. 331, 336-337 (1998). Intelligence gathering for counterterrorism must anticipate threats before they are carried out, while law enforcement typically reacts after the event. However, because terrorism and international crime pose national security threats that transcend both national borders *and* the borders between law enforcement and intelligence collection, coordination and cooperation are required among intelligence agencies and between the intelligence and law enforcement arms of the FBI.

The National Security Act of 1947 declares that the CIA shall have no "internal security" functions. See *supra* p. 357. It was thus determined by Congress that the already functioning FBI would continue to serve as the nation's domestic security agency. At the same time, it was understood early on that the "internal security" prohibition in the 1947 Act would not forbid the CIA from coordinating or collecting *foreign* intelligence information in the United States. However, there was nothing in the Act to provide for CIA and FBI coordination, and there were no rules to say when the CIA could play a counterintelligence role in the United States. Thus, the 1947 Act "cut the man down the middle ... between domestic and foreign counterespionage." Mark Riebling, *Wedge: The Secret War Between the FBI and CIA* 78 (1994).

The 1947 Act also calls on the Director of the CIA to take any actions necessary to "protect intelligence sources and methods from unauthorized disclosure." In addition, the CIA is to "perform such other functions and duties related to intelligence affecting the national security as the President or the National Security Council may direct." See *supra* p. 357. According to Mark Reibling, this language provided "a pair of operational baggy pants," while CIA Counsel Scott Breckinridge called the "other functions" language a "banana-peel clause." Riebling, *supra*, at 79. In fact, efforts to coordinate FBI and CIA operations within the United States occurred from the beginning, with several high and low points in the decades since 1947.

In addition to the 1947 Act, Executive Order No. 12,333 explicitly confirms FBI and CIA joint authority over counterintelligence operations, *id.* §1.8(a), while it sustains the notion of divided FBI and CIA roles by charging the CIA

B. Information Sharing and Agency Reforms

with conducting counterintelligence activities within the United States "without assuming or performing any internal security functions." *Id.* §1.8(c). In spite of continuing efforts at coordinating counterintelligence, the agencies have frequently been at bureaucratic loggerheads. *See Meeting the Espionage Challenge: A Review of United States Counterintelligence and Security Programs,* S. Rep. No. 522, 99th Cong. 5 (1986).

The Aldrich Ames spy scandal prompted serious consideration of counterintelligence reform. Ames, a CIA employee since 1962, was recruited by the Soviet KGB while trying to turn Soviet agents toward the United States. Despite a series of suspicious developments dating at least from 1985 — U.S. agents exposed and killed in the Soviet Union, lavish spending by Ames and his wife, a failed 1991 polygraph test — the CIA declined for years to involve the FBI in a counterintelligence inquiry, and the FBI was not able to open a formal investigation of Ames until May 1993. Riebling, *supra,* at 430-431. Although the CIA had clearly violated a 1988 memorandum of understanding promising that CIA suspicions would be passed along to the Bureau in a timely fashion, CIA officials defended their actions. A Bureau search of Ames's CIA office, followed by telephone taps, mail opening, and various other bugging and surveillance methods, finally led to his arrest in February 1994. *Id.* at 431-433, 441-444.

The spectacle of an open and angry feud between the CIA and the FBI over the handling of the Ames investigation prompted passage of the Counterintelligence and Security Enhancements Act of 1994, Pub. L. No. 103-359, §§801-811, 108 Stat. 3423, amending the National Security Act of 1947. The measure made several changes in the way access to classified information is determined for federal employees. The Act also expanded the ability of federal investigators to gain access to financial and credit information, consumer reports, and travel records "as may be necessary to conduct any authorized law enforcement investigation, counterintelligence inquiry, or security determination." Pub. L. No. 103-359, §802(a). Investigations may be commenced concerning any executive branch employee as a condition of access to classified information. *Id.* The predicate for initiating such an investigation is that "there are reasonable grounds to believe, based on credible information, that the person is, or may be, disclosing classified information in an unauthorized manner to a foreign power or agent of a foreign power." *Id.*

In addition, the Act established a Counterintelligence Policy Board to report to the President through the National Security Council (NSC). *Id.* §811(a). *See Intelligence Authorization Act for Fiscal Year 1995,* H.R. Conf. Rep. No. 103-753, at 35 (1994). The Act provides that

> the head of each department or agency within the executive branch shall ensure that . . . the [FBI] is advised immediately of any information, regardless of its origin, which indicates that classified information is being, or may have been, disclosed in an unauthorized manner to a foreign power or an agent of a foreign power.

Pub. L. No. 103-359, §811(c)(1)(A). Following such a report to the FBI, the Bureau must be "consulted with respect to all subsequent actions" taken by the affected agency, and "given complete and timely access to the employees and records" of the affected agency. *Id.* §811(c)(1)(B), (C).

Another action taken partly in response to the Ames investigation was the establishment by the Attorney General in July 1995 of policies and procedures for internal DOJ coordination of FBI counterintelligence investigations with the Criminal Division. Although additional coordination procedures were promulgated in January 2000, problems persist. *See* General Accounting Office, *FBI Intelligence Investigations: Coordination Within Justice on Counterintelligence Criminal Matters Is Limited* (GAO-01-780) (2001). As with the "primary purpose" doctrine, see *supra* p. 425, limits on cooperation between law enforcement and intelligence gathering reflect a fear that investigators might characterize a law enforcement investigation as a purely intelligence operation in order to avoid the stricter investigative rules that attend the criminal laws, and that a judge could exclude evidence from a criminal trial based on that possibility. *Id.* at 3. Just such a cautionary stance may have thwarted an investigation that could have tipped off officials to the September 11, 2001, attacks before they occurred. See *supra* p. 533. Yet because counterterrorism investigations now regularly become law enforcement and intelligence investigations simultaneously, sorting out the problems of cooperation and coordination remains crucial. See *supra* p. 546. The perception that the "primary purpose" standard had made threat detection and interdiction more difficult before September 11 led to an amendment to FISA in the USA PATRIOT Act requiring that the intelligence purpose of an investigation be "a significant" purpose rather than "the" purpose. See *supra* p. 535.

Another USA PATRIOT Act provision authorizes a greater degree of interagency cooperation and sharing of information than was permitted previously. The Act permits, "[n]otwithstanding any other provision of law...foreign or counterintelligence...information obtained as part of a criminal investigation to be disclosed to any Federal law enforcement, intelligence, protective, immigration, national defense, or national security official in order to assist the official receiving that information in the performance of his official duties." Pub. L. No. 107-56, §203(d)(1), 115 Stat. 272, 281 (2001), amending 50 U.S.C. §403-5(d). The same discretion is given for the sharing of grand jury information. *Id.* §203(a)(1), 115 Stat. 278-279, amending 18 U.S.C. §6(e)(3)(C). In addition, the USA PATRIOT Act amended FISA as follows:

> (1) Federal officers who conduct electronic surveillance [or a physical search] to acquire foreign intelligence information under this title may consult with Federal law enforcement officers to coordinate efforts to investigate or protect against —
> a. actual or potential attack or other grave hostile acts of a foreign power or an agent of a foreign power;
> b. sabotage or international terrorism by a foreign power or an agent of a foreign power;
> c. clandestine intelligence activities by an intelligence service or network of a foreign power or by an agent of a foreign power.
> (2) Coordination authorized [above] shall not preclude the certification required by [FISA] or the entry of an order.... [*Id.* §504(a), (b), 115 Stat. 364-365, amending 50 U.S.C. §1825.]

The Homeland Security Act further amended FISA by permitting intelligence officers to consult with state and local law enforcement officers regarding foreign intelligence information. Pub. L. No. 107-296, §898, 116 Stat. 2258 (2002), amending 50 U.S.C. §1806(k)(1).

B. Information Sharing and Agency Reforms

Likewise, the USA PATRIOT Act amended the National Security Act of 1947 to require the Director of Central Intelligence to "establish requirements and priorities" for disseminating foreign intelligence information collected under FISA, Pub. L. No. 107-56, §901, 115 Stat. 387, and to direct the Attorney General to disclose to the Director of the CIA foreign intelligence acquired by the Department of Justice in the course of a criminal investigation. *Id.* §905(a)(2), 115 Stat. 389. Exceptions to disclosure for classes, matters, or targets of foreign intelligence may be determined by the Attorney General in consultation with the Director of the CIA. *Id.* The same officials are obligated to develop guidelines to help inform the Director of the CIA "within a reasonable period of time" of a determination by the Department of Justice whether a foreign intelligence source will be subject to a criminal investigation. *Id.* §905(b), 115 Stat. 389.

Among the reforms recommended by the 9/11 Commission, *supra* p. 363, was creation of a national counterterrorism center. In August 2004, President Bush adopted the recommendation by executive order. Executive Order No. 13,354, *National Counterterrorism Center*, 69 Fed. Reg. 53,589 (Aug. 27, 2004). A few months later, in the Intelligence Reform and Terrorism Prevention Act of 2004 (IRTPA), Pub. L. No. 108-458, 118 Stat. 3638, Congress created the National Counterterrorism Center (NCTC). *Id.* §1021, 118 Stat. 3672. The Senate-confirmed Director of the NCTC reports to the DNI generally, but to the President on the planning and implementation of joint counterterrorism operations. *Id.* In turn, IRTPA vests in the DNI the "principal authority to ensure maximum availability of and access to intelligence information within the intelligence community consistent with national security." *Id.* §1011(a), 118 Stat. 3650. IRTPA also requires a "coordinated environment" in which intelligence information can be "provided in its more shareable form." *Id.* §1016(b)(2), (d)(1), 118 Stat. at 3665-3666.

In December 2005, the 9/11 Commission, reincarnated as the Public Discourse Project, issued its *Final Report on 9/11 Commission Recommendations*, Dec. 5, 2005, *available at* http://www.9-11pdp.org. The Report gave a grade of "B" to the NCTC, noting that "shared analysis and evaluation of threat information is in progress; joint operational planning is beginning," but that insufficient resources are available to fulfill the intelligence and planning role envisioned.

The NCTC runs three video teleconferences (VTCs) on a daily basis, and its staff posts intelligence on a Web site, which is classified but is accessible to about 5,000 analysts. The NCTC operates alongside the Counterterrorist Center (CTC) at the CIA, in addition to the Information Analysis and Infrastructure Protection (IAIP) Directorate at the Department of Homeland Security (DHS). (IAIP is described and its functions are detailed *infra* p. 961.) The CTC and NCTC have considerable overlap — pursuing al Qaeda operatives worldwide and providing strategic operational planning for counterterrorism activities. Scott Shane, *Year Into Revamped Spying, Troubles and Some Progress*, N.Y. Times, Feb. 28, 2006, at A12. Former National Intelligence Council vice chairman Gregory Treverton described the NCTC-CTC relationship as a "food fight" and called the relationship between federal officials and state and local law enforcement "a complete mess." *Id.*

2. Reforming the FBI

Owing at least in part to its longstanding tradition of performing the federal law enforcement role, FBI intelligence collection and analysis efforts were long regarded inside the Bureau as of secondary importance. Even as additional resources and staff were devoted to intelligence collection and analysis inside the FBI during the 1990s, the intelligence function was still not central to the FBI mission. In addition to the perception among many that engaging heavily in intelligence work would only compromise the effectiveness of FBI law enforcement, the Bureau's reluctance to embrace an intelligence mission wholeheartedly was also due in part to our nation's cultural and historical antipathy to a domestic intelligence service. Images of the sinister omnipresence of the German Gestapo and the Soviet KGB have been firmly etched into the public consciousness.

Post-September 11 critiques describing massive failures of intelligence are outlined *supra* pp. 636-637. Reports by the intelligence committees, the 9/11 Commission, and the Silberman/Robb Commission lamented breakdowns in information sharing and weaknesses in the FBI. *Id.* A few months after Congress created a revised intelligence community structure in December 2004, President Bush issued an order creating a new national security division within the FBI that will be subject to the overall direction of the DNI. Douglas Jehl, *Bush to Create New Unit in F.B.I. for Intelligence*, N.Y. Times, June 30, 2005, at A1. The restructuring was designed to break down historic barriers between the FBI and CIA, while elevating the relative importance of the intelligence mission inside FBI. *Id.* The new division, called the National Security Service (see chart *supra* p. 365) includes counterterrorism and counterintelligence divisions and an intelligence directorate. A new position of assistant attorney general for national security matters, in charge of counterterrorism, counterintelligence, and the Office of Intelligence Policy Review, was approved by Congress in the USA PATRIOT Improvement and Reauthorization Act of 2005, Pub. L. No. 109-177, §506(a), 120 Stat. 192, 247 (2006).

NOTES AND QUESTIONS

1. *Organizing the Intelligence-Sharing Network.* IRTPA places the DNI at the head of the National Intelligence Program and vests in him authority to task intelligence agencies and shape their budgets and spending. See *supra* pp. 362-368. The Act does not, however, prescribe how to organize a network for sharing information or provide much detail concerning the rules for its implementation. How would you advise the DNI to shape an effective information-sharing network that ensures efficient sharing of information while protecting both the security of the information and the rights of those targeted? One model was proposed in 2003 by the Markle Foundation Task Force, *Creating a Trusted Information Network for Homeland Security* (2003), *available at* http://www.markletaskforce.org/reports/TFNS_Master.pdf.

2. *Separate Agencies for Domestic and Foreign Intelligence Activities?* Should there be a strict legal requirement that separate agencies gather intelligence inside

B. Information Sharing and Agency Reforms 639

and outside the United States? What is the value of such a requirement? Is it required by the Constitution? To the extent that such separation exists, are the inevitable compromises in information sharing worth the benefits?

3. *Utility of the Information-Sharing Requirements.* Are the USA PATRIOT Act information-sharing provisions clearly advisable? Do these provisions raise the possibility that the CIA will collect information in the United States about Americans? In light of the complexities of mounting an effective counterterrorism strategy, can you think of any good alternatives to these information-sharing mechanisms? Can you think of ways to create greater accountability for their use?

Is the NCTC likely to promote effective information sharing? How will the Center discourage agencies from hoarding their own intelligence leads? Is the placement of the NCTC just below the DNI a good idea, or is the NCTC simply another layer of bureaucracy, this time at the top? The Public Discourse Project gave a "D" grade to the information-sharing efforts to date by Congress and the Administration and commented that "many complaints about lack of information sharing between federal authorities and state and local level officials" remain. *Final Report, supra,* at 3. What legal measures might improve information sharing across these jurisdictional lines? Between agencies?

4. *9/11 Commission Report Card on the FBI and Information Sharing.* The Public Discourse Project *Final Report* issued a "C" grade on implementing the FBI national security division and commented that the FBI "shift to a counterterrorism posture is far from institutionalized.... Unless there is improvement in a reasonable period of time, Congress will have to look at alternatives." *Final Report, supra,* at 3.

5. *Checks and Balances vs. Efficiency.* Is competition between the CIA and the FBI inevitable? If the coordination and competition problems *can* be solved, *should* they be solved? Or is it part of our nation's character "to chafe at bureaucratic inefficiency... [but] to distrust the centralization of power needed to correct it"? Riebling, *supra* p. 634, at 460. Are the agencies' missions so different that their work cannot be coordinated? Is the reluctance to vest one agency with both foreign and domestic security responsibility a sign of healthy skepticism about the dangers of the accumulation of power in one entity? In the end, is the foreign/domestic dichotomy that continues to dominate the law of internal security workable? Is it constitutionally defensible? Is the better dividing line one between intelligence collection and law enforcement?

6. *Oversight.* Can oversight of intelligence agencies and their information-sharing activities help safeguard the civil liberties that might otherwise be at risk? Oversight might be performed outside the intelligence community—through the intelligence and appropriations committees in Congress—or internally—by agency overseers, inspectors general, or presidential advisory groups such as the NSC, the President's Foreign Intelligence Advisory Board (PFIAB), and the Intelligence Oversight Board (IOB). How do you think the oversight function should be organized? How should it be codified? What agencies and congressional committees would have an interest in this question? What are the implications for democratic government?

Surveillance Abroad — 23

The policy of countering terrorism by detecting and then preventing terrorist acts targeting the United States has as its first line of defense the investigation of terrorism abroad. Indeed, the United States has long conducted law enforcement and intelligence investigations overseas. This chapter examines the question whether, when U.S. investigators go abroad, the Constitution travels with them to limit their activities and, if so, to what extent. It also asks whether any constitutional protections for U.S. citizens abroad extend equally to noncitizens, and how U.S. investigations outside the United States may be constrained by international law. Finally, in this chapter we consider how rules governing such investigations can be implemented practically.

Reid v. Covert
United States Supreme Court, 1957
354 U.S. 1

[The facts and a portion of the opinion in this case are set out *supra* p. 173.]

Mr. Justice BLACK announced the opinion of the Court and delivered an opinion, in which the Chief Justice, Mr. Justice DOUGLAS, and Mr. Justice BRENNAN join.... At the beginning we reject the idea that when the United States acts against citizens abroad it can do so free of the Bill of Rights. The United States is entirely a creature of the Constitution. Its power and authority have no other source. It can only act in accordance with all the limitations imposed by the Constitution. When the Government reaches out to punish a citizen who is abroad, the shield which the Bill of Rights and other parts of the Constitution provide to protect his life and liberty should not be stripped away just because he happens to be in another land....

The rights and liberties which citizens of our country enjoy are not protected by custom and tradition alone, they have been jealously preserved from the encroachments of Government by express provisions of our written Constitution.

Chapter 23. Surveillance Abroad

Among those provisions, Art. III, §2 and the Fifth and Sixth Amendments are directly relevant to these cases. Article III, §2 lays down the rule that:

> "The Trial of all Crimes, except in Cases of Impeachment, shall be by Jury; and such Trial shall be held in the State where the said Crimes shall have been committed; but when not committed within any State, the Trial shall be at such Place or Places as the Congress may by Law have directed."

The Fifth Amendment declares:

> "No person shall be held to answer for a capital, or otherwise infamous crime, unless on a presentment or indictment of a Grand Jury, except in cases arising in the land or naval forces, or in the Militia, when in actual service in time of War or public danger; . . ."

And the Sixth Amendment provides:

> "In all criminal prosecutions, the accused shall enjoy the right to a speedy and public trial, by an impartial jury of the State and district wherein the crime shall have been committed. . . ."

The language of Art. III, §2 manifests that constitutional protections for the individual were designed to restrict the United States Government when it acts outside of this country, as well as here at home. After declaring that all criminal trials must be by jury, the section states that when a crime is "not committed within any State, the Trial shall be at such Place or Places as the Congress may by Law have directed." If this language is permitted to have its obvious meaning, §2 is applicable to criminal trials outside of the States as a group without regard to where the offense is committed or the trial held. From the very first Congress, federal statutes have implemented the provisions of §2 by providing for trial of murder and other crimes committed outside the jurisdiction of any State "in the district where the offender is apprehended, or into which he may first be brought." The Fifth and Sixth Amendments, like Art. III, §2, are also all inclusive with their sweeping references to "no person" and to "all criminal prosecutions."

This Court and other federal courts have held or asserted that various constitutional limitations apply to the Government when it acts outside the continental United States. While it has been suggested that only those constitutional rights which are "fundamental" protect Americans abroad, we can find no warrant, in logic or otherwise, for picking and choosing among the remarkable collection of "Thou shalt nots" which were explicitly fastened on all departments and agencies of the Federal Government by the Constitution and its Amendments. Moreover, in view of our heritage and the history of the adoption of the Constitution and the Bill of Rights, it seems peculiarly anomalous to say that trial before a civilian judge and by an independent jury picked from the common citizenry is not a fundamental right. . . . Trial by jury in a court of law and in accordance with traditional modes of procedure after an indictment by grand jury has served and remains one of our most vital barriers to governmental arbitrariness. These elemental procedural safeguards were embedded in our

Constitution to secure their inviolateness and sanctity against the passing demands of expediency or convenience....

The [holding in In re Ross, 140 U.S. 453 (1891)] that the Constitution has no applicability abroad has long since been directly repudiated by numerous cases. That approach is obviously erroneous if the United States Government, which has no power except that granted by the Constitution, can and does try citizens for crimes committed abroad.... At best, the *Ross* case should be left as a relic from a different era.

[Last term the Court] relied on the "Insular Cases" to support its conclusion that Article III and the Fifth and Sixth Amendments were not applicable to the trial of Mrs. Smith and Mrs. Covert. We believe that reliance was misplaced. The "Insular Cases," which arose at the turn of the [twentieth] century, involved territories which had only recently been conquered or acquired by the United States. These territories, governed and regulated by Congress under Art. IV, §3, had entirely different cultures and customs from those of this country....

Moreover, it is our judgment that neither the cases nor their reasoning should be given any further expansion. The concept that the Bill of Rights and other constitutional protections against arbitrary government are inoperative when they become inconvenient or when expediency dictates otherwise is a very dangerous doctrine and if allowed to flourish would destroy the benefit of a written Constitution and undermine the basis of our government. If our foreign commitments become of such nature that the Government can no longer satisfactorily operate within the bounds laid down by the Constitution, that instrument can be amended by the method which it prescribes. But we have no authority, or inclination, to read exceptions into it which are not there....

Mr. Justice HARLAN, concurring in the result.... As I have already stated, I do not think that it can be said that these safeguards of the Constitution are never operative without the United States, regardless of the particular circumstances. On the other hand, I cannot agree with the suggestion that every provision of the Constitution must always be deemed automatically applicable to American citizens in every part of the world. For *Ross* and the *Insular Cases* do stand for an important proposition, one which seems to me a wise and necessary gloss on our Constitution. The proposition is, of course, not that the Constitution "does not apply" overseas, but that there are provisions in the Constitution which do not *necessarily* apply in all circumstances in every foreign place.... In other words, what *Ross* and the *Insular Cases* hold is that the particular local setting, the practical necessities, and the possible alternatives are relevant to a question of judgment, namely, whether jury trial should be deemed a necessary condition of the exercise of Congress' power to provide for the trial of Americans overseas....

And so I agree with my brother Frankfurter that, in view of *Ross* and the *Insular Cases*, we have before us a question analogous, ultimately, to issues of due process; one can say, in fact, that the question of which specific safeguards of the Constitution are appropriately to be applied in a particular context overseas can be reduced to the issue of what process is "due" a defendant in the particular circumstances of a particular case.

On this basis, I cannot agree with the sweeping proposition that a full Article III trial, with indictment and trial by jury, is required in every case for the trial of a civilian dependent of a serviceman overseas. The Government, it seems to me, has made an impressive showing that at least for the run-of-the-mill offenses committed by dependents overseas, such a requirement would be as impractical and anomalous as it would have been to require jury trial for Balzac in Porto Rico....

So far as capital cases are concerned, I think they stand on quite a different footing than other offenses. In such cases the law is especially sensitive to demands for that procedural fairness which inheres in a civilian trial where the judge and trier of fact are not responsive to the command of the convening authority. I do not concede that whatever process is "due" an offender faced with a fine or a prison sentence necessarily satisfies the requirements of the Constitution in a capital case.... The number of such cases would appear to be so negligible that the practical problems of affording the defendant a civilian trial would not present insuperable problems.

On this narrow ground I concur in the result in these cases.

[The opinions of FRANKFURTER, J., concurring, and of CLARK, J., dissenting, are omitted.]

United States v. Verdugo-Urquidez
United States Supreme Court, 1990
494 U.S. 259

Chief Justice REHNQUIST delivered the opinion of the Court. The question presented by this case is whether the Fourth Amendment applies to the search and seizure by United States agents of property that is owned by a nonresident alien and located in a foreign country. We hold that it does not.

[Respondent Rene Martin Verdugo-Urquidez was a citizen and resident of Mexico who was apprehended by Mexican police and delivered to U.S. border authorities in response to a U.S. warrant for his arrest on drug-smuggling charges. Following his arrest, and while he was incarcerated in the United States, DEA agents searched Verdugo-Urquidez's property in Mexico with the approval of Mexican authorities, but without a U.S. warrant, and seized certain documents that were subsequently offered as evidence against him. The defendant sought to have that evidence excluded.]

The Fourth Amendment provides:

> "The right of the people to be secure in their persons, houses, papers, and effects, against unreasonable searches and seizures, shall not be violated, and no Warrants shall issue, but upon probable cause, supported by Oath or affirmation, and particularly describing the place to be searched, and the persons or things to be seized."

That text, by contrast with the Fifth and Sixth Amendments, extends its reach only to "the people." Contrary to the suggestion of *amici curiae* that the Framers used this phrase "simply to avoid [an] awkward rhetorical redundancy," "the people" seems to have been a term of art employed in select parts of the Constitution. The Preamble declares that the Constitution is ordained and established by "the People of the United States." The Second Amendment protects "the right of the people to keep and bear Arms," and the Ninth and Tenth Amendments provide that certain rights and powers are retained by and reserved to "the people." See also U.S. Const., Amdt. 1 ("Congress shall make no law . . . abridging . . . *the right of the people* peaceably to assemble") (emphasis added); Art. I, §2, cl. 1 ("The House of Representatives shall be composed of Members chosen every second Year *by the People of the several States*") (emphasis added). While this textual exegesis is by no means conclusive, it suggests that "the people" protected by the Fourth Amendment, and by the First and Second Amendments, and to whom rights and powers are reserved in the Ninth and Tenth Amendments, refers to a class of persons who are part of a national community or who have otherwise developed sufficient connection with this country to be considered part of that community. The language of these Amendments contrasts with the words "person" and "accused" used in the Fifth and Sixth Amendments regulating procedure in criminal cases.

What we know of the history of the drafting of the Fourth Amendment also suggests that its purpose was to restrict searches and seizures which might be conducted by the United States in domestic matters. . . . The available historical data show, therefore, that the purpose of the Fourth Amendment was to protect the people of the United States against arbitrary action by their own Government; it was never suggested that the provision was intended to restrain the actions of the Federal Government against aliens outside of the United States territory.

There is likewise no indication that the Fourth Amendment was understood by contemporaries of the Framers to apply to activities of the United States directed against aliens in foreign territory or in international waters. Only seven years after the ratification of the Amendment, French interference with American commercial vessels engaged in neutral trade triggered what came to be known as the "undeclared war" with France. In an Act to "protect the Commerce of the United States" in 1798, Congress authorized President Adams to "instruct the commanders of the public armed vessels which are, or which shall be employed in the service of the United States, to subdue, seize and take any armed French vessel, which shall be found within the jurisdictional limits of the United States, or elsewhere, on the high seas." §1 of An Act Further to Protect the Commerce of the United States, ch. 68, 1 Stat. 578. . . . Some commanders were held liable by this Court for unlawful seizures because their actions were beyond the scope of the congressional grant of authority, *see, e.g.,* Little v. Barreme, 2 Cranch 170, 177-178 (1804); *cf.* Talbot v. Seeman, 1 Cranch 1, 31 (1801) (seizure of neutral ship lawful where American captain had probable cause to believe vessel was French), but it was never suggested that the Fourth Amendment restrained the authority of congress or of United States agents to conduct operations such as this.

The global view taken by the Court of Appeals of the application of the Constitution is also contrary to this Court's decisions in the *Insular Cases,* which held that not every constitutional provision applies to governmental activity even where the United States has sovereign power. In Dorr v. United States, 195 U.S. 138 (1904), we declared the general rule that in an unincorporated territory — one not clearly destined for statehood — Congress was not required to adopt "a system of laws which shall include the right of trial by jury, and that *the*

Chapter 23. Surveillance Abroad

Constitution does not, without legislation and of its own force, carry such right to territory so situated." 195 U.S. at 149 (emphasis added). Only "fundamental" constitutional rights are guaranteed to inhabitants of those territories.... [C]ertainly, it is not open to us in light of the *Insular Cases* to endorse the view that every constitutional provision applies wherever the United States Government exercises its power.

Indeed, we have rejected the claim that aliens are entitled to Fifth Amendment rights outside the sovereign territory of the United States. In Johnson v. Eisentrager, 339 U.S. 763 (1950), the Court held that enemy aliens arrested in China and imprisoned in Germany after World War II could not obtain writs of habeas corpus in our federal courts on the ground that their convictions for war crimes had violated the Fifth Amendment and other constitutional provisions. The *Eisentrager* opinion acknowledged that in some cases constitutional provisions extend beyond the citizenry; "[t]he alien ... has been accorded a generous and ascending scale of rights as he increases his identity with our society." *Id.*, at 770. But our rejection of extraterritorial application of the Fifth Amendment was emphatic:

> "Such extraterritorial application of organic law would have been so significant an innovation in the practice of governments that, if intended or apprehended, it could scarcely have failed to excite contemporary comment. Not one word can be cited. No decision of this Court supports such a view. *Cf.* Downes v. Bidwell, 182 U.S. 244 [(1901)]. None of the learned commentators on our Constitution has even hinted at it. The practice of every modern government is opposed to it." *Id.*, at 784.

If such is true of the Fifth Amendment, which speaks in the relatively universal term of "person," it would seem even more true with respect to the Fourth Amendment, which applies only to "the people."

To support his all-encompassing view of the Fourth Amendment, respondent points to language from the plurality opinion in Reid v. Covert, 354 U.S. 1 (1957).... Four Justices "reject[ed] the idea that when the United States acts *against citizens* abroad it can do so free of the Bill of Rights." *Id.*, at 5 (emphasis added). The plurality went on to say:

> "The United States is entirely a creature of the Constitution. Its power and authority have no other source. It can only act in accordance with all the limitations imposed by the Constitution. When the Government reaches out to punish *a citizen* who is abroad, the shield which the Bill of Rights and other parts of the Constitution provide to protect his life and liberty should not be stripped away just because he happens to be in another land." *Id.*, at 5-6 (emphasis added; footnote omitted).

Respondent urges that we interpret this discussion to mean that federal officials are constrained by the Fourth Amendment wherever and against whomever they act. But the holding of *Reid* stands for no such sweeping proposition: it decided that United States citizens stationed abroad could invoke the protection of the Fifth and Sixth Amendments. The concurring opinions by Justices Frankfurter and Harlan in *Reid* resolved the case on much narrower grounds than the plurality and declined even to hold that United States citizens were entitled to the full range of constitutional protections in all overseas criminal prosecutions. See *id.*, at 75 (Harlan, J., concurring in result) ("I agree with my brother Frankfurter that . . . we have before us a question analogous, ultimately, to issues of due process; one can say, in fact, that the question of which specific safeguards of the Constitution are appropriately to be applied in a particular context overseas can be reduced to the issue of what process is 'due' a defendant in the particular circumstances of a particular case"). Since respondent is not a United States citizen, he can derive no comfort from the *Reid* holding.

Verdugo-Urquidez also relies on a series of cases in which we have held that aliens enjoy certain constitutional rights. *See, e.g.*, Plyler v. Doe, 457 U.S. 202, 211-212 (1982) (illegal aliens protected by Equal Protection Clause); Kwong Hai Chew v. Colding, 344 U.S. 590, 596 (1953) (resident alien is a "person" within the meaning of the Fifth Amendment); Bridges v. Wixon, 326 U.S. 135, 148 (1945) (resident aliens have First Amendment rights); Russian Volunteer Fleet v. United States, 282 U.S. 481 (1931) (Just Compensation Clause of Fifth Amendment); Wong Wing v. United States, 163 U.S. 228, 238 (1896) (resident aliens entitled to Fifth and Sixth Amendment rights); Yick Wo v. Hopkins, 118 U.S. 356, 369 (1886) (Fourteenth Amendment protects resident aliens). These cases, however, establish only that aliens receive constitutional protections when they have come within the territory of the United States and developed substantial connections with this country. Respondent is an alien who has had no previous significant voluntary connection with the United States, so these cases avail him not. . . .

Not only are history and case law against respondent, but as pointed out in Johnson v. Eisentrager, 393 U.S. 763 (1950), the result of accepting his claim would have significant and deleterious consequences for the United States in conducting activities beyond its boundaries. The rule adopted by the Court of Appeals would apply not only to law enforcement operations abroad, but also to other foreign policy operations which might result in "searches or seizures." The United States frequently employs armed forces outside this country—over 200 times in our history—for the protection of American citizens or national security. Congressional Research Service, *Instances of Use of United States Armed Forces Abroad, 1798-1989* (E. Collier ed. 1989). Application of the Fourth Amendment to those circumstances could significantly disrupt the ability of the political branches to respond to foreign situations involving our national interest. Were respondent to prevail, aliens with no attachment to this country might well bring actions for damages to remedy claimed violations of the Fourth Amendment in foreign countries or in international waters. *See* Bivens v. Six Unknown Federal Narcotics Agents, 403 U.S. 388 (1971). . . . The Members of the Executive and Legislative Branches are sworn to uphold the Constitution, and they presumably desire to follow its commands. But the Court of Appeals' global view of its applicability would plunge them into a sea of uncertainty as to what might be reasonable in the way of searches and seizures conducted abroad. Indeed, the Court of Appeals held that absent exigent circumstances, United States agents could not effect a "search or seizure" for law enforcement purposes in a foreign country without first obtaining a warrant—which would be a dead letter outside the United States—from a magistrate in this country. Even if no warrant were required, American agents would have to articulate specific facts giving them probable cause to undertake a search or seizure if they wished to comply with the Fourth Amendment as conceived by the Court of Appeals. . . .

For better or for worse, we live in a world of nation-states in which our Government must be able to "function effectively in the company of sovereign nations." Perez v. Brownell, 356 U.S. 44, 57 (1958). Some who violate our laws may live outside our borders under a regime quite different from that which obtains in this country. Situations threatening to important American interests may arise halfway around the globe, situations which in the view of the political branches of our Government require an American response with armed force. If there are to be restrictions on searches and seizures which occur incident to such American action, they must be imposed by the political branches through diplomatic understanding, treaty, or legislation.

The judgment of the Court of Appeals is accordingly

Reversed.

Justice KENNEDY, concurring.... I take it to be correct, as the plurality opinion in Reid v. Covert sets forth, that the Government may act only as the Constitution authorizes, whether the actions in question are foreign or domestic. *See* 354 U.S., at 6. But this principle is only a first step in resolving this case. The question before us then becomes what constitutional standards apply when the Government acts, in reference to an alien, within its sphere of foreign operations.... [Various cases], as well as United States v. Curtiss-Wright Export Corp., 299 U.S. 304, 318 (1936), stand for the proposition that we must interpret constitutional protections in light of the undoubted power of the United States to take actions to assert its legitimate power and authority abroad. Justice Harlan made this observation in his opinion concurring in the judgment in Reid v. Covert:

> "I cannot agree with the suggestion that every provision of the Constitution must always be deemed automatically applicable to American citizens in every part of the world. For *Ross* and the *Insular Cases* do stand for an important proposition, one which seems to me a wise and necessary gloss on our Constitution. The proposition is, of course, not that the Constitution 'does not apply' overseas, but that there are provisions in the Constitution which do not *necessarily* apply in all circumstances in every foreign place. In other words, it seems to me that the basic teaching of *Ross* and the *Insular Cases* is that there is no rigid and abstract rule that Congress, as a condition precedent to exercising power over Americans overseas, must exercise it subject to all the guarantees of the Constitution, no matter what the conditions and considerations are that would make adherence to a specific guarantee altogether impracticable and anomalous." 354 U.S., at 74.

The conditions and considerations of this case would make adherence to the Fourth Amendment's warrant requirement impracticable and anomalous.... The absence of local judges or magistrates available to issue warrants, the differing and perhaps unascertainable conceptions of reasonableness and privacy that prevail abroad, and the need to cooperate with foreign officials all indicate that the Fourth Amendment's warrant requirement should not apply in Mexico as it does in this country. For this reason, in addition to the other persuasive justifications stated by the Court, I agree that no violation of the Fourth Amendment has occurred in the case before us. The rights of a citizen, as to whom the United States has continuing obligations, are not presented by this case.

I do not mean to imply, and the Court has not decided, that persons in the position of the respondent have no constitutional protection. The United States is prosecuting a foreign national in a court established under Article III, and all of the trial proceedings are governed by the Constitution. All would agree, for instance, that the dictates of the Due Process Clause of the Fifth Amendment protect the defendant. Indeed, as Justice Harlan put it, "the question of which specific safeguards . . . are appropriately to be applied in a particular context . . . can be reduced to the issue of what process is 'due' a defendant in the particular circumstances of a particular case." *Reid, supra*, at 75. Nothing approaching a violation of due process has occurred in this case.

[The opinion of Justice STEVENS, concurring in the judgment on the grounds that, although the Fourth Amendment applied, the search was reasonable, is omitted.]

Justice BRENNAN, with whom Justice MARSHALL joins, dissenting. . . . The Court today creates an antilogy: the Constitution authorizes our Government to enforce our criminal laws abroad, but when Government agents exercise this authority, the Fourth Amendment does not travel with them. This cannot be. At the very least, the Fourth Amendment is an unavoidable correlative of the Government's power to enforce the criminal law. . . .

When we tell the world that we expect all people, wherever they may be, to abide by our laws, we cannot in the same breath tell the world that our law enforcement officers need not do the same. Because we cannot expect others to respect our laws until we respect our Constitution, I respectfully dissent.

Justice BLACKMUN, dissenting. I cannot accept the Court of Appeals' conclusion, echoed in some portions of Justice Brennan's dissent, that the Fourth Amendment governs every action by an American official that can be characterized as a search or seizure. American agents acting abroad generally do not purport to exercise sovereign authority over the foreign nationals with whom they come in contact. The relationship between these agents and foreign nationals is therefore fundamentally different from the relationship between United States officials and individuals residing within this country.

I am inclined to agree with Justice Brennan, however, that when a foreign national is held accountable for purported violations of United States criminal laws, he has effectively been treated as one of "the governed" and therefore is entitled to Fourth Amendment protections. . . . I agree with the Government, however, that an American magistrate's lack of power to authorize a search abroad renders the Warrant Clause inapplicable to the search of a noncitizen's residence outside this country.

The Fourth Amendment nevertheless requires that the search be "reasonable." And when the purpose of a search is the procurement of evidence for a criminal prosecution, we have consistently held that the search, to be reasonable, must be based upon probable cause. Neither the District Court nor the Court of Appeals addressed the issue of probable cause, and I do not believe that a reliable determination could be made on the basis of the record before us. I therefore would vacate the judgment of the Court of Appeals and remand the case for further proceedings.

NOTES AND QUESTIONS

1. *Does Verdugo Limit Reid?* Are *Reid* and *Verdugo* consistent? The *Verdugo* majority argues that *Reid*'s holding is limited to the proposition that U.S. citizens stationed abroad may invoke the protections of the Fifth and Sixth Amendments. But does this invalidate *Reid*'s broader proposition (dictum or not) that the Constitution travels with agents of the U.S. government because they and their government are "entirely a creature of the Constitution"? How can FBI, DEA, or INS agents ever act abroad without drawing their authority and limitations on that authority from the Constitution?

2. *To Which Persons Does the Fourth Amendment Apply?* *Verdugo* indicates that the Fourth Amendment is inapplicable to persons who lack a substantial connection to the United States. Is that conclusion consistent with Justice Kennedy's concurring opinion? Or with Justice Harlan's concurring opinion in *Reid?* Which understanding of the Constitution is more persuasive?

3. *Substantially Connected Aliens.* What is a "substantial connection" to the United States? Could the connection required to invoke the Fourth Amendment be greater than that required by the Due Process Clause for a U.S. criminal court to exercise jurisdiction over a defendant? Verdugo-Urquidez's actual connections were deemed insufficient by the majority. Other cases are inconsistent: one found a two-year illegal stay in the United States insufficient; another found several voluntary trips to negotiate an employment relationship sufficient; and a third found that illegal drug-trafficking to the United States was sufficient. *See generally* Douglas I. Koff, *Post-Verdugo-Urquidez: The Sufficient Connection Test — Substantially Ambiguous, Substantially Unworkable,* 25 Colum. Hum. Rts. L. Rev. 435, 455-465 (1994). The resulting ambiguity makes it difficult for U.S. officials engaged in overseas surveillance of aliens to know how to proceed. The differentiation among aliens also means that disparate standards may apply to codefendants engaged in the same conduct, suspected of the same crimes, and subjected to the same search. Should courts draw a brighter line, and, if so, what should it be? *Compare* Randall K. Miller, *The Limits of U.S. International Law Enforcement After Verdugo-Urquidez: Resurrecting Rochin,* 58 U. Pitt. L. Rev. 867, 885 n.88 (1997) (drawing the line at the border, thus denying Fourth Amendment protections to all aliens searched abroad, regardless of their connection to the United States), *with* Koff, *supra,* at 485 (extending Fourth Amendment protections to all persons except nonresident enemy aliens searched incident to a military confrontation).

4. *Handicapping the Use of Force Abroad?* The majority worries that extension of Fourth Amendment protections to someone like Verdugo-Urquidez would have made U.S. naval searches and seizures on the high seas during the Quasi-War with France unlawful, and even that it "could significantly disrupt the ability of the political branches to respond to foreign situations" with armed force. Are the three kinds of operations truly analogous? Does Johnson v. Eisentrager, cited by the majority, suggest one answer? Does Bas v. Tingy, *supra* p. 94? Or can the approach urged by Justice Kennedy in *Verdugo* and by Justice Harlan in *Reid* be adapted to these situations?

5. *Applying Verdugo to Torture.* Suppose the DEA beats and tortures an "unconnected" alien abroad to force him to reveal the location of invoices, which are then seized and used against him at trial. How, if at all, would you distinguish *Verdugo* in arguing to suppress this evidence on the alien's behalf? In Harbury v. Deutch, 233 F.3d 596 (D.C. Cir. 2000), *supra* p. 451, the plaintiff alleged that the CIA conspired with its "assets" in Guatemala to violate her Guatemalan husband's substantive due process rights by psychologically abusing and physically torturing him for 18 months before executing him. Acknowledging that the alleged conduct "shocks the conscience," the court concluded that the Fifth Amendment does not prohibit torture by the CIA or its assets of nonresident foreign nationals living abroad. In support of its decision, the court quoted *Verdugo* and the discussion of *Eisentrager* in that case, *supra* p. 645. Can you distinguish *Verdugo*? What about *Eisentrager*, insofar as it is quoted in *Verdugo*?

In 2005, Congress enacted the Detainee Treatment Act in two different statutes. Department of Defense, Emergency Supplemental Appropriations to Address Hurricanes in the Gulf of Mexico, and Pandemic Influenza Act, 2006, Pub. L. No. 109-148, §1003(a), 119 Stat. 2680, 2739-2740 (2005); National Defense Authorization Act for Fiscal Year 2006, Pub. L. No. 109-163, §1403(a), 119 Stat. 3136, 3475 (2006). It provides, in part, "No individual in the custody or under the physical control of the United States Government, regardless of nationality or physical location, shall be subject to cruel, inhuman, or degrading treatment or punishment." How important is the "regardless of nationality or physical location" language in determining the scope of the government's investigative authority and the rights of the detainee? Do you think this statute affects the liability of the U.S. government or its officials in cases like *Harbury*? The Detainee Treatment Act is considered in greater detail *infra* p. 798.

United States v. Bin Laden

United States District Court, Southern District of New York, 2000
126 F. Supp. 2d 264

SAND, District Judge. The Defendants are charged with numerous offenses arising out of their alleged participation in an international terrorist organization [Al Qaeda] led by Defendant Usama Bin Laden and that organization's alleged involvement in the August 1998 bombings of the United States Embassies in Nairobi, Kenya and Dar es Salaam, Tanzania. Presently before the Court are Defendant El-Hage's motions which seek the following: suppression of evidence seized from the search of his residence in Nairobi, Kenya in August 1997 and suppression of evidence obtained from electronic surveillance, conducted from August 1996 to August 1997, of four telephone lines in Nairobi, Kenya.

BACKGROUND...

By the late spring of 1996, the United States intelligence community ("Intelligence Community") became aware that persons associated with bin Laden's organization had established an al Qaeda presence in Kenya. In addition, the Intelligence Community had isolated and identified five telephone numbers which were being used by persons associated with al Qaeda. All five of these phone lines were monitored by the Intelligence Community from August 1996 through August 1997. One of these phone lines was located in an office in the same building where the Defendant, El-Hage, and his family resided. (El-Hage, an American citizen, and his family lived in Nairobi from 1994 to 1997.) Another of the phone lines was a cellular phone used by El-Hage and others.

On April 4, 1997, the Attorney General authorized the collection of intelligence specifically targeting El-Hage. This authorization was renewed on July 3, 1997. On August 21, 1997, American and Kenyan officials conducted a search of the Defendant's residence. The Defendant's wife (the Defendant was not present during the search) was shown a document which was identified as a Kenyan warrant authorizing a search for "stolen property." The American officials who participated in the search did not, however, "rely upon the Kenyan warrant as the legal authority for the search." At the end of the search, the Defendant's wife was given an inventory by one of the Kenyan officers present which enumerated the items which had been seized during the search.

ANALYSIS...

El-Hage's suppression motion raises significant issues of first impression concerning the applicability of the full panoply of the Fourth Amendment to searches conducted abroad by the United States for foreign intelligence purposes and which are directed at an American citizen believed to be an agent of a foreign power....

I. APPLICATION OF THE FOURTH AMENDMENT OVERSEAS

Before proceeding to that Fourth Amendment analysis, it is necessary to ascertain whether the Amendment applies in this situation. El-Hage is an American citizen and the searches at issue were conducted in Kenya....

The Supreme Court cases on point suggest that the Fourth Amendment applies to United States citizens abroad. See Reid v. Covert, 354 U.S. 1, 5-6 (1957) (plurality opinion) (stating, in a case involving the Fifth and Sixth Amendments, that the "shield" provided to an American citizen by the Bill of Rights "should not be stripped away just because he happens to be in another land").... Thus, this Court finds that even though the searches at issue in this case occurred in Kenya, El-Hage can bring a Fourth Amendment challenge. However, the extent of the Fourth Amendment protection, in particular the applicability of the Warrant Clause, is unclear.

II. AN EXCEPTION TO THE WARRANT REQUIREMENT FOR FOREIGN INTELLIGENCE SEARCHES

...According to the Government, searches conducted for the purpose of foreign intelligence collection which target persons who are agents of a foreign power do not require a warrant....

The question, for this Court, is twofold. First, it is necessary to evaluate whether there is an exception to the warrant requirement for searches conducted abroad for purposes of foreign intelligence collection. Second, if such an exception exists, the Court must evaluate whether the searches conducted in this case properly fall within the parameters of that exception.

A. The Constitutional and Practical Bases for the Exception...

1. *The President's Power Over Foreign Affairs*

In all of the cases finding an exception to the warrant requirement for foreign intelligence collection, a determinative basis for the decision was the constitutional grant to the Executive Branch of power over foreign affairs....

Warrantless foreign intelligence collection has been an established practice of the Executive Branch for decades.... Congress has legislated with respect to domestic incidents of foreign intelligence collection, *see* FISA, 50 U.S.C. §§1801 et. seq. (1978), but has not addressed the issue of foreign intelligence collection which occurs abroad. The Supreme Court has remained, in the three decades since *Keith* [United States v. United States District Court, 407 U.S. 297 (1972), *supra*, p. 485], essentially silent on both aspects of the issue.... While the fact of this silence is not dispositive of the question before this Court, it is by no means insignificant....

2. *The Costs of Imposing a Warrant Requirement*

It is generally the case that imposition of a warrant requirement better safeguards the Fourth Amendment rights of citizens in the Defendant's position. But several cases direct that when the imposition of a warrant requirement proves to be a disproportionate and perhaps even disabling burden on the Executive, a warrant should not be required. *See* [United States v. Truong Dinh Hung, 629 F.2d 908, 913 (4th Cir. 1980), *supra*, p. 500] (finding that a requirement that officials secure a warrant before these types of searches "would 'unduly frustrate' the President in carrying out his foreign affairs responsibilities"); *Keith*, 407 U.S. at 315 ("We must also ask whether a warrant requirement would unduly frustrate the efforts of Government to protect itself from acts of subversion and overthrow directed against it."). For several reasons, it is clear that imposition of a warrant requirement in the context of foreign intelligence searches conducted abroad would be a significant and undue burden on the Executive.

It has been asserted that the judicial branch is ill-suited to the task of overseeing foreign intelligence collection. Foreign affairs decisions, it has been said, are often particularly complex. *See* Chicago & Southern Airlines [v. Waterman S.S. Corp., 333 U.S. 103, 111 (1948)] (explaining that foreign affairs decisions are "of a kind for which the Judiciary has neither aptitude, facilities nor responsibility"). These arguments have, to some extent, been undercut by both the Supreme Court, in *Keith*, and Congress, in FISA. On the other hand, neither *Keith* nor FISA addresses the particular difficulties attendant to *overseas* foreign intelligence collection. In fact, as mentioned previously, it was precisely these peculiarities which caused Congress to restrain the reach of FISA to domestic searches. The Government makes several persuasive points about the intricacies of foreign intelligence collection conducted abroad. First, the Government cautions that a court would have greater difficulty (than in the domestic context) predicting "the international consequences flowing from a decision on the merits regarding Executive Branch foreign policy decisions." Often these decisions have significant impacts on the essential cooperative relationships between United States officials and foreign intelligence services. In addition, when some members of the government of the country in which the searches are sought to be conducted are perceived as hostile to the United States or sympathetic to the targets of the search, a procedure requiring notification to that government could be self-defeating. The Government also explains that too much involvement could place American courts in an "institutionally untenable position" when the operations which are authorized are violative of foreign law.

These concerns about the complexity of foreign intelligence decisions should not be taken to mean that the judiciary is not capable of making these judgments. Judges will, of course, be called on to assess the constitutionality of these searches ex post. Requiring judicial approval in advance, however, would inevitably mean costly increases in the response time of the Executive Branch....

In addition to concerns about the impact of a warrant requirement on the speed of the executive response, there is an increased possibility of breaches of security when the Executive is required to take the Judiciary into its confidence. The Government emphasizes the detrimental impact that the existence of a warrant requirement for foreign intelligence searches might have on the cooperative relationships which are integral to overseas foreign intelligence collection efforts. As the Government explains, "[t]he mere *perception* that inadvertent disclosure is more likely is sufficient to obstruct the intelligence collection imperative." The United States' heightened dependence on foreign governments for assistance in overseas foreign intelligence collection is a concern that was not addressed by the circuit courts that considered an exception to the warrant requirement for foreign intelligence collection within this country.

3. *The Absence of a Warrant Procedure*

The final consideration which persuades the Court of the need for an exception to the warrant requirement for foreign intelligence collection conducted overseas is that there is presently no statutory basis for the issuance of a warrant to conduct searches abroad. In addition, existing warrant procedures and standards are simply not suitable for foreign intelligence searches....

...As an additional point, the people and agencies upon whom the Executive relies in the foreign intelligence context for information and cooperation would undoubtedly be wary of any warrant procedures that did not adequately protect sensitive foreign intelligence information.

B. Adoption of the Foreign Intelligence Exception to the Warrant Requirement

In light of the concerns outlined here, the Court finds that the power of the Executive to conduct foreign intelligence collection would be significantly frustrated by the imposition of a warrant requirement in this context. Therefore, this Court adopts the foreign intelligence exception to the warrant requirement for searches targeting foreign powers (or their agents) which are conducted abroad....

At the same time, the Court is mindful of the importance of the Fourth Amendment interests at stake. In keeping with the precedents reviewed above, the warrant exception adopted by this Court is narrowly drawn to include only those overseas searches, authorized by the President (or his delegate, the Attorney General), which are conducted primarily for foreign intelligence purposes and which target foreign powers or their agents.... All warrantless searches are still governed by the reasonableness requirement and can be challenged in ex post criminal or civil proceedings.

C. Application of the Exception

Before the Court can find that the exception applies to this case, it is necessary to show, first, that Mr. El-Hage was an agent of a foreign power; second, that the searches in question were conducted "primarily" for foreign intelligence purposes; and finally, that the searches were authorized by the President or the Attorney General.

1. *Agent of a Foreign Power*

It is clear from the Court's review of the evidence contained in the classified DCI declaration and in the materials considered by the Attorney General in issuing authorization for the post-April 4, 1997 surveillance and the August 21, 1997 search of El-Hage's residence that there was probable cause to suspect that El-Hage was an agent of a foreign power. The Court is also persuaded that al Qaeda was properly considered a foreign power. In reaching this conclusion, the Court relies on the definitions of "foreign power" and "agent of a foreign power" which were incorporated by Congress into FISA. *See* 50 U.S.C. §1801(a)-(b) [*supra* p. 522].

2. *Primarily for Foreign Intelligence Purposes*

This exception to the warrant requirement applies until and unless the primary purpose of the searches stops being foreign intelligence collection. *See Truong*, 629 F.2d at 915. If foreign intelligence collection is merely *a* purpose and not the *primary* purpose of a search, the exception does not apply. Similarly, if a reviewing judge finds that the Government officials were "looking for evidence of criminal conduct *unrelated* to the foreign affairs needs of a President, then he would undoubtedly hold the surveillances to be illegal and take appropriate measures." [United States v. Butenko, 494 F.2d 593, 606 (3d Cir. 1974) (en banc), *cert. denied sub nom.* Ivanov v. United States, 419 U.S. 881 (1974) (emphasis added)]....

The Government's submissions establish persuasively that the purpose, throughout the entire electronic surveillance of El-Hage and during the physical search of his Nairobi residence, was primarily the collection of foreign intelligence information about the activities of Usama Bin Laden and al Qaeda. There was no FBI participation in the electronic surveillance that took place. Although there was an FBI agent present during the search of El-Hage's residence, the Court does not find that foreign intelligence collection ceased to be the primary purpose of that search. The Court's determination about the purpose of the residential search is, in part, dependent upon the Government's classified submissions. For that reason, further analysis of this question is included in Classified Appendix A.

In particular, the Government explained that the purpose of its efforts was "to gather intelligence about al Qaeda, including the status of the Kenyan cell, the points of contact for other al Qaeda cells around the world, as well as any indications of the future terrorist plans of al Qaeda." The searches yielded important foreign intelligence information. The electronic surveillance that was conducted revealed that al Qaeda persons in Kenya "were heavily involved in: providing passports and other false documentation to various al Qaeda associates . . . ; passing messages to al Qaeda members and associates . . . ; passing coded telephone numbers to and from al Qaeda headquarters; . . . and passing warnings when al Qaeda members and associates were compromised by authorities." Similarly, the Government asserts that the physical search "recovered documents of great intelligence value from el Hage's computer, including a report in which el Hage's close associate Harun made an explicit admission that the Kenyan cell of Bin Laden's group were responsible for the American military personnel killed in Somalia in 1993." The Court is satisfied that the facts presented here, while perhaps suggestive of an investigation that was driven by multiple motives, clearly establish that the primary purpose of the searches at issue was, from start to finish, foreign intelligence collection.

3. Authorization from the President or the Attorney General

Finally, to apply the exception to the warrant requirement for foreign intelligence searches conducted abroad against an agent of a foreign power, the Court must find that the searches in question were directly authorized by the President or the Attorney General. On April 4, 1997 (and again on July 3, 1997), the Attorney General gave her express authorization for the foreign intelligence collection techniques (including the post-April 4, 1997 electronic surveillance and the August 21, 1997 physical search) that were employed. . . .

The electronic surveillance conducted from August 1996 until April 4, 1997 is, however, not embraced by the foreign intelligence exception to the warrant requirement. The Government does not rely on the foreign intelligence exception and seeks, instead, to distinguish the pre-authorization surveillance by emphasizing that it was directed at the activities of al Qaeda, generally, and not at El-Hage. In the Government's words, although "incidental" interception of El-Hage was "anticipated," he was not the "target" of the collection. For that reason, the Government believed that its only constitutional obligation was to "minimize interception of el-Hage." It is on this basis that the Government suggests that no Fourth Amendment violation occurred. . . .

In the cases which have rejected the Fourth Amendment claims of an incidental interceptee, though, the term "incidental" appears to be reserved for those situations where, at the time the wiretap order was sought, either the identity or the actual involvement of the interceptee was not known. . . .

Ultimately, the Court holds that with respect to the electronic surveillance of the home and cellular phones, El-Hage was not intercepted "incidentally" because he was not an unanticipated user of those telephones and because he was believed to be a participant in the activities being investigated. The Court finds that El-Hage had a reasonable expectation of privacy in his home and cellular phones and the Government should have obtained approval from either the President or the Attorney General before undertaking the electronic surveillance on those phone lines in August 1996.

III. THE EXCLUSIONARY RULE

Despite the fact that this electronic surveillance was unlawful, the Court finds that exclusion of this evidence would be inappropriate because it would not have the deterrent effect which the exclusionary rule requires and because the surveillance was undertaken in good faith....

A. Deterrence

... [T]he main purpose of the exclusionary rule is deterrence....

The Court is satisfied that the goal of the intelligence collection, "to neutralize the Bin Laden threat to national security," overwhelmingly dominated the electronic surveillance conducted prior to April 4, 1997. There was no FBI participation in that surveillance and the Court believes that the surveillance would have been conducted even if there had been an awareness that the material recorded would be inadmissible at a future criminal trial of El-Hage. Although El-Hage suggests that suppression would have the effect of deterring the Government "from improperly merging 'foreign-intelligence gathering' and criminal investigations," the Court did not find that there was any evidence of an impermissible merger in this case....

B. Good Faith

One offshoot of the deterrence analysis has been the development of an exception to the exclusionary rule that is derived from the "good faith" of the officials involved in a particular search.

... The Court is persuaded that the officials who conducted the electronic surveillance operated under an actual and reasonable belief that Attorney General approval was not required prior to April 4, 1997, when El-Hage was specifically identified by the Government as a target of foreign intelligence collection. The surveillance was also conducted in a good faith attempt to conform to the Government's perception of what the law allowed. The Court finds that the officials' interpretation of the caselaw which informs this analysis was reasonable even if in the end it was incorrect. Therefore, the exclusionary rule should not be applied.

IV. THE REASONABLENESS REQUIREMENT

Even if the Government was not required to secure a warrant in advance of the searches, the Fourth Amendment still requires that the searches be reasonable....

A. The Physical Search of the Residence

All of the cases which have established the existence of a foreign intelligence exception to the warrant requirement (and which are relied upon by the Government) arose in the context of electronic surveillance. El-Hage also notes, correctly, that "[n]one of the other 'foreign intelligence-gathering' cases involved a residential search." It is therefore necessary to assess whether the precedents reviewed apply with equal force to a physical search of the home.

The proposition that searches of the home have always merited rigorous Fourth Amendment scrutiny is unassailable. At the same time, numerous cases have emphasized the highly intrusive nature of electronic surveillance. These cases, considering the relative intrusiveness of residential searches and electronic surveillance, generally seem to conclude that neither automatically merits greater protection from the Fourth Amendment.

... For these reasons, the Court finds that the foreign intelligence exception to the warrant requirement applies with equal force to residential searches. El-Hage's argument that the search of his residence was *per se* unreasonable is therefore rejected.

In addition, the limited scope and overall nature of the search indicate that the search was executed in a reasonable manner and was not, as El-Hage alleges, "conducted as if pursuant to a 'general warrant.'" The Government and the Defendant both state that the search was conducted during the daytime, an inventory of the items seized was left at the residence and that an American official was present for the search (and "identified himself... in true name"). The scope of the search was limited to those items which were believed to have foreign intelligence value and retention and dissemination of the evidence acquired during the search were minimized. Therefore, the items seized during the physical search of El-Hage's Kenya residence are not suppressed.

B. The Electronic Surveillance

The Defendant argues that the electronic surveillance undertaken in this case is unreasonable because there were no reasonable durational limits on the surveillance: "the Government continuously and without interruption intercepted any and all of Mr. El-Hage's and his family's telephone conversations and facsimiles from July 1996 through September 1997." Although the excessive length of an electronic surveillance can be a factor tending toward unreasonableness, courts will consider the duration and the continuity within the context of a particular case. As the Government notes, more extensive monitoring and "greater leeway" in minimization efforts are permitted in a case like this given the "world-wide, covert and diffuse nature of the international terrorist group(s) targeted."

In addition, the Government emphasizes that the recorded conversations were conducted in a foreign language and that there was a high likelihood that some of the seemingly innocuous conversations were in code. The Government minimized the electronic surveillance by limiting the conversations for which verbatim transcripts were prepared and by disseminating the Defendant's name only where necessary for foreign intelligence purposes.

Finally, the Government's surveillance was reasonable in light of the use to which the telephones in question were put. Here the Government's assertion that these were "communal" phones which were regularly used by al Qaeda associates is highly relevant. For these reasons this Court finds that the automated recording of the phone lines was not unreasonable....

CONCLUSION

For the foregoing reasons, El-Hage's motion to suppress evidence from the physical search of his Kenya residence and electronic surveillance is denied without a hearing.

SO ORDERED.

DECLASSIFIED APPENDIX A

As outlined in the opinion, the Court finds that the search of El-Hage's residence was undertaken primarily for the purpose of foreign intelligence collection. The mere fact that FBI Agent Coleman [*redacted*] was present during the residential search does not mean that law enforcement displaced foreign intelligence collection as the primary purpose of the search. Coleman's presence was intended to ensure that "if anything of evidentiary value for law enforcement was found, [he] could testify to a chain of custody without involving covert [*redacted*] employees." ([*Name redacted*] Decl. ¶65.) Although [*redacted*] has, at times, "attempted to accommodate law enforcement . . . the primary focus has been collection, disruption, and dissemination of intelligence" on Bin Laden and his organization. (*Id.* ¶38.) The intelligence objective, [*redacted*] was at all times overriding, (*Id.* ¶59.) It was also believed that evidence gleaned from El-Hage's computer would provide [*redacted*] "insight into the Bin Laden infrastructure." (*Id.*) The Government's assertion that [*redacted*] actions were primarily for the purpose of foreign intelligence collection is reinforced by the fact that foreign intelligence collection against Bin Laden and al Qaeda "continues today." (*Id.* ¶38.) As is clear from the [*name redacted*] Declaration, the search of El-Hage's residence yielded important intelligence information about Bin Laden's organization. (¶67.) Finally, in disseminating the information discovered during the search, [*redacted*] followed minimization procedures (*Id.* ¶68).

NOTES AND QUESTIONS

1. *Impracticality of Warrants for Searches Abroad.* Before reaching the "foreign intelligence exception" to the warrant requirement, the court concludes that such a requirement is impractical for searches conducted abroad. Do you agree? How would a warrant requirement be implemented for such searches? *See* Justin M. Sandberg, *The Need for Warrants Authorizing Foreign Intelligence Searches of American Citizens Abroad: A Call for Formalism*, 69 U. Chi. L. Rev. 403 (2002) (urging judicial creation of warrant requirement); Carrie Truehart,

United States v. Bin Laden and the Foreign Intelligence to the Warrant Requirements for Searches of "United States Persons" Abroad, 82 B.U. L. Rev. 555 (2002) (urging statutory implementation of asserted constitutional warrant requirement). The USA PATRIOT Act, enacted shortly after the September 11, 2001, terrorist attacks, now authorizes a federal magistrate "in any district in which activities related to terrorism may have occurred" to issue a warrant for a search of property or a person "within or outside the district." Pub. L. No. 107-56, §219, 115 Stat. 272, 291 (2001). In view of the impracticality of warrants for searches abroad, should this provision be interpreted to reach searches abroad?

2. *Foreign Intelligence Exception.* Even if the warrant requirement otherwise applied, the court adopts a foreign intelligence exception. How are its requirements satisfied in *Bin Laden*? Isn't foreign intelligence collection always a continuing purpose of any overseas surveillance of suspected terrorists? How and when, if ever, would it become a secondary purpose? Suppose several of El-Hage's at-large associates were secretly indicted with him, and surveillance of them continued until they were apprehended. Would the fruits of that surveillance also fall within the foreign intelligence exception?

3. *Reasonableness of Searches Abroad.* The court holds that even though the warrant requirement is inapplicable, searches conducted abroad still must be reasonable. How does the court test for reasonableness? Can you derive a general test from its analysis?

In United States v. Barona, 56 F.3d 1087 (9th Cir. 1995), a divided court came up with different tests for reasonableness of warrantless surveillance of U.S. citizens abroad in a drug-smuggling investigation. The majority looked to good faith compliance with the law of the foreign country where the surveillance was conducted, absent conduct that shocks the conscience. *Id.* at 1103. In fact, the United States has entered into a growing number of bilateral mutual legal assistance treaties (MLATs), which independently require U.S. officials operating abroad to comply with the law of the foreign state. *See, e.g.*, Treaty Between the United States and the Government of Mexico on Mutual Legal Assistance in Criminal Matters, Dec. 9, 1987, U.S.-Mex., art. 12, 1987 U.S.T. LEXIS 208 ("A request for search, seizure, and delivery of any object acquired thereby to the requesting State shall be executed if it includes the information justifying such action *under the laws of the requested Party.*") (emphasis supplied). Such treaties confer no private rights, but their very existence may support the *Barona* court's incorporation of a compliance-with-foreign-law requirement into the Fourth Amendment's reasonableness standard. (They also create formal methods for U.S. law enforcement authorities to obtain help with investigations abroad.)

Judge Reinhardt dissented vigorously. Under the majority's reasoning, he argued, Americans are not only relegated to the "vagaries of foreign law," they are given

> *even less* protection than foreign law since...the Constitution does not even require foreign officials to comply with their own law; all that is required is that American officials have a good faith belief that they did so.... [W]hen Americans

enter Iraq, Iran, Singapore, Kuwait, China, or other similarly inclined foreign lands, they can be treated by the United States government exactly the way those foreign nations treat their own citizens — at least for Fourth Amendment purposes. [56 F.3d at 1101.]

Instead, Judge Reinhardt argued, the government still must have probable cause for a foreign search, even if a warrant is impractical. On a motion to suppress, a court would make a post hoc determination of probable cause based on the government's explanation of why it initiated the search. "Because judicial scrutiny of the search will always take place *after* it has been conducted, there is no conceivable way that imposing such a requirement would hinder law enforcement efforts abroad — except to the extent that those efforts violate our own Constitution." *Id.* at 1102.

Why do you suppose that the government expressly declined to rely on its compliance with a Kenyan warrant as legal authority for the search against El-Hage? If it had not declined, how would that surveillance fare under the two standards set out in *Barona*, based on the facts given and on what those facts reasonably imply? Which of these tests for reasonableness — the *Bin Laden* test, the *Barona* test, or Judge Reinhardt's test — is most nearly faithful to Fourth Amendment values?

4. *The Good Faith Exception.* No matter which test for reasonableness a court employs, it may still decline to exclude evidence by finding that the law enforcement officers made a "good faith" mistake. How did the court apply the good faith exception in *Bin Laden*?

5. *The Silver Platter Doctrine.* Suppose the Kenyan police *alone* had conducted the warrantless surveillance of El-Hage without probable cause and in flagrant violation of their own laws. Should a U.S. court suppress the fruits of such a foreign police surveillance? With two exceptions noted below, the courts have uniformly held no. Because the Bill of Rights does not protect Americans from the acts of foreign sovereigns and because applying the exclusionary rule to such acts would not deter them, such evidence can be turned over to U.S. law enforcement officials on a "silver platter" and admitted in U.S. criminal prosecutions. *See generally* Eric Bentley, *Toward an International Fourth Amendment: Rethinking Searches and Seizures After Verdugo-Urquidez*, 27 Vand. J. Transnatl. L. 329, 374-375 (1994); Robert L. King, *The International Silver Platter and the "Shocks the Conscience" Test: U.S. Law Enforcement Overseas*, 67 Wash. U. L.Q. 489, 511 (1989); Steven H. Theisen, *Evidence Seized in Foreign Searches: When Does the Fourth Amendment Exclusionary Rule Apply?*, 25 Wm. & Mary L. Rev. 161 (1983).

6. *The Joint Venture Exception.* Courts have recognized an exception to the silver platter doctrine for searches that are "joint ventures" between U.S. and foreign officials. Such searches are deemed the acts of the U.S. officials and subject to whatever limitations apply to U.S. searches abroad. Unfortunately, the courts are not agreed on what constitutes a joint venture. Most agree that it is not a joint venture for U.S. agents merely to provide a tip to foreign police, and many hold it insufficient for U.S. agents just to request, be present during, or even participate in the search as long as they did not initiate and control

it. *See* Bentley, *supra*, at 400 nn.297-314; Koff, *supra* p. 649, at 492 n.19. The *Restatement* simply restates the question by requiring application of the exclusionary rule only where "the participation of United States law enforcement officers in the investigation, arrest, search, or interrogation through which the evidence was obtained was so substantial as to render the action that of the United States." *Restatement (Third) of Foreign Relations Law of the United States* §433(3) (1987). A comment explains that such participation is lacking when U.S. officers "only assist, advise, or observe"; they must be "predominantly involved." *Id.* comment a. The Second Circuit has cut its own path by asking whether foreign police are acting as agents of the United States or whether U.S. law enforcement agents are evading our law by using foreign police. *See* United States v. Maturo, 982 F.2d 57, 61 (2d Cir. 1992). How would a court apply this standard? Apparently, U.S. participation in the Kenyan search was so substantial that the government did not contest responsibility. Related questions about the U.S. practice of rendering terrorist suspects to a third country for interrogation (and likely harsh treatment) by that country's police or intelligence officials are considered *infra* pp. 804-816.

7. *The Shocks-the-Conscience Exception.* A second exception to the silver platter doctrine exists for conduct that shocks the conscience. It was articulated in United States v. Toscanino, 500 F.2d 267 (2d Cir. 1974), a forcible abduction case. But while it has been paid lip service in multiple opinions since then, it apparently has been applied to exclude evidence only in United States v. Fernandez-Caro, 677 F. Supp. 893 (S.D. Tex. 1987):

> The Defendant's undisputed evidence is that the [Mexican Federal Judicial Police] threatened to kill him, beat him about the face and body, poured water through his nostrils while he was stripped, bound, and gagged, and applied electrical shocks to his wet body, among other things. The [U.S.] Government does not dispute this evidence. Indeed, Agent Garza confirmed that when the Defendant was physically delivered to American officials by Mexican officials, physical signs of abuse were readily apparent on Defendant's body. Under these circumstances, the motion [to suppress evidence which was the fruit of a confession obtained by the torture conducted by the Mexican police] is easily resolved.... The conduct of the Mexican police officials violated even minimal standards of decency expected in a civilized society. Certainly the abuse of Defendant exceeded the conduct which "shocked the conscience" of the United States Supreme Court in *Rochin v. California*, 342 U.S. 165 (1952). Even more than in *Rochin*, the methods employed here were "too close to the rack and the screw" to be acceptable. [*Id.* at 894-895, quoting *Rochin*, 343 U.S. at 172.]

Exclusion of such evidence is "not based on our Fourth Amendment jurisprudence," said the majority in *Barona*, "but rather on the recognition that we may employ our supervisory powers when absolutely necessary to preserve the integrity of the criminal justice system." 56 F.3d at 1091. Such forced confessions may be excluded even when obtained by foreign officials not acting as agents of the United States. *Maturo, supra*, 982 F.2d at 60-61. *See also* United States v. Nagelberg, 434 F.2d 585, 587 n.1 (2d Cir. 1970) (suggesting that a foreign officer's "rubbing pepper in the eyes" of a prisoner might require exclusion of the prisoner's statement).

The reason the exception has not been applied more often is probably *not* that there are few investigations that could qualify. Many foreign police use investigatory methods that might shock the conscience of a U.S. court. *See, e.g.,* Kevin Sullivan, *Mexico Pledges an End to Torture of Suspects,* Wash. Post, Mar. 6, 2001, at A18. The more likely reason is serious doctrinal confusion in the courts about the shocks-the-conscience exception. After *Verdugo,* for example, does the exception apply at all to unconnected aliens?

There is also confusion about the constitutional basis for the exception. Is the exception grounded in the Fourth Amendment or in the Fifth Amendment's guarantee of substantive due process? The Supreme Court has asserted that "[w]here a particular Amendment provides an explicit textual source of constitutional protection against a particular source of government behavior, that Amendment, not the more generalized notion of substantive due process, must be the guide for analyzing these claims." Graham v. Connor, 490 U.S. 386, 395 (1989) (internal quotation marks omitted). It is unclear whether this confines the shocks-the-conscience test to Fourth Amendment analysis. Moreover, the Supreme Court is deeply divided about whether substantive due process questions in general should be resolved by reference to "our Nation's history, legal traditions, and practices," Washington v. Glucksberg, 521 U.S. 702, 736 (1997), or to "the contemporary conscience [and] an understanding of contemporary practice." Sacramento v. Lewis, 523 U.S. 833, 847 n.8 (1998). Justice Scalia has ridiculed "th' ol' 'shocks-the-conscience' test" in other settings as "the *ne plus ultra,* the Napoleon Brandy, the Mahatma Ghandi, the Celophane of subjectivity." *Id.* at 861 (Scalia, J., concurring in judgment).

Finally, despite the court's statement in *Barona, supra,* there is confusion about the prudential basis for an exclusionary rule aimed at shocking conduct by foreign police. Such a rule would probably have no deterrent effect on the offending police. United States courts have no authority to exercise supervisory power over foreign courts, and, some scholars argue, no reason to exercise it over their own system when the shocking conduct was perpetrated by foreign officials. *See* Theisen, *supra,* at 168 (arguing that because an offending foreign official is incapable of violating the U.S. Constitution, the admission of evidence seized by him does not impair U.S. courts' integrity).

8. *International Prohibitions on Shocking Investigative Conduct.* Arguments against the shocks-the-conscience exception may be unduly parochial. The prohibition against torture is a peremptory norm of international law, or *jus cogens.* See *supra* pp. 197-198. In addition, the United States has ratified the Convention Against Torture and Other Cruel, Inhuman or Degrading Treatment or Punishment, Dec. 10, 1984, S. Treaty Doc. No. 100-20 (1988), 1465 U.N.T.S. 85, which requires states to adopt measures to prevent acts of "torture," defined in relevant part as

> any act by which severe pain or suffering, whether physical or mental, is intentionally inflicted on a person *for such purposes as obtaining from him or a third person information* or a confession . . . when such pain or suffering is inflicted by or at the instigation of or with the consent or acquiescence of a public official or other person acting in an official capacity. [*Id.* art. 1(1) (emphasis added).]

Congress has included a similar definition in the Torture Victim Protection Act, 28 U.S.C. §1350 note (2000), creating a civil cause of action for victims of torture, and in legislation implementing the Convention, 18 U.S.C.A. §§2340-2340B (West 2000 & Supp. 2005), which criminalizes acts of torture. The laws prohibiting torture are considered in greater detail *infra* pp. 792-804.

Thus, sanctions against torture are already part of our law. Excluding evidence obtained by torture — no matter which officials committed the acts — would vindicate international law and "demonstrate that no civilized nations should countenance violations of fundamental human rights." Stephen Saltzburg, *The Reach of the Bill of Rights Beyond the Terra Firma of the United States*, 20 Va. J. Intl. L. 741, 775 (1980). Do you think such exclusions by U.S. courts might even deter foreign police from violating peremptory international law?

9. *Statutory Endorsement of the Silver Platter Doctrine?* Six years after *Verdugo*, Congress authorized the intelligence community to collect information outside the United States against non-U.S. persons at the request of law enforcement agencies, "notwithstanding that the law enforcement agency intends to use the information collected for purposes of a law enforcement investigation or counterintelligence investigation." 50 U.S.C. §403-5a(a) (2000). Does this measure impliedly approve the admission of such information into evidence however it was obtained? *See* Thomas Cooperstein, *The Emerging Interplay Between Law Enforcement and Intelligence Gathering*, Intl. & Natl. Security L. News 3, 9 (1997). Should the law be read to prevail over inconsistent international law forbidding the use of torture to obtain information? See *infra* pp. 181, 194. What effect does the Detainee Treatment Act prohibition of cruel, inhuman, or degrading treatment, *supra* pp. 798-799, have on intelligence collection abroad?

10. *An International Fourth Amendment?* No clear international standard has yet emerged for government searches and seizures, although the International Covenant on Civil and Political Rights, which the United States ratified in 1992, provides that "[n]o one shall be subjected to arbitrary or unlawful interference with his privacy, family, home or correspondence.... Everyone has the right to the protection of the law against such interference or attacks." International Covenant on Civil and Political Rights, Dec. 16, 1966, art. 17, 999 U.N.T.S. 171. Do you think a U.S. court would ever find, based on the Covenant, that a search that complied with foreign law was "arbitrary and unlawful," that probable cause should have been shown, or that a warrant was required? Would it ever find that evidence produced by such a search should be excluded?

24
Civil Detention of Terrorist Suspects

Investigation of the September 11 terrorist attacks (dubbed the PENTTBOM investigation)[1] began even before the last plane crashed, but not simply to identify, apprehend, and convict the perpetrators in the time-honored fashion of criminal investigations. Assistant Attorney General Michael Chertoff explained:

> In past terrorist investigations, you usually had a defined event and you're investigating it after the fact. That's not what we had here.... From the start, there was every reason to believe that there is more to come.... So we thought that we were getting information to prevent more attacks, which was even more important than trying any case that came out of the attacks. [*Quoted in* Toobin, *supra* note 1.]

The FBI immediately checked passenger manifests, airport terminal and parking garage videotapes, car rental agreements, credit card receipts, telephone records, and numerous other data sources to help identify the hijackers. It then extended its investigation to persons who lived or worked with the hijackers or otherwise crossed paths with them.

Most of those interviewed were foreign nationals. The FBI itself detained some or had state and local authorities detain them on suspicion of committing a variety of minor crimes. In addition, the FBI detained a few persons as "material witnesses." The Bureau asked the INS to detain many others who were in technical violation of their immigration status (out-of-status immigrants).

"We're clearly not standing on ceremony, and if there is a basis to hold them we're going to hold them," Chertoff said in reference to the detentions. *Id.* Attorney General Ashcroft was even more blunt: "We have waged a deliberate

---

1. Background about the investigation was drawn from The Constitution Project, *Report on Post-9/11 Detentions*, June 2, 2004; Amnesty International, *United States of America: Amnesty International's Concerns Regarding Post September 11 Detentions in the USA* (AMR 51/044/2002), Mar. 14, 2002; Jeffrey Rosen, *Holding Pattern*, New Republic, Dec. 10, 2001, at 17; *Hearing on DOJ Oversight: Preserving Our Freedom While Defending Against Terrorism, Before the S. Comm. on the Judiciary*, 107th Cong. (2001) (statements of John Ashcroft, Attorney General, and Michael Chertoff, Asst. Attorney General); Dan Eggen, *Many Held on Tenuous Ties to Sept. 11*, Wash. Post, Nov. 29, 2001, at A18; Dept. of Justice, *Attorney General Ashcroft Provides Total Number of Federal Criminal Charges and INS Detainees*, Nov. 27, 2001; Jeffrey Toobin, *Crackdown*, New Yorker, Nov. 5, 2001, at 56; Amy Goldstein, *A Deliberate Strategy of Disruption; Massive, Secretive Detention Effort Aimed Mainly at Preventing More Terror*, Wash. Post, Nov. 4, 2001, at A1.

campaign of arrest and detention to remove suspected terrorists who violate the law from our streets." *Hearing on DOJ Oversight, supra* p. 664.

Within weeks, the media reported that more than 1,100 persons had been or were being detained by law enforcement authorities. Although the government declined to release a breakdown of this number, a newspaper investigation of 235 detainees whom it could identify indicated that the largest number were from Egypt, Saudi Arabia, and Pakistan. By the end of November, federal criminal charges had been brought against 104 individuals (most relating to possession of false identification or other fraud), of whom 55 were then in custody, while the INS had detained 548 persons for immigration violations.

In January 2002, the government initiated the "Absconder Apprehension Initiative" to locate and deport 6,000 Arabs and Muslims with outstanding deportation orders (among more than 300,000 foreign nationals subject to similar orders). As of May 2003, another 2,747 noncitizens were detained as part of a special registration program directed at Arabs and Muslims.

The following affidavit of an FBI agent opposing a detainee's bond request offers a rare insight into the otherwise secretive investigative process.

Affidavit of Michael E. Rolince, U.S. Dept. of Justice, Exec. Office for Immigration Review, Immigration Court

Reprinted in Human Rights Watch, *Presumption of Guilt: Human Rights Abuses of Post-September 11 Detainees,* App. B (Aug. 2002) *available at http://www.hrw.org/reports/2002/us911/USA0802.pdf*

In Bond Proceedings
RE: ALI ABUBAKR ALI AL-MAQTARI

Pursuant to 28 U.S.C. §1736, I, Michael E. Rolince, hereby declare as follows:

1. I have been employed by the Federal Bureau of Investigation (FBI) since September 1974 as a Special Agent, and since August 1998, I have been the Section Chief of the Counterterrorism Division's International Terrorism Operations Section (ITOS) at FBI Headquarters in Washington D.C....

3. As the ITOS Section Chief, I am personally involved in and have significant supervisory responsibilities for the nationwide FBI investigation initiated in response to a series of deadly terrorist attacks which occurred on September 11, 2001. As such, I am privy both to the broad scope of and to particular details from the investigation....

5. The FBI has identified nineteen suspected hijackers, some of whose legal immigration status had expired. Based on a review of intelligence and other source information, the FBI has reason to believe that the hijackers were associated with al Qaeda, aka "the Base," an international network of terrorist cells controlled by Osama bin Laden, which has been formally designated by the Department of State as a foreign terrorist organization since October 8, 1999. Prior to the September 11, 2001 attacks, Osama bin Laden was being sought by the FBI in connection with

the August 7, 1998 bombings of the United States embassies in Dar es Salaam, Tanzania, and Nairobi, Kenya, which killed over 200 individuals.

6. At the direction of President George W. Bush and Attorney General John Ashcroft, the FBI has initiated a nationwide investigation to identify and apprehend individuals involved in the hijackings and to prevent future acts of terrorism within the United States. To date the FBI has received or generated more than 250,000 leads from its web site, special hot line, a toll-free WATTS line, and in the FBI field offices, and additional leads are coming in every day. The investigation has yielded over 300 searches, and more than 100 court orders and 3000 subpoenas. There is still a great deal of information to be collected before the FBI will be in a position to determine the full scope of the terrorist conspiracy and to determine the full extent of damage that the terrorists intended to cause.

7. The FBI has come to believe that associates of the hijackers with connections to foreign terrorist organizations may still be in the United States. The tips received and the leads developed in our field offices have enabled the FBI to identify individuals who may have information about these associates, or, in fact, be among the participants. As explained below, the number of people of interest to the FBI is constantly changing as leads are followed and more information is obtained.

8. Information available to the FBI indicates a potential for additional terrorist incidents. As a result, the FBI has requested that all law enforcement agencies nationwide be on heightened alert. When there is threat information about a specific target, the FBI shares that information with appropriate state and local authorities. Several city and state officials have been contacted over the last few weeks to alert them to potential threats.

9. On September 23, 2001, the FBI issued a nationwide alert based on information indicating the possibility of attacks using crop-dusting aircraft. The FBI assesses the uses of this type of aircraft to distribute chemical or biological weapons of mass destruction as potential threats to Americans. At this point, there is no clear indication of the intended time or place of any such attack. The FBI has confirmed that Mohammed Atta, one of the suspected hijackers, was acquiring knowledge of crop-dusting aircraft prior to the attacks on September 11th. . . .

10. The investigation has also uncovered several individuals, including individuals who may have links to the hijackers, who fraudulently have obtained, or attempted to obtain, licenses to transport hazardous material.

11. In the context of this terrorism investigation, the FBI identified individuals whose activities warranted further inquiry. When such individuals were identified as aliens who were believed to have violated their immigration status, the FBI notified the Immigration and Naturalization Service (INS). The INS detained such aliens under the authority of the Immigration and Nationality Act. At this point, the FBI must consider the possibility that these aliens are somehow linked to, or may possess knowledge useful to the investigation of,

the terrorist attacks on the World Trade Center and the Pentagon. The respondent, Ali Abubakr Ali Al-Maqtari (AL-MAQTARI), is one such individual.

12. As a result of a search previously described to the court, the FBI continues to download the hard drive of a computer. (The computer was found in a car belonging to Al-Maqtari's wife.) When interviewed by the FBI, Al-Maqtari said he had not used the laptop but purchased it used for $250 from a customer at the convenience store where he works. Al-Maqtari said that the customer obtained the computer from a third party. At present, the download of the hard drive is still running. Once this process is completed, the FBI will need several days to review the information obtained.

13. The FBI continues to actively pursue this investigation.

14. The business of counterterrorism intelligence gathering in the United States is akin to the construction of a mosaic. At this stage of the investigation, the FBI is gathering and processing thousands of bits and pieces of information that may seem innocuous at first glance. We must analyze all that information, however, to see if it can be fit into a picture that will reveal how the unseen whole operates. The significance of one item of information may frequently depend upon knowledge of many other items of information. What may seem trivial to some may appear of great moment to those within the FBI or the intelligence community who have a broader context within which to consider a questioned item or isolated piece of information. At the present stage of this vast investigation, the FBI is gathering and culling information that may corroborate or diminish our current suspicions of the individuals that have been detained. The Bureau is approaching that task with unprecedented resources and a nationwide urgency. In the meantime, the FBI has been unable to rule out the possibility that respondent is somehow linked to, or possesses knowledge of, the terrorist attacks on the World Trade Center and the Pentagon. To protect the public, the FBI must exhaust all avenues of investigation while ensuring that critical information does not evaporate pending further investigation.

I declare under penalty of perjury that the foregoing is true and correct. Executed on October 11, 2001, in Washington, D.C.

Michael E. Rolince
Federal Bureau of Investigation

Office of the Inspector General, Department of Justice, Press Release, The September 11 Detainees: A Review of the Treatment of Aliens Held on Immigration Charges in Connection with the Investigation of the September 11 Attacks

June 2, 2003
http://www.usdoj.gov/oig/special/0306/press.pdf

After the September 11 terrorist attacks, the Department of Justice (Department) used federal immigration laws to detain aliens in the United States who were suspected of having ties to the attacks or connections to terrorism, or who were encountered during the course of the Federal Bureau of Investigation's (FBI) investigation into the attacks. In the 11 months after the attacks, 762 aliens were detained in connection with the FBI terrorism investigation for various immigration offenses, including overstaying their visas and entering the country illegally.

The Office of the Inspector General (OIG) examined the treatment of these detainees, including their processing, bond decisions related to them, the timing of their removal from the United States or their release from custody, their access to counsel, and their conditions of confinement....

Among the specific findings in the OIG's report:

ARREST, CHARGING & ASSIGNMENT TO A DETENTION FACILITY

- The FBI in New York City made little attempt to distinguish between aliens who were subjects of the FBI terrorism investigation (called "PENTT-BOM") and those encountered coincidentally to a PENTTBOM lead. The OIG report concluded that, even in the chaotic aftermath of the September 11 attacks, the FBI should have expended more effort attempting to distinguish between aliens who it actually suspected of having a connection to terrorism from [sic] those aliens who, while possibly guilty of violating federal immigration law, had no connection to terrorism but simply were encountered in connection with a PENTTBOM lead.
- The INS did not consistently serve the September 11 detainees with notice of the charges under which they were being held within the INS's stated goal of 72 hours. The review found that some detainees did not receive these charging documents (called a "Notice to Appear" or NTA) for more than a month after being arrested. This delay affected the detainees' ability to understand why they were being held, obtain legal counsel, and request a bond hearing....
- The Department instituted a policy that all aliens in whom the FBI had an interest in connection with the PENTTBOM investigation required clearance by the FBI of any connection to terrorism before they could be removed or released. Although not communicated in writing, this "hold until cleared" policy was clearly understood and applied throughout the Department. The policy was based on the belief—which turned out to be erroneous—that the FBI's clearance process would proceed quickly. FBI agents responsible for clearance investigations often were assigned other duties and were not able to focus on the detainee cases. The result was that detainees remained in custody—many in extremely restrictive conditions of confinement—for weeks and months with no clearance investigations being conducted. The OIG review found that, instead of taking a few days as anticipated, the FBI clearance process took an average of 80 days, primarily because it was understaffed and not given sufficient priority by the FBI.

BOND AND REMOVAL ISSUES

- The Department instituted a "no bond" policy for all September 11 detainees as part of its effort to keep the detainees confined until the FBI could complete its clearance investigations. The OIG review found that the INS raised concerns about this blanket "no bond" policy, particularly when it became clear that the FBI's clearance process was much slower than anticipated and the INS had little information in many individual cases on which to base its continued opposition to bond in immigration hearings. INS officials also were concerned about continuing to hold detainees while the FBI conducted clearance investigations where detainees had received a final removal or voluntary departure order. The OIG review found that the INS and the Department did not timely address conflicting interpretations of federal immigration law about detaining aliens with final orders of removal who wanted and were able to leave the country, but who had not been cleared by the FBI.

- In January 2002, when the FBI brought the issue of the extent of the INS's detention authority to the Department's attention, the Department abruptly changed its position as to whether the INS should continue to hold aliens after they had received a final departure or removal order until the FBI had completed the clearance process. After this time, the Department allowed the INS to remove aliens with final orders without FBI clearance. In addition, in many cases the INS failed to review the detainees' custody determination as required by federal regulations.

The FBI's initial assessment of the September 11 detainees' possible connections to terrorism and the slow pace of the clearance process had significant ramifications on the detainees' conditions of confinement. Our review found that 84 September 11 detainees were housed at the MDC [Metropolitan Detention Center] in Brooklyn under highly restrictive conditions. These conditions included "lock down" for at least 23 hours per day; escort procedures that included a "4-man hold" with handcuffs, leg irons, and heavy chains any time the detainees were moved outside their cells; and a limit of one legal telephone call per week and one social call per month.

Among the OIG review's findings regarding the treatment of detainees held at the MDC and Passaic are:

CONDITIONS OF CONFINEMENT

- BOP officials imposed a communications blackout for September 11 detainees immediately after the terrorist attacks that lasted several weeks. After the blackout period ended, the MDC's designation of the September 11 detainees as "Witness Security" inmates frustrated efforts by detainees' attorneys, families, and even law enforcement officials, to determine where the detainees were being held. We found that MDC staff frequently—and mistakenly—told people who inquired about a specific September 11 detainee that the detainee was not held at the facility when, in fact, the opposite was true.
- The MDC's restrictive and inconsistent policies on telephone access for detainees prevented some detainees from obtaining legal counsel in a timely manner. Most of the September 11 detainees did not have legal representation prior to their detention at the MDC. Consequently, the policy developed by the MDC that permitted detainees one legal call

per week — while complying with broad BOP national standards — severely limited the detainees' ability to obtain and consult with legal counsel. In addition, we found that in many instances MDC staff did not ask detainees if they wanted their one legal call each week. We also found that the list of pro bono attorneys provided to the detainees contained inaccurate and outdated information.
- With regard to allegations of abuse at the MDC, the evidence indicates a pattern of physical and verbal abuse by some correctional officers at the MDC against some September 11 detainees, particularly during the first months after the attacks and during intake and movement of prisoners. Although the allegations of abuse have been declined for criminal prosecution, the OIG is continuing to investigate these matters administratively.
- The OIG review found that certain conditions of confinement at the MDC were unduly harsh, such as subjecting the September 11 detainees to having two lights illuminated in their cells 24 hours a day for several months longer than necessary, even after electricians rewired the cellblock to allow the lights to be turned off individually. We also found that MDC staff failed to inform MDC detainees in a timely manner about the process for filing formal complaints about their treatment.
- By contrast, the OIG review found that the detainees confined at Passaic had much different, and significantly less harsh, experiences than the MDC detainees. According to INS data, Passaic housed 400 September 11 detainees from the date of the terrorist attacks through May 30, 2002, the largest number of September 11 detainees held at any single U.S. detention facility. Passaic detainees housed in the general population were treated like "regular" INS detainees who also were held at the facility. Although we received some allegations of physical and verbal abuse, we did not find the evidence indicated a pattern of abuse at Passaic. However, the INS did not conduct sufficient and regular visits to Passaic to ensure the September 11 detainees' conditions of confinement were appropriate.

"The Justice Department faced enormous challenges as a result of the September 11 terrorist attacks, and its employees worked with dedication to meet these challenges," [Inspector General] Fine said. "The findings of our review should in no way diminish their work. However, while the chaotic situation and the uncertainties surrounding the detainees' connections to terrorism explain some of the problems we found in our review, they do not explain them all," Fine said....

Non-Detention Act
18 U.S.C. §4001(a) (2000)

No citizen shall be imprisoned or otherwise detained by the United States except pursuant to an Act of Congress.

NOTES AND QUESTIONS

a. Constitutional and Statutory Limits on Detention

1. *The Constitutional Standard for Detention.* Generally, the Fourth Amendment requires that police, before making an arrest, have probable cause to believe that a suspect has committed a crime. However, they are allowed to stop a person when there is an "articulable suspicion that the person has been, is, or is about to be engaged in criminal activity." United States v. Place, 462 U.S. 696, 703 (1983). *See* Terry v. Ohio, 392 U.S. 1, 9 (1968). Nevertheless, "reasonable suspicion of criminal activity," short of probable cause, only "warrants a temporary seizure for the purpose of questioning limited to the purpose of the stop." Florida v. Royer, 460 U.S. 491, 498 (1983).

The INS may stop and detain persons for questioning about their citizenship upon a reasonable suspicion that they are illegal aliens. United States v. Brignoni-Ponce, 422 U.S. 873, 882-883 (1975). Congress has authorized the arrest and detention of such aliens pending a decision about their removal. 8 U.S.C. §1226 (2000). The Supreme Court has ruled that after a decision to remove, continued indefinite detention would present a serious due process issue, at least as to aliens already in the country, who enjoy Fifth Amendment protection. Zadvydas v. Davis, 533 U.S. 678 (2001).

Zadvydas, however, did not involve an alien suspected of terrorism. The Court emphasized that the detention there at issue "did not apply narrowly to 'a small segment of particularly dangerous individuals,' say suspected terrorists." *Id.* at 691 (quoting Kansas v. Hendricks, 521 U.S. 346, 368 (1997) (involving preventive detention of convicted sexual predator until he is no longer dangerous)). "Neither do we consider terrorism or other special circumstances," it added, "where special arguments might be made for forms of preventive detention and for heightened deference to the judgments of the political branches with respect to matters of national security." *Zadvydas, supra,* 533 U.S. at 696.

Is the Court suggesting a "national security exception" to the Fifth Amendment guarantee of due process? In the same vein, could there be such an exception to the Fourth Amendment's protection against unreasonable seizure? (Recall that, before enactment of the Foreign Intelligence Surveillance Act (FISA) in 1978, some lower courts found a national security exception to the warrant requirement for some kinds of searches and electronic surveillance. See *supra* pp. 494-505.) How would you define such an exception? What limitations, if any, would the Fourth or Fifth Amendment place on the preventive detention of suspected alien terrorists in the United States?

2. *The Burden of Proof.* In the final analysis, the FBI affidavit sought to justify the detention of Al-Maqtari on the basis that the Bureau was "unable to rule out the possibility that respondent is somehow linked to, or possesses knowledge of, the terrorist attacks on the World Trade Center and the Pentagon." Rolince Aff. ¶14. Is this rationale consistent with the Fourth Amendment? With a presumption of innocence? Or was the FBI suggesting a new standard or presumption for detentions intended to prevent terrorist attacks?

3. *Due Process Requirements for Statutory Detention.* In Denmore v. Hyung Joon Kim, 538 U.S. 510 (2003), Justice Souter summarized the due process requirements for preventive detention as follows:

> [D]ue process requires a "special justification" for physical detention that "outweighs the individual's constitutionally protected interest in avoiding physical restraint" as well as "adequate procedural protections." "There must be a 'sufficiently compelling' governmental interest to justify such an action, usually a punitive interest in imprisoning the convicted criminal or a regulatory interest in forestalling danger to the community." The class of persons subject to confinement must be commensurately narrow and the duration of confinement limited accordingly.... Finally, procedural due process requires, at a minimum, that a detainee have the benefit of an impartial decisionmaker able to consider particular circumstances on the issue of necessity.

Id. at 557 (Souter, J., concurring in part and dissenting in part).

Applying similar standards in United States v. Salerno, 481 U.S. 739 (1987), a divided Supreme Court upheld the provisions of the Bail Reform Act of 1984, 18 U.S.C. §3142(e) (2000), which authorized preventive detention (denial of bail) of arrestees on the grounds of flight risk or future dangerousness. The majority found that the Act authorized a "regulatory," rather than punitive, detention that was reasonably related to compelling government interests. The Court noted that regulatory interests in community safety can outweigh an individual's liberty interest, "[f]or example, in times of war and insurrection." 481 U.S. at 748. But the Court emphasized that the Bail Reform Act authorized detention of an arrestee only when: (a) he has been arrested and indicted on probable cause of having committed one or more specified extremely dangerous offenses, (b) a court conducts a full-blown adversary hearing on the denial of bail, at which the arrestee is entitled to be represented by his own counsel, (c) the government persuades the court by clear and convincing evidence that no conditions of release can assure the presence of the arrestee or the safety of the community, and (d) the arrestee is given a right of appeal from the court's decision.

Do the post-September 11 detentions described above satisfy the Court's due process standards? Even if they do, does the Bail Reform Act occupy the field of preventive detention (leaving aside immigration detentions)?

4. *Cold War Detentions and the Non-Detention Act.* In 1950, Congress passed, over President Truman's veto, the Emergency Detention Act. Pub. L. No. 81-831, 64 Stat. 1019. Following a lengthy litany of the dangers of a "world communist movement," it authorized the President to declare an "Internal Security Emergency" in the event of an invasion, declaration of war by Congress, or "Insurrection within the United States in aid of a foreign enemy." *Id.* §102(a). In such an emergency, the President, acting through the Attorney General, was empowered to "apprehend and by order detain ... each person as to whom there is reasonable ground to believe that such person probably will engage in, or probably will conspire with others to engage in, acts of espionage or of sabotage." *Id.* §103(a). The Justice Department constructed a half-dozen detention "camps" around the country pursuant to the Act, and during the Vietnam era it was suggested that war protests might be regarded for purposes of the Act as an

"Insurrection within the United States in aid of a foreign enemy." *See* Alan M. Dershowitz, *The Role of Law During Times of Crisis: Would Liberty Be Suspended?*, in *Civil Disorder and Violence* 140-141 (Harry M. Cloor ed., 1972).

The Act was repealed unused by Pub. L. No. 92-129, 85 Stat. 348 (1971). The legislative history of the repealer cites First and Fifth Amendment violations and declares that "the concentration camp implications of the legislation render it abhorrent." H.R. Rep. No. 92-116, at 4 (1971), *reprinted in* 1971 U.S.C.C.A.N. 1438. But does the threat of further terrorist attacks after September 11, 2001, justify reenactment of the measure or one like it, permitting preventive detention of citizens and non-citizens alike as a counterterrorist measure? *See* Thomas F. Powers, *When to Hold 'Em*, Legal Aff. (Sept./Oct. 2004) (yes).

At the same time that it repealed the Emergency Detention Act, Congress adopted the Non-Detention Act, 18 U.S.C. §4001(a) (2000), set forth above. Does this Act apply to the detention of suspected terrorists? *See* Louis Fisher, *Detention of U.S. Citizens* (Cong. Res. Serv. RS22130), Apr. 28, 2005 (concluding from legislative history of the Non-Detention Act that Congress "intended the statutory language to restrict all detentions by the executive branch, not merely those by the Attorney General"). *See also* Howe v. Smith, 452 U.S. 473, 479 n.3 (1981) (the Act proscribes "detention of *any kind* by the United States, absent a congressional grant of authority to detain") (emphasis in original). Application of the Non-Detention Act was considered in two recent cases, set out *infra* pp. 721 and 744.

b. "Spitting on the Sidewalk"

1. *"Spitting on the Sidewalk" Detentions.* Explaining the detentions, Attorney General Ashcroft likened some of the arrests for minor crimes to Attorney General Robert Kennedy's policy of "arrest[ing] mobsters [for] spitting on the sidewalk if it would help in the battle against organized crime." Goldstein, *supra* p. 664 n.1. Identity fraud, credit card fraud, forgery, and larceny were among the criminal charges brought against some of the detainees. One difficulty with the spitting-on-the-sidewalk policy, however, is that persons charged with such minor offenses are usually released on bail. Indeed, even *conviction* on such a charge often yields no term of imprisonment. Rising to the occasion, however, one federal magistrate denied bail for an immigrant from El Salvador who had allegedly helped some of the September 11 hijackers obtain false identity papers (apparently without knowing that they were terrorists), explaining that "[o]ne of the unspoken issues today is, after the events of September 11, is it going to be business as usual? I suspect not. The defendant, either wittingly or unwittingly, certainly contributed to [the attacks]." T.R. Reid & Allen Lengel, *Scotland Yard Says Hijackers May Have Trained in Britain; Terror Suspects Arrested in Spain, Holland*, Wash. Post, Sept. 27, 2001, at A18.

2. *PENTTBOM Convictions.* In mid-2005, the Administration asserted that terrorism investigations had resulted in charges against more than 400 suspects, half of whom were convicted. A Washington Post study of the Department of Justice's own list of prosecutions, however, indicated that only 39 of these convictions were for crimes related to terrorism or national security.

Dan Eggen & Julie Tate, *U.S. Campaign Produces Few Convictions of Terrorism Charges*, Wash. Post, June 12, 2005, at A1. The majority were for minor crimes such as fraud, making false statements, and passport violations, for which the median sentence was just eleven months.

The Justice Department defended the numbers by arguing that many defendants were prosecuted for such crimes in exchange for nonpublic information that was valuable in other terrorism probes. *Id.* The former Associate Attorney General who headed the Office of Legal Policy had an additional explanation: "You're talking about a violation of law that may or may not rise to the level of what might usually be called a federal case. But the calculation does not happen in isolation; you are not just talking about the [minor] crime itself, but the suspicion of terrorism.... That skews the calculation in favor of prosecution." *Id.* (quoting Viet D. Dinh). In other words, the Post paraphrased, "the primary strategy is to use 'prosecutorial discretion' to detain suspicious individuals by charging them with minor crimes." *Id.* Replied a defense attorney, "That's fine if you take it as a given that you have the devil there," citing Al Capone (who was eventually prosecuted for income tax evasion) as an example, but "the problem is...[that] you're going to make mistakes and you're going to hurt innocent people." *Id.*

c. Material Witness Detentions

1. *Detaining Material Witnesses.* The material witness statute, 18 U.S.C. §3144 (2000), has been employed extensively by the government in the fight against terrorism. It provides as follows:

> If it appears from an affidavit filed by a party that the testimony of a person is material in a criminal proceeding, and if it is shown that it may become impracticable to secure the presence of the person by subpoena, a judicial officer may order the arrest of the person and treat the person in accordance with the provisions of section 3142 of this title [governing release on bond and requiring a judicial hearing]. No material witness may be detained because of inability to comply with any condition of release if the testimony of such witness can adequately be secured by deposition, and if further detention is not necessary to prevent a failure of justice. Release of a material witness may be delayed for a reasonable period of time until the deposition of the witness can be taken pursuant to the Federal Rules of Criminal Procedure.

The statute apparently was first used in a terrorism investigation to detain Terry Nichols, who was eventually convicted in connection with the Oklahoma City bombing. *See* United States v. McVeigh, 940 F. Supp. 1541, 1562 (D. Colo. 1996) (finding that Nichols' renunciation of U.S. citizenship and his association with Timothy McVeigh sufficiently showed probable cause to believe that it "may become impracticable" to rely on a subpoena to secure his testimony).

2. *Material Witness Detentions in PENTTBOM.* Although the government has not disclosed exactly how many persons it has held as material witnesses in the PENTTBOM and subsequent counterterrorist investigations, Human Rights Watch reported that its research had identified 70 such individuals as of June 2005. Human Rights Watch, *Witness to Abuse: Human Rights Abuses Under the*

Material Witness Law Since September 11, 17 Hum. Rts. Watch 1, June 2005, at 2. What aspect of the procedure for detaining material witnesses might deter the government from making wider use of this legal basis for detention? On the other hand, in view of the fact that criminal arrests require probable cause and that immigration detentions apply only to aliens, when might material witness detention appeal to the government?

3. *Applicability to Grand Jury Investigations.* A Second Circuit Court of Appeals panel rejected a challenge to one of the PENTTBOM detentions, finding that it was lawful to detain a material witness in connection with a grand jury investigation, not just for trial, as the challenger had argued. United States v. Awadallah, 349 F.3d 42, 52 (2d Cir. 2003), *cert. denied,* 543 U.S. 1056 (2005). At the same time, however, the court cautioned that "it would be improper for the government to use [material witness detention] for other ends, such as the detention of persons suspected of criminal activity for which probable cause has not yet been established." *Id.* at 59.

Human Rights Watch found, nevertheless, that fewer than half of the 9/11 material witnesses were ever brought before a grand jury or court to testify; many were apparently held as suspects rather than as witnesses. *Witness to Abuse, supra,* at 2. Yet the government has not been shy about explaining this use of the statute. For example, after acknowledging that the United States has no general preventive detention law, one architect of the post-9/11 detention policy said that "the material witness statute *gives the government effectively the same power....* To the extent that it is a suspect involved in terror, you hold them on a material witness warrant, and you get the information until you find out what's going on." *Id.* at 19 (quoting Mary Jo White, former U.S. Attorney for the Southern District of New York) (emphasis added). In another case in which the material witness's lawyer argued that the government was holding his client as a criminal suspect, not as a witness, the government responded, "Based on evidence collected to date, the government cannot exclude the possibility that [the detainee] was criminally, rather than innocently, involved in how his fingerprint got to Spain." *Quoted in* Ricardo J. Bascuas, *The Unconstitutionality of "Hold Until Clear": Reexamining Material Witness Detentions in the Wake of the September 11th Dragnet,* 58 Vand. L. Rev. 677, 679 (2005) (citation omitted).

Is the use of the statute to detain suspects, rather than witnesses, consistent with the Second Circuit dicta? With the Constitution? *See* Bascuas, *supra,* at 732-736 (no; section 3144 is "facially unconstitutional" and unprecedented for permitting arrests without probable cause or even individualized suspicion of criminal conduct).

4. *Testimony: A Key to the Material Witness's Jail Cell?* The Second Circuit panel also found that the material witness statute made a deposition available as an alternative to detention for obtaining grand jury testimony, effectively giving the detainee a key to his jail cell. *Awadallah,* 349 F.3d at 52. Human Rights Watch reports, however, that the government has consistently opposed depositions or stalled taking them, citing national security reasons. *Witness to Abuse, supra,* at 79. Moreover, the government reportedly failed to advise many detainees of the reasons for their arrests, of their right to an attorney and to have an attorney present at their interrogations, and of their right to remain silent. *Id.* at 4.

d. Immigration Detentions

1. *Immigration Detentions.* Aliens who have been found either inadmissible or removable for terrorist activity are subject to mandatory detention under the immigration laws until their removal can be effected. 8 U.S.C. §§1182(a)(3)(B), 1227(a)(4)(B) (2000). *See generally* 8 Charles Gordon et al., *Immigration Law and Procedure* §108.02[2][b] (2005). Most of the September 11 detainees, however, were not charged with terrorist activity. For example, as the Rolince affidavit, *supra* p. 665, suggests, at ¶11, Al-Maqtari was arrested for a minor immigration violation: overstaying his visa. *See* Goldstein, *supra* p. 664 n.1.

Prolonged detention for minor "overstays" is highly unusual, according to immigration lawyers. Pat Leisner, *Detention After Attacks Challenged*, AP Online, Dec. 1, 2001. INS regulations before the September 11 attacks provided that persons suspected of immigration violations could be held for 24 hours before being charged. After the attacks, the Department of Justice lengthened the period to 48 hours, then authorized the Attorney General to stay for ten days the release of immigrants granted bond in order to allow the government to appeal. 66 Fed. Reg. 54,909 (Oct. 31, 2001). Asked to explain what standard he used for staying releases ordered by immigration judges, Attorney General Ashcroft testified that "if the attorney general develops an understanding that it's against the national interest and would in some way potentially violate or jeopardize the national security, then those orders are overruled." *Hearing on DOJ Oversight, supra* p. 664. *See also* 66 Fed. Reg. 56,967 (Nov. 14, 2001) (providing for indefinite detention of suspected terrorist aliens after expiration of removal period); Jess Bravin, *U.S. Issues Rules to Indefinitely Detain Illegal Aliens Who Are Potentially Terrorists*, Wall St. J., Nov. 15, 2001, at A18. Authorities explained that immigration charges are a good way to detain persons suspected of terrorist connections when the government lacks sufficient evidence to prove the connections. *Id.*

Since March 2003, the government has filed immigration charges against more than 500 people who were under scrutiny in terrorism investigations. Mary Beth Sheridan, *Immigration Law as an Anti-Terrorism Tool*, Wash. Post, June 13, 2005, at A1. The Washington Post reports that 768 suspects were "secretly processed on immigration charges" in the 9/11 investigations, and most were deported after being cleared of terrorism connections. *Id.*

2. *Pretextual Immigration Detention.* In Turkmen v. Ashcroft, 2006 WL 1662663 (E.D.N.Y. June 14, 2006), a group of post-9/11 immigration detainees, all but one of whom were Muslims of Middle Eastern origin, challenged their detention in part on the Fourth Amendment ground that they were really detained for criminal investigation without probable cause. The court rejected the challenge:

> As explained above, plaintiffs' entire detention was authorized by the post-removal period [immigration] detention statute. [8 U.S.C. §1231(a)(2)] That the government may have been motivated by a desire to keep terrorism suspects in jail pending further investigation does not alter the legality of the detention. It is well-established that the government's "[s]ubjective intent . . . does not make otherwise lawful conduct illegal or unconstitutional." Whren v. United States, 517 U.S. 806,

817 (1996) (internal quotation marks omitted). Accordingly, even accepting as true plaintiffs' allegations regarding defendants' motives, the detention of plaintiffs was authorized pursuant to the post-removal detention statute and thus did not violate the Fourth Amendment. [*Turkmen, supra,* slip op. at *41.]

The court's rejection of the detainees' Equal Protection claim is discussed *infra* p. 613.

3. *The USA PATRIOT Act Preventive Detention Provision.* Immediately after the 9/11 attacks, Attorney General Ashcroft asked Congress for authority to hold suspected alien terrorists indefinitely. Bravin, *supra* p. 676. Would such legislation be constitutional? Congress rebuffed this request, providing instead in the USA PATRIOT Act that the INS could hold immigrants for up to seven days before charging them and then hold them while immigration proceedings were pending if the Attorney General certified, at least every six months, that their release would threaten national security. Pub. L. No. 107-56, §412, 115 Stat. 272, 350-351 (2001). How, if at all, might you argue that this legislation affected the legality of subsequent immigration detentions in the PENTTBOM investigation?

4. *The Ethics of Immigration Bond Hearings.* As the OIG report suggests, immigration laws, like the Bail Reform Act, see *supra* p. 672, authorize immigration judges to deny bond for a detained immigrant if the government provides evidence of flight risk or dangerousness. The FBI, however, provided no information to sustain such determinations in many cases. Nevertheless, INS lawyers were apparently ordered to argue the "no bond" position in court without any evidence, using "boilerplate" language like that in the Rolince affidavit, *supra* p. 665. See *The September 11 Detainees: A Review of the Treatment of Aliens Held on Immigration Charges, supra* p. 667, at 78-80. Was this ethical? *See id.* at 79, 81. In some cases, the alien succeeded in obtaining a bond order and in posting bond, but the INS, without appealing the order, continued to hold him anyway. Was this lawful? *See id.* at 87 (reporting that one INS official admitted not knowing what to tell the immigrant's lawyer, "because I cannot bring myself to say that the INS no longer feels compelled to obey the law"). How far may a government lawyer go in defending preventive detention if she is instructed that it is essential to a terrorism investigation?

5. *The Length of Immigration Detentions.* In Denmore v. Hyung Joon Kim, 538 U.S. 510 (2003), the Supreme Court revisited the issue of immigration detention, this time considering a statutory provision for mandatory detention of criminal aliens pending their removal hearings. Admitting that individualized bond hearings might be feasible, the majority nevertheless concluded that "when the Government deals with deportable aliens, the Due Process Clause does not require it to employ the least burdensome means to accomplish its goal." *Id.* at 528. It therefore upheld the mandatory detention law but emphasized that such detentions pending removal were for less than 90 days in the majority of cases. Joining in the opinion, Justice Kennedy noted that if the removal proceedings were unreasonably delayed, "it could become necessary then to inquire whether the detention is not to facilitate deportation, or to

protect against risk of flight or dangerousness, but to incarcerate for other reasons." *Id.* at 532-533 (Kennedy, J., concurring). How would the post-September 11 immigration detentions described in the OIG report fare by these standards?

6. *Rights of Detainees.* Ordinarily, immigrant detainees have a due process right to counsel at their own expense. *See generally* Gordon, *supra* p. 676, §108.04[2][b]. The Department of Justice said it afforded the September 11 detainees that right, although some detainees reportedly found it difficult to exercise it. *See, e.g., Hearing on DOJ Oversight, supra* p. 664 n. 1 (questions by Sen. Feingold to Attorney General Ashcroft); Amnesty International, *supra* p. 664 n. 1, at 4-6 (reporting that many detainees were effectively denied access to a lawyer for substantial periods). Shortly after publication of the OIG report, a divided panel of the D.C. Circuit Court of Appeals found that various public interest groups had no right under the Freedom of Information Act or the First Amendment to assorted information about the post-September 11 detentions, which they sought in part to ascertain the legality of the detentions and conditions of confinement. Center for National Security Studies v. United States Dept. of Justice, 331 F.3d 918 (D.C. Cir. 2003), *cert. denied,* 540 U.S. 1104 (2004). Based presumably on the government's representations, a majority of the panel assumed that the immigrant detainees "have had access to counsel, and the INS has provided detainees with lists of attorneys willing to represent them.... They have also been free to disclose their names to the public." *Id.* In light of the OIG report, were these assumptions warranted?

7. *International Legal Rights of Alien Detainees.* Detainees also have rights under international law. The Vienna Convention on Consular Relations, April 24, 1963, 21 U.S.T. 77, 596 U.N.T.S. 261, which the United States has ratified, gives a foreign arrestee the right to have his government notified of his arrest. *Id.* art. 361(b). *See* Sanchez-Llamas v. Oregon, 126 S. Ct. 2669 (2006) (assuming, without deciding, that Convention grants individuals enforceable rights, violations will not be enforced by applying an exclusionary rule, and enforceability is conditioned on compliance with state procedural rules). What purpose do you think this right serves? State law enforcement authorities have notoriously disregarded this right, *see* Sean D. Murphy, *United States Practice in International Law 1999-2000* (2002), at 39 & n.1, despite the primacy of the Convention under the Supremacy Clause. Apart from the Supremacy Clause, can you think of any policy reason why the United States should honor the Convention's notification requirement?

The International Covenant on Civil and Political Rights art. 9, Dec. 16, 1966, 999 U.N.T.S. 171, ratified by the United States in 1992, states that "[n]o one shall be subjected to arbitrary arrest or detention," and that "[a]nyone who is deprived of his liberty by arrest or detention shall be entitled to take proceedings before a court, in order that that court may decide without delay on the lawfulness of his detention." Were these provisions violated by the PENTTBOM detentions?

e. Military Detentions

The USA PATRIOT Act was not the last word in preventive detention of immigrants. On November 13, 2001, President Bush claimed by "Military Order" the very detention authority he had unsuccessfully sought from Congress. 66 Fed. Reg. 57,833 (Nov. 13, 2001). See *infra* p. 879. The Military Order directs the Secretary of Defense to detain without time limit any noncitizen whom the President has "reason to believe" is a member of Al Qaeda, is involved in international terrorism, or has knowingly harbored such members or terrorists. *Id.* §3. Is the Military Order's detention provision consistent with the USA PATRIOT Act? If not, which prevails? Is the Military Order's detention provision constitutional? Military detention of both citizen and noncitizen "enemy combatants" is discussed in Chapter 26.

f. Profiling?

Even the incomplete numbers reflect the fact that the PENTTBOM detentions have overwhelmingly targeted Arabs and Muslims. The immigration crackdown did the same. Indeed, civil rights lawyers allege that immigration laws are being selectively enforced against Muslims and Arabs and largely ignored with respect to the rest of the immigrant population. "The approach is basically to target the Muslim and Arab community with a kind of zero-tolerance immigration policy. No other community is treated to zero-tolerance enforcement," said Professor David Cole. Sheridan, *supra* p. 676. We address the legality of "profiling" in Chapter 21.

25

Suspending the Great Writ

A case in which an "enemy combatant" held by the United States petitioned a federal court for a writ of habeas corpus prompted the following account of the writ by Justice Scalia:

> The very core of liberty secured by our Anglo-Saxon system of separated powers has been freedom from indefinite imprisonment at the will of the Executive. Blackstone stated this principle clearly:
>
> > "Of great importance to the public is the preservation of this personal liberty: for if once it were left in the power of any, the highest, magistrate to imprison arbitrarily whomever he or his officers thought proper... there would soon be an end of all other rights and immunities.... To bereave a man of life, or by violence to confiscate his estate, without accusation or trial, would be so gross and notorious an act of despotism, as must at once convey the alarm of tyranny throughout the whole kingdom. But confinement of the person, by secretly hurrying him to gaol, where his sufferings are unknown or forgotten; is a less public, a less striking, and therefore a more dangerous engine of arbitrary government....
> >
> > "To make imprisonment lawful, it must either be, by process from the courts of judicature, or by warrant from some legal officer, having authority to commit to prison; which warrant must be in writing, under the hand and seal of the magistrate, and express the causes of the commitment, in order to be examined into (if necessary) upon a *habeas corpus.* If there be no cause expressed, the gaoler is not bound to detain the prisoner. For the law judges in this respect,... that it is unreasonable to send a prisoner, and not to signify withal the crimes alleged against him." 1 W. Blackstone, Commentaries on the Laws of England 132-133 (1765).
>
> These words were well known to the Founders. Hamilton quoted from this very passage in The Federalist No. 84, p. 444 (G. Carey & J. McClellan eds., 2001). The two ideas central to Blackstone's understanding—due process as the right secured, and habeas corpus as the instrument by which due process could be insisted upon by a citizen illegally imprisoned—found expression in the Constitution's Due Process and Suspension Clauses. See Amdt. 5; Art. I, §9, cl. 2.
>
> The gist of the Due Process Clause, as understood at the founding and since, was to force the Government to follow those common-law procedures traditionally deemed necessary before depriving a person of life, liberty, or property. When a

A. Statutory Basis for Habeas Corpus

citizen was deprived of liberty because of alleged criminal conduct, those procedures typically required committal by a magistrate followed by indictment and trial.... [Hamdi v. Rumsfeld, 542 U.S. 507, 554-556 (2004) (Scalia, J., dissenting), *infra* p. 721.]

The Great Writ, as it is called, is mentioned in Article I, §9 of the U.S. Constitution: "The Privilege of the Writ of Habeas Corpus shall not be suspended, unless when in Cases of Rebellion or Invasion the public Safety may require it." Despite this seemingly restrictive language, Congress has long limited the availability of the writ by statute.

We begin this chapter with a look at the statutory basis for habeas corpus jurisdiction in federal courts. We next examine how the writ is suspended or restricted. In the final part of the chapter we consider whether the writ is available to nonresident aliens.

A. STATUTORY BASIS FOR HABEAS CORPUS

Habeas Corpus
28 U.S.C.A. §§2241-2255 (West 1994 & Supp. 2005)
& Pub. L. No. 109-163, §1405(e)(1), 119 Stat. 3136, 3477 (2006)

§2241. POWER TO GRANT WRIT

(a) Writs of habeas corpus may be granted by the Supreme Court, any justice thereof, the district courts and any circuit judge within their respective jurisdictions. The order of a circuit judge shall be entered in the records of the district court of the district wherein the restraint complained of is had.

(b) The Supreme Court, any justice thereof, and any circuit judge may decline to entertain an application for a writ of habeas corpus and may transfer the application for hearing and determination to the district court having jurisdiction to entertain it.

(c) The writ of habeas corpus shall not extend to a prisoner unless—

(1) He is in custody under or by color of the authority of the United States or is committed for trial before some court thereof; or

(2) He is in custody for an act done or omitted in pursuance of an Act of Congress, or an order, process, judgment or decree of a court or judge of the United States; or

(3) He is in custody in violation of the Constitution or laws or treaties of the United States; or

(4) He, being a citizen of a foreign state and domiciled therein is in custody for an act done or omitted under any alleged right, title, authority, privilege, protection, or exemption claimed under the commission, order or sanction of any foreign state, or under color thereof, the validity and effect of which depend upon the law of nations; or

(5) It is necessary to bring him into court to testify or for trial....

§2243. ISSUANCE OF WRIT; RETURN; HEARING; DECISION

A court, justice or judge entertaining an application for a writ of habeas corpus shall forthwith award the writ or issue an order directing the respondent to show cause why the writ should not be granted, unless it appears from the application that the applicant or person detained is not entitled thereto.

The writ, or order to show cause shall be directed to the person having custody of the person detained. It shall be returned within three days unless for good cause additional time, not exceeding twenty days, is allowed.

The person to whom the writ or order is directed shall make a return certifying the true cause of the detention.

When the writ or order is returned a day shall be set for hearing, not more than five days after the return unless for good cause additional time is allowed.

Unless the application for the writ and the return present only issues of law the person to whom the writ is directed shall be required to produce at the hearing the body of the person detained.

The applicant or the person detained may, under oath, deny any of the facts set forth in the return or allege any other material facts. . . .

The court shall summarily hear and determine the facts, and dispose of the matter as law and justice require.

B. SUSPENDING THE WRIT

Although the Suspension Clause appears in that part of the Constitution devoted to an enumeration of legislative powers, there is no other textual clue about who possesses the power to suspend the writ. The question arose in an early Civil War era case, Ex parte Merryman, 17 F. Cas. 144 (C.C.D. Md. 1861) (No. 9487), when Chief Justice Taney, sitting as a circuit court judge, ordered the release of a Southern sympathizer imprisoned at Fort McHenry. Merryman had been seized after President Lincoln signed an order authorizing suspension of the writ of habeas corpus. Said the Chief Justice, "I had supposed it to be one of those points in constitutional law upon which there was no difference of Opinion . . . that the privilege of the writ could not be suspended, except by act of congress." *Id.* at 148. However, Taney's decree was ignored by the President, and Merryman remained in prison for a time. A month later, in a message to a special session of Congress, Lincoln remarked that Taney's interpretation of the constitutional requirement would allow

> all the laws, but one, to go unexecuted, and the government itself go to pieces, lest that one be violated. . . . [T]he Constitution itself, is silent as to which, or who, is to exercise the power; and as the provision was plainly made for a dangerous emergency, it cannot be believed the framers of the instrument intended, that in every case, the danger should run its course, until Congress could be called together; the very assembling of which might be prevented, as was intended in this case, by the rebellion. [4 *The Collected Works of Abraham Lincoln* 430-431 (Roy P. Basler ed., 1953).]

B. Suspending the Writ

Five years later, the full Supreme Court made it clear that under some circumstances the writ can properly be suspended.

Ex parte Milligan
United States Supreme Court, 1866
71 U.S. 2 (4 Wall.)

[Lambdin P. Milligan, a resident of Indiana, was not a member of the armed forces. Nevertheless, on October 5, 1864, he was arrested at his home by order of General Alvin P. Hovey, commander of the military district of Indiana, and held in close confinement. He was then brought before a military tribunal in Indianapolis, tried on charges ranging from conspiracy against the government to inciting insurrection, found guilty, and sentenced to be hanged.

Subsequently, on January 2, 1865, the United States Circuit Court for Indiana met at Indianapolis and empanelled a grand jury to inquire whether any laws of the United States had been broken by anyone, and to make presentments. The grand jury did not find any bill of indictment or make any presentment against Milligan, and on January 27 the court adjourned after discharging the grand jury from further service. Milligan later petitioned the Circuit Court for his release, arguing that the military tribunal had no jurisdiction to try him.

Although only the first part of the resulting opinion treats the suspension of the writ of habeas corpus, we provide an excerpt here of the full majority and concurring opinions in order to convey accurately the Court's view of the importance of the issues it presented. We take up later parts of the majority opinion *infra* pp. 714 and 877.]

Mr. Justice DAVIS delivered the opinion of the court.... The importance of the main question presented by this record cannot be overstated; for it involves the very framework of the government and the fundamental principles of American liberty.

During the late wicked Rebellion, the temper of the times did not allow that calmness in deliberation and discussion so necessary to a correct conclusion of a purely judicial question. *Then*, considerations of safety were mingled with the exercise of power; and feelings and interests prevailed which are happily terminated. *Now* that the public safety is assured, this question, as well as all others, can be discussed and decided without passion or the admixture of any element not required to form a legal judgment....

... Milligan claimed his discharge from custody by virtue of the act of Congress "relating to *habeas corpus* and regulating judicial proceedings in certain cases," approved March 3d, 1863. Did that act confer jurisdiction on the Circuit Court of Indiana to hear this case?

In interpreting a law, the motives which must have operated with the legislature in passing it are proper to be considered. This law was passed in a time of great national peril, when our heritage of free government was in danger. An armed rebellion against the national authority, of greater proportions than history affords an example of, was raging; and the public safety required that the privilege of the writ of *habeas corpus* should be suspended. The President had practically suspended it, and detained suspected persons in custody without trial; but his authority to do this was questioned. It was claimed that Congress alone could exercise this power; and that the legislature, and not the President, should judge of the political considerations on which the right to suspend it rested. The privilege of this great writ had never before been withheld from the citizen; and as the exigence of the times demanded immediate action, it was of the highest importance that the lawfulness of the suspension should be fully established. It was under these circumstances, which were such as to arrest the attention of the country, that this law was passed. The President was authorized by it to suspend the privilege of the writ of *habeas corpus,* whenever, in his judgment, the public safety required; and he did, by proclamation, bearing date the 15th of September, 1863, reciting, among other things, the authority of this statute, suspend it. The suspension of the writ does not authorize the arrest of any one, but simply denies to one arrested the privilege of this writ in order to obtain his liberty.

It is proper, therefore, to inquire under what circumstances the courts could rightfully refuse to grant this writ, and when the citizen was at liberty to invoke its aid.

The second and third sections of the law are explicit on these points. The language used is plain and direct, and the meaning of the Congress cannot be mistaken. The public safety demanded, if the President thought proper to arrest a suspected person, that he should not be required to give the cause of his detention on return to a writ of *habeas corpus.* But it was not contemplated that such person should be detained in custody beyond a certain fixed period, unless certain judicial proceedings, known to the common law, were commenced against him....

Milligan, in his application to be released from imprisonment, averred the existence of every fact necessary under the terms of this law to give the Circuit Court of Indiana jurisdiction. If he was detained in custody by the order of the President, otherwise than as a prisoner of war; if he was a citizen of Indiana and had never been in the military or naval service, and the grand jury of the district had met, after he had been arrested, for a period of twenty days, and adjourned without taking any proceedings against him, *then* the court had the right to entertain his petition and determine the lawfulness of his imprisonment....

The controlling question in the case is this: Upon the *facts* stated in Milligan's petition, and the exhibits filed, had the military commission mentioned in it *jurisdiction,* legally, to try and sentence him?...

No graver question was ever considered by this court, nor one which more nearly concerns the rights of the whole people; for it is the birthright of every American citizen when charged with crime, to be tried and punished according to law. The power of punishment is, alone through the means which the laws have provided for that purpose, and if they are ineffectual, there is an immunity from punishment, no matter how great an offender the individual may be, or how much his crimes may have shocked the sense of justice of the country, or endangered its safety. By the protection of the law human rights are secured; withdraw that protection, and they are at the mercy of wicked rulers, or the clamor of an excited people. If there was law to justify this military trial, it is not our province to interfere; if there was not, it is our duty to declare the nullity of the whole proceedings. The decision of this question does not depend on

B. Suspending the Writ

argument or judicial precedents, numerous and highly illustrative as they are. These precedents inform us of the extent of the struggle to preserve liberty and to relieve those in civil life from military trials. The founders of our government were familiar with the history of that struggle; and secured in a written constitution every right which the people had wrested from power during a contest of ages. By that Constitution and the laws authorized by it this question must be determined. The provisions of that instrument on the administration of criminal justice are too plain and direct, to leave room for misconstruction or doubt of their true meaning. Those applicable to this case are found in that clause of the original Constitution which says, "That the trial of all crimes, except in case of impeachment, shall be by jury;" and in the fourth, fifth, and sixth articles of the amendments. The fourth proclaims the right to be secure in person and effects against unreasonable search and seizure; and directs that a judicial warrant shall not issue "without proof of probable cause supported by oath or affirmation." The fifth declares "that no person shall be held to answer for a capital or otherwise infamous crime unless on presentment by a grand jury, except in cases arising in the land or naval forces, or in the militia, when in actual service in time of war or public danger, nor be deprived of life, liberty, or property, without due process of law." And the sixth guarantees the right of trial by jury, in such manner and with such regulations that with upright judges, impartial juries, and an able bar, the innocent will be saved and the guilty punished....

Time has proven the discernment of our ancestors; for even these provisions, expressed in such plain English words, that it would seem the ingenuity of man could not evade them, are *now*, after the lapse of more than seventy years, sought to be avoided. Those great and good men foresaw that troublous times would arise, when rulers and people would become restive under restraint, and seek by sharp and decisive measures to accomplish ends deemed just and proper; and that the principles of constitutional liberty would be in peril, unless established by irrepealable law. The history of the world had taught them that what was done in the past might be attempted in the future. The Constitution of the United States is a law for rulers and people, equally in war and in peace, and covers with the shield of its protection all classes of men, at all times, and under all circumstances. No doctrine, involving more pernicious consequences, was ever invented by the wit of man than that any of its provisions can be suspended during any of the great exigencies of government. Such a doctrine leads directly to anarchy and despotism, but the theory of necessity on which it is based is false; for the government, within the Constitution, has all the powers granted to it, which are necessary to preserve its existence; as has been happily proved by the result of the great effort to throw off its just authority.

Have any of the rights guaranteed by the Constitution been violated in the case of Milligan? and if so, what are they?

Every trial involves the exercise of judicial power; and from what source did the military commission that tried him derive their authority? Certainly no part of the judicial power of the country was conferred on them; because the Constitution expressly vests it "in one supreme court and such inferior courts as the Congress may from time to time ordain and establish," and it is not pretended that the commission was a court ordained and established by Congress. They cannot justify on the mandate of the President; because he is controlled by law, and has his appropriate sphere of duty, which is to execute, not to make, the laws; and there is "no unwritten criminal code to which resort can be had as a source of jurisdiction."

But it is said that the jurisdiction is complete under the "laws and usages of war."

It can serve no useful purpose to inquire what those laws and usages are, whence they originated, where found, and on whom they operate; they can never be applied to citizens in states which have upheld the authority of the government, and where the courts are open and their process unobstructed. This court has judicial knowledge that in Indiana the Federal authority was always unopposed, and its courts always open to hear criminal accusations and redress grievances; and no usage of war could sanction a military trial there for any offence whatever of a citizen in civil life, in nowise connected with the military service. Congress could grant no such power; and to the honor of our national legislature be it said, it has never been provoked by the state of the country even to attempt its exercise. One of the plainest constitutional provisions was, therefore, infringed when Milligan was tried by a court not ordained and established by Congress, and not composed of judges appointed during good behavior.

Why was he not delivered to the Circuit Court of Indiana to be proceeded against according to law? No reason of necessity could be urged against it; because Congress had declared penalties against the offences charged, provided for their punishment, and directed that court to hear and determine them. And soon after this military tribunal was ended, the Circuit Court met, peacefully transacted its business, and adjourned. It needed no bayonets to protect it, and required no military aid to execute its judgments. It was held in a state, eminently distinguished for patriotism, by judges commissioned during the Rebellion, who were provided with juries, upright, intelligent, and selected by a marshal appointed by the President. The government had no right to conclude that Milligan, if guilty, would not receive in that court merited punishment; for its records disclose that it was constantly engaged in the trial of similar offences, and was never interrupted in its administration of criminal justice. If it was dangerous, in the distracted condition of affairs, to leave Milligan unrestrained of his liberty because he "conspired against the government, afforded aid and comfort to rebels, and incited the people to insurrection," the *law* said arrest him, confine him closely, render him powerless to do further mischief; and then present his case to the grand jury of the district, with proofs of his guilt, and, if indicted, try him according to the course of the common law. If this had been done, the Constitution would have been vindicated, the law of 1863 enforced, and the securities for personal liberty preserved and defended....

... When peace prevails, and the authority of the government is undisputed, there is no difficulty of preserving the safeguards of liberty; for the ordinary modes of trial are never neglected, and no one wishes it otherwise; but if society is disturbed by civil commotion—if the passions of men are aroused and the restraints of law weakened, if not disregarded—these safeguards need, and should receive, the watchful care of those intrusted with the guardianship of the Constitution and laws. In no other way can we transmit to posterity unimpaired the blessings of liberty, consecrated by the sacrifices of the Revolution.

It is claimed that martial law covers with its broad mantle the proceedings of this military commission. The proposition is this: that in a time of war the

B. Suspending the Writ

commander of an armed force (if in his opinion the exigencies of the country demand it, and of which he is to judge), has the power, within the lines of the military district, to suspend all civil rights and their remedies, and subject citizens as well as soldiers to the *rule* of his will; and in the exercise of his lawful authority cannot be restrained, except by his superior officer or the President of the United States.

If this position is sound to the extent claimed, then when war exists, foreign or domestic, and the country is subdivided into military departments for mere convenience, the commander of one of them can, if he chooses, within his limits, on the plea of necessity, with the approval of the Executive, substitute military force for and to the exclusion of the laws, and punish all persons, as he thinks right and proper, without fixed or certain rules.

The statement of this proposition shows its importance; for, if true, republican government is a failure, and there is an end of liberty regulated by law. Martial law, established on such a basis, destroys every guarantee of the Constitution, and effectually renders the "military independent of and superior to the civil power"—the attempt to do which by the King of Great Britain was deemed by our fathers such an offence, that they assigned it to the world as one of the causes which impelled them to declare their independence. Civil liberty and this kind of martial law cannot endure together; the antagonism is irreconcilable; and, in the conflict, one or the other must perish.

This nation, as experience has proved, cannot always remain at peace, and has no right to expect that it will always have wise and humane rulers, sincerely attached to the principles of the Constitution. Wicked men, ambitious of power, with hatred of liberty and contempt of law, may fill the place once occupied by Washington and Lincoln; and if this right is conceded, and the calamities of war again befall us, the dangers to human liberty are frightful to contemplate. If our fathers had failed to provide for just such a contingency, they would have been false to the trust reposed in them. They knew—the history of the world told them—the nation they were founding, be its existence short or long, would be involved in war; how often or how long continued, human foresight could not tell; and that unlimited power, wherever lodged at such a time, was especially hazardous to freemen. For this, and other equally weighty reasons, they secured the inheritance they had fought to maintain, by incorporating in a written constitution the safeguards which *time* had proved were essential to its preservation. Not one of these safeguards can the President, or Congress, or the Judiciary disturb, except the one concerning the writ of *habeas corpus*.

It is essential to the safety of every government that, in a great crisis, like the one we have just passed through, there should be a power somewhere of suspending the writ of *habeas corpus*. In every war, there are men of previously good character, wicked enough to counsel their fellow-citizens to resist the measures deemed necessary by a good government to sustain its just authority and overthrow its enemies; and their influence may lead to dangerous combinations. In the emergency of the times, an immediate public investigation according to law may not be possible; and yet, the peril to the country may be too imminent to suffer such persons to go at large. Unquestionably, there is then an exigency which demands that the government, if it should see fit in the exercise of a proper discretion to make arrests, should not be required to produce the persons arrested in answer to a writ of *habeas corpus*. The Constitution goes no further. It does not say after a writ of *habeas corpus* is denied a citizen, that he shall be tried otherwise than by the course of the common law....

It will be borne in mind that this is not a question of the power to proclaim martial law, when war exists in a community and the courts and civil authorities are overthrown. Nor is it a question what rule a military commander, at the head of his army, can impose on states in rebellion to cripple their resources and quell the insurrection. The jurisdiction claimed is much more extensive. The necessities of the service, during the late Rebellion, required that the loyal states should be placed within the limits of certain military districts and commanders appointed in them; and, it is urged, that this, in a military sense, constituted them the theatre of military operations; and, as in this case, Indiana had been and was again threatened with invasion by the enemy, the occasion was furnished to establish martial law. The conclusion does not follow from the premises. If armies were collected in Indiana, they were to be employed in another locality, where the laws were obstructed and the national authority disputed. On *her* soil there was no hostile foot; if once invaded, that invasion was at an end, and with it all pretext for martial law. Martial law cannot arise from a *threatened* invasion. The necessity must be actual and present; the invasion real, such as effectually closes the courts and deposes the civil administration.

It is difficult to see how the *safety* for the country required martial law in Indiana. If any of her citizens were plotting treason, the power of arrest could secure them, until the government was prepared for their trial, when the courts were open and ready to try them. It was as easy to protect witnesses before a civil as a military tribunal; and as there could be no wish to convict, except on sufficient legal evidence, surely an ordained and established court was better able to judge of this than a military tribunal composed of gentlemen not trained to the profession of the law.

It follows, from what has been said on this subject, that there are occasions when martial rule can be properly applied. If, in foreign invasion or civil war, the courts are actually closed, and it is impossible to administer criminal justice according to law, *then*, on the theatre of active military operations, where war really prevails, there is a necessity to furnish a substitute for the civil authority, thus overthrown, to preserve the safety of the army and society; and as no power is left but the military, it is allowed to govern by martial rule until the laws can have their free course. As necessity creates the rule, so it limits its duration; for, if this government is continued *after* the courts are reinstated, it is a gross usurpation of power. Martial rule can never exist where the courts are open, and in the proper and unobstructed exercise of their jurisdiction. It is also confined to the locality of actual war. Because, during the late Rebellion it could have been enforced in Virginia, where the national authority was overturned and the courts driven out, it does not follow that it should obtain in Indiana, where that authority was never disputed, and justice was always administered. And so in the case of a foreign invasion, martial rule may become a necessity in one state, when, in another, it would be "mere lawless violence."...

If the military trial of Milligan was contrary to law, then he was entitled, on the facts stated in his petition, to be discharged from custody by the terms of the act of Congress of March 3d, 1863....

The CHIEF JUSTICE delivered the following opinion [in which WAYNE, SWAYNE, and MILLER, JJ., concurred].... [The Chief Justice agreed that the military

B. Suspending the Writ

commission was without lawful jurisdiction to try Milligan.] But the opinion which has just been read goes further; and as we understand it, asserts not only that the military commission held in Indiana was not authorized by Congress, but that it was not in the power of Congress to authorize it....

We think that Congress had power, though not exercised, to authorize the Military Commission which was held in Indiana....

...Congress cannot direct the conduct of campaigns, nor can the President, or any commander under him, without the sanction of Congress, institute tribunals for the trial and punishment of offences, either of soldiers or civilians, unless in cases of a controlling necessity, which justifies what it compels, or at least insures acts of indemnity from the justice of the legislature.

We by no means assert that Congress can establish and apply the laws of war where no war has been declared or exists.

Where peace exists the laws of peace must prevail. What we do maintain is, that when the nation is involved in war, and some portions of the country are invaded, and all are exposed to invasion, it is within the power of Congress to determine in what states or district such great and imminent public danger exists as justifies the authorization of military tribunals for the trial of crimes and offences against the discipline or security of the army or against the public safety....

NOTES AND QUESTIONS

1. *Presidential Authority to Suspend the Writ?* Although the privilege of the writ has been suspended on a number of other occasions, the question raised by *Merryman* has not yet reached the full Supreme Court. *But see* Ex parte Bollman, 8 U.S. (4 Cranch) 75, 1010 (1807) ("If at any time the public safety should require the suspension of the powers vested by this act in the courts of the United States, it is for the legislature to say so. That question depends on political considerations, on which the legislature is to decide."). Do you see any danger in allowing the President, acting alone, to suspend the writ, as Lincoln did? *See* Michael Stokes Paulsen, *The Merryman Power and the Dilemma of Autonomous Executive Branch Interpretation,* 15 Cardozo L. Rev. 81, 88-99 (1993); (Chief Justice) William H. Rehnquist, *All the Laws But One: Civil Liberties in Wartime* 11-45 (1998) (criticizing Chief Justice Taney); Harold C. Relyea, *National Emergency Powers: A Brief Overview of Presidential Suspensions of the Habeas Corpus Privilege and Invocations of Martial Law* (Cong. Res. Serv.), Sept. 20, 1976; John T. Sharer, *Power, Idealism, and Compromise: The Coordinate Branches and the Writ of Habeas Corpus,* 26 Emory L.J. 149 (1977); and Martin S. Sheffer, *Presidential Power to Suspend Habeas Corpus: The Taney-Bates Dialogue and Ex parte Merryman,* 11 Okla. City U. L. Rev. 1 (1986). What about a danger in not allowing the President, acting alone, to suspend? How, if at all, could the Suspension Clause be interpreted to balance the dangers?

2. *Congress's Authority to Restrict Suspension by the President?* Is there any limit on Congress's ability to regulate the President's authority to suspend the writ? Did the *Milligan* decision shed any light on this question?

3. *Construing to Avoid the Constitutional Question.* By the usual rules of statutory construction, courts should construe legislation or executive orders,

when "fairly possible," to avoid significant constitutional questions. *See Immigration and Naturalization Service v. St. Cyr*, 533 U.S. 289, 299-300 (2001). It may be especially desirable to avoid having to decide whether the executive alone may cut off access to the courts, because, "[a]t its historical core, the writ of habeas corpus has served as a means of reviewing the legality of executive detention, and it is in that context that its protections have been the strongest." *Id.* at 301. Thus, in *St. Cyr*, the Court construed a statute as allowing access to the courts, even though the statute was entitled "Elimination of Custody Review by Habeas Corpus." The Court insisted that any effort to restrict the privilege of seeking the writ must be clearly stated!

4. *Congressional Limits on Appeals.* Could Congress, exercising its authority under Article III, Section 2 of the Constitution, limit judicial scrutiny of a suspension of the writ either by Congress or by the President? After the *Milligan* decision, Congress expressly provided for appeals to the Supreme Court from lower federal court decisions in habeas corpus proceedings. Act of Feb. 5, 1867, 14 Stat. 385. When a Southern newspaper editor was arrested and held for trial by a military commission on charges of libel and inciting insurrection, he applied for a writ of habeas corpus first to a federal circuit court and then to the Supreme Court. During the pendency of his appeal, Congress repealed the appellate jurisdiction of the Supreme Court under the 1867 Act. 15 Stat. 44 (1868). This apparent end run around *Milligan* was upheld in Ex parte McCardle, 74 U.S. (7 Wall.) 506 (1868), although the Court noted an alternate route to Supreme Court review. The Court then granted a petition for a writ of certiorari in another case involving the trial of a civilian in a military court. Ex parte Yerger, 75 U.S. (8 Wall.) 85 (1868). It based its decision on the appellate jurisdiction conferred on the Supreme Court by the Judicial Act of 1789 and by the Constitution to hear petitions for writs of habeas corpus. *Id.* at 96-106. Uncertainty about the constitutional necessity for an avenue of appeal to the Supreme Court is explored in William W. Van Alstyne, *A Critical Guide to Ex Parte McCardle*, 15 Ariz. L. Rev. 229 (1973); and Leonard G. Ratner, *Congressional Power Over the Appellate Jurisdiction of the Supreme Court*, 109 U. Pa. L. Rev. 157 (1960).

5. *Habeas Corpus After September 11.* In the massive PENTTBOM investigation that followed the terrorist attacks on September 11, 2001, the Justice Department extended by regulation from 24 to 48 hours the time that an alien suspected of an immigration violation could be held without criminal charges, and it provided for indefinite detention of suspected terrorist aliens. See *supra* p. 676. Do you think any of the several hundred persons detained for questioning for an extended period was entitled to a writ of habeas corpus?

C. AVAILABILITY OF THE WRIT TO NONRESIDENT ALIENS

During World War II, the government had to decide what to do with eight German saboteurs who were caught in the United States. President Roosevelt

C. Availability of the Writ to Nonresident Aliens

opted to try them by military commission in Washington, D.C., because a commission could impose death sentences, unlike the civilian courts at the time. *See* David J. Danelski, *The Saboteurs' Case*, 1 J. of S. Ct. Hist. 61 (1996). But the President also told his Attorney General, "I won't hand them over to any United States marshal armed with a writ of habeas corpus. Understand?" *Id.* The presidential proclamation establishing the military commission dealt with this eventuality by providing that defendants "shall not be privileged to seek any remedy or maintain any proceeding directly or indirectly, or to have any such remedy or proceeding brought on their behalf, in the courts of the United States," except under such regulations as the Attorney General might issue. Proclamation No. 2561, 7 Fed. Reg. 5101 (July 2, 1942). This transparent attempt to suspend the writ ultimately fared poorly in court, however. The Supreme Court concluded that nothing in the proclamation "foreclose[d] consideration by the courts of petitioners' contentions that the Constitution and the laws of the United States constitutionally enacted forbid their trial by military commission." Ex parte Quirin, 317 U.S. 1, 25 (1942), *infra* p. 714.

In a later World War II case involving a military commission, the Court added that the Congress "has not withdrawn, and the Executive branch of the government could not, unless there was suspension of the writ, withdraw from the courts the duty and power to make such inquiry into the authority of the commission as may be made by habeas corpus." Application of Yamashita, 327 U.S. 1, 9 (1946). Indeed, Justice Murphy characterized the claim that courts could not make such inquiries as an "obnoxious doctrine," which he said the Court "rejected fully and unquestionably." *Id.* at 30. In both *Quirin* and *Yamashita,* however, the Justices unanimously agreed that habeas corpus was available only to test the legal authority for trial by military commission, and not to question the correctness of a commission's decisions.

Notwithstanding this history, when President George W. Bush issued a military order in November 2001 providing for the military detention and trial by military commission of noncitizens he designated as members of al Qaeda or as persons involved in acts of international terrorism, he included the following provision:

Military Order of November 13, 2001
Detention, Treatment, and Trial of Certain Non-Citizens in the War Against Terrorism
66 Fed. Reg. 57,833 (Nov. 13, 2001)[1]

SECTION 7. RELATIONSHIP TO OTHER LAW AND FORUMS....

(b) With respect to any individual subject to this order—
(1) military tribunals shall have exclusive jurisdiction with respect to offenses by the individual; and

---

[1. Other portions of the order are reproduced *infra* p. 878.]

(2) the individual shall not be privileged to seek any remedy or maintain any proceeding, directly or indirectly, or to have any such remedy or proceeding sought on the individual's behalf, in
  (i) any court of the United States, or any State thereof,
  (ii) any court of any foreign nation, or
  (iii) any international tribunal....

Rasul v. Bush
United States Supreme Court, 2004
542 U.S. 466

Justice STEVENS delivered the opinion of the Court. These two cases present the narrow but important question whether United States courts lack jurisdiction to consider challenges to the legality of the detention of foreign nationals captured abroad in connection with hostilities and incarcerated at the Guantanamo Bay Naval Base, Cuba.

I...

...Acting pursuant to [statutory] authorization [*supra* p. 100], the President sent U.S. Armed Forces into Afghanistan [in late 2001] to wage a military campaign against al Qaeda and the Taliban regime that had supported it.

Petitioners in these cases are 2 Australian citizens and 12 Kuwaiti citizens who were captured abroad during hostilities between the United States and the Taliban. Since early 2002, the U.S. military has held them—along with, according to the Government's estimate, approximately 640 other non-Americans captured abroad—at the Naval Base at Guantanamo Bay. The United States occupies the Base, which comprises 45 square miles of land and water along the southeast coast of Cuba, pursuant to a 1903 Lease Agreement executed with the newly independent Republic of Cuba in the aftermath of the Spanish-American War. Under the Agreement, "the United States recognizes the continuance of the ultimate sovereignty of the Republic of Cuba over the [leased areas]," while "the Republic of Cuba consents that during the period of the occupation by the United States...the United States shall exercise complete jurisdiction and control over and within said areas."[2] In 1934, the parties entered into a treaty providing that, absent an agreement to modify or abrogate the lease, the lease would remain in effect "[s]o long as the United States of America shall not abandon the...naval station of Guantanamo."[3]...

[Petitioners filed various actions in the U.S. District Court for the District of Columbia challenging the legality of their detention and/or seeking to be informed of the charges against them, to be allowed to meet with their families

---

2. Lease of Lands for Coaling and Naval Stations, Feb. 23, 1903, U.S.-Cuba, Art. III, T.S. No. 418 (hereinafter 1903 Lease Agreement)....
3. Treaty Defining Relations with Cuba, May 29, 1934, U. S.-Cuba, Art. III, 48 Stat. 1683, T.S. No. 866 (hereinafter 1934 Treaty).

C. Availability of the Writ to Nonresident Aliens

and with counsel, and to have access to the courts or some other impartial tribunal, and claiming that denial of these rights violated the Constitution, international law, and treaties of the United States.]

Construing all three actions as petitions for writs of habeas corpus, the District Court dismissed them for want of jurisdiction. The court held, in reliance on our opinion in *Johnson v. Eisentrager*, 339 U.S. 763 (1950), that "aliens detained outside the sovereign territory of the United States [may not] invok[e] a petition for a writ of habeas corpus." 215 F. Supp. 2d 55, 68 (D.D.C. 2002). The Court of Appeals affirmed....

II

Congress has granted federal district courts, "within their respective jurisdictions," the authority to hear applications for habeas corpus by any person who claims to be held "in custody in violation of the Constitution or laws or treaties of the United States." 28 U.S.C. §§2241(a), (c)(3)....

Habeas corpus is, however, "a writ antecedent to statute,...throwing its root deep into the genius of our common law." *Williams v. Kaiser*, 323 U.S. 471, 484 n.2 (1945) (internal quotation marks omitted). The writ appeared in English law several centuries ago, became "an integral part of our common-law heritage" by the time the Colonies achieved independence, *Preiser v. Rodriguez*, 411 U.S. 475, 485 (1973), and received explicit recognition in the Constitution, which forbids suspension of "[t]he Privilege of the Writ of Habeas Corpus...unless when in Cases of Rebellion or Invasion the public Safety may require it," Art. I, §9, cl. 2.

As it has evolved over the past two centuries, the habeas statute clearly has expanded habeas corpus "beyond the limits that obtained during the 17th and 18th centuries." *Swain v. Pressley*, 430 U.S. 372, 380 n.13 (1977). But "[a]t its historical core, the writ of habeas corpus has served as a means of reviewing the legality of Executive detention, and it is in that context that its protections have been strongest." *INS v. St. Cyr*, 533 U.S. 289, 301 (2001). As Justice Jackson wrote in an opinion respecting the availability of habeas corpus to aliens held in U.S. custody:

> "Executive imprisonment has been considered oppressive and lawless since John, at Runnymede, pledged that no free man should be imprisoned, dispossessed, outlawed, or exiled save by the judgment of his peers or by the law of the land. The judges of England developed the writ of habeas corpus largely to preserve these immunities from executive restraint." *Shaughnessy v. United States ex rel. Mezei*, 345 U.S. 206, 218-219 (1953) (dissenting opinion).

Consistent with the historic purpose of the writ, this Court has recognized the federal courts' power to review applications for habeas relief in a wide variety of cases involving Executive detention, in wartime as well as in times of peace. The Court has, for example, entertained the habeas petitions of an American citizen who plotted an attack on military installations during the Civil War, *Ex parte Milligan*, 4 Wall. 2 (1866), and of admitted enemy aliens convicted of war crimes during a declared war and held in the United States,

Ex parte Quirin, 317 U.S. 1 (1942), and its insular possessions, *In re Yamashita,* 327 U.S. 1 (1946).

The question now before us is whether the habeas statute confers a right to judicial review of the legality of Executive detention of aliens in a territory over which the United States exercises plenary and exclusive jurisdiction, but not "ultimate sovereignty."

III

Respondents' primary submission is that the answer to the jurisdictional question is controlled by our decision in *Eisentrager*. In that case, we held that a Federal District Court lacked authority to issue a writ of habeas corpus to 21 German citizens who had been captured by U.S. forces in China, tried and convicted of war crimes by an American military commission headquartered in Nanking, and incarcerated in the Landsberg Prison in occupied Germany.... [T]his Court summarized the six critical facts in the case:

> "We are here confronted with a decision whose basic premise is that these prisoners are entitled, as a constitutional right, to sue in some court of the United States for a writ of *habeas corpus*. To support that assumption we must hold that a prisoner of our military authorities is constitutionally entitled to the writ, even though he (a) is an enemy alien; (b) has never been or resided in the United States; (c) was captured outside of our territory and there held in military custody as a prisoner of war; (d) was tried and convicted by a Military Commission sitting outside the United States; (e) for offenses against laws of war committed outside the United States; (f) and is at all times imprisoned outside the United States." 39 U.S. at 777.

On this set of facts, the Court concluded, "no right to the writ of *habeas corpus* appears." *Id.* at 781.

Petitioners in these cases differ from the *Eisentrager* detainees in important respects: They are not nationals of countries at war with the United States, and they deny that they have engaged in or plotted acts of aggression against the United States; they have never been afforded access to any tribunal, much less charged with and convicted of wrongdoing; and for more than two years they have been imprisoned in territory over which the United States exercises exclusive jurisdiction and control.

Not only are petitioners differently situated from the *Eisentrager* detainees, but the Court in *Eisentrager* made quite clear that all six of the facts critical to its disposition were relevant only to the question of the prisoners' *constitutional* entitlement to habeas corpus. *Id.* at 777. The Court had far less to say on the question of the petitioners' *statutory* entitlement to habeas review. Its only statement on the subject was a passing reference to the absence of statutory authorization: "Nothing in the text of the Constitution extends such a right, nor does anything in our statutes." *Id.* at 768....

[Here the Court notes that the *Eisentrager* Court relied on an earlier decision, Ahrens v. Clark, 335 U.S. 188 (1948), holding that the habeas statute did not permit a district court to issue the writ for a detainee outside the court's territorial jurisdiction.]

C. Availability of the Writ to Nonresident Aliens

... [However,] persons detained outside the territorial jurisdiction of any federal district court no longer need rely on the Constitution as the source of their right to federal habeas review. In *Braden v. 30th Judicial Circuit Court of Ky.*, 410 U.S. 484, 495 (1973), this Court held, contrary to *Ahrens,* that the prisoner's presence within the territorial jurisdiction of the district court is not "an invariable prerequisite" to the exercise of district court jurisdiction under the federal habeas statute. Rather, because "the writ of habeas corpus does not act upon the prisoner who seeks relief, but upon the person who holds him in what is alleged to be unlawful custody," a district court acts "within [its] respective jurisdiction" within the meaning of §2241 as long as "the custodian can be reached by service of process." 410 U.S. at 494-495.... *Braden* thus established that *Ahrens* can no longer be viewed as establishing "an inflexible jurisdictional rule," and is strictly relevant only to the question of the appropriate forum, not to whether the claim can be heard at all. 410 U.S. at 499-500.

Because *Braden* overruled the statutory predicate to *Eisentrager*'s holding, *Eisentrager* plainly does not preclude the exercise of §2241 jurisdiction over petitioners' claims.

IV

Putting *Eisentrager* and *Ahrens* to one side, respondents contend that we can discern a limit on §2241 through application of the "longstanding principle of American law" that congressional legislation is presumed not to have extraterritorial application unless such intent is clearly manifested. *EEOC v. Arabian American Oil Co.*, 499 U.S. 244, 248 (1991). Whatever traction the presumption against extraterritoriality might have in other contexts, it certainly has no application to the operation of the habeas statute with respect to persons detained within "the territorial jurisdiction" of the United States. *Foley Bros., Inc. v. Filardo,* 336 U.S. 281, 285 (1949). By the express terms of its agreements with Cuba, the United States exercises "complete jurisdiction and control" over the Guantanamo Bay Naval Base, and may continue to exercise such control permanently if it so chooses. 1903 Lease Agreement, Art. III; 1934 Treaty, Art. III. Respondents themselves concede that the habeas statute would create federal-court jurisdiction over the claims of an American citizen held at the base. Considering that the statute draws no distinction between Americans and aliens held in federal custody, there is little reason to think that Congress intended the geographical coverage of the statute to vary depending on the detainee's citizenship. Aliens held at the base, no less than American citizens, are entitled to invoke the federal courts' authority under §2241.

Application of the habeas statute to persons detained at the base is consistent with the historical reach of the writ of habeas corpus. At common law, courts exercised habeas jurisdiction over the claims of aliens detained within sovereign territory of the realm, as well as the claims of persons detained in the so-called "exempt jurisdictions," where ordinary writs did not run, and all other dominions under the sovereign's control. ...

In the end, the answer to the question presented is clear. Petitioners contend that they are being held in federal custody in violation of the laws of the United States.[15] No party questions the District Court's jurisdiction over petitioners' custodians. Cf. *Braden,* 410 U.S. at 495. Section 2241, by its terms, requires nothing more. We therefore hold that §2241 confers on the District Court jurisdiction to hear petitioners' habeas corpus challenges to the legality of their detention at the Guantanamo Bay Naval Base.

V

In addition to invoking the District Court's jurisdiction under §2241, the *Al Odah* petitioners' complaint invoked the court's jurisdiction under 28 U.S.C. §1331, the federal question statute, as well as §1350, the Alien Tort Statute. The Court of Appeals, again relying on *Eisentrager,* held that the District Court correctly dismissed the claims founded on §1331 and §1350 for lack of jurisdiction, even to the extent that these claims "deal only with conditions of confinement and do not sound in habeas," because petitioners lack the "privilege of litigation" in U.S. courts. 321 F.3d at 1144 (internal quotation marks omitted)....

... But ... nothing in *Eisentrager* or in any of our other cases categorically excludes aliens detained in military custody outside the United States from the "'privilege of litigation'" in U.S. courts. 321 F.3d at 1139. The courts of the United States have traditionally been open to nonresident aliens. And indeed, 28 U.S.C. §1350 explicitly confers the privilege of suing for an actionable "tort ... committed in violation of the law of nations or a treaty of the United States" on aliens alone. The fact that petitioners in these cases are being held in military custody is immaterial to the question of the District Court's jurisdiction over their nonhabeas statutory claims.

VI

Whether and what further proceedings may become necessary after respondents make their response to the merits of petitioners' claims are matters that we need not address now. What is presently at stake is only whether the federal courts have jurisdiction to determine the legality of the Executive's potentially indefinite detention of individuals who claim to be wholly innocent of wrongdoing. Answering that question in the affirmative, we reverse the judgment of the Court of Appeals and remand for the District Court to consider in the first instance the merits of petitioners' claims.

It is so ordered.

Justice KENNEDY, concurring in the judgment. The Court is correct, in my view, to conclude that federal courts have jurisdiction to consider challenges to the legality of the detention of foreign nationals held at the Guantanamo Bay Naval Base in Cuba. While I reach the same conclusion, my analysis follows a

---

15. Petitioners' allegations — that, although they have engaged neither in combat nor in acts of terrorism against the United States, they have been held in Executive detention for more than two years in territory subject to the long-term, exclusive jurisdiction and control of the United States, without access to counsel and without being charged with any wrongdoing — unquestionably describe "custody in violation of the Constitution or laws or treaties of the United States." 28 U.S.C. §2241(c)(3).

different course.... In my view, the correct course is to follow the framework of *Eisentrager*....

The decision in *Eisentrager* indicates that there is a realm of political authority over military affairs where the judicial power may not enter. The existence of this realm acknowledges the power of the President as Commander in Chief, and the joint role of the President and the Congress, in the conduct of military affairs. A faithful application of *Eisentrager*, then, requires an initial inquiry into the general circumstances of the detention to determine whether the Court has the authority to entertain the petition and to grant relief after considering all of the facts presented. A necessary corollary of *Eisentrager* is that there are circumstances in which the courts maintain the power and the responsibility to protect persons from unlawful detention even where military affairs are implicated. See also *Ex parte Milligan*, 4 Wall. 2 (1866).

The facts here are distinguishable from those in *Eisentrager* in two critical ways, leading to the conclusion that a federal court may entertain the petitions. First, Guantanamo Bay is in every practical respect a United States territory, and it is one far removed from any hostilities....

The second critical set of facts is that the detainees at Guantanamo Bay are being held indefinitely, and without benefit of any legal proceeding to determine their status. In *Eisentrager*, the prisoners were tried and convicted by a military commission of violating the laws of war and were sentenced to prison terms. Having already been subject to procedures establishing their status, they could not justify "a limited opening of our courts" to show that they were "of friendly personal disposition" and not enemy aliens. 339 U.S., at 778. Indefinite detention without trial or other proceeding presents altogether different considerations. It allows friends and foes alike to remain in detention. It suggests a weaker case of military necessity and much greater alignment with the traditional function of habeas corpus. Perhaps, where detainees are taken from a zone of hostilities, detention without proceedings or trial would be justified by military necessity for a matter of weeks; but as the period of detention stretches from months to years, the case for continued detention to meet military exigencies becomes weaker.

In light of the status of Guantanamo Bay and the indefinite pretrial detention of the detainees, I would hold that federal-court jurisdiction is permitted in these cases. This approach would avoid creating automatic statutory authority to adjudicate the claims of persons located outside the United States, and remains true to the reasoning of *Eisentrager*. For these reasons, I concur in the judgment of the Court.

Justice SCALIA, with whom the CHIEF JUSTICE and Justice THOMAS join, dissenting.... Today, the Court springs a trap on the Executive, subjecting Guantanamo Bay to the oversight of the federal courts even though it has never before been thought to be within their jurisdiction — and thus making it a foolish place to have housed alien wartime detainees.

II

In abandoning the venerable statutory line drawn in *Eisentrager*, the Court boldly extends the scope of the habeas statute to the four corners of the earth.

Part III of its opinion asserts that *Braden* stands for the proposition that "a district court acts 'within [its] respective jurisdiction' within the meaning of §2241 as long as 'the custodian can be reached by service of process.' " Endorsement of that proposition is repeated in Part IV. ("Section 2241, by its terms, requires nothing more [than the District Court's jurisdiction over petitioners' custodians]").

The consequence of this holding, as applied to aliens outside the country, is breathtaking. It permits an alien captured in a foreign theater of active combat to bring a §2241 petition against the Secretary of Defense. Over the course of the last century, the United States has held millions of alien prisoners abroad. A great many of these prisoners would no doubt have complained about the circumstances of their capture and the terms of their confinement. The military is currently detaining over 600 prisoners at Guantanamo Bay alone; each detainee undoubtedly has complaints — real or contrived — about those terms and circumstances. The Court's unheralded expansion of federal-court jurisdiction is not even mitigated by a comforting assurance that the legion of ensuing claims will be easily resolved on the merits. To the contrary, the Court says that the "[p]etitioners' allegations... unquestionably describe 'custody in violation of the Constitution or laws or treaties of the United States.' " Ante, n.15. From this point forward, federal courts will entertain petitions from these prisoners, and others like them around the world, challenging actions and events far away, and forcing the courts to oversee one aspect of the Executive's conduct of a foreign war.

Today's carefree Court disregards, without a word of acknowledgment, the dire warning of a more circumspect Court in *Eisentrager:*

> "To grant the writ to these prisoners might mean that our army must transport them across the seas for hearing. This would require allocation for shipping space, guarding personnel, billeting and rations. It might also require transportation for whatever witnesses the prisoners desired to call as well as transportation for those necessary to defend legality of the sentence. The writ, since it is held to be a matter of right, would be equally available to enemies during active hostilities as in the present twilight between war and peace. Such trials would hamper the war effort and bring aid and comfort to the enemy. They would diminish the prestige of our commanders, not only with enemies but with wavering neutrals. It would be difficult to devise more effective fettering of a field commander than to allow the very enemies he is ordered to reduce to submission to call him to account in his own civil courts and divert his efforts and attention from the military offensive abroad to the legal defensive at home. Nor is it unlikely that the result of such enemy litigiousness would be conflict between judicial and military opinion highly comforting to enemies of the United States." 339 U.S., at 778-779.

These results should not be brought about lightly, and certainly not without a textual basis in the statute and on the strength of nothing more than a decision dealing with an Alabama prisoner's ability to seek habeas in Kentucky.

III

Part IV of the Court's opinion, dealing with the status of Guantanamo Bay, is a puzzlement....

C. Availability of the Writ to Nonresident Aliens

The Court gives only two reasons why the presumption against extraterritorial effect does not apply to Guantanamo Bay. First, the Court says (without any further elaboration) that "the United States exercises 'complete jurisdiction and control' over the Guantanamo Bay Naval Base [under the terms of a 1903 lease agreement], and may continue to exercise such control permanently if it so chooses [under the terms of a 1934 Treaty]." But that lease agreement explicitly recognized "the continuance of the ultimate sovereignty of the Republic of Cuba over the [leased areas]," Lease of Lands for Coaling and Naval Stations, Feb. 23, 1903, U.S.-Cuba, Art. III, T.S. No. 418, and the Executive Branch — whose head is "exclusively responsible" for the "conduct of diplomatic and foreign affairs," *Eisentrager, supra,* at 789 — affirms that the lease and treaty do not render Guantanamo Bay the sovereign territory of the United States.

The Court does not explain how "complete jurisdiction and control" without sovereignty causes an enclave to be part of the United States for purposes of its domestic laws. Since "jurisdiction and control" obtained through a lease is no different in effect from "jurisdiction and control" acquired by lawful force of arms, parts of Afghanistan and Iraq should logically be regarded as subject to our domestic laws. Indeed, if "jurisdiction and control" rather than sovereignty were the test, so should the Landsberg Prison in Germany, where the United States held the *Eisentrager* detainees.

The second and last reason the Court gives for the proposition that domestic law applies to Guantanamo Bay is the Solicitor General's concession that there would be habeas jurisdiction over a United States citizen in Guantanamo Bay. "Considering that the statute draws no distinction between Americans and aliens held in federal custody, there is little reason to think that Congress intended the geographical coverage of the statute to vary depending on the detainee's citizenship." But the reason the Solicitor General conceded there would be jurisdiction over a detainee who was a United States citizen had *nothing to do* with the special status of Guantanamo Bay: "Our answer to that question, Justice Souter, is that citizens of the United States, because of their constitutional circumstances, may have greater rights with respect to the scope and reach of the Habeas Statute as the Court has or would interpret it." And *that* position — the position that United States citizens throughout the world may be entitled to habeas corpus rights — is precisely the position that this Court adopted in *Eisentrager,* see 339 U.S., at 769-770, even while holding that aliens abroad *did not have* habeas corpus rights. Quite obviously, the Court's second reason has no force whatever....

In sum, the Court's treatment of Guantanamo Bay, like its treatment of §2241, is a wrenching departure from precedent....

Departure from our rule of *stare decisis* in statutory cases is always extraordinary; it ought to be unthinkable when the departure has a potentially harmful effect upon the Nation's conduct of a war. The Commander in Chief and his subordinates had every reason to expect that the internment of combatants at Guantanamo Bay would not have the consequence of bringing the cumbersome machinery of our domestic courts into military affairs. Congress is in session. If it wished to change federal judges' habeas jurisdiction from what this Court had previously held that to be, it could have done so. And it could have done so by intelligent revision of the statute, instead of by today's clumsy, countertextual reinterpretation that confers upon wartime prisoners greater habeas rights than domestic detainees. The latter must challenge their present physical confinement in the district of their confinement, see *Rumsfeld v. Padilla*, [542 U.S. 426 (2004)], whereas under today's strange holding Guantanamo Bay detainees can petition in any of the 94 federal judicial districts. The fact that extraterritorially located detainees lack the district of detention that the statute requires has been converted from a factor that precludes their ability to bring a petition at all into a factor that frees them to petition wherever they wish — and, as a result, to forum shop. For this Court to create such a monstrous scheme in time of war, and in frustration of our military commanders' reliance upon clearly stated prior law, is judicial adventurism of the worst sort. I dissent.

NOTES AND QUESTIONS

1. *Jurisdiction over the Custodian.* In Rumsfeld v. Padilla, 542 U.S. 426 (2004), noted *infra* p. 743, decided the same day as *Rasul,* the Supreme Court ruled that its earlier decision in *Ahrens* prevented a federal district court in New York from exercising jurisdiction over the habeas petition of a detainee in South Carolina, because the immediate custodian of the petitioner was the warden of the Navy brig in Charleston. Can the holdings on this point in *Padilla* and *Rasul* possibly be reconciled?

2. *The Military Order's "Suspension" of the Writ.* Assuming that some of the petitioners in *Rasul* were detained pursuant to Military Order No. 1, why didn't §7 of the order cut off their access to the courts? First, consider whether, in light of §7's pedigree, it was intended to suspend the writ. Next, consider whether, in light of the "clear statement" rule declared in *St. Cyr, supra* p. 690, any such intent was stated with the required clarity.

3. *Eisentrager's "Dire Warning."* Justice Scalia quotes the "dire warning" in Johnson v. Eisentrager, 339 U.S. 763 (1950), to suggest that the Court's ruling in *Rasul* will open the floodgates to habeas petitions by enemy aliens after we capture large numbers in battle. Indeed, alien detainees at Guantánamo quickly pressed habeas petitions in U.S. courts. *See* In re Guantanamo Detainee Cases, 355 F. Supp. 2d 443 (D.D.C. 2005) (reporting that 13 cases involving more than 60 detainees had been filed as of July 2004).

Does the Court have any answer to this concern? *Milligan* and the statute it applied in 1866 supply one answer. What is it? See Detainee Treatment Act of 2005, *infra* Note 6. Another is suggested by the first sentence of part VI of the opinion for the Court. What is it? How might the "further proceedings" in the habeas court, or prior proceedings by the military itself, affect the floodgates claim?

In an apparent effort to control the floodgates, the Pentagon announced shortly after the Supreme Court's decision in *Rasul* that it was creating a Combatant Status Review Tribunal (CSRT), to be staffed by military officers, before which detainees could contest their combatant status. Memorandum from the Deputy Secretary of Defense to the Secretary of the Navy, *Order Establishing Combatant Status Review Tribunal,* July 7, 2004, *available at* http://www.defenselink.mil/news/Jul2004/d20040707review.pdf. Detainees would have the assistance of a "personal representative" assigned by the government, but

C. Availability of the Writ to Nonresident Aliens

not a lawyer, and they would have to overcome a "rebuttable presumption in favor of the government's evidence." *Id.* ¶¶c. and g.(12). Do you think this program will satisfy Justice Stevens's concerns? Justice Scalia's?

Another way to close the floodgates would be to hear an alien detainee's habeas petition, but then simply deny it on the grounds that the detainees have no cognizable constitutional or international rights. Would such an approach be consistent with *Rasul*? *See* footnote 15 therein.

4. *The Inner Realm of Military Affairs: What's Left of Eisentrager?* Justice Kennedy joined in the judgment by preserving part of *Eisentrager*. He found that it approved of "a realm of political authority over military affairs where the judicial power may not enter," but also that the Guantánamo Bay detentions, far removed from hostilities and attended by no status-determining procedures, even by the military, fell outside that realm. How does he define that realm? What detainees from the U.S. military operations in Afghanistan would fall within it? More generally, reading the opinion for the Court and Justice Kennedy's opinion together, what is left of *Eisentrager*?

5. *Contextual Influences.* Even if you are unconvinced or unmoved by Justice Scalia's floodgates concern, would you agree that the Court eviscerated *Eisentrager*? Did it not also ignore the executive's reliance interest and thus upset calculated military and intelligence policy? (The prisoners at Guantánamo Bay are being detained partly for interrogation.) Speculation about the Court's motives is always treacherous. Yet between the oral arguments in *Rasul*, in which the government assured the Court that the detainees were being treated in compliance with basic international human rights principles, and the Court's decision, the press broke the scandal about abuse of prisoners in Iraq and possible use of torture by the United States in the interrogation of detainees. See *infra* pp. 759-764. Might the reports of mistreatment and of possible violations of international laws against torture have influenced the Court's decision on opening access to Article III courts?

6. *Detainee Treatment Act of 2005.* Congress responded quickly to *Rasul* by adding the following provision to the relevant habeas statute:

> (e) Except as provided in section 1005 of the Detainee Treatment Act of 2005, no court, justice, or judge shall have jurisdiction to hear or consider—
> (1) an application for a writ of habeas corpus filed by or on behalf of an alien detained by the Department of Defense at Guantanamo Bay, Cuba; or
> (2) any other action against the United States or its agents relating to any aspect of the detention by the Department of Defense of an alien at Guantanamo Bay, Cuba, who—
> (A) is currently in military custody; or
> (B) has been determined by the United States Court of Appeals for the District of Columbia Circuit in accordance with the procedures set forth in section 1005(e) of the Detainee Treatment Act of 2005 to have been properly detained as an enemy combatant.
>
> [Detainee Treatment Act of 2005, National Defense Authorization Act for Fiscal Year 2006, Pub. L. No. 109-163, §1405(e)(1), 119 Stat. 3136, 3477 (2006) (DTA).]

Section 1005(e) of the Act provided limited judicial review in the D.C. Circuit of the procedural validity of final decisions of CSRTs and of Military Commissions sitting pursuant to Military Order No. 1, but not review of the merits of such decisions. *Id.* §1005(e).

7. *Hamdan and the Military Commissions Act of 2006.* Notwithstanding the apparent intent of the DTA, in Hamdan v. Rumsfeld, 126 S. Ct. 2749 (2006), a divided Supreme Court held that the federal courts still had jurisdiction to hear a Guantánamo detainee's petition for the writ in a challenge to his prospective trial as an enemy combatant by military commission. See generally *infra* Chapter 30. The majority reasoned that Congress had not clearly expressed an intent to withdraw habeas jurisdiction from pending cases like Hamdan's. *Id.* at 2762-2769. After extended negotiations with the Administration in which, according to most observers, the Administration prevailed, Congress responded to *Hamdan* by replacing DTA §1005(e)(1) with the following provision:

> (e)(1) No court, justice, or judge shall have jurisdiction to hear or consider an application for a writ of habeas corpus filed by or on behalf of an alien detained by the United States who has been determined by the United States to have been properly detained as an enemy combatant or is awaiting such determination.
> (2) Except as provided in paragraphs (2) and (3) of section 1005(e) of the Detainee Treatment Act of 2005 [providing for the limited review of final decisions of CSRTs and Military Commissions noted above], no court, justice, or judge shall have jurisdiction to hear or consider any other action against the United States or its agents relating to any aspect of the detention, transfer, treatment, trial, or conditions of confinement of an alien who is or was detained by the United States and has been determined by the United States to have been properly detained as an enemy combatant or is awaiting such determination. [Military Commissions Act of 2006, Pub. L. No. 109-366, §7(a), 120 Stat. 2600, 2636.]

The provision was made effective on the date of the Act's enactment and made applicable, "without exception," to all pending cases relating to "detention, transfer, treatment, trial, or conditions of detention of an alien detained by the United States since September 11, 2001." *Id.* §7(b), 120 Stat. 2636. Has Congress suspended habeas? If so, for what cases? As you read the following chapters on military detention and investigational torture, consider the application of this provision to cases brought by any aliens who have been detained by the military, or tortured or mistreated while in U.S. military or CIA detention, or informally "rendered" by the United States to foreign states that have detained or tortured them. If this provision had been enacted on September 12, 2001, what do you think would be the present state of the case law regarding detention or investigational torture?

8. *After Rasul and the DTA.* Suppose that the United States takes a Syrian-born Canadian off a plane in New York on suspicion that he is a terrorist and asks the Syrian authorities to hold him for us indefinitely. The FBI then transports him to Syria. Assuming that his family would have "next friend" standing to file a habeas corpus petition on his behalf, would a federal court have jurisdiction? To answer this question, you have to consider, *inter alia,* who has custody of him, where the custodian is, whether *Rasul* or *Eisentrager* applies, and whether the MCA has any application. See *infra* p. 804.

Military Detention

During war, national security may require the detention of both noncombatants and combatants for the duration of hostilities, and the military may participate in the detention. Here we consider the law governing such detentions and postpone the overlapping topic of military trials until Chapter 30. Part A of this chapter treats the wartime detention of noncombatants. Part B sets out two seminal pre-9/11 cases regarding military authority over putative enemy combatants. Although these cases deal primarily with military trials rather than detention, their reasoning has influenced the law of military detention and military trials alike because detention is a predicate for trial. Part C considers military detention of citizen enemy combatants after 9/11. Finally, Part D discusses military detention of alien enemy combatants after 9/11 and briefly addresses in the process some applicable international laws of war.

A. WARTIME DETENTION OF NONCOMBATANTS BEFORE 9/11

Alien Enemy Act
50 U.S.C. §21 (2000)

Whenever there is a declared war between the United States and any foreign nation or government, or any invasion or predatory incursion is perpetrated, attempted, or threatened against the territory of the United States by any foreign nation or government, and the President makes public proclamation of the event, all natives, citizens, denizens, or subjects of the hostile nation or government, being of the age of fourteen years and upward, who shall be within the United States and not actually naturalized, shall be liable to be apprehended, restrained, secured, and removed as alien enemies. The President is authorized in any such event, by his proclamation thereof, or other public act, to direct the conduct to be observed, on the part of the United States, toward the aliens who become so liable; the manner and degree of the restraint to which they shall be subject and in what cases, and upon what security their residence shall be permitted, and to provide for the removal of those who, not being permitted to reside within the United States, refuse or neglect to depart therefrom; and to establish any other regulations which are found necessary in the premises and for the public safety.

Korematsu v. United States
United States Supreme Court, 1944
323 U.S. 214

Mr. Justice BLACK delivered the opinion of the Court. The petitioner, an American citizen of Japanese descent, was convicted in a federal district court for remaining in San Leandro, California, a "Military Area," contrary to Civilian Exclusion Order No. 34 of the Commanding General of the Western Command, U.S. Army, which directed that after May 9, 1942, all persons of Japanese ancestry should be excluded from that area. No question was raised as to petitioner's loyalty to the United States. The Circuit Court of Appeals affirmed, and the importance of the constitutional question involved caused us to grant certiorari.

It should be noted, to begin with, that all legal restrictions which curtail the civil rights of a single racial group are immediately suspect. That is not to say that all such restrictions are unconstitutional. It is to say that courts must subject them to the most rigid scrutiny. Pressing public necessity may sometimes justify the existence of such restrictions; racial antagonism never can.

In the instant case prosecution of the petitioner was begun by information charging violation of an Act of Congress, of March 21, 1942, 56 Stat. 173, which provides that

> ...whoever shall enter, remain in, leave, or commit any act in any military area or military zone prescribed, under the authority of an Executive order of the President, by the Secretary of War, or by any military commander designated by the Secretary of War, contrary to the restrictions applicable to any such area or zone or contrary to the order of the Secretary of War or any such military commander, shall, if it appears that he knew or should have known of the existence and extent of the restrictions or order and that his act was in violation thereof, be guilty of a misdemeanor and upon conviction shall be liable to a fine of not to exceed $5,000 or to imprisonment for not more than one year, or both, for each offense.

Exclusion Order No. 34, which the petitioner knowingly and admittedly violated, was one of a number of military orders and proclamations, all of which were substantially based upon Executive Order No. 9066, 7 Fed. Reg. 1407. That order, issued after we were at war with Japan, declared that "the successful prosecution of the war requires every possible protection against espionage and against sabotage to national-defense material, national-defense premises, and national-defense utilities...."

One of the series of orders and proclamations, a curfew order, which like the exclusion order here was promulgated pursuant to Executive Order 9066, subjected all persons of Japanese ancestry in prescribed West Coast military

A. Wartime Detention of Noncombatants Before 9/11

areas to remain in their residences from 8 P.M. to 6 A.M. As is the case with the exclusion order here, that prior curfew order was designed as a "protection against espionage and against sabotage." In Hirabayashi v. United States, 320 U.S. 81, we sustained a conviction obtained for violation of the curfew order. The Hirabayashi conviction and this one thus rest on the same 1942 Congressional Act and the same basic executive and military orders, all of which orders were aimed at the twin dangers of espionage and sabotage.

The 1942 Act was attacked in the *Hirabayashi* case as an unconstitutional delegation of power; it was contended that the curfew order and other orders on which it rested were beyond the war powers of the Congress, the military authorities and of the President, as Commander in Chief of the Army; and finally that to apply the curfew order against none but citizens of Japanese ancestry amounted to a constitutionally prohibited discrimination solely on account of race. To these questions, we gave the consideration which their importance justified. We upheld the curfew order as an exercise of the power of the government to take steps necessary to prevent espionage and sabotage in an area threatened by Japanese attack.

In the light of the principles we announced in the *Hirabayashi* case, we are unable to conclude that it was beyond the war power of Congress and the Executive to exclude those of Japanese ancestry from the West Coast war area at the time they did. True, exclusion from the area in which one's home is located is a far greater deprivation than constant confinement to the home from 8 P.M. to 6 A.M. Nothing short of apprehension by the proper military authorities of the gravest imminent danger to the public safety can constitutionally justify either. But exclusion from a threatened area, no less than curfew, has a definite and close relationship to the prevention of espionage and sabotage....

Here, as in the *Hirabayashi* case, *supra*, at p. 99, "...we cannot reject as unfounded the judgment of the military authorities and of Congress that there were disloyal members of that population, whose number and strength could not be precisely and quickly ascertained. We cannot say that the war-making branches of the Government did not have ground for believing that in a critical hour such persons could not readily be isolated and separately dealt with, and constituted a menace to the national defense and safety, which demanded that prompt and adequate measures be taken to guard against it."...

We uphold the exclusion order as of the time it was made and when the petitioner violated it. In doing so, we are not unmindful of the hardships imposed by it upon a large group of American citizens. But hardships are part of war, and war is an aggregation of hardships. All citizens alike, both in and out of uniform, feel the impact of war in greater or lesser measure. Citizenship has its responsibilities as well as its privileges, and in time of war the burden is always heavier. Compulsory exclusion of large groups of citizens from their homes, except under circumstances of direst emergency and peril, is inconsistent with our basic governmental institutions. But when under conditions of modern warfare our shores are threatened by hostile forces, the power to protect must be commensurate with the threatened danger....

It is said that we are dealing here with the case of imprisonment of a citizen in a concentration camp solely because of his ancestry, without evidence or inquiry concerning his loyalty and good disposition towards the United States.

Our task would be simple, our duty clear, were this a case involving the imprisonment of a loyal citizen in a concentration camp because of racial prejudice. Regardless of the true nature of the assembly and relocation centers — and we deem it unjustifiable to call them concentration camps with all the ugly connotations that term implies — we are dealing specifically with nothing but an exclusion order. To cast this case into outlines of racial prejudice, without reference to the real military dangers which were presented, merely confuses the issue. Korematsu was not excluded from the Military Area because of hostility to him or his race. He *was* excluded because we are at war with the Japanese Empire, because the properly constituted military authorities feared an invasion of our West Coast and felt constrained to take proper security measures, because they decided that the military urgency of the situation demanded that all citizens of Japanese ancestry be segregated from the West Coast temporarily, and finally, because Congress, reposing its confidence in this time of war in our military leaders — as inevitably it must — determined that they should have the power to do just this. There was evidence of disloyalty on the part of some, the military authorities considered that the need for action was great, and time was short. We cannot — by availing ourselves of the calm perspective of hindsight — now say that at that time these actions were unjustified.

Affirmed.

Mr. Justice FRANKFURTER, concurring.... The provisions of the Constitution which confer on the Congress and the President powers to enable this country to wage war are as much part of the Constitution as provisions looking to a nation at peace. And we have had recent occasion to quote approvingly the statement of former Chief Justice Hughes that the war power of the Government is "the power to wage war successfully." Hirabayashi v. United States, supra at 93; and see Home Bldg. & L. Assn. v. Blaisdell, 290 U.S. 398, 426. Therefore, the validity of action under the war power must be judged wholly in the context of war. That action is not to be stigmatized as lawless because like action in times of peace would be lawless. To talk about a military order that expresses an allowable judgment of war needs by those entrusted with the duty of conducting war as "an unconstitutional order" is to suffuse a part of the Constitution with an atmosphere of unconstitutionality. The respective spheres of action of military authorities and of judges are of course very different. But within their sphere, military authorities are no more outside the bounds of obedience to the Constitution than are judges within theirs. "The war power of the United States, like its other powers...is subject to applicable constitutional limitations," Hamilton v. Kentucky Distilleries Co., 251 U.S. 146, 156. To recognize that military orders are "reasonably expedient military precautions" in time of war and yet to deny them constitutional legitimacy makes of the Constitution an instrument for dialectic subtleties not reasonably to be attributed to the hard-headed Framers, of whom a majority had had actual participation in war....

Mr. Justice MURPHY, dissenting. This exclusion of "all persons of Japanese ancestry, both alien and non-alien," from the Pacific Coast area on a plea of military necessity in the absence of martial law ought not to be approved. Such exclusion goes over "the very brink of constitutional power" and falls into the ugly abyss of racism.

A. Wartime Detention of Noncombatants Before 9/11

In dealing with matters relating to the prosecution and progress of a war, we must accord great respect and consideration to the judgments of the military authorities who are on the scene and who have full knowledge of the military facts. The scope of their discretion must, as a matter of necessity and common sense, be wide. And their judgments ought not to be overruled lightly by those whose training and duties ill-equip them to deal intelligently with matters so vital to the physical security of the nation.

At the same time, however, it is essential that there be definite limits to military discretion, especially where martial law has not been declared. Individuals must not be left impoverished of their constitutional rights on a plea of military necessity that has neither substance nor support. Thus, like other claims conflicting with the asserted constitutional rights of the individual, the military claim must subject itself to the judicial process of having its reasonableness determined and its conflicts with other interests reconciled. "What are the allowable limits of military discretion, and whether or not they have been overstepped in a particular case, are judicial questions." Sterling v. Constantin, 287 U.S. 378, 401.

The judicial test of whether the Government, on a plea of military necessity, can validly deprive an individual of any of his constitutional rights is whether the deprivation is reasonably related to a public danger that is so "immediate, imminent, and impending" as not to admit of delay and not to permit the intervention of ordinary constitutional processes to alleviate the danger. United States v. Russell, 13 Wall. 623, 627-628; Mitchell v. Harmony, 13 How. 115, 134-135; Raymond v. Thomas, 91 U.S. 712, 716. Civilian Exclusion Order No. 34, banishing from a prescribed area of the Pacific Coast "all persons of Japanese ancestry, both alien and non-alien," clearly does not meet that test. Being an obvious racial discrimination, the order deprives all those within its scope of the equal protection of the laws as guaranteed by the Fifth Amendment. It further deprives these individuals of their constitutional rights to live and work where they will, to establish a home where they choose and to move about freely. In excommunicating them without benefit of hearings, this order also deprives them of all their constitutional rights to procedural due process. Yet no reasonable relation to an "immediate, imminent, and impending" public danger is evident to support this racial restriction which is one of the most sweeping and complete deprivations of constitutional rights in the history of this nation in the absence of martial law....

Mr. Justice JACKSON, dissenting.... [T]he "law" which this prisoner is convicted of disregarding is not found in an act of Congress, but in a military order. Neither the Act of Congress nor the Executive Order of the President, nor both together, would afford a basis for this conviction. It rests on the orders of General DeWitt. And it is said that if the military commander had reasonable military grounds for promulgating the orders, they are constitutional and become law, and the Court is required to enforce them. There are several reasons why I cannot subscribe to this doctrine.

It would be impracticable and dangerous idealism to expect or insist that each specific military command in an area of probable operations will conform to conventional tests of constitutionality. When an area is so beset that it must be put under military control at all, the paramount consideration is that its measures be successful, rather than legal. The armed services must protect a society, not merely its Constitution. The very essence of the military job is to marshall physical force, to remove every obstacle to its effectiveness, to give it every strategic advantage. Defense measures will not, and often should not, be held within the limits that bind civil authority in peace. No court can require such a commander in such circumstances to act as a reasonable man; he may be unreasonably cautious and exacting. Perhaps he should be. But a commander in temporarily focusing the life of a community on defense is carrying out a military program; he is not making law in the sense that the courts know the term. He issues orders, and they may have a certain authority as military commands, although they may be very bad as constitutional law.

But if we cannot confine military expedients by the Constitution, neither would I distort the Constitution to approve all that the military may deem expedient. That is what the Court appears to be doing, whether consciously or not. I cannot say, from any evidence before me, that the orders of General DeWitt were not reasonably expedient military precautions, nor could I say that they were. But even if they were permissible military procedures, I deny that it follows that they are constitutional. If, as the Court holds, it does follow, then we may as well say that any military order will be constitutional and have done with it.

The limitation under which courts always will labor in examining the necessity for a military order [is] illustrated by this case. How does the Court know that these orders have a reasonable basis in necessity? No evidence whatever on that subject has been taken by this or any other court....

In the very nature of things, military decisions are not susceptible of intelligent judicial appraisal. They do not pretend to rest on evidence, but are made on information that often would not be admissible and on assumptions that could not be proved. Information in support of an order could not be disclosed to courts without danger that it would reach the enemy. Neither can courts act on communications made in confidence. Hence courts can never have any real alternative to accepting the mere declaration of the authority that issued the order that it was reasonably necessary from a military viewpoint.

Much is said of the danger to liberty from the Army program for deporting and detaining these citizens of Japanese extraction. But a judicial construction of the due process clause that will sustain this order is a far more subtle blow to liberty than the promulgation of the order itself. A military order, however unconstitutional, is not apt to last longer than the military emergency. Even during that period a succeeding commander may revoke it all. But once a judicial opinion rationalizes such an order to show that it conforms to the Constitution, or rather rationalizes the Constitution to show that the Constitution sanctions such an order, the Court for all time has validated the principle of racial discrimination in criminal procedure and of transplanting American citizens. The principle then lies about like a loaded weapon ready for the hand of any authority that can bring forward a plausible claim of an urgent need. Every repetition imbeds that principle more deeply in our law and thinking and expands it to new purposes....

I should hold that a civil court cannot be made to enforce an order which violates constitutional limitations even if it is a reasonable exercise of military authority. The courts can exercise only the judicial power, can apply only law, and must abide by the Constitution, or they cease to be civil courts and become instruments of military policy.

A. Wartime Detention of Noncombatants Before 9/11

Of course the existence of a military power resting on force, so vagrant, so centralized, so necessarily heedless of the individual, is an inherent threat to liberty. But I would not lead people to rely on this Court for a review that seems to me wholly delusive. The military reasonableness of these orders can only be determined by military superiors. If the people ever let command of the war power fall into irresponsible and unscrupulous hands, the courts wield no power equal to its restraint. The chief restraint upon those who command the physical forces of the country, in the future as in the past, must be their responsibility to the political judgments of their contemporaries and to the moral judgments of history.

My duties as a justice as I see them do not require me to make a military judgment as to whether General DeWitt's evacuation and detention program was a reasonable military necessity. I do not suggest that the courts should have attempted to interfere with the Army in carrying out its task. But I do not think they may be asked to execute a military expedient that has no place in law under the Constitution. I would reverse the judgment and discharge the prisoner.

[The opinion of Justice ROBERTS, dissenting, is omitted.]

NOTES AND QUESTIONS

1. *Alien Enemies?* Why did the government not invoke the Alien Enemy Act to confine Korematsu and his fellow internees? Could the government have invoked it to justify the PENTTBOM (referring to the 9/11 investigation) detentions of immigrants described *supra* p. 676? If so, has Congress occupied the field of alien detention during war or invasion with the Alien Enemy Act?

2. *Constitutionality of Emergency Actions.* Attorney General Francis Biddle wrote about the decision to create the internments,

> I do not think [President Roosevelt] was much concerned with the gravity or implications of this step.... Nor do I think the constitutional difficulty plagued him. The Constitution has not greatly bothered any wartime President. That was a question of law, which ultimately the Supreme Court must decide. And meanwhile — probably a long meanwhile — we must get on with the war. [Francis Biddle, *In Brief Authority* 219 (1962).]

Whatever the President's regard for fidelity to the Constitution, what is the significance of the Court's and Justice Frankfurter's constitutionalization of actions that in times of peace would be lawless? Consider Justice Jackson's warning on this point in his dissenting opinion. Professor Lobel indicates that throughout the twentieth century, but especially since World War II, the expanding U.S. role in global affairs and a nearly constant state of national crisis have promoted the development of a "relativistic" theory that finds emergency powers within the framework of the Constitution: the Commander in Chief and Executive Clauses, the President's inherent power in foreign affairs, and the presumed power of Congress to make laws anticipating every emergency. Jules Lobel, *Emergency Powers and the Decline of Liberalism*, 98 Yale L.J. 1385, 1399-1409 (1989).

If the Court is to review the constitutionality of emergency actions, what standards are to be applied? Are they found in the Constitution itself, or elsewhere?

These questions and others are considered in the classic contemporaneous criticisms of the principal case: Nanete Dembitz, *Racial Discrimination and the Military Judgment: The Supreme Court's Korematsu and Endo Decisions*, 45 Colum. L. Rev. 175 (1945); and Eugene Rostow, *The Japanese American Cases — A Disaster*, 54 Yale L.J. 489 (1945). *See also* Lobel, *supra*, at 1399-1412.

3. *Possible Effect of Martial Law.* Justice Murphy suggested in his dissent that there might have been greater justification for the expulsion if martial law had been declared. Do you agree? Would a declaration of martial law have been appropriate? *See* Ex parte Milligan, *supra* p. 683. Would the Court have examined the propriety of such a declaration? See generally *infra* pp. 969-972.

4. *Possible Significance of Citizenship and Loyalty.* In Ex parte Endo, 323 U.S. 283 (1944), decided the same day as *Korematsu*, the Court found that a Japanese-American citizen whose loyalty to the United States was conceded by the government could not be detained in a relocation center. The Court noted that

> [t]he Constitution when it committed to the Executive and to Congress the exercise of the war power necessarily gave them wider scope for the exercise of judgment and discretion so that war might be waged effectively and successfully [citing *Hirabayashi*]. At the same time, however, the Constitution is as specific in its enumeration of many of the civil rights of the individual as it is in the enumeration of the powers of his government. . . .
>
> . . . In interpreting a wartime measure we must assume that Congress' purpose was to allow for the greatest possible accommodation between civil liberties and the exigencies of war. [*Id.* at 298-300.]

So saying, the Court refused to find in either the 1942 congressional act or Executive Order No. 9066 any implied authority to detain an admittedly loyal citizen where none was expressly given. Should we infer from the court's holding that internment based on race or ethnic background might be permissible if it were approved either by an act of Congress or a clear presidential directive? Or does *Endo* stand for the proposition that a loyal American may not be locked up, even in time of war? If the latter, are you prepared to say how loyalty can be established, and who has the burden of proving its presence or absence?

5. *Standard of Review.* One commentator argues that careful judicial scrutiny is appropriate, if not essential, in cases like *Hirabayashi* and *Korematsu*, " 'where there is the most at stake in terms of personal freedom and the political branches are most likely to over-react' — when the government deems it necessary to restrict the most cherished liberties of American citizens to guard the nation's security." Eric R. Yamamoto, *Korematsu Revisited — Correcting the Injustice of Extraordinary Government Excess and Lax Judicial Review*, 26 Santa Clara L. Rev. 1, 48 (1986) (citation omitted). Heightened judicial scrutiny is especially important in such cases, he suggests, because "it addresses the inherent weakness in the system of majority rule." *Id.* at 48-49.

A. Wartime Detention of Noncombatants Before 9/11

How is this proposed standard of review different from the one set forth in the second paragraph of the *Korematsu* opinion? What standard of review was actually applied by the *Korematsu* Court? *See* Adarand Constructors, Inc. v. Pena, 515 U.S. 200, 214 (1995) (calling the *Korematsu* Court's application of its "most rigid scrutiny" standard "inexplicab[le]"). How do you think *Korematsu* would be decided today under modern equal protection law? For a description of that law, see *supra* p. 608.

6. *Belated Disclosure of Government Misconduct.* The *Korematsu* Court's extremely deferential review of the government's claim of military necessity enabled a stunning act of official fraud that was not revealed until nearly 40 years later. In 1982, Professor Peter Irons of the University of California at San Diego initiated a Freedom of Information Act request to obtain access to Justice Department records from its prosecution of the *Korematsu* case in 1944. His discoveries encouraged Fred Korematsu to file a petition for a writ of *coram nobis* in the court where he was tried 40 years earlier to vacate his conviction on grounds of government misconduct. The court found that

> the government knowingly withheld information from the courts when they were considering the critical question of military necessity in this case. A series of correspondence regarding what information should be included in the government's brief before the Supreme Court culminated in two different versions of a footnote that was to be used to specify the factual data upon which the government relied for its military necessity justification. The first version read as follows:
>
> > The Final Report of General DeWitt (which is dated June 5, 1943, but which was not made public until January 1944) is relied on in this brief for statistics and other details concerning the actual evacuation and the events that took place subsequent thereto. *The recital of the circumstances justifying the evacuation as a matter of military necessity, however, is in several respects,* particularly with reference to the use of illegal radio transmitters and to shore-to-ship signalling by persons of Japanese ancestry, *in conflict with information in the possession of the Department of Justice. In view of the contrariety of the reports on this matter we do not ask the Court to take judicial notice of the recital of those facts contained in the Report.* Petitioner's Exhibit AA, Memorandum of John L. Burling to Assistant Attorney General Herbert Wechsler, September 11, 1944 [emphasis added]....
>
> The footnote that appeared in the final version of the brief merely read as follows:
>
> > The Final Report of General DeWitt (which is dated June 5, 1943, but which was not made public until January 1944), hereinafter cited as Final Report, is relied on in this brief for statistics and other details concerning the actual evacuation and the events that took place subsequent thereto. *We have specifically recited in this brief the facts relating to the justification for the evacuation, of which we ask the Court to take judicial notice, and we rely upon the Final Report only to the extent that it relates to such facts.*
>
> Brief for the United States, Korematsu v. United States, October Term, 1944, No. 22, at 11. The final version made no mention of the contradictory reports. The record is replete with protestations of various Justice Department officials that the government had the obligation to advise the courts of the contrary facts and opinions. In fact, several Department of Justice officials pointed out to their

superiors and others the "wilful historical inaccuracies and intentional falsehoods" contained in the DeWitt Report.

These omissions are critical. In the original proceedings, before the district court and on appeal, the government argued that the actions taken were within the war-making powers of the Executive and Legislative branches and, even where the actions were directed at a particular class of persons, they were beyond judicial scrutiny so long as they were reasonably related to the security and defense of the nation and the prosecution of the war. . . .

. . . Omitted from the reports presented to the courts was information possessed by the Federal Communications Commission, the Department of the Navy, and the Justice Department which directly contradicted General DeWitt's statements. Thus, the court had before it a selective record. [Korematsu v. United States, 584 F. Supp. 1406, 1417-1419 (N.D. Cal. 1984).]

Setting aside Fred Korematsu's conviction, Judge Marilyn Patel concluded with this warning about the Supreme Court's 1944 decision:

Korematsu remains on the pages of our legal and political history. As a legal precedent it is now recognized as having very limited application. As historical precedent it stands as a constant caution that in times of war or declared military necessity our institutions must be vigilant in protecting constitutional guarantees. It stands as a caution that in times of distress the shield of military necessity and national security must not be used to protect governmental actions from close scrutiny and accountability. It stands as a caution that in times of international hostility and antagonisms our institutions, legislative, executive and judicial, must be prepared to exercise their authority to protect all citizens from the petty fears and prejudices that are so easily aroused. [*Id.* at 1420.]

The circumstances leading up to the 1984 decision are described in Peter Irons, *Justice at War: The Story of the Japanese American Internment Cases* (1983).

7. *The Role of Government Lawyers in Korematsu.* Why do you think the government lawyers behaved the way they did, both initially in approving the executive order, and later in deliberately misleading the Supreme Court? Some possible reasons are set forth in Peter Irons, *Politics and Principle: An Assessment of the Roosevelt Record on Civil Rights and Liberties*, 59 Wash. L. Rev. 693, 716-720 (1984).

8. *Military Necessity or Racism?* In the first *Korematsu* case, the Supreme Court relied heavily on its earlier decision in Hirabayashi v. United States, 320 U.S. 81 (1943). Gordon Hirabayashi's conviction for violating a curfew based on Executive Order No. 9066 was also vacated in a later *coram nobis* proceeding. Hirabayashi v. United States, 828 F.2d 591 (9th Cir. 1987). Evidence introduced in the new case included a report by General Dewitt that evacuation was necessary not because of any military exigency, but because traits peculiar to citizens of Japanese ancestry made it impossible to separate the loyal from the disloyal. *Id.* at 598. The report was later altered to expunge the racist rhetoric and to argue instead that "time is of the essence," and in its altered form the report was presented to the Supreme Court with a request that the Court take judicial notice of the facts recited therein. *Id.* at 596, 598-599. Documents and

commentary on the later proceedings may be found in *Justice Delayed: The Record of the Japanese American Internment Cases* (Peter Irons ed., 1989). *See also* Irons, *supra* Note 6; Yamamoto, *supra*; and Joanne Hirase, Comment, *The Internment of Japanese Americans: The Constitutional Threat Fifty Years Later*, 19 J. Contemp. L. 143 (1993).

9. *Apology and Payment.* On February 19, 1976, President Gerald Ford rescinded Executive Order No. 9066, 34 years to the day after its issuance. Praising the sacrifices and contributions of Japanese Americans, he called upon the American people to affirm with him "this American Promise—that we have learned from the tragedy of that long-ago experience forever to treasure liberty and justice for each individual American, and to resolve that this kind of action shall never again be repeated." Proclamation No. 4417, 41 Fed. Reg. 7741 (Feb. 20, 1976).

In 1980, Congress established the Commission on Wartime Relocation and Internment of Civilians to review the facts and circumstances surrounding Executive Order No. 9066 and its impact on American citizens and permanent resident aliens. Pub. L. No 96-317, 94 Stat. 964. In its report, entitled *Personal Justice Denied* (1982), the Commission found that some 120,000 people were held without judicial review, "despite the fact that not a single documented act of espionage, sabotage, or fifth column activity was committed by an American citizen of Japanese ancestry or by a resident Japanese alien on the West Coast.... [T]here was no justification in military necessity for the exclusion, ... there was no basis for the detention." *Id.* at 3, 10.

In 1948, Congress passed the American-Japanese Evacuation Claims Act, 50 U.S.C. App. §§1981-1987 (2000), authorizing payment of up to $100,000 to each internee for loss of real or personal property occasioned by the evacuation. Forty years later, after protracted debate, Congress voted to give $20,000 and an apology to each of 60,000 surviving internees. The measure was signed into law by President Reagan in 1988. 50 U.S.C. App. §§1989 to 1989c-8 (2000). Acceptance of the $20,000 payment "shall be in full satisfaction of all claims" against the government for damages. *Id.* §1989b-4(a)(6). *See* Chris K. Iijima, *Reparations and the "Model Minority" Ideology of Acquiescence: The Necessity to Refuse the Return to Original Humiliation*, 40 B.C. L. Rev. 385 (1998) (warning that reparations must not be used to excuse the racism that caused the internments); Sarah L. Brew, *Making Amends for History: Legislative Reparations for Japanese Americans and Other Minority Groups*, 8 J.L. & Inequality 179 (1989).

An American of German ancestry who was detained in 1945 complained that compensation of Japanese Americans and Aleuts who were interned, but not of German Americans, denied him equal protection of the laws. His claim was rejected. The court noted that after "three years of testimony from hundreds of witnesses, Congress concluded that Japanese Americans were detained en masse because of racial prejudice and demagoguery, while German Americans were detained in small numbers, and only after individual hearings about their loyalty." Jacobs v. Barr, 959 F.2d 313, 314 (D.C. Cir. 1992).

10. *Could It Happen Again?* On the fiftieth anniversary of the internments, Fred Korematsu remarked, "The constitutional violations that were committed have been cleared. This will never happen again." Katherine Bishop,

Japanese-Americans Treat Pain of Internment in World War II, N.Y. Times, Feb. 19, 1992, at A15. Do you think he was right?

It is suggested that General Dewitt was the evil genius whose singleminded racism was responsible for this sorry turn of events. *See, e.g., Hirabayashi,* 828 F.2d at 599-600. But should General Dewitt be asked to shoulder all or even a major part of the blame? Judge Patel's warning at the end of the opinion in the *coram nobis* case suggests otherwise. Taking her admonition to heart, can you describe some legal mechanism that would make us less likely to repeat our mistake? If you think some broader strategy will be required, can you say what it is?

For a fascinating account of *Korematsu*'s use as precedent since 1944, as well as the use and misuse of narrative in deciding the case, *see* Dean Masaru Hashimoto, *The Legacy of Korematsu v. United States: A Dangerous Narrative Retold,* 4 Asian Pac. Am. L.J. 72 (1996).

B. WARTIME DETENTION OF COMBATANTS BEFORE 9/11

Ex parte Milligan
United States Supreme Court, 1866
71 U.S. (4 Wall.) 2

[The opinion is set forth *supra* p. 683.]

Ex parte Quirin
United States Supreme Court, 1942
317 U.S. 1

[After war was declared between the United States and Germany, seven German nationals, and Herbert Hans Haupt, a dual U.S.-German national, were trained at a German sabotage school near Berlin. German submarines then carried the saboteurs with a supply of explosives to the United States. They landed on U.S. beaches wearing German Marine Infantry uniforms, which they immediately buried. Before they could engage in any act of sabotage, however, they were betrayed to the FBI by one of their number.

After their arrest, President Roosevelt issued an order establishing a military commission and proclaimed its jurisdiction to try nationals of enemy states or those who act under their direction for sabotage, espionage, or "violations of the law of war." Proclamation 2561, 7 Fed. Reg. 5101 (1942). The Military Commission conducted a secret 18-day trial of the saboteurs. Toward the end of the trial, the Supreme Court decided in an extraordinary expedited summer session to hear argument on the saboteurs' appeal from refusal of the lower courts to entertain their petitions for writs of habeas corpus. Less than 24 hours after argument, it ruled *per curiam* that the military commission was lawfully constituted and authorized to try the saboteurs, promising a full opinion later. Six of the saboteurs were executed eight days after the Supreme

B. Wartime Detention of Combatants Before 9/11

Court's *per curiam* ruling (Roosevelt commuted the sentences of the others to imprisonment). The Court issued its full opinion three months later.]

Mr. Chief Justice STONE delivered the opinion of the Court.... We are not here concerned with any question of the guilt or innocence of petitioners. Constitutional safeguards for the protection of all who are charged with offenses are not to be disregarded in order to inflict merited punishment on some who are guilty. Ex parte Milligan, [71 U.S. (4 Wall.) 2 (1866)]. But the detention and trial of petitioners—ordered by the President in the declared exercise of his powers as Commander in Chief of the Army in time of war and of grave public danger—are not to be set aside by the courts without the clear conviction that they are in conflict with the Constitution or laws of Congress constitutionally enacted.

Congress and the President, like the courts, possess no power not derived from the Constitution. But one of the objects of the Constitution, as declared by its preamble, is to "provide for the common defence."...

[The Court then catalogued first Congress's, then the President's, national security authorities under the Constitution.]

The Constitution thus invests the President as Commander in Chief with the power to wage war which Congress has declared, and to carry into effect all laws passed by Congress for the conduct of war and for the government and regulation of the Armed Forces, and all laws defining and punishing offences against the law of nations, including those which pertain to the conduct of war.

By the Articles of War, 10 U.S.C. §§1471-1593, Congress has provided rules for the government of the Army.... But the Articles also recognize the "military commission" appointed by military command as an appropriate tribunal for the trial and punishment of offenses against the law of war not ordinarily tried by court martial. See Arts. 12, 15. Articles 38 and 46 authorize the President, with certain limitations, to prescribe the procedure for military commissions. Articles 81 and 82 authorize trial, either by court martial or military commission, of those charged with relieving, harboring or corresponding with the enemy and those charged with spying. And Article 15 declares that "the provisions of these articles conferring jurisdiction upon courts-martial shall not be construed as depriving military commissions... or other military tribunals of concurrent jurisdiction in respect of offenders or offenses that by statute or by the law of war may be triable by such military commissions... or other military tribunals."...

From the very beginning of its history this Court has recognized and applied the law of war as including that part of the law of nations which prescribes, for the conduct of war, the status, rights and duties of enemy nations as well as of enemy individuals. By the Articles of War, and especially Article 15, Congress has explicitly provided, so far as it may constitutionally do so, that military tribunals shall have jurisdiction to try offenders or offenses against the law of war in appropriate cases....

An important incident to the conduct of war is the adoption of measures by the military command not only to repel and defeat the enemy, but to seize and subject to disciplinary measures those enemies who in their attempt to thwart or impede our military effort have violated the law of war. It is unnecessary for present purposes to determine to what extent the President as

Commander in Chief has constitutional power to create military commissions without the support of Congressional legislation. For here Congress has authorized trial of offenses against the law of war before such commissions.... We may assume that there are acts regarded in other countries, or by some writers on international law, as offenses against the law of war which would not be triable by military tribunal here, either because they are not recognized by our courts as violations of the law of war or because they are of that class of offenses constitutionally triable only by a jury. It was upon such grounds that the Court denied the right to proceed by military tribunal in Ex parte Milligan, supra. But as we shall show, these petitioners were charged with an offense against the law of war which the Constitution does not require to be tried by jury....

... [B]y the reference in the 15th Article of War to "offenders or offenses that... by the law of war may be triable by such military commissions," Congress has incorporated by reference, as within the jurisdiction of military commissions, all offenses which are defined as such by the law of war, and which may constitutionally be included within that jurisdiction. Congress had the choice of crystallizing in permanent form and in minute detail every offense against the law of war, or of adopting the system of common law applied by military tribunals so far as it should be recognized and deemed applicable by the courts. It chose the latter course.

By universal agreement and practice the law of war draws a distinction between the armed forces and the peaceful populations of belligerent nations and also between those who are lawful and unlawful combatants. Lawful combatants are subject to capture and detention as prisoners of war by opposing military forces. Unlawful combatants are likewise subject to capture and detention, but in addition they are subject to trial and punishment by military tribunals for acts which render their belligerency unlawful. The spy who secretly and without uniform passes the military lines of a belligerent in time of war, seeking to gather military information and communicate it to the enemy, or an enemy combatant who without uniform comes secretly through the lines for the purpose of waging war by destruction of life or property, are familiar examples of belligerents who are generally deemed not to be entitled to the status of prisoners of war, but to be offenders against the law of war subject to trial and punishment by military tribunals....

Specification 1 states that petitioners "being enemies of the United States and acting for... the German Reich, a belligerent enemy nation, secretly and covertly passed, in civilian dress, contrary to the law of war, through the military and naval lines and defenses of the United States... and went behind such lines, contrary to the law of war, in civilian dress... for the purpose of committing... hostile acts, and, in particular, to destroy certain war industries, war utilities and war materials within the United States."

This specification... plainly alleges violation of the law of war....

Citizenship in the United States of an enemy belligerent does not relieve him from the consequences of a belligerency which is unlawful because in violation of the law of war. Citizens who associate themselves with the military arm of the enemy government, and with its aid, guidance and direction enter this country bent on hostile acts are enemy belligerents within the meaning of the Hague Convention and the law of war. It is as an enemy belligerent that petitioner Haupt is charged with entering the United States, and unlawful belligerency is the gravamen of the offense of which he is accused....

But petitioners insist that even if the offenses with which they are charged are offenses against the law of war, their trial is subject to the requirement of the Fifth Amendment that no person shall be held to answer for a capital or otherwise infamous crime unless on a presentment or indictment of a grand jury, and that such trials by Article III, §2, and the Sixth Amendment must be by jury in a civil court....

Presentment by a grand jury and trial by a jury of the vicinage where the crime was committed were at the time of the adoption of the Constitution familiar parts of the machinery for criminal trials in the civil courts. But they were procedures unknown to military tribunals, which are not courts in the sense of the Judiciary Article, and which in the natural course of events are usually called upon to function under conditions precluding resort to such procedures....

...[W]e must conclude that §2 of Article III and the Fifth and Sixth Amendments cannot be taken to have extended the right to demand a jury to trials by military commission, or to have required that offenses against the law of war not triable by jury at common law be tried only in the civil courts....

Petitioners, and especially petitioner Haupt, stress the pronouncement of this Court in the *Milligan* case that the law of war "can never be applied to citizens in states which have upheld the authority of the government, and where the courts are open and their process unobstructed." Elsewhere in its opinion, the Court was at pains to point out that Milligan, a citizen twenty years resident in Indiana, who had never been a resident of any of the states in rebellion, was not an enemy belligerent either entitled to the status of a prisoner of war or subject to the penalties imposed upon unlawful belligerents. We construe the Court's statement as to the inapplicability of the law of war to Milligan's case as having particular reference to the facts before it. From them the Court concluded that Milligan, not being a part of or associated with the armed forces of the enemy, was a non-belligerent, not subject to the law of war save as — in circumstances found not there to be present and not involved here — martial law might be constitutionally established.

The Court's opinion is inapplicable to the case presented by the present record. We have no occasion now to define with meticulous care the ultimate boundaries of the jurisdiction of military tribunals to try persons according to the law of war. It is enough that petitioners here, upon the conceded facts, were plainly within those boundaries, and were held in good faith for trial by military commission, charged with being enemies who, with the purpose of destroying war materials and utilities, entered or after entry remained in our territory without uniform — an offense against the law of war. We hold only that those particular acts constitute an offense against the law of war which the Constitution authorizes to be tried by military commission....

It follows that the orders of the District Court should be affirmed, and that leave to file petitions for habeas corpus in this Court should be denied.

Justice MURPHY took no part in the consideration or decision of these cases.

NOTES AND QUESTIONS

1. *Military Necessity.* In Reid v. Covert, 354 U.S. 1, 21 (1957), *supra* p. 640, the Court emphasized that

> the jurisdiction of military tribunals is a very limited and extraordinary jurisdiction derived from the cryptic language of Art. I, §8, and, at most, was intended to be only a narrow exception to the normal and preferred method of trial in courts of law. Every extension of military jurisdiction is an encroachment on the jurisdiction of the civil courts, and, more important, acts as a deprivation of the right to jury trial and of other treasured constitutional protections.

At the same time, the Court found that the "exigencies which have required military rule on the battlefront are not present...where no conflict exists. Military trial of civilians 'in the field' is an extraordinary jurisdiction and it should not be expanded at the expense of the Bill of Rights." *Id.* at 35.

What "exigencies" require military *detention*? Are they geographically limited? Did they apply to the military detention of Milligan? Did the existence of an exigency depend on whether there were reasonable alternatives to his military detention? Were there?

2. *Statutory Authority?* Quirin suggests in several places that there was statutory authority for the commission that tried the German saboteurs. Indeed, articles 81 and 82 of the Articles of War, which it cites, seemed to authorize the trial of spies, at least, by military commission. But the decision places chief reliance on article 15, which it quotes *supra* p. 715. Does article 15, which is now 10 U.S.C. §821 (2000), authorize military commissions or is it merely a savings clause? If the latter, what authority does it save? In another World War II case involving military commissions, Application of Yamashita, 327 U.S. 1 (1946), the Supreme Court explained that "[b]y thus recognizing military commissions in order to preserve their traditional jurisdiction over enemy combatants unimpaired by the Articles, Congress gave sanction, as we held in Ex parte Quirin, to any use of the military commission contemplated by the *common law of war.* " *Id.* at 20 (emphasis added).

Presumably the law of war also authorizes the military detention of enemy combatants. If so, is §821 or any statute necessary to authorize military detention as long as we are at war? *See* Hamdan v. Rumsfeld, 126 S. Ct. 2749, 2774 (2006), *infra* p. 882 (refraining from deciding analogous question). Could Congress by statute regulate or prohibit such detentions? On what specific constitutional authority would Congress rely for such a statute? *See id.*

3. *Declared State of War?* If military detention is authorized by the common law of war, must war be declared for the Commander in Chief to exercise that authority? War had, of course, been declared before *Quirin* and *Yamashita* were decided. One advantage of requiring a declared war to authorize military detention or trial is that the authority then has a temporal limit; it lasts "so long as a state of war exists from its declaration until peace is proclaimed." *Yamashita*, 327 U.S. at 11-12. "A declaration of war draws clear lines. It defines (or at least has traditionally done so) who the enemy is: another state, and all the nationals of

B. Wartime Detention of Combatants Before 9/11

that state. It marks a clear beginning, and (again traditionally) an end, with some act or instrument marking its conclusion." American Bar Assn. Task Force on Terrorism and the Law, *Report and Recommendations on Military Commissions* 5 (Jan. 4, 2002) (*ABA Task Force Report*).

But we have seen that Congress can authorize "imperfect" war without a formal declaration. Writing of one such war (the Quasi-War with France) in Talbot v. Seeman, 5 U.S. 1 (1801), Chief Justice Marshall observed that "congress may authorize general hostilities, in which case the general laws of war apply to our situation; or partial hostilities, in which case the laws of war, so far as they actually apply to our situation, must be noticed." Military detention and trials by military commissions were also common in the field and in occupied Confederate states during the undeclared Civil War.

Yet even those states of war each had a defined and discernible end. Does a war on terrorists have a discernible end? If a state of war triggers common law of war authority, did the Authorization for Use of Military Force (AUMF), Pub. L. No. 107-40, 115 Stat. 224 (2001), *supra* p. 100, approving the use of force against the perpetrators of the September 11 attacks, authorize a state of war permitting the President to direct military detention and to use military commissions? *See* Hamdan v. Rumsfeld, 126 S. Ct. 2749, 2775 (2006), *infra* p. 882 (yes, as to military commissions, but it does not expand the President's existing authority to convene such commissions). War against whom? Does this state of war draw clear lines for the duration of this authority?

4. *Violations of the Law of War.* Were the September 11 attacks acts of war, and did they violate the law of war? Traditionally, states carry out acts of war, and a state's deliberate attack on noncombatant civilians would clearly violate the laws of war. *See, e.g.*, Convention Relative to the Protection of Civilian Persons in Time of War (1949 Geneva Convention IV), Aug. 12, 1949, 6 U.S.T. 3516, 75 U.N.T.S. 287. Opponents of the military commission have argued that "war crimes" must by definition either be committed during an international armed conflict between *states* or in an internal armed conflict, and they assert that the war conducted by terrorists is neither. *See, e.g.*, Joan Fitzpatrick, *Jurisdiction of Military Commissions and the Ambiguous War on Terrorism*, 96 Am. J. Intl. L. 345 (2002).

But the law of war applies also to some nonstate actors, such as insurgents. *ABA Task Force Report, supra*, at 7. It also presumably applies to terrorists with state sponsors. But does one also violate the law of war by conspiring with or aiding and abetting al Qaeda? *See* Association of the Bar of the City of New York, Comm. on Military Aff. & Justice, *Inter Arma Silent Leges: In Times of Armed Conflict, Should the Laws Be Silent?* (*N.Y. City Bar Report*) (Dec. 2001), at 16 (no). In Hamdan v. Rumsfeld, 126 S. Ct. 2749 (2006), a plurality of the Supreme Court found that conspiracy was not a crime traditionally triable under the law of war. *Id.* at 2778-2786. Congress responded by purportedly codifying "offenses that have traditionally been triable by military commissions," but then including not only "conspiracy," but also "providing material support for terrorism." Military Commissions Act of 2006, Pub. L. No. 109-366, §3(a), 120 Stat. 2600, 2630.

5. *Reconciling Milligan and Quirin.* Although Attorney General Biddle at first asked the Court in *Quirin* to overrule *Milligan*, he later backed off from this demand in his oral argument and asserted that the Court could uphold the use of the military commission to try the saboteurs "without touching a hair of the *Milligan* case." George Lardner Jr., *Nazi Saboteurs Captured!*, Wash. Post, Jan. 13, 2002, Magazine, at 23. How *did* the Court distinguish *Milligan*? Did it distinguish the defendants by their citizenship? *See* Mudd v. Caldera, 134 F. Supp. 2d 138 (D.D.C. 2001) (citizens and noncitizens alike may be subject to the jurisdiction of a military commission for violating the laws of war). By their acts? (Recall that Milligan was charged with "Violation of the laws of war."). If *Milligan* survived *Quirin*, as the later opinion suggests, how much of it is left?

Quirin suggests that *Milligan* should be limited to its facts. On the other hand, Justice Black wrote the other Justices in *Quirin* that "[i]n this case I want to go no further than to declare that these particular defendants are subject to the jurisdiction of a military tribunal because of the circumstances." *See* Evan P. Schultz, *Now and Later*, Legal Times, Dec. 24, 2001, at 54. Accordingly, the opinion for the Court stated, "We hold only that these particular facts constitute an offense against the law of nations which the Constitution authorizes to be tried by military commission." *Quirin*, 317 U.S. at 20. Do "these particular facts" include the fact of declared war with its attendant limits (including identification of enemy combatants)?

If *Quirin* is limited to *its* facts, and applicable to military detention (not just trial), could the military constitutionally detain a suspected terrorist apprehended in the United States while civilian courts are open? In view of the Court's characterization of the military commission as a "narrow exception to the normal and preferred method of trial in courts of law," should we read *Quirin* for all that its language may be worth, or as narrowly as possible? *Cf. ABA Task Force Report, supra*, at 16 (recommending that "any use of military commissions should be limited to narrow circumstances in which compelling security interests justify their use" and that they not be used against persons lawfully present in the United States or unconnected with the September 11 attacks absent additional specific authority from Congress); *NY City Bar Report, supra*, at 8 (arguing that *Quirin* should be limited to declared war).

C. DETENTION OF U.S. CITIZENS AS ENEMY COMBATANTS AFTER 9/11

After 9/11, the government placed two U.S. citizens in military detention, citing Ex parte Quirin as authority. We consider first the case of Yaser Hamdi, who reportedly was captured on the battlefield in Afghanistan. We then turn to the military detention of José Padilla, originally arrested in Chicago as a material witness, before being designated an enemy combatant by President George W. Bush and transferred to military custody.

Hamdi v. Rumsfeld
United States Supreme Court, 2004
542 U.S. 507

Justice O'CONNOR announced the judgment of the Court and delivered an opinion, in which THE CHIEF JUSTICE, Justice KENNEDY, and Justice BREYER join. . . .

[During the U.S. military operations in Afghanistan that followed the 9/11 terrorist attacks, petitioner Hamdi was captured by Afghan Northern Alliance forces. He was subsequently transferred to U.S. military custody in Afghanistan and sent to Guantánamo. When it was discovered that he had been born in Louisiana, making him a U.S. citizen, he was transferred to the United States as an enemy combatant and detained at a Navy brig in Charleston, South Carolina. Hamdi's father filed this habeas petition on behalf of his son under 28 U.S.C. §2241, alleging that the government held him in violation of the Fifth and Fourteenth Amendments. In the ensuing proceeding, the government filed an affidavit by Department of Defense official Michael Mobbs, setting forth the foregoing facts as hearsay.]

II

The threshold question before us is whether the Executive has the authority to detain citizens who qualify as "enemy combatants." There is some debate as to the proper scope of this term, and the Government has never provided any court with the full criteria that it uses in classifying individuals as such. It has made clear, however, that, for purposes of this case, the "enemy combatant" that it is seeking to detain is an individual who, it alleges, was "part of or supporting forces hostile to the United States or coalition partners" in Afghanistan and who "engaged in an armed conflict against the United States" there. We therefore answer only the narrow question before us: whether the detention of citizens falling within that definition is authorized.

The Government maintains that no explicit congressional authorization is required, because the Executive possesses plenary authority to detain pursuant to Article II of the Constitution. We do not reach the question whether Article II provides such authority, however, because we agree with the Government's alternative position, that Congress has in fact authorized Hamdi's detention, through the AUMF [*supra* p. 100].

Our analysis on that point, set forth below, substantially overlaps with our analysis of Hamdi's principal argument for the illegality of his detention. He posits that his detention is forbidden by 18 U.S.C. §4001(a). Section 4001(a) states that "[n]o citizen shall be imprisoned or otherwise detained by the United States except pursuant to an Act of Congress." Congress passed §4001(a) in 1971 as part of a bill to repeal the Emergency Detention Act of 1950, 50 U.S.C. §811 *et seq.*, which provided procedures for executive detention, during times of emergency, of individuals deemed likely to engage in espionage or sabotage. Congress was particularly concerned about the possibility that the Act could be used to reprise the Japanese internment camps of World War II. The Government again presses two alternative positions. First, it argues that §4001(a), in light of its legislative history and its location in Title 18, applies only to "the control of civilian prisons and related detentions," not to military detentions. Second, it maintains that §4001(a) is satisfied, because Hamdi is being detained "pursuant to an Act of Congress" — the AUMF. Again, because we conclude that the Government's second assertion is correct, we do not address the first. In other words, for the reasons that follow, we conclude that the AUMF is explicit congressional authorization for the detention of individuals in the narrow category we describe (assuming, without deciding, that such authorization is required), and that the AUMF satisfied §4001(a)'s requirement that a detention be "pursuant to an Act of Congress" (assuming, without deciding, that §4001(a) applies to military detentions).

The AUMF authorizes the President to use "all necessary and appropriate force" against "nations, organizations, or persons" associated with the September 11, 2001, terrorist attacks. 115 Stat. 224. There can be no doubt that individuals who fought against the United States in Afghanistan as part of the Taliban, an organization known to have supported the al Qaeda terrorist network responsible for those attacks, are individuals Congress sought to target in passing the AUMF. We conclude that detention of individuals falling into the limited category we are considering, for the duration of the particular conflict in which they were captured, is so fundamental and accepted an incident to war as to be an exercise of the "necessary and appropriate force" Congress has authorized the President to use.

The capture and detention of lawful combatants and the capture, detention, and trial of unlawful combatants, by "universal agreement and practice," are "important incident[s] of war." *Ex parte Quirin*, 317 U.S. [1 (1942)], at 28. The purpose of detention is to prevent captured individuals from returning to the field of battle and taking up arms once again.

There is no bar to this Nation's holding one of its own citizens as an enemy combatant. In *Quirin*, one of the detainees, Haupt, alleged that he was a naturalized United States citizen. 317 U.S., at 20. We held that "[c]itizens who associate themselves with the military arm of the enemy government, and with its aid, guidance and direction enter this country bent on hostile acts, are enemy belligerents within the meaning of . . . the law of war." *Id.*, at 37-38. While Haupt was tried for violations of the law of war, nothing in *Quirin* suggests that his citizenship would have precluded his mere detention for the duration of the relevant hostilities. See *id.*, at 30-31. Nor can we see any reason for drawing such a line here. A citizen, no less than an alien, can be "part of or supporting forces hostile to the United States or coalition partners" and "engaged in an armed conflict against the United States"; such a citizen, if released, would pose the same threat of returning to the front during the ongoing conflict.

In light of these principles, it is of no moment that the AUMF does not use specific language of detention. Because detention to prevent a combatant's return to the battlefield is a fundamental incident of waging war, in permitting the use of "necessary and appropriate force," Congress has clearly and unmistakably authorized detention in the narrow circumstances considered here. . . .

Hamdi contends that the AUMF does not authorize indefinite or perpetual detention. Certainly, we agree that indefinite detention for the purpose of interrogation is not authorized. Further, we understand Congress' grant of authority for the use of "necessary and appropriate force" to include the authority to detain for the duration of the relevant conflict, and our understanding is

C. Detention of U.S. Citizens as Enemy Combatants After 9/11

based on longstanding law-of-war principles. If the practical circumstances of a given conflict are entirely unlike those of the conflicts that informed the development of the law of war, that understanding may unravel. But that is not the situation we face as of this date. Active combat operations against Taliban fighters apparently are ongoing in Afghanistan. The United States may detain, for the duration of these hostilities, individuals legitimately determined to be Taliban combatants who "engaged in an armed conflict against the United States." If the record establishes that United States troops are still involved in active combat in Afghanistan, those detentions are part of the exercise of "necessary and appropriate force," and therefore are authorized by the AUMF.

Ex parte Milligan, [71 U.S. (4 Wall.) 2 (1866)], does not undermine our holding about the Government's authority to seize enemy combatants, as we define that term today. In that case, the Court made repeated reference to the fact that its inquiry into whether the military tribunal had jurisdiction to try and punish Milligan turned in large part on the fact that Milligan was not a prisoner of war, but a resident of Indiana arrested while at home there. *Id.,* at 118, 131. That fact was central to its conclusion. Had Milligan been captured while he was assisting Confederate soldiers by carrying a rifle against Union troops on a Confederate battlefield, the holding of the Court might well have been different. The Court's repeated explanations that Milligan was not a prisoner of war suggest that had these different circumstances been present he could have been detained under military authority for the duration of the conflict, whether or not he was a citizen....

III

Even in cases in which the detention of enemy combatants is legally authorized, there remains the question of what process is constitutionally due to a citizen who disputes his enemy-combatant status....

A

Though they reach radically different conclusions on the process that ought to attend the present proceeding, the parties begin on common ground. All agree that, absent suspension, the writ of habeas corpus remains available to every individual detained within the United States. U.S. Const., Art. I, §9, cl. 2 ("The Privilege of the Writ of Habeas Corpus shall not be suspended, unless when in Cases of Rebellion or Invasion the public Safety may require it"). Only in the rarest of circumstances has Congress seen fit to suspend the writ.... All agree suspension of the writ has not occurred here. Thus, it is undisputed that Hamdi was properly before an Article III court to challenge his detention under 28 U.S.C. §2241. Further, all agree that §2241 and its companion provisions provide at least a skeletal outline of the procedures to be afforded a petitioner in federal habeas review. Most notably, §2243 provides that "the person detained may, under oath, deny any of the facts set forth in the return or allege any other material facts," and §2246 allows the taking of evidence in habeas proceedings by deposition, affidavit, or interrogatories.

The simple outline of §2241 makes clear both that Congress envisioned that habeas petitioners would have some opportunity to present and rebut facts and that courts in cases like this retain some ability to vary the ways in which they do so as mandated by due process. The Government recognizes the basic procedural protections required by the habeas statute, but asks us to hold that, given both the flexibility of the habeas mechanism and the circumstances presented in this case, the presentation of the Mobbs Declaration to the habeas court completed the required factual development. It suggests two separate reasons for its position that no further process is due.

B

First, the Government urges the adoption of the Fourth Circuit's holding below — that because it is "undisputed" that Hamdi's seizure took place in a combat zone, the habeas determination can be made purely as a matter of law, with no further hearing or factfinding necessary. This argument is easily rejected. As the dissenters from the denial of rehearing en banc noted, the circumstances surrounding Hamdi's seizure cannot in any way be characterized as "undisputed," as "those circumstances are neither conceded in fact, nor susceptible to concession in law, because Hamdi has not been permitted to speak for himself or even through counsel as to those circumstances." 337 F.3d 335, 357 (Luttig, J., dissenting from denial of rehearing en banc). Further, the "facts" that constitute the alleged concession are insufficient to support Hamdi's detention. Under the definition of enemy combatant that we accept today as falling within the scope of Congress' authorization, Hamdi would need to be "part of or supporting forces hostile to the United States or coalition partners" and "engaged in an armed conflict against the United States" to justify his detention in the United States for the duration of the relevant conflict. The habeas petition states only that "[w]hen seized by the United States Government, Mr. Hamdi resided in Afghanistan." An assertion that one *resided* in a country in which combat operations are taking place is not a concession that one was "*captured* in a zone of active combat operations in a foreign theater of war," 316 F.3d, at 459 (emphasis added), and certainly is not a concession that one was "part of or supporting forces hostile to the United States or coalition partners" and "engaged in an armed conflict against the United States." Accordingly, we reject any argument that Hamdi has made concessions that eliminate any right to further process.

C

The Government's second argument requires closer consideration. This is the argument that further factual exploration is unwarranted and inappropriate in light of the extraordinary constitutional interests at stake. Under the Government's most extreme rendition of this argument, "[r]espect for separation of powers and the limited institutional capabilities of courts in matters of military decision-making in connection with an ongoing conflict" ought to eliminate entirely any individual process, restricting the courts to investigating only

C. Detention of U.S. Citizens as Enemy Combatants After 9/11

whether legal authorization exists for the broader detention scheme. At most, the Government argues, courts should review its determination that a citizen is an enemy combatant under a very deferential "some evidence" standard. [Brief for Respondents] 34 ("Under the some evidence standard, the focus is exclusively on the factual basis supplied by the Executive to support its own determination" (citing *Superintendent, Mass. Correctional Institution at Walpole v. Hill,* 472 U.S. 445, 455-457 (1985) (explaining that the some evidence standard "does not require" a "weighing of the evidence," but rather calls for assessing "whether there is any evidence in the record that could support the conclusion")). Under this review, a court would assume the accuracy of the Government's articulated basis for Hamdi's detention, as set forth in the Mobbs Declaration, and assess only whether that articulated basis was a legitimate one. In response, Hamdi emphasizes that this Court consistently has recognized that an individual challenging his detention may not be held at the will of the Executive without recourse to some proceeding before a neutral tribunal to determine whether the Executive's asserted justifications for that detention have basis in fact and warrant in law. See, *e.g., Zadvydas v. Davis,* 533 U.S. 678, 690 (2001)....

...The ordinary mechanism that we use for balancing such serious competing interests, and for determining the procedures that are necessary to ensure that a citizen is not "deprived of life, liberty, or property, without due process of law," U.S. Const., Amdt. 5, is the test that we articulated in *Mathews v. Eldridge,* 424 U.S. 319 (1976). *Mathews* dictates that the process due in any given instance is determined by weighing "the private interest that will be affected by the official action" against the Government's asserted interest, "including the function involved" and the burdens the Government would face in providing greater process. 424 U.S., at 335. The *Mathews* calculus then contemplates a judicious balancing of these concerns, through an analysis of "the risk of an erroneous deprivation" of the private interest if the process were reduced and the "probable value, if any, of additional or substitute safeguards." *Ibid.* We take each of these steps in turn.

1

It is beyond question that substantial interests lie on both sides of the scale in this case. Hamdi's "private interest...affected by the official action," *ibid.,* is the most elemental of liberty interests — the interest in being free from physical detention by one's own government. "In our society liberty is the norm," and detention without trial "is the carefully limited exception." [United States v. Salerno, 481 U.S. 739 (1987)], at 755 ....

Nor is the weight on this side of the *Mathews* scale offset by the circumstances of war or the accusation of treasonous behavior, for "[i]t is clear that commitment for *any* purpose constitutes a significant deprivation of liberty that requires due process protection," *Jones v. United States,* 463 U.S. 354, 361 (1983) (emphasis added; internal quotation marks omitted), and at this stage in the *Mathews* calculus, we consider the interest of the *erroneously* detained individual. Indeed, as *amicus* briefs from media and relief organizations emphasize, the risk of erroneous deprivation of a citizen's liberty in the absence of sufficient process here is very real. See Brief for AmeriCares et al. as *Amici Curiae* 13-22 (noting ways in which "[t]he nature of humanitarian relief work and journalism present a significant risk of mistaken military detentions"). Moreover, as critical as the Government's interest may be in detaining those who actually pose an immediate threat to the national security of the United States during ongoing international conflict, history and common sense teach us that an unchecked system of detention carries the potential to become a means for oppression and abuse of others who do not present that sort of threat....

2

On the other side of the scale are the weighty and sensitive governmental interests in ensuring that those who have in fact fought with the enemy during a war do not return to battle against the United States. As discussed above, the law of war and the realities of combat may render such detentions both necessary and appropriate, and our due process analysis need not blink at those realities. Without doubt, our Constitution recognizes that core strategic matters of warmaking belong in the hands of those who are best positioned and most politically accountable for making them. *Department of Navy v. Egan,* 484 U.S. 518, 530 (1988) (noting the reluctance of the courts "to intrude upon the authority of the Executive in military and national security affairs"); *Youngstown Sheet & Tube Co. v. Sawyer,* 343 U.S. 579, 587 (1952) (acknowledging "broad powers in military commanders engaged in day-to-day fighting in a theater of war").

The Government also argues at some length that its interests in reducing the process available to alleged enemy combatants are heightened by the practical difficulties that would accompany a system of trial-like process. In its view, military officers who are engaged in the serious work of waging battle would be unnecessarily and dangerously distracted by litigation half a world away, and discovery into military operations would both intrude on the sensitive secrets of national defense and result in a futile search for evidence buried under the rubble of war. To the extent that these burdens are triggered by heightened procedures, they are properly taken into account in our due process analysis.

3

Striking the proper constitutional balance here is of great importance to the Nation during this period of ongoing combat. But it is equally vital that our calculus not give short shrift to the values that this country holds dear or to the privilege that is American citizenship. It is during our most challenging and uncertain moments that our Nation's commitment to due process is most severely tested; and it is in those times that we must preserve our commitment at home to the principles for which we fight abroad.

With due recognition of these competing concerns, we believe that neither the process proposed by the Government nor the process apparently envisioned by the District Court below strikes the proper constitutional balance when a United States citizen is detained in the United States as an enemy combatant. That is, "the risk of erroneous deprivation" of a detainee's liberty interest is unacceptably high under the Government's proposed rule, while some of the "additional or substitute procedural safeguards" suggested by the District Court

C. Detention of U.S. Citizens as Enemy Combatants After 9/11

are unwarranted in light of their limited "probable value" and the burdens they may impose on the military in such cases. *Mathews,* 424 U.S., at 335.

We therefore hold that a citizen-detainee seeking to challenge his classification as an enemy combatant must receive notice of the factual basis for his classification, and a fair opportunity to rebut the Government's factual assertions before a neutral decisionmaker. "For more than a century the central meaning of procedural due process has been clear: 'Parties whose rights are to be affected are entitled to be heard; and in order that they may enjoy that right they must first be notified.' It is equally fundamental that the right to notice and an opportunity to be heard 'must be granted at a meaningful time and in a meaningful manner.'" *Fuentes v. Shevin,* 407 U.S. 67, 80 (1972). These essential constitutional promises may not be eroded.

At the same time, the exigencies of the circumstances may demand that, aside from these core elements, enemy combatant proceedings may be tailored to alleviate their uncommon potential to burden the Executive at a time of ongoing military conflict. Hearsay, for example, may need to be accepted as the most reliable available evidence from the Government in such a proceeding. Likewise, the Constitution would not be offended by a presumption in favor of the Government's evidence, so long as that presumption remained a rebuttable one and fair opportunity for rebuttal were provided. Thus, once the Government puts forth credible evidence that the habeas petitioner meets the enemy-combatant criteria, the onus could shift to the petitioner to rebut that evidence with more persuasive evidence that he falls outside the criteria. A burden-shifting scheme of this sort would meet the goal of ensuring that the errant tourist, embedded journalist, or local aid worker has a chance to prove military error while giving due regard to the Executive once it has put forth meaningful support for its conclusion that the detainee is in fact an enemy combatant. In the words of *Mathews,* process of this sort would sufficiently address the "risk of erroneous deprivation" of a detainee's liberty interest while eliminating certain procedures that have questionable additional value in light of the burden on the Government. 424 U.S., at 335.

We think it unlikely that this basic process will have the dire impact on the central functions of warmaking that the Government forecasts. The parties agree that initial captures on the battlefield need not receive the process we have discussed here; that process is due only when the determination is made to *continue* to hold those who have been seized. The Government has made clear in its briefing that documentation regarding battlefield detainees already is kept in the ordinary course of military affairs. Any factfinding imposition created by requiring a knowledgeable affiant to summarize these records to an independent tribunal is a minimal one. Likewise, arguments that military officers ought not have to wage war under the threat of litigation lose much of their steam when factual disputes at enemy-combatant hearings are limited to the alleged combatant's acts. This focus meddles little, if at all, in the strategy or conduct of war, inquiring only into the appropriateness of continuing to detain an individual claimed to have taken up arms against the United States. While we accord the greatest respect and consideration to the judgments of military authorities in matters relating to the actual prosecution of a war, and recognize that the scope of that discretion necessarily is wide, it does not infringe on the core role of the military for the courts to exercise their own time-honored and constitutionally mandated roles of reviewing and resolving claims like those presented here. Cf. *Korematsu v. United States,* 323 U.S. 214, 233-234 (1944) (Murphy, J., dissenting) ("[L]ike other claims conflicting with the asserted constitutional rights of the individual, the military claim must subject itself to the judicial process of having its reasonableness determined and its conflicts with other interests reconciled"); *Sterling v. Constantin,* 287 U.S. 378, 401 (1932) ("What are the allowable limits of military discretion, and whether or not they have been overstepped in a particular case, are judicial questions").

In sum, while the full protections that accompany challenges to detentions in other settings may prove unworkable and inappropriate in the enemy-combatant setting, the threats to military operations posed by a basic system of independent review are not so weighty as to trump a citizen's core rights to challenge meaningfully the Government's case and to be heard by an impartial adjudicator.

D

In so holding, we necessarily reject the Government's assertion that separation of powers principles mandate a heavily circumscribed role for the courts in such circumstances. Indeed, the position that the courts must forgo any examination of the individual case and focus exclusively on the legality of the broader detention scheme cannot be mandated by any reasonable view of separation of powers, as this approach serves only to *condense* power into a single branch of government. We have long since made clear that a state of war is not a blank check for the President when it comes to the rights of the Nation's citizens. *Youngstown Sheet & Tube,* 343 U.S., at 587. Whatever power the United States Constitution envisions for the Executive in its exchanges with other nations or with enemy organizations in times of conflict, it most assuredly envisions a role for all three branches when individual liberties are at stake. *Mistretta v. United States,* 488 U.S. 361, 380 (1989) (it was "the central judgment of the Framers of the Constitution that, within our political scheme, the separation of governmental powers into three coordinate Branches is essential to the preservation of liberty"); *Home Building & Loan Assn. v. Blaisdell,* 290 U.S. 398, 426 (1934) (The war power "is a power to wage war successfully, and thus it permits the harnessing of the entire energies of the people in a supreme cooperative effort to preserve the nation. But even the war power does not remove constitutional limitations safeguarding essential liberties"). Likewise, we have made clear that, unless Congress acts to suspend it, the Great Writ of habeas corpus allows the Judicial Branch to play a necessary role in maintaining this delicate balance of governance, serving as an important judicial check on the Executive's discretion in the realm of detentions. See *INS v. St. Cyr,* 533 U.S. 289, 301 (2001) ("At its historical core, the writ of habeas corpus has served as a means of reviewing the legality of Executive detention, and it is in that context that its protections have been strongest"). Thus, while we do not question that our due process assessment must pay keen attention to the particular burdens faced by the Executive in the context of military action, it would turn our system of checks and balances on its head to suggest that a citizen could not make his way to court with a challenge to the factual basis for his detention by his

C. Detention of U.S. Citizens as Enemy Combatants After 9/11

government, simply because the Executive opposes making available such a challenge. Absent suspension of the writ by Congress, a citizen detained as an enemy combatant is entitled to this process.

Because we conclude that due process demands some system for a citizen detainee to refute his classification, the proposed "some evidence" standard is inadequate. Any process in which the Executive's factual assertions go wholly unchallenged or are simply presumed correct without any opportunity for the alleged combatant to demonstrate otherwise falls constitutionally short. As the Government itself has recognized, we have utilized the "some evidence" standard in the past as a standard of review, not as a standard of proof. That is, it primarily has been employed by courts in examining an administrative record developed after an adversarial proceeding—one with process at least of the sort that we today hold is constitutionally mandated in the citizen enemy-combatant setting. This standard therefore is ill suited to the situation in which a habeas petitioner has received no prior proceedings before any tribunal and had no prior opportunity to rebut the Executive's factual assertions before a neutral decisionmaker.

Today we are faced only with such a case. Aside from unspecified "screening" processes, and military interrogations in which the Government suggests Hamdi could have contested his classification, Hamdi has received no process. An interrogation by one's captor, however effective an intelligence-gathering tool, hardly constitutes a constitutionally adequate factfinding before a neutral decisionmaker. Compare Brief for Respondents 42-43 (discussing the "secure interrogation environment," and noting that military interrogations require a controlled "interrogation dynamic" and "a relationship of trust and dependency" and are "a critical source" of "timely and effective intelligence") with *Concrete Pipe* [and Products of California, Inc. v. Construction Laborers Pension Trust], 508 U.S. 602, 617-618 (1993) ("one is entitled as a matter of due process of law to an adjudicator who is not in a situation which would offer a possible temptation to the average man as a judge... which might lead him not to hold the balance nice, clear and true" (internal quotation marks omitted)). That even purportedly fair adjudicators "are disqualified by their interest in the controversy to be decided is, of course, the general rule." *Tumey v. Ohio*, 273 U.S. 510, 522 (1927). Plainly, the "process" Hamdi has received is not that to which he is entitled under the Due Process Clause.

There remains the possibility that the standards we have articulated could be met by an appropriately authorized and properly constituted military tribunal. Indeed, it is notable that military regulations already provide for such process in related instances, dictating that tribunals be made available to determine the status of enemy detainees who assert prisoner-of-war status under the Geneva Convention. See Enemy Prisoners of War, Retained Personnel, Civilian Internees and Other Detainees, Army Regulation 190-8, §1-6 (1997). In the absence of such process, however, a court that receives a petition for a writ of habeas corpus from an alleged enemy combatant must itself ensure that the minimum requirements of due process are achieved.... As we have discussed, a habeas court in a case such as this may accept affidavit evidence like that contained in the Mobbs Declaration, so long as it also permits the alleged combatant to present his own factual case to rebut the Government's return. We anticipate that a District Court would proceed with the caution that we have indicated is necessary in this setting, engaging in a factfinding process that is both prudent and incremental. We have no reason to doubt that courts faced with these sensitive matters will pay proper heed both to the matters of national security that might arise in an individual case and to the constitutional limitations safeguarding essential liberties that remain vibrant even in times of security concerns.

IV

Hamdi asks us to hold that the Fourth Circuit also erred by denying him immediate access to counsel upon his detention and by disposing of the case without permitting him to meet with an attorney. Since our grant of certiorari in this case, Hamdi has been appointed counsel, with whom he has met for consultation purposes on several occasions, and with whom he is now being granted unmonitored meetings. He unquestionably has the right to access to counsel in connection with the proceedings on remand. No further consideration of this issue is necessary at this stage of the case....

The judgment of the United States Court of Appeals for the Fourth Circuit is vacated, and the case is remanded for further proceedings.

It is so ordered.

Justice SOUTER, with whom Justice GINSBURG joins, concurring in part, dissenting in part, and concurring in the judgment.... The plurality rejects [the government's "some evidence"] limit on the exercise of habeas jurisdiction and so far I agree with its opinion. The plurality does, however, accept the Government's position that if Hamdi's designation as an enemy combatant is correct, his detention (at least as to some period) is authorized by an Act of Congress as required by §4001(a), that is, by the Authorization for Use of Military Force, 115 Stat. 224 (hereinafter Force Resolution). Here, I disagree and respectfully dissent....

II

The threshold issue is how broadly or narrowly to read the Non-Detention Act, the tone of which is severe: "No citizen shall be imprisoned or otherwise detained by the United States except pursuant to an Act of Congress."... For a number of reasons, the prohibition within §4001(a) has to be read broadly to accord the statute a long reach and to impose a burden of justification on the Government.

First, the circumstances in which the Act was adopted point the way to this interpretation. The provision superseded a cold-war statute, the Emergency Detention Act of 1950, which had authorized the Attorney General, in time of emergency, to detain anyone reasonably thought likely to engage in espionage or sabotage. That statute was repealed in 1971 out of fear that it could authorize a repetition of the World War II internment of citizens of Japanese ancestry; Congress meant to preclude another episode like the one described in *Korematsu v. United States*, 323 U.S. 214 (1944)....

C. Detention of U.S. Citizens as Enemy Combatants After 9/11

...To appreciate what is most significant, one must only recall that the internments of the 1940's were accomplished by Executive action. Although an Act of Congress ratified and confirmed an Executive order authorizing the military to exclude individuals from defined areas and to accommodate those it might remove, see *Ex parte Endo,* 323 U.S. 283, 285-288 (1944), the statute said nothing whatever about the detention of those who might be removed; internment camps were creatures of the Executive, and confinement in them rested on assertion of Executive authority. When, therefore, Congress repealed the 1950 Act and adopted §4001(a) for the purpose of avoiding another *Korematsu,* it intended to preclude reliance on vague congressional authority (for example, providing "accommodations" for those subject to removal) as authority for detention or imprisonment at the discretion of the Executive (maintaining detention camps of American citizens, for example). In requiring that any Executive detention be "pursuant to an Act of Congress," then, Congress necessarily meant to require a congressional enactment that clearly authorized detention or imprisonment.

Second, when Congress passed §4001(a) it was acting in light of an interpretive regime that subjected enactments limiting liberty in wartime to the requirement of a clear statement and it presumably intended §4001(a) to be read accordingly. This need for clarity was unmistakably expressed in *Ex parte Endo, supra,* decided the same day as *Korematsu....* The petitioner was held entitled to habeas relief in an opinion that set out this principle for scrutinizing wartime statutes in derogation of customary liberty:

> "In interpreting a wartime measure we must assume that [its] purpose was to allow for the greatest possible accommodation between...liberties and the exigencies of war. We must assume, when asked to find implied powers in a grant of legislative or executive authority, that the law makers intended to place no greater restraint on the citizen than was clearly and unmistakably indicated by the language they used." *Id.,* at 300.

Congress's understanding of the need for clear authority before citizens are kept detained is itself therefore clear, and §4001(a) must be read to have teeth in its demand for congressional authorization.

Finally, even if history had spared us the cautionary example of the internments in World War II, even if there had been no *Korematsu,* and *Endo* had set out no principle of statutory interpretation, there would be a compelling reason to read §4001(a) to demand manifest authority to detain before detention is authorized. The defining character of American constitutional government is its constant tension between security and liberty, serving both by partial helpings of each. In a government of separated powers, deciding finally on what is a reasonable degree of guaranteed liberty whether in peace or war (or some condition in between) is not well entrusted to the Executive Branch of Government, whose particular responsibility is to maintain security. For reasons of inescapable human nature, the branch of the Government asked to counter a serious threat is not the branch on which to rest the Nation's entire reliance in striking the balance between the will to win and the cost in liberty on the way to victory; the responsibility for security will naturally amplify the claim that security legitimately raises. A reasonable balance is more likely to be reached on the judgment of a different branch, just as Madison said in remarking that "the constant aim is to divide and arrange the several offices in such a manner as that each may be a check on the other—that the private interest of every individual may be a sentinel over the public rights." The Federalist No. 51, p. 349 (J. Cooke ed. 1961). Hence the need for an assessment by Congress before citizens are subject to lockup, and likewise the need for a clearly expressed congressional resolution of the competing claims.

III

Under this principle of reading §4001(a) robustly to require a clear statement of authorization to detain, none of the Government's arguments suffices to justify Hamdi's detention.

A

First, there is the argument that §4001(a) does not even apply to wartime military detentions, a position resting on the placement of §4001(a) in Title 18 of the United States Code, the gathering of federal criminal law.... [The] legislative history indicates that Congress was aware that §4001(a) would limit the Executive's power to detain citizens in wartime to protect national security, and it is fair to say that the prohibition was thus intended to extend not only to the exercise of power to vindicate the interests underlying domestic criminal law, but to statutorily unauthorized detention by the Executive for reasons of security in wartime, just as Hamdi claims.[1]

B

Next, there is the Government's claim, accepted by the Court, that the terms of the Force Resolution are adequate to authorize detention of an enemy combatant under the circumstances described,[2] a claim the Government fails to support sufficiently to satisfy §4001(a) as read to require a clear statement of authority to detain. Since the Force Resolution was adopted one week after the attacks of September 11, 2001, it naturally speaks with some generality, but its focus is clear, and that is on the use of military power. It is fairly read to

---

1. Nor is it possible to distinguish between civilian and military authority to detain based on the congressional object of avoiding another *Korematsu v. United States,* 323 U.S. 214 (1944). Although a civilian agency authorized by Executive order ran the detention camps, the relocation and detention of American citizens was ordered by the military under authority of the President as Commander in Chief. See *Ex parte Endo,* 323 U.S. 283, 285-288 (1944). The World War II internment was thus ordered under the same Presidential power invoked here and the intent to bar a repetition goes to the action taken and authority claimed here.

2. ... [T]he Government argues that a required Act of Congress is to be found in a statutory authorization to spend money appropriated for the care of prisoners of war and of other, similar prisoners, 10 U.S.C. §956(5). It is enough to say that this statute is an authorization to spend money if there are prisoners, not an authorization to imprison anyone to provide the occasion for spending money.

C. Detention of U.S. Citizens as Enemy Combatants After 9/11

authorize the use of armies and weapons, whether against other armies or individual terrorists. But, like the statute discussed in *Endo*, it never so much as uses the word detention, and there is no reason to think Congress might have perceived any need to augment Executive power to deal with dangerous citizens within the United States, given the well-stocked statutory arsenal of defined criminal offenses covering the gamut of actions that a citizen sympathetic to terrorists might commit. See, *e.g.*, 18 U.S.C. §2339A (material support for various terrorist acts); §2339B (material support to a foreign terrorist organization); §2332a (use of a weapon of mass destruction, including conspiracy and attempt); §2332b(a)(1) (acts of terrorism "transcending national boundaries," including threats, conspiracy, and attempt); 18 U.S.C.A. §2339C (financing of certain terrorist acts); see also 18 U.S.C. §3142(e) (pretrial detention).

C

Even so, there is one argument for treating the Force Resolution as sufficiently clear to authorize detention of a citizen consistently with §4001(a). Assuming the argument to be sound, however, the Government is in no position to claim its advantage.

Because the Force Resolution authorizes the use of military force in acts of war by the United States, the argument goes, it is reasonably clear that the military and its Commander in Chief are authorized to deal with enemy belligerents according to the treaties and customs known collectively as the laws of war. Accordingly, the United States may detain captured enemies, and *Ex parte Quirin*, 317 U.S. 1 (1942), may perhaps be claimed for the proposition that the American citizenship of such a captive does not as such limit the Government's power to deal with him under the usages of war. Thus, the Government here repeatedly argues that Hamdi's detention amounts to nothing more than customary detention of a captive taken on the field of battle: if the usages of war are fairly authorized by the Force Resolution, Hamdi's detention is authorized for purposes of §4001(a)....

By holding him incommunicado, however, the Government obviously has not been treating him as a prisoner of war, and in fact the Government claims that no Taliban detainee is entitled to prisoner of war status. This treatment appears to be a violation of the Geneva Convention provision that even in cases of doubt, captives are entitled to be treated as prisoners of war "until such time as their status has been determined by a competent tribunal." Art. 5, 6 U.S.T., at 3324....

Whether, or to what degree, the Government is in fact violating the Geneva Convention and is thus acting outside the customary usages of war are not matters I can resolve at this point. What I can say, though, is that the Government has not made out its claim that in detaining Hamdi in the manner described, it is acting in accord with the laws of war authorized to be applied against citizens by the Force Resolution. I conclude accordingly that the Government has failed to support the position that the Force Resolution authorizes the described detention of Hamdi for purposes of §4001(a).

It is worth adding a further reason for requiring the Government to bear the burden of clearly justifying its claim to be exercising recognized war powers before declaring §4001(a) satisfied. Thirty-eight days after adopting the Force Resolution, Congress passed the statute entitled Uniting and Strengthening America by Providing Appropriate Tools Required to Intercept and Obstruct Terrorism Act of 2001 (USA PATRIOT ACT), 115 Stat. 272; that Act authorized the detention of alien terrorists for no more than seven days in the absence of criminal charges or deportation proceedings, 8 U.S.C. §1226a(a)(5) (2000 ed., Supp. I). It is very difficult to believe that the same Congress that carefully circumscribed Executive power over alien terrorists on home soil would not have meant to require the Government to justify clearly its detention of an American citizen held on home soil incommunicado.

D

Since the Government has given no reason either to deflect the application of §4001(a) or to hold it to be satisfied, I need to go no further; the Government hints of a constitutional challenge to the statute, but it presents none here. I will, however, stray across the line between statutory and constitutional territory just far enough to note the weakness of the Government's mixed claim of inherent, extrastatutory authority under a combination of Article II of the Constitution and the usages of war. It is in fact in this connection that the Government developed its argument that the exercise of war powers justifies the detention, and what I have just said about its inadequacy applies here as well. Beyond that, it is instructive to recall Justice Jackson's observation that the President is not Commander in Chief of the country, only of the military. *Youngstown Sheet & Tube Co. v. Sawyer,* 343 U.S. 579, 643-644 (1952) (concurring opinion); see also *id.,* at 637-638 (Presidential authority is "at its lowest ebb" where the President acts contrary to congressional will).

There may be room for one qualification to Justice Jackson's statement, however: in a moment of genuine emergency, when the Government must act with no time for deliberation, the Executive may be able to detain a citizen if there is reason to fear he is an imminent threat to the safety of the Nation and its people (though I doubt there is any want of statutory authority). This case, however, does not present that question, because an emergency power of necessity must at least be limited by the emergency; Hamdi has been locked up for over two years. Cf. *Ex parte Milligan,* 4 Wall. 2, 127 (1866) (martial law justified only by "actual and present" necessity as in a genuine invasion that closes civilian courts)....

IV ...

It should go without saying that in joining with the plurality to produce a judgment, I do not adopt the plurality's resolution of constitutional issues that I would not reach. It is not that I could disagree with the plurality's determinations (given the plurality's view of the Force Resolution) that someone in Hamdi's position is entitled at a minimum to notice of the Government's claimed factual basis for holding him, and to a fair chance to rebut it before a neutral decision maker; nor, of course, could I disagree with the plurality's

C. Detention of U.S. Citizens as Enemy Combatants After 9/11

affirmation of Hamdi's right to counsel. On the other hand, I do not mean to imply agreement that the Government could claim an evidentiary presumption casting the burden of rebuttal on Hamdi, or that an opportunity to litigate before a military tribunal might obviate or truncate enquiry by a court on habeas.

Subject to these qualifications, I join with the plurality in a judgment of the Court vacating the Fourth Circuit's judgment and remanding the case.

Justice SCALIA, with whom Justice STEVENS joins, dissenting.... Where the Government accuses a citizen of waging war against it, our constitutional tradition has been to prosecute him in federal court for treason or some other crime. Where the exigencies of war prevent that, the Constitution's Suspension Clause, Art. I, §9, cl. 2, allows Congress to relax the usual protections temporarily. Absent suspension, however, the Executive's assertion of military exigency has not been thought sufficient to permit detention without charge. No one contends that the congressional Authorization for Use of Military Force, on which the Government relies to justify its actions here, is an implementation of the Suspension Clause. Accordingly, I would reverse the decision below.

I

The very core of liberty secured by our Anglo-Saxon system of separated powers has been freedom from indefinite imprisonment at the will of the Executive. Blackstone stated this principle clearly:

> "Of great importance to the public is the preservation of this personal liberty: for if once it were left in the power of any, the highest, magistrate to imprison arbitrarily whomever he or his officers thought proper... there would soon be an end of all other rights and immunities.... To bereave a man of life, or by violence to confiscate his estate, without accusation or trial, would be so gross and notorious an act of despotism, as must at once convey the alarm of tyranny throughout the whole kingdom. But confinement of the person, by secretly hurrying him to gaol, where his sufferings are unknown or forgotten; is a less public, a less striking, and therefore a more dangerous engine of arbitrary government....
>
> "To make imprisonment lawful, it must either be, by process from the courts of judicature, or by warrant from some legal officer, having authority to commit to prison; which warrant must be in writing, under the hand and seal of the magistrate, and express the causes of the commitment, in order to be examined into (if necessary) upon a *habeas corpus*. If there be no cause expressed, the gaoler is not bound to detain the prisoner. For the law judges in this respect,... that it is unreasonable to send a prisoner, and not to signify withal the crimes alleged against him." 1 W. Blackstone, Commentaries on the Laws of England 132-133 (1765) (hereinafter Blackstone).

These words were well known to the Founders. Hamilton quoted from this very passage in The Federalist No. 84, p. 444 (G. Carey & J. McClellan eds. 2001). The two ideas central to Blackstone's understanding—due process as the right secured, and habeas corpus as the instrument by which due process could be insisted upon by a citizen illegally imprisoned—found expression in the Constitution's Due Process and Suspension Clauses. See Amdt. 5; Art. I, §9, cl. 2.

The gist of the Due Process Clause, as understood at the founding and since, was to force the Government to follow those common-law procedures traditionally deemed necessary before depriving a person of life, liberty, or property. When a citizen was deprived of liberty because of alleged criminal conduct, those procedures typically required committal by a magistrate followed by indictment and trial....

II

The allegations here, of course, are no ordinary accusations of criminal activity. Yaser Esam Hamdi has been imprisoned because the Government believes he participated in the waging of war against the United States. The relevant question, then, is whether there is a different, special procedure for imprisonment of a citizen accused of wrongdoing *by aiding the enemy in wartime.*

A

Justice O'CONNOR writing for a plurality of this Court, asserts that captured enemy combatants (other than those suspected of war crimes) have traditionally been detained until the cessation of hostilities and then released. That is probably an accurate description of wartime practice with respect to enemy *aliens.* The tradition with respect to American citizens, however, has been quite different. Citizens aiding the enemy have been treated as traitors subject to the criminal process....

The modern treason statute is 18 U.S.C. §2381; it basically tracks the language of the constitutional provision. Other provisions of Title 18 criminalize various acts of warmaking and adherence to the enemy. The only citizen other than Hamdi known to be imprisoned in connection with military hostilities in Afghanistan against the United States *was* subjected to criminal process and convicted upon a guilty plea. See *United States v. Lindh,* 212 F. Supp. 2d 541 (E.D. Va. 2002) (denying motions for dismissal).

B

There are times when military exigency renders resort to the traditional criminal process impracticable. English law accommodated such exigencies by allowing legislative suspension of the writ of habeas corpus for brief periods. Blackstone explained:

> "And yet sometimes, when the state is in real danger, even this [*i.e.,* executive detention] may be a necessary measure. But the happiness of our constitution is, that it is not left to the executive power to determine when the danger of the state is so great, as to render this measure expedient. For the parliament only, or legislative power, whenever it seems proper, can authorize the crown, by suspending the *habeas corpus* act for a short and limited time, to imprison suspected persons without giving any reason for so doing.... In like manner this experiment ought

C. Detention of U.S. Citizens as Enemy Combatants After 9/11

only to be tried in case of extreme emergency; and in these the nation parts with it[s] liberty for a while, in order to preserve it for ever." 1 Blackstone 132....

Our Federal Constitution contains a provision explicitly permitting suspension, but limiting the situations in which it may be invoked: "The privilege of the Writ of Habeas Corpus shall not be suspended, unless when in Cases of Rebellion or Invasion the public Safety may require it." Art. I, §9, cl. 2. Although this provision does not state that suspension must be effected by, or authorized by, a legislative act, it has been so understood, consistent with English practice and the Clause's placement in Article I.

The Suspension Clause was by design a safety valve, the Constitution's only "express provision for exercise of extraordinary authority because of a crisis," *Youngstown Sheet & Tube Co. v. Sawyer*, 343 U.S. 579, 650 (1952) (Jackson, J., concurring)....

III...

Writings from the founding generation also suggest that, without exception, the only constitutional alternatives are to charge the crime or suspend the writ. In 1788, Thomas Jefferson wrote to James Madison questioning the need for a Suspension Clause in cases of rebellion in the proposed Constitution. His letter illustrates the constraints under which the Founders understood themselves to operate:

> "Why suspend the Hab. corp. in insurrections and rebellions? The parties who may be arrested may be charged instantly with a well defined crime. Of course the judge will remand them. If the publick safety requires that the government should have a man imprisoned on less probable testimony in those than in other emergencies; let him be taken and tried, retaken and retried, while the necessity continues, only giving him redress against the government for damages." 13 Papers of Thomas Jefferson 442 (July 31, 1788) (J. Boyd ed. 1956)....

Further evidence comes from this Court's decision in *Ex parte Milligan*, [71 U.S. (4 Wall.) 2] (1866). There, the Court issued the writ to an American citizen who had been tried by military commission for offenses that included conspiring to overthrow the Government, seize munitions, and liberate prisoners of war. The Court rejected in no uncertain terms the Government's assertion that military jurisdiction was proper "under the 'laws and usages of war,'" *id.*, at 121:

> "It can serve no useful purpose to inquire what those laws and usages are, whence they originated, where found, and on whom they operate; they can never be applied to citizens in states which have upheld the authority of the government, and where the courts are open and their process unobstructed." *Ibid.*[1]

---

1. As I shall discuss presently, the Court purported to limit this language in *Ex parte Quirin*, 317 U.S. 1, 45 (1942). Whatever *Quirin*'s effect on *Milligan*'s precedential value, however, it cannot undermine its value as an indicator of original meaning. Cf. *Reid v. Covert*, 354 U.S. 1, 30 (1957) (plurality opinion) (*Milligan* remains "one of the great landmarks in this Court's history").

Milligan is not exactly this case, of course, since the petitioner was threatened with death, not merely imprisonment. But the reasoning and conclusion of *Milligan* logically cover the present case. The Government justifies imprisonment of Hamdi on principles of the law of war and admits that, absent the war, it would have no such authority. But if the law of war cannot be applied to citizens where courts are open, then Hamdi's imprisonment without criminal trial is no less unlawful than Milligan's trial by military tribunal.

Milligan responded to the argument, repeated by the Government in this case, that it is dangerous to leave suspected traitors at large in time of war:

> "If it was dangerous, in the distracted condition of affairs, to leave Milligan unrestrained of his liberty, because he 'conspired against the government, afforded aid and comfort to rebels, and incited the people to insurrection,' the *law* said arrest him, confine him closely, render him powerless to do further mischief; and then present his case to the grand jury of the district, with proofs of his guilt, and, if indicted, try him according to the course of the common law. If this had been done, the Constitution would have been vindicated, the law of 1863 enforced, and the securities for personal liberty preserved and defended." *Id.,* at 122.

Thus, criminal process was viewed as the primary means—and the only means absent congressional action suspending the writ—not only to punish traitors, but to incapacitate them.

The proposition that the Executive lacks indefinite wartime detention authority over citizens is consistent with the Founders' general mistrust of military power permanently at the Executive's disposal. In the Founders' view, the "blessings of liberty" were threatened by "those military establishments which must gradually poison its very fountain." The Federalist No. 45, p. 238 (J. Madison). No fewer than 10 issues of the Federalist were devoted in whole or part to allaying fears of oppression from the proposed Constitution's authorization of standing armies in peacetime. Many safeguards in the Constitution reflect these concerns. Congress's authority "[t]o raise and support Armies" was hedged with the proviso that "no Appropriation of Money to that Use shall be for a longer Term than two Years." U.S. Const., Art. 1, §8, cl. 12. Except for the actual command of military forces, all authorization for their maintenance and all explicit authorization for their use is placed in the control of Congress under Article I, rather than the President under Article II. . . . A view of the Constitution that gives the Executive authority to use military force rather than the force of law against citizens on American soil flies in the face of the mistrust that engendered these provisions.

IV

The Government argues that our more recent jurisprudence ratifies its indefinite imprisonment of a citizen within the territorial jurisdiction of federal courts. It places primary reliance upon *Ex parte Quirin,* 317 U.S. 1 (1942), a World War II case upholding the trial by military commission of eight German saboteurs, one of whom, Hans Haupt, was a U.S. citizen. The case was not this Court's finest hour. The Court upheld the commission and denied relief in a brief *per curiam* issued the day after oral argument concluded; a week later the Government carried out the commission's death sentence upon six saboteurs,

C. Detention of U.S. Citizens as Enemy Combatants After 9/11

including Haupt. The Court eventually explained its reasoning in a written opinion issued several months later.

Only three paragraphs of the Court's lengthy opinion dealt with the particular circumstances of Haupt's case. The Government argued that Haupt, like the other petitioners, could be tried by military commission under the laws of war. In agreeing with that contention, *Quirin* purported to interpret the language of *Milligan* quoted above (the law of war "can never be applied to citizens in states which have upheld the authority of the government, and where the courts are open and their process unobstructed") in the following manner:

> "Elsewhere in its opinion... the Court was at pains to point out that Milligan, a citizen twenty years resident in Indiana, who had never been a resident of any of the states in rebellion, was not an enemy belligerent either entitled to the status of a prisoner of war or subject to the penalties imposed upon unlawful belligerents. We construe the Court's statement as to the inapplicability of the law of war to Milligan's case as having particular reference to the facts before it. From them the Court concluded that Milligan, not being a part of or associated with the armed forces of the enemy, was a nonbelligerent, not subject to the law of war...." 317 U.S., at 45.

In my view this seeks to revise *Milligan* rather than describe it. *Milligan* had involved (among other issues) two separate questions: (1) whether the military trial of Milligan was justified by the laws of war, and if not (2) whether the President's suspension of the writ, pursuant to congressional authorization, prevented the issuance of habeas corpus. The Court's categorical language about the law of war's inapplicability to citizens where the courts are open (with no exception mentioned for citizens who were prisoners of war) was contained in its discussion of the first point. See 4 Wall., at 121. The factors pertaining to whether Milligan could reasonably be considered a belligerent and prisoner of war, while mentioned earlier in the opinion, were made relevant and brought to bear in the Court's later discussion of whether Milligan came within the statutory provision that effectively made an exception to Congress's authorized suspension of the writ for (as the Court described it) "all parties, not prisoners of war, resident in their respective jurisdictions,... who were citizens of states in which the administration of the laws in the Federal tribunals was unimpaired," *id.* at 116. *Milligan* thus understood was in accord with the traditional law of habeas corpus I have described: Though treason often occurred in wartime, there was, absent provision for special treatment in a congressional suspension of the writ, no exception to the right to trial by jury for citizens who could be called "belligerents" or "prisoners of war."

But even if *Quirin* gave a correct description of *Milligan,* or made an irrevocable revision of it, *Quirin* would still not justify denial of the writ here. In *Quirin* it was uncontested that the petitioners were members of enemy forces. They were "*admitted* enemy invaders," 317 U.S., at 47 (emphasis added), and it was "undisputed" that they had landed in the United States in service of German forces, *id.,* at 20. The specific holding of the Court was only that, "upon the *conceded* facts," the petitioners were "plainly within [the] boundaries" of military jurisdiction, *id.,* at 46 (emphasis added). But where those jurisdictional facts are *not* conceded — where the petitioner insists that he is *not* a belligerent — *Quirin* left the pre-existing law in place: Absent suspension of the writ, a citizen held where the courts are open is entitled either to criminal trial or to a judicial decree requiring his release.

V

It follows from what I have said that Hamdi is entitled to a habeas decree requiring his release unless (1) criminal proceedings are promptly brought, or (2) Congress has suspended the writ of habeas corpus. A suspension of the writ could, of course, lay down conditions for continued detention, similar to those that today's opinion prescribes under the Due Process Clause. But there is a world of difference between the people's representatives' determining the need for that suspension (and prescribing the conditions for it), and this Court's doing so.

The plurality finds justification for Hamdi's imprisonment in the Authorization for Use of Military Force, 115 Stat. 224.... This is not remotely a congressional suspension of the writ, and no one claims that it is. Contrary to the plurality's view, I do not think this statute even authorizes detention of a citizen with the clarity necessary to satisfy the interpretive canon that statutes should be construed so as to avoid grave constitutional concerns; with the clarity necessary to comport with cases such as *Ex parte Endo,* 323 U.S. 283, 300 (1944), and *Duncan v. Kahanamoku,* 327 U.S. 304, 314-316, 324 (1946); or with the clarity necessary to overcome the statutory prescription that "[n]o citizen shall be imprisoned or otherwise detained by the United States except pursuant to an Act of Congress." 18 U.S.C. §4001(a).[5] But even if it did, I would not permit it to overcome Hamdi's entitlement to habeas corpus relief. The Suspension Clause of the Constitution, which carefully circumscribes the conditions under which the writ can be withheld, would be a sham if it could be evaded by congressional prescription of requirements *other than the common-law requirement of committal for criminal prosecution* that render the writ, though available, unavailing. If the Suspension Clause does not guarantee the citizen that he will either be tried or released, unless the conditions for suspending the writ exist and the grave action of suspending the writ has been taken; if it merely guarantees the citizen that he will not be detained unless Congress by ordinary legislation says he can be detained; it guarantees him very little indeed.

It should not be thought, however, that the plurality's evisceration of the Suspension Clause augments, principally, the power of Congress. As usual, the major effect of its constitutional improvisation is to increase the power of the Court. Having found a congressional authorization for detention of citizens where none clearly exists; and having discarded the categorical procedural protection of the Suspension Clause; the plurality then proceeds, under the guise of the Due Process Clause, to prescribe what procedural protections *it* thinks appropriate....

---

5. The plurality rejects any need for "specific language of detention" on the ground that detention of alleged combatants is a "fundamental incident of waging war." Its authorities do not support that holding in the context of the present case. Some are irrelevant because they do not address the detention of *American citizens.* The plurality's assertion that detentions of citizen and alien combatants are equally authorized has no basis in law or common sense. Citizens and noncitizens, even if equally dangerous, are not similarly situated. See, *e.g., Milligan, supra; Johnson v. Eisentrager,* 339 U.S. 763 (1950); Rev. Stat. 4067, 50 U.S.C. §21 (Alien Enemy Act). That captivity may be consistent with the principles of international law does not prove that it also complies with the restrictions that the Constitution places on the American Government's treatment of its own citizens....

C. Detention of U.S. Citizens as Enemy Combatants After 9/11

... This judicial remediation of executive default is unheard of. The role of habeas corpus is to determine the legality of executive detention, not to supply the omitted process necessary to make it legal....

There is a certain harmony of approach in the plurality's making up for Congress's failure to invoke the Suspension Clause and its making up for the Executive's failure to apply what it says are needed procedures—an approach that reflects what might be called a Mr. Fix-it Mentality. The plurality seems to view it as its mission to Make Everything Come Out Right, rather than merely to decree the consequences, as far as individual rights are concerned, of the other two branches' actions and omissions. Has the Legislature failed to suspend the writ in the current dire emergency? Well, we will remedy that failure by prescribing the reasonable conditions that a suspension should have included. And has the Executive failed to live up to those reasonable conditions? Well, we will ourselves make that failure good, so that this dangerous fellow (if he is dangerous) need not be set free. The problem with this approach is not only that it steps out of the courts' modest and limited role in a democratic society; but that by repeatedly doing what it thinks the political branches ought to do it encourages their lassitude and saps the vitality of government by the people.

VI

Several limitations give my views in this matter a relatively narrow compass. They apply only to citizens, accused of being enemy combatants, who are detained within the territorial jurisdiction of a federal court. This is not likely to be a numerous group; currently we know of only two, Hamdi and Jose Padilla. Where the citizen is captured outside and held outside the United States, the constitutional requirements may be different. Cf. *Johnson v. Eisentrager,* 339 U.S. 763, 769-771 (1950); *Reid v. Covert,* 354 U.S. 1, 74-75 (1957) (Harlan, J., concurring in result); *Rasul v. Bush,* [542 U.S. 466 (2004)] (Scalia, J., dissenting). Moreover, even within the United States, the accused citizen-enemy combatant may lawfully be detained once prosecution is in progress or in contemplation....

... If the situation demands it, the Executive can ask Congress to authorize suspension of the writ—which can be made subject to whatever conditions Congress deems appropriate, including even the procedural novelties invented by the plurality today. To be sure, suspension is limited by the Constitution to cases of rebellion or invasion. But whether the attacks of September 11, 2001, constitute an "invasion," and whether those attacks still justify suspension several years later, are questions for Congress rather than this Court....

Justice THOMAS, dissenting. The Executive Branch, acting pursuant to the powers vested in the President by the Constitution and with explicit congressional approval, has determined that Yaser Hamdi is an enemy combatant and should be detained. This detention falls squarely within the Federal Government's war powers, and we lack the expertise and capacity to second-guess that decision. As such, petitioners' habeas challenge should fail, and there is no reason to remand the case.... I do not think that the Federal Government's war powers can be balanced away by this Court. Arguably, Congress could provide for additional procedural protections, but until it does, we have no right to insist upon them. But even if I were to agree with the general approach the plurality takes, I could not accept the particulars. The plurality utterly fails to account for the Government's compelling interests and for our own institutional inability to weigh competing concerns correctly. I respectfully dissent....

Order by President George W. Bush to the Secretary of Defense

June 9, 2002
Appendix A, Padilla v. Rumsfeld, 352 F.2d 695 (2d Cir. 2003)

TO THE SECRETARY OF DEFENSE:

Based on the information available to me from all sources,
REDACTED
In accordance with the Constitution and consistent with the laws of the United States, including the Authorization for Use of Military Force Joint Resolution (Public Law 107-40);

I, GEORGE W. BUSH, as President of the United States and Commander in Chief of the U.S. armed forces, hereby DETERMINE for the United States of America that:

(1) Jose Padilla, who is under the control of the Department of Justice and who is a U.S. citizen, is, and at the time he entered the United States in May 2002 was, an enemy combatant;

(2) Mr. Padilla is closely associated with al Qaeda, an international terrorist organization with which the United States is at war;

(3) Mr. Padilla engaged in conduct that constituted hostile and war-like acts, including conduct in preparation for acts of international terrorism that had the aim to cause injury to or adverse effects on the United States;

(4) Mr. Padilla possesses intelligence, including intelligence about personnel and activities of al Qaeda, that, if communicated to the U.S., would aid U.S. efforts to prevent attacks by al Qaeda on the United States or its armed forces, other governmental personnel, or citizens;

(5) Mr. Padilla represents a continuing, present and grave danger to the national security of the United States, and detention of Mr. Padilla is necessary to prevent him from aiding al Qaeda in its efforts to attack the United States or its armed forces, other governmental personnel, or citizens;

(6) it is in the interest of the United States that the Secretary of Defense detain Mr. Padilla as an enemy combatant; and

(7) it is REDACTED consistent with U.S. law and the laws of war for the Secretary of Defense to detain Mr. Padilla as an enemy combatant.

Accordingly, you are directed to receive Mr. Padilla from the Department of Justice and to detain him as an enemy combatant.

Padilla challenged his detention by filing a habeas petition in the Southern District of New York. The district court held that the government was authorized to detain him if it could adduce "some evidence" that he was an enemy combatant, but that he was entitled to an evidentiary hearing in court on that question and to have access to counsel in order to participate meaningfully in such hearing. Padilla *ex rel.* Newman v. Bush, 233 Fed. Supp. 2d 564 (S.D.N.Y. 2002).

In a decision reached before the Supreme Court decided *Hamdi*, the Second Circuit Court of Appeals reversed on the merits. Padilla v. Rumsfeld, 352 F.3d 695 (2d Cir. 2003), *rev'd and remanded for lack of jurisdiction*, 542 U.S. 426 (2004). It found that the President "lacks inherent constitutional authority as Commander-in-Chief to detain American citizens on American soil outside a zone of combat." 352 F.3d at 712. It reasoned that the Constitution's explicit grant of powers to Congress by the Offenses Clause, U.S. Const. art. II, §8, cl. 10, the Suspension Clause (which it found to lodge the suspension power only in Congress), and the Third Amendment is "a powerful indication that, absent express congressional authorization, the President's Commander-in-Chief powers do not support Padilla's confinement." *Id.* at 715. *Quirin* was not to the contrary, it explained, because there Congress had authorized the military detention and trial of the saboteurs. Finally, the Court found that the 2001 AUMF did not meet the clear statement standard of the Non-Detention Act, 18 U.S.C. §4001(a), to authorize "the detention of an American citizen already held in a federal correctional institution and not 'arrayed against our troops' in the field of battle." *Id.* at 723. Is this reasoning invalidated by the subsequent decision in *Hamdi*?

The Supreme Court reversed on jurisdictional grounds by a 5-4 vote, ruling that Padilla had chosen the wrong court for filing his habeas petition. The following is an excerpt of the dissenting opinion from that decision.

Rumsfeld v. Padilla
United States Supreme Court 2004
542 U.S. 426

Justice STEVENS, with whom Justice SOUTER, Justice GINSBURG, and Justice BREYER join, dissenting.... In sum, respondent properly filed his petition against Secretary Rumsfeld in the Southern District of New York.

III

Whether respondent is entitled to immediate release is a question that reasonable jurists may answer in different ways.[8] There is, however, only one possible answer to the question whether he is entitled to a hearing on the justification for his detention.[9]

---

8. Consistent with the judgment of the Court of Appeals, I believe that the Non-Detention Act, 18 U.S.C. §4001(a), prohibits—and the Authorization for Use of Military Force Joint Resolution, 115 Stat. 224, adopted on September 18, 2001, does not authorize—the protracted, incommunicado detention of American citizens arrested in the United States.

9. Respondent's custodian has been remarkably candid about the Government's motive in detaining respondent: "'[O]ur interest really in his case is not law enforcement, it is not punishment because he was a terrorist or working with the terrorists. Our interest at the moment is to try

At stake in this case is nothing less than the essence of a free society. Even more important than the method of selecting the people's rulers and their successors is the character of the constraints imposed on the Executive by the rule of law. Unconstrained Executive detention for the purpose of investigating and preventing subversive activity is the hallmark of the Star Chamber. Access to counsel for the purpose of protecting the citizen from official mistakes and mistreatment is the hallmark of due process.

Executive detention of subversive citizens, like detention of enemy soldiers to keep them off the battlefield, may sometimes be justified to prevent persons from launching or becoming missiles of destruction. It may not, however, be justified by the naked interest in using unlawful procedures to extract information. Incommunicado detention for months on end is such a procedure. Whether the information so procured is more or less reliable than that acquired by more extreme forms of torture is of no consequence. For if this Nation is to remain true to the ideals symbolized by its flag, it must not wield the tools of tyrants even to resist an assault by the forces of tyranny.

I respectfully dissent.

Taking into account this dissent, as well as the lineup of the Justices in *Hamdi*, how many votes would you count for finding that the military detention of Padilla was unlawful? (Of course, the Court's composition has since changed.)

After the Supreme Court's decision, Padilla filed a new habeas petition in the proper federal court in South Carolina. The district court granted the petition, and the government appealed to the Fourth Circuit Court of Appeals, with the following result.

Padilla v. Hanft

United States Court of Appeals, Fourth Circuit, 2005
423 F.3d 386, *cert. denied*, 126 S. Ct. 1649 (2006)

LUTTIG, Circuit Judge.... The exceedingly important question before us is whether the President of the United States possesses the authority to detain militarily a citizen of this country who is closely associated with al Qaeda, an entity with which the United States is at war; who took up arms on behalf of that enemy and against our country in a foreign combat zone of that war; *and* who thereafter traveled to the United States for the avowed purpose of further prosecuting that war on American soil, against American citizens and targets.

We conclude that the President does possess such authority pursuant to the Authorization for Use of Military Force Joint Resolution enacted by Congress in the wake of the attacks on the United States of September 11, 2001. Accordingly, the judgment of the district court is reversed.

---

and find out everything he knows so that hopefully we can stop other terrorist acts.'" 233 F. Supp. 2d 564, 573-574 (S.D.N.Y. 2002) (quoting News Briefing, Dept. of Defense (June 12, 2002), 2002 WL 22026773).

C. Detention of U.S. Citizens as Enemy Combatants After 9/11

I.

Al Qaeda operatives recruited Jose Padilla, a United States citizen, to train for jihad in Afghanistan in February 2000, while Padilla was on a religious pilgrimage to Saudi Arabia.[1] Subsequently, Padilla met with al Qaeda operatives in Afghanistan, received explosives training in an al Qaeda-affiliated camp, and served as an armed guard at what he understood to be a Taliban outpost. When United States military operations began in Afghanistan, Padilla and other al Qaeda operatives moved from safehouse to safehouse to evade bombing or capture. Padilla was, on the facts with which we are presented, "armed and present in a combat zone during armed conflict between al Qaeda/Taliban forces and the armed forces of the United States."

Padilla eventually escaped to Pakistan, armed with an assault rifle. Once in Pakistan, Padilla met with Khalid Sheikh Mohammad, a senior al Qaeda operations planner, who directed Padilla to travel to the United States for the purpose of blowing up apartment buildings, in continued prosecution of al Qaeda's war of terror against the United States. After receiving further training, as well as cash, travel documents, and communication devices, Padilla flew to the United States in order to carry out his accepted assignment.

Upon arrival at Chicago's O'Hare International Airport on May 8, 2002, Padilla was detained by FBI agents, who interviewed and eventually arrested him pursuant to a material witness warrant issued by the district court for the Southern District of New York in conjunction with a grand jury investigation of the September 11 attacks. Padilla was transported to New York, where he was held at a civilian correctional facility until, on June 9, 2002, the President designated him an "enemy combatant" against the United States and directed the Secretary of Defense to take him into military custody. Since his delivery into the custody of military authorities, Padilla has been detained at a naval brig in South Carolina....

II.

A.

The Authorization for Use of Military Force Joint Resolution (AUMF), upon which the President explicitly relied in his order that Padilla be detained by the military and upon which the government chiefly relies in support of the President's authority to detain Padilla, was enacted by Congress in the immediate aftermath of the September 11, 2001, terrorist attacks on the United States. It provides as follows:

> [T]he President is authorized to use all necessary and appropriate force against those nations, organizations, or persons he determines planned, authorized, committed, or aided the terrorist attacks that occurred on September 11, 2001,

---

1. For purposes of Padilla's summary judgment motion, the parties have stipulated to the facts as set forth by the government. It is only on these facts that we consider whether the President has the authority to detain Padilla.

or harbored such organizations or persons, in order to prevent any future acts of international terrorism against the United States by such nations, organizations or persons.

Pub. L. No. 107-40, §2(a), 115 Stat. 224 (September 18, 2001)....

As the AUMF authorized Hamdi's detention by the President, so also does it authorize Padilla's detention. Under the facts as presented here, Padilla unquestionably qualifies as an "enemy combatant" as that term was defined for purposes of the controlling opinion in *Hamdi*. Indeed, under the definition of "enemy combatant" employed in *Hamdi*, we can discern no difference in principle between Hamdi and Padilla. Like Hamdi, Padilla associated with forces hostile to the United States in Afghanistan. And, like Hamdi, Padilla took up arms against United States forces in that country in the same way and to the same extent as did Hamdi. Because, like Hamdi, Padilla is an enemy combatant, and because his detention is no less necessary than was Hamdi's in order to prevent his return to the battlefield, the President is authorized by the AUMF to detain Padilla as a fundamental incident to the conduct of war.

Our conclusion that the AUMF as interpreted by the Supreme Court in *Hamdi* authorizes the President's detention of Padilla as an enemy combatant is reinforced by the Supreme Court's decision in *Ex parte Quirin*, 317 U.S. 1 (1942), on which the plurality in *Hamdi* itself heavily relied. In *Quirin*, the Court held that Congress had authorized the military trial of Haupt, a U.S. citizen who entered the country with orders from the Nazis to blow up domestic war facilities but was captured before he could execute those orders. The Court reasoned that Haupt's citizenship was no bar to his military trial as an unlawful enemy belligerent....

Like Haupt, Padilla associated with the military arm of the enemy, and with its aid, guidance, and direction entered this country bent on committing hostile acts on American soil. Padilla thus falls within *Quirin*'s definition of "enemy belligerent," as well as within the definition of the equivalent term accepted by the plurality in *Hamdi*. Compare *Quirin*, 317 U.S. at 37-38 (holding that "[c]itizens who associate themselves with the military arm of the enemy government, and with its aid, guidance and direction enter this country bent on hostile acts, are enemy belligerents within the meaning of . . . the law of war"), *with Hamdi*, 124 S. Ct. at 2639 (accepting for purposes of the case the government's definition of "enemy combatants" as those who were "'part of or supporting forces hostile to the United States or coalition partners' in Afghanistan and who 'engaged in an armed conflict against the United States' there").

We understand the plurality's *reasoning* in *Hamdi* to be that the AUMF authorizes the President to detain all those who qualify as "enemy combatants" within the meaning of the laws of war, such power being universally accepted under the laws of war as necessary in order to prevent the return of combatants to the battlefield during conflict. Given that Padilla qualifies as an enemy combatant under both the definition adopted by the Court in *Quirin* and the definition accepted by the controlling opinion in *Hamdi*, his military detention as an enemy combatant by the President is unquestionably authorized by the AUMF as a fundamental incident to the President's prosecution of the war against al Qaeda in Afghanistan.

C. Detention of U.S. Citizens as Enemy Combatants After 9/11

B. . . .

1.

Recognizing the hurdle to his position represented by the Supreme Court's decision in *Hamdi,* Padilla principally argues that his case does not fall within the "narrow circumstances" considered by the Court in that case because, although he too stood alongside Taliban forces in Afghanistan, he was seized on American soil, whereas Hamdi was captured on a foreign battlefield. In other words, Padilla maintains that capture on a foreign battlefield was one of the "narrow circumstances" to which the plurality in *Hamdi* confined its opinion. We disagree. When the plurality articulated the "narrow question" before it, it referred simply to the permissibility of detaining "an individual who . . . was 'part of or supporting forces hostile to the United States or coalition partners' in Afghanistan and who 'engaged in an armed conflict against the United States' there." Nowhere in its framing of the "narrow question" presented did the plurality even mention the locus of capture.

The actual reasoning that the plurality thereafter employed is consistent with the question having been framed so as to render locus of capture irrelevant. That reasoning was that Hamdi's detention was an exercise of "necessary and appropriate force" within the meaning of the AUMF because "detention to prevent a combatant's return to the battlefield is a fundamental incident of waging war." *Id.* at 2641. This reasoning simply does not admit of a distinction between an enemy combatant captured abroad and detained in the United States, such as Hamdi, and an enemy combatant who escaped capture abroad but was ultimately captured domestically and detained in the United States, such as Padilla. As we previously explained, Padilla poses the same threat of returning to the battlefield as Hamdi posed at the time of the Supreme Court's adjudication of Hamdi's petition. Padilla's detention is thus "necessary and appropriate" to the same extent as was Hamdi's. . . .

Our conclusion that the reasoning in *Hamdi* does not support a distinction based on the locus of capture is buttressed by the plurality's analysis of *Quirin.* Although at issue in *Quirin* was the authority of the President to subject a United States citizen who was also an enemy combatant to military trial, the plurality in *Hamdi* went to lengths to observe that Haupt, *who had been captured domestically,* could instead have been permissibly *detained* for the duration of hostilities. That analysis strongly suggests, if it does not confirm, that the plurality did not regard the locus of capture (within or without the United States) as relevant to the President's authority to detain an enemy combatant who is also a citizen, and that it believed that the detention of such a combatant is not more or less a necessary incident of the President's power to wage war depending upon the locus of eventual capture. . . .

2.

Padilla also argues, and the district court held, that Padilla's military detention is "neither necessary nor appropriate" because he is amenable to criminal prosecution. . . .

As to the fact that Padilla can be prosecuted, the availability of criminal process does not distinguish him from Hamdi. If the mere availability of criminal prosecution rendered detention unnecessary within the meaning of the AUMF, then Hamdi's detention would have been unnecessary and therefore unauthorized, since he too was detained in the United States and amenable to criminal prosecution. We are convinced, in any event, that the availability of criminal process cannot be determinative of the power to detain, if for no other reason than that criminal prosecution may well not achieve the very purpose for which detention is authorized in the first place — the prevention of return to the field of battle. Equally important, in many instances criminal prosecution would impede the Executive in its efforts to gather intelligence from the detainee and to restrict the detainee's communication with confederates so as to ensure that the detainee does not pose a continuing threat to national security even as he is confined — impediments that would render military detention not only an appropriate, but also the necessary, course of action to be taken in the interest of national security. . . .

3.

Padilla, citing *Ex parte Endo,* 323 U.S. 283 (1944), and relying upon *Quirin,* next argues that only a clear statement from Congress can authorize his detention, and that the AUMF is not itself, and does not contain, such a clear statement.

In *Endo,* the Court did state that, when asked to find implied powers in a wartime statute, it must assume that "the law makers intended to place no greater restraint on the citizen than was clearly and unmistakably indicated by the language [the law makers] used." The Court almost immediately thereafter observed, however, that the "fact that the Act" at issue was "silent on detention [did] not of course mean that any power to detain [was] lacking," an observation that proves that the Court did not adopt or even apply in that case a "clear statement" rule of the kind for which Padilla argues.

Padilla contends that *Quirin* also supports the existence of a clear statement rule. However, in no place in *Quirin* did the Court even purport to establish a clear statement rule. In its opinion, the Court did note that Congress had "explicitly" authorized Haupt's military trial. But to conclude from this passing note that the Court required a clear statement as a matter of law would be unwarranted. In fact, to the extent that *Quirin* can be understood to have addressed the need for a clear statement of authority from Congress at all, the rule would appear the opposite:

> [T]he detention and trial of petitioners — ordered by the President in the declared exercise of his powers as Commander in Chief of the Army in time of war and of grave public danger — are not to be set aside by the courts without the clear conviction that they are in conflict with the Constitution or laws of Congress constitutionally enacted.

Of course, even were a clear statement by Congress required, the AUMF constitutes such a clear statement according to the Supreme Court. In *Hamdi,* stating that "it [was] of no moment that the AUMF does not use specific

C. Detention of U.S. Citizens as Enemy Combatants After 9/11

language of detention," the plurality held that the AUMF "clearly and unmistakably authorized" Hamdi's detention. Nothing in the AUMF permits us to conclude that the Joint Resolution clearly and unmistakably authorized Hamdi's detention but not Padilla's. To the contrary, read in light of its purpose clause ("in order to prevent any future acts of international terrorism against the United States") and its preamble (stating that the acts of 9/11 "render it both necessary and appropriate ... to protect United States citizens both at home and abroad"), the AUMF applies even more clearly and unmistakably to Padilla than to Hamdi. Padilla, after all, in addition to supporting hostile forces in Afghanistan and taking up arms against our troops on a battlefield in that country like Hamdi, *also* came to the United States in order to commit future acts of terrorism against American citizens and targets....

4.

Finally, Padilla argues that, even if his detention is authorized by the AUMF, it is unlawful under *Ex parte Milligan*, 71 U.S. (4 Wall.) 2 (1866). In *Milligan*, the Supreme Court held that a United States citizen associated with an anti-Union secret society but unaffiliated with the Confederate army could not be tried by a military tribunal while access to civilian courts was open and unobstructed. *Milligan* purported to restrict the power of Congress as well as the power of the President. ("[N]o usage of war could sanction a military trial ... for any offence whatever of a citizen in civil life, in nowise connected with the military service. Congress could grant no such power...."). *Quirin*, however, confirmed that *Milligan* does not extend to enemy combatants. As the Court in *Quirin* explained, the *Milligan* Court's reasoning had "particular reference to the facts before it," namely, that Milligan was not "a part of or associated with the armed forces of the enemy." The *Hamdi* plurality in turn reaffirmed this limitation on the reach of *Milligan*, emphasizing that *Quirin*, a unanimous opinion, "both postdates and clarifies *Milligan*." Thus confined, *Milligan* is inapposite here because Padilla, unlike Milligan, associated with, and has taken up arms against the forces of the United States on behalf of, an enemy of the United States....

III.

The detention of petitioner being fully authorized by Act of Congress, the judgment of the district court that the detention of petitioner by the President of the United States is without support in law is hereby reversed.

Reversed.

NOTES AND QUESTIONS

1. *Hamdi After Remand.* After the Supreme Court remanded, Hamdi and the government negotiated an agreement for his release to his family in Saudi Arabia. The government asserted that he no longer had any intelligence value and posed no threat. Under the agreement, Hamdi gave up his U.S. citizenship, renounced terrorism, waived any civil claim he had for his detention,

and accepted certain travel restrictions, including a ten-year ban on returning to the United States. *See* Motion to Stay Proceedings, Hamdi v. Rumsfeld, No. 2:02CV439 (E.D. Va. Sept. 24, 2004), *available at* http://notablecases.vaed.uscourts.gov/2:02-cv-00439/docs/70223/0.pdf.

2. *The Greater Includes the Lesser?* In both *Hamdi* and *Padilla* the courts assume that Supreme Court precedents concerning trial by military commission, especially *Quirin*, are apposite to the legality of military detention. *Quirin* did say that both lawful and unlawful combatants "are subject to capture and *detention*," and that unlawful combatants are additionally subject to military trial and punishment, *supra* p. 716 (emphasis supplied). This the lower court in *Padilla* understood to reflect the Supreme Court's belief that "detention alone... [is] certainly the lesser of the consequences an unlawful combatant could face." Padilla *ex rel.* Newman v. Bush, 233 F. Supp. 2d 564, 595 (S.D.N.Y. 2002), *rev'd*, 352 F.3d 685 (2d Cir. 2003), *rev'd and remanded*, 542 U.S. 426 (2004).

But is that always true? The unlawful combatant who is tried at least will see a resolution of his status. *See Rasul, supra* p. 697 (Kennedy, J., concurring in the judgment) (distinguishing *Eisentrager*, involving aliens being detained after having been convicted by military commission, from *Rasul*, involving aliens "being held indefinitely, and without benefit of any legal proceeding to determine their status"). What about the combatant who is detained indefinitely by the military without trial or even charges, or until the political branches determine that the war is over? If detention is not the "lesser" consequence for such a combatant, is case law establishing the legality of a military *trial* really apposite to the legality of *detention*?

3. *Necessity for Military Detention in Hamdi.* Detention under the law of war is based on military necessity, a premise echoed in the AUMF authorization for use of "*necessary* and appropriate force." *See* §2(a), *supra* p. 100 (emphasis supplied). What is that necessity?

"The purpose of detention is to prevent captured individuals from returning to the field of battle and taking up arms once again," Justice O'Connor noted in *Hamdi*. They are detained, in other words, both to enable U.S. forces to carry out their mission and to provide force protection. In addition, such individuals are detained to obtain operational intelligence by interrogation. Indeed, their detention may itself be instrumental to a successful interrogation, because the isolation of the detainees and their consequent dependence on their captors may induce them to talk. Bringing such persons before a judge, or even holding some kind of hearing, may be impracticable in the midst of hostilities, while the bullets are flying. Moving detainees back from the front lines may not be a cure, because it is often still impractical to withdraw troops from the front to give testimony or to preserve evidence during the fighting. *Cf.* Odah v. United States, 321 F.3d 1134, 1150 (D.C. Cir. 2003) (Randolph, J., concurring) (asserting with respect to military detainees at Camp X-Ray in Guantánamo Naval Base, Cuba, that "[t]he historical meaning of 'in the field' was not restricted to the field of battle. It applied as well to 'organized camps stationed in remote places where civil courts did not exist.' "), *rev'd and remanded by* Rasul v. Bush, 542 U.S. 466 (2004), *supra* p. 692.

C. Detention of U.S. Citizens as Enemy Combatants After 9/11

How, if at all, did the Court in *Hamdi* respond to such arguments of military necessity? Do you agree? Would it make a difference whether Hamdi—a U.S. citizen allegedly fighting alongside the enemy—was one of a kind or one of a thousand?

4. *Necessity for Military Detention in Padilla.* If the arguments of necessity apply to Hamdi, do they also apply to Padilla? What if the government believes Padilla to be an imminent threat to set off a dirty bomb but lacks probable cause to arrest him? What response does Justice Souter suggest for such an emergency? Here's the District Court's answer, after Padilla refiled his habeas petition on remand from the Supreme Court:

> Simply stated, this is a law enforcement matter, not a military matter.... At the time that [Padilla] was arrested pursuant to the material arrest warrant, any alleged terrorist plans that he harbored were thwarted. From then on, he was available to be questioned—and was indeed questioned—just like any citizen accused of criminal conduct....
>
> There can be no debate that this country's laws amply provide for the investigation, detention and prosecution of citizen and non-citizen terrorists alike....
>
> ... The difference between invocation of the criminal process and the power claimed by the President here, however, is one of accountability. The criminal justice system requires that defendants and witnesses be afforded access to counsel, imposes judicial supervision over government action, and places congressionally imposed limits on incarceration.

[Padilla v. Hanft, 389 F. Supp. 2d 678, 691-692 (D.S.C.), *rev'd*, 423 F.3d 387 (4th Cir. 2005), *cert. denied*, 126 S. Ct. 1649 (2006) (quoting *amici curiae* in Rumsfeld v. Padilla, 542 U.S. 426 (2004)).]

As the principal case shows, Fourth Circuit Court of Appeals disagreed. Barely three weeks later and just two business days before the government's brief in response to Padilla's petition for certiorari was due to be filed in the Supreme Court of the United States, the government announced Padilla's indictment on charges considerably less serious than those for which he had been militarily detained. It then moved to transfer him to civilian custody. The Court of Appeals, in an opinion by the visibly angry author of the earlier opinion that had accepted the government's claim of military necessity in upholding the military detention, denied the motion and refused to vacate its decision. Padilla v. Hanft, 432 F.3d 582 (4th Cir. 2005). The court asserted that the timing of the indictment gave an appearance that it had been driven by the government's desire to avoid consideration of the Fourth Circuit's favorable decision by the Supreme Court, *id.* at 585, and it stated that the issues raised by Padilla's military detention were sufficiently important to warrant consideration by the Supreme Court. *Id.* at 587. As to claims of military necessity, it commented:

> [A]s the government surely must understand, although the various facts it has asserted are not necessarily inconsistent or without basis, its actions have left not only the impression that Padilla may have been held for these years, even if justifiably, by mistake—an impression we would have thought the government could ill afford to leave extant. They have left the impression that the government may even have come to the belief that the principle in reliance upon which it has

detained Padilla for this time, that the President possesses the authority to detain enemy combatants who enter into this country for the purpose of attacking America and its citizens from within, can, in the end, yield to expediency with little or no cost to its conduct of the war against terror — an impression we would have thought the government likewise could ill afford to leave extant. And these impressions have been left, we fear, at what may ultimately prove to be substantial cost to the government's credibility before the courts, to whom it will one day need to argue again in support of a principle of assertedly like importance and necessity to the one that it seems to abandon today. While there could be an objective that could command such a price as all of this, it is difficult to imagine what that objective would be. [*Id.* at 587.]

Do *Korematsu* and the last Court of Appeals decision in *Padilla* cast any doubt on judicial deference to executive claims of military necessity for military detention? If so, how should the courts view such claims? How would you reframe the authority for military detention to confine it strictly to situations of bona fide military necessity? Does the length of the detention affect the necessity, and, if so, how would you reflect this consideration in your specification of detention authority?

The issue of necessity figured prominently in the Supreme Court's 2006 decision about the jurisdiction of a military commission to try an alien charged with violations of the law of war. *See* Hamdan v. Rumsfeld, 126 S. Ct. 2749, 2772-2786 (2006), *infra* p. 882.

5. *The Non-Detention Act — Section 4001(a).* A plurality in *Hamdi* assumes, but does not decide, that §4001(a) applies to military detentions and then finds it satisfied by the AUMF. If §4001(a) does apply and the AUMF is invoked as a statutory exception within its contemplation, should we apply the clear statement requirement to the AUMF as Justices Souter and Ginsburg insist in *Hamdi*, and the Second Circuit did in *Padilla*? Why does the Fourth Circuit not apply that rule? What rebuttal to a clear statement claim could you pose based on analogies to the Posse Comitatus Act, 18 U.S.C. §1385, *infra* p. 945, and the War Powers Resolution §8(a), *supra* p. 242? Who was right about the application of the clear statement rule — the Fourth Circuit or the Second Circuit?

On the other hand, even without insisting on a clear statement, does a natural reading of the AUMF embrace uses of force (and, by implication, military detention) *within* the United States, or just in Afghanistan or wherever else the armed forces are deployed in combat? *See* Stephen I. Vladeck, Comment, *A Small Problem of Precedent: 18 U.S.C. §4001(a) and the Detention of U.S. Citizen "Enemy Combatants,"* 112 Yale L.J. 961, 967 (2003) (arguing that the AUMF fails to satisfy §4001(a)).

6. *"Plenary" Military Authority.* In *Hamdi*, the government argued that the executive has plenary authority under Article II to detain enemy combatants, presumably a "war power" of the Commander in Chief. Though the plurality did not reach this claim, it agreed that the capture and military detention of combatants are "important incident[s] of war," quoting *Quirin,* and Justice Thomas dissented on the ground that Hamdi's "detention falls squarely within the Federal Government's war powers" vested in the executive branch. This assertion of war power presents several thorny questions.

C. Detention of U.S. Citizens as Enemy Combatants After 9/11

First, if the war power presupposes a war, is a state of war as the Supreme Court defined that term in *The Prize Cases, supra* p. 67, sufficient, or must the war be expressly authorized by Congress? Was a war authorized by the AUMF, *supra* p. 100? If so, what is its scope, both geographical and temporal? Does the AUMF trigger all the war powers of the President, or just some? *See* Hamdan v. Rumsfeld, 126 S. Ct. 2749, 2775 (2006), *infra* p. 886 (declaring that "there is nothing in the text or legislative history of the AUMF even hinting that Congress intended to expand or alter" the President's existing authority to convene a military commission). Note that a use-of-force authorization would apparently not trigger the Alien Enemy Act, *supra* p. 703. Does the AUMF override the Alien Enemy Act? If not, does this mean that the President has war power under the AUMF to detain U.S. citizen combatants but not aliens in the United States?

Second, how should we define "enemy combatants" subject to military detention under the law of war? How does the *Hamdi* Court define them? Recall the differences in the status of Milligan and of Quirin. Is Hamdi more like Milligan or like Quirin? In this regard, note that the saboteurs in *Quirin*, unlike Hamdi, did not contest their status as enemy soldiers. (This was one basis on which the Second Circuit distinguished *Quirin*. Another was that *Quirin* was decided before the Non-Detention Act.) What about Padilla? What definition of "enemy combatant" would you construct from *Milligan, Quirin,* and *Hamdi*?

Or are we looking in the wrong place? If war is authorized by declaration or by a use-of-force statute, shouldn't we look to the authorization for a definition of the enemy? Suppose Congress had not authorized the use of force against terrorist organizations like Al Qaeda, but the President had gone ahead anyway on the theory of repelling attack. Would military detention of combatants in that war be authorized? How would they be defined? What about persons detained as terrorists generally in an undeclared "war on terrorism"?

Third, even if the AUMF suffices to authorize military detention in the field, does it apply in the United States? The Fourth Circuit reasoned that the "locus of capture [is] irrelevant" to the military necessity for Padilla's detention. Should the court have considered the availability of criminal law and open civilian courts to that end, or should the court have considered the constitutional authorities that the Second Circuit identified as vesting explicit legislative power in the Congress?

7. *Determining the Combatant Status of U.S. Citizens.* The plurality in *Hamdi* decided what procedures were required for determining his status by conducting a due process balancing. To test your understanding of where they came out, consider the alternatives.

First, why was combatant status not an issue in *Quirin*? All are agreed that the answer is that the German saboteurs admitted their status. If there is no factual dispute, then even a due process balancing presumably does not require any procedure to decide that status. Why did the Court reject the government's argument that Hamdi's status was undisputed?

If the detainee's combatant status *is* disputed and he is entitled to petition for a writ of habeas corpus, then the habeas corpus statute, 28 U.S.C. §2243, *supra* p. 682, itself suggests some evidentiary proceeding. Can you see why from examining the statute?

But what evidence and what kind of proceeding? The government suggested that "some evidence" would suffice, a conclusion reached by the district court in *Padilla* as well. The government therefore argued that the court's role in a habeas corpus proceeding was only to decide whether the evidence stated in the Mobbs Declaration was sufficient standing alone. Is that consistent with the habeas corpus statute? Or with due process?

The Court rejected the "some evidence" standard partly on the grounds that "it primarily has been employed by courts in examining an administrative record developed after an adversarial proceeding. . . ." But the government *has* asserted that it has developed an administrative record after an elaborate internal process for determining combatant status of U.S. citizens that incorporated information developed by the Department of Defense, the Central Intelligence Agency, and the Department of Justice, written assessments by the same agencies, a formal legal opinion by the Office of Legal Counsel, recommendations by the Attorney General and the Secretary of Defense, and a final recommendation to and briefing for the President by the White House Counsel.[2] If such procedures were actually used to designate Hamdi and Padilla as enemy combatants and to generate the factual predicates for their military detention, why isn't the "some evidence" standard sufficient?

Finally, consider the procedures that the plurality in *Hamdi* found were required by a due process balancing. Are these sufficient to reduce the risk of inaccuracy in light of the interests at stake? What more would Justices Souter and Ginsburg require if they found that Congress had authorized military detention? What would you find necessary if you performed the balancing?

In light of the foregoing, are Justices Scalia and Stevens right — is this a job for Congress? If so, what procedures would you recommend that Congress require?

8. *The Right to Assistance of Counsel.* Is any proceeding for determining a detainee's status fair without his input? Can he give that input without a lawyer? Many have argued that the right to assistance of counsel is the most important right of a person detained or prosecuted by the government because it is essential to effectively asserting every other right.

The government responded to such concerns by insisting that "[t]he rights the Constitution affords persons in the criminal justice system simply do not apply in the context of detention of enemy combatants." Letter from Daniel J. Bryant (Asst. Attorney General, U.S. Dept. of Justice) to Carl Levin (Chairman of the Senate Committee on Armed Services), Nov. 26, 2002, at 4. But doesn't this beg the question whether a detainee *is* an "enemy combatant"? Even if military detention and trial operate in some legal universe parallel to the Constitution, does it follow that the President alone is gatekeeper to that universe? If the court has some gatekeeping function as well, how can it fulfill that function without help from the detainee and his counsel?

---

2. Alberto R. Gonzales, Counsel to the President, Remarks at the American Bar Assn. Standing Comm. on Law and Natl. Security (Feb. 24, 2004) (transcript *available at* http://www.fas.org/irp/news/2004/02/Gonzales.pdf) (asserting also, however, that neither these procedures nor any other specific procedures were required by law, but that they were adopted instead simply by administrative grace).

D. Military Detention of Alien Enemy Combatants After 9/11

Consider the following recommendations from the American Bar Association Task Force on Treatment of Enemy Combatants:

> RESOLVED, That the American Bar Association urges that U.S. citizens and residents who are detained within the United States based on their designation as "enemy combatants" be afforded the opportunity for meaningful judicial review of their status, under a standard according such deference to the designation as the review court determines to be appropriate to accommodate the needs of the detainee and the requirements of national security; and
>
> FURTHER RESOLVED, That the American Bar Association urges that U.S. citizens and residents who are detained within the United States based on their designations as "enemy combatants" not be denied access to counsel in connection with the opportunity for such review, subject to appropriate conditions as may be set by the court to accommodate the needs of the detainee and the requirements of national security....

ABA Task Force on Treatment of Enemy Combatants, *Report to the House of Delegates* (2003).

Shortly before the argument in the Supreme Court in *Hamdi*, but not earlier, Hamdi was permitted to meet with counsel appointed to represent him. The timing of the government's action suggested to some a desire to avoid a ruling by the high court on this issue. The Court asserted that Hamdi "unquestionably has the right to access to counsel in connection with proceedings on remand. No further consideration of this issue is necessary at this stage of the case." 542 U.S. at 539. Did the plurality decide that access to counsel is part of the procedure owed Hamdi by due process? How would you decide that question?

D. MILITARY DETENTION OF ALIEN ENEMY COMBATANTS AFTER 9/11

The decisions in *Hamdi* and *Padilla* might suggest that the military detention of *alien* enemy combatants after 9/11 would be comparatively less controversial, as least as a matter of domestic law. First, aliens outside the United States have fewer, if any, constitutional rights. *See, e.g.*, United States v. Verdugo-Urquidez, 494 U.S. 259 (1990), *supra* p. 643. Second, the Non-Detention Act, *supra* p. 670, does not apply to them.

President George W. Bush presumably was so advised when, just a month after the 9/11 attacks, he issued Military Order No. 1, which authorizes military detention of aliens whom he believes to be members of al Queda or who have "engaged in, aided or abetted, or conspired to commit, acts of international terrorism, or acts in preparation therefor," directed at the United States or its people. Military Order of November 13, 2001, *Detention, Treatment, and Trial of Certain Non-Citizens in the War Against Terrorism*, 66 Fed. Reg. 57,833 (Nov. 13, 2001), reproduced in relevant part *supra* p. 691 and *infra* p. 878. When military operations in Afghanistan began to yield captives in the fall of 2001, the government decided to transfer many of them to a detention facility at the U.S. Naval Base at Guantánamo Bay, Cuba, pursuant to the military order.

Applications for writs of habeas corpus, as well as other suits, soon followed, leading to the decision in Rasul v. Bush, 542 U.S. 466 (2004), *supra* p. 692, holding that the federal courts had statutory "jurisdiction to determine the legality of the Executive's potentially indefinite detention of individuals [including Rasul and other alien detainees held at Guantánamo Bay] who claim to be wholly innocent of wrongdoing." 542 U.S. at 485.

The *Rasul* ruling paved the way for conflicting decisions in the lower courts. In Hamdan v. Rumsfeld, 344 F. Supp. 2d 152 (D.D.C. 2004), *rev'd,* 435 F.3d 582 (D.C. Cir. 2005), *rev'd,* 126 S. Ct. 2749 (2006), a district court found that the proposed trial of a Guantánamo Bay detainee by military commission pursuant to Military Order No. 1 violated the Geneva Conventions. In In re Guantánamo Detainee Cases, 355 F. Supp. 2d 443 (D.D.C. 2005), a different district court adopted the lower court's reasoning in *Hamdan* to find that the Geneva Conventions applied to fighters for the Taliban, then held that the Conventions were not satisfied by the hearings held by Combatant Status Review Tribunals (CSRTs) to determine whether detainees were enemy combatants. In addition, relying on footnote 15 in *Rasul, supra* p. 696, the court held that detainees had stated valid claims under the Fifth Amendment when they asserted that the procedures used by the CSRTs violated due process. However, a third district court reached the opposite conclusions in Khalid v. Bush, 355 F. Supp. 2d 311 (D.D.C. 2005). Reasoning that *Rasul* decided only the jurisdictional question, not the question whether detainees in Guantánamo Bay have constitutional rights, the *Khalid* court, relying on *Eisentrager,* found that they did not. The court also held that the detention and treatment of individuals held at Guantánamo violated no U.S. laws and that international laws were either inapplicable or not privately enforceable.

The case law generated by the Guantánamo Bay detainees continues to metastasize, making it difficult to assert what the law of any circuit is, let alone the law more generally concerning military detention. At this writing, both In re Guantanamo Detainee Cases and Khalid v. Bush are being appealed. In Hamdan v. Rumsfeld, 435 F.3d 582 (D.C. Cir. 2005), a D.C. Circuit Court of Appeals panel reversed the lower court's holding that the Geneva Conventions applied to Guantánamo detainees. *Hamdan,* however, involved a challenge to the trial of detainees by military commission, rather than to a status determination by a CSRT, and the D.C. Circuit panel did not rule on the applicability of the Constitution. In the meantime, Congress enacted the Detainee Treatment Act of 2005, *supra* p. 701, limiting habeas corpus jurisdiction and the attendant scope of judicial review over claims by Guantánamo Bay detainees. Subsequently, the Supreme Court ruled in *Hamdan* that the Detainee Treatment Act did not apply to pending cases, and that trial of detainees by military commission was not authorized. (Trials by military commission and the Supreme Court's *Hamdan* decision are examined in depth in Chapter 30.) It very pointedly declined to rule on the propriety of the detentions.

Shortly before this book went to press, Congress passed the Military Commissions Act of 2006, Pub. L. No. 109-366, 120 Stat. 2600. Aimed in part at avoiding the Supreme Court's ruling in *Hamdan,* the Act also purports to allow indefinite detention of persons designated "enemy combatants," without the benefit of habeas corpus or any other judicial review.

D. Military Detention of Alien Enemy Combatants After 9/11

NOTES AND QUESTIONS

1. *CSRTs.* Reread the final paragraph of part III of the Supreme Court's opinion in Hamdi v. Rumsfeld, *supra* p. 729. Can you see why CSRTs were created? Between August 2004 and March 2005, CSRTs reviewed the status of 558 detainees and deemed 520 to be enemy combatants. *See Combatant Status Review Summary,* Mar. 29, 2005 (reporting review by Convening Authority Rear Adm. James M. McGarrah), *available at* http://www.dod.mil/news/Mar2005/d20050329csrt.pdf.

2. *The Constitutional Rights of Aliens.* Recall, and, if necessary, reread *Verdugo-Urquidez, supra* p. 643. It held that alien Verdugo-Urquidez had no constitutional protection under the Fourth Amendment from a warrantless search of his property in Mexico. Why did that decision not resolve the question of the constitutional rights of aliens generally? If that question was left open, does *Rasul* shed light on the substantive constitutional rights of the alien detainees, or is it just a jurisdictional ruling on their access to habeas corpus? If they have no substantive rights, is such a procedural right a cruel hoax? *See* Amnesty International, *Guantánamo and Beyond: The Continuing Pursuit of Unchecked Executive Power,* May 13, 2005, at 46 (characterizing the government's claim that *Rasul* conferred only "procedural rights" on alien detainees as an argument that "the detainees could file *habeas corpus* petitions, but only in order to have them necessarily dismissed"), *available at* http://web.amnesty.org/library/Index/ENGAMR510632005?open&of=ENG-USA. What other rights could they assert in their petition?

Al-Marri v. Hanft, 378 F. Supp. 2d 673 (D.S.C. 2005), may help put some of these questions into sharper relief. Al-Marri is a Qatari national who earned a bachelor's degree during the 1990s from Bradley University in Illinois and legally returned to the United States with his family to pursue a master's degree from the same university. Unfortunately for him, he returned on September 10, 2001, and was subsequently arrested on December 12 as a material witness and later indicted for making false statements and for credit card fraud before being designated an enemy combatant by President Bush on June 23, 2003. The criminal case was dismissed with prejudice, and al-Marri was transferred to military detention at the Naval Consolidated Brig in South Carolina.

Does al-Marri have any constitutional rights that he can assert to challenge his military detention? Is he differently situated from the Guantánamo detainees or Khalid? The court that rejected his petition for a writ of habeas corpus cited *Eisentrager* in concluding that the Supreme Court had limited "a resident alien enemy's use of our courts . . . 'as necessary to prevent use of the courts to accomplish a purpose which might hamper our own war efforts or to give aid to the enemy.'" *Id.* at 678 (quoting *Eisentrager,* 339 U.S. at 776) (internal citation omitted)). Should the court have discussed *Verdugo-Urquidez*?

The *al-Marri* court also reasoned that the Alien Enemy Act, *supra* p. 703, confirmed that during war even resident enemy aliens receive protections different from those enjoyed by citizens, although the court conceded that the Act had no direct application absent a declared war against a foreign nation or government. 378 F. Supp. 2d at 679. What contrary argument could you make based upon the existence of that Act?

3. *The Value of Due Process Rights.* The report cited in Note 2, above, indicates that in 520 of 558 cases the CSRT upheld the designations of detainees as "enemy combatants." Thirty-two of the 38 cases that rejected that designation were decided *after* the decision in In re Guantanamo Detainee Cases. Amnesty International, *supra*, at 50. However, it is not clear whether these results reflect a change in procedures or the way in which procedures were applied.

4. *AUMF vs. Treaty.* Does it really matter whether the Geneva Conventions are self-executing or whether they apply? They preceded in time the AUMF, passed by Congress after 9/11. Why is not the AUMF simply *lex posterior*—a last-in-time controlling statute? *See supra* pp. 181, 194-195.

5. *Synthesis?* The cases in this subchapter present the following variables, among others:

- citizen or alien?
- admitted enemy combatant or contested?
- detention in mainland United States or Guantánamo Bay?
- capture on the Afghan battlefield or in the United States?
- member of al Qaeda or fighter for the Taliban?

Can you distinguish the outcomes of the cases using these variables or others? Can you synthesize the cases to state the present law of military detention in the war on terrorism? If not, do you think this is an appropriate issue for resolution by the courts as opposed to the political branches? Do the courts have a choice?

Interrogating Terrorist Suspects   27

As early as December 2002, U.S. military and civilian interrogators are reported to have abused individuals captured and detained in the war on terrorism by beating them and subjecting them to prolonged sleep and sensory deprivation, as well as to sexual humiliation. The abuse began in Afghanistan, then in Guantánamo Bay, Cuba, and other offshore U.S. interrogation centers, and later in Iraq. Several investigations of these abuses revealed that serious injuries and deaths occurred among the detainees.

Our objective in the first two parts of this chapter is to tell the interrogation story from September 11 to the present, then to introduce the legal regime for U.S. interrogation and treatment of detainees abroad. We consider both the sources of applicable rules and the limits those rules impose on interrogation techniques. We also try to determine whether the President enjoys constitutional or other powers that would excuse him from compliance with the rules. The raw materials for this analysis—internal government legal memoranda—provide a remarkable view of the work of lawyers in a wartime executive branch.

In the third part of the chapter we examine a controversial variant of U.S. detention and interrogation activities. Through "extraordinary rendition" the United States allegedly has transferred detainees to foreign countries in circumstances where it is more likely than not that the individuals will be subjected to torture or to cruel, inhuman, or degrading treatment. Whether undertaken by military or intelligence operatives, on secret orders of the President or without authorization, extraordinary rendition requires a careful assessment of international and domestic law limits.

A. THE EVOLVING HISTORY OF DETAINEE INTERROGATION IN THE WAR ON TERRORISM

In October 1996, Secretary of Defense William Perry spoke at a meeting of Western Hemisphere defense ministers in Argentina. Responding to criticisms of so-called "torture manuals" used to train Latin American intelligence officers at the U.S. Army School of the Americas in the 1980s and to a 1996 Intelligence Oversight Board report describing intelligence activities in Latin America, Perry said he was shocked when he found out about the manuals. He also declared that the Defense Department would never again advocate torture or other inhumane treatment in its training programs.[1]

Secretary Perry's assertion could not have taken into account September 11 and the war on terrorism. According to Cofer Black, former director of the CIA's counterterrorism unit, "after 9/11, the gloves came off."[2] Beginning with the capture in Afghanistan of senior al Qaeda operatives, the Bush administration had to determine how best to extract intelligence information from individuals detained by U.S. forces. "Setting" the methods and parameters of interrogation thus became an integral part of counterterrorism planning. Should al Qaeda figures be questioned by the FBI, using traditional methods? By military interrogators, following service branch rules? By the CIA, perhaps using harsher techniques in secret locations?

The Bush administration decided early on to detain indefinitely a number of persons seized in Afghanistan and elsewhere and to create a new detention facility at the U.S. base at Guantánamo Bay to hold at least some of them. The first detainees taken there in January 2002 were designated "unlawful combatants" by President Bush.

Initially, the Administration contended that Taliban and al Qaeda fighters held at Guantánamo were not eligible for the protections of the Geneva Conventions, the principal set of international legal norms for wartime detainees created by the international community after World War II. The internal debate attending this decision is reflected in memoranda from the Justice Department, the White House Counsel, and the State Department excerpted *infra* pp. 764-774. The Administration eventually decided that captured Taliban fighters would be protected by the Third Geneva Convention, although not as "prisoners of war." Captured members of al Qaeda would be treated "humanely," although the Geneva Conventions would not apply to them. In any case, according to the Defense Department, at least until December 2002 interrogations at Guantánamo were conducted in accordance with rules set out in Department of the Army, *Intelligence Interrogation* (FM 34-52) (1992).[3]

In the summer of 2002, however, the Justice Department was asked to advise what interrogation techniques would violate U.S. or international law. In August, the Office of Legal Counsel (OLC) opined that

> for an act to constitute torture as defined in [the Torture Statute], it must inflict pain that is difficult to endure. Physical pain amounting to torture must be equivalent in intensity to the pain accompanying serious physical injury, such as organ failure, impairment of bodily function, or even death. For purely mental pain or suffering to amount to torture . . . it must result in significant psychological harm of significant duration, e.g., lasting for months or even years. We conclude

---

1. Linda D. Kozaryn, *Perry Bans U.S. Training in Inhumane Techniques*, American Forces Information Serv., Oct. 9, 1996, *available at* http://www.defenselink.mil/news/Oct1996/n10091996_9610095.html.
2. John Barry, Michael Hirsh & Michael Isikoff, *The Roots of Terror*, Newsweek, May 24, 2004, at 26.
3. Dept. of Defense News Release, *DoD Provides Details on Interrogation Process*, June 22, 2004, *at* http://www.defenselink.mil/releases/2004/nr20040622-0930.html.

A. The Evolving History of Detainee Interrogation in the War on Terrorism

that the mental harm also must result from one of the predicate acts listed in the statute, namely: threats of imminent death; threats of the infliction of the kind of pain that would amount to physical torture; infliction of such physical pain as a means of psychological torture; use of drugs or other procedures designed to deeply disrupt the senses, or fundamentally alter an individual's personality; or threatening to do any of these things to a third party.[4]

The memorandum suggested that a one-time kick to a prisoner's stomach with military boots while forcing him into a kneeling position would not amount to "torture" that would be subject to prosecution. The OLC memorandum even concluded that torture might be justified in some circumstances.[5]

Reacting to what was characterized as "tenacious resistance by some detainees to existing interrogation techniques,"[6] in October 2002 the commander at Guantánamo Bay sought permission to use new interrogation techniques that were more coercive than those authorized in the Army field manual, including the "use of stress positions (like standing), for a maximum of four hours"; isolation for up to 30 days; "deprivation of light and auditory stimuli"; hooding; removal of clothing; "forced grooming (shaving of facial hair, etc.)"; and using "fear of dogs... to induce stress."[7] A separate legal opinion by Army Lt. Col. Diane Beaver evaluated a range of even more aggressive techniques—from exposure to cold weather or water to threats of death or severe pain to inducing the "misperception of asphyxiation" and "mild noninjurious physical contact."[8] Lt. Col. Beaver found that these techniques were consistent with existing legal standards if they could "plausibly have been thought necessary... to achieve a legitimate governmental objective" and the force was applied "in a good faith effort and not maliciously or sadistically for the very purpose of causing harm."[9]

By December 2002, the media began reporting that so-called "stress and duress" tactics or "high pressure methods" were being used in secret detention centers overseas by Defense Department and CIA interrogators in pursuit of "actionable intelligence." Those methods included forcing detainees to stand or kneel for hours in black hoods or spray-painted goggles, bombarding the detainees with lights 24 hours a day, withholding painkillers from wounded detainees, confining them in tiny rooms or binding them in painful positions, subjecting them to loud noises, and depriving them of

---

4. Office of Legal Counsel, U.S. Dept. of Justice, *Memorandum for Alberto R. Gonzales, Counsel to the President, Re: Standards of Conduct for Interrogation Under 18 U.S.C. §§2340-2340A*, Aug. 1, 2002 (commonly referred to as the Bybee Memo, for Asst. Atty. General Jay S. Bybee, who signed it), at 1, *available at* http://www.gwu.edu/~nsarchiv/NSAEBB/NSAEBB127/02.08.01.pdf. The "organ failure" passage relies on public health statutes of questionable applicability to the interrogation setting.

5. The memo took the position that the statutory prohibition on torture cannot be applied to actions taken by the President as Commander in Chief. *Id.* at 33-39.

6. *Final Report of the Independent Panel to Review DoD Detention Operations* 35, Aug. 24, 2004 (hereinafter *Schlesinger Report*), at http://www.dod.gov/news/Aug2004/d20040824finalreport.pdf.

7. Memorandum for Chairman of the Joint Chiefs of Staff from James T. Hill, General, U.S. Army, *Counter-Resistance Techniques*, Oct. 25, 2002, *available at* http://www.gwu.edu/~nsarchiv/NSAEBB/NSAEBB127/02.10.25.pdf. The techniques were outlined in Diane E. Beaver, Joint Task Force 170, Dept. of Defense, *Legal Brief on Proposed Counter-Resistance Strategies*, Oct. 11, 2002, *available at* http://www.gwu.edu/~nsarchiv/NSAEBB/NSAEBB127/02.10.11.pdf.

8. Beaver, *supra* note 7.

9. *Id.*

sleep.[10] A June 2004 statement from the Department of Defense confirmed that similarly harsh interrogation techniques were approved by Secretary Donald Rumsfeld on December 2, 2002, for use in Guantánamo but were rescinded on January 15, 2003.[11] An August 2004 Army report found that interrogators in Afghanistan employed similar techniques beginning in December 2002.[12]

By early 2003, the apparent failure to obtain useful information from certain detainees at Guantánamo led Secretary Rumsfeld to charge an "Interrogation Working Group" of senior Defense Department lawyers to develop guidance on parameters for interrogation. In April 2003, the Working Group advised that the President as Commander in Chief could authorize torture despite legal prohibitions. Excerpts from the Working Group's report are set forth *infra* p. 774. Based at least in part on advice in the report, Secretary Rumsfeld approved interrogation techniques that included reversing detainees' sleep patterns, exposing them to heat, cold, loud noise, and bright lights, and extending interrogation sessions to 20 hours or more.[13] In June 2004, however, the Defense Department stated:

> It is the policy and practice of the Department of Defense to treat detainees in the War on Terrorism humanely and, to the extent appropriate and consistent with military necessity, in a manner consistent with the principles of the Geneva Convention.
>
> No procedures approved for use ordered, authorized, permitted, or tolerated torture. Individuals who have abused the trust and confidence placed in them will be held accountable.[14]

After the United States and its allies invaded Iraq in March 2003, there reportedly was widespread confusion about permissible techniques for interrogating prisoners there. The U.S. command authority initially ordered that standard FM 34-52 rules be followed. In August 2003, however, Secretary Rumsfeld sent the military overseer of interrogation at Guantánamo, Major General Geoffrey Miller, to Iraq to "rapidly exploit internees for actionable intelligence."[15] General Miller brought with him the list of techniques approved by Secretary Rumsfeld for Guantánamo, although he noted that the Geneva Conventions were supposed to apply in Iraq. In September, the military commander in Iraq approved a policy on interrogation that included portions of the Guantánamo policy and elements of policies then used by special forces.[16] Central Command disapproved the September policy, however, and in October

---

10. *See* Dana Priest & Barton Gellman, *U.S. Decries Abuse But Defends Interrogations*, Wash. Post, Dec. 26, 2002, at A1.

11. Dept. of Defense News Release, *DoD Provides Details on Interrogation Process*, June 22, 2004, available at http://www.defenselink.mil/releases/2004/nr 20040622-0930.html.

12. Maj. Gen. George R. Fay, *AR 15-6 Investigation of the Abu Ghraib Prison and 205th Military Intelligence Brigade* 29, Aug. 25, 2004 (hereinafter *Fay Report*), at http://www.dod.gov/news/Aug2004/d20040825fay.pdf.

13. *See* Jess Bravin, *Pentagon Report Sought to Justify Use of Torture*, Wall St. J., June 7, 2004, at 1.

14. *DoD Provides Details on Interrogation Process*, *supra* note 11.

15. General Antonio M. Taguba, *Article 15-6 Investigation of the 800th Military Police Brigade* (hereinafter *Taguba Report*), Jan. 31, 2004, at 7, available at http://news.findlaw.com/hdocs/docs/iraq/tagubarpt.html.

16. Subsequent investigators described a migration to Iraq of Guantánamo techniques — such as the use of dogs and forced nudity — to intimidate and dehumanize detainees. *See Schlesinger Report*, *supra* note 6, at 36; *Fay Report*, *supra* note 12, at 10.

A. The Evolving History of Detainee Interrogation in the War on Terrorism

approved rules that mirrored an outdated version of FM 34-52, which permitted interrogators to control "lighting and heating, as well as food, clothing, and shelter given to detainees."[17] The policy on interrogation in Iraq changed again in October, the third amendment in less than 30 days.[18]

In January 2004, following public reports of detainee abuse, Lt. Gen. Ricardo S. Sanchez, Commander of Combined Joint Task Force Seven in Iraq, requested an investigation of the operations of the 800th Military Police Brigade, the unit in charge of Abu Ghraib prison near Baghdad. Major General Antonio M. Taguba, who was appointed to conduct the investigation, found "numerous incidents of sadistic, blatant, wanton criminal abuses" at the prison, "intentionally perpetrated by several members of the military police guard force." The abuses included "punching, slapping, and kicking detainees," a litany of sexual and vulgar insults and attacks, and threats with loaded weapons.[19] In February 2004, the International Committee of the Red Cross (ICRC) issued a report detailing a number of serious human rights abuses by coalition forces in Iraq between March and November 2003.[20] Finally, in May 2004, public attention focused on Abu Ghraib after graphic photos of prisoner abuse were exposed by the media.[21]

A July 2004 Army report found 94 cases of "confirmed or possible abuse" in Iraq.[22] The report determined that the abuses "resulted from the failure of individuals to follow known standards of discipline and Army values and, in some cases, the failure of a few leaders to enforce those standards of discipline."[23] The Army decided not to charge any of those leaders with wrongdoing, however, finding some senior officers "responsible" but not "culpable."[24] By contrast, an investigation led by former Defense Secretary Schlesinger found that the abuses were "more than the failure of a few leaders to enforce proper discipline. There is both institutional and personal responsibility at higher levels."[25]

On March 22, 2006, an Army spokesman reported more than 600 accusations of detainee abuse in Iraq and Afghanistan since October 2001 and disciplinary actions against 251 soldiers. Only 11 soldiers had been convicted on criminal charges, the highest-ranking an Army captain.[26] Four of the five officers investigated by the Army for their role in the Abu Ghraib abuses were cleared;

---

17. *Schlesinger Report, supra* note 6, at 37-38; *see* Dept. of the Army, *Intelligence Interrogation* (FM 34-52), Sept. 28, 1992, at ch. 3.
18. *Fay Report, supra* note 12, at 28.
19. *Taguba Report, supra* note 15.
20. *Report of the International Committee of the Red Cross (ICRC) on the Treatment by the Coalition Forces of Prisoners of War and Other Protected Persons by the Geneva Conventions in Iraq During Arrest, Internment and Interrogation*, Feb. 2004, *available at* http://www.informationclearinghouse.info/pdf/icrc_iraq.pdf.
21. The Abu Ghraib photos are collected at http://www.salon.com/news/abu_ghraib/2006/03/14/introduction.
22. Inspector General, Dept. of the Army, *Detainees Operation Inspection Report*, July 21, 2004, at foreword, *at* http://www4.army.mil/ocpa/reports/ArmyIGDetaineeAbuse/index.html.
23. *Id.*
24. Josh White & Thomas E. Ricks, *Officers Won't Be Charged in Prison Scandal*, Wash. Post, Aug. 27, 2004, at A17.
25. *Schlesinger Report, supra* note 6, at 5.
26. Eric Schmitt, *Iraq Abuse Trial Is Again Limited to Lower Ranks*, N.Y. Times, Mar. 23, 2006, at A1; Eric Schmitt, *Army Dog Handler Is Convicted in Detainee Abuse at Abu Ghraib*, N.Y. Times, Mar. 22, 2006, at A1.

Brig. Gen. Janis Karpinski, Commander of the 800th Military Police Brigade, was demoted to the rank of colonel.[27] No one has been criminally prosecuted in U.S. civilian courts for detainee abuse.

The following materials trace this tangled history. They include portions of the legal memorandum prepared in early 2002 by Justice Department lawyers that purports to spell out legal requirements for interrogation and treatment of al Qaeda and Taliban detainees. Also included is follow-on correspondence from the White House Counsel, the Attorney General, and the Legal Adviser to the Department of State, along with part of an April 2003 memorandum from the Defense Department "Interrogation Working Group" and portions of another April 2003 memorandum from Defense Secretary Rumsfeld expanding the permissible interrogation techniques at Guantánamo. These materials are followed in turn by extensive notes and questions.

B. THE LEGAL STANDARDS AND THEIR APPLICATION

Application of Treaties and Laws to al Qaeda and Taliban Detainees

U.S. Department of Justice, Office of Legal Counsel
January 9, 2002
http://www.gwu.edu/~nsarchiv/NSAEBB/NSAEBB127/02.01.09.pdf

Memorandum for: William J. Haynes II, General Counsel, Department of Defense

From: John Yoo, Deputy Asst. Attorney General
Robert J. Delahunty, Special Counsel

You have asked for our Office's views concerning the effect of international treaties and federal laws on the treatment of individuals detained by the U.S. Armed Forces during the conflict in Afghanistan. In particular, you have asked whether the laws of armed conflict apply to the conditions of detention and the procedures for trial of members of al Qaeda and the Taliban militia. We conclude that these treaties do not protect members of the al Qaeda organization, which as a non-State actor cannot be a party to the international agreements governing war. We further conclude that these treaties do not apply to the Taliban militia. This memorandum expresses no view as to whether the President should decide, as a matter of policy, that the U.S. Armed Forces should adhere to the standards of conduct in those treaties with respect to the treatment of prisoners.

We believe it most useful to structure the analysis of these questions by focusing on the War Crimes Act, 18 U.S.C. §2441 (Supp. III 1997) ("WCA"). The WCA directly incorporates several provisions of international treaties

---

27. U.S. Army News Release, *Army Releases Findings in Detainee Abuse Investigations*, May 5, 2005, *at* http://www4.army.mil/ocpa/read.php?story_id_key=7293.

B. The Legal Standards and Their Application

governing the laws of war into the federal criminal code. Part I of this memorandum describes the WCA and the most relevant treaties that it incorporates: the four 1949 Geneva Conventions, which generally regulate the treatment of non-combatants, such as prisoners of war ("POWs"), the injured and sick, and civilians.[1]

Part II examines whether al Qaeda detainees can claim the protections of these agreements. Al Qaeda is merely a violent political movement or organization and not a nation-state. As a result, it is ineligible to be a signatory to any treaty. Because of the novel nature of this conflict, moreover, we do not believe that al Qaeda would be included in non-international forms of armed conflict to which some provisions of the Geneva Conventions might apply. Therefore, neither the Geneva Conventions nor the WCA regulate[s] the detention of al Qaeda prisoners captured during the Afghanistan conflict.

Part III discusses whether the same treaty provisions, as incorporated through the WCA, apply to the treatment of captured members of the Taliban militia. We believe that the Geneva Conventions do not apply for several reasons. First, the Taliban was not a government and Afghanistan was not — even prior to the beginning of the present conflict — a functioning State during the period in which they engaged in hostilities against the United States and its allies. Afghanistan's status as a failed state is ground alone to find that members of the Taliban militia are not entitled to enemy POW status under the Geneva Conventions. Further, it is clear that the President has the constitutional authority to suspend our treaties with Afghanistan pending the restoration of a legitimate government capable of performing Afghanistan's treaty obligations. Second, it appears from the public evidence that the Taliban militia may have been so intertwined with al Qaeda as to be functionally indistinguishable from it. To the extent that the Taliban militia was more akin to a non-governmental organization that used military force to pursue its religious and political ideology than a functioning government, its members would be on the same legal footing as al Qaeda.

In Part IV, we address the question whether any customary international law of armed conflict might apply to the al Qaeda or Taliban militia members detained during the course of the Afghanistan conflict. We conclude that customary international law, whatever its source and content, does not bind the President, or restrict the actions of the United States military, because it does not constitute federal law recognized under the Supremacy Clause of the Constitution. The President, however, has the constitutional authority as Commander in Chief to interpret and apply the customary or common laws of war in such a way that they would extend to the conduct of members of both al Qaeda and the Taliban, and also to the conduct of the U.S. Armed Forces towards members of those groups taken as prisoners in Afghanistan.

---

1. The four Geneva Conventions for the Protection of Victims of War, dated August 12, 1949, were ratified by the United States on July 14, 1955. These are the Convention for the Amelioration of the Condition of the Wounded and Sick in Armed Forces in the Field, 6 U.S.T. 3115 ("Geneva Convention I"); the Convention for the Amelioration of the Condition of Wounded, Sick and Shipwrecked Members of the Armed Forces at Sea, 6 U.S.T. 3219 ("Geneva Convention II"); the Convention Relative to the Treatment of Prisoners of War, 6 U.S.T. 3517 ("Geneva Convention III"); and the Convention Relative to the Protection of Civilian Persons in Time of War, 6 U.S.T. 3317 ("Geneva Convention IV").

I. BACKGROUND AND OVERVIEW OF THE WAR CRIMES ACT AND THE GENEVA CONVENTIONS

... We believe that the WCA provides a useful starting point for our analysis of the application of the Geneva Conventions to the treatment of detainees captured in the Afghanistan theater of operations.[4] Section 2441 of Title 18 renders certain acts punishable as "war crimes." The statute's definition of that term incorporates, by reference, certain treaties or treaty provisions relating to the laws of war, including the Geneva Conventions.

A. SECTION 2441: AN OVERVIEW

Section 2441 reads in full as follows:

War crimes

    (a) Offense.—Whoever, whether inside or outside the United States, commits a war crime, in any of the circumstances described in subsection (b), shall be fined under this title or imprisoned for life or any term of years, or both, and if death results to the victim, shall also be subject to the penalty of death.

    (b) Circumstances.—The circumstances referred to in subsection (a) are that the person committing such war crime or the victim of such war crime is a member of the Armed Forces of the United States or a national of the United States....

    (c) Definition.—As used in this section the term "war crime" means any conduct—

        (1) defined as a grave breach in any of the international conventions signed at Geneva 12 August 1949, or any protocol to such convention to which the United States is a party;

        (2) prohibited by Article 23, 25, 27, or 28 of the Annex to the Hague Convention IV, Respecting the Laws and Customs of War on Land, signed 18 October 1907;

        (3) which constitutes a violation of common Article 3 of the international conventions signed at Geneva, 12 August 1949, or any protocol to such convention to which the United States is a party and which deals with non-international armed conflict; or

        (4) of a person who, in relation to an armed conflict and contrary to the provisions of the Protocol on Prohibitions or Restrictions on the Use of Mines, Booby-Traps and Other Devices as amended at Geneva on 3 May 1996 (Protocol II as amended on 3 May 1996), when the United States is a party to such Protocol, willfully kills or causes serious injury to civilians.

18 U.S.C. §2441.

...A House Report states that the original legislation "carries out the international obligations of the United States under the Geneva Conventions

---

4. The rule of lenity requires that the WCA be read so as to ensure that prospective defendants have adequate notice of the nature of the acts that the statute condemns. *See, e.g., Castillo v. United States*, 530 U.S. 120, 131 (2000). In those cases in which the application of a treaty incorporated by the WCA is unclear, therefore, the rule of lenity requires that the interpretative issue be resolved in the defendant's favor.

B. The Legal Standards and Their Application

of 1949 to provide criminal penalties for certain war crimes." H.R. Rep. No. 104-698 at 1 (1996), *reprinted in* 1996 U.S.C.C.A.N. 2166, 2166. Each of those four conventions includes a clause relating to legislative implementation and to criminal punishment.[5]

In enacting section 2441, Congress also sought to fill certain perceived gaps in the coverage of federal criminal law. The main gaps were thought to be of two kinds: subject matter jurisdiction and personal jurisdiction. First, Congress found that "[t]here are major gaps in the prosecutability of individuals under federal criminal law for war crimes committed against Americans." H.R. Rep. No. 104-698 at 6, *reprinted in* 1996 U.S.C.C.A.N. at 2171. For example, "the simple killing of a[n American] prisoner of war" was not covered by any existing Federal statute. *Id.* at 5, *reprinted in* 1996 U.S.C.C.A.N. at 2170.[6] Second, Congress found that "[t]he ability to court martial members of our armed services who commit war crimes ends when they leave military service. [Section 2441] would allow for prosecution even after discharge." *Id.* at 7, *reprinted in* 1996 U.S.C.C.A.N. at 2172.[7] Congress considered it important to fill this gap, not only in the interest of the victims of war crimes, but also of the accused. "The Americans prosecuted would have available all the procedural protections of the American justice system. These might be lacking, if the United States extradited the individuals to their victims' home countries for prosecution." *Id.*[8] Accordingly, Section 2441 criminalizes forms of conduct in which a U.S. national or a member of the Armed Forces may be either a victim or a perpetrator.

B. GRAVE BREACHES OF THE GENEVA CONVENTIONS . . .

The Geneva Conventions . . . structure legal relationships between Nation States, not between Nation States and private, subnational groups or organizations. All four Conventions share the same Article 2, known as "common Article 2." It states:

> In addition to the provisions which shall be implemented in peacetime, the present Convention shall apply to all cases of declared war or of any other armed

---

5. That common clause reads as follows:

The [signatory Nations] undertake to enact any legislation necessary to provide effective penal sanctions for persons committing, or ordering to be committed, any of the grave breaches of the present Convention. . . . Each [signatory nation] shall be under the obligation to search for persons alleged to have committed, or to have ordered to be committed, such grave breaches, and shall bring such persons, regardless of their nationality, before its own courts. . . . It may also, if it prefers, . . . hand such persons over for trial to another [signatory nation], provided such [nation] has made out a *prima facie* case.

Geneva Convention I, art. 49; Geneva Convention II, art. 50; Geneva Convention III, art. 129; Geneva Convention IV, art. 146.

6. In projecting our criminal law extraterritorially in order to protect victims who are United States nationals, Congress was apparently relying on the international law principle of passive personality. . . .

7. In *United States ex rel. Toth v. Quarles*, 350 U.S. 11 (1955), the Supreme Court had held that a former serviceman could not constitutionally be tried before a court martial under the Uniform Code for Military Justice (the "UCMJ") for crimes he was alleged to have committed while in the armed services.

8. The principle of nationality in international law recognizes that (as Congress did here) a State may criminalize acts performed extraterritorially by its own nationals. *See, e.g, Skiriotes v. Florida*, 313 U.S. 69, 73 (1941); *Steele v. Bulova Watch Co.*, 344 U.S. 280, 282 (1952).

conflict *which may arise between two or more of the High Contracting Parties*, even if the state of war is not recognized by one of them.

The Convention shall also apply to all cases of partial or total occupation of the territory of a High Contracting Party, even if the said occupation meets with no armed resistance.

Although one of the Powers in conflict may not be a party to the present Convention, the Powers who are parties thereto shall remain bound by it in their mutual relations. They shall furthermore be bound by the Convention in relation to the said Power, if the latter accepts and applies the provisions thereof.

(Emphasis added.)

As incorporated by §2441(c)(1), the four Geneva Conventions similarly define "grave breaches." Geneva Convention III on POWs defines a grave breach as:

> willful killing, torture or inhuman treatment, including biological experiments, willfully causing great suffering or serious injury to body or health, compelling a prisoner of war to serve in the forces of the hostile Power, or willfully depriving a prisoner of war of the rights of fair and regular trial prescribed in this Convention.

Geneva Convention III, art. 130. . . .

Thus, the WCA does not criminalize all breaches of the Geneva Conventions. Failure to follow some of the regulations regarding the treatment of POWs, such as difficulty in meeting all of the conditions set forth for POW camp conditions, does not constitute a grave breach within the meaning of Geneva Convention III, art. 130. Only by causing great suffering or serious bodily injury to POWs, killing or torturing them, depriving them of access to a fair trial, or forcing them to serve in the Armed Forces, could the United States actually commit a grave breach. Similarly, unintentional, isolated collateral damage on civilian targets would not constitute a grave breach within the meaning of Geneva Convention IV, art. 147. Article 147 requires that for a grave breach to have occurred, destruction of property must have been done "wantonly" and without military justification, while the killing or injury of civilians must have been "wilful."

D. COMMON ARTICLE 3 OF THE GENEVA CONVENTIONS

Section 2441(c)(3) also defines as a war crime conduct that "constitutes a violation of common Article 3" of the Geneva Conventions. Article 3 is a unique provision that governs the conduct of signatories to the Conventions in a particular kind of conflict that is *not* one between High Contracting Parties to the Conventions. Thus, common Article 3 may require the United States, as a High Contracting Party, to follow certain rules even if other parties to the conflict are not parties to the Conventions. On the other hand, Article 3 requires state parties to follow only certain minimum standards of treatment toward prisoners, civilians, or the sick and wounded, rather than the Conventions as a whole.

Common Article 3 reads in relevant part as follows:

> In the case of armed conflict not of an international character occurring in the territory of one of the High Contracting Parties, each

B. The Legal Standards and Their Application

Party to the conflict shall be bound to apply, as a minimum, the following provisions:

(1) Persons taking no active part in the hostilities, including members of armed forces who have laid down their arms and those placed *hors de combat* by sickness, wounds, detention, or any other cause, shall in all circumstances, be treated humanely, without any adverse distinction founded on race, color, religion or faith, sex, birth or wealth, or any other similar criteria.

To this end, the following acts are and shall remain prohibited at any time and in any place whatsoever with respect to the above-mentioned persons:

(a) violence to life and person, in particular murder of all kinds, mutilation, cruel treatment and torture;

(b) taking of hostages;

(c) outrages upon personal dignity, in particular humiliating and degrading treatment;

(d) the passing of sentences and the carrying out of executions without previous judgment pronounced by a regularly constituted court, affording all the judicial guarantees which are recognized as indispensable by civilized peoples....

The application of the preceding provisions shall not affect the legal status of the Parties to the conflict.

Common Article 3 complements common Article 2. Article 2 applies to cases of declared war or of any other armed conflict that may arise between two or more of the High Contracting Parties, even if the state of war is not recognized by one of them. Common Article 3, however, covers "armed conflict not of an international character"—a war that does not involve cross-border attacks—that occurs within the territory of one of the High Contracting Parties. There is substantial reason to think that this language refers specifically to a condition of civil war, or a large-scale armed conflict between a State and an armed movement within its own territory.

To begin with, Article 3's text strongly supports the interpretation that it applies to large-scale conflicts between a State and an insurgent group. First, the language at the end of Article 3 states that "[t]he application of the preceding provisions shall not affect the legal status of the Parties to the conflict." This provision was designed to ensure that a Party that observed Article 3 during a civil war would not be understood to have granted the "recognition of the insurgents as an adverse party." Frits Kalshoven, *Constraints on the Waging of War* 59 (1987). Second, Article 3 is in terms limited to "armed conflict... occurring *in the territory of one of the High Contracting Parties*" (emphasis added). This limitation makes perfect sense if the Article applies to civil wars, which are fought primarily or solely within the territory of a single state. The limitation makes little sense, however, as applied to a conflict between a State and a transnational terrorist group, which may operate from different territorial bases, some of which might be located in States that are parties to the Conventions and some of which might not be. In such a case, the Conventions would apply to a single armed conflict in some scenes of action but not in others—which seems inexplicable....

Analysis of the background to the adoption of the Geneva Conventions in 1949 confirms our understanding of common Article 3. It appears that the drafters of the Conventions had in mind only the two forms of armed conflict that were regarded as matters of general *international* concern at the time: armed conflict between Nation States (subject to Article 2), and large-scale civil war within a Nation State (subject to Article 3)....

Decision re Application of the Geneva Convention on Prisoners of War to the Conflict with Al Qaeda and the Taliban
January 25, 2002
http://www.gwu.edu/~nsarchiv/NSAEBB/NSAEBB127/02.01.25.pdf

Memorandum for: The President

From: Alberto R. Gonzales [Counsel to the President]

PURPOSE

On January 18, I advised you that the Department of Justice had issued a formal legal opinion concluding that the Geneva Convention III on the Treatment of Prisoners of War (GPW) does not apply to the conflict with al Qaeda. I also advised you that DOJ's opinion concludes that there are reasonable grounds for you to conclude that GPW does not apply with respect to the conflict with the Taliban. I understand that you decided that GPW does not apply and, accordingly, that al Qaeda and Taliban detainees are not prisoners of war under the GPW.

The Secretary of State has requested that you reconsider that decision.[28] Specifically, he has asked that you conclude that GPW does apply to both al Qaeda and the Taliban. I understand, however, that he would agree that al Qaeda and Taliban fighters could be determined not to be prisoners of war (POWs) but only on a case-by-case basis following individual hearings before a military board.

This memorandum outlines the ramifications of your decision and the Secretary's request for reconsideration....

RAMIFICATIONS OF DETERMINATION THAT GPW DOES NOT APPLY

The consequences of a decision to adhere to what I understood to be your earlier determination that the GPW does not apply to the Taliban include the following:

POSITIVE:

Preserves flexibility:

- As you have said, the war against terrorism is a new kind of war. It is not the traditional clash between nations adhering to the laws of war that formed the backdrop for GPW. The nature of the new war places a high premium on other factors, such as the ability to quickly obtain information from captured terrorists and their sponsors in order to avoid further atrocities

[28. Judge Gonzales was reacting to an earlier Department of State memorandum, the essence of which is contained in the memorandum from State Department Legal Adviser William H. Taft, IV, *infra* p. 773.]

B. The Legal Standards and Their Application

against American civilians, and the need to try terrorists for war crimes such as wantonly killing civilians. In my judgment, this new paradigm renders obsolete Geneva's strict limitations on questioning of enemy prisoners and renders quaint some of its provisions requiring that captured enemy be afforded such things as commissary privileges, scrip (i.e., advances of monthly pay), athletic uniforms, and scientific instruments.

- Although some these provisions do not apply to detainees who are not POWs, a determination that GPW does not apply to al Qaeda and the Taliban eliminates any argument regarding the need for case-by-case determinations of POW status. It also holds open options for the future conflicts in which it may be more difficult to determine whether an enemy force as a whole meets the standard for POW status.

- By concluding that GPW does not apply to al Qaeda and the Taliban, we avoid foreclosing options for the future, particularly against nonstate actors.

Substantially reduces the threat of domestic criminal prosecution under the War Crimes Act (18 U.S.C. 2441)

- ...A determination that the GPW is not applicable to the Taliban would mean that Section 2441 would not apply to actions taken with respect to the Taliban.

- Adhering to your determination that GPW does not apply would guard effectively against misconstruction or misapplication of Section 2441 for several reasons.

  —First, some of the language of the GPW is undefined (it prohibits, for example, "outrages upon personal dignity" and "inhuman treatment"), and it is difficult to predict with confidence what actions might be deemed to constitute violations of the relevant provisions of GPW.
  —Second, it is difficult to predict the needs and circumstances that could arise in the course of the war on terrorism.
  —Third, it is difficult to predict the motives of prosecutors and independent counsels who may in the future decide to pursue unwarranted charges based on Section 2441. Your determination would create a reasonable basis in law that Section 2441 does not apply, which would provide a solid defense to any future prosecution.

NEGATIVE:

On the other hand, the following arguments would support reconsideration and reversal of your decision that the GPW does not apply to either al Qaeda or the Taliban:

- Since the Geneva Conventions were concluded in 1949, the United States has never denied their applicability to either U.S. or opposing forces engaged in armed conflict, despite several opportunities to do so. During the last Bush Administration, the United States stated that it "has a policy of applying the Geneva Conventions of 1949 whenever armed hostilities occur with regular foreign armed forces, even if arguments could be made that the threshold standards for the applicability of the Conventions . . . are not met."

- The United States could not invoke the GPW if enemy forces threatened to mistreat or mistreated U.S. or coalition forces captured during operations in Afghanistan, or if they denied Red Cross access or other POW privileges.

- The War Crimes Act could not be used against the enemy, although other criminal statutes and the customary law of war would still be available.

- Our position would likely provoke widespread condemnation among our allies and in some domestic quarters, even if we make clear that we will comply with the core humanitarian principles of the treaty as a matter of policy.

- Concluding that the Geneva Convention does not apply may encourage other countries to look for technical "loopholes" in future conflicts to conclude that they are not bound by GPW either.

- Other countries may be less inclined to turn over terrorists or provide legal assistance to us if we do not recognize a legal obligation to comply with the GPW.

- A determination that GPW does not apply to al Qaeda and the Taliban could undermine U.S. military culture which emphasizes maintaining the highest standards of conduct in combat, and could introduce an element of uncertainty in the status of adversaries.

RESPONSE TO ARGUMENTS FOR APPLYING GPW TO THE AL QAEDA AND THE TALIBAN

On balance, I believe that the arguments for reconsideration and reversal are unpersuasive.

- The argument that the U.S. has never determined that GPW did not apply is incorrect. In at least one case (Panama in 1989) the U.S. determined that GPW did not apply even though it determined for policy reasons to adhere to the convention. More importantly, as noted above, this is a new type of warfare — one not contemplated in 1949 when the GPW was framed — and requires a new approach in our actions towards captured terrorists. Indeed, as the statement quoted from the administration of President George Bush makes clear, the U.S. will apply GPW "whenever hostilities occur *with regular foreign armed forces.*" By its terms, therefore, the policy does not apply to a conflict with terrorists, or with irregular forces, like the Taliban, who are armed militants that oppressed and terrorized the people of Afghanistan.

- In response to the argument that we should decide to apply GPW to the Taliban in order to encourage other countries to treat captured U.S. military personnel in accordance with the GPW, it should be noted that your policy of providing humane treatment to enemy detainees gives us the credibility to insist on like treatment for our soldiers. Moreover, even if GPW is not applicable, we can still bring war crimes charges against anyone who mistreats U.S. personnel. Finally, I note that our adversaries in several recent conflicts have not been deterred by GPW in their mistreatment of captured U.S. personnel, and terrorists will not follow GPW rules in any event.

- The statement that other nations would criticize the U.S. because we have determined that GPW does not apply is undoubtedly true. It is even possible that some nations would point to that determination as a basis for failing to cooperate with us on specific matters in the war against terrorism. On the other hand, some international and domestic criticism is already likely to flow from your previous decision not to treat the detainees as POWs. And we can facilitate cooperation with other nations by reassuring them that we fully support GPW where it is applicable and by acknowledging that in this conflict the U.S. continues to respect other recognized standards.

- In the treatment of detainees, the U.S. will continue to be constrained by (i) its commitment to treat the detainees humanely and, to the extent appropriate and consistent with military necessity, in a manner consistent with the principles of GPW, (ii) its applicable treaty obligations, (iii) minimum standards of treatment universally recognized by the nations of the world, and (iv) applicable military regulations regarding the treatment of detainees.

- Similarly, the argument based on military culture fails to recognize that our military remain bound to apply the principles of GPW because that is what you have directed them to do.

Comments on Your Paper on the Geneva Convention
February 2, 2002
http://www.fas.org/sgp/othergov/taft.pdf

Memorandum to: Counsel to the President

From: William H. Taft, IV [Legal Adviser, Department of State]

The paper should make clear that the issue for decision by the President is whether the Geneva Conventions apply to the conflict in Afghanistan in which U.S. armed forces are engaged. The President should know that a decision that the Conventions do apply is consistent with the plain language of the Conventions and the unvaried practice of the United States in introducing its forces into conflict over fifty years. It is consistent with the advice of DOS lawyers and, as far as is known, the position of every other party to the Conventions. It is consistent with UN Security Council Resolution 1193 affirming that "All parties to the conflict [in Afghanistan] are bound to comply with their obligations under international humanitarian law and in particular the Geneva Conventions...." It is not inconsistent with the DOJ opinion that the Conventions generally do not apply to our world-wide effort to combat terrorism and to bring al Qaeda members to justice.

From a policy standpoint, a decision that the Conventions apply provides the best legal basis for treating the al Qaeda and Taliban detainees in the way we intend to treat them. It demonstrates that the United States bases its conduct not just on its policy preference but on its international legal obligations. Agreement by all lawyers that the War Crimes Act does not apply to our conduct means that the risk of prosecution under that statute is negligible. Any small benefit from reducing it further will be purchased at the expense of the men and women in our armed forces that we send into combat. A decision that the Conventions do not apply to the conflict in Afghanistan in which our armed forces are engaged deprives our troops there of any claim to the protection of the Convention in the event they are captured and weakens the protections afforded by the Conventions to our troops in future conflicts.

The structure of the paper suggesting a distinction between our conflict with al Qaeda and our conflict with the Taliban does not conform to the structure of the Conventions. The Conventions call for a decision whether they apply to the conflict in Afghanistan. If they do, their provisions are applicable to all persons involved in that conflict—al Qaeda, Taliban, Northern Alliance, U.S. troops, civilians, etc. If the Conventions do not apply to the conflict, no one involved in it will enjoy the benefit of their protections as a matter of law....

Working Group Report On Detainee Interrogations in the Global War on Terrorism[29]

April 4, 2003
http://www.defenselink.mil/news/Jun2004/d20040622doc8.pdf

II. INTERNATIONAL LAW...

B. THE 1994 CONVENTION AGAINST TORTURE

(U)[30] The United States' primary obligation concerning torture and related practices derives from the Convention Against Torture and Other Cruel, Inhuman, or Degrading Treatment or Punishment (commonly referred to as "the Torture Convention"). The United States ratified the Convention in 1994, but did so with a variety of Reservations and Understandings.

(U) Article 1 of the Convention defines the term "torture" for purpose of the treaty.[3] The United States conditioned its ratification of the treaty on an understanding that:

> ...in order to constitute torture, an act must be specifically intended to inflict severe physical or mental pain or suffering and that mental pain or suffering refers

---

[29. The Working Group, consisting of Defense Department officials, was tasked to prepare this report in a January 15, 2003, order from Secretary Donald Rumsfeld.]

[30. The expression "(U)" means that the adjacent material is unclassified.]

3. (U) Article 1 provides: "For the purposes of this Convention, the term 'torture' means any act by which severe pain or suffering, whether physical or mental, is intentionally inflicted on a person for such purposes as obtaining from him or a third person information or a confession, punishing him for an act he or a third person has committed or is suspected of having committed, or intimidating or coercing him or a third person, or for any reason based on discrimination of any kind, when such pain or suffering is inflicted by or at the instigation of or with the consent or acquiescence of a public official acting in an official capacity. It does not include pain or suffering arising only from, inherent in or incidental to lawful sanctions."

B. The Legal Standards and Their Application

to prolonged mental harm caused by or resulting from (1) the intentional infliction or threatened infliction of severe physical pain or suffering; (2) the administration or application, or threatened administration or application, of mind altering substances or other procedures calculated to disrupt profoundly the senses or the personality; (3) the threat of imminent death; or (4) the threat that another person will imminently be subjected to death, severe physical pain or suffering, or the administration or application of mind altering substances or other procedures calculated to disrupt profoundly the senses or personality.[4]

(U) Article 2 of the Convention requires the Parties to "take effective legislative, administrative, judicial and other measures to prevent acts of torture in any territory under its jurisdiction." The U.S. Government believed existing state and federal criminal law was adequate to fulfill this obligation, and did not enact implementing legislation. Article 2 also provides that acts of torture cannot be justified on the grounds of exigent circumstances, such as a state of war or public emergency, or on orders from a superior officer or public authority.[5] The United States did not have an Understanding or Reservation relating to this provision (however the U.S. issued a declaration stating that Article 2 is not self-executing).

(U) Article 3 of the Convention contains an obligation not to expel, return, or extradite a person to another state where there are "substantial grounds" for believing that the person would be in danger of being subjected to torture. The U.S. understanding relating to this article is that it only applies "if it is more likely than not" that the person would be tortured.

(U) Under Article 5, the Parties are obligated to establish jurisdiction over acts of torture when committed in any territory under its jurisdiction or on board a ship or aircraft registered in that state, or by its nationals wherever committed. The U.S. has criminal jurisdiction over territories under U.S. jurisdiction and onboard U.S. registered ships and aircraft by virtue of the special maritime and territorial jurisdiction of the United States (the "SMTJ") established under 18 U.S.C. §7. Acts that would constitute torture are likely to be criminal acts under the SMTJ.... Accordingly, the U.S. has satisfied its obligation to establish jurisdiction over such acts in territories under U.S. jurisdiction or on board a U.S. registered ship or aircraft. However, the additional requirement of Article 5 concerning jurisdiction over acts of torture by U.S. nationals "wherever committed" needed legislative implementation. Chapter 113C of Title 18 of the U.S. Code provides federal criminal jurisdiction over an extraterritorial act or attempted act of torture if the offender is a U.S. national. The statute defines "torture" consistent with the U.S. Understanding on Article 1 of the Torture Convention.

(U) The United States is obligated under Article 10 of the Convention to ensure that law enforcement and military personnel involved in interrogations are educated and informed regarding the prohibition against torture. Under Article 11, systematic reviews of interrogation rules, methods, and practices are also required.

---

4. 18 U.S.C. §2340 tracks this language. For a further discussion of the U.S. understandings and reservations, see the Initial Report of the U.S. to the U.N. Committee Against Torture, dated October 15, 1999.

5. (U) See discussion to the contrary at the Domestic Law section on the necessity defense.

(U) In addition to torture, the Convention prohibits cruel, inhuman and degrading treatment or punishment within territories under a Party's jurisdiction (Art 16). Primarily because the meaning of the term "cruel, inhuman and degrading treatment or punishment" was vague and ambiguous, the United States imposed a Reservation on this article to the effect that it is bound only to the extent that such treatment or punishment means the cruel, unusual and inhuman treatment or punishment prohibited by the 5th, 8th, and 14th Amendments to the U.S. Constitution....

(U) An additional treaty to which the United States is a party is the International Covenant on Civil and Political Rights, ratified by the United States in 1992. Article 7 of this treaty provides that "No one shall be subjected to torture or to cruel, inhuman or degrading treatment or punishment." The United States' ratification of the Covenant was subject to a Reservation that "the United States considers itself bound by Article 7 only to the extent that cruel, inhuman, or degrading treatment or punishments means the cruel and unusual treatment or punishment prohibited by the Fifth, Eighth, and/or Fourteenth Amendments to the Constitution of the United States." Under this treaty, a "Human Rights Committee" may, with the consent of the Party in question, consider allegations that such Party is not fulfilling its obligations under the Covenant. The United States has maintained consistently that the Covenant does not apply outside the United States or its special maritime and territorial jurisdiction, and that it does not apply to operations of the military during an international armed conflict....

III. DOMESTIC LAW

A. FEDERAL CRIMINAL LAW

1. Torture Statute

(U) 18 U.S.C. §2340 defines as torture any "*act committed by a person acting under the color of law specifically intended to inflict severe physical or mental pain....*" The intent required is the intent to inflict severe physical or mental pain. 18 U.S.C. §2340A requires that the offense occur "outside the United States." Jurisdiction over the offense extends to any national of the United States or any alleged offender present in the United States, and could, therefore, reach military members, civilian employees of the United States, or contractor employees.[8] The "United States" is defined to include all areas under the jurisdiction of the United States, including the special maritime and territorial jurisdiction (SMTJ) of the United States. SMTJ is a statutory creation[9] that extends the criminal jurisdiction of the United States for designated crimes to defined areas.[10] The effect is to grant federal court criminal jurisdiction for the specifically identified crimes....

---

8. (U) Section 2340A provides "*Whoever outside* the United States commits or attempts to commit torture shall be fined or imprisoned...." (emphasis added).
9. (U) 18 USC §7, "Special maritime and territorial jurisdiction of the United States" includes any lands under the exclusive or concurrent jurisdiction of the United States.
10. (U) Several paragraphs of 18 USC §7 are relevant to the issue at hand. Paragraph 7(3) provides: [SMTJ includes:] "Any lands reserved or acquired for the use of the United States, and

B. The Legal Standards and Their Application

(U) By its terms, the plain language of new subsection 9 includes Guantanamo Bay Naval Station (GTMO) within the definition of the SMTJ, and accordingly makes GTMO within the United States for purposes of §2340. As such, the Torture Statute does not apply to the conduct of U.S. personnel at GTMO. Prior to passage of the Patriot Act in 2001, GTMO was still considered within the SMTJ as manifested by (i) the prosecution of civilian dependents and employees living in GTMO in Federal District Courts based on SMTJ jurisdiction, and (ii) a Department of Justice opinion[11] to that effect....

(U) Although Section 2340 does not apply to interrogations at GTMO, it could apply to U.S. operations outside U.S. jurisdiction, depending on the facts and circumstances of each case involved. The following analysis is relevant to such activities.

(U) To convict a defendant of torture, the prosecution must establish that: (1) the torture occurred outside the United States; (2) the defendant acted under color of law; (3) the victim was within the defendant's custody or physical control; (4) the defendant specifically intended to cause severe physical or mental pain or suffering; and (5) that the act inflicted severe physical or mental pain or suffering. *See also* S. Exec. Rep. No. 101-30, at 6 (1990)....

3. Legal doctrines under the Federal Criminal Law that could render specific conduct, otherwise criminal, *not* unlawful...

a. *Commander-in-Chief Authority*

(U) As the Supreme Court has recognized, and as we will explain further below, the President enjoys complete discretion in the exercise of his Commander-in-Chief authority including in conducting operations against hostile forces. Because both "[t]he executive power and the command of the military and naval forces [are] vested in the President," the Supreme Court has unanimously stated that it is "*the President alone* who is constitutionally invested with the *entire charge of hostile operations.*" *Hamilton v. Dillin*, 88 U.S. (21 Wall.) 73, 87 (1874) (emphasis added).

(U) In light of the President's complete authority over the conduct of war, without a clear statement otherwise, criminal statutes are not read as infringing on the President's ultimate authority in these areas. The Supreme Court has established a canon of statutory construction that statutes are to be construed in a manner that avoids constitutional difficulties so long as a reasonable alternative construction is available. *See, e.g., Edward J. DeBartolo Corp. v. Florida Gulf Coast Bldg. & Constr. Trades Council*, 485 U.S. 568, 575 (1988) (citing *NLRB v. Catholic*

---

under the exclusive or concurrent jurisdiction thereof, or any place...." Paragraph 7(7) provides: [SMTJ includes:] "Any place outside the jurisdiction of any nation to an offense by or against a national of the United States. Similarly, paragraphs 7(1) and 7(5) extend SMTJ jurisdiction to, "the high seas, any other waters within the admiralty and maritime jurisdiction of the United States and out of the jurisdiction of any particular state, and any vessel belonging in whole or in part to the United States..." and to "any aircraft belonging in whole or in part to the United States... while such aircraft is in flight over the high seas, or over any other waters within the admiralty and maritime jurisdiction of the United States and out of the jurisdiction of any particular State."

11. (U) 6 Op. OLC 236 (1982). The issue was the status of GTMO for purposes of a statute banning slot machines on "any land where the United States government exercises exclusive or concurrent jurisdiction."

Bishop of Chicago, 440 U.S. 490, 499-501, 504 (1979)) ("[W]here an otherwise acceptable construction of a statute would raise serious constitutional problems, [courts] will construe [a] statute to avoid such problems unless such construction is plainly contrary to the intent of Congress."). This canon of construction applies especially where an act of Congress could be read to encroach upon powers constitutionally committed to a coordinate branch of government. . . .

(U) In the area of foreign affairs, and war powers in particular, the avoidance canon has special force. *See, e.g., Dept. of Navy v. Egan*, 484 U.S. 518, 530 (1988) ("unless Congress specifically has provided otherwise, courts traditionally have been reluctant to intrude upon the authority of the Executive in military and national security affairs."); *Japan Whaling Ass'n v. American Cetacean Socy*, 478 U.S. 221, 232-33 (1986) (construing federal statutes to avoid curtailment of traditional presidential prerogatives in foreign affairs). It should not be lightly assumed that Congress has acted to interfere with the President's constitutionally superior position as Chief Executive and Commander-in-Chief in the area of military operations. *See Egan*, 484 U.S. at 529 (quoting *Haig v. Agee*, 1453 U.S. 280, 293-94 (1981). *See also Agee*, 453 U.S. at 291 (deference to Executive Branch is "especially" appropriate "in the area of national security").

(U) In order to respect the President's inherent constitutional authority to manage a military campaign, 18 U.S.C. §2340A (the prohibition against torture) as well as any other potentially applicable statute must be construed as inapplicable to interrogations undertaken pursuant to his Commander-in-Chief authority. Congress lacks authority under Article I to set the terms and conditions under which the President may exercise his authority as Commander-in-Chief to control the conduct of operations during a war. The President's power to detain and interrogate enemy combatants arises out of his constitutional authority as Commander-in-Chief. A construction of Section 2340A that applied the provision to regulate the President's authority as Commander-in-Chief to determine the interrogation and treatment of enemy combatants would raise serious constitutional questions. Congress may no more regulate the President's ability to detain and interrogate enemy combatants than it may regulate his ability to direct troop movements on the battlefield. Accordingly, we would construe Section 2340A to avoid this constitutional difficulty and conclude that it does not apply to the President's detention and interrogation of enemy combatants pursuant to his Commander-in-Chief authority. . . .

(U) One of the core functions of the Commander in Chief is that of capturing, detaining, and interrogating members of the enemy. It is well settled that the President may seize and detain enemy combatants, at least for the duration of the conflict, and the laws of war make clear that prisoners may be interrogated for information concerning the enemy, its strength, and its plans. Numerous Presidents have ordered the capture, detention, and questioning of enemy combatants during virtually every major conflict in the Nation's history, including recent conflicts in Korea, Vietnam, and the Persian Gulf. Recognizing this authority, Congress has never attempted to restrict or interfere with the President's authority on this score.

(U) Any effort by Congress to regulate the interrogation of unlawful combatants would violate the Constitution's sole vesting of the Commander-in-Chief authority in the President. There can be little doubt that intelligence operations, such as the detention and interrogation of enemy combatants and leaders, are

B. The Legal Standards and Their Application

both necessary and proper for the effective conduct of a military campaign. Indeed, such operations may be of more importance in a war with an international terrorist organization than one with the conventional armed forces of a nation-state, due to the former's emphasis on secret operations and surprise attacks against civilians. It may be the case that only successful interrogations can provide the information necessary to prevent the success of covert terrorist attacks upon the United States and its citizens....

b. Necessity

(U) The defense of necessity could be raised, under the current circumstances, to an allegation of a violation of a criminal statute. Often referred to as the "choice of evils" defense, necessity has been defined as follows:

> Conduct that the actor believes to be necessary to avoid a harm or evil to himself or to another is justifiable, provided that:
> (a) the harm or evil sought to be avoided by such conduct is greater than that sought to be prevented by the law defining the offense charged; and
> (b) neither the Code nor other law defining the offense provides exceptions or defenses dealing with the specific situation involved; and
> (c) a legislative purpose to exclude the justification claimed does not otherwise plainly appear.

Model Penal Code §3.02. *See also* Wayne R. LaFave & Austin W. Scott, 1 Substantive Criminal Law §5.4 at 627 (1986 & 2002 supp.) ("LaFave & Scott"). Although there is no federal statute that generally establishes necessity or other justifications as defenses to federal criminal laws, the Supreme Court has recognized the defense. *See United States v. Bailey*, 444 U.S. 394, 410 (1980) (relying on LaFave & Scott and Model Penal Code definitions of necessity defense)....

(U) Legal authorities identify an important exception to the necessity defense. The defense is available "only in situations wherein the legislature has not itself, in its criminal statute, made a determination of values." [LaFave & Scott] at 629. Thus, if Congress explicitly has made clear that violation of a statute cannot be outweighed by the harm avoided, courts cannot recognize the necessity defense. LaFave and Israel provide as an example an abortion statute that made clear that abortions even to save the life of the mother would still be a crime; in such cases the necessity defense would be unavailable. *Id.* at 630. Here, however, Congress has not explicitly made a determination of values vis-a-vis torture. In fact, Congress explicitly removed efforts to remove torture from the weighing of values permitted by the necessity defense.[21]

---

21. In the CAT [Convention Against Torture], torture is defined as the intentional infliction of severe pain or suffering "for such purposes as obtaining from him or a third person information or a confession." CAT art 1.1. One could argue that such a definition represented an attempt to indicate that the good of obtaining information — no matter what the circumstances — could not justify an act of torture. In other words, necessity would not be a defense. In enacting Section 2340, however, Congress removed the purpose element in the definition of torture, evidencing an intention to remove any fixing of values by statute. By leaving Section 2340 silent as to the harm done by torture in comparison to other harms, Congress allowed the necessity defense to apply when appropriate.

Further, the CAT contains an additional provision that "no exceptional circumstances whatsoever, whether a state of war or a threat of war, internal political instability or any other public

c. Self-Defense

(U) Even if a court were to find that necessity did not justify the violation of a criminal statute, a defendant could still appropriately raise a claim of self-defense. The right to self-defense, even when it involves deadly force, is deeply embedded in our law, both as to individuals and as to the nation as a whole.... Self-defense is a common-law defense to federal criminal law offenses, and nothing in the text, structure or history of Section 2340A precludes its application to a charge of torture. In the absence of any textual provision to the contrary, we assume self-defense can be an appropriate defense to an allegation of torture....

(U) There can be little doubt that the nation's right to self-defense has been triggered under our law. The Constitution announces that one of its purposes is "to provide for the common defense." U.S. Const., Preamble. Article I, §8 declares that Congress is to exercise its powers to "provide for the common defense." *See also* 2 Pub. Papers of Ronald Reagan 920, 921 (1988-89) (right to self-defense recognized by Article 51 of the U.N. Charter). The President has particular responsibility and power to take steps to defend the nation and its people. *In re Neagle*, 135 U.S. at 64. *See also* U.S. Const. art. IV, §4 ("The United States shall... protect [each of the States] against Invasion"). As Commander-in-Chief and Chief Executive, he may use the Armed Forces to protect the nation and its people. *See, e.g., United States v. Verdugo-Urquidez*, 494 U.S. 259, 273 (1990). And he may employ secret agents to aid in his work as Commander-in-Chief. *Totten v. United States*, 92 U.S. 105, 106 (1876). As the Supreme Court observed in *The Prize Cases*, 67 U.S. (2 Black) 635 (1862), in response to an armed attack on the United States "the President is not only authorized but bound to resist force by force... without waiting for any special legislative authority." *Id.* at 668. The September 11 events were a direct attack on the United States, and as we have explained above, the President has authorized the use of military force with the support of Congress.

(U) As DOJ has made clear in opinions involving the war on al Qaida, the nation's right to self-defense has been triggered by the events of September 11. If a government defendant were to harm an enemy combatant during an interrogation in a manner that might arguably violate criminal prohibition, he would be doing so in order to prevent further attacks on the United States by the al Qaida terrorist network. In that case, DOJ believes that he could argue that the executive branch's constitutional authority to protect the nation from attack justified his actions. This national and international version of the right to self-defense could supplement and bolster the government defendant's individual right....

---

emergency, may be invoked as a justification of torture," CAT art. 2.2. Aware of this provision of the treaty and of the definition of the necessity defense that allows the legislature to provide *for* an exception to the defense, see Model Penal Code §3.02(b), Congress did not incorporate CAT article 2.2 into Section 2-4. Given that Congress omitted CAT's effort to bar a necessity or wartime defense, Section 2340 could be read as permitting the defense.

B. The Legal Standards and Their Application

B. FEDERAL CIVIL STATUTES

1. 28 U.S.C. §1350

(U) 28 U.S.C. §1350 extends the jurisdiction of the U.S. District Courts to "*any civil action by an alien for a tort only, committed in violation of the law of nations or a treaty of the United States.*"[33] Section 1350 is a vehicle by which victims of torture and other human rights violations by their native government and its agents have sought judicial remedy for the wrongs they've suffered. However, all the decided cases we have found involve foreign nationals suing in U.S. District Courts for conduct by foreign actors/governments.[34] The District Court for the District of Columbia has determined that section 1350 actions, by the GTMO detainees, against the United States or its agents acting within the scope of employment fail. This is because (1) the United States has not waived sovereign immunity to such suits like those brought by the detainees, and (2) the *Eisentrager* doctrine barring habeas access also precludes other potential avenues of jurisdiction.[35] This of course leaves interrogators vulnerable in their individual capacity for conduct a court might find to constitute torture. Assuming a court would take jurisdiction over the matter and grant standing to the detainee,[36] it is possible that this statute would provide an avenue of relief for actions of the United States or its agents found to violate customary international law....

2. Torture Victims Protection Act (TVPA)

(U) In 1992, President Bush signed into law the Torture Victims Protection Act of 1991.[37] Appended to the U.S. Code as a note to section 1350, the TVPA specifically creates a cause of action for individuals (or their successors) who have been subjected to torture or extra-judicial killing by "an individual who, under actual or apparent authority, or color of law, *of any foreign nation*— (1) subjects an individual to torture shall, in a civil action, be liable for damages to that individual; or (2) subjects an individual to extra-judicial killing shall, in a civil action, be liable for damages...." (emphasis added).[38] Thus, the TVPA does not apply to the conduct of U.S. agents acting under the color of law....

---

33. (U) 28 U.S.C. §1350, the Alien Tort Claim Act (ATCA).
34. (U) See, for example, *Abebe-Jira v. Negewo*, No. 93-9133, United States Court of Appeals, Eleventh Circuit, Jan. 10, 1996. In this case the 11th Circuit concluded, "the Alien Tort Claims Act establishes a federal forum where courts may fashion domestic common law remedies to give effect to violations of customary international law."
35. (U) *Al Odah v. United States* (D.D.C., 2002).
36. (U) *Filartiga v. Pena-Irala*, 630 F.2d 876 (2nd Cir. 1980) 885, note 18, "conduct of the type alleged here [torture] would be actionable under 42 U.S.C. §1983, or undoubtedly the Constitution, if performed by a government official."
37. Pub. L. No. 102-256, 106 Stat. 73, 28 U.S.C. §1350 (note).
38. (U) The definition of torture used in PL 102-256 is: "any act, directed against an individual in the offender's custody or physical control, by which severe pain or suffering (other than pain or suffering arising only from or inherent in, or incidental to lawful sanctions) whether physical or mental, is intentionally inflicted on that individual for such purposes as obtaining from that individual or a third person information or a confession, punishing that individual for an act that individual or a third person has committed or is suspected of having committed, intimidating or coercing that individual or a third person, or for any reason based on discrimination of any kind." This is similar, but broader, than the definition in the Torture Statute. The definition of mental pain and suffering is the same as in the Torture Statute.

Counter-Resistance Techniques in the War on Terrorism
April 16, 2003
http://www.defenselink.mil/news/Jun2004/d20040622doc9.pdf

Memorandum for: Commander, US Southern Command

From: Donald Rumsfeld, Secretary of Defense

(U) I have considered the report of the Working Group that I directed be established on January 15, 2003.

(U) I approve the use of specified counter-resistance techniques, subject to the following:

(U) a. The techniques I authorize are those lettered A-X, at Tab A.

(U) b. These techniques must be used with all the safeguards described at Tab B.

(U) c. Use of these techniques is limited to interrogations of unlawful combatants held at Guantanamo Bay, Cuba.

(U) d. Prior to the use of these techniques, the Chairman of the Working Group on Detainee Interrogations in the Global War on Terrorism must brief you and your staff.

(U) I reiterate that US Armed Forces shall continue to treat detainees humanely and, to the extent appropriate and consistent with military necessity, in a manner consistent with the principles of the Geneva Conventions. In addition, if you intend to use techniques B, I, O, or X, you must specifically determine that military necessity requires its use and notify me in advance.

(U) If, in your view, you require additional interrogation techniques for a particular detainee, you should provide me, via the Chairman of the Joint Chiefs of Staff, a written request describing the proposed technique, recommended safeguards, and the rationale for applying it with an identified detainee.

(U) Nothing in this memorandum in any way restricts your existing authority to maintain good order and discipline among detainees.

Tab A
Interrogation Techniques

(U) The use of techniques A-X is subject to the general safeguards as provided below as well as specific implementation guidelines to be provided by the appropriate authority. Specific implementation guidance with respect to techniques A-Q is provided in Army Field Manual 34-52. Further implementation guidance with respect to techniques R-X will need to be developed by the appropriate authority.

(U) Of the techniques set forth below, the policy aspects of certain techniques should be considered to the extent those policy aspects reflect the views of other major U.S. partner nations. Where applicable, the description of the technique is annotated to include a summary of the policy issues that should be considered before application of the technique.

A. (U) Direct: Asking straightforward questions.

B. The Legal Standards and Their Application

B. (U) Incentive/Removal of Incentive: Providing a reward or removing a privilege, above and beyond those that are required by the Geneva Convention, from detainees. (Caution: Other nations that believe that detainees are entitled to POW protections may consider that provision and retention of religious items (e.g., the Koran) are protected under international law (see, Geneva III, Article 34). Although the provisions of the Geneva Convention are not applicable to the interrogation of unlawful combatants, consideration should be given to these views prior to the application of the technique.)

C. (U) Emotional Love: Playing on the love a detainee has for an individual or group.

D. (U) Emotional Hate: Playing on the hatred a detainee has for an individual or group.

E. (U) Fear Up Harsh: Significantly increasing the fear level in a detainee.

F. (U) Fear Up Mild: Moderately increasing the fear level in a detainee.

G. (U) Reduced Fear: Reducing the fear level in a detainee.

H. (U) Pride and Ego Up: Boosting the ego of a detainee.

I. (U) Pride and Ego Down: Attacking or insulting the ego of a detainee, not beyond the limits that would apply to a POW. (Caution: Article 17 of the Geneva III provides, "Prisoners of war who refuse to answer may not be threatened, insulted, or exposed to any unpleasant or disadvantageous treatment of any kind." Other nations that believe that detainees are entitled to POW protections may consider this technique inconsistent with the provisions of Geneva. Although the provisions of Geneva are not applicable to the interrogation of unlawful combatants, consideration should be given to these views prior to application of the technique.)

J. (U) Futility: Invoking the feeling of futility of a detainee.

K. (U) We Know All: Convincing the detainee that the interrogator knows the answer to questions he asks the detainee.

L. (U) Establish Your Identity: Convincing the detainee that the interrogator has mistaken the detainee for someone else.

M. (U) Repetition Approach: Continuously repeating the same question to the detainee within interrogation periods of normal duration.

N. (U) File and Dossier: Convincing the detainee that the interrogator has a damning and inaccurate file, which must be fixed.

O. (U) Mutt and Jeff: A team consisting of a friendly and harsh interrogator. The harsh interrogator might employ the Pride and Ego Down technique. (Caution: Other nations that believe that POW protections apply to detainees may view this technique as inconsistent with the Geneva III, Article 13 which provides that POWs must be protected against acts of intimidation. Although the provisions of Geneva are not applicable to the interrogation of unlawful combatants, consideration should be given to these views prior to application of the technique.)

P. (U) Rapid Fire: Questioning in rapid succession without allowing detainee to answer.

Q. (U) Silence: Staring at the detainee to encourage discomfort.

R. (U) Change of Scenery Up: Removing the detainee from the standard interrogation setting (generally to a location more pleasant, but no worse).

S. (U) Change of Scenery Down: Removing the detainee from the standard interrogation setting and placing him in a setting that may be less comfortable; would not constitute a substantial change in environmental quality.
T. (U) Dietary Manipulation: Changing the diet of a detainee; no intended deprivation of food or water; no adverse medical or cultural effect and without intent to deprive subject of food or water, e.g., hot rations to MREs.
U. (U) Environmental Manipulation: Altering the environment to create moderate discomfort (e.g., adjusting temperature or introducing an unpleasant smell). Conditions would not be such that they would injure the detainee. Detainee would be accompanied by interrogator at all times. (Caution: Based on court cases in other countries, some nations may view application of this technique in certain circumstances to be inhumane. Consideration of these views should be given to use of this technique.)
V. (U) Sleep Adjustment: Adjusting the sleeping times of the detainee (e.g., reversing sleep cycles from night to day.) This technique is NOT sleep deprivation.
W. (U) False Flag: Convincing the detainee that individuals from a country other than the United States are interrogating him.
X. (U) Isolation: Isolating the detainee from other detainees while still complying with basic standards of treatment. (Caution: The use of isolation as an interrogation technique requires detailed implementation instructions, including specific guidelines regarding the length of isolation, medical and psychological review, and approval for extensions of the length of isolation by the appropriate level in the chain of command. This technique is not known to have been generally used for interrogation purposes for longer than 30 days. Those nations that believe detainees are subject to POW protections may view use of this technique as inconsistent with the requirements of Geneva III, Article 13 which provides that POWs must be protected against acts of intimidation; Article 14 which provides that POWs are entitled to respect for their person; Article 34 which prohibits coercion and Article 126 which ensures access and basic standards of treatment. Although the provisions of Geneva are not applicable to the interrogation of unlawful combatants, consideration should be given to these views prior to application of the technique.)

Tab B
General Safeguards

(U) Application of these interrogation techniques is subject to the following general safeguards: (i) limited to use only at strategic interrogation facilities; (ii) there is a good basis to believe that the detainee possesses critical intelligence; (iii) the detainee is medically and operationally evaluated as suitable (considering all techniques to be used in combination); (iv) interrogators are specifically trained for the technique(s); (v) a specific interrogation plan

B. The Legal Standards and Their Application

(including reasonable safeguards, limits on duration, intervals between applications, termination criteria and the presence or availability of qualified medical personnel) has been developed; (vi) there is appropriate supervision; and (vii) there is appropriate specified senior approval for use with any specific detainee (after considering the foregoing and receiving legal advice)....

NOTES AND QUESTIONS

a. Torture in General

1. *Detainee Investigations.* Several collections of documents relating to U.S. interrogation of its detainees may be found online. Among the most extensive are New York Times, *A Guide to the Memos on Torture* (n.d.), *at* http://www.nytimes.com/ref/international/24MEMO-GUIDE.html; National Security Archive, *Interrogation Documents: Debating U.S. Policy and Methods* (updated July 13, 2004), *at* http://www.gwu.edu/~nsarchiv/NSA EBB/NSAEBB127; and American Civil Liberties Union, *Government Documents on Torture* (n.d.), *at* http://action.aclu.org/torturefoia/. The Department of Defense Web site also provides links to DOD reports, independent panel and inspector general reports, briefing transcripts, and news releases and articles, *at* http://www.defenselink.mil/news/detainee_investigations.html. Many of the key documents are collected in Mark Danner, *Torture and Truth: America, Abu Ghraib, and the War on Terror* (2004); and *The Torture Papers: the Road to Abu Ghraib* (Karen J. Greenberg & Joshua L. Dratel eds., 2005).

A February 2006 U.N. report on the Guantánamo Bay detentions, compiled by U.N. envoys who interviewed former detainees, their families, and their lawyers, along with U.S. officials, concluded that U.S. treatment of detainees there violated the detainees' rights to physical and mental health and, in some cases, constituted torture. United Nations Commission on Human Rights, *Situation of Detainees at Guantanamo Bay*, Feb. 15, 2006, *available at* http://www.ohchr.org/english/bodies/chr/docs/62chr/E.CN.4.2006.120_.pdf. The United States replied to the U.N. report with a factual and legal defense, *Reply of the Government of the United States of America to the Report of the Five UNCHR Special Rapporteurs on Detainees in Guantanamo Bay, Cuba*, Mar. 10, 2006, *available at* http://www.asil.org/pdfs/ilib0603212.pdf.

2. *Definitions.* What constitutes "torture"? Not surprisingly, torture is forbidden by a number of written treaties and international conventions, by customary international law, and by U.S. statutory and constitutional law. There is, however, no universally accepted definition of "torture." Torture may be physical or psychological, and a variety of interrogation techniques may be forbidden as torture.

What are the elements of the Torture Convention's definition of "torture"? See *supra* p. 774. Of the U.S. understanding upon ratification? See *supra* p. 774. Do any of the techniques in Defense Secretary Rumsfeld's April 16, 2003, memo on Guantánamo exceed the limits set out in either? See *supra* pp. 782-785. Which techniques? Would the same methods be lawful in Iraq? At some undisclosed offshore location?

The Torture Statute, 18 U.S.C. §§2340-2340B, is supposed to implement the Torture Convention. *See* Working Group Report, *supra* p. 774 (noting that the statute tracks the U.S. reservation to Article 1 of the Torture Convention). Recall that in August 2002 the Justice Department's OLC offered a very narrow definition of "torture," see *supra* p. 761, and argued that the President could authorize torture. It also indicated that interrogation activities "may be cruel, inhuman, or degrading, but still not produce pain and suffering of the requisite intensity" to violate §2340. Bybee Memo, *supra* p. 761 n.4, at 1. The memorandum also asserted that a specific intent to torture is required to violate the torture statute. *Id.* at 4. How would you rate this definition of the key terms against those set out in the Torture Convention and the U.S. understanding? According to some commentators, the interpretations of relevant law by Defense Department and Justice Department lawyers amounted to endorsements of what has been referred to as "torture lite." *See* Seth F. Kreimer, *"Torture Light," "Full Bodied" Torture, and the Insulation of Legal Conscience*, 1 J. Natl. Security L. & Poly. 187 (2005); Duncan Campbell, *U.S. Interrogators Turn to "Torture Lite,"* The Guardian, Jan. 25, 2003, at 17.

Two months after the public disclosure of abuses at Abu Ghraib, the August 2002 memorandum was withdrawn by OLC head Jack Goldsmith, and a new opinion superseding it was delivered to the new Deputy Attorney General for OLC on December 30, 2004. Memorandum for James B. Comey, Deputy Atty. General, from Daniel Levin, Acting Asst. Atty. General, *Legal Standards Applicable Under 18 U.S.C. 2340-2340A*, Dec. 30, 2004, *at* http://www.usdoj.gov/olc/dagmemo.pdf. The new memorandum questioned "the appropriateness and relevance of the non-statutory discussion . . . and various aspects of the statutory analysis" in the earlier memo — namely, the assertion that torture required organ failure, impaired bodily function, or death. *Id.* at 1-2. However, the new memorandum did not disagree with any substantive conclusions offered by the 2002 memorandum. *Id.* at 2 n.8. The 2004 memorandum continued to maintain that it was unlikely that a person who "acted in good faith, and only after reasonable investigation establishing that his conduct would not inflict severe physical or mental pain or suffering," would possess the specific intent required to violate the torture statute. *Id.* at 17. Do you agree?

Would a universal definition of the key terms be a good idea? Would it matter? *See* Oren Gross, *Are Torture Warrants Warranted? Pragmatic Absolutism and Official Disobedience*, 88 Minn. L. Rev. 101, 109 (2004) ("preventive interrogational torture is far too complex to be addressed by definitional juggling"); Jeremy Waldron, *Torture and Positive Law: Jurisprudence for the White House*, 105 Colum. L. Rev. 1681, 1698 (2005) (a precise definition of torture is advisable, because "if the terms are . . . indeterminate, the person to whom the prohibition is addressed may not know exactly what is required of him"). *Compare* John T. Parry, *"Just For Fun": Understanding Torture and Understanding Abu Ghraib*, 1 J. Natl. Security L. & Poly. 253, 262-270 (2005) (asserting that the United States and other nations play a "definitional game" where governments parse language and deny responsibility for conduct that goes too far).

Do you think the legal ambiguities described here contributed to abuses at Abu Ghraib or elsewhere?

B. The Legal Standards and Their Application

3. *Assigning Responsibility.* Guidance for interrogations at Abu Ghraib prison came from three different sources at different times—from Army field manuals, from personnel who had worked earlier in Afghanistan, and from Guantánamo. Craig Gordon, *High-Pressure Tactics: Critics Say Bush Policies— Post 9/11—Gave Interrogators Leeway to Push Beyond Normal Limits*, Newsday, May 23, 2004, at A5. General Taguba found that operating procedures and copies of the Geneva Conventions were not distributed to the guards handling the prisoners. To complicate matters, senior military commanders called for interrogators to isolate and manipulate detainees who might have "significant intelligence value." R. Jeffrey Smith, *Memo Gave Intelligence Bigger Role: Increased Pressure Sought on Prisoners*, Wash. Post, May 21, 2004, at A17.

The overall detention and interrogation picture that has emerged from official statements and documents reveals "a trail of fitful ad hoc policymaking" where interrogation techniques were authorized, then rescinded or modified, at times leading to decisions made in the field or at the Pentagon on a case-by-case basis. Dana Priest & Bradley Graham, *U.S. Struggled Over How Far to Push Tactics*, Wash. Post, June 24, 2004, at A1. Unlike CIA requests for expanded interrogation authority that were reviewed by the Department of Justice and the National Security Council, Defense Department interrogation policy decisions were not subjected to outside review. *Id.*

A March 2004 classified report by the CIA Inspector General, however, concluded that some of the interrogation techniques approved for CIA use by the Department of Justice in 2002 may violate the Convention Against Torture prohibition on "cruel, inhuman, or degrading" treatment. Douglas Jehl, *Report Warned on CIA's Tactics in Interrogation*, N.Y. Times, Nov. 9, 2005, at A1. A March 2006 news story described the existence of a temporary, top-secret detention site at Camp Nana, near Baghdad, that since early 2004 included a "Black Room" where placards posted by soldiers stated, "No blood, no foul." Eric Schmitt & Carolyn Marshall, *In Secret Unit's "Black Room," a Grim Portrait of U.S. Abuse*, N.Y. Times, Mar. 19, 2006, at A1. Detainee abuse attributed to the Special Operations unit at Camp Nana reflected "confusion over and, in some cases, disregard for" interrogation rules and standards for treatment of detainees. *Id.*

The Army announced in April 2005 that it was preparing to issue a new field manual to replace *Intelligence Interrogation* (FM 34-52), Sept. 28, 1992. The new manual reportedly will specifically prohibit the harsh techniques that came to light in the Abu Ghraib scandal and will include safeguards to prevent future misconduct. Eric Schmitt, *In New Manual, Army Limits Tactics in Interrogation*, N.Y. Times, April 28, 2005, at A1. The new manual apparently will also forbid physical and mental torture, slapping, and humiliation. Additional units trained in detention operations are planned, including 9,000 new military intelligence personnel. *Id.*

In June 2005 the Defense Department promoted or nominated for promotion the former deputy commander of U.S. forces in Iraq and the senior military lawyer for the U.S. command in Baghdad, both involved in overseeing or advising detention and interrogation operations during the Abu Ghraib scandal. The top intelligence officer in Iraq at that time was promoted earlier in the year. Eric Schmitt, *Army Moves to Advance 2 Linked to Abu Ghraib*, N.Y. Times, June 29, 2005, at A20. The *Schlesinger Report, supra* p. 761 n.6, found those officers to be among those responsible for the abuses at Abu Ghraib, and the Fay Report, *supra* p. 762 n.12, faulted the commanders for issuing and revising the interrogation rules three times in 30 days and their legal staff for giving bad legal advice — not warning that practices permitted at Guantánamo and in Afghanistan might not be lawful in Iraq. Nevertheless, the Army Inspector General cleared them of any wrongdoing. Inspector General, Dept. of the Army, *Detainee Operations Inspection*, July 21, 2004, *at* http://www4.army.mil/ocpa/reports/ArmyIGDetaineeAbuse/index.html.

Thus far, only low-level interrogators and handlers have been disciplined for interrogation abuses in Afghanistan and at Guantánamo. A review by Air Force Lt. Gen. Randall M. Schmidt of three years' practice and over 24,000 interrogations at Guantánamo led to a recommendation of reprimand for Army Maj. Gen. Geoffrey C. Miller, commander of the Guantánamo facility in 2002 and 2003, for failing to oversee the interrogation of a high-value detainee who was subjected to abusive treatment. *Army Regulation 15-6: Final Report, Investigation into FBI Allegations of Detainee Abuse at Guantanamo Bay, Cuba Detention Facility*, Apr. 1, 2005, amended June 9, 2005. Nevertheless, the Army's Inspector General decided that Miller had not violated the law or Defense Department policy. David S. Cloud, *Guantanamo Reprimand Was Sought, An Aide Says*, N.Y. Times, July 13, 2005, at A16. One suggested reason for the failure to hold senior officials accountable is the lack of an independent prosecutor inside the military, equivalent to a district attorney, who would have command authority to investigate up the chain of command. Eric Schmitt, *Iraq Abuse Trial Is Again Limited to Lower Ranks*, N.Y. Times, March 23, 2006, A1.

At a news conference called in response to the Abu Ghraib publicity in June 2004, White House Counsel Alberto Gonzales denied that "the president...authorized ordered or directed" violations of "the standards of the torture conventions or the torture statute." *Transcript of Press Briefing by Alberto Gonzales*, June 22, 2004. What legal wiggle room does the Gonzales statement leave for the President? Does it mean that President Bush was not responsible for the reported abuses?

Who do you think is responsible for the abuses at Abu Ghraib and Camp Nana? If you are unsure of the answer, how do you think it will be possible to find out?

4. *Who Decides What Interrogation Conduct Is Unlawful?* The official policy of the United States is to condemn and prohibit torture. *See generally* U.S. Dept. of State, *Initial Report of the United States of America to the UN Committee Against Torture*, Oct. 15, 1999, *available at* http://www.state.gov/www/global/human_rights/torture_intro.html ("Torture is prohibited by law throughout the United States. It is categorically denounced as a matter of policy and as a tool of state authority."); *Second Periodic Report of the United States of America to the Committee Against Torture*, May 6, 2005, *available at* http://www.state.gov/g/drl/rls/45738.htm ("United States is unequivocally opposed to the use and practice of torture.... No circumstance whatsoever... may be invoked as a justification for or defense to committing torture.") Who decides how to translate the policy into enforceable rules?

5. *Outsourcing and Hiding Torture?* Article 49 of the Fourth Geneva Convention prohibits "the deportations of protected persons from occupied

B. The Legal Standards and Their Application

territory." Such a deportation or transfer or unlawful confinement of a protected person is a "grave breach" of the convention. Art. 147. On March 19, 2004, the OLC drafted a memo indicating that the CIA could transfer detainees out of Iraq for interrogation, despite the Geneva Convention, by construing the ban not to apply to illegal aliens who have no legal right to remain in Iraq. The memo concluded that the temporary relocation of persons not charged with a crime to face interrogation at another location outside Iraq is not akin to the wartime practices the Geneva Convention provision was designed to forbid. Draft Memorandum from Jack Goldsmith, Asst. Attorney General, to Alberto R. Gonzales, Counsel to the President, *Permissibility of Relocating Certain "Protected Persons" From Occupied Iraq*, Mar. 19, 2004, *available at* http://www.washingtonpost.com/wp-srv/nation/documents/doj_memo031904.pdf. The CIA then transported as many as a dozen detainees from Iraq to other countries between March and October of 2004. *See* Dana Priest, *Memo Lets CIA Take Detainees Out of Iraq*, Wash. Post, Oct. 24, 2004, at A1. (The practice of "extraordinary rendition" is addressed *infra* pp. 804-816.)

The CIA also reportedly held dozens, perhaps up to 100, persons in Iraq as "ghost detainees." In June or July 2003, for example, Hiwa Abdul Rahman Rashul, a suspected member of the Iraqi Al-Ansar terrorist group who was nicknamed "Triple X" by CIA and military officials, was captured by Kurdish fighters. He was turned over to the CIA, which rendered him to Afghanistan for interrogation, then brought him back to Iraq. Then-DCI George Tenet asked Defense Secretary Rumsfeld not to give Rashul a prisoner number and to hide him from the Red Cross. Rashul was then lost in the Iraqi prison system for seven months. When asked about the legal basis for hiding Rashul, Rumsfeld replied, "We know from our knowledge that [Tenet] has authority to do this." *Id.*; Eric Schmitt & Thom Shanker, *Rumsfeld Issued an Order to Hide Detainee in Iraq*, N.Y. Times, June 17, 2004, at A1. In late 2005, Human Rights Watch provided a list of 26 "ghost detainees" believed to be in U.S. custody. *U.S. Holding at Least Twenty-Six "Ghost Detainees,"* Dec. 1, 2005. One secret CIA prison is reportedly codenamed Bright Light, where the most important Al Qaeda detainees are held in an undisclosed location. James Risen, *State of War: The Secret History of the CIA and the Bush Administration* 31 (2006).

What could be wrong with hiding a detainee in this fashion? How would you respond to the OLC's legal justification for rendering "ghost detainees"?

6. *The Moral Dimension.* What *should* the U.S. position on torture be? One perspective emphasizes a range of practical problems that seriously limit the value of information obtained through torture. *See* Jeannine Bell, *One Thousand Shades of Gray: The Effectiveness of Torture*, Ind. U. School of Law-Bloomington Res. Paper No. 37, Oct. 2005, *available at* http://ssrn.com/abstract=820467. Still, there is an undoubted and morally complex tension between the need to obtain information that could save many lives through coercive interrogation of a suspect and the condoning of torture.

Is it *ever* justifiable to torture a detainee? Assume that authorities have in custody someone whom they are certain has placed an especially destructive explosive device somewhere in a large shopping mall. The explosive may go off at any time, and there may not be enough time to evacuate the mall. If the bomb detonates, thousands will die. The detainee is the only person with knowledge of the bomb, and he will not talk. Should the interrogators torture the detainee in hopes of learning the location of the bomb before it is too late? *Compare* Alan Dershowitz, *Why Terrorism Works* 142-149 (2002) (torture techniques may be morally and legally justified in some circumstances), *with* Association of the Bar of the City of New York, Comm. on Intl. Human Rights, Comm. on Military Affairs and Justice, *Human Rights Standards Applicable to the United States' Interrogation of Detainees*, Apr. 30, 2004, at 8-9, *available at* http://www.abcny.org/pdf/HUMANRIGHTS.pdf ("Condoning torture under any circumstances erodes one of the most basic principles of international law and human rights and contradicts our values as a democratic state"), *and* David Luban, *Liberalism, Torture, and the Ticking Bomb*, 91 Va. L. Rev. 1425 (2005) (ticking-bomb scenarios may be used to rationalize institutionalized practices and procedures of torture). *See also* Kim Lane Scheppele, *Hypothetical Torture in the "War on Terrorism,"* 1 J. Natl. Security L. & Poly. 285 (2005) (taking a "hard line" against torture on sociological grounds). The Convention Against Torture, to which the United States is a party, says torture can never be justified. See *infra* p. 774.

7. *Torture Warrants?* Professor Dershowitz would recognize a qualified prohibition on torture. He suggests a form of judicial "torture warrant" before permitting torture of suspected terrorists in interrogations. Dershowitz, *supra*, at 148-149, 158-163. What might be the criteria for issuing such warrants? Should a judge, for example, try to balance the credibility or gravity of a threat against the suffering or injury to be inflicted on the recalcitrant detainee? Can you articulate a process that would be helpful to the court in doing that?

Another approach to making exceptions to a ban on torture has been recommended by Professors Philip Heymann and Juliette Kayyem. They advocate an "emergency exception" to a ban on torture based on a written finding by the President of "an urgent and extraordinary need" reported "within a reasonable period" to appropriate congressional committees, that states the reason to believe that the information is known by the person to be interrogated, that it "concerns a specific plan that threatens U.S. lives," and that there are "no reasonable alternatives to save the lives in question." Philip B. Heymann & Juliette N. Kayyem, *Long-Term Strategy Project for Preserving Security and Democratic Freedoms in the War on Terrorism* 25-26 (2004). Is this "findings" approach preferable in the ticking bomb case to a torture warrant?

Professor Jeremy Waldron would not allow the authorization of torture even in the ticking bomb scenario. Waldron argues that a line on what techniques are permitted has to be drawn "somewhere, and I say we should draw it where the law requires it, and where the human rights tradition has insisted that it should be drawn." Waldron, *supra*, at 1715.

Alternatively, should we expect government officials confronted with the ticking bomb case to engage in a form of official disobedience, hoping for ratification of the disobedient conduct after the fact? *See* Gross, *supra*, at 107; *see also supra* pp. 85-87. Could Congress or the President make lawful through ratification torture that was undertaken in disobedience of the law?

Which of these approaches is best? If you think torture might be permissible in some circumstances, can you think of other methods for keeping its "qualified" use in check?

B. The Legal Standards and Their Application

8. *Defenses of Torture Offered by the Government.*

a. *Necessity.* Bush administration lawyers argued that self-defense and necessity may legitimate torture. Does the presence of an arguable defense to an act of torture nullify the requirement that the torture be legally authorized? *See* William C. Banks & Peter Raven-Hansen, *Targeted Killing and Assassination: The U.S. Legal Framework*, 37 U. Richmond L. Rev. 667, 668 (2003) (basic rule of law requires positive legal authority for government actions). Would a necessity defense be available even where Congress clearly proscribed the conduct so defended? *See* Wayne R. LaFave & Austin W. Scott, I *Substantive Criminal Law* §5.4 (1986), at 629. Might a defense be available to someone charged with carrying out even a specious legal authorization of torture? *See* Public Committee Against Torture in Israel v. State of Israel, H.C. 5100/94, 53(4) P.D. 817 (1999).

b. *Self-Defense.* The criminal law doctrine of self-defense permits the use of force to prevent harm to another person. Does that doctrine apply in this setting to exculpate otherwise unlawful torture or inhumane treatment by an interrogator of a prisoner? Is an individual claim of self-defense portable to the executive branch in the war on terrorism? How would you rebut the argument made by the Working Group, *supra* p. 774, that the Commander in Chief's defensive war powers legitimate what might otherwise be proscribed as torture? Unlike the Bybee Memo, *supra* p. 761 n.4, the December 30, 2004, OLC memo, *supra* p. 764, made no mention of the constitutional authority of the President to disregard statutory or treaty obligations regarding torture. Of what significance is the revision?

c. *Article II as a Trump Card?* The January 2002 OLC memo, *supra* p. 764, at 36, 39, asserted that "Congress can no more interfere with the President's conduct of the interrogation of enemy combatants than it can dictate strategic or tactical decisions on the battlefield." In what particular settings is the Article II argument most persuasive? *See* Michael D. Ramsey, *Torturing Executive Power*, 93 Geo. L.J. 1213 (2005). Compare detention and on-the-spot interrogations of those seized on the battlefield during combat with long-term detentions in remote locations away from the battle. Al Qaeda reportedly continues to plan and carry out terrorist acts that threaten national security. Does that ongoing threat give the Commander in Chief a tactical choice to capture and interrogate al Qaeda operatives using torture?

If you agree that there is a constitutional limit to the authority of Congress to regulate interrogation, can you construe the laws reviewed in this section to avoid the potential constitutional problem? Did the Working Group Report persuasively apply the avoidance canon? Can Congress prohibit at least some particular interrogatory techniques?

9. *Lawyers and Their Role.* Many of the legal opinions in the Justice Department and Defense Department memoranda excerpted above are highly controversial. Some commentators argue that the memoranda were designed primarily to protect potentially culpable officials from prosecution for interrogation abuses. See *Lawyers' Statement on Bush Administration's Torture Memos*, Aug. 4, 2004, *at* http://www.allianceforjustice.org/spotlight/collection/spotlight_statement0804.html (letter signed by about 130 prominent lawyers); *Letter Sent to the United States Congress Regarding Recent Human Rights Issues in Iraq,*

June 16, 2004, *at* http://www.lawprofessorblogs.com/taxprof/linkdocs/harvardimpeach.pdf#search=iraqletter.com (letter signed by more than 500 university professors). Others, including Defense Department investigators of detention and interrogation practices, found that the confusion and ambiguity fostered by these memoranda may have contributed to the abusive practices or to a "permissive climate in which abuses were more likely." Richard B. Bilder & Detlev F. Vagts, *Speaking Law to Power: Lawyers and Torture*, 98 Am. J. Intl. L. 689, 691 (2004) (citing, e.g., John Barry, Michael Hirsh & Michael Isikoff, *The Roots of Torture*, Newsweek, May 24, 2004, at 28). What are the legal and ethical responsibilities of government lawyers in the war on terror? *See* Bilder & Vagts, *supra*, at 691-695; *Symposium: Lawyers' Roles and the War on Terror*, 1 J. Natl. Security L. & Poly. 357 (2005).

The *Schlesinger Report, supra* p. 761 n.6, found that in the development of Defense Department detention and interrogation policies in 2002 and 2003 "the legal resources of the Services' Judge Advocate General and General Counsels were not utilized to their full potential. Had the Secretary of Defense had a wider range of legal opinions and more robust debate regarding detainee policies and operations," the frequent policy changes between December 2002 and April 2003 might have been avoided. *Id.* at 8. Why would the Secretary not have sought more advice from JAG lawyers and General Counsels? What would have been gained by their perspectives?

At a Senate hearing in July 2005, the judge advocates general for the Army, Air Force, and Marines stated that they complained about the Justice Department's definition of "torture" and how it would be applied in the Working Group process early in 2003. Their objections apparently were overruled by the Defense Department general counsel's office. Neil A. Lewis, *Military's Opposition to Harsh Interrogation Is Outlined*, N.Y. Times, July 28, 2005, at A21; Josh White, *Military Lawyers Fought Policy on Interrogations, JAGs Recount Objections to Definition of Torture*, Wash. Post, July 15, 2005, at A1. Why do you think the Secretary failed to heed the advice that was offered?

Apparently, on March 17, 2005, the General Counsel of the Defense Department wrote a memo that rescinded the Working Group Report and concluded that the report "does not reflect now-settled executive branch views of the relevant law.... [T]he [report] is to be considered a historical document with no standing in policy, practice, or law." White, *supra*. What do you suppose happened between April 2003 and March 2005 to change the executive branch's views of the relevant law? In what specific ways is the new understanding different from the old one?

b. (Incorporated?) International Law on Torture

1. *The U.N. Convention Against Torture and Other Cruel, Inhuman, or Degrading Treatment or Punishment (CAT).* The instruments of ratification submitted by the United States for the CAT include a declaration making it clear that it regards CAT Articles 1 through 16 as not self-executing. *See* Office of the High Commissioner for Human Rights, *Declarations and Reservations* (as of 23 April 2004) ("United States of America" at ¶III(1)), *at* http://www.unhchr.ch/html/menu2/6/cat/treaties/convention-reserv.htm. What is the legal significance of such a declaration?

B. The Legal Standards and Their Application

The prohibitions against torture in the CAT, qualified by the various U.S. reservations, understandings, and declarations attached to it, have been implanted in domestic law in a range of settings, and its provisions underlie the Alien Tort Claims Act and Torture Victim Protection Act, both addressed *infra.* What are the important elements of "torture" as defined in the CAT? Does it apply to military and civilian interrogators? To private persons?

Recall that in ratifying the CAT the United States specified that "torture" as mental pain or suffering refers to

> prolonged mental harm caused by or resulting from: (1) the intentional infliction or threatened infliction of severe physical pain or suffering; (2) the administration or application, or threatened administration or application, of mind-altering substances or other procedures calculated to disrupt profoundly the senses or the personality; (3) the threat of imminent death; or (4) the threat that another person will imminently be subjected to death, severe physical pain or suffering, or the administration or application of mind-altering substances or other procedures calculated to disrupt profoundly the senses or personality. [*Id.* at ¶II(1)(a).]

What is the practical significance of this understanding? Consistent with this understanding, what interrogation techniques are permitted by the CAT? Sleep deprivation? Starvation? Sensory deprivation or bombardment? Do any of the techniques approved by the Secretary of Defense, *supra* p. 782, constitute "torture" or "cruel, inhuman, or degrading treatment" under the CAT?

Article 2(2) of the CAT provides that "[n]o exceptional circumstances whatsoever, whether a state of war or a threat of war, internal political instability, or any other public emergency, may be invoked as a justification of torture." What is the legal significance of this "no exceptions" provision?

Article 2(1) requires parties to take preventive measures "in any territory under its jurisdiction." How does extension of the CAT to the special maritime and territorial jurisdiction of the United States affect the rules for interrogation at Guantánamo? How do you think this Article 2 provision applies in Afghanistan or in Iraq?

2. *Cruel, Inhuman, or Degrading Treatment.* How does the prohibition against cruel, inhuman, or degrading treatment differ from the rule barring torture? As noted in the Working Group Report, the United States reserved its commitment to the prevention of "cruel, inhuman, or degrading treatment or punishment" under CAT Article 16 to acts that would be forbidden by the Fifth, Eighth, and/or Fourteenth Amendments. See *supra* p. 776. Why would the United States make such a reservation? Because the case law interpreting those amendments arises in domestic criminal justice proceedings, how would you measure U.S. compliance with the "cruel, inhuman, or degrading" proviso? *See* Kreimer, *supra* p. 786, at 201-224. Do the techniques described in the *Taguba Report, supra* p. 762 n.15, or the Rumsfeld memorandum fall within the definition?

3. *Criminalizing Torture Under the CAT.* The criminal sanction in 18 U.S.C. §2340 was included to meet the CAT requirement that each ratifying country criminalize torture. Compare the definitions in the treaty and the Act, *supra*

pp. 774-777. Do you see any important differences? In an August 1, 2002, letter to the White House Counsel, OLC asserted that "interrogation methods that comply with Section 2340 would not violate our international obligations under the Torture Convention." Letter to Alberto R. Gonzales, Counsel to the President, from John C. Yoo, Deputy Asst. Atty. General, Aug. 1, 2002, at 1, *available at* http://www.gwu.edu/~nschariv/NSAEBB/NSAEBB127/02.08.01.pdf. If the measures of compliance with the CAT prohibition against "cruel, inhuman, or degrading treatment" are the Fifth, Eighth, and Fourteenth Amendments, do aliens held by the United States overseas have any protection from cruel, inhuman, or degrading treatment by U.S. officials under the CAT? Does the lack of domestic criminal enforcement authority extinguish U.S. obligations under the Torture Convention not to engage in "cruel, inhuman, and degrading treatment"? *See* Arar v. Ashcroft, 414 F. Supp. 2d 250 (E.D.N.Y. 2006), *infra* p. 804.

In 18 U.S.C. §2340 (2000), Congress forbade conduct that is "specifically intended to inflict severe physical or mental pain or suffering." Without further statutory definitions, how would you define the key words and phrases — "severe," "severe physical pain or suffering," "severe mental pain or suffering," and "specifically intended"? See *Memorandum for James B. Comey, supra* p. 786, at 5-17.

4. *Application of the Geneva Conventions.* Apply the language of the Geneva Conventions, as incorporated through the War Crimes Act (WCA), *supra* pp. 766-770, to the detentions and interrogation described in these materials. What threshold determinations must be made, and by whom?

a. *What Conflicts?* Was the conflict with the Taliban and al Qaeda in Afghanistan covered by the Geneva Conventions? Do you agree with the January 9, 2002, OLC opinion, *supra* p. 764, that Geneva Convention III for the protection of POWs should not apply because Afghanistan was a "failed" state? Despite the Taliban's violent and harsh measures against Afghan citizens, its government controlled nearly all of Afghanistan when U.S. and British forces invaded that country in December 2001. *See* Hamdan v. Rumsfeld, 415 F.3d 33 (D.C. Cir. 2005). In *Hamdan,* a panel of the D.C. Circuit Court of Appeals ruled that the conflict was neither an international conflict between a signatory state and an opposing power that has accepted the provisions of the convention, nor an Article 3 "armed conflict not of an international character occurring in the territory of one of the High Contracting Parties," because the President had determined that the conflict was "international in scope." Does this ruling affirm the OLC's analysis? Does it make sense? Is there a third category of conflict that falls outside the convention altogether and therefore escapes the convention rules?

What do you think was the effect, if any, of the election of the Karzai government in Afghanistan in June 2002? Before that date, the conflict arguably was subject to the Geneva Conventions by virtue of Common Article 2, which provides that the conventions "apply to all cases of...armed conflict" between two or more parties to the Convention. Signatories are bound regardless of whether an additional party to the conflict is a signatory. After formation of the Karzai government, the conflict seemingly became internal, and U.S. and other foreign forces were present in Afghanistan with the consent of the government.

Whatever the applicability of Article 2, in Hamdan v. Rumsfeld, 126 S. Ct. 2749 (2006), the Supreme Court reversed the Court of Appeals and found that

B. The Legal Standards and Their Application

Common Article 3 affords some protection to persons who are not associated with a signatory or nonsignatory "Power" but who are involved in a conflict "in the territory of" a signatory. The Court construed the phrase "not of an international character" literally to distinguish conflicts between nations. The *Hamdan* decision is presented *infra* p. 882. In light of the Supreme Court interpretation, what do you think of the OLC analysis of Common Article 3? *See* Waldron, *supra*, at 1694 (the OLC opinion "proceeds as though the methods of analogy, inference, and reasoned elaboration—the ordinary tools of our lawyerly trade—are utterly inappropriate in this case.... The Geneva Conventions... respond to a strongly felt and well-established sense that certain abuses are beyond the pale.")

Do you think it likely, as the Yoo/Delahunty memorandum argues, that the signers of the 1949 Geneva Conventions meant to exclude "small-scale" civil wars from their coverage? If so, was the conflict between U.S. and Taliban and al Qaeda forces "small-scale"?

b. *Which Combatants?* Can you say on what basis any persons detained during wartime are wholly outside the protections of the Geneva Conventions? *See* Sean D. Murphy, *Contemporary Practice of the United States Relating to International Law*, 96 Am. J. Intl. L. 461, 476-477 (2002).

The Bush administration first took the position that al Qaeda and Taliban prisoners are "unlawful combatants" and thus not protected at all by the conventions. The White House, President George W. Bush, *Memorandum to National Security Advisors Re: Humane Treatment of al Qaeda and Taliban Detainees*, Feb. 7, 2002, *available at* http://www.gwu.edu/~nsarchiv/NSAEBB/NSAEBB127/02.02.07.pdf. The Administration also reasoned that the Geneva Conventions have no application to non-state organizations such as al Qaeda, that the conflict was internal, and further that al Qaeda members failed to meet the criteria in Article 4 of Geneva Convention III. Under Article 4, combatants earn POW status if they are members of the armed forces other than medical or chaplain personnel. The general criteria include being subject to command authority, having a "fixed distinctive sign recognizable at a distance," carrying arms openly, and conducting operations in accordance with the laws and customs of war. The Taliban also were not entitled to Geneva Convention protections, according to the Administration, because Afghanistan was not a functioning state during the conflict and because the Taliban were not recognized as a legitimate government. *Id.*

After Secretary of State Powell objected and requested that the Administration reconsider its position, President Bush announced that Geneva Convention III was applicable to the Taliban but not to al Qaeda. But because the Taliban violated the laws of war and associated with al Qaeda, he determined that Taliban detainees do not qualify as POWs. *See White House Fact Sheet: Status of Detainees at Guantanamo*, Feb. 7, 2002. Do you find support for the Administration's position in the memoranda excerpted here? If not, in what respects does the argument come up short? *Cf.* United States v. Lindh, 212 F. Supp. 2d 541 (E.D. Va. 2002) (concluding that the Taliban were not covered by Geneva Convention III because they had an insufficient internal system of military command, wore no distinctive sign, and regularly targeted civilian populations).

In cases of doubt, Article 5 of Geneva Convention III entitles detainees to a "competent tribunal" to determine their status. Does it offer a reasonable way to accommodate both sides in this debate? *See* Jennifer Elsea, *Treatment of*

"Battlefield Detainees" in the War on Terrorism (Cong. Res. Serv. RL31367) 36, Mar. 27, 2006 (asserting that the United States has in the past required an individualized assessment of detainee status before denying POW status). Why do you suppose POW determination tribunals have not been established? Does the U.S. stance itself constitute a violation of the laws of war, thus providing an enemy with an argument for denying captured U.S. soldiers POW status?

The OLC asserted in a March 28, 2002, letter to the State Department Legal Adviser that there can be no doubt about the POW status of any individual affiliated with the Taliban, because the organization was found not to meet the requirements of Article 4. Letter to William H. Taft IV, Legal Adviser, Dept. of State, from John C. Yoo, Deputy Asst. Atty. General, Mar. 28, 2002, *available at* http://www.cartoonbank.com/newyorker/slideshows/05YooTaft.pdf. Does it necessarily follow that the categorical denial of POW status to a military organization makes any person allegedly a member of that organization ineligible for an Article 5 tribunal? *See* Waldron, *supra*, at 1695 (it is "discouraging... to see American lawyers arguing for the inapplicability of the Conventions on grounds that are strikingly similar... to those invoked by Germany" during World War II.)

c. *Which Other Persons?* Defense Secretary Rumsfeld acknowledged in early 2002 in comments about the detention facility at Guantánamo Bay that "[s]ometimes when you capture a big, large group there will be someone who just happened to be in there that didn't belong in there." *Secretary Rumsfeld Media Availability En Route to Camp X-Ray*, Jan. 27, 2002, *available at* http://www.defenselink.mil/transcripts/2002/t01282002_ t0127sd2.html. What rights do such innocent bystanders have, once detained? Do Articles 4 and 5 of Geneva Convention III and Geneva Convention IV apply? Does it matter for the purposes of qualifying for Geneva Convention IV that a person may have unlawfully participated in a conflict?

d. *What Conduct Is Covered?* What constitutes a "grave breach" under the Geneva Conventions? If "torture or inhuman treatment" is such a breach, what aspects of the conventions remain in dispute concerning detainees in the war on terrorism? For POWs, Article 17 of Geneva Convention III provides that "no physical or mental torture, nor any other form of coercion, may be inflicted on prisoners of war to secure from them information of any kind whatever." For protected civilians, Article 31 of Geneva Convention IV provides that "[n]o physical or moral coercion shall be exercised against [them], in particular to obtain information from them or from third parties." What interrogation techniques would be proscribed by these rules? How do the techniques recommended by the Working Group and approved by Secretary Rumsfeld, *supra* p. 774, measure up under the Geneva Conventions? *See* Jennifer K. Elsea, *Lawfulness of Interrogation Techniques under the Geneva Conventions* (Cong. Res. Serv. RL32567) 23-35, Sept. 8, 2004.

e. *Liability for U.S. Personnel?* The documents excerpted above expose an underlying tension in setting the interrogation policy—providing maximum flexibility to pressure detainees to talk while ensuring immunity from criminal sanctions if lawful boundaries are crossed. Compare the arguments on the amenability of U.S. personnel to criminal prosecution in the OLC opinion of January 9, 2002, and by State Department General Counsel Taft. Which side has the better view in light of the Geneva Conventions?

B. The Legal Standards and Their Application

f. *Are the Conventions Judicially Enforceable?* Salim Ahmed Hamdan was captured by Afghan militia forces in November 2001. He was turned over to the U.S. military and transported to Guantánamo Bay. In July 2003, President Bush determined "that there was reason to believe that [Hamdan] was a member of al Qaeda or was otherwise involved in terrorism directed against the United States," and Hamdan was designated for trial before a military commission. After Hamdan filed a petition for habeas corpus in federal district court, he was charged with a variety of terrorism-related offenses stemming from his alleged role as the personal driver for Osama bin Laden. In November 2004, the district court granted Hamdan's petition in part, holding that he could not be tried by a military commission unless a competent tribunal determined that he was not a POW under Geneva Convention III. Hamdan v. Rumsfeld, 344 F. Supp. 2d 152 (D.D.C. 2004).

On July 15, 2005, a D.C. Circuit Court of Appeals panel reversed. In Hamdan v. Rumsfeld, 415 F.3d 33 (D.C. Cir. 2005), the court found that Geneva Convention III confers upon Hamdan no right to enforce its provisions in court. *Id.* at 40. In 2006, the Supreme Court reversed the judgment of the Court of Appeals. In Hamdan v. Rumsfeld, 126 S. Ct. 2749, 2795 (2006), the Court found that Common Article 3 is applicable to the conflict with al Qaeda. Even though its protections fall "short of full protection under the Conventions," *id.* at 2796, Hamdan must be tried by a " 'regularly constituted court affording all the judicial guarantees which are recognized as indispensable by civilized peoples.' " *Id.* at 2795, quoting from Common Article 3. What effect will the *Hamdan* decision likely have on future disputes about interrogation and treatment of detainees? *See infra* p. 882.

In February 2006, a federal district court dismissed most of a lawsuit for damages brought by Guantánamo Bay detainees who alleged that they were tortured in violation of the Geneva Conventions, the law of nations, and the Constitution. Rasul v. Rumsfeld, 414 F. Supp. 2d 26 (D.D.C. 2006). The court held that sovereign immunity barred the law of nations and Geneva Conventions claims and that qualified immunity required dismissal of the constitutional claims because the rights at stake were not "clearly established." For sovereign immunity to apply to the international law claims, however, the court had to find that the defendants were acting within their scope of employment. How could U.S. officials act within their scope of employment when they torture detainees? The status of U.S. constitutional law regarding torture-related claims is assessed *infra* p. 799.

5. *The New Paradigm?* White House Counsel Gonzales argued that the "nature of the new war" and the "new paradigm render[] obsolete Geneva's strict limitations" on questioning and make other Geneva provisions "quaint." How would you rebut Gonzales's interpretation? Do Gonzales's arguments apply with equal force in Afghanistan and in Iraq? To detainees captured elsewhere? *See* Derek Jinks & David Sloss, *Is the President Bound by the Geneva Conventions?*, 90 Cornell L. Rev. 97 (2004) (concluding that he is). By contrast, the Office of Legal Counsel argued that the Geneva Conventions are "quite clear" and that the President correctly determined that the Taliban and al Qaeda detainees cannot meet the clear requirements of Geneva Convention III. *Letter to Taft from Yoo, supra* p. 796. Is the OLC position more or less persuasive than that of the former White House Counsel?

6. *The International Covenant on Civil and Political Rights.* The ICCPR, like the CAT, forbids torture and cruel, inhuman, and degrading conduct, and it was subject to Senate approval. The ICCPR is non-self-executing, and lower federal courts have found that the ICCPR creates no privately enforceable rights in U.S. courts. However, some courts cite the ICCPR as evidence that customary international law prohibits arbitrary arrest, prolonged detention, and torture. See *supra* p. 776. What is the legal basis for the Working Group position that the ICCPR does not apply to U.S. activities abroad during an armed conflict? *See* Elsea, *supra* p. 795, at 12-13 (U.S. "has not officially proclaimed an emergency or named measures that would derogate from the ICCPR.")

7. *The Role of Customary International Law and Jus Cogens.* The substantive content of customary international law on the subject of torture is embodied in the CAT and ICCPR, among other instruments. The torture prohibition is also part of *jus cogens* and is so recognized by U.S. courts. *See Restatement (Third) of Foreign Relations Law of the United States* §702 (1986). It remains unclear, however, whether the prohibition against cruel, inhuman, or degrading treatment is also part of *jus cogens*. For a refresher on the role of custom and *jus cogens* as U.S. law, see *supra* pp. 182-185.

c. Domestic Law on Torture

1. *A Congressional Prohibition.* In 2005, over the strenuous objection of the Bush administration, Congress enacted the Detainee Treatment Act in two different statutes. Department of Defense, Emergency Supplemental Appropriations to Address Hurricanes in the Gulf of Mexico, and Pandemic Influenza Act, 2006, Pub. L. No. 109-148, §§1001-1006, 119 Stat. 2680, 2739-2744 (2005); National Defense Authorization Act for Fiscal Year 2006, Pub. L. No. 109-163, §§1401-1406, 119 Stat. 3136, 3474-3480 (2006). It provides, in part:

Prohibition on Cruel, Inhuman, or Degrading Treatment or Punishment of Persons Under Custody or Control of the United States Government.

(a) In General. — No individual in the custody or under the physical control of the United States Government, regardless of nationality or physical location, shall be subject to cruel, inhuman, or degrading treatment or punishment.

(b) Construction. — Nothing in this section shall be construed to impose any geographical limitation on the applicability of the prohibition against cruel, inhuman, or degrading treatment or punishment under this section.

(c) Limitation on Supersedure. — The provisions of this section shall not be superseded, except by a provision of law enacted after the date of the enactment of this Act which specifically repeals, modifies, or supersedes the provisions of this section.

(d) Cruel, Inhuman, or Degrading Treatment or Punishment Defined. — In this section, the term "cruel, inhuman, or degrading treatment or punishment" means the cruel, unusual, and inhumane treatment or punishment prohibited by the Fifth, Eighth, and Fourteenth Amendments to the Constitution of the United States, as defined in the United States Reservations, Declarations and Understandings to the United Nations Convention Against Torture and Other

B. The Legal Standards and Their Application

Forms of Cruel, Inhuman or Degrading Treatment or Punishment done at New York, December 10, 1984. [Pub. L. No. 109-148, §1003, 119 Stat. 2739-2740; Pub. L. No. 109-163, §1403, 119 Stat. 3475.]

How important is the "regardless of nationality or physical location" language in determining the scope of the government's investigative authority and the rights of the detainee? The definition of "cruel, inhuman, or degrading treatment" mirrors that stated in the U.S. reservation to Article 16 of the CAT and covers only acts prohibited by the Fifth, Eighth, and Fourteenth Amendments. Does the Detainee Treatment Act thus require that persons (including aliens) in U.S. custody or control abroad not be subjected to treatment that would be unconstitutional if it occurred in the United States? If the meaning of the constitutional protections changes over time, the treatment forbidden by the Act presumably will change as well. How would you advise those responsible for supervising interrogations to keep abreast of their responsibilities?

The Detainee Treatment Act also forbids exposure of persons in the custody or under the effective control of DOD to any interrogation techniques not listed in the *Army Field Manual on Intelligence Interrogation*. Pub. L. No. 109-148, §1002(a), 119 Stat. 2739; Pub. L. No. 109-163, §1402(a), 119 Stat. 3475. What is the legal significance of limiting DOD interrogators to techniques in the *Army Field Manual*? Why do you suppose that non-DOD interrogators are not subject to the same or some similar restriction?

In a signing statement for the legislation containing the Detainee Treatment Act, President Bush declared that he would construe the provisions set forth above

> in a manner consistent with the constitutional authority of the President to supervise the unitary executive branch and as Commander in Chief and consistent with the constitutional limitations on the judicial power, which will assist in achieving the shared objective of the Congress and the President...of protecting the American people from further terrorist attacks. [Statement on Signing the Department of Defense, Emergency Supplemental Appropriations to Address Hurricanes in the Gulf of Mexico, and Pandemic Influenza Act, 2006, 41 Weekly Comp. Pres. Doc. 1918, Jan. 2, 2006.]

Do you think this declaration alters the President's obligation to comply with the statute?

2. *Applying the Constitution.* The U.S. reservation to Article 16 of the CAT limits "cruel, inhuman or degrading conduct" to that which violates that Fifth, Eighth, and/or Fourteenth Amendments. What is the content of those constitutional protections? For contrasting views, see Seth F. Kreimer, *Too Close to the Rack and the Screw: Constitutional Constraints on Torture in the War on Terror*, 6 U. Penn. J. Constl. L. 278 (2003); and John T. Parry, *What Is Torture, Are We Doing It, and What If We Are?*, 64 U. Pitt. L. Rev. 237 (2003).

In Chavez v. Martinez, 538 U.S. 760 (2003), a badly fractured Supreme Court ruled on claims of liability asserted by a plaintiff who had been subjected to persistent police questioning while he was in the hospital incapacitated by extreme pain. Five Justices voted to remand the question of whether the plaintiff could pursue a claim for violation of his substantive due process rights, but the Court could not agree about the scope and applicability of those rights or the related right against self-incrimination.

Three Justices joined in part of an opinion by Justice Thomas asserting that the interrogation was not egregious or conscience-shocking enough to violate the plaintiff's substantive due process rights. They reasoned that "freedom from unwanted police questioning is [not] a right so fundamental that it cannot be abridged absent a 'compelling state interest.'" *Id.* at 776. For them, it was enough that the questioning was justified by *some* government interest—here the need to preserve critical evidence concerning a shooting by a police officer—and that it was not "conduct intended to injure in some way unjustifiable by any government interest." *Id.* at 774.

Justice Stevens concluded that "the interrogation of respondent was the functional equivalent of an attempt to obtain an involuntary confession from a prisoner by torturous methods," which is "a classic example of a violation of a constitutional right 'implicit in the concept of ordered liberty.'" *Id.* at 788 (Stevens, J., concurring in part, dissenting in part).

Justice Kennedy (joined on this point by Justices Stevens and Ginsburg) agreed that the use of investigatory torture violates a person's fundamental right to liberty but noted that interrogating suspects who are in pain or anguish is not necessarily torture when the police have "legitimate reasons, borne of exigency... [such as] [l]ocating the victim of a kidnapping, ascertaining the whereabouts of a dangerous assailant or accomplice, or determining whether there is a rogue police officer." *Id.* at 796 (Kennedy, J., concurring in part, dissenting in part). On the other hand, he added, the police may not prolong or increase the suspect's suffering or threaten to do so to elicit a statement. The test for a constitutional violation, in Justice Kennedy's view, was whether the police "exploited" the suspect's pain to secure his statement. He found that they had done so in *Chavez*.

Under any of the tests in *Chavez* would torture in the United States of a suspected terrorist to obtain information about an imminent terrorist attack violate substantive due process? How about practices such as hooding and sleep deprivation? Do military or civilian investigators in the war on terrorism have broader authority than the police do to use coercive interrogation techniques because of their different goals in an interrogation? *See* Marcy Strauss, *Torture*, 48 N.Y.L. Sch. L. Rev. 201, 251 (2003) (maintaining that it is unclear whether torture used to gain information violates the Fifth Amendment privilege against self-incrimination if the information is not used in a criminal prosecution; if so used, the right is violated).

Does the Eighth Amendment ban on "cruel and unusual punishment" supply an interpretive standard in the coercive interrogation context? If no judicially imposed punishment is contemplated by the interrogators, does the Eighth Amendment even apply? *See* Ingraham v. Wright, 430 U.S. 651, 671 n.40 (1977) ("[T]he State does not acquire the power to punish with which the Eighth Amendment is concerned until after it has secured a formal adjudication of guilt in accordance with due process of law.").

3. *Extraterritorial Application of the Constitution.* Are U.S. interrogators in Iraq, Afghanistan, or elsewhere outside the United States subject to the same

B. The Legal Standards and Their Application 801

constitutional constraints on their interrogation methods that limit their conduct in the United States? Are they subject to any U.S. laws? See *supra* pp. 173-198. If aliens held at Guantánamo have *some* U.S. constitutional rights, *see* Rasul v. Bush, 542 U.S. 466 (2004), *supra* p. 692, do aliens held by U.S. forces in Afghanistan or Iraq have *any*? If they do not, are U.S. interrogators therefore not constrained by Article 16 of the CAT? How, if at all, is your answer affected by the Detainee Treatment Act of 2005, *supra* p. 701?

4. *"Shocks the Conscience" Redux.* Consider the "shocks the conscience" standard described *supra* p. 661. Applying this standard, would the most abusive techniques used at Abu Ghraib ever be permitted in the United States? How about in the "ticking bomb" situation? Would your answer be different if the treatment occurred abroad? *See* Oren Gross, *The Prohibition on Torture and the Limits of the Law* 2 (2004).

5. *Criminal Sanctions.* The Torture statute, 18 U.S.C. §§2340-2340B (2000 & Supp. IV 2004), imposes criminal sanctions for torture, purportedly in accordance with U.S. obligations under the Convention Against Torture. It applies, however, only to U.S. nationals or others present in the United States who commit or conspire to commit torture "outside the United States." The Working Group took pains to assert that Guantánamo is included within the special maritime jurisdiction of the United States and thus that the U.S. personnel conducting interrogations there are not subject to the Torture statute. At the same time, the government rejected claims of sovereignty over Guantánamo for the purpose of federal court jurisdiction to hear claims by detainees held there. *See* Rasul v. Bush, 542 U.S. 466 (2004), *supra* p. 692. Can the two positions be reconciled?

The Torture statute was amended in 2004 to extend the definition of "United States" to include the several states, the District of Columbia, and the commonwealths, territories, and possessions of the United States. Pub. L. No. 108-375, §1089, 118 Stat. 2067, amending 18 U.S.C. §2340(3). In any case, it appears that the United States has never prosecuted a U.S. agent or foreign agent suspected of engaging in torture outside the United States. *See* Amnesty Intl. USA, *United States of America: A Safe Haven for Torturers*, 2002, *available at* http://www.amnestyusa.org/stoptorture/safehaven.pdf; Michael John Garcia, *U.N. Convention Against Torture (CAT): Overview and Application to Interrogation Techniques* (Cong. Res. Serv. RL34238) 11-12, Feb. 10, 2005.

Why do you suppose Congress has not enacted a statute specifically outlawing torture within the United States?

The Uniform Code of Military Justice (UCMJ) provides for courts-martial to prosecute torture or inhumane acts committed within or outside the United States by members of the military and certain accompanying civilians. 10 U.S.C. §805 (UCMJ applies worldwide); *id.* §802 (to any service member); *id.* §802(a)(10) (to certain accompanying civilians); *id.* §818 (for an offense against the laws of war); *id.* §855 (torture or cruel or unusual punishment); *id.* §934 ("disorders and neglects to the prejudice of good order and discipline in the armed forces"). To date, ten low-ranking soldiers and one captain have been convicted under the UCMJ of abusing detainees at Abu Ghraib, while 251 other soldiers and officers have been punished in some way for detainee abuse in Iraq and Afghanistan. Eric Schmitt, *Iraq Abuse Trial Is Again Limited to Lower Ranks*, N.Y. Times, Mar. 23, 2006, at A1.

One part of the Detainee Treatment Act, *supra* p. 701, provides a legal defense for U.S. personnel in any criminal or civil action brought against them based on their involvement in an authorized interrogation of suspected foreign terrorists. The defense exists when the U.S. interrogator "did not know that the [interrogation] practices were unlawful and a person of ordinary sense and understanding would not know the practices were unlawful." Pub. L. No. 109-148, §1004(a), 119 Stat. 2740; Pub. L. No. 109-163, §1404, 119 Stat. 3475-3476. A good faith reliance on the advice of counsel may be "an important factor" in measuring the accused's culpability. *Id.* Why do you think these provisions were added to the Act? What is their likely impact?

6. *Prosecuting Civilian Contractors.* In June 2004 a federal grand jury in North Carolina indicted a contractor employed by the CIA on assault charges for allegedly beating a detainee in Afghanistan over two days in 2003. The detainee died the next day. Richard A. Oppel Jr. & Ariel Hart, *Contractor Indicted in Afghan Detainee's Beating*, N.Y. Times, June 17, 2004, at A1. The CIA refused to acknowledge whether the agency was aware that the accused had been arrested on felony assault charges before his employment by the Agency. *Id.* How might the War Crimes Act, 18 U.S.C. §2441, *supra* pp. 766-770, apply to the accused in this case?

Generally, the UCMJ has not been applied to civilians accompanying military units in peacetime. *See, e.g.,* Willenburg v. Neurauter, 48 M.J. 152, 157 (C.A.A.F. 1998). The Military Extraterritorial Jurisdiction Act of 2000 (MEJA), however, provides for federal jurisdiction over crimes committed abroad by civilians who are "accompanying or employed by" the U.S. military. 18 U.S.C. §§3261-3267 (2000 & Supp. IV 2004). Still, after the *Taguba Report, supra* p. 762 n.15, named the contracting firms Titan Corporation and CACI International, Inc. as having provided translators and interrogators accused of engaging in detainee abuse at the Abu Ghraib prison, it appeared that the jurisdictional provisions of the MEJA would not reach the contractors that employed the accused individuals. Moreover, CACI's contract is with the Department of Interior rather than with the Department of Defense (DOD). Scott Shane, *Some U.S. Prison Contractors May Avoid Charges*, Balt. Sun, May 24, 2004, at A1. In response to this jurisdictional gap, the 2005 Defense Authorization Act broadened the range of potential defendants under MEJA to include civilian employees, contractors or subcontractors, and their employees, of DOD or "any other Federal agency, or any provisional authority, to the extent such employment relates to supporting the mission of the Department of Defense overseas." Pub. L. No. 108-375, §1088, 118 Stat. 1811, 2066-2067 (2004). Do these amendments to MEJA plug all the holes? Would it reach State Department or FBI contractors? CIA contractors? *See* Frederick A. Stein, *Have We Closed the Barn Door Yet? A Look at the Current Loopholes in the Military Extraterritorial Jurisdiction Act*, 27 Hous. J. Intl. L. 579 (2005).

MEJA creates no substantive crimes but incorporates a range of existing offenses, such as murder, assault, sexual abuse, and deprivation of rights under color of law. What ordinary crimes might be charged against civilian contractors working in facilities like Abu Ghraib? Could CIA operatives engaged in

B. The Legal Standards and Their Application

interrogational torture while operating with military units be prosecuted under the UCMJ? Do these problems with the use of civilian contractors suggest broader issues that should be considered in privatizing national security activities of the government? How might these issues be addressed? *See* Jon D. Michaels, *Beyond Accountability: The Constitutional, Democratic, and Strategic Problems with Privatizing War*, 82 Wash. U. L.Q. 1001 (2004).

7. *Civil Sanctions.* The Foreign Claims Act (FCA), 10 U.S.C. §2734(a) (2000), permits recovery of up to $100,000 from the United States for a claim brought by a resident of a foreign country where the injury occurred outside the United States "and is caused by, or is otherwise incident to [the] noncombat activities of" the U.S. military. *Id.* "Noncombat activity" is defined to include any "activity, other than combat, war or armed conflict, that is particularly military in character and has little parallel in the civilian community." 32 C.F.R. §842.41(c) (2005). Under the Act, claims commissions, consisting of commissioned officers, are established for each service branch, and are in place wherever the military has a significant presence. However, experience with the FCA in Iraq suggests that complex procedures and stringent policies have prevented most injured Iraqis from obtaining compensation for their injuries. Scott Borrowman, *Sosa v. Alvarez-Machain and Abu Ghraib — Civil Remedies for Victims of Extraterritorial Torts by U.S. Military Personnel and Civilian Contractors*, 2005 B.Y.U. L. Rev. 371, 376 (2005).

The Alien Tort Claims Act (ATCA), 28 U.S.C. §1350 (2000), confers jurisdiction on federal district courts over tort suits by aliens where a violation of the law of nations or a treaty of the United States is alleged. In Sosa v. Alvarez-Machain, 542 U.S. 692 (2004), *supra* p. 187, the Supreme Court rejected the ATCA as a basis for jurisdiction in the federal courts over a tort claim related to the abduction of Alvarez-Machain by a Mexican national who acted with the approval of the DEA. The Court reasoned that the ATCA was intended to create jurisdiction to hear suits based on current international norms, but only those whose "content and acceptance among civilized nations" is no less definite than the small number of "historical paradigms" familiar when the statute was passed in 1789. *Id.* at 718. In the course of its opinion, however, the Court cited with evident approval the decision in Filartiga v. Peña-Irala, 630 F.2d 876 (2d Cir. 1980), noted *supra* p. 781, which applied the ATCA in a torture case.

The Torture Victim Protection Act (TVPA), Pub. L. No. 102-256, 106 Stat. 73 (1992), codified at 28 U.S.C. §1350 Note (2000), provides a civil remedy in the federal courts for individuals, including U.S. persons, who have been victims of torture or extrajudicial killing. See *supra* p. 781. The TVPA thus may offer relief for U.S. persons that would be unavailable under the ATCA. However, the TVPA only provides a cause of action for torture or extrajudicial killing "under color of law, of any foreign nation." *Id.* §2a. Do you think that the TVPA would support an action for improper removal by U.S. officials of an individual who might be subjected to torture abroad? Would it apply where U.S. officials allegedly direct foreign officials to carry out acts of torture against a non-U.S. citizen? *See* Arar v. Ashcroft, 414 F. Supp. 2d 250 (E.D.N.Y. 2006), *infra* p. 804.

What would be the measure of "torture" under these civil mechanisms? Relying on the ATCA, in 2004 the Center for Constitutional Rights sued the two prime security contractors operating for the United States in Iraq — CACI

International, Inc. and Titan Corp. — on behalf of Iraqi prisoners, alleging that the contractors conspired with government officials to abuse the detainees and failed adequately to supervise their employees. *See* Renae Merle, *CACI and Titan Sued Over Iraq Operations*, Wash. Post, June 10, 2004, at E3. The suit seeks damages and an injunction to prevent the contractors from obtaining new government contracts. What problems can you foresee for the plaintiffs in this lawsuit? *See* Saleh v. Titan Corp., 353 F. Supp. 2d 1087 (S.D. Cal. 2004); 361 F. Supp. 2d 1152 (S.D. Cal. 2005); *see also* Ibrahim v. Titan Corp., 391 F. Supp. 2d 10 (D.D.C. 2005). In other civil suits U.S. courts have found that defendants committed actionable torture by subjecting detainees to interrogation sessions lasting 14 hours, Xuncax v. Gramajo, 886 F. Supp. 162, 170 (D. Mass. 1995); beating with hands, Tachiaona v. Mugabe, 234 F. Supp. 2d 401, 420-423 (S.D.N.Y. 2002); striking with blunt objects and boots, Mehinovic v. Vuckovic, 198 F. Supp. 2d 1322 (N.D. Ga. 2002); threatening with death, Adebe-Jira v. Negewo, 72 F.3d 844, 845 (11th Cir. 1996); and using techniques to increase pain or injury. *Id.*

C. EXTRAORDINARY RENDITION

Rendition is generally understood to be the surrender of a person from one state to another state that has requested him, typically pursuant to an agreement or extradition treaty, for the purpose of criminal prosecution. In recent years, however, the United States has begun transferring detainees to foreign countries without the request of the transferee country in circumstances where it is more likely than not that the individuals will be subjected to torture or to cruel, inhuman, or degrading treatment. The practice is called "irregular rendition" or "extraordinary rendition," because it involves no treaty or formal agreement and is attended by no judicial process. Whether authorized by secret presidential directive or simply done by government officials without authorization, extraordinary rendition has apparently been used as an integral adjunct to coercive interrogation in the war on terrorism.

Arar v. Ashcroft
United States District Court, Eastern District of New York, 2006
414 F. Supp. 2d 250

TRAGER, District Judge. Plaintiff Maher Arar brings this action against defendants, U.S. officials, who allegedly held him virtually incommunicado for thirteen days at the U.S. border and then ordered his removal to Syria for the express purpose of detention and interrogation under torture by Syrian officials. He brings claims under the Torture Victim Prevention Act and the Fifth Amendment to the U.S. Constitution.

Defendants have filed motions to dismiss the complaint.... The questions presented by these motions are whether the facts alleged can give rise to any theory of liability under those provisions of law and, if so, whether those claims

C. Extraordinary Rendition

can survive on prudential grounds in light of the national-security and foreign policy issues involved.

BACKGROUND

All statements contained in parts (1) through (4) in this background section of the opinion are taken from the complaint, attached exhibits, or documents referred to in the complaint and are presumed true for the limited purposes of these motions to dismiss....

(1) Plaintiff Maher Arar ("Arar" or "plaintiff") is a 33-year-old native of Syria who immigrated to Canada with his family when he was a teenager. He is a dual citizen of Syria and Canada and presently resides in Ottawa. In September 2002, while vacationing with family in Tunisia, he was called back to work by his employer to consult with a prospective client. He purchased a return ticket to Montreal with stops in Zurich and New York and left Tunisia on September 25, 2002.

On September 26, 2002, Arar arrived from Switzerland at John F. Kennedy Airport ("JFK Airport") in New York to catch a connecting flight to Montreal. Upon presenting his passport to an immigration inspector, he was identified as "the subject of a...lookout as being a member of a known terrorist organization." He was interrogated by various officials for approximately eight hours. The officials asked Arar if he had contacts with terrorist groups, which he categorically denied. Arar was then transported to another site at JFK Airport, where he was placed in solitary confinement. He alleges that he was transported in chains and shackles and was left in a room with no bed and with lights on throughout the night....

[Arar was detained and interrogated for 13 days in the United States. He alleges that during that time he was physically and psychologically abused by U.S. officials.]

... [On] October 7, 2002, the INS Regional Director, J. Scott Blackman, determined from classified and unclassified information that Arar is "clearly and unequivocally" a member of al Qaeda and..."that there are reasonable grounds to believe that [Arar] is a danger to the security of the United States." At approximately 4:00 a.m. on October 8, 2002, Arar learned that, based on classified information, INS regional director Blackman had ordered that Arar be sent to Syria and that his removal there was consistent with Article 3 of the United Nations Convention Against Torture and Other Cruel, Inhuman, or Degrading Treatment or Punishment ("CAT"). Arar pleaded for reconsideration but was told by INS officials that the agency was not governed by the "Geneva Conventions."...

Later that day, Arar was taken in chains and shackles to a New Jersey airfield, where he boarded a small jet bound for Washington, D.C. From there, he was flown to Amman, Jordan, arriving there on October 9, 2002. He was then handed over to Jordanian authorities, who delivered him to the Syrians later that day. At this time, U.S. officials had not informed...Canadian Consulate official[s]...that Arar had been removed to Syria. Arar alleges that Syrian officials refused to accept Arar directly from the United States....

(2) During his ten-month period of detention in Syria, Arar alleges that he was placed in a "grave" cell measuring six-feet long, seven feet high, and three feet wide. The cell was located within the Palestine Branch of the Syrian Military Intelligence ("Palestine Branch"). The cell was damp and cold, contained very little light, and was infested with rats, which would enter the cell through a small aperture in the ceiling. Cats would urinate on Arar through the aperture, and sanitary facilities were nonexistent. Arar was allowed to bathe himself in cold water once per week. He was prohibited from exercising and was provided barely edible food. Arar lost forty pounds during his ten-month period of detention in Syria.

During his first twelve days in Syrian detention, Arar was interrogated for eighteen hours per day and was physically and psychologically tortured. He was beaten on his palms, hips and lower back with a two-inch-thick electric cable. His captors also used their fists to beat him on his stomach, face and back of his neck. He was subjected to excruciating pain and pleaded with his captors to stop, but they would not. He was placed in a room where he could hear the screams of other detainees being tortured and was told that he, too, would be placed in a spine-breaking "chair," hung upside down in a "tire" for beatings and subjected to electric shocks. To lessen his exposure to the torture, Arar falsely confessed, among other things, to having trained with terrorists in Afghanistan, even though he had never been to Afghanistan and had never been involved in terrorist activity.

Arar alleges that his interrogation in Syria was coordinated and planned by U.S. officials, who sent the Syrians a dossier containing specific questions. As evidence of this, Arar notes that the interrogations in the U.S. and Syria contained identical questions, including a specific question about his relationship with a particular individual wanted for terrorism. In return, the Syrian officials supplied U.S. officials with all information extracted from Arar; plaintiff cites a statement by one Syrian official who has publicly stated that the Syrian government shared information with the U.S. that it extracted from Arar.

(3) The Canadian Embassy contacted the Syrian government about Arar on October 20, 2002, and, the following day, Syrian officials confirmed that they were detaining him. At this point, the Syrian officials ceased interrogating and torturing Arar.

Canadian officials visited Arar at the Palestine Branch five times during his ten-month detention. Prior to each visit, Arar was warned not to disclose that he was being mistreated. He complied but eventually broke down during the fifth visit, telling the Canadian consular official that he was being tortured and kept in a grave....

On October 5, 2003, Syria, without filing any charges against Arar, released him into the custody of Canadian Embassy officials in Damascus. He was flown to Ottawa the following day and reunited with his family.

Arar contends that he is not a member of any terrorist organization, including al Qaeda, and has never knowingly associated himself with terrorists, terrorist organizations or terrorist activity....

Arar alleges that he continues to suffer adverse effects from his ordeal in Syria. He claims that he has trouble relating to his wife and children, suffers from

C. Extraordinary Rendition

nightmares, is frequently branded a terrorist and is having trouble finding employment due to his reputation and inability to travel in the United States.

(4) The complaint alleges on information and belief that Arar was removed to Syria under a covert U.S. policy of "extraordinary rendition," according to which individuals are sent to foreign countries to undergo methods of interrogation not permitted in the United States. The extraordinary rendition policy involves the removal of "non-U.S. citizens detained in this country and elsewhere and suspected—reasonably or unreasonably—of terrorist activity to countries, including Syria, where interrogations under torture are routine." Arar alleges on information and belief that the United States sends individuals "to countries like Syria precisely because those countries can and do use methods of interrogation to obtain information from detainees that would not be morally acceptable or legal in the United States and other democracies."...

This extraordinary rendition program is not part of any official or declared U.S. public policy; nevertheless, it has received extensive attention in the press, where unnamed U.S. officials and certain foreign officials have admitted to the existence of such a policy....

Arar alleges that defendants directed the interrogations by providing information about Arar to Syrian officials and receiving reports on Arar's responses. Consequently, the defendants conspired with, and/or aided and abetted, Syrian officials in arbitrarily detaining, interrogating and torturing Arar. Plaintiff argues in the alternative that, at a minimum, defendants knew or at least should have known that there was a substantial likelihood that he would be tortured upon his removal to Syria.

(5) Arar's claim that he faced a likelihood of torture in Syria is supported by U.S. State Department reports on Syria's human rights practices. *See, e.g.,* Bureau of Democracy, Human Rights, and Labor, United States Department of State, 2004 Country Reports on Human Rights Practices (Released February 28, 2005) ("2004 Report"). According to the State Department, Syria's "human rights record remained poor, and the Government continued to commit numerous, serious abuses... includ[ing] the use of torture in detention, which at times resulted in death." 2004 Report at 1....

[The court first held that Arar failed to show sufficient continuing injury to establish standing to sue for declaratory relief, and that the Torture Victim Protection Act, *supra* p. 781, does not create a private right of action for rendition leading to torture and, in any case, does not apply where U.S. officials are alleged to direct foreign officials to torture a non-U.S. citizen.]

DUE PROCESS CLAIMS FOR DETENTION AND TORTURE IN SYRIA

Counts 2 and 3 of plaintiff's complaint allege that defendants violated Arar's rights to substantive due process by removing him to Syria and subjecting him to both torture and coercive interrogation (Count 2) and arbitrary and indefinite detention (Count 3). He seeks damages under *Bivens v. Six Unknown Named Agents of Fed. Bureau of Narcotics,* 403 U.S. 388 (1971), claiming deprivation of Fifth Amendment due process rights.

Bivens establishes "that the victims of a constitutional violation by a federal agent have a right to recover damages against the official in federal court despite the absence of any statute conferring such a right." *Carlson v. Green*, 446 U.S. 14, 18 (1980). The threshold inquiry is whether Arar alleges a violation of federal law that can be vindicated in his *Bivens* claim....

Arar argues that the treatment he allegedly suffered unquestionably constitutes a violation of substantive due process. However, defendants question whether robust Fifth Amendment protections can extend to someone like Arar, who, for juridical purposes, never actually entered the United States. Moreover, they cite precedent rejecting extraterritorial Fifth Amendment protections to non-U.S. citizens.

While one cannot ignore the "shocks the conscience" test established in *Rochin v. California*, 342 U.S. 165, 172-73 (1952), that case involved the question whether torture could be used to extract evidence for the purpose of prosecuting criminal conduct, a very different question from the one ultimately presented here, to wit, whether substantive due process would erect a *per se* bar to coercive investigations, including torture, for the purpose of preventing a terrorist attack. Whether the circumstances here ultimately cry out for immediate application of the Due Process clause, or, put differently, whether torture always violates the Fifth Amendment under established Supreme Court case law prohibiting government action that "shocks the conscience"—a question analytically prior to those taken up in the parties' briefing—remains unresolved from a doctrinal standpoint. Nevertheless, because both parties seem (at least implicitly) to have answered this question in the affirmative, it will be presumed for present purposes that the Due Process clause would apply to the facts alleged.

Defendants argue that Arar's claims alleging torture and unlawful detention in Syria are *per se* foreclosed under *Johnson v. Eisentrager*, 339 U.S. 763 (1950) [see *supra* p. 646], and its progeny. These cases, they claim, unequivocally establish that non-resident aliens subjected to constitutional violations on non-U.S. soil are prohibited from bringing claims under the Due Process clause....

However, there are obvious distinctions between *Eisentrager* and the case at bar. The *Eisentrager* petitioners had a trial pursuant to the laws of war. Although that trial might not have afforded them the panoply of rights provided in the civilian context, one cannot say that the petitioners had no fair process. Moreover, the *Eisentrager* detainees had "never been or resided in the United States," were "captured outside of our territory and there held in military custody as [ ] prisoner[s] of war," were "tried by a Military Commission sitting outside the United States," and were "at all times imprisoned outside the United States." *Eisentrager*, 339 U.S. at 777. Arar, by contrast, was held virtually incommunicado—moreover, on U.S. soil—and denied access to counsel and process of any kind. Owing to these factual distinctions, *Eisentrager* is not squarely applicable to the case at bar.

Defendants also cite *United States v. Verdugo-Urquidez*, 494 U.S. 259 (1990), in which the Supreme Court revisited the question of the extraterritoriality of the U.S. Constitution to non-U.S. citizens.... After foreclosing the possibility of any extraterritorial application of the Fourth Amendment, the *Verdugo-Urquidez* court explored in dicta the same question with regard to the Fifth Amendment.

C. Extraordinary Rendition

Relying on dicta in *Eisentrager,* the Supreme Court held that prior case law foreclosed such possibility [*supra* p. 643]....

However, *Verdugo-Urquidez,* which involved a search and seizure of a home in Mexico, can be distinguished from the case at bar. As Justice Kennedy observed in his concurring opinion, Mexico's different legal regime compounded (and perhaps created) the Fourth Amendment violations. "The absence of local judges or magistrates available to issue warrants, the differing and perhaps unascertainable conceptions of reasonableness and privacy that prevail abroad, and the need to cooperate with foreign officials all indicate that the Fourth Amendment's warrant requirement should not apply in Mexico as it does in this country." *Verdugo-Urquidez,* 494 U.S. at 278 (Kennedy, J., concurring).

Verdugo-Urquidez is further distinguishable from the instant case by the fact that the defendant in that case was prosecuted in an Article III court, where "all of the trial proceedings are governed by the Constitution. All would agree, for instance, that the dictates of the Due Process Clause of the Fifth Amendment protect the defendant." *Id.* Thus, any anxiety over the lack of Fourth Amendment protection [was] minimized by the fact that the trial would ultimately proceed in accordance with Fifth Amendment guarantees.

After *Verdugo-Urquidez,* the Court of Appeals for the District of Columbia Circuit considered a case, more directly applicable to the facts at issue here, involving a Guatemalan citizen and high-ranking member of a Guatemalan rebel organization who was allegedly tortured in Guatemala at the behest of CIA officials, who had ordered and directed the torture and then engaged in an eighteen-month cover-up. *Harbury v. Deutch,* 233 F.3d 596 (D.C. Cir. 2000), *rev'd on other grounds sub nom. Christopher v. Harbury,* 536 U.S. 403 (2002) [*supra* p. 451]. The constitutional violations at issue in *Harbury* included torture. Moreover, the torture was allegedly planned and orchestrated by U.S. officials acting within the United States. Thus, unlike *Eisentrager* and *Verdugo-Urquidez,* the factual background of *Harbury* is closely related to the case at bar.

The D.C. Circuit relied heavily on dicta in *Verdugo-Urquidez,* particularly its reading of *Eisentrager,* to ultimately hold that the decedent's wife (a U.S. citizen) could not bring a Fifth Amendment claim on his behalf for the torture he suffered in Guatemala. The D.C. Circuit noted, first, that *Verdugo-Urquidez* did not attach constitutional significance to the fact "that the search was both planned and ordered from within the United States. Instead, it focused on the location of the primary constitutionally significant conduct at issue: the search and seizure itself." *Harbury,* 233 F.3d at 603. Because of this, the D.C. Circuit found that "the primary constitutionally relevant conduct at issue here—[the deceased's] torture—occurred outside the United States." *Id.* at 603.

The D.C. circuit further noted that *Verdugo-Urquidez* read *Eisentrager* to "emphatically" reject the notion of any extraterritorial application of the Fifth Amendment. That language, although "dicta...is firm and considered dicta that binds this court." *Harbury,* 233 F.3d at 604.

Still, the case at bar, unlike *Harbury,* presents a claim of torture by an alien apprehended at the U.S. border and held here pending removal; furthermore, the fact that Arar's alleged torture began with his removal from the territory of the United States makes this case factually different from *Harbury.* Nevertheless, by answering the question "whether the Fifth Amendment prohibits torture of non-resident foreign nationals living abroad" in the negative, *id.* at 602, *Harbury* appears to have important implications for the case at bar.

However, in *Rasul v. Bush,* 542 U.S. 466 (2004) [*supra* p. 692], the Supreme Court issued a ruling potentially favorable to Arar....

Rasul only considered the question "whether the federal courts have jurisdiction to determine the legality of the Executive's potentially indefinite detention of individuals who claim to be wholly innocent of wrongdoing." *Id.* at 485. Moreover, the Supreme Court reached its decision by noting that "the United States exercises 'complete jurisdiction and control' over the Guantanamo Bay Naval Base, and may continue to exercise such control permanently if it so chooses." *Id.* at 480.

To be sure, there is no argument that the United States exercises the same control over the Syrian officials alleged to have detained and tortured Arar as it does in the case of Guantanamo Bay. Nevertheless, one might read *Rasul* as extending habeas jurisdiction to a group of aliens with even less of a connection to the United States than Arar.

Defendants reject that contention, arguing that, in light of the above-cited cases, the substantive due process violations asserted in Arar's complaint "are predicated upon a constitutional protection that has never been extended to arriving aliens, much less aliens whom the executive has determined pursuant to legislative authorization have terrorist connections." But Arar — who received none of the procedural and substantive protections afforded the petitioners in *Eisentrager* — has a connection to the United States lacking in *Eisentrager, Verdugo-Urquidez, Harbury* and *Rasul*. All of Arar's claims against U.S. officials allegedly arise out of actions taken or initiated by them while Arar was on U.S. soil. Moreover, the factual scenario presented in this case makes it more difficult to simply apply the precedents established in the *Eisentrager* line of cases.

As already noted, the *Eisentrager* detainees had "never been or resided in the United States," were "captured outside of our territory and there held in military custody as [ ] prisoner[s] of war, were 'tried by a Military Commission sitting outside the United States' " and were "at all times imprisoned outside the United States." *Eisentrager,* 339 U.S. at 777. Arar, by contrast, was held virtually incommunicado in *this* country and denied access to counsel and a meaningful process of any kind. Moreover, as the *Rasul* court noted, the Guantanamo detainees "are not nationals of countries at war with the United States, and they deny that they have engaged in or plotted acts of aggression against the United States; they have never been afforded access to any tribunal, much less charged with and convicted of wrongdoing...." *Id.* at 476.

Another difference between *Rasul* and the case at bar is that *Rasul* based its jurisdiction on the statutory habeas provision (28 U.S.C. §2241), not the U.S. Constitution. Arar, by contrast, alleges substantive constitutional claims not addressed in *Rasul. See In re Guantanamo Detainee Cases,* 355 F. Supp. 2d 443, 463 (D.D.C. 2005) (citing language in *Rasul* as "stand[ing] in sharp contrast to the declaration in *Verdugo-Urquidez...* that the Supreme Court's 'rejection of extraterritorial application of the Fifth Amendment [has been] emphatic' ").

At this juncture, the question whether the Due Process Clause vests Arar with substantive rights is unresolved. Assuming, without resolving, the existence of some substantive protection, Arar's claims are foreclosed under an exception to the *Bivens* doctrine.

C. Extraordinary Rendition

SPECIAL FACTORS COUNSELING HESITATION

The substantive due process analysis notwithstanding, the Supreme Court's creation of a *Bivens* remedy for alleged constitutional violations by federal officials is subject to certain prudential limitations and exceptions. The Supreme Court has "expressly cautioned . . . that such a remedy will not be available when 'special factors counseling hesitation' are present." *Chappell v. Wallace*, 462 U.S. 296, 298 (1983) (quoting *Bivens*, 403 U.S. at 396). Those factors do not concern "the merits of the particular remedy [being] sought." *Bush v. Lucas*, 462 U.S. 367, 380 (1983). Rather, they involve "the question of who should decide whether such a remedy should be provided." *Id.* . . . Moreover, courts will refrain from extending a *Bivens* claim if doing so trammels upon matters best decided by coordinate branches of government. *See Lucas*, 462 U.S. at 378-80 (discussing case law according to which courts have deferred to coordinate branches). . . .

This case undoubtedly presents broad questions touching on the role of the Executive branch in combating terrorist forces — namely the prevention of future terrorist attacks within U.S. borders by capturing or containing members of those groups who seek to inflict damage on this country and its people. Success in these efforts requires coordination between law-enforcement and foreign-policy officials; complex relationships with foreign governments are also involved. In light of these factors, courts must proceed cautiously in reviewing constitutional and statutory claims in that arena, especially where they raise policy-making issues that are the prerogative of coordinate branches of government.

A number of considerations must be noted here. First, Article I, Section 8 of the U.S. Constitution places the regulation of aliens squarely within the authority of the Legislative branch. Congress has yet to take any affirmative position on federal-court review of renditions; indeed, by withholding any explicit grant of a private cause of action under the Torture Victim Protection Act to plaintiffs like Arar . . . the opposite is the more reasonable inference.

Second, this case raises crucial national-security and foreign policy considerations, implicating "the complicated multilateral negotiations concerning efforts to halt international terrorism." *Doherty v. Meese*, 808 F.2d 938, 943 (2d Cir. 1986). The propriety of these considerations, including supposed agreements between the United States and foreign governments regarding intelligence-gathering in the context of the efforts to combat terrorism, are most appropriately reserved to the Executive and Legislative branches of government. Moreover, the need for much secrecy can hardly be doubted. One need not have much imagination to contemplate the negative effect on our relations with Canada if discovery were to proceed in this case and were it to turn out that certain high Canadian officials had, despite public denials, acquiesced in Arar's removal to Syria. More generally, governments that do not wish to acknowledge publicly that they are assisting us would certainly hesitate to do so if our judicial discovery process could compromise them. Even a ruling sustaining state-secret-based objections to a request for interrogatories, discovery demand, or questioning of a witness could be compromising. Depending on the context it could be construed as the equivalent of a public admission that the alleged conduct had occurred in the manner claimed — to the detriment of our relations with foreign countries, whether friendly or not. Hence, extending a *Bivens* remedy "could significantly disrupt the ability of the political branches to respond to foreign situations involving our national interest." *Verdugo-Urquidez*, 494 U.S. 259, 273-274. It risks "produc[ing] what the Supreme Court has called in another context 'embarrassment of our government abroad' through 'multifarious pronouncements by various departments on one question.'" *Sanchez-Espinoza v. Reagan*, 770 F.2d 202, 208 (D.C. Cir. 1985) (Scalia, J.) (quoting *Baker v. Carr*, 369 U.S. 186, 226, 217 (1962))....

Third, with respect to these coordinate branch concerns, there is a fundamental difference between courts evaluating the legitimacy of actions taken by federal officials in the domestic arena and evaluating the same conduct when taken in the international realm. In the former situation...judges have not only the authority vested under the Constitution to evaluate the decision-making of government officials that goes on in the domestic context, whether it be a civil or a criminal matter, but also the experience derived from living in a free and democratic society, which permits them to make sound judgments. In the international realm, however, most, if not all, judges have neither the experience nor the background to adequately and competently define and adjudge the rights of an individual vis-à-vis the needs of officials acting to defend the sovereign interests of the United States, especially in circumstances involving countries that do not accept our nation's values or may be assisting those out to destroy us....

Accordingly, the task of balancing individual rights against national-security concerns is one that courts should not undertake without the guidance or the authority of the coordinate branches, in whom the Constitution imposes responsibility for our foreign affairs and national security. Those branches have the responsibility to determine whether judicial oversight is appropriate. Without explicit legislation, judges should be hesitant to fill an arena that, until now, has been left untouched — perhaps deliberately — by the Legislative and Executive branches. To do otherwise would threaten "our customary policy of deference to the President in matters of foreign affairs." [Jama v. Immmigration and Customs Enforcement, 543 U.S. 335 (2005)], at 348. In sum, whether the policy be seeking to undermine or overthrow foreign governments, or rendition, judges should not, in the absence of explicit direction by Congress, hold officials who carry out such policies liable for damages even if such conduct violates our treaty obligations or customary international law.

For these reasons, I conclude that a remedy under *Bivens* for Arar's alleged rendition to Syria is foreclosed. Accordingly, Counts 2 and 3 of the complaint are dismissed....

[The court also dismissed Arar's claim of substantive due process violations based on his treatment while in the United States, but the dismissal without prejudice allows Arar to refile and supply more detail concerning the physical mistreatment he alleges occurred.]

NOTES AND QUESTIONS

1. *Arar v. Ashcroft and the Availability of Judicial Remedies.* On March 30, 2005, media sources reported the discovery of flight records that appear to

C. Extraordinary Rendition

corroborate at least part of Arar's story. *See* Scott Shane, Stephen Grey & Ford Fessenden, *Detainee's Suit Gains Support from Jet's Log*, N.Y. Times, Mar. 30, 2005, at A1. In an omitted portion of Arar v. Ashcroft, the court ruled that the TVPA creates no private right of action for rendition of a person who may be subjected to torture. Nor does the TVPA apply where U.S. officials allegedly direct foreign officials to torture a non-U.S. citizen. 414 F. Supp. 2d at 266. Of what value, then, is the TVPA to victims of torture?

Why did the court decline to decide Arar's claim for damages arising out of the alleged due process violations? What is the basis for the exception to the *Bivens* constitutional torts doctrine, where "foreign policy and national security" concerns suggest that the claims asserted should "be left to the political branches of government"? *Id.* at 283. Can you identify a rationale from the political question doctrine cases, *supra* pp. 134-149, to support the court's decision? Is the potential embarrassment of Canadian government officials a good reason for the court not to decide the case? Are the political branches better suited than the court to resolve Arar's dispute with the United States?

2. *Due Process.* If the court had reached the merits on Arar's due process claim, what should the outcome have been? Which precedents provide guideposts that are most portable to the *Arar* setting—Reid v. Covert, *supra* p. 173; Verdugo-Urquidez v. United States, *supra* p. 643; Johnson v. Eisentrager, noted *supra* p. 646; Harbury v. Deutch, *supra* p. 452; or Rasul v. Bush, *supra* p. 692?

3. *Availability of Habeas Corpus.* In Abu Ali v. Ashcroft, 350 F. Supp. 2d 28 (D.D.C. 2004), U.S. citizen Omar Abu Ali challenged his ongoing detention in a prison in Saudi Arabia allegedly at the direction and with the ongoing supervision of the United States. When Abu Ali's parents sought habeas corpus for their son, the United States argued that the suit must be dismissed for lack of jurisdiction, "no matter how extensive a role the United States might have played and continues to play" in Abu Ali's detention, "for the sole reason that he is presently in a foreign prison." *Id.* at 40. The court held that the United States may not avoid habeas corpus jurisdiction by enlisting a foreign nation to detain an American citizen:

> This position is as striking as it is sweeping. The full contours of the position would permit the United States, at its discretion and without judicial review, to arrest a citizen of the United States and transfer her to the custody of allies overseas in order to avoid constitutional scrutiny; to arrest a citizen of the United States through the intermediary of a foreign ally and ask the ally to hold the citizen at a foreign location indefinitely at the direction of the United States; or even to deliver American citizens to foreign governments to obtain information through the use of torture. In short, the United States is in effect arguing for nothing less than the unreviewable power to separate an American citizen from the most fundamental of his constitutional rights merely by choosing where he will be detained or who will detain him." [*Id.*]

How, if at all, does the court's answer to the government affect those in a situation similar to Arar's?

4. *Scope of the Operations.* No one knows for sure how many extraordinary renditions have occurred. Rendition of suspected terrorists to other nations apparently has been part of U.S. counterterrorism activities since the late 1990s, and perhaps since a directive from President Ronald Reagan in 1986. Some estimate that more than 100 persons have been thus rendered by the United States since the September 11 attacks. Dana Priest, *CIA's Assurances on Transferred Suspects Doubted,* Wash. Post, Mar. 17, 2005, at A1. Reported destinations for extraordinary rendition include Egypt, Jordan, Morocco, Saudi Arabia, Yemen, and Syria, all condemned by the U.S. State Department as employing torture in interrogation. *See* Jane Mayer, *Outsourcing Torture,* New Yorker, Feb. 14, 2005, at 106. In March 2005, it was reported that President Bush issued a classified directive following the September 11 attacks that broadened the CIA's authority to render suspected terrorists to other states. The White House has neither confirmed nor denied the report. Douglas Jehl & David Johnston, *Rule Change Lets CIA Freely Send Suspects Abroad to Jails,* N.Y. Times, Mar. 6, 2005, at A1. In June 2005, Italian police officials issued arrest warrants for 22 alleged U.S. intelligence operatives in connection with the rendering of an Islamic cleric from Italy to Egypt without the consent of the Italian government. Although some reported that Italian authorities knew of and consented to the rendition, the Italian government denied those reports. Craig Whitlock, *Italy Denies Complicity in Alleged CIA Action,* Wash. Post, July 1, 2005, at A14. In April 2006, however, the Italian justice minister declined to forward a prosecutor's extradition request to Washington for the 22 accused CIA officers. Peter Kiefer, *Italian Minister Declines to Seek Extradition of C.I.A. Operatives,* N.Y. Times, Apr. 13, 2006, at A6. Other examples of alleged extraordinary renditions, compiled from news sources, are summarized in Committee on International Human Rights of the Assn. of the Bar of the City of New York and Center for Human Rights and Global Justice, N.Y.U. School of Law, *Torture by Proxy: International and Domestic Law Applicable to "Extraordinary Renditions"* 9-13 (2004), *available at* http://www.nyuhr.org/docs/TortureByProxy.pdf. *See also* Amnesty Intl., *Below the Radar: Secret Flights to Torture and "Disappearance,"* Apr. 5, 2006, *available at* http://web.amnesty.org/library/Index/ENGAMR510512006.

5. *CIA Charter Flights.* Some extraordinary renditions have reportedly been carried out by the CIA pursuant to broadly worded findings approved by the President. Douglas Jehl & David Johnston, *Rule Change Lets CIA Freely Send Suspects Abroad to Jails,* N.Y. Times, Mar. 6, 2005, at A1. An apparently private charter company, Aero Contractors, is actually a domestic centerpiece of the CIA secret air service, which conducts flights to render suspects abroad. *See* Scott Shane, *CIA Expanding Terror Battle Under Guise of Charter Flights,* N.Y. Times, May 31, 2005, at A1. One 2005 analysis of 26 planes operated by CIA companies showed 307 flights in Europe since September 2001. Ian Fisher, *Reports of Secret U.S. Prisons in Europe Draw Ire and Otherwise Red Faces,* N.Y. Times, Dec. 1, 2005, at A14. Assuming that the President's findings complied with the National Security Act, *supra* p. 355, are the renditions lawful? Does it matter legally if Congress is not notified about individual cases?

6. *Why Do It?* Why would the United States sponsor or participate in extraordinary renditions? One unnamed official with experience in so

C. Extraordinary Rendition

rendering detainees explained: "We don't kick the [expletive] out of them. We send them to other countries so they can kick the [expletive] out of them." Dana Priest & Barton Gellman, *U.S. Decries Abuse but Defends Interrogations; "Stress and Duress" Tactics Used on Terrorism Suspects Held in Secret Overseas Facilities*, Wash. Post, Dec. 26, 2002, at A1.

7. *Official Policy?* The Bush administration has not denied that persons have been rendered to foreign nations reputed to practice torture. However, officials have denied that renditions have occurred for the purpose of torture. *See* R. Jeffrey Smith, *Gonzales Defends Transfer of Detainees*, Wash. Post, Mar. 8, 2005, at A3 (quoting Attorney General Gonzales as stating that it is not U.S. policy to send persons "to countries where we believe or we know that they're going to be tortured"); Joel Brinkley, *U.S. Interrogations Are Saving European Lives, Rice Says*, N.Y. Times, Dec. 6, 2005, at A3 (quoting Secretary of State Condoleezza Rice as stating that "[t]he United States does not transport and has not transported detainees from one country to another for the purpose of interrogation using torture."). How much legal wiggle room do these statements preserve for the Administration? How, if at all, should these statements of U.S. policy affect Arar's likelihood of gaining relief in his lawsuit?

8. *The CAT and Implementing Legislation.* Review the discussion of the Convention Against Torture and its implementing legislation, *supra* pp. 774-781. CAT Article 3 provides that "[n]o State Party shall expel, return ('refouler') or extradite a person to another State where there are substantial grounds for believing that he would be in danger of being subjected to torture." An understanding attached to the convention by the Senate upon its advice and consent states that the requirement in Article 3 would apply when it is "more likely than not" that torture would follow such a rendition. Sen. Exec. Rpt. No. 101-30, *Resolution of Advice and Consent to Ratification* (1990), at ¶II(2). What information should lawyers take into account when asked to advise on a "more likely than not" determination? The CAT lacks a parallel provision regarding cruel, inhuman, or degrading treatment. What is the legal significance of this omission? *See* Michael John Garcia, *Renditions: Constraints Imposed by Laws on Torture* (Cong. Res. Serv. RL32890) 7, Sept. 22, 2005.

In 1998, Congress approved legislation implementing Article 3 of the CAT. Pub. L. No. 105-277, §2242(a)-(b), 112 Stat. 2681, 2681-822. Although Congress gave immigration officials administrative discretion in excluding from CAT protection certain classes of aliens, current Department of Homeland Security regulations prohibit the removal of all persons to states where they more likely than not would be tortured. 8 C.F.R. §§208.16-18, 1208.16-18 (2005). CIA regulations concerning renditions, if any, are not publicly available. Garcia, *supra*, at 9.

The criminal sanctions implementing Articles 4 and 5 of the CAT forbid torture outside the United States. Review the specific intent required by the statute. See *supra* p. 794. Would the torturer be liable if the torture occurred, say, in Syria? How about the CIA official who arranged for the extraordinary rendition?

CAT Article 4 and its implementing legislation would, in any case, provide criminal penalties for U.S. officials who conspire with others to render a person to facilitate torture. Recall, however, Attorney General Gonzales's comment in

Note 7 above. Would a mere belief that a suspect might be tortured in the destination state be sufficient to attach criminal responsibility to U.S. officials for any torture that occurs there?

9. *Geneva Convention Limits on Rendition.* An involuntary transfer of "protected persons" to another state is forbidden by Geneva Convention IV, Article 49. A violation constitutes a "grave breach" and is thus a war crime. *Id.* art. 147. Recall the Bush administration's arguments concerning the applicability of the Geneva Conventions in the post-September 11 campaign. Which persons in what places are protected from rendition under the Geneva Conventions? Would these provisions be helpful to Maher Arar in his lawsuit?

10. *Effect of the Detainee Treatment Act.* Review the language of the Detainee Treatment Act set forth *supra* p. 701. If this provision had been in effect when Arar was rendered to Syria, would the Act have been violated? Does the Act establish rights for detainees that they otherwise would not enjoy?

Criminalizing Terrorism and Material Support 28

Generally, First Amendment protections for freedom of speech, assembly, and association pose no obstacle to prosecution of terrorists for committing terrorist acts. Murder and maiming enjoy no constitutional protection. But the prosecution of such primary offenders — if they survive the terrorist attack and are successfully hunted down — comes too late to prevent the harm. Nor is such prosecution likely to deter others who are religiously or politically motivated to commit terrorist attacks. Counterterrorist criminal law therefore necessarily searches up the chain of causation to secondary defendants who aid and abet, conspire, harbor, or otherwise assist the terrorists. And prosecution of either primary or secondary defendants is complicated when their conduct takes place abroad, given the normal presumption against extraterritorial application of U.S. law.

In Part A of this chapter, we consider a case that suggests that the hoary criminal laws of treason and sedition may be a poor fit for such prosecutions. In the 1990s, Congress therefore criminalized providing "material support" to terrorists or designated foreign terrorist organizations. See *supra* pp. 467-468 (describing the effects and mechanics of designation). In Part B, we consider these laws and the issues they raise about criminalizing advocacy and association as well as personal guilt. Finally, in Part C, we consider the extraterritorial application of U.S. counterterrorism laws.

A. TREASON AND SEDITION

United States v. Rahman
United States Court of Appeals, Second Circuit, 1999
189 F.3d 88

PER CURIAM: These are appeals by ten defendants convicted of seditious conspiracy and other offenses arising out of a wide-ranging plot to conduct a campaign of urban terrorism. Among the activities of some or all of the defendants were rendering assistance to those who bombed the World Trade Center, planning to bomb bridges and tunnels in New York City, murdering Rabbi Meir Kahane, and planning to murder the President of Egypt. We affirm the convictions of all the defendants....

The Government adduced evidence at trial showing the following: Abdel Rahman, a blind Islamic scholar and cleric, was the leader of the seditious conspiracy, the purpose of which was *"jihad,"* in the sense of a struggle against the enemies of Islam. Indicative of this purpose, in a speech to his followers Abdel Rahman instructed that they were to "do *jihad* with the sword, with the cannon, with the grenades, with the missile...against God's enemies." Abdel Rahman's role in the conspiracy was generally limited to overall supervision and direction of the membership, as he made efforts to remain a level above the details of individual operations. However, as a cleric and the group's leader, Abdel Rahman was entitled to dispense *"fatwas,"* religious opinions on the holiness of an act, to members of the group sanctioning proposed courses of conduct and advising them whether the acts would be in furtherance of *jihad*.

According to his speeches and writings, Abdel Rahman perceives the United States as the primary oppressor of Muslims worldwide, active in assisting Israel to gain power in the Middle East, and largely under the control of the Jewish lobby. Abdel Rahman also considers the secular Egyptian government of Mubarak to be an oppressor because it has abided Jewish migration to Israel while seeking to decrease Muslim births. Holding these views, Abdel Rahman believes that *jihad* against Egypt and the United States is mandated by the Qur'an. Formation of a *jihad* army made up of small "divisions" and "battalions" to carry out this *jihad* was therefore necessary, according to Abdel Rahman, in order to beat back these oppressors of Islam including the United States....

I. CONSTITUTIONAL CHALLENGES

A. SEDITIOUS CONSPIRACY STATUTE AND THE TREASON CLAUSE

Defendant Nosair (joined by other defendants) contends that his conviction for seditious conspiracy, in violation of 18 U.S.C. §2384, was illegal because it failed to satisfy the requirements of the Treason Clause of the U.S. Constitution, Art. III, §3.

Article III, Section 3 provides, in relevant part:

> Treason against the United States, shall consist only in levying War against them, or in adhering to their Enemies, giving them Aid and Comfort. No Person shall be convicted of Treason unless on the Testimony of two Witnesses to the same overt Act, or on Confession in open Court.

The seditious conspiracy statute provides:

> If two or more persons in any State or Territory, or in any place subject to the jurisdiction of the United States, conspire to overthrow, put down or to destroy by force the Government of the United States, or to levy war against them, or to oppose by force the authority thereof, or by force to prevent, hinder or delay the execution of any law of the United States, or by force to seize, take, or possess

A. Treason and Sedition

any property of the United States contrary to the authority thereof, they shall each be fined under this title or imprisoned not more than twenty years, or both.

18 U.S.C. §2384.

Nosair contends that because the seditious conspiracy statute punishes conspiracy to "levy war" against the United States without a conforming two-witness requirement, the statute is unconstitutional. He further claims that because his conviction for conspiracy to levy war against the United States was not based on the testimony of two witnesses to the same overt act, the conviction violates constitutional standards.

It is undisputed that Nosair's conviction was not supported by two witnesses to the same overt act. Accordingly the conviction must be overturned if the requirement of the Treason Clause applies to this prosecution for seditious conspiracy.

The plain answer is that the Treason Clause does not apply to the prosecution. The provisions of Article III, Section 3 apply to prosecutions for "treason." Nosair and his co-appellants were not charged with treason. Their offense of conviction, seditious conspiracy under Section 2384, differs from treason not only in name and associated stigma, but also in its essential elements and punishment....

Seditious conspiracy by levying war includes no requirement that the defendant owe allegiance to the United States, an element necessary to conviction of treason. *See* 18 U.S.C. §2381 (defining "allegiance to United States" as an element of treason)....

The reference to treason in the constitutional clause necessarily incorporates the elements of allegiance and betrayal that are essential to the concept of treason.... Nosair was thus tried for a different, and lesser, offense than treason. We therefore see no reasonable basis to maintain that the requirements of the Treason Clause should apply to Nosair's prosecution.

B. SEDITIOUS CONSPIRACY STATUTE AND THE FIRST AMENDMENT

Abdel Rahman, joined by the other appellants, contends that the seditious conspiracy statute, 18 U.S.C. §2384, is an unconstitutional burden on free speech and the free exercise of religion in violation of the First Amendment. First, Abdel Rahman argues that the statute is facially invalid because it criminalizes protected expression and that it is overbroad and unconstitutionally vague. Second, Abdel Rahman contends that his conviction violated the First Amendment because it rested solely on his political views and religious practices.

1. Facial Challenge

a. *Restraint on Speech.* ... As Section 2384 proscribes "speech" only when it constitutes an agreement to use force against the United States, Abdel Rahman's generalized First Amendment challenge to the statute is without merit. Our court has previously considered and rejected a First Amendment challenge to Section 2384. *See* United States v. Lebron, 222 F.2d 531, 536 (2d Cir. 1955). Although *Lebron*'s analysis of the First Amendment issues posed by

Section 2384 was brief, the panel found the question was squarely controlled by the Supreme Court's then-recent decision in Dennis v. United States, 341 U.S. 494 (1951). In *Dennis*, the Court upheld the constitutionality of the Smith Act, which made it a crime to advocate, or to conspire to advocate, the overthrow of the United States government by force or violence. *See* 18 U.S.C. §2385; *Dennis*, 341 U.S. at 494. The *Dennis* Court concluded that, while the "element of speech" inherent in Smith Act convictions required that the Act be given close First Amendment scrutiny, the Act did not impermissibly burden the expression of protected speech, as it was properly "directed at advocacy [of overthrow of the government by force], not discussion." *See id.* at 502.

After *Dennis*, the Court broadened the scope of First Amendment restrictions on laws that criminalize subversive advocacy. It remains fundamental that while the state may not criminalize the expression of views — even including the view that violent overthrow of the government is desirable — it may nonetheless outlaw encouragement, inducement, or conspiracy to take violent action. Thus, in Yates v. United States, 354 U.S. 298, 318 (1957), overruled in part on other grounds, Burks v. United States, 437 U.S. 1, 7 (1978), the Court interpreted the Smith Act to prohibit only the advocacy of concrete violent action, but not "advocacy and teaching of forcible overthrow as an abstract principle, divorced from any effort to instigate action to that end." And in Brandenburg v. Ohio, 395 U.S. 444, 447 (1969) (per curiam), the Court held that a state may proscribe subversive advocacy only when such advocacy is directed towards, and is likely to result in, "imminent lawless action."

The prohibitions of the seditious conspiracy statute are much further removed from the realm of constitutionally protected speech than those at issue in *Dennis* and its progeny. To be convicted under Section 2384, one must conspire to *use* force, not just to *advocate* the use of force. We have no doubt that this passes the test of constitutionality. . . .

b. *Vagueness and Overbreadth*. Abdel Rahman also contends that Section 2384 is overbroad and void for vagueness.

(i) *Overbreadth*. A law is overbroad, and hence void, if it "does not aim specifically at evils within the allowable area of State control, but, on the contrary, sweeps within its ambit other activities that . . . constitute an exercise of freedom of speech or of the press." Thornhill v. Alabama, 310 U.S. 88, 97 (1940). . . .

We recognize that laws targeting "sedition" must be scrutinized with care to assure that the threat of prosecution will not deter expression of unpopular viewpoints by persons ideologically opposed to the government. But Section 2384 is drawn sufficiently narrowly that we perceive no unacceptable risk of such abuse.

Abdel Rahman argues that Section 2384 is overbroad because Congress could have achieved its public safety aims "without chilling First Amendment rights" by punishing only "substantive acts involving bombs, weapons, or other violent acts." One of the beneficial purposes of the conspiracy law is to permit arrest and prosecution before the substantive crime has been accomplished. The Government, possessed of evidence of conspiratorial planning, need not

A. Treason and Sedition

wait until buildings and tunnels have been bombed and people killed before arresting the conspirators. Accordingly, it is well established that the Government may criminalize certain preparatory steps towards criminal action, even when the crime consists of the use of conspiratorial or exhortatory words. Because Section 2384 prohibits only conspiratorial agreement, we are satisfied that the statute is not constitutionally overbroad.

(ii) *Vagueness.* Abdel Rahman also challenges the statute for vagueness. A criminal statute, particularly one regulating speech, must "define the criminal offense with sufficient definiteness that ordinary people can understand what conduct is prohibited and in a manner that does not encourage arbitrary and discriminatory enforcement." Kolender v. Lawson, 461 U.S. 352, 357 (1983). Abdel Rahman argues that Section 2384 does not provide "fair warning" about what acts are unlawful, leaving constitutionally protected speech vulnerable to criminal prosecution.

There is indeed authority suggesting that the word "seditious" does not sufficiently convey what conduct it forbids to serve as an essential element of a crime. *See* Keyishian v. Board of Regents, 385 U.S. 589, 598 (1967) (noting that "dangers fatal to First Amendment freedoms inhere in the word 'seditious,'" "and invalidating law that provided, *inter alia,* that state employees who utter "seditious words" may be discharged). But the word "seditious" does not appear in the prohibitory text of the statute; it appears only in the caption. The terms of the statute are far more precise. The portions charged against Abdel Rahman and his co-defendants — conspiracy to levy war against the United States and to oppose by force the authority thereof — do not involve terms of such vague meaning. Furthermore, they unquestionably specify that agreement *to use force* is an essential element of the crime. Abdel Rahman therefore cannot prevail on the claim that the portions of Section 2384 charged against him criminalize mere expressions of opinion, or are unduly vague.

2. Application of Section 2384 to Abdel Rahman's Case

Abdel Rahman also argues that he was convicted not for entering into any conspiratorial agreement that Congress may properly forbid, but "solely for his religious words and deeds" which, he contends, are protected by the First Amendment. In support of this claim, Abdel Rahman cites the Government's use in evidence of his speeches and writings.

There are two answers to Abdel Rahman's contention. The first is that freedom of speech and of religion do not extend so far as to bar prosecution of one who uses a public speech or a religious ministry to commit crimes. Numerous crimes under the federal criminal code are, or can be, committed by speech alone. As examples: Section 2 makes it an offense to "counsel[ ]," "command[ ]," "induce[ ]" or "procure[ ]" the commission of an offense against the United States. 18 U.S.C. §2(a). Section 371 makes it a crime to "conspire ... to commit any offense against the United States." 18 U.S.C. §371. Section 373, with which Abdel Rahman was charged, makes it a crime to "solicit[ ], command[ ], induce[ ], or otherwise endeavor[ ] to persuade" another person to commit a crime of violence. 18 U.S.C. §373(a). Various other statutes, like Section 2384, criminalize conspiracies of specified objectives, *see, e.g.*, 18 U.S.C. §1751(d) (conspiracy to kidnap); 18 U.S.C. §1951 (conspiracy to interfere with commerce through robbery, extortion, or violence); 21 U.S.C. §846 (conspiracy to violate drug laws). All of these offenses are characteristically committed through speech. Notwithstanding that political speech and religious exercise are among the activities most jealously guarded by the First Amendment, one is not immunized from prosecution for such speech-based offenses merely because one commits them through the medium of political speech or religious preaching. Of course, courts must be vigilant to insure that prosecutions are not improperly based on the mere expression of unpopular ideas. But if the evidence shows that the speeches crossed the line into criminal solicitation, procurement of criminal activity, or conspiracy to violate the laws, the prosecution is permissible.

The evidence justifying Abdel Rahman's conviction for conspiracy and solicitation showed beyond a reasonable doubt that he crossed this line. His speeches were not simply the expression of ideas; in some instances they constituted the crime of conspiracy to wage war on the United States under Section 2384 and solicitation of attack on the United States military installations, as well as of the murder of Egyptian President Hosni Mubarak under Section 373.

For example: Abdel Rahman told Salem he "should make up with God... by turning his rifle's barrel to President Mubarak's chest, and kill[ing] him." Tr. 4633.

On another occasion, speaking to Abdo Mohammed Haggag about murdering President Mubarak during his visit to the United States, Abdel Rahman told Haggag, "Depend on God. Carry out this operation. It does not require a fatwa.... You are ready in training, but do it. Go ahead." Tr. 10108.

The evidence further showed that Siddig Ali consulted with Abdel Rahman about the bombing of the United Nations Headquarters, and Abdel Rahman told him, "Yes, it's a must, it's a duty." Tr. 5527-5529.

On another occasion, when Abdel Rahman was asked by Salem about bombing the United Nations, he counseled against it on the ground that it would be "bad for Muslims," Tr. 6029, but added that Salem should "find a plan to destroy or to bomb or to... inflict damage to the American Army." Tr. 6029-6030.

Words of this nature — ones that instruct, solicit, or persuade others to commit crimes of violence — violate the law and may be properly prosecuted regardless of whether they are uttered in private, or in a public speech, or in administering the duties of a religious ministry. The fact that his speech or conduct was "religious" does not immunize him from prosecution under generally-applicable criminal statutes.

Abdel Rahman also protests the Government's use in evidence of his speeches, writings, and preachings that did not in themselves constitute the crimes of solicitation or conspiracy. He is correct that the Government placed in evidence many instances of Abdel Rahman's writings and speeches in which Abdel Rahman expressed his opinions within the protection of the First Amendment. However, while the First Amendment fully protects Abdel Rahman's right to express hostility against the United States, and he may not be prosecuted for so speaking, it does not prevent the use of such speeches or writings in evidence when relevant to prove a pertinent fact in a criminal prosecution. The Government was free to demonstrate Abdel Rahman's

A. Treason and Sedition

resentment and hostility toward the United States in order to show his motive for soliciting and procuring illegal attacks against the United States and against President Mubarak of Egypt.

Furthermore, Judge Mukasey properly protected against the danger that Abdel Rahman might be convicted because of his unpopular religious beliefs that were hostile to the United States. He explained to the jury the limited use it was entitled to make of the material received as evidence of motive. He instructed that a defendant could not be convicted on the basis of his beliefs or the expression of them — even if those beliefs favored violence. He properly instructed the jury that it could find a defendant guilty only if the evidence proved he committed a crime charged in the indictment.

We reject Abdel Rahman's claim that his conviction violated his rights under the First Amendment. . . .

NOTES AND QUESTIONS

1. *Treason.* "Treason" is the only crime expressly identified in the Constitution, which states that "Treason against the United States, shall consist only in levying War against them, or in adhering to their Enemies, giving them Aid and Comfort." U.S. Const. art. III, §3. Furthermore, the text supplies a special evidentiary rule for treason prosecutions: "No Person shall be convicted of Treason unless on the Testimony of two Witnesses to the same overt Act, or on Confession in open Court." *Id.* Why did the Framers single out treason for special mention and write an evidentiary rule for treason prosecutions directly into the Constitution, while leaving other crimes to legislative definition and evidentiary rules to the courts through the medium of the common law?

The restrictive nature of the constitutional rule of evidence suggests an answer: the Framers feared that the state would use treason prosecutions to suppress dissent.

> The treason clause is a product of the awareness of the Framers of the "numerous and dangerous excrescences" which had disfigured the English law of treason and was therefore intended to put it beyond the power of Congress to "extend the crime and punishment of treason." The debate in the Convention, remarks in the ratifying conventions, and contemporaneous public comment make clear that a restrictive concept of the crime was imposed and that ordinary partisan divisions within political society were not to be escalated by the stronger into capital charges of treason, as so often had happened in England. [S. Doc. No. 92-82, Congressional Research Service, *The Constitution of the United States of America: Analysis and Interpretation* (1973) (citations omitted), *updated version available at* http://www.law.cornell.edu/anncon/authorship.html.]

Indeed, the Framers provided additional protections for such partisan divisions by prohibiting Congress from enacting any law abridging freedom of speech, the press, assembly, petition, and (by judicial implication) association. U.S. Const. amend. I. *See* Ronald D. Rotunda & John E. Nowak, *Treatise on Constitutional Law*

§20.41 (3d ed. Pocket Part 2005) (describing case law regarding freedom of association).

Why did Abdel Rahman argue that he was effectively convicted of treason? Did the court's answer to his claim bypass the protections that the Framers built into the Treason Clause?

2. *Inciting Imminent Harm.* The *Rahman* court's synopsis of the constitutional law governing advocacy of lawless action makes it sound more consistent than it is. *See, e.g.,* Christina E. Wells, *Fear and Loathing in Constitutional Decision-Making,* 2005 Wis. L. Rev. 115. In a World War I case under the 1918 Sedition Act, the Supreme Court declared that the government could constitutionally criminalize the utterance of "words...used in such circumstances...as to create a clear and present danger that they will bring about the substantive evils that Congress has a right to prevent." Schenck v. United States, 249 U.S. 47, 52 (1919). The Court seemed to relax the clear-and-present-danger test in Dennis v. United States, 341 U.S. 494 (1951), by finding that the harm from an overthrow of the government would be so grave that the government need not show its imminence or probability in order to punish advocacy of the overthrow. Dennis and his co-defendants were convicted and sentenced to long prison terms for violating the Smith Act, which made it unlawful "to knowingly or willfully advocate, abet, advise, or teach the duty, necessity, desirability, or propriety of overthrowing or destroying any government in the United States by force or violence...." Act of June 28, 1940, 54 Stat. 670, 671 (1940). What were their criminal acts? Apparently, according to the evidence adduced by the government, assembling to discuss and plan future teaching of books by Stalin, Marx and Engels, and Lenin. Finally, without disavowing these chilling precedents, the Court reversed a conviction for "criminal syndicalism" in Brandenberg v. Ohio, 395 U.S. 444 (1969). There, the defendant had given a racist and anti-Semitic speech at a Ku Klux Klan rally. The Court held that a State could not criminalize "advocacy of the use of force or violation of law except where such advocacy is directed to inciting or producing imminent lawless action *and* is *likely* to incite or produce such action." *Id.* at 447 (emphasis added).

How does Section 2384 fare under these tests? Did the *Rahman* court apply them correctly? *See* John Alan Cohan, *Seditious Conspiracy, the Smith Act, and Prosecution for Religious Speech Advocating the Violent Overthrow of Government,* 17 St. John's J. Legal Comment. 199 (2003).

3. *Expression as Evidence.* Are not Rahman's religious expressions, quoted in the case, quintessentially protected speech? Why was it constitutional to base his criminal prosecution in part on them? *See generally* Cohan, *supra.*

B. MATERIAL SUPPORT CRIMES

The material support statutes set out below have been invoked often recently in criminal prosecutions growing out of the war on terrorism. They

B. Material Support Crimes

have also been amended a number of times. Note that the italicized language was added by the Intelligence Reform and Terrorism Prevention Act of 2004, Pub. L. No. 108-458, §6603(c)(2), 118 Stat. 3638, 3763, *after* and partly in response to the decisions in the two cases that follow the statutory excerpts.

18 U.S.C. §2339A. Providing material support to terrorists

(a) Offense.—Whoever provides material support or resources or conceals or disguises the nature, location, source, or ownership of material support or resources, knowing or intending that they are to be used in preparation for, or in carrying out, a violation of [various specific terrorist crimes] or in preparation for, or in carrying out, the concealment of an escape from the commission of any such violation, or attempts or conspires to do such an act, shall be fined under this title, imprisoned not more than 15 years, or both, and, if the death of any person results, shall be imprisoned for any term of years or for life. A violation of this section may be prosecuted in any Federal judicial district in which the underlying offense was committed, or in any other Federal judicial district as provided by law.

(b) Definitions.—As used in this section—

(1) the term "material support or resources" means *any property, tangible or intangible, or service, including* currency or monetary instruments or financial securities, financial services, lodging, training, expert advice or assistance, safehouses, false documentation or identification, communications equipment, facilities, weapons, lethal substances, explosives, personnel *(1 or more individuals who may be or include oneself)*, and transportation, except medicine or religious materials.

(2) the term "training" means instruction or teaching designed to impart a specific skill, as opposed to general knowledge; and

(3) the term "expert advice or assistance" means advice or assistance derived from scientific, technical or other specialized knowledge.

18 U.S.C. §2339B. Providing material support or resources to designated foreign terrorist organizations

(a) (1) Unlawful conduct.—Whoever knowingly provides material support or resources to a foreign terrorist organization, or attempts or conspires to do so, shall be fined under this title or imprisoned not more than 15 years, or both, and, if the death of any person results, shall be imprisoned for any term of years or for life. *To violate this paragraph, a person must have knowledge that the organization is a designated terrorist organization..., that the organization has engaged or engages in terrorist activity..., or that the organization has engaged or engages in terrorism....*

(g) Definitions.—As used in this section— ... (4) the term "material support or resources" has the same meaning given that term in section 2339A....

18 U.S.C. §2339C. Prohibitions against the financing of terrorism

(a) Offenses.—(1) In general.—Whoever, in a circumstance described in subsection (b) [prescribing jurisdictional attributes of crime], by any means, directly or indirectly, unlawfully and willfully provides or collects funds with the intention that such funds be used, or with the knowledge that such funds are to be used, in full or in part, in order to carry out... (B) any... act intended to cause death or serious bodily injury to a civilian, or to any other person not taking an active part in the hostilities in a situation of armed conflict, when the purpose of such act, by its nature or context, is to intimidate a population, or to compel a government or an international organization to do or to abstain from doing any act, shall be punished as prescribed in subsection (d)(1)....

Humanitarian Law Project v. Reno
United States Court of Appeals, Ninth Circuit, 2000
205 F.3d 1130 (*Humanitarian I*)

KOZINSKI, Circuit Judge: We consider whether Congress may, consistent with the First Amendment, prohibit contributions of material support to certain foreign terrorist organizations.

The Antiterrorism and Effective Death Penalty Act of 1996, Pub. L. No. 104-132, 110 Stat. 1214, known among the cognoscenti as AEDPA, authorizes the Secretary of State to "designate an organization as a foreign terrorist organization... if the Secretary finds that (A) the organization is a foreign organization; (B) the organization engages in terrorist activity...; and (C) the terrorist activity of the organization threatens the security of United States nationals or the national security of the United States." AEDPA §302(a), 110 Stat. at 1248 (codified at 8 U.S.C. §1189(a)).

This provision has teeth. AEDPA decrees punishment by fine, imprisonment for up to 10 years or both on "[w]hoever, within the United States or subject to the jurisdiction of the United States, knowingly provides material support or resources to a foreign terrorist organization, or attempts or conspires to do so...." AEDPA §303(a), 110 Stat. at 1250 (codified at 18 U.S.C. §2339B(a)(1)). The phrase "material support or resources" is broadly defined as "currency or other financial securities, financial services, lodging, training, safehouses, false documentation or identification, communications equipment, facilities, weapons, lethal substances, explosives, personnel, transportation, and other physical assets, except medicine or religious materials." AEDPA §323, 110 Stat. at 1255 (codified at 18 U.S.C. §2339A(b)).

Pursuant to those guidelines, the Secretary had, as of October 1997, designated 30 organizations as foreign terrorist organizations. Two such entities are the Kurdistan Workers' Party ("PKK") and the Liberation Tigers of Tamil Eelam

B. Material Support Crimes

("LTTE"). Plaintiffs, six organizations and two United States citizens, wish to provide what they fear would be considered material support to the PKK and LTTE. Plaintiffs claim that such support would be directed to aid only the non-violent humanitarian and political activities of the designated organizations. Being prohibited from giving this support, they argue, infringes their associational rights under the First Amendment. Because the statute criminalizes the giving of material support to an organization regardless of whether the donor intends to further the organization's unlawful ends, plaintiffs claim it runs afoul of the rule set forth in cases such as NAACP v. Claiborne Hardware Co., 458 U.S. 886 (1982). That rule, as succinctly stated in *Claiborne Hardware*, is "[f]or liability to be imposed by reason of association alone, it is necessary to establish that the group itself possessed unlawful goals and that the individual held a specific intent to further those illegal aims." *Id.* at 920. Plaintiffs further complain that AEDPA grants the Secretary unfettered and unreviewable authority to designate which groups are listed as foreign terrorist organizations, a violation of the First and Fifth Amendments. Lastly, plaintiffs maintain that AEDPA is unconstitutionally vague.

Plaintiffs sought a preliminary injunction barring enforcement of AEDPA against them. The district court denied the injunction, for the most part. However, it agreed with plaintiffs that AEDPA was impermissibly vague, specifically in its prohibition on providing "personnel" and "training." The court therefore enjoined the enforcement of those prohibitions. Each side appeals its losses.

A. Plaintiffs try hard to characterize the statute as imposing guilt by association, which would make it unconstitutional under cases such as *Claiborne Hardware*. But *Claiborne Hardware* and similar cases address situations where people are punished "by reason of association alone," *Claiborne Hardware*, 458 U.S. at 920—in other words, merely for membership in a group or for espousing its views. AEDPA authorizes no such thing. The statute does not prohibit being a member of one of the designated groups or vigorously promoting and supporting the political goals of the group. Plaintiffs are even free to praise the groups for using terrorism as a means of achieving their ends. What AEDPA prohibits is the act of giving material support, and there is no constitutional right to facilitate terrorism by giving terrorists the weapons and explosives with which to carry out their grisly missions. Nor, of course, is there a right to provide resources with which terrorists can buy weapons and explosives.

B. Plaintiffs also insist that AEDPA is unconstitutional because it proscribes the giving of material support even if the donor does not have the specific intent to aid in the organization's unlawful purposes. They rely on American-Arab Anti-Discrimination Comm. v. Reno, 70 F.3d 1045 (9th Cir. 1995) (ADC I), where we declared that "[t]he government must establish a 'knowing affiliation' and a 'specific intent to further those illegal aims'" in order to punish advocacy. *Id.* at 1063 (quoting Healy v. James, 408 U.S. 169, 186 (1972)). But advocacy is far different from making donations of material support. Advocacy is always protected under the First Amendment whereas making donations is protected only in certain contexts. *See* Section C. *infra*. Plaintiffs here do not contend they are prohibited from advocating the goals of the foreign terrorist organizations, espousing their views or even being members of such groups. They can do so without fear of penalty right up to the line established by Brandenburg v. Ohio, 395 U.S. 444 (1969)....

Material support given to a terrorist organization can be used to promote the organization's unlawful activities, regardless of donor intent. Once the support is given, the donor has no control over how it is used. We therefore do not agree that the First Amendment requires the government to demonstrate a specific intent to aid an organization's illegal activities before attaching liability to the donation of funds.

C. Plaintiffs make a separate First Amendment argument based on the fact that the terrorist organizations in question also engage in political advocacy. Pointing to cases such as Buckley v. Valeo, 424 U.S. 1 (1976), and In re Asbestos Sch. Litig., 46 F.3d 1284 (3d Cir. 1994), plaintiffs argue that providing money to organizations engaged in political expression is itself both political expression and association. *See Buckley*, 424 U.S. at 44-45 ("[T]he constitutionality of [the restrictions on contributions to political candidates] turns on whether the government interests advanced in its support satisfy the exacting scrutiny applicable to limitations on core First Amendment rights of political expression."). However, the cases equating monetary support with expression involved organizations whose overwhelming function was political advocacy. *Buckley* is the quintessential example, where the contributions were made to candidates for political office for the purpose of helping them engage in electioneering. Under those circumstances, money, and the things money can buy, do indeed serve as a proxy for speech and demonstrate one's association with the organization. However, even in *Buckley*, the Court treated limits on donations differently from limits on candidates' expenditures of personal funds. While the First Amendment protects the expressive component of seeking and donating funds, expressive *conduct* receives significantly less protection than pure speech. *See* Texas v. Johnson, 491 U.S. 397, 406 (1989) ("The government generally has a freer hand in restricting expressive conduct than it has in restricting the written or spoken word.") (citing United States v. O'Brien, 391 U.S. 367, 376-377 (1968)). The government may thus regulate contributions to organizations that engage in lawful — but non-speech related — activities. And it may certainly regulate contributions to organizations performing unlawful or harmful activities, even though such contributions may also express the donor's feelings about the recipient.

Contrary to plaintiffs' argument, the material support restriction here does not warrant strict scrutiny because it is not aimed at interfering with the expressive component of their conduct but at stopping aid to terrorist groups. *Compare O'Brien*, 391 U.S. at 376-377 (applying intermediate scrutiny to regulation prohibiting the burning of any draft card) *with Johnson*, 491 U.S. at 406 (applying strict scrutiny to law prohibiting only the burning of flags which offended witnesses). Intermediate scrutiny applies where, as here, "a regulation ... serves purposes unrelated to the content of expression." Ward v. Rock Against Racism, 491 U.S. 781, 791 (1989).

When we review under the intermediate scrutiny standard, we must ask four questions: Is the regulation within the power of the government? Does it promote an important or substantial government interest? Is that interest unrelated

B. Material Support Crimes

to suppressing free expression? And, finally, is the incidental restriction on First Amendment freedoms no greater than necessary? *See O'Brien*, 391 U.S. at 377.

Here all four questions are answered in the affirmative. First, the federal government clearly has the power to enact laws restricting the dealings of United States citizens with foreign entities; such regulations have been upheld in the past over a variety of constitutional challenges. Second, the government has a legitimate interest in preventing the spread of international terrorism, and there is no doubt that that interest is substantial.[1] Third, this interest is unrelated to suppressing free expression because it restricts the actions of those who wish to give material support to the groups, not the expression of those who advocate or believe the ideas that the groups support.

So the heart of the matter is whether AEDPA is well enough tailored to its end of preventing the United States from being used as a base for terrorist fundraising. Because the judgment of how best to achieve that end is strongly bound up with foreign policy considerations, we must allow the political branches wide latitude in selecting the means to bring about the desired goal....

Congress explicitly incorporated a finding into the statute that "foreign organizations that engage in terrorist activity are so tainted by their criminal conduct that any contribution to such an organization facilitates that conduct." AEDPA §301(a)(7), 110 Stat. at 1247. It follows that all material support given to such organizations aids their unlawful goals. Indeed, as the government points out, terrorist organizations do not maintain open books. Therefore, when someone makes a donation to them, there is no way to tell how the donation is used. Further, as amicus Anti-Defamation League notes, even contributions earmarked for peaceful purposes can be used to give aid to the families of those killed while carrying out terrorist acts, thus making the decision to engage in terrorism more attractive. More fundamentally, money is fungible; giving support intended to aid an organization's peaceful activities frees up resources that can be used for terrorist acts. We will not indulge in speculation about whether Congress was right to come to the conclusion that it did. We simply note that Congress has the fact-finding resources to properly come to such a conclusion. Thus, we cannot say that AEDPA is not sufficiently tailored....

E. Finally, Plaintiffs challenge AEDPA on vagueness grounds.... When a criminal law implicates First Amendment concerns, the law must be "sufficiently clear so as to allow persons of 'ordinary intelligence a reasonable opportunity to know what is prohibited.'" Foti v. City of Menlo Park, 146 F.3d 629, 638 (9th Cir. 1998) (quoting Grayned v. City of Rockford, 408 U.S. 104, 108 (1972)). It is easy to see how someone could be unsure about what AEDPA prohibits with the use of the term "personnel," as it blurs the line between protected expression and unprotected conduct. Someone who advocates the cause of the PKK could be

---

1. Plaintiffs complain that the statute allows the designation not only of groups who threaten our "national defense," but also those groups that imperil our "foreign relations" or "economic interests." But "[p]rotection of the foreign policy of the United States is a governmental interest of great importance, since foreign policy and national security considerations cannot neatly be compartmentalized." Haig v. Agee, 453 U.S. 280, 307 (1981). The same, of course, is true of our economic interests.

seen as supplying them with personnel; it even fits under the government's rubric of freeing up resources, since having an independent advocate frees up members to engage in terrorist activities instead of advocacy. But advocacy is pure speech protected by the First Amendment.

In order to keep the statute from trenching on such advocacy, the government urges that we read into it a requirement that the activity prohibited be performed "under the direction or control" of the foreign terrorist organization. While we construe a statute in such a way as to avoid constitutional questions, *see* Crowell v. Benson, 285 U.S. 22, 62 (1932), we are not authorized to rewrite the law so it will pass constitutional muster....

The term "training" fares little better. Again, it is easy to imagine protected expression that falls within the bounds of this term. For example, a plaintiff who wishes to instruct members of a designated group on how to petition the United Nations to give aid to their group could plausibly decide that such protected expression falls within the scope of the term "training." The government insists that the term is best understood to forbid the imparting of skills to foreign terrorist organizations through training. Yet, presumably, this definition would encompass teaching international law to members of designated organizations. The result would be different if the term "training" were qualified to include only military training or training in terrorist activities. Because plaintiffs have demonstrated that they are likely to succeed on the merits of their claim with respect to the terms "training" and "personnel," we conclude that the district court did not abuse its discretion in issuing its limited preliminary injunction.

The judgment of the district court is Affirmed.

United States v. Al-Arian
United States District Court, Middle District of Florida, 2004
308 F. Supp. 2d 1322

Moody, J. . . .

I. BACKGROUND

A. FACTUAL AND PROCEDURAL BACKGROUND

This is a criminal action against alleged members of the Palestinian Islamic Jihad-Shiqaqi Faction (the "PIJ") who purportedly operated and directed fundraising and other organizational activities in the United States for almost twenty years. The PIJ is a foreign organization that uses violence, principally suicide bombings, and threats of violence to pressure Israel to cede territory to the Palestinian people. On February 19, 2003, the government indicted the Defendants in a 50 count indictment that included counts for... (3) conspiracy to provide material support to or for the benefit of foreign terrorists (Counts 3 and 4)....

B. Material Support Crimes

II. DISCUSSION...

A. STATUTORY CONSTRUCTION AND CONSTITUTIONAL ISSUES

1. Statutory Construction of AEDPA[2]...

b. *Standards for interpreting a statute*...

In [*United States v.*] *X-Citement Video* [513 U.S. 64 (1994)], the Supreme Court faced almost the same statutory interpretation issues faced in this case. There, the Supreme Court considered the Protection of Children Against Sexual Exploitation Act, 18 U.S.C. §2252. 513 U.S. at 65-66. Section 2252 of that Act made it unlawful for any person to "knowingly" transport, ship, receive, distribute, or reproduce a visual depiction involving a "minor engaging in sexually explicit conduct." *Id.* at 68. The Ninth Circuit had interpreted "knowingly" to only modify the surrounding verbs, like transport or ship. *See id.* Under this construction, whether a defendant knew the minority of the performer(s) or even knew whether the material was sexually explicit was inconsequential. *See id.* at 68-69. The Supreme Court reversed, concluding that, while the Ninth Circuit's construction of Section 2252 complied with the plain meaning rule, the construction caused absurd results. *See id.* at 69. Under the Ninth Circuit's construction, the Court noted that a Federal Express courier who knew that there was film in a package could be convicted even though the courier had no knowledge that the film contained child pornography. *See id.* To avoid such results, the Court utilized the cannons of statutory construction to imply a "knowing" requirement to each element, including the age of the performers and the sexually explicit nature of the material. *See id.* at 70-78. The Court stated that in criminal statutes "the presumption in favor of a scienter requirement should apply to each of the statutory elements that criminalize otherwise innocent conduct." *Id.* at 72.

c. *Statutory Construction of AEDPA*

Turning now to AEDPA, Section 2339B(a)(1) makes it unlawful for a person to "knowingly provide[ ] material support or resources to a foreign terrorist organization, or attempts or conspires to do so...." 18 U.S.C. §2339B(a)(1). The Ninth Circuit has twice in a single case interpreted Section 2339B and found portions to be unconstitutionally vague as applied to the plaintiffs in that case. *See* [Humanitarian Law Project v. United States Dept. of Justice, 352 F.3d 382 (9th Cir. 2003)] *Humanitarian II*, 352 F.3d at 385, 393; [Humanitarian Law Project v. Reno, 205 F.3d 1130 (9th Cir. 2000), *cert. denied sub nom.* Humanitarian Law Project v. Ashcroft, 532 U.S. 904 (2001),] *Humanitarian I*, 205 F.3d at 1133-36. *Humanitarian* involved a civil action for declaratory and injunctive relief brought by six organizations and two United States citizens who wished to provide the Kurdistan Workers' Party (the "PKK") and the Liberation Tigers of Tamil Eelam (the "LTTE") with support for the political and nonviolent humanitarian activities of each organization....

On subsequent appeal in *Humanitarian II*, the Ninth Circuit reaffirmed its prior rulings on the plaintiffs' First Amendment arguments. 352 F.3d at 385, 393. However, the *Humanitarian II* panel faced a new Fifth Amendment

---

[2. Anti-Terrorism and Effective Death Penalty Act of 1996, Pub. L. No. 104-132.]

challenge by the plaintiffs, who argued that the lack of personal guilt requirement in Section 2339B rendered it unconstitutional. *See id.* at 385. Therefore, the Ninth Circuit reconsidered its interpretation of the *mens rea* requirement in *Humanitarian I. See id.* Under its new interpretation, the Ninth Circuit concluded that Section 2339B also required proof that a person either knew: (a) that an organization was a FTO [foreign terrorist organization]; or (b) of an organization's unlawful activities that caused it to be designated as a FTO. *See id.* at 400. The Ninth Circuit then reaffirmed its prior holding on the vagueness of "personnel" and "training" without analyzing how the change in the *mens rea* requirement affected its prior vagueness analysis. *See id.* at 403-05.

This Court agrees with the Ninth Circuit in *Humanitarian I* that a purely grammatical reading of the plain language of Section 2339B(a)(1) makes it unlawful for any person to knowingly furnish any item contained in the material support categories to an organization that has been designated a FTO. And like *Humanitarian II*, this Court agrees that this construction renders odd results and raises serious constitutional concerns. For example, under *Humanitarian I*, a donor could be convicted for giving money to a FTO without knowledge that an organization was a FTO or that it committed unlawful activities, and without an intent that the money be used to commit future unlawful activities.[28]

Humanitarian II attempted to correct this odd result and accompanying constitutional concerns by interpreting "knowingly" to mean that a person knew: (a) an organization was a FTO; or (b) an organization committed unlawful activities, which caused it to be designated a FTO. *See* 352 F.3d at 400. But, *Humanitarian II*'s construction of Section 2339B only cures some of the Fifth Amendment concerns. First, *Humanitarian II* fails to comply with *X-Citement Video*'s holding that a *mens rea* requirement "should apply to each of the statutory elements that criminalize otherwise innocent conduct." 513 U.S. at 72. *Humanitarian II* implies only a *mens rea* requirement to the FTO element of Section 2339B(a)(1) and not to the material support element. Under *Humanitarian II*'s construction, a cab driver could be guilty for giving a ride to a FTO member to the UN, if he knows that the person is a member of a FTO or the member or his organization at some time conducted an unlawful activity in a foreign country. Similarly, a hotel clerk in New York could be committing a crime by providing lodging to that same FTO member under similar circumstances as the cab driver. Because the *Humanitarian II*'s construction fails to avoid potential Fifth Amendment concerns, this Court rejects its construction of Section 2339B.

Second, the *Humanitarian II* construction does not solve the constitutional vagueness concerns of Section 2339B(a)(1), which can be avoided by implying a *mens rea* requirement to the "material support or resources" element of Section 2339(B)(a)(1). If this Court accepted the *Humanitarian II* construction, it would likely have to declare many more categories of "material support" (in addition to "training" and "personnel" determined to be unconstitutionally vague in the *Humanitarian* cases) unconstitutionally vague for impinging on advocacy rights, including "financial services," "lodging," "safe houses," "communications

---

28. Similarly, a bank teller who cashes the donor's check for a FTO could also be guilty despite a similar lack of knowledge.

B. Material Support Crimes

equipment," "facilities," "transportation" and "other physical assets." Using the Ninth Circuit's vagueness example on "training,"[30] the statute could likewise punish other innocent conduct, such as where a person in New York City (where the United Nations is located) gave a FTO member a ride from the airport to the United Nations before the member petitioned the United Nations. Such conduct could be punished as providing "transportation" to a FTO under Section 2339B.[31] The end result of the Ninth Circuit's statutory construction in *Humanitarian II* is to render a substantial portion of Section 2339B unconstitutionally vague.

But, it is not necessary to do such serious damage to the statute if one follows the analysis used by the United States Supreme Court in *X-Citement Video*.[32] This Court concludes that it is more consistent with Congress's intent, which was to prohibit material support from FTOs to the "fullest possible basis," to imply a *mens rea* requirement to the "material support" element of Section 2339B(a)(1). Therefore, this Court concludes that to convict a defendant under Section 2339B(a)(1) the government must prove beyond a reasonable doubt that the defendant knew that: (a) the organization was a FTO or had committed unlawful activities that caused it to be so designated; and (b) what he was furnishing was "material support." To avoid Fifth Amendment personal guilt problems, this Court concludes that the government must show more than a defendant knew something was within a category of "material support" in order to meet (b). In order to meet (b), the government must show that the defendant knew (had a specific intent) that the support would further the illegal activities of a FTO.

This Court does not believe this burden is that great in the typical case.[34] Often, such an intent will be easily inferred. For example, a jury could infer a specific intent to further the illegal activities of a FTO when a defendant knowingly provides weapons, explosives, or lethal substances to an organization that he knows is a FTO because of the nature of the support. Likewise, a jury could infer a specific intent when a defendant knows that the organization continues to commit illegal acts and the defendant provides funds to that organization knowing that money is fungible and, once received, the donee can use the funds for any purpose it chooses. That is, by its nature, money carries an inherent danger for furthering the illegal aims of an organization. Congress said as much when it found that FTOs were "so tainted by their criminal conduct that any

---

30. The Ninth Circuit utilized the example of "a plaintiff who wishes to instruct members of a designated group on how to petition the United Nations to give aid to their group...." *Humanitarian I*, 205 F.3d at 1138.

31. Other examples of innocent conduct that could be prohibited include the same person allowing the FTO member to spend the night at his house, cashing a check, loaning the member a cell phone for use during the stay, or allowing the member to use the fax machine or laptop computer in preparing the petition. And, the additional phrase "expert advice or assistance" added by the Patriot Act in 2002 could also fail as unconstitutionally vague. *See, e.g., Humanitarian Law Project v. Ashcroft*, 2004 WL 112760, at *12-14 (C.D. Cal. Jan. 22, 2004) (holding that "expert advice or assistance" added by the Patriot Act to definition of "material support" was unconstitutionally vague).

32. The Supreme Court has repeatedly recognized that a *scienter* or *mens rea* requirement may mitigate a law's vagueness. *See, e.g., Posters 'N' Things, Ltd. v. United States*, 511 U.S. 513, 526 (1994).

34. Indeed, Congress recently added 18 U.S.C. §2339C, which criminalized raising funds with the specific intent that the funds will be or are used to cause the death or serious bodily injury of a civilian with the purpose of intimidating the population or compelling a government to do or abstain from doing any act. *See* 18 U.S.C. §2339C.

contribution to such an organization facilitates that conduct." Pub. L. No. 104-132, §301(a)(7).

This opinion in no way creates a safe harbor for terrorists or their supporters to try and avoid prosecution through utilization of shell "charitable organizations" or by directing money through the memo line of a check towards lawful activities.[35] This Court believes that a jury can quickly peer through such facades when appropriate. This is especially true if other facts indicate a defendant's true intent, like where defendants or conspirators utilize codes or unusual transaction practices to transfer funds. Instead, this Court's holding works to avoid potential constitutional problems and fully accomplish congressional intent....

... Therefore, this Court denies Defendants' motions to dismiss the Indictment for alleged due process violations of the PIJ's rights....

[The court denied defendants' motions to dismiss particular counts insofar as they were based on the aforementioned constitutional grounds and dismissed some other counts on other grounds.]

NOTES AND QUESTIONS

1. *The Anti-Terrorist Prosecutor's Weapon of Choice?* As we noted above, the apparent expansion of the suicide terrorist threat in the nineties, and the difficulty of identifying and arresting would-be suicide terrorists in time, has caused the government to begin searching more vigorously up the chain of causation not only for those who plan, but also for those who support, acts of terrorism. Abdel Rahman's prosecution was a way station in this shift in prosecutorial focus to "precursor crimes," because he was prosecuted for "overall supervision and direction of the membership," as the *Rahman* court put it, not for involvement in "individual operations." But the "seditious conspiracy" crime that the government there charged was anachronistic, notwithstanding the eventual success of the prosecution. *But see* Carlton F.W. Larson, *The Forgotten Constitutional Law of Treason and the Enemy Combatant Problem*, 154 U. Pa. L. Rev. 863 (2006) (urging prosecution of enemy combatants for treason and noting the historical applicability of the offense not just to citizens, but to anyone within the United States). Prosecutors needed a tool better suited to interdicting material support and, thereby, suicide terrorism.

When Congress responded by enacting the material support provision of AEDPA in 1996 and expanding material support liability in subsequent legislation, prosecutors used their new weapon enthusiastically. The material support charge is increasingly the government's weapon of choice against suspected terrorists. Data through October 2004 indicate that material support charges ranked second only to document fraud in charges and convictions in the war on terrorism. Center on Law and Security, *Terrorist Trials: A Report Card* 6-7, Feb. 2005, *available at* http://www.law.nyu.edu/centers/lawsecurity/publications/terroristtrialreportcard.pdf. *See generally* Norman Abrams, *The Material Support*

---

35. For example, a donation to a suicide bomber's family given with the intent to encourage others to engage in such activities or support such activities would satisfy this specific intent requirement.

B. Material Support Crimes

Terrorism Offenses: Perspectives Derived from the (Early) Model Penal Code, 1 J. Natl. Security L. & Pol'y. 5 (2005); Robert M. Chesney, *The Sleeper Scenario: Terrorism-Support Laws and the Demands of Prevention*, 42 Harv. J. Legis. 3 (2005); Wayne McCormack, *Inchoate Terrorism: Liberalism Clashes With Fundamentalism*, 37 Geo. J. Intl. L. 1 (2005).

2. *Constitutional Issues in Criminalizing Material Support: An Overview.* When the government targets support, it risks hitting advocacy and association. The *Rahman* case foreshadowed the resulting constitutional issues, but they have since surfaced more fully in material support prosecutions.

Vagueness and Overbreadth. Vagueness is one issue: does the law give fair notice of the conduct it prohibits? Overbreadth is a related issue: does the law sweep so broadly that it may reach or at least chill activity that is protected by the First Amendment? Critics charge that "'[m]aterial support' has been used as a catch-all category in terrorism cases ... and has failed to provide clarity or consistency as to the use of these statutes." Center on Law and Security, *supra*, at 2.

Scienter. The material support statutes carry different scienter requirements. This raises the further question whether they comport with the Fifth Amendment's implicit insistence on personal guilt for a criminal prosecution. These issues are complicated by their interaction, as *Al-Arian* suggests: a vague or overbroad statute may be saved by a narrow scienter requirement.

Regulation of Protected Expression. Of course, the material support provisions are *intended* to reach some activities usually protected by the First Amendment, such as fundraising, in order to achieve the government purpose of preventing terrorism. This poses an issue about the level of First Amendment protection to which such activity is entitled and the corresponding level of judicial scrutiny of government regulation of the activity.

Collateral Attack on FTO Designation. Finally, 18 U.S.C. §2339B poses its own due process issue by criminalizing material support for an entity that has been designated an FTO. Does a criminal defendant have the right to mount a collateral challenge to the FTO designation in his criminal case?

Keeping in mind the interrelationship of many of these problems, we treat them separately in the following notes.

3. *Vagueness and Overbreadth.* "Because First Amendment freedoms need breathing space to survive, government may regulate in the area only with narrow specificity." NAACP v. Button, 371 U.S. 415, 433 (1963). Criminal laws that impact such freedoms are therefore always subject to attack for vagueness or overbreadth. A law is unconstitutionally vague if a reasonable person cannot tell what expression is prohibited and what is permitted. A law is unconstitutionally overbroad if it "regulates substantially more speech than the Constitution allows to be regulated and a person to whom the law constitutionally can be applied can argue that it would be unconstitutional as applied to others." Erwin Chemerinsky, *Constitutional Law* 943 (3d ed. 2006). Because the overbreadth doctrine creates substantial social costs by prohibiting enforcement of a criminal statute even for behavior that it could otherwise constitutionally reach, the Supreme Court has "insisted that the law's application to protected speech be 'substantial,' not only in an absolute sense, but also

relative to the scope of the law's plainly legitimate applications" for the statute to be struck down for overbreadth. Virginia v. Hicks, 539 U.S. 113, 119-120 (2003).

Applying just these principles for the moment, consider the case of a lawyer for a convicted terrorist who meets periodically with her client in prison and secretly conveys messages between him and his associates (including members of an FTO) outside of prison. Is this term unconstitutionally vague as applied to prosecute that lawyer for providing *herself* as "personnel" to a terrorist or FTO? *See* United States v. Sattar, 272 F. Supp. 2d 348 (S.D.N.Y. 2003) (*Sattar I*) (yes; government's assertion in oral argument that "you know it when you see it" is an "insufficient guide by which a person can predict the legality of that person's conduct," whatever merit it may have as a way to identify obscenity). Is it too vague for prosecuting the lawyer for supplying *her client* as "personnel" to the FTO, by making him "available" through communications that she conveys? *See* United States v. Sattar, 314 F. Supp. 2d 279, 300 (S.D.N.Y. 2004) (*Sattar II*) (no; "the 'provision' of 'personnel'—in this case, by making the imprisoned Sheik Abdel Rahman available as a co-conspirator in a conspiracy to kill and kidnap persons in a foreign country—is conduct that plainly is prohibited by the statute" with sufficient definiteness). How about a U.S. citizen who joins the Taliban to fight alongside Al Qaeda fighters against U.S. armed forces in Afghanistan? *See* United States v. Lindh, 212 F. Supp. 2d 541, 574 (E.D. Va. 2002) (no; "personnel" is not unconstitutionally vague as applied to "employees" or "employee-like operatives" who were under the "direction and control" of an FTO). *See* James P. Fantetti, Comment, *John Walker Lindh, Terrorist? Or Merely a Citizen Exercising His Constitutional Freedom: The Limits of the Freedom of Association in the Aftermath of September Eleventh*, 71 U. Cinn. L. Rev. 1373 (2003).

Can you think of applications of the "training" or "expert advice or assistance" forms of material support that would invite vagueness or overbreadth challenges? In footnote 30 in *Al-Arian*, the court recalls the Ninth Circuit's characterization of "expert advice or assistance" as unconstitutionally vague if it applied to "a plaintiff who wishes to instruct members of a designated group on how to petition the United Nations to give aid to their group." But suppose this person styled himself as a "trainer" in lobbying and called the instruction "Training in Dealing with the UN"? Has the vagueness problem been cured? Is it still vague if applied to a person who trains members of an FTO in car bomb assembly? In either case, is the problem vagueness or overbreadth? *See Humanitarian I*, 205 F.3d at 1138. *See generally* McCormack, *supra*, at 40-43.

4. *Scienter and Guilt by Association?* Congress has not made it a crime to be a member of an FTO. What legal reasons might explain why it has not?

In the Smith Act, Congress criminalized knowing membership in any organization that advocates the overthrow of the government by force or violence. 18 U.S.C. §2385 (2000). The Act came before the Supreme Court in Scales v. United States, 367 U.S. 203 (1961), in which the Court upheld a conviction for membership on proof of *knowing* membership or affiliation and *specific intent* to further the group's unlawful goals. The Court explained its insistence on these elements of proof by rejecting the concept of guilt by association:

B. Material Support Crimes

> In our jurisprudence guilt is personal, and when the imposition of punishment on a status or on conduct can only be justified by reference to the relationship of that status or conduct to other concededly criminal activity (here advocacy of violent overthrow), that relationship must be sufficiently substantial to satisfy the concept of personal guilt in order to withstand attack under the Due Process Clause of the Fifth Amendment. [*Id.* at 224-225.]

Specific intent implements the requirement of personal guilt by "tying the imposition of guilt to an individually culpable act." David Cole, *Hanging With the Wrong Crowd: Of Gangs, Terrorists, and the Right of Association*, 1999 Sup. Ct. Rev. 203, 217. In First Amendment terms, the specific intent requirement "identifies the only narrowly tailored way to punish individuals for group wrongdoing (essentially by requiring evidence of individual wrongdoing), just as the *Brandenburg* test [*supra* p. 824] sets forth the narrowly tailored way to respond to advocacy of illegal conduct." Cole, *supra*, at 218.

But the material support statute does not criminalize membership in, or even support for the political goals of, an FTO. It criminalizes

> the act of giving material support, and there is no constitutional right to facilitate terrorism by giving terrorists the weapons and explosives with which to carry out their grisly mission... [or] to provide resources with which terrorists can buy weapons and explosives. [*Humanitarian I*, 205 F.3d at 1133.]

Humanitarian II did not read a specific intent requirement into the statute. The court found instead that knowledge of the FTO's designation or of its terrorist activities sufficed for criminal liability. The court in *Al-Arian*, on the other hand, thought a heightened scienter requirement was necessary to offset the vagueness of the "material support" definition. Other courts disagree. "The statute's vagueness as applied to the allegations in the Indictment concerning the provision of personnel is a fatal flaw that the Court cannot cure by reading into the statute a stricter definition of the material support provision than the statute itself provides." *Sattar I*, 272 F. Supp. 2d at 360.

Should the *Al-Arian* court have read 18 U.S.C. §§2339A, 2339B, and 2339C *in pari materia* in construing §2339B? What does such a reading suggest about the legislative intent regarding scienter? *See Sattar II*, 314 F. Supp. 2d at 301.

5. *Humanitarian II or Al-Arian? Congress's Answer.* Would applying the *Humanitarian II* scienter requirement to the hypotheticals set out by the court in *Al-Arian* in footnote 31 and the related text be consistent with "the concept of personal guilt" mentioned in *Scales* or the "presumption in favor of a scienter requirement" declared in *X-Citement Video*? In that regard, consider the fact that some FTOs engage in both terrorism and social work. *Cf.* Michael Whidden, Note, *Unequal Justice: Arabs in America and United States Antiterrorism in Legislation*, 69 Fordham L. Rev. 2825, 2873 (2001) (asserting that FTOs Hamas and Hezbollah operate orphanages, hospitals, schools, and medical clinics for indigent Palestinians in addition to conducting terrorist activities).

On the other hand, doesn't the court's solution in *Al-Arian* undercut congressional intent? *See Aiding Terrorists—An Examination of the Material Support Statute: Hearing Before the S. Judiciary Comm.*, 108th Cong. (May 5, 2004) (statement of Asst. Prof. Robert Chesney, Wake Forest Univ. School of Law), *available at* http://judiciary.senate.gov/print_testimony.cfm?id=1172&wit_id=3394 ("By interpreting the statute to require proof of specific intent to further the illegal ends of the recipient organization in all its applications, the district court in effect rejected the Congressional determination that all forms of support for a foreign terrorist organization, however well-intentioned, enhance the overall capacity of the organization to engage in activities harmful to U.S. national security and foreign policy"). Congress apparently thought so, because it amended §2339B(a)(1) after *Al-Arian* to add the italicized language *supra* p. 825. Does this solve the problem that *Al-Arian* identified?

6. *Donating Money as Protected Expression.* Donating money is not membership, but it is also unlike donating weapons, safe houses, or transportation. "The right to join together 'for the advancement of beliefs and ideas' is diluted," the Supreme Court explained, "if it does not include the right to pool money through contributions, for funds are often essential if 'advocacy' is to be truly or optimally 'effective.'" Buckley v. Valeo, 424 U.S. 1, 65-66 (1974) (quoting NAACP v. Alabama ex rel. Patterson, 357 U.S. 449, 460 (1958)). Why is donating money to an FTO not protected political expression?

One answer is that it *is* protected expression, but that the protection is not absolute. What degree of scrutiny should a court then give to its regulation? *Compare* Cole, *supra*, at 237-238 (urging strict scrutiny—requiring a close relationship to a compelling government interest—when government's purpose is to regulate association as such), *with Al-Arian*, *supra* (apparently applying intermediate scrutiny—requiring a "sufficiently important government interest"). Does it matter, given the government interest in regulating material support? *See generally* Nina J. Crimm, *High Alert: The Government's War on the Financing of Terrorism and Implications for Donors, Domestic Charitable Organizations, and Global Philanthropy*, 45 Wm. & Mary L. Rev. 1341 (2004); David Cole, *The New McCarthyism: Repeating History in the War on Terrorism*, 38 Harv. C.R.-C.L. L. Rev. 1, 11 (2003).

7. *Collaterally Challenging the FTO Designation.* The D.C. Circuit has held that some FTOs have a due process right, in connection with their designation as FTOs, to notice, disclosure of at least unclassified parts of the administrative record underlying their designation, and an opportunity to be heard. See *supra* p. 473. *See generally* Sahar Aziz, *The Laws on Providing Material Support to Terrorist Organizations: Erosion of Constitutional Rights or a Legitimate Tool for Preventing Terrorism?*, 9 Tex. J. C.L. & C.R. 45 (2003). Is Al-Arian bound by the designation when he is prosecuted for violating 2339B? The *Al-Arian* court said yes because, as a third party to the designation, he lacked standing, and the designation had been made with due process. In any case, section 2339B requires only that the recipient of the material support have been designated an FTO, not that the designation have been valid. It was not disputed that the PIJ had been designated an FTO.

C. THE LONG ARM OF THE LAW: EXTRATERRITORIAL CRIMINAL JURISDICTION

Congress has enacted a variety of statutes aimed at international terrorism. *See, e.g.*, 18 U.S.C. §§31-32 (2000) (hijacking or sabotaging aircraft); *id.* §§175-178 (developing or possessing biological or toxin weapons); *id.* §§2331-2332 (killing or injuring U.S. citizens abroad); *id.* §2332a (directing weapons of mass destruction against Americans abroad or against anyone within the United States); *id.* §2339A (providing material support to terrorists); and 49 U.S.C. §§46501-46507 (2000 & Supp. III 2003) (committing air piracy). Most of these are now expressly extraterritorial in application. But some older criminal statutes are not. The following case discusses the interpretative principles governing extraterritorial application of U.S. criminal laws.

United States v. Bin Laden
United States District Court, Southern District of New York, 2000
92 F. Supp. 2d 189

SAND, District Judge. The sixth superseding indictment in this case ("the Indictment") charges fifteen defendants with conspiracy to murder United States nationals, to use weapons of mass destruction against United States nationals, to destroy United States buildings and property, and to destroy United States defense utilities. The Indictment also charges defendants Mohamed Sadeek Odeh, Mohamed Rashed Daoud al-'Owhali, and Khalfan Khamis Mohamed, among others, with numerous crimes in connection with the August 1998 bombings of the United States Embassies in Nairobi, Kenya, and Dar es Salaam, Tanzania, including 223 counts of murder....

I. EXTRATERRITORIAL APPLICATION

Odeh argues that Counts 5-8, 11-237, and 240-244 must be dismissed because (a) they concern acts allegedly performed by Odeh and his co-defendants outside United States territory, yet (b) are based on statutes that were not intended by Congress to regulate conduct outside United States territory. More specifically, Odeh argues that "the statutes that form the basis for the indictment fail clearly and unequivocally to regulate the conduct of foreign nationals for conduct outside the territorial boundaries of the United States."...

A. GENERAL PRINCIPLES OF EXTRATERRITORIAL APPLICATION

It is well-established that Congress has the power to regulate conduct performed outside United States territory. It is equally well-established, however, that courts are to presume that Congress has not exercised this power—i.e., that statutes apply only to acts performed within United States territory—unless

Congress manifests an intent to reach acts performed outside United States territory. This "clear manifestation" requirement does not require that extraterritorial coverage should be found only if the statute itself explicitly provides for extraterritorial application. Rather, courts should consider "all available evidence about the meaning" of the statute, e.g., its text, structure, and legislative history.

Furthermore, the Supreme Court has established a limited exception to this standard approach for "criminal statutes which are, as a class, not logically dependent on their locality for the Government's jurisdiction, but are enacted because of the right of the Government to defend itself against obstruction, or fraud wherever perpetrated, especially if committed by its own citizens, officers, or agents." United States v. Bowman, 260 U.S. 94, 98 (1922). As regards statutes of this type, courts may infer the requisite intent "from the nature of the offense" described in the statute, and thus need not examine its legislative history.[3] *Id.* The Court further observed that "to limit the [ ] locus [of such a statute] to the strictly territorial jurisdiction [of the United States] would be greatly to curtail the scope and usefulness of the statute and leave open a large immunity for frauds as easily committed by citizens on the high seas and in foreign countries as at home...."

Odeh argues that *Bowman* is "not controlling precedent" because it "involved the application of [a] penal statute[ ] to United States citizens," i.e., not to foreign nationals such as himself. This argument is unavailing....

...Under international law, the primary basis of jurisdiction is the "subjective territorial principle," under which "a state has jurisdiction to prescribe law with respect to...conduct that, wholly or in substantial part, takes place within its territory." Restatement (Third) of the Foreign Relations Law of the United States §402(1)(a) (1987). International law recognizes five other principles of jurisdiction by which a state may reach conduct *outside* its territory: (1) the objective territorial principle; (2) the protective principle; (3) the nationality principle; (4) the passive personality principle; and (5) the universality principle. The objective territoriality principle provides that a state has jurisdiction to prescribe law with respect to "conduct outside its territory that has or is intended to have substantial effect within its territory." Restatement §402(1)(c). The protective principle provides that a state has jurisdiction to prescribe law with respect to "certain conduct outside its territory by *persons not its nationals* that is directed against *the security of the state* or against a limited class of other state interests." *Id.* §402(3) (emphasis added). The nationality principle provides that a state has jurisdiction to prescribe law with respect to "the activities, interests, status, or relations of its nationals outside as well as within its territory." *Id.* §402(2). The passive personality principle provides that "a state may apply law—particularly criminal law—to an act committed outside its territory by a person not its national where the victim of the act was its national." *Id.* §402, cmt. g. The universality principle provides that, "[a] state

---

3. This is not necessarily to say, however, that legislative history is entirely irrelevant under the *Bowman* exception to the standard approach. Given that the *Bowman* rule is ultimately concerned with congressional intent, if the legislative history clearly indicates that Congress intended the statute in question to apply only within the United States, it would be inconsistent with *Bowman* to ignore this evidence, and conclude—in reliance on *Bowman*—that Congress intended the statute to apply extraterritorially....

C. The Long Arm of the Law: Extraterritorial Criminal Jurisdiction

has jurisdiction to define and prescribe punishment for certain offenses recognized by the community of nations as of universal concern, such as piracy, slave trade, attacks on or hijacking of aircraft, genocide, war crimes, and perhaps *certain acts of terrorism,*" regardless of the locus of their occurrence. *Id.* §404 (emphasis added). Because Congress has the power to override international law if it so chooses, Restatement §402, cmt. I., none of these five principles places ultimate limits on Congress's power to reach extraterritorial conduct. At the same time, however, "[i]n determining whether a statute applies extraterritorially, [courts] presume that Congress does not intend to violate principles of international law ... [and] in the absence of an explicit Congressional directive, courts do not give extraterritorial effect to any statute that violates principles of international law." United States v. Vasquez-Velasco, 15 F.3d 833, 839 (9th Cir. 1994) (citing McCulloch v. Sociedad Nacional de Marineros de Honduras, 372 U.S. 10, 21-22 (1963)). Hence, courts that find that a given statute applies extraterritorially typically pause to note that this finding is consistent with one or more of the five principles of extraterritorial jurisdiction under international law.

The *Bowman* rule would appear to be most directly related to the protective principle, which, as noted, explicitly authorizes a state's exercise of jurisdiction over "conduct outside its territory *by persons not its nationals.*" Restatement §402(3). Hence, an application of the *Bowman* rule that results in the extraterritorial application of a statute to the conduct of foreign nationals is consistent with international law. . . .

In light of the preceding general principles, we find that Congress intended each of the following statutory provisions to reach conduct by foreign nationals on foreign soil. . . .

The Indictment predicates Count 5 on 18 U.S.C. §§844(f). . . . Subsection 844(f)(1) provides:

> Whoever maliciously damages or destroys, or attempts to damage or destroy, by means of fire or an explosive, any building, vehicle, or other personal or real property in whole or in part owned or possessed by, or leased to, the United States, or any department or agency thereof, shall be imprisoned for not less than 5 years and not more than 20 years, fined under this title, or both. [18 U.S.C. §844(f)(1).]

Given (i) that this provision is explicitly intended to protect United States property, (ii) that a significant amount of United States property is located outside the United States, and (iii) that, accordingly, foreign nationals are in at least as good a position as are United States nationals to damage such property, we find, under *Bowman*, that Congress intended Section 844(f)(1) to apply extraterritorially—irrespective of the nationality of the perpetrator. . . .

Odeh argues that the Counts based on 18 U.S.C. §§2332 and 2332a must be dismissed because these statutes are unconstitutional in that they exceed Congress's authority to legislate under the Constitution. As noted above, Subsection 2332(b) provides in relevant part that "[w]hoever outside the United States . . . engages in a conspiracy to kill[ ] a national of the United States shall [be punished as further provided]," 18 U.S.C. §2332(b); and Section 2332a(a) provides in relevant part that, "[a] person who . . . uses, threatens, or attempts or conspires to use, a weapon of mass destruction . . . (1) against a national of the

United States while such national is outside of the United States;...or (3) against any property that is owned, leased or used by the United States..., whether the property is within or outside of the United States, shall [be punished as further provided]." 18 U.S.C. §2332a(a).

Odeh suggests that there is but one constitutional grant of authority to legislate that could support these two statutory provisions: Article I, Section 8, Clause 10. Clause 10 grants Congress the authority "[t]o define and punish Piracies and Felonies committed on the high Seas, and Offenses against the Law of Nations." U.S. Const. art. I, §8, cl. 10. Odeh argues that, as "[t]he acts described in these two statutes... are not widely regarded as offenses 'against the law of nations,' " these statutes exceed Congress's authority under Clause 10.

There are two problems with this argument. First, even assuming that the acts described in Sections 2332 and 2332a are not *widely* regarded as violations of international law, it does not necessarily follow that these provisions exceed Congress's authority under Clause 10. Clause 10 does not merely give Congress the authority to punish offenses against the law of nations; it also gives Congress the power to "define" such offenses. Hence, provided that the acts in question are recognized by at least some members of the international community as being offenses against the law of nations, Congress arguably has the power to criminalize these acts pursuant to its power *to define* offenses against the law of nations. *See* United States v. Smith, 18 U.S. (5 Wheat.) 153, 159 (1820) (Story, J.) ("Offenses... against the law of nations, cannot, with any accuracy, be said to be completely ascertained and defined in any public code recognized by the common consent of nations.... [T]herefore..., there is a peculiar fitness in giving the power to define as well as to punish.").

Second, and more important, it is not the case that Clause 10 provides the only basis for Sections 2332 and 2332a. The Supreme Court has recognized that, with regard to foreign affairs legislation, "investment of the federal Government with the powers of external sovereignty did not depend upon the affirmative grants of the Constitution." United States v. Curtiss-Wright Export Corp., 299 U.S. 304, 318 (1936). Rather, Congress's authority to regulate foreign affairs "exist[s] as inherently inseparable from the conception of nationality." *Id.* (citations omitted). More specifically, this "concept of essential sovereignty of a free nation clearly requires the existence and recognition of an inherent power in the state to protect itself from destruction." United States v. Rodriguez, 182 F. Supp. 479, 491 (S.D. Cal. 1960), *aff'd in part sub nom.* Rocha v. United States, 288 F.2d 545 (9th Cir.), *cert. denied*, 366 U.S. 948 (1961).

In penalizing extraterritorial conspiracies to kill nationals of the United States, Section 2332(b) is clearly designed to protect a vital United States interest. And, indeed, Congress expressly identified this protective function as the chief purpose of Section 2332. Therefore, we conclude, under *Curtiss-Wright*, that Congress acted within its authority in enacting these provisions....

Odeh argues that interpreting Section 930(c)[3] to reach "the deaths of Kenyan and Tanzanian citizens [as opposed to United States citizens] would be

---

[3. 18 U.S.C. §930(c) provides that "[a] person who kills or attempts to kill any person in the course of a violation of subsection (a) or (b) [involving knowing possession of firearms or other dangerous weapons in a federal facility], or in the course of an attack on a Federal facility involving the use of a firearm or other dangerous weapon, shall be punished [as further provided]."]

C. The Long Arm of the Law: Extraterritorial Criminal Jurisdiction

contrary to established principles of international law." More specifically, Odeh advances the following two arguments. First, given (i) that "[u]nder 18 U.S.C. §930(c), the only arguable basis for jurisdiction over the deaths of foreign citizens is the principle of universality," (ii) that "[u]niversal jurisdiction results where there is *universal* condemnation of an offense, and a general interest in cooperating to suppress them, as reflected in *widely accepted* international agreements," and (iii) that "the universality principle does not encompass terrorist actions resulting in the deaths of individuals who are not diplomatic personnel," it follows that applying Section 930(c) to the deaths of "ordinary" foreign nationals on foreign soil would constitute a violation of international law.

There are two problems with this argument. First, because "universal jurisdiction is increasingly accepted for certain acts of terrorism, such as...indiscriminate violent assaults on people at large," Restatement §404, cmt. a, a plausible case could be made that extraterritorial application of Section 930(c) in this case *is* supported by the universality principle.

Second, it is not the case that the universality principle is the "only arguable basis for jurisdiction over the deaths of foreign citizens." As indicated by our conclusion...that Section 930(c) is designed to *protect* vital United States interests, the protective principle is also an "arguable basis" for the extraterritorial application of Section 930(c).... In providing for the death penalty where death results in the course of an attack on a Federal facility, Section 930(c) is clearly designed to deter attacks on Federal facilities. Given the likelihood that foreign nationals will be in or near Federal facilities located in foreign nations, this deterrent effect would be significantly diminished if Section 930(c) were limited to the deaths of United States nationals....

Odeh argues, second, that, even if the universality principle (or one of the four other principles) did authorize the application of Section 930(c) to the deaths of ordinary foreign nationals on foreign soil, such application would violate international law nevertheless, because (i) "[e]ven where one of the principles authorizes jurisdiction, a nation is nevertheless precluded from exercising jurisdiction where jurisdiction would be 'unreasonable,'" and (ii) application of Section 930(c) to the deaths of ordinary foreign nationals on foreign soil would be unreasonable. *Id.* (citations omitted).

According to the Restatement, the following factors are to be taken into account for the purpose of determining whether exercise of extraterritorial jurisdiction is reasonable:

> (a) the link of the activity to the territory of the regulating state, i.e., the extent to which the activity takes place within the territory, or has substantial, direct, and foreseeable effect upon or in the territory;
> (b) the connections, such as nationality, residence, or economic activity, between the regulating state and the person principally responsible for the activity to be regulated, or between that state and those whom the regulation is designed to protect;
> (c) the character of the activity to be regulated, the importance of regulation to the regulating state, the extent to which other states regulate such activities, and the degree to which the desirability of such regulation is generally accepted;

(d) the existence of justified expectations that might be protected or hurt by the regulation;

(e) the importance of the regulation to the international political, legal, or economic system;

(f) the extent to which the regulation is consistent with the traditions of the international system;

(g) the extent to which another state may have an interest in regulating the activity; and

(h) the likelihood of conflict with regulation by another state.

Restatement §403(2). Given that factor (a) alludes to the subjective territorial principle and the objective territorial principle, it is not especially relevant to a statute, such as Section 930(c), based primarily on the protective principle. Much the same can be said of factor (b), as it alludes to the nationality principle, the subjective territorial principle, and the objective territorial principle. Factor (c), in contrast, is highly relevant to Section 930(c). It is important both to the United States and other nations to prevent the destruction of their facilities — regardless of their location; and such regulation is accordingly widely accepted among the nations of the world. As for factor (d), Section 930(c) protects the expectation of foreign nationals that they will be free of harm while on the premises of United States facilities. We can think of no "justified" expectation, however, that would be hurt by the extraterritorial application of Section 930(c). As for factor (e), in light of the prominent role played by the United States in "the international political, legal, and economic systems," the protection of United States facilities — regardless of their location — is highly important to the stability of these systems. Turning to factor (f), as indicated by the preceding discussion of factor (c), most, if not all, nations are concerned about protecting their facilities, both at home and abroad. Hence, Section 930(c) is highly consistent "with the traditions of the international system." As for (g), it must be acknowledged that when the United States facility is on foreign soil, and when the victims of the attack are nationals of the host nation, the host nation "has a keen interest in regulating and punishing [the] offenders." This is not to say, however, that the host nation has a greater interest than does the United States. Furthermore, even if it were the case that the host nation had a greater interest than the United States, this single factor would be insufficient to support the conclusion that application of Section 930(c) to the bombings of the two Embassies is unreasonable. Coming, finally, to factor (h), Odeh does not argue that application of Section 930(c) to the bombings would conflict with Kenyan and/or Tanzanian law, nor are we otherwise aware of such conflict. On the contrary, the Government informs the Court that "[t]he Kenyan Government voluntarily rendered Odeh (and [co-defendant] al-'Owhali) to the United States, and neither the Kenyan nor the Tanzanian Government has asserted any objection to the United States' exercise of jurisdiction in this case." Factor (h) thus counts in favor of the reasonableness of applying Section 930(c) to the bombings....

NOTES AND QUESTIONS

1. *Extraterritoriality and the Constitution.* No one questions a sovereign state's authority to prescribe laws for its own territory, and the Constitution quite clearly vests limited authority to do so in Congress. But can Congress

constitutionally make laws that apply abroad? The Constitution is silent on this question, but Article III states that when a crime is "not committed within any State," trial for the crime shall be conducted where Congress directs. U.S. Const. art. III, §2, cl. 3. Thus, the Framers clearly contemplated criminal sanctions against acts committed outside any state of the union. Moreover, they vested Congress with the authority to define and punish "Offenses against the Law of Nations." *Id.* art. I, §8, cl. 10. See *supra* pp. 196-197. Because such offenses may be committed abroad, this provision gives Congress extraterritorial lawmaking authority. On what basis does Odeh argue that 18 U.S.C. §§2332 and 2332a exceed Congress's lawmaking authority? Is the court's response consistent with a federal government of limited lawmaking authority?

Assuming that Congress can enact laws with extraterritorial effect, does the Constitution place any limit on extraterritoriality? Civil procedure students may suspect that some "minimum contact" by the defendant or her acts with the United States might be required as a matter of due process. Beyond that, however, customary international law principles of prescriptive jurisdiction might also establish limits as a part of our federal common law. See *supra* p. 194. Indeed, one commentator asserts that "[i]t is arguable that the Constitution permits Congress to make acts committed abroad crimes under United States law only to the extent permitted by international law." Andreas Lowenfeld, *U.S. Law Enforcement Abroad: The Constitution and International Law*, 83 Am. J. Intl. L. 880, 881 (1989). How does the *Bin Laden* court regard this assertion?

If international law does not limit extraterritorial lawmaking by Congress, what role, if any, does it play, according to the court? What rule of statutory construction is implicated by applicable international laws?

2. *Presumption Against Extraterritoriality.* Why should the courts presume that a statute applies locally only, unless Congress clearly manifests an intent to reach acts performed abroad? Sometimes such an intent is manifested by the plain language of the statute. The statute that makes it a crime to develop, produce, stockpile, transfer, acquire, retain, or possess any biological agent, toxin, or delivery system for use as a weapon, for example, expressly provides that "[t]here is extraterritorial Federal jurisdiction over an offense under this section committed by or against a national of the United States." 18 U.S.C. §175 (2000). Similarly, 18 U.S.C. §2332(b) (2000), expressly makes it a crime to engage in a conspiracy "outside the United States" to kill U.S. nationals. *Bowman* created an exception to the presumption against extraterritoriality. Why?

3. *The Territoriality and Nationality Principles of Extraterritorial Jurisdiction.* The court in *Bin Laden* catalogued principles of jurisdiction under customary international law, but such principles are not equally accepted by all nations, and they may not be helpful for other reasons. See generally Christopher L. Blakesley, *Extraterritorial Jurisdiction*, in II *International Criminal Law* 33 (M. Cherif Bassiouni ed., 2d ed. 1999). The territorial principle, for example, applies both to actors within a sovereign's territory ("subjective territoriality") and to effects in such territory resulting from acts abroad ("objective territoriality"), and it is reflected in *Restatement* §402(1). But while it is the most common and widely accepted principle of jurisdiction, it often will be unavailable for terrorist or other criminal acts performed abroad, including inchoate acts intended ultimately to cause injury in the United States. The nationality principle — allowing

a sovereign to exercise jurisdiction over its nationals for their acts performed abroad — is also accepted by the practice of nations. Roman Boed, *United States Legislative Approach to Extraterritorial Jurisdiction in Connection with Terrorism*, in II *International Criminal Law, supra*, at 147. But international terrorists may not be U.S. nationals, just as most of the *Bin Laden* defendants were not.

4. *The Protective Principle of Extraterritorial Jurisdiction.* The protective principle is more likely to apply to acts of international terrorism, but it is limited to offenses against the security of the state or acts that threaten the integrity of government functions. *Restatement* §402(3) & cmt. f. (1981). It thus is easily applied to the embassy bombings. Would it apply to terrorist acts committed against private U.S. nationals abroad? "The lack of definition of the range of conduct encompassed by the protective principle and the principle's malleability," Professor Boed worries, "could lead to the principle's justification of a wide-ranging exercise of extraterritorial jurisdiction." Boed, *supra*, at 148.

5. *The Passive Personality Principle of Extraterritorial Jurisdiction.* Even if the protective principle does not apply to terrorist acts against private U.S. nationals, such acts would clearly fall under the passive personality principle. But this principle has not traditionally found wide support in the practice of states, Boed, *supra*, at 149, and it was squarely rejected by the United States until recently. *See* Blakesley, *supra*, at 69-70 ("The passive-personality theory traditionally has been anathema to U.S. law and practice.").

In the Omnibus Diplomatic Security and Antiterrorism Act of 1986, however, Congress made it a crime to kill or conspire to kill or cause physical violence to a U.S. national while such national is outside the United States. Pub. L. No. 99-399, §1202, 100 Stat. 853, 896, now codified at 18 U.S.C. §2332 (2000). The *Bin Laden* defendants were charged with this crime, and it would apply as well to acts of homicide or physical violence against private U.S. nationals traveling abroad. Does that mean that the United States could prosecute an Italian pickpocket for pushing a U.S. tourist in Rome as he extracted the tourist's wallet? Even Congress had doubts about reaching so far, so it added a limitation forbidding any prosecution except upon written certification by the Attorney General or his Deputy that "such offense was intended to coerce, intimidate, or retaliate against a government or a civilian population." 18 U.S.C. §2332(d). Here Congress attempted to narrow the offenses to terrorist offenses without defining them and thus to avoid extending the statute to barroom brawls or ordinary street crimes. But what new problem does this provision arguably create? Who creates jurisdiction under this law, and when is it created? *See* Lowenfeld, *supra*, at 891 (opining that the statute is unconstitutional).

Congress came back to passive personality jurisdiction in the Antiterrorism and Effective Death Penalty Act of 1996. Pub. L. No. 104-132, 110 Stat. 1214 (1996). In a section of that act entitled "Clarification and Extension of Criminal Jurisdiction Over Certain Terrorism Offenses Overseas," Congress systematically amended multiple sections of the criminal code to supply the "clear manifestation" of extraterritoriality that is needed to overcome the presumption against extraterritoriality. *Id.* §721. These sections address aircraft piracy, destruction of aircraft, violence at international airports, murder of foreign officials and other persons, protection of the same, threats and extortion against

C. The Long Arm of the Law: Extraterritorial Criminal Jurisdiction

the same, kidnaping of internationally protected persons, and developing or possessing biological weapons. *See* Boed, *supra*, at 159-173.

6. *The Universality Principle of Extraterritorial Jurisdiction.* Universality is perhaps the most controversial of the principles of extraterritorial jurisdiction, because it could theoretically result in a state prosecuting a non-national for acts performed abroad against other non-nationals. *See* Kenneth C. Randall, *Universal Jurisdiction Under International Law*, 66 Tex. L. Rev. 785 (1988). It rests on the assumption that there are some crimes so widely regarded as heinous that their perpetrators are enemies of mankind, subject to prosecution the world over. The prosecuting nation acts for all nations to protect their collective interest. See *supra* p. 197 (discussing *jus cogens*).

To which crimes does this principle apply, according to the *Bin Laden* court? Do they include terrorism? In 1984, Judge Edwards of the D.C. Circuit Court of Appeals asserted that he was unable to conclude "that the law of nations... outlaws politically motivated terrorism, no matter how repugnant it might be to our legal system." Tel-Oren v. Libyan Arab Republic, 726 F.2d 774, 796 (D.C. Cir. 1984), *cert. denied*, 470 U.S. 1003 (1985). Why do you suppose that the law of nations might not subject terrorism to universal jurisdiction? On the other hand, the law of nations is not static. *Restatement* §404 (quoted in *Bin Laden*, *supra* p. 841) would include "*perhaps* certain acts of terrorism" (emphasis supplied). Professor Blakesley argues that the law of nations has *already* condemned individual offenses (such as air piracy and hostage-taking) for which "terrorism" is merely a composite term. Blakesley, *supra*, at 72. What was the *Bin Laden* court's conclusion in 2000?

7. *The Rule of Reasonableness.* The *Restatement* suggests that traditional principles of extraterritoriality are not to be mechanically applied; a court must always consider whether exercising jurisdiction in the particular circumstances would be reasonable. Indeed, the malleability and overlap of the traditional principles of extraterritorial jurisdiction under international law have caused some to suggest that reasonableness is today the overriding principle, under which the availability or nonavailability of the traditional principles is just a factor in the equation. Blakesley, *supra*, at 41. Is extraterritorial jurisdiction in *Bin Laden* reasonable? Why or why not?

8. *"Substantial Nexus."* We suggested that the civil procedure student might speculate whether the Due Process Clause imposes a "minimum contacts" requirement for extraterritorial jurisdiction. In fact, a few cases have spoken of the need for a substantial nexus between the defendant or his acts and the state exercising extraterritorial jurisdiction. *See, e.g.*, United States v. Davis, 905 F.2d 245 (9th Cir. 1990), *cert. denied*, 498 U.S. 1047 (1991). Most courts, however (including the *Bin Laden* court in a portion of the opinion not reproduced here), have concluded that if extraterritorial jurisdiction is justified by the international principles of extraterritorial jurisdiction, Due Process is satisfied. 905 F.2d at 249. This seems persuasive when jurisdiction is supported by the territoriality, nationality, or protective principle, because each presumes "contact." Can you explain how? But does it work for jurisdiction supported only by the passive personality or universality principle?

Secret Evidence — 29

It is not just the crimes that pose legal problems in prosecuting terrorists, but also the evidence. In 1996, Congress for the first time authorized the intelligence community, "upon the request of a United States law enforcement agency, [to] collect information outside the United States about individuals who are not United States persons . . . notwithstanding that the law enforcement agency intends to use the information collected for purposes of a law enforcement investigation or counterintelligence investigation." 50 U.S.C. §403-5a(a) (2000). Moreover, after 9/11, Congress expressly authorized and encouraged more sharing of information among intelligence and law enforcement agencies. See *supra* pp. 634-639. When intelligence agencies are tasked with information collection for law enforcement and those agencies share their information, the information collected may be used or sought in administrative or judicial proceedings against alleged terrorists or their supporters. *See generally* Note, *Secret Evidence in the War on Terror*, 118 Harv. L. Rev. 1962 (2005). However, such use or access may compromise the security of the information itself, as well as the sources and methods by which it was collected.

An immigration or criminal court dealing with alleged terrorists or their supporters thus may confront several difficult choices. First, the government may itself want to use information obtained by classified intelligence sources and methods as evidence against a suspected terrorist or other criminal. The government may have to decide whether to proceed and release that evidence into the public trial record, unless the law permits it to use secret evidence. Some immigration regulations, in fact, have been interpreted to permit the government to rely on secret evidence in certain proceedings against aliens with suspected terrorist connections. The use of secret evidence generally, and its employment in immigration proceedings in particular, as well as the potential for a secret immigration court, are discussed in Part A of this chapter.

Second, in criminal cases, a defendant may invoke her constitutional, statutory, and rule-based rights of discovery to gain access to classified information in government hands that she says she needs to defend herself. Alternatively, she may already possess classified information as a current or former government employee, and she may threaten to use that information at trial to rebut or explain the charged conduct. To deal with the discovery and use of classified information in criminal cases, Congress enacted the Classified Information Procedures Act (CIPA) in 1980. We consider CIPA in Part B.

In Part C of this chapter we review these statutory and constitutional issues in the context of the recent criminal prosecution of Zacarias Moussaoui, who was accused of involvement in the 9/11 terrorist attacks.[1]

A. USING SECRET EVIDENCE AGAINST TERROR SUSPECTS

American-Arab Anti-Discrimination Committee v. Reno
United States Court of Appeals, Ninth Circuit, 1995
70 F.3d 1045

[Barakat and Sharif, resident aliens, applied for legalization of their status under the immigration laws. They were denied because the Immigration and Naturalization Service (INS), using undisclosed classified information, found them excludable under a statute that provides for the exclusion of aliens who advocate or teach or are members of organizations that advocate or teach the duty, necessity, or propriety of unlawfully assaulting or killing officers of government or unlawfully damaging property. *See* 8 U.S.C. §1182(a)(28)(F), explanatory notes for 1990 amendments.[2] The classified information was said to link Barakat and Sharif to the Popular Front for the Liberation of Palestine (PFLP). Barakat and Sharif then sued in district court to challenge the use of secret information and won an injunction. This appeal followed.]

D.W. NELSON, Circuit Judge: ...

B. THE DUE PROCESS CHALLENGE TO THE USE OF CLASSIFIED INFORMATION. . . .

2. APPROPRIATENESS OF THE PERMANENT INJUNCTION

a. Applicability of Due Process Protections to Aliens

Aliens who reside in this country are entitled to full due process protections. The Government does not dispute that the Due Process Clause protects Barakat and Sharif, but it contends that reliance on undisclosed information to determine legalization satisfies the demands of due process.

---

1. We defer until Chapter 35 the related issue of the public's right of access to adjudicative proceedings and the government's desire to close them in order to protect national security information.
2. The Immigration and Nationality Act has been amended almost annually, rendering most case citations to the Act obsolete. At this writing, the INA excludes aliens who have engaged in "terrorist activities." 8 U.S.C. §1182(a)(3)(B) (2000).

b. Statutory and Regulatory Authority for Summary Process...

At the time that Barakat and Sharif applied for legalization, the INS regulations required that all issues of statutory eligibility for immigration benefits, including legalization, be determined solely on the basis of information in the record disclosed to the applicant. However, after a three-year delay, the INS finally issued Notices of Intent to Deny to Barakat and Sharif in March 1991, pursuant to amended regulations, effective upon publication as interim rules in January 1991, that extended the confidential use of classified information to statutory entitlement determinations. The INS claimed that the information's "protection from unauthorized disclosure is required in the interests of national security, as provided in [the interim regulations]."

The Government cites section 235(c) of the Immigration and Nationality Act, 8 U.S.C. §1225(c) (as amended), as authority for use of the undisclosed classified information in the legalization determination. That statute establishes the powers of INS officers to inspect aliens "seeking admission or readmission," 8 U.S.C. §1225(a), to temporarily detain aliens who are not entitled to enter "at the port of arrival," 8 U.S.C. §1225(b), and to exclude aliens on the particular finding by the Attorney General that confidential information supports that exclusion, 8 U.S.C. §1225(c) (allowing summary process for exclusion).[3] We do not, however, accept the proposition that denying a resident alien legalization is the same thing as "exclusion."

Use of summary process in settings other than exclusion raises troubling due process concerns. *See, e.g.,* Kwong Hai Chew, 344 U.S. 590 (barring the INS from using summary process to exclude a resident alien returning from abroad, because he was entitled to a hearing as of constitutional right). Thus, even reentering permanent resident aliens, who enjoy few rights because of the admitted power of Congress over entry into the country, are entitled to additional due process safeguards when subjected to the summary exclusion process. Rafeedie v. INS, 880 F.2d 506, 512 (D.C. Cir. 1989), *on remand,* 795 F. Supp. 13, 20 (D.D.C. 1992) (applying the *Mathews* balancing test[4] to determine that subjecting a returning resident alien, who was accused of being a PFLP officer, to summary exclusion proceedings utilizing secret information violated due process)....

[3. This section of the INA still, at this writing, provides for the "removal without further hearing" of certain aliens on security grounds, if, on review of the removal order, the Attorney General "is satisfied on the basis of confidential information that the alien is inadmissible [on security grounds] and, after consulting with appropriate security agencies of the United States Government, concludes that disclosure of the information would be prejudicial to the public interest, safety, or security...." 8 U.S.C. §1225(c)(1)-(2) (2000).]

[4. In Mathews v. Eldridge, 424 U.S. 319 (1976), the Supreme Court explained that the process constitutionally due before the government deprives a person of life, liberty, or property is determined by balancing (1) the private interest that will be affected by the government action; (2) the risk of erroneous deprivation of that interest through the procedures the government is using, as well as the probable value of additional or substitute procedures; and, finally, (3) the government's interest in the action and in avoiding the additional administrative or fiscal burdens that additional or substitute procedures would impose. *Mathews* balancing is now commonly used to decide procedural due process once a person has shown that government action implicates a private interest protected by the Due Process Clause. *See, e.g.,* Najjar v. Reno, 97 F. Supp. 2d 1329, 1352-1360 (S.D. Fl. 2000) (applying *Mathews* balancing to decide process due in hearings in which the government relied on undisclosed classified information to deny bail to a detained alien alleged to be a supporter of a terrorist organization).]

A. Using Secret Evidence Against Terror Suspects

c. The Mathews Balancing Test

(1) The Private Interest Affected. Aliens who have resided for more than a decade in this country, even those whose status is now unlawful because of technical visa violations, have a strong liberty interest in remaining in their homes. Similarly, the denial of legalization impacts the opportunity of an alien to work, which also raises constitutional concerns. The statute provides an entitlement not subject to denial according to the discretion of the Attorney General, as long as the eligibility requirements are satisfied. 8 U.S.C. §1255a(a). Thus, the district court did not err in finding that the private interests affected are truly substantial.

(2) The Risk of Erroneous Deprivation and Value of Safeguards. There is no direct evidence in the record to show what percentage of decisions utilizing undisclosed classified information result in error; yet, as the district court below stated, "One would be hard pressed to design a procedure more likely to result in erroneous deprivations." *See, e.g.,* Goss v. Lopez, 419 U.S. 565, 580 (1975) (finding that "the risk of error is not at all trivial" in summary discipline in school settings). Without any opportunity for confrontation, there is no adversarial check on the quality of the information on which the INS relies. *See* Knauff v. Shaughnessy, 338 U.S. 537, 551 (1950) (Jackson, J., dissenting) ("The plea that evidence of guilt must be secret is abhorrent to free men, because it provides a cloak for the malevolent, the misinformed, the meddlesome, and the corrupt to play the role of informer undetected and uncorrected.") (citation omitted).

Although not all rights of criminal defendants are applicable to the civil context, the procedural due process notice and hearing requirements have "ancient roots" in the rights to confrontation and cross-examination. Greene v. McElroy, 360 U.S. 474, 496 (1959).

> Certain principles have remained relatively immutable in our jurisprudence. One of these is that where governmental action seriously injures an individual, and the reasonableness of the action depends on fact findings, the evidence used to prove the Government's case must be disclosed to the individual so that he has an opportunity to show that it is untrue.

Id. As judges, we are necessarily wary of one-sided process: "democracy implies respect for the elementary rights of men...and must therefore practice fairness; and fairness can rarely be obtained by secret, one-sided determination of facts decisive of rights." Anti-Fascist Committee v. McGrath, 341 U.S. 123, 170 (1951) (Frankfurter, J., concurring). "It is therefore the firmly held main rule that a court may not dispose of the merits of a case on the basis of *ex parte, in camera* submissions." Abourezk v. Reagan, 785 F.2d 1043, 1061 (D.C. Cir. 1986). Thus, the very foundation of the adversary process assumes that use of undisclosed information will violate due process because of the risk of error. We conclude that the district court did not err in finding that there is an exceptionally high risk of erroneous deprivation when undisclosed information is used to determine the merits of the admissibility inquiry.

(3) The Governmental Interest. The Government seeks to use undisclosed information to achieve its desired outcome of prohibiting these individuals whom it perceives to be threats to national security from remaining in the United States while protecting its confidential sources involved in the investigation of terrorist organizations. Yet the Government has offered no evidence to demonstrate that these particular aliens threaten the national security of this country. In fact, the Government claims that it need not. It relies on general pronouncements in two State Department publications about the PFLP's involvement in global terrorism and on the President's recent broad Executive Order prohibiting "any United States persons" from transacting business with the PFLP. *See* Exec. Order No. 12947 (January 23, 1995) (finding "that grave acts of violence committed by foreign terrorists that disrupt the Middle East peace process constitute an unusual and extraordinary threat to the national security, foreign policy, and economy of the United States"). We take judicial notice of these government documents on appeal for the limited purpose of assessing the strength of the Government's interest, yet we find these data insufficient to tip the *Mathews* scale towards the Government. These aliens have been free since the beginning of this litigation almost eight years ago, without criminal charges being brought against them for their activities. According to the district court, the government's *in camera* submission targets the PFLP: although it indicates that the PFLP advocates prohibited doctrines and that the aliens are members, it does not indicate that either alien has personally advocated those doctrines or has participated in terrorist activities.

If Barakat and Sharif engage in any deportable activities, the government is not precluded from contesting their legalization or from instituting deportation on the basis of non-secret information. If the Government chooses not to reveal its information in order to protect its sources, the only risk it faces is that attendant to tolerance of Barakat's and Sharif's presence so long as they do not engage in deportable activities. Thus, although the Government undoubtedly has a legitimate interest in protecting its confidential investigations, it has not demonstrated a strong interest in this case in accomplishing its goal of protecting its information while prohibiting these aliens' legalization.

The Government's attempt to bolster its interest by relying on permitted uses of undisclosed information is misguided. Although the courts have allowed the Government to keep certain information confidential, the exceptions to full disclosure are narrowly circumscribed. For example, a formal claim of a "state secrets privilege" may prevent discovery and shield the use of materials against the Government in tort litigation for damages. [*Abourezk*, 785 F.2d at 1061]; *see also* United States v. Reynolds, 345 U.S. 1, 6-7 (1953) (in a tort suit against the Government, permitting nonproduction of an Air Force accident investigation report because of national security concerns); Ellsberg v. Mitchell, 709 F.2d 51 (D.C. Cir. 1983) (in a constitutional tort suit for damages against officials, allowing the Government to withhold production of wiretap information), *cert. denied*, 465 U.S. 1038 (1984). However, the failure to disclose information prevents its use in the adversary proceeding: the effect of upholding the privilege is "that the evidence is unavailable, as though a witness had died." *Ellsberg*, 709 F.2d at 64. Even in those rare cases when the privilege operates as a complete shield to the government and results in the dismissal of a plaintiff's suit, the information is simply unavailable and may not be used by either side. Here, the Government

A. Using Secret Evidence Against Terror Suspects

does not seek to shield state information from disclosure in the adjudication of a tort claim against it; instead, it seeks to use secret information as a sword against the aliens.

Because of the danger of injustice when decisions lack the procedural safeguards that form the core of constitutional due process, the *Mathews* balancing suggests that use of undisclosed information in adjudications should be presumptively unconstitutional. Only the most extraordinary circumstances could support one-sided process. We cannot in good conscience find that the President's broad generalization regarding a distant foreign policy concern and a related national security threat suffices to support a process that is inherently unfair because of the enormous risk of error and the substantial personal interests involved. "[T]he fact that a given law or procedure is efficient, convenient, and useful in facilitating functions of government, standing alone, will not save it if it is contrary to the Constitution." [Immigration and Naturalization Service v.] Chadha, 462 U.S. 919, 944 (1983) [see *supra* pp. 128-129]. Therefore, we find that the district court did not err in deciding that use of undisclosed classified information under these circumstances violates due process. . . .

Affirmed in part, reversed and remanded in part [on other grounds].

NOTES AND QUESTIONS

1. *The State Secrets Privilege.* Proposed Federal Rule of Evidence 509 (which Congress rejected for reasons not relevant to our study) described in pertinent part the common law privilege for "state secrets" as follows: "The government has a privilege to refuse to give evidence and to prevent any person from giving evidence upon a showing of reasonable likelihood of danger that the evidence will disclose a secret of state. . . ." 26 Charles Alan Wright & Kenneth W. Graham, *Federal Practice and Procedure* 416 (1992). The rule defined "state secret" as "a governmental secret relating to the national defense or the international relations of the United States." *Id.* at 415. The rule embodied a privilege recognized by the Supreme Court in United States v. Reynolds, 345 U.S. 1, 6 (1953), but otherwise only generally articulated by lower court decisions. *See generally* Louis Fisher, *In the Name of National Security: Unchecked Presidential Power and the Reynolds Case* (2006).

How would an immigration judge or court determine whether "state secrets" were involved in a deportation case? Usually a party in litigation who invokes an evidentiary privilege has the obligation to lay a foundation sufficient for other parties and the court to assess the applicability of the privilege. *See, e.g.,* Fed. R. Civ. P. 26(b)(5). Should the state secrets privilege be handled differently? These questions and the use of the state secrets privilege in civil litigation are addressed *infra* pp. 1037-1050.

2. *Statutory Authorization for Using Secret Evidence.* The rights of aliens in immigration proceedings traditionally depended on their status (e.g., resident or nonresident, entering or reentering, etc.), the nature of the proceeding (e.g., exclusion, removal, suspension of deportation, etc.), and the corresponding statutes and INS regulations. In Jay v. Boyd, 351 U.S. 345 (1956), cited by the government to support its use of secret evidence in *American-Arab*

Anti-Discrimination Committee, the Supreme Court found implied authority in INS regulations for the Attorney General to use undisclosed "confidential information" to make the entirely discretionary decision whether to suspend an alien's deportation. Why is *Jay* not controlling in the instant case? In neither case was there express statutory or regulatory authority for using undisclosed classified information against the alien. If the statute is silent or ambiguous about authority to use secret evidence, how should the court resolve the ambiguity? *See* Greene v. McElroy, *supra* p. 105. Does footnote 3, *supra,* make a difference in your analysis? Note that *Greene* was decided after *Jay.* Is *Jay* still good law?

3. *The Risk of Inaccuracy from Using Secret Evidence.* Boyd, from Jay v. Boyd, had permanently resided in the United States since 1914 and had never engaged in any misconduct during his 65 years, although he had *legally* been a member of the Communist Party from 1935 to 1940. He alleged on information and belief that the "confidential information" the Attorney General used against him was that his name had appeared on a list circulated by an organization deemed subversive by the Attorney General. The majority opinion dealt only with the issue of statutory and regulatory authority, asserting in a footnote without elaboration that "the constitutionality of [the regulation] as herein interpreted gives us no difficulty." *Jay,* 351 U.S. at 357 n.21.

It gave dissenters Warren, Black, Frankfurter, and Douglas great difficulty, however. Justice Black asked:

> What is meant by "confidential information"? According to officers of the Immigration Service it may be "merely information we received off the street"; or "what might be termed as hearsay evidence, which could not be gotten into the record..."; or "information from persons who were in a position to give us the information that might be detrimental to the interests of the Service to disclose that person's name ..." or "such things, perhaps, as income-tax returns, or maybe a witness who didn't want to be disclosed, or where it might endanger their life, or something of that kind...." No nation can remain true to the ideal of liberty under law and at the same time permit people to have their homes destroyed and their lives blasted by the slurs of unseen and unsworn informers. There is no possible way to contest the truthfulness of anonymous accusations. The supposed accuser can neither be identified nor interrogated. He may be the most worthless and irresponsible character in the community. What he said may be wholly malicious, untrue, unreliable, or inaccurately reported. In a court of law the triers of fact could not even listen to such gossip, much less decide the most trifling issue on it. [*Id.* at 365.]

Illustrating these points, a former Director of Central Intelligence, representing a group of detained Iraqis, found "serious errors" in previously secret evidence used against his clients, including mistranslations, ethnic and religious stereotyping, and rumors derived from inter-group rivalry. *See* Susan M. Akram, *Scheherezade Meets Kafka: Two Dozen Sordid Tales of Ideological Exclusion,* 14 Geo. Immigr. L.J. 51, 87-88 (1999).

Jay was decided not only before Greene v. McElroy, but also before the explosion of due process decisions in the Supreme Court, including Mathews v. Eldridge. In light of these cases, should the constitutionality of the procedure used against Boyd now give judges any difficulty? How would

Boyd have fared under a *Mathews* balancing analysis? *See generally* Michael J. Whidden, *Unequal Justice: Arabs in America and United States Antiterrorism Legislation*, 69 Fordham L. Rev. 2825, 2845-2849, 2874-2879 (2001); Akram, *supra*, at 51-52; Michael Scaperlanda, *Are We That Far Gone? Due Process and Secret Deportation Proceedings*, 7 Stan. L. & Poly. Rev. 23, 27-29 (1996).

The risk of inaccuracy from using secret evidence also may be illustrated by a case described in the Washington Post as "the only criminal case since the Sept. 11 attacks in which secret evidence was presented against the defendant." *See* Dale Russakoff, *N.J. Judge Unseals Transcript in Controversial Terror Case*, Wash. Post, June 25, 2003, at A3. Reportedly, local (nonfederal) prosecutors convinced a state judge during a bail hearing that evidence against a defendant whom they alleged had ties to terrorists was so sensitive that the defendant could not be allowed to see it. Months later, an appellate judge ruled that prosecutors had not shown the defendant to be a security risk, and the trial judge then unsealed the bail hearing transcript. *Id.*; Robert Hanley & Jonathan Miller, *4 Transcripts Are Released in Case Tied to 9/11 Hijackers*, N.Y. Times, June 25, 2003, at B5; Jennifer V. Hughes, *Supposed Links to Terrorism Revealed*, The Record, June 25, 2003, at A1. Most of the evidence consisted of testimony by a detective about what he had heard from FBI agents regarding the defendant. Federal authorities, however, contradicted or denied knowledge of some of this information after release of the transcripts, and the defendant's attorney dismissed it as "slanderous, hearsay, double- and triple-hearsay, evidence which he claimed he could have rebutted if only he and the defendant had been allowed to see it." Russakoff, *supra*. "To think that they kept me in jail on this," the defendant said, after being held for six months as a suspected terrorist. *Id.* The state dropped all but one of 25 counts of selling fraudulent documents to Hispanic immigrants (none tied to terrorism).

4. *The Probable Value of Additional Process*. Short of unconditionally disclosing all the evidence to Barakat and Sharif, what additional procedures, if any, would satisfy due process? Would supplying them with an unclassified one-page summary of the evidence suffice? *See* Kiareldeen v. Reno, 71 F. Supp. 2d 402 (D.N.J. 1999) (rejecting this alternative because summary failed to identify a single source and was barely two pages long). Would a more detailed summary, which the judge checked ex parte and in camera for accuracy and completeness against the classified information? *See* Najjar v. Reno, 97 F. Supp. 2d 1329, 1359 (S.D. Fla. 2000) (suggesting such a procedure on remand). Should immigration judges have security clearances to perform this function? Should we require the alien's counsel to be cleared as well? Alternatively, would an independent verification of the information internal to the Department of Justice, but without disclosure to or participation of the defendant or his counsel, suffice? *See Hearing on H.R. 2121 Before the H. Judiciary Subcomm. on Immigration and Claims*, 106th Cong. 47 (2000) (prepared testimony of Larry R. Parkinson, General Counsel, FBI, explaining that "[b]efore any final decision is made to use classified information in immigration proceedings, the information and the case are subjected to rigorous review at high levels of all affected Justice Department components to ensure that it is necessary and appropriate to use the information.").

5. *The Alien Terrorist Removal Court*. The 1996 Anti-Terrorism and Effective Death Penalty Act established a special alien terrorist "Removal Court" (ATRC)

as another way of removing alien terrorists from the United States. *See* 8 U.S.C. §§1531-1537 (2000). Article III judges are appointed to the ATRC, like the Foreign Intelligence Surveillance Court (see *supra* p. 524), and the alien is represented by counsel, but only counsel who has been selected from a specially cleared panel. The government may submit classified evidence to the court *in camera* and *ex parte*, "and neither [an] alien [who is not a permanent resident] nor the public shall be informed of such evidence or its sources" except by an unclassified summary approved by the court as "sufficient to enable the alien to prepare a defense." *Id.* §1534(e)(3). If the court cannot give such approval, the removal hearing is terminated unless the court also finds that the alien's continued presence in the United States, and the provision of a summary to the alien, would both cause "serious and irreparable harm to the national security or death or serious bodily injury to any person." *Id.* §1534(e)(3)(D). Thus, the ATRC is authorized to remove a nonpermanent resident alien suspected of terrorism on the basis of secret evidence of which he is completely uninformed. How would such a removal fare under the *Mathews* balancing test? *Compare* Jennifer A. Beall, *Are We Only Burning Witches? The Antiterrorism and Effective Death Penalty Act of 1996's Answer to Terrorism*, 73 Ind. L.J. 693, 705-708 (1998) (contending that it would fail), and David B. Kopel & Joseph Olson, *Preventing a Reign of Terror: Civil Liberties Implications of Terrorism Legislation*, 21 Okla. City U.L. Rev. 247, 332-335 (1996) (same), *with* Scaperlanda, *supra*, at 225-229 (contending that it would pass). Note that, apart from the Foreign Intelligence Surveillance Court, the United States last used a secret court to prosecute and condemn to death German saboteurs in World War II. *Ex Parte Quirin*, 317 U.S. 1 (1942), *supra* p. 714. *See* Sam Skolnik, *Death Sentences Before Closed Doors*, Legal Times, Dec. 20, 1999, at 20.

It may be that constitutional doubts about the extraordinary Star Chamber quality of this special court are why the government has never used it. Another reason may be that ordinary criminal prosecutions of terrorists in open court have generally been successful, as the Bin Laden case demonstrates. But a less benign explanation for the neglect of the ATRC to date may simply be that administrative immigration proceedings using secret evidence have afforded a simpler solution. Although the Attorney General has imposed some internal departmental review procedures (see *supra* Note 4),

> there remains no statutory or regulatory obligation for the INS to disclose an unclassified summary, for cleared counsel to be permitted to see the testimony, nor (in some cases) for judicial review by Article III judges before exhausting administrative remedies. The INS administrative use of classified information, outside the ATRC, is thus easier and simpler since fewer rights are afforded the alien. The non-ATRC use of classified information is the faster—albeit less legitimate—approach. [Juliette Kayyem, *Whatever Happened to the Alien Terrorist Removal Court?*, ABA Natl. Security L. Rep. 3 (Mar.-Apr. 2000).]

See also Whidden, *supra* p. 855, at 2846 (contending that Antiterrorism and Effective Death Penalty Act (AEDPA) "signaled to the INS that there was political support to apply INS secret evidence proceedings more aggressively"). If this is correct, then opinions like *American-Arab Anti-Discrimination Committee* may perversely encourage recourse to the ATRC, unless, of course, it too is found wanting by their due process analysis.

B. CLASSIFIED INFORMATION PROCEDURES ACT

Classified Information Procedures Act
18 U.S.C.A. app. 3 §§1-16 (West 2000 & Supp. 2006)

§4. DISCOVERY OF CLASSIFIED INFORMATION BY DEFENDANTS

The court, upon a sufficient showing, may authorize the United States to delete specified items of classified information from documents to be made available to the defendant through discovery under the Federal Rules of Criminal Procedure, to substitute a summary of the information for such classified documents, or to substitute a statement admitting relevant facts that the classified information would tend to prove. The court may permit the United States to make a request for such authorization in the form of a written statement to be inspected by the court alone....

§5. NOTICE OF DEFENDANT'S INTENTION TO DISCLOSE CLASSIFIED INFORMATION

(a) Notice by defendant. If a defendant reasonably expects to disclose or to cause the disclosure of classified information in any manner in connection with any trial or pretrial proceeding involving the criminal prosecution of such defendant, the defendant shall, within the time specified by the court or, where no time is specified, within thirty days prior to trial, notify the attorney for the United States and the court in writing. Such notice shall include a brief description of the classified information. Whenever a defendant learns of additional classified information he reasonably expects to disclose at any such proceeding, he shall notify the attorney for the United States and the court in writing as soon as possible thereafter and shall include a brief description of the classified information....

§6. PROCEDURE FOR CASES INVOLVING CLASSIFIED INFORMATION

(a) Motion for hearing. Within the time specified by the court for the filing of a motion under this section, the United States may request the court to conduct a hearing to make all determinations concerning the use, relevance, or admissibility of classified information that would otherwise be made during the trial or pretrial proceeding. Upon such a request, the court shall conduct such a hearing. Any hearing held pursuant to this subsection (or any portion of such hearing specified in the request of the Attorney General) shall be held in camera if the Attorney General certifies to the court in such petition that a public proceeding may result in the disclosure of classified information. As to each item of classified information, the court shall set forth in writing the basis for its determination. Where the United States' motion under this subsection is filed prior to the trial or pretrial proceeding, the court shall rule prior to the commencement of the relevant proceeding.

(b) Notice.

(1) Before any hearing is conducted pursuant to a request by the United States under subsection (a), the United States shall provide the defendant with notice of the classified information that is at issue. Such notice shall identify the specific classified information at issue whenever that information previously has been made available to the defendant by the United States. When the United States has not previously made the information available to the defendant in connection with the case, the information may be described by generic category, in such form as the court may approve, rather than by identification of the specific information of concern to the United States.

(2) Whenever the United States requests a hearing under subsection (a), the court, upon request of the defendant, may order the United States to provide the defendant, prior to trial, such details as to the portion of the indictment or information at issue in the hearing as are needed to give the defendant fair notice to prepare for the hearing.

(c) Alternative procedure for disclosure of classified information

(1) Upon any determination by the court authorizing the disclosure of specific classified information under the procedures established by this section, the United States may move that, in lieu of the disclosure of such specific classified information, the court order—

(A) the substitution for such classified information of a statement admitting relevant facts that the specific classified information would tend to prove; or

(B) the substitution for such classified information of a summary of the specific classified information.

The court shall grant such a motion of the United States if it finds that the statement or summary will provide the defendant with substantially the same ability to make his defense as would disclosure of the specific classified information. The court shall hold a hearing on any motion under this section. Any such hearing shall be held in camera at the request of the Attorney General.

(2) The United States may, in connection with a motion under paragraph (1), submit to the court an affidavit of the Attorney General certifying that disclosure of classified information would cause identifiable damage to the national security of the United States and explaining the basis for the classification of such information. If so requested by the United States, the court shall examine such affidavit in camera and ex parte....

(e) Prohibition on disclosure of classified information by defendant, relief for defendant when United States opposes disclosure

(1) Whenever the court denies a motion by the United States that it issue an order under subsection (c) and the United States files with the court an affidavit of the Attorney General objecting to disclosure of the classified information at issue, the court shall order that the defendant not disclose or cause the disclosure of such information.

(2) Whenever a defendant is prevented by an order under paragraph (1) from disclosing or causing the disclosure of classified information, the court shall dismiss the indictment or information; except that, when the court determines that the interests of justice would not be served by dismissal of the indictment or information, the court shall order such other action, in lieu

of dismissing the indictment or information, as the court determines is appropriate. Such action may include, but need not be limited to —
    (A) dismissing specified counts of the indictment or information;
    (B) finding against the United States on any issue as to which the excluded classified information relates; or
    (C) striking or precluding all or part of the testimony of a witness....

United States v. Lee

United States District Court, District of New Mexico, 2000
90 F. Supp. 2d 1324

CONWAY, Chief Judge. This matter came on for consideration of the Motion of Dr. Wen Ho Lee for a Declaration that Sections 5 and 6 of the Classified Information Procedures Act (CIPA) are Unconstitutional as Applied.... [Wen Ho Lee was being prosecuted on charges of espionage and mishandling of classified information at the Los Alamos National Laboratory.]

I. CIPA FRAMEWORK

The Classified Information Procedures Act (CIPA), 18 U.S.C. app. III §§1-16 (1988), provides for pretrial procedures to resolve questions of admissibility of classified information in advance of its use in open court.[1] Under CIPA procedures, the defense must file a notice briefly describing any classified information that it "reasonably expects to disclose or to cause the disclosure of" at trial. 18 U.S.C. app. III §5(a). Thereafter, the prosecution may request an *in camera* hearing for a determination of the "use, relevance and admissibility" of the proposed defense evidence. *Id.* at §6(a). If the Court finds the evidence admissible, the government may move for, and the Court may authorize, the substitution of unclassified facts or a summary of the information in the form of an admission by the government.[2] *See id.* at §6(c)(1). Such a motion may be granted if the Court finds that the statement or summary will provide the defendant with "substantially the same ability to make his defense as would disclosure of the specific classified information." *Id.* If the Court does not authorize the substitution, the government can require that the defendant not disclose classified information. *See id.* at §6(e). However, under §6(e)(2), if the government prevents a defendant from disclosing classified information at trial, the court may: (A) dismiss the entire indictment or specific counts,

---

    1. Classified information is defined as including "information and material" subject to classification or otherwise requiring protection from public disclosure. *See* 18 U.S.C. app. III §1. Thus, CIPA applies to classified testimony as well as to classified documents.
    2. If the court finds that the evidence is not admissible at trial, CIPA is no longer implicated. When determining the use, relevance and admissibility of the proposed evidence, the court may not take into account that the evidence is classified; relevance of classified information in a given case is governed solely by the standards set forth in the Federal Rules of Evidence.

(B) find against the prosecution on any issue to which the excluded information relates, or (C) strike or preclude the testimony of particular government witnesses. *See* 18 U.S.C. app. III §6(e)(2). Finally, CIPA requires that the government provide the defendant with any evidence it will use to rebut the defendant's revealed classified information evidence. *See id.* at §6(f).

II. CONSTITUTIONALITY OF CIPA

Defendant Lee contends that, as applied to him, the notice and hearing requirements of §5 and §6 of CIPA are unconstitutional.... Although I find Defendant's claims unjustified, I will nevertheless address them in turn.[3]

A. DEFENDANT'S PRIVILEGE AGAINST SELF-INCRIMINATION

Defendant Lee's first contention is that the notice and hearing requirements of §5 and §6 violate his Fifth Amendment privilege against self-incrimination because they force him to reveal classified aspects of his own trial testimony. Defendant argues that by forcing him to reveal portions of his potential testimony, CIPA unconstitutionally infringes upon his right to remain silent until and unless he decides to testify. Similarly, Defendant argues that if he chooses not to comply with the notice requirements, under the penalty of not being able to offer such testimony at trial, CIPA unconstitutionally denies him the right to testify on his own behalf. In either case, Defendant contends that CIPA forces him to pay a price in the form of a costly pretrial decision in order to preserve his constitutional rights at trial.

CIPA does not require that a defendant specify whether or not he will testify or what he will testify about. Instead, CIPA requires "merely a general disclosure as to what classified information the defense expects to use at trial, regardless of the witness or the document through which that information is to be revealed." United States v. Poindexter, 725 F. Supp. 13, 33 (D.D.C. 1989). Defendant's argument that if he discloses the classified information his right to remain silent has been compromised (or in the alternative that if he refuses to disclose the classified information his right to testify has been compromised) is misplaced. Despite CIPA's requirements, Defendant still has the option of not testifying. Similarly, if the defense does not disclose classified information as required by CIPA, the defendant retains the option of testifying, albeit with the preclusion of any classified information.

In addition, the pretrial disclosure of certain aspects of a criminal defense is hardly a novel concept. Examples of such requirements include Fed. R. Crim. P. 12.1 (alibi defense); Fed. R. Crim. P. 12.2 (insanity defense); Fed. R. Crim. P. 12.3 (public authority defense); and Fed. R. Crim. P. 16 (medical and scientific tests, and tangible objects and certain documents). Such provisions have consistently been held constitutional.... CIPA merely provides a mechanism for determining the admissibility of classified information so that classified information is not inadvertently disclosed during open proceedings. Defendant still

---

3. Other courts that have considered the constitutionality of CIPA are in accord....

B. Classified Information Procedures Act

has the choice of presenting the evidence during trial or not, after it has been deemed admissible. "That the defendant faces...a dilemma demanding a choice between complete silence and presenting a defense has never been thought an invasion of the privilege against compelled self-incrimination." Williams v. Florida, 399 U.S. 78, 84 (1970).

Defendant also argues that the burdens placed upon him by CIPA unconstitutionally violate his Fifth Amendment rights in that they do not advance any interests related to the fairness and accuracy of the criminal trial. However, Defendant's argument is unconvincing. CIPA is designed to "assure the fairness and reliability of the criminal trial" while permitting the government to "ascertain the potential damage to national security of proceeding with a given prosecution before trial." *See* United States v. Ivy, 1993 WL 316215 at *4 (citations omitted). As the Supreme Court has noted, "it is obvious and unarguable that no governmental interest is more compelling than the security of the Nation." *Poindexter*, 725 F. Supp. at 34 (quoting Haig v. Agee, 453 U.S. 280, 307 (1981)). CIPA serves that interest "by providing a mechanism for protecting both the unnecessary disclosure of sensitive national security information and by helping to ensure that those with significant access to such information will not escape the sanctions of the law applicable to others by use of the greymail route."[5] *Id.* at 34. Accordingly, I find that CIPA does not violate Defendant's privilege against self-incrimination by infringing upon either his right to remain silent or his right to testify on his own behalf.

B. DEFENDANT'S RIGHT TO CONFRONT AND CROSS-EXAMINE WITNESSES

Defendant Lee next argues that §5 and §6 of CIPA violate his Sixth Amendment right to confront and cross-examine government witnesses by forcing him to notify the government pretrial (and explain the significance) of all the classified information he reasonably expects to elicit from prosecution witnesses on cross-examination and all such information that will be contained in defense counsel's questions to those witnesses.[6]

Defendant contends that under CIPA, the "prosecution can shape its case-in-chief to blunt the force of the defense cross examination" and that the advance notice under CIPA "will impede effective defense cross-examination." However, the Confrontation Clause does not guarantee the right to undiminished surprise with respect to cross-examination of prosecutorial witnesses....

CIPA does not require that the defense reveal its plan of cross-examination to the government. CIPA also does not require that the defendant reveal what questions his counsel will ask, in which order, and to which witnesses. Likewise, the defendant need not attribute the information to any particular witness. CIPA merely requires that the defendant identify the classified information

---

5. Greymail refers to a tactic employed by a defendant who threatens to disclose classified information with the hopes that the prosecution will choose not to prosecute in order to keep the information protected.

6. Under the Sixth Amendment, a criminal defendant "shall enjoy the right...to be confronted with the witnesses against him." U.S. Const. amend. VI. Pursuant to the right to confront the witnesses against him, a criminal defendant has the "fundamental right" to cross examine witnesses for the prosecution.

he reasonably intends to use. Because the only cited tactical disadvantage that may accrue, minimization of surprise, is slight, defendant has failed to demonstrate that the requirements under CIPA render his opportunity for cross-examination ineffective.

C. DEFENDANT'S RIGHT TO DUE PROCESS

Defendant's due process argument is based on the contention that CIPA's disclosure requirements violate the Due Process Clause by imposing a one-sided burden on the defense, without imposing a mandatory reciprocal duty on the prosecution. However, due process is only denied where the balance of discovery is tipped against the defendant and in favor of the government....

Here, the CIPA burdens are not one-sided. First, the government has already agreed to allow Defendant and his counsel access to all classified files at issue in the indictment. Second, the government must produce all discoverable materials before the defense is required to file a §5(a) notice. Third, before a §6 hearing is conducted, the government must reveal details of its case so as to give the defense fair notice to prepare for the hearing. *See* 18 U.S.C. app. III §6(b)(2). Specifically, the government must provide the defense with any portions of any material it may use to establish the "national defense" element of any charges against Lee. Fourth, under §6(f), the government is required to provide notice of any evidence it will use to rebut classified information that the court permits the defense to use at trial. Finally, in addition to the discovery obligations under §6 of CIPA, the government must also comply with the Federal Rules of Criminal Procedure and Brady v. Maryland, 373 U.S. 83 (1963).

Despite the fact that the government's reciprocal duties under CIPA are not triggered until it decides to request a §6 hearing, the overall balance of discovery is not tipped against Lee....

III. CONCLUSION

In summary, Defendant Lee has failed to show that the carefully balanced framework for determining the use of classified information by the defense set forth in CIPA violates his Fifth Amendment privilege against self-incrimination, his Fifth Amendment right to remain silent or his Fifth and Sixth Amendment rights to testify on his own behalf. Defendant has also failed to demonstrate that CIPA violates his Fifth Amendment right to due process of law or his Sixth Amendment right to confront and cross-examine witnesses.

NOTES AND QUESTIONS

1. *The Decision to Prosecute.* As we noted above, when the government decides whether to mount a criminal prosecution or initiate an immigration proceeding against an alleged terrorist or international criminal, it must evaluate the risk that going forward will expose state secrets or classified information. Consequently, the Attorney General has instructed federal prosecutors, in

B. Classified Information Procedures Act

deciding whether to prosecute, to weigh (a) the likelihood of such exposure, (b) the resulting damage to national security, (c) the likelihood of success if the case is brought, and (d) the nature and importance of other federal interests that prosecution would promote. U.S. Dept. of Justice, *Attorney General's Guidelines for Prosecutions Involving Classified Information* 4-6 (1981). Sometimes this weighing will dictate not prosecuting. How, if at all, would the enactment of CIPA have affected this process? The decision to prosecute and the government's conduct of the trial of Wen Ho Lee are dealt with extensively in Dan Stober & Ian Hoffman, *A Convenient Spy: Wen Ho Lee and the Politics of Nuclear Espionage* (2001).

2. *Is It Classified?* How did the *Lee* court decide whether CIPA was applicable — that is, whether the information Wen Ho Lee was planning to use was "classified"? Must the court simply defer to the government's classification stamp? If so, "the government could make CIPA applicable whenever it suited its purpose simply by rubber-stamping documents that have no relevance to the national security." 26 Wright & Graham, *supra* p. 853, at 748. Rules for classifying information are examined in Chapter 33.

3. *Greymail.* In United States v. Reynolds, 345 U.S. 1, 12 (1953), the Supreme Court said that "it is unconscionable to allow [the government] to undertake prosecution and then invoke its governmental privileges to deprive the accused of anything which might be material to his defense." Rejected Federal Rule of Evidence 509 therefore provided that when the state secrets privilege is sustained and a party is thereby deprived of material evidence, the court should make whatever orders "the interests of justice require, including striking the testimony of a witness, declaring a mistrial, finding against the government upon an issue as to which the evidence is relevant, or dismissing the action." 26 Wright & Graham, *supra*, at 417. *See generally* Fisher, *supra* p. 853 (reviewing the history of the rule).

Can you see how these principles from civil litigation help set the stage for greymail in criminal trials? How does it work? Is it an unfair tactic by unscrupulous defendants or lawyers? Former Assistant Attorney General Philip Heymann has noted that "[i]t would be a mistake... to view the 'greymail' problem as limited to instances of unscrupulous or questionable conduct by defendants since wholly proper defense attempts to obtain or disclose classified information may present the government with the same 'disclose or dismiss' dilemma." S. Rep. No. 96-823, at 3 (1980), *reprinted in* 1980 U.S.C.C.A.N. 4294, 4296-4297. Into which category would the disclose-or-dismiss dilemma in the Wen Ho Lee case fall? *See* Bob Drogin, *Nuke Secrets Deemed Vital to Scientist's Case*, L.A. Times, June 16, 2000, at 28 (reporting that a member of Lee's legal team characterized as "graymailing the government" his request for complete computer records and 400,000 pages of classified data for nearly every U.S. nuclear weapon). Has the enactment of CIPA eliminated the possibility of greymail?

4. *Prosecutor's Use of Secret Evidence?* Look closely at the CIPA provisions. Do they permit the prosecutor to use classified information *to make the government's case* against the defendant, either secretly or in substituted or summarized form? If you are not sure, how should we resolve any ambiguity? *See* Greene v. McElroy, 360 U.S. 474 (1959), *supra* p. 105.

5. *Defendant's Discovery in Criminal Cases*. In criminal cases, defendants have certain limited rights to discovery. The Supreme Court has held that the prosecution must disclose evidence that is favorable to defendant and "is material either to guilt or to punishment." Brady v. Maryland, 373 U.S. 83-87 (1963). Specific defense requests thus require the prosecution to turn over all exculpatory evidence, which may include classified information in national security prosecutions. *See* United States v. Rezaq, 156 F.R.D. 514, 516-517 (D.D.C. 1994). In addition, the Jencks Act, 18 U.S.C. §3500 (2000), requires the prosecution to produce statements in its possession by witnesses who have testified on direct examination at trial in order to facilitate cross-examination by the defense. Such statements could include ones made by secret intelligence assets. For example, in the case that prompted enactment of the Act, the statements were confidential reports by paid government informants who were members of the Communist Party. Jencks v. United States, 353 U.S. 657 (1957). Finally, Federal Rule of Criminal Procedure 16(a)(1) permits criminal defendants to discover their own statements, as well as documents and tangible objects in the possession, custody, or control of the government that are material to the defendant's defense, are intended for use by government as evidence, or were obtained from or belong to the defendant. Here again, the documents or tangible objects might include classified information, or their disclosure might reveal intelligence courses and methods. *See generally* Jonathan M. Fredman, *Intelligence Agencies, Law Enforcement, and the Prosecution Team*, 16 Yale L. & Poly. Rev. 331 (1998).

Of course, intelligence agencies may hold back classified information or sources and methods and provide only unclassified information to the prosecution. Could the prosecution then argue that it had only the latter in its possession, custody, or control, thus avoiding discovery of classified information by the defense? The cases are neither clear nor consistent, but in general they hold that "federal discovery obligations extend to those government agencies that are so closely 'aligned' with the prosecution of a specific matter that justice requires their records be subject to the respective discovery obligations." *Id.* at 347. The *United States Attorneys' Manual* states that "an investigative or prosecutive agency becomes aligned with the government prosecutor when it becomes actively involved in the investigation or the prosecution of a particular case." *United States Attorneys' Manual* tit. 9-90.210(D)(1) (1997).

Does the tasking of an intelligence agency by the FBI under the 1996 law (quoted *supra* p. 848) constitute sufficient "active involvement" to align it with the prosecution? *See* Fredman, *supra* at 364 (opining that "a court could well [so] conclude"). Suppose the intelligence community on its own initiative forwards to the FBI foreign surveillance information suggesting criminal wrongdoing. Has it thereby aligned itself with the prosecutors if a criminal prosecution results? *Id.* (probably not). The *United States Attorneys' Manual* suggests that its role must first "exceed the role of providing mere tips or leads based on information generated independently of the criminal case." *United States Attorneys' Manual* tit. 9-90.210(d)(1) (1997).

6. *CIPA and Discovery*. CIPA permits the government to argue ex parte against the discovery of classified information, 18 U.S.C. app. 3 §4, but it does not purport to change discovery standards. Nevertheless, some courts and

B. Classified Information Procedures Act

commentators have read CIPA to narrow a defendant's rights or balance them against governmental interests. *See* 26 Wright & Graham, *supra* p. 853, §5672. In United States v. Yunis, 867 F.2d 617 (D.C. Cir. 1989), for example, the court arguably crafted a new relevancy standard for discovery of classified information by holding that "mere . . . theoretical relevance" was not enough; defendant was obliged to show that the information is "at least 'helpful to the defense of [the] accused.'" *Id.* at 623 (*quoting* Roviaro v. United States, 353 U.S. 53, 60-61 (1957) (involving informer's privilege)).

When a court in a section 4 proceeding *does* find that classified information is discoverable, the government is afforded the option of substituting a summary or a statement admitting relevant facts that the classified information would tend to prove. The courts have also inferred authority from CIPA to order defense counsel to obtain security clearances as a condition of seeing classified information or participating in hearings at which it may be disclosed. *See* United States v. Bin Laden, 58 F. Supp. 2d 113 (S.D.N.Y. 1999) (rejecting the claim that this requirement unconstitutionally interferes with defendant's choice of counsel).

7. *CIPA Notice and the Admissibility Hearing.* A defendant who wishes to disclose classified information in the case must give specific prior notice to the government pursuant to section 5, on penalty of having the court exclude any classified information omitted from the notice. 18 U.S.C. app. 3 §5. Why is it not unconstitutional to thus require a defendant to tip his hand, according to *Lee*?

Following a §5 notice, the government may request a hearing concerning the use, relevancy, or admissibility of the identified information. 18 U.S.C. app. 3 §6. This hearing is usually held in camera. CIPA's legislative history is quite clear that it was not intended to change existing rules of evidence applicable in this hearing. *See* 26 Wright & Graham, *supra*, §5672 (discussing history). Some courts have taken this history to heart and even stated that they must disregard the classified nature of the information in ruling on its relevancy and admissibility. Others — notably the Fourth Circuit — have found that CIPA established "a more strict rule of admissibility" for classified information. United States v. Smith, 780 F.2d 1102, 1105 (4th Cir. 1985). *See* Note, *United States v. Smith: Construing the Classified Information Procedures Act as Restricting the Admissibility of Evidence*, 44 Wash. & Lee L. Rev. 720 (1987). Moreover, other courts have obtained the same results as *Smith* by narrowly construing defenses, such as reliance on CIA authority (*see* United States v. Lopez-Lima, 738 F. Supp. 1404 (S.D. Fla. 1990), *supra* p. 376), in order to rule the classified information irrelevant. *See* 26 Wright & Graham, *supra*, §5672.

8. *CIPA Substitution.* Courts may find classified information to be relevant and material. CIPA §6 then affords the government the option of moving to substitute an unclassified statement of admissions or an unclassified summary for the classified information. The court must grant that motion "if it finds that the statement or summary will provide the defendant with substantially the same ability to make his defense as would disclosure." 18 U.S.C. app. 3 §6(c)(1). Is this procedure constitutional under a *Mathews* balancing?

9. *CIPA: Disclose or Dismiss.* If, on the other hand, the court denies the motion, then the Attorney General must decide whether to disclose the information. *Id.* §6(e)(1). If she decides against disclosure, the court may dismiss all or part of the indictment, find against the government on an issue to which the withheld information relates, or strike testimony. *Id.* §6(e)(2). In deciding among these alternatives, the court is not supposed to balance interests, but instead to take whatever action is necessary "to make the defendant whole again." S. Rep. No. 96-823, at 9 (1980). For example, in United States v. Fernandez, 913 F.2d 148 (4th Cir. 1990), a prosecution of the CIA station chief in Costa Rica growing out of the Iran-Contra Affair, the defendant sought to introduce classified documents purporting to show the truth of statements he had made concerning the CIA's role in the resupply of the Contras. Using CIPA procedures, the Independent Counsel proposed that an unclassified summary of evidence be used in substitution for the documents, but the court found that the summary would not provide Fernandez with substantially the same ability to make his defense as would disclosure of the classified information. When the Attorney General refused to declassify the information, the court dismissed the indictment over the strenuous objections of the Independent Counsel. The government also ended the Wen Ho Lee prosecution by accepting his plea to a single count of the multi-count indictment, partly, it is reported, because senior Energy Department officials feared that the judge would order disclosure of classified information to Lee for use in his defense. *See* Bob Drogin, *How FBI's Flawed Case Against Lee Unraveled*, L.A. Times, Sept. 13, 2000, at 1.

10. *Another Option: Lying?* In 1983, a former CIA officer named Edwin P. Wilson was tried and convicted for illegally exporting explosives to Libya. He claimed that he was still working for the Agency and acting on its authority. During Wilson's trial, the government introduced an affidavit from a high-ranking CIA official denying Wilson's continued employment. The affidavit was a deliberate falsehood. Before Wilson was sentenced, attorneys at the CIA and the Justice Department learned of the fabrication, yet they failed to inform either the trial court or the appellate court. When the truth came to light 20 years later, Wilson's conviction was vacated. United States v. Wilson, 289 F. Supp. 2d 801 (S.D. Tex. 2003). A clearly incensed judge wrote, "Honesty comes hard to the government." *Id.* at 809.

C. HANDLING SECRET EXCULPATORY TESTIMONY

United States v. Moussaoui
United States Court of Appeals, 4th Circuit, 2004
365 F.3d 292, *amended on reh'g*, 382 F.3d 453,
cert. denied, 544 U.S. 931

[Zacarias Moussaoui was arrested before the 9/11 attacks, then later indicted for acts in connection with those attacks. The government sought

C. Handling Secret Exculpatory Testimony

the death penalty on several of these charges. Subsequently, Witness * * * * (the ellipsis is used by the court), a suspected member of al Qaeda, was captured by the United States. Moussaoui moved for access to Witness * * * *, asserting that the witness would be an important part of his defense. Ultimately, he sought access from two additional witnesses in U.S. custody. The government opposed these requests.

The District Court found that the requested witnesses were material witnesses who might support Moussaoui's claim that he was not involved in the 9/11 attacks and that he should not receive the death penalty if convicted. It ordered their deposition by remote video, but the government appealed. The Court of Appeals remanded for the District Court to determine whether any substitution existed that would place Moussaoui in substantially the same position as would a deposition. The District Court rejected the government's proposed substitutions and again ordered deposition of the witnesses. When the government refused to comply with this order, the District Court dismissed the death notice and prohibited the government "from making any argument, or offering any evidence, suggesting that the defendant had any involvement in, or knowledge of, the September 11 attacks." This appeal followed.]

WILLIAM W. WILKINS, Chief Judge: . . .

III. . . .

A. PROCESS POWER

The Sixth Amendment guarantees that "[i]n all criminal prosecutions, the accused shall enjoy the right . . . to have compulsory process for obtaining witnesses in his favor." U.S. Const. amend. VI. The compulsory process right is circumscribed, however, by the ability of the district court to obtain the presence of a witness through service of process. The Government maintains that because the enemy combatant witnesses are foreign nationals outside the boundaries of the United States, they are beyond the process power of the district court and, hence, unavailable to Moussaoui. . . .

The Government's argument overlooks the critical fact that the enemy combatant witnesses are in the custody of an official of the United States Government. Therefore, we are concerned not with the ability of the district court to issue a subpoena to the witnesses, but rather with its power to issue a writ of habeas corpus *ad testificandum* ("testimonial writ") to the witnesses' custodian. . . .

[The court found that Secretary Rumsfeld was the proper custodian and that he was within the process power of the district court.]

IV.

The Government next argues that even if the district court would otherwise have the power to order the production of the witnesses, the

January 30 and August 29 orders are improper because they infringe on the Executive's warmaking authority, in violation of separation of powers principles....

B. GOVERNING PRINCIPLES...

This is not a case involving arrogation of the powers or duties of another branch. The district court orders requiring production of the enemy combatant witnesses involved the resolution of questions properly — indeed, exclusively — reserved to the judiciary. Therefore, if there is a separation of powers problem at all, it arises only from the burden the actions of the district court place on the Executive's performance of its duties.

The Supreme Court has explained on several occasions that determining whether a judicial act places impermissible burdens on another branch of government requires balancing the competing interests. *See, e.g., Nixon v. Admin'r of Gen. Servs.*, 433 U.S. 425, 443 (1977)....

C. BALANCING

1. The Burden on the Government

The Constitution charges the Congress and the Executive with the making and conduct of war. It is not an exaggeration to state that the effective performance of these duties is essential to our continued existence as a sovereign nation. Indeed, "no governmental interest is more compelling than the security of the Nation." *Haig v. Agee*, 453 U.S. 280, 307 (1981)....

The Government alleges — and we accept as true — that * * * * the enemy combatant witnesses is critical to the ongoing effort to combat terrorism by al Qaeda. The witnesses are al Qaeda operatives * * * * Their value as intelligence sources can hardly be overstated. And, we must defer to the Government's assertion that interruption * * * * will have devastating effects on the ability to gather information from them. * * * *, it is not unreasonable to suppose that interruption * * * * could result in the loss of information that might prevent future terrorist attacks.

The Government also asserts that production of the witnesses would burden the Executive's ability to conduct foreign relations. The Government claims that if the Executive's assurances of confidentiality can be abrogated by the judiciary, the vital ability to obtain the cooperation of other governments will be devastated.

The Government also reminds us of the bolstering effect production of the witnesses might have on our enemies.... For example, al Qaeda operatives are trained to disrupt the legal process in whatever manner possible; indications that such techniques may be successful will only cause a redoubling of their efforts.

In summary, the burdens that would arise from production of the enemy combatant witnesses are substantial.

C. Handling Secret Exculpatory Testimony

2. Moussaoui's Interest

The importance of the Sixth Amendment right to compulsory process is not subject to question — it is integral to our adversarial criminal justice system:

> The need to develop all relevant facts in the adversary system is both fundamental and comprehensive. The ends of criminal justice would be defeated if judgments were to be founded on a partial or speculative presentation of the facts. The very integrity of the judicial system and public confidence in the system depend on full disclosure of all the facts, within the framework of the rules of evidence. To ensure that justice is done, it is imperative to the function of the courts that compulsory process be available for the production of evidence needed either by the prosecution or by the defense.

United States v. Nixon, 418 U.S. 683, 709 (1974).

The compulsory process right does not attach to any witness the defendant wishes to call, however. Rather, a defendant must demonstrate that the witness he desires to have produced would testify "in his favor." Thus, in order to assess Moussaoui's interest, we must determine whether the enemy combatant witnesses could provide testimony material to Moussaoui's defense.

In the CIPA context,[12] we have adopted the standard articulated by the Supreme Court in *Roviaro v. United States*, 353 U.S. 53 (1957), for determining whether the government's privilege in classified information must give way. Under that standard, a defendant becomes entitled to disclosure of classified information upon a showing that the information "'is relevant and helpful to the defense... or is essential to a fair determination of a cause.'" [United States v. Smith, 780 F.2d 1102 (4th Cir. 1985)], at 1107 (quoting *Roviaro*, 353 U.S. at 60-61).

Because Moussaoui has not had — and will not receive — direct access to any of the witnesses, he cannot be required to show materiality with the degree of specificity that applies in the ordinary case. Rather, it is sufficient if Moussaoui can make a "plausible showing" of materiality. However, in determining whether Moussaoui has made a plausible showing, we must bear in mind that Moussaoui *does* have access to the * * * * summaries....

... [T]he Government argues that even if the witnesses' testimony would tend to exonerate Moussaoui of involvement in the September 11 attacks, such testimony would not be material because the conspiracies with which Moussaoui is charged are broader than September 11. Thus, the Government argues, Moussaoui can be convicted even if he lacked any prior knowledge of September 11. This argument ignores the principle that the scope of an alleged conspiracy is a jury question, and the possibility that Moussaoui may assert that the conspiracy culminating in the September 11 attacks was distinct from any conspiracy in which he was involved. Moreover, even if the jury accepts the Government's

---

12. We adhere to our prior ruling that CIPA does not apply because the January 30 and August 29 orders of the district court are not covered by either of the potentially relevant provisions of CIPA: §4 (concerning deletion of classified information from *documents* to be turned over to the defendant during discovery) or §6 (concerning the disclosure of classified information by the defense during pretrial or trial proceedings). *See Moussaoui I,* 333 F.3d at 514-15. Like the district court, however, we believe that CIPA provides a useful framework for considering the questions raised by Moussaoui's request for access to the enemy combatant witnesses.

claims regarding the scope of the charged conspiracy, testimony regarding Moussaoui's non-involvement in September 11 is critical to the penalty phase. If Moussaoui had no involvement in or knowledge of September 11, it is entirely possible that he would not be found eligible for the death penalty.

We now consider the rulings of the district court regarding the ability of each witness to provide material testimony in Moussaoui's favor.

* * * * * *

The district court did not err in concluding that Witness * * * * could offer material evidence on Moussaoui's behalf. * * * * Several statements by Witness * * * * tend to exculpate Moussaoui. For example, the * * * * summaries state that * * * * This statement tends to undermine the theory (which the Government may or may not intend to advance at trial) that Moussaoui was to pilot a fifth plane into the White House. Witness * * * * has also * * * * This statement is significant in light of other evidence * * * * indicating that Moussaoui had no contact with any of the hijackers. * * * * This is consistent with Moussaoui's claim that he was to be part of a post-September 11 operation....

...Moussaoui has made a sufficient showing that evidence from Witness * * * * would be more helpful than hurtful, or at least that we cannot have confidence in the outcome of the trial without Witness * * * * evidence....

3. Balancing

Having considered the burden alleged by the Government and the right claimed by Moussaoui, we now turn to the question of whether the district court should have refrained from acting in light of the national security interests asserted by the Government. The question is not unique; the Supreme Court has addressed similar matters on numerous occasions. In all cases of this type — cases falling into "what might loosely be called the area of constitutionally guaranteed access to evidence," *Arizona v. Youngblood,* 488 U.S. 51, 55 (1988) (internal quotation marks omitted) — the Supreme Court has held that the defendant's right to a trial that comports with the Fifth and Sixth Amendments prevails over the governmental privilege. Ultimately, as these cases make clear, the appropriate procedure is for the district court to order production of the evidence or witness and leave to the Government the choice of whether to comply with that order. If the government refuses to produce the information at issue — as it may properly do — the result is ordinarily dismissal....

In addition to the pronouncements of the Supreme Court in this area, we are also mindful of Congress' judgment, expressed in CIPA, that the Executive's interest in protecting classified information does not overcome a defendant's right to present his case. Under CIPA, once the district court determines that an item of classified information is relevant and material, that item must be admitted unless the government provides an adequate substitution. If no adequate substitution can be found, the government must decide whether it will prohibit the disclosure of the classified information; if it does so, the district court must impose a sanction, which is presumptively dismissal of the indictment.

In view of these authorities, it is clear that when an evidentiary privilege — even one that involves national security — is asserted by the Government in the

C. Handling Secret Exculpatory Testimony

context of its prosecution of a criminal offense, the "balancing" we must conduct is primarily, if not solely, an examination of whether the district court correctly determined that the information the Government seeks to withhold is material to the defense. We have determined that the enemy combatant witnesses can offer material testimony that is essential to Moussaoui's defense, and we therefore affirm the January 30 and August 29 orders. Thus, the choice is the Government's whether to comply with those orders or suffer a sanction.

V.

As noted previously, the Government has stated that it will not produce the enemy combatant witnesses for depositions (or, we presume, for any other purpose related to this litigation). We are thus left in the following situation: the district court has the power to order production of the enemy combatant witnesses and has properly determined that they could offer material testimony on Moussaoui's behalf, but the Government has refused to produce the witnesses. Under such circumstances, dismissal of the indictment is the usual course. Like the district court, however, we believe that a more measured approach is required. Additionally, we emphasize that no punitive sanction is warranted here because the Government has rightfully exercised its prerogative to protect national security interests by refusing to produce the witnesses.

Although, as explained above, this is not a CIPA case, that act nevertheless provides useful guidance in determining the nature of the remedies that may be available. Under CIPA, dismissal of an indictment is authorized only if the government has failed to produce an adequate substitute for the classified information, and the interests of justice would not be served by imposition of a lesser sanction. CIPA thus enjoins district courts to seek a solution that neither disadvantages the defendant nor penalizes the government (and the public) for protecting classified information that may be vital to national security.

A similar approach is appropriate here. Under such an approach, the first question is whether there is any appropriate substitution for the witnesses' testimony. Because we conclude, for the reasons set forth below, that appropriate substitutions are available, we need not consider any other remedy....

C. INSTRUCTIONS

... [W]e conclude that the district court erred in ruling that any substitution for the witnesses' testimony is inherently inadequate to the extent it is derived from the * * * * reports. To the contrary, we hold that the * * * * summaries (which, as the district court determined, accurately recapitulate the * * * * reports) provide an adequate basis for the creation of written statements that may be submitted to the jury in lieu of the witnesses' deposition testimony.

The crafting of substitutions is a task best suited to the district court, given its greater familiarity with the facts of the case and its authority to manage the presentation of evidence. Nevertheless, we think it is appropriate to provide some guidance to the court and the parties.

First, the circumstances of this case — most notably, the fact that the substitutions may very well support Moussaoui's defense — dictate that the crafting of substitutions be an interactive process among the parties and the district court. Second, we think that accuracy and fairness are best achieved by crafting substitutions that use the exact language of the * * * * summaries to the greatest extent possible. We believe that the best means of achieving both of these objectives is for defense counsel to identify particular portions of the * * * * summaries that Moussaoui may want to admit into evidence at trial. The Government may then argue that additional portions must be included in the interest of completeness.... If the substitutions are to be admitted at all (we leave open the possibility that Moussaoui may decide not to use the substitutions in his defense), they may be admitted only by Moussaoui. Based on defense counsel's submissions and the Government's objections, the district court could then create an appropriate set of substitutions....

As previously indicated, the jury must be provided with certain information regarding the substitutions. While we leave the particulars of the instructions to the district court, the jury must be informed, at a minimum, that the substitutions are what the witnesses would say if called to testify; that the substitutions are derived from statements obtained under conditions that provide circumstantial guarantees of reliability; that the substitutions contain statements obtained * * * * ; and that neither the parties nor the district court has ever had access to the witnesses....

Affirmed in part, vacated in part, and remanded.

[The opinions of WILLIAMS, Circuit Judge, and GREGORY, Circuit Judge, each concurring in part and dissenting in part, are omitted.]

NOTES AND QUESTIONS

1. *Guilty Plea and Sentence.* On April 22, 2005, Moussaoui surprised everyone by pleading guilty to the key charges against him, while at the same time denying having any intention to commit mass murder. *See Moussaoui Pleads Guilty to Terror Charges,* CNN.com, Apr. 23, 2005, *at* http://www.cnn.com/2005/LAW/04/22/moussaoui/index.html. He was subsequently sentenced to life in prison. United States v. Moussaoui, No. 1:01CR00455-001, Judgment in a Criminal Case at 2 (E.D. Va. May 14, 2006).

2. *Deciding a Clash Between Branches: Formalism or Balancing?* The court concluded that the appropriate separation of powers analysis required by Moussaoui's insistence on access to * * * * is balancing, as prescribed by Nixon v. Administrator of General Services, 433 U.S. 425, 443 (1977) (stating that "the proper inquiry focuses on the extent to which [the judicial act of ordering access, in this instance] prevents the Executive Branch from accomplishing its constitutionally assigned functions,... [and whether] that impact is justified by an overriding need to promote objectives within the constitutional authority of [the court]"). See *supra* p. 55. But in Public Citizen v. United States Department of Justice, 491 U.S. 440, 485 (1989), noted *supra* p. 55, Justice Kennedy indicated that there is "a line of cases of equal weight and authority,... where

C. Handling Secret Exculpatory Testimony

the Constitution by explicit text commits the power at issue to the exclusive control of the President, . . . [and the Court has] refused to tolerate *any* intrusion by [the courts]." Why is not *Moussaoui* controlled by the latter line of cases? Doesn't the Commander in Chief Clause of Article II commit command of the armed forces in war to the President, and isn't the interrogation of enemy combatants in war part of that command? Does *Hamdi, supra* p. 721, or *Padilla, supra* p. 744, suggest any answers to these questions?

What other cases would you rely on in making the formalist argument for the government, or, by a balancing analysis, in arguing the extent to which court-ordered access to * * * would prevent the President from conducting the war? In this regard, consider *Keith, supra* p. 485, *Korematsu, supra* p. 704, and *Zadvydas, supra* p. 671, Note 1. If the *Moussaoui* jury had been the target of serious threats of harm, how would you balance his Sixth Amendment right to trial by jury against the government's interest in protecting jurors by empaneling them secretly in a secure location to hear the trial by video?

3. *CIPA by Analogy.* In deciding the alternatives, the court determined that CIPA (see *supra* p. 857) did not apply but relied on it anyway for a "useful framework." *See also* United States v. Paracha, 2006 WL 12768 (S.D.N.Y. 2006) (using CIPA by analogy to impose *Moussaoui*-type solution to terror defendant's demand for access to witnesses in U.S. custody in Afghanistan). Why did CIPA not apply? By what authority did the court undertake the relevance and balancing inquiries and order access to the summaries? Did the court, in effect, create a "wartime exception" to the Sixth Amendment after all? Is this another example of what Justice Scalia condemned as the "Mr. Fix-It Mentality" of courts? If CIPA is to be amended to cover the *Moussaoui* problem, why not leave that job to Congress?

4. *Switching Fora?* The district court invited the government to "reconsider whether the civilian criminal courts are the appropriate fora" for trying someone like Moussaoui. United States v. Moussaoui, No. Cr-01-455-A (E.D. Va. Mar. 10, 2003). The alternative is trial by military commission, which we explore in Chapter 30. Indeed, even Moussaoui's standby counsel appears to have invited this alternative, gratuitously conceding that the government's authority to try enemy combatants by military commission is "settled," and implying that the government can simply dismiss the criminal prosecution and proceed instead by a military commission to resolve the tension between Moussaoui's Sixth Amendment rights and the war powers. Brief of the Appellee at 3-4, United States v. Moussaoui, No. 03-4162 (4th Cir. May 13, 2003).

After you read the materials on military commissions, you can decide for yourself whether this was a wise concession. Do you agree with the apparent assumption upon which that concession and the District Court's invitation rested — that the government can switch fora in midstream? Even assuming that the government could lawfully have tried Moussaoui by military commission *ab initio*, does it necessarily follow that the government may start in a civilian court and then dismiss in favor of a military commission when it is unhappy with the civilian court's rulings? Would it matter how far the criminal prosecution had progressed beyond the indictment? If such a switch survived constitutional challenges, would it nevertheless violate the spirit of the law?

The government did, in fact, make a switch — actually a double switch — in Al-Marri v. Hanft, 378 F. Supp. 2d 673 (D.S.C. 2005), noted *supra* p. 757. After Al-Marri lawfully entered the United States with his family to obtain a master's degree, he was initially arrested as a material witness in the 9/11 investigation. In the first switch, he was then rearrested and indicted for making false statements and for credit card fraud. More than two years later, President Bush interrupted the course of normal criminal proceedings (trial had not yet begun) by designating Al-Marri an enemy combatant, after which he was transferred to military detention in South Carolina. The government then successfully moved to drop the criminal indictment with prejudice. At this writing, Al-Marri remains in military detention without charges.

Al-Marri argued that his criminal detention was sufficient to thwart any terrorist acts and that there was no necessity for military detention. The district court rejected his argument in part on the reasoning that when a federal investigation of criminal charges pending in state court reveals a federal crime, the state charges can be dismissed and the matter can be transferred to federal jurisdiction. *Id.* at 681. Is the analogy sound?

Al-Marri also protested that while he might have been acquitted of the criminal charges, he had no opportunity to prove his innocence in military detention. The court rejected this claim as well, reasoning that the purpose of military detention is preventive.

> This Court recognizes the natural response to this reasoning that, when a defendant is acquitted of criminal charges, society should not assume that he ever did nor that he will, in the future, engage in the activities for which he was charged. In this case, however, Petitioner was not charged with crimes of terrorism, and thus, an acquittal of various fraud charges does not lead to the conclusion that he will not, in the future, engage in acts of terrorism as alleged by the government.

Id. at 681 n.8.

5. *A Military Brig — the Better Forum?* The following assessment was written before the conclusion of the Moussaoui trial.

> The United States should drop all criminal charges against Zacarias Moussaoui, not because he is innocent, but because he is a foreign citizen who is (or was) a terrorist bent on killing innocent Americans, destroying American property, and disrupting American society. For less than a nanosecond, Moussaoui should be a free man again....
>
> Before the nanosecond of Moussaoui's freedom ends, he should be transferred to the custody of the United States Department of Defense. After that, based on recommendations coordinated by the National Security Council (NSC) for the President, the Executive Branch should implement a well-conceived decision about Moussaoui's next address. The NSC, rather than a particular United States agency, such as the Justice Department or the Defense Department, is the appropriate forum to vet such policies because they transcend the boundaries between domestic and international spheres, going beyond law enforcement and military issues.... The President, in making this decision on Moussaoui's next address, should consider our relations with foreign countries and the safety of our homeland. But whatever happens to Moussaoui, he did not — and does not — belong in

C. Handling Secret Exculpatory Testimony

criminal custody. [John Radsan, *The Moussaoui Case: The Mess From Minnesota*, 31 Wm. Mitchell L. Rev. 1417 (2005).]

Do you agree? Did the system work? Or was the system distorted to accommodate national security? Do you think accused terrorists like Moussaoui should be tried by military commissions (a subject to which we turn in the next chapter)?

30
Trial by Military Commission

Before deploying "necessary and appropriate force" against al Qaeda and the Taliban in Afghanistan in November 2001, the Bush administration had to decide what it would do with those whom U.S. forces and their allies captured in the fight. Apart from simply detaining them, one possibility was trying them in U.S. criminal courts. But the problems of secret evidence, which we explored in the previous chapter, not to mention concerns about security and efficiency, given the sheer numbers of anticipated captives, made this option impractical. A second option was trying them before some ad hoc international tribunal. The surrender of control that this would entail, coupled with the Administration's repudiation of the International Criminal Court, made this option unappealing. A third option was trying them by court-martial, using the same rules applicable to U.S. servicemen. This option would have used fair and time-tested procedures at the same time that it conformed with the laws of war. But the very fairness of the procedures may have been a strike against them; they may have seemed too fair and, partly as a result, too cumbersome for terrorists charged with horrific war crimes against civilians. *See* Jane Mayer, *The Hidden Power*, New Yorker, May 3, 2006, at 44 (quoting Vice President Cheney on military commissions: "We think it guarantees that we'll have the kind of treatment of these individuals that we believe they deserve."). Their conformity with the laws of war could have been another strike against them, as long as the administration insisted that such laws did not apply to terrorists. See Chapter 27.

Whatever the precise reasons, the administration chose a fourth option: to try selected captives by "military commission" under procedures devised for the occasion. Military commissions are tribunals of military officers who sit as judge and jury. Historically, they have been used in the field to try spies, saboteurs, and others who violate the laws of war, and in occupied territories to try common crimes as well. In Chapter 26, we considered two pre-9/11 cases in reviewing the legal authority for *detention* by the military. In Part A of this chapter, we revisit these cases in exploring the legal authority for *trial* by military commission. In Part B, we examine the Military Order of November 13, 2001, which adopted the military commission option and the procedures implementing it, before turning to the Supreme Court's 2006 decision in *Hamdan v. Rumsfeld* about the legal authority for military commissions.

A. TRIAL BY MILITARY COMMISSION BEFORE 9/11

Ex parte Milligan
United States Supreme Court, 1866
71 U.S. (4 Wall.) 2

[The opinion is set forth *supra* p. 683.]

Ex parte Quirin
United States Supreme Court, 1942
317 U.S. 1

[The opinion is set forth *supra* p. 714.]

NOTES AND QUESTIONS

[The notes and questions are set forth *supra* pp. 718-720.]

B. TRIAL BY MILITARY COMMISSION AFTER 9/11

By the following Military Order, President Bush authorized trial by military commissions of persons he designated. The order delegated to the Secretary of Defense the task of promulgating procedures for such trials. Secretary Rumsfeld and the Department of Defense subsequently issued a host of implementing orders and instructions, some of which were later revised. *See* Dept. of Defense, *Military Commission Order No. 1*, Mar. 21, 2002; Dept. of Defense, *Military Commissions Instructions Nos. 1-10* (various dates). The flow chart *infra* p. 882 generally depicts the resulting military commission process, while the most relevant military commission procedures and characteristics are summarized in *Hamdan v. Rumsfeld*, 126 S. Ct. 2749, 2786-2787 (2006), *infra* p. 882, which follows the chart.

Military Order of November 13, 2001
Detention, Treatment, and Trial of Certain Non-Citizens in the War Against Terrorism
66 Fed. Reg. 57,833 (Nov. 13, 2001)

By the authority vested in me as President and as Commander in Chief of the Armed Forces of the United States by the Constitution and the laws of the United States of America, including the Authorization for Use of Military Force Joint Resolution (Public Law 107-40, 115 Stat. 224) and sections 821 and 836 of title 10, United States Code, it is hereby ordered as follows:

SECTION 1. *FINDINGS.*

(a) International terrorists, including members of al Qaeda, have carried out attacks on United States diplomatic and military personnel and activities abroad and on citizens and property within the United States on a scale that has created a state of armed conflict that requires the use of the United States Armed Forces.

(b) In light of grave acts of terrorism and threats of terrorism, including the terrorist attacks on Sept. 11, 2001, on the headquarters of the United States Department of Defense in the national capital region, on the World Trade Center in New York, and on civilian aircraft such as in Pennsylvania, I proclaimed a national emergency on Sept. 14, 2001 (Proclamation 7463, Declaration of National Emergency by Reason of Certain Terrorist Attacks).

(c) Individuals acting alone and in concert involved in international terrorism possess both the capability and the intention to undertake further terrorist attacks against the United States that, if not detected and prevented, will cause mass deaths, mass injuries, and massive destruction of property, and may place at risk the continuity of the operations of the United States government.

(d) The ability of the United States to protect the United States and its citizens, and to help its allies and other cooperating nations protect their nations and their citizens, from such further terrorist attacks depends in significant part upon using the United States Armed Forces to identify terrorists and those who support them, to disrupt their activities, and to eliminate their ability to conduct or support such attacks.

(e) To protect the United States and its citizens, and for the effective conduct of military operations and prevention of terrorist attacks, it is necessary for individuals subject to this order pursuant to section 2 hereof to be detained, and, when tried, to be tried for violations of the laws of war and other applicable laws by military tribunals.

(f) Given the danger to the safety of the United States and the nature of international terrorism, and to the extent provided by and under this order, I find consistent with section 836 of title 10, United States Code, that it is not practicable to apply in military commissions under this order the principles of law and the rules of evidence generally recognized in the trial of criminal cases in the United States district courts.

B. Trial by Military Commission After 9/11

(g) Having fully considered the magnitude of the potential deaths, injuries, and property destruction that would result from potential acts of terrorism against the United States, and the probability that such acts will occur, I have determined that an extraordinary emergency exists for national defense purposes, that this emergency constitutes an urgent and compelling government interest, and that issuance of this order is necessary to meet the emergency.

SECTION 2. DEFINITION AND POLICY.

(a) The term "individual subject to this order" shall mean any individual who is not a United States citizen with respect to whom I determine from time to time in writing that:
    (1) there is reason to believe that such individual, at the relevant times,
        (i) is or was a member of the organization known as al Qaeda;
        (ii) has engaged in, aided or abetted, or conspired to commit, acts of international terrorism, or acts in preparation therefor, that have caused, threaten to cause, or have as their aim to cause, injury to or adverse effects on the United States, its citizens, national security, foreign policy, or economy; or
        (iii) has knowingly harbored one or more individuals described in subparagraphs (i) or (ii) of subsection 2(a)(1) of this order; and
    (2) it is in the interest of the United States that such individual be subject to this order.

(b) It is the policy of the United States that the secretary of defense shall take all necessary measures to ensure that any individual subject to this order is detained in accordance with section 3, and, if the individual is to be tried, that such individual is tried only in accordance with section 4.

(c) It is further the policy of the United States that any individual subject to this order who is not already under the control of the Secretary of Defense but who is under the control of any other officer or agent of the United States or any state shall, upon delivery of a copy of such written determination to such officer or agent, forthwith be placed under the control of the Secretary of Defense.

SECTION 3. DETENTION AUTHORITY OF THE SECRETARY OF DEFENSE.

Any individual subject to this order shall be —
(a) detained at an appropriate location designated by the Secretary of Defense outside or within the United States;
(b) treated humanely, without any adverse distinction based on race, color, religion, gender, birth, wealth, or any similar criteria;
(c) afforded adequate food, drinking water, shelter, clothing, and medical treatment;
(d) allowed the free exercise of religion consistent with the requirements of such detention; and

(e) detained in accordance with such other conditions as the Secretary of Defense may prescribe.

SECTION 4. *AUTHORITY OF THE SECRETARY OF DEFENSE REGARDING TRIALS OF INDIVIDUALS SUBJECT TO THIS ORDER.*

(a) Any individual subject to this order shall, when tried, be tried by military commission for any and all offenses triable by military commission that such individual is alleged to have committed, and may be punished in accordance with the penalties provided under applicable law, including life imprisonment or death.

(b) As a military function and in light of the findings in section 1, including subsection (f) thereof, the Secretary of Defense shall issue such orders and regulations, including orders for the appointment of one or more military commissions, as may be necessary to carry out subsection (a) of this section.

(c) Orders and regulations issued under subsection (b) of this section shall include, but not be limited to, rules for the conduct of the proceedings of military commissions, including pretrial, trial, and post-trial procedures, modes of proof, issuance of process, and qualifications of attorneys, which shall at a minimum provide for—

(1) military commissions to sit at any time and any place, consistent with such guidance regarding time and place as the Secretary of Defense may provide;

(2) a full and fair trial, with the military commission sitting as the triers of both fact and law;

(3) admission of such evidence as would, in the opinion of the presiding officer of the military commission (or instead, if any other member of the commission so requests at the time the presiding officer renders that opinion, the opinion of the commission rendered at that time by a majority of the commission), have probative value to a reasonable person;

(4) in a manner consistent with the protection of information classified or classifiable under Executive Order 12958 of April 17, 1995, as amended, or any successor Executive Order, protected by statute or rule from unauthorized disclosure, or otherwise protected by law, (A) the handling of, admission into evidence of, and access to materials and information, and (B) the conduct, closure of, and access to proceedings;

(5) conduct of the prosecution by one or more attorneys designated by the Secretary of Defense and conduct of the defense by attorneys for the individual subject to this order;

(6) conviction only upon the concurrence of two-thirds of the members of the commission present at the time of the vote, a majority being present;

(7) sentencing only upon the concurrence of two-thirds of the members of the commission present at the time of the vote, a majority being present; and

(8) submission of the record of the trial, including any conviction or sentence, for review and final decision by me or by the Secretary of Defense if so designated by me for that purpose.

B. Trial by Military Commission After 9/11

SECTION 5. *OBLIGATION OF OTHER AGENCIES TO ASSIST THE SECRETARY OF DEFENSE.*

Departments, agencies, entities, and officers of the United States shall, to the maximum extent permitted by law, provide to the Secretary of Defense such assistance as he may request to implement this order.

SECTION 6. *ADDITIONAL AUTHORITIES OF THE SECRETARY OF DEFENSE.*

(a) As a military function and in light of the findings in section 1, the Secretary of Defense shall issue such orders and regulations as may be necessary to carry out any of the provisions of this order.

(b) The Secretary of Defense may perform any of his functions or duties, and may exercise any of the powers provided to him under this order (other than under section 4(c)(8) hereof) in accordance with section 113(d) of title 10, United States Code.

SECTION 7. *RELATIONSHIP TO OTHER LAW AND FORUMS.*

(a) Nothing in this order shall be construed to—

(1) authorize the disclosure of state secrets to any person not otherwise authorized to have access to them;

(2) limit the authority of the President as Commander in Chief of the Armed Forces or the power of the President to grant reprieves and pardons; or

(3) limit the lawful authority of the Secretary of Defense, any military commander, or any other officer or agent of the United States or of any State to detain or try any person who is not an individual subject to this order.

(b) With respect to any individual subject to this order—

(1) military tribunals shall have exclusive jurisdiction with respect to offenses by the individual; and

(2) the individual shall not be privileged to seek any remedy or maintain any proceeding, directly or indirectly, or to have any such remedy or proceeding sought on the individual's behalf, in

(i) any court of the United States, or any State thereof,

(ii) any court of any foreign nation, or

(iii) any international tribunal.

(c) This order is not intended to and does not create any right, benefit, or privilege, substantive or procedural, enforceable at law or equity by any party, against the United States, its departments, agencies, or other entities, its officers or employees, or any other person.

(d) For purposes of this order, the term "state" includes any State, district, territory, or possession of the United States.

(e) I reserve the authority to direct the Secretary of Defense, at any time hereafter, to transfer to a governmental authority control of any individual subject to this order. Nothing in this order shall be construed to limit the authority of any such governmental authority to prosecute any individual for whom control is transferred.

SECTION 8. PUBLICATION.

This order shall be published in the *Federal Register*.

George W. Bush

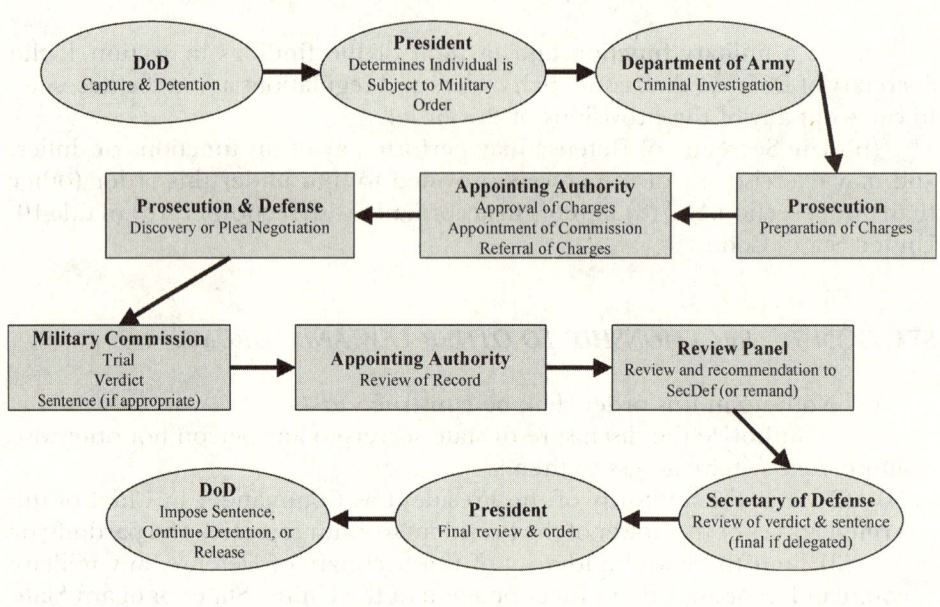

Hamdan v. Rumsfeld
United States Supreme Court, 2006
126 S. Ct. 2749

[Salim Ahmed Hamdan, a Yemeni national, was captured in November 2001 by militia forces in Afghanistan and turned over to the U.S. military. In June 2002, he was transported to the military prison at Guantánamo Bay, Cuba. On July 3, 2003, President Bush determined that Hamdan (and five other detainees at Guantánamo Bay) were subject to the Military Order of November 13, 2001, and therefore triable by military commission. Military counsel was appointed for him, and his counsel promptly filed demands for charges and for a speedy trial pursuant to the Uniform Code of Military Justice (UCMJ), 10 U.S.C. §801-946 (2000 & Supp. III 2003). The demands were

[1. U.S. Dept. of Defense, *Department of Defense Fact Sheet: Military Commission Procedures*, Aug. 2003. The appeals process depicted in the chart is substantially changed by the Military Commissions Act of 2006, Pub. L. No. 109-366, 120 Stat. 2600. See *infra* p. 906.]

denied by a military official on the ground that Hamdan was not entitled to any of the protections of the UCMJ. On July 13, 2004, Hamdan was charged with conspiring with members of al Qaeda to commit the offenses of "attacking civilians; attacking civilian objects; murder by an unprivileged belligerent; and terrorism." Among the overt acts listed in the charges was the claim that Hamdan acted as Osama bin Laden's "bodyguard and personal driver."

Before his trial could begin, Hamdan challenged the legality of the commission by habeas and mandamus petitions. The district court granted his petition for a writ of habeas corpus, but the Court of Appeals, in an opinion by then Judge Roberts, reversed. The Supreme Court granted certiorari and issued the following opinion.]

JUSTICE STEVENS announced the judgment of the Court and delivered the opinion of the Court with respect to Parts I through IV, Parts VI through VI-D-iii, Part VI-D-v, and Part VII, and an opinion with respect to Parts V and VI-D-iv, in which JUSTICE SOUTER, JUSTICE GINSBURG, and JUSTICE BREYER join.... [Hamdan] concedes that a court-martial constituted in accordance with the Uniform Code of Military Justice (UCMJ) would have authority to try him. His objection is that the military commission the President has convened lacks such authority, for two principal reasons: First, neither congressional Act nor the common law of war supports trial by this commission for the crime of conspiracy—an offense that, Hamdan says, is not a violation of the law of war. Second, Hamdan contends, the procedures that the President has adopted to try him violate the most basic tenets of military and international law, including the principle that a defendant must be permitted to see and hear the evidence against him....

For the reasons that follow, we conclude that the military commission convened to try Hamdan lacks power to proceed because its structure and procedures violate both the UCMJ and the Geneva Conventions. Four of us also conclude, see Part V, *infra,* that the offense with which Hamdan has been charged is not an "offens[e] that by ... the law of war may be tried by military commissions." 10 U.S.C. §821....

II

[The Court found that the Detainee Treatment Act, *supra* p. 701, did not preclude review.]

III

[The Court refused to abstain pending completion of the military commission proceedings against Hamdan, noting that the comity considerations favoring abstention in Schlesinger v. Councilman, 420 U.S. 738 (1975), did not apply to Hamdan's case.]....

... First, Hamdan is not a member of our Nation's Armed Forces, so concerns about military discipline do not apply. Second, the tribunal convened to try Hamdan is not part of the integrated system of military courts, complete with independent review panels, that Congress has established. Unlike the officer in

Councilman, Hamdan has no right to appeal any conviction to the civilian judges of the Court of Military Appeals (now called the United States Court of Appeals for the Armed Forces, see Pub. L. 103-337, 108 Stat. 2831). Instead, under Dept. of Defense Military Commission Order No. 1 (Commission Order No. 1), which was issued by the President on March 21, 2002, and amended most recently on August 31, 2005, and which governs the procedures for Hamdan's commission, any conviction would be reviewed by a panel consisting of three military officers designated by the Secretary of Defense. Commission Order No. 1 §6(H)(4). Commission Order No. 1 provides that appeal of a review panel's decision may be had only to the Secretary of Defense himself, §6(H)(5), and then, finally, to the President, §6(H)(6).

We have no doubt that the various individuals assigned review power under Commission Order No. 1 would strive to act impartially and ensure that Hamdan receive all protections to which he is entitled. Nonetheless, these review bodies clearly lack the structural insulation from military influence that characterizes the Court of Appeals for the Armed Forces, and thus bear insufficient conceptual similarity to state courts to warrant invocation of abstention principles....

IV

The military commission, a tribunal neither mentioned in the Constitution nor created by statute, was born of military necessity. See W. Winthrop, Military Law and Precedents 831 (rev. 2d ed. 1920) (hereinafter Winthrop)....

...As further discussed below, each aspect of that seemingly broad [military commission] jurisdiction was in fact supported by a separate military exigency. Generally, though, the need for military commissions during this period—as during the Mexican War—was driven largely by the then very limited jurisdiction of courts-martial: "The *occasion* for the military commission arises principally from the fact that the jurisdiction of the court-martial proper, in our law, is restricted by statute almost exclusively to members of the military force and to certain specific offences defined in a written code." *Id.,* at 831 (emphasis in original).

Exigency alone, of course, will not justify the establishment and use of penal tribunals not contemplated by Article I, §8 and Article III, §1 of the Constitution unless some other part of that document authorizes a response to the felt need. See *Ex parte Milligan,* [71 U.S.] 4 Wall. 2, 121 (1866) ("Certainly no part of the judicial power of the country was conferred on [military commissions]"). And that authority, if it exists, can derive only from the powers granted jointly to the President and Congress in time of war. See *In re Yamashita,* 327 U.S. 1, 11 (1946).

The Constitution makes the President the "Commander in Chief" of the Armed Forces, Art. II, §2, cl. 1, but vests in Congress the powers to "declare War...and make Rules concerning Captures on Land and Water," Art. I, §8, cl. 11, to "raise and support Armies," *id.,* cl. 12, to "define and punish...Offences against the Law of Nations," *id.,* cl. 10, and "To make Rules for the Government and Regulation of the land and naval Forces," *id.,* cl. 14. The interplay between

B. Trial by Military Commission After 9/11

these powers was described by Chief Justice Chase in the seminal case of *Ex parte Milligan:*

> "The power to make the necessary laws is in Congress; the power to execute in the President. Both powers imply many subordinate and auxiliary powers. Each includes all authorities essential to its due exercise. But neither can the President, in war more than in peace, intrude upon the proper authority of Congress, nor Congress upon the proper authority of the President.... Congress cannot direct the conduct of campaigns, nor can the President, or any commander under him, without the sanction of Congress, institute tribunals for the trial and punishment of offences, either of soldiers or civilians, unless in cases of a controlling necessity, which justifies what it compels, or at least insures acts of indemnity from the justice of the legislature." 4 Wall., at 139-140.

Whether Chief Justice Chase was correct in suggesting that the President may constitutionally convene military commissions "without the sanction of Congress" in cases of "controlling necessity" is a question this Court has not answered definitively, and need not answer today. For we held in [Ex parte Quirin, 317 U.S. 1 (1942), *supra* p. 714] that Congress had, through Article of War 15, sanctioned the use of military commissions in such circumstances. 317 U.S., at 28 ("By the Articles of War, and especially Article 15, Congress has explicitly provided, so far as it may constitutionally do so, that military tribunals shall have jurisdiction to try offenders or offenses against the law of war in appropriate cases"). Article 21 of the UCMJ, the language of which is substantially identical to the old Article 15 and was preserved by Congress after World War II, reads as follows:

> "Jurisdiction of courts-martial not exclusive."
> "The provisions of this code conferring jurisdiction upon courts-martial shall not be construed as depriving military commissions, provost courts, or other military tribunals of concurrent jurisdiction in respect of offenders or offenses that by statute or by the law of war may be tried by such military commissions, provost courts, or other military tribunals." 64 Stat. 115.

We have no occasion to revisit *Quirin*'s controversial characterization of Article of War 15 as congressional authorization for military commissions. Contrary to the Government's assertion, however, even *Quirin* did not view the authorization as a sweeping mandate for the President to "invoke military commissions when he deems them necessary." Rather, the *Quirin* Court recognized that Congress had simply preserved what power, under the Constitution and the common law of war, the President had had before 1916 to convene military commissions — with the express condition that the President and those under his command comply with the law of war. See 317 U.S., at 28-29.[23] That much is evidenced by the Court's inquiry, *following* its conclusion that Congress

---

23. Whether or not the President has independent power, absent congressional authorization, to convene military commissions, he may not disregard limitations that Congress has, in proper exercise of its own war powers, placed on his powers. See *Youngstown Sheet & Tube Co. v. Sawyer*, 343 U.S. 579, 637 (1952) (Jackson, J., concurring). The Government does not argue otherwise.

had authorized military commissions, into whether the law of war had indeed been complied with in that case.

The Government would have us dispense with the inquiry that the *Quirin* Court undertook and find in either the AUMF [Authorization for Use of Military Force, Pub. L. No. 107-40, 115 Stat. 224 (2001), *supra* p. 100] or the DTA [Detainee Treatment Act of 2005, Pub. L. 109-148, 119 Stat. 2739, *supra* p. 701] specific, overriding authorization for the very commission that has been convened to try Hamdan. Neither of these congressional Acts, however, expands the President's authority to convene military commissions. First, while we assume that the AUMF activated the President's war powers, see *Hamdi v. Rumsfeld*, 542 U.S. 507 (2004) (plurality opinion), and that those powers include the authority to convene military commissions in appropriate circumstances, there is nothing in the text or legislative history of the AUMF even hinting that Congress intended to expand or alter the authorization set forth in Article 21 of the UCMJ.[24]

Likewise, the DTA cannot be read to authorize this commission. Although the DTA, unlike either Article 21 or the AUMF, was enacted after the President had convened Hamdan's commission, it contains no language authorizing that tribunal or any other at Guantanamo Bay. The DTA obviously "recognize[s]" the existence of the Guantanamo Bay commissions in the weakest sense because it references some of the military orders governing them and creates limited judicial review of their "final decision[s]," DTA §1005(e)(3), 119 Stat. 2743. But the statute also pointedly reserves judgment on whether "the Constitution and laws of the United States are applicable" in reviewing such decisions and whether, if they are, the "standards and procedures" used to try Hamdan and other detainees actually violate the "Constitution and laws."

Together, the UCMJ, the AUMF, and the DTA at most acknowledge a general Presidential authority to convene military commissions in circumstances where justified under the "Constitution and laws," including the law of war. Absent a more specific congressional authorization, the task of this Court is, as it was in *Quirin,* to decide whether Hamdan's military commission is so justified. It is to that inquiry we now turn.

V

The common law governing military commissions may be gleaned from past practice and what sparse legal precedent exists. Commissions historically have been used in three situations. First, they have substituted for civilian courts at times and in places where martial law has been declared. Their use in these circumstances has raised constitutional questions, see *Duncan v. Kahanamoku*, 327 U.S. 304 (1946); *Milligan*, 4 Wall., at 121-122, but is well recognized. Second, commissions have been established to try civilians "as part of a temporary

---

24. On this point, it is noteworthy that the Court in *Ex parte Quirin*, 317 U.S. 1 (1942), looked beyond Congress' declaration of war and accompanying authorization for use of force during World War II, and relied instead on Article of War 15 to find that Congress had authorized the use of military commissions in some circumstances. Justice Thomas' assertion that we commit "error" in reading Article 21 of the UCMJ to place limitations upon the President's use of military commissions ignores the reasoning in *Quirin*.

B. Trial by Military Commission After 9/11

military government over occupied enemy territory or territory regained from an enemy where civilian government cannot and does not function." *Duncan,* 327 U.S., at 314; see *Milligan,* 4 Wall., at 141-142 (Chase, C.J., concurring in judgment) (distinguishing "martial law proper" from "military government" in occupied territory)....

The third type of commission, convened as an "incident to the conduct of war" when there is a need "to seize and subject to disciplinary measures those enemies who in their attempt to thwart or impede our military effort have violated the law of war," *Quirin,* 317 U.S., at 28-29, has been described as "utterly different" from the other two. Not only is its jurisdiction limited to offenses cognizable during time of war, but its role is primarily a factfinding one — to determine, typically on the battlefield itself, whether the defendant has violated the law of war. The last time the U.S. Armed Forces used the law-of-war military commission was during World War II. In *Quirin,* this Court sanctioned President Roosevelt's use of such a tribunal to try Nazi saboteurs captured on American soil during the War. 317 U.S. 1. And in *Yamashita,* we held that a military commission had jurisdiction to try a Japanese commander for failing to prevent troops under his command from committing atrocities in the Philippines. 327 U.S. 1.

Quirin is the model the Government invokes most frequently to defend the commission convened to try Hamdan. That is both appropriate and unsurprising. Since Guantanamo Bay is neither enemy-occupied territory nor under martial law, the law-of-war commission is the only model available. At the same time, no more robust model of executive power exists; *Quirin* represents the high-water mark of military power to try enemy combatants for war crimes.

The classic treatise penned by Colonel William Winthrop, whom we have called "the 'Blackstone of Military Law,' " *Reid v. Covert,* 354 U.S. 1, 19, n.38 (1957) (plurality opinion), describes at least four preconditions for exercise of jurisdiction by a tribunal of the type convened to try Hamdan. First, "[a] military commission, (except where otherwise authorized by statute), can legally assume jurisdiction only of offenses committed within the field of the command of the convening commander." Winthrop 836. The "field of command" in these circumstances means the "theatre of war." *Ibid.* Second, the offense charged "must have been committed within the period of the war." *Id.,* at 837. No jurisdiction exists to try offenses "committed either before or after the war." *Ibid.* Third, a military commission not established pursuant to martial law or an occupation may try only "[i]ndividuals of the enemy's army who have been guilty of illegitimate warfare or other offences in violation of the laws of war" and members of one's own army "who, in time of war, become chargeable with crimes or offences not cognizable, or triable, by the criminal courts or under the Articles of war." *Id.,* at 838. Finally, a law-of-war commission has jurisdiction to try only two kinds of offense: "Violations of the laws and usages of war cognizable by military tribunals only," and "[b]reaches of military orders or regulations for which offenders are not legally triable by court-martial under the Articles of war." *Id.,* at 839....

...The question is whether the preconditions designed to ensure that a military necessity exists to justify the use of this extraordinary tribunal have been satisfied here.

The charge against Hamdan...alleges a conspiracy extending over a number of years, from 1996 to November 2001.[30] All but two months of that more than 5-year-long period preceded the attacks of September 11, 2001, and the enactment of the AUMF—the Act of Congress on which the Government relies for exercise of its war powers and thus for its authority to convene military commissions.[31] Neither the purported agreement with Osama bin Laden and others to commit war crimes, nor a single overt act, is alleged to have occurred in a theater of war or on any specified date after September 11, 2001. None of the overt acts that Hamdan is alleged to have committed violates the law of war.

These facts alone cast doubt on the legality of the charge and, hence, the commission; as Winthrop makes plain, the offense alleged must have been committed both in a theater of war and *during,* not before, the relevant conflict. But the deficiencies in the time and place allegations also underscore—indeed are symptomatic of—the most serious defect of this charge: The offense it alleges is not triable by law-of-war military commission.

There is no suggestion that Congress has, in exercise of its constitutional authority to "define and punish... Offences against the Law of Nations," U.S. Const., Art. I, §8, cl. 10, positively identified "conspiracy" as a war crime. As we explained in *Quirin,* that is not necessarily fatal to the Government's claim of authority to try the alleged offense by military commission; Congress, through Article 21 of the UCMJ, has "incorporated by reference" the common law of war, which may render triable by military commission certain offenses not defined by statute. 317 U.S., at 30. When, however, neither the elements of the offense nor the range of permissible punishments is defined by statute or treaty, the precedent must be plain and unambiguous. To demand any less would be to risk concentrating in military hands a degree of adjudicative and punitive power in excess of that contemplated either by statute or by the Constitution....

At a minimum, the Government must make a substantial showing that the crime for which it seeks to try a defendant by military commission is acknowledged to be an offense against the law of war. That burden is far from satisfied here. The crime of "conspiracy" has rarely if ever been tried as such in this country by any law-of-war military commission not exercising some other form of jurisdiction, and does not appear in either the Geneva Conventions or the Hague Conventions—the major treaties on the law of war....

...[T]he only "conspiracy" crimes that have been recognized by international war crimes tribunals (whose jurisdiction often extends beyond war crimes proper to crimes against humanity and crimes against the peace)

---

30. The elements of this conspiracy charge have been defined not by Congress but by the President. See Military Commission Instruction No. 2, 32 C.F.R. §11.6 (2005).

31. Justice Thomas would treat Osama bin Laden's 1996 declaration of jihad against Americans as the inception of the war. But even the Government does not go so far; although the United States had for some time prior to the attacks of September 11, 2001, been aggressively pursuing al Qaeda, neither in the charging document nor in submissions before this Court has the Government asserted that the President's *war powers* were activated prior to September 11, 2001. Justice Thomas' further argument that the AUMF is "backward looking" and therefore authorizes *trial by military commission* of crimes that occurred prior to the inception of war is insupportable. If nothing else, Article 21 of the UCMJ requires that the President comply with the law of war in his use of military commissions. As explained in the text, the law of war permits trial only of offenses "committed within the period of the war." Winthrop 837; see also *Quirin,* 317 U.S., at 28-29 (observing that law-of-war military commissions may be used to try "those enemies *who in their attempt to thwart or impede our military effort* have violated the law of war" (emphasis added))....

B. Trial by Military Commission After 9/11

are conspiracy to commit genocide and common plan to wage aggressive war, which is a crime against the peace and requires for its commission actual participation in a "concrete plan to wage war." 1 Trial of the Major War Criminals Before the International Military Tribunal: Nuremberg, 14 November 1945-1 October 1946, p. 225 (1947)....

In sum, the sources that the Government and Justice Thomas rely upon to show that conspiracy to violate the law of war is itself a violation of the law of war in fact demonstrate quite the opposite. Far from making the requisite substantial showing, the Government has failed even to offer a "merely colorable" case for inclusion of conspiracy among those offenses cognizable by law-of-war military commission. Cf. *Quirin*, 317 U.S., at 36. Because the charge does not support the commission's jurisdiction, the commission lacks authority to try Hamdan.

The charge's shortcomings are not merely formal, but are indicative of a broader inability on the Executive's part here to satisfy the most basic precondition—at least in the absence of specific congressional authorization—for establishment of military commissions: military necessity. Hamdan's tribunal was appointed not by a military commander in the field of battle, but by a retired major general stationed away from any active hostilities. Cf. *Rasul v. Bush*, 542 U.S., at 487 (Kennedy, J., concurring in judgment) (observing that "Guantanamo Bay is... far removed from any hostilities"). Hamdan is charged not with an overt act for which he was caught redhanded in a theater of war and which military efficiency demands be tried expeditiously, but with an *agreement* the inception of which long predated the attacks of September 11, 2001 and the AUMF. That may well be a crime,[41] but it is not an offense that "by the law of war may be tried by military commissio[n]." 10 U.S.C. §821. None of the overt acts alleged to have been committed in furtherance of the agreement is itself a war crime, or even necessarily occurred during time of, or in a theater of, war. Any urgent need for imposition or execution of judgment is utterly belied by the record; Hamdan was arrested in November 2001 and he was not charged until mid-2004. These simply are not the circumstances in which, by any stretch of the historical evidence or this Court's precedents, a military commission established by Executive Order under the authority of Article 21 of the UCMJ may lawfully try a person and subject him to punishment.

VI

Whether or not the Government has charged Hamdan with an offense against the law of war cognizable by military commission, the commission lacks power to proceed. The UCMJ conditions the President's use of military commissions on compliance not only with the American common law of war, but also with the rest of the UCMJ itself, insofar as applicable, and with the "rules and precepts of the law of nations," *Quirin*, 317 U.S., at 28—including, *inter alia*,

---

41. Justice Thomas' suggestion that our conclusion precludes the Government from bringing to justice those who conspire to commit acts of terrorism is therefore wide of the mark. That conspiracy is not a violation of the law of war triable by military commission does not mean the Government may not, for example, prosecute by court-martial or in federal court those caught "plotting terrorist atrocities like the bombing of the Khobar Towers."

the four Geneva Conventions signed in 1949. The procedures that the Government has decreed will govern Hamdan's trial by commission violate these laws.

A

The commission's procedures are set forth in Commission Order No. 1, which was amended most recently on August 31, 2005—after Hamdan's trial had already begun. Every commission established pursuant to Commission Order No. 1 must have a presiding officer and at least three other members, all of whom must be commissioned officers. §4(A)(1). The presiding officer's job is to rule on questions of law and other evidentiary and interlocutory issues; the other members make findings and, if applicable, sentencing decisions. §4(A)(5). The accused is entitled to appointed military counsel and may hire civilian counsel at his own expense so long as such counsel is a U.S. citizen with security clearance "at the level SECRET or higher." §§4(C)(2)-(3).

The accused also is entitled to a copy of the charge(s) against him, both in English and his own language (if different), to a presumption of innocence, and to certain other rights typically afforded criminal defendants in civilian courts and courts-martial. See §§5(A)-(P). These rights are subject, however, to one glaring condition: The accused and his civilian counsel may be excluded from, and precluded from ever learning what evidence was presented during, any part of the proceeding that either the Appointing Authority or the presiding officer decides to "close." Grounds for such closure "include the protection of information classified or classifiable...; information protected by law or rule from unauthorized disclosure; the physical safety of participants in Commission proceedings, including prospective witnesses; intelligence and law enforcement sources, methods, or activities; and other national security interests." §6(B)(3). Appointed military defense counsel must be privy to these closed sessions, but may, at the presiding officer's discretion, be forbidden to reveal to his or her client what took place therein. *Ibid.*

Another striking feature of the rules governing Hamdan's commission is that they permit the admission of *any* evidence that, in the opinion of the presiding officer, "would have probative value to a reasonable person." §6(D)(1). Under this test, not only is testimonial hearsay and evidence obtained through coercion fully admissible, but neither live testimony nor witnesses' written statements need be sworn. See §§6(D)(2)(b), (3). Moreover, the accused and his civilian counsel may be denied access to evidence in the form of "protected information" (which includes classified information as well as "information protected by law or rule from unauthorized disclosure" and "information concerning other national security interests," §§6(B)(3), 6(D)(5)(a)(v)), so long as the presiding officer concludes that the evidence is "probative" under §6(D)(1) and that its admission without the accused's knowledge would not "result in the denial of a full and fair trial." §6(D)(5)(b).[43] Finally,

---

43. As the District Court observed, this section apparently permits reception of testimony from a confidential informant in circumstances where "Hamdan will not be permitted to hear the testimony, see the witness's face, or learn his name. If the government has information developed by interrogation of witnesses in Afghanistan or elsewhere, it can offer such evidence in transcript form, or even as summaries of transcripts." 344 F. Supp. 2d 152, 168 (D.D.C. 2004).

B. Trial by Military Commission After 9/11

a presiding officer's determination that evidence "would not have probative value to a reasonable person" may be overridden by a majority of the other commission members. §6(D)(1).

Once all the evidence is in, the commission members (not including the presiding officer) must vote on the accused's guilt. A two-thirds vote will suffice for both a verdict of guilty and for imposition of any sentence not including death (the imposition of which requires a unanimous vote). §6(F). Any appeal is taken to a three-member review panel composed of military officers and designated by the Secretary of Defense, only one member of which need have experience as a judge. §6(H)(4). The review panel is directed to "disregard any variance from procedures specified in this Order or elsewhere that would not materially have affected the outcome of the trial before the Commission." *Ibid.* Once the panel makes its recommendation to the Secretary of Defense, the Secretary can either remand for further proceedings or forward the record to the President with his recommendation as to final disposition. §6(H)(5). The President then, unless he has delegated the task to the Secretary, makes the "final decision." §6(H)(6). He may change the commission's findings or sentence only in a manner favorable to the accused. *Ibid.* ...

C

In part because the difference between military commissions and courts-martial originally was a difference of jurisdiction alone, and in part to protect against abuse and ensure evenhandedness under the pressures of war, the procedures governing trials by military commission historically have been the same as those governing courts-martial....

The uniformity principle is not an inflexible one; it does not preclude all departures from the procedures dictated for use by courts-martial. But any departure must be tailored to the exigency that necessitates it. See Winthrop 835, n.81. That understanding is reflected in Article 36 of the UCMJ, which provides:

> "(a) The procedure, including modes of proof, in cases before courts-martial, courts of inquiry, military commissions, and other military tribunals may be prescribed by the President by regulations which shall, so far as he considers practicable, apply the principles of law and the rules of evidence generally recognized in the trial of criminal cases in the United States district courts, but which may not be contrary to or inconsistent with this chapter.
>
> "(b) All rules and regulations made under this article shall be uniform insofar as practicable and shall be reported to Congress." 70A Stat. 50.

Article 36 places two restrictions on the President's power to promulgate rules of procedure for courts-martial and military commissions alike. First, no procedural rule he adopts may be "contrary to or inconsistent with" the UCMJ—however practical it may seem. Second, the rules adopted must be "uniform insofar as practicable." That is, the rules applied to military commissions must be the same as those applied to courts-martial unless such uniformity proves impracticable....

... Without reaching the question whether any provision of Commission Order No. 1 is strictly "contrary to or inconsistent with" other provisions of the UCMJ, we conclude that the "practicability" determination the President has made is insufficient to justify variances from the procedures governing courts-martial. Subsection (b) of Article 36 was added after World War II, and requires a different showing of impracticability from the one required by subsection (a). Subsection (a) requires that the rules the President promulgates for courts-martial, provost courts, and military commissions alike conform to those that govern procedures in *Article III courts,* "so far as *he considers* practicable." 10 U.S.C. §836(a) (emphasis added). Subsection (b), by contrast, demands that the rules applied in courts-martial, provost courts, and military commissions — whether or not they conform with the Federal Rules of Evidence — be "uniform *insofar as practicable.*" §836(b) (emphasis added). Under the latter provision, then, the rules set forth in the Manual for Courts-Martial must apply to military commissions unless impracticable.

The President here has determined, pursuant to subsection (a), that it is impracticable to apply the rules and principles of law that govern "the trial of criminal cases in the United States district courts," §836(a), to Hamdan's commission. We assume that complete deference is owed that determination. The President has not, however, made a similar official determination that it is impracticable to apply the rules for courts-martial. And even if subsection (b)'s requirements may be satisfied without such an official determination, the requirements of that subsection are not satisfied here.

Nothing in the record before us demonstrates that it would be impracticable to apply court-martial rules in this case. There is no suggestion, for example, of any logistical difficulty in securing properly sworn and authenticated evidence or in applying the usual principles of relevance and admissibility. Assuming *arguendo* that the reasons articulated in the President's Article 36(a) determination ought to be considered in evaluating the impracticability of applying court-martial rules, the only reason offered in support of that determination is the danger posed by international terrorism. Without for one moment underestimating that danger, it is not evident to us why it should require, in the case of Hamdan's trial, any variance from the rules that govern courts-martial.

The absence of any showing of impracticability is particularly disturbing when considered in light of the clear and admitted failure to apply one of the most fundamental protections afforded not just by the Manual for Courts-Martial but also by the UCMJ itself: the right to be present. See 10 U.S.C.A. §839(c) (Supp. 2006). Whether or not that departure technically is "contrary to or inconsistent with" the terms of the UCMJ, 10 U.S.C. §836(a), the jettisoning of so basic a right cannot lightly be excused as "practicable."

Under the circumstances, then, the rules applicable in courts-martial must apply. Since it is undisputed that Commission Order No. 1 deviates in many significant respects from those rules, it necessarily violates Article 36(b).

The Government's objection that requiring compliance with the court-martial rules imposes an undue burden both ignores the plain meaning of Article 36(b) and misunderstands the purpose and the history of military commissions. The military commission was not born of a desire to dispense a more summary form of justice than is afforded by courts-martial; it developed, rather, as a tribunal of necessity to be employed when courts-martial lacked jurisdiction over either the accused or the subject matter. See Winthrop 831. Exigency lent the commission its legitimacy, but did not further justify the wholesale jettisoning of procedural protections. That history explains why the military commission's procedures typically have been the ones used by courts-martial. That the jurisdiction of the two tribunals today may sometimes overlap does not detract from the force of this history. Article 21 did not transform the military commission from a tribunal of true exigency into a more convenient adjudicatory tool. Article 36, confirming as much, strikes a careful balance between uniform procedure and the need to accommodate exigencies that may sometimes arise in a theater of war. That Article not having been complied with here, the rules specified for Hamdan's trial are illegal.

D

The procedures adopted to try Hamdan also violate the Geneva Conventions. The Court of Appeals dismissed Hamdan's Geneva Convention challenge on three independent grounds: (1) the Geneva Conventions are not judicially enforceable; (2) Hamdan in any event is not entitled to their protections; and (3) even if he is entitled to their protections, ... abstention is appropriate. ...

i ...

... We may assume that "the obvious scheme" of the 1949 Conventions is identical in all relevant respects to that of the 1929 Convention,[57] and even that that scheme would, absent some other provision of law, preclude Hamdan's invocation of the Convention's provisions as an independent source of law binding the Government's actions and furnishing petitioner with any enforceable right. For, regardless of the nature of the rights conferred on Hamdan, cf. *United States v. Rauscher,* 119 U.S. 407 (1886), they are, as the Government does not dispute, part of the law of war. And compliance with the law of war is the condition upon which the authority set forth in Article 21 is granted.

ii ...

The conflict with al Qaeda is not, according to the Government, a conflict to which the full protections afforded detainees under the 1949 Geneva Conventions apply because Article 2 of those Conventions (which appears in all four Conventions) renders the full protections applicable only to "all cases of declared war or of any other armed conflict which may arise between two or more of the High Contracting Parties." 6 U.S.T., at 3318. Since Hamdan was captured and detained incident to the conflict with al Qaeda and not the conflict with the Taliban, and since al Qaeda, unlike Afghanistan, is not a "High

---

57. But see, *e.g.,* 4 Int'l Comm. of Red Cross, Commentary: Geneva Convention Relative to the Protection of Civilian Persons in Time of War 21 (1958) (hereinafter GCIV Commentary) (the 1949 Geneva Conventions were written "first and foremost to protect individuals, and not to serve State interests"); GCIII Commentary 91 ("It was not ... until the Conventions of 1949 ... that the existence of 'rights' conferred in prisoners of war was affirmed").

Contracting Party" — *i.e.,* a signatory of the Conventions, the protections of those Conventions are not, it is argued, applicable to Hamdan.[60]

We need not decide the merits of this argument because there is at least one provision of the Geneva Conventions that applies here even if the relevant conflict is not one between signatories. Article 3, often referred to as Common Article 3 because, like Article 2, it appears in all four Geneva Conventions, provides that in a "conflict not of an international character occurring in the territory of one of the High Contracting Parties, each Party to the conflict shall be bound to apply, as a minimum," certain provisions protecting "[p]ersons taking no active part in the hostilities, including members of armed forces who have laid down their arms and those placed *hors de combat* by . . . detention." *Id.,* at 3318. One such provision prohibits "the passing of sentences and the carrying out of executions without previous judgment pronounced by a regularly constituted court affording all the judicial guarantees which are recognized as indispensable by civilized peoples." *Ibid.*

The Court of Appeals thought, and the Government asserts, that Common Article 3 does not apply to Hamdan because the conflict with al Qaeda, being "'international in scope,'" does not qualify as a "'conflict not of an international character.'" That reasoning is erroneous. The term "conflict not of an international character" is used here in contradistinction to a conflict between nations. So much is demonstrated by the "fundamental logic [of] the Convention's provisions on its application." [415 F.3d 33, 44 (D.C. Cir. 2005) (Williams, J., concurring).] Common Article 2 provides that "the present Convention shall apply to all cases of declared war or of any other armed conflict which may arise between two or more of the High Contracting Parties." 6 U.S.T., at 3318 (Art. 2, ¶1). High Contracting Parties (signatories) also must abide by all terms of the Conventions vis-à-vis one another even if one party to the conflict is a nonsignatory "Power," and must so abide vis-à-vis the nonsignatory if "the latter accepts and applies" those terms. *Ibid.* (Art. 2, ¶3). Common Article 3, by contrast, affords some minimal protection, falling short of full protection under the Conventions, to individuals associated with neither a signatory nor even a nonsignatory "Power" who are involved in a conflict "in the territory of" a signatory. The latter kind of conflict is distinguishable from the conflict described in Common Article 2 chiefly because it does not involve a clash between nations (whether signatories or not). In context, then, the phrase "not of an international character" bears its literal meaning. See, *e.g.,* J. Bentham, Introduction to the Principles of Morals and Legislation 6, 296 (J. Burns & H. Hart eds. 1970) (using the term "international law" as a "new though not inexpressive appellation" meaning "betwixt nation and nation"; defining "international" to include "mutual transactions between sovereigns as such"). . . .

iii

Common Article 3, then, is applicable here and, as indicated above, requires that Hamdan be tried by a "regularly constituted court affording all

---

60. The President has stated that the conflict with the Taliban is a conflict to which the Geneva Conventions apply.

the judicial guarantees which are recognized as indispensable by civilized peoples." 6 U.S.T., at 3320 (Art. 3, ¶1(d)). While the term "regularly constituted court" is not specifically defined in either Common Article 3 or its accompanying commentary, other sources disclose its core meaning. The commentary accompanying a provision of the Fourth Geneva Convention, for example, defines "'regularly constituted'" tribunals to include "ordinary military courts" and "definitely exclud[e] all special tribunals." GCIV Commentary 340 (defining the term "properly constituted" in Article 66, which the commentary treats as identical to "regularly constituted")....

The Government offers only a cursory defense of Hamdan's military commission in light of Common Article 3. As Justice Kennedy explains, that defense fails because "[t]he regular military courts in our system are the courts-martial established by congressional statutes." At a minimum, a military commission "can be 'regularly constituted' by the standards of our military justice system only if some practical need explains deviations from court-martial practice." As we have explained, see Part VI-C, *supra*, no such need has been demonstrated here.

iv

Inextricably intertwined with the question of regular constitution is the evaluation of the procedures governing the tribunal and whether they afford "all the judicial guarantees which are recognized as indispensable by civilized peoples." 6 U.S.T., at 3320 (Art. 3, ¶1(d)). Like the phrase "regularly constituted court," this phrase is not defined in the text of the Geneva Conventions. But it must be understood to incorporate at least the barest of those trial protections that have been recognized by customary international law....

We agree with Justice Kennedy that the procedures adopted to try Hamdan deviate from those governing courts-martial in ways not justified by any "evident practical need," and for that reason, at least, fail to afford the requisite guarantees. We add only that, as noted in Part VI-A, *supra*, various provisions of Commission Order No. 1 dispense with the principles, articulated in Article 75 [of Protocol I to the Geneva Conventions of 1949, June 8, 1977, 1125 U.N.T.S. 3, 16 I.L.M. 1391] and indisputably part of the customary international law, that an accused must, absent disruptive conduct or consent, be present for his trial and must be privy to the evidence against him. See §§6(B)(3), (D). That the Government has a compelling interest in denying Hamdan access to certain sensitive information is not doubted. But, at least absent express statutory provision to the contrary, information used to convict a person of a crime must be disclosed to him....

VII

We have assumed, as we must, that the allegations made in the Government's charge against Hamdan are true. We have assumed, moreover, the truth of the message implicit in that charge—viz., that Hamdan is a dangerous individual whose beliefs, if acted upon, would cause great harm and even death to innocent civilians, and who would act upon those beliefs if given the opportunity. It bears emphasizing that Hamdan does not challenge, and we do not today address, the Government's power to detain him for the duration of active hostilities in order to prevent such harm. But in undertaking to try Hamdan and subject him to criminal punishment, the Executive is bound to comply with the Rule of Law that prevails in this jurisdiction.

The judgment of the Court of Appeals is reversed, and the case is remanded for further proceedings.

It is so ordered.

THE CHIEF JUSTICE took no part in the consideration or decision of this case.

JUSTICE BREYER, with whom JUSTICE KENNEDY, JUSTICE SOUTER, and JUSTICE GINSBURG join, concurring. The dissenters say that today's decision would "sorely hamper the President's ability to confront and defeat a new and deadly enemy." They suggest that it undermines our Nation's ability to "preven[t] future attacks" of the grievous sort that we have already suffered. That claim leads me to state briefly what I believe the majority sets forth both explicitly and implicitly at greater length. The Court's conclusion ultimately rests upon a single ground: Congress has not issued the Executive a "blank check." Cf. *Hamdi v. Rumsfeld*, 542 U.S. 507, 536 (2004) (plurality opinion). Indeed, Congress has denied the President the legislative authority to create military commissions of the kind at issue here. Nothing prevents the President from returning to Congress to seek the authority he believes necessary.

Where, as here, no emergency prevents consultation with Congress, judicial insistence upon that consultation does not weaken our Nation's ability to deal with danger. To the contrary, that insistence strengthens the Nation's ability to determine — through democratic means — how best to do so. The Constitution places its faith in those democratic means. Our Court today simply does the same.

JUSTICE KENNEDY, with whom JUSTICE SOUTER, JUSTICE GINSBURG, and JUSTICE BREYER join as to Parts I and II, concurring in part. Military Commission Order No. 1, which governs the military commission established to try petitioner Salim Hamdan for war crimes, exceeds limits that certain statutes, duly enacted by Congress, have placed on the President's authority to convene military courts. This is not a case, then, where the Executive can assert some unilateral authority to fill a void left by congressional inaction. It is a case where Congress, in the proper exercise of its powers as an independent branch of government, and as part of a long tradition of legislative involvement in matters of military justice, has considered the subject of military tribunals and set limits on the President's authority. Where a statute provides the conditions for the exercise of governmental power, its requirements are the result of a deliberative and reflective process engaging both of the political branches. Respect for laws derived from the customary operation of the Executive and Legislative Branches gives some assurance of stability in time of crisis. The Constitution is best preserved by reliance on standards tested over time and insulated from the pressures of the moment....

I join the Court's opinion, save Parts V and VI-D-iv. To state my reasons for this reservation, and to show my agreement with the remainder of the Court's analysis by identifying particular deficiencies in the military commissions at issue, this separate opinion seems appropriate.

I

Trial by military commission raises separation-of-powers concerns of the highest order. Located within a single branch, these courts carry the risk that offenses will be defined, prosecuted, and adjudicated by executive officials without independent review. Concentration of power puts personal liberty in peril of arbitrary action by officials, an incursion the Constitution's three-part system is designed to avoid. It is imperative, then, that when military tribunals are established, full and proper authority exists for the Presidential directive. . . .

II . . .

These structural differences between the military commissions and courts-martial — the concentration of functions, including legal decisionmaking, in a single executive official; the less rigorous standards for composition of the tribunal; and the creation of special review procedures in place of institutions created and regulated by Congress — remove safeguards that are important to the fairness of the proceedings and the independence of the court. Congress has prescribed these guarantees for courts-martial; and no evident practical need explains the departures here. For these reasons the commission cannot be considered regularly constituted under United States law and thus does not satisfy Congress' requirement that military commissions conform to the law of war.

Apart from these structural issues, moreover, the basic procedures for the commissions deviate from procedures for courts-martial, in violation of §836(b). As the Court explains, the Military Commission Order abandons the detailed Military Rules of Evidence, which are modeled on the Federal Rules of Evidence in conformity with §836(a)'s requirement of presumptive compliance with district-court rules. . . .

In sum, as presently structured, Hamdan's military commission exceeds the bounds Congress has placed on the President's authority in §§836 and 821 of the UCMJ. Because Congress has prescribed these limits, Congress can change them, requiring a new analysis consistent with the Constitution and other governing laws. At this time, however, we must apply the standards Congress has provided. By those standards the military commission is deficient.

III

In light of the conclusion that the military commission here is unauthorized under the UCMJ, I see no need to consider several further issues addressed in the plurality opinion by Justice Stevens and the dissent by Justice Thomas. . . .

JUSTICE SCALIA, with whom JUSTICE THOMAS and JUSTICE ALITO join, dissenting.... [Justice Scalia found that the DTA deprived the Court of jurisdiction to hear Hamdan's case at this time. He then considered, assuming that the Court had jurisdiction, whether it should abstain from exercising it.]

... The principal opinion on the merits makes clear that it does not believe that the trials by military commission involve any "military necessity" *at all:* "The charge's shortcomings... are indicative of a broader inability on the Executive's part here to satisfy the most basic precondition... for establishment of military commissions: military necessity." This is quite at odds with the views on this subject expressed by our political branches. Because of "military necessity," a joint session of Congress authorized the President to "use all necessary and appropriate force," including military commissions, "against those nations, organizations, or persons [such as petitioner] he determines planned, authorized, committed, or aided the terrorist attacks that occurred on September 11, 2001." Authorization for Use of Military Force, §2(a), 115 Stat. 224, note following 50 U.S.C. §1541 (2000 ed., Supp. III). In keeping with this authority, the President has determined that "[t]o protect the United States and its citizens, and for the effective conduct of military operations and prevention of terrorist attacks, it is necessary for individuals subject to this order... to be detained, and, when tried, to be tried for violations of the laws of war and other applicable laws by military tribunals." Military Order of Nov. 13, 2001, 3 C.F.R. §918(e) (2002). It is not clear where the Court derives the authority—or the audacity—to contradict this determination. If "military necessities" relating to "duty" and "discipline" required abstention in *Councilman, supra,* at 757, military necessities relating to the disabling, deterrence, and punishment of the mass-murdering terrorists of September 11 require abstention all the more here.

The Court further seeks to distinguish *Councilman* on the ground that "the tribunal convened to try Hamdan is not part of the integrated system of military courts, complete with independent review panels, that Congress has established."...

Even if we were to accept the Court's extraordinary assumption that the President "lack[s] the structural insulation from military influence that characterizes the Court of Appeals for the Armed Forces,"[8] the Court's description of the review scheme here is anachronistic. As of December 30, 2005, the "fina[l]" review of decisions by military commissions is now conducted by the D.C. Circuit pursuant to §1005(e)(3) of the DTA, and by this Court under 28 U.S.C. §1254(1). This provision for review by Article III courts creates, if anything, a review scheme *more* insulated from Executive control than that in *Councilman*....

Moreover, a third consideration counsels strongly in favor of abstention in this case.... Here, apparently for the first time in history, a District Court enjoined ongoing military commission proceedings, which had been deemed "necessary" by the President "[t]o protect the United States and its citizens, and for the effective conduct of military operations and prevention of terrorist

---

8. The very purpose of Article II's creation of a *civilian* Commander in Chief in the President of the United States was to generate "structural insulation from military influence." See The Federalist No. 28 (A. Hamilton); *id.,* No. 69 (same). We do not live under a military junta. It is a disservice to both those in the Armed Forces and the President to suggest that the President is subject to the undue control of the military.

B. Trial by Military Commission After 9/11

attacks." Military Order of Nov. 13, 3 C.F.R. §918(e). Such an order brings the Judicial Branch into direct conflict with the Executive in an area where the Executive's competence is maximal and ours is virtually nonexistent. We should exercise our equitable discretion to *avoid* such conflict. Instead, the Court rushes headlong to meet it....

I would abstain from exercising our equity jurisdiction, as the Government requests....

JUSTICE THOMAS, with whom JUSTICE SCALIA joins, and with whom JUSTICE ALITO joins in all but parts I, II-C-1, and III-B-2, dissenting.... [T]he President's decision to try Hamdan before a military commission for his involvement with al Qaeda is entitled to a heavy measure of deference. In the present conflict, Congress has authorized the President "to use all necessary and appropriate force against those nations, organizations, or persons *he determines* planned, authorized, committed, or aided the terrorist attacks that occurred on September 11, 2001 ... in order to prevent any future acts of international terrorism against the United States by such nations, organizations or persons." Authorization for Use of Military Force (AUMF), 115 Stat. 224, note following 50 U.S.C. §1541 (2000 ed., Supp. III) (emphasis added). As a plurality of the Court observed in *Hamdi*, the "capture, detention, and *trial* of unlawful combatants, by 'universal agreement and practice,' are 'important incident[s] of war,'" *Hamdi*, 542 U.S., at 518 (quoting *Quirin, supra*, at 28, 30; emphasis added), and are therefore "an exercise of the 'necessary and appropriate force' Congress has authorized the President to use." *Hamdi*, 542 U.S., at 518; *id.*, at 587 (Thomas, J., dissenting). *Hamdi*'s observation that military commissions are included within the AUMF's authorization is supported by this Court's previous recognition that "[a]n important incident to the conduct of war is the adoption of measures by the military commander, not only to repel and defeat the enemy, but to seize and subject to disciplinary measures those enemies who, in their attempt to thwart or impede our military effort, have violated the law of war." *In re Yamashita*, 327 U.S. 1, 11 (1946)....

... Nothing in the language of Article 21 ... suggests that it outlines the entire reach of congressional authorization of military commissions in all conflicts—quite the contrary, the language of Article 21 presupposes the existence of military commissions under an independent basis of authorization. Indeed, consistent with *Hamdi*'s conclusion that the AUMF itself authorizes the trial of unlawful combatants, the original sanction for military commissions historically derived from congressional authorization of "the initiation of war" with its attendant authorization of "the employment of all necessary and proper agencies for its due prosecution." W. Winthrop, Military Law and Precedents 831 (2d ed. 1920) (hereinafter Winthrop). Accordingly, congressional authorization for military commissions pertaining to the instant conflict derives not only from Article 21 of the UCMJ, but also from the more recent, and broader, authorization contained in the AUMF.[2] ...

---

2. Although the President very well may have inherent authority to try unlawful combatants for violations of the law of war before military commissions, we need not decide that question because Congress has authorized the President to do so. Cf. *Hamdi v. Rumsfeld*, 542 U.S. 507, 587 (2004) (Thomas, J., dissenting) (same conclusion respecting detention of unlawful combatants).

II...

A

... [A] law-of-war military commission may only assume jurisdiction of "offences committed within the field of the command of the convening commander," and ... such offenses "must have been committed within the period of the war." See *id.*, at 836, 837. Here, as evidenced by Hamdan's charging document, the Executive has determined that the theater of the present conflict includes "Afghanistan, Pakistan and other countries" where al Qaeda has established training camps, and that the duration of that conflict dates back (at least) to Usama bin Laden's August 1996 "*Declaration of Jihad Against the Americans.*" Under the Executive's description of the conflict, then, every aspect of the charge, which alleges overt acts in "Afghanistan, Pakistan, Yemen and other countries" taking place from 1996 to 2001, satisfies the temporal and geographic prerequisites for the exercise of law-of-war military commission jurisdiction. And these judgments pertaining to the scope of the theater and duration of the present conflict are committed solely to the President in the exercise of his commander-in-chief authority. See [*The Prize Cases*, 67 U.S. (2 Black) 635, 670 (1863), *supra* p. 67] (concluding that the President's commander-in-chief judgment about the nature of a particular conflict was "a question to be decided *by him,* and this Court must be governed by the decisions and acts of the political department of the Government to which this power was entrusted")....

... The starting point of the present conflict (or indeed any conflict) is not determined by congressional enactment, but rather by the initiation of hostilities. See *Prize Cases, supra,* at 668 (recognizing that war may be initiated by "invasion of a foreign nation," and that such initiation, and the President's response, usually *precedes* congressional action). Thus, Congress' enactment of the AUMF did not mark the beginning of this Nation's conflict with al Qaeda, but instead authorized the President to use force in the midst of an ongoing conflict. Moreover, while the President's "war powers" may not have been activated until the AUMF was passed, the date of such activation has never been used to determine the scope of a military commission's jurisdiction.[3]...

---

3. Even if the formal declaration of war were generally the determinative act in ascertaining the temporal reach of the jurisdiction of a military commission, the AUMF itself is inconsistent with the plurality's suggestion that such a rule is appropriate in this case. The text of the AUMF is backward looking, authorizing the use of "all necessary and appropriate force against those nations, organizations, or persons he determines planned, authorized, committed, or aided the terrorist attacks that occurred on September 11, 2001." Thus, the President's decision to try Hamdan by military commission—a use of force authorized by the AUMF—for Hamdan's involvement with al Qaeda prior to September 11, 2001, fits comfortably within the framework of the AUMF. In fact, bringing the September 11 conspirators to justice is the *primary point* of the AUMF. By contrast, on the plurality's logic, the AUMF would not grant the President the authority to try Usama bin Laden himself for his involvement in the events of September 11, 2001.

B. Trial by Military Commission After 9/11

c

[Justice Thomas also concluded that, under the law of war, Hamdan could properly be charged with membership in a war-criminal enterprise and with conspiracy to commit war crimes.]

3

Ultimately, the plurality's determination that Hamdan has not been charged with an offense triable before a military commission rests not upon any historical example or authority, but upon the plurality's raw judgment of the "inability on the Executive's part here to satisfy the most basic precondition...for establishment of military commissions: military necessity." This judgment starkly confirms that the plurality has appointed itself the ultimate arbiter of what is quintessentially a policy and military judgment, namely, the appropriate military measures to take against those who "aided the terrorist attacks that occurred on September 11, 2001." AUMF §2(a), 115 Stat. 224. The plurality's suggestion that Hamdan's commission is illegitimate because it is not dispensing swift justice on the battlefield is unsupportable. Even a cursory review of the authorities confirms that law-of-war military commissions have wide-ranging jurisdiction to try offenses against the law of war in exigent and nonexigent circumstances alike. Traditionally, retributive justice for heinous war crimes is as much a "military necessity" as the "demands" of "military efficiency" touted by the plurality, and swift military retribution is precisely what Congress authorized the President to impose on the September 11 attackers in the AUMF.

Today a plurality of this Court would hold that conspiracy to massacre innocent civilians does not violate the laws of war. This determination is unsustainable. The judgment of the political branches that Hamdan, and others like him, must be held accountable before military commissions for their involvement with and membership in an unlawful organization dedicated to inflicting massive civilian casualties is supported by virtually every relevant authority, including all of the authorities invoked by the plurality today. It is also supported by the nature of the present conflict. We are not engaged in a traditional battle with a nation-state, but with a worldwide, hydra-headed enemy, who lurks in the shadows conspiring to reproduce the atrocities of September 11, 2001, and who has boasted of sending suicide bombers into civilian gatherings, has proudly distributed videotapes of beheadings of civilian workers, and has tortured and dismembered captured American soldiers. But according to the plurality, when our Armed Forces capture those who are plotting terrorist atrocities like the bombing of the Khobar Towers, the bombing of the U.S.S. *Cole*, and the attacks of September 11—even if their plots are advanced to the very brink of fulfillment—our military cannot charge those criminals with any offense against the laws of war. Instead, our troops must catch the terrorists "redhanded" in the midst of *the attack itself*, in order to bring them to justice. Not only is this conclusion fundamentally inconsistent with the cardinal principal of the law of war, namely protecting non-combatants, but it would sorely hamper the President's ability to confront and defeat a new and deadly enemy....

III

[Justice Thomas concluded that the Court should defer to the President's determination that court martial procedures are not "practicable" for military commissions and therefore reject any requirement for uniformity of procedures. He also concluded that Common Article 3 was not judicially enforceable; that, if it were, the Court should defer to the President's "reasonable" interpretation of Common Article 3 as inapplicable to the "international" conflict with al Qaeda; and, finally, that any claim Hamdan might have under Common Article 3 was not ripe.]

For these reasons, I would affirm the judgment of the Court of Appeals.

JUSTICE ALITO, with whom JUSTICES SCALIA and THOMAS join in parts I-III, dissenting. For the reasons set out in Justice Scalia's dissent, which I join, I would hold that we lack jurisdiction. On the merits, I join Justice Thomas' dissent with the exception of Parts I, II-C-1, and III-B-2, which concern matters that I find unnecessary to reach....

I...

In order to determine whether a court has been properly appointed, set up, or established, it is necessary to refer to a body of law that governs such matters. I interpret Common Article 3 as looking to the domestic law of the appointing country because I am not aware of any international law standard regarding the way in which such a court must be appointed, set up, or established, and because different countries with different government structures handle this matter differently. Accordingly, "a regularly constituted court" is a court that has been appointed, set up, or established in accordance with the domestic law of the appointing country....

III...

A...

In sum, I believe that Common Article 3 is satisfied here because the military commissions (1) qualify as courts, (2) that were appointed and established in accordance with domestic law, and (3) any procedural improprieties that might occur in particular cases can be reviewed in those cases.

B

The commentary on Common Article 3 supports this interpretation. The commentary on Common Article 3, ¶1(d)...states: "... *We must be very clear about one point: it is only 'summary' justice which it is intended to prohibit....*" GCIV Commentary 39 (emphasis added).

B. Trial by Military Commission After 9/11

It seems clear that the commissions at issue here meet this standard. Whatever else may be said about the system that was created by Military Commission Order No. 1 and augmented by the Detainee Treatment Act, §1005(e)(1), 119 Stat. 2742, this system—which features formal trial procedures, multiple levels of administrative review, and the opportunity for review by a United States Court of Appeals and by this Court—does not dispense "summary justice."

For these reasons, I respectfully dissent.

NOTES AND QUESTIONS

1. *Holding?* What, precisely, did *Hamdan* hold? Note that Justice Kennedy's vote is necessary to form a majority. Which parts of the decision are those of the plurality alone? Note also that the Chief Justice—who wrote the opinion for the Court of Appeals in *Hamdan*—did not participate. If he had, how might it have changed any of the Court's conclusions (not that our speculation would have much predictive power, in light of his or the dissenters' possible views about stare decisis)?

2. *Military Necessity Redux.* We saw in Chapter 26 that the military commission exception to the "preferred" method of civilian trial is justified by necessity. What is the necessity that the majority identified in *Hamdan*? Is it limited by time or place? Is it limited to acts for which a person is "caught redhanded in a theater of war and which military efficiency demands be tried expeditiously," as the plurality suggests? See *supra* p. 889. If so, is necessity a wasting justification? If necessity for trying Hamdan by military commission is no longer present, is there any necessity for continuing to detain him? What does the Court say and why? See *supra* p. 896.

Reread section 1 of the Military Order, especially section 1(e), *supra* p. 878. Has not the President already found military commissions necessary? Why doesn't the Court defer to his finding, as it did to the finding of military necessity in *Korematsu*, *supra* p. 704? Reread the AUMF, *supra* p. 100. Hasn't Congress found necessity and authorized the President to use all "necessary and appropriate force," as he determines? Why doesn't the Court defer to Congress? Which branch is best equipped to decide necessity?

When there is a "controlling necessity," does the President *need* any statutory authority to use military commissions? That is, does he have inherent authority to establish them? What does the majority say? What does Justice Thomas say? If so, is there any limit on that authority?

3. *Statutory Authority.* The Court does not reach the question of inherent presidential authority for military commissions because it found that Article 21 preserved or incorporated the common law of war authority for military commissions.

Recall that the Court found that the AUMF authorized the military detention of Yaser Hamdi. *See* Hamdi v. Rumsfeld, 542 U.S. 507 (2004), *supra* p. 721. Why does it not also authorize trial of Hamdan by military commission, especially since the AUMF was enacted after Article 21? Alternatively, why doesn't the DTA authorize such a trial?

4. *The Law-of-War Limits on Military Commissions.* Article 21 is a two-headed coin: if it incorporates the common law of war and thus authorizes military commissions, it also incorporates any jurisdictional and procedural limits set by that law. What are they? By what constitutional authority may Congress directly, or by implication, impose any limits on the President's use of military commissions?

One law-of-war limit is temporal — military commission jurisdiction is only for charges committed within the period of war. When did that period commence? If it commenced by attack, was the attack on 9/11 or on the earliest date that al Qaeda attacked U.S. persons or property? Is Justice Thomas correct in arguing that *The Prize Cases* commits this decision to the President's conclusive discretion? If Congress took a different view by enacting the AUMF and referring to the 9/11 attacks, which branch prevails? *See generally* Barbara Salazar Torreon, *Periods of War* (Cong. Res. Serv. RS21405), May 1, 2006.

5. *The UCMJ and the Uniformity Principle.* Article 36 of the UCMJ authorizes the President to prescribe procedures for military commissions. *See generally* Jennifer Elsea, *The Department of Defense Rules for Military Commissions: Analysis of Procedural Rules and Comparison with Proposed Legislation and the Uniform Code of Military Justice* (Cong. Res. Serv. RL31600), Jan. 18, 2005. What two restrictions does it place on the President's procedural power? Why were these restrictions not met by sections 1(f) and 1(g) of the Military Order of November 13, 2001? See *supra* pp. 878-879. If the President had simply added "or the procedures of courts-martial recognized by the UCMJ" at the end of section 2(f), would that have satisfied the restriction? If not, what else would he have to find?

6. *The Geneva Conventions.* International treaties also impose procedural law-of-war limitations on military commissions. The majority in *Hamdan* held that Common Article 3 of the Geneva Conventions of 1949 applied to the conflict with al Qaeda. It requires trial by a tribunal that is "regularly constituted . . . ." Why does the majority think that a military commission established by the President's military order and operating under procedures promulgated with his authority is not such a court? How are courts "regularly constituted" in the United States? Could a military commission ever be "regularly constituted"? What is Justice Alito's answer to these questions?

Common Article 3 also forbids "cruel treatment and torture," as well as "outrages upon personal dignity, in particular humiliating and degrading treatment." See *supra* pp. 768-769. Does Common Article 3 now clearly govern investigatory torture of persons captured in the conflict against al Qaeda, or can you distinguish *Hamdan*?

7. *Military Commission Procedures and Due Process.* In In re Yamashita, 327 U.S. 1 (1946), a military commission gave General Yamashita less than three weeks to prepare for a massive trial that ultimately heard more than 200 witnesses; the commission permitted the government to add 59 new specifications to the 64 pending specifications just two days before trial, then denied his

B. Trial by Military Commission After 9/11

defense any extra time to meet them; it denied Yamashita access to the Army's investigative reports, which might have contained exculpatory materials; it admitted the rankest hearsay; and it even cut back cross-examination "as a means of saving time." *See* Stephen B. Ives Jr., *Vengeance Did Not Deliver Justice,* Wash. Post, Dec. 30, 2001, at B2. Most observers concluded that Yamashita did not receive a fair trial, but the Supreme Court refused to review the commission's rulings on the evidence or its conduct of the proceedings and therefore found it "unnecessary to consider what, in other situations, the Fifth Amendment might require." *Yamashita,* 327 U.S. at 23.

Justice Murphy dissented vehemently:

> The immutable rights of the individual, including those secured by the due process clause of the Fifth Amendment, belong not alone to the members of those nations that excel on the battlefield or that subscribe to the democratic ideology. They belong to every person in the world, victor or vanquished, whatever may be his race, color or beliefs. They rise above any status of belligerency or outlawry. They survive any popular passion or frenzy of the moment. No court or legislature or executive, not even the mightiest army in the world, can destroy them....
>
> The failure of the military commission to obey the dictates of the due process requirements of the Fifth Amendment is apparent in this case.... No military necessity or other emergency demanded the suspension of the safeguards of due process. Yet petitioner was rushed to trial under an improper charge, given insufficient time to prepare an adequate defense, deprived of the benefits of some of the most elementary rules of evidence, and summarily sentenced to be hanged. [*Id.* at 27-28.]

Justice Rutledge agreed with Justice Murphy in dissent.

Does the Fifth Amendment apply to trial by military commission? Does it depend on where the defendant is captured or whether the military commission sits here or abroad? *See* Rasul v. Bush, 542 U.S. 466, 483 n.15 (2004), *supra* p. 692; Zadvydas v. Davis, 533 U.S. 678, 693 (2001) ("[T]he Due Process Clause applies to all 'persons' within the United States, including aliens, whether their presence here is lawful, temporary, or permanent."); *cf.* United States v. Verdugo-Urquidez, 494 U.S. 259 (1990), *supra* p. 643.

The district court found it unnecessary to reach the question whether Hamdan has any constitutional rights, although it noted that the Supreme Court's decision in *Rasul* "may contain some hint that non-citizens held at Guanánamo Bay have some Constitutional protection." 355 F. Supp. 2d 152, 173 n.19 (D.D.C. 2004), *rev'd,* 415 F.3d 33 (D.C. Cir. 2005), *rev'd and remanded,* 126 S. Ct. 2749 (2006). The question of Hamdan's right to due process, if any, was therefore not before the Supreme Court.

In In re Guantanamo Detainee Cases, 355 F. Supp. 2d 443 (D.D.C. 2005), however, Judge Joyce Hens Green found that the Due Process Clause applied to the procedures followed in Combatant Status Review Tribunals (CSRTs) for detainees held at the Guantánamo Bay Naval Base. *Contra,* Khalid v. Bush, 355 F. Supp. 2d 311 (D.D.C. 2005). If Judge Green is right, would it apply also to military commission trials held at Guantánamo Bay? She noted that the military commission procedures, unlike the CSRT procedures, authorize withholding of classified information only from the defendant, not from defense counsel. Would this difference save a commission hearing from a due process challenge, if due process applied to military commission proceedings?

A strict reading of the November 13 Military Order might suggest that military commissions could use information obtained through torture or coercion, if it "would have probative value to a reasonable person." Military Order of November 13, 2001, §4(c)(3), *supra* p. 399. If a military commission relies on such evidence, would it violate due process?

8. *Answering the Court's Call.* Congress responded to *Hamdan* by enacting the Military Commissions Act of 2006, Pub. L. No. 109-366, 120 Stat. 2600. The Act delegates authority to the President to establish military commissions to try unlawful enemy combatants, and it defines offenses triable by such commissions. It also amends the Uniform Code of Military Justice to establish procedures and rules of evidence for trial by military commissions. The Act excludes from such trials any statement obtained by torture, but it permits admission of some statements obtained by coercion if the totality of the circumstances renders the statement reliable and probative. While the Act provides limited post-trial administrative review and more limited subsequent review by the federal courts, it also strips all courts of habeas jurisdiction for petitions brought by enemy combatant detainees. In addition, it prohibits persons from invoking the Geneva Conventions as a source of rights in habeas or other civil proceedings to which the United States or its agents are party. Finally, it amends the War Crimes Act, 18 U.S.C. §2441 (*supra* p. 766) and declares that "[n]o foreign or international source of law shall supply a basis for a rule of decision in the courts of the United States interpreting" parts of that act. Pub. L. No. 109-366, §6(a)(2), 120 Stat. 2632. Indeed, it provides that the President may interpret the meaning and application of the Geneva Conventions by an executive order that shall be "authoritative." *Id.* §6(a)(3)(C), 120 Stat. 2632. Are the last provisions constitutionally vulnerable in light of the Supremacy Clause, Article III, and the materials on incorporation of international law in Chapter 7? More generally, does *Hamdan* leave room for constitutional challenges to trial by military commission now that Congress has expressly authorized such trial?.

Managing a WMD Attack —31

> America will become increasingly vulnerable to hostile attack on our homeland, and our military superiority will not protect us.... States, terrorists, and other disaffected groups will acquire weapons of mass destruction, and some will use them. Americans will likely die on American soil, possibly in large numbers.[1]

This grim prediction appeared in a 1999 federal commission report. It was tragically prescient, as the events of September 11, 2001, made clear. Long before the terrorist attacks on the World Trade Center and the Pentagon, however, the United States government had begun to develop extensive plans for a response to such an unhappy development. In earlier chapters we examined the elaborate federal apparatus for detecting and interdicting terrorist threats. Here we consider what to do if those prophylactic efforts fail.

Planning by all levels of government for a response to a weapon of mass destruction (WMD) attack has evolved rapidly since September 11, 2001. In this chapter we approach that response functionally. We begin with a broad look at the planning process, then consider a range of issues raised by a bioterrorist attack. Next we examine the roles of first responders — firefighters, police officers, EMTs, and others — who are necessarily first on the scene in a great emergency, even one that implicates national security. The federal government's plans and authorities are then assessed. Finally, we look at various restrictions on personal liberties (isolation, quarantine, vaccination) that may be required by the government's response to a WMD attack.

It should be noted that almost all the legal and practical issues considered in this chapter may be raised by government responses to other great emergencies, such as hurricanes or influenza pandemics. Such natural disasters may call for similar tactics using many of the same resources. They also may pose serious threats to national security.

---

1. United States Commn. on National Security/21st Century (Hart/Rudman Commission), *New World Coming: American Security in the 21st Century* 141 (1999).

A. THINKING THE UNTHINKABLE: PLANNING A RESPONSE TO A TERRORIST ATTACK

Is planning for a response to a terrorist attack a good idea, given the need for flexibility in responding to a great national crisis? Is it worth the considerable effort currently being devoted to it, especially considering the relatively low probability of an attack with chemical, biological, or radiological weapons? Is any conceivable plan likely to be effective in reducing the loss of life and property in light of the creativity of terrorists who would use airliners as weapons of mass destruction? If we do engage in planning, is there any reason to think that a future President will feel constrained by any plans if she is convinced that the threat of a terrorist attack is real, or if an attack has already created panic in the population?

Concerning the need for flexibility, legislatures and bureaucrats constantly engage in planning about a wide range of issues. These plans lend an element of predictability to government and enable us to lead more orderly and productive lives while at the same time leaving room for adjustments to accommodate currently unpredictable developments. Planning for the response to a terrorist attack is no different in principle from, say, zoning, involving as it does the same difficult judgments about just how much government officials should be constrained in the future by decisions we make today.

Will plans that we make now be followed in the crisis precipitated by a terrorist attack? We might hope that the President would do whatever is reasonably necessary to protect us — perhaps even declaring martial law or relying on some claim to inherent emergency power. Yet the potential for mischief — or mistake — is great. The President might exercise such awesome authority on the basis of erroneous information or when other less drastic alternatives are available. There could be no assurance of how that authority would be exercised or for how long. Unlike a declared war against a foreign state, a "war" against terrorists may have no clear end point: "emergency" authority for the "duration" could last indefinitely. And government officials would not be accountable for their actions during such an emergency, at least until some time later. Recall Justice Jackson's concern, in the *Steel Seizure Case*, supra p. 28, about the claim of inherent presidential powers *ex necessitate*.

One reason for planning, then, is that the more carefully we plan ahead and the more diligently we rehearse those plans, the more likely it is that in a great crisis the President will see adherence to the plan as a reasonable option and the more nearly the President's response will reflect deliberate choices we make now about how to strike the proper balance between physical security and civil liberties.

Another reason to plan carefully for a great emergency — especially for a terrorist attack — is that an effective response will require the cooperation of the public. During the Cold War, Americans became very familiar with this occasional radio and TV message:

> This is a test. This station is conducting a test of the Emergency Broadcasting System. This is only a test.
> [A tone is broadcast to trigger special receivers or alert listeners.]

> This is a test of the Emergency Broadcast System. The broadcasters of your area in voluntary cooperation with Federal, state, and local authorities have developed this system to keep you informed in the event of an emergency. If this had been an actual emergency, the Attention Signal you just heard would have been followed by official information, news, or instructions. This concludes this test of the Emergency Broadcast System.[2]

Without ever mentioning the possibility of a nuclear attack, it reminded us of the direst possible national emergency. But we were not told under what circumstances short of an actual attack the Emergency Broadcast System might be activated. Neither was it revealed what sort of instructions might be broadcast, or upon whose authority.

To achieve the necessary cooperation, members of the public must expect and understand that: (1) a program exists to deal effectively with the crisis, (2) the plan is legitimate, and (3) someone is in charge to execute the plan. Analyzing a simulated terrorist attack using a smallpox virus, a House subcommittee warned that the "slightest indication of ill preparation, confusion, or conflict among local, State, and Federal agencies—particularly federal—will lead our nation's citizens into a state of chaos and contribute to anarchy." *Combating Terrorism: Federal Response to a Biological Weapons Attack: Hearing Before the Subcomm. on National Affairs, Veterans Affairs, and Intl. Relations of the H. Comm. on Government Reform,* 107th Cong. 4 (2001). Public confidence will require public education (more than the Emergency Broadcast System tests or the single page the Federal Emergency Management Agency (FEMA) used to put in phone books to explain what to do in the event of a nuclear attack). It will also take reliable communications during an actual crisis. Moreover, citizen involvement in the planning process may promote public acceptance and actually improve the quality of the plan.

A third reason for planning is to "deter terrorism through a clear public position that our policies will not be affected by terrorist acts."[3] This goal can only be achieved if the "clear public position" is credible. In other words, a potential terrorist has to be convinced that his destructive acts will not precipitate a collapse of basic government structures, and convinced as well that the American people will not lose faith in their government even in the worst of times. Needless to say, the potential terrorist will be persuaded only if the American people are.

NOTES AND QUESTIONS

1. *Balancing Security and Liberty.* Finding the right balance between security and liberty in planning a response to a threatened or actual terrorist attack is especially daunting, because it is complicated by uncertainty about the timing

---

2. Federal Communications Commn., EBS Checklist 9 (1987). Although the warning system is still operational, it was not activated on September 11, 2001. Americans turned instead to CNN and broadcast media for information about the attacks.

3. Presidential Decision Directive 39 (PDD-39), *U.S. Policy on Counterterrorism* 3, June 21, 1995, *available at* http://www.fas.org/irp/offdocs/pdd39.htm (partially redacted).

and character of such an attack. Whom should we entrust with the responsibility for striking that balance? What do you know about the practical capabilities of the executive and legislative branches, respectively, that recommend them for the job?

2. *Transparency in Planning.* Planning for a response to a terrorist attack has always been conducted behind closed doors, and details of the plans themselves are closely guarded. Obviously, every detail cannot be made public, lest terrorists exploit those plans in mounting an attack. But where should the line be drawn between what to publicize and what to keep secret? And who should draw the line? Can you describe a planning process that would provide needed security and yet some measure of public accountability? What are the implications of these questions for democratic government?

B. A HYPOTHETICAL WORST-CASE SCENARIO

Thomas V. Inglesby, Rita Grossman & Tara O'Toole, A Plague on Your City: Observations from TOPOFF

32 Clinical Infectious Diseases 436 (2001)
available at http://www.journals.uchicago.edu/CID/journal/issues/v32n3/001347/001347.html

May 17: An aerosol of pneumonic plague (*Yersinia pestis*) bacilli is released covertly from a fire extinguisher at a benefit concert in the Denver Performing Arts Center.

May 20: The Colorado Department of Public Health and Environment receives information that increasing numbers of persons began seeking medical attention at Denver area hospitals for cough and fever during the evening of May 19th. By early afternoon on May 20, 500 persons with these symptoms have received medical care, and 25 of those have died.

The Health Department notifies the CDC of the increased volume of sick. Plague is identified first by the state laboratory and subsequently confirmed in a patient specimen by the CDC lab at Ft. Collins. A public health emergency is declared by the State Health Officer, who immediately requests support from DHHS's Office of Emergency Preparedness. The Governor's Emergency Epidemic Response Committee assembles to respond to the unfolding crisis.

Thirty-one CDC staff are sent to Denver. Hospitals and clinics around the Denver area that just a day earlier were dealing with what appeared to be an unusual increase in influenza cases are now recalling staffs, implementing emergency plans, and seeking assistance in determining treatment protocols and protective measures. By late afternoon, hospital staff are beginning to call in sick, and antibiotics and ventilators are becoming more scarce. Some hospital staff have donned respiratory protective equipment.

B. A Hypothetical Worst-Case Scenario

The CDC and the FBI are notified by Denver police that a dead man has been found with terrorist literature and paraphernalia in his possession; his cause of death is unknown.

The Governor issues an executive order that restricts travel—including bus, rail and air travel—into or out of 14 Denver Metro counties, and commandeers all antibiotics that can be used to prevent or treat plague. At a press conference, the Governor informs the public that there is a plague outbreak in Denver as a result of a terrorist attack, and he announces his executive order. Citizens are instructed to seek treatment at a medical facility if feeling ill or if they have been in contact with a known or suspected case of plague. Those who are well are directed to stay in their homes and avoid public gatherings. The public is told that the disease is spread from person to person only "if you are within 6 feet of someone who is infected and coughing," and told that dust masks are effective at preventing the spread of disease.

Confirmed cases of plague are identified in Colorado locations other than Denver. Patient interviews suggest that most victims were at the Performing Arts Center days earlier. It is announced that the Governor is working with the President of the United States to resolve the crisis and that federal resources are being brought in to support the state agencies. By the end of the day, 783 cases of pneumonic plague have occurred, and 123 persons have died.

May 21: Broadcast media report that a "national crash effort" is underway to move large quantities of antibiotics to the region, as the CDC brings in its "national stockpile," but the quantity of available antibiotics is uncertain. The report explains that early administration of antibiotics is effective in treating plague but that antibiotics must be started within 24 hours of developing symptoms. A news story a few hours later reports that hospitals are running out of antibiotics.

A shipment from the National Pharmaceutical Stockpile (NPS) arrives in Denver, but there are great difficulties moving antibiotics from the airport to the persons who need it for treatment and prophylaxis. Out-of-state cases begin to be reported. The CDC officially notifies bordering states of the epidemic. Cases are reported in England and Japan. Both Japan and the World Health Organization request technical assistance from the CDC.

A number of hospitals in Denver are full to capacity and by the end of the day are unable to see or admit new patients. Thirteen hundred ventilators from the NPS are flown to Colorado. Bodies in hospital morgues are reported to have reached critical levels. The U.S. Surgeon General flies to Colorado to facilitate communications. Many states now are requesting supplies from the NPS. By the end of the day, 1,871 plague cases have been diagnosed throughout the U.S. and abroad. Of these, 389 persons have died.

May 22: Hospitals are under-staffed and have insufficient antibiotics, ventilators, and beds to meet demand. They cannot manage the influx of sick patients into the hospitals. Medical care is "beginning to shut down" in Denver.

Officials from the Health Department and the CDC have determined that a secondary spread of disease is occurring. The population in Denver is encouraged to wear face masks. The CDC advises that Colorado state borders be cordoned off in order to limit further spread of plague throughout the U.S. and other countries. Colorado officials express concern about their ability to get food and supplies into the state. The Governor's executive order is extended to prohibit travel into or out of the state of Colorado. By noon, there are 3,060 U.S. and international cases of pneumonic plague, 795 of whom have died.

The following day, May 23, 2000, this frightening exercise, called TOP-OFF, was terminated. It had been organized by the Justice Department to test the ability of top officials at all levels of government to respond to a bioterrorist attack. Among the sobering results was the revelation that local health services — medical personnel, hospitals, and pharmaceutical supplies — were not nearly prepared to treat an outbreak of an infectious disease on such a large scale. Communications among local, state, and federal officials were unreliable. And responses were slowed by cumbersome decisionmaking processes or by a perception that no one was in charge. Other conclusions are described below.

> The unfolding situation precipitated a series of increasingly stringent containment measures. By the end of the first day, [a travel advisory was issued] . . . that restricted travel in 16 Denver Metro counties. . . . Some people, in fact, were reported to be racing out of the state. As part of the travel advisory, persons were advised to stay home unless they were close contacts of diagnosed cases or were feeling sick; in the case of the latter they were directed to seek medical care. . . . [T]he police and National Guard admitted . . . that they would be unable to keep people at home. . . . [B]y the end of the exercise, "people had been asked to stay in their homes for 72 hours. . . . How were they supposed to get food or medicine?"
>
> Throughout the unfolding epidemic, determining what information the public should be given and how quickly was an important and difficult issue. . . . It was clear that the public message itself would affect the capacity to control the epidemic, in that worried or panicked people might not seek the care they needed or, alternatively, might dangerously crowd health care facilities.
>
> Balancing the rights of the uninfected with the rights of the infected was considered a critical issue. One observer commented that a citizen might be expected to respond to the series of advisories by saying, "You've told me I should just stay in my home, now you have an obligation to give me antibiotics." But there were not enough antibiotics to do this. . . .
>
> Sometime into the exercise, (notional) civil unrest broke out. People had not been allowed to shop. Stores were closed. Food ran out because no trucks were being let into the state. Rioting began to occur. Gridlock occurred around the city, including around health care facilities. The use of snow-plows was proposed as a way of clearing the road of cars. Given the constraints of the exercise, it was not possible to gauge the true extent of social disorder that a bioterrorist attack might evoke, but most observers and participants agreed that serious civil disruption would be a genuine risk in such a crisis.
>
> The wide spectrum of disease containment measures which were considered or implemented illustrated the uncertainty surrounding what measures would, in fact, be feasible and effective. One senior health participant said that sufficient

legal powers seemed to exist to carry out the decisions that were being made, and noted that legal authorities were not the problem. The critical issue was having access to the necessary scientific, technical, practical and political expertise, and having sufficient reliable and timely information available (e.g., the number and location of sick persons, etc.) to make sound decisions about how to contain the epidemic....

...Perhaps the most striking observation overall is the recognition that the systems and resources now in place would be hard-pressed to successfully manage a bioweapons attack like that simulated in TOPOFF.... [*Id.*]

While the TOPOFF exercise was underway in Denver in May 2000, simulated terrorist attacks were also occurring in Portsmouth, New Hampshire (positing the use of a chemical weapon) and Washington, DC (radiological weapon). Another exercise in June 2001 that simulated an attack using smallpox virus reached similar conclusions, including this one: "Inherent conflicts already exist and will become exacerbated between health and law enforcement officials, military officials, etc. Priority to save victims and protect potential victims was given to the medical community, usurping law enforcement's jurisdiction in investigative matters." *Combating Terrorism: Federal Response to a Biological Weapons Attack, supra* p. 909, at 2-3. The smallpox exercise is described in Anser Institute for Homeland Security, *Dark Winter* (n.d.), *at* http://www.homelanddefense.org/darkwinter/index.cfm.

A subsequent exercise, in May 2003, is described in Dept. of Homeland Security, *Top Officials (TOPOFF) Exercise Series: TOPOFF 2—After Action Summary Report* (Dec. 19, 2003). It featured a simulated radiological attack in Seattle, a dispersal of plague bacilli in Chicago, a cyber attack, and terrorism threats in other locations. One conclusion was that "additional clarity...would be helpful" regarding authorities and resources available to the federal government. *Id.* at 4. Unlike the earlier TOPOFF exercise, however, in TOPOFF 2 participants were notified well in advance. The resulting lack of unpredictability and spontaneity may have reduced its value as either a test of preparedness or an aid in planning. A similar TOPOFF 3 exercise was conducted in early 2005. It involved 27 federal, 30 state, and 44 local departments and agencies, plus 156 private sector organizations. *See* Dept. of Homeland Security, Office of Inspector General, *A Review of the Top Officials 3 Exercise* (OIG-06-07), Nov. 2005; Eric Lipton, *Fictional Doomsday Team Plays Out Scene After Scene*, N.Y. Times, Mar. 26, 2005, at A11.

In 2005, DHS worked with other federal agencies to develop 15 all-hazards scenarios for use in homeland security preparedness activities. The scenarios represent high-consequence terrorist attacks that might be caused by foreign or state-sponsored terrorists, domestic groups, or even single disgruntled individuals. *See* Dept. of Homeland Security/Homeland Security Council, *National Planning Scenarios* (Version 20.1 Draft, Apr. 2005), *available at* http://media.washingtonpost.com/wp-srv/nation/nationalsecurity/earlywarning/NationalPlanningScenariosApril2005.pdf.

NOTES AND QUESTIONS

1. *Varying Effects of Terrorist Weapons.* Terrorist attacks using biological or radiological weapons might be carried out covertly (as in TOPOFF), with the results not manifesting themselves in health effects until days or even weeks later. A covert attack using a contagious pathogen could have a wide impact even before it is detected, since a person infected might become contagious long before she begins to exhibit serious symptoms. By contrast, an attack using chemical weapons, high explosives, or (as on September 11) a civilian airliner would be immediately apparent. A weaponized, noncontagious biological agent, like the anthrax spores mailed to Senators Tom Daschle and Patrick Leahy in October 2001, see *infra* p. 942, falls somewhere in between, because it can be widely dispersed like a chemical or radiological material, but its effects might not be felt for some time. Can you describe other practical differences in attacks using different kinds of weapons of mass destruction that would complicate efforts by government officials to minimize the resulting harm, restore essential public services, maintain public order, and prevent another attack? What different legal issues would be raised?

2. *Assessing the Emergency.* The escalating crisis in the TOPOFF exercise shows the importance of rapid recognition of the nature of an emergency. According to a recent DHS study,

> ER physicians, local hospital staff, infectious disease physicians, medical examiners, epidemiologists, and other public health officials should rapidly recognize the seriousness of the incident. Although laboratory methods to suspect preliminary diagnosis of the plague are available at many local public and private laboratories, there may be delayed recognition of the plague since most hospital ER and laboratory personnel in the United States and Canada have limited or no experience in identifying and/or treating plague.
> ... A rapid onset with large numbers of persons presenting at ERs with pneumonia should create high suspicion of a terrorist incident utilizing the plague. Detection of the plague should also initiate laboratory identification of the plague strain and a determination of the potentiality of known antimicrobial drug resistance.... [*National Planning Scenarios, supra*, at 4-4.]

The CDC has developed a standard protocol for reporting possible outbreaks of diseases that might be weaponized by terrorists. *Interim Recommended Notification Procedures for Local and State Public Health Department Leaders in the Event of a Bioterrorist Incident,* Feb. 1, 2001, at http://www.bt.cdc.gov/EmContact/Protocols.asp. If a local health official suspects that an outbreak of common symptoms might have been caused by a biological weapon, the official must inform the state's health department, which will then notify CDC. If a terrorist source is confirmed or thought by the state health department to be probable, the FBI and other predetermined response partners are to be notified. The CDC reporting protocol is not mandatory, however, and state and local governments have adopted it with some variations that might cause delay or confusion in a crisis. Is there any justification for the variations?

B. A Hypothetical Worst-Case Scenario

3. *First Response.* As soon as a bioterrorist attack is detected, a concerted, immediate response will be required to limit the loss of life. What measures would the first responders to such an attack take? A DHS study includes this partial catalog:

> Persons with primary aerosol exposure to plague need to receive antibiotic therapy within 24 hours in order to prevent near certain fatality. The potential secondary person-to-person spread by fleeing victims will be a challenge. Epidemiological assessments, including contact investigation and notification, will be needed. Actions of incident-site personnel tested after the attack include hazard identification and site control, establishment and operation of the [federal] Incident Command System (ICS), isolation and treatment of exposed victims, mitigation efforts, obtainment of PPE [personal protective equipment] and prophylaxis for responders, site remediation and monitoring, notification of airlines and other transportation providers, provision of public information, and effective coordination with national and international public health and governmental agencies....
>
> Evacuation and treatment of some victims will be required. Self-quarantine through shelter-in-place may be instituted....
>
> Tens of thousands of people will require treatment or prophylaxis with ventilators and antibiotics. Plague prompts antimicrobial prophylaxis of exposed persons, responders, and pertinent health care workers. Thousands will seek care at hospitals with many needing advanced critical care due to pneumonia caused by plague. Exposed persons will also need to be informed of signs and symptoms suggestive of plague as well as measures to prevent person-to-person spread. PPE (e.g., masks) for responders and health care providers should be available. Mobilization of the Strategic National Stockpile for additional critical supplies and antibiotics will be necessary. Public information activities will be needed to promote awareness of potential signs and symptoms of plague. Proper control measures will include the need for rapid treatment; contact tracing; and, potentially, self-quarantine through shelter-in-place or other least restrictive means. Actions of incident-site personnel tested after the attack include protective action decisions, recognition of the hazard and scope, providing emergency response, communication, protection of special populations, treating victims with additional ventilators at hospitals, providing patient screening clinics, and providing treatment or drug distribution centers for prophylactic antibiotics. Mortuary requirements, animal-based surveillance to monitor potential spread of plague via natural methods, and veterinary services also will need to be considered. Since this is an international incident, the U.S. Department of State's Bureau of Consular Affairs will need to be involved in order to assist foreign populations residing in the United States, foreign nationals in the United States, or U.S. citizens exposed or ill abroad. [*National Planning Scenarios, supra,* at 4-6.]

Who should be expected to perform all these tasks? What legal problems can you foresee in implementing these measures?

4. *Civil Unrest.* In the TOPOFF exercise, civil unrest (notionally, but predictably) broke out after a day or two. Can you suggest ways to avoid domestic violence in the wake of a terrorist attack? If such unrest is unavoidable, what government entity should be charged with responsibility for restoring order?

5. *Controlling Public Information.* When word began to spread about the September 11, 2001, attacks on the World Trade Center and the Pentagon, Americans turned immediately to their televisions for news. They were rewarded with days of nonstop pictures, government press releases, and expert speculation about what had happened. If an attack affects a wider area, as a chemical or radiological weapon might, or involves an infectious biological agent like plague, can you think of reasons that the government might want to regulate media coverage? Do you think it should be able to impose limits on the dissemination of news? If so, can you say under what circumstances? See Chapter 37.

6. *Preventing Another Attack.* A WMD attack would obviously trigger massive intelligence efforts and criminal investigations. One objective would be to bring those responsible for the attack to justice. Another would be to prevent a subsequent attack. Who would be in charge of these activities, and what means would be employed? How would the criminal and intelligence investigations be coordinated with immediate measures to protect the public health?

7. *Secondary Effects.* A WMD attack like the one described in TOPOFF is likely to have widespread ripple effects, including disruptions of the nation's financial infrastructure.

> As the financial world... begins to realize the likelihood of an epidemic, a sell-off occurs in the markets. There is a high absentee rate at banks, other financial institutions, and major corporations. Adding to these complications is the fact that bank and other financial customers may be staying home, afraid to venture into public places and trying instead to conduct business on the phone. As a result, the phone systems at financial institutions may become completely tied up, with far fewer transactions than normal occurring. Automatic teller machines (ATMs), especially drive-up machines, may run out of cash before they can be replenished. The fear of plague has raised memories of the anthrax incidents of 2001, which may cause many citizens to be afraid to open their mail. [*National Planning Scenarios, supra,* at 6.]

How could these kinds of impacts be limited?

C. FIRST RESPONDERS: ROLES AND AUTHORITIES

If terrorists launch an attack in the United States using chemical, biological, radiological, or nuclear weapons or high explosives, local police, EMTs, hospital and other public health personnel, firefighters, and HAZMAT teams will be the first responders — seeking to contain the damage, ministering to the injured, and collecting evidence for a criminal prosecution. *See* Sydney J. Freedberg Jr., *Beyond the Blue Canaries,* Natl. J., Mar. 10, 2001.

Our consideration of the roles and authorities of first responders is framed by the response to the September 11, 2001, terrorist attack on the Pentagon. Although that attack was overshadowed by the more dramatic calamity at the

World Trade Center, the reaction of state and local officials in Virginia and surrounding areas demonstrated that intergovernmental planning and cooperation can pay off during a crisis.

The 9/11 Commission Report: Final Report of the National Commission on Terrorist Attacks Upon the United States
Pages 311-315 (2004)

If it had happened on any other day, the disaster at the Pentagon would be remembered as a singular challenge and an extraordinary national story. Yet the calamity at the World Trade Center [on September 11, 2001] included catastrophic damage 1,000 feet above the ground that instantly imperiled tens of thousands of people. The two experiences are not comparable....

The emergency response at the Pentagon represented a mix of local, state, and federal jurisdictions and was generally effective. It overcame the inherent complications of a response across jurisdictions because the Incident Command System, a formalized management structure for emergency response, was in place in the National Capital Region on 9/11.

Because of the nature of the event—a plane crash, fire, and partial building collapse—the Arlington County Fire Department served as incident commander. Different agencies had different roles. The incident required a major rescue, fire, and medical response from Arlington County at the U.S. military's headquarters—a facility under the control of the secretary of defense. Since it was a terrorist attack, the Department of Justice was the lead federal agency in charge (with authority delegated to the FBI for operational response). Additionally, the terrorist attack affected the daily operations and emergency management requirements of Arlington County and all bordering and surrounding jurisdictions.

At 9:37, the west wall of the Pentagon was hit by hijacked American Airlines Flight 77, a Boeing 757. The crash caused immediate and catastrophic damage. All 64 people aboard the airliner were killed, as were 125 people inside the Pentagon (70 civilians and 55 military service members). One hundred six people were seriously injured and transported to area hospitals....

Local, regional, state, and federal agencies immediately responded to the Pentagon attack. In addition to county fire, police, and sheriff's departments, the response was assisted by the Metropolitan Washington Airports Authority, Ronald Reagan Washington National Airport Fire Department, Fort Myer Fire Department, the Virginia State Police, the Virginia Department of Emergency Management, the FBI, FEMA, a National Medical Response Team, the Bureau of Alcohol, Tobacco, and Firearms, and numerous military personnel within the Military District of Washington.

Command was established at 9:41. At the same time, the Arlington County Emergency Communications Center contacted the fire departments of Fairfax County, Alexandria, and the District of Columbia to request mutual aid. The incident command post provided a clear view of and access to the crash site, allowing the incident commander to assess the situation at all times.

At 9:55, the incident commander ordered an evacuation of the Pentagon impact area because a partial collapse was imminent; it occurred at 9:57, and no first responder was injured.

At 10:15, the incident commander ordered a full evacuation of the command post because of the warning of an approaching hijacked aircraft passed along by the FBI. This was the first of three evacuations caused by reports of incoming aircraft, and the evacuation order was well communicated and well coordinated.

Several factors facilitated the response to this incident, and distinguish it from the far more difficult task in New York. There was a single incident, and it was not 1,000 feet above ground. The incident site was relatively easy to secure and contain, and there were no other buildings in the immediate area. There was no collateral damage beyond the Pentagon.

Yet the Pentagon response encountered difficulties that echo those experienced in New York. As the "Arlington County: After-Action Report" notes, there were significant problems with both self-dispatching and communications: "Organizations, response units, and individuals proceeding on their own initiative directly to an incident site, without the knowledge and permission of the host jurisdiction and the Incident Commander, complicate the exercise of command, increase the risks faced by bonafide responders, and exacerbate the challenge of accountability." With respect to communications, the report concludes: "Almost all aspects of communications continue to be problematic, from initial notification to tactical operations. Cellular telephones were of little value.... Radio channels were initially oversaturated.... Pagers seemed to be the most reliable means of notification when available and used, but most firefighters are not issued pagers."

It is a fair inference, given the differing situations in New York City and Northern Virginia, that the problems in command, control, and communications that occurred at both sites will likely recur in any emergency of similar scale. The task looking forward is to enable first responders to respond in a coordinated manner with the greatest possible awareness of the situation.

NOTES AND QUESTIONS

1. *Who Are the First Responders?* Which officials and private citizens were actually the first responders in the 9/11 attack on the Pentagon? What agencies and jurisdictions did they represent? Pursuant to what authority did they operate?

Given the gravity, scale, and complexity of the consequences, coordination of the various responses was critically important. Who did the coordinating, and how well was it done?

2. *Regional Cooperation.* Pentagon responders from various agencies and jurisdictions had prior experience working together in different settings, and they benefited from the existence of an incident command center, described above. This permitted regional coordination that was extremely beneficial. Mutual above agreements—formal, pre-negotiated, interjurisdictional agreements for mutual assistance—also allowed most of the first responders to

share a common radio frequency so they could receive assignments by radio and get to work immediately upon arrival. *9/11 Commission Report, supra,* at 315.

Thirteen states have entered into a congressionally approved compact of mutual assistance, including help with evacuations. *See, e.g.,* Emergency Management Assistance Compact, Pub. L. No. 104-321, 110 Stat. 3877 (1996). Regional mechanisms for response to disasters, or the lack thereof, were the focus of reports assessing the response in 2005 to Hurricane Katrina. *See* The White House, *The Federal Response to Hurricane Katrina: Lessons Learned,* Feb. 2006, *available at* http://www.whitehouse.gov/report/katrina-lessons-learned.pdf; *A Failure of Initiative: Final Report of the Select Bipartisan Committee to Investigate the Preparation for and Response to Hurricane Katrina,* H.R. Rep. No. 109-377 (2006), *available at* http://a257.g.akamaitech.net/7/257/2422/15feb20061230/www.gpoaccess.gov/katrinareport/fullreport.pdf.

What advantages do such regional response structures offer? Do you see any legal obstacles to their creation or implementation? How can these obstacles be overcome?

3. *State and Local Response Plans.* What plans do you think cities, counties, and states have made in preparation for terrorist attacks? How would you find out about such plans? If a city is unable to respond fully to a terrorist attack, a state might provide assistance to it. What rules would govern such assistance? Who would be in charge of the state assets deployed to a city under attack? A review and assessment of the status of catastrophic and evacuation planning for all states, as well as major cities and urban areas, may be found at Dept. of Homeland Security, *Nationwide Plan Review—Phase 2 Report,* June 16, 2006, *available at* http://www.dhs.gov/interweb/assetlibrary/Prep_NationwidePlan Review.pdf.

D. SECOND RESPONDERS: THE FEDERAL ROLE

From 1950, when the Soviet Union tested its first atomic weapon, until the end of the Cold War, the American people lived in constant fear of a nuclear attack. (That fear has now abated, despite the fact that Russia and the United States each still maintain more than 6,000 strategic nuclear weapons on high alert.) For more than 40 years, the Civil Defense Act of 1950, ch. 1228, 64 Stat. 1245 (1951), as amended, directed the creation of a program to minimize the effects of such an attack on the civilian population and to deal with the resulting emergency conditions. Included in the program were planning for continuity of government, recruitment of emergency personnel, stockpiling of critical materials, and provision of warning systems and shelters. The act purported to give the President broad powers in a civil defense emergency, for example, to take property "without regard to the limitation of any existing law," *id.* §303(a), 64 Stat. 1252, and to provide the government with immunity from suits for damages to property, death, or personal injury based on its actions during such an emergency. *Id.* §304, 64 Stat. 1253. The civil defense program, administered since 1979 by FEMA, was supposed to convince the American people and the Soviet leadership that the United States could not only survive a nuclear war, but also win one.

Among the plans developed by FEMA under the Civil Defense Act was one called "Crisis Relocation." The plan called for evacuation to the countryside of 145 million Americans living in big cities or near key military bases in anticipation of a nuclear attack. In each of 400 target areas the exodus would be guided by instructions printed in local telephone directories. According to the plan, evacuees would be welcomed by their rural hosts and housed in schools, churches, and other public buildings until the trouble blew over. As recently as 1981, FEMA asserted that a "moderate-cost, balanced civil defense program...could enable survival of roughly 80 percent of the U.S. population in a heavy attack." FEMA, U.S. Crisis Relocation Planning (P&P-7 1981). Critics of the plan were numerous, with some warning that as soon as word of an impending attack got out, target populations would evacuate spontaneously and chaotically. *See, e.g., Counterfeit Ark: Crisis Relocation for Nuclear War* (Jennifer Leaning & Langley Keyes eds., 1984). Presumably, some of these plans have been or will be recycled for possible use if terrorists attack again using weapons of mass destruction.

The Civil Defense Act also provided for federal responses to natural disasters, such as floods and hurricanes. It was augmented in 1974 by the Robert T. Stafford Disaster Relief and Emergency Assistance Act (Stafford Act), 42 U.S.C.A. §§5121-5206 (West 2003 & Supp. 2006). That statute provides broadly for federal assistance to states affected by various disasters. In 1994, the Civil Defense Act was repealed, then partially reenacted as an amendment to the Stafford Act. National Defense Authorization Act for Fiscal Year 1995, Pub. L. No. 103-337, §§3411, 3412, 108 Stat. 2663, 3100-3111 (1994). A House Armed Services Committee report declared at the time, ironically, that "the program has lost its defense emphasis.... Rather, the chief threats today come from tornadoes, earthquakes, floods, chemical spills, and the like." H.R. Rep. No. 103-499, at 5 (1994), *reprinted in* U.S.C.C.A.N. 2091, 2182-2183.

The Stafford Act may be invoked in the event of a presidentially declared major disaster or emergency, including "any natural catastrophe...or, regardless of cause, any fire, flood, or explosion," or on "any occasion for which, in the determination of the President, Federal assistance is needed to supplement State and local efforts and capabilities to save lives and to protect property and public health and safety, or to lessen or avert the threat of a catastrophe." 42 U.S.C. §§5122, 5170, 5191(a). While the President's declaration will usually be based on a state governor's request for help, the President may act without such a request when "the primary responsibility for response rests with the United States." *Id.* §5191(b). Moreover, the President may direct the DOD to perform any emergency work "essential for the preservation of life and property" for up to ten days. *Id.* §5170b(c). President Clinton declared an emergency under the Stafford Act on April 19, 1995, in response to the terrorist bombing that day of the Alfred P. Murrah Federal Building in Oklahoma City, and he ordered FEMA to direct and coordinate responses by other federal agencies and provide needed federal assistance. 60 Fed. Reg. 22,579 (May 8, 1995). *See also* 60 Fed. Reg. 21,819 (May 3, 1995) (declaring a "major disaster" and providing public and individual assistance). The Stafford Act was also invoked on September 11, 2001, when President Bush declared a "major

D. Second Responders: The Federal Role

disaster" in the State of New York in order to make available various forms of public and individual assistance, 66 Fed. Reg. 48,682-01, and was invoked on August 31, 2005, for Louisiana, Mississippi, and Alabama following the landfall of Hurricane Katrina. The White House, *The Federal Response to Hurricane Katrina: Lessons Learned* 33, Feb. 2006.

In July 2002, the White House Office of Homeland Security published the *National Strategy for Homeland Security*, available at http://www.whitehouse.gov/homeland/book/. In line with earlier recommendations, this document recognized a need to "clarify lines of responsibility for homeland security in the executive branch, . . . mobilize our entire society, . . . and manage risk and allocate resources judiciously." *Id.* at 3. It called for planning to defend against terrorist attacks using conventional weapons as well as weapons of mass destruction, and against cyber attacks and new or unexpected tactics. To accomplish these goals, it proposed the establishment of a new Department of Homeland Security (DHS), which would assume primary responsibility for intelligence and warning of a domestic attack, border and transportation security, domestic counterterrorism, protection of critical infrastructure, and response and recovery from any future terrorist attack. DHS would also respond to natural disasters and consolidte emergency activities into one "genuinely all-discipline, all-hazard plan." *Id.* at 42.

The new department was created later the same year with passage of the Homeland Security Act of 2002, Pub. L. No. 107-296, 116 Stat. 2135 (2002), 6 U.S.C. §§101-557 and scattered sections of other titles. The Act merges all or portions of 22 federal agencies and 170,000 employees into the DHS. Included are the Coast Guard, Customs Service, Transportation Security Administration, FEMA, Secret Service, parts of the Immigration and Naturalization Service, and a long list of less well-known federal entities. The startup of this huge new enterprise is traced in Harold C. Relyea, *Homeland Security: Department Organization and Management — Implementation Phase* (Cong. Res. Serv. RL31751), Jan. 3, 2005.

One of the principal goals of DHS is to provide a unified federal response to a terrorist incident as well as to natural disasters. DHS is now the focal point for communications between and among federal, state, and local agencies, and it is supposed to provide an authoritative voice of the government in keeping the public informed about emergency responses.

In February 2003, the White House published Homeland Security Presidential Directive/HSPD-5, entitled *Management of Domestic Incidents*. It is meant to "ensure that all levels of the government across the Nation have the capability to work efficiently and effectively together, using a national approach to domestic incident management," *id.* ¶(3), and it declares that the Secretary of Homeland Security is the "principal Federal official for domestic incident management." *Id.* at ¶(4). On the other hand, the Secretary of Health and Human Services (HHS) shares responsibility with DHS for biological incidents, Sarah A. Lister, *An Overview of the U.S. Public Health System in the Context of Emergency Preparedness* (Cong. Res. Serv. RL31719) 22, May 17, 2005, while the Attorney General is given lead responsibility for criminal investigations of terrorist threats or acts within the United States, and she is directed to "coordinate the activities of other members of the law enforcement community to detect, prevent, preempt, and disrupt terrorist attacks against the United States." HSPD-5 at ¶(8). In addition, the Defense Department may provide military support to civil authorities in a domestic incident, but always under the command of the Secretary of Defense. *Id.* at ¶(9). The DHS responsibilities are triggered when a federal agency acting under its own authority has requested DHS assistance, when state and local resources are overwhelmed and federal assistance has been requested by state and local authorities, when more than one federal agency has become involved in responding to the incident, or when the President directs the Secretary of Homeland Security to assume management of the incident. *Id.* at ¶(4).

HSPD-5 also ordered the creation of a National Incident Management System (NIMS), to provide a flexible national framework within which governments at all levels and private entities could work together to manage domestic "incidents." The NIMS was rolled out a year later. Dept. of Homeland Security, *National Incident Management System*, Mar. 1, 2004, *available at* http://www.dhs.gov/interweb/assetlibrary/NIMS-90-web.pdf.

Finally, HSPD-5 called for development of a National Response Plan (NRP) to replace existing national emergency response plans. The new NRP was published in January 2005. Dept. of Homeland Security, *National Response Plan*, Dec. 2004, *available at* http://www.dhs.gov/interweb/assetlibrary/NRP_FullText.pdf. Like earlier plans, the NRP provides for a coordinated, all-hazards approach to "incident management," spelling out in broad terms the roles of all relevant elements of the national government and calling for communications and operational coordination by offices within DHS. It also sets out a framework for federal interaction with state, local, and tribal governments and with the private sector in an emergency. In addition, it includes 12 Emergency Support Functions (ESFs), described in annexes to the NRP that supply details on the mission, policies, and concept of operations of the federal agencies involved in support to state and local agencies.

A related document, *National Preparedness* (HSPD-8), Dec. 17, 2003, "describes the way Federal departments and agencies will prepare for...a response [to a terrorist attack or major natural disaster], including prevention activities during the early stages of a terrorism incident."

Federal emergency planning is extensively evaluated in *Nationwide Plan Review—Phase 2 Report*, *supra* p. 919, at 70-78.

NOTES AND QUESTIONS

1. *Adequacy of Emergency Response Authority.* Federal plans for responses to terrorist attacks and other catastrophes are described here in very general terms. In part that is because such plans, as well as the organizations that draw them up, have changed dramatically since September 11, 2001, and are continuing to evolve rapidly. Some current details may be found on the Web site of the Department of Homeland Security, at http://www.dhs.gov/dhspublic/.

Do you think there is adequate authority to execute existing plans? To do whatever else might be required? How will a federal official in charge of responding to a terrorist attack determine whether she has the authority she thinks she

D. Second Responders: The Federal Role

needs? Can you suggest a strategy for making it more likely that such an official would act only within the limits of her authority?

2. *Assigning Agency Responsibilities.* If the inherent unpredictability of these crises makes it impossible to anticipate every appropriate response, it is important to at least have an agreement about who will have overall responsibility for making necessary decisions based on contemporaneous information. The National Response Plan is supposed to reflect that agreement, indicating which agencies will be responsible for discharging what federal responsibilities in any given crisis.

In the aftermath of Hurricane Katrina, however, White House investigators of the flawed federal response to the storm found that, while the NRP is sufficiently "flexible and scalable" to meet any threat or event, "the specific triggers" for the NRP and its components "are unclear." *The Federal Response to Hurricane Katrina, supra,* at 14. DHS Secretary Michael Chertoff declared Katrina to be an incident of national significance (INS) on August 30, 2005, when two of the four triggering criteria listed in HSPD-5 ¶(4), noted above, had been met. *Id.* Yet there reportedly was confusion about whether the INS was triggered earlier by the President's emergency declaration under the Stafford Act. And according to the White House report, the NRP failed to articulate what actions should be taken by which agencies once an INS was declared. The lack of clear guidance was said to compromise the response. *Id.* at 15. If instead of a hurricane the City of New Orleans had been struck by a bioterrorist attack, the federal response presumably would have been equally ineffectual. Can you guess why it has been so difficult to make federal plans more detailed and concrete?

3. *Critical Infrastructure Protection.* In 2003, President Bush signed *Critical Infrastructure Identification, Prioritization, and Protection* (HSPD-7), Dec. 17, 2003, setting out policy for protection of the nation's telecommunications, finance, transportation, postal, and other vital services. These services have become highly automated and interdependent, and they may be especially vulnerable to cyber attacks. Every federal agency is charged by the directive with assessing the vulnerability of its own critical infrastructures and taking appropriate precautions.

Homeland Security Act §201(d)(5) charged DHS to "develop a comprehensive national plan for securing the key resources and critical infrastructure of the United States." The plan, including a letter agreement signed by heads of various relevant federal agencies, was completed on June 30, 2006. Dept. of Homeland Security, *National Infrastructure Protection Plan* (2006). Private sector operators — banks, public utilities, airlines, Internet service providers, and others — are enlisted in the effort to guard against terrorist attacks that could dramatically interrupt the routine of daily life as well as threaten national security. What legal and practical challenges do you think might be presented by this collaboration between government and nongovernment entities?

4. *Secrecy in Planning?* As recently as 1988, the President had prepared and made ready for immediate signature a series of 48 Presidential Emergency Action Documents (PEADs), some of them Top Secret "option documents," others standby executive orders dealing with border controls, detention of aliens, mobilization for a conventional war, and other matters. These were

premised not on the Civil Defense Act or the Stafford Act but on the President's "implied authority." Many more recent emergency planning documents are either partly or entirely classified. Should the content of these documents, or in some instances the very existence of the documents, be made public? What are the practical consequences of keeping them secret? The implications for constitutional government?

5. *Coordination with First Responders.* Federal planning documents call for the national government to furnish guidance to state and local authorities in planning responses to man-made and natural disasters and to provide direct assistance to those authorities when they are overwhelmed. The planning documents also call for federal agencies to maintain control over uniquely federal functions in a crisis. Can you tell from the authorities reviewed so far exactly how federal agencies would work with or support state and local authorities and first responders in responding to a WMD attack or massive natural disaster? If first responders are necessarily first on the scene, when, to what extent, and upon whose order would responsibility for overall management of an incident shift to federal control? How long would that federal primacy continue? Do you think it is important to try to answer these questions in advance of a crisis?

6. *Communications in a Crisis.* How would you rate the importance of ensuring clear and reliable communications in a terrorist crisis among the relevant federal, state, and local government agencies? What about providing authoritative current information and instructions to the public? Are the two tasks related? Considering the terrorist attack scenarios set forth earlier in this chapter, can you describe strategies for achieving both of these objectives?

7. *A Military Role?* Each state's National Guard has elements trained and equipped to assist, under the direction of the state governor, in the response to a WMD attack or a large natural disaster. See *infra* p. 966. At the federal level, the Stafford Act, the NRP, and other planning documents assign the Defense Department a supporting role in responding to a terrorist attack, including one involving a weapon of mass destruction. Should the military be given a larger role, or even lead agency responsibility? Consideration was given to such proposals in the wake of the flawed response to Hurricane Katrina. *See* David E. Sanger, *Bush Wants to Consider Broadening of Military's Powers During Natural Disasters*, N.Y. Times, Sept. 27, 2005, at A1. Do you think either state or federal governments could mount a fully effective response to such a calamity without the assistance of military forces? These questions are explored in Chapter 32.

E. QUARANTINES AND LIKE RESPONSES TO A TERRORIST ATTACK

Terrorist attacks using some kinds of weapons of mass destruction would present government responders with challenges not encountered with high explosives or a hostage-taking. A chemical, nuclear, or radiological weapon

E. Quarantines and Like Responses to a Terrorist Attack

might require exclusion of persons from a contaminated area. If a biological weapon were used, public health officials might need to prevent infected persons, whether sick or asymptomatic, from spreading the disease to others by isolating them, especially if the infectious agent had been altered to make it drug- or vaccine-resistant. They might also have to be given medicine. Others who might have been exposed to the disease could require vaccination or have their movements restricted. *See* Edward A. Fallone, *Preserving the Public Health: A Proposal to Quarantine Recalcitrant AIDS Carriers*, 68 B.U. L. Rev. 441, 460-461 (1988). The federal government has authority to impose interstate and foreign quarantines and to take other protective measures, while state and local health departments may exercise quarantine and isolation authority as part of the first response to a terrorist attack. These overlapping authorities, as well as some practical concerns, are examined here.

1. State and Local Responses to a Terrorist Attack

Jew Ho v. Williamson
Circuit Court, N.D. California, 1900
103 F. 10

MORROW, Circuit Judge.... On the 28th day of May, 1900, the board of health of the city and county of San Francisco adopted [a] resolution [noting nine deaths due to bubonic plague in a San Francisco district and requesting the board of supervisors to authorize quarantine of the district.]...

Thereafter... the board of supervisors passed [an] ordinance:...

..."The board of health... is hereby authorized and empowered to quarantine persons, houses, places, and districts within this city and county, when in its judgment it is deemed necessary to prevent the spreading of contagious or infectious diseases."...

... [O]n the 29th day of May, 1900, at a special meeting of the board of health, a resolution was passed, which... provided as follows:

"And whereas, after a careful and minute investigation had during a period of three months last past, and from the result of investigation made by Drs. Kellogg, bacteriologist to the board of health, Montgomery, of the University of California, Ophulf, of the Cooper Medical College, and J.J. Kinyoun, of the U.S. marine hospital service, each and all of whom have reported to this board that bubonic plague has existed in the district hereafter mentioned, and that nine deaths have occurred within said period within said district from said disease; and whereas, this board has reason to believe and does believe that danger does exist to the health of the citizens of the city and county of San Francisco by reason of the existence of germs of the said disease remaining in the district hereafter mentioned: Now, therefore, be it resolved: That the health officer be and is hereby instructed to place in quarantine until further notice that particular district of the city bounded north by Broadway, northeast by Montgomery avenue, east by Kearney, south by California, and west by Stockton streets; and that the chief of police is hereby requested to furnish such assistance as may be necessary to establish and maintain said quarantine...."

Thereafter, on May 31, 1900, the board of supervisors passed another ordinance... [that] provided for the establishment of quarantine regulations in the district named, and directed the chief of police to furnish such assistance as might be necessary to establish and maintain this quarantine.

The complainant in this case, Jew Ho, alleges... that he resides... within the limits of said quarantined district, and is engaged in the business of conducting a grocery store, as the proprietor and manager thereof, at his said place of residence, and that a great number of the patrons and customers of his said business reside at various places in the city and county of San Francisco outside the boundaries of said quarantined district, and are now, and ever since the 29th day of May, 1900, have been, prevented and prohibited by the defendants from visiting, patronizing, and dealing with the complainant in his said grocery store; that the complainant has been prevented and prohibited since the said 29th day of May, 1900, from selling his goods, wares, and merchandise, and from otherwise carrying on the business in which he is engaged.... The complainant alleges that there is not now, and never has been, any case of bubonic plague within the limits of said quarantined district, nor any germs or bacteria of bubonic plague, and that other diseases caused the illness and death of the persons claimed by defendants to have died of the bubonic plague within the 30 days next preceding the filing of this complaint.... The prayer of the bill is that an injunction be granted, enjoining and restraining the defendants from interfering with the personal rights and privileges of the complainant....

It is... contended that the acts of the defendants in establishing a quarantine district in San Francisco are authorized by the general police power of the state, intrusted to the city of San Francisco. The defendants rely upon a number of cases in support of this asserted jurisdiction and authority....

The case of *Lawton v. Steel*, 152 U.S. 133 (1894), had relation to a regulation concerning the fisheries. The court said with respect to the police power of the state:

> "The extent and limits of what is known as the 'police power'... [are] universally conceded to include everything essential to the public safety, health, and morals, and to justify the destruction or abatement by summary proceedings of whatever may be regarded as a public nuisance. Under this power it has been held that the state may order the destruction of a house falling to decay, or otherwise endangering the lives of passers-by; the demolition of such as are in the path of a conflagration; the slaughter of diseased cattle; the destruction of decayed or unwholesome food; the prohibition of wooden buildings in cities; the regulation of railways and other means of public conveyance, and of interment in burial grounds; the restriction of objectionable trades to certain localities; the compulsory vaccination of children; the confinement of the insane or those afflicted with contagious diseases; the restraint of vagrants, beggars, and habitual drunkards; the suppression of obscene publications and houses of ill fame; and the prohibition of gambling houses and places where intoxicating liquors are sold. Beyond this, however, the state may interfere wherever the public interests demand it; and in this particular a large discretion is necessarily vested in the legislature to determine, not only what the interests of the public require, but what measures are necessary for the protection of such interests. To justify the state in thus

E. Quarantines and Like Responses to a Terrorist Attack

interposing its authority in behalf of the public, it must appear—First, that the interests of the public generally, as distinguished from those of a particular class, require such interference; and, second, that the means are reasonably necessary for the accomplishment of the purpose, and not unduly oppressive upon individuals. The legislature may not, under the guise of protecting the public interests, arbitrarily interfere with private business, or impose unusual and unnecessary restrictions upon lawful occupations. In other words, its determination as to what is a proper exercise of its police powers is not final or conclusive, but is subject to the supervision of the courts." . . .

Affidavits have been filed on behalf of the complainant in this case,—one of them by Dr. J. I. Stephen . . . .

I read that affidavit for the purpose of showing the method adopted by the board of health for the suppressing of this so-called plague, namely, the quarantining of a large territory in the city of San Francisco,—some 10 or 12 blocks,—in which there are located about 10,000 people. It must necessarily follow that, where so many have been quarantined, the danger of the spread of the disease would not diminish. The purpose of quarantine and health laws and regulations with respect to contagious and infectious diseases is directed primarily to preventing the spread of such diseases among the inhabitants of localities. In this respect these laws and regulations come under the police power of the state, and may be enforced by quarantine and health officers, in the exercise of a large discretion, as circumstances may require. The more densely populated the community, the greater danger there is that the disease will spread, and hence the necessity for effectual methods of protection. To accomplish this purpose, persons afflicted with such diseases are confined to their own domiciles until they have so far recovered as not to be liable to communicate the disease to others. The same restriction is imposed upon victims of such diseases found traveling. The object of all such rules and regulations is to confine the disease to the smallest possible number of people; and hence when a vessel in a harbor, a car on a railroad, or a house on land, is found occupied by persons afflicted with such a disease, the vessel, the car, or the house, as the case may be, is cut off from all communication with the inhabitants of adjoining houses or contiguous territory, that the spread of the disease may be arrested at once and confined to the least possible territory. This is a system of quarantine that is well recognized in all communities, and is provided by the laws of the various states and municipalities: That, when a contagious or infectious disease breaks out in a place, they quarantine the house or houses first; the purpose being to restrict the disease to the smallest number possible, and that it may not spread to other people in the same locality. It must necessarily follow that, if a large section or a large territory is quarantined, intercommunication of the people within that territory will rather tend to spread the disease than to restrict it. . . . If we are to suppose that this bubonic plague has existed in San Francisco since the 6th day of March, and that there has been danger of its spreading over the city, the most dangerous thing that could have been done was to quarantine the whole city, as to the Chinese, as was substantially done in the first instance. [In an omitted portion of the opinion, the court found that the quarantine was enforced against members of the Chinese community but not against others.] The next most dangerous thing to do was to quarantine any considerable portion of the city, and not restrict intercommunication within the quarantined district. The quarantined district comprises 12 blocks. It is not claimed that in all the 12 blocks of the quarantined district the disease has been discovered. There are, I believe, 7 or 8 blocks in which it is claimed that deaths have occurred on account of what is said to be this disease. In 2 or 3 blocks it has not appeared at all. Yet this quarantine has been thrown around the entire district. The people therein obtain their food and other supplies, and communicate freely with each other in all their affairs. They are permitted to go from a place where it is said that the disease has appeared, freely among the other 10,000 people in that district. It would necessarily follow that, if the disease is there, every facility has been offered by this species of quarantine to enlarge its sphere and increase its danger and its destructive force.... The court cannot but see the practical question that is presented to it as to the ineffectiveness of this method of quarantine against such a disease as this. So, upon that ground, the court must hold that this quarantine is not a reasonable regulation to accomplish the purposes sought. It is not in harmony with the declared purpose of the board of health or of the board of supervisors....

There is one other feature of this case, and that is as to whether or not the bubonic plague has existed in this city, and whether it does now exist....

The evidence of Dr. Stephen and these other physicians shows that, at most, there have been 11 deaths in the quarantined district which on autopsy have disclosed some of the symptoms of the bubonic plague. But there has been no living case under the examination of the physicians from which a clinical history has been obtained, and it does not appear that there has been any transmission of the disease from any of those who have died. From all of which the court infers that the suspected cases were not contagious or infectious, or, if contagious and infectious, they were but sporadic in their nature, and had no tendency to spread or disseminate in the city. If it were within the province of this court to determine this issue, I think, upon such testimony as that given by these physicians, I should be compelled to hold that the plague did not exist and has not existed in San Francisco. But this testimony is contradicted by the physicians of the board of health. They have furnished the testimony of reputable physicians that the bubonic plague has existed, and that the danger of its development does exist. In the face of such testimony the court does not feel authorized to render a judicial opinion as to whether or not the plague exists or has existed in this city. Indeed, that is one of the questions that courts, under ordinary circumstances, are disposed to leave to boards of health to determine, upon such evidence as their professional skill deems satisfactory. If they believe, or if they have even a suspicion, that there is an infectious or contagious disease existing within the city, it is unquestionably the duty of such boards to act and protect the city against it, not to wait always until the matter shall be established to the satisfaction of all the physicians or all the persons who may examine into the question. It is the duty of the court to leave such question to be determined primarily by the authority competent for that purpose....

... [T]his quarantine cannot be continued, by reason of the fact that it is unreasonable, unjust, and oppressive, and therefore contrary to the laws limiting the police powers of the state and municipality in such matters .... The counsel for complainant will prepare an injunction, which shall, however, permit the board to maintain a quarantine around such places as it may have reason to believe are infected by contagious or infectious diseases, but that the

E. Quarantines and Like Responses to a Terrorist Attack

general quarantine of the whole district must not be continued, and that the people residing in that district, so far as they have been restricted or limited in their persons and their business, have that limitation and restraint removed....

Jacobson v. Massachusetts
United States Supreme Court, 1905
197 U.S. 11

Mr. Justice HARLAN delivered the opinion of the court. This case involves the validity, under the Constitution of the United States, of certain provisions in the statutes of Massachusetts relating to vaccination.

The Revised Laws of that Commonwealth, c. 75, §137, provide that "the board of health of a city or town, if, in its opinion, it is necessary for the public health or safety, shall require and enforce the vaccination and revaccination of all the inhabitants thereof, and shall provide them with the means of free vaccination. Whoever, being over twenty-one years of age and not under guardianship, refuses or neglects to comply with such requirement shall forfeit five dollars."

An exception is made in favor of "children who present a certificate, signed by a registered physician, that they are unfit subjects for vaccination." §139.

Proceeding under the above statutes, the Board of Health of the city of Cambridge, Massachusetts, on the twenty-seventh day of February, 1902, adopted the following regulation: "Whereas, smallpox has been prevalent to some extent in the city of Cambridge, and still continues to increase; and whereas, it is necessary for the speedy extermination of the disease that all persons not protected by vaccination should be vaccinated; and whereas, in the opinion of the board, the public health and safety require the vaccination or revaccination of all the inhabitants of Cambridge; be it ordered, that all the inhabitants of the city who have not been successfully vaccinated since March 1st, 1897, be vaccinated or revaccinated."

Subsequently, the Board adopted an additional regulation empowering a named physician to enforce the vaccination of persons as directed by the Board at its special meeting of February 27.

The above regulations being in force, the plaintiff in error, Jacobson, was proceeded against by a criminal complaint in one of the inferior courts of Massachusetts. The complaint charged that on the seventeenth day of July, 1902, the Board of Health of Cambridge, being of the opinion that it was necessary for the public health and safety, required the vaccination and revaccination of all the inhabitants thereof who had not been successfully vaccinated since the first day of March, 1897, and provided them with the means of free vaccination; and that the defendant, being over twenty-one years of age and not under guardianship, refused and neglected to comply with such requirement....

The defendant... asked numerous instructions to the jury, among which were the following:...

> That [section 137 of chapter 75 of the Revised Laws of Massachusetts] was in derogation of the rights secured to the defendant by the Fourteenth Amendment of the Constitution of the United States, and especially of the clauses of that

amendment providing that no state shall make or enforce any law abridging the privileges or immunities of citizens of the United States, nor deprive any person of life, liberty, or property without due process of law, nor deny to any person within its jurisdiction the equal protection of the laws....

Each of defendant's prayers for instructions was rejected .... A verdict of guilty was thereupon returned.

The case was then continued for the opinion of the Supreme Judicial Court of Massachusetts [, which] sustained the action of the trial court....

We come, then, to inquire whether any right given or secured by the Constitution is invaded by the statute as interpreted by the state court. The defendant insists that his liberty is invaded when the state subjects him to fine or imprisonment for neglecting or refusing to submit to vaccination; that a compulsory vaccination law is unreasonable, arbitrary, and oppressive, and, therefore, hostile to the inherent right of every freeman to care for his own body and health in such way as to him seems best; and that the execution of such a law against one who objects to vaccination, no matter for what reason, is nothing short of an assault upon his person. But the liberty secured by the Constitution of the United States to every person within its jurisdiction does not import an absolute right in each person to be, at all times and in all circumstances, wholly freed from restraint. There are manifold restraints to which every person is necessarily subject for the common good. On any other basis organized society could not exist with safety to its members. Society based on the rule that each one is a law unto himself would soon be confronted with disorder and anarchy. Real liberty for all could not exist under the operation of a principle which recognizes the right of each individual person to use his own, whether in respect of his person or his property, regardless of the injury that may be done to others. This court has more than once recognized it as a fundamental principle that "persons and property are subjected to all kinds of restraints and burdens in order to secure the general comfort, health, and prosperity of the state; of the perfect right of the legislature to do which no question ever was, or upon acknowledged general principles ever can be, made, so far as natural persons are concerned." Railroad Co. v. Husen, 95 U.S. 465, 471....

Applying these principles to the present case, it is to be observed that the legislature of Massachusetts required the inhabitants of a city or town to be vaccinated only when, in the opinion of the Board of Health, that was necessary for the public health or the public safety. The authority to determine for all what ought to be done in such an emergency must have been lodged somewhere or in some body; and surely it was appropriate for the legislature to refer that question, in the first instance, to a Board of Health composed of persons residing in the locality affected, and appointed, presumably, because of their fitness to determine such questions. To invest such a body with authority over such matters was not an unusual, nor an unreasonable or arbitrary, requirement. Upon the principle of self-defense, of paramount necessity, a community has the right to protect itself against an epidemic of disease which threatens the safety of its members. It is to be observed that when the regulation in question was adopted smallpox, according to the recitals in the regulation adopted by the Board of Health, was prevalent to some extent in the city of Cambridge, and the disease was increasing. If such was the situation — and nothing is asserted or

E. Quarantines and Like Responses to a Terrorist Attack

appears in the record to the contrary—if we are to attach any value whatever to the knowledge which, it is safe to affirm, is common to all civilized peoples touching smallpox and the methods most usually employed to eradicate that disease, it cannot be adjudged that the present regulation of the Board of Health was not necessary in order to protect the public health and secure the public safety. Smallpox being prevalent and increasing at Cambridge, the court would usurp the functions of another branch of government if it adjudged, as matter of law, that the mode adopted under the sanction of the State to protect the people at large was arbitrary, and not justified by the necessities of the case....

Whatever may be thought of the expediency of this statute, it cannot be affirmed to be, beyond question, in palpable conflict with the Constitution. Nor, in view of the methods employed to stamp out the disease of smallpox, can anyone confidently assert that the means prescribed by the state to that end [have] no real or substantial relation to the protection of the public health and the public safety. Such an assertion would not be consistent with the experience of this and other countries whose authorities have dealt with the disease of smallpox. And the principle of vaccination as a means to prevent the spread of smallpox has been enforced in many states by statutes making the vaccination of children a condition of their right to enter or remain in public schools.

... The matured opinions of medical men everywhere, and the experience of mankind, as all must know, negative the suggestion that it is not possible in any case to determine whether vaccination is safe. Was defendant exempted from the operation of the statute simply because of his dread of the same evil results experienced by him when a child, and which he had observed in the cases of his son and other children? Could he reasonably claim such an exemption because "quite often," or "occasionally," injury had resulted from vaccination, or because it was impossible, in the opinion of some, by any practical test, to determine with absolute certainty whether a particular person could be safely vaccinated?

It seems to the court that an affirmative answer to these questions would practically strip the legislative department of its function to care for the public health and the public safety when endangered by epidemics of disease....

... We are unwilling to hold it to be an element in the liberty secured by the Constitution of the United States that one person, or a minority of persons, residing in any community and enjoying the benefits of its local government, should have the power thus to dominate the majority when supported in their action by the authority of the State....

... Until otherwise informed by the highest court of Massachusetts, we are not inclined to hold that the statute establishes the absolute rule that an adult must be vaccinated if it be apparent or can be shown with reasonable certainty that he is not at the time a fit subject of vaccination, or that vaccination, by reason of his then condition, would seriously impair his health, or probably cause his death. No such case is here presented. It is the [case] of an adult who, for aught that appears, was himself in perfect health and a fit subject of vaccination, and yet, while remaining in the community, refused to obey the statute and the regulation adopted in execution of its provisions for the protection of the public health and the public safety, confessedly endangered by the presence of a dangerous disease.

We now decide only that the statute covers the present case, and that nothing clearly appears that would justify this court in holding it to be unconstitutional and inoperative in its application to the plaintiff in error.

The judgment of the court below must be affirmed.

It is so ordered.

Mr. Justice Brewer and Mr. Justice Peckham dissent.

NOTES AND QUESTIONS

1. *Reconciling the Cases.* Can the outcomes in *Jew Ho* and *Jacobson* be reconciled? Can you extract from the two decisions principles to guide state and local decision makers seeking to impose a health-related detention, quarantine, or forced vaccination program in response to a terrorist threat?

In what respects was the San Francisco quarantine legally insufficient? Why was the *Jew Ho* court competent to decide the reasonableness of the quarantine but not whether the plague existed in San Francisco? Could the San Francisco regulation have been revised to cure its defects while still serving its public health objective? If so, how?

2. *Quarantine Authority.* The Supreme Court has long recognized the authority of the government to erect quarantines — both to confine persons and to exclude them — in order to prevent the spread of contagious or infectious diseases. For example, in a recent case approving the confinement of a violent sexual predator, the Court declared that

> we have never held that the Constitution prevents a State from civilly detaining those for whom no treatment is available, but who nevertheless pose a danger to others. A State could hardly be seen as furthering a "punitive" purpose by involuntarily confining persons afflicted with an untreatable, highly contagious disease. [Kansas v. Hendricks, 521 U.S. 346, 366 (1997).]

And while the Court has called the constitutional right to travel from one state to another "firmly imbedded in our jurisprudence," Saenz v. Roe, 526 U.S. 489, 498 (1999), other courts have held that the right may be curtailed in an emergency. *See, e.g.,* Smith v. Avino, 91 F.3d 105 (11th Cir. 1996) (upholding a curfew in South Florida in the wake of Hurricane Andrew). *See generally* Kathleen S. Swendiman & Jennifer K. Elsea, *Federal and State Quarantine and Isolation Authority* (Cong. Res. Serv. RL33201), Dec. 12, 2005; 16B Am. Jur. 2d *Constitutional Law* §617 (1998).

3. *Erring on the Side of Caution?* How widely may government officials establish a cordon around an area suspected of containing infected persons or hazardous chemicals? More generally, how should doubts be resolved about the possible exposure of individuals to a contagious disease? A due process case involving a quarantine of poultry to combat avian influenza may be instructive. In Empire Kosher Poultry, Inc. v. Hallowell, 816 F.2d 907 (3d Cir. 1987), the court said that evidence of disease need not be shown before the quarantine is

E. Quarantines and Like Responses to a Terrorist Attack

erected, because tests might not immediately reveal the existence of infection. Moreover, said the court, a broad buffer zone could be established to prevent the inadvertent movement of infected poultry out of the quarantine area.

4. *Enforcing a Quarantine.* One analysis of the federal TOPOFF exercise, *supra* p. 910, calls the quarantine of large groups of people "impractical," citing concern about the level of force needed for enforcement:

> Not only were local officials uncertain about their statutory authority to proceed with a quarantine, they believed that the public would probably not cooperate with compulsory orders to commandeer property, restrict movement of people, or forcibly remove them to designated locations. Traditionally, governments have counted upon the public to comply with public health orders on the basis that the good of the community overrides the rights of the individual. These days, however, citizens get angry at forced evacuations for such visible calamities as hurricanes, floods, and wildfires, not to mention a stay-at-home order for a microscopic killer that they may doubt is in their midst. Police also questioned whether their colleagues would recognize the authority of the public health officer to declare a quarantine or would even stick around to enforce the order. Finally, some wondered whether there were enough local and state police to quarantine a large metropolitan area in the first place. [Amy E. Smithson & Leslie-Anne Levy, *Ataxia: The Chemical and Biological Terrorism Threat and the U.S. Response* 269 (Henry L. Stimson Center 2000).]

According to one police captain, "If police officers knew that a biological agent had been released, 99 percent of the cops would not be here. They would grab their families and leave." *Id.* at 270 n.225. Do these practical problems have legal solutions?

5. *Commerce Clause Limits?* Are state or local quarantine restrictions potentially vulnerable to legal challenge under the dormant Commerce Clause? As early as Gibbons v. Ogden, 22 U.S. 1 (1824), the Supreme Court recognized that quarantine laws may be construed as "laws of commerce." *Id.* at 25. In Compagnie Francaise de Navigation a Vapeur v. State Board of Health, 186 U.S. 380 (1902), however, the Court rejected a charge that a quarantine of the City of New Orleans unduly burdened commerce because it prevented the landing there of passengers from a French ship. The Court stated that "the health and quarantine laws of the several states are not repugnant to the Constitution of the United States, although they affect foreign and domestic commerce... until Congress has acted under the authority conferred upon it by the Constitution." *Id.* at 391. Although state and local health laws that do not favor residents over nonresidents have generally been upheld when challenged under the Commerce Clause, the possibility remains that a state or local restriction could be viewed as unconstitutionally burdensome on interstate or foreign commerce. *See* Erwin Chemerinsky, *Constitutional Law: Principles and Policies* §5.3 (2d ed. 2002).

6. *Federal/State Conflicts.* According to one analysis, in the event of a bioterrorist attack, "[a]lmost certainly, a clash would occur between public health and legal officials at the local, state, and national levels about the measures necessary

and the entity with jurisdiction to act." Smithson & Levy, *supra*, at 269. Why might that be so? How could such conflicts be avoided?

Legally, if state or local efforts come directly into conflict with federal measures, the former presumably would have to give way under the Supremacy Clause. Federal preemption would be based on a federal right to regulate. Can you describe limits to the federal government's power to respond to a terrorist attack using a biological weapon? How about a chemical or radiological weapon? Would your answer turn on whether a biological agent was contagious? Can you think of constitutional provisions other than the Commerce Clause that would enable preemptive federal action?

7. *Other Constraints on Individual Liberties.* In addition to quarantines, involuntary evacuations, and forced inoculations, government responses to a WMD attack might include compulsory physical examinations to determine whether individuals are infected with a contagious disease, inspections of private property, and reviews of personal medical records. The Court has held that searches of individuals not related to a criminal prosecution will not offend the Fourth Amendment if the state's interest in the result is sufficiently compelling. *See, e.g.,* Vernonia Sch. Dist. 47J v. Acton, 515 U.S. 646, 653 (1995) (upholding random drug tests of student athletes when "special needs, beyond the normal need for law enforcement, make the warrant and probable-cause requirement impracticable"); National Treasury Employees Union v. Von Raab, 489 U.S. 656 (1989) (approving drug tests of Customs Service employees); *cf.* Ferguson v. City of Charleston, 532 U.S. 67 (2001) (rejecting nonconsensual drug testing of obstetrics patients when results were to be given to police). In Camara v. Municipal Court of San Francisco, 387 U.S. 523, 539 (1967), the Court observed that warrantless inspections are "traditionally upheld in emergency situations." In the wake of a bioterrorist attack, the government's interest in examining individuals and their property would be strong and immediate. Do you think it would outweigh individual privacy interests? *See* Barry Kellman, *Biological Terrorism: Legal Measures for Preventing Catastrophe,* 24 Harv. J.L. & Pub. Poly. 417, 478-485 (2001).

In a portion of the *Jew Ho* decision omitted here, the Court noted that one reason for striking down the San Francisco quarantine regulation was its enforcement in a racially discriminatory manner against members of the Chinese community. The health crisis, or purported crisis, furnished a pretext for discrimination with other motivations. This was "the administration of a law 'with an evil eye and an unequal hand,' " in violation of the Fourteenth Amendment to the U.S. Constitution. 103 F. at 24, quoting Yick Wo v. Hopkins, 118 U.S. 356 (1886). Recall that in Korematsu v. United States, 323 U.S. 214 (1944), *supra* p. 704, involving the exclusion and internment of 120,000 Japanese-Americans during World War II, the Supreme Court was far more credulous in accepting government assertions that racial discrimination was required by military necessity.

In Wong Wai v. Williamson, 103 F. 1 (1900), a companion case to *Jew Ho,* the court struck down a San Francisco compulsory vaccination program aimed at combating plague but enforced only against Chinese residents. Apart from the explicitly race-based administration of the program, the court found, based on expert testimony, that the vaccine could itself be life-threatening if given to a person already exposed to the plague; it was only effective before exposure.

E. Quarantines and Like Responses to a Terrorist Attack

Absent the racial criterion, do you think the court would have been willing to scrutinize closely the efficacy of the drug? Should either the efficacy of a drug or the risk it poses to an individual be considered today in a program of compulsory inoculation?

2. A Model State Response: The MSEHPA?

The *Jew Ho* and *Jacobson* cases may be seen as representative of antiquated state quarantine and vaccination laws, many of which are several decades old, do not reflect current disease or treatment science, and are often targeted at particular diseases. *See* Lawrence O. Gostin, *The Law and the Public's Health: A Study of Infectious Disease Law in the United States*, 99 Colum. L. Rev. 59, 102-106 (1999).

Spurred by the 9/11 and anthrax attacks in 2001, states and cities began to reconsider a range of emergency response issues, including quarantine and isolation authorities. The Model State Emergency Health Powers Act (MSEHPA) (draft Dec. 21, 2001), *at* http://www.publichealthlaw.net/MSEHPA/MSEHPA2.pdf, was drawn up in 2001 by public health experts at Georgetown and Johns Hopkins Universities. *See* Center for Law & the Public's Health, *Model State Public Health Laws* (n.d.), *at* http://www.publichealthlaw.net/Resources/Modellaws.htm.

The MSEHPA borrows from various state laws and provides a template for sweeping state authorities that may be invoked in a public health emergency. It authorizes governors to declare a "public health emergency" after consulting with public health authorities or, in the absence of such consultation, "when the situation calls for prompt and timely action." §401. A "public health emergency" is defined as "an occurrence or imminent threat" of illness that is "believed to be caused" by bioterrorism or other disasters and poses "a high probability" of a large number of deaths, serious or long-term disabilities, or widespread exposure "that poses a significant risk of substantial harm to a large number of people in the affected population." §104(m). During a public health emergency, a governor may suspend any statute concerning state government procedures or any agency rule or orders "to the extent that strict compliance with the same would prevent, hinder, or delay necessary action" in response to the public health emergency. §403(a)(1). The public health emergency "shall" be terminated by a governor by executive order "upon finding that the occurrence of an illness or health condition that caused the emergency no longer poses a high probability of a large number of deaths in the affected population . . . or a significant risk of substantial future harm to a large number of people in the affected population." §405(a). Otherwise, a public health emergency will terminate automatically after 30 days unless renewed by the governor or terminated earlier by majority vote of both chambers of a state legislature. §405(b), (c).

In addition, during a public health emergency the MSEHPA authorizes state officials to close, evacuate, or decontaminate "any facility" or decontaminate or destroy "any material" where "there is a reasonable cause to believe that it may endanger the public health." §501. Public health authorities are also given power to condemn or assume control over private property, control and manage health care facilities, and control routes and modes of transportation "if such action is reasonable and necessary to respond to the public health emergency." §502.

The MSEHPA includes these provisions concerning vaccination, treatment, isolation, and quarantine:

Model State Emergency Health Powers Act
Draft Dec. 21, 2001
at http://www.publichealthlaw.net/MSEHPA/MSEHPA2.pdf

ARTICLE VI. SPECIAL POWERS DURING A STATE OF PUBLIC HEALTH EMERGENCY: PROTECTION OF PERSONS

Section 603. Vaccination and treatment.

During a state of public health emergency the public health authority may exercise the following emergency powers over persons as necessary to address the public health emergency—

(a) Vaccination. To vaccinate persons as protection against infectious disease and to prevent the spread of contagious or possibly contagious disease.

(1) Vaccination may be performed by any qualified person authorized to do so by the public health authority.

(2) A vaccine to be administered must not be such as is reasonably likely to lead to serious harm to the affected individual.

(3) To prevent the spread of contagious or possibly contagious disease the public health authority may isolate or quarantine, pursuant to Section 604, persons who are unable or unwilling for reasons of health, religion, or conscience to undergo vaccination pursuant to this Section.

(b) Treatment. To treat persons exposed to or infected with disease.

(1) Treatment may be administered by any qualified person authorized to do so by the public health authority.

(2) Treatment must not be such as is reasonably likely to lead to serious harm to the affected individual.

(3) To prevent the spread of contagious or possibly contagious disease the public health authority may isolate or quarantine, pursuant to Section 604, persons who are unable or unwilling for reasons of health, religion, or conscience to undergo treatment pursuant to this Section.

Section 604. Isolation and quarantine.

(a) Authorization. During the public health emergency, the public health authority may isolate...or quarantine...an individual or groups of individuals.... The public health authority may also establish and maintain places of isolation and quarantine, and set rules and make orders. Failure to obey these rules, orders, or provisions shall constitute a misdemeanor.

(b) Conditions and principles. The public health authority shall adhere to the following conditions and principles when isolating or quarantining individuals or groups of individuals:

E. Quarantines and Like Responses to a Terrorist Attack

(1) Isolation and quarantine must be by the least restrictive means necessary to prevent the spread of a contagious or possibly contagious disease to others and may include, but are not limited to, confinement to private homes or other private and public premises.

(2) Isolated individuals must be confined separately from quarantined individuals.

(3) The health status of isolated and quarantined individuals must be monitored regularly to determine if they require isolation or quarantine.

(4) If a quarantined individual subsequently becomes infected or is reasonably believed to have become infected with a contagious or possibly contagious disease he or she must promptly be removed to isolation.

(5) Isolated and quarantined individuals must be immediately released when they pose no substantial risk of transmitting a contagious or possibly contagious disease to others.

(6) The needs of persons isolated and quarantined shall be addressed in a systematic and competent fashion, including, but not limited to, providing adequate food, clothing, shelter, means of communication with those in isolation or quarantine and outside these settings, medication, and competent medical care.

(7) Premises used for isolation and quarantine shall be maintained in a safe and hygienic manner and be designed to minimize the likelihood of further transmission of infection or other harms to persons isolated and quarantined.

(8) To the extent possible, cultural and religious beliefs should be considered in addressing the needs of individuals, and establishing and maintaining isolation and quarantine premises.

(c) Cooperation. Persons subject to isolation or quarantine shall obey the public health authority's rules and orders; and shall not go beyond the isolation or quarantine premises. Failure to obey these provisions shall constitute a misdemeanor.

(d) Entry into isolation or quarantine premises.

(1) Authorized entry. The public health authority may authorize physicians, health care workers, or others access to individuals in isolation or quarantine as necessary to meet the needs of isolated or quarantined individuals.

(2) Unauthorized entry. No person, other than a person authorized by the public health authority, shall enter isolation or quarantine premises. Failure to obey this provision shall constitute a misdemeanor.

(3) Potential isolation or quarantine. Any person entering an isolation or quarantine premises with or without authorization of the public health authority may be isolated or quarantined pursuant to Section 604(a).

Section 605. Procedures for isolation and quarantine.

During a public health emergency, the isolation and quarantine of an individual or groups of individuals shall be undertaken in accordance with the following procedures.

(a) Temporary isolation and quarantine without notice.

(1) Authorization. The public health authority may temporarily isolate or quarantine an individual or groups of individuals through a written

directive if delay in imposing the isolation or quarantine would significantly jeopardize the public health authority's ability to prevent or limit the transmission of a contagious or possibly contagious disease to others....

(4) Petition for continued isolation or quarantine. Within ten (10) days after issuing the written directive, the public health authority shall file a petition pursuant to Section 605(b) for a court order authorizing the continued isolation or quarantine of the isolated or quarantined individual or groups of individuals.

[Section 605(b) permits the public health authority to petition for isolation or quarantine with notice to affected individuals and a hearing within five days, with a ten-day extension possible in "extraordinary circumstances." The court will grant the state's petition if a preponderance of the evidence shows that isolation or quarantine is "reasonably necessary to prevent or limit that transmission of a contagious or possibly contagious disease to others."]

NOTES AND QUESTIONS

1. *Status of State Legislation.* According to the Center for Law and the Public's Health, as of April 2006, 37 states and the District of Columbia have enacted legislation that includes provisions from or closely related to the MSEHPA. A table documenting state legislative activity is available at http://www.publichealthlaw.net/Resources/Modellaws.htm.

2. *Revisiting the Old Cases.* Does the MSEHPA respond to the problems confronted by the courts in *Jew Ho* and *Jacobson*? Would the portions of the Model Act set out above survive a challenge to their constitutionality?

3. *Commandeering Resources.* Article V of the MSEHPA provides sweeping powers for a state public health authority to commandeer private resources during a public health emergency. In addition to the authority to close, evacuate, or decontaminate facilities or materials, and to gain access to and control of facilities, private property, and transportation modes, state officials would be given control over the procurement, rationing, and distribution of health care supplies. §§501-505. The Model Act anticipates that "just compensation" would be paid to any owner for property lawfully taken during the public health emergency. §506. Under what circumstances would the provisions of Title V be implemented? If enacted, would these provisions be constitutional? Wise? How would you advise a state legislature interested in providing for these contingencies to ensure against the abuse of such powers?

4. *Compulsion of People.* Review the provisions of Article VI of the MSEHPA above. What is the difference between isolation and quarantine? What practical difference does it make whether a person is subject to an isolation or quarantine order? How useful are the conditions and principles set forth in §604(b) in deciding whether to impose isolation or quarantine? Are the public health needs and rights of affected individuals and other persons adequately served? Are the proposed procedures constitutional? Finally, who would actually enforce the quarantine, and how?

E. Quarantines and Like Responses to a Terrorist Attack 939

5. *A Needed Set of Correctives?* Would you advise state legislatures to enact some version of the MSEHPA? What provisions would you say are most controversial, and why? Some scholars have claimed that the Model Act is unnecessary and is an overreaction to the need for incremental public health law reform. LSU Program in Law, Science, and Public Health, *White Paper #2: Review of the Model State Emergency Health Powers Act; Legislative Alternatives to the Model State Emergency Health Powers Act (MSEHPA)*, Apr. 2003, *available at* http://www.biotech.law.lsu.edu/ephl/.

3. The Federal Response to a Bioterrorist Attack

The federal responsibility for biological incidents is shared by several agencies, as noted earlier. Overall coordination is supposed to be provided by DHS. The Department of Health and Human Services, acting through the CDC, will play a leading role based on its specialized experience and expertise. Some of the statutory and regulatory authorities relevant to that role are set out below.

Public Health Service Act
42 U.S.C.A. §§201-300aaa-13 (West 2003 & Supp. 2006)

§243. GENERAL GRANT OF AUTHORITY FOR COOPERATION....

(c) Development of plan to control epidemics and meet emergencies or problems resulting from disasters;...

(1) The Secretary [of Health and Human Services (the "Service")] is authorized to develop (and may take such action as may be necessary to implement) a plan under which personnel, equipment, medical supplies, and other resources of the Service and other agencies under the jurisdiction of the Secretary may be effectively used to control epidemics of any disease or condition and to meet other health emergencies or problems....

§264. REGULATIONS TO CONTROL COMMUNICABLE DISEASES

(a) Promulgation and Enforcement by Surgeon General. The Surgeon General, with the approval of the Secretary, is authorized to make and enforce such regulations as in his judgment are necessary to prevent the introduction, transmission, or spread of communicable diseases from foreign countries into the States or possessions, or from one State or possession into any other State or possession. For purposes of carrying out and enforcing such regulations, the Surgeon General may provide for such inspection, fumigation, disinfection... and other measures, as in his judgment may be necessary.

(b) Apprehension, detention, or conditional release of individuals. Regulations prescribed under this section shall not provide for the apprehension, detention, or conditional release of individuals except for the purpose of preventing the introduction, transmission, or spread of such communicable diseases as may be specified from time to time in Executive orders of the President upon the recommendation of the Secretary, in consultation with the Surgeon General....

(d)(1) Apprehension and examination of persons reasonably believed to be infected. Regulations prescribed under this section may provide for the apprehension and examination of any individual reasonably believed to be infected with a communicable disease in a qualifying stage and (A) to be moving or about to move from a State to another State; or (B) to be a probable source of infection to individuals who, while infected with such disease in a qualifying stage, will be moving from a State to another State. Such regulations may provide that if upon examination any such individual is found to be infected, he may be detained for such time and in such manner as may be reasonably necessary....

HHS has adopted the following regulations to implement this statutory authority:

Interstate Quarantine Regulations
42 C.F.R. part 70 (2005)

§70.2 MEASURES IN THE EVENT OF INADEQUATE LOCAL CONTROL.

Whenever the Director of the Centers for Disease Control and Prevention determines that the measures taken by health authorities of any State or possession (including political subdivisions thereof) are insufficient to prevent the spread of any of the communicable diseases from such State or possession to any other State or possession, he/she may take such measures to prevent such spread of the diseases as he/she deems reasonably necessary, including inspection....

§70.5 CERTAIN COMMUNICABLE DISEASES; SPECIAL REQUIREMENTS.

The following provisions are applicable with respect to any person who is in the communicable period of cholera, plague, smallpox, typhus or yellow fever, or who, having been exposed to any such disease, is in the incubation period thereof:
   (a) Requirements relating to travelers.
      (1) No such person shall travel from one State or possession to another, or on a conveyance engaged in interstate traffic, without a written permit of the Surgeon General or his/her authorized representative....

§70.6 APPREHENSION AND DETENTION OF PERSONS WITH SPECIFIC DISEASES.

Regulations prescribed in this part authorize the detention, isolation, quarantine, or conditional release of individuals, for the purpose of preventing the introduction, transmission, and spread of the communicable diseases listed in an Executive Order setting out a list of quarantinable communicable diseases, as provided under section 361(b) of the Public Health Service Act. Executive Order 13295, of April 4, 2003, contains the current revised list of quarantinable communicable diseases, and may be obtained at http://www.cdc.gov, or at http://www.archives.gov/federal-register/. If this Order is amended, HHS will enforce that amended order immediately and update this reference.

NOTES AND QUESTIONS

1. *Who's in Charge?* Can you tell from the authorities we have examined who will be responsible for coordinating and implementing all these federal, state, and local laws in a great crisis?

2. *Responding to Listed Pathogens.* The HHS regulations set out above have been amended several times since September 11, 2001, to expand the list of infectious agents for which the CDC may erect quarantines or detain persons. The executive order incorporated by reference in §70.6 lists cholera, diphtheria, infectious tuberculosis, plague, smallpox, yellow fever, and viral hemorrhagic fevers (including Lassa, Marburg, and Ebola). It also lists severe acute respiratory syndrome (SARS). Not listed are tularemia, botulism, and other contagions that could be weaponized and used by terrorists. A more recent order aimed at halting the spread of bird flu adds "influenza caused by novel or reemergent influenza viruses that are causing, or have the potential to cause, a pandemic." Exec. Order No. 13,375 (Apr. 1, 2005). CDC issued an extensive and controversial proposed revision to these regulations on November 30, 2005. Dept. of Health and Human Serv., *Control of Communicable Diseases*, 70 Fed. Reg. 71,892-01.

In May 2006, the Homeland Security Council issued its *Pandemic Influenza Implementation Plan*, available at http://www.whitehouse.gov/homeland/nspi_implementation.pdf. At 233 pages, it sets out fairly elaborate guidance for U.S. planning in areas of primary federal responsibility, international efforts, controls of borders and transportation, protection of human and animal health, and public safety, emphasizing the roles of state and local governments wherever possible. *See also* U.S. Dept. of Health and Human Serv., *HHS Pandemic Influenza Plan*, Nov. 2005, *available at* http://www2a.cdc.gov/phlp/docs/PHLP_HHSPandemicInfluenzaPlan.pdf; Sarah A. Lister, *Pandemic Influenza: Domestic Preparedness Efforts* (Cong. Res. Serv. RL331450), Nov. 10, 2005. Because a bird flu pandemic would present many of the legal and practical problems posed by a terrorist attack using plague or some other contagious disease, the *Implementation Plan* probably reflects the latest government thinking about large-scale, integrated planning for both kinds of catastrophe.

3. *Responding to Anthrax.* What measures need to be undertaken by federal officials to address the threat posed by terrorists sending anthrax spores through the mail, as happened in the aftermath of the September 11, 2001, attacks? Recall that anthrax is extremely dangerous but not communicable. Can you explain how various federal agencies might cooperate in this effort? Do HHS and CDC have the authority they need to be helpful? A Defense Department-sponsored report concluded that the anthrax letter attacks "revealed weaknesses in almost every aspect of U.S. biopreparedness and response." David Heyman, *Lessons from the Anthrax Attacks: Implications for U.S. Bioterrorism Preparedness* viii, Apr. 2002, *available at* http://www.fas.org/irp/threat/cbw/dtra02.pdf. *See also* Keith Rhodes, *Diffuse Security Threats: Information on U.S. Domestic Anthrax Attacks* (GAO-03-0323T), Dec. 10, 2002, *available at* pp. 808-822 of another report found at http://www.fas.org/irp/congress/2002_rpt/911rept.pdf; Gen. Acct. Off., *Bioterrorism: Public Health Responses to Anthrax Incidents of 2001* (GAO-04-152), Oct. 2003.

4. *Responding to Smallpox.* Reflecting growing fears that supplies of smallpox virus might fall into the hands of terrorists, the CDC has published a plan for responding to an outbreak of a disease thought to have been eradicated in the 1970s. *See CDC Smallpox Response Plan and Guidelines (Version 3.0)*, Nov. 26, 2002 (with updates), *at* http://www.bt.cdc.gov/agent/smallpox/response-plan/index.asp. The plan calls for employment of a "ring" strategy to isolate confirmed and suspected smallpox cases, vaccinate persons who may have come into contact with them, and keep all possible contacts under close surveillance. The size of a ring is to be determined by state and federal health officials. A different CDC directive declares,

> No one will be forced to be vaccinated, even if they have been exposed to smallpox.... [However, to] prevent smallpox from spreading, anyone who has been in contact with a person with smallpox but who decides not to get the vaccine may need to be isolated for at least 18 days.... People placed in isolation will not be able to go to work. [*Fact Sheet: What You Should Know About a Smallpox Outbreak*, Mar. 29, 2004, *at* http://www.bt.cdc.gov/agent/smallpox/basics/outbreak.asp.]

A companion document provides guidance for state and local government planners. *CDC Guidance for Post-Event Smallpox Planning*, Oct. 29, 2002, *at* http://www.bt.cdc.gov/agent/smallpox/prep/post-event-guidance.asp.

5. *Federal Authority to Constrain Persons.* HHS's enabling legislation states that an "individual believed to be infected with a communicable disease in a communicable stage" may be "apprehended and examined." 42 U.S.C. §264(d). If found to be infected, the individual may then be "detained for such time and in such manner as may be reasonably necessary." *Id.* Do you think this language is meant to give the CDC authority to quarantine an entire city? Or to require vaccinations? What is the relationship between the HHS/CDC authorities and state law, whether or not a state has adopted something like the MSEHPA?

6. *Enforcing a Quarantine.* HHS and CDC have no police force of their own to enforce a federal quarantine. How could such a quarantine be enforced? For one possible answer, see *infra* pp. 963-969.

E. Quarantines and Like Responses to a Terrorist Attack

7. *Intrastate Quarantine.* According to some commentators, no statutory authority exists for a federally mandated quarantine within a single state. *See, e.g.,* National Commission on Terrorism (Bremer Commission), *Countering the Changing Threat of International Terrorism* 27 (2000). Can you see why there might be doubt about this? Considering the language of the Public Health Service Act and its implementing regulations, set out above, do you think these doubts are justified? Statutory and constitutional bases and limits for both state and federal public health regulations dealing with bioterrorism threats are briefed extensively in proposed CDC regulations, Dept. of Health and Human Serv., *Control of Communicable Diseases,* 70 Fed. Reg. 71,892-01, 71,893-71,896 (Nov. 30, 2005).

8. *Triage vs. Equal Protection.* The CDC maintains the Strategic National Stockpile (SNS) program. Within 12 hours of a terrorist attack, the Stockpile can deliver "push packages" containing needed pharmaceuticals and other medical supplies anywhere in the country. See CDC, *Strategic National Stockpile,* Apr. 14, 2005, *at* http://www.bt.cdc.gov/stockpile/. Inventories are nevertheless limited, and they might not be adequate to treat every person affected by an outbreak of some diseases. For example, as of March 2006, 5.5 million doses of antiviral drugs were on hand in case of pandemic influenza, while another 20 million doses were on order. *See* Press Release, Dept. of Health and Human Serv., *HHS Buys Additional Antiviral Medication As Preparations for Potential Influenza Pandemic Continue,* Mar. 1, 2006, *available at* http://www.hhs.gov/news/press/2006pres/20060301.html. Who do you think should receive such limited supplies first? Who should be empowered to choose among potential recipients? Would it be a good idea to decide such questions in advance of a terrorist attack or pandemic? If so, how?

The Domestic Role of the Armed Forces —32

The domestic use of troops has been a fact of life and a matter of controversy at least since President Washington called out the militia to put down the Whiskey Rebellion in 1794. Many other Presidents have deployed federal military forces to help keep the peace, to aid local governments in natural disasters, and to enforce federal and state laws. State governors have called out their militias even more often, especially in the first three decades of the twentieth century.

The precise locus and scope of authority for this use are much disputed. Express constitutional authority for such use appears in Article I, Section 8, which says, "The Congress shall have the power... to provide for calling forth the Militia to execute the Laws of the Union, suppress Insurrections and repel Invasions...." Additional textual authority may be drawn from Article IV, Section 4, which imposes on the federal government the obligation to protect each of the states "against Invasion; and on Application of the Legislature, or of the Executive (when the Legislature cannot be convened) against domestic Violence." The President also claims power from his Article II duties to faithfully execute the laws and to act as Commander in Chief of the armed forces. Congress has enacted a number of relevant measures as well.

This chapter addresses persistent questions about when and how troops can be used within the United States. It also rehearses an urgent current debate about what role the military should play in responding to a threatened or actual terrorist attack or to a great natural disaster.

A. THE MILITARY IN AMERICAN SOCIETY

1. The Posse Comitatus Act as a Background Principle

Bissonette v. Haig
United States Court of Appeals, Eighth Circuit, 1985
776 F.2d 1384, *aff'd*, 800 F.2d 812 (8th Cir. 1986) (en banc),
aff'd, 485 U.S. 264 (1988)

ARNOLD, J. This is an action for damages caused by defendants' alleged violations of the Constitution of the United States....

This case arises out of the occupation of the village of Wounded Knee, South Dakota, on the Pine Ridge Reservation by an armed group of Indians on February 27, 1973. On the evening when the occupation began, members of the Federal Bureau of Investigation, the United States Marshals Service, and the Bureau of Indian Affairs Police sealed off the village by establishing roadblocks at all major entry and exit roads. The standoff between the Indians and the law enforcement authorities ended about ten weeks later with the surrender of the Indians occupying the village....

In their amended complaint, plaintiffs allege three sets of substantive claims. First, they claim that they were unreasonably seized and confined in the village of Wounded Knee contrary to the Fourth Amendment and their rights to free movement and travel. Second, they claim that they were unreasonably searched by ground and aerial surveillance. In both cases, plaintiffs assert that the seizures and searches were unreasonable because "Defendants accomplished or caused to be accomplished those actions by means of the unconstitutional and felonious use of parts of the United States Army or Air Force...." Third, plaintiffs claim they were assaulted, deprived of life in one instance, and deprived of property contrary to their rights under the Fifth and Eighth Amendments. Again, plaintiffs allege that these actions were unconstitutional "for the reason that the arms used in the force or threat of force were parts of the United States Army or Air Force...." This case comes to us on appeal from a dismissal for failure to state a claim, and we therefore accept for present purposes the factual allegations of the complaint.

These allegations must be viewed against the background of the Posse Comitatus Act of 1878, 18 U.S.C. §1385, which plaintiffs claim was violated here. The statue provides:

§1385. Use of Army and Air Force as Posse Comitatus[1]

Whoever, except in cases and under circumstances expressly authorized by the Constitution or Act of Congress, willfully uses any part of the Army or the Air Force as a posse comitatus or otherwise to execute the laws shall be fined not more than $10,000 or imprisoned not more than two years, or both.

[1. The Latin term "posse comitatus" means, literally, "power or authority of the county," but it connotes a body of persons summoned by a sheriff to assist in preserving the peace or enforcing the law. The persons summoned to assist the sheriff might, of course, be either civilian or military.]

A

The first two sets of claims raise the question whether a search or seizure, otherwise permissible, can be rendered unreasonable under the Fourth Amendment because military personnel or equipment were used to accomplish those actions. We believe that the Constitution, certain Acts of Congress, and the decisions of the Supreme Court embody certain limitations on the use of military personnel in enforcing the civil law, and that searches and seizures in circumstances which exceed those limits are unreasonable under the Fourth Amendment.

... Reasonableness is determined by balancing the interests for and against the seizure. Usually, the interests arrayed against a seizure are those of the individual in privacy, freedom of movement, or, in the case of a seizure by deadly force, life. Here, however, the opposing interests are more societal and governmental than strictly individual in character. They concern the special threats to constitutional government inherent in military enforcement of civilian law. That these governmental interests should weigh in the Fourth Amendment balance is neither novel nor surprising. In the typical Fourth Amendment case, the interests of the individual are balanced against those of the government. That some of those governmental interests are on the other side of the Fourth Amendment balance does not make them any less relevant or important.

Civilian rule is basic to our system of government. The use of military forces to seize civilians can expose civilian government to the threat of military rule and the suspension of constitutional liberties. On a lesser scale, military enforcement of the civil law leaves the protection of vital Fourth and Fifth Amendment rights in the hands of persons who are not trained to uphold these rights. It may also chill the exercise of fundamental rights, such as the rights to speak freely and to vote,[6] and create the atmosphere of fear and hostility which exists in territories occupied by enemy forces.

The interest in limiting military involvement in civilian affairs has a long tradition beginning with the Declaration of Independence and continued in the Constitution, certain Acts of Congress, and decisions of the Supreme Court. The Declaration of Independence states among the grounds for severing ties with Great Britain that the King "has kept among us, in times of peace, Standing Armies without Consent of our Legislature ... [and] has affected to render the Military independent of and superior to the Civil power." These concerns were later raised at the Constitutional Convention. Luther Martin of Maryland said, "when a government wishes to deprive its citizens of freedom, and reduce them to slavery, it generally makes use of a standing army."

The Constitution itself limits the role of the military in civilian affairs: it makes the President, the highest civilian official in the Executive Branch, Commander in Chief of the armed services (Art. II, §2); it limits the appropriations for armed forces to two years and grants to the Congress the power to make rules to govern the armed forces (Art. I, §8, cl. 14); and it forbids the involuntary quartering of soldiers in any house in time of peace (Third Amendment).

---

6. Congress has in fact passed two criminal statutes specially dealing with military intimidation at voting places. 18 U.S.C. §§592, 593.

A. The Military in American Society

Congress has passed several statutes limiting the use of the military in enforcing the civil law. [In addition to the Posse Comitatus Act,] Title 10 U.S.C. §§331-335 delimit the circumstances under which the President may call upon the national guard or military to suppress insurrection or domestic violence. See also 32 C.F.R. §215 (1984).

The Supreme Court has also recognized the constitutional limitations placed on military involvement in civilian affairs. A leading case is Ex parte Milligan, 71 U.S. 2, 124 (1866).... More recently, in Laird v. Tatum, 408 U.S. 1, 15-16 (1972), statements the Court made in dicta reaffirm these limitations:

> The concerns of the Executive and Legislative Branches... reflect a traditional and strong resistance of Americans to any military intrusion into civilian affairs.... Indeed, when presented with claims of judicially cognizable injury resulting from military intrusion into the civilian sector, federal courts are fully empowered to consider claims of those asserting such injury; there is nothing in our Nation's history or in this Court's decided cases, including our holding today, that can properly be seen as giving any indication that actual or threatened injury by reason of unlawful activities of the military would go unnoticed or unremedied.

The governmental interests favoring military assistance to civilian law enforcement are primarily twofold: first, to maintain order in times of domestic violence or rebellion; and second, to improve the efficiency of civilian law enforcement by giving it the benefit of military technologies, equipment, information, and training personnel. These interests can and have been accommodated by Acts of Congress to the overriding interest of preserving civilian government and law enforcement. At the time of the Wounded Knee occupation, Congress had prohibited the use of the military to execute the civilian laws, except when expressly authorized. 18 U.S.C. §1385. And it had placed specific limits on the President's power to use the national guard and military in emergency situations. 10 U.S.C. §§331-335. For example, under 10 U.S.C. §332, the President may call upon the military only after having determined that domestic unrest makes it "impracticable to enforce the laws of the United States by the ordinary course of judicial proceedings," and under 10 U.S.C. §334, he may do so only after having issued a proclamation ordering the insurgents to disperse. Those steps were not taken here.

We believe that the limits established by Congress on the use of the military for civilian law enforcement provide a reliable guidepost by which to evaluate the reasonableness for Fourth Amendment purposes of the seizures and searches in question here. Congress has acted to establish reasonable limits on the President's use of military forces in emergency situations, and in doing so has circumscribed whatever, if any, inherent power the President may have had absent such legislation. This is the teaching of Youngstown Sheet & Tube Co. v. Sawyer, 343 U.S. 579 (1952)....

B

... As will be seen shortly when we come to discuss plaintiff's allegations under the Due Process Clause of the Fifth Amendment, the essence of due process is that no governmental power, civilian or military, may be used to restrain the liberty of the citizen or seize his property otherwise than in accordance with the forms of law, including, in most instances, judicial proceedings. In the context of the Fourth Amendment, however, we believe plaintiff's theory that the use of military force is in a class by itself has merit. The legal traditions which we have briefly summarized establish that the use of military force for domestic law-enforcement purposes is in a special category, and that both the courts and Congress have been alert to keep it there. In short, if the use of military personnel is both unauthorized by any statute, and contrary to a specific criminal prohibition, and if citizens are seized or searched by military means in such a case, we have no hesitation in declaring that such searches and seizures are constitutionally "unreasonable." We do not mean to say that every search or seizure that violates a statute of any kind is necessarily a violation of the Fourth Amendment. But the statute prohibiting (if the allegations in the complaint can be proved) the conduct engaged in by defendants here is, as we have attempted to explain, not just any Act of Congress. It is the embodiment of a long tradition of suspicion and hostility towards the use of military force for domestic purposes.

Plaintiffs' Fourth Amendment case, therefore, must stand or fall on the proposition that military activity in connection with the occupation of Wounded Knee violated the Posse Comitatus Act.

In United States v. Casper, 541 F.2d 1275 (8th Cir. 1976) (per curiam), cert. denied, 430 U.S. 970 (1977), ... the District Court had found on a stipulated record that the following activities did not violate the Act: the use of Air Force personnel, planes, and cameras to fly surveillance; the advice of military officers in dealing with the disorder; and the furnishing of equipment and supplies. We affirmed "on the basis of the trial court's thorough and well-reasoned opinion." 541 F.2d at 1276.

... Therefore, unless plaintiffs now allege that the defendants took actions that went beyond those alleged in the *Casper* case, the actions alleged in the complaint now before us cannot violate the Act.

In *Casper*, quoting from Judge VanSickle's opinion for the District Court, 419 F. Supp. at 194, we approved the following standard for determining whether a violation of the Posse Comitatus Act had occurred:

> Were Army or Air Force personnel used by the civilian law enforcement officers at Wounded Knee in such a manner that the military personnel subjected the citizens to the exercise of military power which was regulatory, proscriptive, or compulsory in nature, either presently or prospectively?

541 F.2d at 1278. This formulation, see 419 F. Supp. at 194 n.4, is based on language found in the Supreme Court's opinion in Laird v. Tatum, 408 U.S. 1, 11 (1972). *Laird* involved a claim that First Amendment rights were chilled by the existence of a data-gathering system maintained by Army Intelligence, a system described by plaintiffs in that case as involving the surveillance of lawful civilian political activity. The Court rejected this claim on the ground that no justiciable controversy existed. It held that the mere existence of this challenged data-gathering system infringed no rights of plaintiffs, since there had been no showing of objective harm or threat of specific future harm.

A. The Military in American Society

When this concept is transplanted into the present legal context, we take it to mean that military involvement, even when not expressly authorized by the Constitution or a statute, does not violate the Posse Comitatus Act unless it actually regulates, forbids, or compels some conduct on the part of those claiming relief. A mere threat of some future injury would be insufficient....

... We of course have no way of knowing what plaintiffs would be able to prove if this case goes to trial, but the complaint, considered simply as a pleading, goes well beyond an allegation that defendants simply furnished supplies, aerial surveillance, and advice. It specifically charges that "the several Defendants maintained or caused to be maintained roadblocks and armed patrols constituting an armed perimeter around the village of Wounded Knee...." Defendants' actions, it is charged, "seized, confined, and made prisoners (of plaintiffs) against their will...." These allegations amount to a claim that defendants' activities, allegedly in violation of the Posse Comitatus Act, were "regulatory, proscriptive, or compulsory," in the sense that these activities directly restrained plaintiffs' freedom of movement. No more is required to survive a motion to dismiss....

As to the second set of claims, ... plaintiffs charge that they were searched and subjected to surveillance against their will by aerial photographic and visual search and surveillance. As we have already noted, *Casper* holds that this sort of activity does not violate the Posse Comitatus Act. It is therefore not "unreasonable" for Fourth Amendment purposes....

C

The third set of claims invokes the Due Process Clause of the Fifth Amendment. Plaintiffs argue that they were deprived of liberty, property, and, in the case of the son of one of the plaintiffs, life without due process of law. In the ordinary case, a claimed lack of due process relates to the absence of a notice and hearing or certain other procedural deficiencies. Plaintiffs' theory here is quite different. They claim a due process violation by reason of the mere fact that the confinement and other deprivations inflicted upon them derived from military action instead of civilian. Plaintiffs cite a number of 19th-century cases which they say supports this view. E.g., Ex parte Merryman, 17 Fed. Cas. 144 (No. 9487) (Taney, C.J., in chambers) (1861). We have carefully examined each of these authorities and find in them no clear support for the novel theory advocated by plaintiffs. In *Merryman*, for example, the Chief Justice did mention the Due Process Clause of the Fifth Amendment, and the petitioner in that habeas corpus proceeding was in military custody, but the result in the case would have been exactly the same had the custody been civilian, because Merryman was seized and imprisoned without any judicial process. It was the absence of that process, rather than the military character of Merryman's custodian, that caused the Chief Justice to take the view that the petitioner was unconstitutionally confined.

... [P]laintiffs' complaint here is clearly grounded on the due-process theory that an action by a military officer can violate the Fifth Amendment even though exactly the same thing, if done by a civilian federal official, would not. With this proposition we do not agree....

Our decision to reject plaintiffs' due-process theory is reinforced by the knowledge that all of the proof relevant under such a theory will still come in if and when the Fourth Amendment search-and-seizure theory goes to trial. In other words, plaintiffs do not really need the due-process theory in order to secure relief here, the Court having already held that an unauthorized action by a military officer can be "unreasonable" under the Fourth Amendment even though the same thing, if done by a civilian official, would not....

NOTES AND QUESTIONS

1. *The Military's Role at Wounded Knee.* At Wounded Knee federal law enforcement officials were furnished with vehicles and equipment by the Army and the South Dakota National Guard, with aerial reconnaissance by the Air Force and the Nebraska National Guard, and with Army advisors. Two persons were killed and one U.S. marshal was seriously wounded during the standoff. The ranking Army advisor at the site, Colonel Volney Warner, may have prevented further bloodshed. He convinced federal law enforcement officials to abandon their shoot-to-kill policy, recommended that roadblocks not be tightened, and, perhaps most significantly, consistently advised against the deployment of federal troops. *See* United States v. Jaramillo, 380 F. Supp. 1375, 1379 (D. Neb. 1974), *appeal dismissed,* 510 F.2d 808 (8th Cir. 1975); United States v. Red Feather, 392 F. Supp. 916 (D.S.D. 1975).

2. *Origins of the Posse Comitatus Act.* Early acts of Congress authorized the use of the militia to aid in law enforcement, although such use was never so extensive as it was after the Civil War. Reconstruction era abuses, culminating in the use of federal troops to police polling stations in Southern states (some say to influence the outcome of the presidential election of 1876), led to passage of the Posse Comitatus Act in 1878. The history is set forth in David E. Engdahl, *The New Civil Disturbances Regulations: The Threat of Military Intervention,* 49 Ind. L.J. 581, 597-603 (1974); Gary Felicetti & John Luce, *The Posse Comitatus Act: Setting the Record Straight on 124 Years of Mischief and Misunderstanding Before Any More Damage Is Done,* 175 Mil. L. Rev. 86, 93-127 (2003); Clarence I. Meeks III, *Illegal Law Enforcement: Aiding Civil Authorities in Violation of the Posse Comitatus Act,* 70 Mil. L. Rev. 83, 86-93 (1975); and University of Colorado Law Revision Center, *A Comprehensive Study of the Use of Military Troops in Civil Disorders with Proposals for Legislative Reform,* 43 U. Colo. L. Rev. 399, 402-412 (1972). The Act is described generally in Jennifer Elsea, *The Posse Comitatus Act and Related Matters: A Sketch* (Cong. Res. Serv. RS20590), June 6, 2005; Matthew Carlton Hammond, Note, *The Posse Comitatus Act: A Principle in Need of Renewal,* 75 Wash. U. L.Q. 953 (1997); Sean J. Kealy, *Reexamining the Posse Comitatus Act: Toward a Right to Civil Law Enforcement,* 21 Yale L. & Poly. Rev. 383 (2003); Brian J. Porto, Annotation, *Construction and Application of Posse Comitatus Act,* 141 A.L.R. Fed. 271 (1997); and 53 Am. Jur. 2d *Military & Civil Defense* §§12, 13 (1996).

3. *Elements of a Posse Comitatus Act Violation.* What exactly constitutes use of the armed forces "as a posse comitatus or otherwise to execute the laws"? To the "regulatory, proscriptive, or compulsory" standard set forth in *Bissonette,* we may

A. The Military in American Society

add criteria from other cases growing out of the Wounded Knee incident: whether there was "direct, active" use of the military in civil law enforcement, United States v. Red Feather, *supra*, at 923, or whether the use of the Army or the Air Force "pervaded the activities" of the civil law enforcement officers. United States v. Jaramillo, *supra*, at 1379.

The Posse Comitatus Act may be inapplicable when the primary purpose of armed forces involvement is to enforce the Uniform Code of Military Justice or to achieve some distinctly military goal, and the benefits to civilian authorities are merely incidental, as when the military has concurrent jurisdiction over crimes committed in the civilian community. *See* Applewhite v. United States Air Force, 995 F.2d 997, 1001 (10th Cir. 1993); United States v. Thompson, 33 M.J. 218 (C.M.A. 1991), *cert. denied*, 502 U.S. 1074 (1992).

Do you think the Posse Comitatus Act should be amended to make it easier to predict when the Act would apply? If so, how?

4. *Judicial Remedies for Violations.* There apparently never has been a criminal prosecution of anyone for violation of the Posse Comitatus Act. Paul Jackson Rice, *New Laws and Insights Encircle the Posse Comitatus Act*, 104 Mil. L. Rev. 109, 111 (1984); John D. Gates, Comment, *Don't Call Out the Marines: An Assessment of the Posse Comitatus Act*, 13 Tex. Tech L. Rev. 1467, 1468 (1968).

Violations of the Posse Comitatus Act have often been asserted as a defense to charges under other criminal statutes. For example, in *Red Feather* and *Jaramillo, supra,* individuals at Wounded Knee were charged with interfering with a "law enforcement officer lawfully engaged in the lawful performance of his official duties." *See* 18 U.S.C. §231(a)(3) (2000). The defendants argued that the federal marshals and FBI agents were not performing their duties lawfully, within the meaning of the statute, because they enlisted military forces as a posse comitatus. *See also* United States v. Mendoza-Cecelia, 963 F.2d 1467, 1478 n.9 (11th Cir.), *cert. denied*, 506 U.S. 964 (1992).

Others apprehended by the military while attempting to smuggle drugs into the United States have argued that the evidence obtained in their arrests was inadmissible at trial. However, the federal courts have consistently refused to exclude such evidence in the absence of widespread and repeated Posse Comitatus Act violations. *See, e.g.,* Hayes v. Hawes, 921 F.2d 100, 104 (7th Cir. 1990); United States v. Hartley, 796 F.2d 112, 115 (5th Cir. 1986); United States v. Wolffs, 594 F.2d 77, 85 (5th Cir. 1979). *Cf.* State v. Pattioay, 896 P.2d 911 (Haw. 1995); Taylor v. State, 645 P.2d 522 (Okla. Crim. App. 1982). *See* Timothy J. Saviano, Note, *The Exclusionary Rule's Applicability to Violations of the Posse Comitatus Act*, Army Law., July 1995, at 61. Do you think the admission of such evidence is consistent with the constitutional analysis in *Bissonette?*

In Bissonette v. Haig, the appellants sought damages for infringement of their constitutional rights resulting from Posse Comitatus Act violations. Do such statutory violations give rise to a private cause of action separate and apart from any possible constitutional injury? Does the *Bissonette* opinion suggest the existence of such a right? *See* Robinson v. Overseas Military Sales Corp., 21 F.3d 502 (2d Cir. 1994); Lamont v. Haig, 539 F. Supp. 552 (W.D.S.D. 1982). *See also* O'Brien, Note, *Civil Liability Under the Posse Comitatus Act*, Army Law., July 1995, at 65.

5. *Which Service Branches Are Covered?* Although the Posse Comitatus Act expressly refers only to the Army and Air Force, Navy regulations have long prohibited the use of the Navy and Marine Corps as a posse comitatus, with certain exceptions, as a matter of Defense Department policy. *See* SECNAVINST 5820.7B (Mar. 28, 1988). Several cases have found that the Act does not restrict Navy law enforcement efforts. *Mendoza-Cecelia, supra,* at 1477-1478; United States v. Yunis, 924 F.2d 1086, 1093 (D.C. Cir. 1991); United States v. Roberts, 779 F.2d 565 (9th Cir. 1986). *But cf.* United States v. Chon, 210 F.3d 990 (9th Cir. 2000); United States v. Klimavicius-Viloria, 144 F.3d 1249, 1259 (9th Cir. 1998) ("Congress has extended the substance of the Act to the Navy by a separate statute, 10 U.S.C. §§371-382."); United States v. Kahn, 35 F.3d 426, 431 (9th Cir. 1994); *Hayes, supra,* at 102-103. *See generally* Christopher A. Abel, Note, *Not Fit for Sea Duty: The Posse Comitatus Act, The United States Navy, and Federal Law Enforcement at Sea,* 31 Wm. & Mary L. Rev. 445, 456-485 (1990); John P. Coffey, Note, *The Navy's Role in Interdicting Narcotics Traffic: War on Drugs or Ambush on the Constitution?,* 75 Geo. L.J. 1947 (1987). How do you think the *Bissonette* court would have ruled on this question?

6. *Posse Comitatus Act and the National Guard.* Several courts have held that unfederalized National Guard forces are not subject to the strictures of the Posse Comitatus Act. *See, e.g.,* United States v. Gilbert, 165 F.3d 470 (6th Cir. 1999); United States v. Hutchings, 127 F.3d 1255 (10th Cir. 1997). Moreover, Congress has explicitly approved the states' use of the militia for "drug interdiction and counter-drug activities," so long as they remain under state control. 32 U.S.C.A. §112 (West Supp. 2005). *See* L. Dow Davis, *Reserve Callup Authorities: Time for Recall?,* Army Law., Apr. 1990, at 4.

7. *Extraterritorial Application of the Posse Comitatus Act.* United States statutes are presumed to have no application outside the nation's borders unless Congress makes it clear that they are intended to have extraterritorial effect. The Supreme Court has based that presumption on a desire to avoid unintended entanglements in the diplomatic affairs of other nations. *See* Equal Employment Opportunity Commn. v. Arabian American Oil Co., 499 U.S. 244 (1991); Foley Bros. v. Filardo, 336 U.S. 281 (1949). Does the Posse Comitatus Act limit military involvement in law enforcement abroad? Several courts have answered in the negative. *See, e.g.,* United States v. Yunis, *supra.*

Just weeks before the United States invasion of Panama in 1989, the Justice Department issued an opinion declaring that the Posse Comitatus Act has no application outside the United States. 13 Op. Off. Legal Counsel 321 (1989). It pointed to the text, legislative history, and original purposes of the act, and to the usual presumption against extraterritorial application of statutes. An opinion from the same office a few months earlier had expressed doubt on this question. 13 Op. Off. Legal Counsel 235 (1989).

What do you think Congress had in mind on this point when it passed the Act in 1878? Does the policy basis for the presumption against extraterritorial application of statutes have any relevance to the Posse Comitatus Act? That is, would enforcement of the Act abroad create entanglements in the diplomatic affairs of other nations? What can we infer about Congress's intent from its explicitly limited approval, in 10 U.S.C. §374, of military involvement in the pursuit of drug traffickers offshore? *See* United States v. Kahn, *supra*, at 431 n.6. *See generally* Leroy C. Bryant, *The Posse Comitatus Act, the Military, and Drug Interdiction: Just How Far Can We Go?*, Army Law., Dec. 1990, at 3; Deanne C. Siemer & Andrew S. Effron, *Military Participation in United States Law Enforcement Activities Overseas: The Extraterritorial Effect of the Posse Comitatus Act*, 54 St. John's L. Rev. 1 (1979); Christopher A. Donesa, Note, *Protecting National Interests: The Legal Status of Extraterritorial Law Enforcement by the Military*, 41 Duke L.J. 867 (1992).

2. Exceptions to the Posse Comitatus Act

Recall that the Posse Comitatus Act prohibition applies "except in cases and under circumstances expressly authorized by the Constitution or Act of Congress." 18 U.S.C. §1385 (2000). The most important exception to the act is a set of five statutes, referred to collectively as the Insurrection Act, 10 U.S.C. §§331-335 (2000). They provide, in part:

Insurrection Act
10 U.S.C. §§331-335 (2000) as amended by
Pub. L. No. 109-364, §1076, 120 Stat. 2083, 2404 (2006)

§332. USE OF MILITIA AND ARMED FORCES TO ENFORCE FEDERAL AUTHORITY

Whenever the President considers that unlawful obstructions, combinations, or assemblages, or rebellion against the authority of the United States, make it impracticable to enforce the laws of the United States in any State or Territory by the ordinary course of judicial proceedings, he may call into Federal service such of the militia of any State, and use such of the armed forces, as he considers necessary to enforce those laws or to suppress the rebellion.

§333. MAJOR PUBLIC EMERGENCIES; INTERFERENCE WITH STATE AND FEDERAL LAW

(a) Use of Armed Forces in Major Public Emergencies—
    (1) The President may employ the armed forces, including the National Guard in Federal service, to—
        (A) restore public order and enforce the laws of the United States when, as a result of a natural disaster, epidemic, or other serious public health emergency, terrorist attack or incident, or other condition in any State or possession of the United States, the President determines that—
            (i) domestic violence has occurred to such an extent that the constituted authorities of the State or possession are incapable of maintaining public order; ...
    (b) Notice to Congress—The President shall notify Congress of the determination to exercise the authority in subsection (a)(1)(A) as soon as practicable after the determination and every 14 days thereafter during the duration of the exercise of that authority.

[Section 331 provides for federal military assistance in putting down an insurrection against a state government. Section 334 directs the President to issue a proclamation to disperse. Section 335 makes the statutes applicable to Guam and the Virgin Islands.]

A different set of statutory exceptions to the Posse Comitatus Act was enacted in 1981. Military Cooperation with Law Enforcement Officials Act, Pub. L. No. 97-86, 95 Stat. 1115 (codified as amended at 10 U.S.C. §§371-382). Here are selected provisions:

Military Cooperation with Law Enforcement Officials Act
10 U.S.C. §§371-382 (2000 & Supp. III 2003)

§371. USE OF INFORMATION COLLECTED DURING MILITARY OPERATIONS

(a) The Secretary of Defense may, in accordance with other applicable law, provide to Federal, State, or local civilian law enforcement officials any information collected during the normal course of military training or operations that may be relevant to a violation of any Federal or State law within the jurisdiction of such officials.

(b) The needs of civilian law enforcement officials for information shall, to the maximum extent practicable, be taken into account in the planning and execution of military training or operations.

(c) The Secretary of Defense shall ensure, to the extent consistent with national security, that intelligence information held by the Department of Defense and relevant to drug interdiction or other civilian law enforcement matters is provided promptly to appropriate civilian law enforcement officials....

§375. RESTRICTION ON DIRECT PARTICIPATION BY MILITARY PERSONNEL

The Secretary of Defense shall prescribe such regulations as may be necessary to ensure that any activity (including the provision of any equipment or facility or the assignment or detail of any personnel) under this chapter does not include or permit direct participation by a member of the Army, Navy, Air Force, or Marine Corps in a search, seizure, arrest, or other similar activity unless participation in such activity by such member is otherwise authorized by law....

§382. EMERGENCY SITUATIONS INVOLVING CHEMICAL OR BIOLOGICAL WEAPONS OF MASS DESTRUCTION

(a) In general.—The Secretary of Defense, upon the request of the Attorney General, may provide assistance in support of Department of Justice activities relating to the enforcement of section 175 or 2332c of title 18 during an emergency situation involving a biological or chemical weapon of mass destruction. Department of Defense resources, including personnel of the Department of Defense, may be used to provide such assistance if—

(1) the Secretary of Defense and the Attorney General jointly determine that an emergency situation exists; and

(2) the Secretary of Defense determines that the provision of such assistance will not adversely affect the military preparedness of the United States.

(b) Emergency situations covered.—In this section, the term "emergency situation involving a biological or chemical weapon of mass destruction" means a circumstance involving a biological or chemical weapon of mass destruction—

(1) that poses a serious threat to the interests of the United States; and

(2) in which—

(A) civilian expertise and capabilities are not readily available to provide the required assistance to counter the threat immediately posed by the weapon involved;

(B) special capabilities and expertise of the Department of Defense are necessary and critical to counter the threat posed by the weapon involved; and

(C) enforcement of section 175 or 2332c of title 18 would be seriously impaired if the Department of Defense assistance were not provided.

(c) Forms of assistance.—The assistance referred to in subsection (a) includes the operation of equipment... to monitor, contain, disable, or dispose of the weapon involved or elements of the weapon.

(d) Regulations.—(1) The Secretary of Defense and the Attorney General shall jointly prescribe regulations concerning the types of assistance that may be provided under this section. Such regulations shall also describe the actions that Department of Defense personnel may take in circumstances incident to the provision of assistance under this section.

(2) (A) Except as provided in subparagraph (B), the regulations may not authorize the following actions:

(i) Arrest.

(ii) Any direct participation in conducting a search for or seizure of evidence related to a violation of section 175 or 2332c of title 18.

(iii) Any direct participation in the collection of intelligence for law enforcement purposes.

(B) The regulations may authorize an action described in subparagraph (A) to be taken under the following conditions:

(i) The action is considered necessary for the immediate protection of human life, and civilian law enforcement officials are not capable of taking the action.

(ii) The action is otherwise authorized under subsection (c) or under otherwise applicable law....

Other sections of the 1981 Act, as amended, deal variously with use of military equipment and facilities, training and advising civilian law enforcement officials, maintenance and operation of equipment, reimbursement, the use of Coast Guard personnel for law enforcement, and impacts on military preparedness. References to §§175 and 2332c of title 18 concern prohibitions on the possession or use of biological or chemical weapons, respectively. 18 U.S.C. §2332c has been replaced by 18 U.S.C. §229 (2000).

Additional exceptions to the Posse Comitatus Act are considered in the following Notes and Questions.

NOTES AND QUESTIONS

1. *The Insurrection Act.* The Insurrection Act had its origin in a 1792 law invoked by President Washington in suppressing the Whiskey Rebellion. The history of its component parts is traced in Stephen I. Vladeck, Note, *Emergency Power and the Militia Acts*, 114 Yale L.J. 149, 159-167 (2004). In 1827, the Supreme Court indicated that the President had broad discretion in determining when to use these statutes in calling forth the militia, and that his determination was not subject to judicial review. Martin v. Mott, 25 U.S. (12 Wheat.) 19, 29-32 (1827). *See also* Luther v. Borden, 48 U.S. (7 How.) 1, 43-45 (1849); *The Prize Cases*, 67 U.S. (2 Black) 635, 668 (1863), *supra* p. 67.

Since that time the Insurrection Act has been invoked for a variety of purposes, including the breaking of the Pullman Strike in 1894. More recently, it has been used to help integrate public schools and universities, to control racial unrest, to collect intelligence about citizens, and to enforce a variety of state and federal laws. *See* Dominic J. Campisi, Note, *Honored in the Breech: Presidential Authority to Execute the Laws with Military Force*, 83 Yale L.J. 130, 131, 146-147 (1973); Jack B. Schmetterer, *Military Enforcement of Court Decrees*, 44 A.B.A. J. 727 (1958); and University of Colorado Law Revision Center, *supra* p. 950, at 399-401. It was invoked in 1992 to send federalized California National Guard troops, as well as active duty soldiers from Fort Ord and Marines from Camp Pendleton, to Los Angeles to help control rioting in the wake of the Rodney King trial verdict. Exec. Order No. 12,804, 57 Fed. Reg. 19,361 (May 1, 1992); Proclamation No. 6427, 57 Fed. Reg. 19,359 (May 1, 1992).

Can you think of any domestic emergency that could not be addressed by the President using troops if one of the provisions of the Insurrection Act were invoked? Would the unwillingness of a state governor to ask for assistance ever be a bar to such use? Could troops so deployed make searches and arrests, direct traffic, enforce quarantines? Why do you suppose the Insurrection Act was not invoked at Wounded Knee?

2. *Helping the Secret Service.* Another exception to the Posse Comitatus Act is found in H.R.J. Res. 1292, Pub. L. No. 90-331, 82 Stat. 170 (1968), which directs federal agencies (including the Department of Defense) to assist the Secret Service in the performance of its protective duties. This authority was used by President Johnson to deploy troops in Chicago during the Democratic National Convention in 1968 and by President Nixon to control antiwar demonstrations on several occasions. *See* Campisi, *supra*, at 146.

3. *The Military Cooperation with Law Enforcement Officials Act.* A dramatic surge in illicit drug traffic and related criminal activity during the 1970s and 1980s led President Reagan to declare a "war on drugs." *See* Christopher

A. The Military in American Society

Simpson, *National Security Directives of the Reagan and Bush Administrations* 640-641 (1995). Congress responded in 1981 by enacting the Military Cooperation with Law Enforcement Officials Act, excerpted above, allowing the military to furnish equipment, facilities, and training to civilian law enforcement agencies, and to share relevant intelligence. Department of Defense Authorization Act, 1982, Pub. L. No. 97-86, §905, 95 Stat. 1099, 1114 (codified as amended at 10 U.S.C. §§371-382 (2000 & Supp. IV 2004)). The Act also authorizes military personnel to operate equipment to intercept vessels or aircraft for law enforcement purposes. *Id.* §374. But it expressly forbids "direct participation by a member of the Army, Navy, Air Force, or Marine Corps in a search, seizure, arrest, or other similar activity unless... otherwise authorized by law." *Id.* §375. In separate legislation, the Defense Department was designated lead agency for the detection and monitoring of aerial and maritime shipments of illicit drugs into the United States. 10 U.S.C. §124 (2000). And in 1998 Congress expanded the permitted uses of military personnel to operate loaned equipment to include enforcement of terrorism laws. Pub. L. No. 105-277, Div. B, Tit. II, §201, 112 Stat. 2681, 2681-567 (1998) (amending 10 U.S.C. §374). *See generally* Felicetti & Luce, *supra* p. 950, at 149-153; Peter M. Sanchez, *The "Drug War": The U.S. Military and National Security*, 34 A.F. L. Rev. 109, 137-152 (1991); Thomas S.M. Tudor & Mark E. Garrard, *The Military and the War on Drugs*, 37 A.F. L. Rev. 267 (1994).

Do you think this legislation expanded the role that the military can play in nonmilitary law enforcement? Can you say how? Did it add to powers already enjoyed by the President under the Insurrection Act? If not, why did Congress bother to pass it?

4. *Other Statutory Exceptions.* Congress has approved emergency military assistance in enforcing a prohibition on the unauthorized possession or use of nuclear material. 18 U.S.C. §831(d), (e) (2000). *See also* 42 U.S.C. §1989 (2000) (authorizing federal magistrates to order members of the armed forces to assist in the execution of certain arrest warrants).

5. *The September 18 Authorization for the Use of Military Force.* Review the terms of the congressional resolution, passed in the immediate aftermath of the terrorist attacks of September 11, 2001, authorizing the use of the armed forces to prevent future acts of international terrorism by persons associated with the 9/11 attacks, *supra* p. 100. Does the resolution provide a statutory exception to the Posse Comitatus Act, permitting military assistance to law enforcement? If so, are there any limits to such use?

6. *Constitutional Exceptions.* The Posse Comitatus Act includes an exception for "circumstances expressly authorized by the Constitution." See *supra* p. 945. One possible express constitutional exception may be found in Article IV, Section 4, which provides, "The United States shall guarantee to every State in this Union a Republican Form of Government, and shall protect each of them against Invasion; and on Application of the Legislature, or of the Executive (when the Legislature cannot be convened) against domestic Violence." Can you describe the limits of the President's power to use troops for law enforcement under this provision?

Defense Department regulations entitled "Employment of Military Resources in the Event of Civil Disturbances" refer to two "constitutional exceptions" to the Posse Comitatus Act "based upon the inherent legal right of the U.S. Government—a sovereign national entity under the Federal Constitution—to insure the preservation of public order and the carrying out of governmental operations within its territorial limits, by force if necessary." 32 C.F.R. §215.4(c)(1) (2005). One exception is described as emergency authority to take

> prompt and vigorous Federal action, including use of military forces, to prevent loss of life or wanton destruction of property and to restore governmental functioning and public order when sudden and unexpected civil disturbances, disasters, or calamities seriously endanger life and property and disrupt normal governmental functions to such an extent that duly constituted local authorities are unable to control the situations. [*Id.* §215.4(c)(1)(i).]

The other is for "protection of federal property and functions." *Id.* §215.4(c)(1)(ii). *See also* DOD Dir. 5525.5, *DoD Cooperation with Civilian Law Enforcement Officials* (Dec. 20, 1989), at Encl. 4 §E4.1.2.3. President Johnson apparently believed that he was exercising such inherent powers when he ordered the military to suppress rioting in Washington, D.C., following the assassination of Dr. Martin Luther King Jr. in 1968. *See* Proclamation No. 3840, *Law and Order in the Washington Metropolitan Area*, 33 Fed. Reg. 5495 (Apr. 9, 1968). This regulatory authority closely resembles one for "Immediate Responses," 32 C.F.R. §185.4(e) (2005), noted *infra* p. 966. The powers claimed in the regulations are not "expressly" set out in the constitutional text, of course.

One observer asserts that "Congress could not deprive the President of his inherent constitutional authority to respond to a serious domestic emergency, even if that were its intent." Paul Schott Stevens, *U.S. Armed Forces and Homeland Defense: The Legal Framework* 24 (Center for Strategic and Intl. Studies 2001). Can you find support in our readings for his claim?

7. *Law Enforcement or War Fighting?* José Padilla was confined in a military brig for more than three years as an "enemy combatant" before finally being charged with criminal offenses related to terrorism. See *supra* pp. 742-754. In responding to his petition for a writ of habeas corpus, one court remarked:

> Padilla argues also that his detention by the military violates the Posse Comitatus Act. . . . First, it is questionable whether that statute is enforceable in a habeas corpus proceeding to secure release from custody. *Cf.* Robinson v. Overseas Military Sales Corp., 21 F.3d 502, 511 (2d Cir. 1994) (no private right of action to enforce Posse Comitatus Act). Moreover, the statute bars use of the military in civilian law enforcement. Padilla is not being detained by the military in order to execute a civilian law or for violating a civilian law, notwithstanding that his alleged conduct may in fact violate one or more such laws. He is being detained in order to interrogate him about the unlawful organization with which he is said to be affiliated and with which the military is in active combat, and to prevent him from becoming reaffiliated with that organization. Therefore, his detention by the military does not violate the Posse Comitatus Act. [Padilla v. Bush, 233 Fed. Supp. 2d 564, 588 n.9 (S.D.N.Y. 2002), *rev'd in part*, Padilla v. Rumsfeld, 352 F.3d 695 (2d Cir. 2003).]

Do you think the military can avoid application of the Posse Comitatus Act simply by characterizing a person it suspects of criminal activity as an "enemy combatant"? If you think this practice might be subject to abuse, can you suggest some realistic process for distinguishing between law enforcement and war fighting, at least for this purpose? Or can you articulate some other principled basis for limiting the military's role in activities that involve both law enforcement and war fighting?

8. *Implementing Regulations.* Protocols for the use of troops to quell civil unrest are spelled out in Dept. of the Army, *Civil Disturbance Operations* (FM 3-19.15), Apr. 2005. More detailed guidance is set forth in the *Department of Defense Civil Disurbance Plan (GARDEN PLOT)*, Feb. 15, 1991. *Garden Plot* provides for military missions to restore, not preserve, law and order, including "dispersing unlawful assemblages, patrolling disturbed areas, maintaining essential transportation and communications systems, setting up roadblocks, and cordoning off areas." Center for Law and Military Operations, *Domestic Operations Law (DOPLAW) Handbook for Judge Advocates* 66 (2004). Other regulatory authorities are described *infra* pp. 964-966.

B. THE MILITARY'S ROLE IN HOMELAND SECURITY AND DISASTER RELIEF

Until recently the Defense Department has organized itself almost exclusively to fight a conventional war far from America's shores. In part this reflects the earlier absence of the sort of domestic threats that have emerged in the last decade or so. It also demonstrates the public's strong antipathy, described above, toward any sort of military involvement in domestic affairs. *See* W. Kent Davis, *Swords Into Plowshares: The Dangerous Politicization of the Military in the Post-Cold War Era,* 33 Val. U. L. Rev. 61, 64-77 (1998). Thus, for most of our history the military's domestic role has consisted primarily of preparations for foreign wars, and of occasional support for civilian authorities in curbing civil unrest and fighting the war on drugs.

On September 11, 2001, however, the military's role, like so much else in this country, began to change. The following day the President described the terrorist attacks as "acts of war." The battlefield in this war obviously extends to the U.S. homeland. Should military forces be deployed on this new front? If so, should their "rules of engagement" be different from those that guide military operations abroad? What legal authorities exist or would have to be created to accommodate these needed changes?

In August 2005, with the catastrophic landfall of Hurricane Katrina, new questions were raised about the domestic mission of U.S. military forces in responding to what have come to be called "incidents of national significance." By many measures, the implications for national security were at least as great as those of a major terrorist attack. Should the Defense Department therefore be prepared to act more expansively in natural disasters than it has in the past?

Could any credible plan for recovery from such a disaster omit a leading role for DOD? Are new laws needed to allow the military to play that role?

We address these urgent and difficult questions in this section.

1. The Military's Intelligence Role in Homeland Security

Since the earliest days of the Republic, military intelligence units have supported domestic uses of military force. Chief Justice Marshall reportedly said of Washington, "A general must be governed by his intelligence and must regulate his measures by his information. It is his duty to obtain correct information...." *Quoted in* Tatum v. Laird, 444 F.2d 947, 952-953 (D.C. Cir. 1971), *rev'd*, 408 U.S. 1 (1972).

But military intelligence personnel have also been used occasionally to collect personal information about Americans who posed no real threat to national security. This activity reached a peak in the late 1960s, when the Pentagon compiled data on more than 100,000 politically active Americans, in an effort to quell civil rights and anti-Vietnam War demonstrations and to discredit protestors. The Army deployed 1,500 plainclothes agents to watch demonstrators, infiltrate organizations, and circulate blacklists. Military officials claimed that they were preparing for the use of troops to put down insurrections. *See* Christopher H. Pyle, *Military Surveillance of Civilian Politics, 1961-1971* (1986). In 1976, the Church Committee, looking into a variety of intelligence community abuses, called the Army program "the worst intrusion that military intelligence has ever made into the civilian community." S. Select Comm. to Study Governmental Operations with Respect to Intelligence Activities, *Improper Surveillance of Private Citizens by the Military (Church Committee Report)*, S. Rep. No. 94-755, Book III, at 792 (1976). Today the Pentagon describes what happened then as a classic example of "mission creep."

When these actions were revealed, political activists sued to stop them, claiming that their First Amendment rights of free expression and association were "chilled" by Army surveillance and record collection. They also worried that the improper use of information about their political activities might jeopardize their jobs and reputations. The Supreme Court dismissed the case on standing grounds, however, without directly mentioning the Posse Comitatus Act. Laird v. Tatum, 408 U.S. 1 (1972).

Congress reacted to these and other domestic intelligence abuses by passing the Privacy Act in 1974, 5 U.S.C. §552a (2000), see *infra* pp. 1017-1018, and the Foreign Intelligence Surveillance Act (FISA) in 1978, 50 U.S.C.A §§1801-1862 (West 2003 & Supp. 2005). See *supra* pp. 512-556. Both measures limit the collection, retention, and sharing of information about how individuals exercise rights guaranteed by the First Amendment, as well as information not relevant to the mission of an agency. But serious doubts exist about the efficacy of these laws in safeguarding personal privacy. *See, e.g.,* William C. Banks, *And the Wall Came Tumbling Down: Secret Surveillance After the Terror,* 57 U. Miami L. Rev. 1147 (2002); Steven W. Becker, *Maintaining Secret Government Dossiers on the First Amendment Activities of American Citizens: The Law Enforcement Activity Exception to the Privacy Act,* 50 DePaul L. Rev. 675 (2000).

B. The Military's Role in Homeland Security and Disaster Relief

Several developments in the wake of 9/11 point to a possible expanded domestic role for the military intelligence agencies, which include the Defense Intelligence Agency and intelligence operations within each of the service branches. *See generally* Stephen Dycus, *The Role of Military Intelligence in Homeland Security*, 64 La. L. Rev. 779 (2004). The Department of Homeland Security's Directorate for Information Analysis and Infrastructure Protection (IAIP), *supra* p. 637, receives, analyzes, and disseminates data about possible domestic terrorist threats from government and private sources, including the military's intelligence components. The National Counterterrorism Center (NCTC), *supra* p. 637, performs many of the same functions. Military intelligence personnel work in both of these agencies, where they become both suppliers and recipients of personal information about U.S. persons, some of which may have no clear relevance to the Pentagon's homeland defense mission. Congress has also approved the creation of an Under Secretary of Defense for Intelligence, 10 U.S.C. §137 (Supp. III 2003), who is supposed to provide "more coordinated, better focused intelligence support for pressing national concerns like homeland security." Dept. of Defense, *Report to Congress on the Role of the Department of Defense in Supporting Homeland Security* 3, Sept. 2003.

In 2002, DOD created the Northern Command (NORTHCOM), based in Colorado, to assist in homeland defense. *See generally* http://www.northcom.mil. Like IAIP and NCTC, NORTHCOM receives and "fuses" intelligence and law enforcement information from various sources, then redistributes it widely to federal, state, and local agencies. Unlike the two civilian agencies, however, NORTHCOM also collects domestic data directly, utilizing a Pentagon organization called Counterintelligence Field Activity (CIFA). *See* DOD Dir. 5105.67, *DoD Counterintelligence Field Activity* (Feb. 19, 2002). CIFA is charged to maintain "a domestic law enforcement database" and to develop a data-mining capability. But NORTHCOM has not spelled out any limits on these activities aside from the Pentagon's own domestic intelligence rules. *See* DOD Dir. 5240.1-R, *Procedures Governing the Activities of DoD Intelligence Components That Affect United States Persons* (Dec. 1982). These rules make no provision for outside oversight or accountability, nor do they limit data collection based on activities protected by the First Amendment.

One CIFA activity, Threat and Local Observation Notice (TALON), is officially described as "much like...a 'neighborhood watch' program in which concerned citizens or DoD personnel report suspicious activities." Letter to Hon. Duncan Hunter from Robert W. Rogalski, Acting Dep. Under Secretary of Defense (Counterintelligence and Security), Jan. 27, 2006. TALON has reportedly engaged in surveillance and data collection regarding domestic political activities—for example, by compiling records on the Quakers and others who have protested the Iraq War. *See, e.g.,* Robert Block & Jay Solomon, *Pentagon Steps Up Intelligence Efforts Inside U.S. Borders*, Wall St. J., Apr. 27, 2006, at 1. TALON has also monitored demonstrations against military recruitment on university campuses aimed at DOD's "don't ask, don't tell" policy of excluding homosexuals from military ranks. *See Pentagon Releases Documents Acknowledging Surveillance of Gay Groups*, Servicemembers Legal Defense Network, Apr. 11, 2006 (and linked documents), *at* http://www.sldn.org/templates/press/record.html?record=2859. *See also* Robert Block & Gary Fields, *Is Military Creeping Into Domestic Spying and Enforcement?*, Wall St. J., Mar. 9, 2004, at B1 (describing

CIFA agent's effort to get videotape of law school conference attended by "three Middle Eastern men" who made "suspicious remarks"). The Defense Department says it has removed some information inappropriately stored in its TALON database and ordered "refresher retraining" on relevant collection and privacy laws. Letter to Hon. Duncan Hunter, *supra*.

In June 2005, the Defense Department published *Strategy for Homeland Defense and Civil Support*, declaring that DOD expected to "reorient its intelligence capabilities" to enable it to, *inter alia*, "[c]ollect homeland defense threat information from relevant private and public sector sources, consistent with US constitutional authorities and privacy law," and to "[d]evelop automated tools to improve data fusion, analysis, and management, to track systematically large amounts of data, and to detect, fuse, and analyze aberrant patterns of activity, consistent with US privacy protections." *Id.* at 21. This last is an apparent reference to a data mining system like DARPA's much-maligned Total Information Awareness program. See *supra* p. 583. The document pledges that DOD will work to "diminish existing cultural, technological, and bureaucratic obstacles to information sharing" among federal agencies, with state, local, and tribal governments, with private entities, and with "key foreign partners." *Id.* at 23. Even more broadly, the White House has reportedly considered a proposal to expand CIFA's mission to include investigation of crimes within the United States, such as treason, espionage, and foreign or terrorist sabotage, as well as clandestine operations against potential threats at home. *See* Walter Pincus, *Pentagon Expanding Its Domestic Surveillance Activity*, Wash. Post, Nov. 27, 2005, at A6.

NOTES AND QUESTIONS

1. *A Military Intelligence Charter?* In 1976, the Church Committee proposed a "precisely drawn legislative charter" that would, *inter alia*, "limit military investigations to activities in the civilian community which are necessary and pertinent to the military mission, and which cannot feasibly be accomplished by civilian agencies." *Church Committee Report, supra*, Book II, at 310-311. The committee apparently believed that military intelligence units could make no unique contributions to the domestic security efforts of the FBI, local law enforcement, and other civilian agencies. Its proposal also may have reflected concern about conducting domestic intelligence collection under a military chain of command, whose priority is completion of its military mission, rather than under the Attorney General, whose priority is law enforcement. If these concerns were justified three decades ago, when the threat of terrorism was not such an abiding concern, do you think they are today? Can you outline a charter for domestic military intelligence activities that would avoid its involvement in law enforcement that has nothing to do with homeland defense, or in efforts to suppress political dissent?

2. *Legal Limits.* Do you think that current domestic intelligence activities outlined here, including the role of military personnel in DHS's IAIP Directorate and in the NCTC, fall within the limits imposed by the Posse Comitatus Act? Can you say with confidence which of those activities are related to law

B. The Military's Role in Homeland Security and Disaster Relief

enforcement and which ones are not? Should we distinguish between "receipt" of data from other agencies and data's direct "collection" by military personnel?

If the Posse Comitatus Act is implicated, do any of its constitutional or statutory exceptions apply? Consider in this regard 10 U.S.C. §371, *supra* p. 954. It directs the DOD to give "civilian law enforcement officials any information collected during the normal course of military training or operations that may be relevant to a violation of any Federal or State law," and it declares that the "needs of civilian law enforcement officials for information shall, to the maximum extent practicable, be taken into account in the planning and execution of military training or operations." *Id.* §371(a), (b). In light of this provision, are there any meaningful constraints on military intelligence collection?

3. *Implications for Civil Liberties.* As the military plays a larger domestic intelligence role, how would you weigh possible enhancements in security against possible losses in privacy and related liberties? What civil liberties safeguards apply to civilian intelligence activities that do not apply to the military? Are your answers affected by the availability of new data-mining technology described *supra* pp. 581-584?

2. The Military's Role in Responding to Domestic Crises

Even before September 11, it was assumed that, for practical reasons, the military would be prominently involved in responding to a substantial terrorist attack at home or to other great domestic emergencies. Several qualities recommend the military for such a role. No other agency of government has as much equipment, training, and experience in the use of force as the Defense Department does (although some worry that such force may not be sufficiently refined for use at home). No other agency has such a durable communications system. And no other agency, especially if the National Guard is counted among its forces, is so widely dispersed around the country in places where its services may be urgently needed.

a. *Leading or Supporting Role?*

Some feel that DOD should be assigned an operational leadership role in responding to a great crisis. In the view of one national commission,

> [t]he Department of Defense's ability to command and control vast resources for dangerous, unstructured situations is unmatched by any other department or agency. According to current plans, DoD involvement is limited to supporting the agencies that are currently designated as having the lead in a terrorism crisis, the FBI and the Federal Emergency Management Agency (FEMA). But, in extraordinary circumstances, when a catastrophe is beyond the capabilities of local, state, and other federal agencies, or is directly related to an armed conflict overseas, the President may want to designate DoD as lead federal agency. This may become a critical operational consideration in planning for future conflicts. Current plans

and exercises do not consider this possibility. [National Commission on Terrorism (Bremer Commn.), *Countering the Changing Threat of International Terrorism* 28 (2000).]

See also Fred C. Iklé, *Defending the U.S. Homeland: Strategic and Legal Issues for DOD and the Armed Services* (1999). Another study advocates planning ahead for what it views as inevitable DOD primacy in the most extreme circumstances. Ashton B. Carter, John M. Deutch & Philip D. Zelikow, *Catastrophic Terrorism: Elements of a National Policy* (1998).

Not everyone agrees that handing the reins over to the military would be wise, however. According to a different national commission, the President should "always designate a Federal civilian agency other than the Department of Defense (DoD) as the Lead Federal Agency." Advisory Panel to Assess Domestic Response Capabilities for Terrorism Involving Weapons of Mass Destruction (Gilmore Commn.), *Toward A National Strategy for Combating Terrorism* 28 (2000). The Gilmore Commission worried that "[m]any Americans will not draw the technical distinction between the Department of Defense—the civilian entity—and the U.S. Armed Forces—the military entity," leading to the perception that "the military" is in charge. *Id.* Responding to a suggestion that "active-duty forces should be given complete authority for responding to catastrophic disasters," one National Guard official called that a "policy of domestic regime change." Robert Block, *Local and Federal Authorities Battle to Control Disaster Relief,* Wall St. J., Dec. 8, 2005, at 1.

As of this writing, government planners have prescribed a supporting role for the military. *Homeland Security Presidential Directive/HSPD-5,* Feb. 28, 2003, names the Secretary of Homeland Security as "principal Federal official for domestic incident management," and assigns "lead responsibility for criminal investigations of terrorist acts" to the Attorney General. Current plans call for use of the armed forces only in a supporting role, and then for the most part only when they could be uniquely helpful in responding to a serious emergency: "DOD provides [Defense Support of Civil Authorities (DSCA)] in response to requests for assistance during domestic incidents to include terrorist attacks, major disasters, and other emergencies.... DSCA normally is provided when local, State, and Federal resources are overwhelmed...." Dept. of Homeland Security, *National Response Plan* 41, Dec. 2004.

The Defense Department's own regulations have long described its powers in the midst of a great domestic emergency as subordinate. For example, DOD Dir. 3025.1, *Military Support to Civil Authorities* §4.4.4.2 (Jan. 15, 1993), provides that "DOD resources are provided only when response or recovery requirements are beyond the capabilities of civil authorities (as determined by FEMA or another lead Federal agency for emergency response)." *See generally* Dept. of the Army, *Stability Operations and Support Operations* (FM-3-07), Feb. 20, 2003; DOD Dir. 3025.15, *Military Assistance to Civil Authorities* (Feb. 18, 1997).

In mid-2005, a new DOD policy document appeared that may signal a significantly more expansive domestic role. Dept. of Defense, *Strategy for Homeland Defense and Civil Support,* June 2005. "Our adversaries consider US territory an integral part of a global theater of combat," the document declares. "We must therefore have a strategy that applies to the domestic context the key principles

B. The Military's Role in Homeland Security and Disaster Relief

that are driving the transformation of US power projection and joint expeditionary warfare." *Id.* at 1. The new policy envisions an "active, layered" defense that could deal with "simultaneous, mass casualty attacks." *Id.* at 7, 10. It also calls for significantly expanded domestic intelligence capabilities. *Id.* at 21-23. Finally, while recognizing that "[d]omestic security is primarily a civilian law enforcement function," the strategy declares that when "directed by the President, the Department will execute land-based military operations to detect, deter, and defeat foreign terrorist attacks within the United States." *Id.* at 26. Still, the Pentagon is careful to distinguish between "homeland defense (HD)," such as domestic air defense, for which DOD is the lead agency, and "homeland security." Jt. Pub. 3-26, *Homeland Security*, Aug. 2, 2005, at v-vi. "Except for HD missions," it says, "DOD will serve in a supporting role for domestic incident management." *Id.* at viii.

b. *Controlling Authorities*

A "sense of Congress" provision of the Homeland Security Act of 2002 notes that existing laws, including the Insurrection Acts and the Stafford Act, "grant the President broad powers that may be invoked in the event of domestic emergencies, including an attack against the Nation using weapons of mass destruction, and these laws specifically authorize the President to use the Armed Forces to help restore public order." 6 U.S.C. §466 (a)(5) (Supp. IV 2004).

The Stafford Act, 42 U.S.C.A. §§5121-5206 (West 2003 & Supp. 2005), discussed *supra* p. 920 gives the President authority to use any federal agency, including the Defense Department, to assist state governments in disaster relief operations, *id.* §5192, or specifically to use the armed forces to perform work "essential for the preservation of life and property." *Id.* §5170b(c). It has not been construed to permit the use of those forces to maintain law and order, however. *See* Jennifer K. Elsea, *The Use of Federal Troops for Disaster Assistance* (Cong. Res. Serv. RS22266) 4, Sept. 16, 2005.

Several statutory exceptions to the Posse Comitatus Act, especially the Insurrection Act, 10 U.S.C. §§331-335, *supra* p. 953, give the President wide latitude to use troops for almost any purpose, including law enforcement, in the aftermath of a terrorist attack or natural disaster. The military may turn over to law enforcement officials any information collected during "the normal course of...military operations," and in fact it must take law enforcement needs into account in planning and executing its operations. 10 U.S.C. §371. Treating any attack site as a crime scene, this measure could allow troops to assist in gathering evidence for a criminal prosecution, although a related provision bars any "direct participation" by military personnel in a "search, seizure, arrest, or other similar activity" unless otherwise authorized by law. 10 U.S.C. §375. And during an "emergency situation involving a biological or chemical weapon of mass destruction," military personnel may assist the Department of Justice in the collection of intelligence or in searches or seizures, if it is "necessary for the immediate protection of human life," and civilian law enforcement officials cannot do it. 10 U.S.C. §382. *See also* 18 U.S.C. §831(e) (emergency situation involving nuclear materials). *See generally* Charles Doyle & Jennifer Elsea,

Terrorism: Some Legal Restrictions on Military Assistance to Domestic Authorities Following a Terrorist Attack (Cong. Res. Serv. RS21012), May 27, 2005.

Without reference to any specific enabling legislation, DOD regulations describing "immediate response authority" say that local military commanders may act in an emergency to "save lives, prevent human suffering, or mitigate great property damage." 32 C.F.R. §185.4(e) (2005). *See also id.* at §215.4(c)(1), noted *supra* p. 958, and §501.2(a). This authority was cited when the military furnished medivac aircraft, ambulances, bomb detection dog teams, and various personnel to assist civilian officials following the Oklahoma City bombing in 1995. The regulations would also permit evacuation, restoration of essential public services, and traffic control. *See* Jim Winthrop, *The Oklahoma City Bombing: Immediate Response Authority and Other Military Assistance to Civil Authority (MACA)*, Army Law., July 1997, at 3. Do you think this authority should be spelled out in legislation?

c. *Organizing for a Response*

In 2002, the Defense Department's new Northern Command (NORTHCOM) assumed responsibility for DOD's homeland defense efforts and for provision of military support to civil authorities. *See* Scott Shepherd & Steve Bowman, *Homeland Security: Establishment and Implementation of the United States Northern Command* (Cong. Res. Serv. RS21322), Feb. 10, 2005. It manages military responses to all kinds of threats, from terrorism to hurricanes, working closely with the Department of Homeland Security and directing the activities of the Joint Task Force—Civil Support. Details of NORTHCOM's organization and responsibilities, as well as those of various DOD components, are spelled out in considerable detail in *Report to Congress on the Role of the Department of Defense in Supporting Homeland Security, supra* p. 961; Dept. of Defense, *The DoD Role in Homeland Security: Defense Study and Report to Congress*, July 2003.

The National Guard, with some 450,000 personnel, has a special role to play in the response to a terrorist attack or natural disaster. The nearly 5,000 Army and Air National Guard units scattered across the country have essentially the same relevant training and equipment as active duty military elements, and they have extensive experience in firefighting, rescue, evacuation, and cleanup after storms and floods. The importance of the Guard's role and the need for close coordination of the Guard's activities with those of active duty military forces are spelled out in *Failure of Initiative: Final Report of the [House] Bipartisan Committee to Investigate the Preparation for and Response to Hurricane Katrina*, Feb. 15, 2006 [hereinafter *Failure of Initiative*], at 218-224, 228-231. Unless and until they are federalized by the President's order, however, Guard forces operate under the command of state governors. In this posture, as we have seen, *supra* p. 952, the Posse Comitatus Act does not apply. Thus, there may be an incentive to delay placing these forces under federal command in order to preserve the maximum flexibility in their use. *See generally* the National Guard Bureau home page *at* http://www.ngb.army.mil/; William C. Banks, *The Normalization of Homeland Security After September 11: The Role of the Military in Counterterrorism Preparedness and Response*, 64 La. L. Rev. 735, 762-768 (2004).

B. The Military's Role in Homeland Security and Disaster Relief

The Pentagon has directed Guard forces to provide training and equipment for at least 32 specialized teams of 22 persons each who would be ready on a moment's notice for deployment to the scene of a chemical or biological weapons attack. Equipped with a mobile analytical laboratory and reliable communications gear, a team would assist state and local personnel in identifying dangerous agents, evacuating victims, and controlling access to affected areas. Initially called Rapid Assessment and Initial Detection (RAID) teams, in 2000 they were given a more prosaic name, Weapons of Mass Destruction Civil Support Teams, to emphasize their supporting role. *See* National Guard Bureau, Depts. of the Army and the Air Force, *Weapons of Mass Destruction Civil Support Team Management* (NGR 500-3/ANGI 10-2503), Jan. 16, 2006.

In the aftermath of the September 11 terrorist attacks, National Guard troops, armed and in uniform, were used as extra security at airports across the country. While these personnel were at least nominally under state control, they had to undergo uniform federal training for their new assignments, and their salaries were paid by the federal government. Other National Guard forces were used to beef up security at border crossings into Mexico and Canada.

d. *Preparations for a Natural Disaster*

Because of the military's unique capabilities, it may play a key role in responding to a terrorist attack using weapons of mass destruction. Some of these same attributes historically have allowed Department of Defense and National Guard forces to be helpful in recovering from natural disasters.

Homeland Security Presidential Directive/HSPD-8, Dec. 17, 2003, sets "a national domestic all-hazards preparedness goal" for "improved delivery of Federal preparedness and assistance to State and local governments" in response to "domestic terrorist attacks, major disasters, and other emergencies." The Pentagon, in particular, is directed to furnish "information describing the organizations and functions within the Department of Defense that may be utilized to provide support to civil authorities during a domestic crisis."

When Hurricane Katrina hit New Orleans in the late summer of 2005, local police and other first responders were overwhelmed by the crisis. The federal government generally was very slow to respond. The governor of Louisiana asked the White House for 40,000 soldiers immediately to help in the recovery effort. The White House reportedly decided for political, not legal, reasons not to send in active-duty military forces for another five days, however, and then it deployed only 7,200 troops. Apparently it was felt that the President would have had to federalize Louisiana National Guard forces and invoke the Insurrection Act, and then maintain federal control of the troops to perform law enforcement duties there—to stop looting and other lawlessness. While the Justice Department's Office of Legal Counsel advised that federal military forces could be sent in, even over the objections of local officials, the President wanted to avoid the perception that he was seizing command from a female Southern governor of another party. *See* Eric Lipton, Eric Schmitt & Thom Shanker, *Political Issues Snarled Plans for Troop Aid*, N.Y. Times, Sept. 5, 2005, at A1. The eventual deployment of military forces, said to be the largest in this country since the Civil War, is described in useful detail in *Failure of Initiative, supra*, at pp. 201-238.

Paradoxically, the President almost immediately suggested a need for expanded authority for the use of federal troops in such an emergency. Asked whether DOD should play a larger role, the President responded, "Clearly, in the case of a terrorist attack that would be the case, but is there a natural disaster which — of a certain size that would then enable the Defense Department to become a lead agency in coordinating and leading the response effort? That's going to be a very important consideration for Congress to think about." *President's Remarks During Hurricane Rita Briefing in Texas*, Sept. 25, 2005. A follow-on study, *The Federal Response to Hurricane Katrina: Lessons Learned*, Feb. 2006, declared that "DOD capabilities must be better identified and integrated into the Nation's response plans." *Id.* at 54. Moreover, the study suggested, in "extraordinary circumstances" it will be "appropriate for the Department of Defense to lead the Federal response." *Id.* at 94. DOD and DHS were directed to revise the National Response Plan to reflect this expanded role. *Id.*

Meanwhile, planning is underway for a response to an avian influenza pandemic sometime in the future. One worst-case estimate puts deaths in the United States at 1.9 million people. *See* Ceci Connolly, *U.S. Plan for Flu Pandemic Revealed*, Wash. Post, Apr. 16, 2006, at A1. That figure apparently presumes that the spread of the virus can be sharply limited, since mortality among people infected with the virus has been roughly 50 percent. In an October 4, 2005, press conference, President Bush indicated that troops might be used to enforce quarantines in the event of a bird flu outbreak. The government's *Implementation Plan for the National Strategy for Pandemic Influenza*, May 2006, at 29, 160, however, describes DOD's role only in very general terms as supportive. *See generally* Sarah A. Lister, *Pandemic Influenza: Domestic Preparedness Efforts* (Cong. Res. Serv. RL33145) 21-23, Nov. 10, 2005; Kathleen S. Swendiman & Jennifer K. Elsea, *Federal and State Quarantine and Isolation Authority* (Cong. Res. Serv. RL33201) 16-20, Dec. 12, 2005.

NOTES AND QUESTIONS

1. *How the Military Can Help.* How exactly do you think uniformed military forces could be most helpful in the response to a terrorist attack at home? How could they help in responding to a natural disaster such as a hurricane or earthquake? Which, if any, of these services could be provided only by DOD and not by any other federal agency? Do you agree that we should try to use other federal agencies for this purpose whenever possible? Why or why not?

Should DOD sometimes be expected to play a lead agency role in responding to a domestic emergency? Can you say when? Do you think we can count on civilian leaders to maintain control of the military in such cases? Do you think we can rely on the nation's civilian leadership not to misuse the military in an emergency?

2. *Effect of the Posse Comitatus Act in Various Settings.* One recent study suggests that "[t]here are currently adequate laws and structures in place to facilitate the use of the military in relief efforts in the event of a major catastrophe of whatever kind." ABA Standing Comm. on Law & National Security et al., *Hurricane Katrina Task Force Subcommittee Report* 23, Feb. 2006. Do you agree?

One expert has argued that "use of the military as a posse comitatus and use in event of civil disturbance are fundamentally different," and that "the terms 'civil disturbance' and 'terrorism,' as we use them today, are worlds apart." M.E. Bowman, *The Military Role in Meeting the Threat of Domestic Terrorism*, 39 Naval L. Rev. 209, 211-212 (1990). Do you think it would be a good idea to enact new legislation to resolve any doubts about the definitions of these terms or about the applicability of the Posse Comitatus Act specifically to deployments of military forces in response to different kinds of national crises?

Should the Insurrection Act, *supra* p. 953, be amended to spell out more clearly its availability in the event of a terrorist attack or another natural disaster like Hurricane Katrina? Its use to enforce a quarantine? Would soldiers be permitted to shoot people trying to violate a quarantine?

3. *Cooperation Between DOD and Other Agencies.* Based on the brief description of authorities and plans set out above, how would you rate the chances for a strong, efficient collaboration between the Departments of Defense and Justice in responding to a terrorist attack? What about DOD and FEMA? When the Principal Deputy Assistant Secretary of Defense (Homeland Defense) was asked in August 2005 whether he knew of a document issued by DHS that would help DOD determine the requirements for military assistance to civilian authorities, he replied, "To my knowledge, no such document exists." *See Failure of Initiative, supra* p. 966, at 203. What would you recommend to improve the chances of collaboration? *See generally* Jeffrey D. Brake, *Terrorism and the Military's Role in Domestic Crisis Management: Background and Issues for Congress* (Cong. Res. Serv. RL30938), Jan. 27, 2003.

4. *The National Guard's Role.* How did you react to the presence of armed National Guard troops at airport security checkpoints? Do you think such personal reactions have any legal significance?

What advantages or disadvantages can you see to utilizing Guard forces under the control of state governors, rather than federalizing them, to respond to a terrorist attack? How, if at all, is your answer affected by the fact that Guard personnel in every state receive the same training and equipment prescribed by the Pentagon?

In the wake of Hurricane Katrina, are you convinced that the governor of Louisiana would have had to surrender control of her National Guard forces before active-duty troops could be sent in? Can you imagine an arrangement for cooperation between federal, state, and local forces in the recovery effort? Proposals for shared or unified command of these forces, along with recommendations for more effective coordination, are described in *Failure of Initiative, supra*, at pp. 218-227. What does this experience tell us about federal planning for a response to a great catastrophe like a hurricane or a terrorist attack?

C. MARTIAL LAW: WHEN PLANNING FAILS

If, in the event of an actual or threatened terrorist attack, or a large natural disaster, the execution of federal emergency plans fails to restore order, or if such plans are perceived as inadequate, martial law might be invoked as the option of last resort. Such a drastic step might seem advisable because of the military's extensive, coherent organization, its tradition of discipline, its robust communications systems, and its training in the use of force. Martial law could be declared by the President as Commander in Chief of U.S. armed forces, by a state governor as head of an unfederalized national guard, or by a military officer in the field. Without specific guidance from higher authority, military leaders would then be governed only by rules fashioned by them to fit the situation. The content of the rules and the duration of their enforcement would, by definition, be impossible to predict. So, necessarily, would be the effect on Americans' civil liberties.

In the middle of the eighteenth century, Blackstone described martial law as

> temporary excrescences bred out of the distemper of the state, and not any part of the permanent and perpetual laws of the kingdom. For martial law, which is built upon no settled principles, but is entirely arbitrary in its decisions, is... in truth and reality no law, but something indulged rather than allowed as a law. [2 William Blackstone, *Commentaries* *413.]

A century later, in a Civil War era case, the Supreme Court, in dicta, described the circumstances under which martial law might be invoked.

Ex parte Milligan
United States Supreme Court, 1866
71 U.S. (4 Wall.) 2

[The opinion is set forth *supra* p. 683.]

NOTES AND QUESTIONS

1. *The Necessity for Martial Law.* In an earlier case growing out of a rebellion in Rhode Island, the Court indicated that "a State may use its military power to put down an armed insurrection, too strong to be controlled by the civil authority. The power is essential to the existence of every government, essential to the preservation of order and free institutions, and is as necessary to the States of this Union as to any other government." Luther v. Borden, 48 U.S. (7 How.) 1, 44-45 (1849). In litigation arising in New Orleans, after that city had been captured by the Union Army in 1862 and placed under martial law, the Court declared that "[m]artial law is the law of military necessity in the actual presence of war." United States v. Diekelman, 92 U.S. (2 Otto) 520, 526 (1876). Recall that in his concurring opinion in the *Steel Seizure Case* Justice Jackson was careful to exclude from his discussion of emergency powers based on necessity, "as in a very limited category by itself, the establishment of martial law." 343 U.S. 579, 650 n.19 (1952).

The governor of Hawaii declared martial law immediately after the Japanese attack on Pearl Harbor, as he was authorized to do by the Hawaii Organic Act §67, ch. 339, 31 Stat. 141, 153 (1900). Testing a military tribunal's power to try civilians for ordinary criminal offenses, the Court observed that "the term 'martial law' carries no precise meaning. The Constitution does not refer to 'martial law' at all and no Act of Congress had defined the term. It has been employed in various ways by different people and at different times." Duncan v. Kahanamoku, 327 U.S. 304, 315 (1946). Then, struggling to avoid describing the limits of executive or legislative power, the Court found that in using the term "martial law" Congress had not intended to authorize the supplanting of courts by military tribunals. The story is retold in fascinating detail in Harry N. Scheiber & Jane L. Scheiber, *Bayonets in Paradise: A Half-Century Retrospect on Martial Law in Hawai'i, 1941–1946,* 19 U. Haw. L. Rev. 477 (1997).

2. *Standby Martial Law?* In June 1955, the government conducted a massive civil defense exercise to simulate responses to a nuclear attack. To almost everyone's surprise, President Eisenhower hypothetically declared nationwide martial law, suspended the writ of habeas corpus, and authorized military commanders to stop the functioning of local courts. His action was widely criticized as unnecessary and improper. *See, e.g.,* Robert S. Rankin & Winfried R. Dallmayr, *Freedom and Emergency Powers in the Cold War* 56-60 (1964). Nevertheless, throughout much of the Cold War the government had in place a comprehensive secret plan, called "Plan D," for responding to the threat of a nuclear attack. One element of that plan, Presidential Emergency Action Directive No. 21, apparently included a draft executive order declaring martial law.

In 1987, the Miami Herald reported that Lt. Col. Oliver North and FEMA had drafted a new emergency plan calling for suspension of the Constitution, imposition of martial law, appointment of military commanders to run state and local governments, and detention of dissidents and Central American refugees. Alfonso Chardy, *Reagan Advisors Ran "Secret" Government,* Miami Herald, July 5, 1987, at 1. *See* Jules Lobel, *Emergency Power and the Decline of Liberalism,* 98 Yale L.J. 1385, 1420 (1989) (noting that Lt. Col. North denied drawing up such a plan).

Do you think the President should carry a draft order declaring martial law with her at all times? If so, do you think the terms of the order and criteria for its execution, or at least the fact of its existence, should be publicized?

3. *Conditions for Martial Law.* One scholar argues that the Insurrection Act, 10 U.S.C. §§331-335, delegates to the President the power to impose martial law. Vladeck, *supra* p. 956, at 152-153. If Congress has so conferred this power on the President, it has done no more to clarify the circumstances under which the power might be exercised. The Defense Department, on the other hand, has adopted regulations to cover such an eventuality:

> Martial law depends for its justification upon public necessity. Necessity gives rise to its creation; necessity justifies its exercise; and necessity limits its duration. The extent of the military force used and the actual measures taken, consequently, will depend upon the actual threat to order and public safety which exists at the time. In most instances the decision to impose martial law is made by the President.... However, the decision to impose martial law may be made by the local commander on the spot, if the circumstances demand immediate action, and time and available communications facilities do not permit obtaining prior approval from higher authority. [32 C.F.R. §501.4 (2005).]

How do these regulatory criteria for invocation of martial law compare with those articulated by the Supreme Court in Ex parte Milligan? Would it be possible, or wise, to try to develop more specific guidelines? Could you draft the guidelines? Is there any way to challenge the legitimacy of the DOD regulations before they can be used — or even afterward?

4. *Planning to Avoid Martial Law.* As a practical matter, do you think any statutory or regulatory prescriptions could deter the President or military officials from declaring martial law in the wake of a terrorist attack involving a weapon of mass destruction, or in the aftermath of a great natural disaster? Can you think of any way to limit the resort to martial law in such a crisis?

V
Obtaining and Protecting National Security Information

33

Regulating Access to National Security Information

> If a nation expects to be ignorant and free, in a state of civilization, it expects what never was and never will be.
>
> *Thomas Jefferson*
> Letter to Col. Charles Yancey
> January 6, 1816

> Knowledge will forever govern ignorance, and a people who mean to be their own governors, must arm themselves with the power knowledge gives. A popular government without popular information or the means of acquiring it, is but a prologue to a farce or a tragedy or perhaps both.
>
> *James Madison*
> Letter to W. T. Barry
> August 4, 1822

> Yes, but the whole point of the doomsday machine is lost if you keep it a secret! Why didn't you tell the whole world, eh?
>
> *Dr. Strangelove*
> from the film *Dr. Strangelove, Or: How I Learned to Stop Worrying and Love the Bomb* (1964)

It is no less true today than it was two centuries ago that as citizens we can only make rational decisions about our destinies, indeed can only hope to be in control of our own futures, if we have access to information about the government to which we collectively submit. In 1966, authors of the Freedom of Information Act observed that "[a] democratic society requires an informed, intelligent electorate, and the intelligence of the electorate varies as the quantity and quality of its information varies." H.R. Rep. No. 89-1497, at 12 (1966), *reprinted in* 1966 U.S.C.C.A.N. 2418, 2429.

Of course, there are circumstances when it is in the public interest not to disclose some activities of the government. Among the most compelling are those involving national security and foreign relations. In this democracy we have struck a bargain with ourselves to surrender some knowledge—and with it the power that knowledge gives—to our elected representatives, with the understanding that they will use that knowledge to keep us safe.

Yet the terms of that bargain have always been controversial and are the subject of constant renegotiation. Sissela Bok has observed that

> [t]he contradictions and tensions of secrecy are never stronger than in the military stance of nations. On the one hand, every state requires a measure of secrecy in order to defend itself against enemy forces.... But on the other hand, secrecy is as often a weapon in the hands of the aggressors and an aid in every scheme of oppression.... As Thomas Jefferson pointed out, citizens do assume they have a right to full information about the possibility of war: "It is their sweat which is to earn all the expenses of the war, and their blood which is to flow in expiation of the causes of it." [Sissela Bok, *Secrets: On the Ethics of Concealment and Revelation* 191 (1983).]

This part of the book is concerned with the bargain we have struck to balance secrecy and knowledge, security and self-determination. In this chapter we examine aspects of that dynamic bargain. We also review basic guidelines for withholding government information from public view when the national security is implicated, as set forth in the current executive order on classification. In Chapter 34 we consider several statutes — especially the Freedom of Information Act — that make public access to government records and meetings dependent upon the terms of that order. Chapter 35 addresses public and press rights of access grounded in the common law and the Constitution, as well as the availability of sensitive government information for use in civil litigation. In Chapter 36 we address contractual controls on access to classified information, as well as government responses to leaks. Special attention is given to enforcement of the security clearance system through Espionage Act prosecutions. Finally, in Chapter 37, we review government efforts to prevent the dissemination of information after it has gotten into the hands of the press.

A. BALANCING SECRECY, SECURITY, AND SELF-DETERMINATION

Arvin S. Quist, Security Classification of Information
pages 1-1, 6-1 to 6-3 (Oak Ridge National Laboratory, 1989)
available at http://www.fas.org/sgp/library/quist/

Security classification of information by a nation's government is based on the government's responsibility for the survival of the nation and its people — classification is based on national security reasons. To ensure its survival, a government must sometimes stringently control certain information which, when possessed by the nation and denied to an adversary, (1) gives the nation a significant advantage over adversaries or (2) prevents adversaries from having an advantage that could significantly damage the nation. Governments protect that special information by classifying it, that is, by giving it a special designation such as "Secret," and then by restricting access to it (e.g., by need-to-know requirements and physical security measures). This "right" of a government to keep certain information concerning national security (secrets) from most of the nation's citizens is nearly universally accepted....

A. Balancing Secrecy, Security, and Self-Determination

...However, one of our nation's fundamental principles is the right of its citizens to be informed. We place a high value on open, informed discussion about governmental matters. Therefore, when the U.S. Government keeps secrets from its citizens, that action conflicts with a basic, constitutional right of citizens to be informed of their government's actions so that they can intelligently participate in governmental processes. A democracy's requirement for openness in government is in conflict with a government's need to keep some information secret for reasons of national security. The conflict between secrecy and openness in our government is sharpest when citizens want to have informed influence on governmental decisions that concern national security matters and that have important, long-term implications. It is frequently too easy for government officials (usually in the executive branch of government) to claim special, inside knowledge about a matter and, for alleged national security reasons, not to share that knowledge with all citizens (or even with most members of Congress). Then, citizens (or Congress) are put into a position of having to accept the decision of the governmental official who has the knowledge, the insider's rationale being that, if others knew what the insider knows, they would agree with the insider's judgment.

Problems of secrecy even affect enforcement of federal laws. Criminal charges are sometimes not brought against alleged lawbreakers because our legal system requires an open trial, and in prosecutions concerning national security matters the prosecutor may need to rely on classified information as evidence. [See Chapter 29.]...

Another important aspect of classification is the effect of governmental secrecy on our national character. Congressman Moss, one of the congressional leaders who spearheaded the effort to establish the Freedom of Information Act (FOIA), stated in 1967, "The strength of our nation is not derived from any policy negative in character."...There are other adverse impacts of classification. Economic costs are associated with classification of information—salaries of personnel who classify and declassify information, documents, and materials; costs for security, which include physical security, personnel clearance investigations, and need-to-know restrictions; "extra" costs of preparing classified documents and manufacturing classified hardware in secure areas; costs of classified procurements; and storage and inventorying costs for classified documents and material. Costs are incurred when wrong decisions are made because pertinent information was kept secret from a decision-maker. Classification also creates barriers to the accessibility of knowledge, to friend as well as to foe, and thereby slows down the advance of civilization....

The First Amendment to the Constitution established the principle of an informed public. When information is classified, the public's knowledge of the government's activities is reduced, thereby impeding an informed public evaluation of governmental policies and government officials. Thus, the national security advantages gained by the classification of information are always counterbalanced, to some extent, by the infringement upon our constitutional right to be informed of our government's activities....

A study ordered by Congress concluded that a shift toward greater openness in government might actually make us more secure.

> Even as billions of dollars are spent each year on government secrecy, the classification and personnel security systems have not always succeeded at their core task of protecting those secrets most critical to the national security. The classification system, for example, is used too often to deny the public an understanding of the policymaking process, rather than for the necessary protection of intelligence activities and other highly sensitive matters....
>
> The best way to ensure that secrecy is respected and that the most important secrets *remain* secret, is for secrecy to be returned to its limited but necessary role. Secrets can be protected more effectively if secrecy is reduced overall....
>
> Greater openness permits more public understanding of the Government's actions and also makes it possible for the Government to respond to criticism and justify those actions.... In addition, by allowing for a fuller understanding of the past, it provides opportunities to learn lessons from what has gone before — making it easier to resolve issues concerning the Government's past actions and helping prepare for the future. [Commission on Protecting and Reducing Government Secrecy (Moynihan Commn.), *Secrecy* xxi (1997).]

See also Daniel Patrick Moynihan, *Secrecy: The American Experience* (1998); and *Access Denied: Freedom of Information in the Information Age* (Charles N. Davis & Sigman L. Splichal eds., 2000).

More recently, however, there has been a decided shift away from openness in government. As one high official put it,

> [S]ince the horrific events of September 11 ... and the possibilities for further terrorist activity in their aftermath, federal agencies are concerned with the need to protect critical systems, facilities, stockpiles, and other assets from security breaches and harm.... Such protection efforts, of course, must at the same time include the protection of any agency information that could enable someone to succeed in causing the feared harm. [Memorandum for Heads of All Federal Departments and Agencies from John Ashcroft, Atty. General, *The Freedom of Information Act*, Oct. 15, 2001, *available at* http://www.usdoj.gov/oip/foiapost/2001foiapost19.htm.]

The trend toward greater secrecy is reflected in a report showing that in fiscal year 2005, federal agencies reported that they had classified 14,206,773 documents, compared with 5,790,625 ten years earlier. Information Security Oversight Office [ISOO], *2005 Report to the President*, May 25, 2006, at 13. They declassified 29,680,635 pages, compared with some 96 million in 1996. *Id.* at 15. Other evidence may be found in OpenTheGovernment.Org, *Secrecy Report Card 2005: Quantitative Indicators of Secrecy in the Federal Government*, Sept. 4, 2005; Reporters Committee for Freedom of the Press, *Homefront Confidential: How the War on Terrorism Affects Access to Information and the Public's Right to Know*, Sept. 2005; Scott Shane, *Sharp Increase in the Number of Documents Classified by the Government*, N.Y. Times, July 3, 2005, §1, at 14. Over a period of seven years, intelligence agency personnel even reclassified some 55,000 pages of materials found on open shelves at the National Archives and Records Administration.

See Matthew M. Aid, *Declassification in Reverse: The U.S. Intelligence Community's Secret Historical Document Reclassification Program*, Feb. 21, 2006, *at* http://www.gwu.edu/~nsarchiv/NSAEBB/NSAEBB179/.

NOTES AND QUESTIONS

1. *Negotiating for Democracy.* Arvin Quist, the author of the study excerpted above, was responsible for safeguarding some of the most sensitive U.S. nuclear weapons secrets. Would you call his view of the balance between secrecy and self-determination realistic or romantic? What additional factors need to be considered? How would you describe a proper balance?

Recognizing that the balance is necessarily subject to constant renegotiation, do you think it would be a good idea to codify the bargaining process? What should that process look like? Who should have a say in the negotiation? Should the bargaining always be open and public? Should the process itself be fixed, or subject to review and alteration?

2. *Open Government in an Age of Terrorism.* Does the ongoing "global war on terrorism" justify increased secrecy in government? In what particular respects should the balance between secrecy and self-determination be adjusted? Who should be entrusted with making the adjustment? When do you suppose the earlier balance might be restored?

B. CLASSIFICATION OF NATIONAL SECURITY INFORMATION

Executive Order No. 13,292, Further Amendment to Executive Order No. 12,958, as Amended Classified National Security Information
68 Fed. Reg. 15,315 (Mar. 25, 2003)

This order prescribes a uniform system for classifying, safeguarding, and declassifying national security information, including information relating to defense against transnational terrorism. Our democratic principles require that the American people be informed of the activities of their Government. Also, our Nation's progress depends on the free flow of information. Nevertheless, throughout our history, the national defense has required that certain information be maintained in confidence in order to protect our citizens, our democratic institutions, our homeland security, and our interactions with foreign nations. Protecting information critical to our Nation's security remains a priority.

NOW, THEREFORE, by the authority vested in me as President by the Constitution and the laws of the United States of America, it is hereby ordered as follows:

SEC. 1.1. CLASSIFICATION STANDARDS

(a) Information may be originally classified under the terms of this order only if all of the following conditions are met:
  (1) an original classification authority is classifying the information;
  (2) the information is owned by, produced by or for, or is under the control of the United States Government;
  (3) the information falls within one or more of the categories of information listed in section 1.4 of this order; and
  (4) the original classification authority determines that the unauthorized disclosure of the information reasonably could be expected to result in damage to the national security, which includes defense against transnational terrorism, and the original classification authority is able to identify or describe the damage.

(b) Classified information shall not be declassified automatically as a result of any unauthorized disclosure of identical or similar information.

(c) The unauthorized disclosure of foreign government information is presumed to cause damage to the national security.

SEC. 1.2. CLASSIFICATION LEVELS

(a) Information may be classified at one of the following three levels:
  (1) "Top Secret" shall be applied to information, the unauthorized disclosure of which reasonably could be expected to cause exceptionally grave damage to the national security that the original classification authority is able to identify or describe.
  (2) "Secret" shall be applied to information, the unauthorized disclosure of which reasonably could be expected to cause serious damage to the national security that the original classification authority is able to identify or describe.
  (3) "Confidential" shall be applied to information, the unauthorized disclosure of which reasonably could be expected to cause damage to the national security that the original classification authority is able to identify or describe.

(b) Except as otherwise provided by statute, no other terms shall be used to identify United States classified information.

SEC. 1.3. CLASSIFICATION AUTHORITY

(a) The authority to classify information originally may be exercised only by:
  (1) the President and, in the performance of executive duties, the Vice President;

(2) agency heads and officials designated by the President in the Federal Register; and
(3) United States Government officials delegated this authority...

SEC. 1.4. CLASSIFICATION CATEGORIES

Information shall not be considered for classification unless it concerns:
(a) military plans, weapons systems, or operations;
(b) foreign government information;
(c) intelligence activities (including special activities), intelligence sources or methods, or cryptology;
(d) foreign relations or foreign activities of the United States, including confidential sources;
(e) scientific, technological, or economic matters relating to the national security, which includes defense against transnational terrorism;
(f) United States Government programs for safeguarding nuclear materials or facilities;
(g) vulnerabilities or capabilities of systems, installations, infrastructures, projects, plans, or protection services relating to the national security, which includes defense against transnational terrorism; or
(h) weapons of mass destruction.

SEC. 1.5. DURATION OF CLASSIFICATION

(a) At the time of original classification, the original classification authority shall attempt to establish a specific date or event for declassification based upon the duration of the national security sensitivity of the information. Upon reaching the date or event, the information shall be automatically declassified. The date or event shall not exceed the time frame established in paragraph (b) of this section.
(b) If the original classification authority cannot determine an earlier specific date or event for declassification, information shall be marked for declassification 10 years from the date of the original decision, unless the original classification authority otherwise determines that the sensitivity of the information requires that it shall be marked for declassification for up to 25 years from the date of the original decision....

SEC. 1.6. IDENTIFICATION AND MARKINGS

(a) At the time of original classification, the following shall appear on the face of each classified document, or shall be applied to other classified media in an appropriate manner:
(1) one of the three classification levels defined in section 1.2 of this order;
(2) the identity, by name or personal identifier and position, of the original classification authority;

(3) the agency and office of origin, if not otherwise evident;
(4) declassification instructions...; and
(5) a concise reason for classification that, at a minimum, cites the applicable classification categories in section 1.4 of this order....

SEC. 1.7. CLASSIFICATION PROHIBITIONS AND LIMITATIONS

(a) In no case shall information be classified in order to:
(1) conceal violations of law, inefficiency, or administrative error;
(2) prevent embarrassment to a person, organization, or agency....

SEC. 1.8. CLASSIFICATION CHALLENGES...

(b) ... [A]n agency head or senior agency official shall establish procedures under which authorized holders of information are encouraged and expected to challenge the classification of information that they believe is improperly classified or unclassified. These procedures shall ensure that:
(1) individuals are not subject to retribution for bringing such actions;
(2) an opportunity is provided for review by an impartial official or panel....

SEC. 3.1. AUTHORITY FOR DECLASSIFICATION

(a) Information shall be declassified as soon as it no longer meets the standards for classification under this order.
(b) It is presumed that information that continues to meet the classification requirements under this order requires continued protection. In some exceptional cases, however, the need to protect such information may be outweighed by the public interest in disclosure of the information, and in these cases the information should be declassified....

SEC. 3.3. AUTOMATIC DECLASSIFICATION

(a) Subject to paragraphs (b)-(e) of this section, on December 31, 2006, all classified records that (1) are more than 25 years old and (2) have been determined to have permanent historical value under title 44, United States Code, shall be automatically declassified whether or not the records have been reviewed. Subsequently, all classified records shall be automatically declassified on December 31 of the year that is 25 years from the date of its original classification, except as provided in paragraphs (b)-(e) of this section.
(b) An agency head may exempt from automatic declassification under paragraph (a) of this section specific information, the release of which could be expected to:
(1) reveal the identity of a confidential human source, or a human intelligence source, or reveal information about the application of an intelligence source or method;

(2) reveal information that would assist in the development or use of weapons of mass destruction;

(3) reveal information that would impair U.S. cryptologic systems or activities;

(4) reveal information that would impair the application of state of the art technology within a U.S. weapon system;

(5) reveal actual U.S. military war plans that remain in effect;

(6) reveal information, including foreign government information, that would seriously and demonstrably impair relations between the United States and a foreign government, or seriously and demonstrably undermine ongoing diplomatic activities of the United States;

(7) reveal information that would clearly and demonstrably impair the current ability of United States Government officials to protect the President, Vice President, and other protectees for whom protection services, in the interest of the national security, are authorized;

(8) reveal information that would seriously and demonstrably impair current national security emergency preparedness plans or reveal current vulnerabilities of systems, installations, infrastructures, or projects relating to the national security; or

(9) violate a statute, treaty, or international agreement. . . .

(f) Information exempted from automatic declassification under this section shall remain subject to the mandatory and systematic declassification review provisions of this order. . . .

SEC. 3.4. SYSTEMATIC DECLASSIFICATION REVIEW

(a) Each agency that has originated classified information under this order or its predecessors shall establish and conduct a program for systematic declassification review. . . .

SEC. 3.5. MANDATORY DECLASSIFICATION REVIEW

(a) Except as provided in paragraph (b) of this section, all information classified under this order or predecessor orders shall be subject to a review for declassification by the originating agency if:

(1) the request for a review describes the document or material containing the information with sufficient specificity to enable the agency to locate it with a reasonable amount of effort;

(2) the information is not exempted from search and review under sections 105C, 105D, or 701 of the National Security Act of 1947 (50 U.S.C. 403-5c, 403-5e, and 431); and

(3) the information has not been reviewed for declassification within the past 2 years. . . .

(b) Information originated by:

(1) the incumbent President or, in the performance of executive duties, the incumbent Vice President;

(2) the incumbent President's White House Staff or, in the performance of executive duties, the incumbent Vice President's Staff;

(3) committees, commissions, or boards appointed by the incumbent President; or

(4) other entities within the Executive Office of the President that solely advise and assist the incumbent President

is exempted from the provisions of paragraph (a) of this section....

(c) Agencies conducting a mandatory review for declassification shall declassify information that no longer meets the standards for classification under this order. They shall release this information unless withholding is otherwise authorized and warranted under applicable law.

(d) In accordance with directives issued pursuant to this order, agency heads shall develop procedures to process requests for the mandatory review of classified information.... They also shall provide a means for administratively appealing a denial of a mandatory review request, and for notifying the requester of the right to appeal a final agency decision....

SEC. 3.6. PROCESSING REQUESTS AND REVIEWS

In response to a request for information under the Freedom of Information Act, the Privacy Act of 1974, or the mandatory review provisions of this order, or pursuant to the automatic declassification or systematic review provisions of this order:

(a) An agency may refuse to confirm or deny the existence or nonexistence of requested records whenever the fact of their existence or nonexistence is itself classified under this order or its predecessors....

SEC. 4.1. GENERAL RESTRICTIONS ON ACCESS

(a) A person may have access to classified information provided that:
 (1) a favorable determination of eligibility for access has been made by an agency head or the agency head's designee;
 (2) the person has signed an approved nondisclosure agreement; and
 (3) the person has a need-to-know the information....

George W. Bush
The White House
March 25, 2003

NOTES AND QUESTIONS

1. *The Shifting Balance Between Secrecy and Openness.* Before 1982, there was a discernible trend toward less, rather than more, secrecy in government recordkeeping.

> During the past thirty years, succeeding presidential classification orders have narrowed the bases and discretion for assigning official secrecy to agency records.

B. Classification of National Security Information

However, E.O. 12356 ... clearly reverses this trend by expanding the conditions for classification, requiring the application of official secrecy whenever possible, and maintaining agency records under security protection in perpetuity. [Richard C. Ehlke & Harold C. Relyea, *The Reagan Administration Order on Security Classification: A Critical Assessment*, 30 Fed. Bar News & J. 91 (1983).]

Executive Order No. 12,356, 47 Fed. 14,874 (Apr. 2, 1982), was promulgated by President Reagan. *See also* Steven J. Lepper, Note, *Developments Under the Freedom of Information Act, 1982*, 1983 Duke L.J. 390, 394-401. A possible reason for this change in direction is suggested by a Deputy Assistant Attorney General for the Civil Division of the Justice Department:

We live in a dangerous world. We face adversaries who have military power greater than any enemy this country has ever faced in a time of war. We live with the ever present threat of a nuclear war, which can destroy the world as we know it. We live with the even more insidious threat of international terrorism which because of its very irrationality is so hard for us to comprehend and deal with. These are very serious problems [that] can only be addressed through the careful execution of national security policy by our government; through military preparedness, diplomatic initiative, and perhaps as the foundation of both of those, an effective intelligence system. In order to execute national security policy we simply must have secrecy as to some matters. [Remarks of Richard Willard, in A.B.A. Standing Comm. on Law and National Security, *National Security and the First Amendment* 9 (1983).]

A 1995 executive order promulgated by President Clinton relaxed many of the strictures of the Reagan order. Exec. Order No. 12,958, 60 Fed. Reg. 19,825 (Apr. 17, 1995). For example, it included an instruction to resolve doubts about the need to classify against classification. *Id.* §1.2(b). It also provided for time limits on classification, automatic declassification, and protection for whistleblowers. *Id.* §§1.6, 1.9, and 3.4.

On March 25, 2003, President Bush signed the executive order excerpted above, amending, rather than replacing, the Clinton order. The new order includes a number of important substantive changes. Among them, the categories of information that may be classified have been increased to include "transnational terrorism," §§1.1(a)(4), 1.4(e), "vulnerabilities or capabilities of ... infrastructures," §1.4(f), and "weapons of mass destruction." §1.4(h). No definitions are provided for any of these terms. In addition, information that has been declassified now may be reclassified under certain conditions. §1.7(c). The presumption against classification in the earlier order has been removed.

Were the changes reflected in the 2003 order needed to protect the nation against the increased threat of international terrorism? How might these changes affect agency practice in classifying records or the response of courts to FOIA suits challenging that practice?

2. *Applying the Executive Order.* If you were an agency official with original classification authority, would the executive order provide enough guidance to enable you to determine when information should be classified? What additional instruction might be helpful?

President Reagan's executive order provided that a document "shall" be classified if its unauthorized disclosure "reasonably could be expected to cause damage to the national security." Exec. Order No. 12,356, *supra*, §1.3(b). The Bush order, like President Clinton's, states that information "may" be classified when its unauthorized disclosure "reasonably could be expected to result in damage to the national security... and the original classification authority is able to identify or describe the damage." Exec. Order No. 13,292, §1.1(a)(4). Is there any practical difference in the two tests? Could any federal judge apply either test with confidence in a given case, or is deference to agency professionals a practical necessity? Can you suggest alternative language that would be more helpful?

3. *Weighing the Public Interest.* Section 3.2(b) of the Bush order provides that in "some exceptional cases" the need to protect classified information "may be outweighed by the public interest in disclosure of the information, and in these cases the information should be declassified." The same instruction appeared in the Clinton and Carter (but not the Reagan) orders. In a case decided under the Carter order, one judge remarked:

> It would of course be extremely difficult for judges to "balance" the public's right to know against an acknowledged national security risk, and I do not believe we are currently authorized to do so. However, it seems important in view of recent revelations about past indiscretions in the name of national security, for some government institution, if not the classification system itself, to conduct such a balance. As Emerson explained, "history give[s] value to the present hour and its duty." By not weighing the value to the public of knowing about particularly relevant episodes in the intelligence agency's history, we may undermine the public's ability to assess the government's performance of its duty. [McGehee v. Casey, 718 F.2d 1137, 1150 (D.C. Cir. 1983) (separate statement of Wald, J.).]

But what government institution is better equipped than the courts to do the balancing? *See* United States Dept. of Justice v. Reporters Comm. for Freedom of the Press, 489 U.S. 749, 773 (1989).

4. *Challenging Secrecy.* How can executive branch officials be compelled to comply with the standards and procedures set out in the executive order? How can a decision to classify or refusal to declassify information be challenged?

Agency personnel with knowledge of the information can seek a review of a classification decision under §1.8 of the Bush executive order. Why would a bureaucrat seek such a review? Why would she need protection from retribution, and from whom?

Another way to provoke a review of the classification of a document is to request access to it under the Freedom of Information Act (FOIA) or one of its statutory analogues, as we see in the next chapter.

5. *Secret but Unclassified Information.* In early 2002, the White House Chief of Staff ordered all federal agencies to identify records that were sensitive, although not classified, and protect them from "inappropriate disclosure." Memorandum for the Heads of Executive Departments and Agencies from

B. Classification of National Security Information

Andrew H. Card Jr., *Action to Safeguard Information Regarding Weapons of Mass Destruction and Other Sensitive Documents Relating to Homeland Security*, Mar. 19, 2002. Later the same year, the Homeland Security Act directed the President to develop procedures to "identify and safeguard homeland security information that is sensitive but unclassified." Pub. L. No. 107-296, §892(a)(1)(B), 116 Stat. 2135, 2253 (2002). Neither the Chief of Staff nor Congress, however, defined the term "sensitive" or indicated how access to such information might be restricted.

The term "sensitive but unclassified" (SBU) is one of several used by different agencies to withhold information from disclosure. Other terms include "safeguards information," "sensitive security information," and "for official use only." Each agency has its own definition. A recent White House directive, however, orders federal agencies to adopt uniform standards for designating and handing SBU information. Memorandum for the Heads of Executive Departments and Agencies, *Guidelines and Requirements in Support of the Information Sharing Environment*, Dec. 16, 2005, *available at* http://www.fas.org/sgp/news/2005/12/wh121605-memo.html.

Do you agree that the flexibility provided by this category of data is needed to keep the nation safe? Do you see any danger in allowing the withholding of such information outside the framework of an executive order on classification? Can Congress regulate the handling of SBU information? *See generally* Government Accountability Office, *The Federal Government Needs to Establish Policies and Processes for Sharing Terrorism-Related and Sensitive but Unclassified Information* (GAO-06-385), Mar. 2006; Leslie Gielow Jacobs, *A Troubling Equation in Contracts for Government Funded Scientific Research: "Sensitive But Unclassified" = Secret But Unconstitutional*, 1 J. Natl. Security L. & Poly. 113 (2005); Genevieve Knezo, *"Sensitive but Unclassified" and Other Federal Security Controls on Scientific and Technical Information: History and Current Controversy* (Cong. Res. Serv. RL31845), Feb. 20, 2004; Genevieve Knezo, *"Sensitive but Unclassified" Information and Other Controls: Policy and Options for Scientific and Technical Information* (Cong. Res. Serv. RL33303), Feb. 15, 2006; National Security Archive, *Pseudo-Secrets: A Freedom of Information Audit of the U.S. Government's Policies on Sensitive Unclassified Information*, Mar. 2006.

6. *Sources of Presidential Secrecy Power.* Executive Order No. 10,290, 16 Fed. Reg. 9795 (Sept. 24, 1951), was the first to indicate that the President was relying not upon any specific statutory provision, but rather upon "the authority vested in me by the Constitution and statutes, and as President of the United States." Such reliance upon implied constitutional powers seemed to strengthen the President's discretion to make official secrecy policy by intertwining his responsibility as Commander in Chief with the obligation to "take Care that the Laws be faithfully executed." Ehlke & Relyea, *supra*, at 92.

Does the Commander in Chief Clause of Article II support the President's claim of secrecy authority? See *supra* pp. 343-346. In Department of the Navy v. Egan, 484 U.S. 518, 527 (1988), the Supreme Court suggested in a widely quoted dictum that the President's "authority to classify and control access to information bearing on national security...flows primarily from this constitutional investment of power in the President and exists quite apart from any explicit congressional grant." If the authority mentioned is not found in the Constitution's text, is it nevertheless a fair or even necessary inference?

Is the President authorized to ignore a congressional mandate to release information to the public if she believes that doing so could jeopardize national security? In another part of the *Egan* decision, the Court observed that "*unless Congress specifically has provided otherwise*, courts traditionally have been reluctant to intrude upon the authority of the Executive in military and national security affairs." *Id.* at 530 (emphasis added).

A supplemental defense appropriations measure for FY 2002 provided that the Defense Department should not adopt new restrictions on access to classified national security information without first giving 30 days' notice to congressional defense committees. Pub. L. No. 107-117, §8007, 115 Stat. 2230, 2248 (2002). But in his signing statement President Bush declared that "situations may arise, especially in wartime, in which the President must promptly establish special access controls on classified national security information under his constitutional grants of the executive power and authority as Commander in Chief of the Armed Forces," and that he would act "in a manner consistent with" that authority. *See* Office of the Press Secretary, The White House, *Defense Bill Signing Statement,* Jan. 10, 2002. Can you think of any way for Congress to enforce its mandate?

7. *Testing the Executive Order.* Can you think of any way to test the propriety of the terms of the executive order? In Afshar v. Department of State, 702 F.2d 1125, 1137 (D.C. Cir. 1983), the court remarked, "This court will not, in the absence of any evidence of illegitimate discrimination, and perhaps not even then, question the President's determination that the national security requires increased secrecy." But in American Federal Government Employees, AFL-CIO v. Reagan, 870 F.2d 723 (D.C. Cir. 1989), the court found that an executive order purportedly exerting a statutorily conferred power was entitled only to a rebuttable presumption of regularity.

8. *Cleaning Out Old Secret Files.* The Clinton order, Executive Order No. 12,958, required the automatic declassification by April 17, 2000, of most historically valuable information that was at least 25 years old, a body of material estimated at more than one billion documents. After several delays, that date was extended to December 31, 2006, by §3.3 of the Bush order, although even that extended deadline was not expected to be met. ISOO, *supra* p. 978, at 19. Records may continue to be classified if an agency head determines that their release would jeopardize national security. This happened, for example, when a historian sought FBI files on Gerhard Eisler and Clinton Jencks, suspected Communists investigated by the Bureau during the 1930s and 1940s. *See* Schrecker v. Department of Justice, 254 F.3d 162 (D.C. Cir. 2001). Is there any way to compel agency compliance with §3.3?

34

Statutory Access to National Security Information

It would be difficult to overstate the importance of the Freedom of Information Act (FOIA) and its statutory analogues. Passed in 1966, it opened a window into the operation of the executive branch, transformed the way the government conducts its business, and gave the American people a renewed sense of self-determination. It has special relevance in the national security field, about which information has always been most closely held. In fact, much of the information in this book was obtained through FOIA requests.

In this chapter we examine the structure and operation of FOIA and several other open government laws. In the process we consider the persistent tension between the political branches of government concerning the protection of national security information, as well as the role of courts in resolving questions of access to government records.

A. THE FREEDOM OF INFORMATION ACT

A Citizen's Guide on Using the Freedom of Information Act and the Privacy Act of 1974 to Request Government Records
House Committee on Government Reform,
H.R. Rep. No. 109-226, at 3 (2005)

The Freedom of Information Act (FOIA) establishes a presumption that records in the possession of agencies and departments of the executive branch of the U.S. Government are accessible to the people. This was not always the approach to Federal information disclosure policy. Before enactment of the FOIA in 1966, the burden was on the individual to establish a right to examine these government records. There were no statutory guidelines or procedures to help a person seeking information. There were no judicial remedies for those denied access.

With the passage of the FOIA, the burden of proof shifted from the individual to the government. Those seeking information are no longer required to show a need for information. Instead, the "need to know" standard has been replaced by a "right to know" doctrine. The government now has to justify the need for secrecy.

The FOIA sets standards for determining which records must be disclosed and which records may be withheld. The law also provides administrative and judicial remedies for those denied access to records. Above all, the statute requires Federal agencies to provide the fullest possible disclosure of information to the public.

1. The Statutory Text

Freedom of Information Act
5 U.S.C. §552 (2000 & Supp. III 2003)

§552. PUBLIC INFORMATION; AGENCY RULES, OPINIONS, ORDERS, RECORDS, AND PROCEEDINGS

(a) Each agency shall make available to the public information as follows: . . .

(2) Each agency, in accordance with published rules, shall make available for public inspection and copying—

(A) final opinions, including concurring and dissenting opinions, as well as orders, made in the adjudication of cases;

(B) those statements of policy and interpretations which have been adopted by the agency and are not published in the Federal Register;

(C) administrative staff manuals and instructions to staff that affect a member of the public;

(D) copies of all records, regardless of form or format, which have been released to any person under paragraph (3) and which, because of the nature of their subject matter, the agency determines have become or are likely to become the subject of subsequent requests for substantially the same records; and

(E) a general index of the records referred to under subparagraph (D); unless the materials are promptly published and copies offered for sale. . . . Each agency shall also maintain and make available for public inspection and copying current indexes providing identifying information for the public as to any matter issued, adopted, or promulgated after July 4, 1967, and required by this paragraph to be made available or published. . . . Each agency shall make the index referred to in subparagraph (E) available by computer telecommunications. . . .

(3) (A) Except with respect to the records made available under paragraphs (1) and (2) of this subsection . . . each agency, upon any request for records which (i) reasonably describes such records and (ii) is made in accordance with published rules stating the time, place, fees (if any), and procedures to be followed, shall make the records promptly available to any person.

A. The Freedom of Information Act

(B) In making any record available to a person under this paragraph, an agency shall provide the record in any form or format requested by the person if the record is readily reproducible by the agency in that form or format. Each agency shall make reasonable efforts to maintain its records in forms or formats that are reproducible for purposes of this section.

(C) In responding under this paragraph to a request for records, an agency shall make reasonable efforts to search for the records in electronic form or format....

(E) An agency, or part of an agency, that is an element of the intelligence community (as that term is defined in section 3(4) of the National Security Act of 1947 (50 U.S.C. 401a(4))) shall not make any record available under this paragraph to—

(i) any government entity, other than a State, territory, commonwealth, or district of the United States, or any subdivision thereof; or

(ii) a representative of a government entity described in clause (i).

(4)(A)(i) In order to carry out the provisions of this section, each agency shall promulgate regulations, pursuant to notice and receipt of public comment, specifying the schedule of fees applicable to the processing of requests under this section and establishing procedures and guidelines for determining when such fees should be waived or reduced....

(iii) Documents shall be furnished without any charge or at a charge reduced... if disclosure of the information is in the public interest because it is likely to contribute significantly to public understanding of the operations or activities of the government and is not primarily in the commercial interest of the requester....

(B) On complaint, the district court of the United States in the district in which the complainant resides, or has his principal place of business, or in which the agency records are situated, or in the District of Columbia, has jurisdiction to enjoin the agency from withholding agency records and to order the production of any agency records improperly withheld from the complainant. In such a case the court shall determine the matter de novo, and may examine the contents of such agency records in camera to determine whether such records or any part thereof shall be withheld under any of the exemptions set forth in subsection (b) of this section, and the burden is on the agency to sustain its action....

(E) The court may assess against the United States reasonable attorney fees and other litigation costs reasonably incurred in any case under this section in which the complainant has substantially prevailed.

(F) Whenever the court orders the production of any agency records improperly withheld from the complainant and assesses against the United States reasonable attorney fees and other litigation costs, and the court additionally issues a written finding that the circumstances surrounding the withholding raise questions whether agency personnel acted arbitrarily or capriciously with respect to the withholding, the Special Counsel shall promptly initiate a proceeding to determine whether disciplinary action is warranted against the officer or employee who was primarily responsible for the withholding....

(6) (A) Each agency, upon any request for records... shall—

(i) determine within 20 days... after the receipt of any such request whether to comply with such request and shall immediately notify the person making such request of such determination and the reasons therefor, and of the right of such person to appeal to the head of the agency any adverse determination; and

(ii) make a determination with respect to any appeal within twenty days....

(B) (i) In unusual circumstances... the time limits... may be extended....

(b) This section does not apply to matters that are—

(1) (A) specifically authorized under criteria established by an Executive order to be kept secret in the interest of national defense or foreign policy and (B) are in fact properly classified pursuant to such Executive order;

(2) related solely to the internal personnel rules and practices of an agency;

(3) specifically exempted from disclosure by statute (other than section 552b of this title), provided that such statute (A) requires that the matters be withheld from the public in such a manner as to leave no discretion on the issue, or (B) establishes particular criteria for withholding or refers to particular types of matters to be withheld;

(4) trade secrets and commercial or financial information...;

(5) inter-agency or intra-agency memorandums or letters which would not be available by law to a party other than an agency in litigation with the agency;

(6) personnel and medical files...;

(7) records or information compiled for law enforcement purposes, but only to the extent that the production of such law enforcement records or information (A) could reasonably be expected to interfere with enforcement proceedings, (B) would deprive a person of a right to a fair trial or an impartial adjudication, (C) could reasonably be expected to constitute an unwarranted invasion of personal privacy, (D) could reasonably be expected to disclose the identity of a confidential source,... and, in the case of a record or information compiled by... an agency conducting a lawful national security intelligence investigation, information furnished by a confidential source,... or (F) could reasonably be expected to endanger the life or physical safety of any individual;

(8) ... related to... financial institutions; or

(9) geological and geophysical information....

Any reasonably segregable portion of a record shall be provided to any person requesting such record after deletion of the portions which are exempt under this subsection. The amount of information deleted shall be indicated on the released portion of the record, unless including that indication would harm an interest protected by the exemption in this subsection under which the deletion is made....

(c) ... (3) Whenever a request is made which involves access to records maintained by the Federal Bureau of Investigation pertaining to foreign intelligence or counterintelligence, or international terrorism, and the existence of the records is classified information as provided in subsection (b)(1), the

A. The Freedom of Information Act

Bureau may, as long as the existence of the records remains classified information, treat the records as not subject to the requirements of this section.

(d) This section does not authorize withholding of information or limit the availability of records to the public, except as specifically stated in this section. This section is not authority to withhold information from Congress....

(f) For purposes of this section, the term—
(1) "agency" as defined in section 551(1) of this title includes any executive department, military department, Government corporation, Government controlled corporation, or other establishment in the executive branch of the Government (including the Executive Office of the President), or any independent regulatory agency; and
(2) "record" and any other term used in this section in reference to information includes any information that would be an agency record subject to the requirements of this section when maintained by an agency in any format, including an electronic format.

(g) The head of each agency shall prepare and make publicly available upon request, reference material or a guide for requesting records or information from the agency, subject to the exemptions in subsection (b), including—
(1) an index of all major information systems of the agency;
(2) a description of major information and record locator systems maintained by the agency; and
(3) a handbook for obtaining various types and categories of public information from the agency....

NOTES AND QUESTIONS

1. *Codifying the Balance.* Do you think FOIA achieves a proper balance between public participation in government and legitimate needs for government secrecy? Does it strike the right balance between the political branches concerning control over sensitive information? Should Congress provide the executive with greater flexibility to deal with emerging threats and changes in technology? If so, how could it do that?

In the wake of the terrorist attacks on September 11, 2001, Attorney General Ashcroft issued a new statement of policy on disclosure determinations under FOIA. Memorandum from John Ashcroft to Heads of All Federal Departments and Agencies (Oct. 12, 2001), *available at* http://www.usdoj.gov/oip/foiapost/2001foiapost19.htm. He directed agencies to be much more aggressive in protecting information, instructing them that when they "carefully consider FOIA requests and decide to withhold records, in whole or in part, you can be assured that the Department of Justice will defend your decisions unless they lack a sound legal basis." His instruction superseded one promulgated by Attorney General Reno in 1993 that adopted a "foreseeable harm" standard of review. Can you guess how implementation of this policy might have shifted the balance between openness and secrecy? Do you think the shift is justified by the ongoing "war on terrorism"? If not, how could it be challenged?

2. *Balancing Costs and Benefits.* Can you say how exposure of agency records to public view, or at least the prospect of such exposure, might affect the way the government conducts its business? If your answer is that it makes the government process more costly in some ways, do you think the benefits from a better informed electorate outweigh the increased expense? By one account, the federal government spends roughly the same amount processing FOIA requests that it does on military bands. Charles H. Wichmann III, Note, *Ridding FOIA of Those "Unanticipated Consequences": Repaving a Necessary Road to Freedom,* 47 Duke L.J. 1213, 1255 (1998).

3. *Usability.* Do you believe that a layperson, unassisted by an attorney, is likely to be able to get the information she seeks from a government agency by utilizing FOIA? Should FOIA be amended to make information more nearly accessible without such assistance? If so, how? A 1996 amendment to the Act requires each agency to "prepare and make publically available upon request, reference material or a guide for requesting records or information from the agency." 5 U.S.C. §552(g). Instructions for making a FOIA request are also set out for each agency in the Code of Federal Regulations. *See, e.g.,* 32 C.F.R. pt. 1900 (2005) (Central Intelligence Agency). *See also* General Services Admin., *Your Right to Federal Records: Questions and Answers on the Freedom of Information Act and Privacy Act,* Sept. 2004; and National Security Archive, *FOIA Basics* (n.d.), *available at* http://www.gwu.edu/~nsarchiv/nsa/foia/guide.html.

4. *"Any Request."* Although §552(a)(3) provides that an agency must respond to "any request," it was suggested early on that a requester should demonstrate some good reason for wanting particular information. It now seems well settled in principle that it is not necessary for a requester to make any showing of purpose or relevancy. United States Dept. of Justice v. Reporters Comm. for Freedom of the Press, 489 U.S. 749, 771 (1989). There is evidence, however, that a court might be influenced by a requester's motives. For example, in his dissent in Department of the Air Force v. Rose, 425 U.S. 352 (1976), a case involving information about a cheating scandal at the Air Force Academy, Chief Justice Burger remarked that it was "difficult to attribute to Congress a willingness to subject an individual citizen to the risk of possible severe damage to his reputation simply to permit law students... to prepare a law journal article." *Id.* at 384. Do you suppose that a court might be more reluctant to order release of records if it knew that the requester's intention was to compromise U.S. foreign policy? Should it matter that the release most likely would not have the intended effect? How would you incorporate any concern you have about motive into the statute?

FOIA was amended in 2002 to bar requests from foreign governments, international governmental organizations, or their representatives for records held by elements of the intelligence community. 5 U.S.C. §552(a)(3)(E). This change was reportedly intended to prevent access to intelligence agency records by states that support terrorism. *See* H.R. Rep. No. 107-592, at 27 (2002). Can you think of any other reasons to adopt such a restriction?

5. *Economic Barriers.* Under FOIA §552(a)(4)(A)(iii), the requester's motivation may be taken into account by an agency in deciding whether to reduce or waive its standard charges for document search and duplication "if

disclosure is in the public interest because it is likely to contribute significantly to public understanding of the operations or activities of the government and is not primarily in the commercial interest of the requester." *See generally* Office of Management and Budget, *Uniform Freedom of Information Act Fee Schedule and Guidelines*, 52 Fed. Reg. 10,012 (Feb. 27, 1987). In McClellan Ecological Seepage Situation v. Carlucci, 835 F.2d 1282, 1285-1286 (9th Cir. 1987), the court found that no fee waiver was required because the public interest requester failed to show how it could use the information to contribute to public understanding of the government. But in National Security Archive v. United States Department of Defense, 880 F.2d 1381, 1387-1388 (D.C. Cir. 1989), court rejected, as "contrary to the manifest purpose of [FOIA]...and common sense," DOD's effort to charge "commercial" fees to a not-for-profit organization that compiles government data for scholars, news media, and government researchers. Such charges may, of course, be an effective bar to obtaining the requested information and may even be used by an agency to try to intimidate the requester. But an agency's denial of a waiver is not supposed to be arbitrary or capricious. National Treasury Employees Union v. Griffin, 811 F.2d 644, 646-650 (D.C. Cir. 1987).

The requester's purpose may also affect the decision to award attorney's fees and costs, under FOIA §552(a)(4)(E), when a requester has "substantially prevailed."

> The district court's award of fees under the Freedom of Information Act is discretionary, but in its exercise of discretion the court must consider (1) the public benefit resulting from disclosure; (2) the commercial benefit to the complainant resulting from disclosure; (3) the nature of the complainant's interest in the records sought; and (4) whether the government's withholding of records had a reasonable basis in law. [United Assn. of Journeymen and Apprentices, Local 598 v. Department of the Army, Corps of Engineers, 841 F.2d 1459, 1461 (9th Cir. 1988).]

See also Miller v. United States Dept. of State, 779 F.2d 1378, 1389-1390 (8th Cir. 1985). In Kuzma v. Internal Revenue Service, 821 F.2d 930, 933 (2d Cir. 1987), the court remarked that Congress meant to encourage citizens to act as "private attorneys general" pursuant to "a national policy of disclosure of government information." *Cf.* Burka v. United States Dept. of Health & Human Serv., 142 F.3d 1286 (D.C. Cir. 1998) (denying attorney's fees to successful pro se plaintiff). Will the prospect of a fee award affect the behavior of either agencies or requesters?

6. *"Agency."* What is an "agency" for FOIA purposes? *See* FOIA §552(f)(1). In Rushforth v. Council of Economic Advisers, 762 F.2d 1038, 1040-1043 (D.C. Cir. 1985), the court held that records of a government entity lacking "independent authority" to take "direct action," and whose "sole function is to advise and assist the President," need not be disclosed under FOIA. *See also* Meyer v. Bush, 981 F.2d 1288 (D.C. Cir. 1993); Matthew J. Matule, Note, *Congress, the Courts, and Regulatory Oversight After Meyer v. Bush*, 18 Vt. L. Rev. 823 (1994). Can you square this judicial definition with the statutory one?

In Armstrong v. Executive Office of the President, 90 F.3d 553 (D.C. Cir. 1996), the court determined that the National Security Council (NSC) is not an "agency" within the meaning of FOIA because the NSC staff exercises "no substantial authority either to make or to implement policy" and no "significant non-advisory function." *Id.* at 561, 565. Can you reconcile what the *Armstrong* court said about the NSC with what you read in Chapter 15 concerning its involvement in the Iran-Contra Affair or with the description of its duties in Executive Order No. 12,333, *supra* p. 397? *See* R. Kevin Bailey, Note, *"Did I Miss Anything?": Excising the National Security Council From FOIA Coverage,* 46 Duke L.J. 1475 (1997).

7. *"Agency Records."* Do you understand what is included in the term "agency records"? In the words of one court, "For requested materials to qualify as 'agency records,' two requirements must be satisfied: (i) an agency must 'either create or obtain' the requested materials, and (ii) the agency must be in control of the requested materials at the time the FOIA request is made." Grand Central Pship., Inc. v. Cuomo, 166 F.3d 473, 479 (2d Cir. 1999) (citations omitted). Thus, materials in agency files have been ruled exempt on grounds that they were not covered by FOIA when created, Kissinger v. Reporters Committee for Freedom of the Press, 445 U.S. 136 (1980) (exempting notes in State Department files of the Secretary's telephone conversations while he was National Security Adviser), or because Congress (which is not an "agency" for FOIA purposes) had not given up control of the materials. Goland v. CIA, 607 F.2d 339 (D.C. Cir. 1978) (exempting transcript of secret congressional hearing in CIA files). *Compare* Paisley v. CIA, 712 F.2d 686 (D.C. Cir. 1983) (investigative report created by the CIA for a Senate committee is an agency record). Information collected by an agency illegally has been held not subject to a FOIA request. Marzen v. United States Dept. of Health and Human Services, 632 F. Supp. 785 (N.D. Ill. 1986), *aff'd,* 825 F.2d 1148 (7th Cir. 1987). Nor must records be disclosed that have been improperly disposed of by an agency. *Kissinger, supra,* 445 U.S. at 146-155.

8. *"Reasonably" Described.* FOIA §552(a)(3) requires an agency to make available records "reasonably" described by the requester. A description is sufficient if it enables a professional employee of the agency who is familiar with the subject area of the request to locate the record with a reasonable amount of effort. H.R. Rep. No. 93-876, at 5-6 (1974), *reprinted in* 1974 U.S.C.C.A.N. 6271. *See* Goland v. CIA, 607 F.2d 339, 353 (D.C. Cir. 1978). Nevertheless, the court in Kowalczyk v. Department of Justice, 73 F.3d 386, 389 (D.C. Cir. 1996), declared that the agency is "not obliged to look beyond the four corners of the request for leads to the location of responsive documents." Since a requester usually will not have seen any responsive documents (or even know whether they exist) and will have no way to guess their location, what can she do to improve her chances of getting what she wants?

9. *E-FOIA and E-Government.* In 1996 Congress amended FOIA to reflect increasing reliance on electronic media for both recordkeeping and communication, to make more information available to the public, and to make that information easier to obtain. Electronic Freedom of Information Act Amendments of 1996 (E-FOIA), Pub. L. No. 104-231, 110 Stat. 3048. By requiring

agencies to search electronic databases and to furnish requested records in electronic form, Congress hoped that requests could be processed much more quickly. Equally important, by requiring that frequently requested materials be posted in electronic "reading rooms," Congress thought that the volume of requests might be dramatically reduced. *See generally* James X. Dempsey, *Electronic FOIA Act Adopted: Will Affect Paper Records Too,* Oct. 22, 1996, *at* http://www.gwu.edu/∼nsaarchiv/nsa/efoiacom.html; Joaquin Ferrao, *E-FOIA Law Increases Access for the Public and Brings Challenges to Agencies,* LLRX, Nov. 15, 1999, *at* http://www.llrx.com/features/e-foia.htm. The CIA's electronic reading room may be found at http://www.foia.cia.gov/default.asp.

The E-Government Act of 2002, Pub. L. No. 107-347, 116 Stat. 2899 (2002), furthers the goals of E-FOIA by pushing agencies to make better use of the Internet to provide information and services to citizens. It requires regulatory agencies to conduct rule-making online, for example, and to post everything on their Web sites that they publish in the Federal Register. It also calls for creation of an online directory of all government Web sites, so that a searcher can locate information on a given topic without having to know what agency holds it. Can you think of other ways to use advances in technology to improve public access to agency records?

10. *Other Statutes Requiring Secrecy.* FOIA *permits withholding* of classified data when it is requested. Other acts *require withholding* of data from public view — for example, the Atomic Energy Act of 1954, 42 U.S.C. §2162 (2000) (protecting the secrecy of "restricted" nuclear weapons data unless disclosure would not create an unreasonable risk to the common defense and security of the United States), or *criminalize disclosure* of certain information — for example, Intelligence Identities Protection Act of 1982, 50 U.S.C. §421 (2000) (disclosure of classified information that identifies a covert agent is punishable by fine or imprisonment).

2. Statutory Exemptions and Judicial Review

The following cases reveal some of the history of FOIA and describe the application of two exemptions bearing on the national security. In particular, they address the role of courts in deciding whether to withhold sensitive data from the public.

Ray v. Turner
United States Court of Appeals, District of Columbia Circuit, 1978
587 F.2d 1187

PER CURIAM: This appeal presents the question whether the district court erred in dismissing a lawsuit under the Freedom of Information Act (FOIA) upon the basis of affidavits supplied by an official of the Central Intelligence Agency (CIA). We find there was error and remand.

I. PROCEDURAL BACKGROUND OF LITIGATION

Plaintiffs (appellants) Ellen Ray and William Schaap sent identical letters to the CIA requesting "a copy of any file you may have on me." The CIA replied that while it did not have files on plaintiffs, there were documents in CIA files that referred to plaintiffs. The CIA refused to release those documents, and after administrative appeals were exhausted, plaintiffs brought this action under the FOIA. The CIA subsequently released portions of the withheld documents, and the government then moved for summary judgment, relying principally on affidavits of one Eloise Page... [purporting] to describe the documents at issue and the grounds for the government's claims of exemption.

The district court granted the government's motion for summary judgment and denied plaintiffs' motion for *in camera* inspection.... It found that the withheld documents were exempt from disclosure under the FOIA on the basis of Exemption 1 alone, Exemption 3 alone, or the two exemptions coupled together. As to Exemption 1, 5 U.S.C. §552(b)(1), the court found that the affidavit showed that the documents were properly classified under Executive Order 11,652, 3 C.F.R. 339 (1974). As to Exemption 3, 5 U.S.C. §552(b)(3), the court found that the affidavits stated that the release of the information could reasonably be expected to reveal intelligence sources and methods as well as organizational data, and that 50 U.S.C. §§403(d)(3), 403g justified the CIA invocation of Exemption 3....

II. RELEVANT CONSIDERATIONS IN FOIA CASES INVOLVING NATIONAL SECURITY ISSUES

The FOIA was passed in 1966, as an amendment to the Administrative Procedure Act, in order to increase disclosure of government information to the American people. Agencies were required to disclose all records that did not come within one of nine explicit exemptions specified by Congress. In the event of agency nondisclosure, the Act provided for court review. In any such case, "the court shall determine the matter de novo...and the burden is on the agency to sustain its action."[7]

A. JUDICIAL INTERPRETATIONS AND LEGISLATIVE MODIFICATIONS

In EPA v. Mink, 410 U.S. 73, 81-84 (1973), the Court considered Exemption 1, which at that time covered matters "specifically required by Executive order to be kept secret in the interest of the national defense or foreign policy." 5 U.S.C. §552(b)(1) (1970). It held that a court should not review the substantive propriety of the classification or go behind an agency affidavit stating that the

---

7. 5 U.S.C. §552(a)(3) (1976). Courts were given authority to review de novo any denial of access "in order that the ultimate decision as to the propriety of the agency's action is made by the court and [to] prevent [review] from becoming meaningless judicial sanctioning of agency discretion." S. Rep. No. 813, 89th Cong., 1st Sess. 8 (1965).

A. The Freedom of Information Act

requested documents had been duly classified pursuant to Executive order.[8] The Court said that "Congress chose to follow the Executive's determination in these matters," and *in camera* inspection to test the propriety of the classification was not authorized. 410 U.S. at 81.

In 1974 Congress overrode a presidential veto and amended the FOIA for the express purpose of changing this aspect of the *Mink* case. Exemption 1 was modified to exempt only matters that are "(A) specifically authorized under criteria established by an Executive order to be kept secret in the interest of national defense or foreign policy and (B) are in fact properly classified pursuant to such Executive order." 5 U.S.C. §552(b)(1) (1976).

Furthermore, the 1974 revision changed the FOIA language describing the role of a reviewing court considering *any* claim of exemption. It provided that "the court shall determine the matter de novo, and may examine the contents of such agency records in camera to determine whether such records or any part thereof shall be withheld under any of the exemptions set forth in subsection (b) of this section, and the burden is on the agency to sustain its action." 5 U.S.C. §552(a)(4)(B) (1976). The Conference Report accompanying the amendments explained that "[w]hile *in camera* examination need not be automatic, in many situations it will plainly be necessary and appropriate." S. Rep. No. 93-1200, 93d Cong., 2d Sess. 9 (1974), U.S. Code Cong. & Admin. News 1974, p. 6287.

Exemption 3 originally exempted matters "specifically exempted from disclosure by statute." 5 U.S.C. §552(b)(3) (1970). In FAA Administrator v. Robertson, 422 U.S. 255 (1975), the Court held that a statute could "specifically exempt" matters from disclosure even if the statute gave an agency broad discretion to determine whether the information should be withheld. Concerned about excessive agency discretion, Congress in 1976 passed an amendment to change the result reached in *Robertson*. Exemption 3 now authorizes nondisclosure of matters "specifically exempted from disclosure by statute... provided that such statute (A) requires that the matters be withheld from the public in such a manner as to leave no discretion on the issue, or (B) establishes particular criteria for withholding or refers to particular types of matters to be withheld." 5 U.S.C. §552(b)(3) (1976).

B. THE NATURE OF DE NOVO REVIEW

Procedures to Be Observed

In Vaughn v. Rosen, 484 F.2d 820 (1973), cert. denied, 415 U.S. 977 (1974), this court sought to cope with the difficulty of providing de novo review of exemptions claimed by the government. It initiated procedures designed to mitigate the administrative burden on the courts and ensure that the burden

---

8. *Mink* involved a request for documents prepared by various government officials for the President in connection with a scheduled nuclear test. The documents were withheld under Exemptions 1 and 5. Those seeking the information had not disputed the government's claim that proper classification procedures had been followed, 410 U.S. at 84, and the Court held that the substantive propriety of the classification had been committed by Congress to Executive discretion. The Court therefore reversed the order of the court of appeals that the district court examine the documents *in camera* and release any segregable nonsecret portions....

of justifying claimed exemptions would in fact be borne by the agencies to whom it had been assigned by Congress.

The court took its cue from a portion of the Supreme Court's *Mink* opinion that was not overruled by Congress — the portion discussing how a court should proceed when there is a factual dispute concerning the nature of the materials being withheld.[11] "Expanding" on the Supreme Court's "outline," the court established the following procedures: (1) A requirement that the agency submit a "relatively detailed analysis [of the material withheld] in manageable segments." "[C]onclusory and generalized allegations of exemptions" would no longer be accepted by reviewing courts. 484 F.2d at 826. (2) "[A]n indexing system [that] would subdivide the document under consideration into manageable parts cross-referenced to the relevant portion of the Government's justification." 484 F.2d at 827. This index would allow the district court and opposing counsel to locate specific areas of dispute for further examination and would be an indispensable aid to the court of appeals reviewing the district court's decision. (3) "[A]dequate adversary testing" would be ensured by opposing counsel's access to the information included in the agency's detailed and indexed justification and by *in camera* inspection, guided by the detailed affidavit and using special masters appointed by the court whenever the burden proved to be especially onerous. 484 F.2d at 828.[12]

In proposing the 1974 amendments, the Senate Committee outlined the ruling in *Vaughn* and added, "The committee supports this approach...."[13]

The Judicial Function as Emphasized by 1974 Amendments

In some of the decisions involving national security issues, there has been confusion about the nature of the evidentiary burdens and the scope of the district judge's discretion. This uncertainty is due to a misunderstanding of the legislative history of the 1974 amendments. There were differences in 1974 between the Senate Committee and the House, between the Senate and its Committee, and between the Legislative and Executive Branches. For an authoritative exposition of the purpose and effect of the 1974 amendments, it suffices for present purposes to quote a few key paragraphs of the Conference Committee report:[15]

> The conference substitute follows the Senate amendment, providing that in determining *de novo* whether agency records have been properly withheld, the court may examine records *in camera* in making its determination under any of the nine categories of exemptions under section 552(b) of the law. In Environmental Protection Agency v. Mink, et al., 410 U.S. 73 (1973), the Supreme Court

---

11. See EPA v. Mink, 410 U.S. at 92-94....
12. A remaining problem noted by the court in *Vaughn* — the failure of the district court's opinion to reveal the court's reasoning — was dealt with in Schwartz v. IRS, 511 F.2d 1303, 1307 (1975). *Schwartz* held that the district court had abused its discretion by not granting a plaintiff/appellant's request for a clarification of the legal grounds of its opinion affirming the agency's refusal to disclose information sought under the FOIA....
13. S. Rep. No. 93-854, 93d Cong., 2d Sess. 15 (1974).
15. S. Rep. No. 93-1200, 93d Cong., 2d Sess. 9, 12 (1974), U.S. Code Cong. & Admin. News 1974, pp. 6267, 6287, 6290.

A. The Freedom of Information Act

ruled that *in camera* inspection of documents withheld under section 552(b)(1) of the law, authorizing the withholding of classified information, would ordinarily be precluded in Freedom of Information cases, unless Congress directed otherwise. H.R. 12471 amends the present law to permit such *in camera* examination at the discretion of the court. While *in camera* examination need not be automatic, in many situations it will plainly be necessary and appropriate. Before the court orders *in camera* inspection, the Government should be given the opportunity to establish by means of testimony or detailed affidavits that the documents are clearly exempt from disclosure. The burden remains on the Government under this law....

When linked with the authority conferred upon the Federal courts in this conference substitute for *in camera* examination of contested records as part of their *de novo* determination in Freedom of Information cases, this clarifies Congressional intent to override the Supreme Court's holding in the case of E.P.A. v. Mink, et al., supra, with respect to *in camera* review of classified documents.

However, the conferees recognize that the Executive departments responsible for national defense and foreign policy matters have unique insights into what adverse effects might occur as a result of public disclosure of a particular classified record. Accordingly, the conferees expect that Federal courts, in making *de novo* determinations in section 552(b)(1) cases under the Freedom of Information law, will accord substantial weight to an agency's affidavit concerning the details of the classified status of the disputed record.

The legislative history underscores that the intent of Congress regarding de novo review stood in contrast to, and was a rejection of, the alternative suggestion proposed by the Administration and supported by some Senators: that in the national security context the court should be limited to determining whether there was a reasonable basis for the decision by the appropriate official to withhold the document.[16] In proposing a "reasonable basis" standard, the Administration and supporting legislators argued that de novo responsibility and *in camera* inspection could not properly be assigned to judges, in part because of logistical problems, and in part because of their lack of relevant experience and meaningful appreciation of the implications of the material involved. Those who prevailed in the legislature both resisted the Administration proposal on first consideration and voted to override President Ford's veto of the bill containing the provision for de novo review and *in camera* inspection. They stressed the need for an objective, independent judicial determination, and insisted that judges could be trusted to approach

---

16. See, e.g., Message from President Gerald R. Ford Vetoing H.R. 12471, H. Doc. No. 93-383, 93d Cong., 2d Sess. (1974):

> As the legislation now stands, a determination by the Secretary of Defense that disclosure of a document would endanger our national security would, even though reasonable, have to be overturned by a district judge who thought the plaintiff's position just as reasonable. Such a provision would violate constitutional principles, and give less weight before the courts to an executive determination involving the protection of our most vital national defense interests than is accorded determinations involving routine regulatory matters.
>
> I propose, therefore, that where classified documents are requested the courts could review the classification, but would have to uphold the classification if there is reasonable basis to support it. In determining the reasonableness of the classification, the courts would consider all attendant evidence prior to resorting to an *in camera* examination of the document.

the national security determinations with common sense, and without jeopardy to national security.[18] They emphasized that in reaching a de novo determination the judge would accord substantial weight to detailed agency affidavits and take into account that the executive had "unique insights into what adverse affects might occur as a result of public disclosure of a particular classified record."[19]

The salient characteristics of de novo review in the national security context can be summarized as follows: (1) The government has the burden of establishing an exemption. (2) The court must make a de novo determination. (3) In doing this, it must first "accord substantial weight to an agency's affidavit concerning the details of the classified status of the disputed record."[20] (4) Whether and how to conduct an *in camera* examination of the documents rests in the sound discretion of the court, in national security cases as in all other cases.[21] To these observations should be added an excerpt from our opinion in *Weissman* (as revised): "If exemption is claimed on the basis of national security the District Court must, of course, be satisfied that proper procedures have been followed, and that by its sufficient description the contested document logically falls into the category of the exemption indicated."[22]

---

18. See 120 Cong. Rec. 36,870 (1974) (Sen. Muskie):

> As a practical matter, I cannot imagine that any Federal judge would throw open the gates of the Nation's classified secrets, or that they would substitute their judgment for that of an agency head without carefully weighing all the evidence in the arguments presented by both sides.
>
> On the contrary, if we constrict the manner in which courts perform this vital review function, we make the classifiers themselves privileged officials, immune from the accountability necessary for Government to function smoothly.

Id. at 17,030 (Sen. Ervin):

> The court ought not be required to find anything except that the matter affects or does not affect national security. If a judge does not have enough sense to make that kind of decision, he ought not to be a judge. We ought not to leave that decision to be made by the CIA or any other branch of the Government.

Id. at 17,028 (Sen. Chiles):

> If, as the Senator from Mississippi said, there is a reason, why are judges going to be so unreasonable? We say that four-star generals or admirals will be reasonable but a Federal district judge is going to be unreasonable. I cannot buy that argument, especially when I see that general or that admiral has participated in covering up a mistake, and the Federal judge sits there without a bias one way or another. I want him to be able to decide without blinders or having to go in one direction.

19. S. Rep. No. 93-1200, 93d Cong., 2d Sess. 12 (1974), U.S. Code Cong. & Admin. News 1974, p. 6290.
20. Id.
21. The Senate Committee Report on the 1974 amendments emphasizes the procedural flexibility available to a district judge.

> In making this [exemption] determination, the court must *first* attempt to resolve the matter "on the basis of affidavits and other information submitted by the parties." If it does decide to examine the contested records in camera, the court may consider further argument by both parties, may take further expert testimony, and may in some cases of a particularly sensitive nature decide to entertain an ex parte showing by the government.

S. Rep. No. 93-854, 93d Cong., 2d Sess. 15-16 (1974) (emphasis added)....

22. Weissman v. CIA, 565 F.2d 692, 697 (1977). Whether there is a "sufficient description" to establish the exemptions is, of course, a key issue.

A. The Freedom of Information Act

In part, the foregoing considerations were developed for Exemption 1. They also apply to Exemption 3 when the statute providing criteria for withholding is in furtherance of national security interests.

In Camera Inspection

In the case at bar, the district court observed: "With respect to documents withheld under exemption 3, in camera inspection is seldom, if ever, necessary or appropriate." The legislative history does not support that conclusion. Congress left the matter of *in camera* inspection to the discretion of the district court, without any indication of the extent of its proper use. The ultimate criterion is simply this: Whether the district judge believes that *in camera* inspection is needed in order to make a responsible de novo determination on the claims of exemption.

In camera inspection requires effort and resources and therefore a court should not resort to it routinely on the theory that "it can't hurt." When an agency affidavit or other showing is specific, there may be no need for *in camera* inspection.

On the other hand, when the district judge is concerned that he is not prepared to make a responsible de novo determination in the absence of *in camera* inspection, he may proceed *in camera* without anxiety that the law interposes an extraordinary hurdle to such inspection. The government would presumably prefer *in camera* inspection to a ruling that the case stands in doubt or equipoise and hence must be resolved by a ruling that the government has not sustained its burden.

The issue of bad faith merits a word. The memorandum of the district court noted that there was no evidence of bad faith on the part of the Agency's officials. Where the record contains a showing of bad faith, the district court would likely require *in camera* inspection. But the government's burden does not mean that all assertions in a government affidavit must routinely be verified by audit. Reasonable specificity in affidavits connotes a quality of reliability. When an affidavit or showing is reasonably specific and demonstrates, if accepted, that the documents are exempt, these exemptions are not to be undercut by mere assertion of claims of bad faith or misrepresentation.

In camera inspection does not depend on a finding or even tentative finding of bad faith. A judge has discretion to order *in camera* inspection on the basis of an uneasiness, on a doubt he wants satisfied before he takes responsibility for a de novo determination. Government officials who would not stoop to misrepresentation may reflect an inherent tendency to resist disclosure, and judges may take this natural inclination into account.

III. RULINGS FOR THE CASE AT BAR

Two affidavits were executed by Eloise Page, Chief, Operations Staff of the Directorate of Operations of the CIA. The first is a general statement about the dangers at large of disclosure, background and local color rather than any attempt to link these concerns with specific documents. It is of little aid in the task of deciding whether the nine specific documents now sought come within the claimed exemptions....

Page's second affidavit... purports to link specific exemptions to specific documents. A glaring defect is that it lumps the exemptions together and fails to identify whether different exemptions are claimed as to different parts of each document. The statement for document 2 reads:

> This document is a three-page memorandum the subject of which is "Rennie Davis and Friends." It is essentially the debriefing report of a sensitive intelligence source. The majority of the information concerns individuals other than the plaintiffs.
>
> This document has been denied in its entirety, primarily to protect intelligence sources and methods since the release of any meaningful portion would disclose the identity of the source, and further, to protect cryptonyms, names of CIA personnel and CIA organizational data. Thus exemptions (b)(1), (b)(3) and (b)(6) apply.

The statement for documents 3, 4 and 5 reads:

> These documents are one-page cables from an overseas CIA installation which advise Headquarters of the receipt of documents and information from a foreign intelligence service and which concern the plaintiffs and other individuals. They are denied in their entirety pursuant to Freedom of Information Act exemptions (b)(1), (b)(3) and (b)(6).

In reviewing the judgment on documents 2-6, we encounter a complex of difficulties. Exemption 3 permits a withholding under the provisions of 50 U.S.C. §403g (1970), which specifies that "in order further to implement the proviso of section 403(d)(3) of this title that the Director of Central Intelligence shall be responsible for protecting intelligence sources and methods from unauthorized disclosure, the Agency shall be exempted from... the provisions of any... law which require the publication or disclosure of the organization, functions, names, official titles, salaries, or numbers of personnel employed by the Agency...." Goland v. CIA, [607 F.2d 339, 349 (D.C. Cir. 1978)]; cf. Weissman v. CIA, 565 F.2d 692, 694 (1977). However, in *Goland,* the affidavit demonstrated "in nonconclusory and detailed fashion" (slip op. at 21), that the deleted material disclosed intelligence sources and methods. The CIA's affidavit as to documents 2-6 is not a specific presentation such as that in *Goland.* The statement that the release of any meaningful portion of document 2 would disclose the identity of a "sensitive intelligence source" has some particularity, but it runs into a failure to address specifically whether the disclosure of substantive information may be possible without the disclosure of source, and if not why not.

As to Exemption 1, the information that document 2 relates to "Rennie Davis and Friends," might be some indication that it was reasonable for the official involved to have classified it in the first instance. But that mere reference is not enough information to permit a judge to make an independent ruling that the classification was proper....

Overall, we have a critical problem of segregability, that some portion of the document(s) may be exempt, but that the FOIA might contemplate disclosure in part. The difficulty arises from the CIA's proffer of multiple exemptions for each withheld document, and is maintained by the district court's conclusory rulings.

The reviewing court should not be required to speculate on the precise relationship between each exemption claim and the contents of the specific document. The district judge is not called upon to take on the role of censor—going through a line-by-line analysis for each document and removing particular words. If, however, the problematic material appears in a particular place or places that can be manageably identified, indexing is not to be bypassed because it is something of a chore....

... [T]he CIA ... has not been responsive to the requirement that it provide specific affidavits that segregate each of its claims. The "exemption by document" approach has been rejected by our opinions, notably *Vaughn*, 484 F.2d at 825-826, and Mead Data Central, Inc. v. Dept. of the Air Force, 566 F.2d 242, 259-262 (1977). The agency may not rely on that approach even in a national security context. The agency must provide a reasonable segregation as to the portions of the document that are involved in each of its claims for exemption. As indicated in *Mead*, it is important that the affidavit indicate the extent to which each document would be claimed as exempt under each of the exemptions. The courts cannot meaningfully exercise their responsibility under the FOIA unless the government affidavits are as specific as possible....

We remand for reconsideration of the CIA's exemption claims in light of clarification of the affidavits and for further proceedings not inconsistent with this opinion.

[The concurring opinion of WRIGHT, C.J., is omitted.]

Bassiouni v. Central Intelligence Agency
United States Court of Appeals, Seventh Circuit, 2004
392 F.3d 244

EASTERBROOK, Circuit Judge. Professor M. Cherif Bassiouni, a member of DePaul Law School's faculty since 1964, is the head of DePaul's International Human Rights Law Institute and a frequent participant in human-rights activities sponsored by the United States, the European Union, and the United Nations. In 1983 Bassiouni asked the Central Intelligence Agency for copies of all documents that mention him. The agency replied that it had some but would not reveal any details. In 1999 Bassiouni tried again, invoking both the Freedom of Information Act and the Privacy Act. Again the agency replied that it has documents bearing his name. Some of these, the CIA stated, had come from the State Department, to which it dispatched copies.... But he is dissatisfied with the CIA's refusal to hand over or even describe documents it generated internally or received from sources other than the State Department. The district court concluded that the CIA is entitled to keep mum.

Both the FOIA and the Privacy Act contain exceptions for classified information. 5 U.S.C. §552(b)(1) (FOIA); 5 U.S.C. §552a(k) (Privacy Act).... The agency does not contend that the *contents* of all documents mentioning Bassiouni are classified; it could hardly do so, given not only its refusal to identify which documents it holds but also the certainty that its files contain many U.N. reports, newspaper clippings, and other non-classified materials. Instead the agency maintains that providing a list of the documents that mention Bassiouni, and claiming document-by-document exemptions for those whose contents are classified, would reveal details about intelligence-gathering methods. These methods are classified independently of the information in materials the CIA collects.

It is easy to appreciate the basis of this concern. A list of documents could show clusters of dates that reveal when the agency acquired the information. Knowing which documents entered the files, and when, could permit an astute inference *how* the information came to the CIA's attention—and, in the intelligence business, "how" often means "from whom." A *Vaughn* index (named after *Vaughn v. Rosen*, 484 F.2d 820 (D.C. Cir. 1973)) thus could blow an agent's cover. Painstaking analysis of the patterns reflected in the agency's holdings might reveal that the person named in the request is *himself* a source of information. That would not be worrisome if people could request information only about themselves; Bassiouni knows whether he has ever been on the CIA's payroll (or has provided unpaid assistance). But any member of the public may invoke the FOIA, and the agency must disregard the requester's identity. See *Department of Justice v. Reporters Committee for Freedom of the Press*, 489 U.S. 749, 771 (1989). Thus any information available to Bassiouni is available to North Korea's secret police and Iran's counterintelligence service too. These and other hostile entities would be greatly interested in learning who is assisting the CIA. Even allies could be unpleasantly surprised by information that discloses espionage operations. And when the dates, numbers, and general subjects of documents (the information required in a *Vaughn* index) would not help anyone learn who supplied the information, it could help them learn how the CIA is deploying its resources and what subjects it is investigating; that knowledge could be useful to both nations and terrorists.

Because lists of documents could assist foreign intelligence services—whose powers of inference and deduction rise with their own stock of information, which helps them to identify patterns that professors, newspaper reporters, and judges may miss—the CIA refuses to reveal its holdings. It does this even when disclosure could be innocuous. There are two risks in disclosing when the request is harmless (as Bassiouni's may well be) and keeping silent when the CIA sees a danger. The first risk is that whoever makes the decision on behalf of the CIA may miss some clue that foreign intelligence services would catch, and thus inadvertently reveal secrets. The second risk is that people would draw an inference from disparate treatment: if, for example, the CIA opens its files most of the time and asserts the state-secrets privilege only when the information concerns a subject under investigation or one of its agents, then the very fact of asserting the exemption reveals that the request has identified a classified subject or source. When a pattern of responses itself reveals classified information, the only way to keep secrets is to maintain silence uniformly. And this is what the CIA has done. Today the agency's silence is called a "*Glomar* response," taking its name from the *Hughes Glomar Explorer,* a ship built (we now know) to recover a sunken Soviet submarine, but disguised as a private vessel for mining manganese nodules from the ocean floor. See *Phillippi v. CIA*, 546 F.2d 1009 (D.C. Cir. 1976). Every

A. The Freedom of Information Act

appellate court to address the issue has held that the FOIA permits the CIA to make a "*Glomar* response" when it fears that inferences from *Vaughn* indexes or selective disclosure could reveal classified sources or methods of obtaining foreign intelligence. See, e.g., *Frugone v. CIA,* 169 F.3d 772 (D.C. Cir. 1999); *Minier v. CIA,* 88 F.3d 796 (9th Cir. 1996).

Bassiouni does not take issue with these decisions. Instead he contends that the CIA waived its right to make a *Glomar* response when it revealed that its files contain at least one document bearing his name. Instead of responding to the 1999 request with stony silence, the CIA conceded again that it had some responsive documents and made what it calls a "no number, no list" response, which amounts to the same thing: the requester gets no details. How this can be a "waiver" we do not grasp. The risk to intelligence sources and methods comes from the details that would appear in a *Vaughn* index; it is these details — both the documents that appear in a list and the documents that the CIA might have gathered but did not — that permit crafty observers to infer what the CIA is investigating, what it has and how (and from whom) it gleans information. Bassiouni does not contend that the statement "we have some responsive documents" let the cat out of the bag. Both the first response and the second response leave to the imagination whether there is a cat to let out. The public is as much in the dark about the agency's sources and methods as it ever was. And Bassiouni is better off under a system that permits the CIA to reveal some things (such as the documents routed to the State Department) without revealing everything; if even a smidgen of disclosure required the CIA to open its files, there would be no smidgens. See *Public Citizen v. Department of State,* 11 F.3d 198, 203 (D.C. Cir. 1993)....

Affirmed.

NOTES AND QUESTIONS

1. *The Government's Strategy.* From the opinion in Ray v. Turner, can you outline the government's strategy in responding to the FOIA request? Determined to protect sensitive information from disclosure, government lawyers must be able to draw the line between zealous advocacy and abuse of process. Did they draw it in the right place in this case?

2. *Standards for Reviewing Exemption 1 Claims.* The 1974 amendments to FOIA represent a mid-course legislative correction in response to the holding in the Supreme Court's decision in EPA v. Mink, 410 U.S. 73 (1973), as the *Ray* court noted. *See* H. Comm. on Govt. Operations & Senate Comm. on the Judiciary, *Freedom of Information Act and Amendments of 1974,* 94th Cong. (Jt. Comm. Print 1975). Section 552(a)(4)(B) clearly aimed to withdraw authority from the executive branch and place it in the hands of the courts. In light of the broad delegation of authority to the President in Exemption 1, however, and the expansively drawn standards of Executive Order No. 13,292, did the 1974 amendment really diminish the power of the executive? Put another way, will a court ever be in a position to refute an agency determination that release of certain information "reasonably could be expected to result in damage to the national security"?

Despite the declaration of House and Senate conferees that a reviewing federal court should "accord substantial weight to an agency's affidavit," Ray v. Turner, 587 F.2d at 1193, there remains a wide range of opinion, sometimes even within the same Circuit, about standards for judicial review in national security cases. Yet there is a strong tendency among courts to apply the "reasonable basis" standard of review rejected by Congress in 1974. According to one court, for example, "It appears that Congress did not intend that the courts would make a true de novo review of classified documents." Stein v. Department of Justice, 662 F.2d 1245, 1253 (7th Cir. 1981). Another has stated, "In view of the knowledge, experience and positions held by the three [government] affiants regarding military secrets, military planning and national security, their affidavits were entitled to 'the utmost deference.'" Taylor v. Department of the Army, 684 F.2d 99, 109 (D.C. Cir. 1982). The *Bassiouni* court's very deferential response is far more typical in Exemption 1 and 3 cases today than the response in *Ray*. See Robert P. Deyling, *Judicial Deference and De Novo Review in Litigation Over National Security Information Under the Freedom of Information Act*, 37 Vill. L. Rev. 67, 82-94 (1992); Scott A. Faust, Note, *National Security Information Disclosure Under the FOIA: The Need for Effective Judicial Enforcement*, 25 B.C. L. Rev. 611, 628-637 (1984).

There are notable exceptions. *See, e.g.,* American Civil Liberties Union v. Department of Defense, No. 04 Civ. 4151 (AKH), 2006 WL 1638025 (S.D.N.Y. June 9, 2006) (ordering release of photographic images of abuses of U.S. prisoners in Iraq).

Can you guess why there is a tendency toward greater judicial deference to executive secrecy claims? Could Exemption 1 be more clearly drawn to eliminate any confusion about this point? Can you suggest amending language?

3. *In Camera Inspection.* The district court in Ray v. Turner abused its discretion by *not* conducting an in camera inspection of the requested documents. *See also* Quinon v. Federal Bureau of Investigation, 86 F.3d 1222, 1230 (D.C. Cir. 1996) ("where the agency cannot describe the document fully enough to show that it is exempt from disclosure without in the course of doing so disclosing the very information that warrants exemption, the solution is for the court to review the document in camera"). Under what circumstances should an affirmative decision to conduct such an inspection be reversed? *Compare* Donovan v. FBI, 806 F.2d 55, 59 (2d Cir. 1986), *and* Salisbury v. United States, 690 F.2d 966, 973 n.3 (D.C. Cir. 1982) (district court had broad discretion to make such an inspection, even though the case could have been resolved on the public affidavit alone), *with* Doherty v. Department of Justice, 775 F.2d 49, 53 (2d Cir. 1985), *and* King v. Department of Justice, 586 F. Supp. 286, 290 (D.D.C. 1983) ("In camera proceedings are a last resort").

4. *Vaughn Affidavit.* The *Vaughn* affidavit procedure is supposed to represent a practical alternative to the particular burden that courts face in inspecting numerous or voluminous contested documents. It is also designed to give the requester some idea about what is contained in the withheld record so that there will be "adequate adversary testing" of agency exemption claims, as the court put it in Ray v. Turner. *See* Halpern v. FBI, 181 F.3d 279, 285 (2d Cir. 1999) (rejecting as inadequate a *Vaughn* affidavit purporting to justify withholding of

A. The Freedom of Information Act

files on surveillance of the meat-packing industry: although affiant "wrote much, she said little"); Wiener v. Federal Bureau of Investigation, 943 F.2d 972 (9th Cir. 1991) (FBI files on Beatle John Lennon).

The *Vaughn* affidavit must not reveal too much, of course, as the *Bassiouni* court pointed out, lest the cat be let out of the bag. But should the court in that case have kept the bag entirely closed?

If the court considers ex parte government affidavits, Hayden v. National Security Agency/Cent. Security Serv., 608 F.2d 1381 (D.C. Cir. 1979), or even secret testimony from government witnesses, Pollard v. FBI, 705 F.2d 1151 (9th Cir. 1983), sometimes without even examining the contested documents, Doyle v. FBI, 722 F.2d 554 (9th Cir. 1983), is any meaningful adversary testing possible? In the absence of requester's counsel, must the court play "devil's advocate" and rehearse the arguments for the requester? In Arieff v. United States Dept. of the Navy, 712 F.2d 1462, 1470-1471 (D.C. Cir. 1983), the court said government affidavits should be considered ex parte and in camera only "where absolutely necessary."

5. *The "Glomar" Principle.* Some agency records are so sensitive, as the *Bassiouni* court observes, that disclosure of their very existence could injure the national security. Executive Order No. 12,958 repeats this caution at §3.7(a). In Hudson River Sloop Clearwater v. Department of the Navy, 891 F.2d 414 (2d Cir. 1989), the *Glomar* principle allowed the Navy to conceal from a FOIA requester the possible presence of nuclear weapons on ships based in New York Harbor. And in Minier v. CIA, 88 F.3d 796 (9th Cir. 1996), the CIA invoked the principle when asked to confirm that it had employed a man who claimed involvement in President Kennedy's assassination. Are you convinced by the *Bassiouni* court's analysis that the CIA was entitled to withhold all records relevant to the professor's request? Applying the court's reasoning, is there any record in any agency file that could not be withheld?

The *Glomar* principle, as applied by the *Bassiouni* court, is related to the "mosaic" theory, which has seen increasing use since 9/11. It is invoked in a variety of contexts to withhold bits and pieces of unclassified information that might, according to the theory, be aggregated by an enemy to reveal some important secret. For example, in Center for National Security Studies v. United States Dept. of Justice, 331 F.3d 918, 928 (D.C. Cir. 2003), the court declared that "[a] complete list of names informing terrorists of every suspect detained by the government at any point during the September 11 investigation" could "allow terrorists to better evade the ongoing investigation and more easily formulate or revise counter-efforts." Can you see a potential for abuse with this theory? See David E. Pozen, Note, *The Mosaic Theory, National Security, and the Freedom of Information Act*, 115 Yale L.J. 628 (2005).

6. *Classification Procedure.* Exemption 1 permits withholding of materials that "are in fact properly classified" under the relevant executive order. Ray v. Turner makes it clear that this requirement has substantive as well as procedural content. But since an agency can classify a record or correct an error in the classification procedure at any time, even after receipt of a FOIA request, *see, e.g.*, Miller v. United States Dept. of State, 779 F.2d 1378, 1388 (8th Cir. 1985), does the procedural part of the requirement have any practical

significance? *See* Armstrong v. Executive Office of the President, 897 F. Supp. 10, 13 (D.D.C. 1995) (holding that agency is free to correct its earlier error in classification: "It would be unwise for us to punish flexibility, lest we provide the motivation for intransigence."), *rev'd on other grounds*, 90 F.3d 553 (D.C. Cir. 1996).

7. *Exemption 3.* What is the purpose of Exemption 3? Does it provide any protection for national security secrets not already afforded by Exemption 1?

In CIA v. Sims, 471 U.S. 159 (1985), the Supreme Court applied FOIA Exemption 3 to permit withholding of information under §102(d)(3) of the National Security Act of 1947, currently codified at 50 U.S.C. §403-1(i)(1), which states that the Director of National Intelligence shall "protect intelligence sources and methods from unauthorized disclosure." Based on its reading of "the express intention of Congress [and] the practical necessities of modern intelligence gathering," 471 U.S. at 169, the Court found plenary power in the Director to protect *all* intelligence sources from disclosure, not merely those "who supplied the Agency with information unattainable without guaranteeing confidentiality." *Id.* at 174. Said the Court:

> If potentially valuable intelligence sources come to think that the Agency will be unable to maintain the confidentiality of its relationship to them, many could well refuse to supply information to the Agency in the first place....
>
> We seriously doubt whether a potential intelligence source will rest assured knowing that judges, who have little or no background in the delicate business of intelligence gathering, will order his identity revealed only after examining the facts of the case to determine whether the Agency actually needed to promise confidentiality in order to obtain the information.... Moreover, a court's decision whether an intelligence source will be harmed if his identity is revealed will often require complex political, historical, and psychological judgments. There is no reason for a potential intelligence source, whose welfare and safety may be at stake, to have great confidence in the ability of judges to make those judgments correctly. [*Id.* at 175-176.]

In a separate opinion, Justice Marshall worried that there might be no limit to the information thus shielded from disclosure. "It is difficult to conceive of anything the Central Intelligence Agency might have within its many files that might not disclose or enable an observer to discover something about where the Agency gathers information." *Id.* at 191 (Marshall, J., concurring). *See also* Maynard v. Central Intelligence Agency, 986 F.2d 547, 555 (1st Cir. 1993) ("The CIA, not the judiciary, is better able to weigh the risks that disclosure of such information may reveal intelligence sources and methods so as to endanger national security."); *cf.* Hunt v. Central Intelligence Agency, 981 F.2d 1116, 1120 (9th Cir. 1992) (relying on *Sims*, but declaring, "we are now 'only a short step [from] exempting all CIA records' from FOIA. That result may well be contrary to what Congress intended."). Can the Supreme Court's reading of Exemption 3 be squared with the 1976 amendment to FOIA described in Ray v. Turner?

8. *Exemption of Particular Classes of Records.* In 1984, Congress passed the CIA Information Act, 50 U.S.C.A. §431 (West 2003 & Supp. 2006), exempting most

A. The Freedom of Information Act

of the CIA's "operational" files, those that describe foreign intelligence and counterintelligence activities, from the search and review requirements of FOIA. Proponents of the measure, including the American Civil Liberties Union, argued that by exempting the agency from searching for files that are almost invariably exempt from disclosure under Exemption 1 or 3 anyway, long delays in answering other requests would be reduced. Judicial review is available for complaints that records were improperly placed in exempt operational files, but only based on the requester's "personal knowledge or other admissible evidence." *Id.* §431(f)(3). *See* Karen A. Winchester & James W. Zirkle, *Freedom of Information and the CIA Information Act*, 21 U. Rich. L. Rev. 231 (1987). Practical application of the exemption is described in Sullivan v. Central Intelligence Agency, 992 F.2d 1249 (1st Cir. 1993).

More recently, Congress amended FOIA to provide that the FBI need not reveal the existence of classified records pertaining to "foreign intelligence or counterintelligence, or international terrorism." 5 U.S.C. §552(c)(3). Other exemptions apply to operational files of the National Geospatial-Intelligence Agency, National Security Agency, National Reconnaissance Office, and Defense Intelligence Agency. *See An Operational Files Exemptions for DIA*, Secrecy News, Jan. 5, 2006.

Do you see any potential for abuse in any of these specific exemptions? If so, can you suggest any way to reduce that potential?

9. *Exemption 5.* FOIA Exemption 5 does not, by its terms, address issues of national security. However, requests for information about national defense and foreign policy are often frustrated by its application. The Supreme Court has interpreted this "somewhat Delphic provision" as "incorporat[ing] the privileges which the Government enjoys under the relevant statutory and case law in the pretrial discovery context." United States Dept. of Justice v. Julian, 486 U.S. 1, 11 (1988). The general purpose of Exemption 5 is to withhold "from a member of the public documents which a private party could not discover in litigation with the agency." National Labor Relations Board v. Sears, Roebuck & Co., 421 U.S. 132, 148 (1975).

The most important of these discovery privileges for our purposes is the "executive privilege" (see *supra* pp. 88-92), one aspect of which prevents releases of predecisional communications that would be injurious to the consultative functions of government. For example, in Russell v. Department of the Air Force, 682 F.2d 1045 (D.C. Cir. 1982), the court decided that portions of a draft Air Force historical study of the use of the herbicide Agent Orange in Vietnam need not be disclosed to a veterans' organization or a college student writing an honors thesis.

> Exemption (b)(5) shields from the mandatory disclosure requirements of the FOIA the deliberative process that precedes most decisions of government agencies. Jordan v. United States Dept. of Justice, 591 F.2d 753, 773 (D.C. Cir. 1978). Thus, the exemption protects not only communications which are themselves deliberative in nature, but all communications which, if revealed, would expose to public view the deliberative process of an agency.... In *Jordan,* Judge Wilkey articulates well the policies behind Exemption (b)(5)'s protection of the deliberative process. He states:

There are essentially three policy bases for this privilege. First, it protects creative debate and candid consideration of alternatives within an agency, and, thereby, improves the quality of agency policy decisions. Second, it protects the public from the confusion that would result from premature exposure to discussions occurring before the policies affecting it had actually been settled upon. And third, it protects the integrity of the decision-making process itself by confirming that "officials should be judged by what they decided[,] not for matters they considered before making up their minds."

[*Russell*, 682 F.2d at 1047-1048.]

The *Russell* court suggested that any record may, in a sense, be deemed "antecedent to future...decisions," *Id.* at 1049 n.l. If it is true, as Antonius maintained, that what's past is also prologue, will a requester ever succeed in obtaining a historical report if the agency chooses not to release it? The elements and application of Exemption 5 are described generally in National Council of La Raza v. Department of Justice, 411 F.3d 350 (2d Cir. 2005); Grand Central Pship. Inc. v. Cuomo, 166 F.3d 473, 481-482 (2d Cir. 1999).

Concerning the characterization of a communication as "inter-agency or intra-agency," the Supreme Court has ruled that a document prepared for an agency by a truly independent outside consultant may be protected by the exemption, but that advice from an outside entity that has some interest in the agency's decision will not be. Department of the Interior and Bureau of Indian Affairs v. Klamath Water Users Protective Assn., 532 U.S. 1 (2001). The decision could affect the availability of information about agency contacts with, say, defense contractors or public interest groups.

10. *Exemption 7.* FOIA Exemption 7 is designed to protect certain "records or information compiled for law enforcement purposes." For example, Church of Scientology v. United States Department of the Army, 611 F.2d 738 (9th Cir. 1979), was concerned with records compiled by the Naval Investigative Service (NIS) of the Office of Naval Intelligence. The court found that if NIS had no "law enforcement purpose based upon properly delegated enforcement authority" when it collected the information, Exemption 7 would not permit its withholding. *Id.* at 748. But the Supreme Court held in John Doe Agency v. John Doe Corp., 493 U.S. 146, 153 (1989), *reh'g denied*, 493 U.S. 1064 (1990), that the exemption covers "documents already collected by the government originally for non-law-enforcement purposes." They need only have been "compiled," said the Court, "when the Government invokes the Exemption." *Id.* Should the public disclosure of information in government hands be linked with the purpose for which it was originally collected?

Center for National Security Studies v. United States Dept. of Justice, 331 F.3d 918 (D.C. Cir. 2003), concerned a request for information about persons detained and questioned after 9/11—more than 700 for immigration law violations, 134 on criminal charges, and others as material witnesses. See *supra* p. 665. The FOIA plaintiffs sought the names of the detainees and their attorneys, dates of their arrest and release, and reasons for their detention. The court agreed with the government that this was "law enforcement" information, the production of which "could reasonably be expected to interfere with enforcement proceedings," within the meaning of Exemption 7(A). The terrorism investigation, said the court, concerned "a heinous violation of federal law as well as a breach of this nation's security." *Id.* at 926. The court also declared that "the judiciary is in an extremely poor position to second-guess the executive's judgment in this area of national security." *Id.* at 928.

Subsection (D) of Exemption 7 is often invoked in national security or foreign policy cases to prevent disclosure of confidential sources or information furnished by those sources. The importance of secret informants to the conduct of our government can hardly be overstated. Recall the Supreme Court's declaration to this effect in Central Intelligence Agency v. Sims, noted above. A "confidential" source need not be a paid informer; it may be anyone given an express or implied assurance of confidentiality by the agency. Pope v. United States, 599 F.2d 1383, 1386-1387 (5th Cir. 1979). However, in United States Dept. of Justice v. Landano, 508 U.S. 165 (1993), the Supreme Court rejected a presumption that all sources supplying information to the FBI in a criminal investigation are confidential sources under Exemption 7(D). *See also* Billington v. United States Dept. of Justice, 233 F.3d 581 (2000) (rejecting an unelaborated statement that confidentiality was assured).

11. *Bad Faith.* Agencies do sometimes seem to act in bad faith. In McGehee v. CIA, 697 F.2d 1095 (D.C. Cir. 1983), for example, the agency immediately conducted a search that revealed materials relevant to a FOIA request, then waited two and a half years to respond to the requester, after suit was filed in federal court. The agency also searched for records on only one narrow topic requested ("People's Temple") and ignored others ("Jonestown" and "Jim Jones") that were obviously related and relevant to the request. *Id.* at 1098-1100. On rehearing the court decided that the agency nevertheless had not acted in bad faith. 711 F.2d 1076 (D.C. Cir. 1983).

As the *Ray* decision indicates, evidence of agency bad faith may trigger a more thorough judicial review of the requester's complaint. *See* Meeropol v. Meese, 790 F.2d 942, 958 (D.C. Cir. 1986). FOIA §552(a)(4)(F) also requires consideration of disciplinary action against agency personnel who act arbitrarily or capriciously in withholding information. *See* Paul M. Winters, Note, *Revitalizing the Sanctions Provision of the Freedom of Information Act Amendments of 1976*, 84 Geo. L.J. 617 (1996). Is this provision likely to deter misbehavior by agency officials?

12. *Fruits of FOIA.* Is FOIA of any real value in obtaining information about national security or foreign policy matters? District court orders to turn over classified material have rarely been upheld on appeal. *But see* Donovan v. FBI, 806 F.2d 55 (2d Cir. 1986). Yet the prospect of having to justify its actions before a reviewing court has undoubtedly persuaded some agencies to disclose information that otherwise would not have been made available. For example, in Miller v. United States Dept. of State, 779 F.2d 1378, 1388 (8th Cir. 1985), the requester initially received only seven documents from the agency. Another 56 were released when he filed suit, 72 more when he demanded a pretrial conference, and a total of 232 additional documents before the district court's decision in the case, even though the agency repeatedly insisted that it had already sent all responsive records.

This photographic record of an historic 1970 meeting in the White House was obtained through a FOIA request by the National Security Archive from the National Archives and Records Administration. See http://www.gwu.edu/nsarchiv/nsa/elvis/elnix.html.

Disclosures resulting from 500 FOIA requests, touching on subjects as diverse as UFOs and Billy Carter's Libyan contacts, are indexed in Evan Hendricks, *Former Secrets: Government Records Made Public Through the Freedom of Information Act* (1982). Others are described in *A Culture of Secrecy: The Government Versus the People's Right to Know* (Athan G. Theoharis ed., 1998); Herbert N. Foerstel, *Freedom of Information and the Right to Know: The Origins and Applications of the Freedom of Information Act* 123-161(1999); and Center for National Security Studies, *From Official Files: Abstracts of Documents on National Security and Civil Liberties* (1985). In 1985, former Washington Post reporter Scott Armstrong and others founded the National Security Archive in Washington, D.C. Funded by grants, the Archive uses FOIA to collect materials from various agencies, index them, and make them available to the public and Congress. Many of these materials are available online at http://www.gwu.edu/~nsarchiv/. Other materials relating to national security that were obtained from FOIA requests may be found on the Web site of the Federation of American Scientists, http://www.fas.org/.

13. *Other Sources.* In addition to sources cited elsewhere in these notes, the following general references will be helpful to the reader: *Litigation Under the Federal Open Government Laws* (Harry A. Hammitt, David L. Sobel & Mark S. Zaid eds., 21st ed. 2002); James T. O'Reilly, *Federal Information Disclosure* (3d ed. 2000, with updates); and several publications of the Justice Department's Office of Information and Privacy, including *Freedom of Information Act Guide*, May 2004, *Overview of the Privacy Act of 1974*, May 2004, and a newsletter called *FOIA* Post, all *available at* http://www.usdoj.gov/oip/oip.html.

B. OTHER OPEN GOVERNMENT LAWS

1. Presidential Records Act

The Presidential Records Act of 1978, 44 U.S.C. §§2201-2207 (2000), requires the President to "assure that the activities, deliberations, decisions, and policies that reflect the performance of his constitutional, statutory, or other official or ceremonial duties are adequately documented" and maintained. *Id.* §2203(a). At the end of the President's term the documents are to be turned over to the Archivist of the United States, who is to make them "available to the public as rapidly and completely as possible consistent with the provisions of this Act." *Id.* §2203(f)(1). However, the outgoing President may require that documents falling into categories roughly paralleling the FOIA exemptions be withheld for up to 12 years. *Id.* §2204(a). Thereafter, public access is controlled by the Freedom of Information Act, except that Exemption 5 is not applicable. *Id.* §2204(c)(1).

Litigation growing out of the Iran-Contra Affair tests the limits of the Act. On January 19, 1989, the final day of the Reagan presidency, the National Security Archive filed FOIA requests for all the material stored on White House electronic communications systems. Simultaneously, the Archive and other plaintiffs filed suit to enjoin the destruction of documents contained in those systems on grounds that they were entitled to protection under the Presidential Records Act and the Federal Records Act, 44 U.S.C. §§2101-2118, 2501-2506, 2901-2910, 3101-3107, 3301-3324 (2000 & Supp. III 2003), the latter setting out requirements for the preservation and disposal of "agency" records. The court held that the Presidential Records Act impliedly precludes judicial review of the President's creation, management, and disposal of records covered by that Act. Armstrong v. Bush, 924 F.2d 282, 288-291 (D.C. Cir. 1991). In a subsequent appeal, the same court ruled that the National Security Council, whose records were particularly at issue, is not an "agency" within the meaning of FOIA, Armstrong v. Executive Office of the President, 90 F.3d 553 (D.C. Cir. 1996) (see *supra* p. 995), thus consigning NSC records to administration under the Presidential Records Act and delaying public scrutiny of them. Some of the electronic records at issue in the *Armstrong* case are reproduced in National Security Archive, *White House e-mail* (1995). The lengthy litigation is analyzed in Philip G. Schrag, *Working Papers as Federal Records: The Need for New Legislation to Preserve the History of Federal Policy*, 46 Admin. L. Rev. 95 (1994); James D. Lewis, Note, *White House Electronic Mail and Federal Recordkeeping Law: Press "D" to Delete History*, 93 Mich. L. Rev. 794 (1995).

In the wake of the Watergate scandal, just as in *Armstrong*, concern arose that President Nixon or members of his staff might seek to destroy important historical records that could prove embarrassing or even indicate criminal conduct. Of special interest were Oval Office tape recordings of conversations and telephone calls spanning more than five years. In late 1974, Congress passed the Presidential Recordings and Materials Preservation Act, 44 U.S.C. §2111 note (2000), directing the Archivist to take charge of all materials relating to the Nixon presidency and adopt regulations for public access to them, taking into account, among other factors, "the need to provide the public with the full truth, at the earliest reasonable date, of the abuses of governmental power popularly identified under the generic term 'Watergate.'" *Id.* §104(a)(1). In Nixon v. Administrator of General Services, 433 U.S. 425 (1977), the Supreme Court balanced the intrusion into presidential prerogatives against Congress's desire to preserve the materials and make them available to the public, upholding the validity of the Act against charges that it violated the separation of powers, the executive privilege, and the former President's First Amendment rights, as well as the Bill of Attainder Clause, art. I, §9. *See also* Nixon v. Freeman, 670 F.2d 346 (D.C. Cir.), *cert. denied*, 459 U.S. 1035 (1982) (Act did not violate presidential privilege of confidentiality, right to political association, or Fourth Amendment privacy rights).

Again, on January 19, 1993, just hours before President Clinton's inauguration, outgoing President Bush signed a secret agreement with then-Archivist Don W. Wilson (soon to become head of the George Bush Presidential Studies Center at Texas A&M University) to take charge of thousands of tapes and disks containing White House electronic communications. Presidential information in the materials was to be disposed of only in accordance with instructions from George Bush or his designee. The agreement was struck down as violative of the Presidential Records Act procedure for handling of such materials at the conclusion of a President's term. American Historical Assn. v. Peterson, 876 F. Supp. 1300 (D.D.C. 1995).

Twelve years after President Ronald Reagan left office, when the National Archives and Records Administration announced the impending release of some 68,000 pages of previously undisclosed "confidential communications" of the Reagan presidency, President George W. Bush ordered the release delayed to give him time to decide whether to invoke "a constitutionally based privilege or take other appropriate action." *See* George Lardner Jr., *Bush Clamping Down on Presidential Papers*, Wash. Post., Nov. 1, 2001, at A33. The Presidential Records Act provides that "[n]othing in this Act shall be construed to confirm, limit, or expand any constitutionally-based privilege which may be available to an incumbent or former President." 44 U.S.C. §2204(c)(2). Critics accused Bush of seeking to withhold information that might prove embarrassing to his father, who served as Reagan's Vice-President, or to several members of his own administration who also held important positions under President Reagan.

President Bush then issued an order invoking various presidential privileges, including the deliberative process privilege, see *supra* p. 89, and the state secrets privilege, see *infra* p. 1037, and barring release of any presidential records over the objection of either the incumbent President or the one whose papers are sought. Executive Order No. 13,233, 66 Fed. Reg. 56,025 (Nov. 1, 2001). A coalition of historians and organizations filed suit to compel the release of withheld documents, none of which was subject to withholding under any FOIA exemption. The court ruled against disclosure, declaring that "a president's assertion of constitutional privilege can only be overcome with some 'demonstrated, specific need' on the part of the party seeking the privileged documents." American Historical Assn. v. National Archives and Records Admin., 402 F. Supp. 2d 171, 182 (D.D.C. 2005). Can you guess who could demonstrate a specific need sufficient to overcome a presidential claim of privilege in this context? Has the court effectively nullified the congressional policy to release presidential records?

B. Other Open Government Laws

2. Privacy Act

The Privacy Act of 1974, 5 U.S.C. §552a (2000), was adopted in the wake of revelations that the government compiled secret dossiers on thousands of Americans during the Vietnam War. See *supra* p. 960. Its purpose is

> to promote governmental respect for the privacy of citizens by requiring all departments and agencies of the executive branch and their employees to observe certain constitutional rules in the computerization, use, and disclosure of personal information about individuals.... It is designed to prevent the kind of illegal, unwise, overbroad investigation and record surveillance of law-abiding citizens produced in recent years from actions of some over-zealous investigators, and the curiosity of some government administrators, or the wrongful disclosure and use, in some cases, of personal files held by Federal agencies.... It is to prevent the secret gathering of information on people or the creation of secret information systems or data banks on Americans.... [S. Rep. No. 93-1183 (1974), *reprinted in* 1974 U.S.C.C.A.N. 6916-6917.]

The Act accomplishes this purpose in five basic ways:

> It requires agencies to publicly report the existence of all systems of records maintained on individuals. It requires that the information contained in these record systems be accurate, complete, relevant, and up-to-date. It provides procedures whereby individuals can inspect and correct inaccuracies in almost all Federal files about themselves. It specifies that information about an individual gathered for one purpose not be used for another without the individual's consent. And, finally, it requires agencies to keep an accurate accounting of the disclosure of records and, with certain exceptions, to make these disclosures available to the subject of the record. In addition, the [Act] provides sanctions to enforce these provisions. [H. Comm. on Government Operations, *A Citizen's Guide on How to Use the Freedom of Information Act and the Privacy Act in Requesting Government Documents*, H.R. Rep. No. 95-793, at 16 (1977).]

An individual may utilize the Privacy Act or FOIA or both, as Professor Bassiouni did, see *supra* p. 1005, to seek access to information about herself in agency records, and she is entitled to the cumulative total of access rights under the two acts. Martin v. Office of Special Counsel, 819 F.2d 1181, 1184 (D.C. Cir. 1987). *See* Thomas M. Susman, *The Privacy Act and the Freedom of Information Act: Conflict and Resolution*, 21 J. Marshall L. Rev. 703 (1988).

By giving access to information about the requester, the Privacy Act may also furnish an alternate route to disclosure of national security information. Privacy Act provisions for access to agency records and for judicial relief generally follow the pattern established in FOIA. Thus, agency heads are authorized to withhold information that would be subject to FOIA Exemption 1, 5 U.S.C. §552a(k)(1), or that comprises investigatory material for law enforcement purposes. *Id.* §552a(k)(2). Other Privacy Act exemptions generally parallel those in FOIA. Unlike FOIA, however, the Privacy Act enables the CIA and law enforcement agencies to deny access to any "system of records" (e.g., all wiretap transcripts maintained at the FBI indexed by the names of the investigative targets). 5 U.S.C. §552a(j). Can you see why these agencies, which may have the greatest potential for the abuses at which the Act is aimed, are given special protection under the Act? For a suggestion that these "general" exemptions may be so broadly drawn that they threaten constitutional due process rights, *see* Note, *The Privacy Act of 1974: An Overview*, 1976 Duke L.J. 301, 318-320.

The Privacy Act forbids agencies to maintain any record "describing how any individual exercises rights guaranteed by the First Amendment unless expressly authorized by statute or by the individual about whom the record is maintained or unless pertinent to or within the scope of an authorized law enforcement activity." 5 U.S.C. §552a(e)(7). This provision was invoked by Professor Bassiouni in his request for information about himself in CIA files:

> He contends that between 1970 and 1975 the FBI investigated his political beliefs (including his criticism of American foreign policy) and shared with the CIA the results of this investigation. The CIA does not doubt that Bassiouni has made a sufficient preliminary showing that the FBI gathered information about Bassiouni's politics and has not replied that its maintenance of these records (if indeed it *is* maintaining them, which it will not confirm or deny) is authorized by any of the "unless" clauses in subsection (e)(7). It does not follow, however, that Bassiouni is entitled to a *Vaughn* index. Exemption 1 [of FOIA] would not mean much if all anyone had to do, to see the full list of the CIA's holdings, was allege that the agency had some documents showing how he "exercises rights guaranteed by the First Amendment." Almost anyone whose activities come to the CIA's attention could make such an assertion.
>
> Subsection (e)(7) says that the agency may not *maintain* records unless it meets certain conditions. It does not say that the agency must *disclose* records to the subject when that step would reveal classified intelligence sources and methods. See 5 U.S.C. §552a(g)(2), (4); *Irons v. Bell*, 596 F.2d 468, 470 (1st Cir. 1979). Bassiouni could have asked the district judge to order the CIA to reveal *in camera* what records (if any) it received from the FBI about Bassiouni between 1970 and 1975 (and has clung to for 30 years), and either purge them from its files or give a statutory justification for keeping them. Yet Bassiouni has never made such a request—not of the CIA, not in the district court, and not in this court. He wants disclosure rather than erasure, and disclosure is the one thing that he cannot have. [Bassiouni v. Central Intelligence Agency, 392 F.3d 244, 247-248 (7th Cir. 2004).]

How meaningful is the protection of subsection (e)(7) under the *Bassiouni* court's reading of it? Conflicting interpretations of this provision in other courts may be found in Becker v. Internal Revenue Serv., 34 F.3d 398 (7th Cir. 1994), and J. Roderick MacArthur Found. v. FBI, 102 F.3d 600 (D.C. Cir. 1996). See Steven W. Becker, Comment, *Maintaining Secret Government Dossiers on the First Amendment Activities of American Citizens: The Law Enforcement Activity Exception to the Privacy Act*, 50 DePaul L. Rev. 675 (2000).

3. Open Meetings Laws

The Government in the Sunshine Act, 5 U.S.C. §552b (2000), and the Federal Advisory Committee Act, 5 U.S.C. App. (2000), are designed to open up the government decision-making process by giving members of the public an

B. Other Open Government Laws

opportunity to attend and perhaps participate in the meetings of deliberative bodies. Each act contains exemptions analogous to those found in FOIA, permitting meetings to be closed or their transcripts to be withheld. Public access to such meetings may improve the quality of decision making or may stifle creative debate about grave matters of state, depending on one's point of view. *See* Anessa Abrams, *The First Lady: Federal Employee or Citizen-Representative Under FACA?*, 62 Geo. Wash. L. Rev. 855 (1994); Note, *The Government in the Sunshine Act — An Overview*, 1977 Duke L.J. 565, 571-572.

A case involving the Federal Advisory Committee Act (FACA) came before the Supreme Court in 2004. Cheney v. United States District Court, 542 U.S. 367 (2004). Public interest groups sought various records of the Vice President's energy policy task force, appointed by President Bush early in his administration. Suing under the Mandamus Act, 28 U.S.C. §1361, and the Administrative Procedure Act, 5 U.S.C. §706, to enforce the disclosure provisions of FACA, the plaintiffs asserted that individuals in the private sector worked so closely with the task force that they became de facto members of it, thereby making it an advisory committee subject to FACA's requirements. To establish this factual predicate, the plaintiffs sought discovery that the Court called "overly broad," since the request covered more information than FACA itself would require to be disclosed. 542 U.S. at 377. Distinguishing its holding in United States v. Nixon, 418 U.S. 683 (1974), noted *supra* p. 90, the Court ruled that the Vice President (or the President) was not necessarily required to invoke executive privilege to avoid discovery, because of the burden that requirement would impose on the executive. "Special considerations" control discovery requests, said the Court, "when the Executive Branch's interests in maintaining the autonomy of its office and safeguarding the confidentiality of its communications are implicated." 542 U.S. at 385. After all, the Court remarked, "[e]ven if FACA embodies important congressional objectives, the only consequence from [plaintiffs'] inability to obtain the discovery they seek is that it would be more difficult for private complainants to vindicate Congress' policy objectives under FACA." *Id.* at 384-385. So saying, the Court remanded the case for reconsideration of the discovery request. On remand, the Court of Appeals reasoned that the alleged de facto private sector members of the Vice President's energy policy group were not members of an advisory committee covered by FACA, because they had no vote or veto over committee decisions, and the internal communications of the task force could therefore remain confidential. In re Cheney, 406 F.3d 723, 728 (D.C. Cir. 2005) (en banc). What, if any, are the implications of the *Cheney* litigation for government decisionmaking that affects national security?

For additional information on the Privacy Act and the open meetings laws, *see Litigation Under the Federal Open Government Laws* (Harry A. Hammitt, David L. Sobel & Mark S. Zaid, eds., 21st ed. 2002); James T. O'Reilly, *Federal Information Disclosure* (3d ed. 2000); Office of Information and Privacy, Dept. of Justice, *Overview of the Privacy Act of 1974*, May 2004.

Access to National Security Information in Civil Litigation

> You can't always get what you want.
>
> *Mick Jagger*

The Freedom of Information Act (FOIA) and its statutory analogues are supposed to enable almost anyone to obtain information about the workings of government for any purpose whatsoever. Nonetheless, exemptions in each statute make many agency records inaccessible. Moreover, none of the open government laws provides for access to government records held by the judicial or legislative branches, or even by some parts of the executive branch.

In this chapter we examine other avenues for obtaining government information relating to national security. Here Congress moves to the sidelines, as we consider a right of public access grounded in the common law, then address a First Amendment-based "right to know." We also take up the state secrets privilege — the ability of government in civil litigation to avoid discovery or resist the introduction into evidence of information that could be helpful to the nation's enemies. These rights of access, and the correlative government ability to prevent disclosure, are narrower in some respects and broader in others than the ones provided by statute, and the procedures are mostly different. But in the end we are left with the same basic questions about security and accountability in a democracy.

A. COMMON LAW RIGHT TO KNOW

Schwartz v. United States Department of Justice
United States District Court, District of Columbia, 1977
435 F. Supp. 1203, *aff'd,* 595 F.2d 888 (D.C. Cir. 1979)

PRATT, J. This is an action in which plaintiff seeks certain records from the Department of Justice and Peter A. Rodino, Jr., Chairman of the Committee on the Judiciary of the United States House of Representatives, on the investigation of one Peter R. Schlam. The Department of Justice is sued under the Freedom of

A. Common Law Right to Know

Information Act. Mr. Rodino is sued under the common law right of access to public records. The matter is now before the Court on Mr. Rodino's motion to dismiss. Mr. Rodino claims that Congress is not subject to the common law rule which gives citizens a right of access to public records.

The historic common law right to inspect and copy public records is recognized in this jurisdiction. United States v. Mitchell, 551 F.2d 1252, 1257 (1976). The general rule is that all three branches of government, legislative, executive, and judicial, are subject to the common law right. Courier-Journal & Louisville Times Co. v. Curtis, 335 S.W.2d 934, 936 (Ky. 1959), cert. denied, 364 U.S. 910 (1960).

Defendant Rodino has set forth no persuasive reason why Congress should be exempted from the common law rule. It is true that Congress has exempted itself from the requirements of the Freedom of Information Act, 5 U.S.C. §552, by 5 U.S.C. §551(1)(A). That Act, however, is not coextensive with the common law rule under discussion. It applies to *all* matters in Government files; the common law rule applies only to "public records." Moreover, we can find no inconsistency or conflict between the Freedom of Information Act and the common law rule. Even if there were an inconsistency or conflict, the Act would have to be construed narrowly, favoring application of the common law, because the Freedom of Information Act is in derogation of the common law.

Accordingly, we hold that Congress is subject to the common law rule which guarantees the public a right to inspect and copy public records. Absent a showing that the matters sought by plaintiff are not "public records" within the meaning of the common law rule or that plaintiff does not possess any "interest" required by the rule, we cannot grant defendant Rodino's motion for dismissal.

If Congress wishes to exempt itself from the common law rule or to impose standards for its application, it has the means to do so readily at its disposal. It has, however, not done so and therefore remains subject to the common law rule.

An order will issue accordingly.

NOTES AND QUESTIONS

1. *FOIA and Common Law Right Compared.* FOIA provides public access to records of "agencies" as that word is defined in 5 U.S.C. §552(f) (2000). The common law right gives access to information in government hands that is broader in one sense but narrower in another. Can you say how?

In Center for National Security Studies v. United States Dept. of Justice, 331 F.3d 918 (D.C. Cir. 2003), plaintiffs asserted a common law right to information about more than 700 post-September 11 detainees held inside the United States. (The detentions are addressed *supra* p. 665.) The government argued that the common law right is limited to judicial records and that, even if that right might otherwise apply to executive records, FOIA has displaced it. The court rejected the government's first argument but accepted the second one:

> FOIA provides an extensive statutory regime for plaintiffs to request the information they seek. Not only is it uncontested that the requested information meets the

general category of information for which FOIA mandates disclosure, but for the reasons set forth above, we have concluded that it falls within an express statutory exemption as well. It would make no sense for Congress to have enacted the balanced scheme of disclosure and exemption, and for the court to carefully apply that statutory scheme, and then to turn and determine that the statute had no effect on a preexisting common law right of access. Congress has provided a carefully calibrated statutory scheme, balancing the benefits and harms of disclosure. That scheme preempts any preexisting common law right.... [331 F.3d at 936-937.]

Can you reconcile the court's conclusion with the statement in *Schwartz* that "we can find no inconsistency or conflict between the Freedom of Information Act and the common law rule"? Do you think Congress intended for FOIA to provide the exclusive means for access to executive branch records?

2. *"Public Record."* Do you know what a "public record" is? One court calls it "a government document created and kept for the purpose of memorializing or recording an official action, decision, statement, or other matter of legal significance, broadly conceived." Washington Legal Found. v. United States Sentencing Commn., 89 F.3d 897, 905 (D.C. Cir. 1996). The common law right has been invoked a number of times in federal courts to gain access to evidence in criminal cases. *See, e.g.,* United States v. Amodeo, 71 F.3d 1044 (2d Cir. 1995). Also subject to the common law right are records in civil cases, *see, e.g.,* Hagestad v. Tragesser, 49 F.3d 1430 (9th Cir. 1995), and nonjudicial records, *see, e.g., Washington Legal Found., supra.* As to whether a report of a congressional investigation is a "public record," compare *Schwartz* with Pentagen Technologies v. Committee on Appropriations, 20 F. Supp. 2d 41 (D.D.C. 1998).

Do you think the "public record" requirement will present an obstacle to disclosure of records addressing national security issues? In United States v. George, 786 F. Supp. 11 (D.D.C. 1991), the court recognized the common law right in granting a former CIA Deputy Director of Operations access to classified court records for use in his trial on charges growing out of the Iran-Contra Affair, when he held an appropriate security clearance.

3. *Presumption Favoring Public Access.* Nixon v. Warner Communications, 435 U.S. 589 (1978), involved a broadcaster's assertion of the common law right to obtain from a federal district court copies of Oval Office tape recordings used earlier in the Watergate criminal trials. The Supreme Court found that the plaintiff did not need to demonstrate a proprietary interest in the tapes: "The interest necessary to support the issuance of a writ compelling access has been found, for example, in the citizen's desire to keep a watchful eye on the workings of public agencies, and in a newspaper publisher's intention to publish information concerning the operation of government." *Id.* at 597-598. On the other hand, said the Court, while there is a presumption in favor of public access to judicial records, the right of access is not absolute. A court has discretion to balance that right against proprietary, privacy, and privilege interests of parties resisting release. The Supreme Court decided that the balance was tipped against release because, in its view, Congress intended that the Presidential Recordings and Materials Preservation Act, Pub. L. No. 93-526, 88 Stat. 1695

(1974), set out in a note following 44 U.S.C. §2111 (2000), provides the exclusive means for access to materials of the Nixon presidency. See *supra* p. 1015. Lower courts are divided on the strength of the presumption. *Compare* United States v. Myers, 635 F.2d 945, 952 (2d Cir. 1980) ("only the most compelling circumstances should prevent... public access"), *with* United States v. McDougal, 103 F.3d 651 (8th Cir. 1996) (rejecting the strong presumption standard).

When the common law right of access to public records is invoked, should a court weigh national security implications in balancing the competing interests? If so, what standards should it apply in deciding? Concerning the release of records of FBI investigations into terrorist acts, *compare* In re Four Search Warrants, 945 F. Supp. 1563 (N.D. Ga. 1996) (balancing governmental and public interests and ordering partial release of search warrant affidavits in connection with Atlanta Olympic Park bombing), *with* United States v. McVeigh, 119 F.3d 806 (10th Cir. 1997) (sealing FBI reports and other materials related to bombing of Oklahoma City Murrah Federal Building).

B. CONSTITUTIONAL RIGHT TO KNOW

The First Amendment to the U.S. Constitution provides, "Congress shall make no law... abridging the freedom of speech, or of the press...." While neither a public nor a press right of access to government information is apparent in this language, Professor Emerson argued that

> [t]he public, as sovereign, must have all information available in order to instruct its servants, the government. As a general proposition, if democracy is to work, there can be no holding back of information; otherwise, ultimate decisionmaking by the people, to whom that function is committed, becomes impossible. Whether or not such a guarantee of the right to know is the sole purpose of the first amendment, it is surely a main element of that provision and should be recognized as such. [Thomas I. Emerson, *Legal Foundations of the Right to Know*, 1976 Wash. U. L.Q. 1, 14.]

Yet the Supreme Court declared in a 1978 jail access case that "[n]either the First Amendment nor the Fourteenth Amendment mandates a right of access to government information or sources of information within the government's control." Houchins v. KQED, Inc., 438 U.S. 1, 15 (1978). Concerning the media, the Court remarked earlier that "the First Amendment does not guarantee the press a constitutional right of special access to information not available to the public generally." Branzburg v. Hayes, 408 U.S. 665, 684 (1972).

In 1980, however, the Court recognized a press right to attend criminal trials. Richmond Newspapers v. Virginia, 448 U.S. 555 (1980). Then, in a similar case two years later, the Court observed that "the First Amendment serves to ensure that the individual citizen can effectively participate in and contribute to our republican system of self-government." Globe Newspapers v. Superior Court, 457 U.S. 596, 604 (1982). More recently, in a case involving records of a criminal proceeding, the Supreme Court explained that public access to "governmental processes" will be granted: (1) when "there is a tradition of accessibility"—that is, when "the place and process have historically been open to the press and general public," (2) when "public access plays a significant positive role in the functioning of the particular process," and (3) when there is no showing that "closure is essential to preserve higher values and is narrowly tailored to serve that interest." Press-Enterprise Co. v. Superior Court, 478 U.S. 1, 8, 9 (1986). *See* Eugene Cerruti, *"Dancing in the Courthouse": The First Amendment Right of Access Opens a New Round,* 29 U. Rich. L. Rev. 237 (1995). *See also* Timothy B. Dyk, *Newsgathering, Press Access, and the First Amendment,* 44 Stan. L. Rev. 927 (1992) (arguing that the press should enjoy greater access to government information than the public).

Despite the broad language in *Press-Enterprise,* there is considerable uncertainty about the scope of the First Amendment right of access, and the Supreme Court has not addressed the issue again. *Compare* WPIX, Inc. v. League of Women Voters, 595 F. Supp. 1484, 1489 (S.D.N.Y. 1984) ("Under the first amendment, press organizations have a limited right of access to newsworthy events"), *with* Foto USA, Inc. v. Board of Regents, 141 F.3d 1032, 1035 (11th Cir. 1998) ("There is no First Amendment right of access to public information."). Some courts have expressed doubt about the existence of a broader right of access but applied the *Press-Enterprise* criteria anyway. *See, e.g.,* Capital Cities Media v. Chester, 797 F.2d 1164 (3d Cir. 1986) (finding no tradition of public access to agency records).

Against this background, courts have recently addressed the scope and applicability of a First Amendment right of access in several cases implicating national security. We consider two of them here—one dealing with media access to the battlefield in wartime, the other with a right of access to immigration hearings.

Nation Magazine v. United States Department of Defense
United States District Court, Southern District of New York, 1991
762 F. Supp. 1558

SAND, District Judge. This is an action by various members of the press challenging regulations promulgated by the United States Department of Defense ("DOD") to govern coverage of military activities of American armed forces overseas during periods of open hostilities. These regulations, adopted after the Vietnam War, were in effect in some form during the Grenada and Panama military operations. In revised form, they were in effect during American military operations Desert Shield (American military presence in the Persian Gulf) and Desert Storm (open hostilities). They were lifted on March 4, 1991, upon the informal cessation of hostilities in the Persian Gulf.

... [P]laintiffs' fundamental claim is that the press has a First Amendment right to unlimited access to a foreign arena in which American military forces are engaged. Plaintiffs urge that the DOD "pooling" regulations, which limit access to the battlefield to a specified number of press representatives and subject them to certain restrictions, infringe on news gathering privileges accorded by the First Amendment. The primary focus of plaintiffs' challenge is on the question

B. Constitutional Right to Know

of access and not primarily on those restrictions which limit, for national security reasons, the information that pool members may publish....

The gravamen of plaintiffs' complaint is that, under the First Amendment, the press has a right to gather and report news that involves United States military operations and that DOD's pool regulations are an unconstitutional limitation on access to observe events as they occur. Plaintiffs suggest that this action does not seek to establish a new right or open new constitutional frontiers since no access is sought that involves military plans, secrets, operational information or strategic sessions. In other words, plaintiffs claim that no affirmative assistance from the government is being requested, only the freedom from interference to report on what is overtly happening in an allegedly open area. Contrary to what plaintiffs suggest, this Court finds the question to be one of first impression, the answer to which would require charting new constitutional territory.

The Supreme Court has on a number of occasions considered the relationship between the First Amendment and national security. See Near [v. Minnesota, 283 U.S. 697 (1931),] at 716; New York Times Co. [v. United States, 403 U.S. 713 (1971),] at 722-723; Snepp v. United States, 444 U.S. 507, 514-515 (1980). None of these cases, however, has addressed directly the role and limits of news gathering under the First Amendment in a military context abroad. Nonetheless, there is no dearth of case law on questions involving the access rights of the press and public in other circumstances. As in most cases involving novel issues, the Court must reason by analogy. It is certain that there is no right of access of the press to fora which have traditionally been characterized as private or closed to the public, such as meetings involving the internal discussions of government officials. See United States v. Nixon, 418 U.S. 683, 705 n.15 (1974). Limitations may also be placed on access to government controlled institutions, such as prisons and military bases. See Houchins v. KQED, Inc., 438 U.S. 1, 16 (1978); Greer [v. Spock, 424 U.S. 828 (1976),] at 838; Saxbe v. Washington Post Company, 417 U.S. 843, 850 (1974); Pell v. Procunier, 417 U.S. 817, 828 (1974).

On the other hand, there is an almost absolute right of access to open places, including such fora as streets and parks. See Hague v. C.I.O., 307 U.S. 496, 515 (1939). In recent times the Supreme Court has been particularly generous in interpreting the scope of the public's right under the First Amendment to know about government functioning, at least in such fora as a criminal trial. See Richmond Newspapers, Inc. [v. Virginia, 448 U.S. 555 (1980),] at 564. In these cases, there appears to be some indication that the basis for such a right of access could apply more broadly. See Globe Newspaper Co. v. Superior Court for County of Norfolk, 457 U.S. 596, 606 (1982).

A fundamental theme in *Richmond* and *Globe* was the importance of an informed American citizenry. As the Court wrote, guaranteed access of the public to occurrences in a courtroom during a criminal trial assures "freedom of communication on matters relating to the functioning of government." *Richmond Newspapers*, 448 U.S. at 575. Learning about, criticizing and evaluating government, the Supreme Court has reasoned, requires some "right to receive" information and ideas. Martin v. City of Struthers, 319 U.S. 141, 143 (1943). In *Globe*, the Court devoted extensive attention to the importance of this "checking function" against abuse of government power. See Blasi, "The Checking Value in First Amendment Theory," 1977 Am. B. Found. Research J. 521, 593. This theme has been echoed by the Supreme Court even when the government has suggested that national security concerns were implicated. See *New York Times Co.*, 403 U.S. at 728 (Stewart, J. concurring) ("... [w]ithout an informed and free press, there can not be an enlightened people.")

Given the broad grounds invoked in these holdings, the affirmative right to gather news, ideas and information is certainly strengthened by these cases. By protecting the press, the flow of information to the public is preserved. As the Supreme Court has observed, "the First Amendment goes beyond protection of the press and the self-expression of individuals to prohibit government from limiting the stock of information from which members of the public may draw." First National Bank v. Bellotti, 435 U.S. 765, 783 (1978). Viewing these cases collectively, it is arguable that generally there is at least some minimal constitutional right to access. See Branzburg v. Hayes, 408 U.S. 665, 681 (1972) ("without some protection for seeking out the news, freedom of the press could be eviscerated.")

If the reasoning of these recent access cases were followed in a military context, there is support for the proposition that the press has at least some minimal right of access to view and report about major events that affect the functioning of government, including, for example, an overt combat operation. As such, the government could not wholly exclude the press from a land area where a war is occurring that involves this country. But this conclusion is far from certain since military operations are not closely akin to a building such as a prison, nor to a park or a courtroom.

In order to decide this case on the merits, it would be necessary to define the outer constitutional boundaries of access. Pursuant to long-settled policy in the disposition of constitutional questions, courts should refrain from deciding issues presented in a highly abstract form, especially in instances where the Supreme Court has not articulated guiding standards. See *Rescue Army* [v. Municipal Court of City of Los Angeles, 331 U.S. 549, 575-585 (1947)]. Since the principles at stake are important and require a delicate balancing, prudence dictates that we leave the definition of the exact parameters of press access to military operations abroad for a later date when a full record is available, in the unfortunate event that there is another military operation. Accordingly, the Court declines to exercise its power to grant plaintiffs' request for declaratory relief on their right of access claim....

NOTES AND QUESTIONS

1. *Tradition of Battlefield Access.* For more than two centuries—from the American Revolution until the invasion of Grenada in 1983—the press enjoyed virtually unrestricted access to America's battlefields, with no apparent breaches of security. *See* Michael D. Steger, *Slicing the Gordian Knot: A Proposal to Reform Military Regulation of Media Coverage of Combat Operations*, 28 U.S.F. L. Rev. 957, 960-967 (1994); C. Robert Zelnick, *Military Secrets and First Amendment Values*, 1 J. Natl. Security L. 21, 23-26 (1997). The Defense Department noted, however, that the Persian Gulf conflict was "the first major American war to be covered by news media able to broadcast reports instantaneously to the world, including the

B. Constitutional Right to Know

enemy." Department of Defense, *Conduct of the Persian Gulf War: Final Report to Congress* (PB92-163674) (Apr. 1992), at S-2. It worried that "reporters might not realize the sensitivity of certain information and might inadvertently divulge details of military plans, capabilities, operations, or vulnerabilities that would jeopardize the outcome of an operation or the safety of U.S. or other Coalition forces." *Id.* at S-4. Has the advent of satellite uplink TV broadcasts and instant Internet news altered the "tradition of accessibility" that marked press access to battlefields until 1983? Can DOD's concerns be addressed while preserving this tradition?

In JB Pictures, Inc. v. Department of Defense, 86 F.3d 236 (D.C. Cir. 1996), media demanded access to a hangar at Dover Air Force Base where the bodies of service personnel killed in the Persian Gulf War were held. The court rejected the claim of a First Amendment-based right on grounds that members of the public generally are not provided access to the hangar.

2. *A "Significant Role" in the Process?* Does public (or press) access to the battlefield play a "significant role in the functioning of the particular process"? According to one view, the First Amendment protects

> a social interest in the attainment of truth, so that the country may not only adopt the wisest course but carry it out in the wisest way. This social interest is especially important in war time.... Truth can be sifted out from falsehood only if the government is vigorously and constantly cross-examined, so that the fundamental issues of the struggle may be clearly defined, and the war may not be diverted to improper ends, or conducted with an undue sacrifice of life and liberty, or prolonged after its just purposes are accomplished. [Zechariah Chafee Jr., *Free Speech in the United States* 33 (1941).]

Aside from its management of the press pool during the Persian Gulf War, the Pentagon conducted its own carefully orchestrated public relations campaign, with daily press briefings and film footage of precision bombing raids. *See, e.g.*, Marianne D. Short & Jodene Pope, *History and Scope of the Press' Right of Access to Foreign Battlefields*, 41 Naval L. Rev. 1, 8 (1993). Do you think it is important for the public (and Congress) to be able to receive current information about military operations from nongovernment sources?

3. *Narrow Tailoring of Press Restrictions?* Members of the press covering the Persian Gulf War complained bitterly about the Pentagon press pool rules. Pool members had to be accompanied at all times by military escorts, whom they viewed as attempting to control rather than facilitate news coverage. Escorts reportedly interrupted interviews, intimidated military personnel who might have spoken to reporters, and physically prevented reporters' access to certain areas. The total number of media representatives in the war zone was severely restricted, and major media were favored over foreign and freelance journalists. In addition, there were many reports of news stories dispatched from the front but delayed—sometimes for days—at the military press center in Dhahran. These complaints are summarized in John R. MacArthur, *Second Front: Censorship and Propaganda in the Gulf War* (1992); Kevin P. Kenealey, Comment, *The Persian Gulf War and the Press: Is There a Constitutional Right of Access to Military Operations?*,

87 Nw. U. L. Rev. 287, 289-293 (1992). Are you persuaded that press pool restrictions were "essential to preserve higher values and ... narrowly tailored to serve that interest"?

4. *Media Access in Other Wars.* Media coverage of U.S. military operations in Afghanistan following the September 11, 2001, terrorist attacks was said to be even more restricted than in the Persian Gulf War. *See* Carol Morello, *Tight Control Marks Coverage of Afghan War,* Wash. Post, Dec. 7, 2001. Defense Secretary Rumsfeld said he was "committed to the principle that the media should have access to both the good and the bad in this effort." *Id.* But reporters in a small group allowed into Afghanistan were

> not permitted to accompany troops..., were prohibited from reporting much of what they saw, were diverted toward feature stories such as church services and promotion ceremonies, were not allowed to speak to [most] senior commanders, and were barred from reporting details even after they were leaked — and announced — by the Pentagon. [*Id.*]

In late 2001, the publisher of *Hustler* magazine filed suit on First Amendment grounds when one of his journalists was denied, at least temporarily, the right not only to travel with U.S. troops in Afghanistan, but also "to be accommodated and otherwise facilitated by the military in their reporting efforts during combat, subject only to reasonable security and safety restrictions." Flynt v. Rumsfeld, 355 F.3d 697, 703 (D.C. Cir. 2004). Observing that neither the Supreme Court nor the D.C. Circuit had ever applied the *Richmond Newspapers* test of press access outside the context of criminal judicial proceedings, the court refused to do so in this case. *Id.* at 704. It also found no history of media access like that claimed, and it ruled that restrictions imposed by the military in Afghanistan were reasonable. *Id.* 704-705.

The Pentagon dramatically revised its rules for press access to the battlefield during the 2003 invasion of Iraq. It "embedded" some 775 print and broadcast journalists into a number of military units, although only about 50 or 60 had "front row seats" for combat. Embed "slots" were allocated to media organizations, 80 percent of them domestic, rather than to individual journalists. *See Public Affairs Guidance on Embedding Media,* Feb. 10, 2003 (*Guidelines*), at http://www.defenselink.mil/news/Feb2003/d20030228pag.pdf. Live television coverage from the battlefield was extensive, yet apparently none of the reporting revealed any sensitive information or endangered any personnel.

In return for this extensive access, reporters were obliged to follow broad guidelines about what could be covered (e.g., "military targets and objectives previously under attack") and what could not (e.g., "information regarding future operations"). *Guidelines* ¶ 4. Unit commanders could "impose temporary restrictions on electronic transmissions for operational security reasons," and reporters had to "seek approval to use electronic devices in a combat/hostile environment." *Id.* ¶ 2.C.4. Disputes about coverage of particular events were left to be worked out between reporters and unit commanders. *Id.* ¶ 6. Commanders were to "ensure that media are provided with every opportunity to observe actual combat operations," but reporters could be given "escorts." *Id.* ¶¶ 3.F., 3.G. There was no general review process for media products, as there was during the 1991 Persian Gulf War, but embargoes could be imposed "to protect operational security." *Id.* ¶¶3.R., 4.E. If you believe that there is a First Amendment-based right of battlefield access, do these restrictions (in the form of conditions for access) impermissibly infringe that right?

A large number of "unilateral" journalists operated without the limitations of embedding but also without its physical protections or preferred access to information. They were free to move about independently of the troops, as well as to interview Iraqis and report on the Iraqi view of the war. They were, however, reportedly a "nightmare" for the military, which worried that they might be captured or killed by enemy forces or perhaps come under "friendly" fire.

A detailed description and critique of media coverage of the 2003 Iraq War may be found in Alicia C. Shepard, *Narrowing the Gap: Military, Media, and the Iraq War* (McCormick Tribune Found. 2004).

North Jersey Media Group, Inc. v. Ashcroft
United States Court of Appeals, Third Circuit, 2002
308 F.3d 198, *cert. denied,* 538 U.S. 1056 (2003)

BECKER, Chief Judge. This civil action was brought in the District Court for the District of New Jersey by a consortium of media groups seeking access to "special interest" deportation hearings involving persons whom the Attorney General has determined might have connections to or knowledge of the September 11, 2001 terrorist attacks. This category was created by a directive issued by Michael Creppy, the Chief United States Immigration Judge, outlining additional security measures to be applied in this class of cases, including closing hearings to the public and the press. Named as defendants in the suit were Attorney General John Ashcroft and Chief Judge Creppy....

As we will now explain in detail, we find that the application of the *Richmond Newspapers* [Richmond Newspapers, Inc. v. Virginia, 448 U.S. 555 (1980)] experience and logic tests does not compel us to declare the Creppy Directive unconstitutional....

III. UNDER *RICHMOND NEWSPAPERS*, IS THERE A FIRST AMENDMENT RIGHT TO ATTEND DEPORTATION HEARINGS?...

A. THE "EXPERIENCE" TEST

1. Is there an historical right of access to government proceedings generally?

In *Richmond Newspapers,* 448 U.S. at 575, the Supreme Court acknowledged the State's argument that the Constitution nowhere explicitly guarantees the public's right to attend criminal trials, but it found that right implicit because the Framers drafted the Constitution against a backdrop of longstanding popular access to criminal trials.... Likewise, in *Publicker* [Industries, Inc. v. Cohen, 733 F.2d 1059 (3d Cir. 1984),] at 1059, we found a First Amendment right of access to civil trials because at common law, such access had been "beyond dispute."

The history of access to political branch proceedings is quite different. The Government correctly notes that the Framers themselves rejected any unqualified right of access to the political branches for, as we explained in *Capital Cities Media* [Inc. v. Chester, 797 F.2d 1164 (3d Cir. 1986)], at 1168-1171, the evidence on this point is extensive and compelling....

This tradition of closing sensitive proceedings extends to many hearings before administrative agencies. For example, although hearings on Social Security disability claims profoundly affect hundreds of thousands of people annually, and have great impact on expenditure of government funds, they are open only to "the parties and to other persons the administrative law judge considers necessary and proper." 20 C.F.R. §404.944. Likewise, administrative disbarment hearings are often presumptively closed....

Faced with this litany of administrative hearings that are closed to the public, the Newspapers...submit that, despite frequent closures throughout the administrative realm, deportation proceedings in particular boast a history of openness sufficient to meet the *Richmond Newspapers* requirement....

2. Is the history of open deportation proceedings sufficient to satisfy the *Richmond Newspapers* "experience" prong?

For a First Amendment right of access to vest under *Richmond Newspapers*, we must consider whether "the place and process have historically been open to the press and general public," because such a "tradition of accessibility implies the favorable judgment of experience." *Press-Enterprise II*, 478 U.S. at 8. Noting preliminarily that the question whether a proceeding has been "historically open" is only arguably an objective inquiry, we nonetheless find that based on both Supreme Court and Third Circuit precedents, the tradition of open deportation hearings is too recent and inconsistent to support a First Amendment right of access.

The strongest historical evidence of open deportation proceedings is that since the 1890s, when Congress first codified deportation procedures, "[t]he governing statutes have always expressly closed *exclusion* hearings, but have *never* closed deportation hearings." (Newspapers' Br. at 30-31.) In 1893, the Executive promulgated the first set of immigration regulations, which expressly stated that exclusion proceedings shall be conducted "separate from the public." *See* Treasury Dept., *Immigration Laws and Regulations* 4 (Washington D.C., Gov't Printing Office 1893). Congress codified those regulations in 1903 and, since that time, it has repeatedly reenacted provisions closing exclusion hearings. In contrast, although Congress codified the regulations governing deportation proceedings in 1904 and has reenacted them many times since, it has never authorized the general closure that has long existed in the exclusion context....

...[T]here is also evidence that, in practice, deportation hearings have frequently been closed to the general public. From the early 1900s, the government has often conducted deportation hearings in prisons, hospitals, or private homes, places where there is no general right of public access. Even in recent times, the government has continued to hold thousands of deportation hearings each year in federal and state prisons. Moreover, hearings involving abused alien children are closed by regulation no matter where they are held,

B. Constitutional Right to Know

and those involving abused alien spouses are closed presumptively. *See* 8 C.F.R. §3.27(c).

We ultimately do not believe that deportation hearings boast a tradition of openness sufficient to satisfy *Richmond Newspapers*....

IV. DOES THE *RICHMOND NEWSPAPERS* "LOGIC" PRONG, PROPERLY APPLIED, SUPPORT A RIGHT OF ACCESS?

Even if we could find a right of access under the *Richmond Newspapers* logic prong, absent a strong showing of openness under the experience prong, a proposition we do not embrace, we would find no such right here. The logic test compels us to consider "whether public access plays a significant positive role in the functioning of the particular process in question." *Press-Enterprise II*, 478 U.S. at 8....

... Under the reported cases, whenever a court has found that openness serves community values, it has concluded that openness plays a "significant positive role" in that proceeding. But that cannot be the story's end, for to gauge accurately whether a role is positive, the calculus must perforce take account of the flip side—the extent to which openness impairs the public good. We note in this respect that, were the logic prong only to determine whether openness serves some good, it is difficult to conceive of a government proceeding to which the public would not have a First Amendment right of access. For example, public access to *any* government affair, even internal CIA deliberations, would "promote informed discussion" among the citizenry. It is unlikely the Supreme Court intended this result.

In this case the Government presented substantial evidence that open deportation hearings would threaten national security....

The Government's security evidence is contained in the declaration of Dale Watson, the FBI's Executive Assistant Director for Counterterrorism and Counterintelligence. Watson presents a range of potential dangers, the most pressing of which we [d]escribe here.

First, public hearings would necessarily reveal sources and methods of investigation. That is information which, "when assimilated with other information the United States may or may not have in hand, allows a terrorist organization to build a picture of the investigation." (Watson Dec. at 4.) Even minor pieces of evidence that might appear innocuous to us would provide valuable clues to a person within the terrorist network, clues that may allow them to thwart the government's efforts to investigate and prevent future acts of violence. *Id.*

Second, "information about how any given individual entered the country (from where, when, and how) may not divulge significant information that would reveal sources and methods of investigation. However, putting entry information into the public realm regarding all 'special interest cases' would allow the terrorist organization to see patterns of entry, what works and what doesn't." *Id.* That information would allow it to tailor future entries to exploit weaknesses in the United States immigration system.

Third, "[i]nformation about what evidence the United States has against members of a particular cell collectively will inform the terrorist organization as to what cells to use and which not to use for further plots and attacks." *Id.* A related concern is that open hearings would reveal what evidence the government lacks. For example, the United States may disclose in a public hearing certain evidence it possesses about a member of a terrorist organization. If that detainee is actually involved in planning an attack, opening the hearing might allow the organization to know that the United States is not yet aware of the attack based on the evidence it presents at the open hearing. *Id.*

Fourth, if a terrorist organization discovers that a particular member is detained, or that information about a plot is known, it may accelerate the timing of a planned attack, thus reducing the amount of time the government has to detect and prevent it. If acceleration is impossible, it may still be able to shift the planned activity to a yet-undiscovered cell. *Id.* at 7.

Fifth, a public hearing involving evidence about terrorist links could allow terrorist organizations to interfere with the pending proceedings by creating false or misleading evidence. Even more likely, a terrorist might destroy existing evidence or make it more difficult to obtain, such as by threatening or tampering with potential witnesses. Should potential informants not feel secure in coming forward, that would greatly impair the ongoing investigation. *Id.* . . .

Finally, Watson represents that "the government cannot proceed to close hearings on a case-by-case basis, as the identification of certain cases for closure, and the introduction of evidence to support that closure, could itself expose critical information about which activities and patterns of behavior merit such closure." (Watson Dec. at 8-9.) Moreover, he explains, given judges' relative lack of expertise regarding national security and their inability to see the mosaic, we should not entrust to them the decision whether an isolated fact is sensitive enough to warrant closure.

The Newspapers are undoubtedly correct that the representations of the Watson Declaration are to some degree speculative, at least insofar as there is no concrete evidence that closed deportation hearings have prevented, or will prevent, terrorist attacks. But the *Richmond Newspapers* logic prong is unavoidably speculative, for it is impossible to weigh objectively, for example, the community benefit of emotional catharsis against the security risk of disclosing the United States' methods of investigation and the extent of its knowledge. We are quite hesitant to conduct a judicial inquiry into the credibility of these security concerns, as national security is an area where courts have traditionally extended great deference to Executive expertise. *See, e.g., Zadvydas v. Davis,* 533 U.S. 678, 696 (2001) (noting that "terrorism or other special circumstances" might warrant "heightened deference to the judgments of the political branches with respect to matters of national security"). *See also Dep't of the Navy v. Egan,* 484 U.S. 518, 530 (1988) (noting that "courts traditionally have been reluctant to intrude upon the authority of the Executive in military and national security affairs"). The assessments before us have been made by senior government officials responsible for investigating the events of September 11th and for preventing future attacks. These officials believe that closure of special interest hearings is necessary to advance these goals, and their concerns, as expressed in the Watson Declaration, have gone unrebutted. To the extent that the Attorney General's national security concerns seem credible, we will not lightly second-guess them.

We are keenly aware of the dangers presented by deference to the executive branch when constitutional liberties are at stake, especially in times of national crisis, when those liberties are likely in greatest jeopardy. On balance, however, we are unable to conclude that openness plays a positive role in special interest deportation hearings at a time when our nation is faced with threats of such profound and unknown dimension.

V. CONCLUSION...

Because we find that open deportation hearings do not pass the two-part *Richmond Newspapers* test, we hold that the press and public possess no First Amendment right of access....

[The opinion of SCIRICA, Circuit Judge, dissenting, is omitted.]

NOTES AND QUESTIONS

1. *Closing the Door on Democracy?* In a Sixth Circuit case on identical facts that was decided at almost the same moment, the court reached a dramatically different result. Detroit Free Press v. Ashcroft, 303 F.3d 681 (6th Cir. 2002). Concerning the "experience" prong of the *Richmond Newspapers* test, the court found that deportation hearings have historically been open. Moreover, said the court,

> to paraphrase the Supreme Court, deportation hearings "walk, talk, and squawk" very much like a judicial proceeding. Substantively, we look to other proceedings that have the same effect as deportation. Here, the only other federal court that can enter an order of removal is a United States District Court during sentencing in a criminal trial. *See* 8 U.S.C.A. §1228(c) (2002). At common law, beginning with the Transportation Act of 1718, the English criminal courts could enter an order of transportation or banishment as a sentence in a criminal trial. As *Richmond Newspapers* discussed in great length, these types of criminal proceedings have historically been open. *Richmond Newspapers*, 448 U.S. at 564-74. [303 F.3d at 702.]

As for the "logic" prong, the Sixth Circuit panel declared that public access "undoubtedly enhances the quality of deportation proceedings." *Id.* at 703.

> First, public access acts as a check on the actions of the Executive by assuring us that proceedings are conducted fairly and properly. In an area such as immigration, where the government has nearly unlimited authority, the press and the public serve as perhaps the only check on abusive government practices.
> Second, openness ensures that government does its job properly; that it does not make mistakes....
> Third, after the devastation of September 11 and the massive investigation that followed, the cathartic effect of open deportations cannot be overstated. They serve a "therapeutic" purpose as outlets for "community concern, hostility, and emotions."...

Fourth, openness enhances the perception of integrity and fairness. "The value of openness lies in the fact that people not actually attending trials can have confidence that standards of fairness are being observed...."...

Fifth, public access helps ensure that "the individual citizen can effectively participate in and contribute to our republican system of self-government." *Globe Newspaper,* 457 U.S. at 604. "[A] major purpose of [the First Amendment] was to protect the free discussion of governmental affairs." *Id.* Public access to deportation proceedings helps inform the public of the affairs of the government. Direct knowledge of how their government is operating enhances the public's ability to affirm or protest government's efforts. When government selectively chooses what information it allows the public to see, it can become a powerful tool for deception.... [303 F.3d at 703-705.]

Finding a First Amendment right of access, the Sixth Circuit panel then decided that "the Creppy directive is neither narrowly tailored, nor does it require particularized findings [in individual cases]. Therefore, it impermissibly infringes on the Newspaper Plaintiffs' First Amendment right of access." *Id.* at 705. The court punctuated its ruling with this widely quoted passage:

> In our democracy, based on checks and balances, neither the Bill of Rights nor the judiciary can second-guess government's choices. The only safeguard on this extraordinary governmental power is the public, deputizing the press as the guardians of their liberty. "An informed public is the most potent of all restraints upon misgovernment[.]" Grosjean v. Am. Press Co., 297 U.S. 233, 250 (1936). "[They] alone can here protect the values of democratic government." New York Times v. United States, 403 U.S. 713, 728 (1971) (per curiam) (Stewart, J., concurring).
>
> Today, the Executive Branch seeks to take this safeguard away from the public by placing its actions beyond public scrutiny. Against non-citizens, it seeks the power to secretly deport a class if it unilaterally calls them "special interest" cases. The Executive Branch seeks to uproot people's lives, outside the public eye, and behind a closed door. Democracies die behind closed doors. The First Amendment, through a free press, protects the people's right to know that their government acts fairly, lawfully, and accurately in deportation proceedings. When government begins closing doors, it selectively controls information rightfully belonging to the people. Selective information is misinformation. The Framers of the First Amendment "did not trust any government to separate the true from the false for us." Kleindienst v. Mandel, 408 U.S. 753, 773 (1972) (quoting Thomas v. Collins, 323 U.S. 516, 545 (Jackson, J., concurring)). They protected the people against secret government. [303 F.3d at 683.]

How would you compare the general attitudes of the Third and Sixth Circuit courts about their roles in cases implicating the national security? Should the *North Jersey Media* court have been more skeptical about government assertions of danger from opening deportation hearings? What about claims that some "special interest" cases involved aliens associated with Al Qaeda or with the September 11 hijackers? Should the court have demanded proof of these assertions?

In evaluating "whether public access plays a significant positive role in the functioning of the particular process in question," the two courts had very different ideas about the public interests involved. Which court do you think

B. Constitutional Right to Know

struck the better balance between the public's interest in openness and the risk to national security, and why?

Because of the importance of these two cases, as well as the sharp split between the circuits, many were surprised by the Supreme Court's decision to deny certiorari in the *North Jersey Media* case. What, if anything, do you think this portends for First Amendment-based access to government activities and information in the future?

2. *The Detainees Redux.* In a suit seeking information about more than 700 persons detained inside the United States in the wake of the September 11 attacks, see *supra* p. 665, the court considered and rejected First Amendment grounds for releasing the names of the detainees. Center for National Security Studies v. United States Dept. of Justice, 331 F.3d 918 (D.C. Cir. 2003).

> The narrow First Amendment right of access to information recognized in *Richmond Newspapers* does not extend to non-judicial documents that are not part of a criminal trial, such as the investigatory documents at issue here....
>
> We will not convert the First Amendment right of access to criminal judicial proceedings into a requirement that the government disclose information compiled during the exercise of a quintessential executive power—the investigation and prevention of terrorism.... To be sure, the Sixth Circuit recently held that the public has a constitutional right of access to INS deportation hearings involving the same INS detainees at issue in this case. *See Detroit Free Press; but see North Jersey Media Group* (finding no right of access). However, the Sixth Circuit applied *Richmond Newspapers* only after extensively examining the similarity between deportation proceedings and criminal trials, *Detroit Free Press*, 303 F.3d at 696-99, and noting the crucial distinction between "*investigatory* information" and "access to information relating to a governmental *adjudicative* process," *Id.* at 699. Inasmuch as plaintiffs here request investigatory—not adjudicative—information, we find *Detroit Free Press* distinguishable. We therefore will not expand the First Amendment right of public access to require disclosure of information compiled during the government's investigation of terrorist acts. [331 F.3d at 933-934.]

Does the First Amendment right of access turn on the distinction between "investigatory information" and "information relating to a governmental adjudicative process"? Assuming a history of public access, is exclusion of the public or the media from government functions other than criminal trials consistent with the observation of the Supreme Court in *Globe Newspapers* that "the First Amendment serves to ensure that the individual citizen can effectively participate in and contribute to our republican system of self-government"? 457 U.S. at 604.

3. *Media Access to Terrorism Trials.* During the criminal prosecution of Zacarias Moussaoui for his alleged involvement in the September 11 terrorist attacks, see *supra* p. 866, a consortium of media companies asserted common law and First Amendment rights of access to sealed records of pleadings, discovery materials, and oral arguments that included some information classified top secret. The court rejected the government's argument that the Classified Information Procedures Act (CIPA), 18 U.S.C. App. 3 §§1-16 (2000), analyzed in Chapter 29, could alone override a constitutional right of access. United States v. Moussaoui,

65 Fed. Appx. 881, 887-888 (4th Cir. 2003). Instead, the court determined that the "interest of the public in the flow of information is protected by our exercising independent judgment concerning redactions" of materials from the records. *Id.* at 888. As for access to appellate proceedings, the court ordered bifurcated hearings. Arguments not involving the discussion of classified information would be open to the public, while others would be conducted in a sealed courtroom, followed by the prompt release of a redacted transcript. *Id.* at 890. The litigation is analyzed in Cameron Stracher, *Eyes Tied Shut: Litigating for Access Under CIPA in the Government's "War on Terror,"* 48 N.Y.L. Sch. L. Rev. 173 (2003).

In civil litigation growing out of the terrorist attacks on the World Trade Center in 2001, a court refused to order service of process on several individuals alleged to be in U.S. custody. Federal Insurance Co. v. Al Qaida, No. 03-Civ.-6978, 2004 U.S. Dist. LEXIS 10944 (S.D.N.Y., May 28, 2004). Responding to government concerns that returns of the service in court records would publicly reveal the identity of the individuals served, the court declared that it "defers to the judgment of the executive branch with respect to issues of national security. . . ." *Id.* at *5.

4. *The Case That Didn't Exist.* In what may (or may not) be a common occurrence, a federal district court and court of appeals recently conducted secret hearings and issued secret rulings in a habeas corpus case that appeared on no public record. M.K.B. v. Warden, 540 U.S. 1213 (2004), concerned an Algerian waiter in south Florida who was detained by immigration authorities and questioned by the FBI. The case was discovered by a reporter only because of an appeals court clerk's docketing error. Despite arguments by news organizations that the First Amendment and a common law right of access required unsealing the records, the Supreme Court refused, without comment, to grant certiorari, following submission of a sealed brief by the Solicitor General. Thus, the government's theory of the case, like the fate of the detainee, is completely unknown, although we might assume that it included the arguments made earlier in *North Jersey Media*. The story is reported in Linda Greenhouse, *News Groups Seek to Open Secret Case,* N.Y. Times, Jan. 5, 2004, at A12; Dan Christensen, *Plea for Openness,* Miami Daily Bus. Rev., Nov. 5, 2003. Other cases totally or partially "off the record" are described in *"Sealed v. Sealed": How Courts Confront State Secrets,* Secrecy News, June 29, 2006; Julia Preston, *Judge Issues Secret Ruling in Case of 2 at Mosque,* N.Y. Times, Mar. 11, 2006, at A10.

5. *Common Law and First Amendment Rights Compared.* Could the First Amendment ever provide access to government information when the common law or open government statutes would not? *See* In re State-Record Co., Inc., 917 F.2d 124, 127 (4th Cir. 1990) ("the common law right does not provide as much access to the press and public as does the First Amendment"). One court observed that while "public interests underlying the First Amendment and the FOIA are closely aligned . . . the showing required to close judicial proceedings or records under the First Amendment is more substantial than the showing required to exempt information under the FOIA." Dayton Newspapers, Inc. v. United States Dept. of the Navy, 109 F. Supp. 2d 768, 772-773 (S.D. Ohio 1999). A different court has declared that the "determination of who should have access to particular government held information . . . is 'clearly a legislative task which the Constitution

has left to the political processes.'" Calder v. Internal Revenue Service, 890 F.2d 781, 784 (5th Cir. 1989) (quoting *Houchins, supra*, 438 U.S. at 12). *See also* Capital Cities Media v. Chester, 797 F.2d 1164, 1168-1173 (3d Cir. 1986). Do you agree that the determination of access is "clearly a legislative task"? How could such legislation be tested for its fidelity to the First Amendment?

C. PROTECTING "STATE SECRETS" IN CIVIL LITIGATION

The vindication of constitutional or other legal rights may depend on the ability of litigants to discover or to introduce into evidence information the government wishes, for national security reasons, to protect. The government may invoke one of its evidentiary privileges to withhold the information in a suit between private parties or in a civil suit involving the government as a party. Or a court may be persuaded that the very trial of a case would pose unacceptable risks that sensitive national security information would be exposed. See also Chapter 29, describing the use of classified information in criminal cases.

The following case, introduced in Chapter 16, illustrates the problem for private plaintiffs deprived of critical documentary evidence or testimony in a damages suit for infringement of their civil liberties.

Halkin v. Helms
United States Court of Appeals, District of Columbia Circuit, 1982
690 F.2d 977

[The first part of the opinion is set forth *supra* p. 433.]

A. THE STATE SECRETS PRIVILEGE

...Because the state secrets privilege, like other evidentiary privileges, operates to foreclose relief for violations of rights that may well have occurred by foreclosing the discovery of evidence that they did occur, it is a privilege "not to be lightly invoked." United States v. Reynolds, 345 U.S. 1, 7 (1953). Its invocation must be carefully considered to assure that the proper balance is struck between the interest of the public and the litigant in vindicating private rights and the public's interest in safeguarding of the national security. We turn to that consideration.

1. GENERAL PRINCIPLES

The starting point for any analysis of a claim of the state secrets privilege is United States v. Reynolds, 345 U.S. 1 (1953). That case establishes that secrets of state — matters the revelation of which reasonably could be seen as a threat to the military or diplomatic interests of the nation — are *absolutely privileged* from disclosure in the courts. Although the courts in evaluating claims of the privilege may take cognizance of the need for the information demonstrated by the party seeking disclosure, such need is a factor only in determining the extent of the court's inquiry into the appropriateness of the claim. Once the court is satisfied that the information poses a reasonable danger to secrets of state, "even the most compelling necessity cannot overcome the claim of privilege...." Id. at 11.

Therefore, the critical feature of the inquiry in evaluating the claim of privilege is not a balancing of ultimate interests at stake in the litigation. That balance has already been struck. Rather, the determination is whether the *showing* of the harm that might reasonably be seen to flow from disclosure is adequate in a given case to trigger the absolute right to withhold the information sought in that case....

Reynolds set forth three threshold requirements for claims of the state secrets privilege: that there be "a *formal* claim of privilege, lodged by the *head of the department* which has control over the matter, after *actual personal consideration* by that officer." 345 U.S. at 7-8 (emphasis added). It is undisputed that these requisites are met here. Beyond this, "the court must be satisfied from all the evidence and circumstances, and 'from the implications of the question, in the setting in which it is asked, that a responsive answer to or an explanation of why it cannot be answered might be dangerous because injurious disclosure might result.'" Id. at 9....

Appellants' attack on the showing made by the CIA to justify the privilege with respect to CHAOS information is three-fold. First, appellants argue that the Director's *public* affidavit was too vague to establish the privilege. Second, they contend that the court's reliance upon the Director's *in camera* affidavit improperly deprived them of an opportunity to litigate the privilege question. Third, with particular regard to the refusal to produce (and the redaction of) CHAOS documents, appellants argue that the government should have been compelled to supply a more detailed explanation of *each* withholding and redaction than the letter-and-number code provided. These contentions are considered in order.

1. The value of rules for determining the adequacy of the sort of affidavits involved here varies inversely with the breadth of such rules. As the court in *Reynolds* recognized, it is the circumstances in which a demand for information is made and the "implications of the (demand) in the setting in which it is asked," 345 U.S. at 9, that will provide the commonsense guide to resolving the adequacy question. We think that the Director's public affidavit, read against the background of the widespread public disclosures about the conduct of Operation CHAOS on the one hand and the undeniable sensitivity of our diplomatic relations on the other, alone suffices to satisfy the requirements of the privilege.

It is evident from the descriptions of the CHAOS program found in the Rockefeller Commission and Senate reports that the CIA's conduct of Operation CHAOS extended to the surveillance of foreign citizens both here and abroad. It relied upon the cooperation of foreign intelligence services, and upon the information supplied by CIA agents who were undercover both here and abroad. The Director's public affidavit, while necessarily unspecific, set forth the grounds requiring secrecy in this context.

C. Protecting "State Secrets" in Civil Litigation

It is self-evident that the disclosures sought here pose a "reasonable danger" to the diplomatic and military interests of the United States. Revelation of particular instances in which foreign governments assisted the CIA[57] in conducting surveillance of dissidents could strain diplomatic relations in a number of ways — by generally embarrassing foreign governments who may wish to avoid or may even explicitly disavow allegations of CIA or United States involvements, or by rendering foreign governments or their officials subject to political or legal action by those among their own citizens who may have been subjected to surveillance in the course of dissident activity.

Similarly, the identities of CIA operatives who contributed information to CHAOS (both those hired by CHAOS itself and those attached to other departments within the agency) are self-evidently the sort of information which if disclosed could harm national security or diplomatic interests. Without considering the risk to the individuals involved, it is obvious that the exposure of one who acted — and indeed may still be acting — as a CIA operative here and abroad would pose a threat to our diplomatic and military interests. See Military Audit Project v. Casey, 656 F.2d 724, 749 (D.C. Cir. 1981). Information that permitted one of the appellants to determine that he, she, or it had been the subject of surveillance might also be sufficient, when combined with knowledge of the individual's other activities, to identify CIA operatives as having participated in activities abroad that were heretofore assumed free of such involvement, or as having had access to information previously assumed to have been secure....

2. Because we find the Director's public affidavit adequate to support the district court's decision to uphold the claim of privilege we need not reach appellants' contentions regarding the *in camera* affidavit. Specifically, we need not consider appellants' claim that the court should have required a more complete articulation of the Director's claim on the public record in order to permit full adversary development of the issue of its adequacy.... Appellants offer no reasons to suspect the Director's public affidavit of bad faith or inaccuracy.... Therefore, although the claim of privilege could in this instance have been upheld without reference to the *in camera* affidavit, the district court was free to satisfy itself of the credibility of the public affidavit by resort to the *in camera* submission....

---

57. Appellants argue that they have never sought the identities of any CIA operatives or liaison services, but only the identities of the *plaintiffs* who were subjected to surveillance. However, it is clear that armed with this information and the mass of facts to be culled from the public record of CHAOS activities, it might well be possible for appellants and others to deduce such identities based upon their personal knowledge of their own contacts, activities and whereabouts. We have said that intelligence gathering is "akin to the construction of a mosaic [in which] [t]housands of bits and pieces of seemingly innocuous information can be analyzed and fitted into place to reveal with startling clarity how the unseen whole must operate." *Halkin I* [Halkin v. Helms, 598 F.2d 1 (D.C. Cir. 1978)] at 8. This is no less true of attempts to penetrate the practice of intelligence-gathering itself. In *Halkin I*, we barred discovery of the identity of plaintiffs whose communications had been intercepted by NSA, noting that "the identity of particular individuals whose communications have been acquired can be useful information to a sophisticated intelligence analyst." Id. at 9. Surely that is no less true in the case of the surveillance conducted by CHAOS agents than it is of the eavesdropping performed by NSA computers.

3. Appellants are of the view that a claim of the state secrets privilege with respect to *documents* must be justified in accordance with the same procedures and the same ultimate burdens that obtain in cases seeking disclosure under the Freedom of Information Act. They contend that the refusal of the CIA to produce CHAOS documents or more fully to explain the redactions made in those which were produced violated these requirements. We disagree.

Appellants contend that the withholdings and deletions here should have been justified by a showing of the type required in FOIA cases by Vaughn v. Rosen, 484 F.2d 820 (D.C. Cir. 1973), cert. denied, 415 U.S. 977 (1974). *Vaughn* mandates that government agencies claiming one or more of the statutory exemptions from the FOIA submit "a relatively detailed analysis in manageable segments" that "correlate(s) statements made in the Government's refusal justification with the actual portions of the document" sought to be withheld. 484 F.2d at 826-827. The customary means of complying with this mandate has been for the government to submit a "*Vaughn* index" itemizing each instance of claimed exemption, describing the document involved, and stating the specific exemption(s) asserted to apply. The index may be supplemented with representative exhibits illustrating the nature of the documents and the context of redactions made, and in some cases with *in camera* submissions which make evident the need for confidentiality.

We take note at the outset of the substantial effort already made by the Director in the case to provide the kind of specific explanation contemplated by *Vaughn* and its progeny.... We agree with appellees and the district court that further justification was not called for.

First, the discovery sought here takes place in a context different from the statutory system of mandatory disclosure established by FOIA. Although the scope of civil discovery may well exceed the scope of FOIA-mandated disclosure in some instances, the *nature of the decision* to withhold information in the case of a claim of the state secrets privilege fundamentally differs from the decision to claim a FOIA exemption. The most important difference is that the claim of the state secrets privilege is a decision of *policy* made at the *highest level* of the executive branch after consideration of the facts of the *particular case*. The *Reynolds* requirements compel that it fulfill these requisites. Consequently, the risk of permitting relatively unaccountable "invisible" bureaucratic decisions as to the national security value of information (specifically, the decisions to classify information that trigger FOIA Exemption 1) to bar disclosure of information on a wholesale basis is not presented in a state secrets case.[69]

Second, the unique status of national security information under *both* FOIA and general civil discovery practice militates against requiring broader disclosure here. In their zeal to impose the requirements of *Vaughn* indexing beyond the FOIA context, appellants largely ignore the purposes *Vaughn* itself sought to serve.

---

69. It bears noting that the state secrets privilege applies regardless of whether the information has actually been classified pursuant to the substantive and procedural requirements of applicable statutes or executive orders.... Although matter qualifying as a secret of state will presumably always qualify for classified status, the privilege operates on premises, rooted in the careful consideration by an executive officer in a policymaking role, entirely different from those governing the routine classification of information by lesser officials.

C. Protecting "State Secrets" in Civil Litigation

A *Vaughn*-type index of the withheld documents and redactions involved here would in fact serve little purpose. The *raison d'etre* of the *Vaughn* index is to permit a fuller adversarial examination of the justifications for withholding information which is presumed by statute to be available to the public. In cases where there is frequently doubt as to whether documents meet the threshold requirements of the asserted exemption—e.g., the "investigatory record compiled for a law enforcement purpose" threshold of Exemption 7 or the "medical or personnel files or similar files" threshold of Exemption 6—the *Vaughn* index permits the court, with the assistance of the requesting party, to determine whether the information qualifies for exemption. However, as *Vaughn itself recognized*, where the only question is whether information has been deemed by the executive to be so sensitive as to pose a risk to national security were it disclosed, a more detailed statement of the characteristics of the withheld information would serve no useful end. The executive's resolution of the issue in favor of secrecy *terminates the inquiry under FOIA* just as it does under the state secrets privilege. See *Vaughn*, 484 F.2d at 824....

NOTES AND QUESTIONS

1. *Plaintiffs' Goals.* What exactly do you think were the goals of the plaintiffs and their lawyers in the *Halkin* litigation? Should they have foreseen the outcome? Do you think they felt in the end that it was worth all the trouble and expense?

2. *Scope of the Privilege.* At the outset, the Supreme Court extended state secrets privilege protection only to "military matters which, in the interest of national security, should not be divulged." United States v. Reynolds, 345 U.S. 1, 10 (1953). More recently, however, "[p]ossibly because the state secrets doctrine pertains generally to *national security* concerns, the privilege has been viewed as both expansive and malleable." Ellsberg v. Mitchell, 709 F.2d 51, 57 (D.C. Cir. 1983). Can you say from your reading of *Halkin* what additional matters are covered by its invocation?

3. *FOIA and State Secrets Compared.* The potential for harm to the nation seems as great in litigation involving sensitive information, either through discovery or by introduction of such information into evidence, as in FOIA requests. Should the courts respond to that risk by adopting the same standards and procedures as in FOIA cases? *See* Baldridge v. Shapiro, 455 U.S. 345, 360 n.15 (1982). Is that what the court did in *Halkin*?

4. *State Secrets in Discovery.* Unlike the requester in a FOIA case, a litigant seeking discovery who is faced with a state secrets claim must demonstrate that "the information is relevant to a material aspect of the litigant's case and that the litigant is unable to obtain the crucial data (or adequate substitute) from any other source." Ellsberg v. Mitchell, *supra*, 709 F.2d at 59 n.37.

The *Ellsberg* court noted that "the more compelling a litigant's showing of need for the information in question, the deeper 'the court should probe in satisfying itself that the occasion for invoking the privilege is appropriate'" (quoting from *Reynolds, supra*). *Id.* at 58-59. In an earlier case, another court declared:

> [A] party's showing of need often compels the district court to conduct an in camera review of documents allegedly covered by the privilege in order to determine whether the records are properly classified "secret" by the Government. Any other rule would permit the Government to classify documents just to avoid their production even though there is need for their production and no true need for secrecy. [American Civil Liberties Union v. Brown, 619 F.2d 1170, 1173 (7th Cir. 1980).]

On the other hand, as the *Halkin* court observed, "[o]nce the court is satisfied that the information poses a reasonable danger to secrets of state, even the most compelling necessity cannot overcome the claim of privilege." 690 F.2d at 990.

5. *Judicial Deference.* Just how much should courts defer to the judgment of the executive in these matters?

> It has been argued that certain limitations on the capacity of the judicial branch safely and reliably to evaluate invocations of the state secrets privilege should induce the courts to renounce any role in this area, i.e., to accept without question a privilege claim made by a ranking officer. Such an extreme solution, however, would have grave drawbacks.... [T]he Supreme Court has declared that "[j]udicial control over the evidence in a case cannot be abdicated to the caprice of executive officers" [citing *Reynolds*, 345 U.S. at 9-10]. Thus, to insure that the state secrets privilege is asserted no more frequently and sweepingly than necessary, it is essential that the courts continue critically to examine instances of its invocation. [*Ellsberg, supra,* 709 F.2d at 57-58.]

See In re United States, 872 F.2d 472, 475 (D.C. Cir. 1989). Do you think the courts should conduct a de novo review of the executive's determination of the national interest, as in FOIA cases, without an express mandate from Congress? Adopting an intermediate position, the *Ellsberg* court observed:

> [I]t is frequently noted that the trial judge should accord considerable deference to recommendations from the executive department.... [W]hen assessing claims of a state secrets privilege, a trial judge properly may rely on affidavits and other secondary sources more often than he might when evaluating assertions of other evidentiary privileges.... [T]he more plausible and substantial the government's allegations of danger to national security, in the context of all the circumstances surrounding the case, the more deferential should be the judge's inquiry into the foundation and scope of the claim. [*Ellsberg, supra,* 709 F.2d at 58-59.]

The *Halkin* court concluded that when a risk to national security is asserted, "[t]he executive's resolution of the issue in favor of secrecy terminates the inquiry under FOIA just as it does under the state secrets privilege," 690 F.2d at 996, citing Vaughn v. Rosen. Could the court's position possibly permit abuse of the privilege? Can the court possibly have overlooked the 1974 amendments to FOIA? See *supra* p. 1000.

C. Protecting "State Secrets" in Civil Litigation

6. *Reynolds Revisited.* The Supreme Court's landmark 1953 decision in United States v. Reynolds, 345 U.S. 1, the first recognizing the state secrets privilege, grew out of the crash in 1948 of a B-29 bomber. Surviving family members of three civilian engineers who perished brought suit for damages under the Federal Tort Claims Act. When they sought access through discovery to the official accident report, the Supreme Court accepted without question the Air Force's assertion that disclosure of the report would "seriously hamper[] national security." 345 U.S. at 5. The Court refused even to order in camera review of the report. When the report was declassified many years later, it was found to contain nothing that could apparently have been helpful to the nation's enemies, but instead to show pilot error, a failure to carry out special safety orders, and a history of maintenance problems with the B-29.

In early 2003, surviving *Reynolds* plaintiffs and their heirs asked the Supreme Court to set aside its half-century-old ruling on grounds that the Court was defrauded by government misrepresentation of the contents of the report. *See* Timothy Lynch, *An Injustice Wrapped In a Pretense,* Wash. Post, June 22, 2003; David A. Churchill & Elaine J. Goldenberg, *Who Will Guard the Guardians? Revisiting the State Secrets Privilege of United States v. Reynolds,* 72 U.S.L.W. 2227 (2003). However, the Court denied without comment a motion for leave to file the petition for a writ of error *coram nobis* on June 23, 2003. In re Herring, 539 U.S. 940 (2003). Can you guess why the Court refused to reopen the case? Do you think the Court would have reacted differently to an effort to reopen its 1944 decision in Korematsu v. United States, 323 U.S. 214 (1944), *supra* p. 704, in light of the revelations of government fraud in that case 40 years after it was decided? *See* Korematsu v. United States, 584 F. Supp. 1406 (N.D. Cal. 1984), noted *supra* p. 711.

The *Reynolds* survivors subsequently filed a new action in the federal district court where the case had been heard 54 years earlier, asking for a ruling that the government had perpetrated a fraud on the court, and for damages. They were denied relief. A panel of the Third Circuit Court of Appeals remarked that "[t]he presumption against the reopening of a case that has gone through the appellate process all the way to the United States Supreme Court and reached final judgment must be not just a high hurdle to climb but a steep cliff-face to scale." Herring v. United States, 424 F.3d 384, 386 (3d Cir. 2005). This meant the plaintiffs had to show that government officials in 1953 had committed intentional fraud on the court, something the plaintiffs could not do, because of the "near impossibility of determining with any level of certainty what seemingly insignificant pieces of information would have been of keen interest to a Soviet spy fifty years ago." *Id.* at 391 n.3.

The plaintiffs then petitioned the Supreme Court for a writ of certiorari, claiming that the 1944 decision "rests on a lie." Petition for Writ of Certiorari, Herring v. United States, No.___(U.S. filed Dec. 21, 2005), at 2, *available at* http://www.fas.org/sgp/jud/herring1205.pdf. That petition was denied. 126 S. Ct. 1909 (2006). The *Reynolds* litigation is extensively analyzed in Louis Fisher, *In the Name of National Security: Unchecked Presidential Power and the Reynolds Case* (2006).

Do you think these developments will have any bearing on the way courts consider state secrets privilege claims in the future? Should they?

7. *Public Affidavit.* The government's public affidavit in *Halkin* was sufficiently detailed to make in camera inspection of the requested documents unnecessary. In the *Ellsberg* case, the court declared:

> [I]n camera proceedings should be preceded by as full as possible a public debate over the basis and scope of a privilege claim.... The more specific the public explanation, the greater the ability of the opposing party to contest it. The ensuing arguments assist the judge in assessing the risk of harm posed by dissemination of the information in question. This kind of focused debate is of particular aid to the judge when fulfilling his duty to disentangle privileged from non-privileged materials — to ensure that no more is shielded than is necessary to avoid the anticipated injuries.... [However, the] government's public statement need be no more (and no less) specific than is practicable under the circumstances. [709 F.2d at 63-64.]

How, if at all, does this formulation differ from the requirements for a *Vaughn* affidavit set forth in Ray v. Turner, *supra* p. 997?

8. *Significance of Classification.* Could the state secrets privilege ever cover unclassified material? Is the test for state secrets articulated by the *Halkin* court different in any important way from the one set out in Executive Order No. 13,292 for classification of documents, *supra* p. 979?

9. *"Mosaic" Theory.* Doesn't the "mosaic" theory, that an apparently innocuous piece of information may be combined with other pieces to create a larger picture damaging to the national security, *Halkin*, 690 F.2d at 993 n.57, potentially doom any effort to discover or introduce evidence the government wishes to protect? Is there a practical solution? The mosaic theory is also invoked by the government in FOIA litigation. *See supra* p. 1009.

10. *Growing Reliance on the State Secrets Privilege.* The government seemingly has invoked the state secrets privilege more frequently recently, a practice that some say "has short-circuited judicial scrutiny and public debate of some central controversies of the post-9/11 era." Scott Shane, *Invoking Secrets Privilege Becomes More Popular Legal Tactic by U.S.*, N.Y. Times, June 4, 2006, §1, at 24; *see also* Tom Blanton, Op-Ed., *The Lie Behind the Secrets*, L.A. Times, May 21, 2006, §M, at 1 (the privilege "was invoked only four times in the first 23 years after the U.S. Supreme Court created the privilege in 1953, but now the government is claiming the privilege to dismiss lawsuits at a rate of more than three a year."); *State Secrets Privilege Shuts Courthouse Doors*, Secrecy News, May 22, 2006. For example, one suit was dismissed without trial when the court found that

> the question is whether El-Masri's claims could be fairly litigated without disclosure of the state secrets absolutely protected by the United States' privilege.... [T]his question is easily answered in the negative. To succeed on his claims, El-Masri would have to prove that he was abducted, detained, and subjected to cruel and degrading treatment, all as part of the United States' extraordinary rendition program. [El-Masri v. Tenet, No. 1:05cv1417, 2006 WL 1391390, at *6 (E.D. Va. May 12, 2006).]

C. Protecting "State Secrets" in Civil Litigation

Should a court's decision to grant the privilege be affected by the political controversy surrounding the subject matter of a suit? If so, how?

Tenet v. Doe
United States Supreme Court, 2005
544 U.S. 1

Chief Justice REHNQUIST delivered the opinion of the Court.... Respondents, a husband and wife who use the fictitious names John and Jane Doe, brought suit in the United States District Court for the Western District of Washington.[1] According to respondents, they were formerly citizens of a foreign country that at the time was considered to be an enemy of the United States, and John Doe was a high-ranking diplomat for the country. After respondents expressed interest in defecting to the United States, CIA agents persuaded them to remain at their posts and conduct espionage for the United States for a specified period of time, promising in return that the Government "would arrange for travel to the United States and ensure financial and personal security for life." After "carrying out their end of the bargain" by completing years of purportedly high-risk, valuable espionage services, respondents defected (under new names and false backgrounds) and became United States citizens, with the Government's help. The CIA... began providing financial assistance and personal security.

With the CIA's help, respondent John Doe obtained employment in the State of Washington. As his salary increased, the CIA decreased his living stipend until, at some point, he agreed to a discontinuation of benefits while he was working. Years later, in 1997, John Doe was laid off after a corporate merger. Because John Doe was unable to find new employment as a result of CIA restrictions on the type of jobs he could hold, respondents contacted the CIA for financial assistance. Denied such assistance by the CIA, they claim they are unable to properly provide for themselves. Thus, they are faced with the prospect of either returning to their home country (where they say they face extreme sanctions), or remaining in the United States in their present circumstances.

Respondents assert, among other things, that the CIA violated their procedural and substantive due process rights by denying them support and by failing to provide them with a fair internal process for reviewing their claims. They seek injunctive relief ordering the CIA to resume monthly financial support pending further agency review. They also request a declaratory judgment stating that the CIA failed to provide a constitutionally adequate review process, and detailing the minimal process the agency must provide. Finally, respondents seek a mandamus order requiring the CIA to adopt agency procedures, to give them fair review, and to provide them with security and financial assistance....

A divided panel of the Court of Appeals for the Ninth Circuit... reasoned that *Totten* [v. United States, 92 U.S. 105 (1876)] posed no bar to reviewing some

---

1. The Government has neither confirmed nor denied any of respondents' allegations. We therefore describe the facts as asserted in respondents' second amended complaint. They are, of course, no more than allegations.

of respondents' claims and thus that the case could proceed to trial, subject to the Government's asserting the evidentiary state secrets privilege and the District Court's resolving that issue. 329 F.3d [1135 (2003)], at 1145-1155.... The Government sought review, and we granted certiorari.[4]

In *Totten*, the administrator of William A. Lloyd's estate brought suit against the United States to recover compensation for services that Lloyd allegedly rendered as a spy during the Civil War. Lloyd purportedly entered into a contract with President Lincoln in July 1861 to spy behind Confederate lines on troop placement and fort plans, for which he was to be paid $200 a month. The lower court had found that Lloyd performed on the contract but did not receive full compensation. After concluding with "no difficulty" that the President had the authority to bind the United States to contracts with secret agents, we observed that the very essence of the alleged contract between Lloyd and the Government was that it was secret, and had to remain so:

> "The service stipulated by the contract was a secret service; the information sought was to be obtained clandestinely, and was to be communicated privately; the employment and the service were to be equally concealed. Both employer and agent must have understood that the lips of the other were to be for ever sealed respecting the relation of either to the matter. This condition of the engagement was implied from the nature of the employment, and is implied in all secret employments of the government in time of war, or upon matters affecting our foreign relations, where a disclosure of the service might compromise or embarrass our government in its public duties, or endanger the person or injure the character of the agent." [92 U.S. at 106.]

Thus, we thought it entirely incompatible with the nature of such a contract that a former spy could bring suit to enforce it.

We think the Court of Appeals was quite wrong in holding that *Totten* does not require dismissal of respondents' claims. That court, and respondents here, reasoned first that *Totten* developed merely a contract rule, prohibiting breach-of-contract claims seeking to enforce the terms of espionage agreements but not barring claims based on due process or estoppel theories. In fact, *Totten* was not

---

4. Preliminarily, we must address whether *Steel Co. v. Citizens for Better Environment*, 523 U.S. 83 (1998), prevents us from resolving this case based on the *Totten* issue. In *Steel Co.*, we adhered to the requirement that a court address questions pertaining to its or a lower court's jurisdiction before proceeding to the merits. 523 U.S., at 94-95. In the lower courts, in addition to relying on *Totten*, the Government argued that the Tucker Act, 28 U.S.C. §1491(a)(1), required that respondents' claims be brought in the Court of Federal Claims, rather than in the District Court. The District Court and the Court of Appeals rejected this argument, and the Government did not seek review on this question in its petition for certiorari.

We may assume for purposes of argument that this Tucker Act question is the kind of jurisdictional issue that *Steel Co.* directs must be resolved before addressing the merits of a claim. Nevertheless, application of the *Totten* rule of dismissal, like the abstention doctrine of *Younger v. Harris*, 401 U.S. 37 (1971), or the prudential standing doctrine, represents the sort of "threshold question" we have recognized may be resolved before addressing jurisdiction. See *Ruhrgas AG v. Marathon Oil Co.*, 526 U.S. 574, 585 (1999) ("It is hardly novel for a federal court to choose among threshold grounds for denying audience to a case on the merits"). It would be inconsistent with the unique and categorical nature of the *Totten* bar—a rule designed not merely to defeat the asserted claims, but to preclude judicial inquiry—to first allow discovery or other proceedings in order to resolve the jurisdictional question. Thus, whether or not the Government was permitted to waive the Tucker Act question, we may dismiss respondents' cause of action on the ground that it is barred by *Totten*.

C. Protecting "State Secrets" in Civil Litigation

so limited: "[P]ublic policy forbids the maintenance of *any suit* in a court of justice, the trial of which would inevitably lead to the disclosure of matters which the law itself regards as confidential." *Id.,* at 107 (emphasis added); see also *ibid.* ("The secrecy which such contracts impose precludes *any action* for their enforcement" (emphasis added).) No matter the clothing in which alleged spies dress their claims, *Totten* precludes judicial review in cases such as respondents' where success depends upon the existence of their secret espionage relationship with the Government.

Relying mainly on *United States v. Reynolds,* 345 U.S. 1 (1953), the Court of Appeals also claimed that *Totten* has been recast simply as an early expression of the evidentiary "state secrets" privilege, rather than a categorical bar to their claims....

When invoking the "well established" state secrets privilege, we indeed looked to *Totten. Reynolds, supra,* at 7, n.11 (citing *Totten, supra,* at 107). But that in no way signaled our retreat from *Totten's* broader holding that lawsuits premised on alleged espionage agreements are altogether forbidden. Indeed, our opinion in *Reynolds* refutes this very suggestion: Citing *Totten* as a case "where the very subject matter of the action, a contract to perform espionage, was a matter of state secret," we declared that such a case was to be "dismissed *on the pleadings without ever reaching the question of evidence,* since it was so obvious that the action should never prevail over the privilege." 345 U.S., at 11, n.26 (emphasis added)....

Nor does *Webster v. Doe,* 486 U.S. 592 (1988), support respondents' claim. There, we held that §102(c) of the National Security Act of 1947, 61 Stat. 498, 50 U.S.C. §403(c), may not be read to exclude judicial review of the constitutional claims made by a former CIA employee for alleged discrimination. In reaching that conclusion, we noted the "'serious constitutional question' that would arise if a federal statute were construed to deny any judicial forum for a colorable constitutional claim." But there is an obvious difference, for purposes of *Totten,* between a suit brought by an acknowledged (though covert) employee of the CIA and one filed by an alleged former spy. Only in the latter scenario is *Totten's* core concern implicated: preventing the existence of the plaintiff's relationship with the Government from being revealed. That is why the CIA regularly entertains Title VII claims concerning the hiring and promotion of its employees, as we noted in *Webster,* yet *Totten* has long barred suits such as respondents'.

There is, in short, no basis for respondents' and the Court of Appeals' view that the *Totten* bar has been reduced to an example of the state secrets privilege....

We adhere to *Totten.* The state secrets privilege and the more frequent use of *in camera* judicial proceedings simply cannot provide the absolute protection we found necessary in enunciating the *Totten* rule. The possibility that a suit may proceed and an espionage relationship may be revealed, if the state secrets privilege is found not to apply, is unacceptable: "Even a small chance that some court will order disclosure of a source's identity could well impair intelligence gathering and cause sources to 'close up like a clam.'" *CIA v. Sims,* 471 U.S. 159, 175 (1985). Forcing the Government to litigate these claims would also make it vulnerable to "graymail," *i.e.,* individual lawsuits brought to induce the CIA to settle a case (or prevent its filing) out of fear that any effort to litigate the action would reveal classified information that may undermine ongoing covert operations. And requiring the Government to invoke the privilege on a case-by-case basis risks the perception that it is either confirming or denying relationships with individual plaintiffs.

The judgment of the Court of Appeals is reversed.
It is so ordered.

[The concurring opinions of STEVENS, J., joined by GINSBURG, J., and of SCALIA, J., are omitted.]

NOTES AND QUESTIONS

1. *In re Totten and Its Progeny.* An increasing number of lower courts in recent years have invoked In re Totten to dismiss claims without trial. In 1987, for example, during the Iran-Iraq War, an Iraqi Mirage fighter fired two Exocet missiles at the U.S. frigate *Stark* in the Persian Gulf, killing 37 American sailors. Surviving family members filed suit for damages against several defense contractors, alleging that the Phalanx missile defense system on the ill-fated ship was defectively designed and manufactured. The court refused to allow the case to go forward, fearing that, discovery aside, a trial on the merits might lead to the inadvertent disclosure of state secrets.

> [T]he danger that witnesses might divulge some privileged material during cross-examination is great because the privileged and non-privileged material are inextricably linked. We are compelled to conclude that the trial of this case would inevitably lead to a significant risk that highly sensitive information concerning this defense system would be disclosed. [Bareford v. General Dynamics Corp., 973 F.2d 1138, 1144 (5th Cir. 1992).]

Other cases dismissed on the same grounds include Sterling v. Tenet, 416 F.3d 338 (4th Cir. 2005) (racial discrimination claim against the CIA); Edmonds v. United States Dept. of Justice, 323 F. Supp. 2d 65 (D.D.C. 2004), *cert. denied*, 126 S. Ct. 734 (2005) (fired FBI whistleblower's suit for damages); Burnett v. Al Baraka Investment & Development Corp., 323 F. Supp. 2d 82 (D.D.C. 2004) (deposition in damage suit by 9/11 victims); Trulock v. Lee, 66 Fed. Appx. 472 (4th Cir. 2003) (defamation suit growing out of the Wen Ho Lee case); McDonnell Douglas Corp. v. United States, 323 F.3d 1006 (Fed. Cir. 2003) (defense contract dispute); Tilden v. Tenet, 140 F. Supp. 2d 623 (E.D. Va. 2000) (alleged gender discrimination by CIA); Guong v. United States, 860 F.2d 1063 (Fed. Cir. 1988) (employment contract with CIA); Fitzgerald v. Penthouse International, Ltd., 776 F.2d 1236 (4th Cir. 1985) (alleged Navy and CIA use of dolphins for military and intelligence purposes); Salisbury v. United States, 690 F.2d 966 (D.C. Cir. 1982) (NSA intercepts of electronic communications); Weinberger v. Catholic Action of Hawaii, 454 U.S. 139 (1981) (possible storage of nuclear weapons on Oahu); and Farnsworth Cannon, Inc. v. Grimes, 635 F.2d 268 (4th Cir. 1980) (Navy cancellation of a defense contract). Some of these cases and their significance are analyzed in Sean C. Flynn, Note, *The Totten Doctrine and Its Poisoned Progeny*, 25 Vt. L. Rev. 793 (2001).

C. Protecting "State Secrets" in Civil Litigation

2. *Grounds for Abstention?* Did the Tenet v. Doe Court refuse to hear the case because it lacked jurisdiction to decide it, or was its ruling based instead on prudential considerations? One court recently described the "*Totten* bar" as "a rule of non-justiciability that deprives courts of their ability to hear 'suits against the Government' even in the absence of a formal claim of privilege." El-Masri v. Tenet, No. 1:05cv1417, 2006 WL 1391390, at *7 (E.D. Va. May 12, 2006). Does it matter which theory a court adopts?

3. *The State Secrets Alternative.* In In re United States, 872 F.2d 472, 477 (D.C. Cir. 1989), the court declared, "Dismissal of a suit, and the consequent denial of a forum without giving the plaintiff her day in court... is indeed draconian." The court avoided outright dismissal, concluding that "an item-by-item determination of privilege will amply accommodate the Government's concerns. First, the information remains in the Government's custody.... Thirdly, the case will be tried to the bench, a circumstance that will reduce the threat of unauthorized disclosure of confidential material." *Id.* at 478.

In Tenet v. Doe, a Ninth Circuit panel ruled that "because the net result of refusing to adjudicate the Does' claims is to sacrifice their asserted constitutional interests to the security of the nation as a whole, both the government and the courts need to consider discretely, rather than by formula, whether this is a case in which there is simply no acceptable alternative to that sacrifice." Doe v. Tenet, 329 F.3d 1135, 1146 (9th Cir. 2003), *reh'g and reh'g en banc denied*, 353 F.3d 1141 (9th Cir. 2004). "*Totten* permits dismissal of cases in which it is asserted that the very subject matter is a state secret only *after* complying with the formalities and court investigation requirements that have developed since *Totten* within the framework of the state secrets doctrine." *Id.* at 1149. Thus, the court directed the government to formally assert its state secrets privilege, leaving the court to test that assertion by conducting in camera and ex parte review of documents.

Why do you suppose the government in the principal case was so determined to avoid application of the procedures associated with the state secrets privilege? What did the Supreme Court have to say about the sacrifices of the plaintiffs in the name of national security?

4. *Secure Adjudication?* The Court of Appeals in the principal case said it would make "every effort" to find ways to adjudicate the plaintiffs' claims while protecting the national security, including in camera proceedings, sealing or redaction of records, requiring security clearances for court personnel and attorneys, protective orders, and a bench trial. *Id.* at 1148-1149, 1153. A number of courts have adopted similar protective tactics in cases involving sensitive information. *See, e.g.*, Loral Corp. v. McDonnell Douglas Corp., 558 F.2d 1130 (2d Cir. 1977) (special master); In re Under Seal, 945 F.2d 1285 (4th Cir. 1992) (protective orders); Halpern v. United States, 258 F.2d 36 (2d Cir. 1958) (secret trial). *See generally* Frank Askin, *Secret Justice and the Adversary System*, 18 Hastings Const. L.Q. 745 (1991); Stephen Dycus, *NEPA Secrets*, 2 N.Y.U. Envtl. L.J. 300 (1993). A special court, organized along the lines of the Foreign Intelligence Surveillance Court (see *supra* p. 524), might be created to deal with these difficult cases. Can you think of other ways to try such cases without undue risk? Would any of these resolutions raise separation of powers concerns?

5. *Scope of the Totten Doctrine?* The trial court in the principal case distinguished "purely contractual" claims, trial of which would be precluded by *Totten*, from constitutional claims based on procedural and substantive due process violations, which would not. Doe v. Tenet, 99 F. Supp. 2d 1284, 1289-1290 (W.D. Wash. 2000). *But see* Kielczynski v. United States Central Intelligence Agency, 128 F. Supp. 2d 151, 161-164 (E.D.N.Y. 2001), *aff'd sub nom.* Kielczynski v. Does 1-2, 56 Fed. Appx. 540 (2d Cir. 2003) (on similar facts, due process claim "cannot arise independent of plaintiff's contractual claims"). What importance, if any, did the Supreme Court attach to the distinction?

Will the precedential value of Tenet v. Doe be confined to factually similar disputes — that is, to those involving alleged "covert espionage agreements"? Or will the *Totten* doctrine of nonjusticiability be extended — even without the showing of state secrets required by *Reynolds* — to a wider range of cases involving allegedly sensitive information, as we have witnessed recently in lower court decisions? If so, what do you think remains of the state secrets privilege?

Restraining Unauthorized Disclosures of National Security Information 36

Every contemporary presidential administration has entered office obsessed with unauthorized "leaks"—intentional disclosures of government secrets to the media by present or past employees—or with the publication of such secrets by past employees. The worry is that such disclosures may chill the candor of executive branch communications, warp the development of sound policies by exposing them prematurely, undermine the discipline of good decision making, interfere with political strategies to keep the administration "on message," and, sometimes, injure the national security by compromising classified information.

Some leaks of classified information to the media are in fact authorized. Three decades ago, a court pointed to examples in

> [the] disclosure of this country's development of Multiple Independently Targeted Reentry Vehicles and the release of information about North Vietnamese forces operating in South Vietnam, including the identity of units, their strength and the routes they took to reach their operating areas. These . . . were the result of high level executive decisions that disclosure was in the public interest, to counter popular and congressional pressure for more missiles, in the first instance, and, in the second instance, to bolster domestic support for our own military effort in South Vietnam. They are instances of declassification by official public disclosure. [Alfred A. Knopf, Inc. v. Colby, 509 F.2d 1362, 1369 (4th Cir. 1975).]

More recently, President Bush approved the clandestine disclosure of portions of the then-classified 2002 National Intelligence Estimate in an effort to shore up support for administration claims that Iraq was trying to obtain nuclear weapons. *See* David Johnston & David E. Sanger, *Cheney's Aide Says President Approved Leak*, N.Y. Times, Apr. 7, 2006, at A1. See also *infra* p. 1080.

One way to control unauthorized leaks is to screen persons to whom secrets are entrusted. Every administration conducts some form of political screening, or vetting, for its high-level appointees. In addition, as a condition of access to classified information (and therefore employment), many government employees and defense contractor personnel must obtain security clearances based on background investigations that vary in intensity depending on the classification level of the information to which they will have access. *See generally* Stephen

Dycus, Arthur L. Berney, William C. Banks & Peter Raven-Hansen, *National Security Law* 678-736 (2d ed. 1997). A security breach, such as a leak, can lead to revocation of a security clearance and attendant loss of employment.

The threat of a job loss alone has not proven adequate, however, to stanch the steady leak of national security information to the media. The government has therefore looked to the courts and to Congress for help. The courts have applied contract theories to prevent past employees from publishing putative national security secrets or, at least, from profiting from such publication. Part A of this chapter examines those contract theories, as well as the secrecy and prepublication review agreements upon which they rest. The government mounted an Espionage Act prosecution against one former government employee who sold information to the press by using federal criminal laws that more traditionally have been invoked against spies in the service of foreign states, and the government has used different statutes to punish and deter other leakers. Part B of the chapter examines these prosecutions and looks at recurring efforts to criminalize unauthorized leaks more directly. At the end of the chapter we examine an extremely controversial case involving so-called authorized leaks.

A. RESTRAINING LEAKS BY CONTRACT

1. The CIA Precedents

United States v. Marchetti
United States Court of Appeals, Fourth Circuit, 1972
466 F.2d 1309, *cert. denied*, 409 U.S. 1063 (1972)

[Victor Marchetti, a former employee of the Central Intelligence Agency (Agency or CIA), signed a secrecy agreement promising not to reveal classified information or information relating to intelligence matters when he joined the Agency, and he signed a similar secrecy oath when he resigned.]

HAYNSWORTH, C.J.... After his resignation, Marchetti published a novel, entitled *The Rope Dancer*, concerning an agency called the "National Intelligence Agency." [He] also published an article in the April 3, 1972 issue of... The Nation [magazine]... criticiz[ing] some policies and practices of the Agency. In March, 1972, Marchetti submitted to Esquire magazine and to six other publishers an article in which he reports some of his experiences as an agent. According to the United States, this article contains classified information concerning intelligence sources, methods and operations.... He has submitted to a publishing house an outline of a book he proposes to write about his intelligence experiences....

[Relying on Marchetti's earlier agreements, the District Court ordered him not to release to any person or corporation any writing, fictional or nonfictional, relating to the Agency or to intelligence without prior authorization from the

A. Restraining Leaks by Contract

CIA. Marchetti was also ordered to return any writings or other property of the United States he had acquired while employed at the Agency.]

We readily agreed with Marchetti that the First Amendment limits the extent to which the United States, contractually or otherwise, may impose secrecy requirements upon its employees and enforce them with a system of prior censorship. It precludes such restraints with respect to information which is unclassified or officially disclosed, but we are here concerned with secret information touching upon the national defense and the conduct of foreign affairs, acquired by Marchetti while in a position of trust and confidence and contractually bound to respect it....

Gathering intelligence information and the other activities of the Agency, including clandestine affairs against other nations, are all within the President's constitutional responsibility for the security of the Nation as the Chief Executive and as Commander in Chief of our Armed Forces. Const., art. II, §2. Citizens have the right to criticize the conduct of our foreign affairs, but the Government also has the right and the duty to strive for internal secrecy about the conduct of governmental affairs in areas in which disclosure may reasonably be thought to be inconsistent with the national interest.

The Supreme Court recognized the need for secrecy in government in United States v. Curtiss-Wright Export Corp., 229 U.S. 304, 320 where it said that the President

> has his confidential sources of information. He has his agents in the form of diplomatic, consular and other officials. Secrecy in respect of information gathered by them may be highly necessary, and the premature disclosure of it productive of harmful results....

Congress has imposed on the Director of Central Intelligence the responsibility for protecting intelligence sources and methods. 50 U.S.C. §403(d)(3) [see 50 U.S.C. §403-1(i)(1), *supra* p. 356, now imposing the same duty on the Director of National Intelligence]. In attempting to comply with this duty, the Agency requires its employees as a condition of employment to sign a secrecy agreement, and such agreements are entirely appropriate to a program in implementation of the congressional direction of secrecy....

...One may speculate that ordinary criminal sanctions might suffice to prevent unauthorized disclosure of such information, but the risk of harm from disclosure is so great and maintenance of the confidentiality of the information so necessary that greater and more positive assurance is warranted. Some prior restraints in some circumstances are approvable of course. See Freedman v. Maryland, 380 U.S. 51.

...Marchetti by accepting employment with the CIA and by signing a secrecy agreement did not surrender his First Amendment right of free speech. The agreement is enforceable only because it is not a violation of those rights. We would decline enforcement of the secrecy oath signed when he left the employment of the CIA to the extent that it purports to prevent disclosure of unclassified information, for, to that extent, the oath would be in contravention of his First Amendment rights....

Because we are dealing with a prior restraint upon speech, we think that the CIA must act promptly to approve or disapprove any material which may be submitted to it by Marchetti. Undue delay would impair the reasonableness of the restraint.... We should think that, in all events, the maximum period for responding after the submission of material for approval should not exceed thirty days.

Furthermore, since First Amendment rights are involved, we think Marchetti would be entitled to judicial review of any action by the CIA disapproving publication of the material.... See Freedman v. Maryland, 380 U.S. 51. Because of the sensitivity of the area and confidentiality of the relationship in which the information was obtained, however, we find no reason to impose the burden of obtaining judicial review upon the CIA. It ought to be on Marchetti.

Indeed, in most instances, there ought to be no practical reason for judicial review since, because of its limited nature, there would be only narrow areas for possible disagreement.

... The CIA is one of the executive agencies whose activities are closely related to the conduct of foreign affairs and to the national defense.... If in the conduct of its operations the need for secrecy requires a system of classification of documents and information, the process of classification is part of the executive function beyond the scope of judicial review. See Oetjen v. Central Leather Co., 246 U.S. 297; United States v. Belmont, 301 U.S. 324; Zemel v. Rusk, 381 U.S. 1.

There is a practical reason for avoidance of judicial review of secrecy classifications. The significance of one item of information may frequently depend upon knowledge of many other items of information.... The courts... are ill-equipped to become sufficiently steeped in foreign intelligence matters to serve effectively in the review of secrecy classifications in that area.

Information, though classified, may have been publicly disclosed. If it has been, Marchetti should have as much right as anyone else to republish it. Rumor and speculation are not the equivalent of prior disclosure, however, and the presence of that kind of surmise should be no reason for avoidance of restraints upon confirmation from one in a position to know officially....

Generally, therefore, we approve the injunctive order issued by the District Court. The case will be remanded, however, for the purpose of revising the order to limit its reach to classified information and for the conduct of such further proceedings as may be necessary if Marchetti contends that the CIA wrongfully withheld approval of the publication of any information under the standards we have laid down....

CRAVEN, J. (concurring).... I concur in the opinion of the court except for the statement that the classification of documents and information by the executive is not subject to judicial review. Because the national security may be involved and because of the expertise of the executive, I would resolve any doubt about the reasonableness of a classification in favor of the government. If the burden were put upon one who assails the classification, and surely it ought to be, much of the difficulty envisioned in the court's opinion would presumably disappear. Indeed, I would not object to a presumption of reasonableness, and a requirement that the assailant demonstrate by clear and convincing evidence that a classification is arbitrary and capricious before it may be invalidated....

Snepp v. United States
United States Supreme Court, 1980
444 U.S. 507

PER CURIAM. . . . Based on his experiences as a CIA agent, Snepp published a book about certain CIA activities in South Vietnam. Snepp published the account without submitting it to the Agency for prepublication review. As an express condition of his employment with the CIA in 1968, however, Snepp had executed an agreement promising that he would "not . . . publish . . . any information or material relating to the Agency, its activities or intelligence activities generally, either during or after the term of [his] employment . . . without specific prior approval by the Agency." . . . Thus, Snepp had pledged not to divulge *classified* information and not to publish *any* information without prepublication clearance. The Government brought this suit to enforce Snepp's agreement. . . .

The District Court found that Snepp had "wilfully, deliberately and surreptitiously breached his position of trust with the CIA and the [1968] secrecy agreement" . . . . The court also found that Snepp deliberately misled CIA officials into believing that he would submit the book for prepublication clearance. Finally, the court determined as a fact that publication of the book had "caused the United States irreparable harm and loss." The District Court therefore enjoined future breaches of Snepp's agreement and imposed a constructive trust on Snepp's profits.

The Court of Appeals accepted the findings of the District Court and agreed that Snepp had breached a valid contract.[3] . . . The court, however, concluded that the record did not support imposition of a constructive trust. The conclusion rested on the court's perception that Snepp had a First Amendment right to publish unclassified information and the Government's concession — for the purposes of this litigation — that Snepp's book divulged no classified intelligence. . . .

Whether Snepp violated his trust does not depend upon whether his book actually contained classified information. The Government does not deny — as a general principle — Snepp's right to publish unclassified information. . . . The Government simply claims that, in light of the special trust reposed in him and the agreement that he signed, Snepp should have given the CIA an opportunity to determine whether the material he proposed to publish would compromise classified information or sources. Neither of the Government's concessions undercuts its claim that Snepp's failure to submit to prepublication review was a breach of his trust.

Both the District Court and the Court of Appeals found that a former intelligence agent's publication of unreviewed material relating to intelligence

---

3. . . . He does not claim that he executed this agreement under duress. . . . Moreover, this Court's cases make clear that — even in the absence of an express agreement — the CIA could have acted to protect substantial government interests by imposing reasonable restrictions on employee activities that in other contexts might be protected by the First Amendment. The Government has a compelling interest in protecting both the secrecy of information important to our national security and the appearance of confidentiality so essential to the effective operation of our foreign intelligence service. The agreement that Snepp signed is a reasonable means for protecting this vital interest.

activities can be detrimental to vital national interests even if the published information is unclassified. When a former agent relies on his own judgment about what information is detrimental, he may reveal information that the CIA—with its broader understanding of what may expose classified information and confidential sources—could have identified as harmful....

Undisputed evidence in this case shows that a CIA agent's violation of his obligation to submit writings about the Agency for prepublication review impairs the CIA's ability to perform its statutory duties. Admiral Turner, Director of CIA, testified without contradiction that Snepp's book and others like it have seriously impaired the effectiveness of American intelligence operations. He said:

> Over the last six to nine months, we have had a number of sources discontinue work with us. We have had more sources tell us they are very nervous about continuing work with us....

In view of this and other evidence in the record, both the District Court and the Court of Appeals recognized that Snepp's breach of his explicit obligation to submit his material—classified or not—for prepublication clearance has irreparably harmed the United States Government....

The Government could not pursue the only remedy that the Court of Appeals left it without losing the benefit of the bargain it seeks to enforce. Proof of the tortious conduct necessary to sustain an award of punitive damages might force the Government to disclose some of the very confidences that Snepp promised to protect. The trial of such a suit, before a jury if the defendant so elects, would subject the CIA and its officials to probing discovery into the Agency's highly confidential affairs. Rarely would the Government run this risk. In a letter introduced at Snepp's trial, former CIA Director Colby noted the analogous problem in criminal cases. Existing law, he stated, "requires the revelation in open court of confirming or additional information of such a nature that the potential damage to the national security precludes prosecution."... [1]

A constructive trust, on the other hand, protects both the Government and the former agent from unwarranted risks.... If the agent publishes unreviewed material in violation of his fiduciary and contractual obligation, the trust remedy simply requires him to disgorge the benefits of his faithlessness. Since the remedy is swift and sure, it is tailored to deter those who would place sensitive information at risk. And since the remedy reaches only funds attributable to the breach, it cannot saddle the former agent with exemplary damages out of all proportion to his gain.... We therefore reverse the judgment of the Court of Appeals insofar as it refused to impose a constructive trust on Snepp's profits....

Mr. Justice STEVENS, with whom Mr. Justice BRENNAN and Mr. Justice MARSHALL join, dissenting.... In this case Snepp admittedly breached his duty to submit the manuscript of his book, Decent Interval, to the CIA for prepublication review. However, the Government has conceded that the book contains

---

[1. After *Snepp* was decided, Congress addressed this problem by enacting the Classified Information Procedures Act. 18 U.S.C. App. §§1-16 (2000). See Chapter 29.]

A. Restraining Leaks by Contract

no classified, nonpublic material. Thus, by definition, the interest in confidentiality that Snepp's contract was designed to protect has not been compromised. Nevertheless, the Court today grants the Government unprecedented and drastic relief in the form of a constructive trust....

The rule of law the Court announces today is not supported by statute, by the contract, or by the common law. Although Congress has enacted a number of criminal statutes punishing the unauthorized dissemination of certain types of classified information, it has not seen fit to authorize the constructive trust remedy the Court creates today. Nor does either of the contracts Snepp signed with the Agency provide for any such remedy in the event of a breach. The Court's per curiam opinion seems to suggest that its result is supported by a blend of the law of trusts and the law of contracts. But neither of these branches of the common law supports the imposition of a constructive trust under the circumstances of this case....

... Snepp did not breach his duty to protect confidential information. Rather, he breached a contractual duty, imposed in aid of the basic duty to maintain confidentiality, to obtain prepublication clearance. In order to justify the imposition of a constructive trust, the majority attempts to equate this contractual duty with Snepp's duty not to disclose, labeling them both as "fiduciary." I find nothing in the common law to support such an approach.

Employment agreements often contain covenants designed to ensure in various ways that an employee fully complies with his duty not to disclose or misuse confidential information. One of the most common is a covenant not to compete. Contrary to the majority's approach in this case, the courts have not construed such covenants broadly simply because they support a basic fiduciary duty; nor have they granted sweeping remedies to enforce them. On the contrary, because such covenants are agreements in restraint of an individual's freedom of trade, they are enforceable only if they can survive scrutiny under the "rule of reason." That rule, originally laid down in the seminal case of Mitchel v. Reynolds, 1 P. Wms. 181, 24 Eng. Rep. 347 (1711), requires that the covenant be reasonably necessary to protect a legitimate interest of the employer (such as an interest in confidentiality), that the employer's interest not be outweighed by the public interest, and that the covenant not be of any longer duration or wider geographical scope than necessary to protect the employer's interest.

The Court has not persuaded me that a rule of reason analysis should not be applied to Snepp's covenant.... Like an ordinary employer, the CIA has a vital interest in protecting certain types of information; at the same time, the CIA employee has a countervailing interest in preserving a wide range of work opportunities (including work as an author) and in protecting his First Amendment rights. The public interest lies in a proper accommodation that will preserve the intelligence mission of the Agency while not abridging the free flow of unclassified information. When the Government seeks to enforce a harsh restriction on the employee's freedom, despite its admission that the interest the agreement was designed to protect — the confidentiality of classified information — has not been compromised, an equity court might well be persuaded that the case is not one in which the covenant should be enforced.

... If an employee has used his employer's confidential information for his own personal profit, a constructive trust ... is obviously an appropriate remedy because the profits are the direct result of the breach. But Snepp admittedly did not use confidential information in his book; nor were the profits from his book in any sense a product of his failure to submit the book for prepublication review. For, even if Snepp had submitted the book to the Agency for prepublication review, the Government's censorship authority would surely have been limited to the excision of classified material. In this case, then, it would have been obliged to clear the book for publication in precisely the same form as it now stands.[5] Thus, Snepp has not gained any profits as a result of his breach; the Government, rather than Snepp, will be unjustly enriched if he is required to disgorge profits attributable entirely to his own legitimate activity.

...I do not believe... that the Agency has any authority to censor its employees' publication of unclassified information on the basis of its opinion that publication may be "detrimental to vital national interests" or otherwise "identified as harmful." The CIA never attempted to assert such power over Snepp in either of the contracts he signed; rather, the Agency itself limited its censorship power to preventing the disclosure of "classified" information. Moreover, even if such a wide-ranging prior restraint would be good national security policy, I would have great difficulty reconciling it with the demands of the First Amendment....

... [T]he Court seems unaware of the fact that its drastic new remedy has been fashioned to enforce a species of prior restraint on a citizen's right to criticize his government.[6] Inherent in this prior restraint is the risk that the reviewing agency will misuse its authority to delay the publication of a critical work or to persuade an author to modify the contents of his work beyond the demands of secrecy. The character of the covenant as a prior restraint on free speech surely imposes an especially heavy burden on the censor to justify the remedy it seeks. It would take more than the Court has written to persuade me that that burden has been met....

NOTES AND QUESTIONS

1. *Comparing the Cases.* Which case is a greater inroad on freedom of expression and freedom of the press, *Marchetti* or *Snepp*? How would you compare the two cases on the basis of the kinds of information protected? How would you compare the remedies?

2. *Restraining the Publishers?* Notwithstanding the discussion of Marchetti's constitutional freedom of expression, the court in his case determined that by

---

5. ...[D]espite its reference in footnote 3...to the Government's so-called compelling interest in protecting "the appearance of confidentiality"...and despite some ambiguity in the Court's reference to "detrimental" and "harmful" as opposed to "classified,"...I do not understand the Court to imply that the Government could obtain an injunction against the publication of unclassified information.

6. The mere fact that the Agency has the authority to review the text of a critical book in search of classified information before it is published is bound to have an inhibiting effect on the author's writing. Moreover, the right to delay publication until the review is completed is itself a form of prior restraint that would not be tolerated in other contexts. See, e.g., New York Times Co. v. United States, 403 U.S. 713; Nebraska Press Assn. v. Stuart, 427 U.S. 539. In view of the national interest in maintaining an effective intelligence service, I am not prepared to say that the restraint is necessarily intolerable in this context. I am, however, prepared to say that, certiorari having been granted, the issue surely should not be resolved in the absence of full briefing and argument.

A. Restraining Leaks by Contract

his confidential employment relationship and his secrecy agreement, Marchetti had effectively relinquished his First Amendment rights. Should the injunction against Marchetti have affected his publisher's press freedom? After the decision set out above, Marchetti and a former State Department employee named John Marks prepared a manuscript for a book, entitled *The C.I.A. and the Cult of Intelligence*, from which the CIA insisted on deleting a number of items. The same court barred publication of classified information that the authors obtained during their government employment, even though that information was already in the publisher's hands. Alfred A. Knopf, Inc. v. Colby, 509 F.2d 1362, 1370 (4th Cir. 1975). Could the profits of Snepp's publishers be applied to the trust declared in *Snepp*?

After the *Marchetti* and *Snepp* rulings, are publishers likely to shy away from national security exposés? Or will they instead pressure the author of such an exposé to make any cuts the government demands? Suppose a television producer wants to do a TV miniseries on some CIA intelligence failure or past covert operation, like the ill-fated invasion at the Bay of Pigs in Cuba. If the producer relies partly on a former CIA official for technical advice, would she have to submit the miniseries for prepublication review?

3. *Reviewing Prepublication Review.* In its decision in *Alfred A. Knopf, supra*, the Fourth Circuit panel claimed to back away from its earlier view that "executive decisions respecting the classifying of information are not subject to judicial review." 509 F.2d at 1367. Citing the 1974 amendments to FOIA, 5 U.S.C. §552(a)(4)(B), *supra* p. 991, it acknowledged that deletions could be sustained only if they were found to be both classified and classifiable. 509 F.2d at 1367. The court proceeded to rob this statement of its meaning, however, by indulging the general "presumption of regularity in the performance by a public official of his public duty." *Id.* at 1368. Thus, "the government was required to show no more than that each deletion item disclosed information which was required to be classified in any degree and which was contained in a document bearing a classification stamp." *Id.* Whether the classifier had ever focused on the relevant item's classifiability was considered irrelevant.

The court also found that previous but unofficial public disclosure of classified information would not bear on the efficacy of the censorship. The court reasoned that to allow Marchetti to use such material, as long as he originally had access to it when he was an agent, would enhance the credence of information that might otherwise have only the present force of conjecture or speculation. Thus, Marchetti could not republish material that everyone else might have. In response to this decision, Anthony Lewis noted that Marchetti became "the only person in the history of the United States who has been subjected to a licensing system like that of Tudor and Stuart England." *In the Censor's Grip*, N.Y. Times, Nov. 10, 1977, at A23.

4. *Should Motive Matter?* If the motive for revealing the activities of the CIA is personal gain, it is easy to see why the constructive trust remedy strikes some as apt. What if the individual expects no financial reward and simply believes it is in the public interest to divulge the information? That kind of motive dramatizes the constitutional clash that underlies all these cases — namely, the legitimate power of the government to protect the national security versus the interest of

the public in knowing what its government is doing. Is it ever appropriate to resolve that clash by the application of contract or agency principles? *Cf.* New York Times v. Sullivan, 376 U.S. 254 (1964), where the Court established the principle that libel law doctrine must yield to constitutional law standards where criticism of government officials is involved. Another way of looking at this same question is to ask whether the government can legitimately "purchase" the waiver of constitutional rights. Do you think the media, for example, would be bound by an agreement to submit their copy to military censors in exchange for access to a war zone? See *supra* pp. 1024-1029.

2. Nondisclosure Agreements and Lifetime Prepublication Review

The force of the CIA precedents was not lost on the Reagan administration. In 1983, President Reagan issued National Security Decision Directive 84 (NSDD 84), directing executive agencies that handle classified information to require all persons with access to it to sign nondisclosure agreements, and those with access to Sensitive Compartmented Information (SCI) to sign prepublication agreements as well. NSDD 84, *Safeguarding National Security Information, reprinted in Hearing Before the S. Comm. on Governmental Affairs*, 98th Cong., at 85-86 (1983). By 1987, 2.5 million current and former employees had signed nondisclosure agreements, and 453,000 (in addition to an undisclosed number of CIA and National Security Agency (NSA) employees) had signed prepublication review agreements. Excerpts of the original agreements follow.

Classified Information Nondisclosure Agreement (SF 189)[2]
Information Security Oversight Office

An Agreement Between _____ and the United States
(*Name—Printed or Typed*)

1. Intending to be legally bound, I hereby accept the obligations contained in this Agreement in consideration of my being granted access to classified information. As used [herein,] classified information is information that is either classified or classifiable under the standards of Executive Order 12356, or under any other Executive order or statute that prohibits the unauthorized disclosure of information in the interest of national security....

3. I have been advised ... that direct or indirect unauthorized disclosure, unauthorized retention, or negligent handling of classified information by me could cause irreparable injury to the United States or could be used to advantage by a foreign nation....

[2. SF 189 has been superseded by SF 312, which is substantially identical, except for the deletion of the reference to "classifiable" information from the definition of "classified" in paragraph 1.]

A. Restraining Leaks by Contract

4. I have been advised...that any breach of this Agreement may result in the termination of any security clearances I hold; removal from any position of special confidence and trust requiring such clearances; and the termination of my employment.... In addition, I have been advised...that any unauthorized disclosure of classified information by me may constitute a violation or violations of United States criminal laws....

5. I hereby assign to the United States Government all royalties, remunerations, and emoluments that have resulted, will result or may result from any disclosure, publication, or revelation not consistent with the terms of this Agreement.

6. I understand that the United States Government may seek any remedy available to it to enforce this Agreement including, but not limited to, application for a court order prohibiting disclosure of information in breach of this Agreement.

7. I understand that all information to which I may obtain access by signing this Agreement is now and will forever remain the property of the United States Government. I do not now, nor will I ever, possess any right, interest, title, or claim whatsoever to such information....

8. Unless and until I am released in writing by an authorized representative of the United States Government, I understand that all conditions and obligations imposed upon me by this Agreement apply during the time I am granted access to classified information, and at all times thereafter....

10. I have read this Agreement carefully and my questions, if any, have been answered to my satisfaction. I acknowledge that the briefing officer has made available to me Sections 641, 793, 794, 798 and 952 of Title 18, United States Code, Section 783(b) of Title 50, United States Code, the Intelligence Identities Protection Act of 1982, and Executive Order 12356, so that I may read them at this time, if I so choose.

11. I make this Agreement without mental reservation or purpose of evasion....

Sensitive Compartmented Information Nondisclosure Agreement (SF 4193)[3]
Information Security Oversight Office

4. In consideration of being granted access to [Sensitive Compartmented Information (SCI)]...I hereby agree to submit for security review...all information or materials, including works of fiction, which contain or purport to contain any [SCI] or description of activities that produce or relate to [SCI] or that I have reason to believe are derived from [SCI], that I contemplate disclosing to any person not authorized to have access to [SCI] or that I have prepared for public disclosure. I understand and agree that my obligation to submit such information and materials for review applies during the course of my access to [SCI] and at all times thereafter....

[3. SF 4193 was identical to SF 189, except for the two additional paragraphs set forth here. SF 4193 has since been replaced by SF 4414, which is similar.]

5. I understand that the purpose of the review described in paragraph 4 is to give the United States a reasonable opportunity to determine whether the information or materials submitted... sets forth any [SCI].... [T]he Department or Agency to which I have made a submission will act upon it, coordinating with the Intelligence Community when appropriate, and make a response to me within a reasonable time, not to exceed 30 working days from date of receipt.

NOTES AND QUESTIONS

1. *Authority for Agreements.* The CIA secrecy agreements upheld in *Marchetti* and *Snepp* were explicitly tied to "the CIA Director's statutory mandate to 'protec[t] intelligence sources and methods from unauthorized disclosure,' 50 U.S.C. §403(d)(3)." *Snepp*, 444 U.S. at 509 n.3. See *supra* p. 356. Can you identify the source of the President's authority to promulgate NSDD 84 to cover federal officials and employees other than CIA and NSA personnel?

May prepublication review be extended throughout the executive department? Are there any constitutional limits on that extension? May it be extended to civilian contract employees? To members of Congress and the judiciary?

What administrative control does or should the President have over people after they leave government? Should there be any time limit on the control? Not even Justice Holmes's acerbic remark that "Petitioner may have a constitutional right to talk politics, but he has no constitutional right to be a policeman," McAuliffe v. Mayor of New Bedford, 155 Mass. 216, 220, 29 N.E. 517 (1892), is as far-reaching as NSDD 84. At least the policeman could quit and then talk.

2. *Waiving First Amendment Rights.* One difference between censoring the press and censoring government employees is simply that the restraint in the latter case is based on knowing consent. Can First Amendment rights be waived just as, for example, an accused may waive a right to a jury trial?

Applying cost-benefit analysis to *Snepp*, one commentator concluded that since Snepp entered into his agreement without fraud or coercion, he had made a judgment that he was better off with the agreement than without it. "[One] value of a right... is that it can be sold and both parties to the bargain made better off." Frank H. Easterbrook, *Insider Trading, Secret Agents, Evidentiary Privileges, and the Production of Information,* 1981 Sup. Ct. Rev. 309, 347. Does *any* First Amendment right exist with respect to sensitive information that would not have been gained but for the employment? *See* Jonathan C. Medow, *The First Amendment and the Secrecy State: Snepp v. United States,* 130 U. Pa. L. Rev. 775, 811 (1982).

3. *Impacts on an Informed Electorate?* As a form of prior restraint, prepublication review seems constitutionally more dubious than the nondisclosure requirements. Yet is it not possible that the simple nondisclosure contract, covering millions of federal employees, might actually pose the more serious threat to public debate of government matters? The nondisclosure agreements are absolute, whereas the prepublication requirements contain some procedural safeguards. For example, Department of Justice guidelines require a substantive response to a review request within 30 working days, with priority

for material that the author wishes to publish on an expedited basis, such as speeches or newspaper articles. Administrative appeals must be processed within 15 working days. Authors who are dissatisfied with the administrative decision may seek judicial relief or, upon 30 days' notice, may seek an injunction against the government. 28 C.F.R. §17.18(i) (2005).

Of course, these procedural safeguards are only meaningful if the agency abides by them. After an employee of the Los Alamos National Laboratory, Danny Stillman, submitted his manuscript, *Inside China's Nuclear Weapons Program*, to the Defense Intelligence Agency for prepublication review, he waited 20 months for an answer. Finally, he sued to dislodge the manuscript, only to learn in discovery that almost a year earlier the DOD had already concluded, without telling him, that no excisions could correct the "problems" of the manuscript. *See* William J. Broad, *Author to Sue U.S. Over Book on China's Nuclear Advances*, N.Y. Times, June 18, 2001, at A6. Two weeks after suit was filed, the government released 85 percent of the manuscript.

4. *Timing the Release of Information.* Professor Powe noted that the prepublication review process, "beyond getting lots of speech within the net," shifted "the timing of speech . . . from the speaker to the censor." *Review of the President's NSDD 84 and the Proposed Department of Defense Directive on Polygraph Use: Hearing Before a Subcomm. of H. Comm. on Govt. Operations*, 98th Cong., at 132 (1983) (*Brooks Hearing*) (testimony of L.A. Scot Powe Jr.). He recalled that a 1983 Senate vote on application of the War Powers Resolution in Lebanon came just 31 days after the first two marines were killed in Beirut. An official who had relevant information to contribute to the Senate debate still might have been waiting for his 30-working-day clearance by the time the critical vote was taken. *Id.* at 141. In a similar vein, Bob Schieffer of CBS said that the timeliness of news could be severely affected: "[L]et's say you had a fast breaking news event and you wanted to get comment from some former government official . . . like . . . Kissinger. . . . [He] would have to ask you in advance what questions you intended to ask . . . so [he] could call [his] censor. . . ." *Id.* at 102.

5. *Scope of Prepublication Review.* Both Department of Justice and CIA prepublication review guidelines cover everything from newspaper columns and letters to the editor, to works of fiction. *See* 28 C.F.R. §17.18(f) (2005); 57 Fed. Reg. 54,564 ¶(e)(1) (Nov. 19, 1992) (proposed update of CIA Headquarters Reg. 6-2). The CIA helpfully exempts "material that is totally unrelated to intelligence or employment matters, such as cooking, gardening, or purely domestic political matters." 57 Fed. Reg. 54,564 ¶(f)(1). Both sets of guidelines also treat the special risk of inadvertent oral disclosures. Justice Department guidelines, for example, provide that

> [o]ral statements are also within the scope of a prepublication review requirement when based upon written materials, such as an outline of the statements to be made. There is no requirement to prepare written materials for review, however, unless there is reason to believe in advance that oral statements may contain Sensitive Compartmented Information [SCI] or other information required to be submitted for review under the terms of the nondisclosure agreement. Thus, a person may participate in an oral presentation where there is no opportunity for

prior presentation (e.g., news interview, panel discussion) without violating the provisions of this paragraph. [28 C.F.R. §17.18(g) (2005).]

See also 57 Fed. Reg. 54,564 ¶(g). A since-deleted Justice guideline allowed the expression of "personal views, opinions or judgments" without prior review, unless they contain or imply statements of facts that would themselves be subject to prepublication review. 28 C.F.R. §17.44(l) (1995).

6. *Statutory Restrictions on Nondisclosure Agreements.* SF 189 forbade employees from disclosing classified or "classifiable" information. What is "classifiable" information? How would a risk-averse federal employee interpret this term?

Read literally, the agreement prohibited disclosure not only to unauthorized persons outside the government, but disclosure also to Congress. Congress responded with an appropriations rider prohibiting the use of certain funds to enforce either SF 189 or SF 4193 insofar as they: (1) contained the term "classifiable," (2) concerned information other than that specifically marked as classified or known by the employee to be in the process of a classification determination, or (3) interfered in any way with the right of an employee to petition or communicate with Congress or the right of Congress "to obtain executive branch information in a secure manner" under its rules. Omnibus Continuing Resolution for Fiscal Year 1988, Pub. L. No. 100-202, §630, 101 Stat. 1329, 1329-432 (1987). Federal employees thereafter sued to enforce the rider and declare enforcement of the agreements unconstitutional. *See* National Federation of Federal Employees v. United States (*NFFE I*), 688 F. Supp. 671 (D.D.C. 1988), *vacated sub nom.* American Foreign Service Assn. v. Garfinkel, 490 U.S. 153 (1989). The government (or, more accurately, the executive branch) defended on the ground that the *rider* was unconstitutional.

Citing *Curtiss-Wright, supra* p. 60, the District Court found that the rider "impermissibly restricts the President's power to fulfill obligations imposed upon him by his express constitutional powers and the role of the Executive in foreign relations." 688 F. Supp. at 685. The court found it especially "troubling" that Congress intruded on the President by "a budgetary enactment."

> Section 630 is merely an appropriations measure by which no substantive rights or causes of action are created. By such a measure, Congress cannot accomplish that which by direct legislative action would be beyond its constitutional authority. Cf. United States v. Lovett, 328 U.S. 303, 316 (1946). [*Id.* at 683 n.16.]

Is *Lovett*, noted *supra* p. 124, apposite? Should the court have considered Nixon v. Administrator of General Services, 433 U.S. 425, noted *supra* p. 1016, and the balancing test that it sets forth? What exactly was the intrusion on the President's authority, and what was Congress's need and objective? *See* Peter Raven-Hansen & William C. Banks, *Pulling the Purse Strings of the Commander in Chief,* 80 Va. L. Rev. 833, 923-942 (1994); *Brooks Hearing, supra* p. 1063, at 237.

Professor Glennon called *NFFE I* "the only decision in American case law in which a court has invalidated an exercise of Congress' power over the purse as an unconstitutional encroachment on executive power," and he described the decision as "an ill considered exercise of judicial activism" that "disregards time honored doctrines of Anglo-American jurisprudence." H. Comm. on Govt.

A. Restraining Leaks by Contract

Operations, *Legislation Needed to Curb Secrecy Contracts*, H.R. Rep. No. 100-991, at 15 (1988). Was this strong language warranted? Consider Professor Glennon's argument from history:

> [The appropriations clause] was framed against the backdrop of 150 years of struggle between the King and Parliament for control over the purse, often centering on military matters.... [T]he Framers were well aware of the tradition of parliamentary power over the purse and its use to check unwanted "national security" activities.... Accordingly, the Framers chose, in the words of Jefferson, to transfer the war power "from the executive to the legislative body, from those who are to spend to those who are to pay." [*Congress and the Administration's Secrecy Pledges: Hearing Before a Subcomm. of H. Comm. on Govt. Operations,* 100th Cong., at 150-151 (1988).]

In light of your own studies, particularly Chapters 4 and 5, do you think the court's separation of powers holding is sustainable? *See generally* Louis Fisher, *Congressional-Executive Struggles Over Information: Secrecy Pledges,* 42 Admin. L. Rev. 89, 100-106 (1990).

On appeal, the Supreme Court found some of the issues in *NFFE I* moot and some inadequately explored by the lower court. The Court also admonished the District Court to exercise restraint in addressing the "separation of powers" question:

> In spite of the importance of the constitutional question whether §630 impermissibly intrudes upon the Executive's authority to regulate the disclosure of national security information — indeed partly because of it — we remand this case... without expressing an opinion on that issue....
>
> ... In doing so, we emphasize that the District Court should not pronounce upon the relative constitutional authority of Congress and the Executive Branch unless it finds it imperative to do so. Particularly where, as here, a case implicates the fundamental relationship between the Branches, courts should be extremely careful not to issue unnecessary constitutional rulings. On remand, the District Court should decide first whether the controversy is sufficiently live and concrete to be adjudicated and whether it is an appropriate case for equitable relief, and then decide whether the statute and forms are susceptible of a reconciling interpretation; if they are not, the court may turn to the constitutional question.... [490 U.S. at 158, 161.]

7. *First Amendment Challenges to SF 4193.* Do you think that the admonition to defer consideration of constitutional questions applies equally to the First Amendment challenges raised in *NFFE I*? In a companion case, National Federation of Federal Employees v. United States (*NFFE II*), 695 F. Supp. 1196 (D.D.C. 1988), the district court upheld the prepublication provisions of the SCI agreements but declared that the reference to "classifiable information" in all the original nondisclosure agreements was unconstitutionally vague and overbroad.

Judge Gasch's conclusion in *NFFE II* that the prepublication agreements were constitutional rested squarely on *Snepp*. Could *Snepp* be distinguished on the ground that the prepublication restriction was limited to CIA employees? Judge Gasch rejected the distinction on the basis that the "gravity of the government's interest in assuring the secrecy of national security information" was the same in both cases. 695 F. Supp. at 1201. Even as the judge said this, however, he quoted from that portion of the *Snepp* opinion that emphasized the "CIA Director's statutory mandate to 'protec[t] intelligence sources and methods from unauthorized disclosure.'" *Id.* Do you think the absence of a similar, broad statutory mandate should have given the court pause in *NFFE II?*

Wasn't it contradictory for the court to hold in *NFFE I* that Congress exceeded its power when it refused to fund agreements containing the term "classifiable" and then rule in *NFEE II* that the use of that term in the agreements was unconstitutional? One reason Congress gave for its decision to withhold funding was that restrictions on information not marked classified were unconstitutionally vague. Does a court owe deference to the legislature's constitutional doubts?

The *NFFE II* court did finally embrace the government's narrowing construction of "classifiable," according to which employees could be held liable for disclosure if "they have reason to believe that unmarked information is classified or should be classified and is in the process of becoming so." 695 F. Supp. at 1203-1204. Do you consider that construction of "classifiable" sufficiently precise to meet First Amendment concerns of chilling effect?

B. RESTRAINING LEAKS BY ESPIONAGE PROSECUTIONS

Espionage and Censorship
18 U.S.C. §§793-798 (2000)

§793. GATHERING, TRANSMITTING, OR LOSING DEFENSE INFORMATION

(a) Whoever, for the purpose of obtaining information respecting the national defense with intent or reason to believe that the information is to be used to the injury of the United States, or to the advantage of any foreign nation, goes upon, enters, flies over, or otherwise obtains information concerning [any defense facility or property]; or

(b) Whoever, for the purpose aforesaid, and with like intent or reason to believe, copies, takes, makes, or obtains, or attempts to copy, take, make, or obtain, any sketch, photograph, photographic negative, blueprint, plan, map, model, instrument, appliance, document, writing, or note of anything connected with the national defense; or

(c) Whoever, for the purpose aforesaid, receives or obtains or agrees or attempts to receive or obtain from any person, or from any source whatever, any document [or tangible thing, such as a code book] connected with the national defense, knowing or having reason to believe, at the time he receives or obtains, or agrees or attempts to receive or obtain it, that it has been or will be obtained, taken, made, or disposed of by any person contrary to the provisions of this chapter; or

B. Restraining Leaks by Espionage Prosecutions

(d) Whoever, lawfully having possession of, access to, control over, or being entrusted with any document [or tangible thing] or information relating to the national defense which information the possessor has reason to believe could be used to the injury of the United States or to the advantage of any foreign nation, willfully communicates, delivers, transmits or causes to be communicated, delivered, or transmitted or attempts to communicate, deliver, transmit or cause to be communicated, delivered or transmitted the same to any person not entitled to receive it, or willfully retains the same and fails to deliver it on demand to the officer or employee of the United States entitled to receive it; . . .

(e) [Substantially identical to §793(d), except that it provides punishment for one having "unauthorized" possession of sensitive materials.]

(f) [Punishes the loss of such materials through gross negligence or the failure to report their loss, theft, or destruction.]

Shall be fined under this title or imprisoned not more than ten years, or both. . . .

§794. GATHERING OR DELIVERING DEFENSE INFORMATION TO AID FOREIGN GOVERNMENT

(a) Whoever, with intent or reason to believe that it is to be used to the injury of the United States or to the advantage of a foreign nation, communicates, delivers, or transmits, or attempts to communicate, deliver, or transmit, to any foreign government, or to any faction or party or military or naval force within a foreign country . . . or to any representative, officer, agent, employee, subject, or citizen thereof, either directly or indirectly, any document, writing, code book, signal book, sketch, photograph, photographic negative, blueprint, plan, map, model, note, instrument, appliance, or information relating to the national defense, shall be punished. . . .

[Sections 795-797 criminalize the disclosure of several specific categories of national security information, including photographs or sketches of defense installations.]

§798. DISCLOSURE OF CLASSIFIED INFORMATION

(a) Whoever knowingly and willfully communicates, furnishes, transmits, or otherwise makes available to an unauthorized person, or publishes, or uses in any manner prejudicial to the safety or interest of the United States or for the benefit of any foreign government to the detriment of the United States any classified information—

(1) concerning the nature, preparation, or use of any code, cipher, or cryptographic system of the United States or any foreign government; or

(2) concerning the design, construction, use, maintenance, or repair of any device, apparatus, or appliance used or prepared or planned for use by the United States or any foreign government for cryptographic or communication intelligence purposes; or

(3) concerning the communication intelligence activities of the United States or any foreign government; or

(4) obtained by the processes of communication intelligence from the communications of any foreign government, knowing the same to have been obtained by such processes —

shall be fined under this title or imprisoned....

(b) As used in subsection (a) of this section — ...

The term "communication intelligence" means all procedures and methods used in the interception of communications and the obtaining of information from such communications by other than the intended recipients;...

These laws seem clearly to apply to classical spies — persons acting on behalf of foreign governments to obtain national security secrets for the purpose of harming the United States. Do they also apply to officials who leak or sell national security information to the media? In the alternative, should we treat leaks as theft of government property? Here is another statute used in the prosecution of leaks.

Embezzlement and Theft
18 U.S.C.A. §§641-669 (West 2000 & Supp. 2006)

§641. PUBLIC MONEY, PROPERTY OR RECORDS

Whoever embezzles, steals, purloins, or knowingly converts to his use or the use of another, or without authority, sells, conveys or disposes of any record, voucher, money, or thing of value of the United States or of any department or agency thereof...; or

Whoever receives, conceals, or retains the same with intent to convert it to his use or gain, knowing it to have been embezzled, stolen, purloined or converted — shall be fined under this title or imprisoned....

United States v. Morison
United States District Court, District of Maryland, 1985
604 F. Supp. 655, *appeal dismissed*, 774 F.2d 1156 (4th Cir. 1985)

[Samuel Loring Morison was charged with violation of two provisions of the Espionage Act, 18 U.S.C. §793(d) and (e) (2000), and of 18 U.S.C. §641 (2000) for theft or conversion of government property. Morison was employed as an analyst with "Top Secret-Sensitive Compartmented Information" security clearance at the Naval Intelligence Support Center (NISC). With the Navy's knowledge, he also worked on a free-lance basis for Jane's Defence Weekly (Jane's), a British publication. Count I of the indictment charged Morison with willfully transmitting classified satellite photographs of a Soviet nuclear-powered carrier under construction to Jane's, one "not entitled to receive them," in violation of

B. Restraining Leaks by Espionage Prosecutions

§793(d). Count II charged Morison with the theft or conversion of these same photographs in violation of §641. The photographs were stamped "Secret" and contained a warning notice, "Intelligence Sources or Methods Involved," imprinted on their borders.

Morison was also found in possession of an NISC analysis of an explosion that had taken place at Severomorsk, a Soviet naval base. The analysis was based on classified information, and concerned the nature and extent of damage to the base. When apprehended, Morison was apparently preparing to send this information to his contact at Jane's. Count III charged Morison with unauthorized possession of secret intelligence reports and willfully retaining them without delivering them to an officer entitled to receive them, in violation of §793(e). Count IV charged Morison with theft and disposal or conversion of government property, namely the "Weekly Wires" containing the intelligence analysis of the Severomorsk incident, in violation of §641. Morison moved to dismiss the indictment on all four counts.]

YOUNG, J. . . . Morison's first attack on Sections 793(d) and (e) is that the term "relating to the national defense" is impermissibly vague. . . . This argument relies heavily on the Supreme Court's reasoning in Gorin v. United States, 312 U.S. 19 (1941), which arose under the predecessor statute to §793. In that case, the Court held there was no uncertainty in a statute prohibiting the delivery of information relating to the national defense where the statute contained obvious "delimiting words" requiring intent or reason to believe that the information is to be used to the injury of the United States. Morison argues that the Court in *Gorin* declined to hold the statute void for vagueness only because of the presence of the intent requirement, and that because §§793(d) and (e) do not contain such an intent requirement, the statutory provisions are void for vagueness.

The government has responded to this assertion by noting that the statute does contain an intent requirement, although not the same requirement that was contained in the *Gorin* statute. Sections 793(d) and (e) require that the acts be done "wilfully"; if the transmitted item is "information" "which information the possessor had reason to believe could be used to the injury of the United States." That requirement is not present for the delivery or retention of photographs or documents. The government contends that if a defendant, "such as Morison, wilfully transmits photographs relating to the national defense to someone who is known by the defendant not to be entitled to receive it, the defendant has violated §793(d) no matter how laudable his motives." According to the plain language of the statute, the government's interpretation is correct.

. . . [Because] the "delimiting" intent to injure the United States is not present in this statute . . . defendant argues that it is therefore impermissibly vague. . . . [T]he Fourth Circuit has addressed this issue and found that a similar statute was not unconstitutionally vague. In United States v. Dedeyan, 584 F.2d 36 (4th Cir. 1978), the Fourth Circuit construed 18 U.S.C. §793(f), which provides that anyone with authorized possession of documents or writing relating to the national defense, having knowledge that the same had been illegally removed or abstracted and failed to report it, is guilty of a violation of the statute. The statute does not require any intent to injure the United States or any "guilty knowledge" that the document or writing was removed or abstracted by an enemy of the United States. Defendant in that case was charged with knowing that his cousin, later found to be a Russian agent, had photographed classified information, and with failing to report it. On appeal, the defendant charged that the term "relating to the national defense" was impermissibly vague unless a scienter requirement was added. The Court found that the scienter requirement in the statute was sufficient: knowledge of the document's illegal abstraction. The Court concluded, "[t]he defendant's claim of vagueness is directed at the phrase 'relating to the national defense' in the statute. We do not find this phrase vague in the constitutional sense." That holding applies with equal force in this case, where the only scienter required is the wilful transmission or delivery to one not entitled to receive it. As the District Court noted in *Dedeyan*, "[c]ertainly injury to the United States could be inferred from conduct of the sort charged," whether that conduct involves photographing documents by one foreign agent or release of national defense information to the press and public, where many foreign agents and governments can have access to the information.

... [D]efendant argues that the holding in *Dedeyan* should not be controlling because *Dedeyan* involved the classic espionage situation.... Here, the situation is slightly different because it does not involve a foreign agent or the classic spy scenario. Rather, the defendant is accused of releasing classified information to the press, thus exposing that classified information to every foreign agent and government, hostile or not, in the world.

Defendant cites an impressive wealth of legislative history suggesting that §793 was only meant to apply in the classic espionage setting....

While it is, of course, impossible to determine exactly what Congress meant when it passed the statute, it is more likely that the type of activity that defendant allegedly engaged in was meant to be covered. Congress could very easily have meant, when it used the word "spy" [in the legislative history], one who used his position and classified security clearance to obtain information to which he would not otherwise be entitled and release it to the world.

If Congress had intended this situation to apply only to the classic espionage situation, where the information is leaked to an agent of a foreign and presumably hostile government, then it could have said so by using the words "transmit . . . to an agent of a foreign government." In 18 U.S.C. §794, Congress did precisely that, proscribing the gathering or delivering of national defense information to a foreign government or to an agent, employee, subject or citizen thereof. Section 793, on the other hand, proscribes disclosure of national defense information to those "not entitled to receive it."

... The fear in releasing this type of information is that it gives other nations information concerning the intelligence gathering capabilities of the United States. That fear is realized whether the information is released to the world at large or whether it is released only to specific spies.

Defendant claims that by enforcing this statute in the present case involving the release of information to the press, this Court would be writing a new law, a task, it is argued, better left to the legislature. On the contrary, to read into the statute the requirement that it apply only in "classic espionage" cases where the disclosure is to an agent of a foreign government would be to ignore the plain language of the law as presently written....

B. Restraining Leaks by Espionage Prosecutions

Defendant also contends that Sections 793(d) and (e) are unconstitutionally overbroad because they proscribe disclosure and retention of documents relating to the national defense "which are perfectly harmless and clearly protected by the First Amendment as well as those which might lawfully be regulated because of a compelling governmental interest in secrecy." This argument has been considered and rejected by the Fourth Circuit. When faced with this issue in *Dedeyan*, the Court attempted to cure any possible overbreadth by using a limiting jury instruction. The definition of "relating to the national defense" which, following *Dedeyan*, would be used in the Fourth Circuit would cure any possible defect of overbreadth.... Such an instruction would alleviate the possibility that any harmless material would be covered by the statute, as defendant has claimed.

Defendant next argues that the phrase "not entitled to receive" is also unconstitutionally vague, in that it fails to inform a citizen of whether his conduct is prohibited.... The government has responded by pointing out that under no circumstances is that statute unconstitutionally vague when applied to this defendant, who clearly knew by virtue of his security clearance and his signing of an agreement that classified information and documents were not to be transmitted to outsiders.... The phrase "not entitled to receive" may therefore be given content by reference to the classification system....

Defendant argues that the classification system should not be used to give content to the phrase "not entitled to receive" because Congress has on several occasions declined to enforce the classification system with criminal sanctions, and the court in giving the phrase that construction would do what Congress had declined to do. On the contrary, the President has established a system of classification and this Court may enforce it. Congress has recognized the classification system and given its support to the determination by Executive Order of who is authorized to possess and who is not authorized to possess classified information, i.e., in the Freedom of Information Act, the Internal Security Act of 1950, and in 50 U.S.C. §783(b), which makes criminal the communication of classified information to certain persons unless authorized by the President or relevant officials.... Since these executive orders are issued in fulfillment of the President's Constitutional responsibilities, they have the force and effect of law....

... [T]he defendant has argued that the Indictment should be dismissed because the government has no intention of proving the requisite level of culpability. This is evident, argues the defendant, from the government's contention that it must only show that the disclosure or retention was done "wilfully," which the government defines as "an intentional violation of a known legal duty." Morison argues that the word "wilfully" connotes some evil purpose...

... He urges this Court to adopt a construction of the word wilfully used in Hartzel v. United States, 322 U.S. 680, 686 (1944). In that case, the court, noting that the statute was a highly penal one restricting freedom of expression, held that the word "wilful" must be taken to mean "deliberately and with a specific purpose to do the acts proscribed by Congress." In another sentence, the Court referred to this "evil purpose"; however, in the rest of the opinion the court refers only to the specific intent to do the evil prohibited by the statute, i.e., causing or attempting to cause insubordination, disloyalty, or mutiny. That case did not require "evil purpose" as the defendant reads it, but only required that the prohibited acts be done deliberately and with a specific purpose to do that which was prohibited....

Defendant has also argued that even if §641 can be applied to the unauthorized taking of government information in this case, it should not be applied where the taking involves public disclosure in circumstances which implicate First Amendment issues. Defendant argues again that in all cases in which §641 has been applied to the theft of information, the information was being acquired for private, covert use in illegal enterprises. He argues that... the government may not use a general law not specifically aimed at expressive conduct to regulate such conduct. Defendant argues that using §641 to regulate the disclosure of government information gives executive branch officials unbridled discretion to enforce the statute and thereby control the flow of government information to the public.... Thus, government officials would be free to enforce their own information control policy, and liability may turn on nothing more than the fact that the disclosure embarrasses them or subjects them to public criticism.

These arguments have little to do with this case. It is most doubtful that Morison was asserting a First Amendment right in selling photographs and documents to Jane's. Where the phrase "without authority" is given content by reference to the classification system, then the disclosures that could be punished under §641 would be those where the government has asserted an interest in secrecy by classifying a document or information "secret." It is clear that having decided that disclosures of classified information may be prosecuted under §641, the defendant's motive in disclosing classified information is irrelevant....

NOTES AND QUESTIONS

1. *Threat to the Media?* Morison was tried and found guilty on all four counts, and the conviction was affirmed on appeal. United States v. Morison, 844 F.2d 1057 (4th Cir.), *cert. denied*, 488 U.S. 908 (1988). *Morison* marked the first successful prosecution under the Espionage Act of a person not accused of being a spy. What do you think the effect of this development has been on government employees who would use classified documents to publicize government misbehavior or mismanagement, or on the editors of the New York Times if they receive a leaked classified document?

Unauthorized leaks have in fact continued, and leakers have occasionally been identified, fired, and even criminally prosecuted. The government has sought to learn their identities or at least to deter additional leaks by bringing journalists before grand juries under threat of contempt to force the revelation of sources. *See* Branzburg v. Hayes, 408 U.S. 665 (1972). In one recent case, described *infra* p. 1093, a reporter was jailed for 85 days for refusing to cooperate. *See* Don Van Natta Jr., Adam Liptak & Clifford J. Levy, *The Miller Case: A Notebook, a Cause, a Jail Cell and a Deal*, N.Y. Times, Oct. 16, 2005, §1, at 1.

In United States v. New York Times, 328 F. Supp. 324, 328-329 (S.D.N.Y. 1971), federal District Judge Gurfein held that §793(e) did not cover "publication." See *infra* p. 1089. The *Morison* case nevertheless worried the press sufficiently to prompt almost all the major press organs in the country to join in an

B. Restraining Leaks by Espionage Prosecutions

amici curiae (friends of court) appeal brief on behalf of Morison (hereinafter Amici Brief). The press underlined its interest in the case in the heading of its main argument: "The Espionage Statute Does Not Prohibit The Dissemination of Information *To* or *By* the Press." Amici Brief, *supra,* at 11 (emphasis added).

The media apparently were right to be concerned. Disclosure by the New York Times and other media of secret (and possibly illegal) domestic surveillance programs in 2005 and 2006 have led to calls for direct criminal prosecution of the paper and its staff. See *infra* p. 1079.

2. *The "Plain Meaning" of "National Defense."* The *Morison* court appears to apply a "plain meaning" approach to §793(d) and (e). The court saw no particular ambiguity in the phrases "relating to the national defense" or "persons entitled to receive." Plain meaning is often in the eye of the beholder, however. In United States v. Heine, 151 F.2d 813, 815 (2d Cir. 1945), Judge Learned Hand, referring to the term "national defense" in an earlier version of the Espionage Act, wrote, "It seems plain that the section cannot cover information about all those activities which become tributary to 'the national defense' in time of war; for in modern war there are none which do not."

Do you understand and agree with the position taken in the *Gorin* precedent, relied on by Judge Young, that the requirement of scienter somehow instilled the term "national defense" with increased certainty of meaning? Do the scienter provisions of 18 U.S.C. §793(a) and (b), which make it a crime to communicate to a foreign agent information "respecting the national defense with intent, or reason to believe that the information is to be used to the injury of the United States, or to the advantage of any foreign nation," narrow the operative meaning of "national defense"?

Suppose a U.S. government employee of Pakistani background learns through secret intelligence sources, to which he has gained access in his work, that India is contemplating a preemptive strike against a Pakistan nuclear facility. With the motive of warning Pakistan, he publishes a letter in the Karachi Times disclosing the information. Would he be guilty of violating §793(d)? Would your answer be the same if he had secretly sent the information to his cousin in the Pakistanti embassy in Washington? This hypothetical is loosely based on an alleged "leak." *See Report of the Congressional Committees Investigating the Iran-Contra Affair,* H.R. Rep. No. 100-433, S. Rep. No. 100-216, at 577 (1987) (*Minority Report*).

3. *The Jury's Role.* While denying that the term "national defense" was fatally vague, the *Morison* trial court did give a narrowing instruction to the jury, to wit: To establish that the photographs relate to the national defense, the government must prove: (1) that the "disclosure...would be potentially damaging to the United States or might be useful to an enemy..." and (2) that they "have not been made public and are not available to the general public." 844 F.2d at 1071-1072. On appeal, Circuit Judge James Dickson Phillips, concurring specially, wrote, "Jury instructions on a case-by-case basis are a slender reed upon which to rely for constitutional application of these critical statutes;...the instructions we find necessary here...press to the limit the judiciary's right...to narrow, without 'reconstructing,' statutes whose constitutionality is drawn in

question." *Id.* at 1086. Do you think the trial court pressed or exceeded the limit? Compare the instruction to the text of §793(d) and (e) and to their sister provisions, §793(a) and (b), and §794, *supra* pp. 1066-1067.

A closely related question is what value the jury should have placed on the fact that the material was clearly classified secret and known by the defendant to be so. Should the fact of classification be dispositive of whether information relates to the national defense? Or should it be treated only as evidence of defense-relatedness? *See Gorin,* 312 U.S. at 33. Can one reasonably expect a jury to view classification in a dispassionate fashion? For a careful analysis of these questions, *see* Harold Edgar & Benno L. Schmidt Jr., *The Espionage Statutes and Publication of Defense Information,* 73 Colum. L. Rev. 929, 980-985 (1973). They conclude that the "best way to treat the problem . . . is to permit classification to be used for purposes of showing Government intent to maintain secrecy, but to instruct specially that the Government can and does maintain secrecy as to a substantial number of matters which have no 'relation to national defense' . . . ." *Id.* at 985.

4. *Was It a Crime to Violate Classification Restrictions?* The District Court in *Morison* relied on the classification system to counter Morison's argument that the phrase "not entitled to receive" was vague and overbroad when applied to a case not involving a "subversive purpose." The court concluded that "authorization to possess documents and entitlement to receive them may be determined by reference to the classification system. . . ." 604 F. Supp. at 661. The appellate court agreed: "Any omission in the statute is clarified and supplied by the government's classification system. . . ." 844 F.2d at 1074.

These conclusions directly contradicted the two major themes of the defense: (1) that Congress had consistently refused to provide criminal sanctions for general violations of the classification restrictions, and (2) that Congress never intended under the Espionage Act to reach leaks to the press. Because the words of §793(d) and (e) do not foreclose application of the classification system, and since they "declare no exemption in favor of one who leaks to the press," 844 F.2d at 1063, Morison had to base his argument on the following comparative statutory analysis and legislative history:

(a) The Espionage Act was passed in the midst of war fever in 1917. Several bills that would have given the President full power to restrict the divulgence of government secrets were proposed that year. Edgar & Schmidt, *supra,* at 946. A provision enabling the President to issue and enforce regulations on publication of defense information received particularly vigorous debate. *Id. See also* James A. Goldston *et al.,* Comment, *A Nation Less Secure: Diminished Public Access to Information,* 21 Harv. C.R.-C.L. L. Rev. 409, 422 n.70 (1986). Despite President Wilson's support, all of the bills were rejected. Amici Brief, *supra,* at 13-19. The Court of Appeals responded that this "history" was not specifically relevant to §793. 844 F.2d at 1066 n.15. For an extended discussion of the legislative history, *see* Edgar & Schmidt, *supra,* at 939-942, 946-966, 969-974, 998-1031. *See also* David M. Rabban, *The Emergence of Modern First Amendment Doctrine,* 50 U. Chi. L. Rev. 1205, 1217-1227 (1983).

(b) A 1950 amendment to §793 provided that "nothing in this Act shall be construed . . . to limit or infringe upon freedom of the press." 64 Stat. 987 (1950). *See* Edgar & Schmidt, *supra,* at 1026-1028.

B. Restraining Leaks by Espionage Prosecutions

(c) On the occasions when Congress did adopt prohibitions against disclosure of classified information, it always opted for narrow restrictions. For example, a proposed section of 18 U.S.C. §798 would have prohibited the disclosure of any classified information. *See* S. 805, 79th Cong., 91 Cong. Rec. 3196 (1945). As finally adopted, the statute proscribes only the knowing and willful disclosure of any classified information regarding "communication intelligence"—a relatively small category of classified matter. *Enhancing Security: Report of the House Judiciary Comm.*, H.R. Rep. No. 81-1895, at 2 (1950). *See* Goldston *et al.*, *supra*, at 423 n.76. Implicit in the passage of such special purpose legislation is the assumption that the general provisions of §793 did not cover such disclosures. The same point can be made with respect to the subsequent passage of the Atomic Energy Act 42 U.S.C.A §§2011-2297g-4 (West 2003 & Supp. 2006), *infra* p. 1108, and the Intelligence Identities Protection Act, 50 U.S.C. §§421-426 (2000 & Supp. III 2003), *infra* p. 1080. *See also* Edgar & Schmidt, *supra*, at 1020, 1066, 1072.

One provision of the law does prohibit the disclosure of *any* classified material, whether or not it is "related to the national defense," *id.* at 1074, and whether or not classification is substantively proper. *See* Scarbeck v. United States, 317 F.2d 546, 558 (D.C. Cir.), *cert. denied*, 374 U.S. 856 (1963). That provision is 50 U.S.C. §783(a) (2000), which in pertinent part states:

> It shall be unlawful for any...employee of the United States...to communicate in any manner or by any means, to any other person whom such...employee knows or has reason to believe to be an agent...of any foreign government...any information of a kind which shall have been classified by the President [or by the President's delegates] as affecting the security of the United States, knowing or having reason to know that such information has been so classified...

This statute was passed along with §793(d) and (e) as part of the Internal Security Act of 1950, 64 Stat. 991 (1950). *See* Edgar & Schmidt, *supra*, at 1073-1074.

(d) The fact that succeeding administrations sought legislation protecting specific categories of classified information is testimony to the general understanding that neither §793 nor any other act generally prohibited the disclosure of classified information. In 1957 a commission on government security proposed to make it a crime "for any person willfully to disclose without proper authorization, for any purpose whatever, information classified 'secret' or 'top secret,' knowing...such information to have been so classified." *Report of Commission on Government Security* 619-620 (1957). *See also* Amici Brief, *supra*, at 23; *National Security Secrets and the Administration of Justice: Report of the S. Select Comm. on Intelligence*, 95th Cong., at 18 (1978) (summarizing past legislative initiatives). The proposal was "abandoned by the Executive as politically untenable." Edgar & Schmidt, *supra*, at 1056. *See also Espionage Laws and Leaks: Hearings Before the Subcomm. on Legislation of the H. Permanent Select Comm. on Intelligence*, 96th Cong., at 22 (1979).

Do you find any of this history sufficient to overcome the court's reliance on the text of the statutes?

Following news reports of secret government surveillance programs concerning overseas telecommunications and banking transactions in 2005 and 2006, see *infra* p. 1091 and *supra* p. 548, there were calls for criminal prosecution both of the leakers and of the media that published the information. See *infra* p. 1079. Reviewing this history as well as the language of the relevant statutes, do you think the leakers might be found guilty of violating §793? Could they be guilty of violating §798, *supra* p. 1067? See *infra* p. 1091. Possible criminal prosecution of the media is considered *infra* p. 1092.

5. *Is Leaking Theft?* Do you agree that 18 U.S.C. §641, *supra* p. 1068, a statute that was adopted to make remedies for the common law crimes of larceny, embezzlement, and conversion applicable to the theft of government property, Morissette v. United States, 342 U.S. 246, 266 n.28 (1952), is equally applicable to the unauthorized dissemination of information? The *Morison* court apparently thought so, holding that "information" fit within the meaning of the statutory term "a thing of value," which value could be measured by the payment Morison received, citing, for example, United States v. Girard, 601 F.2d 69 (2d Cir.), *cert. denied*, 444 U.S. 871 (1979) ("theft" of confidential information from a Drug Enforcement Agency computer terminal). *See also* United States v. Collins, 56 F.3d 1416, 1420 (D.C. Cir. 1995) ("[E]very circuit, except one ... has held that intangible property falls within the purview of section 641."). But the absence of the language "intent to injure the United States" or some similar culpability standard led another federal judge to question whether §641 could be constitutionally applied to the unauthorized release of classified information. *See* United States v. Truong Dinh Hung, 629 F.2d 908, 924-925 (4th Cir. 1980), *cert. denied*, 454 U.S. 1144 (1982) (dissenting opinion of Judge Winter; the case was decided on other grounds). *See also* United States v. Tobias, 836 F.2d 449, 451 (9th Cir. 1988) (stating that §641 does not apply to intangible goods like classified information).

The theft statute was used to prosecute Daniel Ellsberg for his disclosure of the Pentagon Papers to the press. *See infra* p. 1082. Ironically, the prosecution was dismissed when it was learned during the Watergate investigation that the government had itself tried to steal files from Ellsberg's psychiatrist's office in an effort to discredit Ellsberg. *See* United States v. Russo, No. 9373-(WMB)-CD (filed Dec. 29, 1971), *dismissed* (C.D. Cal. May 11, 1973). *See* Morton H. Halperin & Daniel Hoffman, *Freedom vs. National Security* 242-248 (1977); Melville B. Nimmer, *National Security Secrets vs. Free Speech: The Issues Left Undecided in the Ellsberg Case*, 26 Stan. L. Rev. 311 (1974).

6. *Does Motive Matter?* Are motives really irrelevant? Morison claimed he had disclosed the information in order to reveal the progress of a Soviet naval buildup. The government charged that his motives were more selfish — money and ambition. 844 F.2d at 1062. Does that explain the government's decision to prosecute?

The government certainly knew that the 1984 edition of *Soviet Military Power*, a Pentagon publication, had openly published detailed drawings of the photographed carrier and the shipyard. It also knew that a CIA employee had sold the Soviets a technical manual detailing the satellite surveillance system (KH-11) six years earlier. *See* United States v. Kampiles, 609 F.2d 1233 (7th Cir. 1979). Moreover, the government did not seriously attempt to refute the testimony of a defense witness, a former CIA official familiar with the KH-11 system, that photographic reproductions in Jane's were so degraded in quality from the originals that they gave no clues as to the capabilities of the system that produced them. *See* Roland S. Inlow, *An Appraisal of the Morison Espionage Trial*, 11 First Principles 1, 5 (May 1986). In light of all this, why do you think the government decided to prosecute Morison? Does the subject of the last-mentioned testimony suggest a reason why the government may be concerned with the disclosure of classified information even when disclosure of the information, standing alone, apparently would not jeopardize national security?

7. *Leak Prosecutions — Inherently Selective?* Morison claimed that he was the victim of selective prosecution. The key witness for the defense later noted, "One of the most telling bits of testimony during the trial was by Morison's superior... when he acknowledged that he began an investigation... only after first checking with the Chief of Naval Intelligence... that no senior Department of Defense official had released the photographs." *Id.* at 5. As a prosecutor, how would you decide when to prosecute leaks like those involved in *Morison*? Should the official level of the suspected leakers affect your decision? Are there some officials beyond your reach or the reach of the law?

Leaks can undermine the decision-making process:

> [T]he lesson [Presidents] learn in order to avoid leaks is to turn inward: involve the minimum number of advisors... and compartmentalize so that technicians will not know how the pieces are going to be fitted together. The problem... as Jody Powell pointed out, is that "the damage done by leaks must be carefully balanced against the damage done by excluding people who can contribute to the decision-making process." [Earnest L. Abel, *Leaking: Who Does It? Who Benefits? At What Cost?* 65 (1987), *quoting from* Stephen Hess, *The Government/Press Connection* 93-94 (1984).]

The most basic argument against leaks, of course, is that they sometimes really do cause harm to the national security. In Eric E. Ballou & Kyle E. McSlarrow, Note, *Plugging the Leak: The Case for a Legislative Resolution of the Conflict Between the Demands of Secrecy and the Need for an Open Government*, 71 Va. L. Rev. 801 (1985), the authors describe a leak that might have deprived the government of "the biggest single intelligence coup in history." The leak concerned a secret CIA operation, code named "Project Jennifer," to salvage a sunken Soviet submarine that supposedly carried nuclear missiles, cryptographic information, and code-books. The project was abandoned when the Soviet Union was alerted by the disclosure of the project in the Los Angeles Times. *Id.* at 801-802.

NOTE ON A PROPOSAL TO CRIMINALIZE ALL UNAUTHORIZED LEAKS

There have been repeated attempts to criminalize all unauthorized leaks of any kind of classified information, as we have seen. Congress took a step in that direction in 1994 when it enacted a measure that provides punishment for "an officer, employee, contractor, or consultant of the United States... [who, entitled to possess] documents or materials containing classified information of the

United States, knowingly removes such documents or materials without authority and with the intent to retain such documents or materials at an unauthorized location." 18 U.S.C. §1924(a) (2000 & Supp. III 2003). The unauthorized provision of documents and materials to Congress is not an offense under the 1994 measure. *Id.* §1924(b).

The statute does not cover oral communications. Whether it requires knowledge that the materials removed were classified is unclear. Also unclear is whether improper classification would constitute a defense to prosecution.

Several years ago, an employee of the super-secret National Reconnaissance Office removed classified budget information showing that the Office accumulated more than $1 billion in slush funds without informing its supervisors at the Pentagon or overseers in Congress, for the purpose of leaking the information to the Washington Post. *See* Walter Pincus, *Spy Agency Hoards Secret $1 Billion*, Wash. Post, Sept. 24, 1995, at A1. Could she be prosecuted under 18 U.S.C. §1924?

In 2000, Congress passed a bill that included the following provision:

Prohibition on Unauthorized Disclosure of Classified Information

(a) Prohibition — Whoever, being [a present or former] officer or employee of the United States, . . . or any other person with authorized access to classified information, knowingly and wilfully discloses, or attempts to disclose, any classified information to a person who is not both an officer or employee of the United States and who is not authorized access to classified information shall be fined not more than $10,000, imprisoned not more than 3 years or both.

(b) [Exempts disclosures "in accordance with applicable law" to federal judges, or committees or members of Congress.] [H.R. 4392, Intelligence Authorization Act for Fiscal Year 2001, 106th Cong. (2000).]

President Clinton vetoed the bill, partly because it had been passed without public hearings and partly because he thought it was "overbroad and may unnecessarily chill legitimate activities that are at the heart of a democracy." *Statement by the President on the Veto of HR 4392*, Nov. 4, 2000, *at* http://clinton6.nara.gov/2000/11/2000-11-04-statement-by-the-president-on-the-veto-of-hr.html.

> A desire to avoid the risk that their good faith choice of words — their exercise of judgment — could become the subject of a criminal referral for prosecution might discourage Government officials from engaging even in appropriate public discussion, press briefings, or other legitimate official activities. Similarly, the legislation may unduly restrain the ability of former Government officials to teach, write, or engage in any activity aimed at building public understanding of complex issues. *Id.*

Two years later, President Bush's Attorney General declared that "current statutes provide a legal basis to prosecute those who engage in unauthorized disclosures. . . . [We] do not require additional legislation." Letter from Attorney General John Ashcroft to J. Dennis Hastert, Speaker of the House of Representatives, Oct. 15, 2002, *available at* http://www.fas.org/sgp/othergov/dojleaks.html.

Efforts to enact such legislation persist, however. In 2005, the Chair of the House Intelligence Committee declared, "The time has come for a comprehensive law that will make it easier for the government to prosecute wrongdoers and increase the penalties, which will hopefully act as a deterrent for people thinking about disclosing information." Peter Hoekstra, *Secrets and Leaks: The Costs and Consequences for National Security*, Heritage Found., July 29, 2005, *at* http://www.heritage.org/Research/HomelandDefense/wm809.cfm. And in 2006, following news accounts of two secret government surveillance programs, see *supra* p. 548, the House Intelligence Committee reported that

> prosecution under current laws relating to unauthorized disclosure has not been an effective deterrent tool, although it remains unclear whether this lack of effectiveness requires changes in the law or is due to other factors. In either event, the Committee believes that additional and more creative steps to deter unauthorized disclosures are warranted. [H.R. Rep. No. 109-411 (2006).]

Assuming that there will be continuing unauthorized leaks of classified information, do you believe that existing criminal and administrative remedies can effectively punish or deter those disclosures that truly threaten national security? What are those existing remedies, and what gaps, if any, do they leave in the protection against such disclosures? Or is new legislation needed to keep the nation safe? What would a new bill accomplish that existing laws do not already do?

What would be the costs of criminalizing all unauthorized leaks of unclassified information? How would those costs compare with whatever benefits might be derived from the leaks? Can you think of some way to codify this cost-benefit analysis, either in the classification of information, see *supra* pp. 976-979, or in the decision to prosecute a leaker? How could you account for the possibility of selective prosecution of leakers and of media (for example, as aiders and abettors, or co-conspirators) who publish or broadcast such leaks?

NOTE ON "AUTHORIZED" LEAKS: THE VALERIE PLAME AFFAIR

The executive branch engages in clandestine leaking of otherwise classified information for its own presumably benign purposes, as we observed at the beginning of this chapter. Members of Congress leak, too. But these unofficial disclosures may not always be entirely harmless. A former Director of Central Intelligence noted:

> [T]he White House staff tends to leak when doing so may help the President politically. The Pentagon leaks, primarily to sell its programs to the Congress and the public. The State Department leaks when it's being forced into a policy move that its people dislike. The CIA leaks when some of its people want to influence policy but know that's a role they're not allowed to play openly. The Congress is most likely to leak when the issue has political ramifications domestically. [Stansfield Turner, *Secrecy and Democracy* 149 (1985).]

See also Martin Linsky, *Impact: How the Press Affects Federal Policymaking* 172, 238-239 (1986); Abel, *supra* p. 1077. Some writers go even further, worrying not only about the government's ability to manage and control information through selective leaks, but also about "plants" of deliberate disinformation. *See* Abel, *supra*, at 31, 43; I.F. Stone, *Schorr Case: The Real Dangers*, N.Y. Rev. of Books, Apr. 1976, at 6.

Not long after the beginning of the war in Iraq, former ambassador Joseph C. Wilson IV wrote an op-ed piece for the New York Times reporting that he had been dispatched to Niger by the CIA in early 2002 to investigate claims that Iraq was seeking to purchase nuclear weapons materials there. *What I Didn't Find in Africa*, N.Y. Times, July 6, 2003, §4, at 9. He said that he found the claims "highly doubtful," and that he reported his findings to the CIA. Because his report questioned one of the central rationales for the war, the President and Vice President allegedly instructed the Vice President's Chief of Staff, I. Lewis "Scooter" Libby, to counter it by covertly releasing portions of the then-classified 2002 National Intelligence Estimate, which contained language supporting this rationale. *See* David Johnston & David E. Sanger, *Cheney's Aide Says President Approved Leak*, N.Y. Times, Apr. 7, 2006, at A1. Libby reportedly was advised that the President's instruction "amounted to declassification of the document," and he did as he was told. *Id.*

At about the same moment, Libby also disclosed to reporters for Newsweek, the New York Times, and perhaps others that Wilson was married to an undercover CIA operative named Valerie Plame. This leak allegedly was intended to discredit Wilson's account by suggesting that his trip to Niger was a junket arranged by his wife that resulted from nepotism. Libby reportedly was given this information by Vice President Cheney, among others. *See* Murray Waas, *Bush Directed Cheney to Counter War Critic*, Natl. J., July 3, 2006. The story was broken on July 14, 2003, by syndicated columnist Robert D. Novak, who allegedly got the information from Karl Rove, the President's deputy chief of staff, and others. *See* David Johnston, *Novak Told Prosecutors His Sources in Leak Case*, N.Y. Times, July 12, 2006, at A16.

Disclosure of the name of a CIA operative can be a felony under certain circumstances. The Intelligence Identities Protection Act, 50 U.S.C. §§421-426 (2000 & Supp. III 2003), provides in part:

> Whoever, having or having had authorized access to classified information that identifies a covert agent, intentionally discloses any information identifying such covert agent to any individual not authorized to receive classified information, knowing that the information disclosed so identifies such covert agent and that the United States is taking affirmative measures to conceal such covert agent's intelligence relationship to the United States, shall be fined ... or imprisoned....
> [*Id.* §421(a).]

Subsections 421(b) and (c) punish, respectively, knowing disclosure by a person with authorized access who *learns* the identity of a covert agent and discloses it, and knowing disclosure pursuant to a *pattern of activities* intended to expose covert agents. *See generally* Elizabeth B. Bazen, *Intelligence Identities Protection Act* (Cong. Res. Serv. RS21636), Oct. 3, 2003.

After the publication of Plame's name, a special prosecutor was named to look into the case. Two years later, Libby was indicted by a federal grand jury, not for violation of the Intelligence Identities Protection Act, but on five felony counts of making false statements, perjury, and obstruction of justice. *See*

B. Restraining Leaks by Espionage Prosecutions

David Johnston & Richard W. Stevenson, *Cheney Aide Charged with Lying in Leak Case*, N.Y. Times, Oct. 29, 2005, at A1. Can you guess why Libby was charged this way? Why do you suppose Libby allegedly was so circumspect with investigators about how he learned of Plame's identity, and with whom he shared this information? *See* Waas, *supra.*

Should the Intelligence Identities Protection Act be amended to make it easier to use in cases like this one? If so, how? Should journalists who publish the names also be subject to prosecution? Could the President or Vice President lawfully release the name of a covert CIA agent?

At this writing, in mid-2006, there have been no other indictments, and Libby is awaiting trial in early 2007.

Restraints on Publication of National Security Information

> You were satisfied to serve the power of your nation
> and we dreamed of giving ours her truth.
>
> Albert Camus, Letters to a German Friend[1]

In the modern age, when technology and sophisticated intelligence-gathering methods seem so inextricably linked to the security of the State, the government has become increasingly concerned with restricting access to sensitive information, even access by loyal citizens, lest such information also fall into the hands of foes or potential adversaries. In the previous four chapters we considered various ways to protect sensitive government information from disclosure. In this chapter we explore the power of the federal government, especially the executive branch, to suppress information to which members of the public, most particularly the press, have already gained access. This question relates to the central role of the press in our society—to keep the public informed—and in turn to a more fundamental question: whether ultimate sovereignty in our democracy resides in the executive, the Congress, or the people.

A. CASE STUDY: THE PENTAGON PAPERS LITIGATION[2]

1. The Roles of Lawyers and Journalists

In 1971, a former Defense Department employee named Daniel Ellsberg surreptitiously provided members of the press with unauthorized copies of a Defense Department study entitled *United States-Vietnam Relations 1945-1967*.

---

1. Translated and republished in *Resistance, Rebellion, and Death* 13 (Justin O'Brien trans., 1961).
2. Much of the information and many of the insights that follow are drawn from Daniel Ellsberg, *Secrets: A Memoir of Vietnam and the Pentagon Papers* (2002); Anthony Lewis, *The Constitution and the Press* (1974) (unpublished course materials, Harvard Law School); David Rudenstine, *The Day the Presses Stopped: A History of the Pentagon Papers Case* (1996); *Inside the Pentagon Papers* (John Prados & Margaret Pratt Porter eds., 2004); Sanford Ungar, *The Papers & The Papers: An Account of the Legal and Political Battle Over the Pentagon Papers* (1989); and John Cary Sims, *Triangulating the Boundaries of Pentagon Papers*, 2 Wm. & Mary Bill of Rights J. 341 (1993). See also Floyd Abrams, *Speaking Freely: Trials of the First Amendment* (2005); Anthony Lewis, *More Than Fit to Print*, N.Y. Rev. of Books, Apr. 7, 2005, at 8.

A. Case Study: The Pentagon Papers Litigation

Each of the 7,000 pages of analysis and documents was stamped Secret, Top Secret, or Top Secret-Sensitive. The decision to publish the *Pentagon Papers*, as they came to be called, and thus to precipitate the most important modern case involving government censorship, was heralded on the front page of the Sunday New York Times on June 13, 1971. Neil Sheehan, *Vietnam Archive: Pentagon Study Traces 3 Decades of Growing U.S. Involvement*. There it was revealed that American involvement in the Vietnam War did not begin with an attack on American ships in the Gulf of Tonkin, as the government had led the public to believe, but as far back as 1950, with large-scale shipments of military equipment to the French by the Truman and Eisenhower administrations. In 1954, U.S. personnel began engaging in sabotage and terror warfare against North Vietnam. The study also reported on U.S. complicity in the overthrow and perhaps in the assassination of South Vietnamese President Ngo Dinh Diem in 1963, on planning for a wider war in the months before the Tonkin Gulf incident in August 1964, and on the careful cultivation of public opinion for support of an expanded conflict. What was particularly provocative about the study was the revelation that the government had deliberately misled the public for several years about the nature and extent of U.S. involvement in Southeast Asia. Other details of the history are set out *supra* pp. 202-208.[3]

It is difficult to assess, let alone impart, the full significance and impact of the publication of these documents. There is, however, little doubt that it had a profound effect on the growing antiwar movement. The disclosures in the detailed study undermined the credibility of the government, and the Nixon administration's effort to suppress the record did nothing to restore public confidence. Indeed, it is arguable that the *Pentagon Papers,* together with subsequent press accounts of the events we now refer to as "Watergate," irreversibly changed the relationship between citizens and government—from one of trust to one of skepticism, if not distrust.[4]

Journalists thought it was extremely important to print portions of the study and to resist government pressure to desist from publication. It offered, one wrote, "the first good look since the end of World War II at the inner workings of the machinery of the Executive Branch that has grown up under the American Presidency." Sheehan et al., *supra* note 3, at xii. The study showed that the White House manipulated releases of information and appealed to patriotic stereotypes, and regarded "Congress, the news media, the citizenry, even international opinion as a whole . . . as elements to be influenced." *Id.* at xiii. It also revealed an "absence of emotional anguish or moral questioning" by policymakers. *Id.* at xv.

---

3. The unabridged Times series was republished in book form: Neil Sheehan, Hedrick Smith, E.W. Kenworthy & Fox Butterfield, *The Pentagon Papers* (1971). More nearly complete versions of the Pentagon study may be found in *The Senator Gravel Edition—The Pentagon Papers: The Defense Department History of United States Decisionmaking in Vietnam* (1971); and *United States-Vietnam Relations, 1945-67: Study Prepared by the Department of Defense* (U.S. Govt. Printing Office 1971).

4. The burglary in June 1972 of the Democratic National Committee headquarters in the Watergate complex in Washington, D.C., by former CIA operatives working for the Republican Committee for the Re-election of President Nixon provided the name "Watergate" for the process that ultimately led to the only "forced" resignation of an American President.

The unauthorized release of the *Pentagon Papers* apparently became an obsession with the Nixon administration. One of the crimes of the so-called White House plumbers, who were supposed to detect and prevent such "leaks," revealed in the course of the Watergate investigation, was a break-in at the office of Daniel Ellsberg's psychiatrist. See *supra* pp. 495, 1076.

Excerpts from the study, along with analyses by several New York Times reporters, were published in a series of daily installments. Following the second installment, the government sought an injunction against further publication. During the pendency of restraining orders imposed while the courts reviewed the matter, the Times editorialized that "Congress and the American people were kept in the dark about fundamental policy decisions affecting the very life of this democracy during the most critical period of the war." *The Pentagon Papers,* June 21, 1971, *reprinted in* Sheehan et al., *supra* note 3, at 646. Moreover, the editorial observed, almost no one inside the government seemed to question the assumption that control of South Vietnam by the Saigon regime justified such a massive U.S. military commitment. A full and open debate in Congress and elsewhere about the reasons for that commitment might, according to the Times, have moved the country in a different direction. What the study demonstrated was "an arrogant disregard for the Congress, for the public, and for the inherent obligation of the responsibilities of leadership in a democratic society." *Id.*

From the beginning, the decision to publish or not to publish was recognized as a truly momentous one, both politically and legally. The journalists, nevertheless, felt very certain about the overriding duty to publish. At the early stages the only lawyer involved in the decision making was James Goodale, general counsel of the Times. He too apparently was convinced from the outset that the Times had a constitutional right, if not a duty, to publish the papers, and he remained a strong voice for that course.

Chief Justice Burger, dissenting in the case that arose out of these facts, said:

> To me it is hardly believable that a newspaper long regarded as a great institution in American life would fail to perform one of the basic and simple duties of every citizen with respect to the discovery or possession of stolen property or secret government documents. That duty, I had thought — perhaps naively — was to report forthwith, to responsible public officers. This duty rests on taxi drivers, Justices, and the New York Times. [New York Times Co. v. United States, 403 U.S. 713, 751 (1971) (Burger, C.J., dissenting).]

What would you have done if you had been an editor of the Times? Would you have returned the government documents unread? Or would you have read them before making your decision? Perhaps out of a journalist's natural curiosity, or arrogance, the Times editors did not react in the fashion suggested by the Chief Justice. In fact, even before the question of what to do with the documents was formally considered at the editorial level, Neil Sheehan, the reporter who had originally received the papers, holed up in a Washington hotel and pored over them for weeks. Only then, as the decision to publish approached, and the legal ramifications, including fines, imprisonment, and injunctions, loomed larger, did the editors apprise the publisher of the project and seek the advice of outside counsel.

> [The] lawyers . . . came to a meeting at the Times and angrily told Sulzberger [the publisher] and his colleagues that it would be a criminal offense to publish any of the material or stories based on it. Indeed, they said, possession of the papers was a crime at that moment. They refused to look at the documents themselves because, they said, they would then be committing an offense. . . . They advised the Times to return the documents and cancel the project. [Lewis, *The Constitution and the Press, supra* p. 1082, at 34.]

A. Case Study: The Pentagon Papers Litigation

How would you have reacted as an attorney for the Justice Department? For an extensive description of government deliberations about how to proceed against the Times, see Rudenstine, *supra* p. 1082, at 77-95. As it turned out, the advice of the newspaper's law firm, Lord, Day & Lord, headed by former Attorney General Herbert Brownell, was correct—at least as far as then-Attorney General John Mitchell was concerned. After the first two installments of the *Pentagon Papers* were published, the Times received a telegram (reproduced on the following page) from Mr. Mitchell containing a thinly veiled threat of prosecution under the Espionage Act.[5] Both the telegram and the advice of counsel were based on the premise that the publication of *any* classified material was a *per se* violation of the criminal law no matter what the reports actually contained. As far as the lawyers on both sides were concerned, whether the material was properly classified or, if properly classified, whether the public interest in the information overrode the need for secrecy, were irrelevant questions.

NOTES AND QUESTIONS

1. *Role of the Media Lawyer.* Is it ever appropriate for an attorney to refuse to examine any material relevant to the case against her client? Should it matter that the client asks the attorney to make such an examination? Of course, lawyers must understand their clients and to some degree empathize with them. As outside counsel for generations to the nation's leading newspaper, should the firm of Lord, Day & Lord have been influenced in their advice by broader considerations of the role of the press in American society?

2. *Institutional Role of the Press.* Consider the following observations of Justice Potter Stewart in 1974:

> [The Court] has uniformly reflected its understanding that the Free Press guarantee is, in essence, a *structural* provision of the Constitution. Most of the other provisions in the Bill of Rights protect specific liberties or ... rights.... In contrast, the Free Press Clause extends protection to an institution. The publishing business is, in short, the only organized private business that is given explicit constitutional protection....
>
> ... If the Free Press guarantee meant no more than freedom of expression, it would be a constitutional redundancy.... [M]any of the state constitutions contained clauses protecting freedom of the press while at the same time recognizing no general freedom of speech. By including both guarantees in the First Amendment, the Founders quite clearly recognized the distinction between the two.
>
> It is also a mistake to suppose that the only purpose of the constitutional guarantee of a free press is to insure that a newspaper will serve as a neutral forum for debate, a "market place for ideas".... A related theory sees the press as a neutral conduit of information between the people and their elected leaders.

---

5. This copy of the original telegram was furnished by Floyd Abrams, Esq., of Cahill, Gordon & Reindel.

NY K TIMES NY
X
NY K TIMES NY
ARTHUR OCHSSULZBERGER
PRESIDENT AND PUBLISHER
THE NEW YORK TIMES
NEW YORK, NEW YORK

1971 JUN 14 PM 8:34

I HAVE BEEN ADVISED BY THE SECRETARY OF DEFENSE THAT THE MATERIAL PUBLISHED IN THE NEW YORK TIMES ON JUNE 13, 14, 1971

CAPTIONED "KEY TEXTS FROM PENTAGON'S VIETNAM STUDY" CONTAINS INFORMATION RELATING TO THE NATIONAL DEFENSE OF THE UNITED STATES AND BEARS A TOP SECRET CLASSIFICATION.

AS, SUCH, PUBLICATION OF THIS INFORMATION IS DIRECTLY PROHIBITED BY THE PROVISIONS OF THE ESPIONAGE LAW, TITLE 18, UNITED STATES CODE, SECTION 793.

MOREOVER, FURTHER PUBLICATION OF INFORMATION OF THIS CHARACTER WILL CAUSEIREXXX IRREPARABLE INJURY TO THE DEFENSE INTERESTS OF THE UNITED STATES.

ACCORDINGLY, I RESPECTFULLY REQUEST THAT YOU PUBLISH NO FURTHER INFORMATION OF THIS CHARACTER AND ADVISE ME THAT YOU HAVE MADE ARRANGEMENTS FOR THE RETURN OF THESE DOCUMENTS TO THE DEPARTMENT OF DEFENSE.

JOHN N. MITCHELL
ATTORNEY GENERAL

These theories, in my view, again give insufficient weight to the institutional autonomy of the press....

In setting up the three branches of... Government, the Founders deliberately created an internally competitive system....

The primary purpose of the constitutional guarantee of a free press was a similar one: to create a fourth institution outside the Government as an additional check on the three official branches....

...[The] autonomy cuts both ways. The press is free to do battle against secrecy and deception.... But the press cannot expect from the Constitution any guarantee that it will succeed.... The Constitution itself is neither a Freedom of Information Act nor an Official Secrets Act.

The Constitution, in other words, establishes the contest, not its resolution. Congress may provide a resolution, at least in some instances, through carefully drawn legislation. For the rest, we must rely, as so often in our system we must, on the tug and pull of the political forces in American society. [Potter Stewart, *Or of the Press,* 26 Hastings L.J. 631, 633-636 (1975).]

Chief Justice Burger did not agree with Justice Stewart's view of the "institutional press." Concurring in First National Bank v. Bellotti, 435 U.S. 765, 797 (1978), the Chief Justice contended that there was no historical or precedential basis for conferring "special and extraordinary privileges or status on the 'institutional press.'" The commentators are similarly divided. *Compare* David Lange, *The Speech and Press Clauses,* 23 UCLA L. Rev. 77 (1975), *and* Anthony Lewis, *A Preferred Position for Journalism?,* 7 Hofstra L. Rev. 595 (1979), *with* Melville B. Nimmer, *Speech and Press: A Brief Reply,* 23 UCLA L. Rev. 120 (1975), Randall P. Bezanson, *The New Free Press Guarantee,* 63 Va. L. Rev. 731 (1977), *and* Floyd Abrams, *The Press Is Different: Reflections on Justice Stewart and the Autonomous Press,* 7 Hofstra L. Rev. 563 (1979). One commentator lifts the idea of the "checking function" to the level of a general First Amendment theory. *See* Vincent Blasi, *The Checking Value in First Amendment Theory,* 1977 Am. B. Found. Res. J. 523.

3. *Relations Between Press and Government.* Is the Stewart view of the relationship between press and government accurate or realistic? Is the relationship perhaps more symbiotic than antagonistic, or sometimes even mutually exploitive? Consider the following excerpt from an affidavit filed by Max Frankel, then Washington Bureau Chief of the New York Times, in the *Pentagon Papers Case*:

> The Government's unprecedented challenge to The Times... cannot be understood, or decided, without an appreciation of the manner in which a small and specialized corps of reporters and a few hundred American officials regularly make use of so-called classified, secret, and top secret information and documentation. It is a cooperative, competitive, antagonistic and arcane relationship....
>
> Without the use of "secrets"... there could be no adequate diplomatic, military and political reporting of the kind our people take for granted, either abroad or in Washington, and there could be no mature system of communication between the Government and the people. That is one reason why the sudden complaint by one party to these regular dealings strikes us as monstrous and hypocritical....[6]

---

6. The affidavit was supplied by Floyd Abrams, Esq., of Cahill, Gordon & Reindel.

Are you comfortable with an arrangement for guarding the nation's secrets that depends so heavily on the sound judgment of unelected officials and professional journalists? In this regard recall two leaks in 2003: one purportedly unauthorized, revealing the identity of a CIA intelligence operative, another authorized by President Bush of a hitherto classified *National Intelligence Estimate*. See *supra* p. 1080. What effect, if any, should this relationship have had on the outcome of the government's case for injunctive relief in the instant case? The subject of leaks is addressed extensively in the preceding chapter.

4. *Press Self-Restraint.* Anthony Lewis recounts the following history from a 1966 speech by Clifton Daniel, then the Times's managing editor.

> The Times had a story for the paper of April 7, 1961, saying that the United States was training an army of Cuban exiles to attack Fidel Castro and that an invasion was imminent. The publisher then, Orvil Dryfoos, was "gravely troubled by the security implications. He could envision failure for the invasion, and he could see The New York Times being blamed for a bloody fiasco." After discussion, the story was given less prominent play and mention of the imminence of the invasion deleted. The Bay of Pigs invasion occurred 10 days later. Despite the downplaying of that story, President Kennedy scolded The Times. At one newspaper association meeting he suggested that editors, in addition to asking whether a story was news, start asking: "Is it in the interest of national security?" But privately he told a Times editor, "If you had printed more about the operation you would have saved us from a colossal mistake." On Sept. 13, 1962, in a conversation with Orvil Dryfoos at the White House, Kennedy remarked, "I wish you had run everything on Cuba." [Lewis, *The Constitution and the Press, supra* p. 1082, at 41.]

In the case of the *Pentagon Papers*, the New York Times opted not to print portions of the history that were identified in an off-the-record briefing and in in camera court proceedings as most potentially damaging. Whitney North Seymour Jr., *Press Paranoia—Delusions of Persecution in the Pentagon Papers Case*, 66 N.Y. St. B.J. 10, 11 (1994).

Following scathing criticism of their publication in 2006 of information about secret government monitoring of international banking transfers, editors of the Los Angeles Times and New York Times wrote that there is "no magic formula, no neat metric" for measuring either the public interest in a story or the danger its publication might pose to the nation. But, they insisted, the responsibility to decide is "not one we can surrender to the government." Dean Baquet & Bill Keller, Op-Ed., *When Do We Publish a Secret?*, N.Y. Times, July 1, 2006, at A15.

What are the implications of this editorial autonomy for the judiciary's prior or subsequent review of a decision to publish? What are the implications for democratic government?

2. The Threat of Criminal Prosecution

Recall that in his June 14, 1971, telegram to the New York Times, Attorney General Mitchell asserted that publication of the Pentagon study was "directly

A. Case Study: The Pentagon Papers Litigation

prohibited by the provisions of the Espionage Law." On June 15, 1971, following publication of the second installment of the *Pentagon Papers* in the Times, the government filed a petition in the federal district court seeking an injunction against further publication, in part to prevent a violation of the Espionage and Censorship Act. Excerpts of that law are set forth *supra* p. 1066. Federal District Court Judge Gurfein responded to that particular claim in the following way:

> Assuming the right of the United States and, indeed, its duty in this case to attempt to restrain the further publication of these documents, the Government claims and the Times denies that there is any statute which *proscribes* such publication.... The Government relies [on §793(e)].
>
> ...It will be noted that the word "publication" does not appear in this section. The Government contends that the word "communicates" covers the publication by a newspaper of the material interdicted by the subsection. A careful reading of the section would indicate that this is truly an espionage section where what is prohibited is the secret or clandestine communication to a person not entitled to receive it where the possessor has reason to believe that it may be used to the injury of the United States or the advantage of any foreign nation. This conclusion is fortified by the circumstance that in other sections of [the Act] there is specific reference to publication. The distinction is sharply made in Section 794 entitled "Gathering or delivering defense information to aid foreign government." Subsection (a) deals with peace-time communication of documents, writings, code books, etc. relating to national defense. It does not use the word "publication." Subsection (b) on the other hand which deals with "in time of war" does punish anyone who "publishes" specific information "with respect to the movement, numbers, description, condition, or disposition of any of the Armed Forces, ships, [etc.]...."
>
> Similarly, in Section 797 one who publishes photographs, sketches, etc. of vital military and naval installations or equipment is subject to punishment.... [F]inally, in Section 798 which deals with "Disclosure of Classified Information" there is a specific prohibition against one who "publishes" any classified information. This classified information is limited to the nature, preparation, or use of any code, cipher, or cryptographic system...for...communications intelligence purposes....
>
> ...The Government does not contend, nor do the facts indicate, that the publication of the documents in question would disclose the types of classified information specifically prohibited by the Congress. Aside from the internal evidence of the language of the various sections as indicating that newspapers were not intended by Congress to come within the purview of Section 793, there is Congressional history to support the conclusion. Section 793 derives from the original espionage act of 1917 (Act of June 15, 1917, Chap. 30, Title I, Sections 1, 2, 4, 6, 40 Stat. 217, 218, 219). At that time there was proposed in H.R. 291 a provision that "(d)uring any national emergency resulting from a war to which the United States is a party or from threat of such a war, the President may, by proclamation, prohibit the publishing or communicating of, or the attempting to publish or communicate any information relating to the national defense, which in his judgment is of such character that it is or might be useful to the enemy." This provision for prior restraint on publication for security reasons limited to war time or threat of war was voted down by the Congress. [United States v. New York Times, 328 F. Supp. 324, 328-329 (S.D.N.Y. 1971).]

NOTES AND QUESTIONS

1. *Lawyer as Advisor.* After reviewing the various provisions of the Espionage Act excerpted and paraphrased *supra* pp. 1066-1068, and described in Judge Gurfein's opinion above, what do you think of the advice counsel offered the Times respecting the criminality of retaining and studying, or publishing, the papers? Could you answer this question without also reviewing the contents of the *Pentagon Papers* in the context of the ongoing national debate over the Vietnam War? How does Judge Gurfein's construction of the statute affect your answer?

2. *More Legislative History.* When the *Pentagon Papers Case* reached the Supreme Court, Justice Douglas commended Judge Gurfein's statutory interpretation as "pre-eminently sound." New York Times Co. v. United States, 403 U.S. 713, 722 (1971) (concurring opinion). Indeed, Justice Douglas supplemented the district judge's analysis of the history of §793 by recalling that the Internal Security Act of 1950, Pub. L. No. 81-831, 64 Stat. 987, which amended and recodified §793, declared, "Nothing in this Act shall be construed to authorize, require, or establish military or civilian censorship or in any way to limit or infringe upon freedom of the press or of speech as guaranteed by the Constitution and no regulation shall be promulgated hereunder having that effect." 403 U.S. at 722 (Douglas, J., concurring). In light of the foregoing, was there any justification for the charge respecting §793 made by the Attorney General in his telegram? A history of efforts to criminalize publication of all classified information can be found in Jennifer K. Elsea, *Protection of National Security Information* (Cong. Res. Serv. RL33502) 15-23, June 30, 2006.

3. *Criminal State of Mind.* Justice White, concurring in the *Pentagon Papers Case*, 403 U.S. at 737, stated that:

> Section 793(e) makes it a criminal act for any unauthorized possessor of a document "relating to the national defense" either (1) willfully to communicate... that document to any person not entitled to receive it or (2) willfully to retain the document and fail to deliver it to an officer... entitled to receive it.

Is this an accurate paraphrase of the statute? See *supra* p. 1067. Didn't the Times plainly violate Justice White's understanding of the statute? Would his reading of §793(e) require an inquiry into either the motive or the culpability of the newspaper or its staff?

In the leading precedent construing §793 the Court said:

> The obvious delimiting words in the statute are those requiring "intent or reason to believe that the information to be obtained *is* to be used to the injury of the United States, or to the advantage of any foreign nation." This requires those prosecuted to have acted in bad faith. The sanctions apply only when scienter is established. [Gorin v. United States, 312 U.S. 19, 27-28 (1941) (emphasis added) Gorin was a Soviet national who obtained defense information from a Naval Intelligence investigator and relayed it to the Soviet Union.]

Under this construction would the Court be required to look into the motives either of the Times or of Daniel Ellsberg in determining the applicability of

§793(e)? The *Gorin* case involved the violation of that section of the 1917 Espionage Act, later incorporated into §793(a) and (b), which explicitly requires proof of a culpable state of mind, namely "intent" or "reason to believe." See *supra* p. 1066. Section 793(e) does not expressly include the same scienter (criminal state of mind) or culpability requirement, but instead concerns "national defense information which information the possessor has reason to believe *could* be used to the injury of the United States" (emphasis added). In an exhaustive and authoritative analysis of the legislative history of the espionage laws, two commentators opined that courts should hold that §793(d) and (e) "are not applicable to communication or retention activities incidental to the non-culpable revelations of defense information." Harold Edgar & Benno C. Schmidt Jr., *The Espionage Statutes and the Publication of Defense Information*, 73 Colum. L. Rev. 930, 1058 (1973).

In the wake of publication by the New York Times and other papers of stories about domestic surveillance of overseas telecommunications without court orders, see *supra* p. 548, and about secret monitoring of international banking transfers, Eric Lichtblau & James Risen, *Bank Data Sifted in Secret by U.S. to Block Terror*, N.Y. Times, June 23, 2006, at A1, there were calls for criminal prosecution of the Times and its staff. *See, e.g.,* Peter Baker, *Surveillance Disclosure Denounced*, Wash. Post, June 27, 2006, at A1. Would any of the statutes reviewed so far support a conviction? What, if any, state of mind would have to be proved?

4. *Extending the Reach of §793?* A closely watched case pending at this writing involves two lobbyists for the American Israel Public Affairs Committee (AIPAC) charged with conspiring to violate §793(d) and (e) by delivering classified information (given them orally by a Department of Defense (DOD) official) to persons not entitled to receive it, including journalists and foreign government officials. United States v. Rosen, Crim. No. 1:05CR225 (E.D. Va. filed Aug. 4, 2005). If the prosecution succeeds, it will mark the first-ever conviction of non-government employees not engaged in espionage for receiving and transmitting national defense information. Do you think it matters that the information was not in writing? Can you distinguish this case from *Gorin, supra?* Can you distinguish it from the case of the New York Times reporters who wrote stories based on leaked classified information? Can you make an argument that the prosecution violates one or more parts of the First Amendment?

5. *Statutes That Expressly Criminalize Publication.* A number of other provisions of the federal criminal code expressly criminalize disclosure of specific, identified kinds of classified information. *See* Elsea, *supra*, at 2-11. Justice White cited some of these—for example, 18 U.S.C. §797 (2000), which prohibits publication of photographs or other graphic representations of military installations, and 18 U.S.C. §798 (2000), *supra* p. 1067, which prohibits publication of "any classified information...concerning communication intelligence activities of the United States" (codes, for example) or information obtained from such activities. It was suggested in the district court hearing in the *Pentagon Papers Case* that some of the material in the 47 volumes could have revealed information about the U.S. intelligence system or codes. If you were counsel for the Times, how would you have responded to such suggestions?

When the New York Times broke the story in late 2005 of a secret (and possibly illegal) National Security Agency (NSA) program to monitor overseas telecommunications traffic, see *supra* p. 548, one commentator argued that the newspaper and its reporters could be prosecuted under §798. Gabriel Schoenfeld, *Has the New York Times Violated the Espionage Act?*, Commentary, March 2006. *See also* Adam Liptak, *Gonzales Says Prosecutions of Journalists Are Possible*, N.Y. Times, May 22, 2006, at A14 (reporting statement by Attorney General Gonzales that prosecution of journalists "is a possibility."); Scott Sherman, *Chilling the Press*, The Nation, July 17, 2006. How would you expect the Times to defend itself in such a prosecution?

According to one court, "Under section 798, the propriety of the classification is irrelevant. The fact of classification of a document . . . is enough to satisfy the classification element of the offense." United States v. Boyce, 594 F.2d 1246, 1251 (9th Cir. 1979). Do you think that holding is consistent with the purpose of the Espionage Act? What are its implications for a defendant?

Justice White also said that 18 U.S.C. §794(b) (2000), the statute under which Julius and Ethel Rosenberg were convicted of spying for the Soviet Union, United States v. Rosenberg, 195 F.2d 583 (2d Cir. 1952), might be relevant:

> Subsection (b) thereof forbids in time of war the collection or publication, with intent that it shall be communicated to the enemy, of any information with respect to the movements of military forces, "or with respect to the plans or conduct . . . of any . . . military operation . . . or any other information relating to the public defense, which might be useful to the enemy. . . ." [*Pentagon Papers Case*, 403 U.S. at 740 n.10.]

Do you agree that newspaper publication of the *Pentagon Papers* for the general edification of the public might be proscribed by §794(b)? If the information and circumstances were plainly the kind contemplated by the statute, how could the government prove the "intent that it shall be communicated to the enemy"? Do you think that publication of materials found in open government files or obtained through a FOIA request could be the subject of a §794(b) prosecution? Would the release of the material by the government operate as an estoppel? Would anyone who gains possession of information colorably within the scope of §794(b) but fails to seek official release of it forfeit the presumption that publication of it was in good faith?

Why do you suppose Congress forbade the disclosure of certain specified kinds of information in some sections of the Espionage Act while in other sections it described protected information in more general terms?

6. *The Decision Not to Prosecute*. While disclaiming any intimation that the Times had "committed a crime, or that [it] would commit a crime if it published the material in its possession," Justice White gave the strong impression that if the government had proceeded by way of criminal prosecution, instead of seeking injunctive relief, he would have found against the newspaper. *See Pentagon Papers*, 403 U.S. at 737-740, particularly n.9. At least two other Justices, Burger and Marshall, recognized force in Justice White's statutory analysis. Why do you suppose the government did not undertake a criminal

prosecution of the Times? How would such a prosecution, successful or not, affect press freedoms?

7. *Shooting the Messenger's Messenger?* Threatening criminal prosecution of a newspaper and its reporters is only one way to discourage publication of information that the government wants to keep secret. Another is to cut off the flow of that information by unmasking and prosecuting the reporters' sources. For example, when a Washington Post reporter wrote that the CIA operated a covert network of prisons for terrorism suspects in Eastern Europe and elsewhere, Dana Priest, *CIA Holds Terror Suspects in Secret Prisons*, Nov. 2, 2005, at A1 (a story for which she was awarded a Pulitzer prize), the CIA asked the Justice Department to open a criminal investigation to determine the reporter's source. David Johnston & Carl Hulse, *C.I.A. Asks Criminal Inquiry Over Secret-Prison Article*, N.Y. Times, Nov. 9, 2005, at A18. And when New York Times reporter Judith Miller refused to disclose to a grand jury her source of information about another leak, she was jailed for contempt for 85 days. *See* Don Van Natta Jr., Adam Liptak & Clifford J. Levy, *The Miller Case: A Notebook, a Cause, a Jail Cell and a Deal*, N.Y. Times, Oct. 16, 2005, §1, at 1. Can you think of other ways for the government to make it more difficult for reporters to gain access to classified information? Criminal prosecution of the leakers themselves is considered in some detail *supra* pp. 1066-1079.

3. The Inherent Power of the Executive to Censor

With some trepidation the Times made the following telegraphic response to the Attorney General's demand that it halt publication:

> We have received the telegram from the Attorney General asking the Times to cease further publication of the Pentagon's Vietnam study. The Times must respectfully decline the request of the Attorney General, believing that it is in the interest of the people of this country to be informed of the material contained in the series of articles. We have also been informed of the Attorney General's intention to seek an injunction against further publication. We believe that it is properly a matter for the courts to decide. The Times will oppose any request for an injunction for the same reason that led us to publish the articles in the first place. We will of course abide by the final decision of the court. [Lewis, *The Constitution and the Press, supra* p. 1082, at 62.]

The next morning, June 15, 1971, the Times, represented by Professor Alexander Bickel, who was brought in at the last minute when the Times's regular counsel declined to appear on behalf of its client, appeared in federal court to defend the newspaper's right to continue publication of one of the most significant news stories of the Vietnam period. The request for a temporary restraining order was supported solely by an affidavit from an assistant attorney general declaring that he had "reviewed" the 47-volume study, that the study was classified "top secret-sensitive," and that its publication would prejudice the defense interests of the United States and result in "irreparable injury" to the national defense.

At the hearing the government stressed that a delay in publication was required to give the government and the court time to review the documents. Professor Bickel resisted pressure from the court to agree to a voluntary suspension of publication, arguing that to do so would be to yield to a classic form of censorship. Judge Gurfein granted the restraining order on the ground that he needed a more thorough briefing than there had been opportunity to provide. He added that any temporary harm to the Times was far outweighed by the "irreparable harm" that could be done to the interests of the United States. It is worth noting that this was the very first case heard by Judge Gurfein following his appointment to the federal bench. James L. Oakes, *Judge Gurfein and the Pentagon Papers*, 2 Cardozo L. Rev. 5, 14 (1980).

Judge Gurfein's concern was understandable. He had no way of knowing what the documents contained. On the other hand, so was the reaction of Times editor James Reston understandable: "The fate of this institution is at stake." Lewis, *supra*, at 72.

The hearing on the preliminary injunction was set for three days later, Friday, June 18, in order to give the government time to document its claim that publication threatened the national security. On June 17 the government unsuccessfully argued a motion for the production of documents under Rule 34 of the Federal Rules of Civil Procedure. Apparently Judge Gurfein agreed with the Times that since the government already had the documents, its real purpose was to discover the source of the Times's copy. The Times argued that it was entitled to keep its source confidential. Recent cases addressing the protection of media sources are reviewed in Marc A. Franklin, David A. Anderson & Fred H. Cate, *Mass Media Law*, ch. IX (2000).

At the hearing on the 18th the government shifted its legal posture. The Espionage Act, §793(e), was cited merely as implicitly supporting the primary argument that the government has "inherent power" to "protect the public interest 'in matters...entrusted to the care of the Nation.'" Lewis, *supra*, at 74. For this proposition the U.S. Attorney for the Southern District of New York, Whitney North Seymour Jr., relied on the old and controversial case of In re Debs, 158 U.S. 564, 586 (1895). In that case the Court had upheld the contempt conviction of socialist leader Eugene Debs for violating an injunction against the Chicago Pullman strike. The Court in *Debs* recognized an inherent executive power, without explicit statutory authority, to seek equitable relief in federal court to forestall interference with interstate commerce and the federal mails. See *supra* p. 84.

The government argued that the mere fact of classification amounted to a prima facie case that the national interest would be disserved by the document's release and that to prevent the unauthorized, unilateral declassification of documents, the government may seek the aid of its courts.

Judge Gurfein rejected the presumption argument and put the government to its proof. In open court the government offered only conclusory generalities about the risk of harm to the nation. For example, one government witness explained that Senator Fulbright's earlier request for the papers had been rejected because security matters were so "entwined" in the study that it could not be declassified.

The judge, in a persistent effort to discover whether there was substance in the government's case, agreed, over the objection of the Times's counsel, to an

A. Case Study: The Pentagon Papers Litigation

in camera proceeding. Even then, government witnesses failed to satisfy the judge's repeated requests for specificity. The U.S. Attorney was obviously in a bind. In a memoir published later he explained, "Impossible as it may be to believe, the Defense and State Department representatives simply would not explain to the Government lawyers which of the documents in the 47 volumes of the *Pentagon Papers* presented specific risks to national security although they were absolutely positive that such documents existed." Whitney North Seymour Jr., *United States Attorney* 199-200 (1975). Seymour said Fred Buzhardt, Defense Department counsel, forbade the witnesses to testify in those terms — for security reasons — unless everyone but the judge left the courtroom. Lewis, *supra*, at 85.

On Saturday, June 19, after working through the night, Judge Gurfein wrote an opinion denying the preliminary injunction and dissolving the restraining order, subject to continuation "until such time during the day as the Government may seek a stay from a Judge of the Court of Appeals...." United States v. New York Times, 328 F. Supp. at 331.

When the Wednesday, June 16th, issue of the Times appeared without the *Pentagon Papers* continuation, Daniel Ellsberg was very upset. He was afraid that Judge Gurfein's stay was only the beginning of interminable legal delays. After being rebuffed by the national television networks, Ellsberg turned to the Washington Post. He supplied the Post with substantial portions of the *Papers*. Following a pitched battle between its journalists and its lawyers, the Post picked up on Friday, June 18, where the Times had left off. Ungar, *supra* p. 1082, at 127-147.

The government moved with more alacrity against the Post, possibly to counter the argument by the Times's lawyers that it would be unfair to enjoin it while other newspapers were publishing. By 5:15 that afternoon the Post was in federal district court before Judge Gerhard A. Gesell. Within a few hours Judge Gesell denied a temporary restraining order. The government immediately appealed to a three-judge panel of the District of Columbia Circuit Court, and at 1:20 A.M. Saturday morning, by a vote of 2-1, Judge J. Skelly Wright dissenting, the panel reversed Judge Gesell. United States v. Washington Post Co., 446 F.2d 1322 (D.C. Cir. 1971). The decision reflected an element of compromise. Though it called for "an opportunity for the Government to substantiate its claims at [an evidentiary] hearing on its request for a preliminary injunction," the appeals court directed Judge Gesell to hold a hearing and reach a decision by 5:00 P.M. Monday. *Id.* at 1325.

Later that Saturday in New York, the government obtained an extension of the stay of Judge Gurfein's order in favor of the Times until a panel of the Second Circuit Court of Appeals could review the district court's ruling, at noon on Monday, June 21. In other words, both newspapers now had received favorable trial court rulings, but both still were restrained from publication.

On Monday Judge Gesell began the hearing promptly at 8:00 A.M. He reluctantly granted a secret hearing but refused to bar Post reporters who had expertise in the area of national security. At 4:30 P.M. he delivered an oral opinion in which he found that the government had failed to show

> that there will be a definite break in diplomatic relations, that there will be an armed attack on the United States, that there will be an armed attack on an ally,

that there will be a war, that there will be a compromise of military or defense plans, a compromise of intelligence operations, or a compromise of scientific and technological materials. [Ungar, *supra*, at 173.]

The cases before the two circuit courts of appeal proceeded pretty much in tandem. The D.C. Circuit ruled 7-2 in favor of the Post, finding that "the government's proof, judged by the standard suggested in Near v. Minnesota . . . does not justify an injunction." 446 F.2d at 1328. The *Near* case concerned the restraint of publication under a Minnesota statute of a "malicious, scandalous and defamatory newspaper." 283 U.S. 697, 701 (1931). The case stands for the proposition that no prior restraint is permissible except in extreme circumstances. The most often quoted dictum in *Near* is:

> [L]imitation [on publication] has been recognized only in exceptional cases. "When a nation is at war many things that might be said in time of peace are such a hindrance to its effort that their utterance will not be endured so long as men fight and that no court could regard them as protected by any constitutional right." Schenck v. United States, 249 U.S. 47, 52. No one would question but that a government might prevent actual obstruction to its recruiting service or the publication of the sailing dates of transports or the number and location of troops. [283 U.S. at 716.]

In the Second Circuit a 4-4 tie was narrowly averted when a compromise was hammered out, apparently in response to a controversial tactic by U.S. Attorney Seymour. He submitted new affidavits from "defense agencies" to buttress the government's case, and he attached to his brief a "special appendix" that highlighted certain testimony from the secret proceedings and listed specific pages of the *Pentagon Papers* that he said created "particularly grave" risks. The appendix, alleging damaging revelations in the study about, *inter alia*, U.S. intelligence estimates, SEATO contingency war plans, encryption, and the Tonkin Gulf Affair, is reproduced at National Security Archive, *Special Appendix for the Second Circuit*, at http://www.gwu.edu/~nsarchiv/NSAEBB/NSAEBB48/appendix.html. The court ruled that the government's "special appendix," and any additional material the Justice Department claimed was especially dangerous to national security, should be remanded for further secret hearings before Judge Gurfein. United States v. New York Times Co., 444 F.2d 544 (2d Cir. 1971).

NOTES AND QUESTIONS

1. *Submission to Censorship?* At the time, especially at the height of the antiwar movement, many thought the newspapers should have published in defiance of court injunctions. What could the government have done, realistically, about such defiance? Newspaper men and women go to jail frequently for their principles, most often to honor promises of confidentiality. Were the principles at stake here less important? Was the Times's promise to abide by court orders a mistake?

Almost certainly the decision to abide was based on the "collateral bar" rule that an injunction "must be obeyed . . . however erroneous the action of the court may be" until the court's decision is reversed by orderly and timely review. Walker v. Birmingham, 388 U.S. 307, 314 (1967), *quoting* Howat v. Kansas, 258 U.S. 181, 189-190 (1922). *See* John Calvin Jeffries Jr., *Rethinking Prior Restraint,* 92 Yale L.J. 409, 433 (1983) (supporting rule only if expedited appellate review allows testing of injunction and if timely publication still possible after lifting of injunction); Martin H. Redish, *The Proper Role of the Prior Restraint Doctrine in First Amendment Theory,* 70 Va. L. Rev. 53, 93-94 (1984) (supporting rule when injunction follows full and fair trial). A television network was found guilty of criminal contempt when it broadcast tape recordings of conversations between Panamanian General Manuel Noriega and his defense lawyers in deliberate violation of a court order not to do so before an appeal of the order could be decided. United States v. Cable News Network, Inc., 865 F. Supp. 1549 (S.D. Fla. 1994).

2. *Demonstrating the Danger.* During the oral argument before the Second Circuit, in an apparent effort to meet the demand for specificity, U.S. Attorney Seymour offered to submit affidavits pointing out with more particularity the material in the 47 volumes that raised serious national security risks. Attorney Bickel objected on the ground that this evidence should have been offered during the in camera evidentiary hearing in the trial court. Bickel said: "I view this as a reopening of the record, not subject to cross-examination." Lewis, *The Constitution and the Press, supra* p. 1082, at 101. The court allowed the affidavits in. Should it have done so?

These same affidavits had been introduced in Judge Gesell's closed session the day before in Washington. Because the Washington federal courts had allowed Post journalists to attend the closed sessions, the affidavits were subjected to rather telling cross-examination. For instance, Vice Admiral Gayler had submitted an affidavit averring that disclosure of the *Papers* threatened to reveal the U.S. capacity to intercept secret messages of other countries. Judge Gesell thought this allegation unconvincing because it was lacking in specifics. Before the D.C. appellate bench the government sought to rehabilitate the admiral's affidavit by citing a specific radio intercept purportedly proving that North Vietnamese vessels had fired on U.S. ships in the Gulf of Tonkin in August 1964. The Post's Pentagon correspondent, George Wilson, to everyone's amazement, remembered the precise place the same information had appeared in a public transcript of an executive session of the Senate Foreign Relations Committee more than two years earlier. *See* Ungar, *supra,* at 204.

On Thursday, June 24, the New York Times sought a writ of certiorari from the Supreme Court, and the government sought Supreme Court review of the D.C. Circuit Court judgment. On June 25, five Justices voted to grant review in the consolidated cases on an expedited basis. These five also voted to extend restraint pending the Supreme Court resolution, at least as to all material in the "Special Appendix" and additionally specified "especially sensitive" items. That was to be the last of a long chain of restraining orders the newspapers had to face in connection with publication of the *Pentagon Papers.* The case was set for oral argument the very next day, June 26, and the Supreme Court issued the following decision four days later, on June 30, 1971.

New York Times Co. v. United States
United States Supreme Court, 1971
403 U.S. 713

PER CURIAM. We granted certiorari in these cases in which the United States seeks to enjoin the New York Times and the Washington Post from publishing the contents of a classified study entitled "History of U.S. Decision-Making Process on Vietnam Policy."...

"Any system of prior restraints of expression comes to this Court bearing a heavy presumption against its constitutional validity." Bantam Books, Inc. v. Sullivan, 372 U.S. 58, 70 (1963); see also Near v. Minnesota, 283 U.S. 697 (1931). The Government "thus carries a heavy burden of showing justification for the imposition of such a restraint." Organization for a Better Austin v. Keefe, 402 U.S. 415, 419 (1971). The District Court for the Southern District of New York in the *New York Times* case and the District Court for the District of Columbia and the Court of Appeals for the District of Columbia Circuit in the *Washington Post* case held that the Government had not met that burden. We agree.

The judgment of the Court of Appeals for the District of Columbia Circuit is therefore affirmed. The order of the Court of Appeals for the Second Circuit is reversed.... The stays entered June 25, 1971, by the Court are vacated. The judgments shall issue forthwith. So ordered.

Mr. Justice BLACK, with whom Mr. Justice DOUGLAS joins, concurring.... [E]very moment's continuance of the injunctions against these newspapers amounts to a flagrant, indefensible, and continuing violation of the First Amendment....

In the First Amendment the Founding Fathers gave the free press the protection it must have to fulfill its essential role in our democracy. The press was to serve the governed, not the governors. The Government's power to censor the press was abolished so that the press would remain forever free to censure the Government. The press was protected so that it could bare the secrets of government and inform the people. Only a free and unrestrained press can effectively expose deception in government. And paramount among the responsibilities of a free press is the duty to prevent any part of the government from deceiving the people and sending them off to distant lands to die of foreign fevers and foreign shot and shell. In my view, far from deserving condemnation for their courageous reporting, the New York Times, the Washington Post, and other newspapers should be commended for serving the purpose that the Founding Fathers saw so clearly. In revealing the workings of government that led to the Vietnam war, the newspapers nobly did precisely that which the Founders hoped and trusted they would do.

The Government's case here is based on premises entirely different from those that guided the Framers of the First Amendment.... And the Government argues in its brief that in spite of the First Amendment, "[t]he authority of the Executive Department to protect the nation against publication of information whose disclosure would endanger the national security stems from two interrelated sources: the constitutional power of the President over the conduct of foreign affairs and his authority as Commander-in-Chief."

... To find that the President has "inherent power" to halt the publication of news by resort to the courts would wipe out the First Amendment and destroy the fundamental liberty and security of the very people the Government hopes to make "secure."...

The word "security" is a broad, vague generality whose contours should not be invoked to abrogate the fundamental law embodied in the First Amendment. The guarding of military and diplomatic secrets at the expense of informed representative government provides no real security for our Republic. The Framers of the First Amendment, fully aware of both the need to defend a new nation and the abuses of the English and Colonial governments, sought to give this new society strength and security by providing that freedom of speech, press, religion, and assembly should not be abridged....

Mr. Justice DOUGLAS, with whom Mr. Justice BLACK joins, concurring.... The power to wage war is "the power to wage war successfully." See Hirabayashi v. United States, 320 U.S. 81, 93. But the war power stems from a declaration of war.... Nowhere are presidential wars authorized. We need not decide therefore what leveling effect the war power of Congress might have....

... It is common knowledge that the First Amendment was adopted against the widespread use of the common law of seditious libel to punish the dissemination of material that is embarrassing to the powers-that-be.... The present cases will, I think, go down in history as the most dramatic illustration of that principle. A debate of large proportions goes on in the Nation over our posture in Vietnam. That debate antedated the disclosure of the contents of the present documents. The latter are highly relevant to the debate in progress.

Secrecy in government is fundamentally anti-democratic....

Mr. Justice BRENNAN, concurring.... The relative novelty of the questions presented, the necessary haste with which decisions were reached, the magnitude of the interests asserted, and the fact that all the parties have concentrated their arguments upon the question whether permanent restraints were proper may have justified at least some of the restraints heretofore imposed in these cases. Certainly it is difficult to fault the several courts below for seeking to assure that the issues here involved were preserved for ultimate review by this Court. But even if it be assumed that some of the interim restraints were proper in the two cases before us, that assumption has no bearing upon the propriety of similar judicial action in the future.... [T]he First Amendment stands as an absolute bar to the imposition of judicial restraints in circumstances of the kind presented by these cases.

... [T]he First Amendment tolerates absolutely no prior judicial restraints of the press predicated upon surmise or conjecture that untoward consequences may result.* Our cases, it is true, have indicated that there is a single, extremely narrow class of cases in which the First Amendment's ban on prior judicial restraint may be overridden. Our cases have thus far indicated that such cases

---

*Freedman v. Maryland, 380 U.S. 51 (1965), and similar cases regarding temporary restraints of allegedly obscene materials are not in point. For those cases rest upon the proposition that "obscenity is not protected by the freedoms of speech and press." Roth v. United States, 354 U.S. 476, 481 (1957). Here there is no question but that the material sought to be suppressed is within the protection of the First Amendment....

may arise only when the Nation "is at war," Schenck v. United States, 249 U.S. 47, 52 (1919), during which times "[n]o one would question but that a government might prevent actual obstruction to its recruiting service or the publication of the sailing dates of transports or the number and location of troops." Near v. Minnesota, 283 U.S. 697, 716 (1931). Even if the present world situation were assumed to be tantamount to a time of war, or if the power of presently available armaments would justify even in peacetime the suppression of information that would set in motion a nuclear holocaust, in neither of these actions has the Government presented or even alleged that publication of items from or based upon the material at issue would cause the happening of an event of that nature.... [O]nly governmental allegation and proof that publication must inevitably, directly, and immediately cause the occurrence of an event kindred to imperiling the safety of a transport already at sea can support even the issuance of an interim restraining order. In no event may mere conclusions be sufficient: for if the Executive Branch seeks judicial aid in preventing publication, it must inevitably submit the basis upon which that aid is sought to scrutiny by the judiciary. And therefore, every restraint issued in this case, whatever its form, has violated the First Amendment — and not less so because that restraint was justified as necessary to afford the courts an opportunity to examine the claim more thoroughly. Unless and until the Government has clearly made out its case, the First Amendment commands that no injunction may issue.

Mr. Justice STEWART, with whom Mr. Justice WHITE joins, concurring. In the governmental structure created by our Constitution, the Executive is endowed with enormous power in the two related areas of national defense and international relations. This power, largely unchecked by the Legislative and Judicial branches, has been pressed to the very hilt since the advent of the nuclear missile age....

In the absence of the governmental checks and balances present in other areas of our national life, the only effective restraint upon executive policy and power in the areas of national defense and international affairs may lie in an enlightened citizenry.... For this reason, it is perhaps here that a press that is alert, aware, and free most vitally serves the basic purpose of the First Amendment. For without an informed and free press there cannot be an enlightened people.

Yet it is elementary that the successful conduct of international diplomacy and the maintenance of an effective national defense require both confidentiality and secrecy. Other nations can hardly deal with this Nation in an atmosphere of mutual trust unless they can be assured that their confidences will be kept. And within our own executive departments, the development of considered and intelligent international policies would be impossible if those charged with their formulation could not communicate with each other freely, frankly, and in confidence. In the area of basic national defense the frequent need for absolute secrecy is, of course, self-evident.

I think there can be but one answer to this dilemma if dilemma it be. The responsibility must be where the power is. If the Constitution gives the Executive a large degree of unshared power in the conduct of foreign affairs and the maintenance of our national defense, then under the Constitution the Executive must have the largely unshared duty to determine and preserve the degree of internal security necessary to exercise that power successfully. It is an awesome responsibility, requiring judgment and wisdom of a high order. I should suppose that moral, political, and practical considerations would dictate that a very first principle of that wisdom would be an insistence upon avoiding secrecy for its own sake. For when everything is classified, then nothing is classified, and the system becomes one to be disregarded by the cynical or the careless, and to be manipulated by those intent on self-protection or self-promotion....

This is not to say that Congress and the courts have no role to play. Undoubtedly Congress has the power to enact specific and appropriate criminal laws to protect government property and preserve government secrets. Congress has passed such laws, and several of them are of very colorable relevance to the apparent circumstances of these cases. And if a criminal prosecution is instituted, it will be the responsibility of the courts to decide the applicability of the criminal law under which the charge is brought. Moreover, if Congress should pass a specific law authorizing civil proceedings in this field, the courts would likewise have the duty to decide the constitutionality of such a law as well as its applicability to the facts proved.

But in the cases before us we are asked neither to construe specific regulations nor to apply specific laws.... I am convinced that the Executive is correct with respect to some of the documents involved. But I cannot say that disclosure of any of them will surely result in direct, immediate, and irreparable damage to our Nation or its people....

Mr. Justice WHITE, with whom Mr. Justice STEWART joins, concurring.... I do not say that in no circumstances would the First Amendment permit an injunction against publishing information about government plans or operations. Nor, after examining the materials the Government characterizes as the most sensitive and destructive, can I deny that revelation of these documents will do substantial damage to public interests. Indeed, I am confident that their disclosure will have that result. But I nevertheless agree that the United States has not satisfied the very heavy burden that it must meet to warrant an injunction against publication in these cases, at least in the absence of express and appropriately limited congressional authorization for prior restraints in circumstances such as these.

The Government's position is simply stated: The responsibility of the Executive for the conduct of the foreign affairs and for the security of the Nation is so basic that the President is entitled to an injunction against publication of a newspaper story whenever he can convince a court that the information to be revealed threatens "grave and irreparable" injury to the public interest; and the injunction should issue whether or not the material to be published is classified, whether or not publication would be lawful under relevant criminal statutes enacted by Congress, and regardless of the circumstances by which the newspaper came into possession of the information.

At least in the absence of legislation by Congress, based on its own investigations and findings, I am quite unable to agree that the inherent powers of the Executive and the courts reach so far as to authorize remedies having such sweeping potential for inhibiting publications by the press. Much of the difficulty inheres in the "grave and irreparable danger" standard suggested by the

United States. If the United States were to have judgment under such a standard in these cases, our decision would be of little guidance to other courts in other cases, for the material at issue here would not be available from the Court's opinion or from public records, nor would it be published by the press. Indeed, even today where we hold that the United States has not met its burden, the material remains sealed in court records and it is properly not discussed in today's opinions....

The Criminal Code contains numerous provisions potentially relevant to these cases.... [Justice White devotes five pages to a discussion of the criminal provisions.]

... I am not, of course, saying that either of these newspapers has yet committed a crime or that either would commit a crime if it published all the material now in its possession. That matter must await resolution in the context of a criminal proceeding if one is instituted by the United States. In that event, the issue of guilt or innocence would be determined by procedures and standards quite different from those that have purported to govern these injunctive proceedings.

Mr. Justice MARSHALL, concurring.... In these cases there is no problem concerning the President's power to classify information as "secret" or "top secret." Congress has specifically recognized Presidential authority, which has been formally exercised in Exec. Order 10501 (1953), to classify documents and information....

The problem here is whether in these particular cases the Executive Branch has authority to invoke the equity jurisdiction of the courts to protect what it believes to be the national interest. See In re Debs, 158 U.S. 564, 584 (1895)....

... [The Constitution] did not provide for government by injunction in which the courts and the Executive Branch can "make law" without regard to the action of Congress. It may be more convenient for the Executive Branch if it need only convince a judge to prohibit conduct rather than ask the Congress to pass a law, and it may be more convenient to enforce a contempt order than to seek a criminal conviction in a jury trial. Moreover, it may be considered politically wise to get a court to share the responsibility.... But convenience and political considerations of the moment do not justify a basic departure from the principles of our system of government....

... It is a traditional axiom of equity that a court of equity will not do a useless thing just as it is a traditional axiom that equity will not enjoin the commission of a crime. Here there has been no attempt to make such a showing. The Solicitor General does not even mention in his brief whether the Government considers that there is probable cause to believe a crime has been committed or whether there is a conspiracy to commit future crimes.

If the Government had attempted to show that there was no effective remedy under traditional criminal law, it would have had to show that there is no arguably applicable statute....

On at least two occasions Congress has refused to enact legislation that would have made the conduct engaged in here unlawful and given the President the power that he seeks in this case. In 1917 during the debate over the original Espionage Act, still the basic provisions of 793, Congress rejected a proposal to give the President in time of war or threat of war authority to directly prohibit by proclamation the publication of information relating to national defense that might be useful to the enemy....

In 1957 the United States Commission on Government Security found that "[a]irplane journals, scientific periodicals, and even the daily newspaper have featured articles containing information and other data which should have been deleted in whole or in part for security reasons." In response to this problem the Commission proposed that "Congress enact legislation making it a crime for any person willfully to disclose without proper authorization, for any purpose whatever, information classified 'secret' or 'top secret,' knowing, or having reasonable grounds to believe, such information to have been so classified." Report of Commission on Government Security 619-620 (1957). After substantial floor discussion on the proposal, it was rejected....

Mr. Chief Justice BURGER, dissenting.... The newspapers make a derivative claim under the First Amendment; they denominate this right as the public "right to know"; by implication, the Times asserts a sole trusteeship of that right by virtue of its journalistic "scoop." The right is asserted as an absolute. Of course, the First Amendment right itself is not an absolute, as Justice Holmes so long ago pointed out in his aphorism concerning the right to shout "fire" in a crowded theater if there was no fire. There are other exceptions, some of which Chief Justice Hughes mentioned by way of example in Near v. Minnesota.... Conceivably such exceptions may be lurking in these cases and would have been flushed had they been properly considered in the trial courts, free from unwarranted deadlines and frenetic pressures. An issue of this importance should be tried and heard in a judicial atmosphere conducive to thoughtful, reflective deliberation....

It is not disputed that the Times has had unauthorized possession of the documents for three to four months.... After these months of deferral, the alleged "right to know" has somehow and suddenly become a right that must be vindicated instanter.

Would it have been unreasonable, since the newspaper could anticipate the Government's objections to release of secret material, to give the Government an opportunity to review the entire collection and determine whether agreement could be reached on publication? Stolen or not, if security was not in fact jeopardized, much of the material could no doubt have been declassified, since it spans a period ending in 1968. With such an approach — one that great newspapers have in the past practiced and stated editorially to be the duty of an honorable press — the newspapers and Government might well have narrowed the area of disagreement as to what was and was not publishable, leaving the remainder to be resolved in orderly litigation, if necessary....

I agree generally with Mr. Justice HARLAN and Mr. Justice BLACKMUN but I am not prepared to reach the merits....

Mr. Justice HARLAN, with whom The Chief Justice and Mr. Justice BLACKMUN join, dissenting.... Due regard for the extraordinarily important and difficult questions involved in these litigations should have led the Court to shun such a precipitate timetable....

Forced as I am to reach the merits of these cases, I dissent from the opinion and judgments of the Court....

... It is plain to me that the scope of the judicial function in passing upon the activities of the Executive Branch of the Government in the field of foreign affairs is very narrowly restricted. This view is, I think, dictated by the concept of separation of powers upon which our constitutional system rests. ...

The power to evaluate the "pernicious influence" of premature disclosure is not, however, lodged in the Executive alone. I agree that, in performance of its duty to protect the values of the First Amendment against political pressures, the judiciary must review the initial Executive determination to the point of satisfying itself that the subject matter of the dispute does lie within the proper compass of the President's foreign relations power. Constitutional considerations forbid "a complete abandonment of judicial control." Cf. United States v. Reynolds, 345 U.S. 1, 8 (1953). Moreover, the judiciary may properly insist that the determination that disclosure of the subject matter would irreparably impair the national security be made by the head of the Executive Department concerned — here the Secretary of State or the Secretary of Defense — after actual personal consideration by that officer. This safeguard is required in the analogous area of executive claims of privilege for secrets of state.

But in my judgment the judiciary may not properly go beyond these two inquiries and redetermine for itself the probable impact of disclosure on the national security. ...

Even if there is some room for the judiciary to override the executive determination, it is plain that the scope of review must be exceedingly narrow. I can see no indication in the opinions of either the District Court or the Court of Appeals in the *Post* litigation that the conclusions of the Executive were given even the deference owing to an administrative agency, much less that owing to a co-equal branch of the Government operating within the field of its constitutional prerogative. ...

Pending further hearings in each case conducted under the appropriate ground rules, I would continue the restraints on publication. I cannot believe that the doctrine prohibiting prior restraints reaches to the point of preventing courts from maintaining the status quo long enough to act responsibly in matters of such national importance as those involved here.

Mr. Justice BLACKMUN, dissenting.... [I] would remand these cases to be developed expeditiously, of course, but on a schedule permitting the orderly presentation of evidence from both sides, with the use of discovery, if necessary, as authorized by the rules, and with the preparation of briefs, oral argument, and court opinions of a quality better than has been seen to this point....

I strongly urge, and sincerely hope, that these two newspapers will be fully aware of their ultimate responsibilities to the United States of America. Judge Wilkey, dissenting in the District of Columbia case, after a review of only the affidavits before his court (the basic papers had not then been made available by either party), concluded that there were a number of examples of documents that..."could clearly result in great harm to the nation," and he defined "harm" to mean "the death of soldiers, the destruction of alliances, the greatly increased difficulty of negotiation with our enemies, the inability of our diplomats to negotiate...." I, for one, have now been able to give at least some cursory study not only to the affidavits, but to the material itself. I regret to say that from

A. Case Study: The Pentagon Papers Litigation

this examination I fear that Judge Wilkey's statements have possible foundation. I therefore share his concern. I hope that damage has not already been done. If, however, damage has been done, and if, with the Court's action today, these newspapers proceed to publish the critical documents and there results therefrom [the aforementioned harm] to which list I might add the factors of prolongation of the war and of further delay in the freeing of United States prisoners, then the Nation's people will know where the responsibility for these sad consequences rests.

NOTES AND QUESTIONS

1. *Who Really Won?* One of the ultimate questions always asked about the *Pentagon Papers Case* was whether the press *really* won. Some think the press's lawyers yielded too much ground and actually emerged with a balancing test where previously there had been an absolute rule against prior restraint. *See* Don R. Pember, *The "Pentagon Papers" Decision: More Questions Than Answers,* 48 Journalism Q. 403 (1971). For a defense of the strategies they pursued, see Alexander M. Bickel, *The Morality of Consent* 79-88 (1976); Stanley Godofsky (a Post lawyer), *Protection of the Press from Prior Restraint and Harassment Under Libel Laws,* 29 U. Miami L. Rev. 462, 471-472 (1975). Bickel himself recognized that something had been lost:

> [L]aw can never make us as secure as we are when we do not need it. Those freedoms which are neither challenged nor defined are the most secure.... Before June 15, 1971, through the troubles of 1798, through one civil and two world wars,...there had never been an effort by the federal government to censor a newspaper....That spell was broken, and in a sense freedom was thus diminished....
>
> ...We extend the legal reality of freedom at some cost in its limitless appearance. [Alexander M. Bickel, *The "Uninhibited, Robust, and Wide-Open" First Amendment,* 54 Commentary 60, 61 (Nov. 1972).]

See also Erwin N. Griswold, *Teaching Alone Is Not Enough,* 25 J. Leg. Educ. 251, 258 (1973), for a claim of victory for the government.

2. *The Holding.* The per curiam decision is spare: prior restraint of expression bears a heavy presumption of unconstitutionality. The government did not discharge the burden of overcoming it.

The decision was reached within six days from the date of filing and four days after arguments were heard. There simply was too little time to circulate opinions in order to form majority and minority positions. Instead, each Justice wrote an opinion, and except for a concurrence here and there, no one opinion mustered the support of enough Justices to become the majority opinion. Six Justices, however, could agree on the common denominator expressed in the per curiam opinion, so that opinion became the opinion for the Court. One important question this poses is: what is the precedential value of this case? *See* Louis Henkin, *The Right to Know and the Duty to Withhold: The Case of the Pentagon Papers,* 120 U. Pa. L. Rev. 271, 272 (1971).

After the remand by the three-judge D.C. Appeals panel, Judge Gesell complained that he was uncomfortable in the role of censor, particularly without standards to guide him. *See* Ungar, *supra* p. 1082, at 173. Drawing from the different opinions, can you compile a list of the sort of matters that might be enjoined?

More recently, the Supreme Court was asked to apply a federal wiretap law that provides penalties for the knowing disclosure of an illegally recorded communication. Bartnicki v. Vopper, 532 U.S. 514 (2001). The case arose when a radio broadcaster aired a taped cell phone conversation between labor union officials. The Court ruled that because of the public importance of the content of the tape and because the broadcaster had not participated in the illegal intercept, the broadcast was protected by the First Amendment. How might the application of these criteria have affected the outcome in the *Pentagon Papers Case*? Do you think they would help predict the outcome of another case involving a restraint on publication in the future?

3. *The Secret Pleadings.* The opinions reveal almost nothing about the contents of the *Pentagon Papers* or about the government's efforts to discharge its "heavy burden of showing justification" for a prior restraint. We know that none of the judges or Justices reviewed all of the 7,000-page history. Following Judge Gurfein's continuation of his temporary restraining order, Defense Department and intelligence officials identified what they thought were the most sensitive parts of the document. Those portions were then described in classified appendices to pleadings in the courts of appeal and in a secret brief in the Supreme Court; they have only recently been made available to researchers. The secret pleadings, along with streaming audio and transcripts of taped White House conversations between Nixon and his advisors about the *Papers,* arguments in the Supreme Court, and a trove of related materials, may be found in National Security Archive, *The Pentagon Papers: Secrets, Lies and Audiotapes* (n.d.), *at* http://www.gwu.edu/~nsarchiv/NSAEBB/NSAEBB48/briefs.html. *See also* Sims, *supra* p. 1082. By revealing the justifications for a continuing restraint that were rejected by the Court, these materials may help us to predict the standard that would apply in a future case.

The government was unaware that Daniel Ellsberg had withheld from the Times four volumes of the study devoted to diplomatic negotiations. They were later published separately. *The Secret Diplomacy of the Vietnam War: The Negotiating Volumes of the Pentagon Papers* (George C. Herring ed., 1983). Those four volumes headed the list of items the release of which the government felt would injure national interests. Their publication, the government argued, could prolong negotiations then under way, thus slowing the release of POWs and resulting in further loss of life.

The government's pleadings also warned about disclosure of the U.S. role in the overthrow of President Ngo Dinh Diem, plans for bombing North Vietnam and for fighting elsewhere in Southeast Asia and China, estimates of Soviet involvement, planning for covert operations, intelligence gathering, and U.S. encryption techniques. The study was also said to contain information embarrassing to our allies, especially South Korea, Thailand, and South Vietnam.

But while the secret pleadings contained numerous references to sensitive portions of the history, allegations that their publication would result in serious and immediate harm to United States interests were couched in general and conclusory terms. No specific examples of threatened injuries were provided. And there was no assertion that publication would "inevitably" result in harm, as Justice Brennan would have required.

According to Professor Sims, the government probably established that the nature and magnitude of the threatened injury were constitutionally adequate to justify a prior restraint, and that the injury would likely result from disclosure. But it failed to show that the feared harm would be a "direct" and "immediate" consequence of publication. Sims, *supra*, at 404-415.

4. *Justiciability.* Has the Court implicitly made a determination about what the public needs to know in order to make a reasoned expression of its political will? Or has the Court confined its inquiry to whether the dissemination of certain information is likely to imperil the national security? Are the two questions related? Is any court properly equipped to deal with either question? *See* Henkin, *supra*, at 278-279 (suggesting no). Is the judiciary entitled under the Constitution to make such a determination?

5. *Balancing Freedom and Death.* During oral argument, Justice Stewart addressed this question to New York Times counsel Alexander Bickel:

> Let us assume that when the members of the Court go back and open up this sealed record we find something there that absolutely convinces us that its disclosure would result in the sentencing to death of a hundred young men whose only offense had been that they were 19 years old and had low draft numbers. What should we do?

Professor Bickel reluctantly conceded that such material should not be published. William R. Glendon, lawyer for the Washington Post, tried to brush the question aside by responding that the hypothetical was not the case before the Court. William R. Glendon, *Fifteen Days in June that Shook the First Amendment: A First Person Account of the Pentagon Papers Case*, 65 N.Y. St. B.J. 24, 26 (1993). How would you have answered? How do you suppose Justice Black would have responded to Justice Stewart?

B. NUCLEAR SECRETS AND *THE PROGRESSIVE*: THE EXTREME CASE?[7]

Eight years after Justice Brennan's opinion in the *Pentagon Papers Case*, the government, believing it faced "the *Near* exception in the nuclear age," moved

---

7. Our account of this case draws extensively from the May and November 1979 issues of The Progressive. *See also* Symposium, *Weapons of Mass Destruction, National Security, and a Free Press: Seminal Issues as Viewed Through the Lens of the Progressive Case*, 26 Cardozo L. Rev. 1323 (2005); Erwin Knoll, *National Security: The Ultimate Threat to the First Amendment*, 66 Minn. L. Rev. 161 (1981).

to enjoin publication in The Progressive magazine of an article by Howard Morland entitled *The H-Bomb Secret: How We Got It, Why We're Telling It*. The secret, according to Morland,

> is in the coupling mechanism that enables an ordinary fission bomb...to trigger...the energy of hydrogen fusion. The physical pressure and heat generated by x- and gamma radiation, moving outward from the trigger at the speed of light, bounces against the weapon's inner wall and is reflected with enormous force into the sides of a carrot-shaped "pencil" which contains the fusion fuel.

A number of additional details, along with illustrations, were included in the article. After reviewing the Notes that follow, ask yourself whether the court should have enjoined publication of the article.

In the wake of the first of a series of atomic energy spy cases here and abroad and in the face of the coming "cold war," Congress passed the Atomic Energy Act of 1946, now amended and codified at 42 U.S.C.A §§2011-2297g-4 (West 2003 & Supp. 2006), upon which the government based its case against The Progressive. Although Congress paid lip service in its policy declaration section to the pleas of some scientists for openness,[8] the body of the Act describes a regime of strict governmental control of information pertaining to atomic energy. The government invoked two sections of the Act when it filed suit against the magazine:

> §2274. Whoever, lawfully or unlawfully, having possession of...information involving or incorporating Restricted Data...(b) communicates, transmits, or discloses the same to any...person...with reason to believe such data will be utilized to injure the United States or to secure an advantage to any foreign nation, shall...be punished....

> §2280. Whenever in the judgment of the [Secretary of Energy] any person has engaged or is about to engage in any acts...which [do] or will constitute a violation of any provision of this chapter...the Attorney General...upon a showing [thereof by the Secretary may seek in an appropriate court] a permanent or temporary injunction....

Once the Energy Department concluded that the Morland piece contained "restricted data,"[9] the government asserted that its right to an injunction under the foregoing provisions was plain. It distinguished the *Pentagon Papers Case* on the very grounds cited by several opinions in that case: here was both a relevant criminal proscription and a statutory authorization to enforce the prohibition by injunctive relief.

In United States v. The Progressive, Inc., 467 F. Supp. 990 (W.D. Wis. 1979), Judge Warren issued what he believed to be "the first...prior restraint

---

8. "The dissemination of scientific and technical information relating to atomic energy should be permitted and encouraged so as to provide that free interchange of ideas...essential to scientific and industrial progress and public understanding and to enlarge the fund of technical information." 42 U.S.C. §2161(b).

9. "The term 'Restricted Data' means all data concerning (1) design, manufacture, or utilization of atomic weapons; (2) the production of special nuclear material; or (3) the use of special nuclear material in the production of energy [except data declassified pursuant to section 2162]." 42 U.S.C. §2014(y).

B. Nuclear Secrets and *The Progressive*: The Extreme Case?

against a publication in this fashion in the history of this country," and ruefully added that "[s]uch notoriety is not to be sought." *Id.* at 996. He apparently felt that the gravity of the risk of harm outweighed the First Amendment interests at stake:

> What is involved here is information dealing with the most destructive weapon in the history of mankind, information of sufficient destructive potential to nullify the right to free speech and to endanger the right to life itself....
>
> The Secretary of State states that publication will increase thermonuclear proliferation and that this would "irreparably impair the national security of the United States." The Secretary of Defense says that dissemination of the Morland paper will mean a substantial increase in the risk of thermonuclear proliferation and lead to use or threats that would "adversely affect the national security of the United States."...
>
> A mistake in ruling against The Progressive will seriously infringe cherished First Amendment rights.... It will curtail defendants' First Amendment rights in a drastic and substantial fashion. It will infringe upon our right to know and to be informed as well.
>
> A mistake in ruling against the United States could pave the way for thermonuclear annihilation for us all. In that event, our right to life is extinguished and the right to publish becomes moot.
>
> In the *Near* case, the Supreme Court recognized that publication of troop movements in time of war would threaten national security and could therefore be restrained. Times have changed significantly since 1931 when *Near* was decided. Now war by foot soldiers has been replaced in large part by war by machines and bombs. No longer need there be any advance warning or any preparation time before a nuclear war could be commenced.
>
> In light of these factors, this Court concludes that publication of the technical information on the hydrogen bomb contained in the article is analogous to publication of troop movements or locations in time of war and falls within the extremely narrow exception to the rule against prior restraint.
>
> Because of this "disparity of risk," because the government has met its heavy burden of showing justification for the imposition of a prior restraint...and because the Court is unconvinced that suppression of the objected-to technical portions of the Morland article would in any plausible fashion impede the defendants in their laudable crusade to stimulate public knowledge of nuclear armament and bring about enlightened debate on national policy questions, the Court finds that the objected-to portions of the article fall within the narrow area recognized by the Court in Near v. Minnesota in which a prior restraint on publication is appropriate.
>
> The government has met its burden under section 2274 of The Atomic Energy Act. In the Court's opinion, it has also met the test enunciated by two Justices in the *New York Times* case, namely grave, direct, immediate and irreparable harm to the United States. [467 F. Supp. at 995-996.]

In an opinion that was initially published secretly, the court subsequently refused to vacate its preliminary injunction. United States v. The Progressive, Inc., 486 F. Supp. 5 (W.D. Wis. 1979).

A writ of mandamus for expedited appeal was denied sub nom. Morland v. Sprecher, 443 U.S. 709 (1979). The government withdrew from a subsequent appeal to the Seventh Circuit Court of Appeals when similar information appeared in another publication, and the case was dismissed. United States v.

Progressive, 610 F.2d 819 (7th Cir. 1979). The article was then published in The Progressive, Nov. 1979, at 14.

NOTES AND QUESTIONS

1. *Balancing Openness Against Annihilation.* One can commiserate with the judge who faces a decision entailing such awesome potential consequences. It is fairly clear from the excerpt of the *Progressive* case, above, that the court applied a balancing test, but it is less clear that the *Pentagon Papers Case*, the ruling law, furnished that standard. Even if, counting the dissenters, one concluded that the majority of the *Pentagon Papers* Court voted in favor of a balancing approach, on what basis can a court convince itself, let alone the public, that it has drawn the balance justly? According to one commentator,

> Experts on nuclear proliferation agree that the obstacles preventing production of a nuclear weapon are not informational. Rather, they lie in acquiring the cadre of skilled scientists needed to reduce the information to application, building the sophisticated and expensive facilities needed for production, and obtaining the necessary plutonium or weapons grade uranium. If this is true, then describing the theory of the H-bomb can not be the equivalent of providing an H-bomb nor will it lead directly and immediately to providing one....
>
> Although acknowledging that *New York Times* governed, the trial court in fact succumbed to the danger that the *New York Times* test was designed to prevent. Instead of requiring that the government meet its heavy burden of proof with clear and convincing evidence, the court weighed the interests on both sides. It balanced the gravity of the risk, posited to be death from nuclear annihilation, against the importance to the public of knowing the specific details of hydrogen bomb manufacture. With the issue thus presented, the result was a foregone conclusion. [Mary M. Cheh, *The Progressive Case and the Atomic Energy Act: Waking to the Dangers of Government Information Controls*, 48 Geo. Wash. L. Rev. 163, 199-200 (1980).]

2. *Security Through Openness?* Six years before the *Progressive* case, Edward Teller, the so-called father of the H-bomb, wrote to the New York Times:

> I urge the United States to move... toward unilaterally abandoning all forms of scientific and technical secrecy.... I advocate this in the enlightened self-interest of the United States.... First [because] in science there are very few real secrets.... Second [because of] the long term [adverse] effect of secrecy on scientific progress, especially in the United States. [Letter of May 27, 1973, *as republished in* The Progressive, May 1979, at 33.]

Howard Morland and The Progressive justified the alleged disclosure of the H-bomb secret on similar grounds. By proving that the secret was discoverable, they said they intended to demonstrate that security based on an arsenal of weapons of mass destruction was a false form of security and that dispelling the "mystique of secrecy" was an essential step toward a truly open policy debate on the dangers these weapons posed. Many in the scientific and journalistic communities disagreed with this perspective. The Washington Post, for example, urged The Progressive to delete the material the government objected

B. Nuclear Secrets and *The Progressive*: The Extreme Case?

to, calling the case "John Mitchell's dream case — the one the Nixon administration was never lucky enough to get: a real First Amendment loser." Do you agree? Should the author's or publisher's motives, assuming they could be ascertained, have played a role in the court's decision?

3. *Criminal Liability?* If the Morland article had been published before the government learned of it, do you think The Progressive could have been successfully prosecuted for a violation of 42 U.S.C. §2274? The language preceding the term "information" in §2274 is: "having possession of, access to, control over, or being entrusted with any document, writing, sketch, photograph, plan, model, instrument, appliance, note, or information. . . ." Does the statutory context of the term "information" affect your answer?

Could the information in the article fall within the term "restricted data" if Morland, a layperson with no special access to government facilities, had derived his information entirely from public sources, some as common as the *Encyclopedia Americana*, and consulted no classified documents? The government maintained that the fact that Morland's "synthesis or new information" was his original work product was irrelevant because restricted data may be "born classified."

Defendants argued that there was no violation of §2274 because evidence that publication would "injure the United States or secure an advantage to any foreign nation" was merely speculative, and because the criminal intent required by §2274 could not be established.

Can you imagine a statute addressing this important field of modern scientific knowledge in more sweeping or uncertain terms? What advice could you give a professor of nuclear physics about what subjects she might cover in an advanced seminar on nuclear energy or what thesis subjects she ought to place off limits, particularly for her foreign students? Would the professor have any choice except to steer away from the cutting edges of her field or submit her plans or syllabi to the Department of Energy for clearance?

Appendix

Constitution of the United States

We the People of the United States, in Order to form a more perfect Union, establish Justice, insure domestic Tranquility, provide for the common defence, promote the general Welfare, and secure the Blessings of Liberty to ourselves and our Posterity, do ordain and establish this Constitution for the United States of America.

Article I

Section 1. All legislative Powers herein granted shall be vested in a Congress of the United States, which shall consist of a Senate and House of Representatives.

Section 2. The House of Representatives shall be composed of Members chosen every second Year by the People of the several States, and the Electors in each State shall have the Qualifications requisite for Electors of the most numerous Branch of the State Legislature....

The House of Representatives shall chuse their Speaker and other Officers; and shall have the sole Power of Impeachment.

Section 3. The Senate of the United States shall be composed of two Senators from each State, [chosen by the Legislature thereof,][1] for six Years; and each Senator shall have one Vote....

The Senate shall have the sole Power to try all Impeachments. When sitting for that Purpose, they shall be on Oath or Affirmation. When the President of the United States is tried, the Chief Justice shall preside: And no Person shall be convicted without the Concurrence of two thirds of the Members present.

Judgment in Cases of Impeachment shall not extend further than to removal from Office, and disqualification to hold and enjoy any Office of honor, Trust or Profit under the United States: but the Party convicted shall nevertheless be liable and subject to Indictment, Trial, Judgment and Punishment, according to Law.

---

1. Changed by the Seventeenth Amendment to read "elected by the people thereof."

Section 4. The Times, Places and Manner of holding Elections for Senators and Representatives, shall be prescribed in each State by the Legislature thereof; but the Congress may at any time by Law make or alter such Regulations, except as to the Places of chusing Senators.

The Congress shall assemble at least once in every Year, and such Meeting shall [be on the first Monday in December,]² unless they shall by Law appoint a different Day.

Section 5. . . . Each House shall keep a Journal of its Proceedings, and from time to time publish the same, excepting such Parts as may in their Judgment require Secrecy; and the Yeas and Nays of the Members of either House on any question shall, at the Desire of one fifth of those Present, be entered on the Journal. . . .

Section 6. The Senators and Representatives shall receive a Compensation for their Services, to be ascertained by Law, and paid out of the Treasury of the United States. They shall in all Cases, except Treason, Felony and Breach of the Peace, be privileged from Arrest during their Attendance at the Session of their respective Houses, and in going to and returning from the same; and for any Speech or Debate in either House, they shall not be questioned in any other Place.

. . . [N]o Person holding any Office under the United States, shall be a Member of either House during his Continuance in Office.

Section 7. All Bills for raising Revenue shall originate in the House of Representatives; but the Senate may propose or concur with amendments as on other Bills.

Every Bill which shall have passed the House of Representatives and the Senate, shall, before it becomes a Law, be presented to the President of the United States; If he approve he shall sign it, but if not he shall return it, with his Objections to that House in which it shall have originated, who shall enter the Objections at large on their Journal, and proceed to reconsider it. If after such Reconsideration two thirds of that House shall agree to pass the Bill, it shall be sent, together with the Objections, to the other House, by which it shall likewise be reconsidered, and if approved by two thirds of that House, it shall become a Law. . . . If any Bill shall not be returned by the President within ten Days (Sundays excepted) after it shall have been presented to him, the Same shall be a Law, in like Manner as if he had signed it, unless the Congress by their Adjournment prevent its Return, in which Case it shall not be a Law.

Every Order, Resolution, or Vote to which the Concurrence of the Senate and House of Representatives may be necessary (except on a question of Adjournment) shall be presented to the President of the United States; and before the Same shall take Effect, shall be approved by him, or being disapproved by him, shall be repassed by two thirds of the Senate and House of Representatives, according to the Rules and Limitations prescribed in the Case of a Bill.

---

2. Changed by section 2 of the Twentieth Amendment to read "begin at noon on the 3d day of January."

Appendix. Constitution of the United States

Section 8. [1] The Congress shall have Power To lay and collect Taxes, Duties, Imposts and Excises, to pay the Debts and provide for the common Defence and general Welfare of the United States; but all Duties, Imposts and Excises shall be uniform throughout the United States;

[2] To borrow Money on the credit of the United States;

[3] To regulate Commerce with foreign Nations, and among the several States, and with the Indian Tribes;

[4] To establish an uniform Rule of Naturalization...;

[9] To constitute Tribunals inferior to the supreme Court;

[10] To define and punish Piracies and Felonies committed on the high Seas, and Offences against the Law of Nations;

[11] To declare War, grant Letters of Marque and Reprisal, and make Rules concerning Captures on Land and Water;

[12] To raise and support Armies, but no Appropriation of Money to that Use shall be for a longer Term than two Years;

[13] To provide and maintain a Navy;

[14] To make Rules for the Government and Regulation of the land and naval Forces;

[15] To provide for calling forth the Militia to execute the Laws of the Union, suppress Insurrections and repel Invasions;

[16] To provide for organizing, arming, and disciplining, the Militia, and for governing such Part of them as may be employed in the Service of the United States, reserving to the States respectively, the Appointment of the Officers, and the Authority of training the Militia according to the discipline prescribed by Congress;...

[18] To make all Laws which shall be necessary and proper for carrying into Execution the foregoing Powers, and all other Powers vested by this Constitution in the Government of the United States, or in any Department or Officer thereof.

Section 9.... [2] The Privilege of the Writ of Habeas Corpus shall not be suspended, unless when in Cases of Rebellion or Invasion the public Safety may require it.

[3] No Bill of Attainder or ex post facto Law shall be passed....

[7] No Money shall be drawn from the Treasury, but in Consequence of Appropriations made by Law; and a regular Statement and Account of the Receipts and Expenditures of all public Money shall be published from time to time.

[8] No Title of Nobility shall be granted by the United States: And no Person holding any Office of Profit or Trust under them, shall, without the Consent of the Congress, accept of any present, Emolument, Office, or Title, of any kind whatever, from any King, Prince, or foreign State.

Section 10. [1] No State shall enter into any Treaty, Alliance, or Confederation; grant Letters of Marque and Reprisal; coin Money; emit Bills of Credit; make any Thing but gold and silver Coin a Tender in Payment of Debts; pass any Bill of Attainder, ex post facto Law, or Law impairing the Obligation of Contracts, or grant any Title of Nobility....

[3] No State shall, without the Consent of Congress, lay any Duty of Tonnage, keep Troops, or Ships of War in time of Peace, enter into any Agreement or Compact with another State, or with a foreign Power, or engage in War, unless actually invaded, or in such imminent Danger as will not admit of delay.

Article II

Section 1. The executive Power shall be vested in a President of the United States of America. He shall hold his Office during the Term of four Years, and, together with the Vice President, chosen for the same Term, be elected, as follows...

Before he enter on the Execution of his Office, he shall take the following Oath or Affirmation:—"I do solemnly swear (or affirm) that I will faithfully execute the Office of President of the United States, and will to the best of my Ability, preserve, protect and defend the Constitution of the United States."

Section 2. The President shall be Commander in Chief of the Army and Navy of the United States, and of the Militia of the several States, when called into the actual Service of the United States; he may require the Opinion, in writing, of the principal Officer in each of the executive Departments, upon any Subject relating to the Duties of their respective Offices, and he shall have Power to grant Reprieves and Pardons for Offences against the United States, except in Cases of Impeachment.

He shall have Power, by and with the Advice and Consent of the Senate, to make Treaties, provided two thirds of the Senators present concur; and he shall nominate, and by and with the Advice and Consent of the Senate, shall appoint Ambassadors, other public Ministers and Consuls, Judges of the supreme Court, and all other Officers of the United States, whose Appointments are not herein otherwise provided for, and which shall be established by Law: but the Congress may by Law vest the Appointment of such inferior Officers, as they think proper, in the President alone, in the Courts of Law, or in the Heads of Departments....

Section 3. He shall from time to time give to the Congress Information of the State of the Union, and recommend to their Consideration such Measures as he shall judge necessary and expedient; he may, on extraordinary Occasions, convene both Houses, or either of them, and in Case of Disagreement between them, with Respect to the Time of Adjournment, he may adjourn them to such Time as he shall think proper; he shall receive Ambassadors and other public Ministers; he shall take Care that the Laws be faithfully executed, and shall Commission all the Officers of the United States.

Section 4. The President, Vice President and all civil Officers of the United States, shall be removed from Office on Impeachment for, and Conviction of, Treason, Bribery, or other high Crimes and Misdemeanors.

Article III

Section 1. The judicial Power of the United States, shall be vested in one supreme Court, and in such inferior Courts as the Congress may from time to time ordain and establish. The Judges, both of the supreme and inferior Courts, shall hold their Offices during good Behaviour, and shall, at stated Times, receive for their Services, a Compensation, which shall not be diminished during their Continuance in Office.

Section 2. The judicial Power shall extend to all Cases, in Law and Equity, arising under this Constitution, the Laws of the United States, and Treaties made, or which shall be made, under their Authority; — to all Cases affecting Ambassadors, other public Ministers and Consuls; — to all Cases of admiralty and maritime Jurisdiction; — to Controversies to which the United States shall be a Party; — to Controversies between two or more States; — [between a State and Citizens of another State; —] between Citizens of different States, — between Citizens of the same State claiming Lands under Grants of different States, [and between a State, or the Citizens thereof, and foreign States, Citizens or Subjects.]³

In all Cases affecting Ambassadors, other public Ministers and Consuls, and those in which a State shall be Party, the supreme Court shall have original Jurisdiction. In all the other Cases before mentioned, the supreme Court shall have appellate Jurisdiction, both as to Law and Fact, with such Exceptions, and under such Regulations as the Congress shall make....

Section 3. Treason against the United States, shall consist only in levying War against them, or in adhering to their Enemies, giving them Aid and Comfort. No Person shall be convicted of Treason unless on the Testimony of two Witnesses to the same overt Act, or on Confession in open Court.

The Congress shall have Power to declare the Punishment of Treason, but no Attainder of Treason shall work Corruption of Blood, or Forfeiture except during the Life of the Person attainted.

Article IV...

Section 4. The United States shall guarantee to every State in this Union a Republican Form of Government, and shall protect each of them against Invasion; and on Application of the Legislature, or of the Executive (when the Legislature cannot be convened) against domestic Violence....

Article VI...

This Constitution, and the Laws of the United States which shall be made in Pursuance thereof; and all Treaties made, or which shall be made, under the

---

3. The bracketed material in this section is changed by the Eleventh Amendment.

Authority of the United States, shall be the supreme Law of the Land; and the Judges in every State shall be bound thereby, any Thing in the Constitution or Laws of any State to the Contrary notwithstanding.

The Senators and Representatives before mentioned, and the Members of the several State Legislatures, and all executive and judicial Officers, both of the United States and of the several States, shall be bound by Oath or Affirmation, to support this Constitution; ...

AMENDMENTS TO THE CONSTITUTION OF THE UNITED STATES OF AMERICA

Amendment I

Congress shall make no law respecting an establishment of religion, or prohibiting the free exercise thereof; or abridging the freedom of speech, or of the press, or the right of the people peaceably to assemble, and to petition the Government for a redress of grievances.

Amendment II

A well regulated Militia, being necessary to the security of a free State, the right of the people to keep and bear Arms, shall not be infringed.

Amendment III

No Soldier shall, in time of peace be quartered in any house, without the consent of the Owner, nor in time of war, but in a manner to be prescribed by law.

Amendment IV

The right of the people to be secure in their persons, houses, papers, and effects, against unreasonable searches and seizures, shall not be violated, and no Warrants shall issue, but upon probable cause, supported by Oath or affirmation, and particularly describing the place to be searched, and the persons or things to be seized.

Amendment V

No person shall be held to answer for a capital, or otherwise infamous crime, unless on a presentment or indictment of a Grand Jury, except in cases arising in the land or naval forces, or in the Militia, when in actual service in time of War or public danger; nor shall any person be subject for the same offence to be twice put in jeopardy of life or limb, nor shall be compelled in any criminal case to be a witness against himself, nor be deprived of life, liberty, or property, without due process of law; nor shall private property be taken for public use without just compensation.

Amendment VI

In all criminal prosecutions, the accused shall enjoy the right to a speedy and public trial, by an impartial jury of the State and district wherein the crime shall have been committed; which district shall have been previously ascertained by law, and to be informed of the nature and cause of the accusation; to be confronted with the witnesses against him; to have compulsory process for obtaining witnesses in his favor, and to have the assistance of counsel for his defence....

Amendment VIII

Excessive bail shall not be required, nor excessive fines imposed, nor cruel and unusual punishments inflicted.

Amendment IX

The enumeration in the Constitution of certain rights shall not be construed to deny or disparage others retained by the people.

Amendment X

The powers not delegated to the United States by the Constitution, nor prohibited by it to the States, are reserved to the States respectively, or to the people....

Amendment XIV

Section 1. All persons born or naturalized in the United States and subject to the jurisdiction thereof, are citizens of the United States and of the State wherein they reside. No State shall make or enforce any law which shall abridge the privileges or immunities of citizens of the United States; nor shall any State deprive any person of life, liberty, or property, without due process of law; nor deny to any person within its jurisdiction the equal protection of the laws....

Table of Cases

Principal cases are set in italics. Cases cited in the authors' text, notes, and questions are set in Roman type.

Abu Ali v. Ashcroft, 813
Adarand Constructors, Inc. v. Pena, 607, 711
Adebe-Jira v. Negewo, 781, 804
Afshar v. Department of State, 988
Aftergood v. Central Intelligence Agency, 389
Air France v. Saks, 162
Alfred A. Knopf, Inc. v. Colby, 1051, 1059
Allen v. Wright, 149
All Matters Submitted to the Foreign Intelligence Surveillance Court, In re, 524
Al-Arian, United States v., 830, 835, 837, 838
Al-Marri v. Hanft, 757, 874
Al Odah v. United States, 781
American-Arab Anti-Discrimination Committee v. Reno, 849
American Civil Liberties Union v. Barr, 530
American Civil Liberties Union v. Brown, 1041, 1042
American Civil Liberties Union v. Department of Defense, 1008
American Civil Liberties Union v. National Security Agency, 556
American Civil Liberties Union v. United States, 545
American Federal Govt. Employees, AFL-CIO v. Reagan, 988
American Federation of Government Employees v. Pierce, 130
American Foreign Service Assn. v. Garfinkel, 91, 127, 1064
American Historical Assn. v. National Archives & Records Admin., 1016
American Historical Assn. v. Peterson, 1016
American Manufacturers Mutual Insurance Co. v. Sullivan, 602
American Telephone and Telegraph Co., United States v., 121, 123, 346
Amodeo, United States v., 1022
Ange v. Bush, 145, 146, 312
Applewhite v. United States Air Force, 951
Arar v. Ashcroft, 794, 803, *804,* 813
Arieff v. United States Dept. of the Navy, 1009

Arjona, United States v., 197
Armstrong v. Bush, 1015
Armstrong v. Executive Office of the President, 995, 1010, 1015
Armstrong, United States v., 604
Atlee v. Laird, 224
Atlee v. Richardson, 224
Avery, United States v., 605
Awadallah, United States v., 675

Bailey, United States v., 569, 779
Baker v. Carr, 146, 147, 148, 222
Baldridge v. Shapiro, 1041
Bareford v. General Dynamics Corp., 1048
Barona, United States v., 659
Barrett v. Kunzig, 594
Bartnicki v. Vopper, 1106
Bassiouni v. CIA, 1005, 1009, 1018
Bas v. Tingy, 94, 99, 101, 133, 201, 214, 257, 258, 649
Beacon Products Corp. v. Reagan, 116
Becker v. Internal Revenue Serv., 1018
Belmont, United States v., 54, 171
Berger v. New York, 492
Berk v. Laird, 222, 224
Berlin Democratic Club v. Rumsfeld, 494
Berrigan, United States v., 225
Billington v. United States Dept. of Justice, 1013
Bin Laden, United States v. (58 F. Supp. 2d 113), 865
Bin Laden, United States v. (92 F. Supp. 2d 189), *839*
Bin Laden, United States v. (126 F. Supp. 2d 264), *650*
Bissonette v. Haig, 945, 951
Blitz v. Donovan, 125
Board of Education v. Earls, 551, 552
Boim v. Quranic Literacy Inst. & Holy Land Found. for Relief & Dev., 470
Bollman, Ex parte, 689

1121

Bowan, United States v., 840, 845
Boyce, United States v., 1092
Brady v. Maryland, 864
Brandenberg v. Ohio, 824
Branzburg v. Hayes, 1023, 1072
Brennan v. Hobson, 442
Brignoni-Ponce, United States v., 607, 608, 671
Brown v. Califano, 125
Brown v. Glines, 2
Brown v. United States (1814), 101
Brown, United States v. (1973), 494
Buckley v. Valeo, 57, 838
Burka v. United States Dept. of Health & Human Serv., 995
Burnett v. Al Baraka Investment & Development Corp., 1048
Bush v. Vera, 605
Butenko, United States v., 494

Cable News Network, Inc., United States v., 1097
Cafeteria & Restaurant Workers Union v. McElroy, 271
Calder v. Internal Revenue Serv., 1037
Camara v. Mun. Court of San Francisco, 483, 934
Campbell v. Clinton, 98, 147, 152, 549
Capital Cities Media, Inc. v. Chester, 1024, 1037
Castillo v. United States, 766
Cavanaugh, United States v., 530, 531
Center for Constitutional Studies v. Bush, 556
Center for National Security Studies v. United States Dept. of Justice, 678, 1009, 1012, 1021, 1035
Central Intelligence Agency v. Sims, 1010, 1013
Chavez v. Illinois State Police, 604
Chavez v. Martinez, 799
Cheney, In re, 1019
Cheney v. United States District Court, 1019
Chon, United States v., 952
Christopher v. Harbury, 455
Church of Scientology v. United States Department of the Army, 1012
City of Indianapolis v. Edmond, 551, 589
City of New Haven v. United States, 112
Clark v. Allen, 169, 170
Cleary, United States v., 566
Clinton v. City of New York, 132
Coleman v. Miller, 152
Collins, United States v., 1076
Committee of U.S. Citizens Living in Nicaragua v. Reagan, 176, 182, 225, 456
Compagnie Francaise de Navigation a Vapeur v. State Board of Health, 933
Consumer Energy Council of America v. Federal Energy Regulatory Commission, 129
Coplin v. United States, 163
Crockett v. Reagan, 140, 251
Crowell v. Benson, 125, 418
Curtiss-Wright Export Corp., United States v., 35, 44, 60, 91, 117, 124, 130, 159, 166, 216, 218, 312, 418, 419, 497, 1064

DaCosta v. Laird (DaCosta I), 230
DaCosta v. Laird (DaCosta III), 233
Dames & Moore v. Regan, 3, 47, *48*, 86, 116, 118, 130, 133, *170*, 269, 270, 327, 407, 550
Davis, United States v., 589, 590, 594, 847
Dayton Newspapers, Inc. v. United States Dept. of the Navy, 1036
Debs, In re, 84, 1094
Dellums v. Bush, *134*, 297, 300, 301
Dellums v. Smith, 372
Denmore v. Hyung Joon Kim, 672, 677
Dennis v. United States, 824
Department of the Air Force v. Rose, 994
Department of the Interior and Bureau of Indian Affairs v. Klamath Water Users Protective Assn., 1012
Department of the Navy v. Egan, 87, 726, 778, 987
Detroit Free Press v. Ashcroft, 1033
Dickerson, United States v., 111
Diekelman, United States v., 970
Doe v. Ashcroft (Doe I), *562*, 577, 579, 580, 581
Doe v. Bush, 156, 312
Doe v. Gonzales, 562, *575*, 579
Doe v. Tenet, 1049, 1050
Doherty v. Department of Justice, 1008
Donovan v. FBI, 1008, 1013
Dow Chemical Co. v. United States, 504
Doyle v. FBI, 1009
Duggan, United States v., *513*, 523, 524, 530, 532, 544, 551
Duncan v. Kahanamoku, 971
Duncan, United States v., 482
Durand v. Hollins, *264*, 268, 324, 407, 418, 419

Earth Island Inst. v. Christopher, 166
Edmonds v. United States Dept. of Justice, 1048
Edward J. DeBartolo Corp. v. Florida Gulf Coast Bldg. & Constr. Trades Council, 777
Edwards v. Carter, 180
Edwards, United States v., 483
Ehrlichman, United States v., *495*, 499
Ellsberg v. Mitchell, 1041, 1042, 1044
Elmaghraby v. Ashcroft, 612
El-Masri v. Tenet, 1044, 1049
Empire Kosher Poultry, Inc. v. Hallowell, 932
Endo, Ex parte, 87, 106, 109, 710
EPA v. Mink, 1000, 1007
Equal Employment Opportunity Commission v. Arabian American Oil Co., 952
Ex parte _____. *See* name of party.

Falvey, United States v., 530
Farnsworth Cannon, Inc. v. Grimes, 1048
Federal Insurance Co. v. Al Qaida, 1036
Ferguson v. City of Charleston, 934
Fernandez, United States v., 866
Fernandez-Caro, United States v., 661
Ferrer-Mazorra v. Meese, 196
Field v. Clark, 43, 171
Filartiga v. Peña-Irala, 456, 781, 803
First National Bank v. Bellotti, 1087

Table of Cases

Fitzgerald v. Penthouse Intl., Ltd., 1048
Flast v. Cohen, 151
Fleming v. Page, 70
Florida v. Royer, 671
Flynt v. Rumsfeld, 1028
Foley Bros. v. Filardo, 952
Foster v. Neilson, 180
Foto USA, Inc. v. Board of Regents, 1024
Four Search Warrants, In re, 1023
Freytag v. Commissioner, 57
Frothingham v. Mellon, 151
Fuentes v. Shevin, 727

Garcia-Mir v. Meese, 196
George, United States v., 1022
Gibbons v. Ogden, 933
Gideon Henfield, Trial of, 157
Gilbert, United States v., 952
Gilligan v. Morgan, 148
Gilmore v. Gonzales, 595, 604
Giordano, United States v., 507
Girard, United States v., 1076
Globe Newspapers v. Superior Court, 1023, 1035
Goland v. CIA, 996
Goldwater v. Carter, 140, 148, 166
Gorin v. United States, 1073, 1074, 1090
Graham v. Connor, 662
Grand Central Pshp., Inc. v. Cuomo, 996, 1012
Gravel v. United States, 216
Gray v. United States, 257
Green v. Transportation Security Administration, 602
Greene v. McElroy, *105*, 111, 223, 238, 854, 863
Guantanamo Detainee Cases, In re, 700
Guong v. United States, 1048
Guy W. Capps, United States v., 181

Hagestad v. Tragesser, 1022
Haig v. Agee, 108, 552, 606
Haldeman, United States v., 499
Halkin v. Helms, 92, *433*, 437, *1037*, 1041, 1044
Halpern v. FBI, 1008
Halpern v. United States, 1049
Hamdan v. Rumsfeld (D.D.C. 2004), 756, 794, 797
Hamdan v. Rumsfeld (D.C. Cir. 2005), 756, 794, 797
Hamdan v. Rumsfeld (S. Ct. 2006), 3, 5, 702, 718, 719, 743, 749, 794, 797, 873, 877, *882*
Hamdi v. Rumsfeld, 48, 134, 550, 551, 680, 681, *721*, 750, 757, 903
Hamilton v. Dillin, 777
Hampton & Co. v. United States, 43
Harbury v. Deutch, *451*, 456, 650, 813
Harisiades v. Shaughnessy, 613
Hartley, United States v., 951
Hartwell, United States v., 594
Hayden v. National Security Agency/Cent. Security Serv., 1009
Hayes v. Hawes, 951

Head Money Cases, The, 177, 179
Heine, United States v., 1073
Helvering v. Hallock, 54
Hepting v. AT&T Corp., 556
Herring v. United States, 1043
Hirabayashi v. United States (1943), 705, 710, 712
Hirabayashi v. United States (1987), 712, 714
Hobson v. Wilson, 442
Hollingsworth v. Virginia, 253
Holtzman v. Schlesinger, 225, *235*, 239, 253, 317
Home Building & Loan Assn. v. Blaisdell, 85, 706
Houchins v. KQED, Inc., 1023
Howat v. Kansas, 1097
Howe v. Smith, 673
Hudson River Sloop Clearwater v. Department of the Navy, 1009
Humanitarian Law Project v. Reno (Humanitarian Law I), 826, 836
Humanitarian Law Project v. Reno (Humanitarian Law II), 837
Hunt v. Central Intelligence Agency, 1010
Hutchings, United States v., 952

Ibrahim v. Titan Corp., 804
Idaho v. Horiuchi, 283
Illinois v. McArthur, 551
Immigration & Naturalization Service v. Chadha, 57, 128, 129–131, 161, 166, 426, 427
Immigration & Naturalization Service v. St. Cyr, 551, 690, 693, 700
Ingraham v. Wright, 800
In re _____. *See* name of party.
Irons v. Bell, 1018
Ivanov v. United States, 494

J. Roderick MacArthur Found. v. FBI, 1018
Jacobs v. Barr, 713
Jacobson v. Massachusetts, 929
Japan Whaling Assn. v. American Cetacean Socy., 778
Jaramillo, United States v., 950, 951
Jay v. Boyd, 853, 854
JB Pictures, Inc. v. Department of Defense, 1027
Jencks v. United States, 864
Jew Ho v. Williamson, 925, 932, 935, 938
John Doe Agency v. John Doe Corp., 1012
Johnson v. Eisentrager, 649, 693–695, 700–702, 750, 757, 781, 813
Johnson, United States v., 530–532

Kahn, United States v., 952, 953
Kampiles, United States v., 1076
Kansas v. Hendricks, 671, 932
Kastigar v. United States, 419
Katz v. United States, 482, 484, 492, 498, 504, 506, 549, 559

Kent v. Dulles, 108, 497
Kevork, In re, 530
Khalid v. Bush, 756, 905
Kiareldeen v. Reno, 855
Kielczynski v. Does 1-2, 1050
Kielczynski v. United States Central Intelligence Agency, 1050
King v. Department of Justice, 1008
Kissinger v. Reporters Committee for Freedom of the Press, 996
Klimavicius-Viloria, United States v., 952
Knights, United States v., 551
Knotts, United States v., 504
Koohi v. United States, 249
Korematsu v. United States (1944), 608, *704*, 711, 712, 714, 728, 752, 873, 934, 1043
Korematsu v. United States (1984), 712, 1043
Kowalczyk v. Department of Justice, 996
Koyemajian, United States v., 520
Kucinich v. Bush, 154
Kuzma v. Internal Revenue Service, 995
Kyllo, United States v., 504, 585

Laird v. Tatum, 225, 504, 960
Lamont v. Haig, 951
Lear Siegler Energy Products Div. v. Lehman, 121
Lee, United States v., *859*
Lichter v. United States, 93, *102*, 124, 125, 130
Lindh, United States v., 795, 836
Little v. Barreme, 77, 98, 99, 101, 133, 229, 374, 419
Logan v. Zimmerman Brush Co., 437
Lopez, United States v., 610
Lopez-Lima, United States v., *376*, 865
Loral Corp. v. McDonnell Douglas Corp., 1049
Lovett v. United States, 124–128, 1064
Lowry v. Reagan, 140, 249
Lujan v. Defenders of Wildlife, 149
Luther v. Borden, 956, 970

MacWade v. Kelly, *590*, 599
Made in USA Found. v. United States, 172
Marbury v. Madison, 144, 147, 345
Marchetti, United States v., *1052*, 1059
Martin v. Mott, 70, 216, 956
Martin v. Office of Special Counsel, 1017
Martinez-Fuerte, United States v., 608
Marzen v. United States Dept. of Health and Human Services, 996
Massachusetts v. Laird, 222–224, 232, 312
Mathews v. Diaz, 613
Matta-Ballesteros v. Henman, 181
Matthews v. Eldridge, 603, 725, 850, 854, 865
Maturo, United States v., 661
Maynard v. Central Intelligence Agency, 1010
McAuliffe v. Mayor of New Bedford, 1062
McClellan Ecological Seepage Situation v. Carlucci, 995
McDonnell Douglas Corp. v. United States, 1048
McDougal, United States v., 1023
McGehee v. Casey, 986

McGehee v. CIA, 1013
McGrain v. Daugherty, *118*, 121
McVeigh, United States v., 674, 1023
Meeropol v. Meese, 1013
Megahey, United States v., 530
Mehinovic v. Vuckovic, 804
Mendoza-Cecelia, United States v., 951, 952
Merryman, Ex parte, 498, 682, 689
Meyer v. Bush, 995
Michigan v. Long, 482
Midwest Oil Co., United States v., 55
Milena Ship Management Co. v. Newcomb, 117
Miller v. The Resolution, 16, 257
Miller, United States v., 559, 569, 578, 584
Miller v. United States Dept. of State, 995, 1009, 1013
Milligan, Ex parte, 498, *683*, 689, 690, 693, 697, 710, *714*, 718, 720, 753, *877*, *970*
Minier v. CIA, 1009
Missouri v. Holland, 179
Mistretta v. United States, 43, 58
Mitchell v. Laird, 152, 225, 231, 232
Mitchell v. United States, 224
M.K.B. v. Warden, 1036
Montoya de Hernandez, United States v., 482
Moore v. United States House of Representatives, 154
Mora v. McNamara, 224
Morisette v. United States, 1076
Morison, United States v., *1068*, 1072–1074, 1076
Morland v. Sprecher, 1109
Morrison v. Olson, 57
Morton Salt Co., United States v., 569
Moussaoui, United States v., *866*, 873, 1035
Mudd v. Caldera, 720
Murray v. The Schooner Charming Betsy, 194
Myer v. Bush, 126
Myers v. United States, 46, 835, 1023

NAACP v. State of Alabama ex rel. Patterson, 571, 838
Nagelberg, United States v., 661
Najjar v. Reno, 850, 855
Nardone v. United States, 484
Nation Magazine v. United States Dept. of Defense, *1024*
National Cable Television Assn. v. United States, 110
National Council of La Raza v. Department of Justice, 1012
National Council of Resistance of Iran v. Department of State, 468, 473
National Federation of Federal Employees v. United States (NFFE I), 91, 127, 1064, 1066
National Federation of Federal Employees v. United States (NFFE II), 1065, 1066
National Labor Relations Board v. Sears, Roebuck & Co., 1011
National Security Archive v. United States Dept. of Defense, 995
National Treasury Employees Union v. Griffin, 995

Table of Cases

National Treasury Employees Union v. Von Raab, 934
Neagle, In re, 80, 84, *264,* 268, 325, 492, 780
Near v. Minnesota, 1096
Nebraska Press Assn. v. Stuart, 1058
New York Tel. Co., United States v., 507
New York Times v. Sullivan, 1060
New York Times Co. v. United States, 2, 3, 437, 1058, 1072, 1084, 1090–1092, 1096, 1097, *1098,* 1105, 1106, 1110
New York Times Co., United States v. (2d Cir.), 1096
New York Times Co., United States v. (S.D.N.Y.), 1072, 1089, 1095
Nicaragua v. United States, 225
Nigro, United States v., 482
Nixon v. Administrator of General Services, 872, 1016, 1064
Nixon v. Freeman, 1016
Nixon, United States v., 45, 88, 90, 91, 411, 1019
Nixon v. Warner Communications, Inc., 1022
Noriega, United States v., 181
North Jersey Media Group, Inc. v. Ashcroft, 1029
North, United States v. (D.C. Cir.), 420, 421
North, United States v. (D.D.C.), 411, 416, 419
Northeastern Florida Chapter, General Contractors of America v. City of Jacksonville, 149
Ntakirutimana v. Reno, 171

Odah v. United States, 750
Oklahoma Press Publishing Co. v. Walling, 569
Olmstead v. United States, 483, 492
Orlando v. Laird, 100, *219,* 253, 293
Ott, United States v., 531

Padilla ex rel. Newman v. Bush, 743, 750, 958
Padilla v. Hanft, 744, 751
Padilla v. Rumsfeld, 742, 743, 750, 873, 958
Paisley v. CIA, 996
Panama Refining Co. v. Ryan, 43
Paquete Habana, The, 183, 194, 196
Paracha, United States v., 873
Paradissiotis v. United States, 118
Pascazi v. Verizon Comm., 556
Paul v. Davis, 602
Pelton, United States v., 531
Pentagen Technologies v. Committee on Appropriations, 1022
Pentagon Papers Case (see *New York Times Co. v. United States*)
People's Mojahedin Organization of Iran v. United States Dept. of State, 472, *473,* 476
Philadelphia Yearly Meeting of the Religious Society of Friends v. Tate, 504
Pietsch v. Bush, 150
Pink, United States v., 181
Place, United States v., 671
Plummer, United States v., 116
Poindexter, United States v., 421
Pollard v. FBI, 1009

Pope v. United States, 1013
Powell v. McCormack, 387
Press-Enterprise Co. v. Superior Court, 1024
Prize Cases, The, 67, 87, 214, 216, 246, 256, *260,* 549, 753, 780, 904, 956
Progressive, Inc., The, United States v., 1108–1110
Public Citizen v. United States Department of Justice, 55, 872
Public Committee Against Torture in Israel v. State of Israel, 791

Quinon v. Federal Bureau of Investigation, 1008
Quirin, Ex parte, 714, 691, 694, 720, 743, 753, *877*

Rahman, United States v., 530, 532, *817,* 834
Raines v. Byrd, 152
Rasul v. Bush, 692, 701, 702, 750, 756, 757, 797, 801, 813, 905
Rasul v. Rumsfeld, 797
Ray v. Turner, 997, 1007–1009, 1044
Red Feather, United States v., 950, 951
Regan v. Wald, 117
Reid v. Covert, 86, *173,* 179, *640,* 718, 813
Reno v. American-Arab Anti-Discrimination Committee, 613
Reno v. Catholic Social Services, Inc., 154
Reynolds, United States v., 88, 853, 863, 1041, 1043
Rezaq, United States v., 864
Richardson v. United States (3d Cir.), 386
Richardson, United States v. (S. Ct.), 385
Richmond Newspapers, Inc. v. Virginia, 1023
Robel, United States v., 1, 125
Roberts, United States v., 952
Robinson v. Overseas Military Sales Corp., 951
Robinson, United States v., 482
Rocca v. Thompson, 162
Rockefeller Center Properties v. United States, 118
Rosen, United States v., 1091
Rosenberg, United States v., 1092
Rumsfeld v. Padilla, 700, *743*
Runyon v. McCrary, 609
Rushforth v. Council of Economic Advisers, 995
Russell v. Department of the Air Force, 1011
Russo, United States v., 1076

Sacramento v. Lewis, 662
Saenz v. Roe, 932
Saint Francis College v. Al Khazraji, 609
Saleh v. Titan Corp., 804
Salerno, United States v., 672
Salisbury v. United States, 1008, 1048
Sanchez-Espinoza v. Reagan, 140, 678
Sanchez-Llamas v. Oregon, 678
Sarkissian, United States v., 532
Sattar, United States v., 836, 837

Scales v. United States, 836
Scarbeck v. United States, 1075
Schechter Poultry Corp. v. United States, 43
Schenck v. United States, 824
Schooner Charming Betsy, The, 194, 195
Schrecker v. Department of Justice, 988
Schwartz v. IRS, 1000
Schwartz v. United States Department of Justice, 1020
Sealed Case No. 02-001, 02-002, In re (310 F.3d 717), 533, 549, 551
Sealed Case, In re (121 F.3d 729), 89
See v. City of Seattle, 569
Seery v. United States, 182
Service v. Dulles, 45
Siderman de Blake v. Republic of Argentina, 197
Sierra Club v. Andrus, 111
Sisson, United States v., 225
Skinner v. Mid-America Pipeline Co., 110
Skinner v. Railway Labor Executives' Assn., 482
Skipwith, United States v., 594
Skiriotes v. Florida, 767
Smith v. Avino, 932
Smith v. Maryland, 507, 557–559, 569, 578, 582, 584
Smith v. United States (1806), 258, 259, 372
Smith, United States v. (4th Cir. 1985), 865
Snepp v. United States, 1055, 1059, 1062, 1065, 1066
Socialist Workers Party v. Attorney General, 504
Sosa v. Alvarez-Machain, 187, 803
Spaulding v. Douglas Aircraft Co., 108, 112
Squillicote, United States v., 531
Stanford v. Kuwait Airways Corp., 470
State v. Pattioay, 951
State-Record Co., Inc., In re, 1036
Steele v. Bulova Watch Co., 767
Steel Seizure Case (see *Youngstown Sheet & Tube Co. v. Sawyer*)
Stein v. Dept. of Justice, 1008
Sterling v. Constantin, 707
Sterling v. Tenet, 1048
Stewart v. Kahn, 108
Sullivan v. Central Intelligence Agency, 1011
Swaim v. United States, 125

Tachiaona v. Mugabe, 804
Talbot v. Seeman, 98, 99, 214, 257, 719
Tatum v. Laird, 960
Taylor v. Department of the Army, 1008
Taylor v. State, 951
Tel-Oren v. Libyan Arab Republic, 847
Tenet v. Doe, 1045, 1049, 1050
Tennessee Valley Authority v. Hill, 111
Terkel v. AT&T Corp., 556
Terrell, United States v., 372, 420
Terry v. Ohio, 482, 671
Thompson, United States v., 951
Tilden v. Tenet, 1048
Tobias, United States v., 1076
Toscanino, United States v., 661
Totten, In re, 1048–1050

Train v. City of New York, 112
Travel Campaign v. Newcomb, 117
Trulock v. Lee, 1048
Truong Dinh Hung, United States v., 500, 532, 1076
Turkmen v. Ashcroft, 613, 676

Under Seal, In re, 1049
United Assn. of Journeymen and Apprentices, Local 598 v. Dept. of the Army, Corps of Engineers, 995
United Public Workers v. Mitchell, 154
United States v. _____. *See* name of defendant.
United States, In re, 1042, 1049
United States Dept. of Justice v. Julian, 437, 1011
United States Dept. of Justice v. Landano, 1013
United States Dept. of Justice v. Reporters Comm. for Freedom of the Press, 585, 986, 994
United States District Court, United States v. (Keith), 485, 511, 512, 549, 873
United States ex rel. Toth v. Quarles, 767
United States House of Representatives v. United States, 122
United States Senate v. Federal Trade Commission, 129
United Steelworkers v. United States, 172

Vander Jagt v. O'Neill, 154
Vaughn v. Rosen, 1042
Velvel v. Nixon, 151, 225
Verdugo-Urquidez, United States v., 324, 643, 755, 757, 780, 813, 905
Vernonia Sch. Dist. 47J v. Acton, 551, 934
Villamonte-Marquez, United States v., 482
Virginia v. Hicks, 836

Walker v. Birmingham, 1097
Walsh v. Brady, 117
Ward v. Rock Against Racism, 574
Warth v. Seldin, 149
Washington v. Glucksberg, 662
Washington Legal Found. v. United States Sentencing Commn., 1022
Washington Post Co., United States v., 1095
Weinberger v. Catholic Action of Hawaii, 1048
Weissman v. CIA, 1002
Whalen v. Roe, 586, 600, 602
Whitney v. Robertson, 175, 181
Whren v. United States, 604, 608, 676
Wiener v. Federal Bureau of Investigation, 1009
Will, United States v., 124
Willenburg v. Neurauter, 802
Wilson v. Girard, 171
Wilson, United States v., 866
Wisconsin v. Constantineau, 602
Wolffs, United States v., 951

Table of Cases

Wong Wai v. Williamson, 934
WPIX, Inc. v. League of Women Voters, 1024

Xuncax v. Gramajo, 804

Yamashita, In re, 691, 694, 718
Yick Wo v. Hopkins, 934
Yoshida Intl., Inc., United States v., 117

Youngstown Sheet & Tube Co. v. Sawyer (Steel Seizure Case), 27, *28*, 46, 86, 125, 129, 131, 133, 214, 324, 417, 497, 550, 726, 908
Yousef, United States v., *469*, 471
Yunis, United States v., 865, 952

Zadvydas v. Davis, 551, 613, 671, 725, 873, 905
Zweibon v. Mitchell, 494

Index

Acquiescence, congressional. *See* Congressional acquiescence
Acquiescence, treaty interpretation, 168
Administrative subpoenas, 565, 569, 577, 579
Advice and consent. *See* Treaties
Advisory Committee Act. *See* Federal Advisory Committee Act
Afghanistan, military strikes in, 273–277
Alien Enemy Act, 99, 703–704, 709, 757
Alien Terrorist Removal Court, 855
Alien Tort Statute, 187–198 *passim*
Ambassadors, presidential power to receive, 11
American-Japanese Evacuation Claims Act, 713
Ames, Aldrich, 635
Anthrax. *See* Terrorism, bioterrorism
Anticipatory self-defense. *See* Unilateral self-defense, defensive power
Anti-Deficiency Act, 417
Antiterrorism. *See* Terrorism
Anti-Terrorism and Effective Death Penalty Act of 1996, 274, 846, 855, 856
Appropriations Clause. *See* Appropriations
Appropriations
  as authority for war, 100–101, 123, 223
  authorizations distinguished, 111
  congressional duty to make, 127
  constitutional power to raise and support armies, 9
  history, 13, 22, 113–114
  Jefferson, Thomas, 24
  limitations on executive, 112, 230
  limitations on riders, 124–128
  mandatory, 126, 127
  practical advantages, 113
  presidential circumvention, 127–128
  ratification by, 109
  supply bills, 19, 114
  unconstitutionality of using to avoid direct constitutional limitation, 126–127
Area limitations, 101, 226–230
Armed Forces Security Agency (AFSA), 443
Armed forces. *See* Congress, rules for government and regulation of army
Arms Export Control Act, 406, 407, 408
Articles of Confederation, 11

Articulable facts order, 577, 578
Assassination
  Church Committee recommendations, 393
  decision standards and procedures, 282–283
  definitions, 281–282
  domestic, 283
  Executive Order No. 11,905, 280
  Executive Order No. 12,036, 280–281
  Executive Order No. 12,333, 277–278, 281–282
  force and effect of executive prohibitions, 282
  international law, 282
  Terrorist Elimination Act, 282
  wartime, 280
Association, freedom of. *See also* Expression, freedom of; Material support
  financial donations, 838
  knowing membership and specific intent, 836–838
  Smith Act, 836–837
  vagueness and overbreadth, 835–836
Asymmetric attacks, 340
Atomic Energy Act, 1108, 1111. *See* Nuclear secrets; *Progressive* litigation. *See also* Classified information
Attainder, bill of, 124
Authorization, distinguished from appropriation, 111
Authorization for Use of Military Force
  Jan. 12, 1991 (against Iraq), 298–300
  Sept. 18, 2001 (against Sept. 11 participants), 48, 100, 215, 277, 554, 719, 752
  Oct. 16, 2002 (against Iraq), 155, 298, 305–309
Avoidance, judicial rule of, 125

Bank records, 559
Bay of Pigs, 1088
Biden Condition, 168
Bill of Attainder Clause,
Bioterrorism. *See* Terrorism
Blacklists, 601
Blackstone, 680–681, 970
Boland Amendments, 411–415. *See* Iran-Contra Affair
Border searches, 589

Brady rule, 864
British constitution, 12
Building entry search, 594–595, 599
Burlamaqui, 15–16

Cambodia, 226–230, 235–239
  appropriations cutoff, 227, 235–239
  bombing, 224, 230, 235
  incursion, 227, 229
CAPPS. *See* Computer Assisted Passenger Prescreening Program (CAPPS)
CAPPS II. *See* Computer Assisted Passenger Prescreening Program (CAPPS II)
Case-Zablocki Act, 172–173
CAT. *See* Convention Against Torture
Censorship. *See* Expression, freedom of
Central Intelligence Agency (CIA)
  appropriations, 385–389
  CHAOS, Operation, 433
  charter, 392–394
  domestic law enforcement prohibition, 357
  information sharing, 634–639
  law enforcement information collection, 848
  oversight by Congress, 384–396
  secrecy agreements. *See* Nondisclosure agreements
Central Intelligence Agency Act of 1949, 385–386
Certification, 577, 580
CHAOS, Operation. *See* Central Intelligence Agency
Checks and balances
  English history, 15–16
  Federalist Papers, 23
Chile, covert action in, 382–384
Church Committee Report, 341–343, 347, 374–375, 380, 381, 384, 392, 431–432, 439–442, 447–449, 495, 512–513
CIA. *See* Central Intelligence Agency
CIPA. *See* Classified Information Procedures Act
Civil defense, 919–920. *See also* Terrorism
Classified information, 976–1014 *passim. See also* Expression, freedom of; Nondisclosure agreements
  Alien Terrorist Removal Court, 855
  alignment, 864
  authority to classify, 87–88, 987
  classification levels, 87, 980
  classified vs. classifiable, 979–981, 1060, 1066
  Classified Information Procedures Act. *See* Classified Information Procedures Act
  Congress and, 122, 345–346
  criminal prosecutions, use in. *See* Classified Information Procedures Act
  criteria for classification, 979–981
  decision to prosecute, 862–863
  declassification review, 984, 997–1013
  discovery of, 864, 872–873
  evidentiary use. *See* Classified Information Procedures Act; State secrets privilege
    immigration proceedings, 876–877, 880
    procedures due, 878–879
    risk of inaccuracy, 877–878
  Freedom of Information Act. *See* Freedom of Information Act, Exemption 1
  intelligence sources and methods, 1010, 1062, 1066. *See also* Central Intelligence Agency
  judicial review of classifiability, 977–1013. *See also* Freedom of Information Act
  public interest in, 975–979, 986
  refusal to confirm or deny, 984, 1009
  restricted data, 1108. *See* Atomic Energy Act
  Sensitive Compartmented Information (SCI), 1060, 1061
  state secrets privilege, relation to, 1041, 1042
  unauthorized removal, 1076
Classified Information Procedures Act (CIPA), 857–859
  admissibility hearing, 865
  alignment of government agencies, 864
  disclose or dismiss dilemma, 866
  discovery, 864–865
  greymail, 863
  notice, 865
  substitution, 865
COINTELPRO, 439–443
Collective self-defense, 217, 284–302
  compared to individual self-defense, 287
  Korean "Police Action," 290–294
  military actions outside the U.N. Charter, 287
  NATO, 302
  Persian Gulf War (1991), 294–302
  police actions, 290, 294
  U.N. Charter Article 42, 285, 286–287
  U.N. Charter Article 43, 286
  U.N. Charter Article 51, 286, 287, 294, 311–312
  U.N. Charter Articles 52–53, 301–302
  U.N. Participation Act, 288–289
  Vietnam War, 217
Colonial government experience, 17
Combatant Status Review Tribunal (CSRT), 700, 756, 757, 758
Commander in Chief, 36
  authority for Vietnam War, 209, 213
  domestic power, 46
  Federalist Papers, 23
  first general and admiral, 21, 70
  powers during war summarized, 80
  powers in face of statute, 77–80
  powers outside theater of war, 37, 46
Commission on the Intelligence Capabilities of the United States Regarding Weapons of Mass Destruction (Silberman/Robb Commission), 362, 367, 442, 458, 638
  Curveball, 458
  Report to the President of the United States (transmittal letter), 362
Committee on Detail, 20
Common Defence, providing for, 9
Common law right to know, 1020–1023, 1039
  Freedom of Information Act, relation to, 1021
  public record, 1022
Computer Assisted Passenger Prescreening Program (CAPPS), 588, 589
Computer Assisted Passenger Prescreening Program (CAPPS II), 583, 586
Computer matching, 586–587
Computer Matching and Privacy Protection Act of 1988, 586–587

Index

Concurrent resolution, contrasted with joint resolution, 131, 253
Congress
   Chadha limitations on, 128–132
   committees with national security jurisdiction, 113 n.2
   contempt of Congress, 122
   declaration of war. *See* Declaration of war
   delegation of war-making authority to the President, 47–48, 218, 312
   defining offenses against the law of nations, 196–197, 845
   emergency authority, 114–118, 689
   investigation. *See* Investigation, Congress's power of
   limitations by Congress on presidential authority, 229–239
   limitations on Congress, 124–132
   Necessary and Proper authority, 126
   oversight. *See* Investigation, Congress's power of
   rules for government and regulation of army authority, 9, 271
   war powers, 93–101, 108
Congressional acquiescence
   appropriation as, 111
   as constitutional gloss, 33
   clear statement rule for restrictions on individual liberties, 108–109
   executive practice or usage, 33–34, 55, 71–80
   Frankfurter's theory, 33–34
   inaction by Congress, 12, 55
   Jackson's groupings, 35
   notice to Congress of executive practice, 55
   predicates for, 33–34, 54–55
   significance of congressional refusals, 54, 75
Constitutional Convention, secret journal, 19–20
Constitutional right to know, 1023–1037 *passim*, 1085, 1087
   military operations, 1024–1029
   press vs. public rights, 1023–1027, 1034
Consultation under War Powers Resolution. *See* War Powers Resolution
Content data, 581
Continental Congress, conduct of Revolutionary War by, 17–18
Convention Against Torture (CAT), 774, 785, 815
Cooper-Church Amendment, 227, 230
Counterintelligence, CIA/FBI cooperation, 634–639
Counterintelligence Policy Board, 635
Cruel, inhuman, or degrading treatment, 793
CSRT. *See* Combatant Status Review Tribunal
Customary executive authority. *See* Congressional acquiescence
Customary international law
   Alien Tort Statute, 194
   common law incorporation, 194
   controlling executive act, 195
   controlling judicial act, 195–196, 198
   controlling legislative act, 194–195
   creation, 194
   due process, 197–198
   incorporation by statute, 196–197
   jus cogens, 197–198, 456, 798
   last-in-time rule, 194–198
Customary war powers, 71–77 *passim*, 259–260

Data aggregation, 584–585, 586
Data mining, 445, 559, 582, 584–585, 587
Declaration of war
   against Rumania, 94
   alternatives to, 98, 100–101, 222–223
   declaration by action, 16–17
   Declaration of War Clause, 9, 20–21, 23
      defensive war, 16
      Federalist Papers, 23
      framing of, 20–21
      law of nations, 98
   declared by United States, 255 n.1
   delegation of, 109–110
   domino legal effects, 99, 115–116
   judicial act, 99
   limitations, 101
   obsolescence, 98
   partial declaration, 100
   perfect war, 16
   standby authorities and, 99, 115–116
   state of war, 97–98
   statutory equivalent, 93, 98
   terrorism and, 99–100
Defense appropriations. *See* Appropriations
Defensive war, generally, 67–71. *See also* Collective self-defense; President; Unilateral self-defense
Delegation doctrine, 43, 47–48, 102–114 *passim*
   checks on, 113
   clear statement doctrine, 108–109
   constitutional silence, 12
   foreign affairs, 65, 130
   judicial review, 48, 130–131
   legislative veto, 128–129
   national security authority, 129–131
   standards, 43, 47–48, 109
   war power, 109, 218, 312
Deliberative communication privilege. *See* Freedom of Information Act, Exemption 5
Department of Defense (DOD)
   responsibility for intelligence, 350–355, 365, 443, 960–963
   role in counterterrorism. *See* Terrorism
   role of Defense Intelligence Agency, 459
Department of Homeland Security, 637, 921. *See also* Terrorism
Department of Homeland Security Appropriations Act of 2006, 603
Desert Shield. *See* Persian Gulf War (1991), Operation Desert Shield
Desert Storm. *See* Persian Gulf War (1991), Operation Desert Storm
Detainee Treatment Act of 2005, 650, 700, 701–702, 798–799, 816
Director of National Intelligence (DNI), 355–356, 363, 364, 637
Dirty assets, 384, 451–458

Domestic Security Guidelines, 629. *See also*
    Federal Bureau of Investigation
  full investigations, 630
  mail covers, 631
  preliminary investigations, 630
  pretext interviews, 632
  use of informants, 630

ECHELON, 446, 447
Electronic Communications Privacy Act of 1986
    (ECPA), 563, 566–567, 581
Electronic surveillance, history, 519
Ellsberg, Daniel, 1082, 1095, 1106
Emergency Broadcasting System, 908
Emergency Detention Act, 672–673
Emergency powers. *See also* Habeas corpus
  Congress's power, 86, 114–118, 689
  Constitution, 46, 84–87, 689
  judicial review, 86–87
  martial law, 39, 969–972
  necessity, 38–39, 75–76, 85
  presidential, 10, 38–39, 84–87, 689, 709
  protecting government functions, 269–270
  racial discrimination. *See* Japanese-American internment
  relativistic theory of, 709
  right to travel and, 117
  statutory authority, 86, 114–118
  takings and, 118
  terrorism. *See* Terrorism
Enemy combatants, 719, 720–758 *passim*, 795–796, 876–906 *passim*
Envelope data, 581
Equal protection
  analysis, 608, 710–711
  compelling interest, 608
  ethnicity, 609–611
  national origin, 609–611, 612–613
  race, 609
  strict scrutiny, 608, 710–711
Espionage and Censorship Act, 1066–1079 *passim*, 1088–1093
  codes, cryptography, intelligence gathering methods, 1067, 1089, 1091–1092
  criminal intent, 1076, 1090
  criminalizing leaks, 1066, 1079
  criminalizing publication, 1072, 1088–1093
  legislative history, 1074–1076, 1090
  Rosenberg, Ethyl and Julius, 1092
Ethics in Government Act, 418
Executive agreements
  Case-Zablocki Act, 172–173
  congressional-executive, 170–171
  congressional limits on, 172–173
  criteria for choosing instead of treaty, 172
  domestic legal effect, 173, 181–182
  history, 170
  sole executive, 171
  treaties distinguished, 171–172
  treaty-based, 171
Executive orders
  form, 44–45
  legal vetting of, 45
  No. 10,290, 987

No. 10,340, 28, 30–31
No. 11,905, 396
No. 12,036, 396, 402
No. 12,331, 402
No. 12,333, 277–278, 397–404, 410, 438, 444–445, 459, 616–617, 628, 634–635
No. 12,356, 985–986
No. 12,863, 428
No. 12,949, 628
No. 12,958, 979, 985, 988
No. 13,354, 637
No. 13,375, 941
No. 13,392, 979, 985–986, 988. *See also* Freedom of Information Act, Exemption 1
  presidential proclamation, directive compared, 44
  publication of, 45
  statutory authority for, 45
Executive privilege,
  balancing test, 89, 123
  common law basis, 89–90
  Congress and, 91–92
  constitutional basis, 88–90, 90–91
  definition, 88
  deliberative process, 89
  Freedom of Information Act, relation to. *See* Freedom of Information Act
  history, 90
  inter-branch negotiation, 91–92
  invocation, 92
  law enforcement, 89
  No-Transfer Act as implied recognition, 387
  presidential communication, 89
  state secrets, 88, 436
  types compared, 88–89
Expression, freedom of. *See also* Association, freedom of; *Pentagon Papers* litigation; *Progressive* litigation; Terrorism
  anonymity, 573
  balancing test, 1105, 1110
  censorship, 1090, 1093–1097
  clear and present danger, 824
  content-based speech, 574
  criminal syndicalism, 824
  financial donations as, 838
  imminent harm, 824
  overbreadth, 835, 1073
  Pentagon press pool. *See* Pentagon press pool
  press. *See also* Constitutional right to know
    confidential sources, protection of, 1072, 1093
    institutional or structural role in government, 1085, 1087
  prior restraint, 574, 576, 1058–1059, 1062, 1082–1111 *passim*
    collateral bar rule, 1096
    presumption of unconstitutionality, 1105–1106
  rights of ISP subscribers, 571, 580
  self-restraint of press, 1088
  vagueness and overbreadth, 835
  viewpoint-neutral regulation, 574
  waiver of rights, 1058–1059, 1062
Extraordinary rendition, 456, 804–816 *passim*
  charter flights by CIA, 814

Index

Convention Against Torture, 815
   definitions, 804
   due process, 813
   extradition, 804
   habeas corpus, 813
   irregular, 804
   regular, 804
Extraterritoriality
   Constitution, 640–649 *passim*, 800–801, 844–845
   nationality principle, 845–846
   nexus requirement, 847
   passive personality principle, 846–847
   personal jurisdiction and minimum contacts, 847
   presumption against, 845
   protective principle, 846
   reasonableness, 847
   universality principle, 847

Faithful Execution Clause, 10
False positives, 585, 602–603
Fast-track legislation, 131
Federal Advisory Committee Act, 1018–1019
Federal Bureau of Investigation (FBI). *See also* Terrorism
   Domestic Security Guidelines, 617–621, 629–632
   National Security Investigation (NSI) Guidelines, 622–627, 632–633. *See also* NSI Guidelines
   preliminary investigation, 629
   pretext interviews, 632
   threat assessment, 632
   use of informants, 630
Federal Emergency Management Agency (FEMA). *See* Terrorism
Federal Records Act, 1015
Federal Rule of Criminal Procedure 41, 525, 526, 527
Federalist Papers
   checks and balances, 23
   Commander in Chief Clause, 23
   Declaration of War Clause, 23
   secrecy, 346
Federative power, 14–15
Feed and Forage Act of 1861, 115
FEMA. *See* Terrorism
Fielding break-in, 495–496
Fifth function, 357–360
Final Report of the Independent Panel to Review DoD Detention Operations (Schlesinger Report), 761, 763, 787, 792
First Amendment. *See also* Association, freedom of; Expression, freedom of; Press, freedom of; Constitutional right to know
First General, Commander in Chief as, 11
FISA. *See* Foreign Intelligence Surveillance Act
FOIA. *See* Freedom of Information Act
Foreign affairs power
   domestic power compared, 65
   extra-constitutionality of, 65–66
   foreign policy and, 66–67
   history of, 65–66
Foreign commerce, regulation of, 9

Foreign Intelligence Surveillance Act (FISA), 512–556 *passim*. *See also* USA PATRIOT Act
   agent of a foreign power, 522
   business records, 521, 558, 568, 578, 579, 580
   case or controversy concerns, 530
   confrontation, 531
   Domestic Security Investigation (DSI) Guidelines, 629
   emergency surveillance, 528, 554
   First Amendment, 531–532
   FISA trends, 546
   Foreign Intelligence Surveillance Court (FISC), 524
   foreign power, 522
   Fourth Amendment, 531, 555
   Internet and e-mail, 520
   judicial review, 529, 562–580
   lone-wolf provision, 523
   mechanics of, 519–530
   minimization, 528, 546
   national security letters, 547
   Pen Register Act, 510
   pen registers, 507, 510, 520, 557, 567, 568, 572–573, 584
   primary purpose, 532–533, 636
   probable cause, 525–526
   section 215 orders, 558, 568, 578, 579, 580
   significant purpose, 537–538
   special needs precedents, 546
   surveillance methods, electronic, 519–521
   surveillance methods, physical searches, 521
   targets, 521
   technology, new, 504–505, 527–528
   Terrorist Surveillance Program, 493, 552
   trap and trace devices, 510, 520, 568
   trends and conclusions, 546–548
   use in law enforcement, 532–546
   "wall," 532
   Woods Procedures, 524
Foreign Intelligence Surveillance Court (FISC). *See* Foreign Intelligence Surveillance Act
Foreign policy, President as maker of, 66–67
Foreign terrorist organization, 468, 472–473, 476, 838
Formalism, in separation of powers analysis, 55–57
Forty Committee, 381
Fourth Amendment, 482–483, 492–493, 555
   administrative subpoena standards, 565, 569, 577, 579
   consent, 594
   electronic national security surveillance, 483–485
   expectation of privacy, 557, 559, 584, 593
   grand jury subpoenas, 565–566, 577
   physical entry, 481–482, 492, 495
   reasonableness of subpoenas, 565
   regulatory search, 591
   relevancy standard, 578, 579
   special needs, 591, 607–608
Framers, identity of, 19
Freedom of association. *See* Association, freedom of
Freedom of expression. *See* Expression, freedom of

Freedom of Information Act (FOIA), 989–1014
  agency, 995
  agency record, 996
  attorneys' fees, 995
  bad faith, 1013
  CIA and intelligence budget, 388–389
  common law right to know, relation to, 1021
  de novo review, 1007–1009
  description of record, 996
  E-FOIA, 996–997
  Executive Order No. 13,292, 979–988
  executive privilege, relation to, 1011
  Exemption 1, 1007–1010
  Exemption 3, 1010
  Exemption 5, 1011
  Exemption 7, 1012–1013
  fee waivers, 994
  identity of requester, 994
  in camera inspection, 1008
  Privacy Act compared, 1017–1018
  procedural requirements, 1009
  purpose of request, 994
  segregability, 1004
  standards for judicial review, 1007–1008
  text, 990–993
  Vaughn affidavit, 1008
Freedom of press. *See* Expression, freedom of
Freedom of speech. *See* Expression, freedom of
Functionalism, in separation of powers analysis, 55–57

General war, 201–239
Geneva Conventions
  Common Article 2, 767–768, 794
  Common Article 3, 768–769, 794–795, 904
  generally, 758, 904
  III, 760, 794, 795–796, 797
  IV, 719, 796, 816
Government in the Sunshine Act, 1018–1019
Grand jury subpoenas, 565–566, 577
Gray Fox, 460
Greymail. *See* Classified Information Procedures Act
Grotius, 15–16
Groupthink, 272–273
Guantánamo Bay (GTMO), 755–756
Gulf of Sidra incident, 260
Gulf of Tonkin. *See* Tonkin Gulf incident; Tonkin Gulf Resolution
Gulf War. *See* Persian Gulf War (1991)

Habeas corpus, 680–702 *passim*
  after September 11, 2001, 690
  Blackstone, 680
  clear statement required, 690, 700
  congressional authority, 689, 690
  custodian, 700
  Detainee Treatment Act of 2005, 700, 701–702
  extraordinary rendition, availability to challenge, 813
  hearing, 682
  history, 680–681

Military Commissions Act of 2006, 702
Military Order of Nov. 13, 2001, 691, 700
  nonresident aliens, availability to, 691–702 *passim*
  presidential authority, 682–683, 689, 690
  text, statutory, 681–682
Hamilton, Alexander
  framing of Declaration of War Clause, 21
  marque and reprisal, 257
  militia, 18
  power of judicial branch, 149–150
Hijacking, 589
"Hold until cleared," 668
Homeland Security Act, 529, 636
Horn of Africa Recovery and Food Security Act, 321–322
Hostage Act
  inapplicability to seizure of American Embassy hostages by Iran, 270
  Iran-Contra Affair, 407
  Iran Hostage Rescue mission, 266–269
  legislative history, 270–271
  text, 48
Hughes-Ryan Amendment, 390–392
  Boland II, 411–418
  Ford, Gerald, critique by, 391
  implied authorization of covert war, 390
  plausible deniability, 391–392
Humanitarian and peace/stability operations
  command by foreign officers, 332–333
  consultation with Congress, 333
  definitions, 318–319
  Department of Defense Appropriations Act of 1994, 329, 332, 333
  inherent executive authority, 321, 330–331
  international law, 333
  mission creep, 331
  peacekeeping, 318–319
  peacemaking, 318–319
  Operation Restore Hope (Somalia), 321–333 *passim*
  police actions, 331–332
  private contractors, 335–336
  stability operations, 334–336
  statutory authority, 319–321, 335
  U.N. Participation Act, 288–289
  War Powers Resolution, 332

Identification and identity cards, 588, 599–600, 604, 613, 615
IEEPA. *See* International Emergency Economic Powers Act
Immigration and special interest immigrants
  bond for release, 668–669, 677
  conditions of detention, 669–670
  detainee rights, 678
  detentions, 676
  length of detention, 676, 677–678
  pretextual detention, 676–677
  profiling, 679
  secret evidence, 849–856
  secret hearings, 1029–1036
  USA PATRIOT Act detention, 677
  "zero tolerance" policy, 679

Index

Imminent hostilities. *See* War Powers Resolution
Impeachment, 13, 15, 123, 239
Imperfect war, 16, 255. *See* Collective self-defense; Unilateral self-defense; Humanitarian and peace/stability operations
Impoundment, 111–112
In camera review. *See* Freedom of Information Act; State secrets privilege
Inaction, congressional. *See* Congressional acquiescence
Independent Counsel. *See* Ethics in Government Act
Indochina. *See* Vietnam War
INF Treaty. *See* Intermediate Range Nuclear Forces (INF) Treaty
Information sharing, 634–639
Inherent presidential power. *See* President
Injury in fact, 149
Insurrection Act, 953–954, 956. *See* Posse Comitatus Act
Intelligence Authorization Act for Fiscal Year 1991, 422–425
Intelligence Authorization Act for Fiscal Year 1995, 635
Intelligence collection, 349–353, 357–358
   clandestine, 357
   cycle, 341
   domestic, 431
   imagery intelligence (IMINT), 350
   human intelligence (HUMINT), 352
   nonofficial cover, 458
   open-source intelligence, 353–354
   signals intelligence (SIGINT), 351
   support for military operations, 354
Intelligence Community, 366
Intelligence interrogation (FM 34-52), 787
Intelligence operations
   congressional oversight, 384–386, 421–429
   executive oversight, 374–376, 380–382, 396–404
   plausible deniability, 391–392
Intelligence Oversight Act of 1980, 394–396
   arms sales to Iran, 405–409
   Boland II, 411–418
Intelligence Oversight Board, 396, 428, 456
Intelligence Reform and Terrorism Prevention Act of 2004 (IRTPA), 355, 363, 523, 547, 637, 825
   lone-wolf provision, 523, 547
   national security letters, 547
Intelligence reorganization, 362
   Civil Liberties Protection Officer, 364
   Director of National Intelligence (DNI), 355, 363, 364, 637
   Director of Science and Technology, 364
   National Counterterrorism Center (NCTC), 364, 367, 637
   National Intelligence Council (NIC), 364
Intelligence support activity, 460
Intelligence support for military operations, 354
Intermediate Range Nuclear Forces (INF) Treaty, 159
International Covenant on Civil and Political Rights (ICCPR), 678, 776, 798
International Emergency Economic Powers Act (IEEPA), 116, 117–118
International law
   Cambodia and Laos invasions raising issues of, 230
   consistency with U.S. law, 181–182, 194–196, 197–198
   incorporation into U.S. law, 16–17, 173–198 *passim*
   Vietnam war, issues raised by, 217–218, 225
Internet and e-mail, 520
Interrogation Working Group, 762
Invasion, power to repel. *See* Unilateral self-defense, defensive power
Investigation, Congress's power of, 118–123
   constitutional basis, 121
   enforcement of, 121–123
   intelligence operations, 345–346
   negotiation of, 91, 123
Investigation, extraterritorial, 640–663 *passim*
   exclusionary rule, 661
   good-faith exception, 660
   foreign intelligence exception, 659
   foreign law, 659
   international Fourth Amendment, 555, 663
   joint venture exception, 660–661
   mutual legal assistance treaties, 659
   probable cause, 660
   reasonableness, 659–660
   shocks-the-conscience exception, 661–662
   silver platter doctrine, 660, 663
   substantially connected aliens, 649
   torture, 650, 662–663
   unconnected aliens, 649
   warrants, 658–659
Iran-Contra Affair, 404–421 *passim*
   Arms Export Control Act, 414
   arms for hostages, 405–409
   Boland Amendments, 411–418
   Boland II and fund restriction, 414–415
   chronology, 404–405
   compliance with executive requirements, 410–411
   Independent Counsel, 418–421
   information exchanges with Contras, 414–416
   Neutrality Act, 420
   North, Oliver, 404–421 *passim*
   Poindexter, John, 404–421 *passim*
   presidential findings, 405–409
   prosecutions, 418–421
      criminal conspiracy, 418–419
      following orders defense, 419–420
   solicitation of unappropriated funds, 415–416
Iran Hostage Rescue mission, 266–273
Iraq Sanctions Act of 1990, 296
Iraq War of 2003, 303–317. *See also* Persian Gulf War (1991)
   Article 51, 312
   Authorization for Use of Military Force, 298, 305, 310
   congressional approval, 305, 310–311
   delegation of authority, 312
   duration of authority, 316–317
   insurgency, 334–336
   judicial challenge, 312

Iraq War of 2003 (*continued*)
   justifications, 304–310, 313–316
     National Security Strategy of 2002, 311
     stability operations, 334–336
     U.N. Security Council Resolution 1441, 309
Item veto, 131–132

Jackson, Justice Robert H.
   inherent presidential power, 38–39
   theory of fluctuating presidential powers
     (*Steel Seizure* concurrence), 35–36, 47–58
   twilight zone, 35, 48
Japanese-American internment, 704–714
   American-Japanese Evaluation Claims Act, 713
   Commission on Wartime Relocation and
     Internment of Civilians, 713
   government litigation misconduct, 711–712
   loyalty, 710
   military necessity, 712–713
   racial discrimination, 712–713, 713–714
Jay, John, 23, 165
Jay Treaty, 90
Jencks Act, 864
Joint resolution, contrasted to concurrent
   resolution, 131, 253
Journal, secrecy of congressional, 344–345
Jurisdiction, extraterritorial. *See* Extraterritoriality
Jus cogens, 197–198, 456, 798
Justiciability. *See* Political question doctrine;
   Ripeness; Standing to sue

Kent State protests, 227
Korean War, 290–294
   as "police action," 294
   history, 290–293
   U.N. Charter Article 51 as authority, 294
   U.N. Security Council resolutions as authority,
     293–294
   usage (practice) as authority for, 46
Kosovo, 302
Koszta incident, 84, 269–270

Laos, 227–230
   appropriations cutoff, 230
   bombing and incursion, 228, 230
Law of nations. *See* International law; Offenses
   against the law of nations
Law of war, 718–719, 752–753
Leaks, 1051–1081 *passim. See also Pentagon Papers*
   litigation, Frankel affidavit
Lee, Wen Ho, 859–863
Legislative supremacy in colonial governments, 17
Legislative rules, 45
Legislative veto, 128–132
Lex posterior. See Treaties, last-in-time rule
Library records, 578, 580–581
Libya bombing raid, 260–264
Limited war. *See* Imperfect war
Lincoln, Abraham
   Emancipation Proclamation, 85
   Mexican War of 1846, 213–214
Line of Death, 260

Line-item veto, 131–132
Link analysis, 558, 582
Locke, John, 13–15
Logan Act, 372
Los Angeles riots, 956
Low intensity conflict. *See* Imperfect war
Loyalty screening, 601

Madison, James, 20–22, 23–24
Mail covers, 631
Mansfield Amendment, 234
Marque and Reprisal Clause, 258, 418. *See*
   Unilateral self-defense, marque and
   reprisal
Martial law, 39, 710, 962–972
Material support
   constitutional issues, 835–838
   forms of, 835–836
   prosecutors' weapon of choice, 834–835
   scienter, 836–837
   text, 825–826
Material witness
   detentions, 674–675
   grand jury, 675
   testimony or deposition, 675–676
   text, 674
MATRIX. *See* Multistate Anti-Terrorism
   Information Exchange
McNamara, Robert S., 208
Mexican War, 213–214
Military. *See also* National Guard; Terrorism
   domestic use of troops, 944–972
   immediate response authority, 966
   law enforcement using. *See* Posse Comitatus Act
   surveillance of citizens by, 960–963
   war on drugs, 954, 956–957
Military commissions
   common law of war authority, 718
   due process, 904–908
   extraordinary jurisdiction, 718
   Geneva Convention Common Article 3, 904
   Military Commissions Act of 2006, 906
   Military Order of November 13, 2001,
     878–882
   necessity for, 903
   process before Military Commissions Act of
     2006, 882
   statutory authority, 718, 903–904
   uniformity principle, 904
   war, as predicate, 718–719
   war crimes jurisdiction, 719, 904
Military Commissions Act of 2006, 702, 756, 906
Military Cooperation with Law Enforcement
   Officials Act, 954–955, 956–957
Military detention, 679, 703–758 *passim*
Military Extraterritorial Jurisdiction Act of
   2000, 802
Military necessity, 712–713, 718, 750–751, 903
Military Order of November 13, 2001, 679, 691,
   700, 877, 878–882
Military special operations as intelligence
   operations, 459
   Communications Security Intelligence
     (COMINT), 459

Index

Defense Intelligence Agency (DIA), 459
  Gray Fox, 460
  Intelligence Support Activity (ISA), 460
  National Reconnaissance Office (NRO), 459
  signals intelligence (SIGINT), 459
  special access programs (SAPs), 460
  Special Military Operations (SMO), 460
  Strategic Support Branch, 460
Militia Acts, 70–71
Militia, 20, 148. *See also* National Guard
Militia Clause, 38
Minatory demonstrations of force, 263
Mission creep, 586, 601–602
Mixed government, in English theory, 14–15
Model State Emergency Health Powers Act, 935–939
Mogadishu line, 321
Montesquieu, 15
Mosaic theory, 576, 667
Moussaoui, Zacarias, 533
Multistate Anti-Terrorism Information Exchange (MATRIX), 583
Mutual legal assistance treaties, 659

National Commission on Terrorist Attacks Upon the United States: Final Report on 9/11, 362, 368, 637
National Counterterrorism Center, 601
National Emergencies Act, 116–117
National emergency, 116–117
National Guard, 924, 952, 966–967, 969. *See also* Terrorism
National identity card or other identifier, 599–600, 604, 613, 615
National Intelligence Program, 366, 368
National Intelligence Reorganization and Reform Act of 1978, 393
National Intelligence Strategy of the United States of America, 368
National Reconnaissance Office, 350, 351, 459
National Security Act of 1947, 355–361 *passim*, 372–374, 628. *See also* Central Intelligence Agency Act; Intelligence Oversight Act
National Security Agency (NSA), 443
  ECHELON, 446, 447
  responsibility for collecting SIGINT, 443
  VENONA, 446
National Security Council
  Boland II, 411–15
  Executive Order No. 12,333, 397–400
  functions, 360, 361–362, 373–375, 400–402
  Iran-Contra Affair, 404–405, 410–411
  National Security Decision Directives. *See* National Security Decision Directives
  origins, 360–361, 373
National Security Decision Directives (NSDD), 44–45
National Security Decisions (NSD). *See* National Security Decision Directives
National security letters (NSL), 558, 559–581
NATO. *See* North Atlantic Treaty Organization
Naval regulations, 271–277
Necessary and Proper Clause, 126

Neutrality Act, 371, 420
Nixon tapes, 90–91. *See also* Watergate
No-fly lists, 595, 603–604
Nondelegation doctrine. *See* Delegation doctrine; Congress, delegation of warmaking authority
Non-Detention Act, 670, 672–673, 752
Nondisclosure agreements, 1052–1066 *passim*
  CIA secrecy agreements and oaths, 1052–1060
  Classified Information Nondisclosure Agreement (SF 189), 1060
  Congress, interference with, 1064–1065
  First Amendment limits on, 1065
  National Security Decision Directive (NSDD) 84, 1060
  scope, 1063
  Sensitive Compartmented Information Nondisclosure (SF 4193), 1061
North Atlantic Treaty Organization (NATO), 302
North, Oliver. *See* Iran-Contra Affair
NSI Guidelines, 622–627, 632–633. *See also* Federal Bureau of Investigation
  CIA activities within the United States, 633
  DOD activities within the United States, 633
  extraterritorial investigations, 633
  threat assessments, 632
NSL. *See* National security letters
Nuclear secrets, 1107–1111
Nuclear weapons. *See* Atomic Energy Act; *Progressive* litigation
Nuremberg defense, 419–420

Obstructing a congressional inquiry, 419
Offenses against the law of nations, 196–197, 845
Office of Inspector General (OIG), Department of Justice, 667
Oklahoma City federal building bombing. *See* Terrorism
Omnibus Crime Control and Safe Streets Act of 1968, Title III, 493–494, 530–531
Operation CHAOS. *See* Central Intelligence Agency
Operation Desert Shield, 295–296, 1024–1029
Operation Desert Storm, 296–301, 1024–1029
Outsourcing torture, 788
Overbreadth. *See* Expression, freedom of
Oversight. *See* Investigation, Congress's power of

Padilla, Jose, 368, 480
Paramilitary operations, 369–370
Passenger screening, 589–590, 604
Pattern recognition or analysis, 559, 582, 584
PDD. *See* Presidential Decision Directives
Peace-enforcing. *See* Humanitarian and peace/stability operations
Peacekeeping. *See* Humanitarian and peace/stability operations
Peacemaking. *See* Humanitarian and peace/stability operations
Peace/stability operations. *See* Humanitarian and peace/stability operations

Pen registers, 507, 510, 520, 557, 567, 572–573, 584
Pentagon Papers litigation, 216, 1082–1107
　Frankel affidavit, 1087
　Mitchell, John, Attorney General, 1085–1086
Pentagon press pool, 1024–1029
PENTTBOM convictions, 673–674
PENTTBOM investigation, 664
Perfect war, 16, 201
Persian Gulf War (1991), 294–301. *See also* Iraq War (2003)
　appropriations, 296
　buildup, 296–297
　congressional authorization, 297–301
　Operation Desert Shield, 295–296
　Operation Desert Storm, 297–301
　press coverage, 1024–1029
　U.N. Security Council Resolution 678, 297
　UNSCOM, 303–304
　War Powers Resolution, 296, 299
Piracy, 196–197, 264, 845
Plausible deniability, 391–392
Poindexter, John. *See* Iran-Contra Affair
Political question doctrine, 144–149, 219–224, 230–239
　declaration of war, 214
　foreign affairs, 147
　lack of standards, 147
　potential for embarrassment, 146
　prudential bases, 144–145
　Supreme Court decisions, 148–149
　textual basis, 144–145
　Vietnam War, 219–224, 230–239
Posse Comitatus Act, 945–959, 965, 968–969
　constitutional exceptions, 957–958
　drug laws as exception, 957
　extraterritorial effect, 952–953
　Fourth Amendment rights affected by, 960–963
　immediate response exception, 958
　insurrection statutes as exception, 953–954, 956, 965, 969
　judicial remedies, 951
　origins, 950
　scope, 950–951, 952
　war, 958–959
Preamble to Constitution, 25
Preemptive war, 303–317. *See* Iraq War (2003)
Prerogative powers of the Crown, 13–14
President. *See also* Sole organ; Separation of powers
　as lawmaker, 43–45
　Commander in Chief, authority as, 46–47, 209, 213
　congressionally imposed limits on warmaking power, 77–80, 226–239
　customary powers, 43–44, 71–77, 209, 212, 214, 347–349
　delegated powers, 47
　emergency powers, 46, 80–87, 709
　foreign affairs powers, 60–67
　foreign policy, maker of, 66–67
　impeachment of, 13, 15, 123, 239
　inherent power to prevent publication, 1093–1096
　inherent powers generally, 45–46
　presidential declarations of war, 79–80
　repel attack authority, 20, 21, 213. *See also* Unilateral self-defense, defensive power
　rescue authority. *See* Unilateral self-defense, rescue
　signing statements, 234
　spending power, 127–128
Presidential Decision Directive (PDD), 44. *See also* Terrorism
Presidential Recordings and Materials Preservation Act, 1015–1016, 1022–1023
Presidential Records Act, 1015–1016
President's Foreign Intelligence Advisory Board, 428
Press. *See* Expression, freedom of
Press pool. *See* Pentagon press pool
Preventive detention, 664–679 *passim*
　burden of proof, 671
　Cold War and the Non-Detention Act, 670, 672
　due process requirements, 672
　Fourth Amendment standard, 671
　immigration, 676–678
　material witness, 674–675
　PENTTBOM convictions, 673–674
　PENTTBOM detentions, 664–665, 667
　pretextual detention, 676–677
　rights of detainees, 678
　spitting on the sidewalk, 673
　USA PATRIOT Act preventive detention provision, 677
Primary purpose doctrine, 636
Prior restraint. *See* Expression, freedom of
Privacy, expectation of. *See* Fourth Amendment
Privacy Act, 545, 1017–1018
Private assets, 447–451
Probable cause, criminal, 568, 577
Profiling, 586, 589, 604–613
Progressive litigation, 1107–1111
Proprietaries, 447–451
Protection of American lives and property. *See* Unilateral self-defense, rescue

Quasi-war with France, statutory authorization of, 98

Racial discrimination. *See* Profiling; Japanese-American internment
Rahman, Sheik Omar Abdel, 480
Raise and Support Clause, 37
Ratification of Constitution, 23–25
Ratification of prior acts, 68
Reagan, Ronald, 404–421 *passim*
Real ID Act, 600
Rebellion, power to quell. *See* Unilateral self-defense, defensive power
Regional organizations, 301–302
Regulatory search. *See* Fourth Amendment
Relevancy standard. *See* Fourth Amendment
Rendition. *See* Extraordinary rendition
Repelling attack. *See* President, repel attack authority; Unilateral self-defense, defensive power

Index

Report and wait, 131
Report of the U.S.A. to the UN Committee Against Torture
  Initial Report, 788
  Second Periodic Report, 788
Reprisal. *See* Unilateral self-defense, reprisal
Rescue. *See* Unilateral self-defense, rescue
Reservation, treaty consent and. *See* Treaties, reservation
Resolutions of inquiry, 121–122
Ressam, Ahmed, 480
Ripeness, 154–156
Roosevelt, Theodore, stewardship theory of presidential power, 59
Rules and regulations for armed forces, 9, 271

Saber-rattling. *See* Minatory demonstrations of force
SCI. *See* Nondisclosure agreements
Screening, 589–604
Search, regulatory, 589–590
SEATO, 203, 210, 216
Secrecy, 975–1111 *passim*. *See also* Classified information; Expression, freedom of
Secret but unclassified information, 986
Secret Journal Clause, 387
Secrets
  agreements and oaths. *See* Nondisclosure agreements
  Constitutional Convention, 19
  Crown in England, 13
  Framers and presidential, 343–349
  intelligence community budgets, 388–389
  Statement and Account Clause and, 386–387
Secure Flight, 603
Seditious conspiracy, 834
Selectee lists, 595
Selective prosecution or enforcement, 604
Self-defense. *See* Unilateral self-defense, defensive power
Separation of powers
  balancing test, 57–58
  English origins, 15
  formalist analysis, 57–58
  functional analysis, 57–58
  Montesquieu, 15
  shared powers, 27
  tiered analysis, 58
  twilight zone, 35, 47–58 *passim*
September 11, 2001, terrorist attacks, 466, 557, 562, 568, 573, 576, 579, 588–589, 594, 596–598, 719, 907, 916, 917–919, 920–921
Shocks-the-conscience exception. *See* Investigation, extraterritorial, shocks-the-conscience exception
Significant anticipated intelligence activity. *See* Intelligence Oversight Act of 1980
Signing statements. *See* President, signing statements
Silver platter doctrine. *See* Investigation, extraterritorial
Simple resolutions, 100

Skyjacking, 589
Smith Act, 824
Sole organ for foreign affairs, 66
"Some evidence" standard, 754
Southeast Asia Collective Defense Treaty. *See* SEATO
Special access programs (SAPs), 460
Special activities. *See* Intelligence operations
Special interest immigrants. *See* Immigration and special interest immigrants
Special Maritime and Territorial Jurisdiction of the U.S. (SMTJ), 775
Special military operations, 460
Special needs, 591
Special operations. *See* Intelligence operations
Speech, freedom of. *See* Expression, freedom of
Spitting-on-the-sidewalk detentions, 673–674
Stafford Act. *See* Terrorism
Standby statutory authorities, 114–118
Standing army
  ratification debates, 22–23
  Revolutionary War, 17–18
Standing to sue, 149–154, 224. *See also* Injury in fact
  citizen plaintiffs, 150–151
  congressional plaintiffs, 152–154
  constitutional basis, 149
  separation of powers, 149
  taxpayers, 151
  Vietnam War challenges, 224
State of the Union Clause, 344–345
State secrets privilege, 436, 1037–1050
  classified information, 1044
  definition, 88, 853
  Federal Rule of Evidence 509, 853
  Freedom of Information Act compared, 1041, 1042
  in camera review, 1041–1043
  In re Totten, 1045–1050
  judicial deference to executive, 1041–1043
  public affidavit, 1044
Statement and Account Clause, 385–387
Stewardship theory of presidential power, 59
Stigma-plus, 603–604
Strategic Support Branch, 460
Stress and duress interrogation tactics, 761
Subpoena, congressional, 122. *See also* Resolutions of inquiry
Sudden attack. *See* Unilateral self-defense, defensive power
Sunset provisions, 131
Supply bills. *See* Appropriations
Supremacy Clause, 22, 157, 173
Surveillance technologies (evolving), 504
Syndicalism, 824

Taft, William Howard, strict theory of presidential power, 59
Take Care Clause, 10
Tangible things. *See* Foreign Intelligence Surveillance Act, section 215 order
Tanker War, 248–250
Targeted killing. *See* Assassination
Taxpayer standing. *See* Standing to sue

Terrorism
- as an act of war, 471
- bioterrorism. *See also* Terrorism, weapons of mass destruction
  - anthrax, 914, 942
  - generally, 910–915, 924–943
  - plague, 910–915, 924–929, 941
  - smallpox, 913, 929–932, 942
- Centers for Disease Control, 914, 941–943
- chemical weapons, 913. *See also* Terrorism, weapons of mass destruction
- civil liberties implications, 924–943
- criminalization of, 839
- critical infrastructure protection, 923
- definitions, 467–469, 472
- Department of Defense, 922
- Department of Health and Human Services, 921, 939–942
- Department of Homeland Security, 921–923, 939
- domestic terrorism, 469, 472
- Federal Emergency Management Agency (FEMA), 919–920
- first responders, 916–919
- Foreign Intelligence Surveillance Act. *See* Foreign Intelligence Surveillance Act
- foreign terrorist organizations. *See* Foreign terrorist organizations
- Model State Emergency Health Powers Act, 935–939
- National Guard, 924, 952, 966–967, 969
- National Response Plan, 922, 923
- Nuclear weapons. *See also* Terrorism, weapons of mass destruction
- Office of Homeland Security, 921
- Oklahoma City federal building bombing, 920
- planning a response to an attack, 907–943 *passim*
- purposes, 465–467
- quarantine, 915, 924–934, 935–938, 939–943
- radiological weapons, 913, 914. *See also* Terrorism, weapons of mass destruction
- September 11, 2001, attacks. *See* September 11, 2001, terrorist attacks
- Sixth Amendment, 872–873
- Stafford Act, 920, 965
- TOPOFF, 910–913, 915, 933
- United Nations, 467
- weapons of mass destruction 907–943 *passim. See also* Terrorism, bioterrorism

Terrorist Screening Center (TSC), 601
Terrorist Screening Database, 601
Terrorist Surveillance Program, 493, 548–556
Terrorist Watch and Warning Unit (TWWU), 601
Third Amendment, 37
Tonkin Gulf incident, 205
Tonkin Gulf Resolution, 206, 210–211, 214, 218, 228, 230–233
Torture, 456, 759–816 *passim. See also* Investigation, extraterritorial, torture
- Abu Ghraib prison, 763, 786
- Alien Tort Claims Act (ATCA), 803
- AR 15-6 Investigation of the Abu Ghraib Prison and 205th Military Intelligence Brigade 29 (Fay Report), 762, 788
- Army Regulation 15-6: Final Report, Investigation into FBI Allegations of Detainee Abuse at Guantanamo Bay, Cuba Detention Facility, 788
- Article 15-6 Investigation of the 800th Military Police Brigade (Taguba Report), 762, 763
- Convention Against Torture (CAT), 774, 785
- cruel, inhuman, or degrading treatment, 793
- defenses
  - necessity, 779, 791
  - self-defense, 780, 791
- definitions, 785
- Detainee Treatment Act (DTA), 798, 802, 816
- Department of the Army, Intelligence Interrogation, 760
- extraterritorial application of the Constitution, 800
- Foreign Claims Act (FCA), 803
- Geneva Conventions, 760, 765, 767, 794, 816
  - combatants, 760, 795
  - conduct covered, 796
  - conflicts, 794
  - other persons, 796
  - unlawful combatants, 760, 795
- Guantanamo Bay, Cuba Detention Facility, 788
- lawyers' role, 791
- moral dimension, 789
- outsourcing, 788
- shocks the conscience, 801
- statute (18 U.S.C. §2340), 776, 786, 801
- stress and duress tactics, 761
- warrants, 790

Torture Victims Protection Act, 781, 803, 813
Total Information Awareness Program (TIA), 583
Trading With the Enemy Act, 116
Transactional information or records, 557–558, 559
Trap and trace devices, 510, 520, 567
Travel, right to, 596
Treason, 10, 823
Treaties. *See also* individual treaties by name or subject matter
- avoiding conflict with, 181
- Biden condition, 159, 168
- consent and ratification, 166, 167–168
- constitutional limitations, 20–21
- construing statutes consistently with, 181
- criteria for choosing instead of executive agreement, 171–172
- deference to executive interpretation, 169–170, 791
- definition, 158
- domestic legal effect, 173, 179
- executive agreements compared, 171
- executive testimony about, 168
- framing history, 21–22
- interpretation, 158–170, 198
- last-in-time rule (*lex posterior*), 181, 758
- negotiation, 165, 168–169
- ratification, 166
- record of negotiating, 166, 168–169
- reinterpretation, 169
- reservations, 161, 793
- self-executing, 179–181
- standing to enforce, 181

Index

statute compared to, 181
termination, 166–167
understandings, 161, 793

Undeclared war. *See also* Imperfect war
  pre-constitutional, 16–17
  ratification debates, 23–25
Uniform Code of Military Justice (UCMJ), 801, 802
Unilateral self-defense
  defensive power
    anticipatory self-defense, 276–277
    Caroline standard, 263
    customary defensive power, 71–77, 259–260
    delegated defensive power, 70–71
    inherent self-defense power, 71
    provoking attack, 263–264
    repel attack power, 20–21, 71, 256–257, 258–259, 260–264 *passim*
    scope, 71
    War Powers Resolution, 263
  marque and reprisal, 9, 10–11, 258, 275, 369–370
    obsolescence of, 258
    pre-constitutional, 257–258
    repelling attack distinguished, 275
    targeted killing, 277–283
    War Powers Resolution, 275–276
  reprisals. *See* Unilateral self-defense, marque and reprisal
  rescue
    Hostage Act, 269, 270–271
    Iran Hostage Rescue mission, 266–269, 272
    naval regulations, 271–272
    protection of American lives and property, 84, 269
    repelling attack distinguished, 271
    War Powers Resolution, 246–247, 271, 272–272
  targeted killing or assassination, 277–283. *See also* Assassination
United Kingdom Security Service (MI5), 443
United Nations. *See also* Korean War; Persian Gulf War (1991); United Nations Participation Act
  Charter, 284, 285–286
  Charter Article 2(4), 284
  Charter Article 43, 286–287, 289–290
  Charter Article 51, 286–287,
  Security Council, 286–287
United Nations Convention Against Torture and Other Cruel, Inhuman, or Degrading Treatment or Punishment (CAT), 792, 793
United Nations Participation Act, 288–289
Unlawful combatants. *See* Enemy combatants
USA PATRIOT Act, 520, 524, 527. *See also* Foreign Intelligence Surveillance Act
  emergency surveillance, 528, 554
  Foreign Intelligence Surveillance Court, 524
  information-sharing, 636–637
  national security letters, 564. *See also* National security letters
  Pen Register Act, 510
  pen registers, 507, 510, 520
  roving wiretap, 527
  significant purpose, 537–538
  trap and trace, 510, 520
  warrant authority, 537–541
USA PATRIOT Improvement and Reauthorization Act of 2005, 527, 558, 579, 580, 587
Usage, presidential authority provided by. *See also* Congressional acquiescence; President, customary powers
Use restrictions, 101

Vagueness. *See* Expression, freedom of
Vattel, 15
Vaughn affidavit. *See* Freedom of Information Act
VENONA, 446
Vestiture Clause, 10–11, 36
Veto, legislative, 128–132
Video monitoring, 504–505
Vienna Convention on Consular Relations, 678
Vietnam War, 201–239 *passim*
  bombing of North Vietnam, 207, 233
  Cambodia. *See* Cambodia, bombing and incursion
  Congress's efforts to limit scope of war, 226–239
  Cooper-Church amendment, 227, 230
  declaration of war not required, 212, 214
  delegation of authority by Congress to the President, 218
  Diem, Ngo Dinh, 203–205
  domino theory, 205, 207
  funding cut-off, 234–239
  Geneva Accords, 203, 217
  history, 202–208
  Ho Chi Minh, 203, 228
  international law issues, 217, 225, 230
  justiciability
    political question, 219–224, 230–239
    standing to sue, 224
  Kent State protests. *See* Kent State protests
  Laos. *See* Laos
  Mansfield amendment, 234
  mining of harbors, 233
  Paris peace talks, 208, 233, 235
  Pentagon Papers. *See Pentagon Papers* litigation
  repel attack authority of President, 209, 213
  SEATO Treaty, 203, 210, 216
  standing to challenge, 224
  Tet offensive, 208
  Tonkin Gulf incident, 205
  Tonkin Gulf Resolution, 206, 210–211, 214, 218, 228, 230–233
  usage, President's authority as provided by, 209, 212, 214
  Viet Cong, 203, 205, 208
  Viet Minh, 203
  Vietnamization, 226
Virginia Plan, 20

War. *See* Collective self-defense; General war; Unilateral self-defense

War against terrorism. *See* Terrorism
War Crimes Act, 764, 766
War on drugs, 954, 956–957
War Powers Resolution, 240–254 *passim*
   appropriations as authorization, 253–254
   authorization of force against terrorism, 275–276
   blank check, 252–253
   Chadha, 253
   concurrent resolution of withdrawal, 253
   consultation, 247–248, 272–273
   covert operations, 389
   delegation, 253
   Gulf of Sidra incident, 263
   history, 240, 246–247
   imminent hostilities, 248
   Iran Hostage Rescue mission, 271
   justiciability, 248–250, 215–252
   Libya bombing raid, 261–263
   Operation Desert Shield, 295–296
   Persian Gulf War (1991), 296, 299
   reports under, 250–251
   rescue, 246–247
   rules of construction, 253–254
   Senate versions, 246–247
   sixty-day clock, 251–253
   substantive provisions, 246
   super-statute, 253–254
   Tanker War, 248–250
   text, 240–243
   treaties as authorization, 254
   trigger, 248–251
   veto by President, 240, 243–245
Watch lists, 446, 598, 599–600
Watergate, 1083 n.4. *See also* Nixon tapes
Whig view of government, 14
Wiretapping. *See* Foreign Intelligence Surveillance Act
Wiretapping, criminal, 568
Wounded Knee, 945–950

Zero tolerance immigration policy, 679
Zone of Twilight, 35, 47–58 *passim*